New World Atlas

NEW WORLD ATLAS

GUILD PUBLISHING·LONDON

Edited by
B.M. Willett, B.A., Cartographic Editor, George Philip and Son Ltd
Consultant Cartographer Harold Fullard, M.Sc.
Maps prepared by George Philip Cartographic Services Ltd
under the direction of A.G. Poynter, M.A.,
Director of Cartography

This edition published 1985 by Book Club Associates
by arrangement with George Philip & Son Ltd.,
12-14 Long Acre, London WC2

Acknowledgements
The Landsat images in *The Earth from Space* were provided by: Canada
Center for Remote Sensing, Ottawa; Eros Data Center, US Geological
Survey, South Dakota; National Air Survey Center, Maryland, USA.

Title-page illustration Savannah country in the Samburu Game
Reserve, Kenya (Bruce Coleman Ltd)

Preface

The **New World Atlas** has been designed to provide a compact and convenient reference book which is easy to handle and consult.

The maps in the atlas are arranged in continental sections; each is introduced by a physical and a political map of the whole continent and these are followed by regional maps at medium scales and larger-scale maps of the more densely-populated areas. The contents list to the atlas as a whole not only gives a complete list of maps but also includes an outline map of each of the continents showing the areas covered by the large-scale map pages. This will help the reader to find the page required very quickly. The location of a specific place can, of course, be found via the index, where place names are listed alphabetically and the map page number and geographical coordinates for each entry are given.

The name forms on the maps are those that are used locally, or that have been transcribed according to the accepted systems. In the case of China, the Pinyin system for romanization, which is being increasingly used in the west, has been accepted. Well-known and well-used forms (often English conventions) for foreign place names are cross-referenced to the local form in the index and are often given alongside the local form on the map.

Where there are rival claims to territory, international boundaries are drawn to indicate the *de facto* situation. This does not denote international recognition of these boundaries but shows the limits of administration on either side of the line. Boundaries crossing disputed areas in the eastern Mediterranean have been specifically identified.

The maps are preceded by a series of satellite photographs, or, more accurately, images of the earth. These are false-colour images and have been obtained from the Landsat satellites of the American space agency NASA which have been circling the globe for many years. The images are all on the scale of 1:1M so they are easily compared and each is accompanied by a locational map and a brief descriptive text. There is also a short introduction on how the Landsat images are produced. To date the information from the satellites is mainly used for specialized purposes and research is concentrated in these areas. Before the end of the century, however, it is likely that satellite information will be used to compile and revise the kind of maps that make up the bulk of this atlas.

Contents

The Earth from Space

World Maps 1-128

The Abbey of Baume-les-Messieurs in the Jura, France (Bruce Coleman Ltd)

Europe

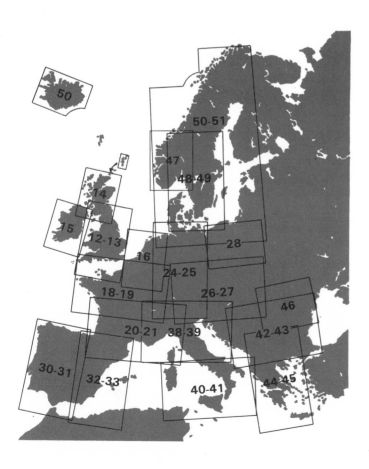

Asia

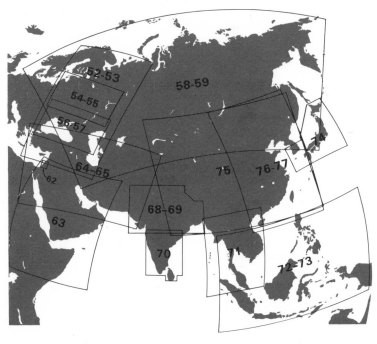

The monastery of Lamayuru Gonpa in Ladakh, Kashmir (Bruce Coleman Ltd)

Africa

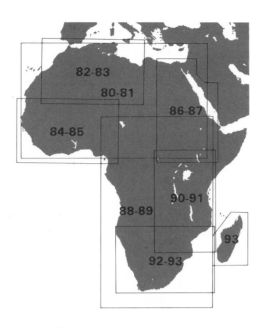

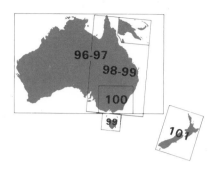

Australasia

Opposite below Ox-bow loop on the Luangwa River, Zambia
(Bruce Coleman Ltd)

Below The Twelve Apostles, Victoria, Australia (Bruce Coleman Ltd)

The Americas

Mt Ausengate, Peru (Bruce Coleman Ltd)

Index

Landsat Images — Introduction

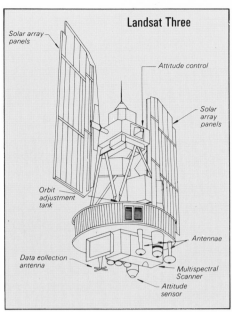

Landsat Three

- Solar array panels
- Attitude control
- Solar array panels
- Orbit adjustment tank
- Antennae
- Data collection antenna
- Multispectral Scanner
- Attitude sensor

The National Aeronautics and Space Administration (NASA) of the United States established its Earth Resources Survey Programme in 1965. It has developed the space programmes of Gemini, Apollo, Skylab and Landsat. The first Landsat was launched in 1972 and the fourth in 1982. The satellite is put into orbit and gathers its information by "remote sensing", that is viewing the Earth from a great height and signalling what it sees back to Earth.

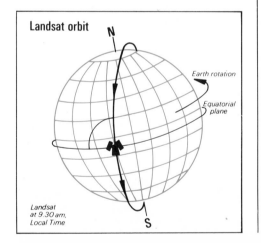

Landsat orbit

- N
- Earth rotation
- Equatorial plane
- Landsat at 9.30 am, Local Time
- S

The Landsat spacecraft circles the Earth at a height of 919km and nearly crosses the Poles, cutting the Equator at 9° from a rightangle. It weighs 959kg. It takes 103 minutes to complete a revolution of the Earth and crosses the Equator at the same local time, about 9.30 in the morning, always therefore on the sunlit side of the Earth. It circles the Earth fourteen times a day and on the fifteenth orbit is overhead, 159km west of its original point. It returns to the original point eighteen days later. When Landsat 2 and 3 were working together this "same image" period was reduced to nine days. The instruments on board record a view of the Earth along its path to a width of 185km and an area of approximately 35,000km² per scene. The fourth Landsat was launched in 1982, flies at an altitude of 705km and has a sixteen day cycle.

Landsat carries a number of instruments and the one responsible for the images on the following pages is the Multi Spectral Scanner (MSS). The word "image" is used rather than photograph because they are not produced by a camera or are they true in colour. On board the spacecraft a

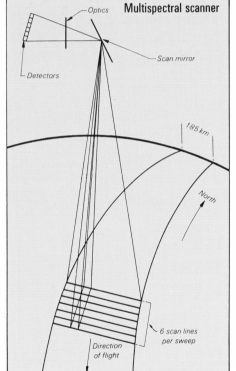

Multispectral scanner

- Optics
- Scan mirror
- Detectors
- 185 km
- North
- 6 scan lines per sweep
- Direction of flight

mirror oscillates slightly, scanning a swathe of the Earth at rightangles to the orbit path. The light from the ground is broken down through filters into four selected parts of the spectrum, two of visible light and two in the infra-red. The intensity in each of these bands for a small area of the Earth is measured and converted into a signal which is sent to the Earth receiving station. If the satellite is out of sight the material is recorded and transmitted when it is in contact with a ground station.

Four black and white images are made for each of the spectral bands by reproducing the intensity for the given area on a grey scale. To produce the false colour images in the following pages, the black and white images of the two visible bands and the longer infra-red are passed through colour filters.

In such a false colour image, growing vegetation being highly reflective in the near infra-red appears in shades of red. Water areas appear as black if clear and deep, but if it has sediment in it, it will be blue. This can be seen at the mouths of rivers and along coastal bays. Soils and rocks appear bluish but can range through yellow and browns; where there is a high water content, as in peats, they will be black. Cities and principal roads which can be detected on the image will be white to blue-grey. These are only indications of the colour for their actual hue can be affected by the angle of illumination of the sun on the original scene, the atmospheric conditions, the season in the vegetational growth cycle and minor variations in the image processing and printing.

Landsat false colour

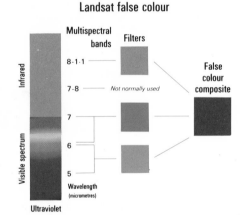

- Infrared
- Visible spectrum
- Ultraviolet
- Multispectral bands
- Filters
- False colour composite
- 8-1·1
- 7-8 — Not normally used
- 7
- 6
- 5
- Wavelength (micrometres)

On each of the following pages are presented a false colour image of part of the Earth at a scale of 1:1 000 000 (1cm = 10km), a map of the same area and a brief description. The map is normally at a scale of 1:2 500 000 (1cm = 25km) but if it is at a smaller scale the image area is shown on the map by a red square.

Some applications of Landsat

Geology	recognition of rock types, landforms and specific minerals
Water resources	area of surface water, water availability; extent of snow cover or ice, glaciers, floods and irrigation; sediment and mapping of shallow waters; shoreline changes
Environment	effects of natural disasters; air pollution; mapping of remote areas
Agriculture	crop, timber, vegetation—surveys and health; soil conditions; crop areas and yield; land-use surveys

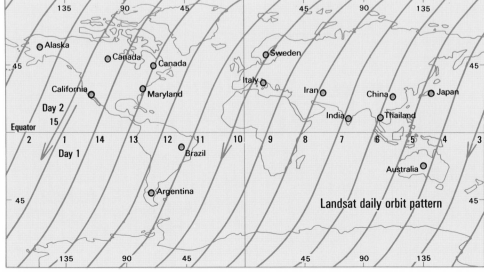

Landsat daily orbit pattern

- Alaska
- Canada
- Canada
- California
- Maryland
- Day 2
- Equator
- Day 1
- Brazil
- Argentina
- Sweden
- Italy
- Iran
- China
- Japan
- India
- Thailand
- Australia

⬤ Ground receiving station

Southwest Iceland

Iceland lies across the Mid-Atlantic Ridge, a great divide in the Earth's crust being forced apart at the rate of a few centimetres per year. The Ridge runs southwestwards across the image, following the lie of the hills and the Hvita valley. It is here that molten lava has poured out across the Earth's surface in volcanic eruptions. The older, dormant cones are topped with ice-caps, but the active Mt. Hekla and the new volcanoes on Heimaey and Surtsey can also be seen. The dark grey lands are bare or thinly-vegetated volcanic rock, but glaciers, rivers and wind have spread soils taken from them across the coastal lowlands. Here, where most Icelanders live, the Arctic climate just allows grass to grow in Summer. *(Image taken in August)*

The Norwegian Fjords

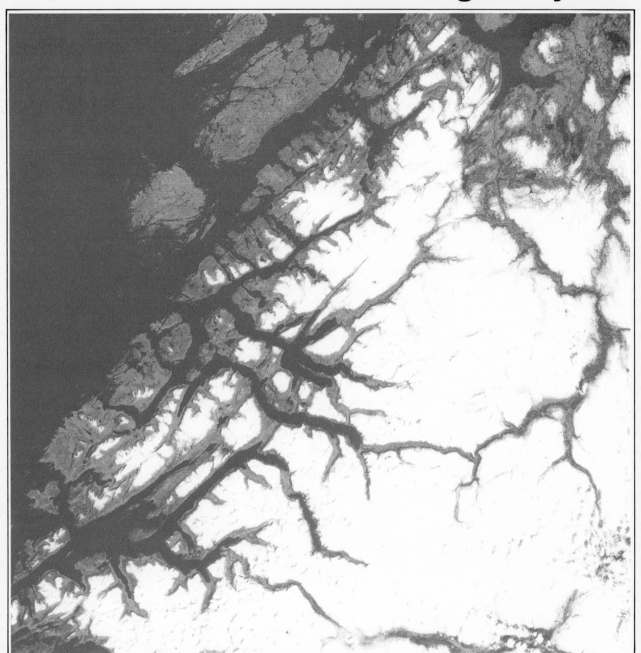

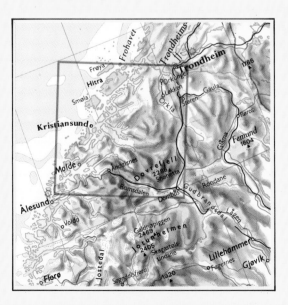

At the end of a long Norwegian winter, the snow has receded to the high moors or *fjeld*, revealing in this image a two-tone red fringe to the coastline. The brighter red traces the *strandflat*, a shelf of lowland hugging the seashore, just wide enough to hold towns and villages, graze cattle and sheep, or grow a few crops. The darker red identifies the spruce and pine of the higher slopes and offshore islands. Viewed from space, the long, thin, black fingers of the sea reach inland. The high, steep-sloping walls of these sea-inlets, or *fjords*, are ancient river-valleys, widened and deepened by glaciers, then later filled by the sea. *(Image taken in May)*

Copenhagen

When the last ice-cap retreated at the end of the Ice Age, it left behind a fertile soils cover overlying Denmark and Southern Sweden, then a continuous plain. The sea-level later rose to separate the two countries and leave Sjælland as an island. Most of the land is now intensively farmed, the fine mosaic texture reflecting the variety of uses to which the land is given at any one time – generally shared between livestock and the crops grown to feed them. Only the larger towns are visible, most notably Copenhagen, which grew up as a port on this important neck of the sea. Moving north-eastwards through Sweden, the character of the land suddenly changes as a fault-line is crossed. The forests and lakes of Scandinavia begin here. *(Image taken in September)*

The Lake Belt of Central Sweden

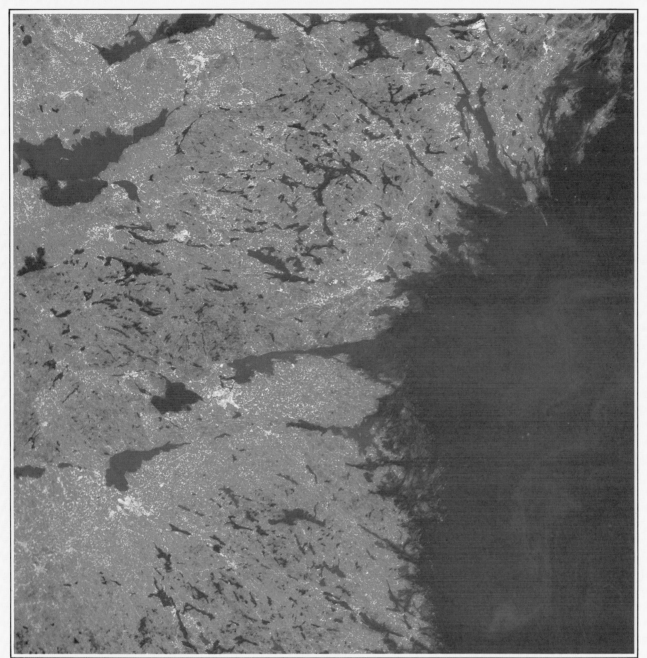

The Lake Belt of Sweden is a region of lowland in a land of mostly inhospitable uplands, and the nation's historic and industrial heart. It is peppered with small towns, a number of which can easily be picked out in this view. A combination of complex faulting and the gouging action of the great ice-cap that once obliterated Northern Europe produced a heavily-cracked surface now containing a myriad of lakes. With the region having once been under sea as well as ice, the variable soil cover has made for a diverse and charming landscape of forest, meadow, moor and farmland. *(Image taken in July)*

London

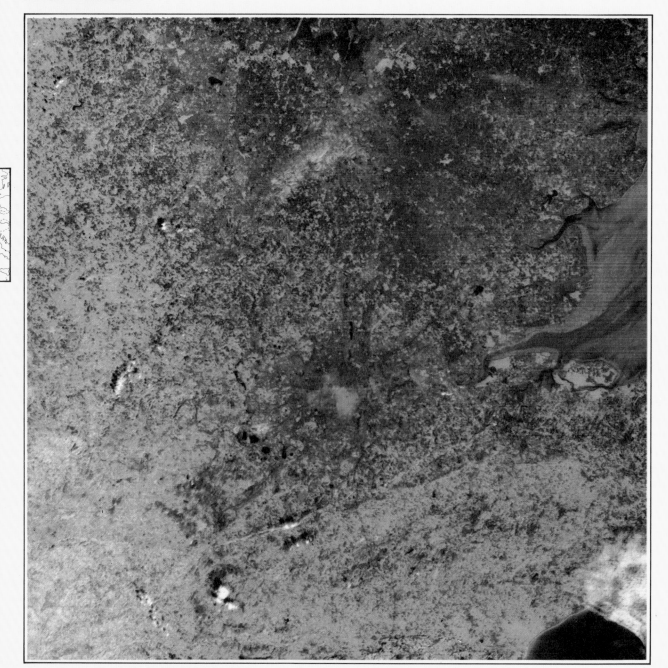

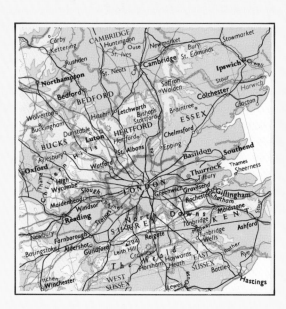

The London Basin, framed within the angle made by the Chiltern Hills and North Downs, comprises 11% of the land area of the United Kingdom, but it is inhabited by some 17 million people, nearly a third of the population, with London itself the established metropolitan core of the country. North of the Thames estuary mudflats is the level, predominantly agricultural countryside of East Anglia, mostly dark-brown ploughed fields just ahead of the growing season, speckled with the pink of occasional grassland. To the south and west, the colours – and use of land – are reversed, apart from in North Kent, where orchards, vegetables and hops supply the London market. *(Image taken in March)*

6

East Midlands, England

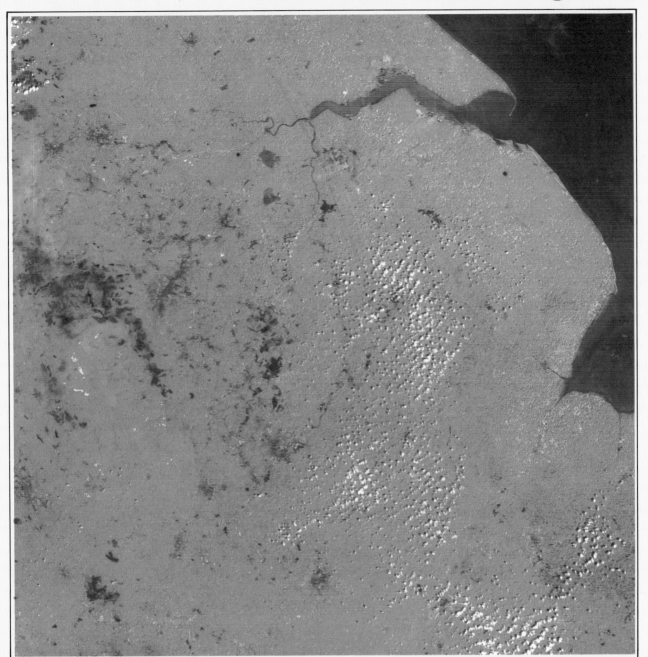

A good part of the industrial heartland of England is covered by this image. From Birmingham to Leeds, from Manchester to Hull, famous manufacturing towns and cities blot the landscape, some so closely packed they begin to merge together, others large enough to exhibit the lighter grey ring of their tree-lined suburbs. To the east, there is farming country, some of the richest in England. Cereals are grown across the flat Lincolnshire countryside; market-gardening occupies the lush Fenland bordering the Wash. Further inland, moving into the pastures of the Midlands, obtrusive dark grey patches appear here and there. They identify the heathlands of Cannock Chase and Sherwood Forest, and the open moorland of the Peak District. *(Image taken in June)*

Paris

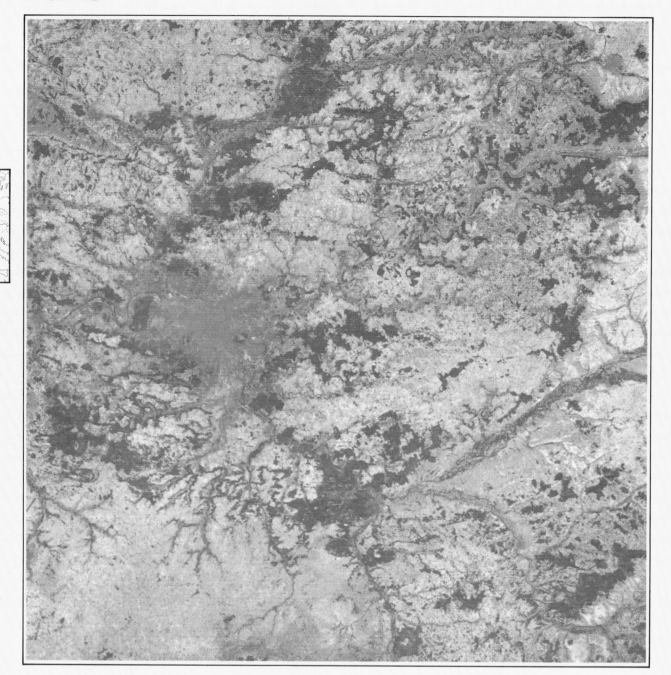

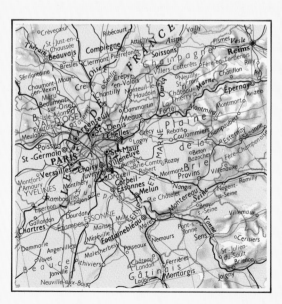

The city of Paris, astride the meandering River Seine, lies at the centre of a giant basin comprising several concentric belts of different rock strata, and containing most of Northern France. The resulting varied landscape is sprinkled with local names *(noms de pays)* that identify regions whose distinctive characters are readily apparent from this early spring scene. In Brie, the clay soils favour dairy farming, while Champagne's dry chalk country is given to cereals and vineyards and the super-fertile plain of Beauce is devoted to wheat and sugar-beet. Elsewhere, especially in Hurepoix, dark areas signify forest, which occupies poor sandy soils. *(Image taken in March)*

Lake Geneva

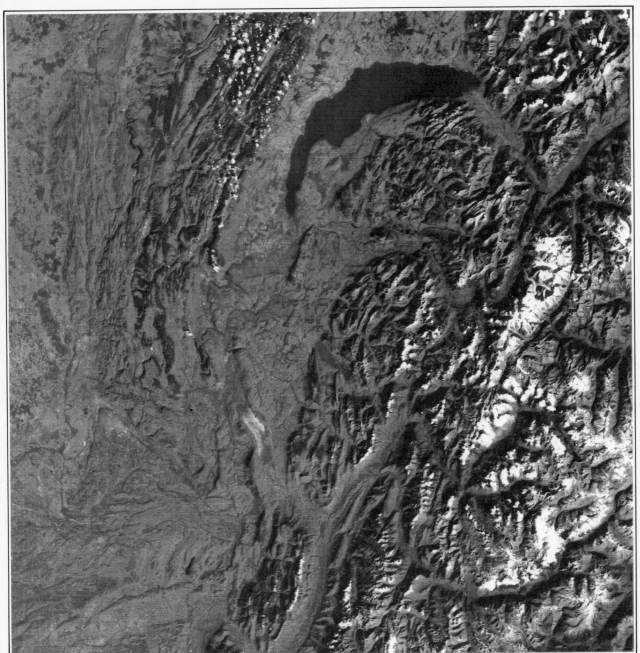

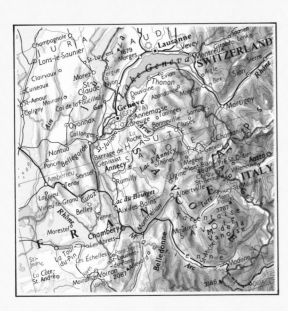

The Alps are the product of the same compressive forces which gave rise to the Himalayas in Asia. Rock strata buckled and overturned, while ice and water carved great valleys across the mountains. The result has been a landscape typified by this scene. Snow-capped summits like Mont Blanc stand highest, on account of their superior resistance to erosive powers. The valleys are fertile ribbons of agriculture reaching into the heart of the Alps, and serve as routes across them. Emerging from Lake Geneva, the Rhône divides the Alps from the Jura, gentler hills to the North, before opening out into lowlands. The region has a pink hue because it is Autumn and crops have been harvested. *(Image taken in October)*

The Po Valley, Italy

Winter in Northern Italy sees the higher summits of the Apennines capped by snow and the fields of the lower Po dark and sodden. Growing crops already show, however, in the Arno basin, the upper Plain and the drained lands near the coast. The Northern Plain is a very flat region, lying between mountain ranges to the north and south. Though watered by the Po and its tributaries, Italy's richest farming land has to be heavily irrigated in the hot and dry summer. The Plain is densely populated, many of the present-day cities being established in Roman times or earlier. Bologna, Modena, Parma and others strung out along the straight Via Emilia, grew up where it was met by roads leading down from Apennine passes. *(Image taken in February)*

The Danube

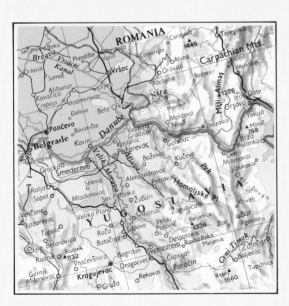

Dominating this view is the course of the River Danube, which winds across the Hungarian Plain, to breach the Carpathian Mountains as a fast-flowing torrent through the "Iron Gate" gorge, before crossing Romania and reaching the Black Sea. Below Belgrade, where it is met by the Sava, and, later, the Morava, the Danube separates two regions, whose differing characters are apparent from their image colouring. Formerly the floor of a huge ancient lake, the lush flat lowlands to the north now constitute Yugoslavia's richest agricultural land, given to a wide range of crops from wheat to market-gardening. The more rugged land on the river's right bank is mostly pasture land and dotted with many small industrial towns. *(Image taken in October)*

Athens

Only a narrow isthmus joins the Peloponnesus to mainland Greece, and this was breached by the construction of the Corinth Ship Canal in 1893. In this summer view, the peninsula is undergoing a long spell of uninterrupted hot and dry weather. It is a mountainous landscape, with little level ground and consists mainly of limestone, a rock highly pervious to rainwater. For a farmer, then, the Peloponnesus is largely unproductive, though orange and olive groves cluster around the southern bays, green vegetables occupy the plain of Argos, and grapes, dried for currants, line the shore of the Gulf of Corinth. Elsewhere, the lower scrub-covered mountain slopes are left to pasture for sheep and goats. *(Image taken in August)*

The Middle East

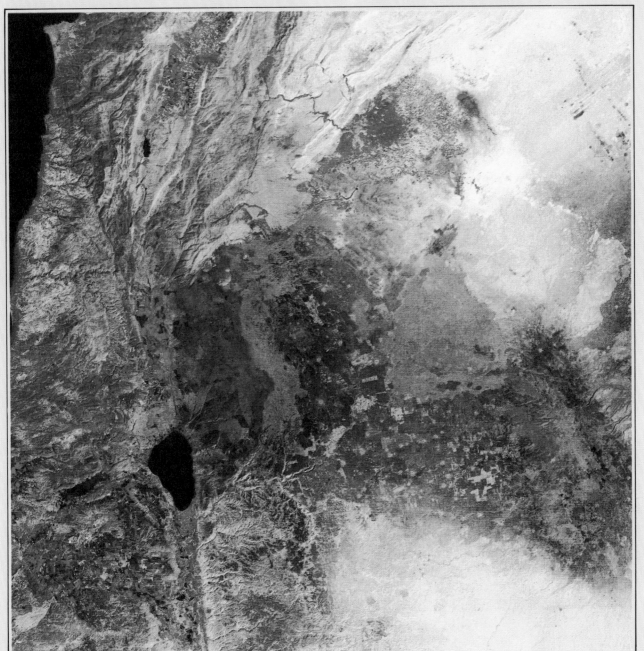

A land where several present-day international boundaries meet, this part of the Middle-East is laden with biblical and historical significance. Famous placenames such as Galilee, Nazareth, Beirut and Damascus can be located here. In more modern times, the region has witnessed military conflict along Israel's border and in Southern Lebanon. Geographically, it is also a frontier between rich Mediterranean farmland and the desert. To the west are the Israeli fruit growing *kibbutzim* of the Upper Jordan and the fertile croplands of the Beqaa valley. To the east, the desert takes over – cultivation is largely confined to oases near Damascus and bordering higher ground further south. *(Image taken in September)*

13

Samarkand

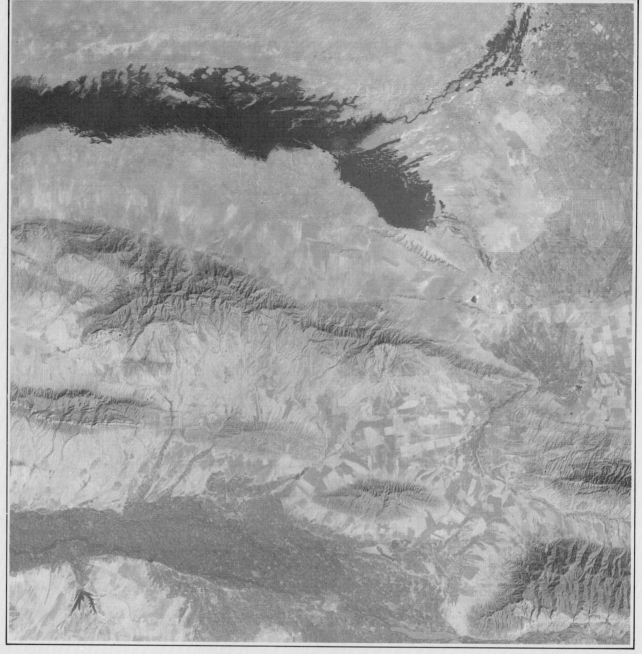

The ancient city of Samarkand, once Tamburlaine's capital, is visible amid the mountains and plains of this typical view of Central Asian Soviet Union. To the north is desert, the Kyzylkum, a name meaning "red sands". Running across the south are mountain chains, western arms of the great Pamirs. From here, rivers water the parched lands as they flow to meet inland lakes – such as Lake Tuzkan, seen here currently in flood – or, like the Zeravshan, to dissipate themselves in the sand. The bleak hues of the desert are thus relieved by lush valleys and oases with fields of cotton, rice, orchards, vineyards and melon plantations. *(Image taken in October)*

The Lower Volga

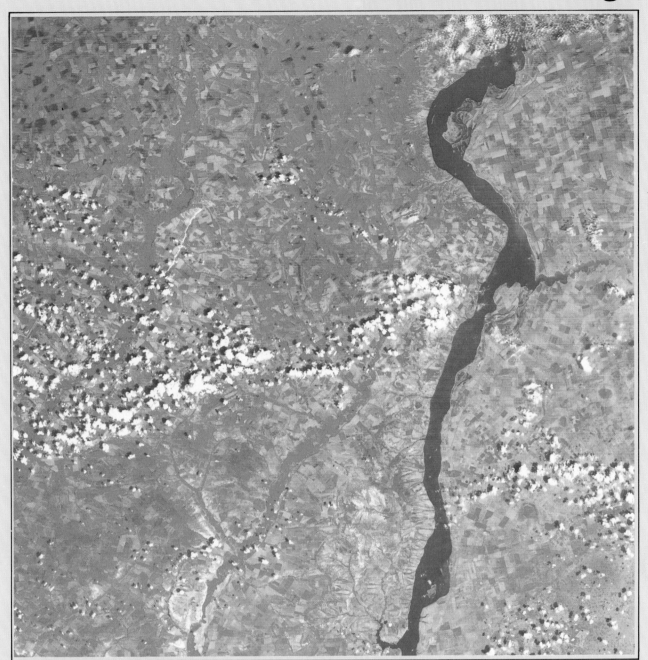

The Volga river, seen here as an elongated lake, is a natural frontier in more than one sense. Geographically, it traces a line where Atlantic climatic influences finally die out and the fertile prairies give way to semi-desert. Historically, it divides the Russian Empire into West and East, a meeting-place for Muscovite and Tatar cultures. In this scene, the contrast is enhanced by the presence of the Volga Heights to the west, where relief and woodland give variety to the mixed farmland. The eastern plains were formerly beneath the salt-waters of a larger Caspian Sea, but are now divided into the huge fields of State collective farms, benefitting from mechanization and irrigation. *(Image taken in July)*

The Himalayas

The Earth's crust is divided into giant "plates", many shifting independently, some actually thrusting into each other. One such area of collision is between India and the rest of Asia. The result has been a crumpling up of rocks on a gigantic scale, known to us as the Himalaya mountains. The range includes many peaks over 8000 m, among them the highest in the world, Mt. Everest, shown here. The image charts the descent from these snow-covered peaks, across the deeply-etched Lesser Himalayas and bamboo-forested Siwalik Hills, to the populous and intensively-farmed Ganges Plain of India, into which flow the gravel-laden streams from the mountains. *(Image taken in December)*

The Rann of Kutch

"Islands" of higher land in this view of Northwest India are welded together by vast expanses of mudflats and marshland known as the Rann of Kutch. There are, in fact, two "Ranns": the Little Rann, an extension of the low, muddy land and maze of channels and inlets at the head of the Gulf, which are occasionally inundated when rains are heavy, and the Great Rann, a vast saltmarsh stretching away to merge with the Thar Desert in the North. Cultivation is possible only on upland areas, particularly the ancient volcanic Kathiawar peninsula to the south, while other areas are elsewhere left to pasture land, scrub or forest. *(Image taken in January)*

The Ganges Delta

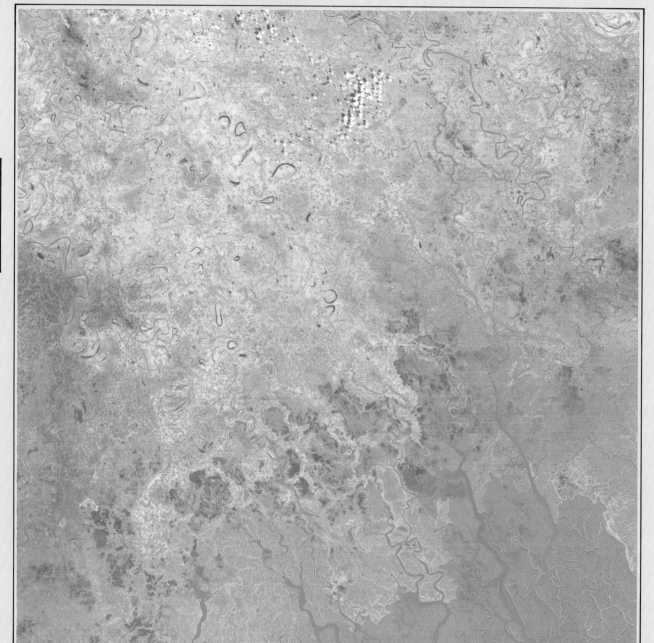

At the head of the Bay of Bengal, where the Ganges and hundreds of minor streams have built an immense delta, there is a land of contrasts. The central portion of the image, comprising the lighter "moribund" delta, strewn with oxbow lakes and abandoned channels, and the saline-forested Sundarbans of the "Mouths" is a region of little or no agricultural use. Eastwards into Bangladesh intensive cultivation on the new, fertile alluvial soils is possible, and millions of people live here, despite regular floods and the changing courses of rivers. The region to the west is also heavily populated, but this time packed into the teeming suburbs of Calcutta lining the banks of the River Hooghly. *(Image taken in November)*

Peking

The distinctive rectangular plan of its Inner City walls identifies the position of Peking, close to the mountains which border the great Eastern plain in the north. A level and fertile region, this plain suffers from a dry climate, though cereals are intensively cultivated in the hot summer growing season. Water for the capital comes from the Kuant'ing Reservoir, dammed from the waters of the Yunting River. This image is a winter scene, a time when cold winds sweep southeastwards from the Mongolian steppes over the mountains of Northern China and the Great Wall that meanders across them – but which is invisible here. *(Image taken in November)*

Canton and Hong Kong

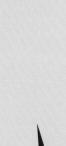

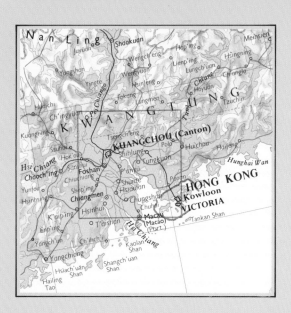

The Kwangtung plains are a meeting-place for rivers flowing down from the Nan Ling mountains. From here, they subdivide and reach the sea as a tangle of tiny channels. Just how much silt and gravel are brought down with them can be seen from the pale blue wash of the estuary – water usually comes out as dark blue or black in Landsat images. Floods have, in the past, spread these deposits across the lowlands, making them very fertile farming land, and still subject the area to frequent inundation. The image shows up water-logged land on the north banks of the Hsi Chiang. Canton itself is situated where a spur of higher ground meets a navigable outlet to the sea. *(Image taken in December)*

Tokyo

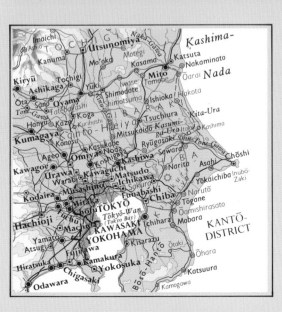

Tokyo's suburbs, strung out along the express-ways, reach like tentacles across the southern plains of the Kantō-Heiya. These fertile lowlands, a carpet of sediments washed down by mountain rivers, were once unproductive swamps, but are now drained to provide valuable farming land. The Tone river has built a classically symmetrical delta into the Pacific Ocean, and in so doing, has linked to the mainland the former island in the south now known as Boso-Hanto, and created Tokyo Bay. Besides serving as an excellent natural harbour, especially for the port of Yokohama, the Bay has paradoxically provided Tokyo with extra land, artificially reclaimed around its shores. *(Image taken in November)*

Canterbury Plains, New Zealand

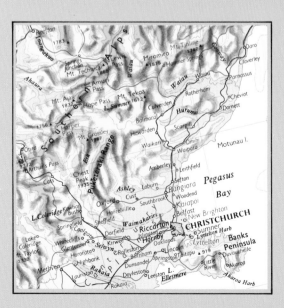

Swollen rivers rushing from the snow-capped Southern Alps carve entrenched courses in the wide alluvial plain which they themselves have built up over the ages. Sheep graze the fertile Canterbury plains and the tussock grass of the Downs rising behind them, although wheat and fodder crops, fruit and vegetables also thrive where the geometrically-laid irrigation channels offset the effects of a rather dry climate. Southeast of Christchurch are the twin volcanoes of the Banks peninsula, into which the sea has created two inlets by drowning deep glacial valleys. *(Image taken in August)*

Perth

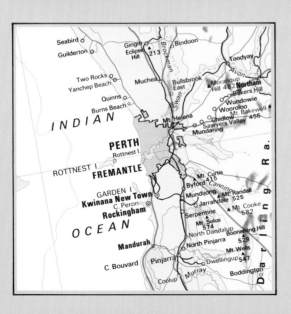

50km short of the coast, the vast ancient granite plateau of Western Australia drops several hundred metres to the coastal plain in a long fault scarp known as the Darling Range. Breaking through the forested uplands are the short perennial rivers with reservoirs built on them to supplement the more seasonal waters of the undulating plateau further inland, enabling extensive wheat and sheep farming to prosper in a favourable "Mediterranean" climate. On the coastal strip, fruit-orchards and vineyards can be seen clustered around Perth and the Swan valley, while the large fields to the north are dairy cattle pastures. *(Image taken in December)*

Sydney

Sydney grew up on the banks of its excellent natural harbour, Port Jackson, which, like other inlets nearby, is the product of deep valley flooding by the sea. Its position on a rare section of the Eastern coastal strip which widens into a substantial plain – the Hunter valley further north is another – has permitted spacious expansion into the valuable farming lands of the Hawkesbury-Nepean lowlands. Rising further inland are the heavily-wrinkled Blue Mountains, an ancient plateau uplifted in geologically recent times into which many streams have cut steep, narrow gorges. *(Image taken in December)*

The Anti Atlas Mountains

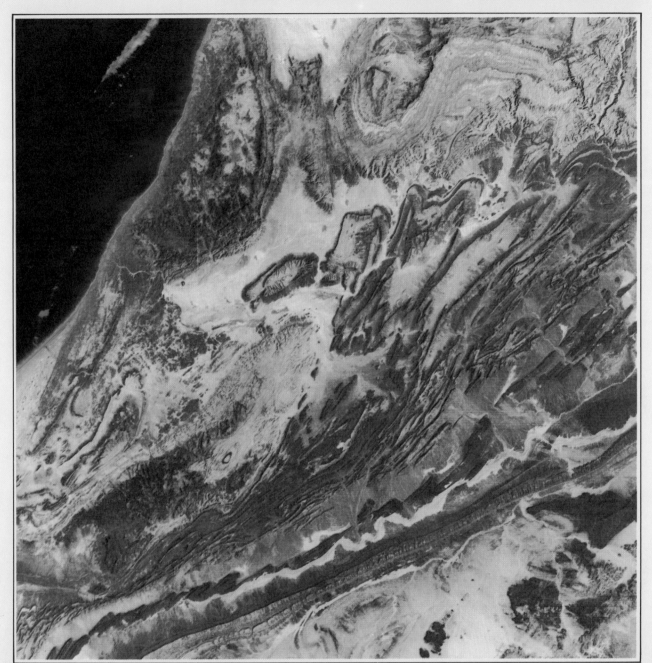

This view of the very edge of the Sahara Desert, where man's influence is confined to mere specks of farmland, captures a beautifully-patterned landscape showing off its geology. In the Anti-Atlas mountains, ancient domes encircled by younger rocks form the southwest guard to the Atlas chain stretching 2000km across Morocco and Algeria. To the south, the succession of ridges in the Djebel Bani are evidence of folded strata becoming more and more compressed as they approach the Oued Draa, the faulted edge of the great Saharan shield itself. *(Image taken in March)*

The Suez Canal

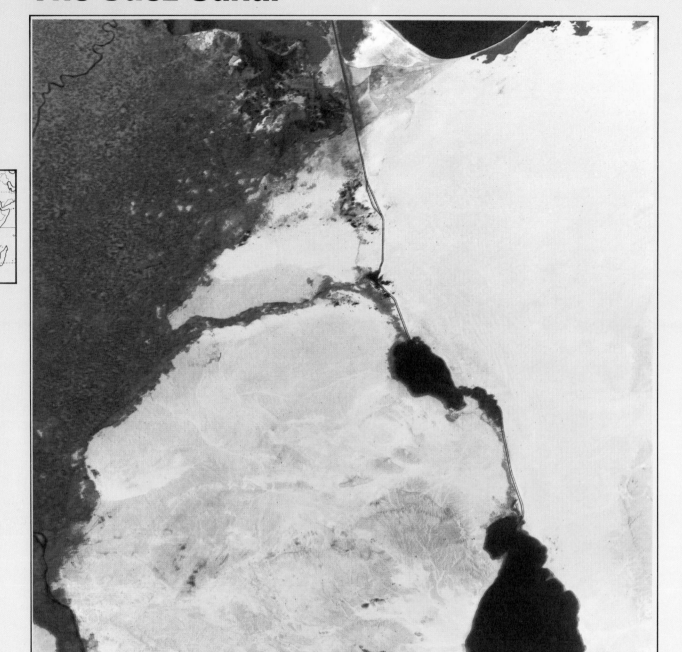

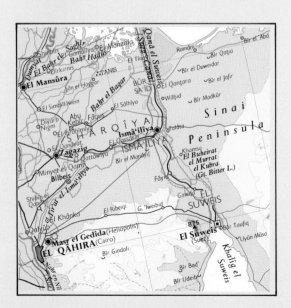

This picture illustrates supremely the impact of fresh water in arid lands. The empty desert, sandy and monotonous in Sinai, rugged and scored by dry valleys west of Suez, suddenly gives way to a region of intensive cultivation, home to millions of people. Responsible for this dramatic contrast is, quite simply, irrigation. Below Cairo, the Nile subdivides into two main branches, a number of smaller streams and hundreds of canals, enabling crops to be grown and the population to be fed. The "arm" of cultivation reaching out to Ismailiya demonstrates this effect in isolation. The larger cities can be picked out from the bright red of the delta – most conspicuously in the case of Cairo, capital of Egypt. *(Image taken in May)*

The Mangueni Plateau, Niger

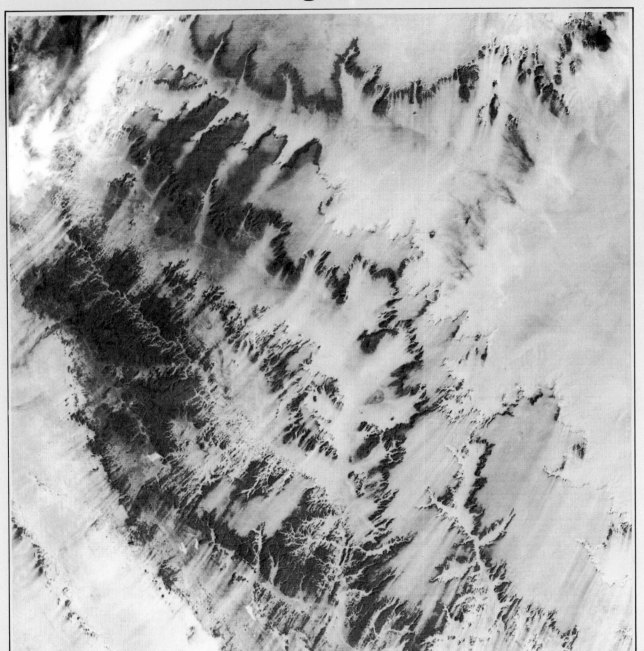

The Mangueni Plateau is a comparatively low "saddle" linking the Ahaggar and Tibesti highland ranges that arc around the southern fringes of the Marzuq sand sea. It is a bleak *hamada* landscape, where rocky platforms rise sharply from level ground, with canyons carved between them – eroded at some time by running water. The region is entirely desert now, but in the past, at the time of the Ice Age in Europe, the Sahara was watered by great rivers, whose valleys became "fossilized" when aridity set in. The streaks in the sand, running across the image at right-angles to the lie of these valleys, give evidence of the strength and direction of northeasterly winds that blow across the desert almost every day. *(Image taken in October)*

Mount Kilimanjaro

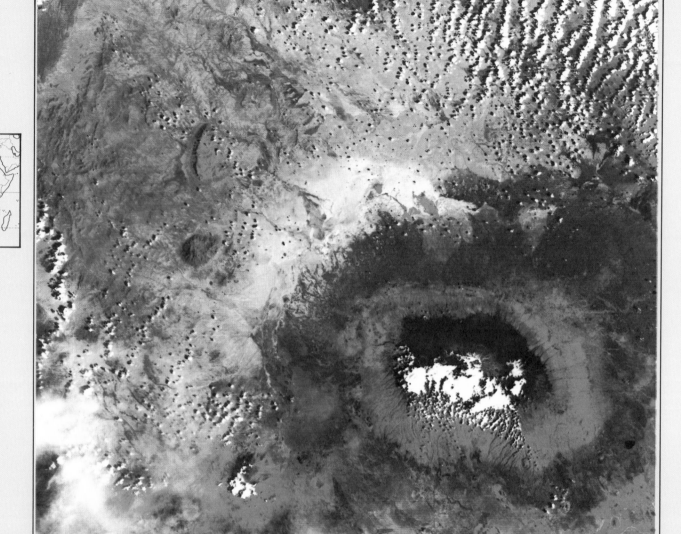

N

It is easy to see that the smears of red on the image correspond to points of high ground on the map. In East Africa, the type of vegetation is ruled by local climate, itself closely controlled by altitude. Here, the general principle – the higher you are, the wetter and cooler it is – takes on a visually stunning aspect, nowhere more so than on Kilimanjaro, the region's – and Africa's – highest mountain. Rising from the savannah and dry lakes of the Nyiri desert, this dormant volcano is encircled by a series of vegetation belts – cultivation, forest, heather – each matching the climate at their respective levels. Around the craters at the summit, just 350 km from the Equator, there are glaciers all year round. *(Image taken in January)*

The Zaire River

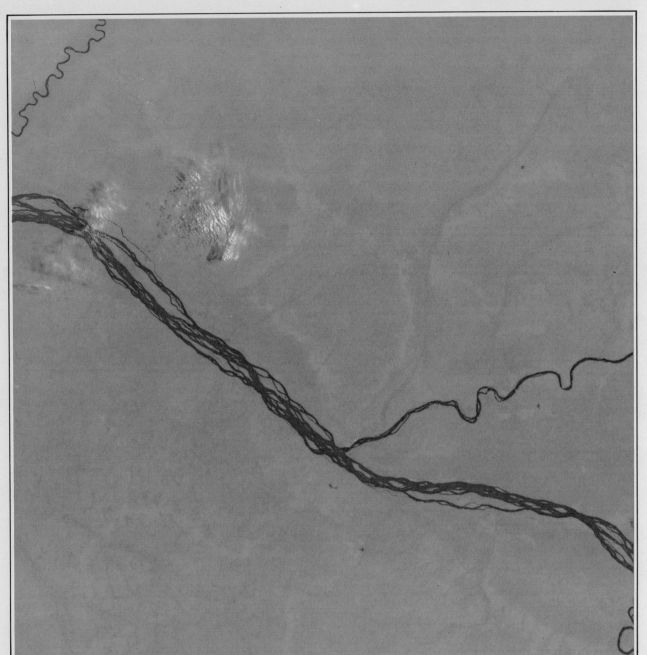

The tropical rain forest of Zaïre is, as the image emphatically demonstrates, monotonous, uniformly flat country, unbroken by sharp changes in relief. The constantly warm, humid and very wet climate sustains the unvaried dense forest cover comprising, however, a wide mix of tree species such as mahogany, ebony, teak and cedar. Across this landscape flows the Zaïre and its many tributaries, some only faintly visible here. With a gradient of only about 10cm per kilometre, the great river flows slowly in a wide, shallow channel, much braided to enable it to carry a heavy sediment load brought down from the mountains to the south and east. *(Image taken in March)*

Prince Edward Island

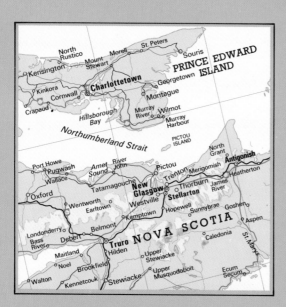

The Appalachian Range extends from the Southern United States as far north as the Gulf of St. Lawrence. Here, it divides, the central trough now flooded by the sea, with slightly higher land becoming islands such as Prince Edward Island. From January to March, its waters are sealed by pack-ice, but summers are long enough and soils sufficiently fertile for dairying and potato growing to take place. The southern arm of uplands forms most of Nova Scotia, a faulted, ice-scoured but even-surfaced plateau almost totally covered by evergreen forest. *(Image taken in January)*

Montreal

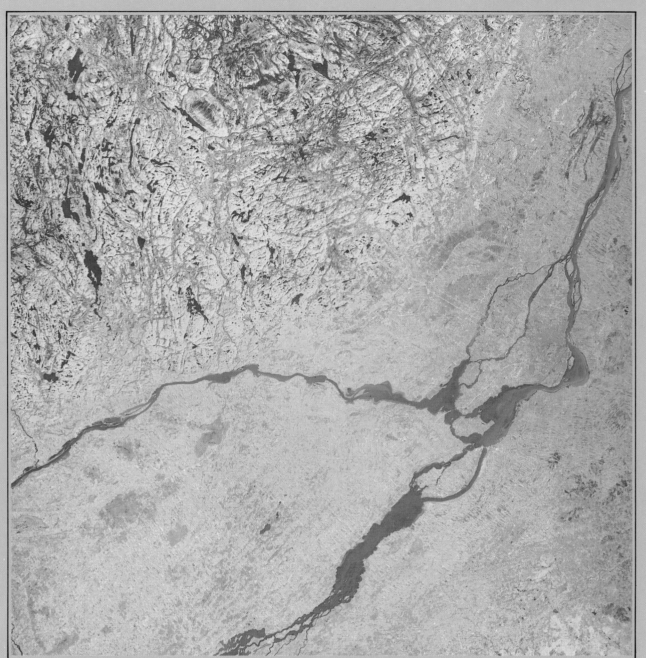

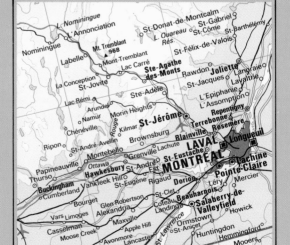

The much-scarred Laurentian Plateau occupies the north part of this scene, a vast shield of ancient rock formations, levelled by millions of years of erosion, finally shaped by Ice-Age glaciation, which scoured the surface and left behind thousands of tiny lakes. The deciduous trees can be distinguished here by their yellow "fall" colours from the red evergreens on higher ground. By contrast is the St. Lawrence plain, where sands and clays deposited by a former inland sea give rise to a productive region with a rich variety of crops. The city of Montreal grew from its command of the river-ways of Canada and routes south to the United States. *(Image taken in October)*

31

The Canadian Rockies

The Rocky Mountain Trench cuts across the Canadian Cordilleras pictured in this image – and for hundreds of miles northwest to the Yukon and southeast to Montana in the United States. This remarkably straight depression, occupied here by the Fraser river sharply divides the Rocky mountains from the Cariboo and Selkirk ranges, though, as the image illustrates, the landscape to either side is one of snow-capped summits and deep valleys with evidence of faulting and glacial erosion. From its linearity and geology, the Trench itself is obviously the product of faulting, but its exact origin is less clear. Could it have been carved by ice along a line of weakness, or was it simply dropped between long parallel cracks in the Earth's surface? *(Image taken in September)*

Cape Cod

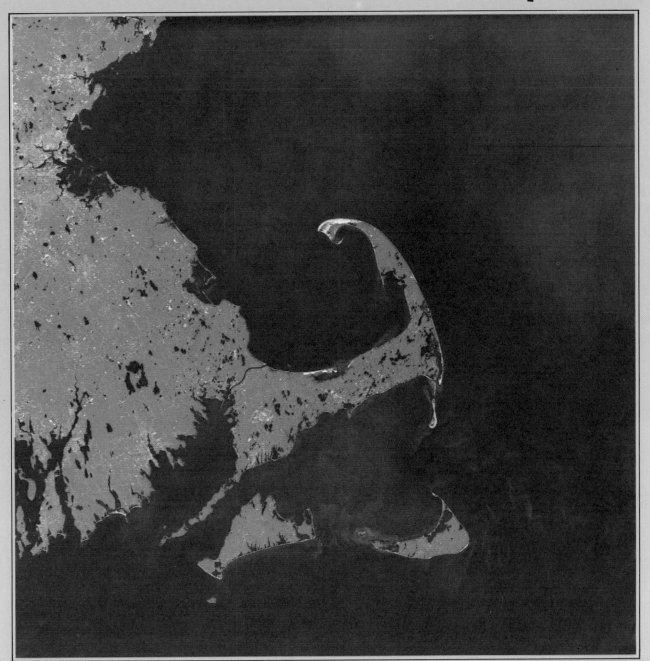

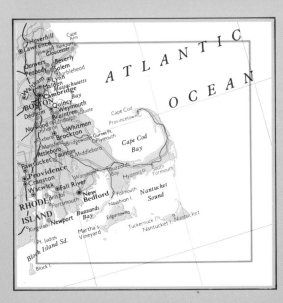

The remarkable outline of Cape Cod, poking out to sea like a scorpion's tail, is the work of two of nature's most potent agents: ice and sea. Ice-transported debris, or *moraine*, piled up where the Ice Age glaciers reached their southernmost extent, were left above the rising sea level as the islands and peninsulas around Nantucket Sound. By steadily removing sand alongshore, ocean waves have subsequently produced bars and spits, Cape Cod being the most spectacular of a number of examples shown in this image. The landscape provides for the nearby East Coast cities in several ways – holiday resorts, fishing harbours, and fertile land for garden produce. *(Image taken in July)*

Washington — Baltimore

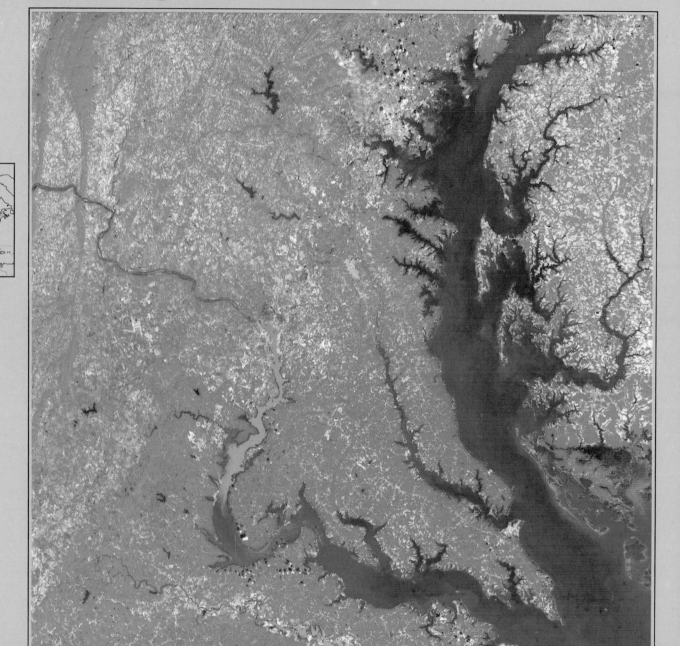

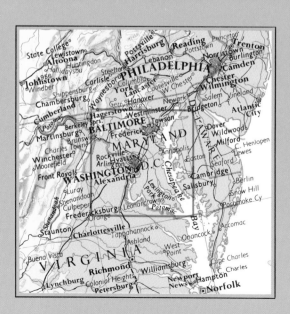

The cities of Washington and Baltimore may be thought of as forming the southern end of a virtually continuous urban agglomeration or *megalopolis* extending as far as Boston in the north. The use of intermediate land not yet swallowed up for urban use is typified here: orchards, vegetable gardens and dairying for city markets lie among stands of dense woodland. Washington's transitional position between the industrial North and agricultural South was considered an important factor when it was chosen as capital of the United States. Some of the city's landmarks are visible here: the Capitol and White House grounds, and the Mall which runs between them. *(Image taken in October)*

The Tennessee Valley

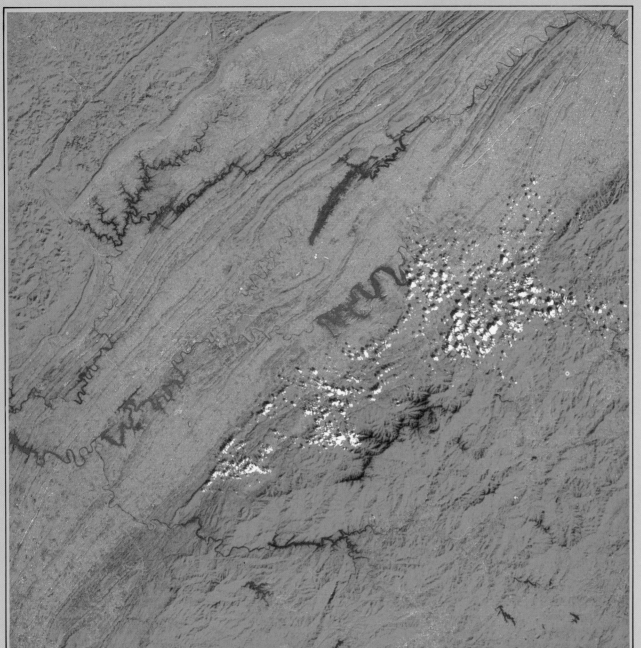

Three regions can be identified running northeast-southwest across this view of the Appalachian Mountains in Tennessee. The heavily-forested Great Smoky Mountains are the highest in Eastern United States, with Clingman's Dome rising above 2000m. Several rivers, many dammed to provide hydroelectric power, meander across the Appalachian Valley, a fertile agricultural corridor characterized by a succession of parallel limestone ridges cloaked in woodland. Separated from the valley by a faulted edge is the isolated Cumberland Plateau, a region of forested upland and limestone gorges, inhabited by poor mining communities. *(Image taken in October)*

Toronto — Buffalo

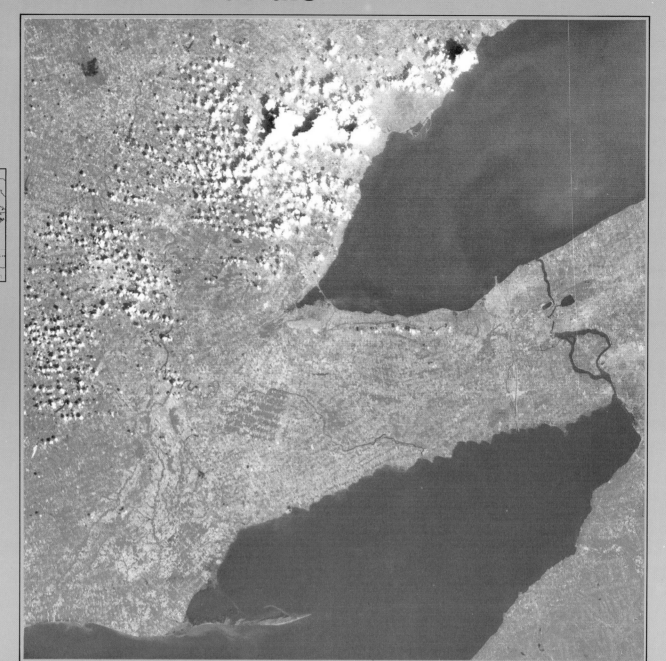

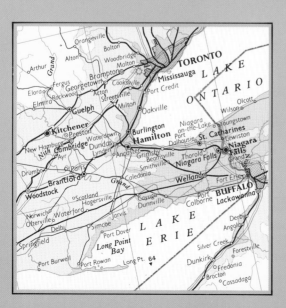

A quarter of a million years ago, a huge ice-cap covered much of North America. When it melted, water collected in huge depressions, becoming what we know as the Great Lakes. The pattern of rivers is now much changed since before the glaciation: the Niagara, between Lakes Erie and Ontario, makes a spectacular waterfall as it flows over the edge of a great limestone escarpment, the product of erosion by an ancient drainage system. Another legacy of the Ice Age has been a coating of fertile clays and sands spread over this region. In consequence, Canada's "Golden Horseshoe", bordering Lake Ontario from Toronto to the U.S. frontier, is rich crop and fruit-growing country, lately experiencing industrial and urban growth. *(Image taken in September)*

St. Louis, Missouri

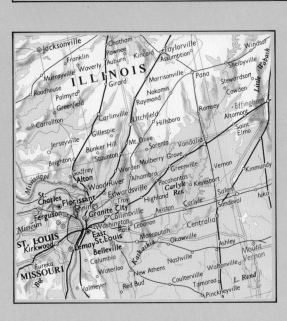

St. Louis, standing at the meeting-place of major rivers and highways, could also be said to lie at the geographical crossroads of the United States. The Mississippi river is generally regarded as the border between the industrialized East and the open country of the West. Below St. Louis, the Mississippi valley opens out into the Gulf Plains of the Deep South. Most of the scene belongs, however, to the continent's agricultural heartland, the lowland prairies that stretch away to the north, beyond the Great Lakes into Canada. Here in Illinois, the corn, wheat and soyabean fields – now harvested – are laced with the deeper red of woods and meadows that follow the river courses and so display their intricate patterns on the landscape. *(Image taken in October)*

The Mississippi River

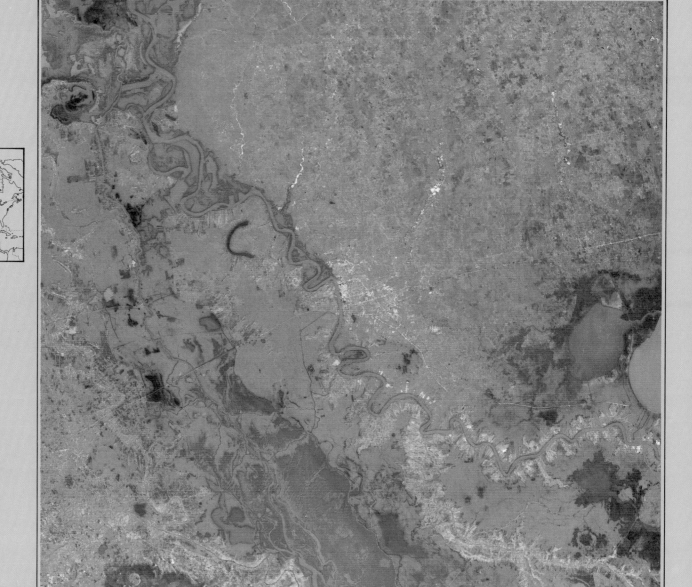

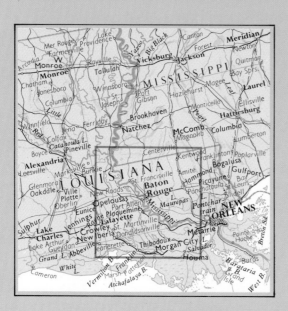

Meandering across the flat plains of Louisiana, the Mississippi is nearing the end of its journey to the Gulf of Mexico. Seen at high water during a spring flood, it is pale blue on the image with the great volume of sediment carried at that time. Especially to the west of the river, there is dense, swampy forest amid a jumble of smaller streams and lakes that represent older courses taken by the Mississippi to the sea. The farmland occupies the areas of higher land that envelop the river course in the southern part of the image. The distinctive field pattern, long strips of land perpendicular to the river-bank, was inherited from early French settlers. *(Image taken in May)*

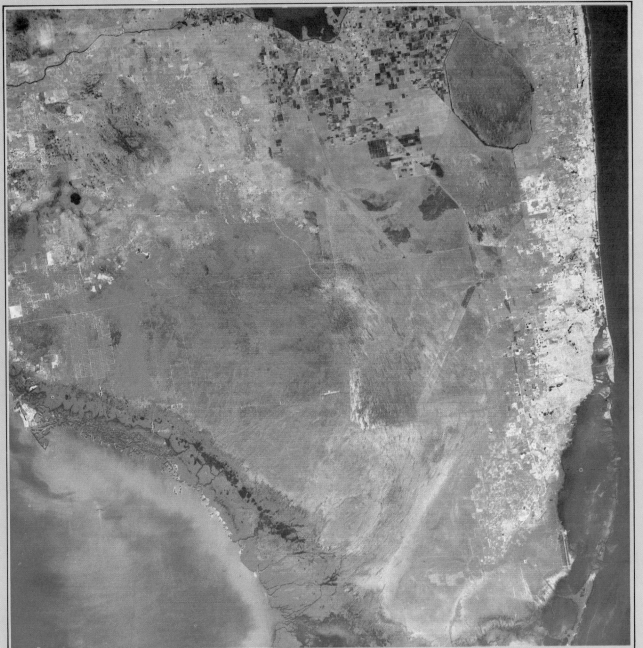

N

Southern Florida is a unique region of the United States. Almost entirely flat lowland, enjoying a tropical climate and covered by swamp and sand, it is also both a tourist boom area and rich farming country. Trapped behind the sand bars thrown up by Atlantic waves, the vast Everglades tall saw-grass swamp dominates this image – a grey mass, flecked with red marking the "tree-islands" of slightly higher rises. Man's shaping of the landscape is betrayed by straight lines and rectangular patterns: the streets and blocks of the Eastern Gold Coast cities from Palm Beach to Miami, the orchards, gardens and sugar-cane fields around the southern shores of Lake Okeechobee. *(Image taken in March)*

The Grand Canyon

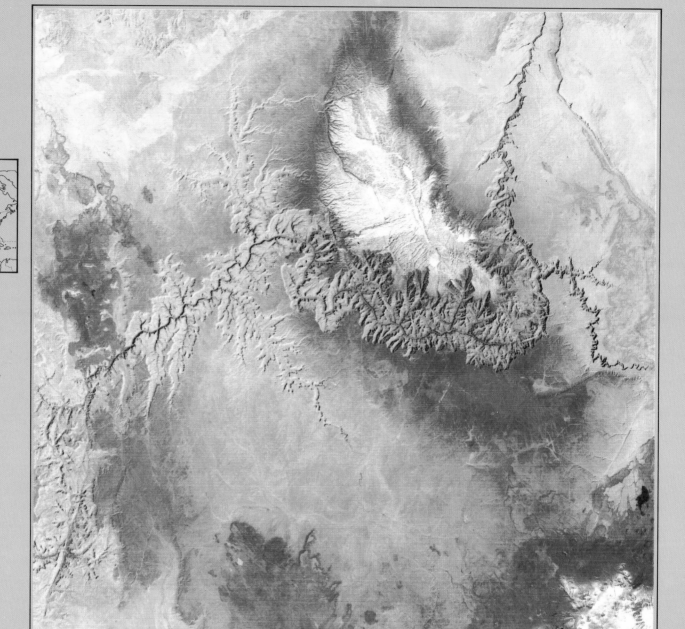

The Colorado River, maintaining its course by cutting deeply into the plateau that has been uplifted in geologically recent times, has sculpted one of the world's most spectacular natural features. 20 km by 1.6 km at its widest and deepest, the Grand Canyon has been hewn from rocks laid down successively in more or less horizontal, undisturbed layers. The resulting profile, weathered back through time, offers both an unparallelled insight into geological history – and breathtaking scenery that draws thousands of tourists every year to this largely semi-desert region. *(Image taken in May)*

The Canyon Lands of Utah

By the same process which created the Grand Canyon further downstream, the upper Colorado and its tributaries have found renewed energy from the uplifting of the Colorado Plateau to carve deep, if less impressive canyons for themselves. The region's climate is not too harsh – there is enough rainfall to support grasslands and dense pine forest on higher ground, masked by snow in this winter scene. It is the ruggedness and inaccessibility that has made farming and settlement difficult. Instead, other potential qualities have been exploited: plentiful supplies of fresh water are dammed in reservoirs, and the natural beauty of the canyonlands draws tourists to the area every year. *(Image taken in February)*

Salton Sea, California

The Colorado River flows well to the East of this image, but its waters are responsible for bringing life to this eternally dry, sun-baked region. A trough between the arid Chocolate Mountains and the scrub-vegetated ranges to the west, its lowest depths reach 80m below sea-level. Here, water was channelled from the Colorado in the early 20th century and collected to form the Salton Sea. A modern irrigation system built from the All-American and Coachella canals that draw water from the Imperial Reservoir, sustains the level of the Sea, and the rich variety of fruit and grain crops filling the Imperial Valley to the south in a bright mosaic. Note how the character of land-use changes across the border at Mexicali. *(Image taken in July)*

San Francisco

Faults, great fissures in the Earth's crust, run the length of America's west coast. Troughs, like San Francisco Bay and San Joaquin Valley, have been created where land has slumped between them. The former was drowned when the sea breached the Golden Gate, creating a magnificent deepwater harbour, around which San Francisco and the Bay Area cities grew up. The San Joaquin Valley, with its fertile soils and perfect Mediterranean climate, produces fruit, vegetables, wine, cotton and rice for sale in the rest of the world. Marking the edge of the redwood-forested Santa Cruz Mountains is the notorious San Andreas fault, responsible for earthquakes which destroyed San Francisco in 1906 and always threaten to do so again. *(Image taken in October)*

Mexico City

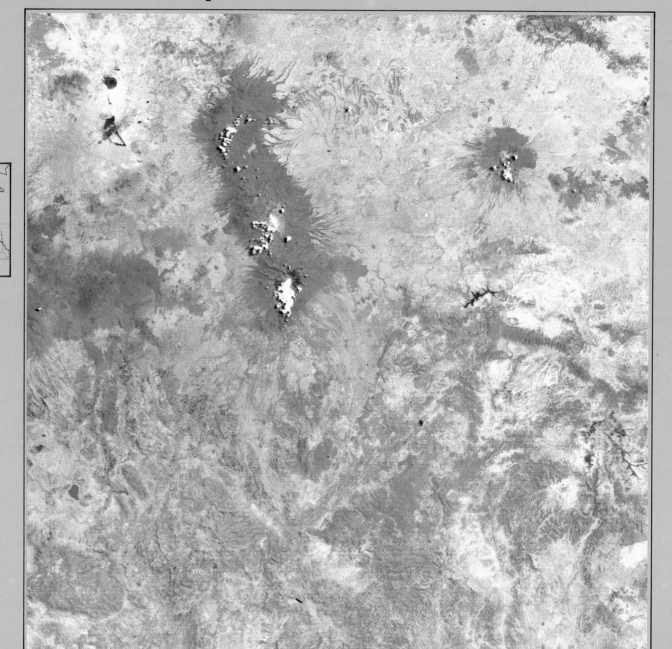

High above the Mesa Central soar the grand volcanoes, Popocatepetl, Iztacihuatl and La Malinche, snow-clad summits atop thickly-forested slopes. To this land of temperate climate and fertile volcanic soils, came the Indians, who farmed the land and founded cities where they settled. The great Aztec civilization originated at Tenochtitlán, by the shores of Lake Texcoco in the Valley of Mexico. Today, as in ancient times, maize and beans are the main crops of the plateau, and the old Aztec city, now called Mexico City, is one of the largest urban areas in the world, with a population of over 10 millions. *(Image taken in May)*

The Bolivian Altiplano

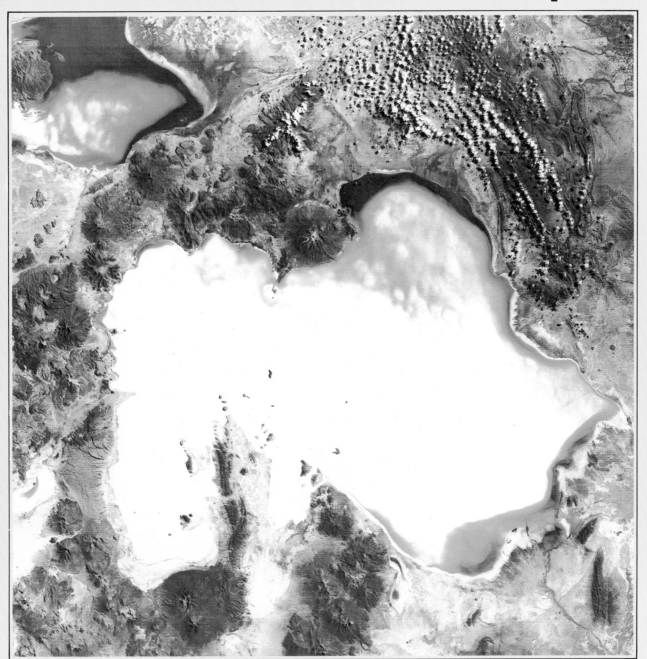

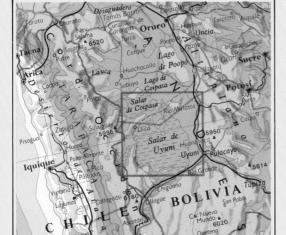

The Altiplano forms a comparatively level plateau at approximately 3000m between the higher peaks of the Andes Mountains, just north of where the Cordillera Occidental meets the Cordillera Oriental. In the centre of this image is the Salar de Uyuni, a vast salt flat fed by mountain streams. The western side of the salt flat is dominated by volcanic cones and lava flows. The environment is arid, remote and inhospitable, though not totally unpopulated – and some cultivation is possible in river valleys protected from the harsh climate. (*Image taken in March*)

Southern Peru

From the Equator to Northern Chile, rivers flowing down the western slopes of the Andes cross a strip of lowland barely 50 km wide, before reaching the Pacific Ocean. This land is desert, one of the driest regions in the World. As the image shows, it is completely unvegetated, apart from the slithers of farmland hugging the streams. Inland, the Western Cordillera of the Andes rises abruptly to over 5000 m, its slopes appearing bright red from a cover of scrub and tussocky grass. Stretching away to the northeast is the rolling upland plateau known as the Altiplano. Between expanses of lighter-grey barren rock above the snowline, lie alpine grass and scrublands, grazed by herds of alpaca and llama. *(Image taken in April)*

Bahía Blanca, Argentina

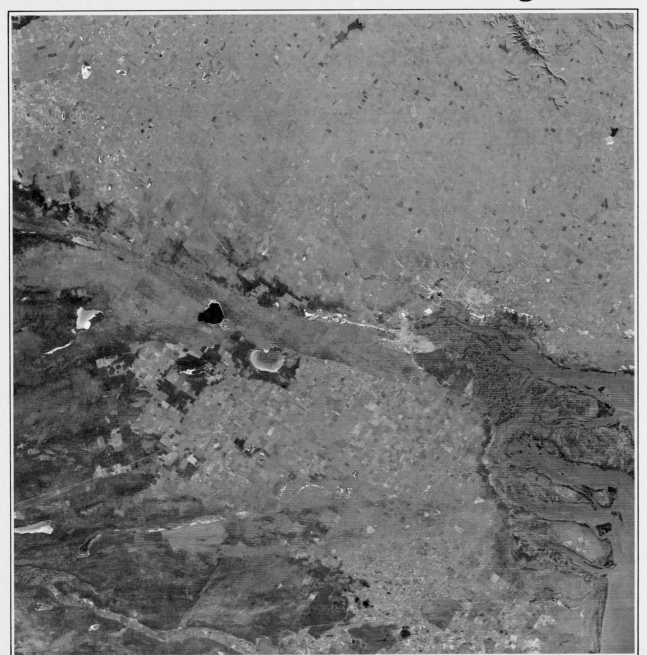

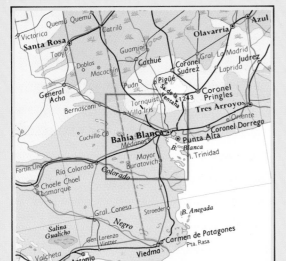

Travelling southwards, Bahía Blanca is the last important town of the fertile, highly-populated Pampas before the dry scrublands of remote Southern Argentina begin. This image captures the transition from one region to another. The north and east, undulating lowlands dotted by small lakes and depressions, is a patchwork of pinks, reds and browns – a reflection of the wide range of crops seen in the fields during their early growing season. To the south and west, there is not enough rainfall to allow cultivation. Watered only by rivers which cross it, the land is left to scrub or occasional livestock ranching where meagre grassland is found. *(Image taken in October)*

Lake Nihuil, Argentina

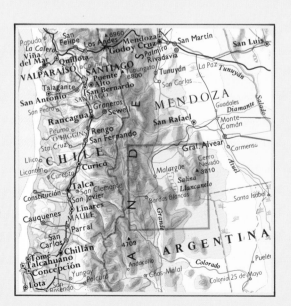

The region surrounding Llancanelo salt lake is a remote part of Argentina. Bleak lowland, broken by volcanic cones and set in the semi-arid rain-shadow of the Andes that tower to the west, it is for the most part uncultivated and uninhabited, largely left to scrub. Vines and fruit-trees grow in the few areas where water is available, close to the banks of the Rio Grande in the south of the image, and where water seeps from beneath a fan of sands and gravels laid down by the Rio Atuel emerging from the mountains. *(Image taken in March)*

GENERAL REFERENCE

Abbreviations of measures used — ft Feet; mm {Millimetres / Millimeters}; cm {Centimetres / Centimeters}; m {Metres / Meters}; Km {Kilometres / Kilometers}; mb Millibars

_ _ _ _ 3386 _ _ _ _ Principal Shipping Routes (Distances in Nautical Miles)

City and Town symbols in order of size

∴ Sites of Archæological or Historical Importance

International Boundaries

International Boundaries (Undemarcated or Undefined)

Internal Boundaries

Principal Roads

Tracks, Seasonal and other Roads

Road Tunnels

Principal Railways

Other Railways

Railways under construction

Railway Tunnels

Principal Canals

Principal Oil Pipelines

✿ Principal Airports

Perennial Streams

Seasonal Streams

Seasonal Lakes, Salt Flats

Swamps, Marshes

Wells in Desert

Permanent Ice

Passes

▲ 8848 Height above sea-level
▼ 8050 Depth below sea-level   } in metres
_1134_ Height of lake-level

CONVERSION SCALE

ft   m
30 000 — 9000
       — 8000
24 000 — 7000
       — 6000
18 000 — 5000
       — 4000
12 000 — 3000
9000   — 2000
6000   — 1000
3000   — 500
Sea-Level 0 — 0 Sea-Level
       — 500
1000   — 1000
       — 2000
2000   — 3000
       — 4000
3000   — 5000
       — 6000
4000   — 7000
       — 8000
5000   — 9000
       — 10 000
6000   — 11 000
       — 12 000
7000
fathoms   m

THE WORLD
Physical
1:150 000 000

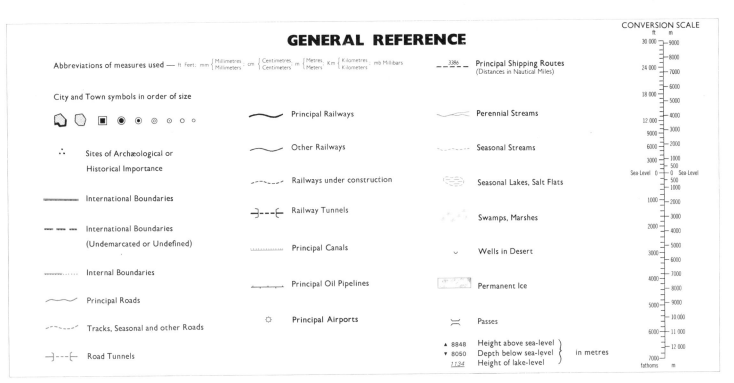

m   4000   2000   200   0   200   2000   4000   m
ft   12 000   6000   600   0   600   6000   12 000   ft

Projection: Hammer Equal Area

Projection: *Hammer Equal Area*

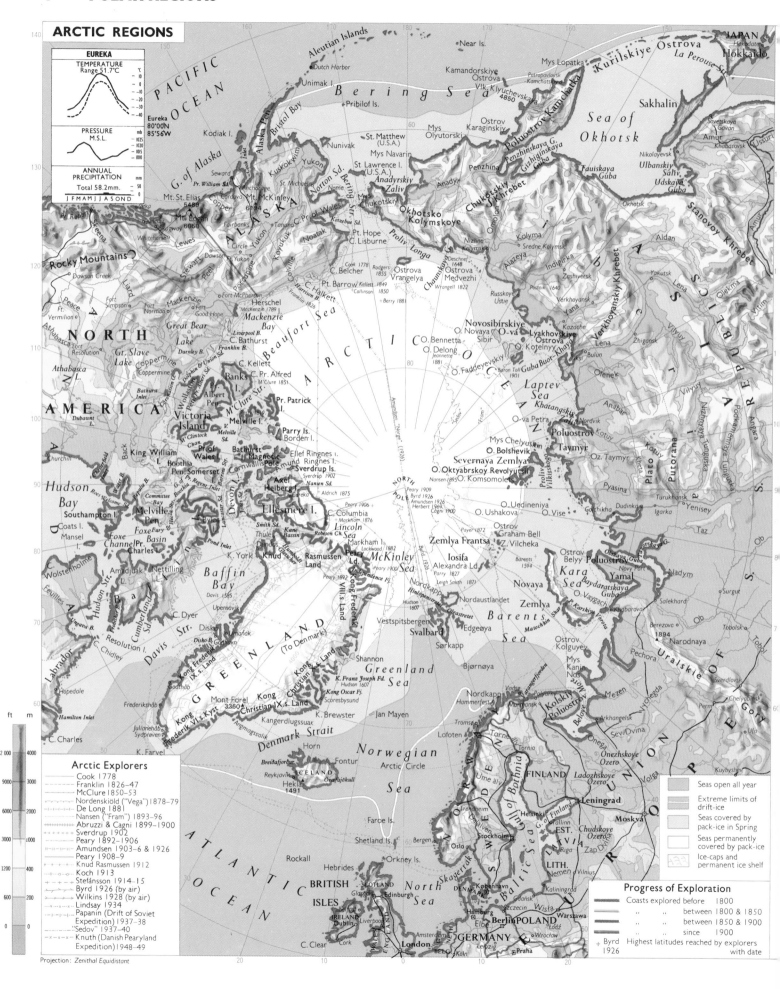

ARCTIC REGIONS

EUREKA
TEMPERATURE
Range 51.7°C

Eureka 80°00'N 85°56'W

PRESSURE
M.S.L.

ANNUAL PRECIPITATION
Total 58.2mm.

J F M A M J J A S O N D

Arctic Explorers

Cook 1778
Franklin 1826–47
McClure 1850–53
Nordenskiöld ("Vega") 1878–79
De Long 1881
Nansen ("Fram") 1893–96
Abruzzi & Cagni 1899–1900
Sverdrup 1902
Peary 1892–1906
Amundsen 1903–6 & 1926
Peary 1908–9
Knud Rasmussen 1912
Koch 1913
Stefánsson 1914–15
Byrd 1926 (by air)
Wilkins 1928 (by air)
Lindsay 1934
Papanin (Drift of Soviet Expedition) 1937–38
"Sedov" 1937–40
Knuth (Danish Pearyland Expedition) 1948–49

Projection: Zenithal Equidistant

Progress of Exploration

Coasts explored before 1800
" " between 1800 & 1850
" " between 1850 & 1900
" " since 1900
+ Byrd 1926 Highest latitudes reached by explorers with date

Seas open all year
Extreme limits of drift-ice
Seas covered by pack-ice in Spring
Seas permanently covered by pack-ice
Ice-caps and permanent ice shelf

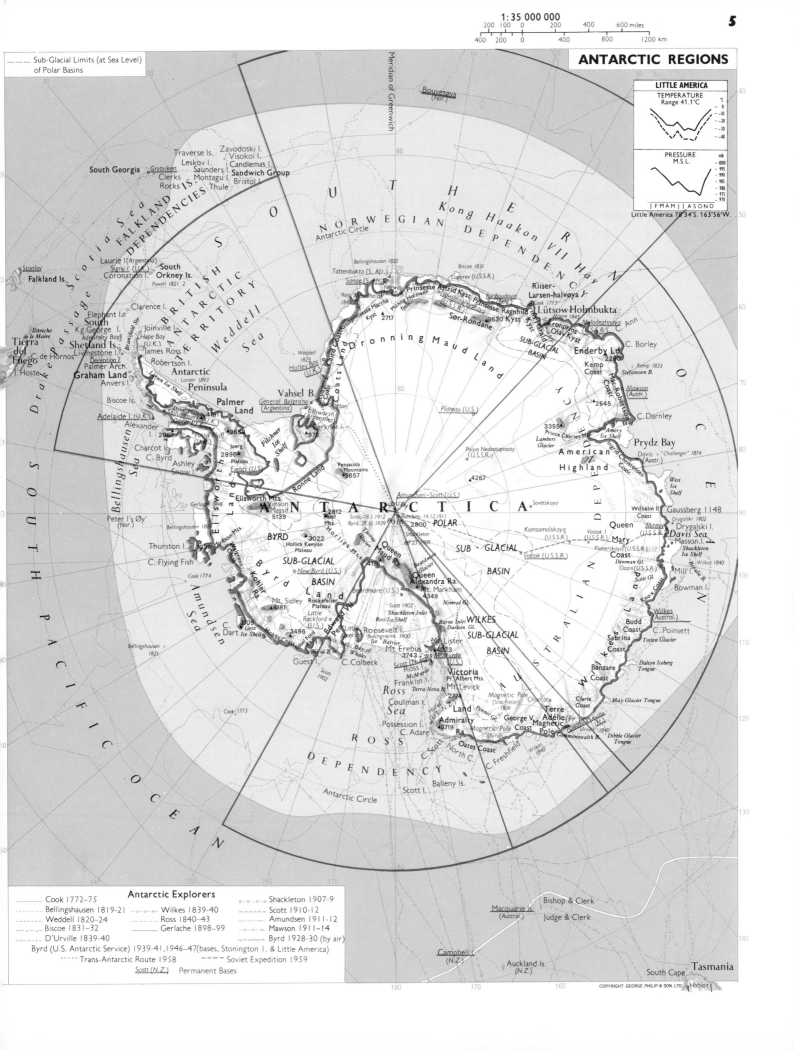

5

ANTARCTIC REGIONS

1 : 35 000 000

LITTLE AMERICA
TEMPERATURE
Range 41.1°C

PRESSURE
M.S.L.

Little America 78°34'S. 163°56'W.

Antarctic Explorers

Cook 1772–75	Shackleton 1907-9
Bellingshausen 1819-21	Wilkes 1839-40	Scott 1910-12
Weddell 1820–24	Ross 1840–43	Amundsen 1911-12
Biscoe 1831–32	Gerlache 1898–99	Mawson 1911–14
D'Urville 1839-40		Byrd 1928-30 (by air)

Byrd (U.S. Antarctic Service) 1939-41,1946-47(bases, Stonington I. & Little America)
Trans-Antarctic Route 1958   Soviet Expedition 1959
Scott (N.Z.)   Permanent Bases

Sub-Glacial Limits (at Sea Level) of Polar Basins

COPYRIGHT. GEORGE PHILIP & SON. LTD.

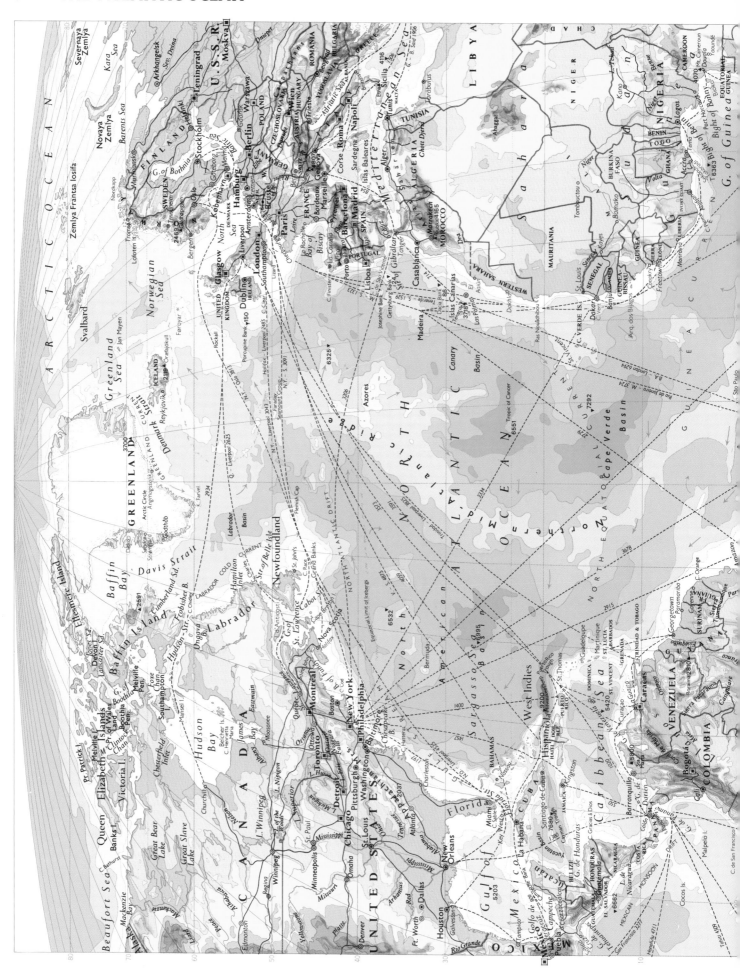

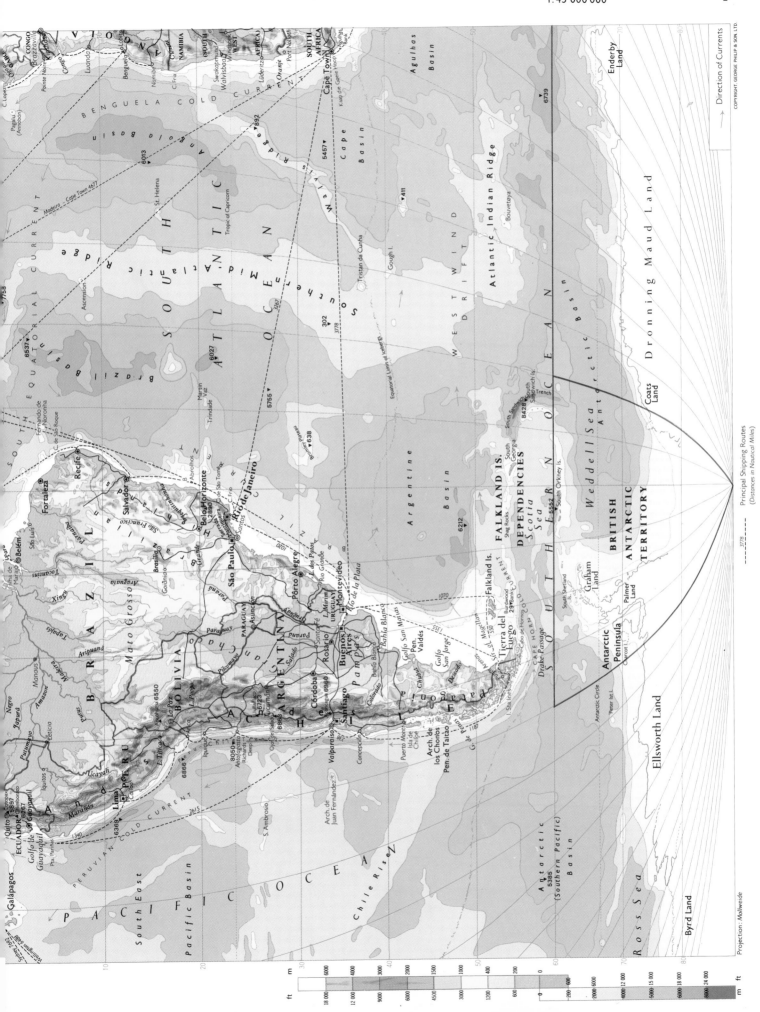

Direction of Currents

COPYRIGHT. GEORGE PHILIP & SON, LTD.

Principal Shipping Routes
(Distances in Nautical Miles)

Projection: Mollweide

PACIFIC OCEAN

Galápagos

ECUADOR
Quito
Guayaquil
Golfo de Guayaquil

PERU
Lima
Callao

Arequipa

BOLIVIA
La Paz
L. Titicaca

CHILE
Antofagasta
Valparaíso
Santiago
Concepción

ARGENTINA
Córdoba
Rosario
Buenos Aires
Bahía Blanca

Arch. de
Juan Fernández

Arch. de
los Chonos
Pen. de Taitao

Tierra del
Fuego
Cabo de Hornos
Drake Passage

B R A Z I L

Recife
Fortaleza
Salvador
Belo Horizonte
Rio de Janeiro
São Paulo
Santos
Pôrto Alegre

URUGUAY
Montevideo
Río de la Plata

PARAGUAY
Asunción

Brasília
Goiânia

Mato Grosso

Amazon

Manaus

S O U T H   A T L A N T I C

O C E A N

St. Helena

Ascension

Tristan da Cunha

Gough I.

FALKLAND IS.
DEPENDENCIES

South Georgia

South Sandwich Is.

South Orkney Is.

South Shetland Is.

Antarctic
Peninsula

Graham
Land

Palmer
Land

BRITISH
ANTARCTIC
TERRITORY

Ellsworth Land

Byrd Land

Ross Sea

CONGO
Brazzaville
Pointe Noire

ANGOLA
Luanda
Benguela

NAMIBIA
(SOUTH WEST
AFRICA)
Walvis Bay
Swakopmund
Lüderitz

SOUTH
AFRICA
Cape Town
Port Nolloth

BENGUELA COLD CURRENT

Angola Basin

Cape Basin

Agulhas
Basin

Mid-Atlantic Ridge

Atlantic Indian Ridge

Dronning Maud Land

Coats
Land

Weddell Sea

S O U T H E R N   O C E A N

Enderby
Land

Antarctic Circle

W E S T   W I N D   D R I F T

Equatorial Limit of Icebergs

Tropic of Capricorn

Brazil Basin

South Equatorial Basin

Peruvian Cold Current

South East Pacific Basin

Chile Rise

Antarctic (Southern Pacific) Basin

Argentine Basin

Scotia Sea

m   ft
18 000   6000
12 000   4000
9000   3000
6000   2000
4500   1500
3000   1000
1200   400
600   200
0   0
200   600
2000   6000
4000   12 000
5000   15 000
6000   18 000
8000   24 000
m   ft

1:17 500 000

100   0   100   200   300   400   500 miles
100   0   200   400   600   800 km

Nordkapp   Nordkinn

Lofoten

L. Inari
Torne älv
Kebnekaise
2123   Lappland

Kanin
Peninsula
Tundra
Kola
Peninsula
d. Pechora
West
Siberian
Plain
Narodnaya
1894
Telpos Iz.
1617
Irtysh
Ob
Tobol

Scandinavia
Indalsälven
Umeälv

White
Sea
Mezen
N. Dvina
Ural   Mountains

Galdhøpiggen
2469

Gulf of Bothnia

Finland

Onega

L. Onega

Oslo
Stockholm
Vänern
Mälaren
Åland Is.
Helsinki
Gulf of Finland
Leningrad
Neva

Lake
Ladoga
Svir
Rybinsk
Res.
Gorkiy
Volga
Kama

Vättern
Gotland

L.
Chudskoye
Valdai
Hills
Volga
Moskva
Oka
Obshchi Syrt
Ural

Kirgiz
Steppe

Skaw
Katte
-gat
København

BALTIC SEA
European
Plain
Dvina
Neman
Vistula
Central
Russian
Uplands
Volga Heights

Elbe
Berlin
Oder
Warszawa
Pripet
Marshes
Pripet
Ukraine
Kiyevo
Dnieper
Don
Tsimlyansk
Res.
Volga

North
Ore
Mts.
Praha
Sudetes
Bohemian Forest
Moravian
Hts.
Tatra
2655
Carpathians
Bug
Dniester
Ust Urt
Plateau
Karagiye Depression
-132

Inn
Wien
Prut
Odessa
Dnieper
Sea of
Azov
Kuban
Caspian
Sea
Kara
Bogaz

Budapest
Bakony Forest
Plain of
Hungary
Drava
Mures
Sava
Transylvanian Alps
Tisza
Mouths
of the
Danube
Crimea
Strait of Kerch
Terek
Caucasus
Elbrus
5633
Baku
-28

Dinaric
Beograd
Danube
Wallachia
Bucureşti
Morava
Black   Sea
Pontine Mts.
Transcaucasia
Kura
Araks

Gran Sasso
2914
Roma
Dalmatia
Dinaric Alps
Adriatic
Sea
Sofiya
Balkans
Rhodope
Istanbul
Bosporus
Balkan
Peninsula
2211
Pindus
Ararat
5165
L. Van
L. Urmia
Elburz Mts.
Tehrān

Strait of Messina
Etna 3263
Sicily
Colabria
C. Spartivento
Ionian
Sea
Ionian Is.
Strt. of
Otranto
Morea
Sea of
Marmara
Aegean
Sea
Dardanelles
Athinai
Anatolia
Ankara
Kizil
L. Tuz
Erciyas
3770
Taurus Mts.
Kurdistan
Mesopotamia
Halab
Euphrates
Tigris
Baghdad

Pantelleria
Malta
5121
C. Matapan
Rhodes
Crete
Cyprus
Bayrut
Syrian   Desert
Tel Aviv-
Yafo
Dead
Sea

MEDITERRANEAN   SEA

Tripoli
Gulf of Sidra
Nile Delta

15   20   25   30   35   40   45

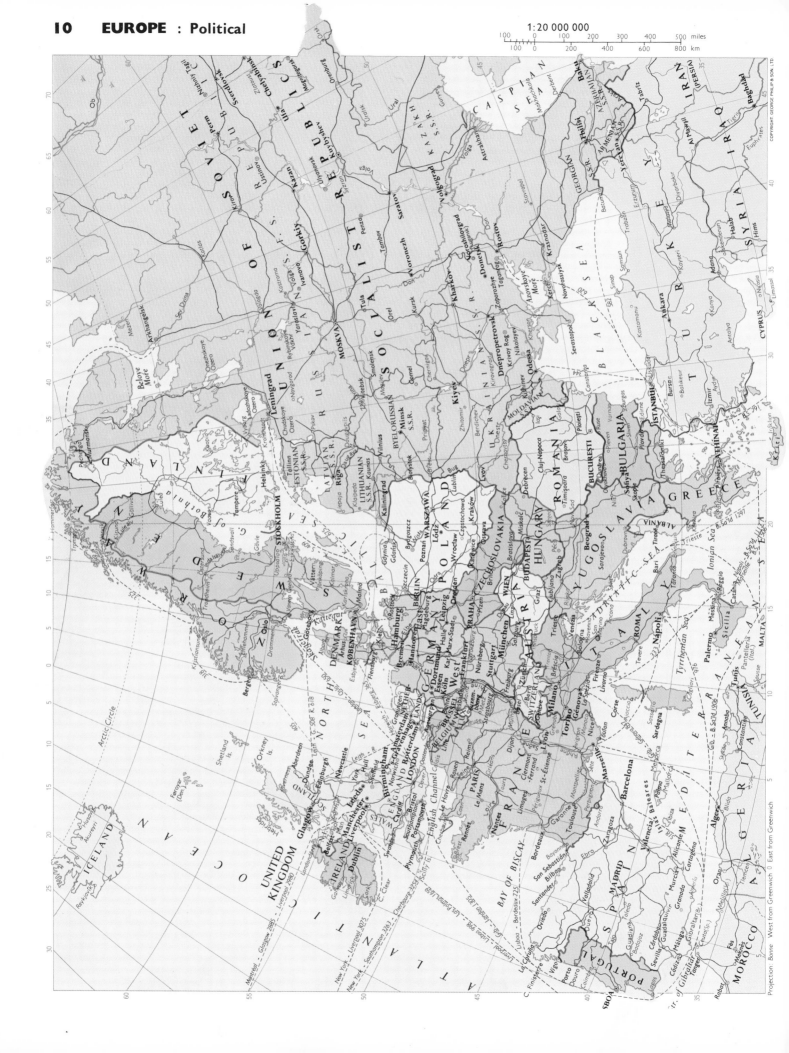

1 : 4 000 000

The DISTRICTS of Northern Ireland have been numbered
and can be identified by reference to this table.

1	Londonderry	14	Craigavon
2	Limavady	15	Armagh
3	Coleraine	16	Newry & Mourne
4	Ballymoney	17	Banbridge
5	Moyle	18	Down
6	Larne	19	Lisburn
7	Ballymena	20	Antrim
8	Magherafelt	21	Newtownabbey
9	Cookstown	22	Carrickfergus
10	Strabane	23	North Down
11	Omagh	24	Ards
12	Fermanagh	25	Castlereagh
13	Dungannon	26	Belfast

1 Merseyside
2 Greater Manchester
3 West Yorkshire
4 South Yorkshire
5 West Glamorgan
6 Mid Glamorgan
7 South Glamorgan

Projection: Conical with two standard parallels

West from Greenwich   East from Greenwich

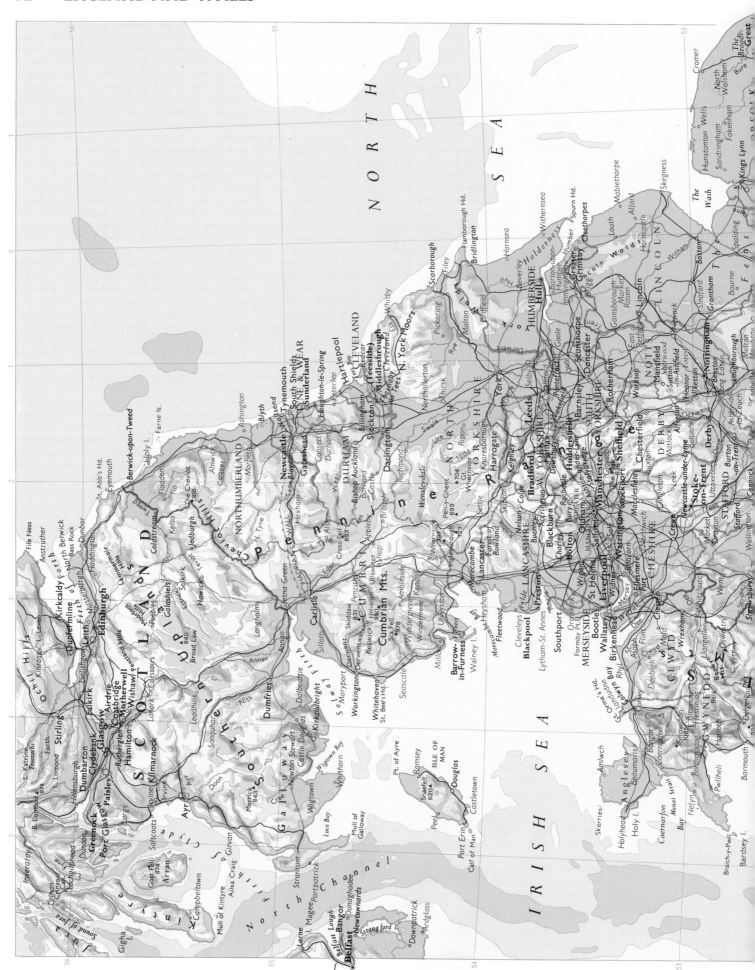

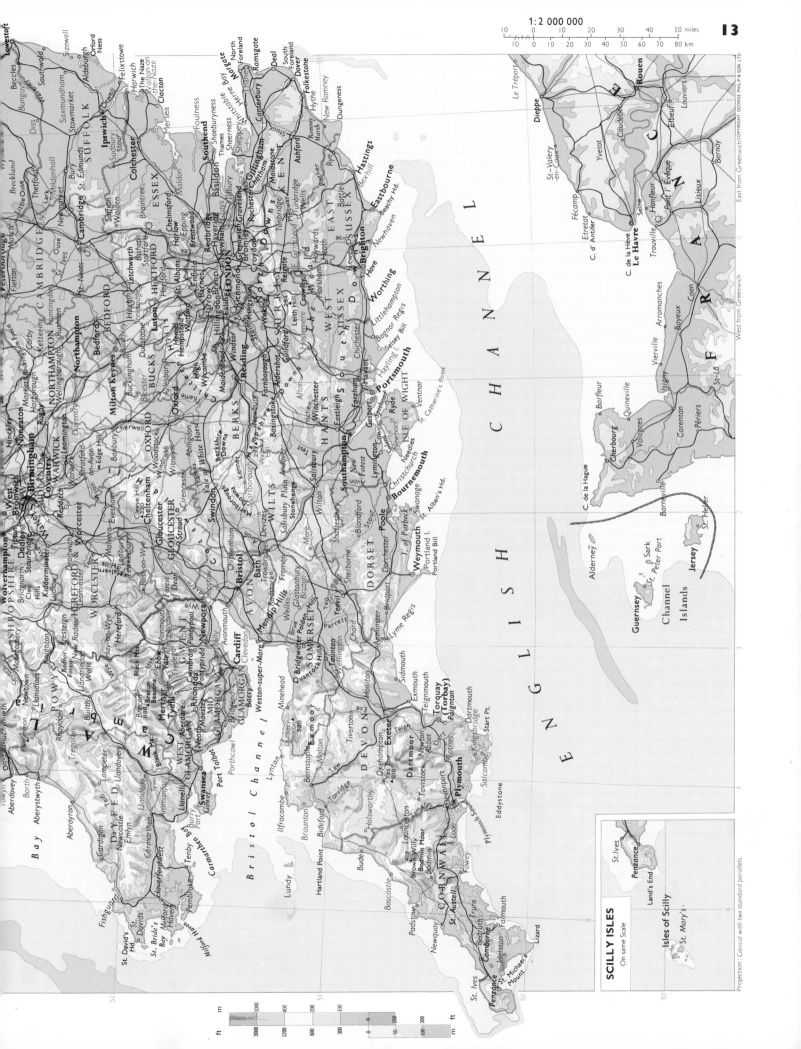

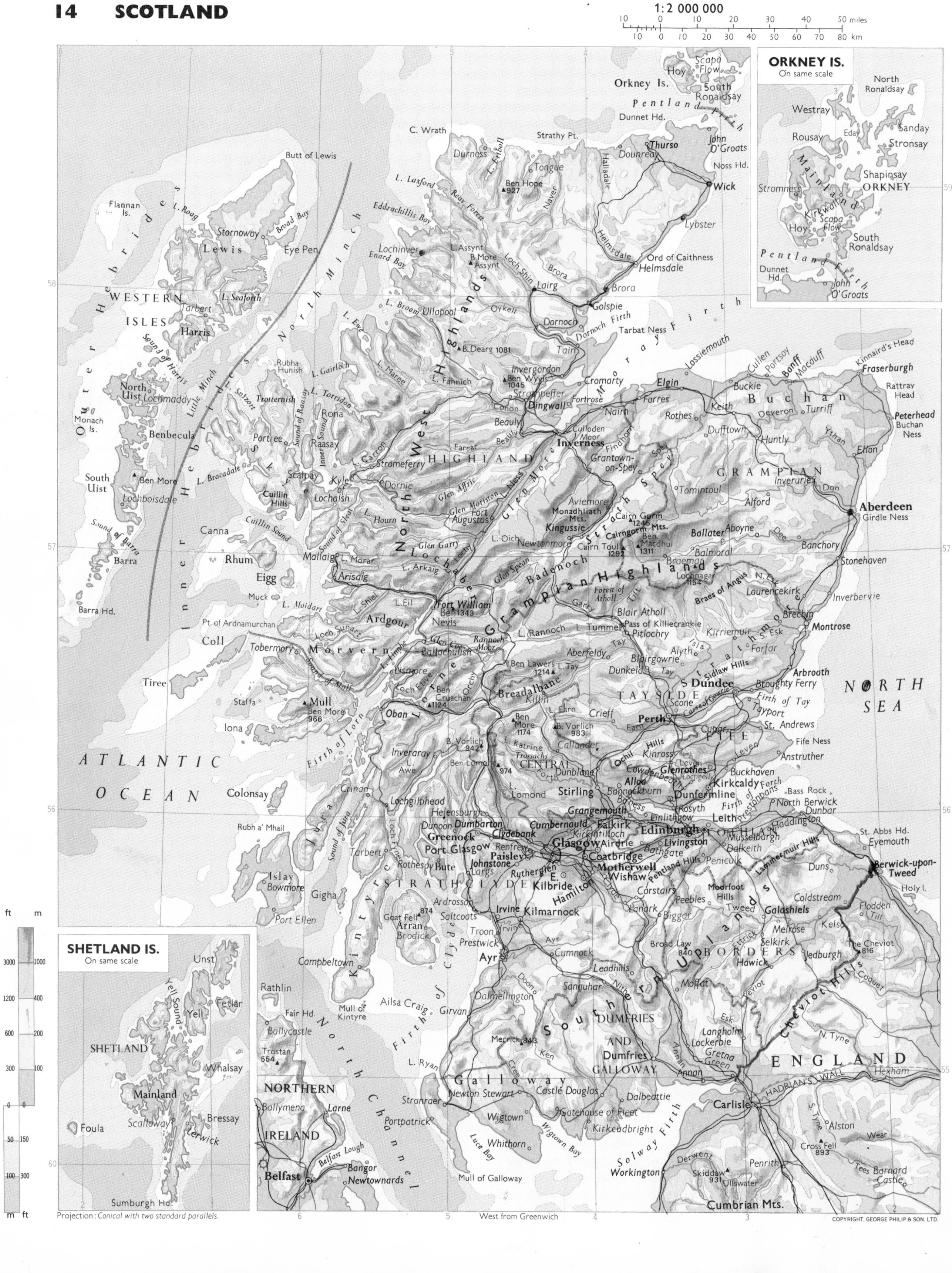

1:2 000 000

10   0   10   20   30   40   50 miles
10   0   10   20   30   40   50   60   70   80 km

ORKNEY IS.
On same scale

North Ronaldsay
Westray
Rousay   Eday   Sanday
Stronsay
Mainland   Shapinsay
Stromness   ORKNEY
Hoy   Scapa   Kirkwall
Flow   South Ronaldsay
Pentland Firth
Dunnet Hd.   John O'Groats

Orkney Is.
Hoy   Scapa Flow   South Ronaldsay
Pentland Firth
Dunnet Hd.   John O'Groats
C. Wrath   Strathy Pt.   Thurso   Dounreay   Noss Hd.   Wick
Durness   L. Fiboll   Tongue   Halladale   Lybster
Ben Hope 927   Naver   Reay Forest   Ord of Caithness
L. Layford   Helmsdale   Helmsdale
Lochinver   Enard Bay   L. Assynt   B. More Assynt   Brora   Brora
L. Shin   Lairg   Golspie
Ullapool   Oykell   Dornoch   Dornoch Firth   Tarbat Ness
L. Broom   B. Dearg 1081   Tain   Moray Firth
Invergordon   Cromarty   Lossiemouth   Cullen   Portsoy
L. Fannich   Ben Wyvis 1045   Elgin   Buckie   Banff   Macduff   Kinnaird's Head   Fraserburgh
Strathpeffer   Dingwall   Fortrose   Nairn   Forres   Keith   Rattray Head
Conon   Beauly   Rothes   Deveron   Turriff   Peterhead   Buchan Ness
Beauly   INVERNESS   Culloden Moor   Findhorn   Dufftown   Huntly   Ython   Ellon
Glen Affric   Grantown-on-Spey   GRAMPIAN   Inverurie   Aberdeen   Girdle Ness
HIGHLAND   Aviemore   Monadhliath Mts.   Cairn Gorm 1245   Alford   Don
Glen Moriston   Fort Augustus   Kingussie   Cairngorm Mts.   Ballater   Aboyne   BANCHORY
Newtonmore   Cairn Toul   Ben Macdhui 1311   Balmoral   Dee   Stonehaven
Glen Garry   L. Oich   Badenoch   Braemar   Lochnagar 1154   Inverbervie
Forest of Atholl   Laurencekirk
Fort William   Ben Nevis 1343   Garry   Blair Atholl   Braes of Angus   Brechin
Ardgour   Glen Coe   L. Rannoch   L. Tummel   Pass of Killiecrankie   Montrose
Ballachulish   Rannoch Moor   Pitlochry   Kirriemuir   Esk
Morvern   Ben Lawers 1214   L. Tay   Aberfeldy   Blairgowrie   Alyth   Forfar   Arbroath
Ben Cruachan 1124   Breadalbane   Killin   Dunkeld   Isla   Sidlaw Hills   Broughty Ferry
Oban   Tay   Scone   DUNDEE   Firth of Tay
Ben More 1174   Crieff   PERTH   Tayport   St. Andrews   Fife Ness
Inveraray   B. Vorlich 942   L. Katrine   Callander   Earn   FIFE   Anstruther
Awe   Ben Lomond 974   Trossachs   CENTRAL   Dunblane   Ochil Hills   Kinross   Leven   Leven   Buckhaven
Lochgilphead   L. Lomond   Stirling   Alloa   Glenrothes   Kirkcaldy   Bass Rock
Helensburgh   Bannockburn   Cowdenbeath   Dunfermline   North Berwick   Dunbar
Dunoon   Dumbarton   Cumbernauld   Falkirk   Rosyth   Leith   Haddington
Greenock   Clydebank   GLASGOW   Airdrie   Linlithgow   EDINBURGH   Musselburgh   St. Abbs Hd.   Eyemouth
Port Glasgow   Paisley   Coatbridge   Livingston   Dalkeith   Duns   Berwick-upon-Tweed
Rothesay   Bute   Johnstone   Rutherglen   Motherwell   Wishaw   Pentland Hills   Penicuik   Lammermuir Hills   Holy I.
Largs   E. Kilbride   Hamilton   Carstairs   Peebles   Moorfoot Hills   Coldstream   Flodden
Ardrossan   Saltcoats   Lanark   Biggar   Tweed   Galashiels   Kelso
Irvine   Kilmarnock   Broad Law 840   Selkirk   Melrose   Jedburgh   The Cheviot 816
Troon   Irvine   BORDERS   Hawick   Coquet
Prestwick   Ayr   Cumnock   Leadhills   Moffat   SOUTHERN UPLANDS   Cheviot Hills
AYR   Doon   Sanquhar   Nith   Esk   Langholm   N. Tyne
Dalmellington   Merrick 843   Ken   Leadhills   DUMFRIES   Lockerbie   Gretna Green   ENGLAND   Hexham
Girvan   Ailsa Craig   DUMFRIES AND GALLOWAY   Annan   Gretna   HADRIAN'S WALL
Stranraer   Newton Stewart   Castle Douglas   Dalbeattie   Carlisle   S. Tyne   Alston
Portpatrick   Wigtown   Gatehouse of Fleet   Kirkcudbright   Wear
L. Ryan   Whithorn   Wigtown Bay   Solway Firth   Cross Fell 893   Penrith
Luce Bay   Workington   Derwent   Skiddaw 931   Ullswater   Tees   Barnard Castle
Mull of Galloway   Cumbrian Mts.

WESTERN ISLES
Butt of Lewis   Flannan Is.   L. Roag   Broad Bay
Lewis   Stornoway   Eye Pen.
Tarbert   L. Seaforth
Harris   Sound of Harris
North Uist   Lochmaddy   Rubha Hunish   Trotternish
Monach Is.   Benbecula   L. Gairloch   L. Torridon
South Uist   Lochboisdale   Ben More   L. Bracadale   Raasay
Sound of Barra   Barra   Cuillin Hills   Kyle of Lochalsh
Barra Hd.   Canna   Cuillin Sound   Sound of Sleat
Rhum   Eigg   L. Morar   Arisaig
Muck   Pt. of Ardnamurchan   L. Moidart   Shiel   L. Eil
Coll   Tobermory   Sound of Mull   MORVERN
Tiree   Staffa   Mull   Ben More 966   L. Etive
Iona   Firth of Lorn
Colonsay
Inner Hebrides
North Minch
Little Minch
Outer Hebrides

NORTH WEST HIGHLANDS
Strome ferry   Dornie
Stromeferry   Portree   Scalpay   Rona
Kyle of Lochalsh   Glen Fort   Augustus   LOCHABER
Mallaig   L. Arkaig   Glen Spean   GRAMPIAN HIGHLANDS

ATLANTIC OCEAN
Rubh' a' Mhail   Colonsay
Crinan   Kintyre   STRATHCLYDE
Jura   Sound of Jura   Firth of Clyde
Islay   Gigha   Goat Fell 874   Arran   Brodick
Bowmore   Campbeltown   Mull of Kintyre
Port Ellen   Ailsa Craig   North Channel

NORTH SEA

SHETLAND IS.
On same scale
Unst
Fetlar
Yell   Yell Sound   Whalsay
SHETLAND   Mainland   Bressay
Foula   Scalloway   Lerwick
Sumburgh Hd.

Rathlin   Fair Hd.   Mull of Kintyre
Ballycastle   Trostan 554
NORTHERN   Ballymena   Larne
IRELAND   Bangor   Newtownards
Belfast   Belfast Lough

ft   m
3000   1000
1200   400
600   200
300   100
0   0
50   150
100   300
m   ft

Projection: Conical with two standard parallels.

West from Greenwich

COPYRIGHT. GEORGE PHILIP & SON LTD.

1:2 000 000

10   0   10   20   30   40   50 miles
10 0 10 20 30 40 50 60 70 80 km

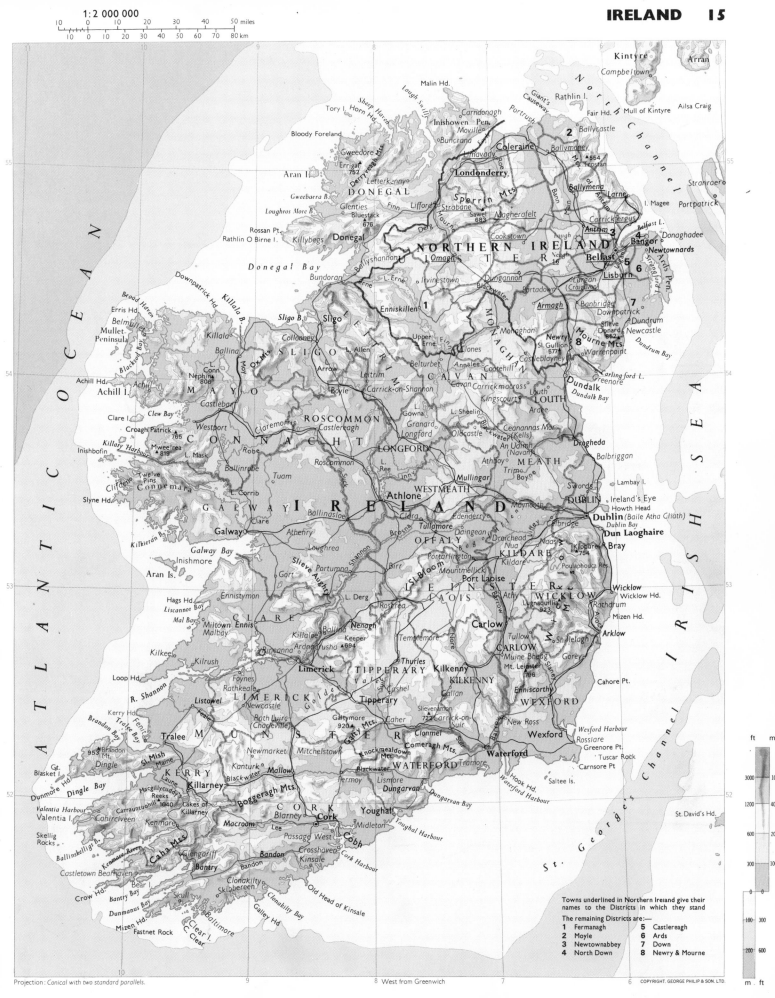

Towns underlined in Northern Ireland give their
names to the Districts in which they stand
The remaining Districts are:—

1 Fermanagh   5 Castlereagh
2 Moyle   6 Ards
3 Newtownabbey   7 Down
4 North Down   8 Newry & Mourne

Projection: Conical with two standard parallels.

West from Greenwich

COPYRIGHT. GEORGE PHILIP & SON. LTD.

1:2 500 000

10   0   10   20   30   40   50 miles
10   0   10   20   30   40   50   60   70   80 km

NORTH

SEA

ENGLAND

WADDENEILANDEN

Terschelling   Ameland   Schiermonnikoog

OSTFRIESISCHE INSELN
Spiekeroog   Wangerooge   Scharhörn
Langeoog   Norderney   Baltrum   Juist   Neuwerk
Borkum

Scharhörn
Neuwerk

Wadden Zee

NETHERLANDS

FRIESLAND   DRENTHE   OVERIJSEL   GELDERLAND

Groningen   Oldenburg   Bremerhaven   Wilhelmshaven

Leeuwarden

Den Helder   Texel   Vlieland

IJsselmeer

AMSTERDAM
Haarlem
Leiden
'sGRAVENHAGE
(The Hague)
Delft
ROTTERDAM
Dordrecht

Utrecht
Arnhem
Nijmegen

GERMANY

Osnabrück
Münster
Dortmund
ESSEN
DUISBURG
DÜSSELDORF
KÖLN
(Cologne)
Bonn

BELGIUM

Antwerpen
BRUSSEL
(Bruxelles)
Gent (Gand)
Brugge
(Bruges)
Oostende
(Ostend)

Maastricht
Liège
Namur

LUXEMBOURG
Luxembourg

Dover
Calais
Dunkerque
Boulogne-sur-Mer

FRANCE

Lille
Roubaix
Amiens
Reims
PARIS
Versailles
Metz
Nancy
Strasbourg

ARDENNES

CHAMPAGNE

SAARLAND
Saarbrücken
Wiesbaden
Mainz

Projection: Conical with two standard parallels

East from Greenwich

COPYRIGHT. GEORGE PHILIP & SON. LTD

ft   m
1200   400
600   200
0
50   150
m   ft

1:5 000 000

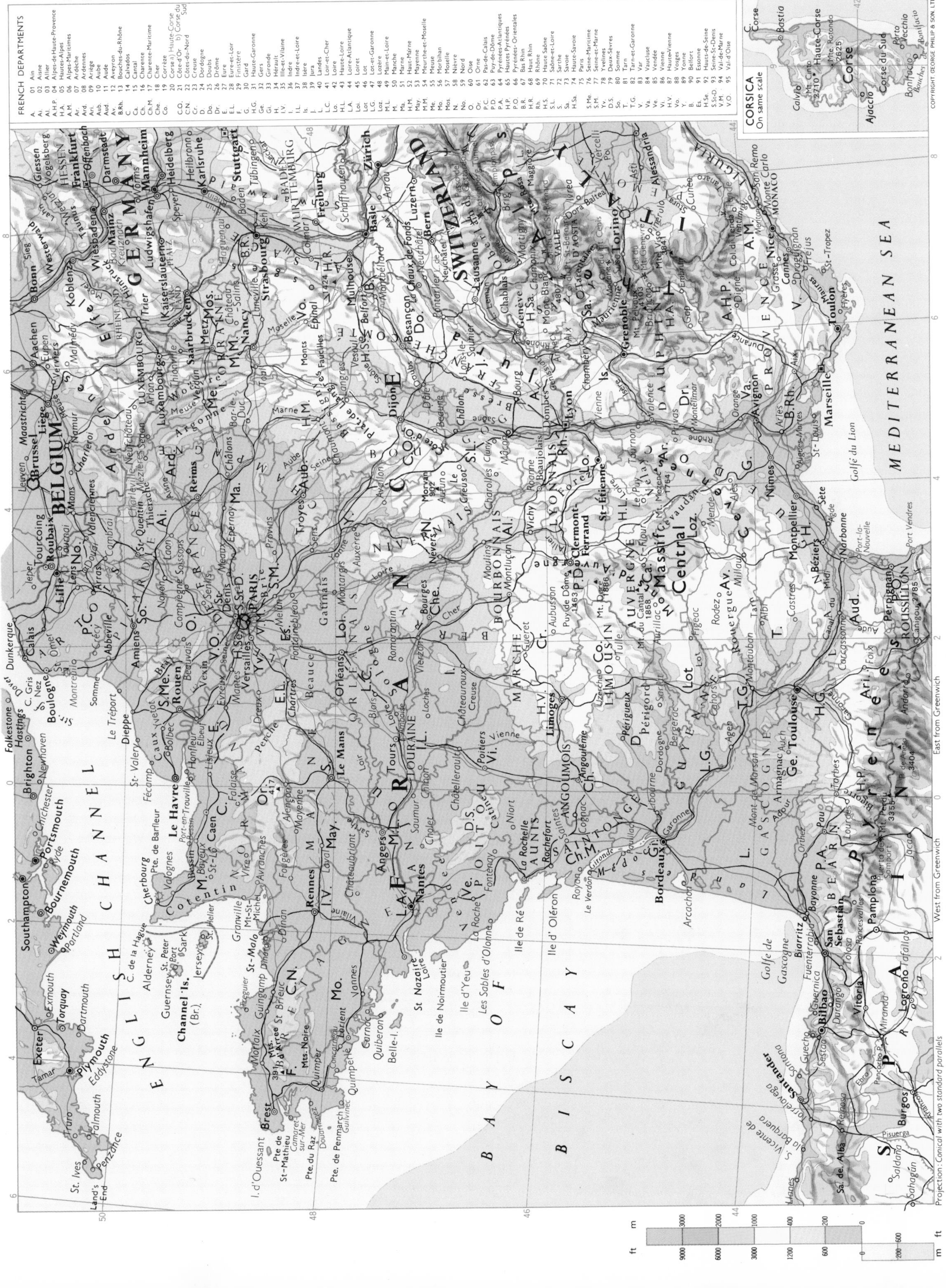

20 10 0 20 40 60 80 100 miles
40 20 0 40 80 120 160 km

FRENCH DEPARTMENTS

A.	01	Ain		
Ai.	02	Aisne		
A.H.P.	03	Alpes-de-Haute-Provence		
H.A.	04	Hautes-Alpes		
A.M.	05	Alpes-Maritimes		
Ard.	06	Ardèche		
Art.	07	Ardennes		
Arg.	08	Ariège		
Aud.	09	Aude		
	10	Aveyron		
B.Rh.	11	Bouches-du-Rhône		
Ch.	12	Calvados		
Ch.M.	13	Cantal		
Ct.	14	Charente		
Che.	15	Charente-Maritime		
	16	Cher		
C.O.	17	Corrèze		
	18	a) Haute-Corse b) Corse du Sud		
C.N.	19	Côtes-du-Nord		
	20	Côte-d'Or		
Cr.	21	Creuse		
D.	22	Dordogne		
Dr.	23	Doubs		
E.	24	Drôme		
E.L.	25	Eure		
Es.	26	Eure-et-Loir		
	27	Finistère		
G.	28	Gard		
H.G.	29	Haute-Garonne		
Ge.	30	Gers		
Gi.	31	Gironde		
H.	32	Hérault		
I.V.	33	Ille-et-Vilaine		
I.	34	Indre		
I.L.	35	Indre-et-Loire		
Is.	36	Isère		
Ju.	37	Jura		
L.	38	Landes		
L.C.	39	Loir-et-Cher		
Lo.	40	Loire		
H.L.	41	Haute-Loire		
Lo.A.	42	Loire-Atlantique		
Loi.	43	Loiret		
Lot	44	Lot		
L.G.	45	Lot-et-Garonne		
Loz.	46	Lozère		
M.L.	47	Maine-et-Loire		
Ma.	48	Manche		
M.	49	Marne		
H.M.	50	Haute-Marne		
May.	51	Mayenne		
M.M.	52	Meurthe-et-Moselle		
Me.	53	Meuse		
Mo.	54	Morbihan		
Mos.	55	Moselle		
N.	56	Nièvre		
No.	57	Nord		
O.	58	Oise		
Or.	59	Orne		
P.C.	60	Pas-de-Calais		
P.D.	61	Puy-de-Dôme		
P.A.	62	Pyrénées-Atlantiques		
H.P.	63	Hautes Pyrénées		
P.O.	64	Pyrénées-Orientales		
B.R.	65	Bas-Rhin		
H.R.	66	Haut-Rhin		
Rh.	67	Rhône		
S.	68	Haute-Saône		
S.	69	Saône-et-Loire		
Sr.	70	Sarthe		
H.Sa.	71	Haute-Savoie		
	72	Savoie		
S.	73	Paris		
S.M.	74	Seine-Maritime		
S.M.	75	Seine-et-Marne		
Y.	76	Yvelines		
D.S.	77	Deux-Sèvres		
So.	78	Somme		
T.	79	Tarn		
T.G.	80	Tarn-et-Garonne		
Va.	81	Var		
Vs.	82	Vaucluse		
Ve.	83	Vendée		
Vi.	84	Vienne		
H.V.	85	Haute-Vienne		
Vo.	86	Vosges		
Y.	87	Yonne		
T.B.	88	Belfort		
Es.	89	Essonne		
H.Se.	90	Hauts-de-Seine		
S.Sr.D.	91	Seine-St-Denis		
V.M.	92	Val-de-Marne		
V.O.	93	Val-d'Oise		

CORSICA
On same scale

CORSE

MEDITERRANEAN SEA

ENGLISH CHANNEL

BAY OF BISCAY

BELGIUM

GERMANY

SWITZERLAND

ITALY

SPAIN

Projection: Conical with two standard parallels

COPYRIGHT GEORGE PHILIP & SON LTD.

Projection: Conical with two standard parallels

West from Greenwich   0   East from Greenwich

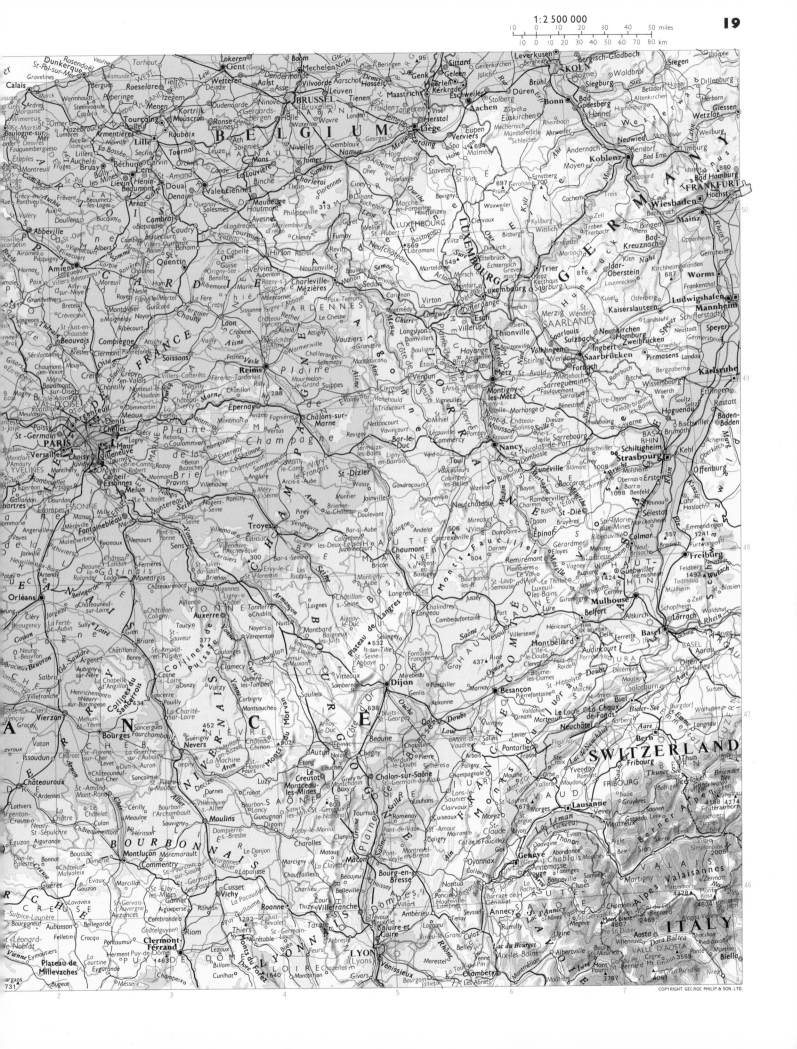

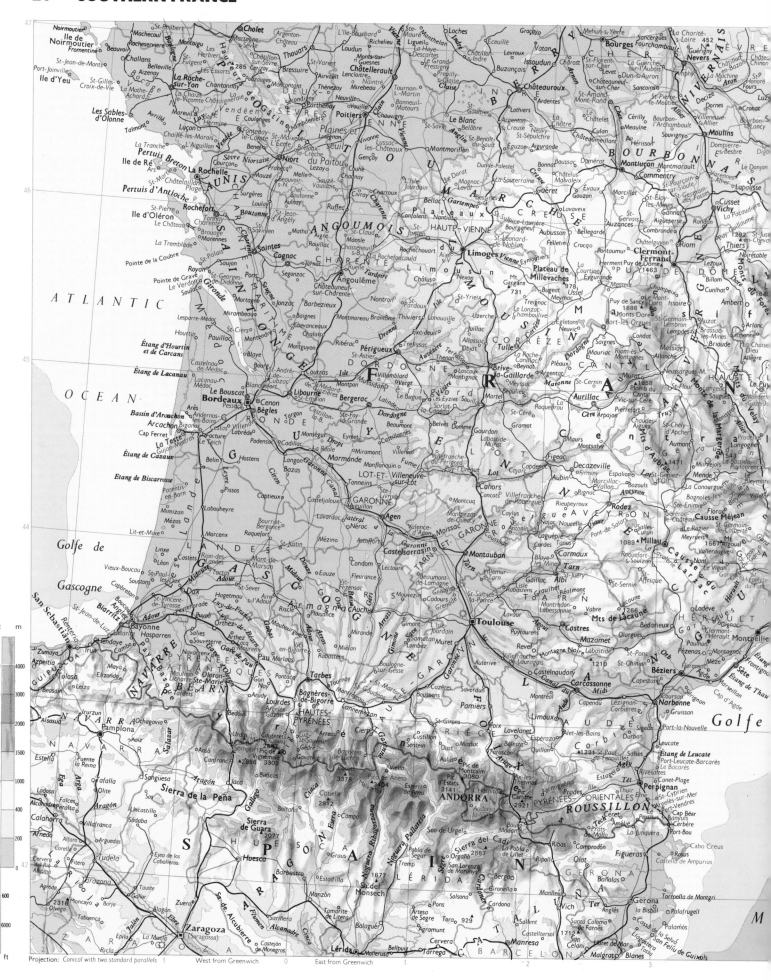

1:2 500 000

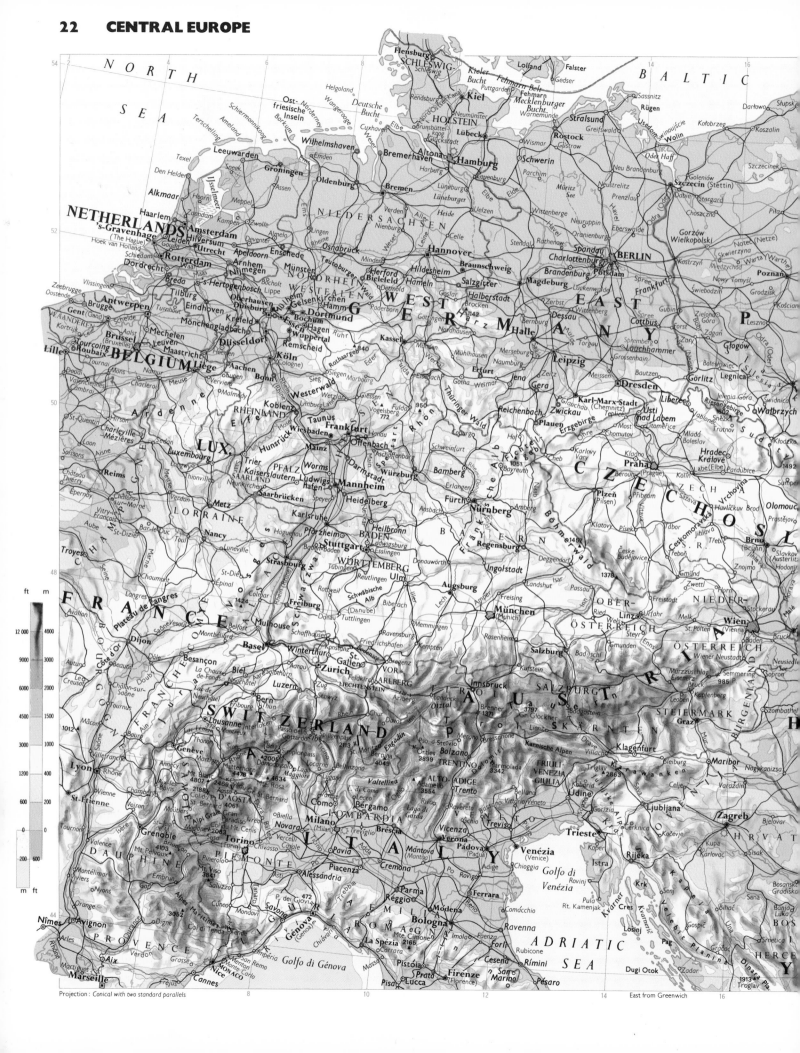

Projection: Conical with two standard parallels

East from Greenwich

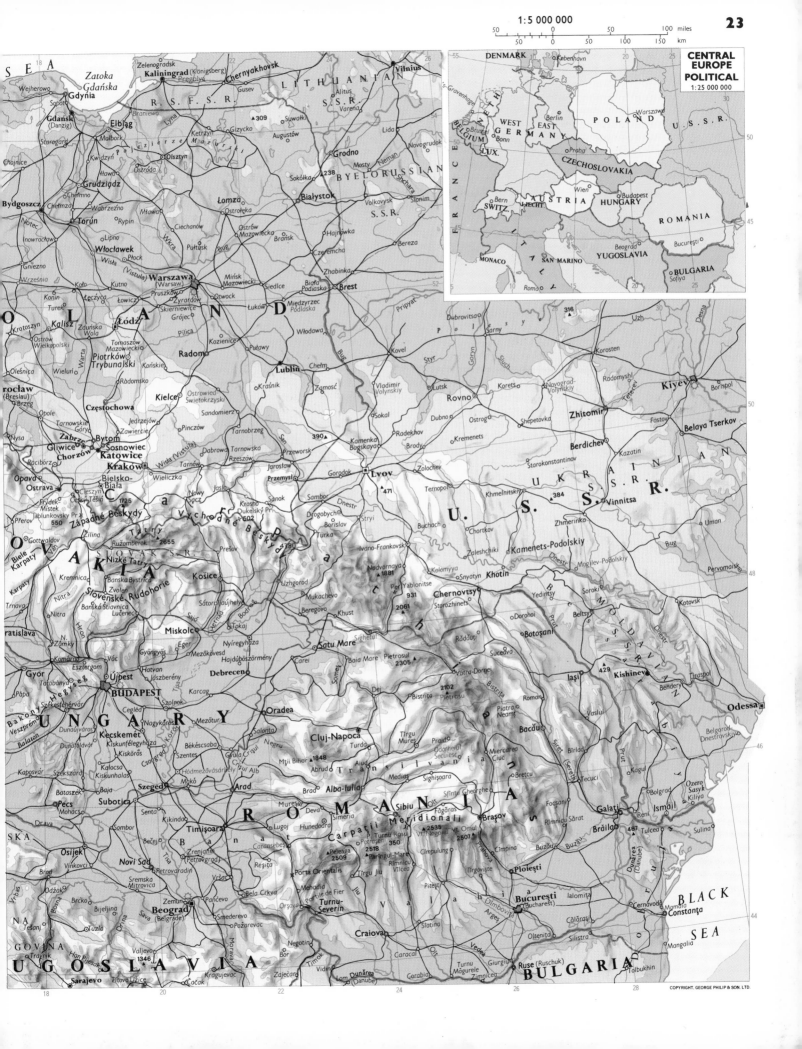

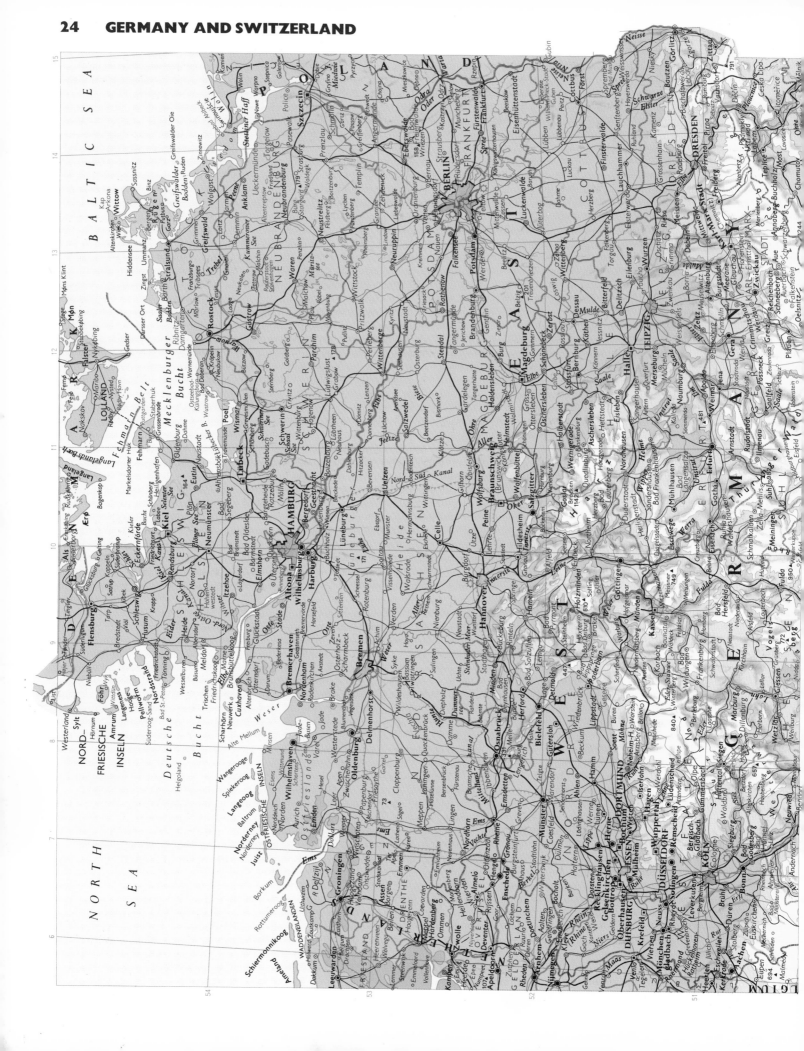

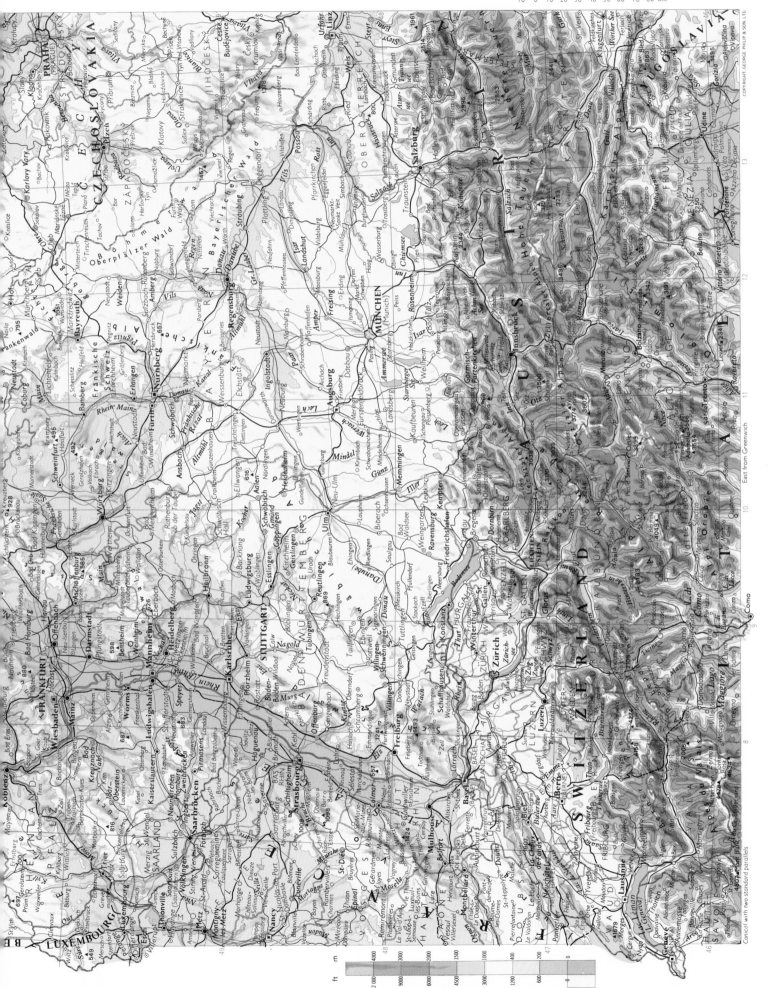

Projection: Conical with two standard parallels

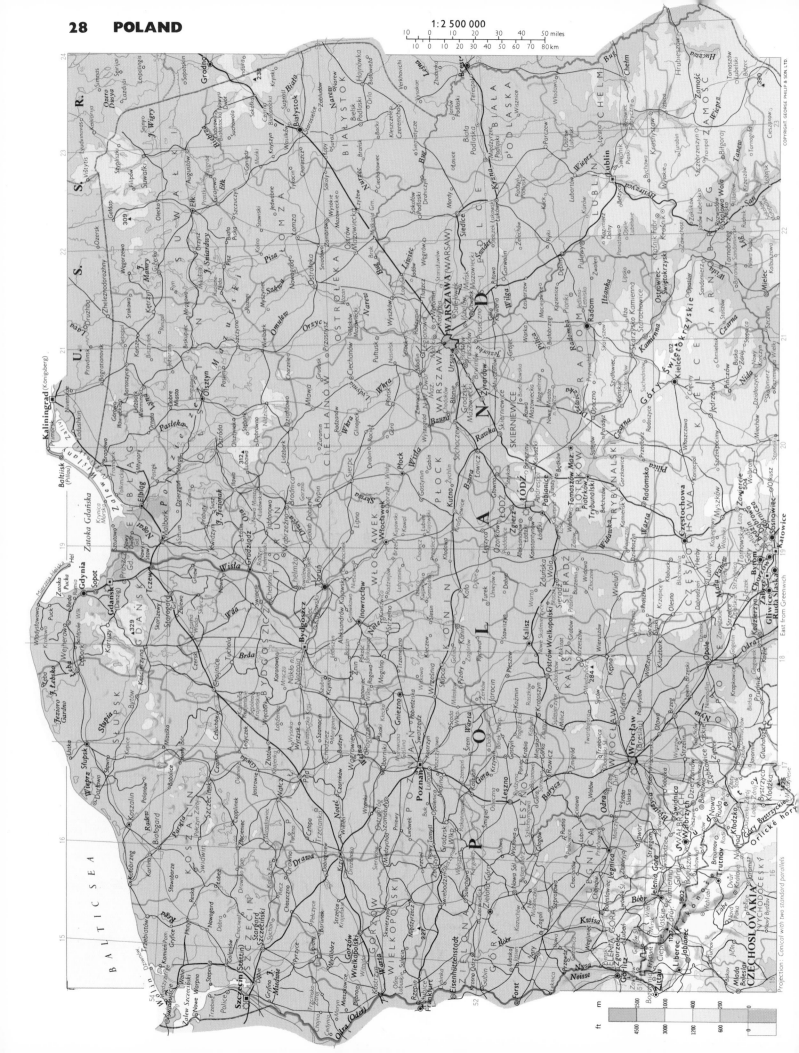

1:2 500 000

Projection: Conical with two standard parallels

East from Greenwich

1:5 000 000

Projection: Conical with two standard parallels

1:2 500 000

MEDITERRANEAN

SEA

MOROCCO

Golfo de Cádiz

Golfo de Almería

Projection : Conical with two standard parallels

COPYRIGHT, GEORGE PHILIP & SON, LTD.

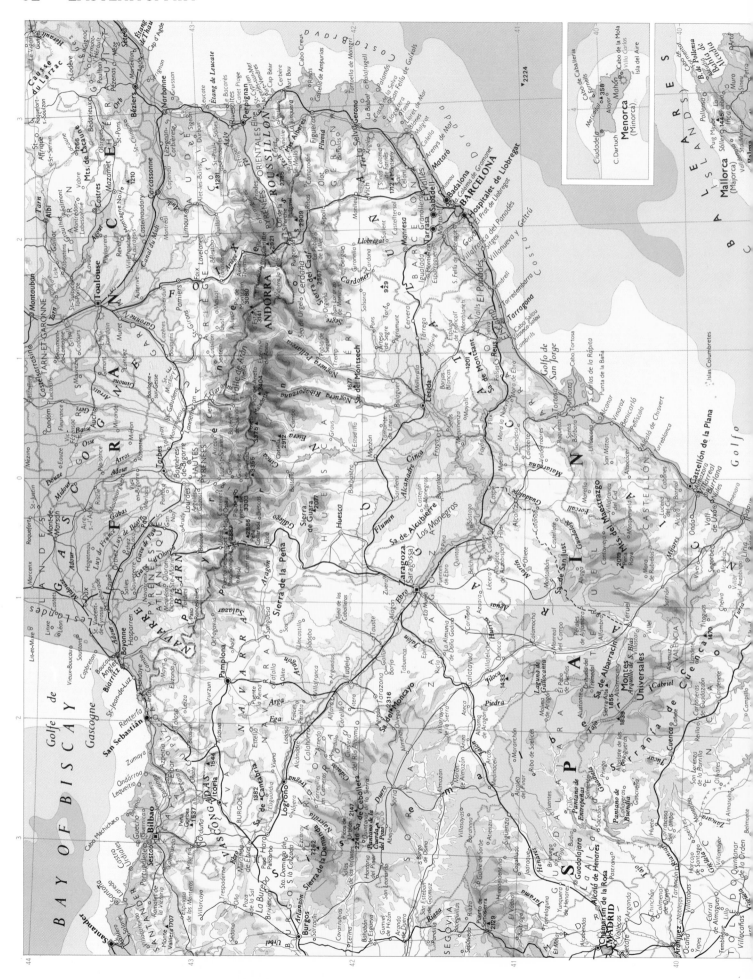

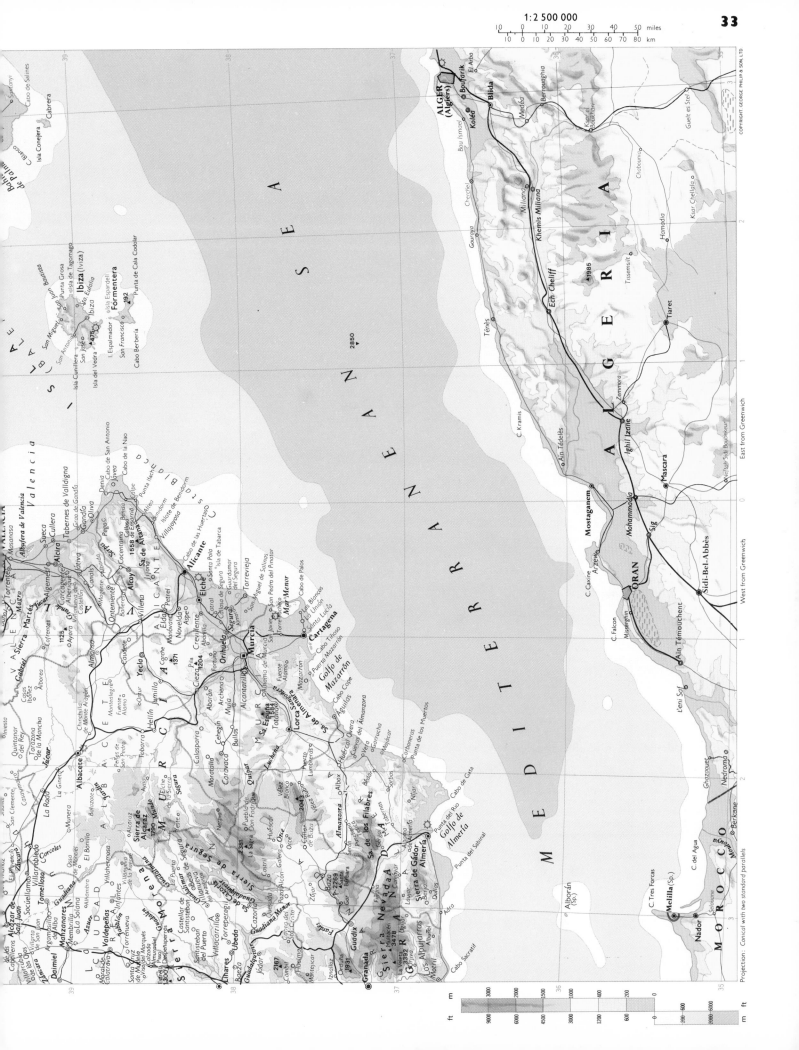

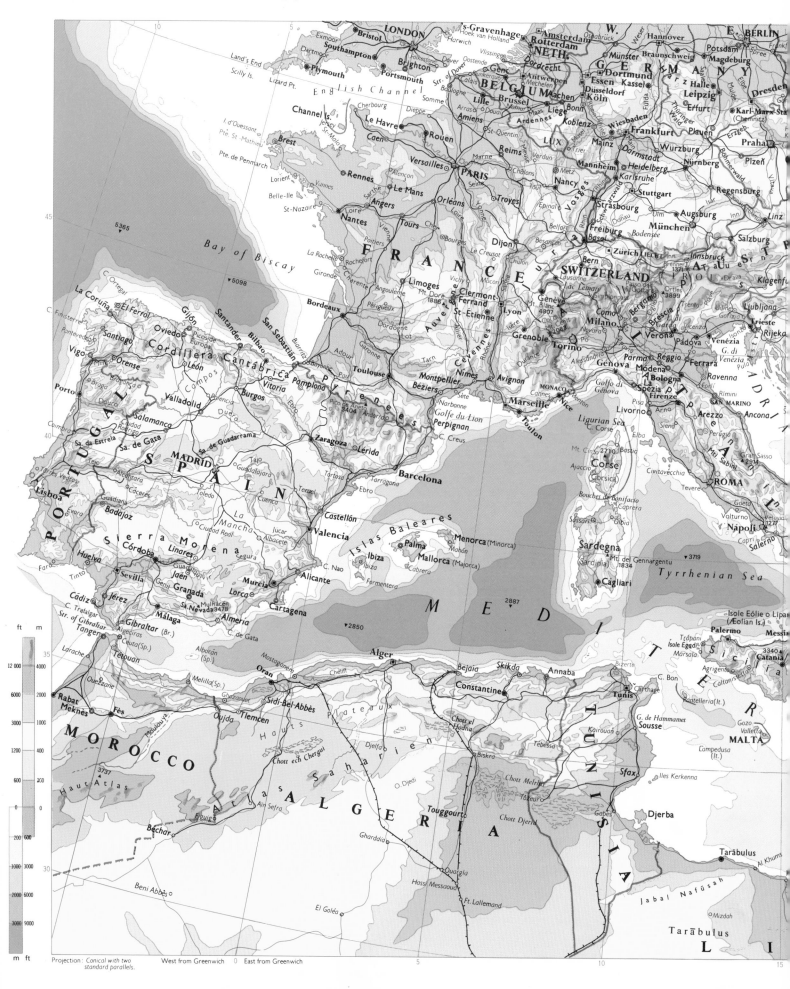

Projection: Conical with two
standard parallels.

West from Greenwich   0   East from Greenwich

S.E. EUROPE
POLITICAL
1:25 000 000

MALTA
1:1 000 000

Projection: Conical with two standard parallels

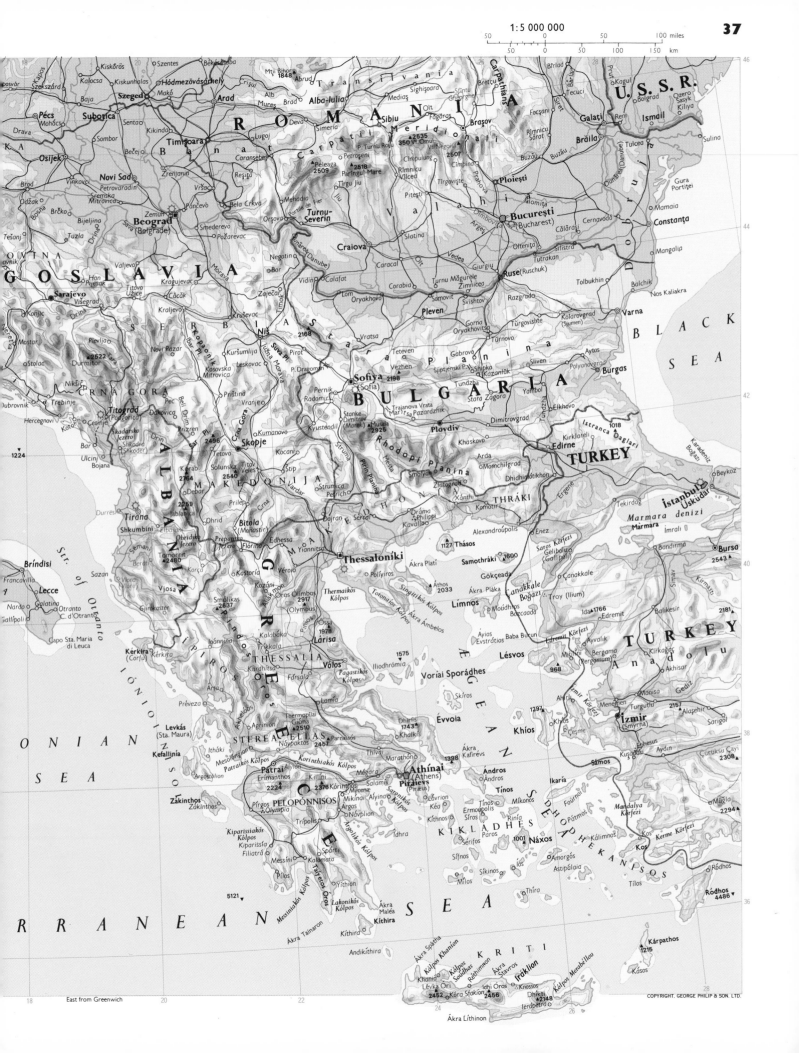

East from Greenwich

Projection: Conical with two standard parallels

East from Greenwich

1:2 500 000

ADRIATIC

SEA

ALBANIA

IONIAN

SEA

MEDITERRANEAN SEA

Golfo di
Táranto

Strait of Otranto

BASILICATA

CALABRIA

SICILIA

Isole Eólie o Lípari (Æolian Is.)

Golfo di
Sant'Eufémia

Golfo di Squillace

G. di Manfredónia

G. di Salerno

G. di
Policastro

G. di Gióia

Kérkira
(Corfu)

1 : 2 500 000

Projection: Conical with two standard parallels

East from Greenwich

Continuation Eastwards on same scale

AEGEAN SEA

SEA OF CRETE (Sea of Candia)

IONIAN SEA

CYCLADES (KIKLÁDHES)

ARKHIPÉLAGOS

DODECANESE (DHODHEKÁNISOS)

KRÍTI (CRETE)

ÍLLAS

PELOPÓNNISOS

AKARNANÍA

AITOLÍA

Khíos (Chios)

Psará

Ikaría

Mikonos

Tínos

Ándros

Náxos

Páros

Síros

Sífnos

Sérifos

Kíthnos

Kéa

Mílos

Íos

Thíra

Skíros

Skópelos

ATHÍNAI (ATHENS)

Piraiévs (Piraeus)

Khalkís (Chalcis)

Thívai (Thebes)

Kórinthos (Corinth)

Corinth Canal

Korinthiakós Kólpos

Saronikós Kólpos

Argolikós Kólpos

Lakonikós Kólpos

Messiniakós Kólpos

Kiparissiakós Kólpos

Pátrai

Pátraikós Kólpos

Taïyetos Oros

Párnon Oros

Spárti (Sparta)

Kalámai

Kíthira (Cerigo)

Ákra Maléa

Ákra Taínaron

Levkás (Santa Maura)

Kefallinía (Cephalonia)

Itháki (Ithaca)

Zákinthos (Zante)

Préveza

Agrínion

Mesolóngion

Amaliás

Pírgos

Trípolis

Megalópolis

Návplion

 Náfplion

Astipálaia

Amorgós

Ródhos (Rhodes)

Kárpathos

Stenón Kárpathos

Kos

Sámos

Kuşadasi Körfezi

Bafa Gölü

Marmaris

Kerme Körfezi

Milétus

Ephesus

Bodrum (Halicarnassus)

Samsun Dağı

TURKEY (TÜRKIYE)

Stenón Kásos

m ft
9000 6000
6000 4500
3000 2000
1500
1000
600
400
200
0

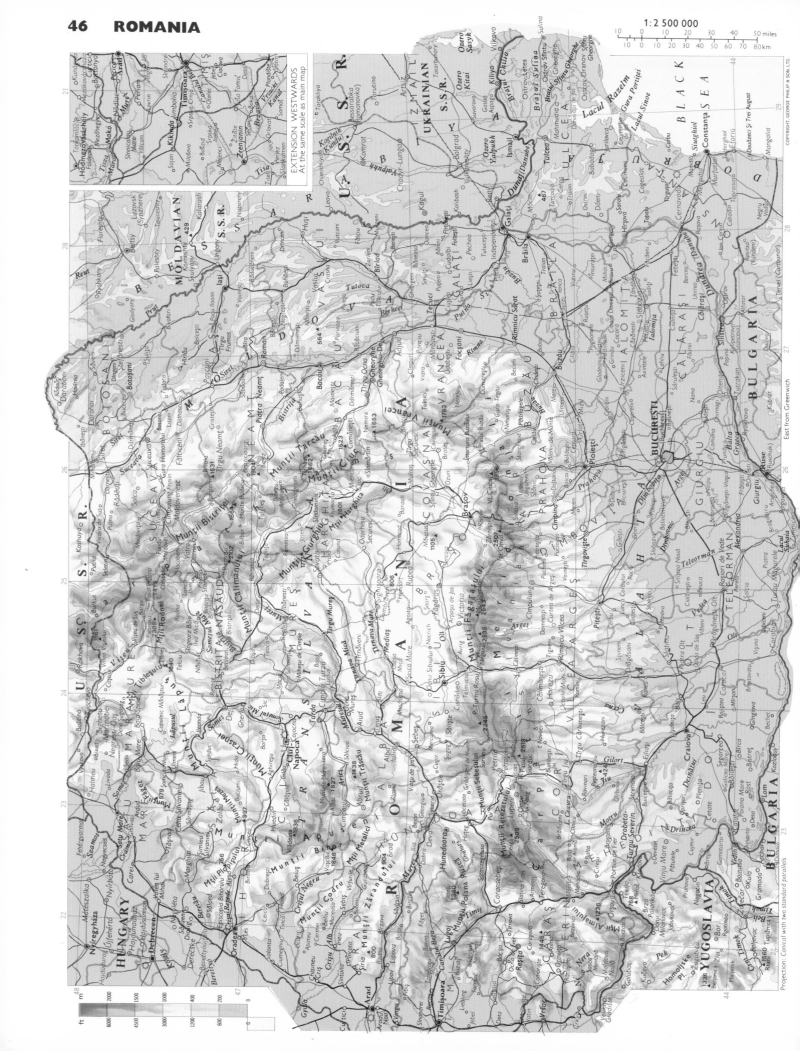

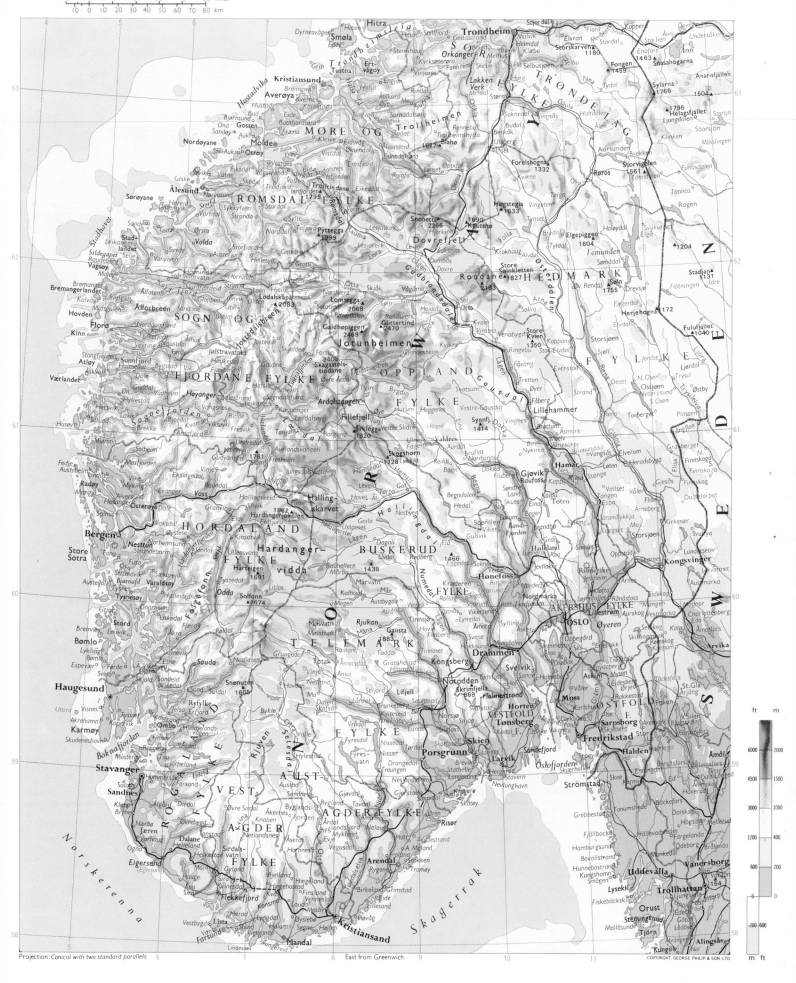

1:2 500 000

Projection: Conical with two standard parallels   East from Greenwich   COPYRIGHT GEORGE PHILIP & SON LTD.

Gulf of Bothnia

1:2 500 000

Projection: Conical with two standard parallels

East from Greenwich

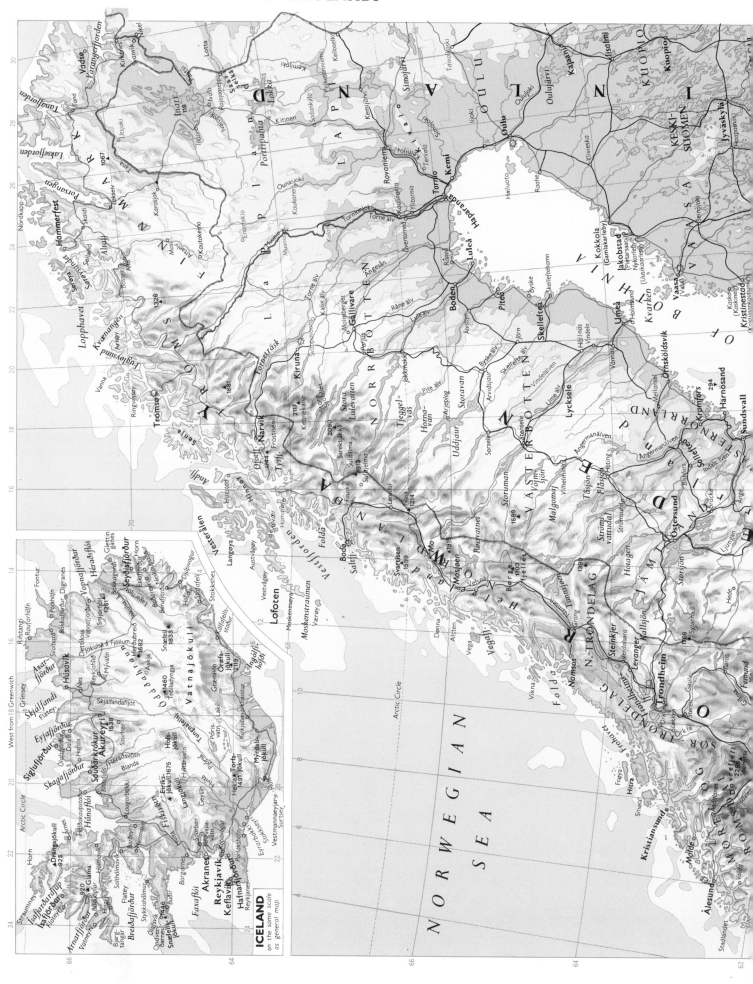

ICELAND
on the same scale
as general map

N O R W E G I A N

S E A

1:5 000 000

20 10 0 20 40 60 80 100 miles
40 20 0 40 80 120 160 km

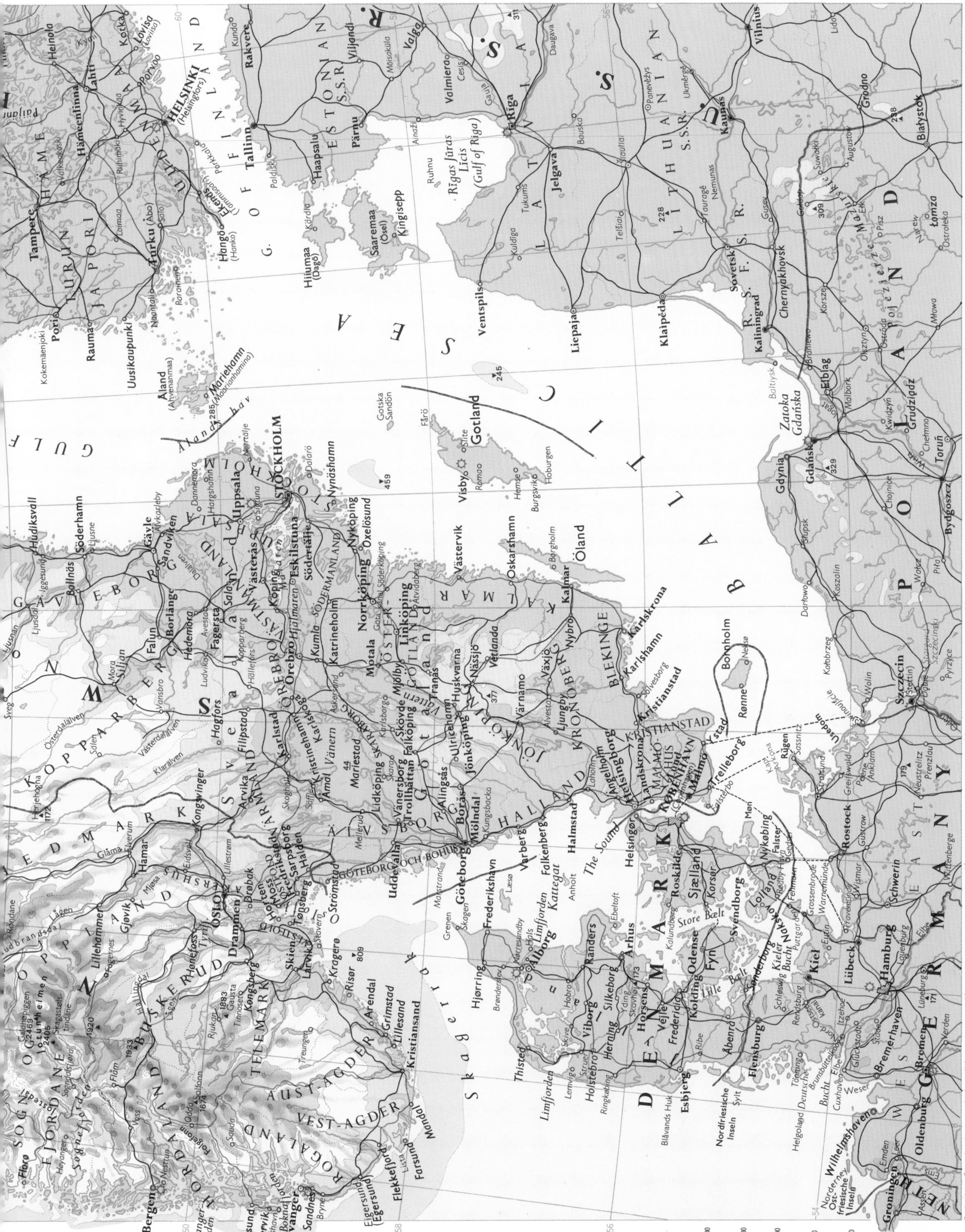

COPYRIGHT. GEORGE PHILIP & SON. LTD.

B A L T I C   S E A

G U L F   O F   F I N L A N D

G U L F   O F   B O T H N I A

S K A G E R R A K

K A T T E G A T T

HELSINKI (Helsingfors)
Tampere · Hämeenlinna · Heinola · Lahti · Kotka (Kotka) · Lovisa (Loviisa)
Turku (Åbo) · Pori · Rauma · Uusikaupunki · Naantali · Hangö (Hanko) · Porvoo
TURUN · JAPORI · HÄME · UUSIMAA

E S T O N I A N   S.S.R.
Tallinn · Haapsalu · Pärnu · Viljandi · Valga
Hiiumaa (Dagö) · Saaremaa (Ösel) · Kingissepp · Ruhnu
Rīgas Jūras Līcis (Gulf of Riga)

L A T V I A N   S.S.R.
Riga · Valmiera · Cēsis · Jelgava · Tukums · Kuldīga · Ventspils · Liepāja

L I T H U A N I A N   S.S.R.
Vilnius · **Kaunas** · Klaipėda · Šiauliai · Panevėžys · Telšiai

R.S.F.S.R.
Kaliningrad · Sovetsk · Chernyakhovsk

P O L A N D
Grodno · Białystok · Łomża · Ostrołęka · Grudziądz · Toruń · Bydgoszcz
Gdańsk · Gdynia · Elbląg · Malbork · Szczecin (Stettin) · Koszalin · Słupsk
Zatoka Gdańska

STOCKHOLM · Uppsala · Västerås · Eskilstuna · Södertälje · Nyköping · Oxelösund
Norrköping · Linköping · Motala · Mjölby · Katrineholm · Nynäshamn
Gävle · Söderhamn · Hudiksvall · Bollnäs · Sandviken · Falun · Borlänge · Hedemora
Mora · Ludvika · Avesta · Fagersta · Hofors
Örebro · Karlskoga · Kristinehamn · Karlstad · Arvika · Filipstad · Kumla · Hallsberg
Göteborg · Borås · Alingsås · Mölndal · Trollhättan · Vänersborg · Uddevalla · Lidköping
Skövde · Falköping · Mariestad · Åmål · Kil · Säffle · Skoghall
Jönköping · Huskvarna · Nässjö · Tranås · Värnamo · Vetlanda · Ljungby · Växjö
Kalmar · Nybro · Oskarshamn · Västervik · Gotland · Visby · Fårö
Karlskrona · Karlshamn · Sölvesborg · Kristianstad · Ystad · Trelleborg
Helsingborg · Landskrona · **MALMÖ** · Lund · Halmstad · Falkenberg · Varberg · Laholm
Öland · Bornholm · Rønne · Nexø

KØBENHAVN · Roskilde · Helsingør · Køge · Næstved · Korsør · Slagelse
Odense · Svendborg · Nyborg · Nykøbing · Kalundborg
DENMARK · Ålborg · Århus · Randers · Horsens · Vejle · Kolding · Fredericia
Viborg · Herning · Silkeborg · Esbjerg · Varde · Ribe · Hjørring · Thisted · Frederikshavn
Sjælland · Fyn · Lolland · Falster · Møn · Langeland
Limfjorden · The Sound

O S L O · Drammen · Kongsberg · Hønefoss · Lillehammer · Hamar · Gjøvik · Kongsvinger
Moss · Fredrikstad · Sarpsborg · Halden · Skien · Larvik · Tønsberg · Sandefjord
Bergen · Haugesund · Stavanger · Sandnes · Egersund · Flekkefjord · Kristiansand
Grimstad · Arendal · Lillesand · Mandal · Farsund · Risør · Kragerø · Porsgrunn
HORDALAND · ROGALAND · VEST-AGDER · AUST-AGDER · TELEMARK · BUSKERUD
AKERSHUS · HEDMARK · OPPLAND · SOGN OG FJORDANE
Hardangerfjorden · Sognefjorden

W E S T   G E R M A N Y
Hamburg · Lübeck · Kiel · Flensburg · Rostock · Schwerin · Wismar · Neustadt
Bremen · Bremerhaven · Oldenburg · Wilhelmshaven · Emden · Verden
Rügen · Usedom · Stralsund · Sassnitz · Greifswald · Anklam · Neubrandenburg
Nordfriesische Inseln · Ostfriesische Inseln · Sylt · Helgoland
Elbe · Weser

N E T H E R L A N D S
Groningen

ft m

Projection: Conical with two standard parallels · East from Greenwich

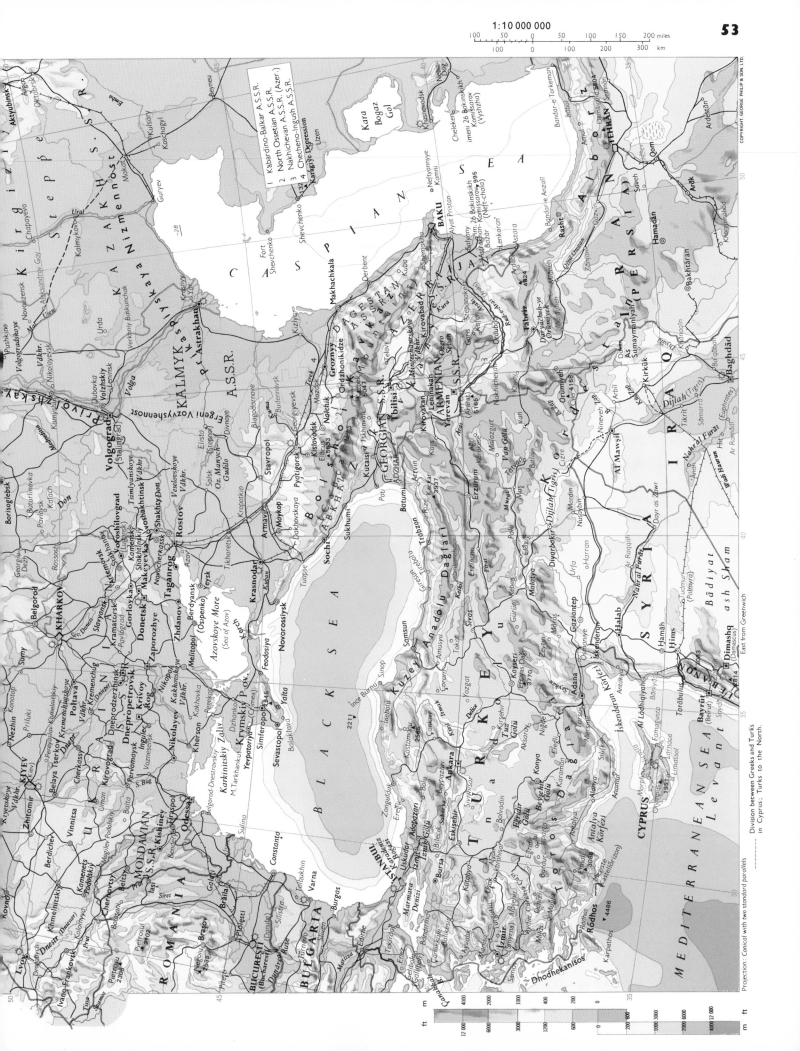

East from Greenwich

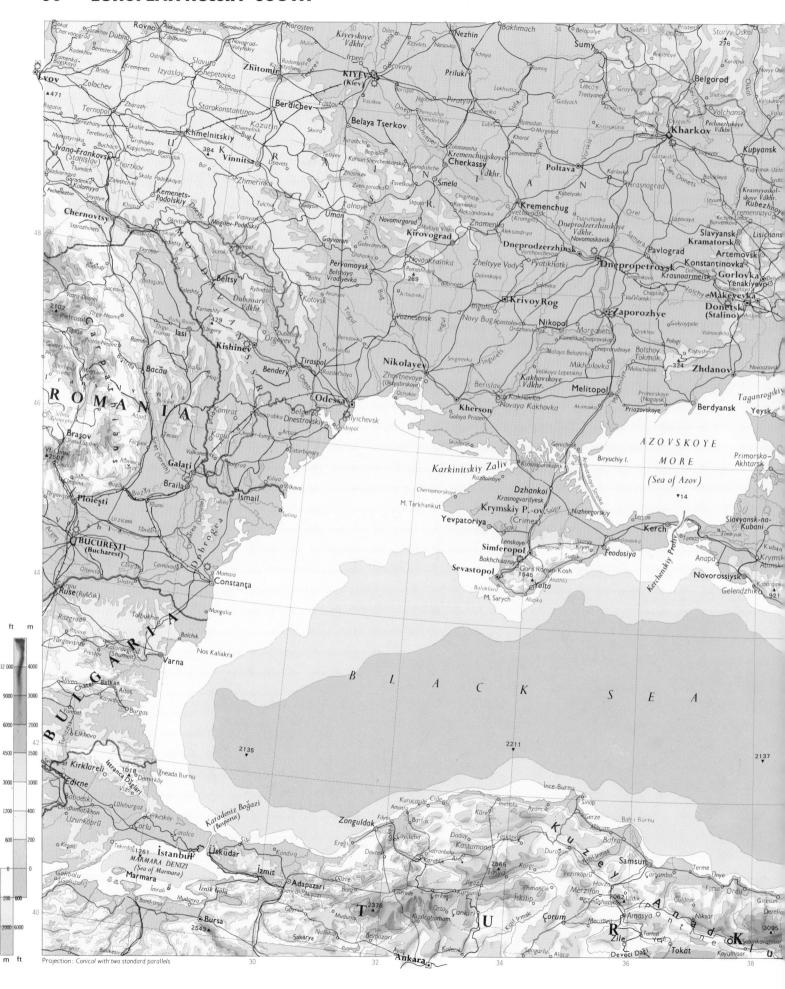

Projection: Conical with two standard parallels

R.S.F.S.R.
1. Daghestan A.S.S.R.
2. Kabardino–Balkar A.S.S.R.
3. Mari A.S.S.R.
4. Mordovian A.S.S.R.
5. North Ossetian A.S.S.R.
6. Tatar A.S.S.R.
7. Udmurt A.S.S.R.
8. Chuvash A.S.S.R.
9. Checheno-Ingush A.S.S.R.
AZERBAIJAN
10. Nakhichevan A.S.S.R.
GEORGIA
11. Abkhaz A.S.S.R.
12. Adzhar A.S.S.R.

Projection: Conical Orthomorphic with two standard parallels

East from Greenwich

1:20 000 000

100   0   100   200   300   400   500 miles
100   0   200   400   600   800 km

OCEAN

East Siberian Sea

Mys Dezhneva
(East C.)

St. Lawrence I.
(U.S.A.)

Severnaya
Zemlya

Poluostrov
Goryu
Taymyr

Nordvik

Verkhoyansk

YAKUT S.S.R.
A.S.S.R.
SOCIALIST REPUBLIC

Vilyuysk

Yakutsk

Olekminsk

Arctic Circle

Bering
Sea

Sea of
Okhotsk

Poluostrov
Kamchatka

Petropavlovsk-
Kamchatskiy

Magadan

Okhotsk

Sakhalin

Yuzhno-Sakhalinsk

Komsomolsk

Khabarovsk

Sovetskaya Gavan

Krasnoyarsk

Nizhneudinsk

Bratsk

Kirensk

Chita

Ulan Ude

Angarsk

Irkutsk

Ulaanbaatar
(Ulan Bator)

MONGOLIA

Hokkaido

Sapporo

Hakodate

Sea of JAPAN

Honshu

Nii-gata

Kanazawa

To-yama

Vladivostok

Ussuriysk

Harbin

Jiamusi

Qiqihar

Jilin

Changchun

Shenyang

Fushun

Anshan

Dandong

Pyongyang

North

South

Sŏul

Pusan

Taejon

Inch'on

Wŏnsan

Chongjin

PEOPLE'S
REPUBLIC

Beijing

Baotou

Zhangjiakou

Lüda

Yingkou

GOBI

COPYRIGHT. GEORGE PHILIP & SON. LTD.

Boundaries of U.S.S.R.
Boundaries of S.S.R.
Boundaries of A.S.S.R.

1:50 000 000

250 0 250 500 750 1000 miles

250 0 500 1000 1500 km

P A C I F I C   O C E A N

Guam Is. 10 822▼

Caroline Is.

New Guinea

Australia

Tropic of Cancer

Bonin Is. 10 554

10 642

Cape Johnson Deep 10 497

Mindanao

Arafura Sea

Philippine Is.

Luzon

Halmahera

Ceram

Banda Sea

Moluccas

Celebes

Celebes Sea

Timor

Flores

Bali

Java Sea

East

Sunda Is.

Java

7822

Aleutian Is.

Bering Sea

Kamchatka Peninsula

Klyuchevsk Vol. 4750

C. Dezhnyova

Bering Str.

Wrangel I.

New Siberian Is.

Severnaya Zemlya

Laptev Sea

Kara Sea

Barents Sea

Novaya Zemlya

Svalbard

A R C T I C   O C E A N

North Cape

Kola Pen.

White Sea

Finland

Scandinavia

Iceland

Greenland

Arctic Circle

British Isles

North Sea

Baltic Sea

Rhine

Elbe

Oder

Vistula

Danube

Carpathians

Adriatic Sea

Mediterranean Sea

Libyan Desert

Nile

Red Sea

Suez Canal

Sinai Pen.

Dead Sea

Syrian Desert

Mesopotamia

Tigris

Euphrates

Cyprus

Anatolia

Taurus Mts.

Ararat 5165

Elbruz 5633

Caucasus

Black Sea

Bosporus

Dnepr

Don

Volga

Ural

Caspian Sea

Elburz Mts.

Plateau of Iran

Zagros

The Gulf

G. of Oman

Arabian Sea

G. of Aden

Gulf of Oman

Ras Asir (C. Guardafui)

Socotra

Somali Peninsula

Rub' al Khali

A r a b i a

Great Salt Desert

Kavir Desert

Hindu Kush 7495

Pamirs

Karakoram Mt. Everest 8861

K2 8611

Himalaya

Plateau of Tibet

Kun-lun Shan

Koko Nor

Tsangpo

Brahmaputra

Ganges

Indus

Sulaiman Ra.

Helmand

Thar Desert

Sutlej

Jumna

Yamuna

Narmada

Godavari

I n d i a

Deccan

Eastern Ghats

Western Ghats

C. Comorin

Ceylon

Palk Strait

Gulf of Mannar

Laccadive Is.

Maldive Is.

Chagos Arch.

Seychelles

Amirantes

I N D I A N   O C E A N

Equator

Bay of Bengal

Godavari

Krishna

Andaman Is.

Nicobar Is.

Sunda Is.

Str. of Malacca

Sumatra

Malay Peninsula

G. of Thailand

Chao Phraya

Salween

Irrawaddy

Mekong

Bangkok

Hong (Red)

Tonkin

G. of Tonkin

Hainan

Si-kiang

South China Sea

Borneo

Sulu Sea

Kinabalu 4101

Palawan

Makasar Strait

Tropic of Cancer

Formosa

Ryukyu Is.

East China Sea

Yellow Sea

Korea Str.

Korea

Japan Sea

Honshu

Shikoku

Kyushu

Japan

Sea of Japan

Hokkaido

Kurile Is.

La Perouse Str.

Sakhalin

Sikhote Alin Ra.

Amur

Sea of Okhotsk

Okhotsk

Sredinny Ra.

Kolyma

Gydan Ra. (Kolyma)

Indigirka

Verkhoyansk Range

Yablonovy Ra.

Stanovoy Ra.

Aldan

Lena

Olekma

Vitim

Central Siberian Plateau

Yenisei

Taimyr Peninsula

Chelyuskin

Lower Tunguska

Angara

Sayan Mts.

Selenga

L. Baikal

Altai

Belukha 4506

Plateau of Mongolia

Great Khingan Mts.

Manchurian Plain

Hwang-ho

Great Plain of China

Pa Hai

C h i n a

Yangtze-kiang

Tsin-ling Shan

Sungari

Ob

Irtysh

Tobol

Tura

L. Balkhash

Ili

Chu

Syr Darya

Amu Darya

Aral Sea

Turgai

Turan Plain

Ural Mountains

1640

Narodnaya 1894

N. Dvina

West Siberian Plain

Turfan Basin

Tarim

Tarim Basin

Takla Makan

Tien Shan

Lop Nor

Communism Pk. 7495

L. Balkhash

S o v i e t   U n i o n

North European Plain

Russian

Central Uplands

Finland

ft m

18 000 6000 4000/20

12 000

6000 3000

1200

600

400 10

200

0

200

2000

4000

6000/6000

8000/18 000

24 000

m ft

Projection: Bonne

1:1 000 000

1949–1974 Armistice lines between Israel and the Arab States.

MEDITERRANEAN SEA

LEBANON

SYRIA

JORDAN

EGYPT

Projection: Conical with two standard parallels

East from Greenwich

COPYRIGHT. GEORGE PHILIP & SON. LTD.

Continuation Southwards 1:2 500 000

ISRAEL

1:15 000 000

100 0 100 200 300 400 miles
100 0 100 200 300 400 500 600 km

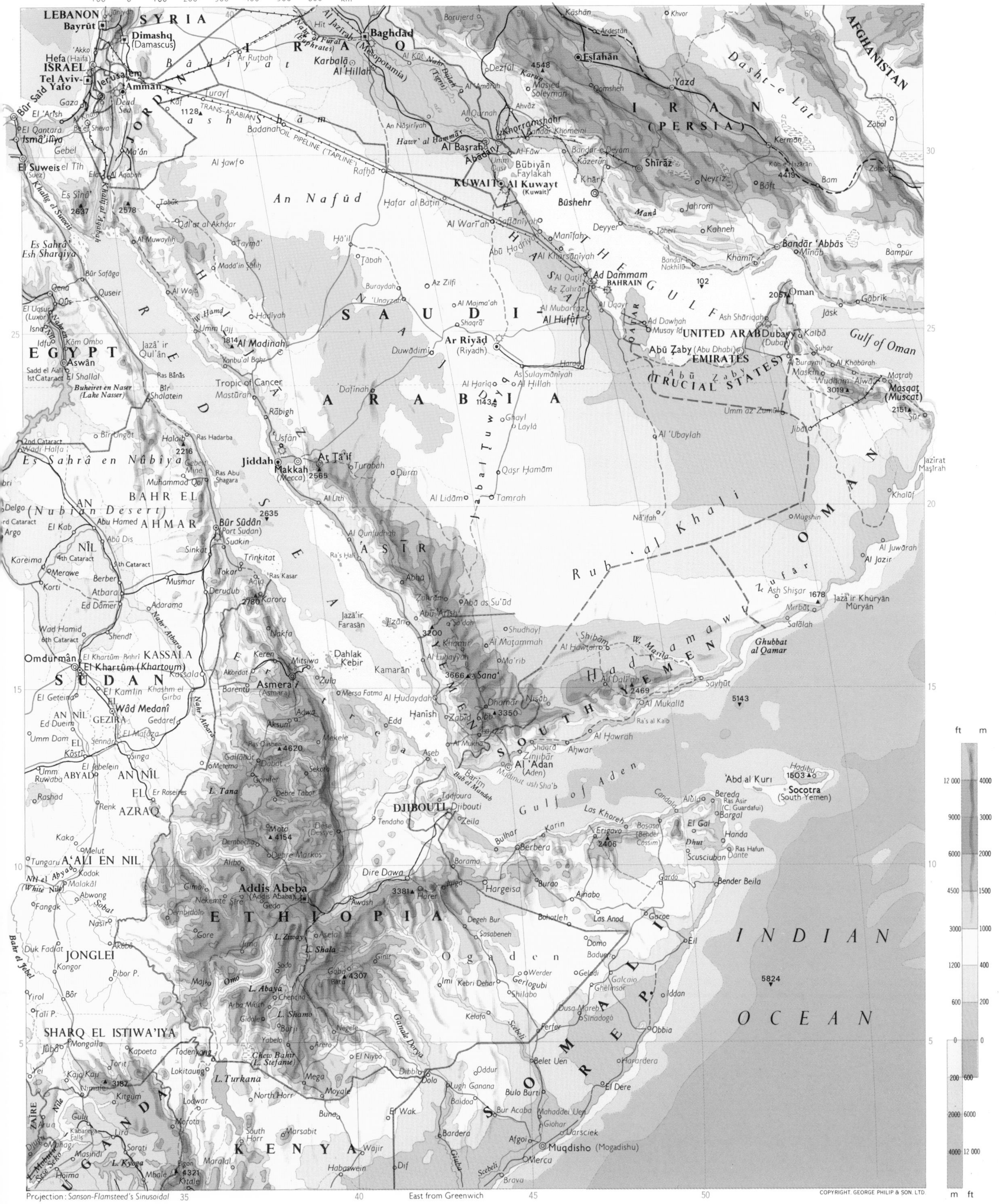

LEBANON
Bayrût
Hefa (Haifa)
ISRAEL
Tel Aviv–Yafo
Bûr Saïd Yafo
'Akko
Jerusalem
Amman
SYRIA
Dimashq (Damascus)
Gaza
Dead Sea
El 'Arîsh
Ismâ'îya
El Qantara
Gebel
El Suweis (Suez)
el Tîh
Es Sîna'
2637
Es Sahrâ
Esh Sharqîya
El 'Aqaba
Tabûk
2578
Qal'at al Akhdar
Al Muwaylih

IRAQ
Baghdad
Karbalâ
Al Hillah
Ar Rutbah
Al Kût
Al 'Amârah
An Nâsirîyah
Hawr' al Hammâr
Al Basrah
Al Fâw
Abadan
Khorramshahr
Bandar-e Khomeini
KUWAIT Al Kuwayt (Kuwait)
Bûbiyân
Faylakah
Hafar al Bâtin
Al Wafrah
Rafhâ

SYRIA
Bâdiyat ash Shâm
Hît
Al Jazîrah
Nahr al Furât (Euphrates)
Mesopotamia

AFGHANISTAN

IRAN (PERSIA)
Esfahân
4548
Yazd
Dasht-e Lût
Kermân
Dezfûl
Ahvâz
Shîrâz
Bûshehr
4419
Bam
Zâbol
Bandar 'Abbâs
Mînâb
Bampûr

An Nafûd
Hâ'il
Taymâ
Tâbah
Buraydah
Az Zilfî
'Unayzah
Al Majma'ah
Shaqrâ

SAUDI
ARABIA
Ar Riyâd (Riyadh)
Duwâdimî
Az Zilfî
As Sulaymânîyah
Al Hillah
Al Hariq
Ad Dammam
BAHRAIN
Az Zahrân
Al Mubarraz
Al Hufûf
Al 'Uqayr
QATAR
Ad Dawhah
UNITED ARAB EMIRATES
Abû Zaby (Abu Dhabi)
Dubayy (Dubai)
TRUCIAL STATES
Al Buraymî

OMAN
Masqat (Muscat)
3019
2151
Sûr
Gulf of Oman
Jâsk
Gâbrik

EGYPT
Aswân
Sadd el 'Alî
1st Cataract El Shallâl
Buheiret en Naser (Lake Nasser)
Kôm Ombo
Idfu
Isna
El Uqsur (Luxor)
Qenâ
Quseir
Bûr Safâga
Ras Banâs
Bîr Shalatein

Tropic of Cancer

RED SEA
Al Madînah
Yanbu' al Bahr
Râbigh
Jiddah
Makkah (Mecca)
2565
At Tâ'if
Turabah
Durm
Qasr Hamâm
Tamrah

Jazâ'ir Farasân
Jîzân
Sa'dah
3200
San'â
3666
Dhamâr
Zabîd
Al Hudaydah
Ta'izz
3350

YEMEN
Ma'rib
Shabwa

Rub' al Khali
Al 'Ubaylah
Mûgshin
5143
Ash Shisar
1678

SUDAN
Omdurmân
El Khartûm (Khartoum)
KASSALA
Kassala
Wâd Medanî
GEZIRA
Sennâr
Gedaref
2nd Cataract
Wâdi Halfa
Delgo
Argo
3rd Cataract
El Kab
Abû Hamed
Berber
Atbara
Ed Dâmer
Shendî
6th Cataract
Wad Hamid
4th Cataract
5th Cataract
Es Sahrâ en Nûbîya
(Nubian Desert)
BAHR EL AHMAR
Bûr Sûdân (Port Sudan)
Suakin
Sinkat
Tokar
Trinkitat
2216
Ras Hadarba
Karora
2780

ETHIOPIA
Asmera (Asmara)
Keren
Mitsiwa
Aksum
Adwa
Mekele
Ras Dashen 4620
Gonder
L. Tana
Debre Tabor
Debre Markos
Addis Abeba (Addis Ababa)
3381
Hârer
Dire Dawa
Awash
Nekemte
Gore
4154
Jima
L. Zway
L. Shala
L. Abaya
4307
L. Shamo
Nazret
Degeh Bur
Ogaden
Imi
Kebri Dehar
Gode

DJIBOUTI
Djibouti
Zeila
Tadjoura
Bab el Mandeb
Berbera
Hargeisa
Burao
Las Anod
Las Khoreh

SOUTH YEMEN
Al 'Adan (Aden)
Al Mukallâ
2469
Ghayl
Sayhût
Ghubbat al Qamar
Salâlah
Mirbat
Jazâ'ir Khûryân Mûryân

Gulf of Aden
'Abd al Kuri
Socotra (South Yemen)
1503
Ras Asir (C. Guardafui)
Bargal
Bereda
Alûla
Scusciuban
Dante
Ras Hafun
Hordio
Bender Beila
Gardo
Eil
Obbia
5824

SOMALI REP.
Mogadishu (Muqdisho)
Baidoa
Merca
Brava
Bardera

KENYA
L. Turkana
Marsabit
Wajir
Moyale
Mandera

UGANDA
L. Kyoga
4321
Mbale

INDIAN OCEAN

Projection: Sanson-Flamsteed's Sinusoidal

East from Greenwich

COPYRIGHT. GEORGE PHILIP & SON. LTD

ft / m
12 000 / 4000
9000 / 3000
6000 / 2000
4500 / 1500
3000 / 1000
1200 / 400
600 / 200
0 / 0
200 / 600
2000 / 6000
4000 / 12 000
m / ft

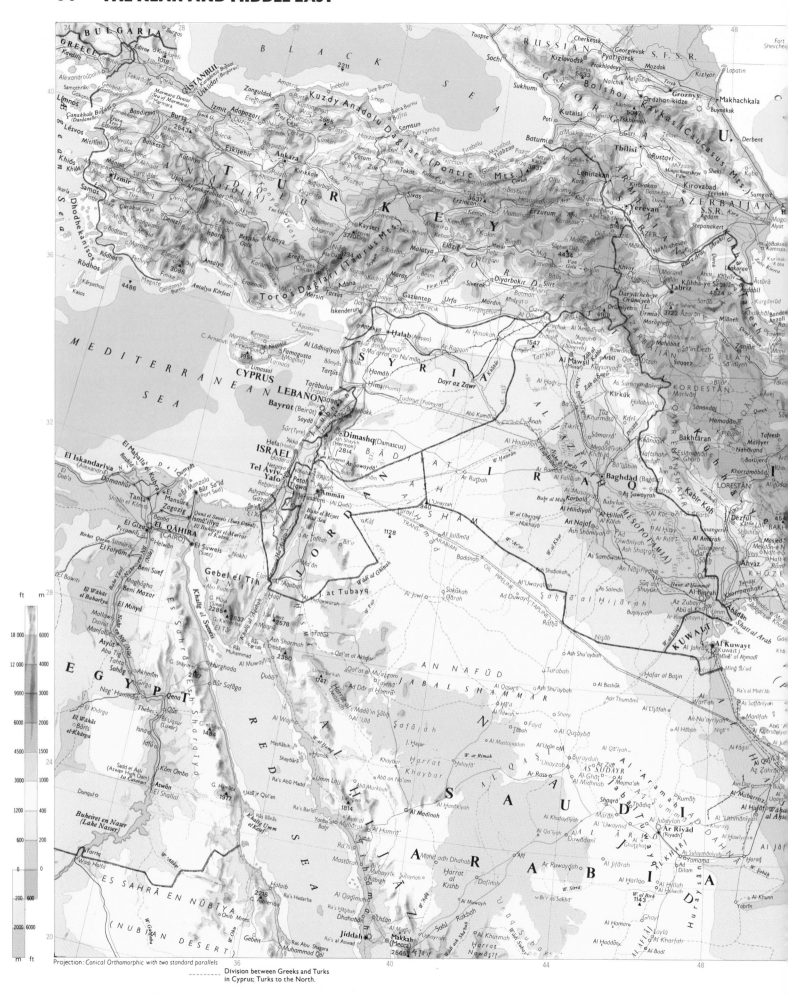

Projection: Conical Orthomorphic with two standard parallels

Division between Greeks and Turks in Cyprus; Turks to the North.

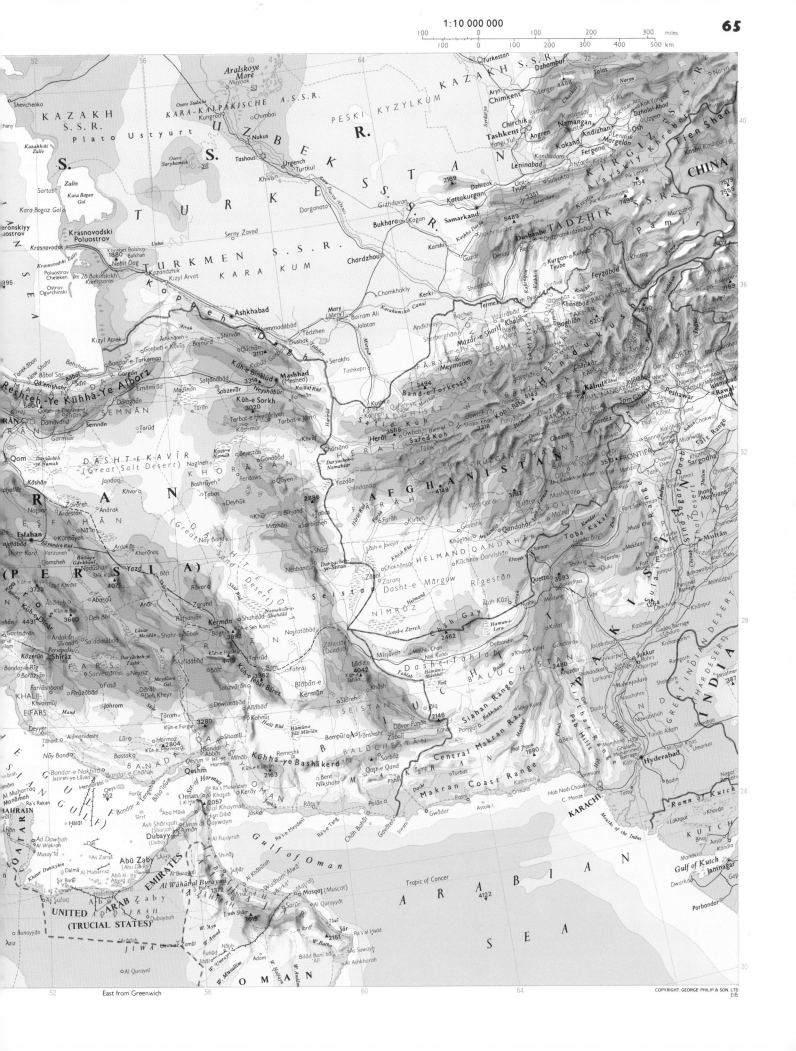

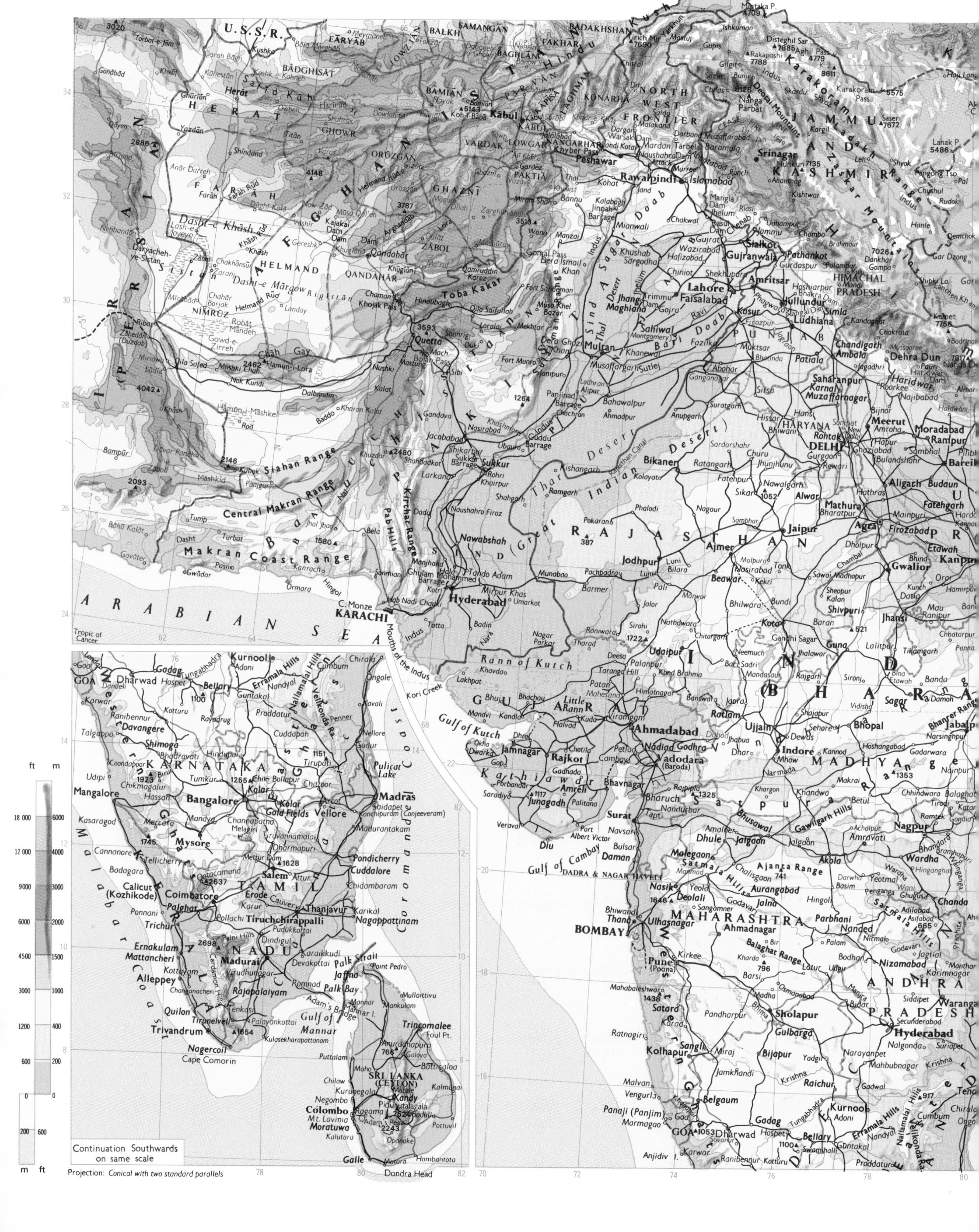

U.S.S.R.

FARYAB BALKH SAMANGAN BADAKHSHAN

BAGHLAN TAKHAR

BADGHISAT JOWZJAN

Herat HERAT GHOWR BAMIAN KAPISA KONARHA NORTH WEST FRONTIER

AFGHANISTAN

Kabul KABUL VARDAK LOWGAR NANGARHAR Khyber Pass Peshawar

PAKTIA Rawalpindi Islamabad JAMMU AND KASHMIR

GHAZNI Srinagar

ORUZGAN ZABOL

QANDAHAR Qandahar PUNJAB HIMACHAL PRADESH

NIMRUZ Lahore Faisalabad Ludhiana Simla Chandigarh Ambala Dehra Dun

BALUCHISTAN Quetta SIND Multan PUNJAB Patiala Haridwar

Makran Coast Range Central Makran Range Siahan Range

ARABIAN SEA

KARACHI Hyderabad

Tropic of Cancer

Sukkur Larkana

Thar Desert (Great Indian Desert) RAJASTHAN Jaipur Agra DELHI New Delhi HARYANA Meerut Moradabad

Jodhpur Ajmer Kota Gwalior

Rann of Kutch Udaipur BHARAT

GUJARAT Ahmadabad MADHYA Bhopal Indore

Gulf of Kutch Jamnagar Rajkot Vadodara (Baroda)

Kathiawar Bhavnagar Surat Bharuch

Gulf of Cambay DADRA & NAGAR HAVELI Daman

Nasik MAHARASHTRA Nagpur

BOMBAY Pune (Poona) Sholapur ANDHRA PRADESH Hyderabad

Kolhapur Gulbarga Bijapur

GOA Belgaum Panaji (Panjim)

Continuation Southwards on same scale

GOA Dharwad Kurnool Gadag Bellary Erramala Hills

KARNATAKA Mangalore Bangalore Kolar Gold Fields Madras Pulicat Lake

Mysore Vellore Kanchipuram (Conjeeveram)

TAMIL NADU Salem Coimbatore Pondicherry Cuddalore

Calicut (Kozhikode) Tiruchchirappalli Thanjavur Nagappattinam

Coromandel Coast

Madurai Palk Strait

Quilon Tirunelveli Gulf of Mannar

Trivandrum Cape Comorin Jaffna

Colombo SRI LANKA (CEYLON) Kandy Trincomalee

Galle Dondra Head

ft m 18 000 6000 12 000 4000 9000 3000 6000 2000 4500 1500 3000 1000 1200 400 600 200 0 200 600 m ft

Projection: Conical with two standard parallels

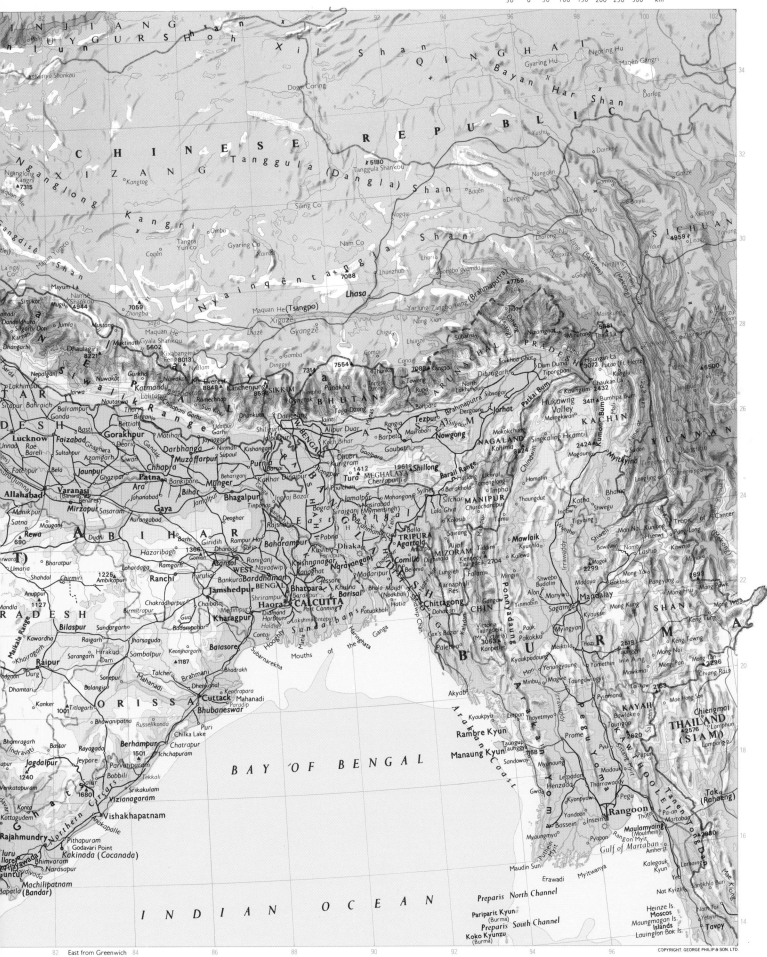

1:10 000 000

50 0 50 100 150 200 miles

50 0 50 100 150 200 250 300 km

C H I N E S E   R E P U B L I C

X I N J I A N G

U Y G U R S H

Kokoxili Shankou

Hoh Xil Shan

Q I N G H A I

Ngoring Hu

Maqên Gangri

Darlag

Gyaring Hu

Bayan Har Shan

X I Z A N G

Tanggula (Dangla) Shan

5180

Yushu

Xinlong

S I C H U A N

Nganglong Kangri

7315

Kangtog

Siling Co

Nagqu

Dêngqên

Baiyü

4959

Litang

Yanjing

Kangdise Shan

Tangra Yumco

Gyaring Co

Nam Co

N y a i n q ê n t a n g l h a   S h a n

Lhari

Pongbo'gyamda

Zhaxize

Gongkar

Ninging

La'nga Co

Ombu

Coqên

Rinbu

7088

Lhünzhub

Zhamo

Xinlong

Mayum La

Namsê Shankou

7059

Zhongba

Saga

Maquan He (Tsangpo)

Xigazê

Lhazê

Gyangzê

Chigu

Yarlung Zangbo Jiang (Brahmaputra)

Nang Xian

Gomai

Jido

Zhongxin

Mili

Dhaulagiri 8221

Muktinath

Kixabangma 8013

Gyala Shankou

5602

Dinggyê

Gamba

7314

7554

Thunka

7089

Kangto

Rupa

Towang

A R U N A C H A L   P R A D E S H

Dibrugarh

Dum Duma

Tipongpani

Hpungan La

3072 Putao (Ft Hertz)

Konglu

5500

B A Y   O F   B E N G A L

I N D I A N   O C E A N

East from Greenwich

COPYRIGHT. GEORGE PHILIP & SON. LTD.

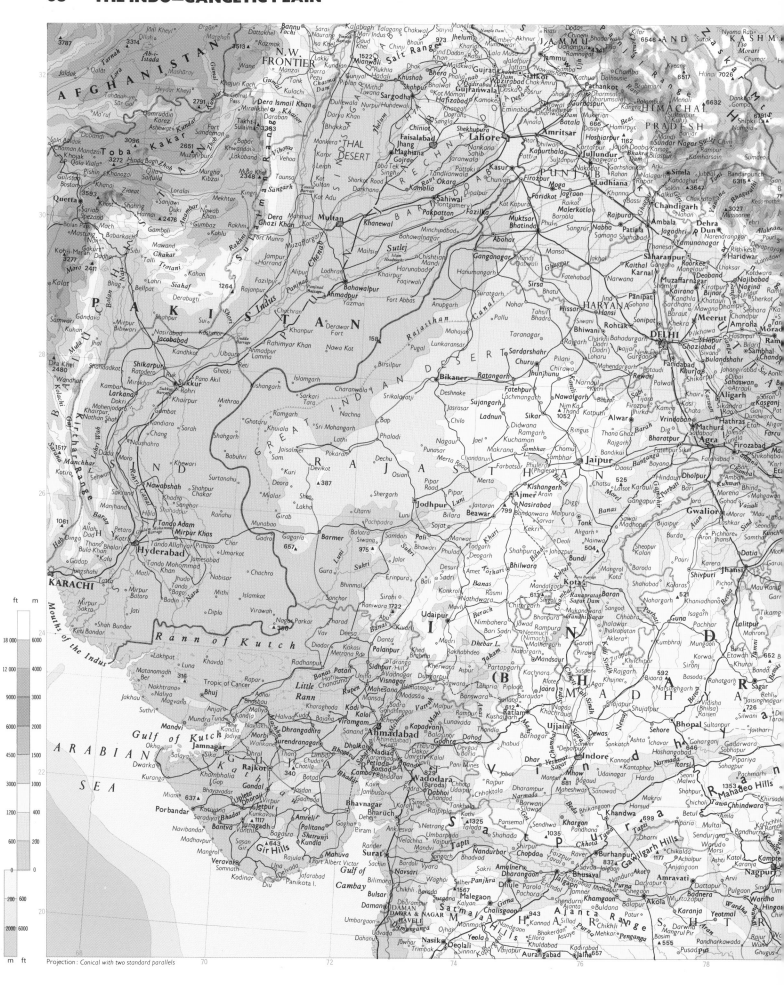

Projection: Conical with two standard parallels

1:6 000 000

50   0   50   100   150 miles
50   0   50 100 150 200 250 km

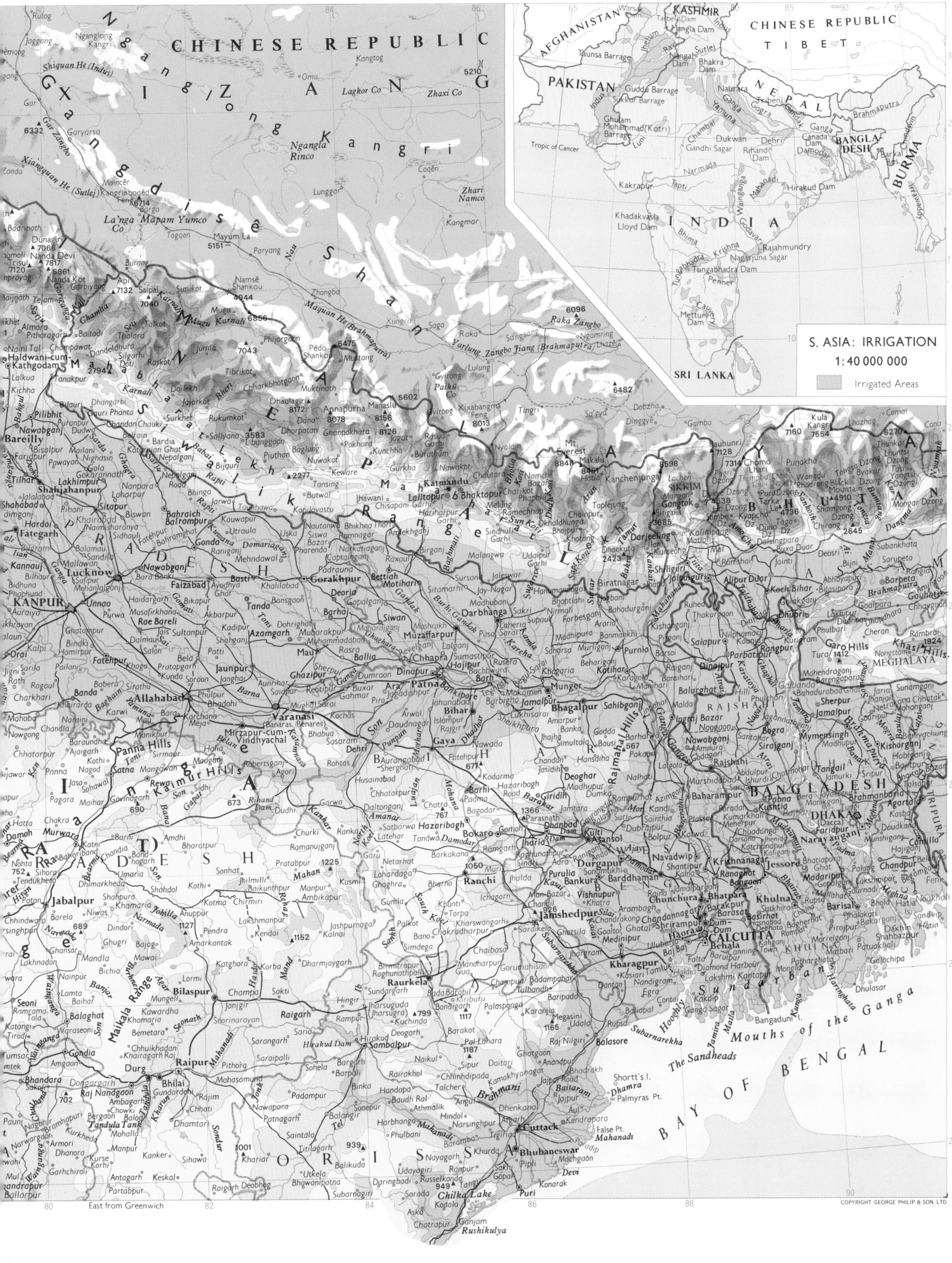

S. ASIA: IRRIGATION
1:40 000 000
Irrigated Areas

CHINESE REPUBLIC

XIZANG

Gangdisê Shan

Himalaya

CHINESE REPUBLIC
TIBET

AFGHANISTAN
PAKISTAN
KASHMIR
NEPAL
BANGLADESH
BURMA
INDIA
SRI LANKA

Tropic of Cancer

Mt. Everest 8848

NEPAL

SIKKIM
BHUTAN
Gangtok
Darjeeling

Katmandu
Bhaktapur

U T T A R   P R A D E S H

Bareilly
Lucknow
KANPUR
Allahabad
Varanasi
Gorakhpur
Faizabad
Jaunpur
Mirzapur-cum-Vindhyachal

M A D H Y A   P R A D E S H

Jabalpur
Bilaspur
Raipur
Bhilai
Durg

Patna
Gaya
BIHAR
Darbhanga
Muzaffarpur
Bhagalpur
Hazaribagh
Ranchi
Jamshedpur
Bokaro
Dhanbad
Asansol
Durgapur

W E S T   B E N G A L

CALCUTTA
Haora
Kharagpur

B A N G L A D E S H

DHAKA (Dacca)
Mymensingh
Khulna
Jessore
Barisal

MEGHALAYA
ASSAM
TRIPURA

R A J S H A H I

O R I S S A

Cuttack
Bhubaneswar
Puri
Balasore
Sambalpur

Chilka Lake
Mouths of the Ganga

BAY OF BENGAL

Sundarbans

East from Greenwich

COPYRIGHT. GEORGE PHILIP & SON LTD.

1:6 000 000

SRI LANKA
On same scale

ARABIAN SEA

BAY OF BENGAL

Gulf of Mannar

(Manaar)

Projection: Conical with two standard parallels

East from Greenwich

COPYRIGHT. GEORGE PHILIP & SON. LTD.

1:10 000 000

PENINSULAR MALAYSIA AND SINGAPORE
1:6 000 000

Projection: Conical with two standard parallels

East from Greenwich

COPYRIGHT. GEORGE PHILIP & SON. LTD.

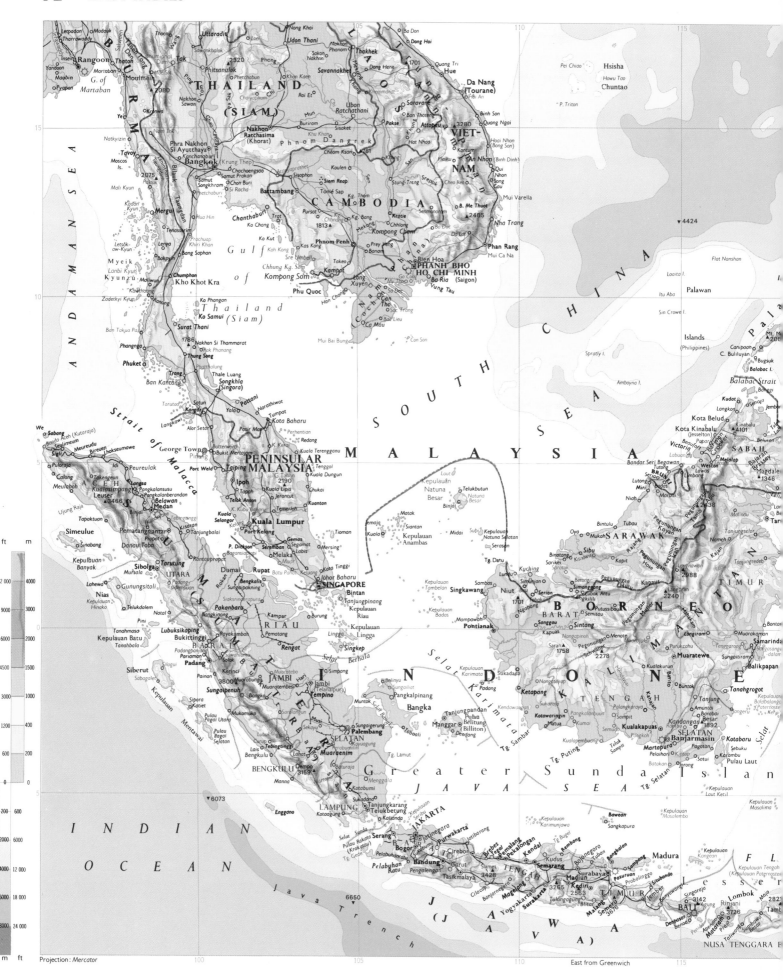

East from Greenwich

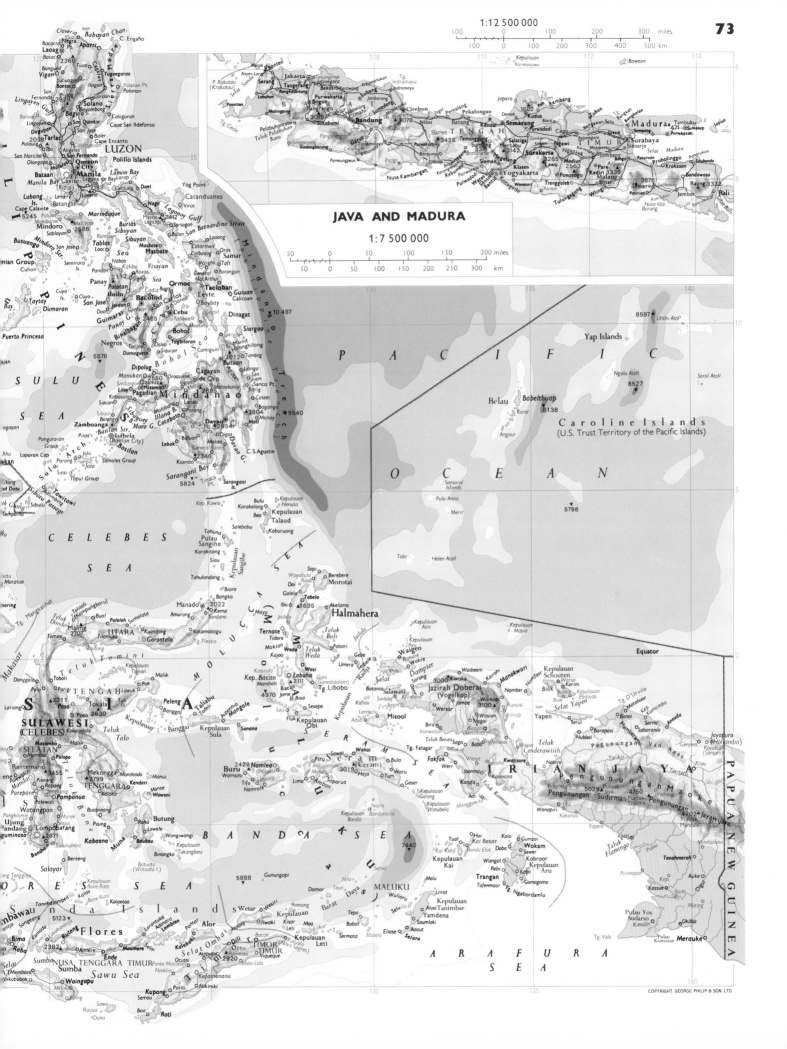

1:12 500 000

100   0   100   200   300 miles
100   0   100   200   300   400   500 km

JAVA AND MADURA

1:7 500 000

50   0   50   100   150   200 miles
50   0   50   100   150   200   250   300 km

LUZON

Manila

PHILIPPINE

SULU

SEA

CELEBES

SEA

Mindanao

Zamboanga

Davao

PACIFIC

OCEAN

Yap Islands

Belau

Caroline Islands
(U.S. Trust Territory of the Pacific Islands)

Babelthuap

Koror

Angaur

Sonsorol Islands

Manado

Gorontalo

Halmahera

Ternate

Tidore

SULAWESI
(CELEBES)

M O L U C C A   S E A

Buru

Seram (Ceram)

SERAM   SEA

Ambon

Misool

Jazirah Doberai
(Vogelkop)

IRIAN   JAYA

Yapen

Jayapura
(Hollandia)

Manokwari

Waigeo

PAPUA   NEW   GUINEA

B A N D A   S E A

Kepulauan Kai

Kepulauan Aru

Trangan

F L O R E S   S E A

Flores

Sumba

NUSA TENGGARA TIMUR

TIMOR TIMUR

Dili

Kupang

A R A F U R A

S E A

Merauke

COPYRIGHT. GEORGE PHILIP & SON. LTD

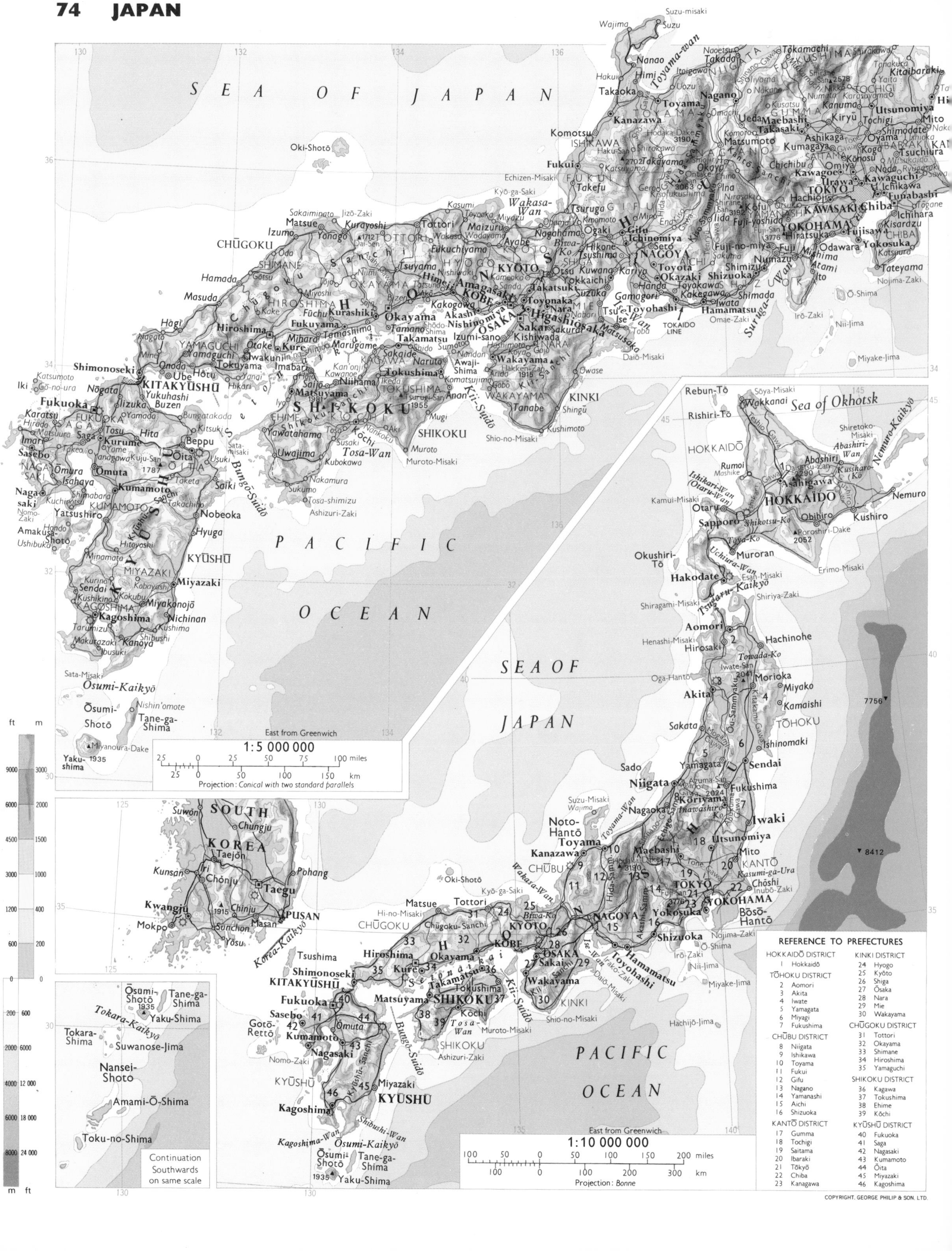

SEA OF JAPAN

PACIFIC OCEAN

SEA OF JAPAN

PACIFIC OCEAN

Sea of Okhotsk

CHŪGOKU

SHIKOKU

KYŪSHŪ

HOKKAIDŌ

TŌHOKU

KANTŌ

CHŪBU

KINKI

SOUTH KOREA

1:5 000 000

| 25 | 0 | 25 | 50 | 75 | 100 miles |

| 25 | 0 | 50 | 100 | 150 | km |

Projection : Conical with two standard parallels

East from Greenwich

1:10 000 000

| 100 | 50 | 0 | 100 | 150 | 200 miles |

| 100 | 0 | 100 | 200 | 300 | km |

Projection : Bonne

East from Greenwich

Continuation Southwards on same scale

Nansei-Shotō

ft   m

9000 3000
6000 2000
4500 1500
3000 1000
1200 400
600   200
0   0
200   600
2000 6000
4000 12 000
6000 18 000
8000 24 000

m   ft

REFERENCE TO PREFECTURES

HOKKAIDŌ DISTRICT	KINKI DISTRICT
1 Hokkaidō	24 Hyogo
TŌHOKU DISTRICT	25 Kyōto
2 Aomori	26 Shiga
3 Akita	27 Ōsaka
4 Iwate	28 Nara
5 Yamagata	29 Mie
6 Miyagi	30 Wakayama
7 Fukushima	**CHŪGOKU DISTRICT**
CHŪBU DISTRICT	31 Tottori
8 Niigata	32 Okayama
9 Ishikawa	33 Shimane
10 Toyama	34 Hiroshima
11 Fukui	35 Yamaguchi
12 Gifu	**SHIKOKU DISTRICT**
13 Nagano	36 Kagawa
14 Yamanashi	37 Tokushima
15 Aichi	38 Ehime
16 Shizuoka	39 Kōchi
KANTŌ DISTRICT	**KYŪSHŪ DISTRICT**
17 Gumma	40 Fukuoka
18 Tochigi	41 Saga
19 Saitama	42 Nagasaki
20 Ibaraki	43 Kumamoto
21 Tōkyō	44 Ōita
22 Chiba	45 Miyazaki
23 Kanagawa	46 Kagoshima

COPYRIGHT. GEORGE PHILIP & SON. LTD.

1:20 000 000

100   0   100   200   300   400 miles
100   0   100   200   300   400   500   600 km

Projection: Bonne

East from Greenwich

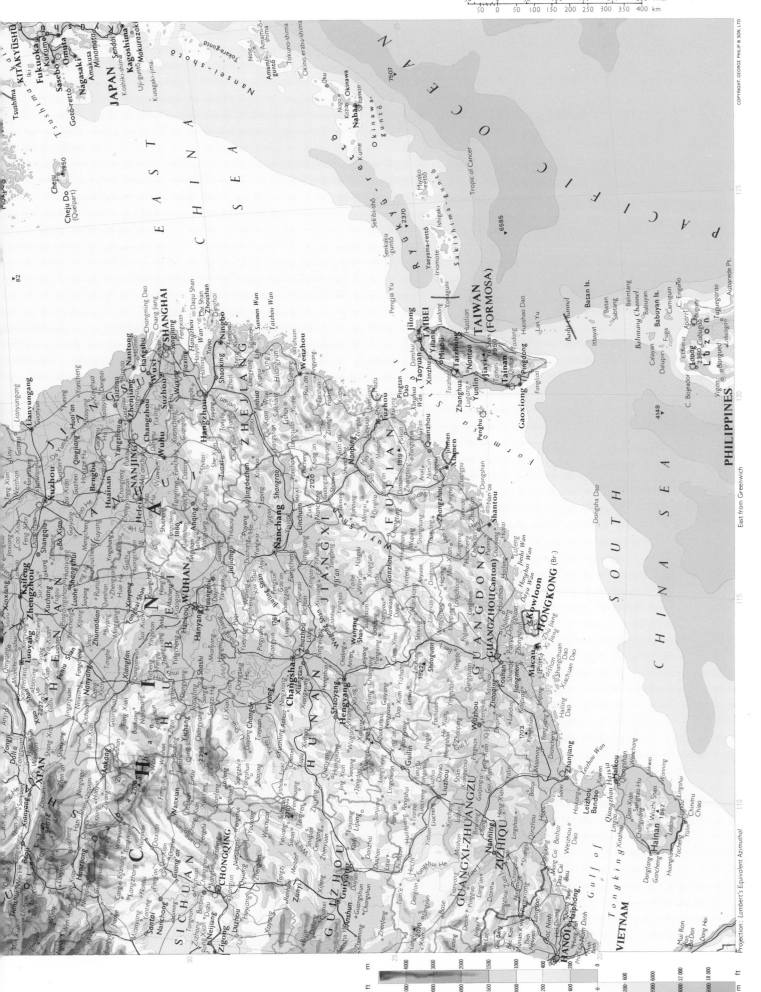

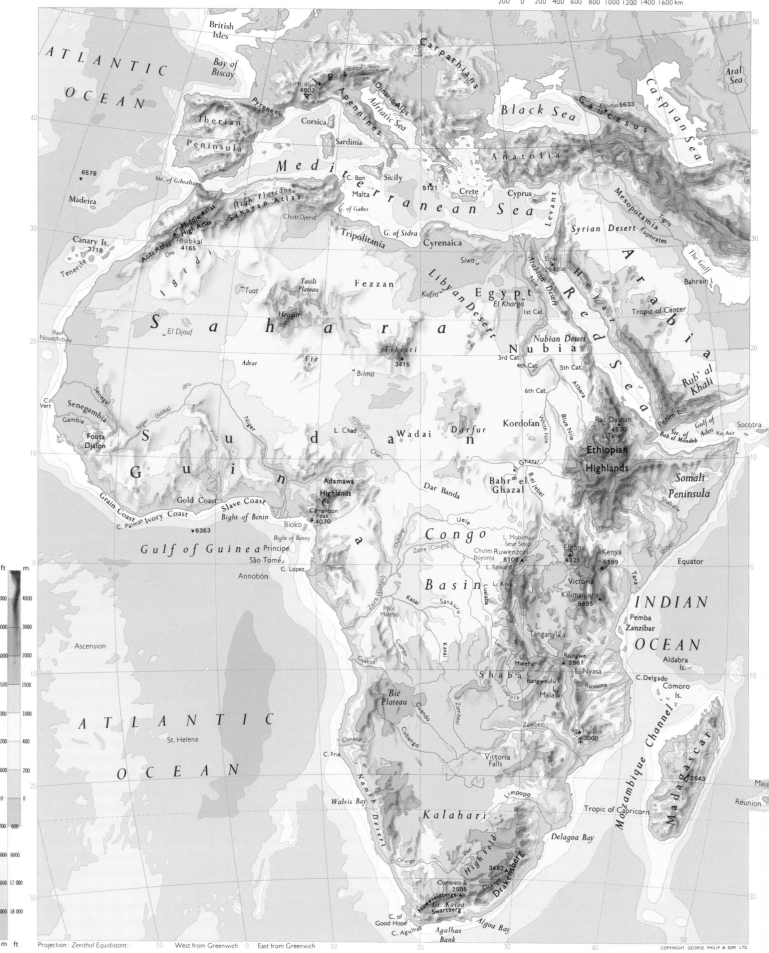

1:40 000 000

Projection: Zenithal Equidistant.

1:40 000 000

200 0 200 400 600 800 1000 miles
200 0 200 400 600 800 1000 1200 1400 1600 km

ATLANTIC OCEAN

UNITED KINGDOM London
NETH. GERMANY POLAND Warszawa
BELG. Praha CZECHOSLOVAKIA Kiyev
Paris W. Wien AUSTRIA HUNGARY
FRANCE SWITZ. ROMANIA Odessa Volgograd
Bay of Biscay AUSTRIA YUGOSLAVIA
Black Sea Aral Sea
U. S. S. R.
PORTUGAL SPAIN Madrid Roma ITALY BULGARIA Istanbul Ankara Baku Caspian Sea
Lisboa Corse Sardegna Adriatic Sea GREECE Athínai TURKEY Tehrān
Madeira (Port) Tanger Tétouan Gibraltar (Br.) Alger Annaba Tunis MALTA Sicilia Kriti CYPRUS Ḥalab Al Mawṣil Esfahān
Casablanca Rabat Fès Oran Constantine Bizerte TUNISIA Sfax Malta-Bûr Saïd SYRIA Dimashq Baghdād IRAN
Islas Canarias Marrakech Essaouira Chatt Djerid Tarābulus El Iskandariya Bûr Saïd Tel Aviv-Yafa JORDAN Al Baṣrah
Tenerife Ifni Dra MOROCCO Ghudāmis Banghāzi El Bayda EL QĀHIRA El Suweis KUWAIT The Gulf
El Aaiun WESTERN SAHARA ALGERIA LIBYA Sahrā' El Faiyūm EGYPT Aswân BAHRAIN QATAR
Dakhla Fdérik In Salah Marzūq El Jawf Siwa Asyūt SAUDI- Al Madīnah Tropic of Cancer
Ras Nouadhibou S a h a r a Ghat Libiya Wadi Halfa ARABIA Makkah Asir
Nouakchott MAURITANIA Agadez Es Sahrâ en Nûbiya Dongola Bûr Sûdân
Tombouctou Gaò NIGER CHAD Abéché Atbara Kassala Asmera Mitsiwa YEMEN
St. Louis SENEGAL Kayes MALI Niamey Sokoto El Fâsher SUDAN Omdurmân El Khartûm SOUTH YEMEN Al 'Adan Socotra
Dakar C. Vert Bamako BURKINA Kano Nguru Lac Tchad Ndjamena (Ft.-Lamy) El Obeid White Nile Blue Nile DJIBOUTI Djibouti Berbera Dante Ras Asir
GAMBIA Banjul GUINEA BISSAU Bissau FASO Ouagadougou Kaduna Maiduguri Bousso El Geneina Malakâl Addis Abeba Harer Hargeisa
Conakry Freetown SIERRA LEONE Tamale NIGERIA Bauchi Benue Sarh CENTRAL AFRICAN REPUBLIC Wâw Bahr el Jebel ETHIOPIA SOMALI REP
Monrovia LIBERIA IVORY COAST Kumasi GHANA BENIN TOGO Ibadan Enugu CAMEROON Ngaoundéré Bangui Ubangi Mongalla Muqdisho
Bouake Abidjan Accra Lagos Porto Novo Port Harcourt Yaoundé Zaïre (Congo) L. Turkana Equator
Sekondi Takoradi Bight of Benin Malabo Douala EQUATORIAL GUINEA L. Mobutu Sese Seko Kisangani UGANDA Kampala KENYA
Gulf of Guinea SÃO TOMÉ & PRINCIPE C. Lopez Libreville GABON CONGO Mbandaka L. Edward RWANDA Victoria Kisumu Nairobi INDIAN
Annobón Brazzaville Kinshasa ZAÏRE L. Kivu BURUNDI Mwanza Mombasa OCEAN
Ascension (Br.) Pointe-Noire Cabinda Kasai Ilebo Mbuji-Mayi Kananga Bujumbura Kigoma Tabora TANZANIA Dodoma Pemba Zanzibar
Luanda Boma Shaba Bukama Kalemie L. Tanganyika Dar-es-Salaam
ATLANTIC ANGOLA Benguela Lobito Huambo Likasi L. Mweru Lubumbashi Kitwe L. Nyasa Ruvuma Cabo Delgado COMOROS Antsiranana
Namibe Lobito Kwanza Cuando Lilongwe L. Malawi MALAWI Moçambique Mahajanga MADAGASCAR
St. Helena (Br.) Cunene ZAMBIA Lusaka Kafue Zambezi Blantyre MOZAMBIQUE Toamasina
OCEAN Kuvango Livingstone Harare Chinde Antananarivo MAURITIUS Réunion (Fr.)
NAMIBIA (SOUTH WEST AFRICA) Windhoek ZIMBABWE Beira Fianarantsoa
Swakopmund Walvis-baai BOTSWANA Bulawayo Limpopo Tropic of Capricorn Toliara Mozambique Channel
Lüderitz Kalahari Gaborone TRANSVAAL Pretoria Maputo (Lourenço Marques) SWAZ.
Oranje Kimberley O.V. Bloemf. NATAL Durban
SOUTH AFRICA CAPE PROVINCE LES.
Cape Town Kaap die Goeie Hoop (Cape of Good Hope) Port Elizabeth East London

Projection: Zenithal Equidistant.
West from Greenwich   East from Greenwich
COPYRIGHT. GEORGE PHILIP & SON. LTD.

LES. Lesotho
O. V. Oranje-Vrystaat
SWAZ. Swaziland

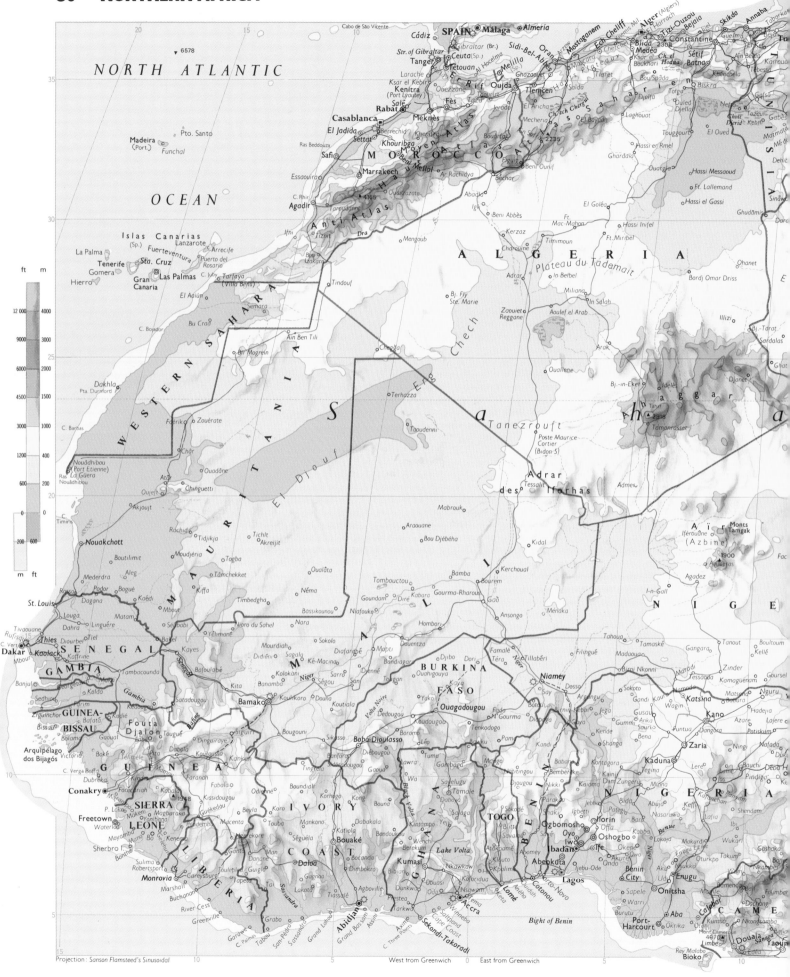

MEDITERRANEAN SEA

TURKEY
CYPRUS
SYRIA
Halab
Al Mawsil
(Mosul)
Hamāh
Hims
LEBANON
Bayrūt
Dimashq (Damascus)
IRAQ
ISRAEL
Tel Aviv-Yafo
Jerusalem (El Quds)
Amman
JORDAN

El Iskandarîya (Alexandria)
El Qâhira (Cairo)
El Gîza
Port Said
Dumyât
Suweis (Suez)

SAUDI
ARABIA
An Nafûd

MALTA
Sicily

Tarâbulus (Tripoli)
Misrâtah
Banghâzî (Benghazi)

L I B Y A
Cyrenaica
Fezzan
Marzûq

Sahrâ
Tibesti
3150
8415

E G Y P T

El Minya
Asyût
El Khârga
Aswân
Lake Nasser
Bûr Sûdân (Port Sudan)
Suakin

RED SEA
Jiddah
Makkah (Mecca)
Al Madinah
At Ta'if

C H A D
Lac Tchad
Ndjamena
(N. Lamy)

S U D A N
ESH SHAMÂLIYA
SHAMÂL DÂRFÛR
SHAMÂL KORDOFAN
El Fâsher
El Obeid
Omdurmân
El Khartûm (Khartoum)
KASSALA
Wad Medanî
AN NIL
EL GEZIRA

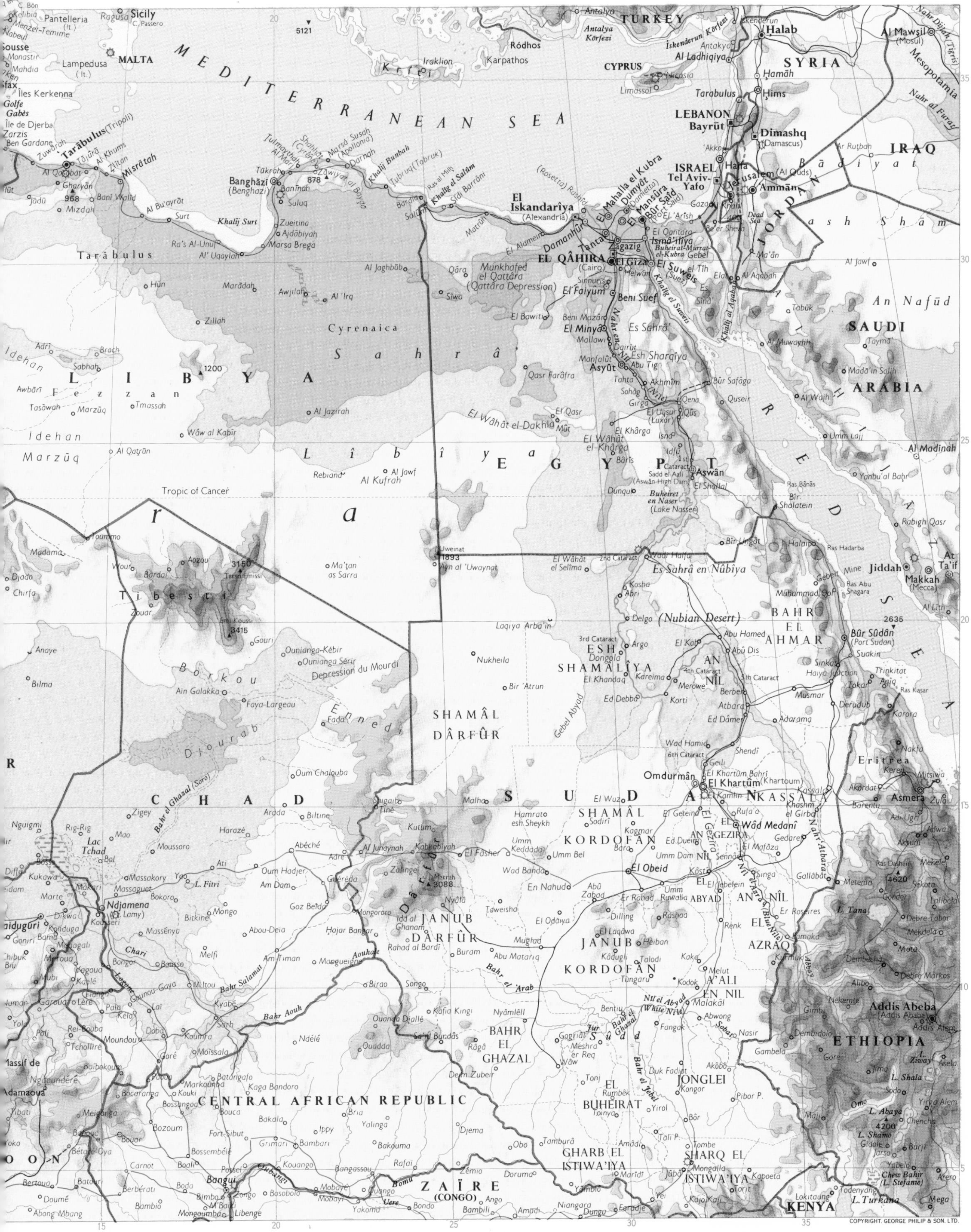

Eritrea
Asmera
Mitsiwa

JANUB DÂRFÛR
JANUB KORDOFAN

CENTRAL AFRICAN REPUBLIC

BAHR EL GHAZAL
EL BUHEIRAT
JONGLEI
Jûba

ETHIOPIA
Addis Abeba (Addis Ababa)
L. Tana
L. Abaya
L. Shamo

GHARB EL ISTIWA'IYA
SHARQ EL ISTIWA'IYA

ZAÏRE (CONGO)
KENYA
L. Turkana

Tropic of Cancer

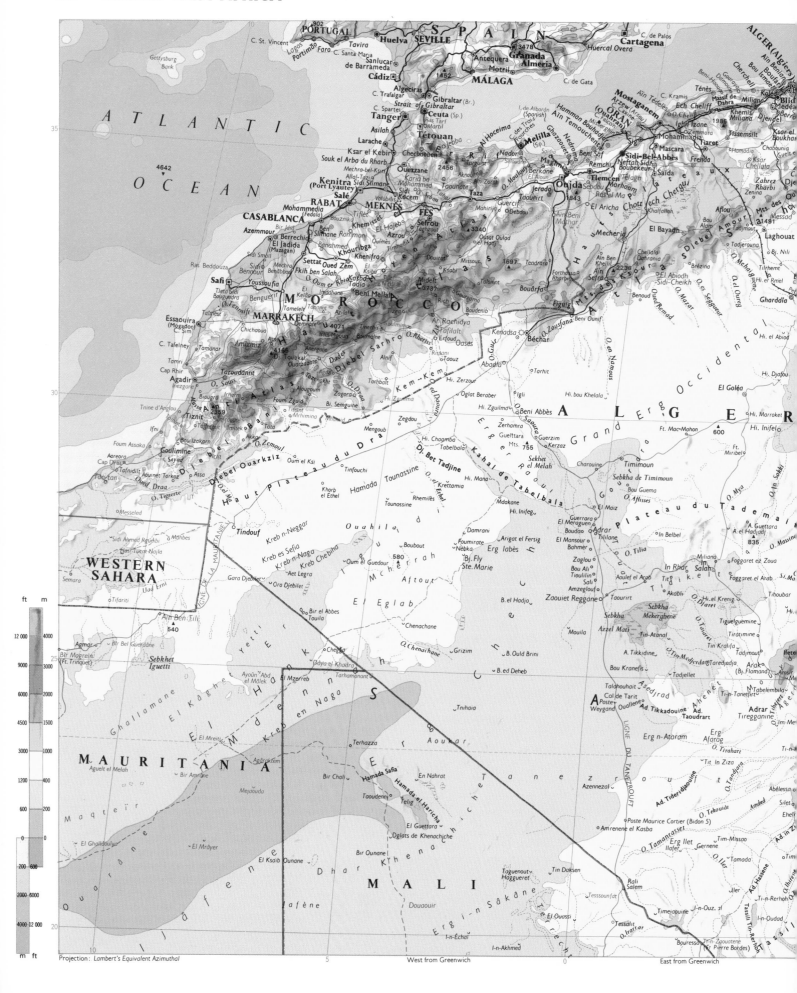

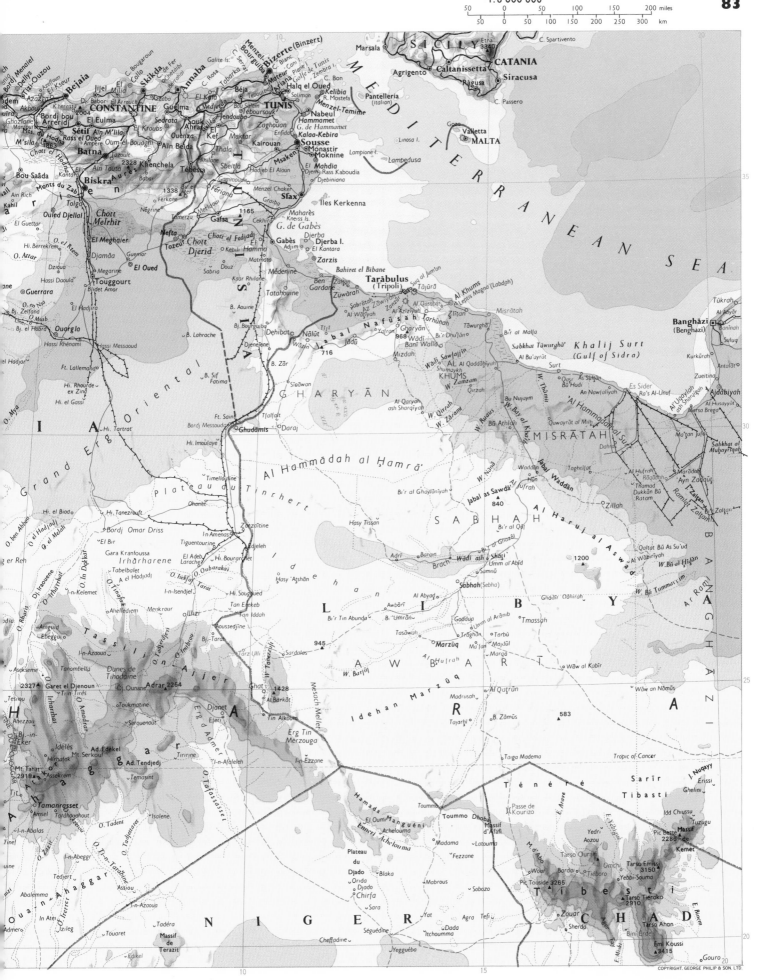

1:8 000 000

50   0   50   100   150   200 miles
50   0   50   100   150   200   250   300 km

MEDITERRANEAN SEA

SICILY
CATANIA
Agrigento Caltanissetta
Ragusa Siracusa
C. Spartivento
Marsala
C. Passero
Pantelleria (Italian)
Linosa I.
Lampione I.
Lampedusa
MALTA
Valletta
Gozo

Menzel-Bourguiba Bizerte (Binzert)
Galite Is.
C. Blanc
Mateur C. Rosa Tabarka Serrat
Annaba Skikda Collo C. de Fer Jijel Mila
Bejaia Azazga El Eulma Azaba El Kala
Tizi-Ouzou Dellys
Menjel El Kseur
Bordj bou Arréridj 2004
Sétif Aïn M'lila
CONSTANTINE Guelma Souk Ahras
M'sila Rass el Oued El Eulma
Batna Aïn Beïda El Kef Maktar
Biskra Khenchela Tébessa Thala
Aurès 2328 Ferkane Kairouan Sousse
Bou Saâda Aïn Touta 1338 Sbeïtla Msaken Monastir
1165 Moknine
Ouled Djellal Négrine Gafsa Mahdia
Chott Melrhir Metlaoui Sfax
El Meghaier Nefta Tozeur Gabès Djerba I.
El Oued Chott Djerid Kebili El Kantara
Touggourt Douz Zarzis
Médenine Ben Gardane

Tarābulus (Tripoli) Al Khums
Az Zawiyah Tarhūnah Leptis Magna (Labdah) Misrātah
Jabal Nafūsah Gharyān 968 Wādī Banī Walīd
Nālūt Jādū 716 Mizdah Al Qaddāhīyah
GHARYĀN Surt Khalij Surt (Gulf of Sidra)
Ghudāmis Banghāzī (Benghazi)
Al Hammādah al Hamrā' Al Jufrah Hūn Waddān
Jabal as Sawdā' 840 SABHAH Al Haruj al Aswad
Plateau du Tinrhert Zillah
Bordj Omar Driss In Amenas 1200
Sabhah (Sebha) LIBYA Tibesti
Tassili n'Ajjer Marzūq AWBĀRĪ
Djanet Idehan Marzūq Tropic of Cancer
Tamanrasset Ahaggar Sarīr Tibastī
Tassili Ténéré Massif du Kemet
NIGER CHAD Tibesti Emi Koussi 3415

COPYRIGHT GEORGE PHILIP & SON. LTD.

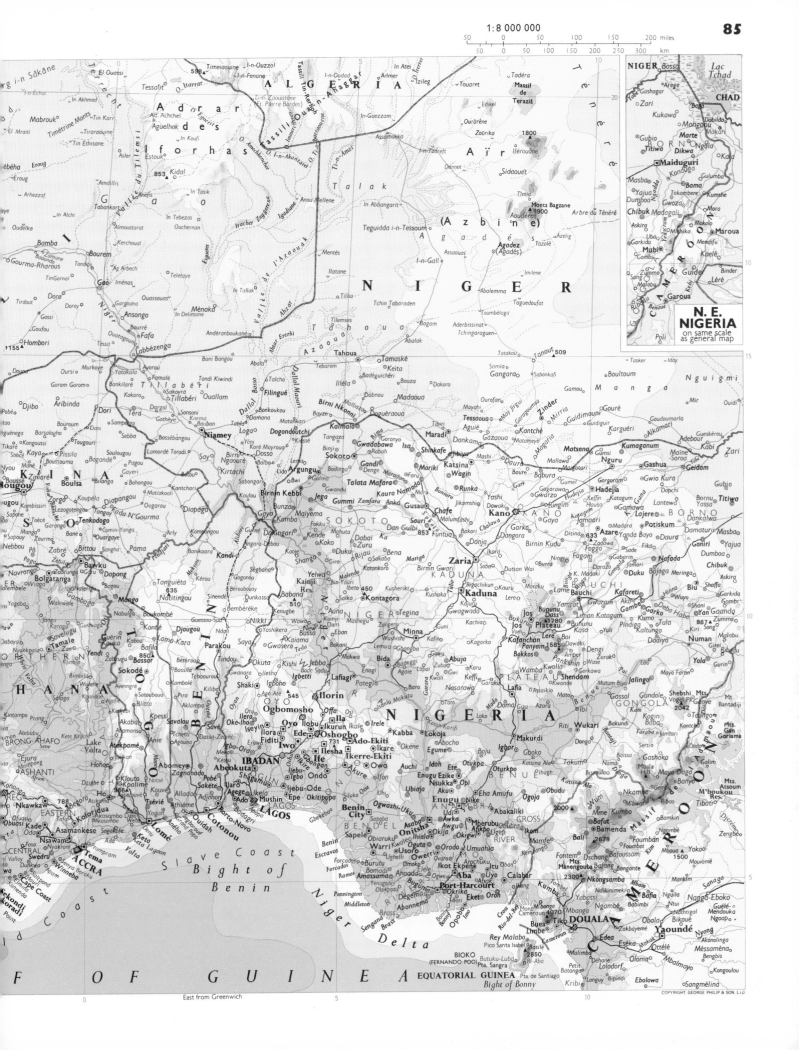

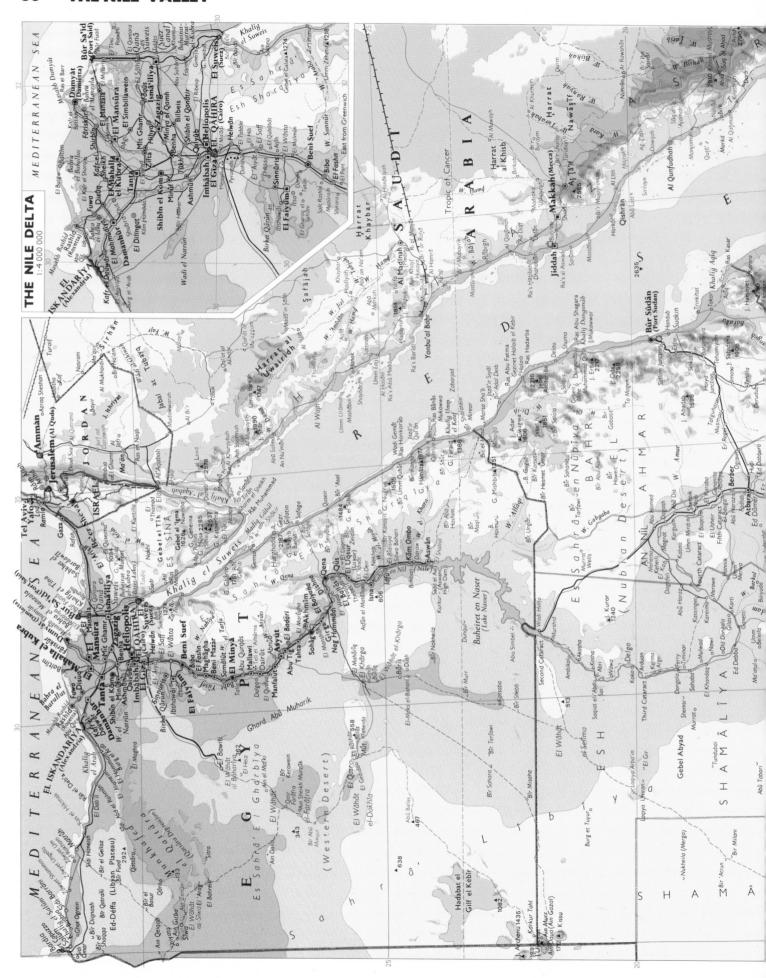

THE NILE DELTA
1:4 000 000

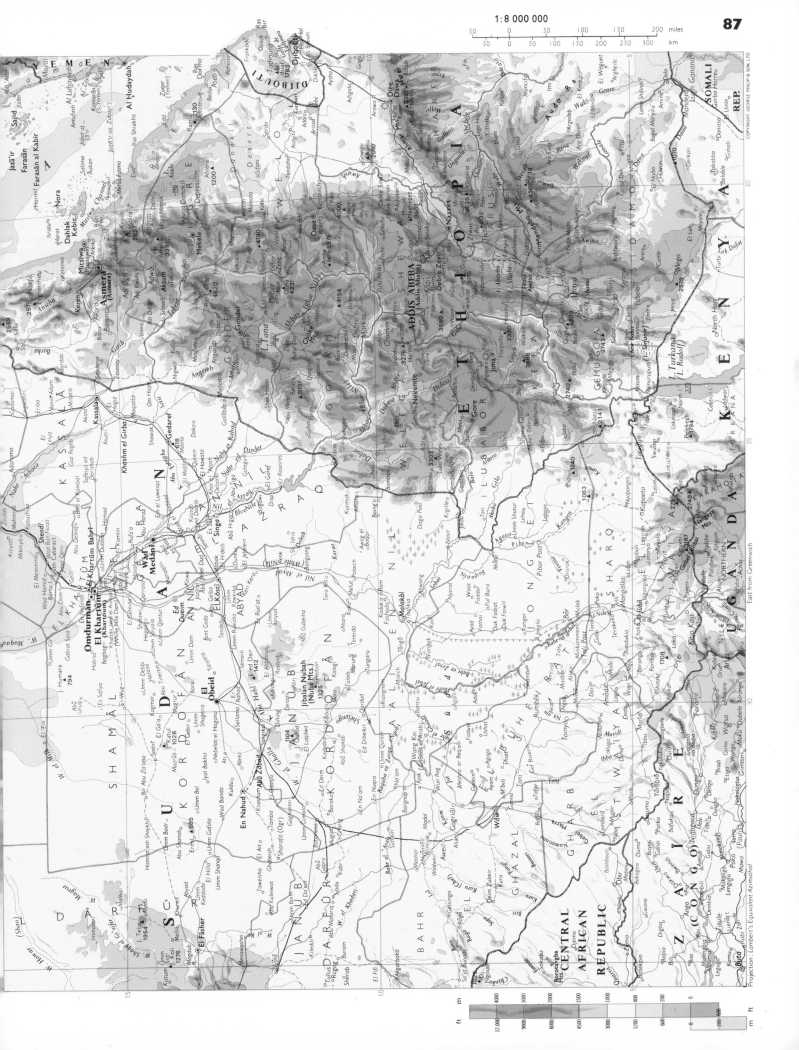

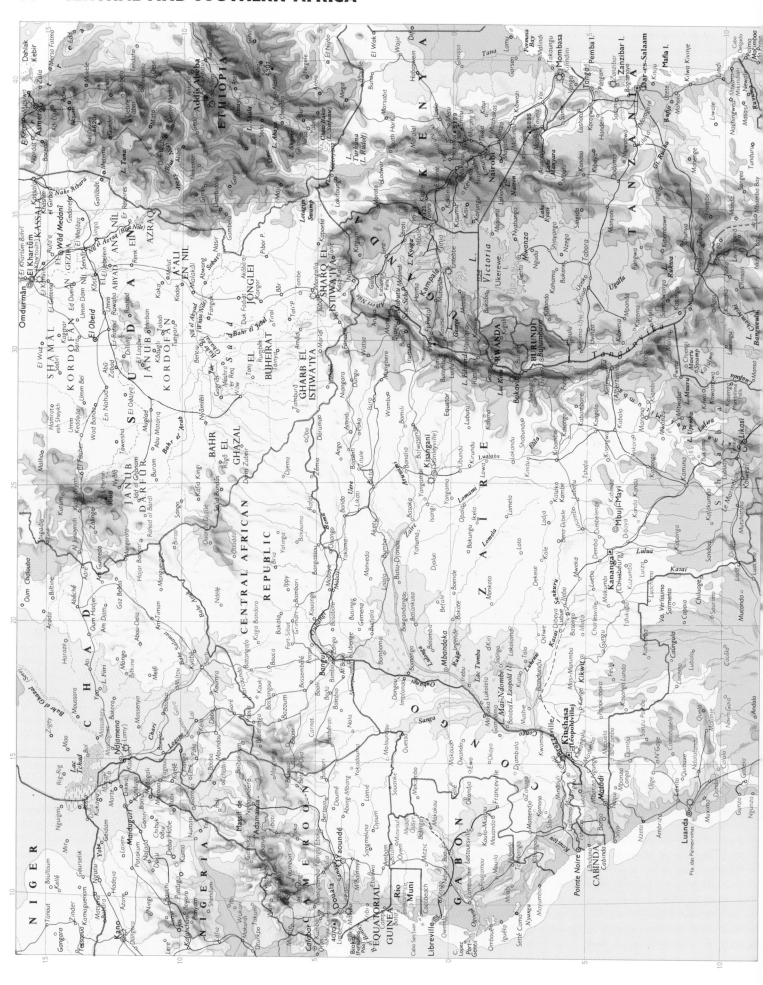

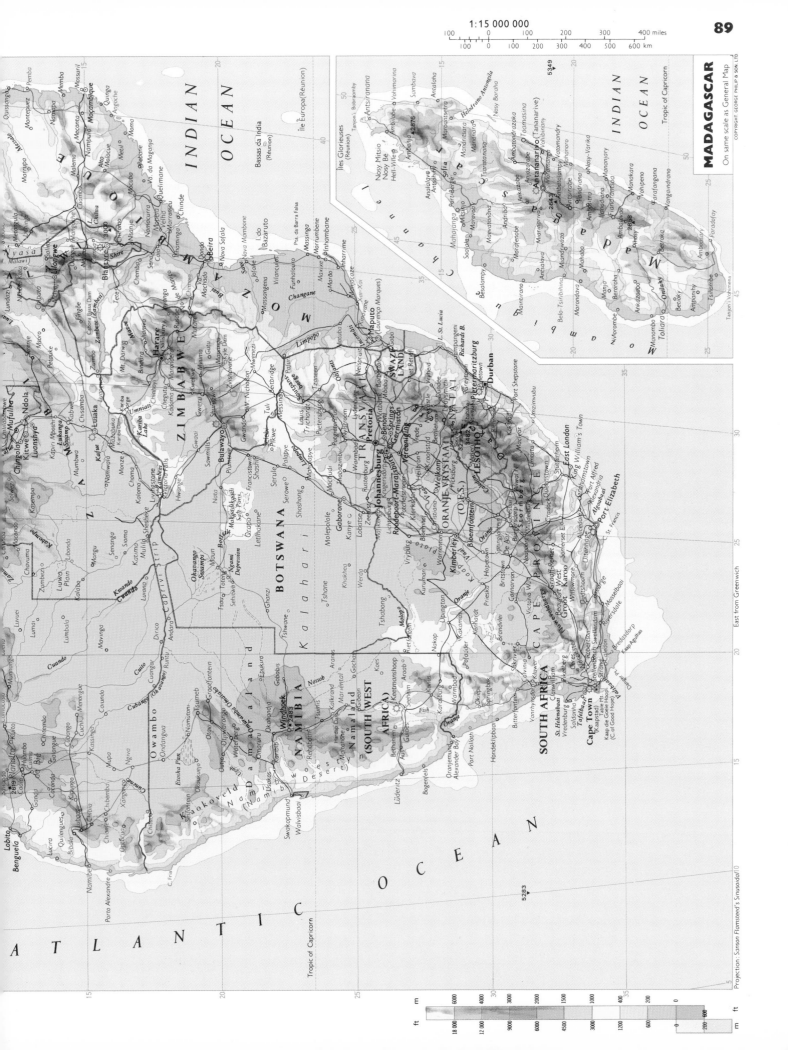

1:15 000 000

100   0   100   200   300   400 miles
100   0   100   200   300   400   500   600 km

MADAGASCAR
On same scale as General Map

COPYRIGHT GEORGE PHILIP & SON LTD

INDIAN   OCEAN

I N D I A N   O C E A N

Tropic of Capricorn

MOÇAMBIQUE

ZIMBABWE

ZAMBIA

BOTSWANA

Kalahari

NAMIBIA
(SOUTH WEST
AFRICA)

Namib Desert

TRANSVAAL

Pretoria
Johannesburg

ORANJE-VRYSTAAT
(O.F.S.)

SWAZI
LAND

NATAL

Durban

LESOTHO

CAPE PROVINCE

SOUTH AFRICA

Cape Town
(Kaapstad)
Kaap die Goeie Hoop
(C. of Good Hope)

East London

Port Elizabeth

A T L A N T I C   O C E A N

Tropic of Capricorn

Projection: Sanson Flamsteed's Sinusoidal

East from Greenwich

m   ft
6000 18 000
4000 12 000
3000 9000
2000 6000
1500 4500
1000 3000
400   1200
200   600
0   0
ft   m

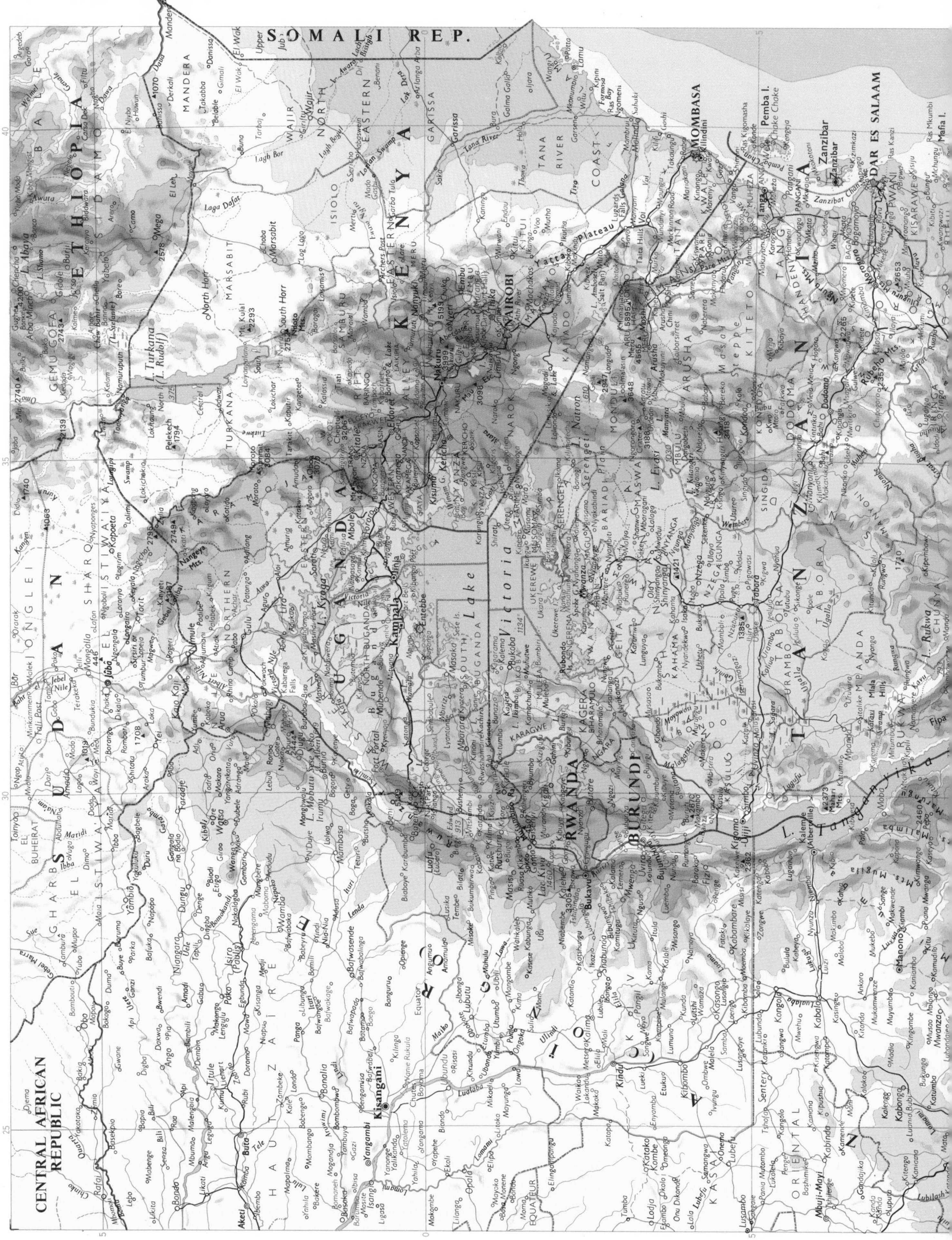

SOMALI REP.

ETHIOPIA

KENYA

UGANDA

SUDAN

ZAIRE

TANZANIA

RWANDA

BURUNDI

CENTRAL AFRICAN REPUBLIC

NAIROBI

MOMBASA

DAR ES SALAAM

Zanzibar

Pemba I.

Mafia I.

Lake Victoria

L. Turkana (L. Rudolf)

L. Mobutu

L. Kivu

L. Tanganyika

Kampala

Entebbe

Kisangani

Equator

1:8 000 000

50 0 50 100 150 200 miles
50 0 100 200 300 km

COPYRIGHT GEORGE PHILIP & SON, LTD.

Projection: Lambert's Equivalent Azimuthal

East from Greenwich

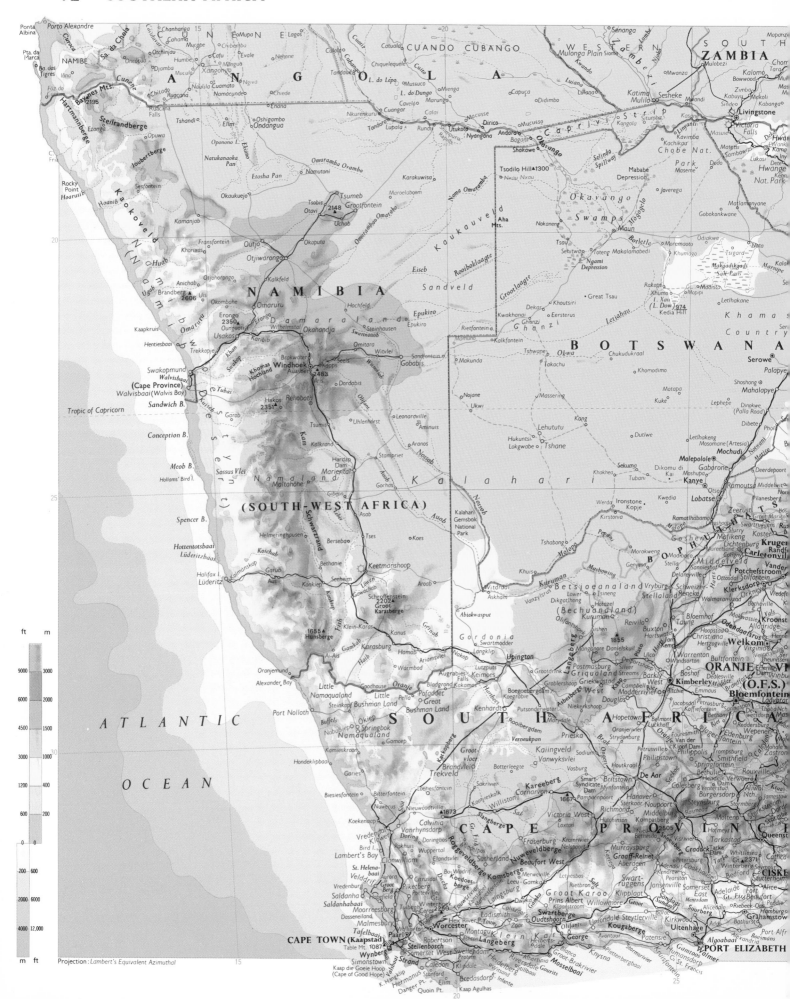

Projection: Lambert's Equivalent Azimuthal

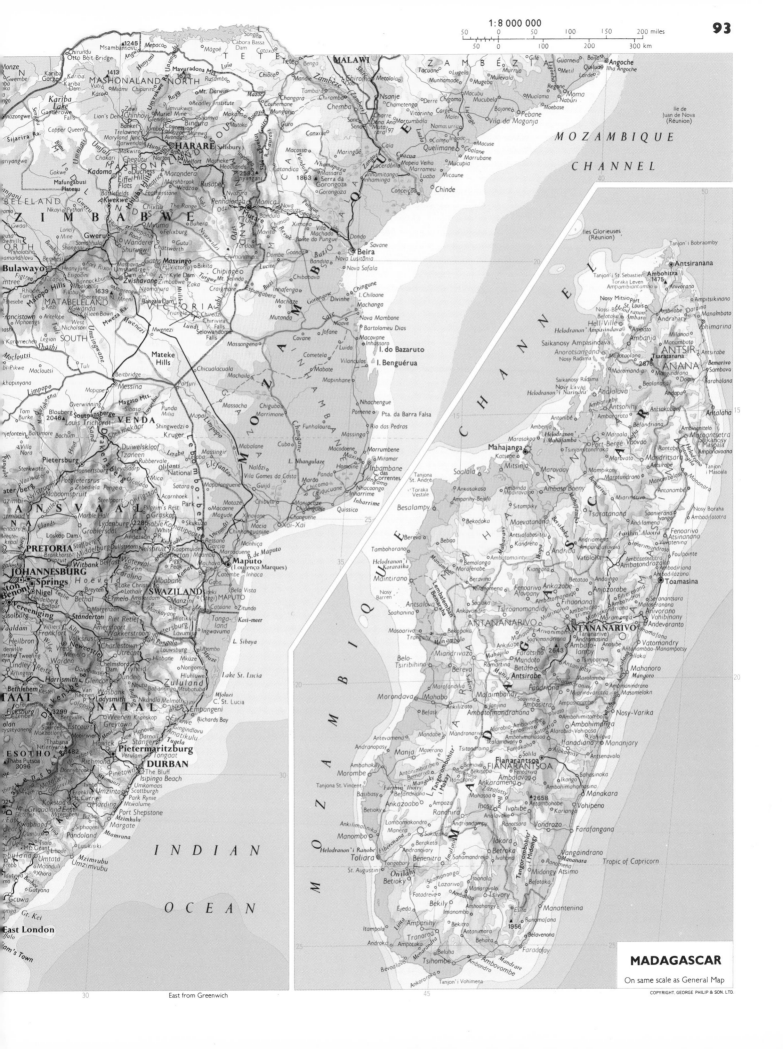

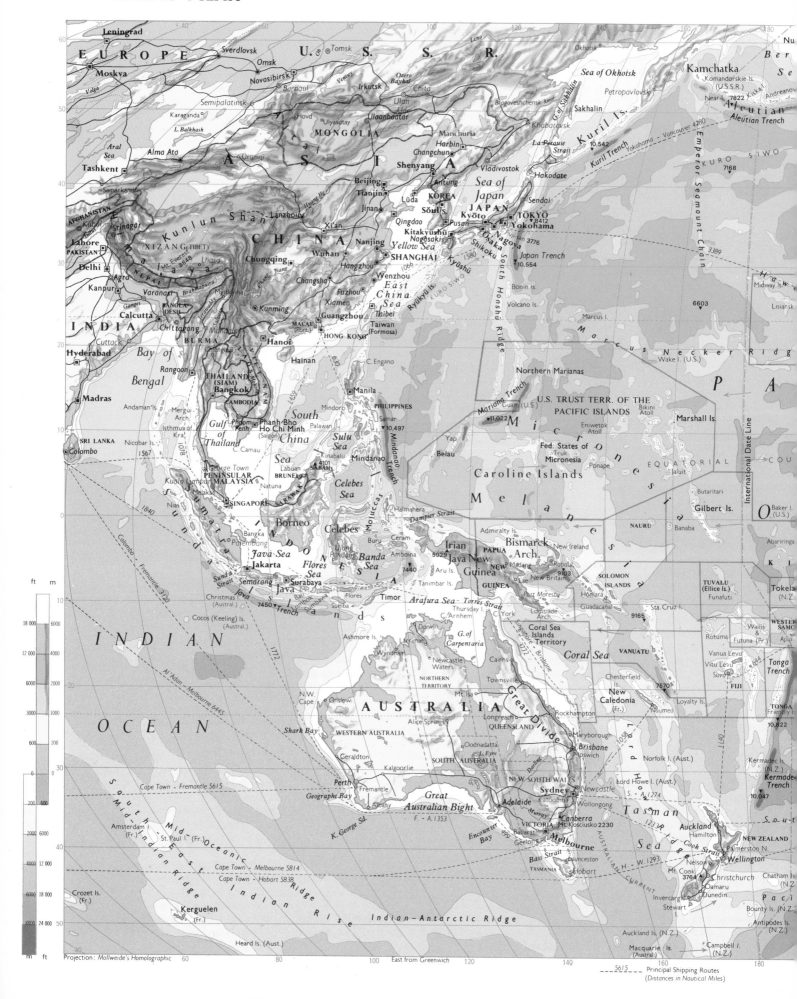

East from Greenwich

‒‒‒5615‒‒‒ Principal Shipping Routes
(Distances in Nautical Miles)

ALASKA
6050
Bristol Bay
nak
IFT
6741

Gulf of Alaska
Juneau
Sitka
Prince of Wales I.
Prince Rupert
Kitimat
Queen Charlotte Is.

Rocky
CANADA
NORTH AMERICA
L. Athabaska
Churchill
Lynn Lake
Belcher Is.
Hudson Bay
James Bay
Scheffferville
Hamilton Inlet

GREENLAND
C. Farewell

Dawson Creek
Edmonton
Prince Albert
Saskatoon
L. Winnipeg
Regina

Labrador
Strait of Belle Isle

NORTH

Vancouver
Vancouver I.
Victoria
Seattle
Tacoma
Portland
C. Blanco

Calgary
Medicine Hat
Winnipeg
Duluth
L. Superior
Ste. Marie
St. Paul
Michigan
L. Huron
L. Ontario
Ottawa
Toronto
Montréal
Québec
Fredericton
Anticosti
G. of St. Lawrence
St. Lawrence
Pr. Edward I.
Saint John
C. Breton I.
Sable I.
New York
Southampton 309I

Newfoundland
C. Race

NORTH

Spokane
Helena
Butte
Boise
Bismarck
Missouri
Snake
Cheyenne
Denver
Salt Lake City
Minneapolis
Milwaukee
CHICAGO
Des Moines
Kansas
St. Louis
Indianapolis
Cincinnati
Detroit
Buffalo
Pittsburgh
Erie
Boston
C. Sable

Mendocino Seascarp
C. Mendocino
Sacramento
Oakland
San Francisco
2419
4418

Mountains
UNITED STATES
Santa Fé
Oklahoma
Little Rock
Memphis
Nashville
Atlanta
Baltimore
Washington
Richmond
Norfolk
C. Hatteras
Philadelphia
NEW YORK

ATLANTIC

2091
Los Angeles
San Diego

Murray Seascarp
CALIFORNIAN CURRENT
Guadalupe
6225
Pto. Eugenia

Sierra Madre
El Paso
Ciudad Juárez
Dallas
Austin
Houston
San Antonio
Galveston
New Orleans
Mobile
Savannah
Jacksonville

New York - Recife
3678
Bermuda (U.K.)

OCEAN

Tropic of Cancer
Clarion Fracture Zone
3777

C. S. Lucas
Gulf of California
Aguascalientes
Guadalajara
Revilla Gigedo Is. (Mexico)
Torreón
Monterrey
San Luis Potosí
Tampico
Veracruz
5700
México
Puebla
5889
Acapulco
Guadalajara

Gulf of Mexico
Tampa
Miami
Florida Strait
Yucatan Channel
Mérida
BAHAMAS
CUBA
La Habana

West Indies
Hispaniola
DOM. REP.
9200
HAITI
JAMAICA
Kingston
Santo Domingo
Puerto Rico (U.S.)
St. Thomas (U.S.)
Virgin Is.
Leeward Is.

N.Y. C. 1972

Hawaiian Is. (U.S.A.)
Ridge
Oahu
Honolulu
Hawaii

4711

Clipperton Fracture Zone
Clipperton I. (Fr.)
3666

BELIZE
GUATEMALA
5895
Guatemala
Honduras
Tegucigalpa
EL SALVADOR
Salvador
NICARAGUA
Managua
CENTRAL AMERICA
COSTA RICA
San José
Colón
PANAMA
Panamá
Canal

Caribbean Sea
Curaçao (Ne.)
Barranquilla
San José
Cartagena
Maracaibo
Caracas
Orinoco
VENEZUELA

Martinique (Fr.)
Guadeloupe (Fr.)
BARBADOS
Windward Is.
TRINIDAD & TOBAGO

S. E. Monsoon Drift
Cocos I.

PACIFIC

CURRENT
Palmyra Is. (U.S.)
Teraina
Tabuaeran
Kiritimati

Christmas Island Ridge

Medellín
Bogotá
Cali
COLOMBIA
C. S. Francisco
835
Quito
ECUADOR
Guayaquil
Chimborazo 6267
Cuenca
Iquitos
Manaus
Amazon
BRAZIL

Jarvis I. (U.S.)
Equator
Galápagos (Ecuador)

SOUTH

EAN
bury I.
enix Is.
IBATI

Malden I.
Starbuck I.

C. Pariñas
Lobos I.
70b
Chiclayo
Trujillo

SOUTH

Marquesas Is.
Tongareva
Penrhyn Is.
Manihiki
Suwarrow Is.
Vostok
Flint I.
Caroline I.

Tahiti - Panamá 4570

6369
PERU
Lima
Callao
Cuzco
L. Titicaca
Ilampu & Ancohuma
6550
La Paz
BOLIVIA

AMERICA

Cook Islands (N.Z.)
1303
Society Is.
Windward Is.
Leeward Is.
Tahiti
Tuamotu Archipelago
FRENCH POLYNESIA

Auckland - Panamá 6510

PERUVIAN CURRENT
Arequipa
6866
Peru
Arica
Iquique
Chile
8050
Antofagasta
Trench

PARAGUAY

Austral
Manuae
Rarotonga

Seamount Chain
Tubuai Is. (Austral Is.)
Rapa Iti

Tuamotu Ridge

Pitcairn I. (U.K.)
Ducie I.

Tropic of Capricorn
Sala-y-Gomez (Chile)
Easter Is. (Chile)
San Félix (Chile)
San Ambrosio (Chile)

Southeast Pacific Basin

East Pacific Ridge

Salta
Tucumán
Corrientes
Pto. Alegre
Asunción

Arch. de Juan Fernández (Chile)
Alejandro Selkirk
Robinson Crusoe
Aconcagua 6960
Valparaíso
Santiago
Concepción
Neuquén

Córdoba
Rosario
Santa Fe
Paysandú
URUGUAY
Paraná
ARGENTINA
Buenos Aires
La Plata
Río de la Plata
Montevideo
Mar del Plata

Basin

Pacific-Antarctic Ridge
Chile Rise

Chonos Arch.
G. of Penas
P. Deseado
Wellington
Sta. Cruz
Punta
Punta Arenas
Str. of Magellan
C. Horn
Tierra del Fuego

Pacific-Antarctic Basin

WEST WIND DRIFT
CAPE HORN CURRENT

P.A. Valparaíso
1414
Buenos Aires - Montevideo
1355 1295
Patagonian
Falkland Is. (U.K.)
Stanley

SOUTH
ATLANTIC

Argentine Basin
6212

OCEAN
South Georgia

160　140　West from Greenwich　100　80　60　40　20

Projection: Bonne

East from Greenwich

Boundaries of the artesian basins

1:12 000 000

AUSTRALASIA
POLITICAL
1:80 000 000

PAPUA NEW GUINEA

1:12 000 000

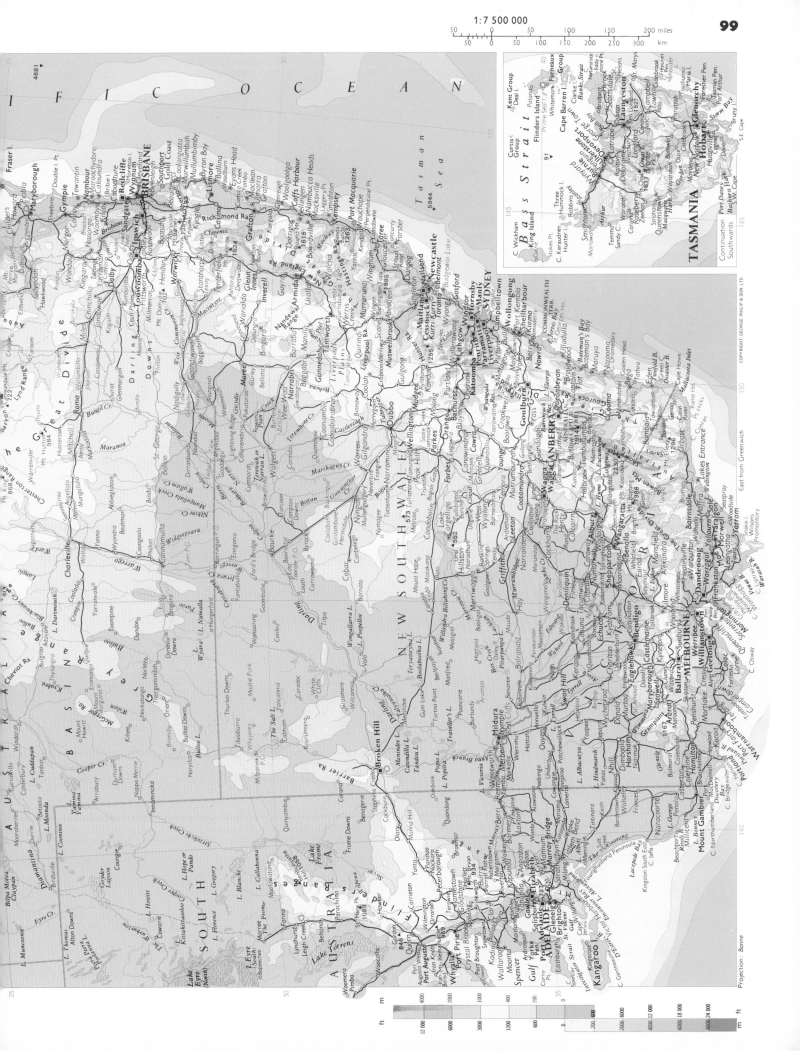

1:4 500 000

20   0   20   40   60   80   100 miles
20   0   40   80   120   160 km

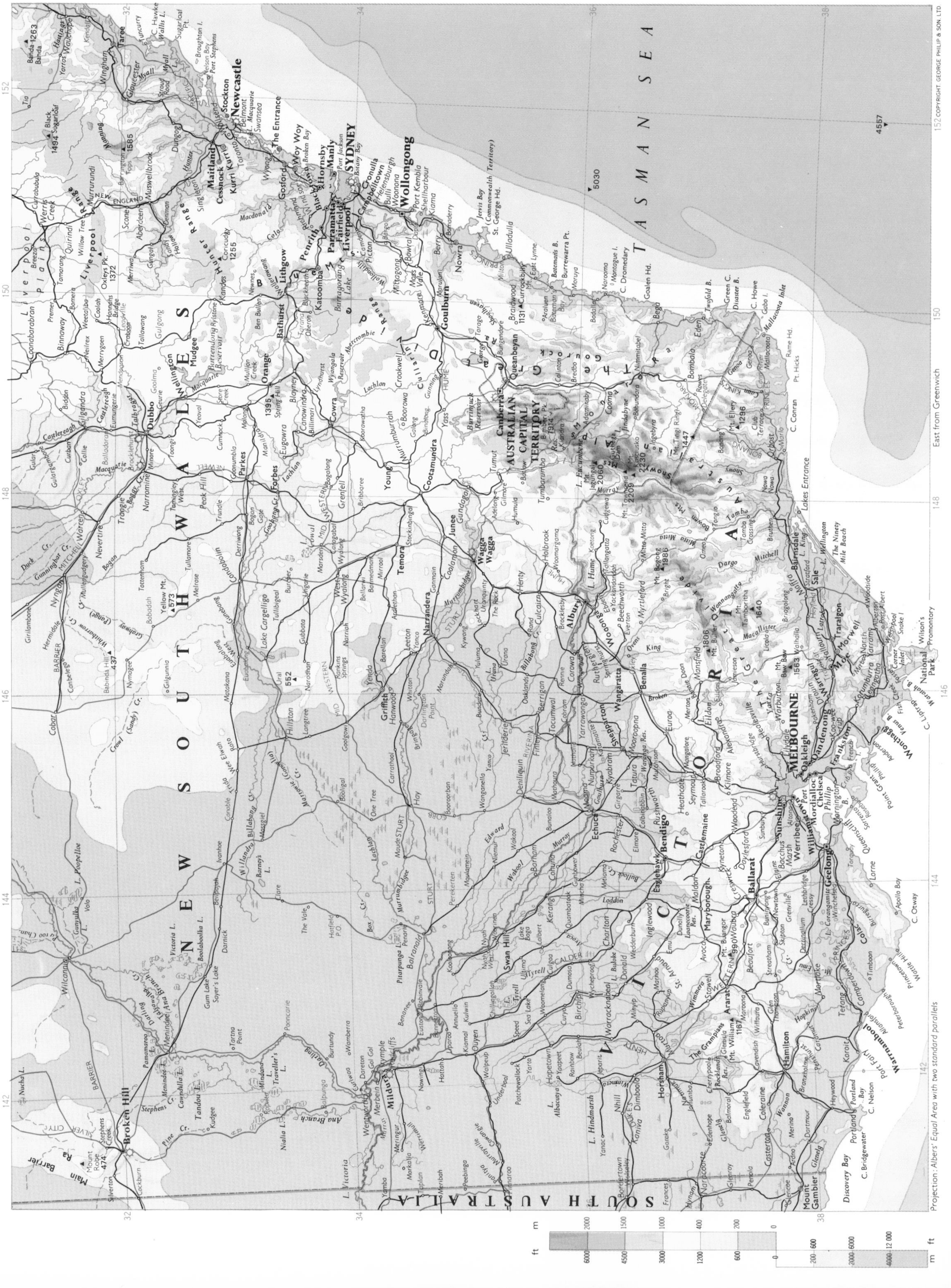

T A S M A N   S E A

N E W   S O U T H   W A L E S

V I C T O R I A

S O U T H   A U S T R A L I A

Liverpool Plain

Liverpool Range

Blue Mts.

Great

Dividing

Range

Australian Alps

Snowy Mts.

Snowy

Wilson's Promontory

The Ninety Mile Beach

East from Greenwich

Major cities and towns:
Newcastle, SYDNEY, Wollongong, Maitland, Cessnock, Kurri Kurri, Stockton, Manly, Hornsby, Parramatta, Fairfield, Liverpool, Penrith, Katoomba, Lithgow, Bathurst, Orange, Dubbo, Mudgee, Wellington, Forbes, Parkes, Cowra, Young, Goulburn, Nowra, Queanbeyan, CANBERRA, Cootamundra, Temora, Wagga Wagga, Junee, Narrandera, Leeton, Griffith, Hanwood, Hay, Deniliquin, Albury, Wangaratta, Benalla, Shepparton, Echuca, Bendigo, Ballarat, MELBOURNE, Geelong, Warrnambool, Portland, Hamilton, Horsham, Swan Hill, Mildura, Wentworth, Broken Hill, Bairnsdale, Sale, Moe, Morwell, Traralgon, Frankston, Dandenong, Oakleigh, Sunshine, Castlemaine, Maryborough, Ararat, Sale

AUSTRALIAN CAPITAL TERRITORY

Projection: Albers' Equal Area with two standard parallels

m   ft
2000   6000
1500   4500
1000   3000
400   1200
200   600
0   0

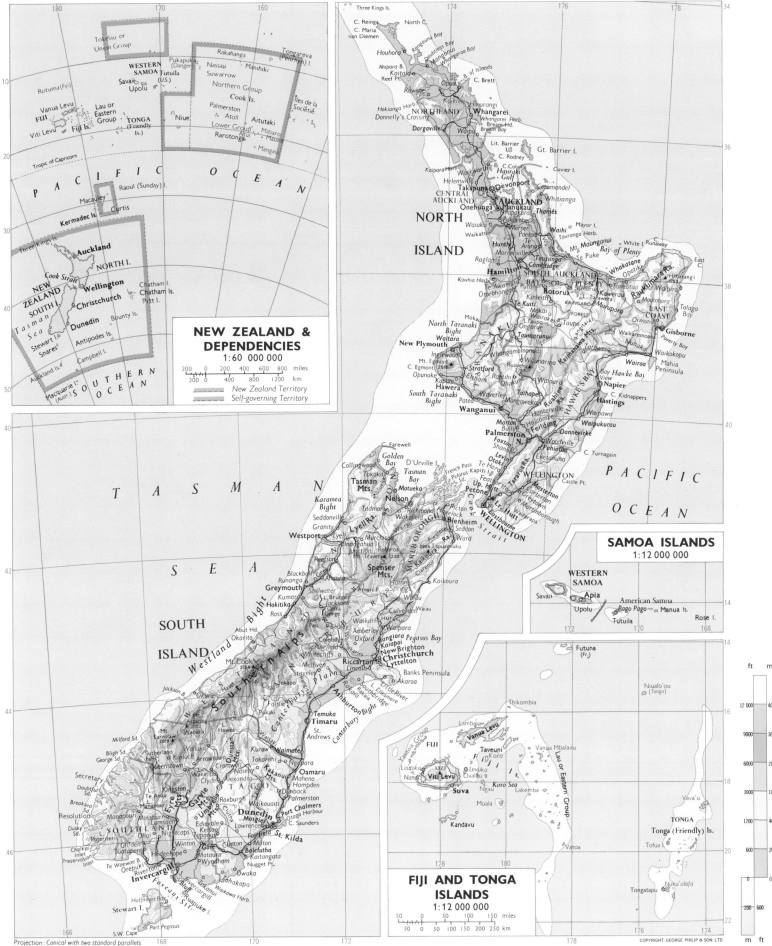

1:6 000 000
20   0   20   40   60   80   100 miles
20   0   40   80   120   160 km

NEW ZEALAND & DEPENDENCIES
1:60 000 000
200 0   200 400 600 800 miles
200 0   400   800   1200 km
New Zealand Territory
Self-governing Territory

SAMOA ISLANDS
1:12 000 000

WESTERN SAMOA

Savaii   Apia
Upolu   American Samoa
          Pago Pago   Manua Is.
          Tutuila   Rose I.

FIJI AND TONGA ISLANDS
1:12 000 000
50   0   50   100   150 miles
50 0 50 100 150 200 250 km

Projection: Conical with two standard parallels

COPYRIGHT GEORGE PHILIP & SON. LTD.

ft   m
12 000   4000
9000   3000
6000   2000
3000   1000
1200   400
600   200
0   0
200   600
m   ft

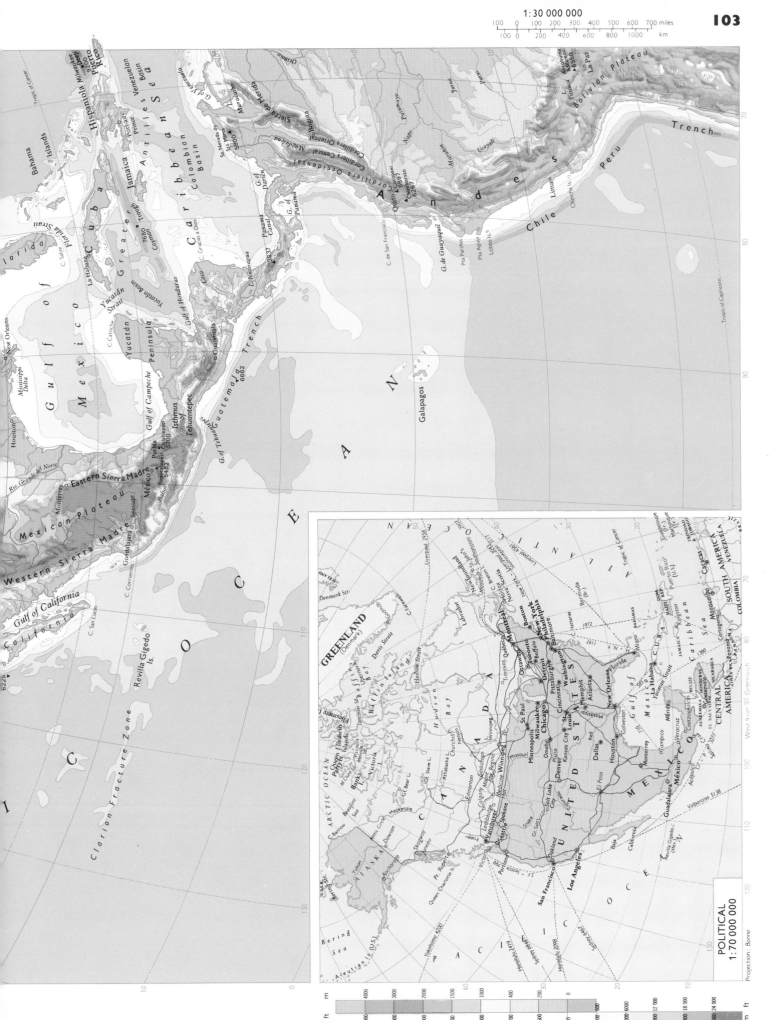

ALASKA
1 : 30 000 000

Projection : Bonne

1:15 000 000

100 50 0   100   200   300   400 miles

100   0   100   200   300   400   500   600
km

N. W. TERRITORIES

MANITOBA

HUDSON BAY

North Belcher Is.
Baker's Dozen Is.
Kugong I.
Belcher Islands
Flaherty I.
Tukarak I.
Innetalling I.

Stupart
Gods
Black Duck
Niskibi
Fort Severn
Echoing
Beaverstone
Severn
Winisk
Wabuk Pt.
C. Lookout
C. Henrietta Maria

Knee L.
Gods L.
Edmund L.
Sharpe L.
Gods L.
Sandy L.
Red Sucker L.
Finger L.
Sachigo L.
Severn
Ponask L.
Bearskin Lake
Favourable Lake
MacDowell L. 396
Casummit Lake
Birch L.
Trout L.
Bowman L.
Cat L.
Central Patricia
Pickle L.
Osnaburgh
Fort Hope
Eabamet L.
Ogoki

Winisk
Shamattawa
Sutton
Kinushseo
Lakitusaki
Lake River
Ekwan Pt.
Attawapiskat
Attawapiskat
Missisa L.
Kapiskau
Akimiski I.
Weston I.
North Twin I.
South Twin I.
Tradely I.
Charlton

L. Minto
Nastapoka Is.
Mélè
Lacs de Loups-M.
L. Guillaume-Delisle
L. à l'Eau Claire
Petite Baleine
Grand Baleine
Lac D'Iberville
Lac Bienville

Merry I.
Poste-de-la-Baleine
Long I.
Pte. Louis-XIV
Burton L.
Roggan
Roggan River
Julian L.
Craven L.
Kanaaupscow
Fort George
Castor L.
Nouveau Comptoir
Duncan L.
La Grande
Sakami L.
Yasinski L.
Fregate L.
L. de la Corvette
Boyd L.
Opinaca
Low L.
Lac Rossignol

JAMES BAY

Ekwan L.
Moosonee
Moose Factory
Moose River
Hannah B.
Fort Albany
Kwataboahegan
Kesagami L.
Rupert B.
Fort Rupert (Rupert House)
Broadback R.
Nottaway
Nemiscau
Eastmain
Némiscou
L. Dana
L. Evans
Rés. Gouin

ONTARIO

Whitewater L.
Wabakimi L.
Ogoki Res.
Little Current
Anikameg L.
Albany
Attawapiskat
Missinaibi
Ogoki
Lansdowne House
Kapiskau

Sioux Lookout
Savant L.
Lac Seul
Ghost River
Allanwater
Caribou L.
Auden
Kowkash
Nakina
Nagagami
Geraldton
Longlac
Calstock
Hearst
Mattice
Smoky Falls
Fraserdale
Island Falls
Cochrane
Norembega
La Reine
La Sarre
Macamic
Iroquois Falls
Taschereau
Amos
Barraute
L. Parent

Hudson
Minnitaki L.
Armstrong
Collins
Ferland
Kenogami
Pagwa River
Opasatika
Mattawishkwia
Kapuskasing
Smooth Rock Falls
South Porcupine
Timmins
Schumacher
Ramore
Kirkland Lake
Nonanda
Rouyn
Cadillac
Senneterre
Val-d'Or
Mégiscane L.

LAKE SUPERIOR

Thunder Bay
Isle Royale
Michipicoten
Lake Superior Prov. Park
Sault Ste. Marie
Sudbury
Copper Cliff
North Bay
Sturgeon Falls
Espanola
Little Current
Manitoulin Is.
Killarney
Georgian Bay
Parry Sound
Pembroke
Renfrew
Arnprior
Ottawa
Hull
Cornwall

WISCONSIN

Duluth
Superior
Ashland
Ironwood
Marquette
Escanaba
Green Bay
Appleton
Oshkosh
Fond du Lac
Sheboygan
Manitowoc
Milwaukee
Madison
Beloit
Rockford
Chicago

MICHIGAN

Iron Mountain
Menominee
Marinette
Traverse City
Cadillac
Manistee
Ludington
Muskegon
Grand Rapids
Big Rapids
Mount Pleasant
Bay City
Saginaw
Flint
Lansing
Battle Creek
Kalamazoo
Detroit
Dearborn
Ann Arbor
Ypsilanti
Port Huron
Pontiac

LAKE HURON
LAKE MICHIGAN
GEORGIAN BAY

Owen Sound
Collingwood
Barrie
Orillia
Midland
Penetanguishene
Wiarton
Goderich
Stratford
Kitchener
Waterloo
Guelph
Cambridge
Brampton
TORONTO
HAMILTON
Burlington
St. Catharines
Niagara Falls
Welland
Brantford
London
Woodstock
Ingersoll
Simcoe
Port Colborne

LAKE ONTARIO
LAKE ERIE

BUFFALO
Rochester
Oswego
Syracuse
Utica
Watertown
Kingston
Belleville
Trenton
Cobourg
Port Hope
Oshawa
Peterborough
Lindsay

CLEVELAND
Toledo
Sandusky
Lorain
Erie
Dunkirk
Jamestown
Bradford
Warren

Windsor
Leamington
Point Pelee
Chatham
Sarnia
Wallaceburg

QUEBEC
MONTRÉAL
Ottawa
Hull
Trois-Rivières
Shawinigan
Grand-Mère
Joliette
St-Jean
Valleyfield
Salaberry-de-Valleyfield
Huntingdon
Cornwall
Brockville
Perth
Smiths Falls
Carleton Place
Renfrew

NEW YORK
Watertown
Ogdensburg
Massena
Malone
Plattsburg
Saranac Lake
Tupper Lake
Lake Placid
Ticonderoga
Glens Falls
Saratoga Springs
Schenectady
Albany
Troy
Amsterdam
Oneida
Rome
Auburn
Geneva
Ithaca
Binghamton
Elmira
Corning
Hornell
Olean
Salamanca

PENNSYLVANIA
OHIO
INDIANA
ILLINOIS

Lambert's Equivalent Azimuthal

ft m
4500 1500
3000 1000
1200 400
600 200
0 0
200 600
2000 6000
4000 12 000
m ft

50   0   50   100   150   200 miles
50   0   50   100   150   200   250   300 km

Z
E
W

South Aulatsivik I.
High I.
Nain
Paul I.
Fraser

Erlandson
Whale
George
L. de la
Hutte
Sauvage
Kogaluk
Voisey B.
Tunungayualok I.
Davis Inlet
Nunaksaluk I.
Big Bay
Hopedale
Kaipokok B.

Fort
McKenzie
L. Nachicapau
Mistastin
Makkovik
Aillik
C. Harrison

C O A S T

Chakonipau L.
Otelnuk L.
Wheeler
Whitegull
L. Tudor
610
Harp L.
Kanairiktok
Nashaupi
Seal L.
Nipishish
Holton
Indian Harbour
Groswater B.

Kaniapiskau
Séringy
Sandy
Attikamagen L.
Schefferville
Smallwood
Reservoir
North-West River
L. Melville
Mealy Mts.
Separation
Point
Cartwright
Island of Ponds
Table B.

O F

Lac Verneuil
L. Néret
Lac
Clairambault
L. Petitsikapau
Grand
1128
Sandwich B.

Nitchequon
Kaniapiskau
L. Bermen
Churchill Falls
Goose
Goose Bay
Happy Valley
Eagle
Paradise
Square Islands

Opiscoteo
Shabogamo L.
Opiskatish L.
Ossokmanuan
Churchill
Alexis

L A B R A D O R
a

Naococane
L.
Winokapau
St. Lewis
St. Mary's
Battle Harbour

Lac Joseph
Atikonak
Minipie
Red
Bay
Belle I.

Péribonca
Opiskatish L.
Burnt
Little Mecatina
St. Paul
St. Lunaire-
Griquet
St. Anthony
Hare B.

Wabush
Labrador City
Ashuanipi
St-Augustin
Brador Bay
Flower's
Cove
Lourdes-de-
Blanc-Sablon
Groais I.
Bell I.

1128
Atikonak
Natashquan
Outer I.
Roddickton
Conche
Englee

Q U E B E C
a
n

Rés.
Manicouagan
Nipissi
1048
West Maine
Musquaro
I. du
Petit-Mécatina
Harrington Harbour
Port
Saunders
White B.
Horse I.
C. St John

Ste-Marguerite
Manitou
Musquaro
Daniel's
Harbour
Great
Harbour
Deep
Deer
Lake

N E W F O U N D L A N D

Manouane
Clarke
City
Sheldrake
Lac
Allard
Etamamu
Kegaska
Gethsémani
Trout River
Bay of Islands
South Brook
Springdale
Seal Cove
Sop's
Arm
Baie
Verte
La Scie
Notre Dame
Twillingate
Fogo I.
Fogo
C. Freels

Pipmuacan
Walker L.
Sept-Îles
Moisie
Mingan
Aguanish Natashquan
Havre-St-Pierre
Corner Brook
814
Howley
Windsor
Springdale
Botwood
Gander
Lewisporte
Glenwood
Glovertown
Bonavista
B.

Péribonca
Res.
Clarke
City
Pte. Ouest
Baie-Trinité
Port-Cartier
Rivière-Pentecôte
Port-Menier
Î. d'Anticosti
Jupiter
Dét. de Jacques-Cartier
Heath Pt.
Long Pt.
Port au Port B.
Stephenville
Red Indian
Buchans
Grand Falls
Bishop's Falls
Dark Cove
Gander
Trinity
Catalina
Bonavista

Godbout
Baie-Trinité
Mont-Louis
Dét.-Vallée
Grande-Vallée
Pte. Sud Ouest
d'Honguedo
Pte. Sud
Port au Port
St. George's B.
Victoria
Grey Res.
White
Bear
Res.
St. Alban's
Terrenceville
Clarenville
Heart's
Content
Bay de Verde
Carbonear

Betsiamites
Forestville
Cap-Chat
Ste-Anne
Rivière-
au-Renard
C. de Gaspé
GULF OF
St. George's
St. David's
South Branch
Belleoram
Fortune
Marystown
Spaniard's
Bay
St. John's

Baie-
Comeau
Mont-
Joli
PARC PROV.
DE LA
GASPÉSIE
1310
Cartier
Gaspé
Douglastown
572
ST. LAWRENCE
St. Andrew's
C. Ray
Channel Port
aux Basques
Burgeo
Ramea
Grand Banks
Placentia
Argentia
Holyrood
Mt.
Pearl

Mts. Chic-Chocs
Pén. de Gaspé
Percé
Grande-Rivière
Chaleur Bay
Rimouski
Sayabec
Amqui
Bonaventure
Chandler
Harbour Breton
Grand Banks
Miquelon
St. Lawrence
St. Mary's B.
C. St. Mary's
Ferryland
Avalon
Peninsula

Bic
Causapscal
Matapédia
Pospébiac
Miscou I.
Î. Brion
Grande-Entrée
St. Paul
Langlade
St-Pierre
C. St. Mary's
C. Pine
C. Race
Trepassey

Trois-Pistoles
Dalhousie
Campbellton
Lamèque
Shippegan
Îs. de la
Madeleine
(Quebec)
Cap-aux-Meules
Fatima
Havre-Aubert
SAINT-PIERRE
ET MIQUELON
(Fr.)

Rivière-du-Loup
Atholville
Kedgwick
St. Arthur
Bathurst
Tracadie
Cap-aux-Meules
Pleasant Bay
NAT'L
PARK
Ingonish

Heath Steele
Miramichi B.
Tignish
Tracadie
Alberton
PRINCE EDWARD
Chéticamp
532
Sydney Mines
New Waterford

Cabano
Van Buren
St. Leonard
819
Grand Falls
Newcastle
Chatham
Richibucto
Rexton
ISLAND
Summerside
Kensington
East Pt.
Souris
Inverness
N. Sydney
Glace Bay

Edmundston
Ft. Kent
Grand Falls
Plaster
Rock
Blackville
Chipman
Dame
Borden
Montague
Murray Hr.
Georgetown
Port
Hawkesbury
Sydney
Louisburg

St-Pacôme
St-Jean-Port-Joli
Allagash
Caribou
Ashland
Presque Isle
Minto
Grand
Notre
Dame
Petitcodiac
Shediac
Tormentine
Pictou
Antigonish
L. Bras
d'Or
Fourchu
Cape Breton
Island

QUEBEC
Lauzon
Lévis
Pamphile
Montmagny
Eagle L.
Houlton
Woodstock
Hartland
Stanley
Gagetown
Sussex
Moncton
Elgin
Amherst
Springhill
Pugwash
New Glasgow
Stellarton
Sherbrooke
Î. Madame
Chedabucto B.
Canso

Deschambault
Ste-Marie
Beauceville
St-Georges
Thetford Mines
Asbestos
Lac-
Mégantic
Island Falls
Chesuncook
Patten
Fredericton
Junc.
Oromocto
Rothesay
St. Martins
Chignecto
B.
Joggins
Parrsboro
Truro
Upper
Stewiacke
Musquodoboit
Sherbrooke

Moosehead
Millinocket
Lincoln
Danforth
Minas
Basin
Windsor
Upper
Musquodoboit
Sheet Hr.

MAINE
East Angus
Sherbrooke
Magog
Coaticook
Mattawamkeag
Greenville
Guilford
Dover-Foxcroft
St. Stephen
St. George
Saint
John
Fundy
Bridgetown
Middleton
Annapolis
Royal
Kentville
Windsor
Dartmouth
Musquodoboit Hr.

Bingham
Skowhegan
Calais
Blacks
Hr.
Eastport
Grand
Manan I.
Bay of
NOVA SCOTIA
Halifax

Moosehead L.
Moosehead
megantic L.
Waterville
Old Town
Brewer
Bar Harbor
Machias
Jonesport
Digby
Weymouth
Bridgewater
Mahone Bay
Lunenburg

Rumford
Berlin
Bethel
Bangor
Belfast
Camden
Rockland
Mt. Desert I.
Yarmouth
St. Mary's B.
Rossignol
Res.
Liverpool
Port Mouton
Shelburne

Johnsbury
1917
Augusta
Bath
Brunswick
Freeport
Wedgeport
Lockeport
Clark's Harbour
C. Sable

Washington
Conway
Laconia
Auburn
Lewiston
Sebago
Portland
ATLANTIC

Rochester
Sanford
Saco
Biddeford
Sable I.
(Nova Scotia)

Concord
Dover
Portsmouth
OCEAN

Manchester
Nashua
Haverhill
Lawrence
Gloucester
C. Ann

Waltham
BOSTON
Lynn

Brockton

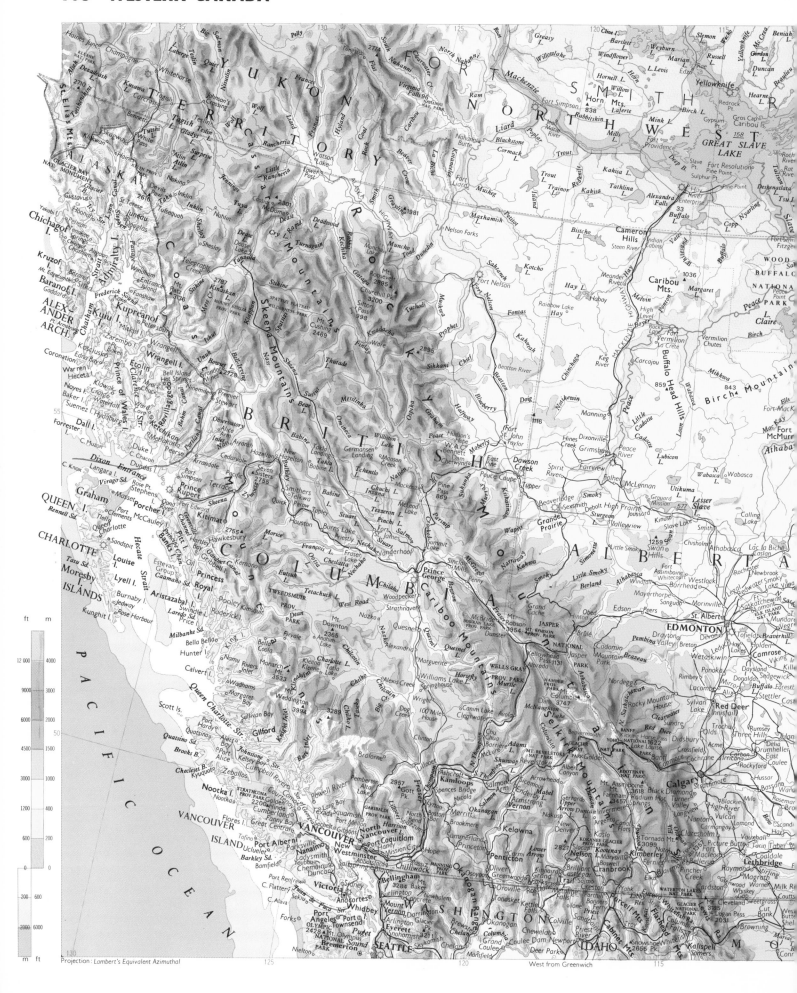

West from Greenwich

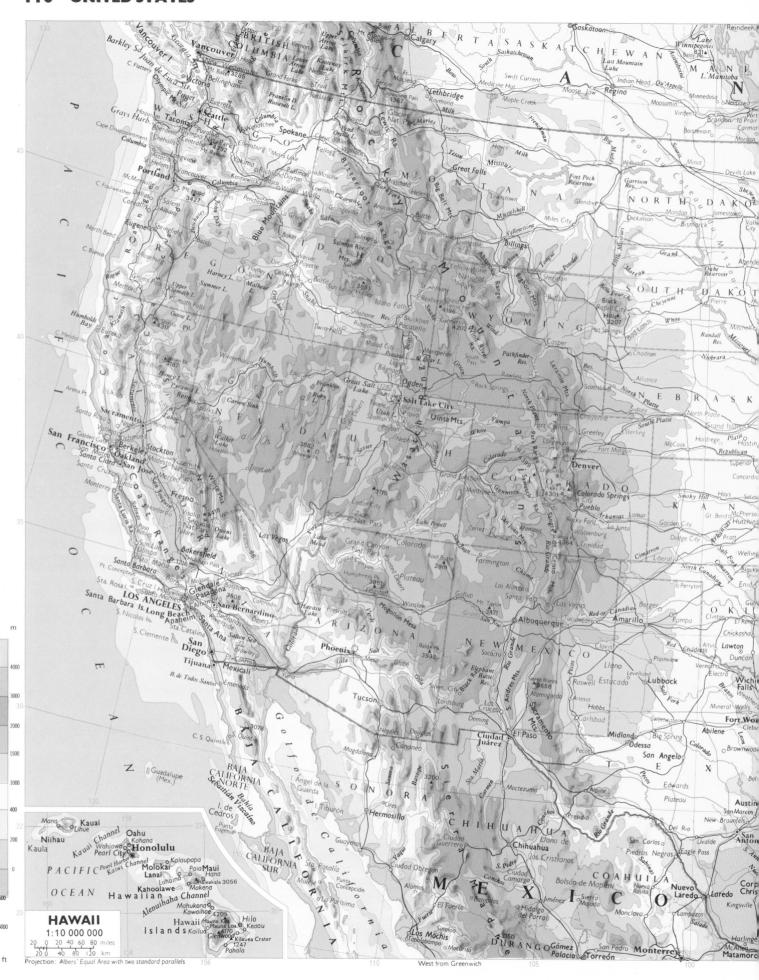

HAWAII
1:10 000 000
20 0 20 40 60 80 miles
20 0 40 80 120 km

Projection: Albers' Equal Area with two standard parallels

West from Greenwich

1:12 000 000

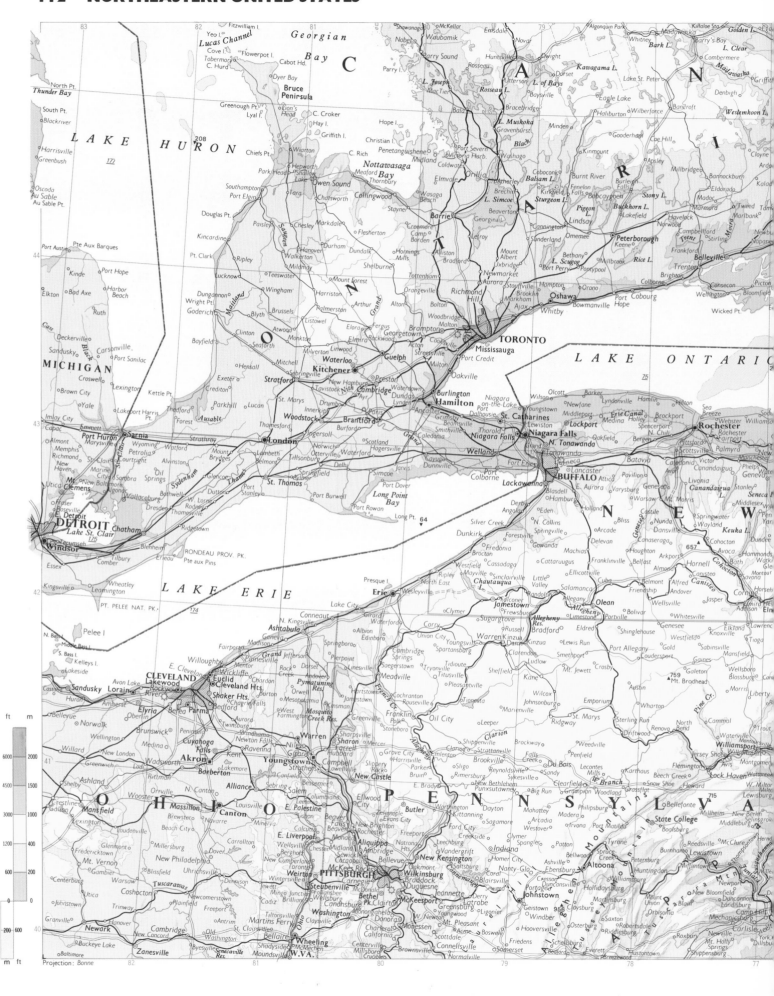

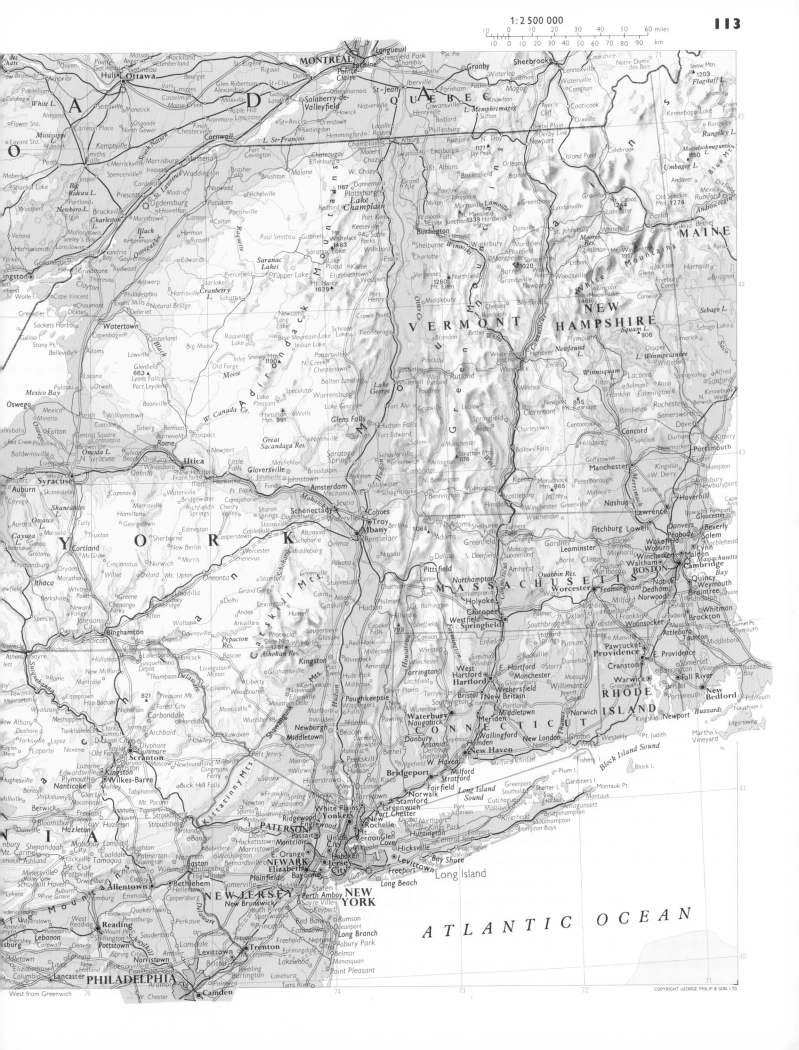

QUEBEC
ONTARIO
MICHIGAN
WISCONSIN
ILLINOIS
INDIANA
OHIO
PENNSYLVANIA
NEW YORK
VERMONT
NEW HAMPSHIRE
MASS.
NEW JERSEY
MARYLAND
DELAWARE
WEST VIRGINIA
VIRGINIA
KENTUCKY
LAKE SUPERIOR
LAKE HURON
LAKE MICHIGAN
LAKE ERIE
LAKE ONTARIO
Georgian Bay
Green Bay
Chesapeake Bay
MONTREAL
OTTAWA
TORONTO
BOSTON
NEW YORK
PHILADELPHIA
BALTIMORE
WASHINGTON D.C.
PITTSBURGH
BUFFALO
CLEVELAND
DETROIT
CHICAGO
MILWAUKEE
INDIANAPOLIS
CINCINNATI
COLUMBUS
DAYTON
TOLEDO

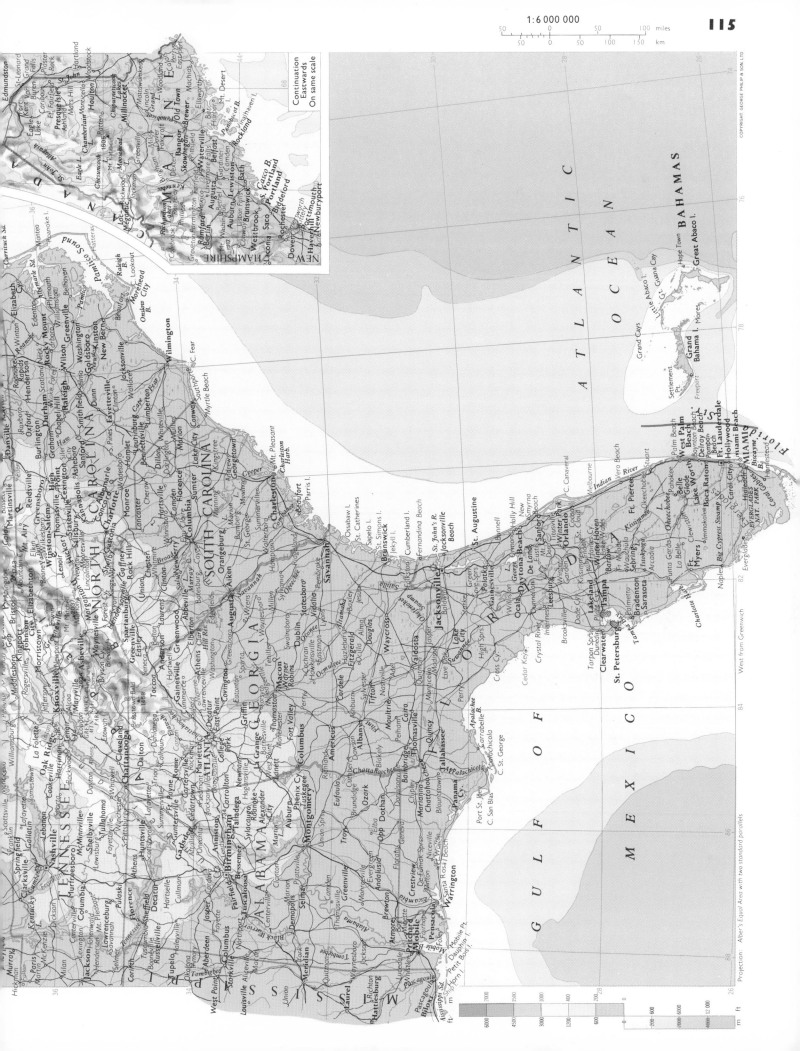

1:6 000 000

50   0   50   100 miles

50   0   50   100   150 km

Continuation
Eastwards
On same scale

ATLANTIC

OCEAN

BAHAMAS

Hope Town
Great Abaco I.
Little Abaco I.
Gt. Guana Cay
Grand Cays
Grand
Bahama I.
Settlement
Pt.
Freeport

MAINE

NEW HAMPSHIRE

CANADA

NORTH CAROLINA

SOUTH CAROLINA

GEORGIA

TENNESSEE

ALABAMA

MISSISSIPPI

FLORIDA

Wilmington

Raleigh

Charlotte

Columbia

Charleston

Savannah

Jacksonville

Orlando

Tampa

St. Petersburg

MIAMI

Atlanta

Birmingham

Montgomery

Mobile

Pensacola

Tallahassee

Knoxville

Chattanooga

Nashville

GULF OF

MEXICO

West from Greenwich

Projection: Alber's Equal Area with two standard parallels

COPYRIGHT GEORGE PHILIP & SON LTD.

ft   m
6000 2000
4500 1500
3000 1000
1200   400
600   200
0   0

m   ft
0   0
200   600
600   2000
1500   6000
4000   12 000

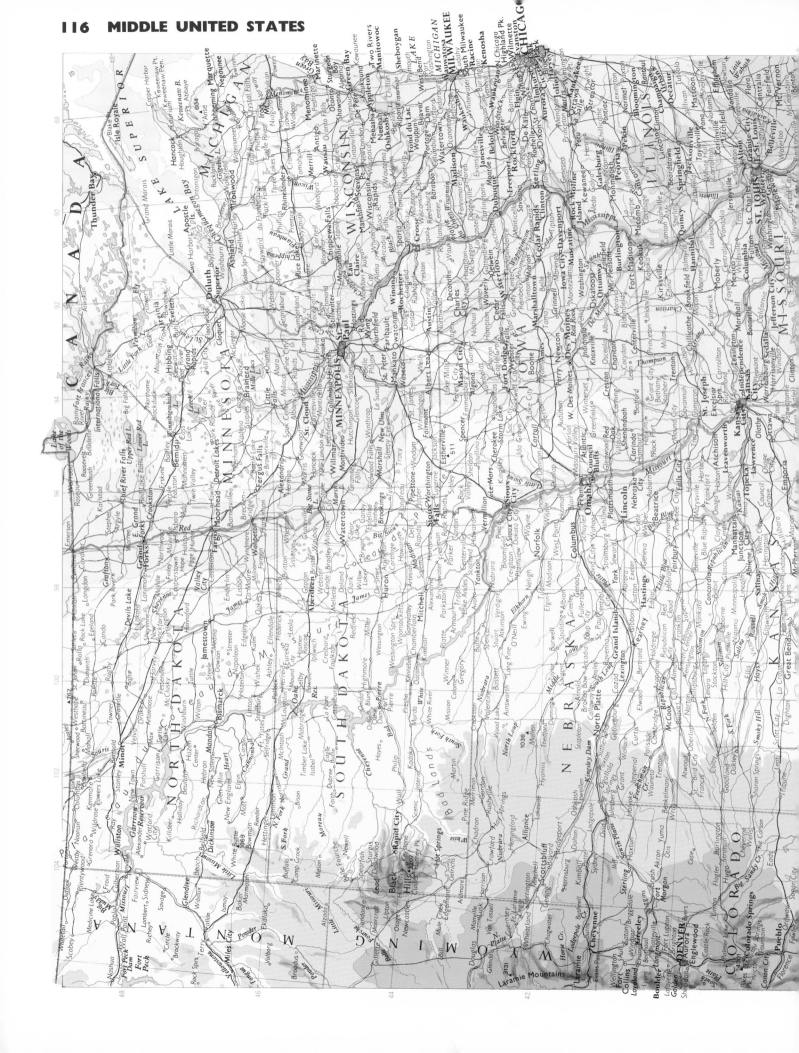

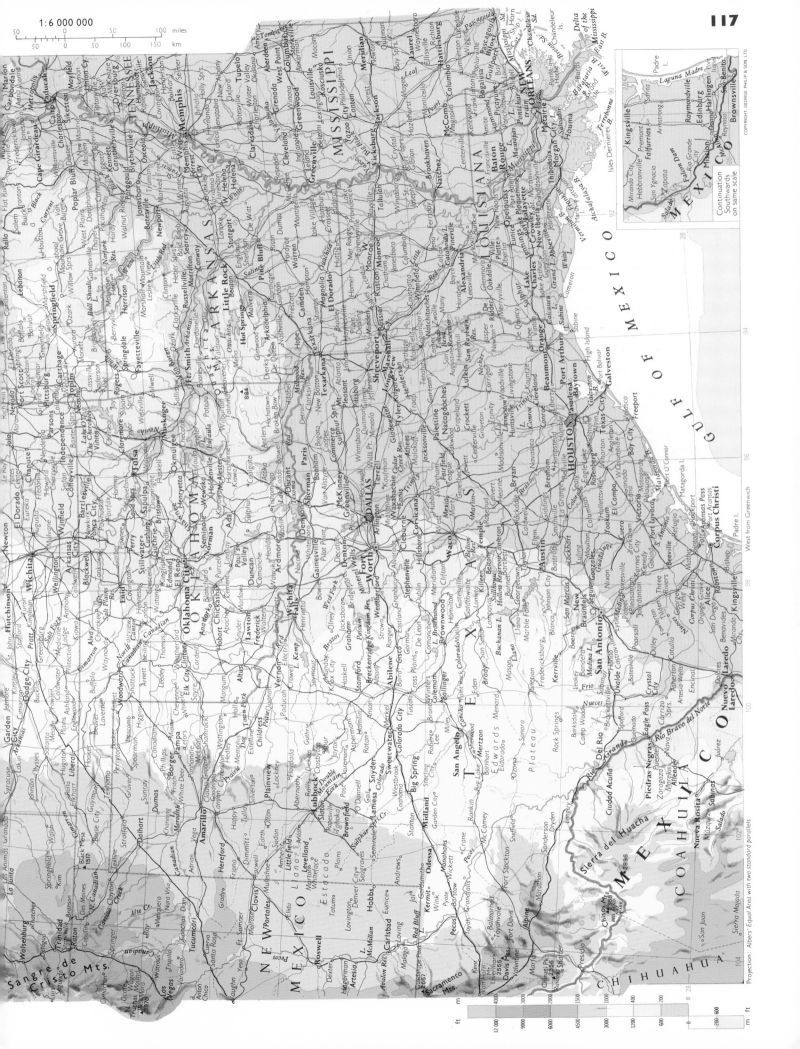

1:6 000 000

50   0   50   100 miles
50 0 50 100 150 km

BRITISH COLUMBIA

SASKATCHEWAN

ALBERTA

MONTANA

WYOMING

IDAHO

WASHINGTON

OREGON

NEVADA

UTAH

CALIFORNIA

Bighorn Mountains

Medicine Bow Range

Park Range

Bitterroot Range

Lemhi Range

Wind River Range

Salmon River Mountains

Clearwater Mountains

Cabinet Mountains

Lewis Range

Big Belt Mts.

Little Belt Mts.

Crazy Mts.

Sapphire Mts.

Wallowa Mts.

Blue Mountains

Shoshone Mountains

Independence Mts.

Ruby Mts.

Stillwater Mts.

Warner Range

Coast Range

Olympic Mts.

Klamath Mts.

GREAT SALT LAKE

Great Salt Lake Desert

YELLOWSTONE NAT. PARK

GLACIER NAT. PARK

Fort Peck Reservoir

VANCOUVER

SEATTLE

Tacoma

PORTLAND

Spokane

Salt Lake City

Ogden

Provo

Reno

Sacramento

Great Falls

Helena

Butte

Billings

Bozeman

Boise

Pocatello

Idaho Falls

Casper

Sheridan

Buffalo

Walla Walla

Pendleton

Yakima

Eugene

Salem

Vancouver

1:12 000 000

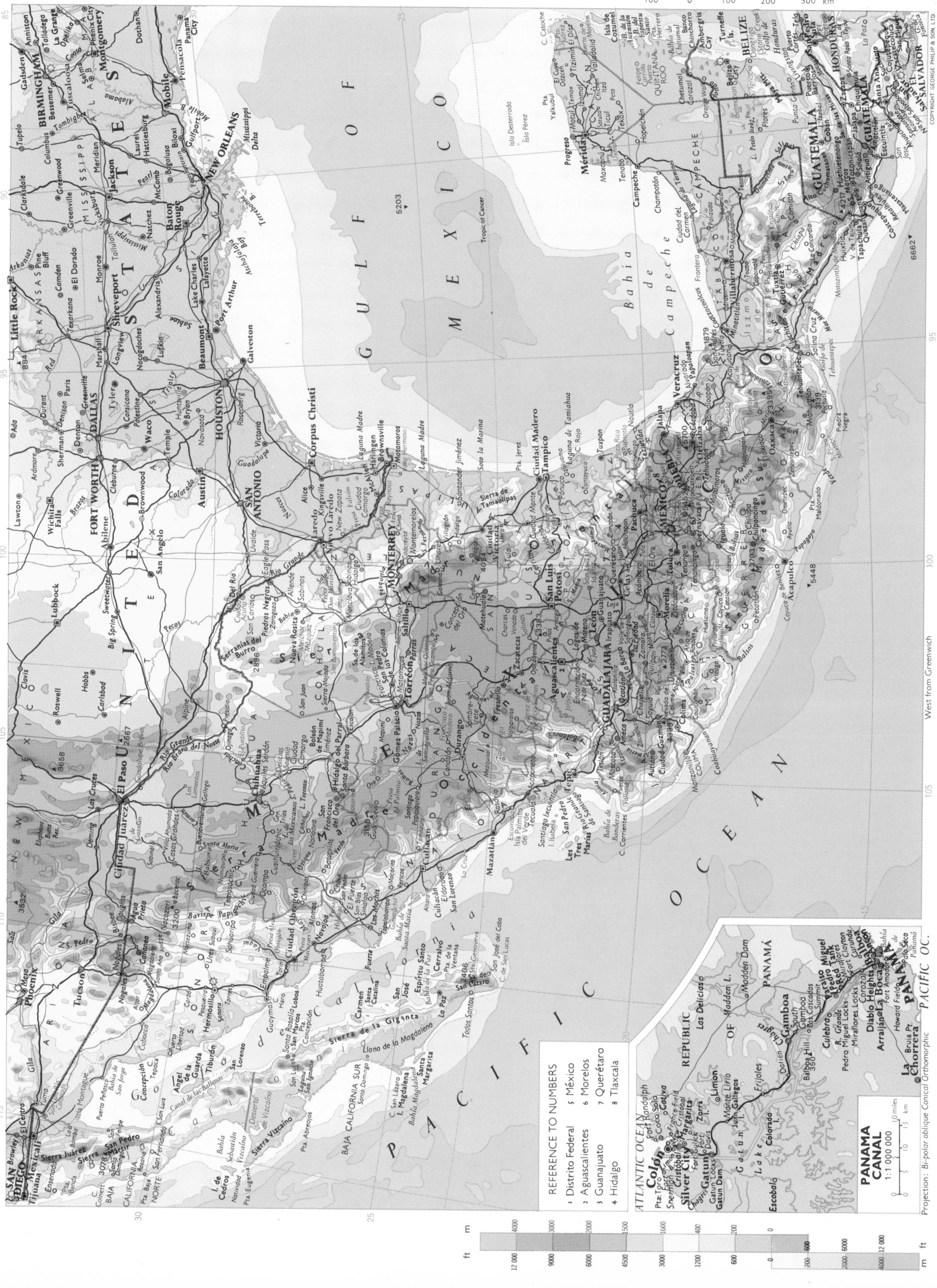

West from Greenwich

COPYRIGHT GEORGE PHILIP & SON LTD.

REFERENCE TO NUMBERS

1 Distrito Federal 5 México
2 Aguascalientes 6 Morelos
3 Guanajuato 7 Querétaro
4 Hidalgo 8 Tlaxcala

PANAMA CANAL
1:1 000 000

Projection: Bi-polar oblique Conical Orthomorphic

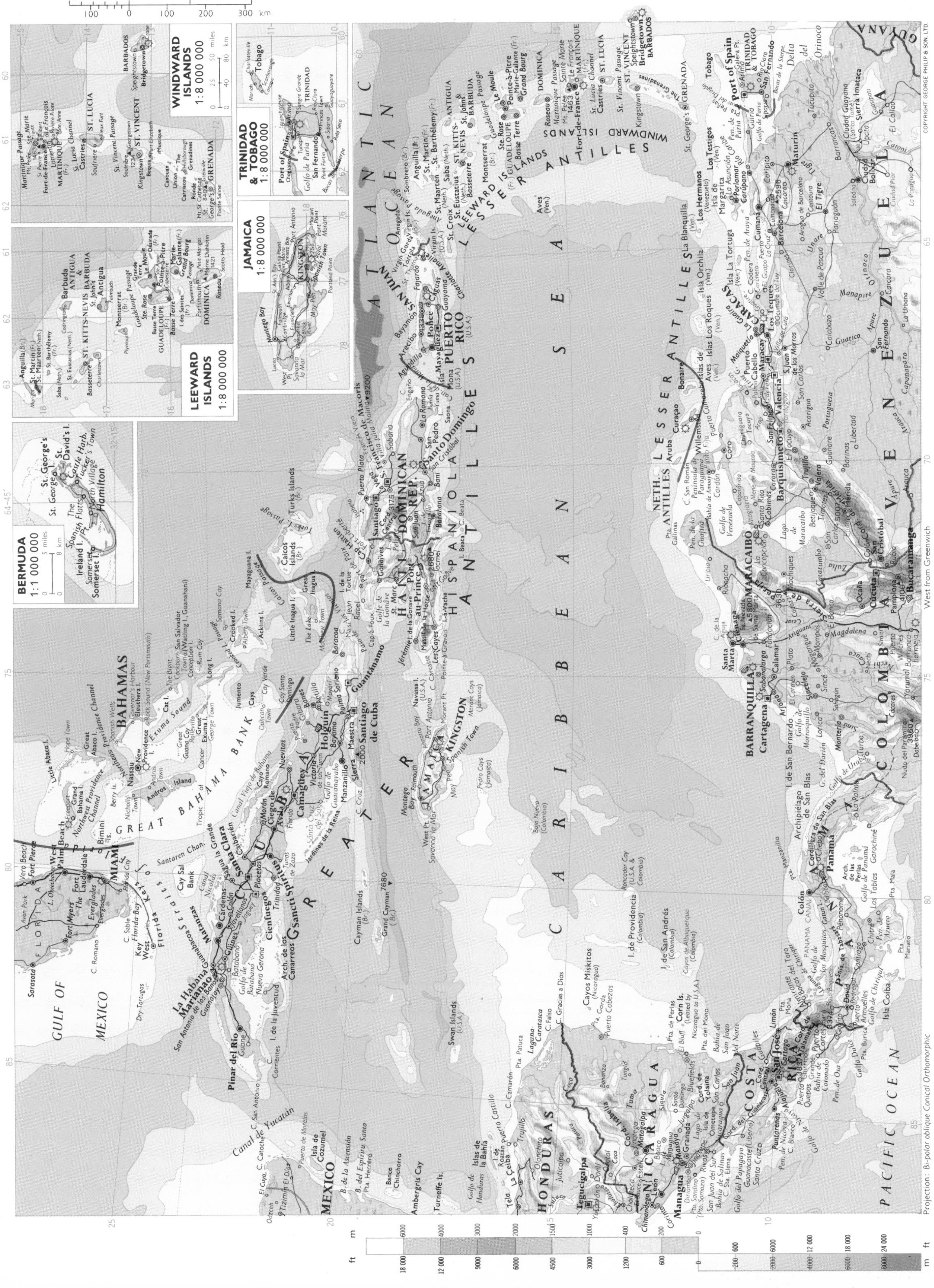

1:12 000 000

100   0   100   200 miles

100   0   100   200   300 km

WINDWARD ISLANDS
1:8 000 000

0   25   50 km

TRINIDAD & TOBAGO
1:8 000 000

LEEWARD ISLANDS
1:8 000 000

JAMAICA
1:8 000 000

BERMUDA
1:1 000 000

0   5 miles

0   8 km

ATLANTIC OCEAN

BAHAMAS

GREAT BAHAMA BANK

GREATER ANTILLES

CARIBBEAN SEA

LESSER ANTILLES

WINDWARD ISLANDS

LEEWARD ISLANDS

NETH. LESSER ANTILLES

GULF OF MEXICO

FLORIDA

MIAMI

CUBA

La Habana

Santiago de Cuba

JAMAICA

Kingston

HAITI

DOMINICAN REP.

Santo Domingo

Port-au-Prince

PUERTO RICO (U.S.A.)

San Juan

HISPANIOLA

GUADELOUPE

MARTINIQUE

ST. LUCIA

ST. VINCENT

GRENADA

BARBADOS

DOMINICA

ANTIGUA

TRINIDAD & TOBAGO

Port of Spain

VENEZUELA

CARACAS

COLOMBIA

Barranquilla

Cartagena

PANAMA

PANAMA CANAL

Colón

COSTA RICA

NICARAGUA

Managua

HONDURAS

Tegucigalpa

MEXICO

PACIFIC OCEAN

Projection: Bi-polar oblique Conical Orthomorphic

COPYRIGHT GEORGE PHILIP & SON LTD.

West from Greenwich

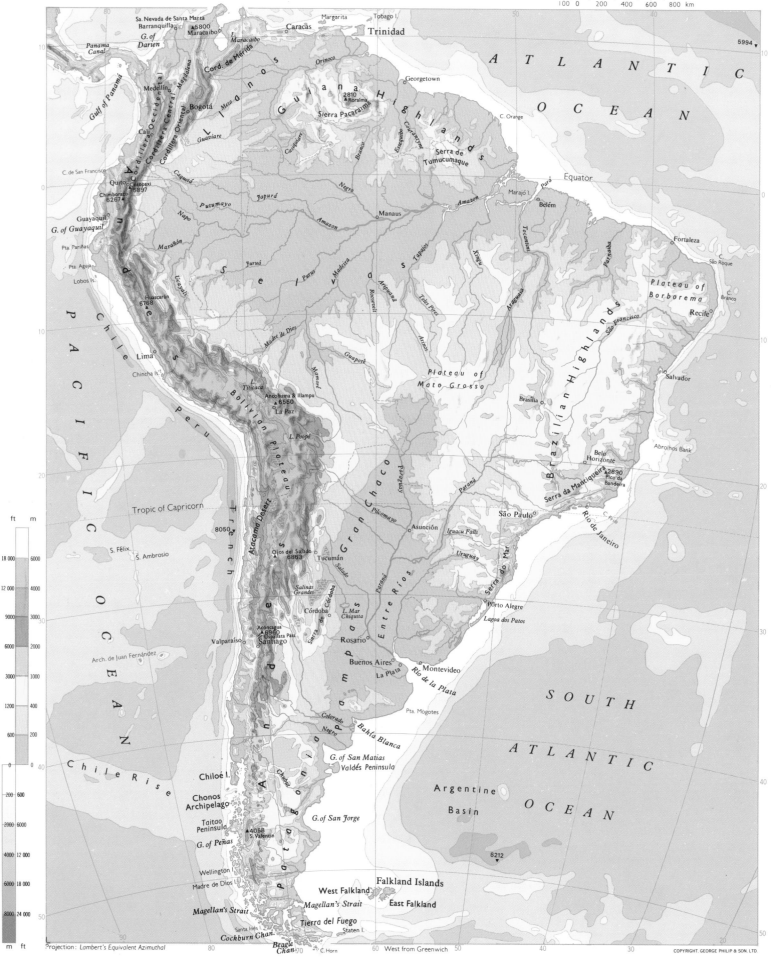

1:30 000 000

100 0 100 200 300 400 500 miles
100 0   200 400 600 800 km

ATLANTIC

OCEAN

5994▾

Sa. Nevada de Santa Marta
Barranquilla ▲5800
Maracaibo
G. of
Darien
Panama
Canal
Gulf of Panamá
Medellín
Cali
Bogotá
C. de San Francisco
Quito Cotopaxi
5897
Chimborazo
6267▲
Guayaquil
G. of Guayaquil
Pta. Pariñas
Pta. Aguja
Lobos Is.
Huascarán
6768▲

Margarita
Tobago I.
Caracas
Trinidad
Cord. de Mérida
Orinoco
L. Maracaibo
Llanos
Meta
Guaviare
Caquetá
Putumayo
Japurá
Napo
Marañón
Ucayali
Juruá
Purús
Madre de Dios

Guiana Highlands
Sierra Pacaraima
2810
Roraima
Serra de
Tumucumaque
Branco
Negro
Amazon
Manaus
Equator
C. Orange
Georgetown

Essequibo
Caroni
Castiquiare

Amazon
Marajó I.
Pará
Belém

Tocantins
Parnaiba
Fortaleza
São Roque

S   e   l   v   a   s

Madeira
Roosevelt
Aripuanã
Tapajos
Teles Pires
Xingú
Araguaia

Plateau of
Borborema
Branco
Recife

Guaporé
Mamoré
Plateau of
Mato Grosso
São Francisco
Salvador

Lima
Chincha Is.
Chile
Peru
L. Titicaca
Ancohuma & Illampu
6550
La Paz
L. Poopó
Bolivian Plateau
Atacama Desert
Tropic of Capricorn
8290
S. Félix
S. Ambrosio
Ojos del Salado
6863
Tucumán
Salinas
Grandes
Sierra de Córdoba
Córdoba
L. Mar
Chiquita
Aconcagua
6960
Uspallata Pass
Valparaíso
Santiago
Rosario
Buenos Aires
La Plata

Brasília
Brazilian Highlands
Belo
Horizonte
2890
Pico da
Bandeira
Serra da Mantiqueira
São Paulo
Serra do Mar
Rio de Janeiro
C. Frío
Abrolhos Bank

Gran Chaco
Pilcomayo
Paraná
Asunción
Iguaçu Falls
Uruguay
Pôrto Alegre
Lagoa dos Patos
Paraguay
Salado
P a m p a s
Entre Ríos

Trench

PACIFIC

OCEAN

Arch. de Juan Fernández

Montevideo
Río de la Plata
Pta. Mogotes

SOUTH

ATLANTIC

OCEAN

Colorado
Negro
Bahía Blanca
G. of San Matias
Valdés Peninsula

Chiloé I.
Chonos
Archipelago
Taitao
Peninsula
G. of Peñas
Wellington
Madre de Dios I.
Chile Rise
S. Valentin
4058
Chubut

Argentine

Basin

6212▾

G. of San Jorge

P a t a g o n i a

A n d e s

Magellan's Strait
Santa Inés I.
Cockburn Chan.
Beagle
Chan.
C. Horn
Tierra del Fuego
Staten I.

Falkland Islands
West Falkland
Magellan's Strait
East Falkland

ft   m
18 000   6000
12 000   4000
9000   3000
6000   2000
3000   1000
1200   400
600   200
0   0
200   600
2000   6000
4000   12 000
6000   18 000
8000   24 000
m   ft

Projection: Lambert's Equivalent Azimuthal

90   80   West from Greenwich   60   50   40   30

COPYRIGHT. GEORGE PHILIP & SON. LTD.

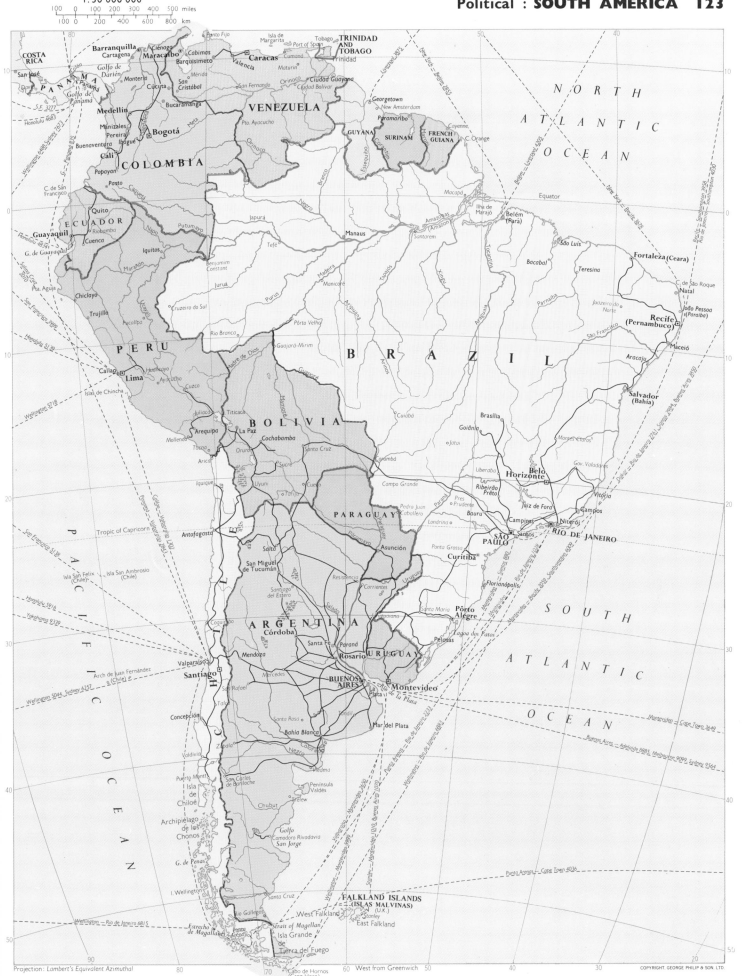

1:30 000 000

West from Greenwich

COPYRIGHT. GEORGE. PHILIP & SON. LTD

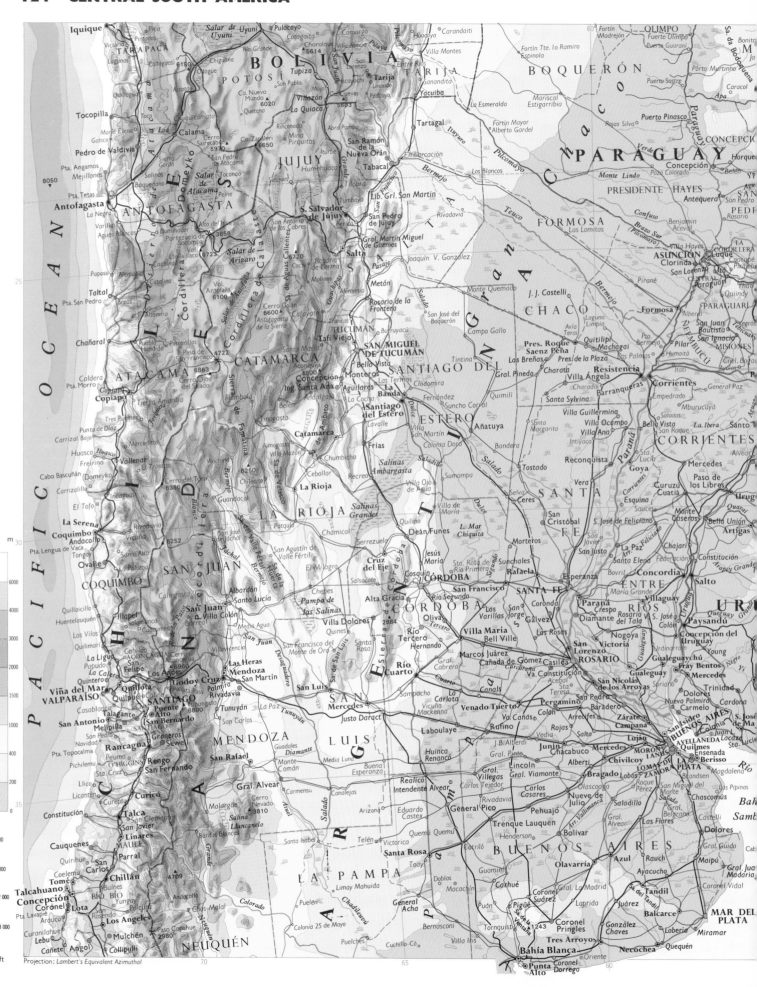

1:8 000 000

50   0   50   100   150 miles
50 0 50 100 150 200 km

BELO HORIZONTE

MATO GROSSO

DO SUL

Nioaque
Maracaju
Dourados
Ponta Porã
Pedro Juan Caballero

Três Lagoas
Andradina
Mirandópolis
Panorama
Xavantina
Pres. Epitácio
Presidente Prudente
Rancharia
Paranavaí
Nova Esperança
Maringá
Mandaguari
Apucarana
Arapongas
Londrina
Cornélio Procópio
Jacarèzinho

Olímpia
S. José do Rio Prêto
Catanduva
Taquaritinga
Rebedouro
Ribeirão Prêto
Jaboticabal
Mococa

SÃO PAULO

Andradina
Adamantina
Tupã
Lins
Penápolis
Birigui
Bauru
Marília
Garça
Jaú
Bariri
São Carlos
Araraquara
Rio Claro
Limeira
Americana
CAMPINAS
Piracicaba
Botucatu
Mogi-Mirim

Assis
Ourinhos
Avaré
Tatuí
Sorocaba
Itu
Jundiaí
Itapetininga
SÃO PAULO
SANTO ANDRÉ
Mogi das Cruzes
S. J. dos Campos
Jacareí
Taubaté

PARANÁ

BRAZIL

Guaíra
Candido de Abreu
Pitanga
Ponta Grossa
Guarapuava
Irati
Palmeira
CURITIBA
Antonina
Paranaguá

Foz do Iguaçu
Iguaçu
Laranjeiras do Sul
União da Vitória
Lapa
Rio Negro
Mafra
São Francisco do Sul
Joinvile
Itajaí
Blumenau
Brusque

SANTA CATARINA
Campos Novos
Rio do Sul
Florianópolis
Ilha de Santa Catarina

Chapecó
Joaçaba
Santa Cecília
Caçador

RIO GRANDE
DO SUL
Erechim
Lajes
Vacaria
Tubarão
Laguna
Criciúma
Araranguá

Passo Fundo
Caràzinho
Cruz Alta
Guaporé
Bento Gonçalves
Caxias do Sul
Santa Maria
Santa Cruz do Sul
Montenegro
Nôvo Hamburgo
Taquara
São Leopoldo
PÔRTO ALEGRE
Osorio

Santana do Livramento
São Gabriel
Dom Pedrito
Bagé
Pelotas
Lagoa dos Patos
Mostardas

Rio Grande

URUGUAY
MONTEVIDEO

Tacuarembó
Melo
Jaguarão
Lagoa Mirim
Treinta y Três
Lagoa Mangueira
Santa Vitória do Palmar
Minas
Rocha
Maldonado

RIO DE JANEIRO
NITERÓI
DUQUE DE CAXIAS
SÃO GONÇALO
Petrópolis
Nova Friburgo
Macaé
Cabo Frio

CAMPOS
Vitória
Vila Velha

Tropic of Capricorn

ATLANTIC

OCEAN

West from Greenwich

COPYRIGHT. GEORGE PHILIP & SON. LTD

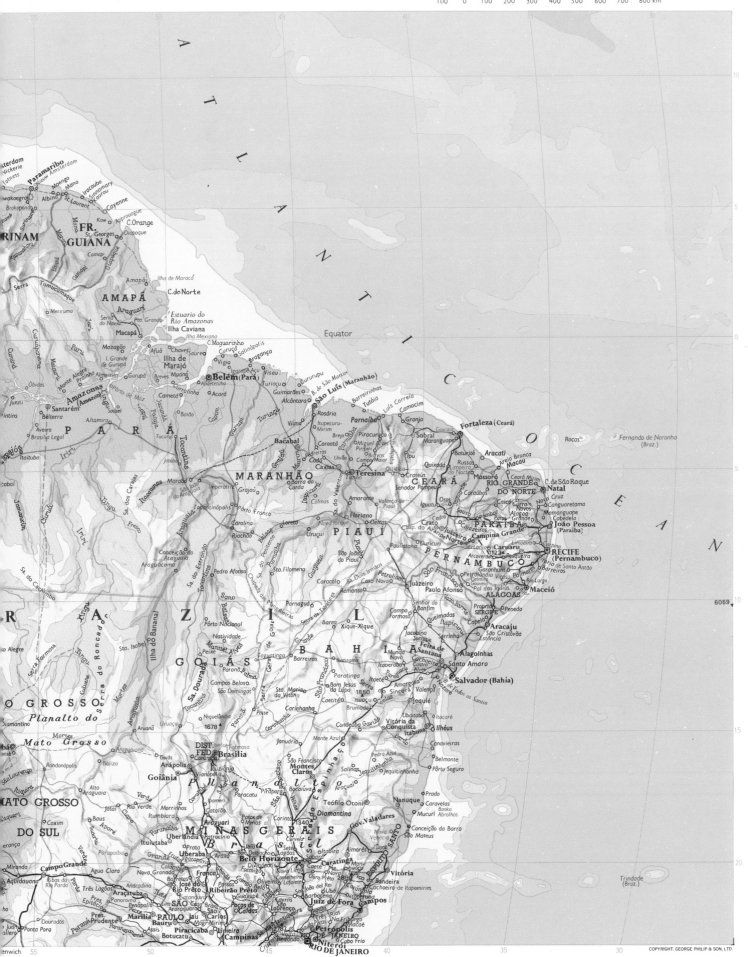

1:16 000 000

100   0   100   200   300   400   500 miles
100   0   100   200   300   400   500   600   700   800 km

A T L A N T I C

O C E A N

Equator

Fernando de Noronha
(Braz.)

RINAM

**FR.
GUIANA**

AMAPÁ

PARÁ

MARANHÃO

CEARÁ

**RIO GRANDE
DO NORTE**

PARAÍBA

PIAUÍ

PERNAMBUCO

RECIFE
(Pernambuco)

João Pessoa
(Paraíba)

Z

Belém (Pará)

Teresina

Fortaleza (Ceará)

Natal

Caruaru

Maceió

ALAGOAS

SERGIPE

Aracaju

B   R   A   Z   I   L

B A H I A

G O I Á S

Salvador (Bahia)

Santo Amaro

**Feira de
Santana**

Alagoinhas

Vitória da
Conquista

Ilhéus

O   GROSSO

Planalto do

Mato Grosso

6059

Pôrto Seguro

**DIST.
FED.** **Brasília**

Anápolis

Goiânia

P l a n a l t o

MATO GROSSO

DO SUL

MINAS GERAIS

**Montes
Claros**

Diamantina

Nanuque

Gov. Valadares

Conceição da Barra

São Mateus

Belo Horizonte

Caratinga

Vitória

Trindade
(Braz.)

Campo Grande

Araçatuba

Ribeirão Prêto

**SÃO
PAULO**

Marília

Bauru

Campinas

Piracicaba

Juiz de Fora

Campos

Petrópolis

Niterói

RIO DE JANEIRO

COPYRIGHT. GEORGE PHILIP & SON, LTD.

1:16 000 000

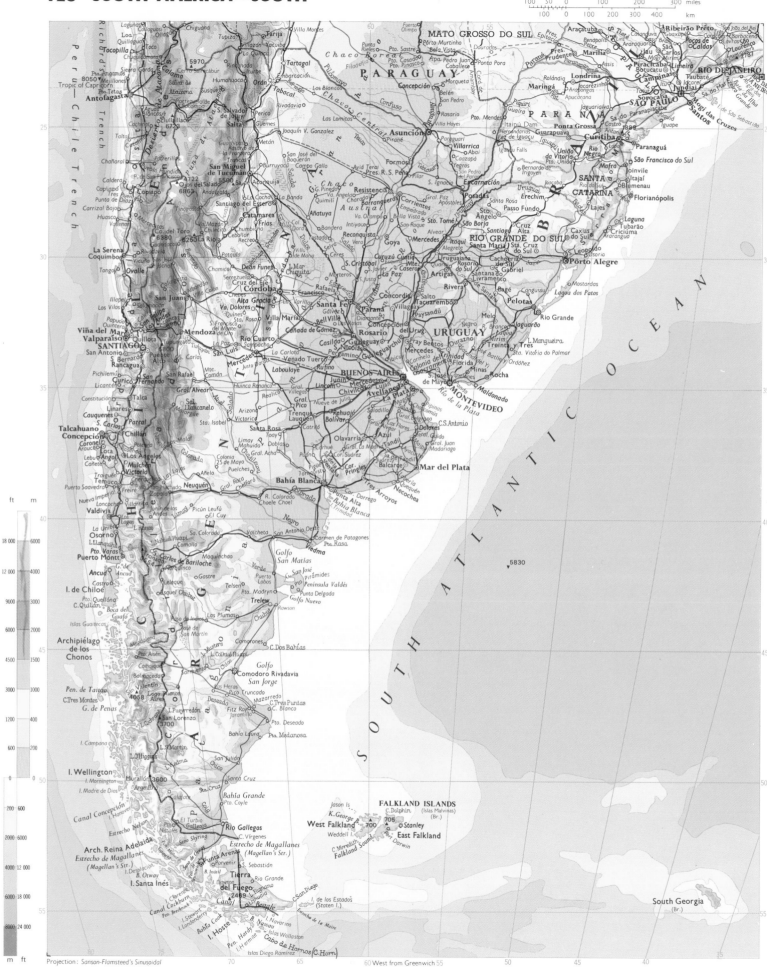

Projection: Sanson-Flamsteed's Sinusoidal

INDEX

The number printed in bold type against each entry indicates the map page where the feature can be found. This is followed by its geographical coordinates. The first coordinate indicates latitude, i.e. distance north or south of the Equator. The second coordinate indicates longitude, i.e. distance east or west of the meridian of Greenwich in England (shown as 0° longitude). Both latitude and longitude are measured in degrees and minutes (with 60 minutes in a degree), and appear on the map as horizontal and vertical gridlines respectively. Thus the entry for Paris in France reads.

Paris, France   **19** 48 50 N   2 20 E

This entry indicates that Paris is on page 19, at latitude 48 degrees 50 minutes north (approximately five-sixths of the distance between horizontal gridlines 48 and 49, marked on either side of the page) and at longitude 2 degrees 20 minutes east (approximately one-third of the distance between vertical gridlines 2 and 3, marked at top and bottom of the page). Paris can be found where lines extended from these two points cross on the page. The geographical coordinates are sometimes only approximate but are close enough for the place to be located. Rivers have been indexed to their mouth or confluence.

An open square □ signifies that the name refers to an administrative subdivision of a country while a solid square ■ follows the name of a country. An arrow ↷ follows the name of a river.

The alphabetical order of names composed of two or more words is governed primarily by the first word and then by the second. This rule applies even if the second word is a description or its abbreviation, R.,L.,I. for example. Names composed of a proper name (Gibraltar) and a description (Strait of) are positioned alphabetically by the proper name. If the same place name occurs twice or more times in the index and all are in the same country, each is followed by the name of the administrative subdivision in which it is located. The names are placed in the alphabetical order of the subdivisions. If the same place name occurs twice or more in the index and the places are in different countries they will be followed by their country names, the latter governing the alphabetical order. In a mixture of these situations the primary order is fixed by the alphabetical sequence of the countries and the secondary order by that of the country subdivisions.

* Please refer to the table at the end of the index for the recent place name changes in India, Iran, Mozambique and Zimbabwe.

Abbreviations used in the index:

A. R.–Autonomous Region
A. S. S. R.–Autonomous Soviet Socialist Republic
Afghan.–Afghanistan
Afr.–Africa
Ala.–Alabama
Alas.–Alaska
Alg.–Algeria
Alta.–Alberta
Amer.–America
And. P.–Andhra Pradesh
Arch.–Archipelago
Argent.–Argentina
Ariz.–Arizona
Ark.–Arkansas
Atl. Oc. – Atlantic Ocean
Austral. – Australia
B. – Baie, Bahía, Bay, Bucht, Bugt
B.A. – Buenos Aires
B.C. – British Columbia
Bangla. – Bangladesh
Barr. – Barrage
Bay. – Bayern
Belg. – Belgium
Berks. – Berkshire
Bol. – Bolshoi
Boliv. – Bolivia
Bots. – Botswana
Br. – British
Bri. – Bridge
Bt. – Bight
Bucks. – Buckinghamshire
Bulg. – Bulgaria
C. – Cabo, Cap, Cape, Coast
C. Prov. – Cape Province
Calif. – California
Camb. – Cambodia
Cambs. – Cambridgeshire
Can. – Canada
Cent. – Central
Chan. – Channel
Co. – Country
Colomb. – Colombia
Colo. – Colorado
Conn. – Connecticut
Cord. – Cordillera
Cr. – Creek
Cumb. – Cumbria
Czech. – Czechoslovakia
D.C. – District of Columbia
Del. – Delaware
Dep. – Dependency
Derby. – Derbyshire
Des. – Desert
Dist. – District
Dj. – Djebel
Dumf. & Gall. – Dumfries and Galloway
E. – East
Eng. – England
Fed. – Federal, Federation
Fla. – Florida
For. – Forest
Fr. – France, French
Fs. – Falls
Ft. – Fort

G. – Golfe, Golfo, Gulf, Guba
Ga. – Georgia
Ger. – Germany
Glam. – Glamorgan
Glos. – Gloucestershire
Gr. – Grande, Great, Greater, Group
H.K. – Hong Kong
H.P. – Himachal Pradesh
Hants. – Hampshire
Harb. – Harbor, Harbour
Hd. – Head
Here. & Worcs. – Hereford and Worcester
Herts. – Hertfordshire
Hts. – Heights
Hung. – Hungary
I.o.M. – Isle of Man
I.(s). – Île, Ilha, Insel, Isla, Island, Isle
Id. – Idaho
Ill. – Illinois
Ind. – Indiana
Ind. Oc. – Indian Ocean
Indon. – Indonesia
J. – Jabal, Jabel, Jazira
Junc. – Junction
K. – Kap, Kapp
K. – Kuala
Kal. – Kalmyk A.S.S.R.
Kans. – Kansas
Kep. – Kepulauan
Ky. – Kentucky
L. – Lac, Lacul, Lago, Lagoa, Lake, Limni, Loch, Lough
La. – Lousiana
Lancs. – Lancashire
Leb. – Lebanon
Leics. – Leicestershire
Lim. – Limerick
Lincs. – Lincolnshire
Lit. – Little
Lr. – Lower
Mad. P. – Madhya Pradesh
Madag. – Madagascar
Malay. – Malaysia
Man. – Manitoba
Manch. – Manchester
Maran. – Maranhão
Mass. – Massachusetts
Md. – Maryland
Me. – Maine
Mend. – Mendoza
Mér. – Méridionale
Mich. – Michigan
Mid. – Middle
Minn. – Minnesota
Miss. – Mississippi
Mo. – Missouri
Mong. – Mongolia
Mont. – Montana
Moroc. – Morocco
Mozam. – Mozambique
Mt.(e). – Mont, Monte, Monti, Montaña, Mountain
Mys. – Mysore
N. – Nord, Norte, North, Northern, Nouveau

N.B. – New Brunswick
N.C. – North Carolina
N.D. – North Dakota
N.H. – New Hampshire
N.I. – North Island
N.J. – New Jersey
N. Mex. – New Mexico
N.S. – Nova Scotia
N.S.W. – New South Wales
N.T. – Northern Territory
N.W.T. – North West Territory
N.Y. – New York
N.Z. – New Zealand
Nat. – National
Nat.Park. – National Park
Nebr. – Nebraska
Neth. – Netherlands
Nev. – Nevada
Newf. – Newfoundland
Nic. – Nicaragua
Northants. – Northamptonshire
Northumb. – Northumberland
Notts. – Nottinghamshire
O. – Oued, ouadi
Occ. – Occidentale
O.F.S. – Orange Free State
Okla. – Oklahoma
Ont. – Ontario
Or. – Orientale
Oreg. – Oregon
Os. – Ostrov
Oxon. – Oxfordshire
Oz. – Ozero
P. – Pass, Passo, Pasul, Pulau
P.E.I. – Prince Edward Island
P.N.G. – Papua New Guinea
P.O. – Post Office
P. Rico. –Puerto Rico
Pa. – Pennsylvania
Pac. Oc. – Pacific Ocean
Pak. – Pakistan
Parag. – Paraguay
Pass. – Passage
Pen. – Peninsula, Peninsule
Phil. – Philippines
Pk. – Peak
Plat. – Plateau
P-ov. – Poluostrov
Port. – Portugal, Portuguese
Prom. – Promontory
Prov. – Province, Provincial
Pt. – Point
Pta. – Ponta, Punta
Pte. – Pointe
Qué. – Québec
Queens. – Queensland
R. – Rio, River
R.I. – Rhode Island
R.S.F.S.R. – Russian Soviet Federative Socialist Republic
Ra.(s). – Range(s)
Raj. – Rajasthan
Reg. – Region
Rep. – Republic
Res. – Reserve, Reservoir
Rhld. – Pfz. – Rheinland– Pfalz

S. – San, South
S. Afr. – South Africa
S. Austral. – South Australia
S.C. – South Carolina
S.D. – South Dakota
S.-Holst. – Schleswig-Holstein
S.I. – South Island
S. Leone–Sierra Leone
S.S.R. – Soviet Socialist Republic
Sa. – Serra, Sierra
Sard. – Sardinia
Sask. – Saskatchewan
Scot. – Scotland
Sd. – Sound
Sept. – Septentrionale
Sev. – Severnaja
Sib. – Siberia
Som. – Somerset
Span. – Spanish
Sprs. – Springs
St. – Saint
Sta. – Santa, Station
Staffs. – Staffordshire
Ste. – Sainte
Sto. – Santo
Str. – Strait, Stretto
Switz. – Switzerland
T.O. – Telegraph Office
Tas. – Tasmania
Tenn. – Tennessee
Terr. – Territory
Tex. – Texas
Tg. – Tanjung
Thai. – Thailand
Tipp. – Tipperary
Trans. – Transvaal
U.K. – United Kingdom
U.S.A. – United States of America
U.S.S.R. – Union of Soviet Socialist Republics
Ukr. – Ukraine
Ut.P. – Uttar Pradesh
Utd. – United
V. – Vorota
Va. – Virginia
Vdkhr. – Vodokhranilishche
Venez. – Venezuela
Vic. – Victoria
Viet. – Vietnam
Vol. – Volcano
Vt. – Vermont
W. – Wadi, West
W.A. – Western Australia
W. Isles–Western Isles
W. Va. – West Virginia
Wash. – Washington
Wilts. – Wiltshire
Wis. – Wisconsin
Wlkp. – Wielkopolski
Wyo. – Wyoming
Yorks. – Yorkshire
Yug. – Yugoslavia
Zap. – Zapadnaja
Zimb. – Zimbabwe

HIA

Aachen
Ain el Mafki

A

Aachen 24 50 47N 6 4 E
Aâlâ en Nîl □ 87 8 50N 29 55 E
Aalen 25 48 49N 10 6 E
Aalsmeer 16 52 17N 4 43 E
Aalst 16 50 56N 4 2 E
Aalten 16 51 56N 6 35 E
Aarau 25 47 23N 8 4 E
Aarberg 25 47 2N 7 16 E
Aare → 25 47 33N 8 14 E
Aargau □ 25 47 26N 8 10 E
Aarschot 16 50 59N 4 49 E
Aba, Nigeria 85 5 10N 7 19 E
Aba, Zaïre 90 3 58N 30 17 E
Âbâ, Jazîrat 87 13 30N 32 31 E
Ābādān 64 30 22N 48 20 E
Abade, Ethiopia 87 9 22N 38 3 E
Abade, Iran 65 31 8N 52 40 E
Abadin 30 43 21N 7 29W
Abadla 82 31 2N 2 45W
Abaetetuba 127 1 40 S 48 50W
Abagnar Qi 76 43 52N 116 2 E
Abai 125 25 58 S 55 54W
Abak 85 4 58N 7 50 E
Abakaliki 85 6 22N 8 2 E
Abakan 59 53 40N 91 10 E
Abal Nam 86 25 20N 38 37 E
Abalemma 85 16 12N 7 50 E
Abanilla 33 38 12N 1 3W
Abano Terme 39 45 22N 11 46 E
Abarán 33 38 12N 1 23W
Abarqū 65 31 10N 53 20 E
'Abasān 62 31 19N 34 21 E
Abashiri 74 44 0N 144 15 E
Abashiri-Wan 74 44 0N 144 30 E
Abau 98 10 11 S 148 46 E
Abaújszántó 27 48 16N 21 12 E
Abay 58 49 38N 72 53 E
Abaya L. 87 6 30N 37 50 E
Abaza 58 52 39N 90 6 E
Abbadia San Salvatore 39 42 53N 11 40 E
Abbay (Nîl el Azraq) → 87 15 38N 32 31 E
Abbaye, Pt. 114 46 58N 88 4W
Abbé, L. 87 11 8N 41 47 E
Abbeville, France 19 50 6N 1 49 E
Abbeville, La., U.S.A. 117 30 0N 92 7W
Abbeville, S.C., U.S.A. 115 34 12N 82 21W
Abbiategrasso 38 45 23N 8 55 E
Abbieglassie 99 27 15 S 147 28 E
Abbotsford, B.C., Can. 108 49 5N 122 20W
Abbotsford, Qué., Can. 113 45 25N 72 53W
Abbotsford, U.S.A. 116 44 55N 90 20W
Abbottabad 66 34 10N 73 15 E
Abd al Kūrī 63 12 5N 52 20 E
Abéché 81 13 50N 20 35 E
Abejar 32 41 48N 2 47W
Abekr 87 12 45N 28 50 E
Abêlessa 82 22 58N 4 47 E
Abengourou 84 6 42N 3 27W
Åbenrå 49 55 3N 9 25 E
Abensberg 25 48 49N 11 51 E
Abeokuta 85 7 3N 3 19 E
Aber 90 2 12N 32 25 E
Aberaeron 13 52 15N 4 16W
Aberayron = Aberaeron 13 52 15N 4 16W
Abercorn 99 25 12 S 151 5 E
Abercorn = Mbala 91 8 46 S 31 17 E
Abercrombie → 100 33 54 S 149 8 E
Aberdare 13 51 43N 3 27W
Aberdare Ra. 90 0 15 S 36 50 E
Aberdeen, Austral. 99 32 9 S 150 56 E
Aberdeen, Can. 109 52 20N 106 8W
Aberdeen, S. Afr. 92 32 28 S 24 2 E
Aberdeen, U.K. 14 57 9N 2 6W
Aberdeen, Ala., U.S.A. 115 33 49N 88 33W
Aberdeen, Idaho, U.S.A. 118 42 57N 112 50W
Aberdeen, S.D., U.S.A. 116 45 30N 98 30W
Aberdeen, Wash., U.S.A. 118 47 0N 123 50W
Aberdovey 13 52 33N 4 3W
Aberfeldy 14 56 37N 3 50W
Abergaria-a-Velha 30 40 41N 8 32W
Abergavenny 13 51 49N 3 1W
Abernathy 117 33 49N 101 49W
Abert L. 118 42 40N 120 8W
Aberystwyth 13 52 25N 4 6W
Abha 86 18 0N 42 34 E
Abhayapuri 69 26 24N 90 38 E
Abidiya 86 18 18N 34 3 E
Abidjan 84 5 26N 3 58W
Abilene, Kans., U.S.A. 116 39 0N 97 16W
Abilene, Texas, U.S.A. 117 32 22N 99 40W
Abingdon, U.K. 13 51 40N 1 17W
Abingdon, Ill., U.S.A. 116 40 53N 90 23W
Abingdon, Va., U.S.A. 115 36 46N 81 56W
Abitau → 109 59 53N 109 3W
Abitau L. 109 60 27N 107 15W
Abitibi L. 106 48 40N 79 40W
Abiy Adi 87 13 39N 39 3 E
Abkhaz A.S.S.R. □ 57 43 0N 41 0 E
Abkit 59 64 10N 157 10 E
Abnûb 86 27 18N 31 4 E
Åbo 51 60 28N 22 15 E
Abo, Massif d' 83 21 41N 16 8 E
Abocho 85 7 35N 6 56 E
Abohar 68 30 10N 74 10 E
Aboisso 84 5 30N 3 5W
Abomey 85 7 10N 2 5 E
Abondance 21 46 18N 6 42 E
Abong-Mbang 88 4 0N 13 8 E
Abonnema 85 4 41N 6 49 E
Abony 27 47 12N 20 3 E
Aboso 84 5 23N 1 57W
Abou-Deïa 81 11 20N 19 20 E
Aboyne 14 57 4N 2 48W
Abra Pampa 124 22 43 S 65 42W
Abrantes 31 39 24N 8 7W
Abraveses 30 40 41N 7 55W
Abreojos, Pta. 120 26 50N 113 40W
Abreschviller 19 48 39N 7 6 E
Abrets, Les 21 45 32N 5 35 E
Abri, Esh Shimâliya, Sudan 86 20 50N 30 27 E
Abri, Janub Kordofân, Sudan 87 11 40N 30 21 E
Abrud 46 46 19N 23 5 E
Abruzzi □ 39 42 15N 14 0 E
Absaroka Ra. 118 44 40N 110 0W
Abū al Khaṣīb 64 30 25N 48 0 E
Abū 'Alī 64 27 20N 49 27 E
Abu 'Arīsh 63 16 53N 42 48 E
Abû Ballas 86 24 26N 27 36 E
Abu Deleiq 87 15 57N 33 48 E
Abū Dhabī 65 24 28N 54 36 E
Abū Dīs 62 31 47N 35 16 E
Abû Dis 86 19 12N 33 38 E
Abû Dom 87 16 18N 32 25 E
Abū Gabra 87 11 2N 26 50 E
Abū Ghaush 62 31 48N 35 6 E
Abû Gubeiha 87 11 30N 31 15 E
Abu Habl, Khawr → 87 12 37N 31 0 E
Abu Hamed 86 19 32N 33 13 E
Abu Haraz 87 14 35N 33 30 E
Abû Haraz 86 19 8N 32 18 E
Abû Higar 87 12 50N 33 59 E
Abū Kamāl 64 34 30N 41 0 E
Abū Madd, Ra's 64 24 50N 37 7 E
Abū Markhah 64 25 4N 38 22 E
Abu Qir 86 31 18N 30 0 E
Abu Qireiya 86 24 5N 35 28 E
Abu Qurqâs 86 28 1N 30 44 E
Abû Rudies 86 29 0N 33 15 E
Abu Salama 86 27 10N 35 51 E
Abû Simbel 86 22 18N 31 40 E
Abu Tig 86 27 4N 31 15 E
Abu Tiga 87 12 47N 34 12 E
Abû Zabad 87 12 25N 29 10 E
Abū Zābī 65 24 28N 54 22 E
Abuja 85 9 16N 7 2 E
Abukuma-Gawa → 74 38 06N 140 52 E
Abunã 126 9 40 S 65 20W
Abunã → 126 9 41 S 65 20W
Aburo, Mt. 90 2 4N 30 53 E
Abut Hd. 101 43 7 S 170 15 E
Abwong 87 9 2N 32 14 E
Åby 49 58 40N 16 10 E
Aby, Lagune 84 5 15N 3 14W
Acámbaro 120 20 0N 100 40W
Acanthus 44 40 27N 23 47 E
Acaponeta 120 22 30N 105 20W
Acapulco 120 16 51N 99 56W
Acatlán 120 18 10N 98 3W
Acayucan 120 17 59N 94 58W
Accéglio 38 44 28N 6 59 E
Accomac 114 37 43N 75 40W
Accra 85 5 35N 0 6W
Accrington 12 53 46N 2 22W
Acebal 124 33 20 S 60 50W
Aceh □ 72 4 15N 97 30 E
Acerenza 41 40 50N 15 58 E
Acerra 41 40 57N 14 22 E
Aceuchal 31 38 39N 6 30W
Achalpur 68 21 22N 77 32 E
Achenkirch 26 47 32N 11 45 E
Achensee 26 47 26N 11 45 E
Acher 68 23 10N 72 32 E
Achern 25 48 37N 8 5 E
Achill 15 53 56N 9 55W
Achill Hd. 15 53 59N 10 15W
Achill I. 15 53 58N 10 5W
Achill Sound 15 53 53N 9 55W
Achim 24 53 1N 9 2 E
Achinsk 59 56 20N 90 20 E
Achol 87 6 35N 31 32 E
Acireale 41 37 37N 15 9 E
Ackerman 117 33 20N 89 8W
Acklins I. 121 22 30N 74 0W
Acland, Mt. 97 24 50 S 148 20 E
Acme 108 51 33N 113 30W
Aconcagua □, Argent. 124 32 50 S 70 0W
Aconcagua □, Chile 124 32 15 S 70 30W
Aconcagua, Cerro 124 32 39 S 70 0W
Aconquija, Mt. 124 27 0 S 66 0W
Açores, Is. dos = Azores 6 38 44N 29 0W
Acquapendente 39 42 45N 11 50 E
Acquasanta 39 42 46N 13 24 E
Acquaviva delle Fonti 41 40 53N 16 50 E
Acqui 38 44 40N 8 28 E
Acre = 'Akko 62 32 55N 35 4 E
Acre □ 126 9 1 S 71 0W
Acre → 126 8 45 S 67 22W
Acri 41 39 29N 16 23 E
Acs 27 47 42N 18 0 E
Actium 44 38 57N 20 45 E
Acton 112 43 38N 80 3W
Ad Dahnā 64 24 30N 48 10 E
Ad Dammām 64 26 20N 50 5 E
Ad Dār al Ḥamrā' 64 27 20N 37 45 E
Ad Dawhah 65 25 15N 51 35 E
Ad Dilam 64 23 55N 47 10 E
Ada, Ghana 85 5 44N 0 40 E
Ada, Minn., U.S.A. 116 47 20N 96 30W
Ada, Okla., U.S.A. 117 34 50N 96 45W
Ada, Yugo. 42 45 49N 20 9 E
Adaja → 30 41 32N 4 52W
Ådalslinden 48 63 27N 16 55 E
Adam 65 22 15N 57 28 E
Adamaoua, Massif de l' 85 7 20N 12 20 E
Adamawa Highlands = Adamaoua, Massif de l' 85 7 20N 12 20 E
Adamello, Mt. 38 46 10N 10 34 E
Adami Tulu 87 7 53N 38 41 E
Adaminaby 99 36 0 S 148 45 E
Adams, Mass., U.S.A. 113 42 38N 73 8W
Adams, N.Y., U.S.A. 114 43 50N 76 3W
Adams, Wis., U.S.A. 116 43 59N 89 50W
Adam's Bridge 70 9 15N 79 40 E
Adams Center 113 43 51N 76 1W
Adams L. 108 51 10N 119 40W
Adams, Mt. 118 46 10N 121 28W
Adam's Peak 70 6 48N 80 30 E
Adamuz 31 38 2N 4 32W
Adana 64 37 0N 35 16 E
Adanero 30 40 56N 4 36W
Adapazarı 64 40 48N 30 25 E
Adarama 87 17 10N 34 52 E
Adare, C. 5 71 0 S 171 0 E
Adaut 73 8 8 S 131 7 E
Adavale 97 25 52 S 144 32 E
Adda → 38 45 8N 9 53 E
Addis Ababa = Addis Abeba 87 9 2N 38 42 E
Addis Abeba 87 9 2N 38 42 E
Addis Alem 87 9 0N 38 17 E
Addison 112 42 9N 77 15W
Adebour 85 13 17N 11 50 E
Adel 115 31 10N 83 28W
Adelaide, Austral. 97 34 52 S 138 30 E
Adelaide, Madag. 93 32 42 S 26 20 E
Adelaide I. 5 67 15 S 68 30W
Adelaide Pen. 104 68 15N 97 30W
Adélie, Terre 5 68 0 S 140 0 E
Ademuz 32 40 5N 1 13W
Aden = Al 'Adan 63 12 45N 45 12 E
Aden, G. of 63 13 0N 50 0 E
Adendorp 92 32 25 S 24 30 E
Adgz 82 30 47N 6 30W
Adhoi 68 23 26N 70 32 E
Adi 73 4 15 S 133 30 E
Adi Daro 87 14 20N 38 14 E
Adi Keyih 87 14 51N 39 22 E
Adi Kwala 87 14 38N 38 48 E
Adi Ugri 87 14 58N 38 48 E
Adieu, C. 96 32 0 S 132 10 E
Adigala 87 10 24N 42 15 E
Adige → 39 45 9N 12 20 E
Adigrat 87 14 20N 39 26 E
Adilabad 70 19 33N 78 20 E
Adin 118 41 10N 121 0W
Adin Khel 65 32 45N 68 5 E
Adirampattinam 70 10 28N 79 20 E
Adirondack Mts. 114 44 0N 74 15W
Adjim 83 33 47N 10 50 E
Adjohon 85 6 41N 2 32 E
Adjud 46 46 7N 27 10 E
Adjumani 90 3 20N 31 50 E
Adlavik Is. 107 55 2N 57 45W
Adler 57 43 28N 39 52 E
Admer 83 20 21N 5 27 E
Admer, Erg d' 83 24 0N 9 5 E
Admiralty B. 5 62 0 S 59 0W
Admiralty G. 96 14 20 S 125 55 E
Admiralty I. 104 57 40N 134 35W
Admiralty Inlet 118 48 0N 122 40W
Admiralty Is. 94 2 0 S 147 0 E
Admiralty Ra. 5 72 0 S 164 0 E
Ado 85 6 36N 2 56 E
Ado Ekiti 85 7 38N 5 12 E
Adok 87 8 10N 30 20 E
Adola 87 11 14N 41 44 E
Adonara 73 8 15 S 123 5 E
Adoni 70 15 33N 77 18W
Adony 27 47 6N 18 52 E
Adour → 20 43 32N 1 32W
Adra, India 69 23 30N 86 42 E
Adra, Spain 33 36 43N 3 3W
Adrano 41 37 40N 14 49 E
Adrar 82 27 51N 0 11W
Adré 81 13 40N 22 20 E
Adrī 83 27 32N 13 2 E
Ádria 39 45 4N 12 3 E
Adrian, Mich., U.S.A. 114 41 55N 84 0W
Adrian, Tex., U.S.A. 117 35 19N 102 37W
Adriatic Sea 34 43 0N 16 0 E
Adua 73 1 45 S 129 50 E
Adur 70 9 8N 76 40 E
Adwa 87 14 15N 38 52 E
Adzhar A.S.S.R. □ 57 42 0N 42 0 E
Adzopé 84 6 7N 3 49W
Ægean Sea 35 37 0N 25 0 E
Æolian Is. = Eólie 41 38 30N 14 50 E
Aerht'ai Shan 75 46 40N 92 45 E
Ærø 49 54 52N 10 25 E
Ærøskøbing 49 54 53N 10 24 E
Aëtós 45 37 15N 21 50 E
Afafi, Massif d' 83 22 11N 15 10 E
Afándou 45 36 18N 28 12 E
Afarag, Erg 82 23 50N 2 47 E
Affreville = Khemis Miliania 82 36 11N 2 14 E
Afghanistan ■ 65 33 0N 65 0 E
Afgoi 63 2 7N 44 59 E
'Afif 64 23 53N 42 56 E
Afikpo 85 5 53N 7 54 E
Aflisses, O. → 82 28 40N 0 50 E
Aflou 82 34 7N 2 3 E
Afognak I. 104 58 10N 152 50W
Afragola 41 40 54N 14 15 E
Afrera 87 13 16N 41 5 E
Africa 78 10 0N 20 0 E
Afton 113 42 14N 75 31W
Aftout 82 26 50N 3 45W
Afuá 127 0 15 S 50 20W
Afula 62 32 37N 35 17 E
Afyonkarahisar 64 38 45N 30 33 E
Aga 86 30 55N 31 10 E
Agadès = Agadez 85 16 58N 7 59 E
Agadez 85 16 58N 7 59 E
Agadir 82 30 28N 9 35W
Agano → 74 37 57N 139 8 E
Agapa 59 71 27N 89 15 E
Agar 68 23 40N 76 2 E
Agaro 87 7 50N 36 38 E
Agartala 67 23 50N 91 23 E
Agăș 46 46 28N 26 15 E
Agassiz 108 49 14N 121 46W
Agats 73 5 33 S 138 0 E
Agattu I. 104 52 25N 172 30 E
Agbélouvé 85 6 35N 1 14 E
Agboville 84 5 55N 4 15W
Agdam 57 40 0N 46 58 E
Agdash 57 40 44N 47 22 E
Agde 20 43 19N 3 28 E
Agde, C. d' 20 43 16N 3 28 E
Agdzhabedi 57 40 5N 47 27 E
Agen 20 44 12N 0 38 E
Ager Tay 83 20 0N 17 41 E
Agersø 49 55 13N 11 12 E
Ageyevo 55 54 10N 36 27 E
Agger 49 56 47N 8 13 E
Aggius 40 40 56N 9 4 E
Aghil Mts. 69 36 0N 77 0 E
Aginskoye 59 51 6N 114 32 E
Agira 41 37 40N 14 30 E
Agly → 20 42 46N 3 3 E
Agnibilékrou 84 7 10N 3 11W
Agnita 46 45 59N 24 40 E
Agnone 41 41 49N 14 20 E
Agofie 85 8 27N 0 15 E
Agogna → 38 45 4N 8 52 E
Agogo 87 7 50N 28 45 E
Agon 18 49 2N 1 34W
Agön 48 61 34N 17 23 E
Agordo 39 46 18N 12 2 E
Agout → 20 43 47N 1 41 E
Agra 68 27 17N 77 58 E
Agramunt 32 41 48N 1 6 E
Agreda 32 41 51N 1 55W
Agri → 41 40 13N 16 44 E
Ağri Daği 64 39 50N 44 15 E
Ağri Karakose 64 39 44N 43 3 E
Agrigento 40 37 19N 13 33 E
Agrinion 45 38 37N 21 27 E
Agrópoli 41 40 23N 14 59 E
Água Clara 127 20 25 S 52 45W
Agua Prieta 120 31 20N 109 32W
Aguadas 126 5 40N 75 38W
Aguadilla 121 18 27N 67 10W
Aguanish 107 50 14N 62 2W
Aguanus → 107 50 13N 62 5W
Aguapey → 124 29 7 S 56 36W
Aguaray Guazú → 124 24 47 S 57 19W
Aguarico → 126 0 59 S 75 11W
Aguas → 32 41 20N 0 30W
Aguas Blancas 124 24 15 S 69 55W
Aguas Calientes, Sierra de 124 25 26 S 66 40W
Aguascalientes 120 21 53N 102 12W
Aguascalientes □ 120 22 0N 102 20W
Agudo 31 38 59N 4 52W
Águeda 30 40 34N 8 27W
Agueda → 30 41 2N 6 56W
Aguié 85 13 31N 7 46 E
Aguilafuente 30 41 13N 4 7W
Aguilar 31 37 31N 4 40W
Aguilar de Campóo 30 42 47N 4 15W
Aguilares 124 27 26 S 65 35W
Aguilas 33 37 23N 1 35W
Agulaa 87 13 40N 39 40 E
Agulhas, Kaap 92 34 52 S 20 0 E
Agung 72 8 20 S 115 28 E
'Agur 62 31 42N 34 55 E
Agur 90 2 28N 32 55 E
Agusan → 73 9 0N 125 30 E
Agvali 57 42 36N 46 8 E
Aha Mts. 92 19 45 S 21 0 E
Ahaggar 83 23 0N 6 30 E
Ahamansu 85 7 38N 0 35 E
Ahar 64 38 35N 47 0 E
Ahaus 24 52 4N 7 1 E
Ahelledjem 83 26 37N 6 58 E
Ahipara B. 101 35 5 S 173 5 E
Ahiri 70 19 30N 80 0 E
Ahlen 24 51 45N 7 52 E
Ahmadabad (Ahmedabad) 68 23 0N 72 40 E
Ahmadnagar (Ahmednagar) 70 19 7N 74 46 E
Ahmadpur 68 29 12N 71 10 E
Ahmar Mts. 87 9 20N 41 15 E
Ahoada 85 5 8N 6 36 E
Ahr → 24 50 33N 7 17 E
Ahrensbök 24 54 0N 10 34 E
Ahrweiler 24 50 31N 7 3 E
Aḥsā', Wāḥat al 64 25 50N 49 0 E
Ahuachapán 120 13 54N 89 52W
Åhus 49 55 56N 14 18 E
Ahvāz 64 31 20N 48 40 E
Ahvenanmaa = Åland 51 60 15N 20 0 E
Ahwar 63 13 30N 46 40 E
Ahzar 85 15 30N 3 20 E
Aichach 25 48 28N 11 9 E
Aichi □ 74 35 0N 137 15 E
Aidone 41 37 26N 14 26 E
Aiello Cálabro 41 39 6N 16 12 E
Aigle 25 46 18N 6 58 E
Aigle, L' 18 48 46N 0 38 E
Aignay-le-Duc 19 47 40N 4 43 E
Aigre 20 45 54N 0 1 E
Aigua 125 34 13 S 54 46W
Aigueperse 20 46 3N 3 13 E
Aigues-Mortes 21 43 35N 4 12 E
Aigues-Mortes, G. d' 21 43 31N 4 3 E
Aiguilles 21 44 47N 6 51 E
Aiguillon 20 44 18N 0 21 E
Aiguillon, L' 20 46 20N 1 16W
Aigurande 20 46 27N 1 49 E
Aihui 75 50 10N 127 30 E
Aija 126 9 50 S 77 45W
Aijal 67 23 40N 92 44 E
Aiken 115 33 34N 81 50W
Aillant-sur-Tholon 19 47 52N 3 20 E
Aillik 107 55 11N 59 18W
Ailly-sur-Noye 19 49 45N 2 20 E
Ailsa Craig 14 55 15N 5 7W
'Ailūn 62 32 18N 35 47 E
Aim 59 59 0N 133 55 E
Aimere 73 8 45 S 121 3 E
Aimogasta 124 28 33 S 66 50W
Aimorés 127 19 30 S 41 4W
Ain □ 21 46 5N 5 20 E
Ain → 21 45 45N 5 11 E
Aïn Banaiyan 65 23 0N 51 0 E
Aïn Beïda 83 35 50N 7 29 E
Ain ben Khellil 82 33 15N 0 49W
Aïn Ben Tili 82 25 59N 9 27W
Aïn Beni Mathar 82 34 1N 2 0W
Aïn Benian 82 36 48N 2 55 E
Ain Dalla 86 27 20N 27 23 E
Ain Dar 64 25 55N 49 10 E
Ain el Mafki 86 27 30N 28 15 E

Aïn Galakka | Alexandria

Aïn Galakka	**81**	18 10N	18 30 E
Aïn Girba	**86**	29 20N	25 14 E
Aïn M'lila	**83**	36 2N	6 35 E
Aïn Qeiqab	**86**	29 42N	24 55 E
Aïn-Sefra	**82**	32 47N	0 37W
Aïn Sheikh Murzûk	**86**	26 47N	27 45 E
Aïn Sukhna	**86**	29 32N	32 20 E
Aïn Tédelès	**82**	36 0N	0 21 E
Aïn-Témouchent	**82**	35 16N	1 8W
Aïn Touta	**83**	35 26N	5 54 E
Aïn Zeitûn	**86**	29 10N	25 48 E
Aïn Zorah	**82**	34 37N	3 32W
Ainabo	**63**	9 0N	46 25 E
Ainaži	**54**	57 50N	24 24 E
Aínos Óros	**45**	38 10N	20 35 E
Ainsworth	**116**	42 33N	99 52W
Aïr	**85**	18 30N	8 0 E
Airaines	**19**	49 58N	1 55 E
Airdrie	**14**	55 53N	3 57W
Aire	**19**	50 37N	2 22 E
Aire →, France	**19**	49 18N	4 55 E
Aire →, U.K.	**12**	53 42N	0 55W
Aire, I. del	**32**	39 48N	4 16 E
Aire-sur-l'Adour	**20**	43 42N	0 15W
Airvault	**18**	46 50N	0 8W
Aisch →	**25**	49 46N	11 1 E
Aisne □	**19**	49 42N	3 40 E
Aisne →	**19**	49 26N	2 50 E
Aitana, Sierra de	**33**	38 35N	0 24W
Aitape	**98**	3 11 S	142 22 E
Aitkin	**116**	46 32N	93 43W
Aitolía Kai Akarnanía □	**45**	38 45N	21 18 E
Aitolikón	**45**	38 26N	21 21 E
Aiud	**46**	46 19N	23 44 E
Aix-en-Provence	**21**	43 32N	5 27 E
Aix-la-Chapelle = Aachen	**24**	50 47N	6 4 E
Aix-les-Bains	**21**	45 41N	5 53 E
Aix-sur-Vienne	**20**	45 48N	1 8 E
Aiyansh	**108**	55 17N	129 2W
Áiyina	**45**	37 45N	23 26 E
Aiyínion	**44**	40 28N	22 28 E
Aiyion	**45**	38 15N	22 5 E
Aizenay	**18**	46 44N	1 38W
Aizpute	**54**	56 43N	21 40 E
Ajaccio	**21**	41 55N	8 40 E
Ajaccio, G. d'	**21**	41 52N	8 40 E
Ajanta Ra.	**70**	20 28N	75 50 E
Ajax	**112**	43 50N	79 1W
Ajdābiyah	**83**	30 54N	20 4 E
Ajdovščina	**39**	45 54N	13 54 E
Ajibar	**87**	10 35N	38 36 E
Ajka	**27**	47 4N	17 31 E
'Ajmān	**65**	25 25N	55 30 E
Ajmer	**68**	26 28N	74 37 E
Ajo	**119**	32 18N	112 54W
Ajok	**87**	9 15N	28 28 E
Ak Dağ	**64**	36 30N	30 0 E
Akaba	**85**	8 10N	1 2 E
Akabli	**82**	26 49N	1 31 E
Akaki Beseka	**87**	8 55N	38 45 E
Akala	**87**	15 39N	36 13 E
Akaroa	**101**	43 49 S	172 59 E
Akasha	**86**	21 10N	30 32 E
Akashi	**74**	34 45N	135 0 E
Akbou	**83**	36 31N	4 31 E
Akelamo	**73**	1 35N	129 40 E
Åkernes	**47**	58 45N	7 30 E
Akershus fylke □	**47**	60 0N	11 10 E
Akeru →	**70**	17 25N	80 0 E
Aketi	**88**	2 38N	23 47 E
Akhaïa □	**45**	38 5N	21 45 E
Akhalkalaki	**57**	41 27N	43 25 E
Akhaltsikhe	**57**	41 40N	43 0 E
Akharnaí	**45**	38 5N	23 44 E
Akhelóös →	**45**	38 36N	21 14 E
Akhendria	**45**	34 58N	25 16 E
Akhéron →	**44**	39 20N	20 29 E
Akhisar	**64**	38 56N	27 48 E
Akhladhókambos	**45**	37 31N	22 35 E
Akhmîm	**86**	26 31N	31 47 E
Akhtopol	**43**	42 6N	27 56 E
Akhtubinsk (Petropavlovskiy)	**57**	48 13N	46 7 E
Akhty	**57**	41 30N	47 45 E
Akhtyrka	**54**	50 25N	35 0 E
Akimiski I.	**106**	52 50N	81 30W
Akimovka	**56**	46 44N	35 0 E
Åkirkeby	**49**	55 4N	14 55 E
Akita	**74**	39 45N	140 7 E
Akita □	**74**	39 40N	140 30 E
Akjoujt	**84**	19 45N	14 15W
Akka	**82**	29 22N	8 9W
'Akko	**62**	32 55N	35 4 E
Akkol	**58**	45 0N	75 39 E
Akköy	**45**	37 30N	27 18 E
Aklampa	**85**	8 15N	2 10 E
Aklavik	**104**	68 12N	135 0W
Akmonte	**31**	37 13N	6 38W
Aknoul	**82**	34 40N	3 55W
Ako	**85**	10 19N	10 48 E
Akobo →	**87**	7 48N	33 3 E
Akola	**68**	20 42N	77 2 E
Akonolinga	**85**	3 50N	12 18 E
Akordat	**87**	15 30N	37 40 E
Akosombo Dam	**85**	6 20N	0 5 E
Akot, India	**68**	21 10N	77 10 E
Akot, Sudan	**87**	6 31N	30 9 E
Akpatok I.	**105**	60 25N	68 8W
Akranes	**50**	64 19N	21 58W
Åkrehamn	**47**	59 15N	5 10 E
Akreïjit	**84**	18 19N	9 11W
Akrítas Venétiko, Ákra	**45**	36 43N	21 54 E
Akron, Colo., U.S.A.	**116**	40 13N	103 15W
Akron, Ohio, U.S.A.	**114**	41 7N	81 31W
Akrotíri, Ákra	**44**	40 26N	25 27 E
Aksai Chih	**69**	35 15N	79 55 E
Aksaray	**64**	38 25N	34 2 E
Aksarka	**58**	66 31N	67 50 E
Aksay	**52**	51 11N	53 0 E
Akşehir	**64**	38 18N	31 30 E
Aksenovo Zilovskoye	**59**	53 20N	117 40 E
Akstafa	**57**	41 7N	45 27 E
Aksu	**75**	41 5N	80 10 E
Aksum	**87**	14 5N	38 40 E
Aktogay	**58**	46 57N	79 40 E
Aktyubinsk	**53**	50 17N	57 10 E
Aku	**85**	6 40N	7 18 E
Akure	**85**	7 15N	5 5 E
Akureyri	**50**	65 40N	18 6W
Akusha	**57**	42 18N	47 30 E
Al Abyār	**83**	32 9N	20 29 E
Al 'Adan	**63**	12 45N	45 0 E
Al Amādaöyah	**64**	37 5N	43 30 E
Al Amārah	**64**	31 55N	47 15 E
Al 'Aqabah	**62**	29 31N	35 0 E
Al 'Aramah	**64**	25 30N	46 0 E
Al Ashkhara	**65**	21 50N	59 30 E
Al 'Ayzarīyah (Bethany)	**62**	31 47N	35 15 E
Al 'Azīzīyah	**83**	32 30N	13 1 E
Al Badī'	**64**	22 0N	46 35 E
Al Barkāt	**83**	24 56N	10 14 E
Al Başrah	**64**	30 30N	47 50 E
Al Bāzūrīyah	**62**	33 15N	35 16 E
Al Bīrah	**62**	31 55N	35 12 E
Al Bu'ayrāt	**83**	31 24N	15 44 E
Al Buqay'ah	**62**	32 15N	35 30 E
Al Dīwanīyah	**64**	32 0N	45 0 E
Al Fallūjah	**64**	33 20N	43 55 E
Al Fāw	**64**	30 0N	48 30 E
Al Fujayrah	**65**	25 7N	56 18 E
Al Ghatghat	**64**	24 40N	46 15 E
Al Hābah	**64**	27 10N	47 0 E
Al Haddār	**64**	21 58N	45 57 E
Al Ḩadīthah	**64**	34 0N	41 13 E
Al Hāmad	**64**	31 30N	39 30 E
Al Ḩamar	**64**	22 23N	46 6 E
Al Hammādah al Ḩamrā'	**83**	29 30N	12 0 E
Al Hamrā'	**64**	24 2N	38 55 E
Al Ḩarīq	**64**	23 29N	46 27 E
Al Harīr, W. →	**62**	32 44N	35 59 E
Al Harūj al Aswad	**83**	27 0N	17 10 E
Al Ḩasakah	**64**	36 35N	40 45 E
Al Ḩawīyah	**64**	24 40N	49 15 E
Al Ḩawrah	**63**	13 50N	47 35 E
Al Ḩawţah	**63**	16 5N	48 20 E
Al Ḩayy	**64**	32 5N	46 5 E
Al Ḩillah, Iraq	**64**	32 30N	44 25 E
Al Ḩillah, Si. Arab.	**64**	23 35N	46 50 E
Al Hindīyah	**64**	32 30N	44 10 E
Al Ḩişnn	**62**	32 29N	35 52 E
Al Hoceïma	**82**	35 8N	3 58W
Al Ḩudaydah	**63**	14 50N	43 0 E
Al Ḩufrah, Awbārī, Libya	**83**	25 32N	14 1 E
Al Ḩufrah, Misrātah, Libya	**83**	29 5N	18 3 E
Al Hūfuf	**64**	25 25N	49 45 E
Al Ḩulwah	**64**	23 24N	46 48 E
Al Husayyāt	**83**	30 24N	20 37 E
Al 'Idwah	**64**	27 15N	42 35 E
Al Irq	**81**	29 5N	21 35 E
Al Ittihad = Madīnat ash Sha'b	**63**	12 50N	45 0 E
Al Jāfūrah	**64**	25 0N	50 15 E
Al Jaghbūb	**81**	29 42N	24 38 E
Al Jahrah	**64**	29 25N	47 40 E
Al Jalāmīd	**64**	31 20N	39 45 E
Al Jawf, Libya	**81**	24 10N	23 24 E
Al Jawf, Si. Arab.	**64**	29 55N	39 40 E
Al Jazir	**63**	18 30N	56 31 E
Al Jazirah, Libya	**81**	26 10N	21 20 E
Al Jazirah, Si. Arab.	**64**	33 30N	44 0 E
Al Jubayl	**64**	27 0N	49 50 E
Al Jubaylah	**64**	24 55N	46 25 E
Al Junaynah	**81**	13 27N	22 45 E
Al Juwārah	**63**	19 0N	57 13 E
Al Khābūrah	**65**	23 57N	57 5 E
Al Khalīl = Hebron	**62**	31 32N	35 6 E
Al Khalūf	**63**	20 30N	58 13 E
Al Kharfah	**64**	22 0N	46 35 E
Al Kharj	**64**	24 0N	47 0 E
Al Khufayfīyah	**64**	24 50N	44 35 E
Al Khums	**83**	32 40N	14 17 E
Al Khums □	**83**	31 20N	14 10 E
Al Khurmah	**64**	21 58N	42 3 E
Al Kufrah	**81**	24 17N	23 15 E
Al Kūt	**64**	32 30N	46 0 E
Al Kuwayt	**64**	29 30N	47 30 E
Al Lādhiqīyah	**64**	35 30N	35 45 E
Al Lidām	**63**	20 33N	44 45 E
Al Līth	**86**	20 9N	40 15 E
Al Lubban	**62**	32 9N	35 14 E
Al Luḩayyah	**63**	15 45N	42 40 E
Al Madīnah	**64**	24 35N	39 52 E
Al-Mafraq	**62**	32 17N	36 14 E
Al Majma'ah	**64**	25 57N	45 22 E
Al Manāmāh	**65**	26 10N	50 30 E
Al Marj	**81**	32 25N	20 30 E
Al Maşīrah	**63**	20 25N	58 50 E
Al Matamma	**63**	16 10N	44 30 E
Al Mawşil	**64**	36 15N	43 5 E
Al Mazra	**62**	31 16N	35 31 E
Al Midhnab	**64**	25 50N	44 18 E
Al Miqdādīyah	**64**	34 0N	45 0 E
Al Mish'āb	**64**	28 12N	48 36 E
Al Mubarraz	**64**	25 30N	49 40 E
Al Muḩarraq	**65**	26 15N	50 40 E
Al Mukallā	**63**	14 33N	49 2 E
Al Mukhā	**63**	13 18N	43 15 E
Al Musayyib	**64**	32 40N	44 25 E
Al Mustajiddah	**64**	26 30N	41 50 E
Al Muwaylih	**64**	27 40N	35 30 E
Al Qaddāhīyah	**83**	31 15N	15 9 E
Al Qaḑīmah	**64**	22 20N	39 13 E
Al Qāmishlī	**64**	37 10N	41 10 E
Al Qaryah ash Sharqīyah	**83**	30 28N	13 40 E
Al Qaşabát	**83**	32 39N	14 1 E
Al Qaţīf	**64**	26 35N	50 0 E
Al Qaţrūn	**83**	24 56N	15 3 E
Al Quaisūmah	**64**	28 10N	46 20 E
Al Quds	**62**	31 47N	35 10 E
Al Qunfidha	**86**	19 3N	41 4 E
Al Quraiyat	**65**	23 17N	58 53 E
Al Qurnah	**64**	31 1N	47 25 E
Al 'Ulá	**64**	26 35N	38 0 E
Al Uqaylah ash Sharqīgah	**83**	30 12N	19 10 E
Al Uqayr	**64**	25 40N	50 15 E
Al 'Uthmānīyahyah	**64**	25 5N	49 22 E
Al 'Uwaynid	**64**	24 50N	46 0 E
Al' 'Uwayqīlah ash Sharqīgah	**64**	30 30N	42 10 E
Al 'Uyūn	**64**	26 30N	43 50 E
Al Wajh	**86**	26 10N	36 30 E
Al Wakrah	**65**	25 10N	51 40 E
Al Warī'āh	**64**	27 51N	47 25 E
Al Wātīyah	**83**	32 28N	11 57 E
Al Yāmūn	**62**	32 29N	35 14 E
Ala	**38**	45 46N	11 0 E
Alabama □	**115**	33 0N	87 0W
Alabama →	**115**	31 8N	87 57W
Alaçati	**45**	38 16N	26 23 E
Alaejos	**30**	41 18N	5 13W
Alagna Valsésia	**38**	45 51N	7 56 E
Alagoa Grande	**127**	7 3 S	35 35W
Alagoas □	**127**	9 0 S	36 0W
Alagoinhas	**127**	12 7 S	38 20W
Alagón	**32**	41 46N	1 12W
Alagón →	**31**	39 44N	6 53W
Alajuela	**121**	10 2N	84 8W
Alakamisy	**93**	21 19 S	47 14 E
Alakurtti	**52**	67 0N	30 30 E
Alameda, Spain	**31**	37 12N	4 39W
Alameda, Idaho, U.S.A.	**118**	43 2N	112 30W
Alameda, N. Mex., U.S.A.	**119**	35 10N	106 43W
Alamitos, Sierra de los	**120**	37 21N	115 10W
Alamo	**119**	36 21N	115 10W
Alamogordo	**119**	32 59N	106 0W
Alamos	**120**	27 0N	109 0W
Alamosa	**119**	37 30N	106 0W
Åland	**51**	60 15N	20 0 E
Aland	**70**	17 36N	76 35 E
Alandroal	**31**	38 41N	7 24W
Alandur	**70**	13 0N	80 15 E
Alange, Presa de	**31**	38 45N	6 18W
Alanis	**31**	38 3N	5 43W
Alanya	**64**	36 38N	32 0 E
Alaotra, Farihin'	**93**	17 30 S	48 30 E
Alapayevsk	**58**	57 52N	61 42 E
Alar del Rey	**30**	42 38N	4 20W
Alaraz	**30**	40 45N	5 17W
Alaşehir	**53**	38 23N	28 30 E
Alaska □	**104**	65 0N	150 0W
Alaska, G. of	**104**	58 0N	145 0W
Alaska Highway	**108**	60 0N	130 0W
Alaska Pen.	**104**	56 0N	160 0W
Alaska Range	**104**	62 50N	151 0W
Alássio	**38**	44 1N	8 10 E
Alataw Shankou	**75**	45 5N	81 57 E
Alatri	**40**	41 44N	13 21 E
Alatyr	**55**	54 45N	46 35 E
Alatyr →	**55**	54 52N	46 36 E
Alausi	**126**	2 0 S	78 50W
Álava □	**32**	42 48N	2 28W
Alava, C.	**118**	48 10N	124 40W
Alaverdi	**57**	41 15N	44 37 E
Alawoona	**99**	34 45 S	140 30 E
Alayor	**32**	39 57N	4 8 E
Alazan →	**57**	41 5N	46 40 E
Alba	**38**	44 41N	8 1 E
Alba □	**46**	46 10N	23 30 E
Alba de Tormes	**30**	40 50N	5 30W
Alba Iulia	**46**	46 8N	23 39 E
Albac	**46**	46 28N	23 1 E
Albacete	**33**	39 0N	1 50W
Albacete □	**33**	38 50N	2 0W
Albacutya, L.	**99**	35 45 S	141 58 E
Ålbæk	**49**	57 36N	10 25 E
Ålbæk Bucht	**49**	57 35N	10 40 E
Albaida	**33**	38 51N	0 31W
Albalate de las Nogueras	**32**	40 22N	2 18W
Albalate del Arzobispo	**32**	41 6N	0 31W
Albania ■	**44**	41 0N	20 0 E
Albano Laziale	**40**	41 44N	12 40 E
Albany, Austral.	**96**	35 1 S	117 58 E
Albany, Ga., U.S.A.	**115**	31 40N	84 10W
Albany, Minn., U.S.A.	**116**	45 37N	94 38W
Albany, N.Y., U.S.A.	**114**	42 35N	73 47W
Albany, Oreg., U.S.A.	**118**	44 41N	123 0W
Albany, Tex., U.S.A.	**117**	32 45N	99 20W
Albany →	**106**	52 17N	81 31W
Albardón	**124**	31 20 S	68 30W
Albarracín	**32**	40 25N	1 26W
Albarracín, Sierra de	**32**	40 30N	1 30W
Albatross B.	**97**	12 45 S	141 30 E
Albegna →	**39**	42 30N	11 11 E
Albemarle	**115**	35 27N	80 15W
Albemarle Sd.	**115**	36 0N	76 30W
Albenga	**38**	44 3N	8 12 E
Alberche →	**30**	39 58N	4 46W
Alberdi	**124**	26 14 S	58 20W
Alberes, Mts.	**32**	42 28N	2 56 E
Alberique	**33**	39 7N	0 31W
Albersdorf	**24**	54 8N	9 19 E
Albert	**19**	50 0N	2 38 E
Albert Canyon	**108**	51 8N	117 41W
Albert L.	**99**	35 30 S	139 10 E
Albert, L. = Mobutu Sese Seko, L.	**90**	1 30N	31 0 E
Albert Lea	**116**	43 32N	93 20W
Albert Nile →	**90**	3 36N	32 2 E
Alberta □	**108**	54 40N	115 0W
Alberti	**124**	35 1 S	60 16W
Albertinia	**92**	34 11 S	21 34 E
Albertirsa	**27**	47 14N	19 37 E
Alberton	**107**	46 50N	64 0W
Albertville	**21**	45 40N	6 22 E
Albertville = Kalemie	**90**	5 55 S	29 9 E
Alberz, Reshteh-Ye Kūhhā-Ye	**65**	36 0N	52 0 E
Albi	**20**	43 56N	2 9 E
Albia	**116**	41 0N	92 50W
Albina	**127**	5 37N	54 15W
Albina, Ponta	**92**	15 52 S	11 44 E
Albino	**38**	45 47N	9 48 E
Albion, Idaho, U.S.A.	**118**	42 21N	113 37W
Albion, Mich., U.S.A.	**114**	42 15N	84 45W
Albion, Nebr., U.S.A.	**116**	41 47N	98 0W
Albion, Pa., U.S.A.	**112**	41 53N	80 21W
Albocácer	**32**	40 21N	0 1 E
Alböke	**49**	56 57N	16 47 E
Alborán	**31**	35 57N	3 0W
Alborea	**33**	39 17N	1 24W
Ålborg	**49**	57 2N	9 54 E
Ålborg B.	**49**	56 50N	10 35 E
Albox	**33**	37 23N	2 8W
Albreda	**108**	52 35N	119 10W
Albuera, La	**31**	38 45N	6 49W
Albufeira	**31**	37 5N	8 15W
Albula →	**25**	46 38N	9 30 E
Albuñol	**33**	36 48N	3 11W
Albuquerque	**119**	35 5N	106 47W
Albuquerque, Cayos de	**121**	12 10N	81 50W
Alburg	**113**	44 58N	73 19W
Alburno, Mte.	**41**	40 32N	15 15 E
Alburquerque	**31**	39 15N	6 59W
Albury	**97**	36 3 S	146 56 E
Alby	**48**	62 30N	15 28 E
Alcácer do Sal	**31**	38 22N	8 33W
Alcaçovas	**31**	38 23N	8 9W
Alcalá de Chisvert	**32**	40 19N	0 13 E
Alcalá de Guadaira	**31**	37 20N	5 50W
Alcalá de Henares	**32**	40 28N	3 22W
Alcalá de los Gazules	**31**	36 29N	5 43W
Alcalá la Real	**31**	37 27N	3 57W
Alcamo	**40**	37 59N	12 55 E
Alcanadre	**32**	42 24N	2 7W
Alcanadre →	**32**	41 43N	0 12W
Alcanar	**32**	40 33N	0 28 E
Alcanede	**31**	39 25N	8 49W
Alcanena	**31**	39 27N	8 40W
Alcañices	**30**	41 41N	6 21W
Alcaníz	**32**	41 2N	0 8W
Alcântara	**127**	2 20 S	44 30W
Alcántara	**31**	39 41N	6 57W
Alcantara L.	**109**	60 57N	108 9W
Alcantarilla	**33**	37 59N	1 12W
Alcaracejos	**31**	38 24N	4 58W
Alcaraz	**33**	38 40N	2 29W
Alcaraz, Sierra de	**33**	38 40N	2 20W
Alcarria, La	**32**	40 31N	2 45W
Alcaudete	**31**	37 35N	4 5W
Alcázar de San Juan	**33**	39 24N	3 12W
Alcira	**33**	39 9N	0 30W
Alcoa	**115**	35 50N	84 0W
Alcobaça	**31**	39 32N	9 0W
Alcobendas	**32**	40 32N	3 38W
Alcolea del Pinar	**32**	41 2N	2 28W
Alcora	**32**	40 5N	0 14W
Alcoutim	**31**	37 25N	7 28W
Alcova	**118**	42 37N	106 52W
Alcoy	**33**	38 43N	0 30W
Alcubierre, Sierra de	**32**	41 45N	0 22W
Alcublas	**32**	39 48N	0 43W
Alcudia	**32**	39 51N	3 7 E
Alcudia, B. de	**32**	39 47N	3 15 E
Alcudia, Sierra de la	**31**	38 34N	4 30W
Aldabra Is.	**3**	9 22 S	46 28 E
Aldan	**59**	58 40N	125 30 E
Aldan →	**59**	63 28N	129 35 E
Aldeburgh	**13**	52 9N	1 35 E
Aldeia Nova	**31**	37 55N	7 24W
Alder	**118**	45 27N	112 3W
Alderney	**18**	49 42N	2 12W
Aldershot	**13**	51 15N	0 43W
Aldersyde	**108**	50 40N	113 53W
Aledo	**116**	41 10N	90 50W
Alefa	**87**	11 55N	36 55 E
Aleg	**84**	17 3N	13 55W
Alegre	**125**	20 50 S	41 30W
Alegrete	**125**	29 40 S	56 0W
Aleisk	**58**	52 40N	83 0 E
Alejandro Selkirk, I.	**95**	33 50 S	80 15W
Aleksandriya, Ukraine S.S.R., U.S.S.R.	**54**	50 37N	26 19 E
Aleksandriya, Ukraine S.S.R., U.S.S.R.	**56**	48 42N	33 3 E
Aleksandriyskaya	**57**	43 59N	47 0 E
Aleksandrov	**55**	56 23N	38 44 E
Aleksandrovac, Srbija, Yugo.	**42**	44 28N	21 13 E
Aleksandrovac, Srbija, Yugo.	**42**	43 28N	21 3 E
Aleksandrovka	**56**	48 55N	32 20 E
Aleksandrovo	**43**	43 14N	24 51 E
Aleksandrovsk-Sakhaliniskiy	**59**	50 50N	142 20 E
Aleksandrovskiy Zavod	**59**	50 40N	117 50 E
Aleksandrovskoye	**58**	60 35N	77 50 E
Aleksandrów Kujawski	**28**	52 53N	18 43 E
Aleksandrów Łódžki	**28**	51 49N	19 17 E
Alekseyevka	**55**	50 43N	38 40 E
Aleksin	**55**	54 31N	37 9 E
Aleksinac	**42**	43 31N	21 42 E
Além Paraíba	**125**	21 52 S	42 41W
Alemania, Argent.	**124**	25 40 S	65 30W
Alemania, Chile	**124**	25 10 S	69 55W
Ålen	**47**	62 51N	11 17 E
Alençon	**18**	48 27N	0 4 E
Alenuihaha Chan.	**110**	20 25N	156 0W
Aleppo = Ḩalab	**64**	36 10N	37 15 E
Aléria	**21**	42 5N	9 26 E
Alert Bay	**108**	50 30N	126 55W
Alès	**21**	44 9N	4 5 E
Aleşd	**46**	47 3N	22 22 E
Alessándria	**38**	44 54N	8 37 E
Ålestrup	**49**	56 42N	9 29 E
Ålesund	**47**	62 28N	6 12 E
Alet-les-Bains	**20**	43 0N	2 14 E
Aleutian Is.	**104**	52 0N	175 0W
Aleutian Trench	**94**	48 0N	180 0
Alexander	**116**	47 51N	103 40W
Alexander Arch.	**104**	57 0N	135 0W
Alexander B.	**92**	28 36 S	16 33 E
Alexander City	**115**	32 58N	85 57W
Alexander I.	**5**	69 0 S	70 0W
Alexandra, Austral.	**99**	37 8 S	145 40 E
Alexandra, N.Z.	**101**	45 14 S	169 25 E
Alexandra Falls	**108**	60 29N	116 18W
Alexandria, B.C., Can.	**108**	52 35N	122 27W
Alexandria, Ont., Can.	**106**	45 19N	74 38W
Alexandria, Romania	**46**	43 57N	25 24 E
Alexandria, S. Afr.	**92**	33 38 S	26 28 E
Alexandria, Ind., U.S.A.	**114**	40 18N	85 40W
Alexandria, La., U.S.A.	**117**	31 20N	92 30W
Alexandria, Minn., U.S.A.	**116**	45 50N	95 20W
Alexandria, S.D., U.S.A.	**116**	43 40N	97 45W
Alexandria, Va., U.S.A.	**114**	38 47N	77 1W

Alexandria **Amursk**

Alexandria = El Iskandarîya **86** 31 0N 30 0 E
Alexandria Bay **114** 44 20N 75 52W
Alexandrina, L. **97** 35 25S 139 10 E
Alexandroúpolis **44** 40 50N 25 54 E
Alexis → **107** 52 33N 56 8W
Alexis Creek **108** 52 10N 123 20W
Alfambra **32** 40 33N 1 5W
Alfândega da Fé **30** 41 20N 6 59W
Alfaro **32** 42 10N 1 50W
Alfatar **43** 43 59N 27 13 E
Alfeld **24** 52 0N 9 49 E
Alfenas **125** 21 20S 46 10W
Alfiós → **45** 37 40N 21 33 E
Alfonsine **39** 44 30N 12 1 E
Alford **14** 57 13N 2 42W
Alfred, Me., U.S.A. **113** 43 28N 70 40W
Alfred, N.Y., U.S.A. **112** 42 15N 77 45W
Alfreton **12** 53 6N 1 22W
Alfta **48** 61 21N 16 4 E
Alga **58** 49 53N 57 20 E
Algaba, La **31** 37 27N 6 1W
Algar **31** 36 40N 5 39W
Ålgård **47** 58 46N 5 53 E
Algarinejo **31** 37 19N 4 9W
Algarve **31** 36 58N 8 20W
Algeciras **31** 36 9N 5 28W
Algemesí **33** 39 11N 0 27W
Alger **82** 36 42N 3 8 E
Algeria ■ **82** 35 10N 3 11 E
Alghero **40** 40 34N 8 20 E
Algiers = Alger **82** 36 42N 3 8 E
Algoabaai **92** 33 50S 25 45 E
Algodonales **31** 36 54N 5 24W
Algodor → **30** 39 55N 3 53W
Algoma, Oreg., U.S.A. **118** 42 25N 121 54W
Algoma, Wis., U.S.A. **114** 44 35N 87 27W
Algona **116** 43 4N 94 14W
Algonac **112** 42 37N 82 32W
Alhama de Almería **33** 36 57N 2 34W
Alhama de Aragón **32** 41 18N 1 54W
Alhama de Granada **31** 37 0N 3 59W
Alhama de Murcia **33** 37 51N 1 25W
Alhambra, Spain **33** 38 54N 3 4W
Alhambra, U.S.A. **119** 34 2N 118 10W
Alhaurín el Grande **31** 36 39N 4 41W
Alhucemas = Al-Hoceïma **82** 35 8N 3 58W
'Alī al Gharbī **64** 32 30N 46 45 E
Ali Bayramly **57** 39 59N 48 52 E
Ali Sabieh **87** 11 10N 42 44 E
Ália **40** 37 47N 13 42 E
'Alīābād **65** 28 10N 57 35 E
Aliaga **32** 40 40N 0 42W
Aliákmon → **44** 40 30N 22 36 E
Alibag **70** 18 38N 72 56 E
Alibo **87** 9 52N 37 5 E
Alibunar **42** 45 5N 20 57 E
Alicante **33** 38 23N 0 30W
Alicante □ **33** 38 30N 0 37W
Alice, S. Afr. **92** 32 48S 26 55 E
Alice, U.S.A. **117** 27 47N 98 1W
Alice →, Queens., Austral. **98** 24 2S 144 50 E
Alice →, Queens., Austral. **98** 15 35S 142 20 E
Alice Arm **108** 55 29N 129 31W
Alice, Punta dell' **41** 39 23N 17 10 E
Alice Springs **96** 23 40S 133 50 E
Alicedale **92** 33 15S 26 4 E
Aliceville **115** 33 9N 88 10W
Alick Cr. → **98** 20 55S 142 20 E
Alicudi, I. **41** 38 33N 14 20 E
Alida **109** 49 25N 101 55W
Aligarh, Raj., India **68** 25 55N 76 15 E
Aligarh, Ut. P., India **68** 27 55N 78 10 E
Alīgūdarz **64** 33 25N 49 45 E
Alijó **30** 41 16N 7 27W
Alimena **41** 37 42N 14 4 E
Alimnia **45** 36 16N 27 43 E
Alingsås **49** 57 56N 12 31 E
Alipur **68** 29 25N 70 55 E
Alipur Duar **69** 26 30N 89 35 E
Aliquippa **114** 40 38N 80 18W
Aliste → **30** 41 34N 5 58W
Alitus **54** 54 24N 24 3 E
Alivérion **45** 38 24N 24 2 E
Aliwal North **92** 30 45S 26 45 E
Alix **108** 52 24N 113 11W
Aljezur **31** 37 18N 8 49W
Aljustrel **31** 37 55N 8 10W
Alkamari **85** 13 27N 11 10 E
Alkmaar **16** 52 37N 4 45 E
All American Canal **119** 32 45N 115 0W
Allada **85** 6 41N 2 9 E
Allah Dad **68** 25 38N 67 34 E
Allahabad **69** 25 25N 81 58 E
Allakh-Yun **59** 60 50N 137 5 E
Allal Tazi **82** 34 30N 6 20W
Allan **109** 51 53N 106 4W
Allanche **20** 45 14N 2 57 E
Allanmyo **67** 19 30N 95 17 E
Allanridge **92** 27 45S 26 40 E
Allanwater **106** 50 14N 90 10W
Allaqi, Wadi → **86** 23 7N 32 47 E
Allariz **30** 42 11N 7 50W
Allassac **20** 45 15N 1 29 E
Allegan **114** 42 32N 85 52W
Allegany **112** 42 6N 78 30W
Allegheny → **114** 40 27N 80 0W
Allegheny Mts. **114** 38 0N 80 0W
Allegheny Res. **112** 42 0N 78 55W
Allègre **20** 45 12N 3 41 E
Allen, Bog of **15** 53 15N 7 0W
Allen, L. **15** 54 12N 8 5W
Allenby (Hussein) Bridge **62** 31 53N 35 33 E
Allende **120** 28 20N 100 50W
Allentown **114** 40 36N 75 30W
Allentsteig **26** 48 41N 15 20 E
Alleppey **70** 9 30N 76 28 E
Aller → **24** 52 57N 9 10 E
Allevard **21** 45 24N 6 5 E
Alliance, Nebr., U.S.A. **116** 42 10N 102 50W
Alliance, Ohio, U.S.A. **114** 40 53N 81 7W
Allier □ **20** 46 25N 3 0 E
Allier → **19** 46 57N 3 4 E
Allingåbro **49** 56 28N 10 20 E
Allinge **49** 55 17N 14 50 E
Alliston **106** 44 9N 79 52W
Alloa **14** 56 7N 3 49W
Allos **21** 44 15N 6 38 E
Alma, Can. **107** 48 35N 71 40W
Alma, Ga., U.S.A. **115** 31 33N 82 28W
Alma, Kans., U.S.A. **116** 39 1N 96 22W
Alma, Mich., U.S.A. **114** 43 25N 84 40W
Alma, Nebr., U.S.A. **116** 40 10N 99 25W
Alma, Wis., U.S.A. **116** 44 19N 91 54W
'Almā ash Sha'b **62** 33 7N 35 9 E
Alma Ata **58** 43 15N 76 57 E
Almada **31** 38 40N 9 9W
Almaden **98** 17 22S 144 40 E
Almadén **31** 38 49N 4 52W
Almagro **31** 38 50N 3 45W
Almanor, L. **118** 40 15N 121 11W
Almansa **33** 38 51N 1 5W
Almanza **30** 42 39N 5 3W
Almanzor, Pico de **30** 40 15N 5 18W
Almanzora → **33** 37 14N 1 46W
Almarcha, La **32** 39 41N 2 24W
Almaş, Mţii. **46** 44 49N 22 12 E
Almazán **32** 41 30N 2 30W
Almazora **32** 39 57N 0 3W
Almeirim, Brazil **127** 1 30S 52 34W
Almeirim, Port. **31** 39 12N 8 37W
Almelo **16** 52 22N 6 42 E
Almenar **32** 41 43N 2 12W
Almenara **32** 39 46N 0 14W
Almenara, Sierra de **33** 37 34N 1 32W
Almendralejo **31** 38 41N 6 26W
Almería **33** 36 52N 2 27W
Almería □ **33** 37 20N 2 20W
Almería, G. de **33** 36 41N 2 28W
Almirante **14** 9 10N 82 30W
Almiropótamos **45** 38 16N 24 11 E
Almirós **45** 39 11N 22 45 E
Almodôvar **31** 37 31N 8 2W
Almodóvar del Campo **31** 38 43N 4 10W
Almogia **31** 36 50N 4 32W
Almonaster la Real **31** 37 52N 6 48W
Almont **112** 42 53N 83 2W
Almonte **113** 45 14N 76 12W
Almonte → **31** 39 41N 6 28W
Almora **69** 29 38N 79 40 E
Almoradi **33** 38 7N 0 46W
Almorox **30** 40 14N 4 24W
Almoustarat **85** 17 35N 0 8 E
Älmult **49** 56 33N 14 8 E
Almuñécar **31** 36 43N 3 41W
Almunia de Doña Godina, La **32** 41 29N 1 23W
Alnif **82** 31 10N 5 8W
Alnwick **12** 55 25N 1 42W
Aloi **90** 2 16N 33 10 E
Alonsa **109** 50 50N 99 0W
Alor **73** 8 15S 124 30 E
Alor Setar **71** 6 7N 100 22 E
Alora **31** 36 49N 4 46W
Alosno **31** 37 33N 7 7W
Alougoum **82** 30 17N 6 56W
Alpedrinha **30** 40 6N 7 27W
Alpena **114** 45 6N 83 24W
Alpes-de-Haute-Provence □ **21** 44 8N 6 10 E
Alpes-Maritimes □ **21** 43 55N 7 10 E
Alpha **97** 23 39S 146 37 E
Alpi Apuane **38** 44 7N 10 14 E
Alpi Lepontine **25** 46 22N 8 27 E
Alpi Orobie **38** 46 7N 10 0 E
Alpi Retiche **25** 46 30N 10 0 E
Alpiarça **31** 39 15N 8 35W
Alpine, Ariz., U.S.A. **119** 33 57N 109 4W
Alpine, Tex., U.S.A. **117** 30 25N 103 35W
Alps **22** 47 0N 8 0 E
Alpujarras, Las **33** 36 55N 3 20W
Alrø **49** 55 52N 10 5 E
Alsace **19** 48 15N 7 25 E
Alsask **109** 51 21N 109 59W
Alsásua **32** 42 54N 2 10W
Alsen **48** 63 23N 13 56 E
Alsfeld **24** 50 44N 9 19 E
Alsónémedi **27** 47 20N 19 15 E
Alsten **50** 65 58N 12 40 E
Alta **50** 69 57N 23 10 E
Alta Gracia **124** 31 40S 64 30W
Alta Lake **108** 50 10N 123 0W
Alta, Sierra **32** 40 31N 1 30W
Altaelva → **50** 69 46N 23 45 E
Altafjorden **50** 70 5N 23 5 E
Altagracia **126** 10 45N 71 30W
Altai = Aerhatai Shan **75** 46 40N 92 45 E
Altamaha → **115** 31 19N 81 17W
Altamira, Brazil **127** 3 12S 52 10W
Altamira, Chile **124** 25 47S 69 51W
Altamira, Cuevas de **30** 43 20N 4 5W
Altamont **113** 42 43N 74 3W
Altamura **41** 40 50N 16 33 E
Altanbulag **75** 50 16N 106 30 E
Altar **120** 30 40N 111 50W
Altata **120** 24 30N 108 0W
Altavista **114** 37 9N 79 22W
Altay **75** 47 48N 88 10 E
Altdorf **25** 46 52N 8 36 E
Alte Mellum **24** 53 45N 8 6 E
Altea **33** 38 38N 0 2W
Altenberg **24** 50 46N 13 47 E
Altenbruch **24** 53 48N 8 44 E
Altenburg **24** 50 59N 12 28 E
Altenkirchen, Germ., E. **24** 54 38N 13 20 E
Altenkirchen, Germ., W. **24** 50 41N 7 38 E
Altenmarkt **26** 47 43N 14 39 E
Altenteptow **24** 53 42N 13 15 E
Alter do Chão **31** 39 12N 7 40W
Altkirch **19** 47 37N 7 15 E
Altmühl → **25** 48 54N 11 54 E
Alto Adige = Trentino-Alto Adige **38** 46 30N 11 0 E
Alto Araguaia **127** 17 15S 53 20W
Alto Chindio **91** 16 19S 35 25 E
Alto Cuchumatanes = Cuchumatanes, Sa. de los **120** 15 30N 91 10W
Alto del Inca **124** 24 10S 68 10W
Alto Ligonha **91** 15 30S 38 11 E
Alto Molocue **91** 15 50S 37 35 E
Alto Paraná □ **125** 25 0S 54 50W
Alton, Can. **112** 43 54N 80 5W
Alton, U.S.A. **116** 38 55N 90 5W
Alton Downs **99** 26 7S 138 57 E
Altona, Austral. **100** 37 51S 144 50 E
Altona, Ger. **24** 53 32N 9 56 E
Altoona **114** 40 32N 78 24W
Altopáscio **38** 43 50N 10 40 E
Altötting **25** 48 14N 12 41 E
Altstätten **25** 47 22N 9 33 E
Altun Shan **75** 38 30N 88 0 E
Alturas **118** 41 36N 120 37W
Altus **117** 34 30N 99 25W
Alucra **57** 40 22N 38 47 E
Aluksne **54** 57 24N 27 3 E
Alùla **63** 11 50N 50 45 E
Alupka **56** 44 23N 34 2 E
Alushta **56** 44 40N 34 25 E
Alusi **73** 7 35S 131 40 E
Alustante **32** 40 36N 1 40W
Alva **117** 36 50N 98 50W
Alvaiázere **30** 39 49N 8 23W
Älvängen **49** 57 58N 12 8 E
Alvarado, Mexico **120** 18 40N 95 50W
Alvarado, U.S.A. **117** 32 25N 97 15W
Alvaro Obregón, Presa **120** 27 55N 109 52W
Alvdal **47** 62 6N 10 37 E
Alvear **124** 29 5S 56 30W
Alverca **31** 38 56N 9 1W
Alvesta **49** 56 54N 14 35 E
Alvie **99** 38 14S 143 30 E
Alvin **117** 29 23N 95 12W
Alvinston **113** 42 49N 81 52W
Alvito **31** 38 15N 8 0W
Älvros **48** 62 3N 14 38 E
Älvsborgs län □ **49** 58 30N 12 30 E
Älvsbyn **50** 65 40N 21 0 E
Älvsered **49** 57 14N 12 51 E
Alwar **68** 27 38N 76 34 E
Alwaye **70** 10 8N 76 24 E
Alxa Zuoqi **76** 38 50N 105 40 E
Alyangula **97** 13 55S 136 30 E
Alyaskitovyy **59** 64 45N 141 30 E
Alyata **57** 39 58N 49 25 E
Alyth **14** 56 38N 3 15W
Alzada **116** 45 3N 104 22W
Alzano Lombardo **38** 45 44N 9 43 E
Alzey **25** 49 48N 8 4 E
Am Dam **81** 12 40N 20 35 E
Am Géréda **81** 12 53N 21 14 E
Am-Timan **81** 11 0N 20 10 E
Amadeus, L. **96** 24 54S 131 0 E
Amâdi **87** 5 29N 30 25 E
Amadi **90** 3 40N 26 40 E
Amadjuak **105** 64 0N 72 39W
Amadjuak L. **105** 65 0N 71 8W
Amadora **31** 38 45N 9 13W
Amagasaki **74** 34 42N 135 20 E
Amager **49** 55 37N 12 35 E
Amakusa-Shotō **74** 32 15N 130 10 E
Åmål **48** 59 3N 12 42 E
Amalapuram **70** 16 35N 81 55 E
Amalfi **41** 40 39N 14 34 E
Amaliás **45** 37 47N 21 22 E
Amalner **68** 21 5N 75 5 E
Amambaí **125** 23 5S 55 13W
Amambaí → **125** 23 22S 53 56W
Amambay □ **125** 23 0S 56 0W
Amambay, Cordillera de **125** 23 0S 55 45W
Amándola **39** 42 59N 13 21 E
Amangeldy **58** 50 10N 65 10 E
Amantea **41** 39 8N 16 3 E
Amapá **127** 2 5N 50 50W
Amapá □ **127** 1 40N 52 0W
Amara **87** 10 25N 34 10 E
Amarante, Brazil **127** 6 14S 42 50W
Amarante, Port. **30** 41 16N 8 5W
Amaranth **109** 50 36N 98 43W
Amaravati → **70** 11 0N 78 15 E
Amareleja **31** 38 12N 7 13W
Amargosa **127** 13 2S 39 36W
Amarillo **117** 35 14N 101 46W
Amaro, Mt. **39** 42 5N 14 6 E
Amarpur **69** 25 5N 87 0 E
Amasra **64** 41 45N 32 30 E
Amassama **85** 5 1N 6 2 E
Amasya **64** 40 40N 35 50 E
Amatikulu **93** 29 3S 31 33 E
Amatitlán **120** 14 29N 90 38W
Amatrice **39** 42 38N 13 16 E
Amazon = Amazonas → **127** 0 5S 50 0W
Amazonas □ **126** 4 0S 62 0W
Amazonas → **127** 0 5S 50 0W
Ambad **70** 19 38N 75 50 E
Ambahakily **93** 21 36S 43 41 E
Ambala **68** 30 23N 76 56 E
Ambalangoda **70** 6 15N 80 5 E
Ambalapuzha **70** 9 25N 76 25 E
Ambalavao **93** 21 50S 46 56 E
Ambam **88** 2 20N 11 15 E
Ambanja **93** 13 40S 48 27 E
Ambarchik **59** 69 40N 162 20 E
Ambarijeby **93** 14 56S 47 41 E
Ambarnath **70** 19 12N 73 22 E
Ambaro, Helodranon' **93** 13 23S 48 38 E
Ambartsevo **58** 57 30N 83 52 E
Ambasamudram **70** 8 43N 77 25 E
Ambato **126** 1 5S 78 42W
Ambato Boeny **93** 16 28S 46 43 E
Ambato, Sierra de **124** 28 25S 66 10W
Ambatofinandrahana **93** 20 33S 46 48 E
Ambatolampy **93** 19 20S 47 35 E
Ambatondrazaka **93** 17 55S 48 28 E
Ambatosoratra **93** 17 37S 48 31 E
Ambenja **93** 15 17S 46 58 E
Amberg **25** 49 25N 11 52 E
Ambergris Cay **120** 18 0N 88 0W
Ambérieu-en-Bugey **21** 45 57N 5 20 E
Amberley **101** 43 9S 172 44 E
Ambert **20** 45 33N 3 44 E
Ambidédi **84** 14 35N 11 47W
Ambikapur **69** 23 15N 83 15 E
Ambikol **86** 21 20N 30 50 E
Ambinanindrano **93** 20 5S 48 23 E
Ambjörnarp **49** 57 25N 13 17 E
Ambleside **12** 54 26N 2 58W
Ambo, Ethiopia **87** 12 20N 37 30 E
Ambo, Peru **126** 10 5S 76 10W
Ambodifototra **93** 16 59S 49 52 E
Ambodilazana **93** 18 6S 49 10 E
Ambohimahasoa **93** 21 7S 47 13 E
Ambohimanga **93** 20 52S 47 36 E
Ambon **73** 3 35S 128 20 E
Amboseli L. **90** 2 40S 37 10 E
Ambositra **93** 20 31S 47 25 E
Ambovombé **93** 25 11S 46 5 E
Amboy **119** 34 33N 115 51W
Amboyna I. **72** 7 50N 112 50 E
Ambridge **112** 40 36N 80 15W
Ambriz **88** 7 48S 13 8 E
Ambur **70** 12 48N 78 43 E
Amby **99** 26 30S 148 11 E
Amchitka I. **104** 51 30N 179 0W
Amderma **58** 69 45N 61 30 E
Ameca **120** 20 30N 104 0W
Ameca → **120** 20 40N 105 15W
Amecameca **120** 19 7N 98 46W
Ameland **16** 53 27N 5 45 E
Amélia **39** 42 34N 12 25 E
Amélie-les-Bains-Palalda **20** 42 29N 2 41 E
Amen **59** 68 45N 180 0 E
Amendolaro **41** 39 58N 16 34 E
American Falls **118** 42 46N 112 56W
American Falls Res. **118** 43 0N 112 50W
American Highland **5** 73 0S 75 0 E
American Samoa **101** 14 20S 170 40W
Americana **125** 22 45S 47 20W
Americus **115** 32 0N 84 10W
Amersfoort, Neth. **16** 52 9N 5 23 E
Amersfoort, S. Afr. **93** 26 59S 29 53 E
Amery **109** 56 34N 94 3W
Amery Ice Shelf **5** 69 30S 72 0 E
Ames **116** 42 0N 93 40W
Amesbury **113** 42 50N 70 52W
Amesdale **109** 50 2N 92 55W
Amfíklia **45** 38 38N 22 35 E
Amfilokhía **45** 38 52N 21 9 E
Amfípolis **44** 40 48N 23 52 E
Ámfissa **45** 38 32N 22 22 E
Amga **59** 60 50N 132 0 E
Amga → **59** 62 38N 134 32 E
Amgu **59** 45 45N 137 15 E
Amgun → **59** 52 56N 139 38 E
Amherst, Burma **67** 16 2N 97 20 E
Amherst, Can. **107** 45 48N 64 8W
Amherst, Mass., U.S.A. **113** 42 21N 72 30W
Amherst, Ohio, U.S.A. **112** 41 23N 82 15W
Amherst, Tex., U.S.A. **117** 34 0N 102 24W
Amherst I. **113** 44 8N 76 43W
Amherstburg **106** 42 6N 83 6W
Amiata, Mte. **39** 42 54N 11 40 E
Amiens **19** 49 54N 2 16 E
Amigdhalokefáli **45** 35 23N 23 30 E
Amindaion **44** 40 42N 21 42 E
Amirante Is. **3** 6 0S 53 0 E
Amisk L. **109** 54 35N 102 15W
Amite **117** 30 47N 90 31W
Amizmiz **82** 31 12N 8 15W
Åmli **47** 58 45N 8 32 E
Amlwch **12** 53 24N 4 21W
Amm Adam **87** 16 20N 36 1 E
'Ammān **62** 31 57N 35 52 E
Ammanford **13** 51 48N 4 0W
Ammerån **48** 63 9N 16 13 E
Ammerån → **48** 63 9N 16 13 E
Ammersee **25** 48 0N 11 7 E
Ammi'ad **62** 32 55N 35 32 E
Amnéville **19** 49 16N 6 9 E
Amorebieta **32** 43 13N 2 44W
Amorgós **45** 36 50N 25 57 E
Amory **115** 33 59N 88 29W
Amos **106** 48 35N 78 5W
Åmot, Buskerud, Norway **47** 59 54N 9 54 E
Åmot, Telemark, Norway **47** 59 34N 8 0 E
Åmotsdal **47** 59 37N 8 26 E
Amour, Djebel **82** 33 42N 1 37 E
Amoy = Xiamen **76** 24 25N 118 4 E
Ampanihy **93** 24 40S 44 45 E
Ampasindava, Helodranon' **93** 13 40S 48 15 E
Ampasindava, Saikanosy **93** 13 42S 47 55W
Amper **85** 9 25N 9 40 E
Amper → **25** 48 30N 11 57 E
Ampère **83** 35 44N 5 27 E
Ampezzo **39** 46 25N 12 48 E
Amposta **32** 40 43N 0 34 E
Ampotaka **93** 25 3S 44 41 E
Ampoza **93** 22 20S 44 44 E
Amqa **62** 32 59N 35 10 E
Amqui **107** 48 28N 67 27W
Amraoti **68** 20 55N 77 45 E
Amreli **68** 21 35N 71 17 E
Amrenene el Kasba **82** 22 10N 0 30 E
Amritsar **68** 31 35N 74 57 E
Amroha **68** 28 53N 78 30 E
Amrum **24** 54 37N 8 21 E
Amsel **83** 22 47N 5 29 E
Amsterdam, Neth. **16** 52 23N 4 54 E
Amsterdam, U.S.A. **114** 42 58N 74 10W
Amsterdam, I. **3** 37 30S 77 30 E
Amstetten **26** 48 7N 14 51 E
Amudarya → **58** 43 40N 59 0 E
Amund Ringnes I. **4** 78 20N 96 25W
Amundsen Gulf **104** 71 0N 124 0W
Amundsen Sea **5** 72 0S 115 0W
Amungen **48** 61 10N 15 40 E
Amuntai **72** 2 28S 115 25 E
Amur → **59** 52 56N 141 10 E
Amurang **73** 1 5N 124 40 E
Amuri Pass **101** 42 31S 172 11 E
Amurrio **32** 43 3N 3 0W
Amursk **59** 50 14N 136 54 E

Amurzet
Arapkir

Amurzet 59 47 50N 131 5 E
Amusco 30 42 10N 4 28W
Amvrakikós Kólpos 45 39 0N 20 55 E
Amvrosiyevka 57 47 43N 38 30 E
Amzeglouf 82 26 50N 0 1 E
An Nafūd 64 28 15N 41 0 E
An Najaf 64 32 3N 44 15 E
An Nāqūrah 62 33 7N 35 8 E
An Nāşirīyah 64 31 0N 46 15 E
An Nawfalīyah 83 30 54N 17 58 E
An Nhon (Binh Dinh) 71 13 55N 109 7 E
An Nīl □ 86 19 30N 33 0 E
An Nīl el Abyad □ 87 14 0N 32 15 E
An Nīl el Azraq □ 87 12 30N 34 30 E
An Nu'ayrīyah 64 27 30N 48 30 E
An Uaimh 15 53 39N 6 40W
Ána-Sira 47 58 17N 6 25 E
Anabar → 59 73 8N 113 36 E
'Anabtā 62 32 19N 35 7 E
Anaconda 118 46 7N 113 0W
Anacortes 118 48 30N 122 40W
Anadarko 117 35 4N 98 15W
Anadia 30 40 26N 8 27W
Anadolu 64 38 0N 30 0 E
Anadyr 59 64 35N 177 20 E
Anadyr → 59 64 55N 176 5 E
Anadyrskiy Zaliv 59 64 0N 180 0 E
Anáfi 45 36 22N 25 48 E
Anafópoulo 45 36 17N 25 50 E
Anagni 40 41 44N 13 8 E
'Ānah 64 34 25N 42 0 E
Anahim Lake 108 52 28N 125 18W
Anáhuac 120 27 14N 100 9W
Anai Mudi, Mt. 70 10 12N 77 4 E
Anaimalai Hills 70 10 20N 76 40 E
Anakapalle 70 17 42N 83 06 E
Anakie 98 23 32 S 147 45 E
Anaklia 57 42 22N 41 35 E
Analalava 93 14 35 S 48 0 E
Anambar → 68 30 15N 68 50 E
Anambas, Kepulauan 72 3 20N 106 30 E
Anamoose 116 47 55N 100 20W
Anamosa 116 42 7N 91 30W
Anamur 64 36 8N 32 58 E
Anan 74 33 54N 134 40 E
Anand 68 22 32N 72 59 E
Anandpur 69 21 16N 86 13 E
Anánes 45 36 33N 24 9 E
Anantapur 70 14 39N 77 42 E
Anantnag 69 33 45N 75 10 E
Ananyev 56 47 44N 29 47 E
Anapa 56 44 55N 37 25 E
Anápolis 127 16 15 S 48 50W
Anār 65 30 55N 55 13 E
Anārak 65 33 25N 53 40 E
Anatolia = Anadolu 64 38 0N 30 0 E
Anatone 118 46 9N 117 4W
Añatuya 124 28 20 S 62 50W
Anaunethad L. 109 60 55N 104 25W
Anaye 81 19 15N 12 50 E
Ancenis 18 47 21N 1 10W
Anchorage 104 61 10N 149 50W
Ancião 30 39 56N 8 27W
Ancohuma, Nevada 126 16 0 S 68 50W
Ancón 126 11 50 S 77 10W
Ancona 39 43 37N 13 30 E
Ancud 128 42 0 S 73 50W
Ancud, G. de 128 42 0 S 73 0W
Anda 76 46 24N 125 19 E
Andacollo, Argent. 124 37 10 S 70 42W
Andacollo, Chile 124 30 5 S 71 10W
Andalgalá 124 27 40 S 66 30W
Åndalsnes 47 62 35N 7 43 E
Andalucía 31 37 35N 5 0W
Andalusia 115 31 19N 86 30W
Andalusia = Andalucía 31 37 35N 5 0W
Andaman Is. 71 12 30N 92 30 E
Andaman Sea 72 13 0N 96 0 E
Andaman Str. 71 12 15N 92 20 E
Andara 92 18 2 S 21 9 E
Andelot 19 48 15N 5 18 E
Andelys, Les 18 49 15N 1 25 E
Andenne 16 50 30N 5 5 E
Andéranboukane 85 15 26N 3 2 E
Andermatt 25 46 38N 8 35 E
Andernach 24 50 24N 7 25 E
Andernos-les-Bains 20 44 44N 1 6W
Anderslöv 49 55 26N 13 19 E
Anderson, Calif., U.S.A. 118 40 30N 122 19W
Anderson, Ind., U.S.A. 114 40 5N 85 40W
Anderson, Mo., U.S.A. 117 36 43N 94 29W
Anderson, S.C., U.S.A. 115 34 32N 82 40W
Anderson → 104 69 42N 129 0W
Anderson, Mt. 93 25 5 S 30 42 E
Anderstorp 49 57 19N 13 39 E
Andes 126 5 40N 75 53W
Andes, Cord de los 126 20 0 S 68 0W
Andfjorden 50 69 10N 16 20 E
Andhra, L. 70 18 54N 73 32 E
Andhra Pradesh □ 70 16 0N 79 0 E
Andikíthira 45 35 52N 23 15 E
Andímilos 45 36 47N 24 12 E
Andíparos 45 37 0N 25 3 E
Andípaxoi 45 39 9N 20 13 E
Andípsara 45 38 30N 25 29 E
Andírrion 45 38 24N 21 46 E
Andizhan 58 41 10N 72 0 E
Andkhvoy 65 36 52N 65 8 E
Andol 70 17 51N 78 4 E
Andong 76 36 40N 128 43 E
Andorra ■ 32 42 30N 1 30 E
Andorra La Vella 32 42 31N 1 32 E
Andover, U.K. 13 51 13N 1 29W
Andover, N.Y., U.S.A. 112 42 11N 77 48W
Andover, Ohio, U.S.A. 112 41 35N 80 35W
Andrahary, Mt. 93 13 37 S 49 17 E
Andraitx 32 39 39N 2 25 E
Andramasina 93 19 11 S 47 35 E
Andranopasy 93 21 17 S 43 44 E
Andreanof Is. 104 52 0N 178 0W
Andreapol 54 56 40N 32 17 E
Andrespol 28 51 45N 19 34 E
Andrews, S.C., U.S.A. 115 33 29N 79 30W
Andrews, Tex., U.S.A. 117 32 18N 102 33W
Ándria 41 41 13N 16 17 E
Andriba 93 17 30 S 46 58 E
Andrijevica 42 42 45N 19 48 E
Andrítsaina 45 37 29N 21 52 E
Androka 93 24 58 S 44 2 E
Ándros 45 37 50N 24 57 E
Andros I. 121 24 30N 78 0W
Andros Town 121 24 43N 77 47W
Andrychów 27 49 51N 19 18 E
Andújar 31 38 3N 4 5W
Aneby 49 57 48N 14 49 E
Anegada I. 121 18 45N 64 20W
Anegada Passage 121 18 15N 63 45W
Aného 85 6 12N 1 34 E
Anergane 82 31 4N 7 14W
Aneto, Pico de 32 42 37N 0 40 E
Ang Thong 71 14 35N 100 31 E
Angamos, Punta 124 23 1 S 70 32W
Ang'angxi 75 47 10N 123 48 E
Angara → 59 58 30N 97 0 E
Angarab 87 13 11N 37 7 E
Angarsk 59 52 30N 104 0 E
Angaston 99 34 30 S 139 8 E
Ånge 48 62 31N 15 35 E
Ángel de la Guarda 120 29 30N 113 30W
Angeles 73 15 9N 120 33 E
Ängelholm 49 56 15N 12 58 E
Angellala 99 26 24 S 146 54 E
Angels Camp 119 38 8N 120 30W
Ängelsberg 48 59 58N 16 0 E
Anger → 87 9 37N 36 6 E
Angereb → 87 13 45N 36 40 E
Ångermanälven → 48 62 40N 18 0 E
Angermünde 24 53 1N 14 0 E
Angers, Can. 113 45 31N 75 29W
Angers, France 18 47 30N 0 35W
Angerville 19 48 19N 2 0 E
Ängesån → 50 66 50N 22 15 E
Anghiari 39 43 32N 12 3 E
Angikuni L. 109 62 0N 100 0W
Angkor 71 13 22N 103 50 E
Anglés 32 41 57N 2 38 E
Anglesey 12 53 17N 4 20W
Anglet 20 43 29N 1 31W
Angleton 117 29 12N 95 23W
Anglin → 20 46 42N 0 52 E
Anglure 19 48 35N 3 50 E
Angmagssalik 4 65 40N 37 20W
Ango 90 4 10N 26 5 E
Angoche 91 16 8 S 40 0 E
Angoche, I. 91 16 20 S 39 50 E
Angol 124 37 56 S 72 45W
Angola, Ind., U.S.A. 114 41 40N 85 0W
Angola, N.Y., U.S.A. 112 42 38N 79 2W
Angola ■ 89 12 0 S 18 0 E
Angoon 108 57 40N 134 40W
Angoram 98 4 4 S 144 4 E
Angoulême 20 45 39N 0 10 E
Angoumois 20 45 50N 0 25 E
Angra dos Reis 125 23 0 S 44 10W
Angren 58 41 1N 70 12 E
Angu 90 3 25N 24 28 E
Anguilla 121 18 14N 63 5W
Angus, Braes of 14 56 51N 3 0W
Anhanduí → 125 21 46 S 52 9W
Anholt 49 56 42N 11 33 E
Anhua 77 28 23N 111 12 E
Anhui □ 75 32 0N 117 0 E
Anhwei □ = Anhui □ 75 32 0N 117 0 E
Ánidhros 45 36 38N 25 43 E
Anie 85 7 42N 1 8 E
Animas 119 31 58N 108 58W
Ånimskog 49 58 53N 12 35 E
Anin 71 15 36N 97 50 E
Anina 42 45 6N 21 51 E
Anivorano 93 18 44 S 48 58 E
Anjangaon 68 21 10N 77 20 E
Anjar 68 23 6N 70 10 E
Anjidiv I. 70 14 40N 74 10 E
Anjou 18 47 20N 0 15W
Anjozorobe 93 18 22 S 47 52 E
Anju 76 39 36N 125 40 E
Anka 85 12 13N 5 58 E
Ankang 75 32 40N 109 1 E
Ankara 64 40 0N 32 54 E
Ankaramena 93 21 57 S 46 39 E
Ankazoabo 93 22 18 S 44 31 E
Ankazobe 93 18 20 S 47 10 E
Ankisabe 93 19 17 S 46 29 E
Anklam 24 53 48N 13 40 E
Anklesvar 68 21 38N 73 3 E
Ankober 87 9 35N 39 40 E
Ankoro 90 6 45 S 26 55 E
Anlu 77 31 15N 113 45 E
Ånn 48 63 19N 12 34 E
Ann Arbor 114 42 17N 83 45W
Ann C., Antarct. 5 66 30 S 50 30 E
Ann C., U.S.A. 113 42 39N 70 37W
Anna, U.S.A. 117 37 28N 89 10W
Anna, U.S.S.R. 55 51 28N 40 23 E
Annaba 83 36 50N 7 46 E
Annaberg-Buchholz 24 50 34N 12 58 E
Annalee → 15 54 3N 7 15W
Annam = Trung-Phan 71 16 30N 107 30 E
Annamitique, Chaîne 71 17 0N 106 0 E
Annan 14 55 0N 3 17W
Annan → 14 54 58N 3 18W
Annapolis 114 38 95N 76 30W
Annapolis Royal 107 44 44N 65 32W
Annapurna 69 28 34N 83 50 E
Anneberg 49 57 32N 12 6 E
Annecy 21 45 55N 6 8 E
Annecy, L. d' 21 45 52N 6 10 E
Annemasse 21 46 12N 6 16 E
Anning 75 24 55N 102 26 E
Anniston 115 33 45N 85 50W
Annobón 79 1 25 S 5 35 E
Annonay 21 45 15N 4 40 E
Annonciation, L' 106 46 25N 74 55W
Annot 21 43 58N 6 38 E
Annotto Bay 121 18 17N 77 3W
Annuello 99 34 53 S 142 55 E
Annville 113 40 18N 76 32W
Annweiler 25 49 12N 7 58 E
Áno Arkhánai 45 35 16N 25 11 E
Áno Porróia 44 41 17N 23 2 E
Áno Viánnos 45 35 2N 25 21 E
Anoka 116 45 10N 93 26W
Anorotsangana 93 13 56 S 47 55 E
Anqing 75 30 30N 117 3 E
Anren 77 26 43N 113 18 E
Ansāb 64 29 11N 44 43 E
Ansai 76 36 50N 109 20 E
Ansbach 25 49 17N 10 34 E
Anse au Loup, L' 107 51 32N 56 50W
Anse, L' 106 46 47N 88 28W
Anseba → 87 16 0N 38 30 E
Anshan 76 41 5N 122 58 E
Anshun 75 26 18N 105 57 E
Ansirabe 93 19 55 S 47 2 E
Ansley 116 41 19N 99 24W
Ansó 32 42 51N 0 48W
Anson 117 32 46N 99 54W
Anson B. 96 13 20 S 130 6 E
Ansongo 85 15 25N 0 35 E
Ansonia 113 41 21N 73 6W
Anstruther 14 56 14N 2 40W
Ansudu 73 2 11 S 139 22 E
Antabamba 126 14 40 S 73 0W
Antakya 64 36 14N 36 10 E
Antalaha 93 14 57 S 50 20 E
Antalya 64 36 52N 30 45 E
Antalya Körfezi 64 36 15N 31 30 E
Antananarivo 93 18 55 S 47 31 E
Antananarivo □ 93 19 0 S 47 0 E
Antanimbaribe 93 21 30 S 44 48 E
Antarctic Pen. 5 67 0 S 60 0W
Antarctica 5 90 0 S 0 0
Antelope 91 21 2 S 28 31 E
Antequera, Parag. 124 24 8 S 57 7W
Antequera, Spain 31 37 5N 4 33W
Antero Mt. 119 38 45N 106 15W
Anthemoûs 44 40 31N 23 15 E
Anthony, Kans., U.S.A. 117 37 8N 98 2W
Anthony, N. Mex., U.S.A. 119 32 1N 106 37W
Anti Atlas, Mts. 82 30 0N 8 30W
Antibes 21 43 34N 7 6 E
Antibes, C. d' 21 43 31N 7 7 E
Anticosti, Î. d' 107 49 30N 63 0W
Antifer, C. d' 18 49 41N 0 10 E
Antigo 116 45 8N 89 5W
Antigonish 107 45 38N 61 58W
Antigua 120 14 34N 90 41W
Antigua & Barbuda ■ 121 17 0N 61 50W
Antilla 121 20 40N 75 50W
Antimony 119 38 7N 112 0W
Antioch 118 38 7N 121 45W
Antioche, Pertuis d' 20 46 6N 1 20W
Antioquia 126 6 40N 75 55W
Antipodes Is. 94 49 45 S 178 40 E
Antler 116 48 58N 101 18W
Antler → 109 49 8N 101 0W
Antlers 117 34 15N 95 35W
Antofagasta 124 23 50 S 70 30W
Antofagasta □ 124 24 0 S 69 0W
Antofagasta de la Sierra 124 26 5 S 67 20W
Antofalla 124 25 30 S 68 5W
Antofalla, Salar de 124 25 40 S 67 45W
Anton 117 33 49N 102 5W
Anton Chico 119 35 12N 105 5W
Antongila, Helodrano 93 15 30 S 49 50 E
Antonibé 93 15 7 S 47 24 E
Antonibé, Presqu'île d' 93 14 55 S 47 20 E
Antonina 125 25 26 S 48 42W
Antonito 119 37 4N 106 1W
Antonovo 57 49 25N 51 42 E
Antrain 18 48 28N 1 30W
Antrim 15 54 43N 6 13W
Antrim □ 15 54 55N 6 20W
Antrim, Mts. of 15 54 57N 6 8W
Antrodoco 39 42 25N 13 4 E
Antropovo 55 58 26N 42 51 E
Antsalova 93 18 40 S 44 37 E
Antsiranana 93 12 25 S 49 20 E
Antsohihy 93 14 50 S 47 59 E
Antwerp 113 44 12N 75 36W
Antwerp = Antwerpen 16 51 13N 4 25 E
Antwerpen 16 51 13N 4 25 E
Antwerpen □ 16 51 15N 4 40 E
Anupgarh 68 29 10N 73 10 E
Anuradhapura 70 8 22N 80 28 E
Anvers = Antwerpen 16 51 13N 4 25 E
Anvers I. 5 64 30 S 63 40W
Anvik 104 62 37N 160 20W
Anxi, Fujian, China 77 25 2N 118 12 E
Anxi, Gansu, China 75 40 30N 95 43 E
Anxious B. 96 33 24 S 134 45 E
Anyama 84 5 30N 4 3W
Anyang 76 36 5N 114 21 E
Anyer-Lor 73 6 6 S 105 56 E
Anyi, Jiangxi, China 77 28 49N 115 25 E
Anyi, Shanxi, China 77 35 2N 111 2 E
Anyuan 77 25 9N 115 21 E
'Anzah 62 32 22N 35 12 E
Anzhero-Sudzhensk 58 56 10N 86 0 E
Ánzio 40 41 28N 12 37 E
Aoiz 32 42 46N 1 22W
Aomori 74 40 45N 140 45 E
Aomori □ 74 40 45N 140 40 E
Aonla 68 28 16N 79 11 E
Aoreora 82 28 51N 10 53W
Aosta 38 45 43N 7 20 E
Aoudéras 85 17 45N 8 20 E
Aouinet Torkoz 82 28 31N 9 46W
Aoukar 82 23 50N 2 45W
Aouker 84 17 40N 10 0W
Aoulef el Arab 82 26 55N 1 2 E
Apa → 124 22 6 S 58 2W
Apache, Ariz., U.S.A. 119 31 46N 109 6W
Apache, Okla., U.S.A. 117 34 53N 98 22W
Apalachee B. 115 30 0N 84 0W
Apalachicola 115 29 40N 85 0W
Apapa 85 6 25N 3 25 E
Apaporis → 126 1 23 S 69 25W
Aparri 73 18 22N 121 38 E
Apateu 46 46 36N 21 47 E
Apatin 42 45 40N 19 0 E
Apátity 52 67 34N 33 22 E
Apatzingán 120 19 0N 102 20W
Apeldoorn 16 52 13N 5 57 E
Apen 24 53 12N 7 47 E
Apenam 72 8 35 S 116 13 E
Apennines 9 44 20N 10 20 E
Apia 101 13 50 S 171 50W
Apiacás, Serra dos 126 9 50 S 57 0W
Apizaco 120 19 26N 98 9W
Aplao 126 16 0 S 72 40W
Apo, Mt. 73 6 53N 125 14 E
Apolda 24 51 1N 11 30 E
Apollo Bay 100 38 45 S 143 40 E
Apollonia 45 36 58N 24 43 E
Apollonia = Marsá Susah 81 32 52N 21 59 E
Apolo 126 14 30 S 68 30W
Apostle Is. 116 47 0N 90 30W
Apóstoles 125 28 0 S 56 0W
Apostolovo 56 47 39N 33 39 E
Apoteri 126 4 2N 58 32W
Appalachian Mts. 114 38 0N 80 0W
Appalachicola → 115 29 40N 85 0W
Appennini 41 41 0N 15 0 E
Appennino Ligure 38 44 30N 9 0 E
Appenzell-Ausser Rhoden □ 25 47 23N 9 23 E
Appenzell-Inner Rhoden □ 25 47 20N 9 25 E
Appiano 39 46 27N 11 17 E
Apple Hill 113 45 13N 74 46W
Appleby 12 54 35N 2 29W
Appleton 114 44 17N 88 25W
Approuague 127 4 20N 52 0W
Aprelevka, U.S.S.R. 55 55 33N 37 4 E
Aprelevka, U.S.S.R. 55 55 34N 37 4 E
Apricena 41 41 47N 15 25 E
Aprigliano 41 39 17N 16 19 E
Aprilia 40 41 38N 12 38 E
Apsheronsk 57 44 28N 39 42 E
Apt 21 43 53N 5 24 E
Apucarana 125 23 55 S 51 33W
Apulia = Púglia 41 41 0N 16 30 E
Apure → 126 7 37N 66 25W
Apurimac → 126 12 17 S 73 56W
Apuseni, Munţii 46 46 30N 22 45 E
Aqabah = Al 'Aqabah 86 29 13N 35 0 E
'Aqabah, Khalīj al 64 28 15N 33 20 E
Āqcheh 65 37 0N 66 5 E
Aqīq 86 18 14N 38 12 E
Aqīq, Khalīg 86 18 20N 38 10 E
Aqrabā 62 32 9N 35 20 E
Aqrah 64 36 46N 43 45 E
Aquidauana 127 20 30 S 55 50W
Áquila, L' 39 42 21N 13 24 E
Aquiles Serdán 120 28 37N 105 54W
Ar Rachidiya 82 31 58N 4 20W
Ar Rafīd 62 32 57N 35 52 E
Ar Ramādī 64 33 25N 43 20 E
Ar Raml 83 26 45N 19 40 E
Ar Ramthā 62 32 34N 36 0 E
Ar Raqqah 64 36 0N 38 55 E
Ar Rass 64 25 50N 43 40 E
Ar Rifā'i 64 31 50N 46 10 E
Ar Riyāḍ 64 24 41N 46 42 E
Ar Rummān 62 32 9N 35 48 E
Ar Ruţbah 64 33 0N 40 15 E
Ar Ruwayḍah 64 23 40N 44 40 E
Arab, Bahr el → 87 9 50N 29 0 E
Arab, Khalîg el 86 30 55N 29 0 E
Arab, Shatt al 64 30 0N 48 31 E
Arabatskaya Strelka 56 45 40N 35 0 E
Arabba 39 46 30N 11 51 E
Arabia 60 25 0N 45 0 E
Arabian Sea 60 16 0N 65 0 E
Arac 64 41 15N 33 21 E
Aracaju 127 10 55 S 37 4W
Aracataca 126 10 38N 74 9W
Aracati 127 4 30 S 37 44W
Araçatuba 125 21 10 S 50 30W
Aracena 31 37 53N 6 38W
Aracena, Sierra de 31 37 50N 6 50W
Araçuai 127 16 52 S 42 4W
'Arad 62 31 15N 35 12 E
Arad 42 46 10N 21 20 E
Arad □ 42 46 20N 22 0 E
Arada 81 15 0N 20 20 E
Aradu Nou 42 46 8N 21 20 E
Arafura Sea 73 9 0 S 135 0 E
Aragats 57 40 30N 44 15 E
Aragón 32 41 25N 1 0W
Aragón → 32 42 13N 1 44W
Aragona 40 37 24N 13 36 E
Araguacema 127 8 50 S 49 20W
Araguaia → 127 5 21 S 48 41W
Araguari 127 18 38 S 48 11W
Araguari → 127 1 15N 49 55W
Arak 82 25 20N 3 45 E
Arāk 64 34 0N 49 40 E
Arakan Coast 67 19 0N 94 0 E
Arakan Yoma 67 20 0N 94 40 E
Arákhova 45 38 28N 22 35 E
Araks = Aras, Rūd-e → 64 39 10N 47 10 E
Aral Sea = Aralskoye More 58 44 30N 60 0 E
Aralsk 58 46 50N 61 20 E
Aralskoye More 58 44 30N 60 0 E
Aramā, Mţii. de 46 47 10N 22 30 E
Aramac 97 22 58 S 145 14 E
Arambagh 69 22 53N 87 48 E
Aran I. 15 55 0N 8 30W
Aran Is. 15 53 5N 9 42W
Aranda de Duero 32 41 39N 3 42W
Arandelovac 42 44 18N 20 27 E
Aranjuez 30 40 1N 3 40W
Aranos 92 24 9 S 19 7 E
Aransas Pass 117 27 55N 97 9W
Araouane 84 18 55N 3 30W
Arapahoe 116 40 22N 99 53W
Arapey Grande → 124 30 55 S 57 49W
Arapkir 64 39 5N 38 30 E

Arapongas Aska

Arapongas 125 23 29 S 51 28W
Araranguá 125 29 0 S 49 30W
Araraquara 127 21 50 S 48 0W
Ararás, Serra das 125 25 0 S 53 10W
Ararat 97 37 16 S 143 0 E
Ararat, Mt. = Ağri Daği 64 39 50N 44 15 E
Araria 69 26 9N 87 33 E
Araripe, Chapada do 127 7 20 S 40 0W
Araruama, Lagoa de 125 22 53 S 42 12W
Aras, Rūd-e → 64 39 10N 47 10 E
Arauca 126 7 0N 70 40W
Arauca → 126 7 24N 66 35W
Arauco 124 37 16 S 73 25W
Arauco □ 124 37 40 S 73 25W
Arawa 87 9 57N 41 58 E
Araxá 127 19 35 S 46 55W
Araya, Pen. de 126 10 40N 64 0W
Arba Minch 87 6 0N 37 30 E
Arbatax 40 39 57N 9 42 E
Arbaza 59 52 40N 92 30 E
Arbīl 64 36 15N 44 5 E
Arboga 48 59 24N 15 52 E
Arbois 19 46 55N 5 46 E
Arbore 87 5 3N 36 50 E
Arborea 40 39 46N 8 34 E
Arborfield 109 53 6N 103 39W
Arborg 109 50 54N 97 13W
Arbrå 48 61 28N 16 22 E
Arbresie, L' 21 45 50N 4 26 E
Arbroath 14 56 34N 2 35W
Arbuckle 118 39 3N 122 2W
Arbus 40 39 30N 8 33 E
Arbuzinka 56 47 0N 31 59 E
Arc 19 47 28N 5 34 E
Arc → 21 45 34N 6 12 E
Arcachon 20 44 40N 1 10W
Arcachon, Bassin d' 20 44 42N 1 10W
Arcade 112 42 34N 78 25W
Arcadia, Fla., U.S.A. 115 27 20N 81 50W
Arcadia, La., U.S.A. 117 32 34N 92 53W
Arcadia, Nebr., U.S.A. 116 41 29N 99 4W
Arcadia, Pa., U.S.A. 112 40 46N 78 54W
Arcadia, Wis., U.S.A. 116 44 13N 91 29W
Arcata 118 40 55N 124 4W
Arcévia 39 43 29N 12 58 E
Archangel = Arkhangelsk 52 64 40N 41 0 E
Archar 42 43 50N 22 54 E
Archbald 113 41 30N 75 31W
Archena 33 38 9N 1 16W
Archer → 97 13 28 S 141 41 E
Archer B. 98 13 20 S 141 30 E
Archers Post 90 0 35N 37 35 E
Archidona 31 37 6N 4 22W
Arci, Monte 40 39 47N 8 44 E
Arcidosso 39 42 51N 11 30 E
Arcila = Asilah 82 35 29N 6 0W
Arcis-sur-Aube 19 48 32N 4 10 E
Arco, Italy 38 45 55N 10 54 E
Arco, U.S.A. 118 43 45N 113 16W
Arcola 109 49 40N 102 30W
Arcos 32 41 12N 2 16W
Arcos de los Frontera 31 36 45N 5 49W
Arcos de Valdevez 30 41 55N 8 22W
Arcot 70 12 53N 79 20 E
Arcoverde 127 8 25 S 37 4W
Arcs, Les 21 43 27N 6 29 E
Arctic Bay 105 73 1N 85 7W
Arctic Ocean 4 78 0N 160 0W
Arctic Red River 104 67 15N 134 0W
Arda →, Bulg. 43 41 40N 26 29 E
Arda →, Italy 38 44 53N 9 52 E
Ardabīl 64 38 15N 48 18 E
Ardahan 64 41 7N 42 41 E
Ardakān 65 30 20N 52 5 E
Årdal, Aust-Agder, Norway 47 58 42N 7 48 E
Årdal, Rogaland, Norway 47 59 9N 6 13 E
Ardales 31 36 53N 4 51W
Årdalstangen 47 61 14N 7 43 E
Ardatov 55 54 51N 46 15 E
Ardea 44 40 58N 22 3 E
Ardèche □ 21 44 42N 4 16 E
Ardèche → 21 44 16N 4 39 E
Ardee 15 53 51N 6 32W
Arden 112 44 43N 76 56W
Arden Stby. 49 56 46N 9 52 E
Ardennes 16 50 0N 5 10 E
Ardennes □ 19 49 35N 4 40 E
Ardentes 19 46 45N 1 50 E
Ardestān 65 33 20N 52 25 E
Ardgour 14 56 45N 5 25W
Árdhas → 44 41 36N 26 25 E
Ardila → 31 38 12N 7 28W
Ardino 43 41 34N 25 9 E
Ardjuno 73 7 49 S 112 34 E
Ardlethan 99 34 22 S 146 53 E
Ardmore, Austral. 98 21 39 S 139 11 E
Ardmore, Okla., U.S.A. 117 34 10N 97 5W
Ardmore, Pa., U.S.A. 113 39 58N 75 18W
Ardmore, S.D., U.S.A. 116 43 0N 103 40W
Ardnacrusha 15 52 43N 8 38W
Ardnamurchan, Pt. of 14 56 44N 6 14W
Ardore Marina 41 38 11N 16 10 E
Ardres 19 50 50N 2 0 E
Ardrossan, Austral. 99 34 26 S 137 53 E
Ardrossan, U.K. 14 55 39N 4 50W
Ards □ 15 54 35N 5 30W
Ards Pen. 15 54 30N 5 25W
Ardud 46 47 37N 22 52 E
Ardunac 57 41 8N 42 5 E
Åre 48 63 22N 13 15 E
Arecibo 121 18 29N 66 42W
Areia Branca 127 5 0 S 37 0W
Aremark 47 59 15N 11 42 E
Arenas 30 43 17N 4 50W
Arenas de San Pedro 30 40 12N 5 5W
Arendal 47 58 28N 8 46 E
Arendsee 24 52 52N 11 27 E
Arenys de Mar 32 41 35N 2 33 E
Arenzano 38 44 24N 8 40 E
Areópolis 45 36 40N 22 22 E
Arequipa 126 16 20 S 71 30W
Arero 87 4 41N 38 50 E
Arès 20 44 47N 1 8W
Arévalo 30 41 3N 4 43W
Arezzo 39 43 28N 11 50 E
Arga → 32 42 18N 1 47W
Argalastí 44 39 13N 23 13 E
Argamasilla de Alba 33 39 8N 3 5W
Arganda 32 40 19N 3 26W
Arganil 30 40 13N 8 3W
Argelès-Gazost 20 43 0N 0 6W
Argelès-sur-Mer 20 42 34N 3 1 E
Argens → 21 43 24N 6 44 E
Argent-sur-Sauldre 19 47 33N 2 25 E
Argenta, Can. 108 50 20N 116 55W
Argenta, Italy 39 44 37N 11 50 E
Argentan 18 48 45N 0 1W
Argentário, Mte. 39 42 23N 11 11 E
Argentat 20 45 6N 1 56 E
Argentera 38 44 23N 6 58 E
Argentera, Monte del 38 44 12N 7 5 E
Argenteuil 19 48 57N 2 14 E
Argentia 107 47 18N 53 58W
Argentiera, C. dell' 40 40 44N 8 8 E
Argentière, L' 21 44 47N 6 33 E
Argentina ■ 128 35 0 S 66 0W
Argentino, L. 128 50 10 S 73 0W
Argenton-Château 18 46 59N 0 27W
Argenton-sur-Creuse 20 46 36N 1 30 E
Argeş □ 46 45 0N 24 45 E
Argeş → 46 44 30N 25 50 E
Arghandab → 66 31 30N 64 15 E
Argo 86 19 28N 30 30 E
Argolikós Kólpos 45 37 20N 22 52 E
Argolís □ 45 37 38N 22 50 E
Argonne 19 49 0N 5 20 E
Árgos 45 37 40N 22 43 E
Árgos Orestikón 44 40 27N 21 26 E
Argostólion 45 38 12N 20 33 E
Arguedas 32 42 11N 1 36W
Arguello, Pt. 119 34 34N 120 40W
Argun → 59 53 20N 121 28 E
Argungu 85 12 40N 4 31 E
Argyle 116 48 23N 96 49W
Argyrádhes 44 39 27N 19 58 E
Århus 49 56 8N 10 11 E
Århus Amtskommune □ 49 56 15N 10 15 E
Ariamsvlei 92 28 9 S 19 51 E
Ariana 83 36 52N 10 12 E
Ariano Irpino 41 41 10N 15 4 E
Ariano nel Polèsine 39 44 56N 12 5 E
Aribinda 85 14 17N 0 52W
Arica, Chile 126 18 32 S 70 20W
Arica, Colomb. 126 2 0 S 71 50W
Arid, C. 96 34 1 S 123 10 E
Aridh 64 25 0N 46 0 E
Ariège □ 20 42 56N 1 30 E
Ariège → 20 43 30N 1 25 E
Arieş → 46 46 24N 23 20 E
Arilje 42 43 44N 20 7 E
Arima 121 10 38N 61 17W
Arinos → 126 10 25 S 58 20W
Ario de Rosales 120 19 12N 102 0W
Aripuanã 126 9 25 S 60 30W
Aripuanã → 126 5 7 S 60 25W
Ariquemes 126 9 55 S 63 6W
Arisaig 14 56 55N 5 50W
Arîsh, W. el → 86 31 9N 33 49 E
Arissa 87 11 10N 41 35 E
Aristazabal I. 108 52 40N 129 10W
Arivaca 119 31 37N 111 25W
Arivonimamo 93 19 1 S 47 11 E
Ariyalur 70 11 8N 79 8 E
Ariza 74 41 19N 2 3W
Arizaro, Salar de 124 24 40 S 67 50W
Arizona 124 35 45 S 65 25W
Arizona □ 119 34 20N 111 30W
Arizpe 120 30 20N 110 11W
Årjäng 48 59 24N 12 8 E
Arjeplog 50 66 3N 18 2 E
Arjona, Colomb. 126 10 14N 75 22W
Arjona, Spain 31 37 56N 4 4W
Arka 59 60 15N 142 0 E
Arkadak 55 51 58N 43 19 E
Arkadelphia 117 34 5N 93 0W
Arkadhía □ 45 37 30N 22 20 E
Arkaig, L. 14 56 58N 5 10W
Arkalyk 58 50 13N 66 50 E
Arkansas □ 117 35 0N 92 30W
Arkansas → 117 33 48N 91 4W
Arkansas City 117 37 4N 97 3W
Árkathos → 44 39 20N 21 4 E
Arkhángelos 45 36 13N 28 7 E
Arkhangelsk 52 64 40N 41 0 E
Arkhangelskoye 55 51 32N 40 58 E
Arkiko 87 15 33N 39 30 E
Arklow 15 52 48N 6 10W
Árkoi 45 37 24N 26 44 E
Arkona, Kap 24 54 41N 13 26 E
Arkonam 70 13 7N 79 43 E
Arkösund 49 58 29N 16 56 E
Arkoúdhi 45 38 33N 20 43 E
Arkticheskiy, Mys 59 81 10N 95 0 E
Arkul 55 57 17N 50 3 E
Arlanc 20 45 25N 3 42 E
Arlanza → 30 42 6N 4 9W
Arlanzón → 30 42 3N 4 17W
Arlberg Pass 25 47 9N 10 12 E
Arlee 118 47 10N 114 4W
Arles 21 43 41N 4 40 E
Arlington, S. Afr. 93 28 1 S 27 53 E
Arlington, Oreg., U.S.A. 118 45 48N 120 6W
Arlington, S.D., U.S.A. 116 44 25N 97 4W
Arlington, Va., U.S.A. 114 38 52N 77 5W
Arlington, Wash., U.S.A. 118 48 11N 122 4W
Arlon 16 49 42N 5 49 E
Arlöv 49 55 38N 13 5 E
Arly 85 11 35N 1 28 E
Armagh 15 54 22N 6 40W
Armagh □ 15 54 18N 6 37W
Armagnac 20 43 44N 0 10 E
Armançon → 19 47 59N 3 30 E
Armavir 57 45 2N 41 7 E
Armenia 126 4 35N 75 45W
Armenian S.S.R. □ 57 40 0N 44 0 E
Armeniş 46 45 13N 22 17 E
Armentières 19 50 40N 2 50 E
Armidale 97 30 30 S 151 40 E
Armour 116 43 20N 98 25W
Armstrong, B.C., Can. 108 50 25N 119 10W
Armstrong, Ont., Can. 106 50 18N 89 4W
Armstrong, U.S.A. 117 26 59N 97 48W
Armur 70 18 48N 78 16 E
Arnaía 44 40 30N 23 40 E
Arnaouti, C. 64 35 0N 32 20 E
Arnarfjörður 50 65 48N 23 40W
Arnaud → 105 60 0N 70 0W
Arnay-le-Duc 19 47 10N 4 27 E
Arnedillo 32 42 13N 2 14W
Arnedo 32 42 12N 2 5W
Årnes 50 66 1N 21 31W
Årnes 47 60 7N 11 28 E
Arnett 117 36 9N 99 44W
Arnhem 16 51 58N 5 55 E
Arnhem B. 96 12 20 S 136 10 E
Arnhem, C. 97 12 20 S 137 30 E
Arnhem Land 96 13 10 S 134 30 E
Arni 70 12 43N 79 19 E
Árnissa 44 40 47N 21 49 E
Arno → 38 43 41N 10 17 E
Arnold, Nebr., U.S.A. 116 41 29N 100 10W
Arnold, Pa., U.S.A. 112 40 36N 79 44W
Arnoldstein 26 46 33N 13 43 E
Arnon → 19 47 13N 2 1 E
Arnot 109 55 56N 96 41W
Arnøy 50 70 9N 20 40 E
Arnprior 106 45 26N 76 21W
Arnsberg 24 51 25N 8 2 E
Arnstadt 24 50 50N 10 56 E
Aroab 92 26 41 S 19 39 E
Aroánia Óri 45 37 56N 22 12 E
Aroche 31 37 56N 6 57W
Arolsen 24 51 23N 9 1 E
Aron → 19 46 50N 3 27 E
Arona 38 45 45N 8 32 E
Arosa, Ria de → 30 42 28N 8 57W
Arpajon, Cantal, France 20 44 54N 2 28 E
Arpajon, Essonne, France 19 48 37N 2 12 E
Arpino 40 41 40N 13 35 E
Arrabury 99 26 45 S 141 0 E
Arrah 69 25 35N 84 32 E
Arraiján 120 8 56N 79 36W
Arraiolos 31 38 44N 7 59W
Arran 14 55 34N 5 12W
Arrandale 108 54 57N 130 0W
Arras 19 50 17N 2 46 E
Arrats → 20 44 6N 0 52 E
Arreau 20 42 54N 0 22 E
Arrecife 80 28 57N 13 37W
Arrecifes 124 34 06 S 60 9W
Arrée, Mts. d' 18 48 26N 3 55W
Arriaga 120 21 55N 101 23W
Arrilalah P.O. 98 23 43 S 143 54 E
Arromanches-les-Bains 18 49 20N 0 38W
Arronches 31 39 8N 7 16W
Arros, R 20 43 40N 0 2W
Arrou 18 48 6N 1 8 E
Arrow, L. 15 54 3N 8 20W
Arrow Rock Res. 118 43 45N 115 50W
Arrowhead 108 50 40N 117 55W
Arrowtown 101 44 57 S 168 50 E
Arroyo de la Luz 31 39 30N 6 38W
Arroyo Grande 119 35 9N 120 32W
Års 49 56 48N 9 30 E
Ars 20 46 13N 1 30W
Ars-sur-Moselle 19 49 5N 6 4 E
Arsenault L. 109 55 6N 108 32W
Arsiero 39 45 49N 11 22 E
Arsikere 70 13 15N 76 15 E
Arsk 55 56 10N 49 50 E
Árta 45 39 8N 21 2 E
Artá 32 39 41N 3 21 E
Árta □ 44 39 15N 21 5 E
Arteaga 120 18 50N 102 20W
Arteijo 30 43 19N 8 29W
Artem, Ostrov 57 40 28N 50 20 E
Artemovsk, R.S.F.S.R., U.S.S.R. 59 54 45N 93 35 E
Artemovsk, Ukraine S.S.R., U.S.S.R. 56 48 35N 38 0 E
Artemovski 57 47 45N 40 16 E
Artenay 19 48 5N 1 50 E
Artern 24 51 22N 11 18 E
Artesa de Segre 32 41 54N 1 3 E
Artesia 117 32 55N 104 25W
Artesia Wells 117 28 17N 99 18W
Artesian 116 44 2N 97 54W
Arthez-de-Béarn 20 43 29N 0 38W
Arthington 84 6 35N 10 45W
Arthur → 99 41 2 S 144 40 E
Arthur Pt. 98 22 7 S 150 3 E
Arthur's Pass 101 42 54 S 171 35 E
Artigas 124 30 20 S 56 30W
Artik 57 40 38N 43 58 E
Artillery L. 109 63 9N 107 52W
Artois 19 50 20N 2 30 E
Artotína 45 38 42N 22 2 E
Artsiz 56 46 4N 29 26 E
Artvin 64 41 14N 41 44 E
Aru, Kepulauan 73 6 0 S 134 30 E
Aru Meru □ 90 3 20 S 36 50 E
Arua 90 3 1N 30 58 E
Aruanã 127 14 54 S 51 10W
Aruba 121 12 30N 70 0W
Arudy 20 43 7N 0 28W
Arun → 69 26 55N 87 10 E
Arunachal Pradesh □ 67 28 0N 95 0 E
Aruppukottai 70 9 31N 78 8 E
Arusha 90 3 20 S 36 40 E
Arusha □ 90 4 0 S 36 30 E
Arusha Chini 90 3 32 S 37 20 E
Arusi □ 87 7 45N 39 00 E
Aruvi → 70 8 48N 79 53 E
Aruwimi → 90 1 13N 23 36 E
Arvada 118 44 43N 106 6W
Arvakalu 70 8 20N 79 58 E
Arvayheer 75 46 15N 102 48 E
Arve → 21 46 11N 6 8 E
Arvi 68 20 59N 78 16 E
Arvida 107 48 25N 71 14W
Arvidsjaur 50 65 35N 19 10 E
Arvika 48 59 40N 12 36 E
Arxan 75 47 11N 119 57 E
Arys 58 42 26N 68 48 E
Arzachena 40 41 5N 9 27 E
Arzamas 55 55 27N 43 55 E
Arzew 82 35 50N 0 23W
Arzgir 57 45 18N 44 23 E
Arzignano 39 45 30N 11 20 E
Aš 26 50 13N 12 12 E
'As Saffānīyah 64 28 5N 48 50 E
Aş Şāfī 62 31 2N 35 28 E
As Salt 62 32 2N 35 43 E
As Samāwah 64 31 15N 45 15 E
As Samū' 62 31 24N 35 4 E
As Sanamayn 62 33 3N 36 10 E
As Sulaymānīyah 64 24 9N 47 18 E
As Sulţan 83 31 4N 17 8 E
As Sumaymānīyah 64 35 35N 45 29 E
As Summān 64 25 0N 47 0 E
As Suwaih 65 22 10N 59 33 E
As Suwaydā' 64 32 40N 36 30 E
Aş Şuwayrah 64 32 55N 45 0 E
Asab 92 25 30 S 18 0 E
Asaba 85 6 12N 6 38 E
Asafo 84 6 20N 2 40W
Asahigawa 74 43 46N 142 22 E
Asale, L. 87 14 0N 40 20 E
Asamankese 85 5 50N 0 40W
Asansol 69 23 40N 87 1 E
Åsarna 48 62 39N 14 22 E
Asbe Teferi 87 9 4N 40 49 E
Asbesberge 92 29 0 S 23 0 E
Asbestos 107 45 47N 71 58W
Asbury Park 114 40 15N 74 1W
Ascensión, B. de la 120 19 50N 87 20W
Ascension I. 7 8 0 S 14 15W
Aschach 26 48 22N 14 2 E
Aschaffenburg 25 49 58N 9 8 E
Aschendorf 24 53 2N 7 22 E
Aschersleben 24 51 45N 11 28 E
Asciano 39 43 14N 11 32 E
Áscoli Piceno 39 42 51N 13 34 E
Áscoli Satriano 41 41 11N 15 32 E
Ascope 126 7 46 S 79 8W
Ascotán 124 21 45 S 68 17W
Aseb 87 13 0N 42 40 E
Åseda 49 57 10N 15 20 E
Asedjrad 82 24 51N 1 29 E
Asela 87 8 0N 39 0 E
Asenovgrad 43 42 1N 24 51 E
Aseral 47 58 37N 7 25 E
Asfeld 19 49 27N 4 5 E
Asfûn el Matâ'na 86 25 26N 32 30 E
Åsgårdstrand 47 59 22N 10 27 E
Ash Fork 119 35 14N 112 32W
Ash Grove 117 37 21N 93 36W
Ash Shām, Bādiyat 64 32 0N 40 0 E
Ash Shāmiyah 64 31 55N 44 35 E
Ash Shāriqah 65 25 23N 55 26 E
Ash Shaţrah 64 31 30N 46 10 E
Ash Shu'aybah 64 27 53N 42 43 E
Ash Shu'bah 64 28 54N 44 44 E
Ash Shūnah ash Shamālīyah 62 32 37N 35 34 E
Asha 52 55 0N 57 16 E
Ashaira 86 21 40N 40 40 E
Ashanti □ 85 7 30N 1 30W
Ashburn 115 31 42N 83 40W
Ashburton 101 43 53 S 171 48 E
Ashburton → 96 21 40 S 114 56 E
Ashby-de-la-Zouch 12 52 45N 1 29W
Ashcroft 108 50 40N 121 20W
Ashdod 62 31 49N 34 35 E
Ashdot Yaaqov 62 32 39N 35 35 E
Asheboro 115 35 43N 79 46W
Asherton 117 28 25N 99 43W
Asheville 115 35 39N 82 30W
Asheweig → 106 54 17N 87 12W
Ashford, Austral. 99 29 15 S 151 3 E
Ashford, U.K. 13 51 8N 0 53 E
Ashford, U.S.A. 118 46 45N 122 2W
Ashikaga 74 36 28N 139 29 E
Ashizuri-Zaki 74 32 44N 133 0 E
Ashkhabad 58 38 0N 57 50 E
Ashland, Kans., U.S.A. 117 37 13N 99 43W
Ashland, Ky., U.S.A. 114 38 25N 82 40W
Ashland, Me., U.S.A. 107 46 34N 68 26W
Ashland, Mont., U.S.A. 118 45 41N 106 12W
Ashland, Nebr., U.S.A. 116 41 5N 96 27W
Ashland, Ohio, U.S.A. 114 40 52N 82 20W
Ashland, Oreg., U.S.A. 118 42 10N 122 38W
Ashland, Pa., U.S.A. 113 40 45N 76 22W
Ashland, Va., U.S.A. 114 37 46N 77 30W
Ashland, Wis., U.S.A. 116 46 40N 90 52W
Ashley, N.D., U.S.A. 116 46 3N 99 23W
Ashley, Pa., U.S.A. 113 41 12N 75 55W
Ashley Snow I. 5 73 35 S 77 6W
Ashmont 108 54 7N 111 35W
Ashmore Reef 96 12 14 S 123 5 E
Ashmûn 86 30 18N 30 55 E
Ashq'elon 62 31 42N 34 35 E
Ashtabula 114 41 52N 80 50W
Ashti 70 18 50N 75 15 E
Ashton, S. Afr. 92 33 50 S 20 5 E
Ashton, U.S.A. 118 44 6N 111 30W
Ashton-under-Lyne 12 53 30N 2 8W
Ashuanipi, L. 107 52 45N 66 15W
Asia 60 45 0N 75 0 E
Asia, Kepulauan 73 1 0N 131 13 E
Asiago 39 45 52N 11 30 E
Asifabad 70 19 20N 79 24 E
Asike 73 6 39 S 140 24 E
Asilah 82 35 29N 6 0W
Asinara, G. dell' 40 41 0N 8 30 E
Asinara I. 40 41 5N 8 15 E
Asino 58 57 0N 86 0 E
'Asīr □ 63 18 40N 42 30 E
Asir, Ras 63 11 55N 51 10 E
Aska 70 19 2N 84 42 E

Asker Babana

Asker 47 59 50N 10 26 E
Askersund 49 58 53N 14 55 E
Askim 47 59 35N 11 10 E
Askja 50 65 3N 16 48W
Asl 86 29 33N 32 44 E
Āsmār 65 35 10N 71 27 E
Asmera (Asmara) 87 15 19N 38 55 E
Asnæs 49 55 40N 11 0 E
Asni 82 31 17N 7 58W
Aso 74 33 0N 131 5 E
Ásola 38 45 12N 10 25 E
Asoteriba, Jebel 86 21 51N 36 30 E
Asotin 118 46 20N 117 3W
Aspe 33 38 20N 0 40W
Aspen 119 39 12N 106 56W
Aspermont 117 33 11N 100 15W
Aspiring, Mt. 101 44 23S 168 46 E
Aspres 21 44 32N 5 44 E
Aspromonte 41 38 10N 16 0 E
Aspur 68 23 58N 74 7 E
Asquith 109 52 8N 107 13W
Assa 82 28 35N 9 6W
Assâba 84 16 10N 11 45W
Assam □ 67 26 0N 93 0 E
Assamakka 85 19 21N 5 38 E
Asse 16 50 24N 4 10 E
Assekrem 83 23 16N 5 49 E
Assémini 40 39 18N 9 0 E
Assen 16 53 0N 6 35 E
Assens, Fyn, Denmark 49 56 41N 10 3 E
Assens, Fyn, Denmark 49 55 16N 9 55 E
Assini 84 5 9N 3 17W
Assiniboia 109 49 40N 105 59W
Assiniboine → 109 49 53N 97 8W
Assis 125 22 40S 50 20W
Assisi 39 43 4N 12 36 E
Ássos 45 38 22N 20 33 E
Assus 44 39 32N 26 22 E
Assynt, L. 14 58 25N 5 15W
Astaffort 20 44 4N 0 40 E
Astakidha 45 35 53N 26 50 E
Astara 53 38 30N 48 50 E
Asti 38 44 54N 8 11 E
Astipálaia 45 36 32N 26 22 E
Astorga 30 42 29N 6 8W
Astoria 118 46 16N 123 50W
Åstorp 49 56 6N 12 55 E
Astrakhan 57 46 25N 48 5 E
Astrakhan-Bazâr 53 39 14N 48 30 E
Astudillo 30 42 12N 4 22W
Asturias 30 43 15N 6 0W
Asunción 124 25 10S 57 30W
Asunción, La 126 11 2N 63 53W
Asutri 87 15 25N 35 45 E
Aswa → 90 3 43N 31 55 E
Aswad, Ras al 86 21 20N 39 0 E
Aswân 86 24 4N 32 57 E
Aswân High Dam = Sadd el Aali 86 24 5N 32 54 E
Asyût 86 27 11N 31 4 E
Asyûti, Wadi → 86 27 11N 31 16 E
Aszód 27 47 39N 19 28 E
At Ţafilah 64 30 45N 35 30 E
At Ta'if 86 21 5N 40 27 E
Aţ Ţur 62 31 47N 35 14 E
Aţ Ţurrah 62 32 39N 35 59 E
Atacama □ 124 27 30S 70 0W
Atacama, Desierto de 124 24 0S 69 20W
Atacama, Salar de 124 23 30N 68 20W
Atakor 83 23 27N 5 31 E
Atakpamé 85 7 31N 1 13 E
Atalándi 45 38 39N 22 58 E
Atalaya 126 10 45S 73 50W
Atami 74 35 5N 139 4 E
Atapupu 73 9 0S 124 51 E
Atâr 80 20 30N 13 5W
Atara 59 63 10N 129 10 E
Ataram, Erg n- 82 23 57N 2 0 E
Atarfe 31 37 13N 3 40W
Atascadero 119 35 32N 120 44W
Atasu 58 48 30N 71 0 E
Atauro 73 8 10S 125 30 E
Atbara 86 17 42N 33 59 E
'Atbara → 86 17 40N 33 56 E
Atbasar 58 51 48N 68 20 E
Atchafalaya B. 117 29 30N 91 20W
Atchison 116 39 40N 95 10W
Atebubu 85 7 47N 1 0W
Ateca 32 41 20N 1 49W
Aterno → 39 42 11N 13 51 E
Atesine, Alpi 38 46 55N 11 30 E
Atessa 39 42 5N 14 27 E
Ath 16 50 38N 3 47 E
Ath Thāmāmi 64 27 45N 44 45 E
Athabasca 108 54 45N 113 20W
Athabasca → 109 58 40N 110 50W
Athabasca, L. 109 59 15N 109 15W
Athboy 15 53 37N 6 55W
Athenry 15 53 18N 8 45W
Athens, Can. 113 44 38N 75 57W
Athens, Ala., U.S.A. 115 34 49N 86 58W
Athens, Ga., U.S.A. 115 33 56N 83 24W
Athens, N.Y., U.S.A. 113 42 15N 73 48W
Athens, Ohio, U.S.A. 114 39 25N 82 6W
Athens, Pa., U.S.A. 113 41 57N 76 36W
Athens, Tenn., U.S.A. 115 35 45N 84 38W
Athens, Tex., U.S.A. 117 32 11N 95 48W
Athens = Athínai 45 37 58N 23 46 E
Atherley 112 44 37N 79 20W
Atherton 97 17 17S 145 30 E
Athiéme 85 6 37N 1 40 E
Athínai 45 37 58N 23 46 E
Athlone 15 53 26N 7 57W
Athni 70 16 44N 75 6 E
Atholl, Forest of 14 56 51N 3 50W
Atholville 107 47 59N 66 43W
Áthos, Mt. 44 40 9N 24 22 E
Athy 15 53 0N 7 0W
Ati, Chad 81 13 13N 18 20 E
Ati, Sudan 87 13 5N 29 2 E
Atiak 90 3 12N 32 2 E
Atico 126 16 14S 73 40W
Atienza 32 41 12N 2 52W
Atikokan 106 48 45N 91 37W
Atikonak L. 107 52 40N 64 32W
Atka 59 60 50N 151 48 E
Atkarsk 55 51 55N 45 2 E
Atkinson 116 42 35N 98 59W
Atlanta, Ga., U.S.A. 115 33 50N 84 24W
Atlanta, Tex., U.S.A. 117 33 7N 94 8W
Atlantic 116 41 25N 95 0W
Atlantic City 114 39 25N 74 25W
Atlantic Ocean 6 0 0 20 0W
Atlin 104 59 31N 133 41W
Atlin, L. 108 59 26N 133 45W
'Atlit 62 32 42N 34 56 E
Atløy 47 61 21N 4 58 E
Atmakur 70 14 37N 79 40 E
Atmore 115 31 2N 87 30W
Atna → 47 61 44N 10 49 E
Atoka 117 34 22N 96 10W
Átokos 45 38 28N 20 49 E
Atouguia 31 39 20N 9 20W
Atoyac → 120 16 30N 97 31W
Atrak → 65 37 50N 57 0 E
Ätran 49 57 7N 12 57 E
Atrauli 68 28 2N 78 20 E
Atri 39 42 35N 14 0 E
Atsbi 87 13 52N 39 50 E
Atsoum, Mts. 85 6 41N 12 57 E
Attalla 115 34 2N 86 5W
Attawapiskat 106 52 56N 82 24W
Attawapiskat → 106 52 57N 82 18W
Attawapiskat, L. 106 52 18N 87 54W
Attendorn 24 51 8N 7 54 E
Attersee 26 47 55N 13 32 E
Attica 114 40 20N 87 15W
Attichy 19 49 25N 3 3 E
Attigny 19 49 28N 4 35 E
Attikamagen L. 107 55 0N 66 30W
Attiki □ 45 38 10N 23 40 E
'Attil 62 32 23N 35 4 E
Attleboro 114 41 56N 71 18W
Attock 66 33 52N 72 20 E
Attopeu 71 14 48N 106 50 E
Attur 70 11 35N 78 30 E
Atuel → 124 36 17S 66 50W
Åtvidaberg 49 58 12N 16 0 E
Atwater 119 37 21N 120 37W
Atwood, Can. 112 43 40N 81 1W
Atwood, U.S.A. 116 39 52N 101 3W
Au Sable → 114 44 25N 83 20W
Au Sable Pt. 106 46 40N 86 10W
Aubagne 21 43 17N 5 37 E
Aube □ 19 48 15N 4 0 E
Aube → 19 48 34N 3 43 E
Aubenas 21 44 37N 4 24 E
Aubenton 19 49 50N 4 12 E
Aubigny-sur-Nère 19 47 30N 2 24 E
Aubin 20 44 33N 2 15 E
Aubrac, Mts. d' 20 44 38N 2 58 E
Auburn, Ala., U.S.A. 115 32 37N 85 30W
Auburn, Calif., U.S.A. 118 38 53N 121 4W
Auburn, Ind., U.S.A. 114 41 20N 85 0W
Auburn, N.Y., U.S.A. 114 42 57N 76 39W
Auburn, Nebr., U.S.A. 116 40 25N 95 50W
Auburn Range 99 25 15S 150 30 E
Auburndale 115 28 5N 81 45W
Aubusson 20 45 57N 2 11 E
Auch 20 43 39N 0 36 E
Auchel 19 50 30N 2 29 E
Auchi 85 7 6N 6 13 E
Auckland 101 36 52S 174 46 E
Auckland Is. 94 50 40S 166 5 E
Aude □ 20 43 8N 2 28 E
Aude → 20 43 13N 3 14 E
Auden 106 50 14N 87 53W
Auderville 18 49 43N 1 57W
Audierne 18 48 1N 4 34W
Audincourt 19 47 30N 6 50 E
Audo Ra. 87 6 20N 41 50 E
Audubon 116 41 43N 94 56W
Aue 24 50 34N 12 43 E
Auerbach 24 50 30N 12 25 E
Auffay 18 49 43N 1 07 E
Augathella 97 25 48S 146 35 E
Augrabies Falls 92 28 35S 20 20 E
Augsburg 25 48 22N 10 54 E
Augusta, Italy 41 37 14N 15 12 E
Augusta, Ark., U.S.A. 117 35 17N 91 25W
Augusta, Ga., U.S.A. 115 33 29N 81 59W
Augusta, Kans., U.S.A. 117 37 40N 97 0W
Augusta, Me., U.S.A. 107 44 20N 69 46W
Augusta, Mont., U.S.A. 118 47 30N 112 29W
Augusta, Wis., U.S.A. 116 44 41N 91 8W
Augustenborg 49 54 57N 9 53 E
Augusto Cardosa 91 12 40S 34 50 E
Augustów 28 53 51N 23 00 E
Augustus Downs 98 18 35S 139 55 E
Augustus, Mt. 96 24 20S 116 50 E
Aukan 87 15 29N 40 50 E
Aulla 38 44 12N 10 0 E
Aulnay 20 46 2N 0 22W
Aulne → 18 48 17N 4 16W
Aulnoye 19 50 12N 3 50 E
Ault 116 40 40N 104 42W
Ault-Onival 18 50 5N 1 29 E
Aulus-les-Bains 20 42 49N 1 19 E
Aumale 19 49 46N 1 46 E
Aumont-Aubrac 20 44 43N 3 17 E
Auna 85 10 9N 4 42 E
Aundh 70 17 33N 74 23 E
Aunis 20 46 5N 0 50W
Auponhia 73 1 58S 125 27 E
Aups 21 43 37N 6 15 E
Auraiya 69 26 28N 79 33 E
Aurangabad, Bihar, India 69 24 45N 84 18 E
Aurangabad, Maharashtra, India 70 19 50N 75 23 E
Auray 18 47 40N 3 0W
Aurès 83 35 8N 6 30 E
Aurich 24 53 28N 7 30 E
Aurillac 20 44 55N 2 26 E
Aurlandsvangen 47 60 55N 7 12 E
Auronza 39 46 33N 12 27 E
Aurora, Can. 112 44 0N 79 28W
Aurora, S. Afr. 92 32 40S 18 29 E
Aurora, Colo., U.S.A. 116 39 44N 104 55W
Aurora, Ill., U.S.A. 114 41 42N 88 12W
Aurora, Mo., U.S.A. 117 36 58N 93 42W
Aurora, Nebr., U.S.A. 116 40 55N 98 0W
Aurora, Ohio, U.S.A. 112 41 21N 81 20W
Aurskog 47 59 55N 11 26 E
Aurukun Mission 98 13 20S 141 45 E
Aus 92 26 35S 16 12 E
Aust-Agder fylke □ 47 58 55N 7 40 E
Austad 47 58 58N 7 37 E
Austerlitz = Slavkov 27 49 10N 16 52 E
Austevoll 47 60 5N 5 13 E
Austin, Minn., U.S.A. 116 43 37N 92 59W
Austin, Nev., U.S.A. 118 39 30N 117 1W
Austin, Pa., U.S.A. 112 41 40N 78 7W
Austin, Tex., U.S.A. 117 30 20N 97 45W
Austin, L. 96 27 40S 118 0 E
Austral Downs 97 20 30S 137 45 E
Austral Is. = Tubuai Is. 95 23 0S 150 0W
Austral Seamount Chain 95 24 0S 150 0W
Australia ■ 94 23 0S 135 0 E
Australian Alps 97 36 30S 148 30 E
Australian Cap. Terr. □ 97 35 30S 149 0 E
Australian Dependency □ 5 73 0S 90 0 E
Austria ■ 26 47 0N 14 0 E
Austvågøy 50 68 20N 14 40 E
Auterive 20 43 21N 1 29 E
Authie → 19 50 22N 1 38 E
Authon 18 48 12N 0 55 E
Autlán 120 19 40N 104 30W
Autun 19 46 58N 4 17 E
Auvergne 20 45 20N 3 15 E
Auvézère → 20 45 12N 0 50 E
Auxerre 19 47 48N 3 32 E
Auxi-le-Château 19 50 15N 2 8 E
Auxonne 19 47 10N 5 20 E
Auzances 20 46 2N 2 30 E
Auzat 20 45 27N 3 19 E
Avallon 19 47 30N 3 53 E
Avalon Pen. 107 47 30N 53 20W
Avalon Res. 117 32 30N 104 30W
Avanigadda 70 16 0N 80 56 E
Avaré 125 23 4S 48 58W
Ávas 44 40 57N 25 56 E
Aveiro, Brazil 127 3 10S 55 5W
Aveiro, Port. 30 40 37N 8 38W
Aveiro □ 30 40 40N 8 35W
Āvej 64 35 40N 49 15 E
Avellaneda 124 34 50S 58 10W
Avellino 41 40 54N 14 46 E
Averøya 47 63 0N 7 35 E
Aversa 41 40 58N 14 11 E
Avery 118 47 22N 115 56W
Aves, I. de 121 15 45N 63 55W
Aves, Is. de 121 12 0N 67 30W
Avesnes-sur-Helpe 19 50 8N 3 55 E
Avesta 48 60 9N 16 10 E
Aveyron □ 20 44 22N 2 45 E
Aveyron → 20 44 7N 1 5 E
Avezzano 39 42 2N 13 24 E
Avgó 45 35 33N 25 37 E
Aviá Terai 124 26 45S 60 50W
Aviano 39 46 3N 12 35 E
Avigliana 38 45 7N 7 13 E
Avigliano 41 40 44N 15 41 E
Avignon 21 43 57N 4 50 E
Ávila 30 40 39N 4 43W
Ávila □ 30 40 30N 5 0W
Ávila, Sierra de 30 40 40N 5 0W
Avilés 30 43 35N 5 57W
Avionárion 45 38 31N 24 8 E
Avisio → 39 46 7N 11 5 E
Aviz 31 39 4N 7 53W
Avize 19 48 59N 4 0 E
Avoca, Austral. 100 37 5S 143 26 E
Avoca, Ireland 15 52 52N 6 13W
Avoca, U.S.A. 112 42 24N 77 25W
Avoca → 100 35 40S 143 43 E
Avola, Can. 108 51 45N 119 19W
Avola, Italy 41 36 56N 15 7 E
Avon, N.Y., U.S.A. 112 43 0N 77 42W
Avon, S.D., U.S.A. 116 43 0N 98 3W
Avon □ 13 51 30N 2 40W
Avon →, Avon, U.K. 13 51 30N 2 43W
Avon →, Hants., U.K. 13 50 44N 1 45W
Avon →, Warwick, U.K. 13 52 0N 2 9W
Avon Downs 97 19 58S 137 25 E
Avon, Îles 97 19 37S 158 17 E
Avon Lake 112 41 28N 82 3W
Avondale 91 17 43S 30 58 E
Avonlea 109 50 0N 105 0W
Avonmore 113 45 10N 74 58W
Avonmouth 13 51 30N 2 42W
Avramov 43 42 45N 26 38 E
Avranches 18 48 40N 1 20W
Avre → 18 48 47N 1 22 E
Avrig 46 45 43N 24 21 E
Avrillé 20 46 28N 1 28W
Avtovac 42 43 9N 18 35 E
Awag el Baqar 87 10 10N 33 10 E
'Awālī 65 26 0N 50 30 E
Awarja → 70 17 5N 76 15 E
'Awartā 62 32 10N 35 17 E
Awasa, L. 87 7 0N 38 30 E
Awash 87 9 1N 40 10 E
Awash → 87 11 45N 41 5 E
Awaso 84 6 15N 2 22W
Awatere → 101 41 37S 174 10 E
Awbārī 83 26 46N 12 57 E
Awbārī □ 83 26 35N 12 46 E
Awe, L. 14 56 15N 5 15W
Aweil 87 8 42N 27 20 E
Awgu 85 6 4N 7 24 E
Awjilah 81 29 8N 21 7 E
Ax-les-Thermes 20 42 44N 1 50 E
Axarfjörður 50 66 15N 16 45W
Axel Heiberg I. 4 80 0N 90 0W
Axim 84 4 51N 2 15W
Axintele 46 44 37N 26 47 E
Axiós → 44 40 57N 22 35 E
Axmarsbruk 48 61 3N 17 10 E
Axminster 13 50 47N 3 1W
Axstedt 24 53 26N 8 43 E
Axvall 49 58 23N 13 34 E
Ay 19 49 3N 4 0 E
Ayabaca 126 4 40S 79 53W
Ayabe 74 35 20N 135 20 E
Ayacucho, Argent. 124 37 5S 58 20W
Ayacucho, Peru 126 13 0S 74 0W
Ayaguz 58 48 10N 80 0 E
Ayakudi 70 10 28N 77 56 E
Ayamonte 31 37 12N 7 24W
Ayan 59 56 30N 138 16 E
Ayancık 56 41 57N 34 18 E
Ayas 56 40 10N 32 14 E
Ayaviri 126 14 50S 70 35W
Āybaq 65 36 15N 68 5 E
Ayenngré 85 8 40N 1 1 E
Ayeritam 71 5 24N 100 15 E
Ayer's Cliff 113 45 10N 72 3W
Ayers Rock 96 25 23S 131 5 E
Aygues → 21 44 7N 4 43 E
Ayiá 44 39 43N 22 45 E
Ayía Ánna 45 38 52N 23 24 E
Áyia Marína 45 35 27N 26 53 E
Ayía Marína 45 37 11N 26 48 E
Ayía Paraskeví 44 39 14N 26 16 E
Ayía Rouméli 45 35 14N 23 58 E
Ayiássos 45 39 5N 26 23 E
Áyion Óros 44 40 25N 24 6 E
Áyios Andréas 45 37 21N 22 45 E
Áyios Evstrátios 44 39 34N 24 58 E
Áyios Evstrátios 44 39 30N 25 0 E
Áyios Ioannis, Ákra 45 35 20N 25 40 E
Áyios Kírikos 45 37 34N 26 17 E
Áyios Matthaíos 44 39 30N 19 47 E
Áyios Mírono 45 35 15N 25 1 E
Áyios Nikólaos 45 35 11N 25 41 E
Áyios Pétros 45 38 38N 20 33 E
Áyios Yeóryios 45 37 28N 23 57 E
Aykathonisi 45 37 28N 27 0 E
Aykin 52 62 15N 49 56 E
Aylesbury 13 51 48N 0 49W
Aylmer 112 42 46N 80 59W
Aylmer L. 104 64 0N 110 8W
'Ayn al Mubārak 64 24 10N 38 10 E
'Ayn 'Arīk 62 31 54N 35 8 E
'Ayn Zaqqūt 83 29 0N 19 30 E
Ayn Zhālah 64 36 45N 42 35 E
Ayna 33 38 34N 2 3W
Ayolas 124 27 10S 56 59W
Ayom 87 7 49N 28 23 E
Ayon, Ostrov 59 69 50N 169 0 E
Ayora 33 39 3N 1 3W
Ayr, Austral. 97 19 35S 147 25 E
Ayr, U.K. 14 55 28N 4 37W
Ayr → 14 55 29N 4 40W
Ayre, Pt. of 12 54 27N 4 21W
Aysha 87 10 50N 42 23 E
Aytos 43 42 42N 27 16 E
Aytoska Planina 43 42 45N 27 30 E
Ayu, Kepulauan 73 0 35N 131 5 E
Ayutla 120 16 58N 99 17W
Ayvalık 64 39 20N 26 46 E
Az Ẓāhirīyah 62 31 25N 34 58 E
Az Ẓahrān 64 26 10N 50 7 E
Az Zarqā 62 32 5N 36 4 E
Az Zāwiyah 83 32 52N 12 56 E
Az-Zilfī 64 26 12N 44 52 E
Az Zubayr 64 30 20N 47 50 E
Azambuja 31 39 4N 8 51W
Azamgarh 69 26 5N 83 13 E
Azaouak, Vallée de l' 85 15 50N 3 20 E
Āzārbāijān □ 64 37 0N 44 30 E
Azare 85 11 55N 10 10 E
Azay-le-Rideau 18 47 16N 0 30 E
Azazga 83 36 48N 4 22 E
Azbine = Aïr 85 18 0N 8 0 E
Azeffoun 83 36 51N 4 26 E
Azemmour 82 33 20N 9 20W
Azerbaijan S.S.R. □ 57 40 20N 48 0 E
Azezo 87 12 28N 37 15 E
Azilal, Beni Mallal 82 32 0N 6 30W
Azimganj 69 24 14N 88 16 E
Aznalcóllar 31 37 32N 6 17W
Azogues 126 2 35S 78 0W
Azor 62 32 2N 34 48 E
Azores 6 38 44N 29 0W
Azov 57 47 3N 39 25 E
Azov Sea = Azovskoye More 56 46 0N 36 30 E
Azovskoye More 56 46 0N 36 30 E
Azovy 58 64 55N 64 35 E
Azpeitia 32 43 12N 2 19W
Azrou 82 33 28N 5 19W
Aztec 119 36 54N 108 0W
Azúa de Compostela 121 18 25N 70 44W
Azuaga 31 38 16N 5 39W
Azuara 32 41 15N 0 53W
Azuer → 31 39 8N 3 36W
Azuero, Pen. de 121 7 30N 80 30W
Azul 124 36 42S 59 43W
Azzaba 83 36 48N 7 6 E
Azzano Décimo 39 45 53N 12 46 E

B

Ba Don 71 17 45N 106 26 E
Ba Ngoi = Cam Lam 71 11 50N 109 10 E
Ba Xian 76 39 8N 116 22 E
Baa 73 10 50S 123 0 E
Baamonde 30 43 7N 7 44W
Baarle Nassau 16 51 27N 4 56 E
Baarn 16 52 12N 5 17 E
Bāb el Māndeb 63 12 35N 43 25 E
Baba 43 42 44N 23 59 E
Baba Burnu 44 39 29N 26 2 E
Baba dag 57 41 0N 48 19W
Babadag 46 44 53N 28 44 E
Babaeski 43 41 26N 27 6 E
Babahoyo 126 1 40S 79 30W
Babana 85 10 31N 3 46 E

Babar Bandula

Babar, Alg. 83 35 10N 7 6 E
Babar, Indon. 73 8 0 S 129 30 E
Babar, Pak. 68 31 7N 69 32 E
Babarkach 68 29 45N 68 0 E
Babayevo 55 59 24N 35 55 E
Babb 118 48 56N 113 27W
Babenhausen 25 49 57N 8 56 E
Babia Gora 27 49 38N 19 38 E
Babile 87 9 16N 42 11 E
Babinda 98 17 20 S 145 56 E
Babine 108 55 22N 126 37W
Babine → 108 55 45N 127 44W
Babine L. 108 54 48N 126 0W
Babo 73 2 30 S 133 30 E
Babócsa 27 46 2N 17 21 E
Bābol 65 36 40N 52 50 E
Bābol Sar 65 36 45N 52 45 E
Baborówo Kietrz 27 50 7N 18 1 E
Baboua 88 5 49N 14 58 E
Babuna 42 41 30N 21 40 E
Babura 85 12 51N 8 59 E
Babušnica 42 43 7N 22 27 E
Babuyan Chan. 73 19 10N 122 0 E
Babylon, Iraq 64 32 40N 44 30 E
Babylon, U.S.A. 113 40 42N 73 20W
Bač 42 45 29N 19 17 E
Bac Kan 71 22 5N 105 50 E
Bac Ninh 71 21 13N 106 4 E
Bac Phan 71 22 0N 105 0 E
Bac Quang 71 22 30N 104 48 E
Bacabal 127 4 15 S 44 45W
Bacan, Kepulauan 73 0 35 S 127 30 E
Bacan, Pulau 73 0 50 S 127 30 E
Bacarès, Le 20 42 47N 3 3 E
Bacarra 73 18 15N 120 37 E
Bacau 73 8 27 S 126 27 E
Bacău 46 46 35N 26 55 E
Bacău □ 46 46 30N 26 45 E
Baccarat 19 48 28N 6 42 E
Bacchus Marsh 100 37 43 S 144 27 E
Bacerac 120 30 18N 108 50W
Băceşti 46 46 50N 27 11 E
Bacharach 25 50 3N 7 46 E
Bachelina 58 57 45N 67 20 E
Bachuma 87 6 48N 35 53 E
Bačina 42 43 42N 21 23 E
Back → 104 65 10N 104 0W
Bačka Palanka 42 45 17N 19 27 E
Bačka Topola 42 45 49N 19 39 E
Bäckefors 49 58 48N 12 9 E
Bački Petrovac 42 45 29N 19 32 E
Backnang 25 48 57N 9 26 E
Backstairs Passage 97 35 40 S 138 5 E
Bacolod 73 10 40N 122 57 E
Bacqueville 18 49 47N 1 0 E
Bacs-Kiskun □ 27 46 43N 19 30 E
Bácsalmás 27 46 8N 19 17 E
Bad → 116 44 22N 100 22W
Bad Aussee 26 47 43N 13 45 E
Bad Axe 106 43 48N 82 59W
Bad Bergzabern 25 49 6N 8 0 E
Bad Bramstedt 24 53 56N 9 53 E
Bad Doberan 24 54 6N 11 55 E
Bad Driburg 24 51 44N 9 0 E
Bad Ems 25 50 22N 7 44 E
Bad Frankenhausen 24 51 21N 11 3 E
Bad Freienwalde 24 52 47N 14 3 E
Bad Godesberg 24 50 41N 7 4 E
Bad Hersfeld 24 50 52N 9 42 E
Bad Hofgastein 26 47 17N 13 6 E
Bad Homburg 25 50 17N 8 33 E
Bad Honnef 24 50 39N 7 13 E
Bad Ischl 26 47 44N 13 38 E
Bad Kissingen 25 50 11N 10 5 E
Bad Kreuznach 25 49 47N 7 47 E
Bad Lands 116 43 40N 102 10W
Bad Langensalza 24 51 6N 10 40 E
Bad Lauterberg 24 51 38N 10 29 E
Bad Leonfelden 26 48 31N 14 18 E
Bad Lippspringe 24 51 47N 8 46 E
Bad Mergentheim 25 49 29N 9 47 E
Bad Münstereifel 24 50 33N 6 46 E
Bad Muskau 24 51 33N 14 43 E
Bad Nauheim 25 50 24N 8 45 E
Bad Oeynhausen 24 52 16N 8 45 E
Bad Oldesloe 24 53 48N 10 22 E
Bad Orb 25 50 16N 9 21 E
Bad Pyrmont 24 51 59N 9 15 E
Bad Reichenhall 25 47 44N 12 53 E
Bad St.-Peter 24 54 23N 8 32 E
Bad Salzuflen 24 52 8N 8 44 E
Bad Segeberg 24 53 58N 10 16 E
Bad Tölz 25 47 43N 11 34 E
Bad Waldsee 25 47 56N 9 46 E
Bad Wildungen 24 51 7N 9 10 E
Bad Wimpfen 25 49 12N 9 10 E
Bad Windsheim 25 49 29N 10 25 E
Badagara 70 11 35N 75 40 E
Badagri 85 6 25N 2 55 E
Badajoz 31 38 50N 6 59W
Badajoz □ 31 38 40N 6 30W
Badakhshan □ 65 36 30N 71 0 E
Badalona 32 41 26N 2 15 E
Badalzai 66 29 50N 65 35 E
Badampahar 69 22 10N 86 10 E
Badanah 64 30 58N 41 30 E
Badas 72 4 33N 114 25 E
Badas, Kepulauan 72 0 45N 107 5 E
Baddo → 66 28 0N 64 20 E
Bade 73 7 10 S 139 35 E
Baden, Austria 27 48 1N 16 13 E
Baden, Can. 112 43 14N 80 40W
Baden, Switz. 25 47 28N 8 18 E
Baden-Baden 25 48 45N 8 15 E
Baden-Württemberg □ 25 48 40N 9 0 E
Badgastein 26 47 7N 13 9 E
Badger 107 49 0N 56 4W
Bādghīsāt □ 65 35 0N 63 0 E
Badia Polèsine 39 45 6N 11 30 E
Badin 68 24 38N 68 54 E
Badnera 68 20 48N 77 44 E
Badogo 84 11 2N 8 13W
Badong 77 31 1N 110 23 E
Badrinath 69 30 45N 79 30 E
Baduen 63 7 15N 47 40 E
Badulla 70 7 1N 81 7 E
Baena 31 37 37N 4 20W
Baeza 33 37 57N 3 25W
Bafa Gölü 45 37 30N 27 29 E
Bafang 85 5 9N 10 11 E
Bafatá 84 12 8N 14 40W
Baffin B. 4 72 0N 64 0W
Baffin I. 105 68 0N 75 0W
Bafia 88 4 40N 11 10 E
Bafilo 85 9 22N 1 22 E
Bafing → 84 13 49N 10 50W
Bafoulabé 84 13 50N 10 55W
Bafoussam 85 5 28N 10 25 E
Bafra 56 41 34N 35 54 E
Bafra, C. 56 41 44N 35 58 E
Bāft, Esfahān, Iran 65 31 40N 55 25 E
Bāft, Kermān, Iran 65 29 15N 56 38 E
Bafut 85 6 6N 10 2 E
Bafwasende 90 1 3N 27 5 E
Bagalkot 70 16 10N 75 40 E
Bagamoyo 90 6 28 S 38 55 E
Bagamoyo □ 90 6 20 S 38 30 E
Baganga 73 7 34N 126 33 E
Bagansiapiapi 72 2 12N 100 50 E
Bagasra 68 21 30N 71 0 E
Bagawi 87 12 20N 34 18 E
Bagdarin 59 54 26N 113 36 E
Bagé 125 31 20 S 54 15W
Bagenalstown = Muine Bheag 15 52 42N 6 57W
Baggs 118 41 8N 107 46W
Baghdād 64 33 20N 44 30 E
Bagheihat 69 22 40N 89 47 E
Bagheria 40 38 5N 13 30 E
Bāghīn 65 30 12N 56 45 E
Baghlān 65 36 12N 69 0 E
Baghlān □ 65 36 0N 68 30 E
Bagley 116 47 30N 95 22W
Bagnacavallo 39 44 25N 11 58 E
Bagnara Cálabra 41 38 16N 15 49 E
Bagnères-de-Bigorre 20 43 5N 0 9 E
Bagnères-de-Luchon 20 42 47N 0 38 E
Bagni di Lucca 38 44 1N 10 37 E
Bagno di Romagna 39 43 50N 11 59 E
Bagnoles-de-l'Orne 18 48 32N 0 25W
Bagnoli di Sopra 39 45 13N 11 55 E
Bagnolo Mella 38 45 27N 10 14 E
Bagnols-les-Bains 20 44 30N 3 40 E
Bagnols-sur-Cèze 21 44 10N 4 36 E
Bagnorégio 39 42 38N 12 7 E
Bagolino 38 45 49N 10 28 E
Bagotville 107 48 22N 70 54W
Bagrdan 42 44 5N 21 11 E
Baguio 73 16 26N 120 34 E
Bahabón de Esgueva 32 41 52N 3 43W
Bahadurgarh 68 28 40N 76 57 E
Bahama, Canal Viejo de 121 22 10N 77 30W
Bahamas ■ 121 24 0N 75 0W
Baharîya, El Wâhât al 86 28 0N 28 50 E
Bahau 71 2 48N 102 26 E
Bahawalnagar 68 30 0N 73 15 E
Bahawalpur 68 29 24N 71 40 E
† Bahawalpur □ 68 29 5N 71 3 E
Baheri 69 28 45N 79 34 E
Bahi 90 5 58 S 35 21 E
Bahi Swamp 90 6 10 S 35 0 E
Bahia = Salvador 127 13 0 S 38 30W
Bahia □ 127 12 0 S 42 0W
Bahía Blanca 124 38 35 S 62 13W
Bahía de Caráquez 126 0 40 S 80 27W
Bahía, Islas de la 121 16 45N 86 15W
Bahía Laura 128 48 10 S 66 30W
Bahía Negra 126 20 5 S 58 5W
Bahir Dar 87 11 37N 37 10 E
Bahmer 82 27 32N 0 10W
Bahönye 27 46 25N 17 28 E
Bahr Aouk → 88 8 40N 19 0 E
Bahr el Ahmar □ 86 20 0N 35 0 E
Bahr el Ghazâl □ 87 7 0N 28 0 E
Bahr el Jebel → 87 7 30N 30 30 E
Bahr Salamat → 81 9 20N 18 0 E
Bahr Yûsef → 86 28 25N 30 35 E
Bahra el Burullus 86 31 28N 30 48 E
Bahraich 69 27 38N 81 37 E
Bahrain ■ 65 26 0N 50 35 E
Bai 84 13 35N 3 28W
Baia Mare 46 47 40N 23 35 E
Baia-Sprie 46 47 41N 23 43 E
Baïbokoum 81 7 46N 15 43 E
Baicheng 76 45 38N 122 42 E
Băicoi 46 45 3N 25 52 E
Baidoa 63 3 8N 43 30 E
Baie Comeau 107 49 12N 68 10W
Baie-St-Paul 107 47 28N 70 32W
Baie Trinité 107 49 25N 67 20W
Baie Verte 107 49 55N 56 12W
Baignes 20 45 23N 0 25W
Baigneux-les-Juifs 19 47 31N 4 39 E
Ba'ījī 64 35 0N 43 30 E
Baikal, L. = Baykal, Oz. 59 53 0N 108 0 E
Bailadila, Mt. 70 18 43N 81 15 E
Baile Atha Cliath = Dublin 15 53 20N 6 18W
Bailei 87 6 44N 40 18 E
Bailén 31 38 8N 3 48W
Băileşti 46 44 01N 23 20 E
Bailhongal 70 15 55N 74 53 E
Bailleul 19 50 44N 2 41 E
Bailundo 89 12 10 S 15 50 E
Baimuru 98 7 35 S 144 51 E
Bain-de-Bretagne 18 47 50N 1 40W
Bainbridge, Ga., U.S.A. 115 30 53N 84 34W
Bainbridge, N.Y., U.S.A. 113 42 17N 75 29W
Baing 73 10 14 S 120 34 E
Bainville 116 48 8N 104 10W
Bā'ir 64 30 45N 36 55 E
Baird 117 32 25N 99 25W
Baird Mts. 104 67 10N 160 15W
Bairin Youqi 76 43 30N 118 35 E
Bairin Zuoqi 76 43 58N 119 15 E
Bairnsdale 97 37 48 S 147 36 E
Baise → 20 44 17N 0 18 E
Baissa 85 7 14N 10 38 E
Baitadi 69 29 35N 80 25 E
Baiyin 76 36 45N 104 14 E
Baiyu Shan 76 37 15N 107 30 E
Baiyuda 86 17 35N 32 07 E
Baja 27 46 12N 18 59 E
Baja California 120 31 10N 115 12W
Baja, Pta. 120 29 50N 116 0W
Bajah, Wadi → 86 23 14N 39 20 E
Bajana 68 23 7N 71 49 E
Bajimba, Mt. 99 29 17 S 152 6 E
Bajina Bašta 42 43 58N 19 35 E
Bajmok 42 45 57N 19 24 E
Bajo Nuevo 121 15 40N 78 50W
Bajoga 85 10 57N 11 20 E
Bajool 98 23 40 S 150 35 E
Bak 27 46 43N 16 51 E
Bakala 88 6 15N 20 20 E
Bakar 39 45 18N 14 32 E
Bakchav 58 57 1N 82 5 E
Bakel 84 14 56N 12 20W
Baker, Calif., U.S.A. 119 35 16N 116 8W
Baker, Mont., U.S.A. 116 46 22N 104 12W
Baker, Nev., U.S.A. 118 38 59N 114 7W
Baker, Oreg., U.S.A. 118 44 50N 117 55W
Baker I. 94 0 10N 176 35W
Baker, L. 104 64 0N 96 0W
Baker Lake 104 64 20N 96 3W
Baker Mt. 118 48 50N 121 49W
Baker's Dozen Is. 106 56 45N 78 45W
Bakersfield, Calif., U.S.A. 119 35 25N 119 0W
Bakersfield, Vt., U.S.A. 113 44 46N 72 48W
Bakhchisaray 56 44 40N 33 45 E
Bakhmach 54 51 10N 32 45 E
Bakhtīārī □ 64 32 0N 49 0 E
Bakinskikh Komissarov, im 26 64 39 20N 49 15 E
Bakırköy 43 40 59N 28 53 E
Bakkafjörður 50 66 2N 14 48W
Bakkagerði 50 65 31N 13 49W
Bakony → 27 47 35N 17 54 E
Bakony Forest = Bakony Hegység 27 47 10N 17 30 E
Bakony Hegység 27 47 10N 17 30 E
Bakori 85 11 34N 7 25 E
Bakouma 88 5 40N 22 56 E
Bakov 26 50 27N 14 55 E
Baku 57 40 25N 49 45 E
Bala 112 45 1N 79 37W
Bal'ā 62 32 20N 35 6 E
Bala, L. = Tegid, L. 12 52 53N 3 38W
Balabac I. 72 8 0N 117 0 E
Balabac, Str. 72 7 53N 117 5 E
Balabakk 64 34 0N 36 10 E
Balabalangan, Kepulauan 72 2 20 S 117 30 E
Bălăciţa 46 44 23N 23 8 E
Balaghat 69 21 49N 80 12 E
Balaghat Ra. 70 18 50N 76 30 E
Balaguer 32 41 50N 0 50 E
Balakhna 55 56 25N 43 32 E
Balaklava, Austral. 99 34 7 S 138 22 E
Balaklava, U.S.S.R. 56 44 30N 33 30 E
Balakleya 56 49 28N 36 55 E
Balakovo 55 52 4N 47 55 E
Balanda 55 51 30N 44 40 E
Balangir 69 20 43N 83 35 E
Balapur 68 20 40N 76 45 E
Balashikha 55 55 49N 37 59 E
Balashov 55 51 30N 43 10 E
Balasinor 68 22 57N 73 23 E
Balasore 69 21 35N 87 3 E
Balassagyarmat 27 48 4N 19 15 E
Balât 86 25 36N 29 19 E
Balaton 27 46 50N 17 40 E
Balatonfüred 27 46 58N 17 54 E
Balatonszentgyörgy 27 46 41N 17 19 E
Balazote 33 38 54N 2 09W
Balboa 120 9 0N 79 30W
Balboa Hill 120 9 6N 79 44W
Balbriggan 15 53 35N 6 10W
Balcarce 124 38 0 S 58 10W
Balcarres 109 50 50N 103 35W
Balchik 43 43 28N 28 11 E
Balclutha 101 46 15 S 169 45 E
Bald Knob 117 35 20N 91 35W
Baldock L. 109 56 33N 97 57W
Baldwin, Fla., U.S.A. 115 30 15N 82 10W
Baldwin, Mich., U.S.A. 114 43 54N 85 53W
Baldwinsville 114 43 10N 76 19W
Bale 39 45 4N 13 46 E
Bale □ 87 6 20N 41 30 E
Baleares □ 32 39 30N 3 0 E
Baleares, Islas 32 39 30N 3 0 E
Balearic Is. = Baleares, Islas 32 39 30N 3 0 E
Băleni 46 45 48N 27 51 E
Baler 73 15 46N 121 34 E
Balfe's Creek 98 20 12 S 145 55 E
Balfour 93 26 38 S 28 35 E
Balfouriyya 62 32 38N 35 18 E
Bali, Camer. 85 5 54N 10 0 E
Bali, Indon. 72 8 20 S 115 0 E
Bali □ 72 8 20 S 115 0 E
Bali, Selat 73 8 30 S 114 35 E
Baligród 27 49 20N 22 17 E
Balikesir 64 39 35N 27 58 E
Balikpapan 72 1 10 S 116 55 E
Balimbing 73 5 10N 120 3 E
Baling 71 5 41N 100 55 E
Balipara 67 26 50N 92 45 E
Baliza 127 16 0 S 52 20W
Balkan Mts. = Stara Planina 43 43 15N 23 0 E
Balkan Pen. 9 42 0N 22 0 E
Balkh 65 36 44N 66 47 E
Balkh □ 65 36 30N 67 0 E
Balkhash 58 46 50N 74 50 E
Balkhash, Ozero 58 46 0N 74 50 E
Ballachulish 14 56 40N 5 10W
Balladoran 100 31 52 S 148 39 E
Ballarat 97 37 33 S 143 50 E
Ballard, L. 96 29 20 S 120 10 E
Ballarpur 70 19 50N 79 23 E
Ballater 14 57 2N 3 2W
Ballenas, Canal de las 120 29 10N 113 45W
Balleny Is. 5 66 30 S 163 0 E
Ballia 69 25 46N 84 12 E
Ballina, Austral. 97 28 50 S 153 31 E
Ballina, Mayo, Ireland 15 54 7N 9 10W
Ballina, Tipp., Ireland 15 52 49N 8 27W
Ballinasloe 15 53 20N 8 12W
Ballinger 117 31 45N 99 58W
Ballinrobe 15 53 36N 9 13W
Ballinskelligs B. 15 51 46N 10 11W
Ballon 18 48 10N 0 14 E
Ballycastle 15 55 12N 6 15W
Ballymena 15 54 53N 6 18W
Ballymena □ 15 54 53N 6 18W
Ballymoney 15 55 5N 6 30W
Ballymoney □ 15 55 5N 6 23W
Ballyshannon 15 54 30N 8 10W
Balmaceda 128 46 0 S 71 50W
Balmazújváros 27 47 37N 21 21 E
Balmoral, Austral. 99 37 15 S 141 48 E
Balmoral, U.K. 14 57 3N 3 13W
Balmorhea 117 31 2N 103 41W
Balonne → 97 28 47 S 147 56 E
Balrampur 69 27 30N 82 20 E
Balranald 97 34 38 S 143 33 E
Balş 46 44 22N 24 5 E
Balsas → 120 17 55N 102 10W
Bålsta 48 59 35N 17 30 E
Balston Spa 113 43 0N 73 52W
Balta, Romania 46 44 54N 22 38 E
Balta, U.S.A. 116 48 12N 100 7W
Balta, R.S.F.S.R., U.S.S.R. 57 42 58N 44 32 E
Balta, Ukraine S.S.R., U.S.S.R. 56 48 2N 29 45 E
Baltanás 30 41 56N 4 15W
Baltic Sea 51 56 0N 20 0 E
Baltîm 86 31 35N 31 10 E
Baltimore, Ireland 15 51 29N 9 22W
Baltimore, U.S.A. 114 39 18N 76 37W
Baltrum 24 53 43N 7 25 E
Baluchistan □ 65 27 30N 65 0 E
Balurghat 69 25 15N 88 44 E
Balygychan 59 63 56N 154 12 E
Bam 65 29 7N 58 14 E
Bama 85 11 33N 13 41 E
Bamako 84 12 34N 7 55W
Bamba 85 17 5N 1 24W
Bambari 88 5 40N 20 35 E
Bamberg, Ger. 25 49 54N 10 53 E
Bamberg, U.S.A. 115 33 19N 81 1W
Bambesi 87 9 45N 34 40 E
Bambey 84 14 42N 16 28W
Bambili 90 3 40N 26 0 E
Bamboo 98 14 34 S 143 20 E
Bamenda 85 5 57N 10 11 E
Bamfield 108 48 45N 125 10W
Bāmīān □ 65 35 0N 67 0 E
Bamiancheng 76 43 15N 124 2 E
Bamkin 85 6 3N 11 27 E
Bampūr 65 27 15N 60 21 E
Ban Aranyaprathet 71 13 41N 102 30 E
Ban Ban 71 19 31N 103 30 E
Ban Bua Chum 71 15 11N 101 12 E
Ban Houei Sai 71 20 22N 100 32 E
Ban Khe Bo 71 19 10N 104 39 E
Ban Khun Yuam 71 18 49N 97 57 E
* Ban Me Thuot 71 12 40N 108 3 E
Ban Phai 71 16 4N 102 44 E
Ban Thateng 71 15 25N 106 27 E
Baña, Punta de la 32 40 33N 0 40 E
Banaba 94 0 45 S 169 50 E
Banadar Daryay Oman □ 65 27 30N 56 0 E
Banalia 90 1 32N 25 5 E
Banam 71 11 20N 105 17 E
Banamba 84 13 29N 7 22W
Banana 98 24 28 S 150 8 E
Bananal, I. do 127 11 30 S 50 30W
Banaras = Varanasi 69 25 22N 83 8 E
Banas →, Gujarat, India 68 23 45N 71 25 E
Banas →, Madhya Pradesh, India 69 24 15N 81 30 E
Bânâs, Ras. 86 23 57N 35 50 E
Banbridge 15 54 21N 6 17W
Banbridge □ 15 54 21N 6 16W
Banbury 13 52 4N 1 21W
Banchory 14 57 3N 2 30W
Bancroft 106 45 3N 77 51W
Band 43 46 30N 24 25 E
Band-e Torkestān 65 35 30N 64 0 E
Banda 68 25 30N 80 26 E
Banda Aceh 72 5 35N 95 20 E
Banda Banda, Mt. 99 31 10 S 152 28 E
Banda Elat 73 5 40 S 133 5 E
Banda, Kepulauan 73 4 37 S 129 50 E
Banda, La 124 27 45 S 64 10W
Banda Sea 73 6 0 S 130 0 E
Bandama → 84 6 32N 5 30W
Bandanaira 73 4 32 S 129 54 E
Bandanwara 68 26 9N 74 38 E
Bandar = Machilipatnam 70 16 12N 81 12 E
Bandār 'Abbās 65 27 15N 56 15 E
Bandar-e Būshehr 65 28 55N 50 55 E
Bandar-e Chārak 65 26 45N 54 20 E
Bandar-e Deylam 64 30 5N 50 10 E
Bandar-e Lengeh 65 26 35N 54 58 E
Bandar-e Ma'shur 64 30 35N 49 10 E
Bandar-e Nakhīlū 65 26 58N 53 30 E
Bandar-e Rīg 65 29 30N 50 45 E
Bandar-e Shāh 65 37 0N 54 10 E
Bandar-e Shāhpūr 64 30 30N 49 5 E
Bandar-i-Pahlavī 64 37 30N 49 30 E
Bandar Seri Begawan 72 4 52N 115 0 E
Bandawe 91 11 58 S 34 5 E
Bande 30 42 3N 7 58W
Bandeira, Pico da 125 20 26 S 41 47W
Bandera, Argent. 124 28 55 S 62 20W
Bandera, U.S.A. 117 29 45N 99 3W
Banderas, Bahía de 120 20 40N 105 30W
Bandia → 70 19 2N 80 28 E
Bandiagara 84 14 12N 3 29W
Bandırma 64 40 20N 28 0 E
Bandon 15 51 48N 8 45W
Bandon → 15 51 40N 8 41W
Bandula 91 19 0 S 33 7 E

† Now part of Punjab □

* Renamed Buon Me Thuot

Bandundu Baume-les-Dames

Bandundu 88 3 15S 17 22 E
Bandung 73 6 54S 107 36 E
Băneasa 46 45 56N 27 55 E
Bañeres 33 38 44N 0 38W
Banes 121 21 0N 75 42W
Bañeza, La 30 42 17N 5 54W
Banff, Can. 108 51 10N 115 34W
Banff, U.K. 14 57 40N 2 32W
Banff Nat. Park 108 51 30N 116 15W
Banfora 84 10 40N 4 40W
Bang Hieng → 71 16 10N 105 10 E
Bang Lamung 71 13 3N 100 56 E
Bang Saphan 71 11 14N 99 28 E
Bangala Dam 91 21 7S 31 25 E
Bangalore 70 12 59N 77 40 E
Bangante 85 5 8N 10 32 E
Bangaon 69 23 0N 88 47 E
Bangassou 88 4 55N 23 7 E
Bangeta, Mt. 98 6 21S 147 3 E
Banggai 73 1 40S 123 30 E
Banggi, P. 72 7 17N 117 12 E
Banghāzī 83 32 11N 20 3 E
Banghāzī □ 83 32 7N 20 4 E
Bangil 73 7 36S 112 50 E
Bangjang 87 11 23N 32 41 E
Bangka, Pulau, Sulawesi, Indon. 73 1 50N 125 5 E
Bangka, Pulau, Sumatera, Indon. 72 2 0S 105 50 E
Bangka, Selat 72 2 30S 105 30 E
Bangkalan 73 7 2S 112 46 E
Bangkinang 72 0 18N 101 5 E
Bangko 72 2 5S 102 9 E
Bangkok = Krung Thep 71 13 45N 100 35 E
Bangladesh ■ 67 24 0N 90 0 E
Bangolo 84 7 1N 7 29W
Bangor, N. Ireland, U.K. 15 54 40N 5 40W
Bangor, Wales, U.K. 12 53 13N 4 9W
Bangor, Me., U.S.A. 107 44 48N 68 42W
Bangor, Pa., U.S.A. 113 40 51N 75 13W
Bangued 73 17 40N 120 37 E
Bangui 88 4 23N 18 35 E
Banguru 90 0 30N 27 10 E
Bangweulu, L. 91 11 0S 30 0 E
Bangweulu Swamp 91 11 20S 30 15 E
Bani 121 18 16N 70 22W
Bani → 84 14 30N 4 12W
Bani Bangou 85 15 3N 2 42 E
Bani, Djebel 82 29 16N 8 0W
Banī Na'īm 62 31 31N 35 10 E
Banī Suhaylah 62 31 21N 34 19 E
Bania 84 9 4N 3 6W
Baniara 98 9 44S 149 54 E
Banīnah 83 32 0N 20 12 E
Bāniyās 64 35 10N 36 0 E
Banja Luka 42 44 49N 17 11 E
Banjar 73 7 24S 108 30 E
Banjarmasin 72 3 20S 114 35 E
Banjarnegara 73 7 24S 109 42 E
Banjul 84 13 28N 16 40W
Bankeryd 49 57 53N 14 6 E
Banket 91 17 27S 30 19 E
Bankilaré 85 14 35N 0 44 E
Bankipore 69 25 35N 85 10 E
Banks I., B.C., Can. 108 53 20N 130 0W
Banks I., N.W.T., Can. 4 73 15N 121 30W
Banks I., P.N.G. 97 10 10S 142 15 E
Banks Pen. 101 43 45S 173 15 E
Banks Str. 99 40 40S 148 10 E
Bankura 69 23 11N 87 18 E
Bankya 42 42 43N 23 8 E
Bann →, Down, U.K. 15 54 30N 6 31W
Bann →, Londonderry, U.K. 15 55 10N 6 34W
Bannalec 18 47 57N 3 42W
Banning 119 33 58N 116 52W
Banningville = Bandundu 88 3 15S 17 22 E
Bannockburn, Can. 112 44 39N 77 33W
Bannockburn, U.K. 14 56 5N 3 55W
Bannockburn, Zimb. 91 20 17S 29 48 E
Bañolas 32 42 16N 2 44 E
Banon 21 44 2N 5 38 E
Baños de la Encina 31 38 10N 3 46W
Baños de Molgas 30 42 15N 7 40W
Bánovce 27 48 44N 18 16 E
Banská Bystrica 27 48 46N 19 14 E
Banská Štiavnica 27 48 25N 18 55 E
Bansko 43 41 52N 23 28 E
Banswara 68 23 32N 74 24 E
Banten 73 6 5S 106 8 E
Bantry 15 51 40N 9 28W
Bantry, B. 15 51 35N 9 50W
Bantul 73 7 55S 110 19 E
Bantva 68 21 29N 70 12 E
Bantval 70 12 55N 75 0 E
Banya 43 42 33N 24 50 E
Banyak, Kepulauan 72 2 10N 97 10 E
Banyo 85 6 52N 11 45 E
Banyuls 20 42 29N 3 8 E
Banyumas 73 7 32S 109 18 E
Banyuwangi 73 8 13S 114 21 E
Banzare Coast 5 68 0S 125 0 E
Banzyville = Mobayi 88 4 15N 21 8 E
Baocheng 77 33 12N 106 56 E
Baode 76 39 1N 111 5 E
Baoding 76 38 50N 115 28 E
Baoji 77 34 20N 107 5 E
Baojing 77 28 45N 109 41 E
Baokang 77 31 54N 111 12 E
Baoshan 75 25 10N 99 5 E
Baotou 76 40 32N 110 2 E
Baoying 77 33 17N 119 20 E
Bap 68 27 23N 72 18 E
Bapatla 70 15 55N 80 30 E
Bapaume 19 50 7N 2 50 E
Bāqa el Gharbīyya 62 32 25N 35 2 E
Ba'qūbah 64 33 45N 44 50 E
Baquedano 124 23 20S 69 52W
Bar, U.S.S.R. 56 49 4N 27 40 E
Bar, Yugo. 42 42 8N 19 8 E
Bar Harbor 107 44 15N 68 20W
Bar-le-Duc 19 48 47N 5 10 E
Bar-sur-Aube 19 48 14N 4 40 E
Bar-sur-Seine 19 48 7N 4 20 E
Barabai 72 2 32S 115 34 E
Barabinsk 58 55 20N 78 20 E
Baraboo 116 43 28N 89 46W
Baracoa 121 20 20N 74 30W
Baradero 124 33 52S 59 29W
Baraga 116 46 49N 88 29W
Barahona, Dom. Rep. 121 18 13N 71 7W
Barahona, Spain 32 41 17N 2 39W
Barail Range 67 25 15N 93 20 E
Baraka → 86 18 13N 37 35 E
Barakhola 67 25 0N 92 45 E
Barakot 69 21 33N 84 59 E
Barakula 99 26 30S 150 33 E
Baralaba 98 24 13S 149 50 E
Baralzon L. 109 60 0N 98 3W
Baramati 70 18 11N 74 33 E
Baramba 69 20 25N 85 23 E
Barameiya 86 18 32N 36 38 E
Baramula 69 34 15N 74 20 E
Baran 68 25 9N 76 40 E
Baranof I. 104 57 0N 135 10W
Baranovichi 54 53 10N 26 0 E
Baranów Sandomierski 28 50 29N 21 30 E
Baranya □ 27 46 0N 18 15 E
Barão de Melgaço 126 11 50S 60 45W
Baraolt 46 46 5N 25 34 E
Barapasi 73 2 15S 137 5 E
Barasat 69 22 46N 88 31 E
Barat Daya, Kepulauan 73 7 30S 128 0 E
Barataria B. 117 29 15N 89 45W
Baraut 68 29 13N 77 7 E
Barbacena 125 21 15S 43 56W
Barbacoas 126 1 45N 78 0W
Barbados ■ 121 13 0N 59 30W
Barban 39 45 5N 14 4 E
Barbastro 32 42 2N 0 5 E
Barbate 31 36 13N 5 56W
Barberino di Mugello 39 44 1N 11 15 E
Barberton, S. Afr. 93 25 42S 31 2 E
Barberton, U.S.A. 114 41 0N 81 40W
Barbezieux 20 45 28N 0 9W
Barbigha 69 25 21N 85 47 E
Barbourville 115 36 57N 83 52W
Barbuda I. 121 17 30N 61 40W
Barca, La 120 20 20N 102 40W
Barcaldine 97 23 43S 145 6 E
Barcarrota 31 38 31N 6 51W
Barcellona Pozzo di Gotto 41 38 8N 15 15 E
Barcelona, Spain 32 41 21N 2 10 E
Barcelona, Venez. 126 10 10N 64 40W
Barcelona □ 32 41 30N 2 0 E
Barcelonette 21 44 23N 6 40 E
Barcelos 126 1 0S 63 0W
Barcin 28 52 52N 17 55 E
Barcoo → 97 25 30S 142 50 E
Barcs 27 45 58N 17 28 E
Barczewo 28 53 50N 20 42 E
Barda 57 40 25N 47 10 E
Bardai 83 21 25N 17 0 E
Bardas Blancas 124 35 49S 69 45W
Bardejov 27 49 18N 21 15 E
Bardera 63 2 20N 42 27 E
Bardi 38 44 38N 9 43 E
Bardi, Ra's 64 24 17N 37 31 E
Bardia 81 31 45N 25 0 E
Bardo 28 50 31N 16 42 E
Bardoli 68 21 12N 73 5 E
Bardolino 38 45 33N 10 43 E
Bardsey I. 12 52 46N 4 47W
Bardstown 114 37 50N 85 29W
Bareilly 69 28 22N 79 27 E
Barentin 18 49 33N 0 58 E
Barenton 18 48 38N 0 50W
Barents Sea 4 73 0N 39 0 E
Barentu 87 15 2N 37 35 E
Barfleur 18 49 40N 1 17W
Barga, China 75 30 40N 81 20 E
Barga, Italy 38 44 5N 10 30 E
Bargal 63 11 25N 51 0 E
Bargara 98 24 50S 152 25 E
Barge 38 44 43N 7 19 E
Barge, La 118 42 12N 110 4W
Bargnop 87 9 32N 28 25 E
Bargteheide 24 53 42N 10 13 E
Barguzin 59 53 37N 109 37 E
Barh 69 25 29N 85 46 E
Barhaj 69 26 18N 83 44 E
Barham 100 35 36S 144 8 E
Barhi 69 24 15N 85 25 E
Bari, India 68 26 39N 77 39 E
Bari, Italy 41 41 6N 16 52 E
Bari Doab 68 30 20N 73 0 E
Bariadi □ 90 2 45S 34 40 E
Barīm 63 12 39N 43 25 E
Barinas 126 8 36N 70 15W
Baring C. 104 70 0N 117 30W
Baringo 90 0 47N 36 16 E
Baringo □ 90 0 55N 36 0 E
Baringo, L. 90 0 47N 36 16 E
Baripada 69 21 57N 86 45 E
Bârîs 86 24 42N 30 31 E
Barisal 69 22 45N 90 20 E
Barisan, Bukit 72 3 30S 102 15 E
Barito → 72 4 0S 114 50 E
Barjac 21 44 20N 4 22 E
Barjols 21 43 34N 6 2 E
Barjūj, Wadi → 83 25 26N 12 12 E
Bark L. 112 45 27N 77 51W
Barka = Baraka → 87 18 13N 37 35 E
Barkalı 65 23 40N 58 0 E
Barker 112 43 20N 78 35W
Barkley Sound 108 48 50N 125 10W
Barkly Downs 98 20 30S 138 30 E
Barkly East 92 30 58S 27 33 E
Barkly Tableland 97 17 50S 136 40 E
Barkly West 92 28 5S 24 31 E
Barkol, Wadi → 86 17 40N 32 0 E
Barksdale 117 29 47N 100 2W
Barlee, L. 96 29 15S 119 30 E
Barlee Ra. 96 23 30S 116 0 E
Barletta 41 41 20N 16 17 E
Barleur, Pointe de 18 49 42N 1 16W
Barlinek 28 53 0N 15 15 E
Barlow L. 109 62 00N 103 0W
Barmedman 99 34 9S 147 21 E
Barmer 68 25 45N 71 20 E
Barmera 99 34 15S 140 28 E
Barmouth 12 52 44N 4 3W
Barmstedt 24 53 47N 9 46 E
Barnagar 68 23 7N 75 19 E
Barnard Castle 12 54 33N 1 55W
Barnato 99 31 38S 145 0 E
Barnaul 58 53 20N 83 40 E
Barne Inlet 5 80 15S 160 0 E
Barnes 99 36 2S 144 47 E
Barnesville 115 33 6N 84 9W
Barnet 13 51 37N 0 15W
Barneveld, Neth. 16 52 7N 5 36 E
Barneveld, U.S.A. 113 43 16N 75 14W
Barneville 18 49 23N 1 46W
Barney, Mt. 97 28 17S 152 44 E
Barngo 99 25 3S 147 20 E
Barnhart 117 31 10N 101 8W
Barnsley 12 53 33N 1 29W
Barnstaple 13 51 5N 4 3W
Barnsville 116 46 43N 96 28W
Baro 85 8 35N 6 18 E
Baro → 87 8 26N 33 13 E
Baroda 68 25 29N 76 35 E
Baroda = Vadodara 68 22 20N 73 10 E
Barpali 69 21 11N 83 35 E
Barqin 83 27 33N 13 34 E
Barques, Pte. aux 114 44 5N 82 55W
Barquinha 31 39 28N 8 25W
Barquísimeto 126 10 4N 69 19W
Barr 19 48 25N 7 28 E
Barra, Brazil 127 11 5S 43 10W
Barra, U.K. 14 57 0N 7 30W
Barra do Corda 127 5 30S 45 10W
Barra do Piraí 125 22 30S 43 50W
Barra Falsa, Pta. da 93 22 58S 35 37 E
Barra Hd. 14 56 47N 7 40W
Barra Mansa 125 22 35S 44 12W
Barra, Sd. of 14 57 4N 7 25W
Barraba 99 30 21S 150 35 E
Barrackpur 69 22 44N 88 30 E
Barrafranca 41 37 22N 14 10 E
Barranca, Lima, Peru 126 10 45S 77 50W
Barranca, Loreto, Peru 126 4 50S 76 50W
Barrancabermeja 126 7 0N 73 50W
Barrancas 126 8 55N 62 5W
Barrancos 31 38 10N 6 58W
Barranqueras 124 27 30S 59 0W
Barranquilla 126 11 0N 74 50W
Barras 127 4 15S 42 18W
Barraute 106 48 26N 77 38W
Barre 114 44 15N 72 30W
Barreal 124 31 33S 69 28W
Barreiras 127 12 8S 45 0W
Barreirinhas 127 2 30S 42 50W
Barreiro 31 38 40N 9 6W
Barreiros 127 8 49S 35 12W
Barrême 21 43 57N 6 23 E
Barren I. 71 12 17N 93 50 E
Barren, Nosy 93 18 25S 43 40 E
Barretos 127 20 30S 48 35W
Barrhead 108 54 10N 114 24W
Barrie 106 44 24N 79 40W
Barrier Ra. 97 31 0S 141 30 E
Barrière 108 51 12N 120 7W
Barrington, Ill., U.S.A. 114 42 8N 88 5W
Barrington, R.I., U.S.A. 113 41 43N 71 20W
Barrington L. 109 56 55N 100 15W
Barrington Tops 97 32 6S 151 28 E
Barrow 104 71 16N 156 50W
Barrow → 15 52 10N 6 57W
Barrow Creek T.O. 96 21 30S 133 55 E
Barrow I. 96 20 45S 115 20 E
Barrow-in-Furness 12 54 8N 3 15W
Barrow Pt. 98 14 20S 144 40 E
Barrow Ra. 96 26 0S 127 40 E
Barrow Str. 4 74 20N 95 0W
Barruecopardo 30 41 4N 6 40W
Barruelo 30 42 54N 4 17W
Barry 13 51 23N 3 19W
Barry's Bay 106 45 29N 77 41W
Barsalogho 85 13 25N 1 3W
Barsi 70 18 10N 75 50 E
Barsø 49 55 7N 9 33 E
Barstow, Calif., U.S.A. 119 34 58N 117 2W
Barstow, Tex., U.S.A. 117 31 28N 103 24W
Barth 24 54 20N 12 36 E
Bartica 126 6 25N 58 40W
Bartin 64 41 38N 32 21 E
Bartle Frere, Mt. 97 17 27S 145 50 E
Bartlesville 117 36 50N 95 58W
Bartlett 117 30 46N 97 30W
Bartlett, L. 108 63 5N 118 20W
Bartolomeu Dias 91 21 10S 35 8 E
Barton-upon-Humber 12 53 41N 0 27W
Bartoszyce 28 54 15N 20 55 E
Bartow 115 27 53N 81 49W
Barumba 90 1 3N 23 37 E
Baruth 24 52 3N 13 31 E
Barvenkovo 56 48 57N 37 0 E
Barwani 68 22 2N 74 57 E
Barycz → 28 51 42N 16 15 E
Barysh 55 53 39N 47 8 E
Bas-Rhin □ 19 48 40N 7 30 E
Bašaid 42 45 38N 20 25 E
Bāsa'idū 65 26 35N 55 20 E
Basankusa 88 1 5N 19 50 E
Bascuñán, C. 124 28 52S 71 35W
Basel (Basle) 25 47 35N 7 35 E
Basel-Stadt □ 25 47 35N 7 35 E
Baselland □ 25 47 26N 7 45 E
Basento → 41 40 21N 16 50 E
Bashkir A.S.S.R. □ 52 54 0N 57 0 E
Basilaki I. 98 10 35S 151 0 E
Basilan 73 6 35N 122 0 E
Basilan Str. 73 6 50N 122 0 E
Basildon 13 51 34N 0 29 E
Basilicata □ 41 40 30N 16 0 E
Basim 70 20 3N 77 0 E
Basin 118 44 22N 108 2W
Basingstoke 13 51 15N 1 5W
Basirhat 69 22 40N 88 54 E
Baška 39 44 58N 14 45 E
Baskatong, Rés. 106 46 46N 75 50W
Baskerville C. 96 17 10S 122 15 E
Basle = Basel 25 47 35N 7 35 E
Basmat 70 19 15N 77 12 E
Basoda 68 23 52N 77 54 E
Basoka 90 1 16N 23 40 E
Basongo 88 4 15S 20 20 E
Basque Provinces = Vascongadas 32 42 50N 2 45W
Basra = Al Başrah 64 30 30N 47 50 E
Bass Rock 14 56 5N 2 40W
Bass Str. 97 39 15S 146 30 E
Bassano 108 50 48N 112 20W
Bassano del Grappa 39 45 45N 11 45 E
Bassar 85 9 19N 0 57 E
Basse Santa-Su 84 13 13N 14 15W
Basse-Terre 121 16 0N 61 40W
Bassée, La 19 50 31N 2 49 E
Bassein 71 19 26N 72 48 E
Basseterre 121 17 17N 62 43W
Bassett, Nebr., U.S.A. 116 42 37N 99 30W
Bassett, Va., U.S.A. 115 36 48N 79 59W
Bassi 68 30 44N 76 21 E
Bassigny 19 48 0N 5 10 E
Bassikounou 84 15 55N 6 1W
Bassum 24 52 50N 8 42 E
Båstad 49 56 25N 12 51 E
Bastak 65 27 15N 54 25 E
Bastar 70 19 15N 81 40 E
Basti 69 26 52N 82 55 E
Bastia 21 42 40N 9 30 E
Bastia Umbra 39 43 4N 12 34 E
Bastide-Puylaurent, La 20 44 35N 3 55 E
Bastogne 16 50 1N 5 43 E
Bastrop 117 30 5N 97 22W
Basuto 92 19 50S 26 25 E
Bat Yam 62 32 2N 34 44 E
Bata, Eq. Guin. 88 1 57N 9 50 E
Bata, Romania 46 46 1N 22 4 E
Bataan 73 14 40N 120 25 E
Batabanó 121 22 40N 82 20W
Batabanó, G. de 121 22 30N 82 30W
Batac 73 18 3N 120 34 E
Batagoy 59 67 38N 134 38 E
Batak 43 41 57N 24 12 E
Batakan 72 4 5S 114 38 E
Batalha 31 39 40N 8 50W
Batama 90 0 58N 26 33 E
Batamay 59 63 30N 129 15 E
Batang, China 75 30 1N 99 0 E
Batang, Indon. 73 6 55S 109 40 E
Batangafo 88 7 25N 18 20 E
Batangas 73 13 35N 121 10 E
Batanta 73 0 55S 130 40 E
Batatais 125 20 54S 47 37W
Batavia 114 43 0N 78 10W
Bataysk 57 47 3N 39 45 E
Batchelor 96 13 4S 131 1 E
Bateman's B. 97 35 40S 150 12 E
Batemans Bay 99 35 44S 150 11 E
Batesburg 115 33 54N 81 32W
Batesville, Ark., U.S.A. 117 35 48N 91 40W
Batesville, Miss., U.S.A. 117 34 17N 89 58W
Batesville, Tex., U.S.A. 117 28 59N 99 38W
Bath, U.K. 13 51 22N 2 22W
Bath, Maine, U.S.A. 107 43 50N 69 49W
Bath, N.Y., U.S.A. 114 42 20N 77 17W
Bathgate 14 55 54N 3 38W
Bathurst, Austral. 97 33 25S 149 31 E
Bathurst, Can. 107 47 37N 65 43W
Bathurst = Banjul 84 13 28N 16 40W
Bathurst B. 97 14 16S 144 25 E
Bathurst, C. 104 70 34N 128 0W
Bathurst Harb. 99 43 15S 146 10 E
Bathurst I., Austral. 96 11 30S 130 10 E
Bathurst I., Can. 4 76 0N 100 30W
Bathurst In. 104 68 10N 108 50W
Bathurst Inlet 104 66 50N 108 1W
Batie 84 9 53N 2 53W
Batinah 65 24 0N 56 0 E
Batlow 99 35 31S 148 9 E
Batman 64 37 55N 41 5 E
Batna 83 35 34N 6 15 E
Batočina 42 44 7N 21 5 E
Batoka 91 16 45S 27 15 E
Baton Rouge 117 30 30N 91 5W
Batopilas 120 27 0N 107 45W
Batouri 88 4 30N 14 25 E
Battambang 71 13 7N 103 12 E
Batticaloa 70 7 43N 81 45 E
Battipáglia 41 40 38N 15 0 E
Battīr 62 31 44N 35 8 E
Battle, Can. 109 52 58N 110 52W
Battle, U.K. 13 50 55N 0 30 E
Battle → 109 52 43N 108 15W
Battle Camp 98 15 20S 144 40 E
Battle Creek 114 42 20N 85 6W
Battle Harbour 107 52 16N 55 35W
Battle Lake 116 46 20N 95 43W
Battle Mountain 118 40 45N 117 0W
Battlefields 91 18 37S 29 47 E
Battleford 109 52 45N 108 15W
Battonya 27 46 16N 21 3 E
Batu 87 6 55N 39 45 E
Batu Gajah 71 4 28N 101 3 E
Batu, Kepulauan 72 0 30S 98 25 E
Batu Pahat 71 1 50N '02 56 E
Batuata 73 6 12S 122 42 E
Batumi 57 41 30N 41 30 E
Baturaja 72 4 11S 104 15 E
Baturité 127 4 28S 38 45W
Bau 72 1 25N 110 9 E
Baubau 73 5 25S 122 38 E
Bauchi 85 10 22N 9 48 E
Bauchi □ 85 10 30N 10 0 E
Baud 18 47 52N 3 1W
Baudette 116 48 46N 94 35W
Baugé 18 47 31N 0 8W
Baule-Escoublac, La 18 47 18N 2 23W
Baume-les-Dames 19 47 22N 6 22 E

Baunatal Benavente

Baunatal 24 51 13N 9 25 E
Baunei 40 40 2N 9 41 E
Bauru 125 22 10S 49 0W
Baús 127 18 22S 52 47W
Bauska 54 56 24N 25 15 E
Bautzen 24 51 11N 14 25 E
Baux, Les 21 43 45N 4 51 E
Bavanište 42 44 49N 20 53 E
Bavaria = Bayern □ 25 49 7N 11 30 E
Båven 48 59 0N 16 56 E
Bavi Sadri 68 24 28N 74 30 E
Bavispe → 120 29 30N 109 11W
Baw Baw, Mt. 100 37 49S 146 19 E
Bawdwin 67 23 5N 97 20 E
Bawean 72 5 46S 112 35 E
Bawku 85 11 3N 0 19W
Bawlake 67 19 11N 97 21 E
Baxley 115 31 43N 82 23W
Baxter Springs 117 37 3N 94 45W
Bay Bulls 107 47 19N 52 50W
Bay City, Mich., U.S.A. 114 43 35N 83 51W
Bay City, Oreg., U.S.A. 118 45 45N 123 58W
Bay City, Tex., U.S.A. 117 28 59N 95 55W
Bay de Verde 107 48 5N 52 54W
Bay, Laguna de 73 14 20N 121 11 E
Bay Minette 115 30 54N 87 43W
Bay St. Louis 117 30 18N 89 22W
Bay Shore 114 40 44N 73 15W
Bay Springs 117 31 58N 89 18W
Bay View 101 39 25S 176 50 E
Baya 91 11 53S 27 25 E
Bayamo 121 20 20N 76 40W
Bayamón 121 18 24N 66 10W
Bayan 76 46 5N 127 24 E
Bayan Har Shan 75 34 0N 98 0 E
Bayan Hot = Alxa Zuoqi 76 38 50N 105 40 E
Bayan Obo 76 41 52N 109 59 E
Bayana 68 26 55N 77 18 E
Bayanaul 58 50 45N 75 45 E
Bayanhongor 75 46 8N 102 43 E
Bayard 116 41 48N 103 17W
Bayázeh 65 33 30N 54 40 E
Baybay 73 10 40N 124 55 E
Bayburt 64 40 15N 40 20 E
Bayerischer Wald 25 49 0N 13 0 E
Bayern □ 25 49 7N 11 30 E
Bayeux 18 49 17N 0 42W
Bayfield, Can. 112 43 34N 81 42W
Bayfield, U.S.A. 116 46 50N 90 48W
Baykal, Oz. 59 53 0N 108 0 E
Baykit 59 61 50N 95 50 E
Baykonur 58 47 48N 65 50 E
Baymak 52 52 36N 58 19 E
Baynes Mts. 92 17 15S 13 0 E
Bayombong 73 16 30N 121 10 E
Bayon 19 48 30N 6 20 E
Bayona 30 42 6N 8 52W
Bayonne, France 20 43 30N 1 28W
Bayonne, U.S.A. 113 40 41N 74 7W
Bayovar 126 5 50S 81 0W
Baypore → 70 11 10N 75 47 E
Bayram-Ali 58 37 37N 62 10 E
Bayreuth 25 49 56N 11 35 E
Bayrischzell 25 47 39N 12 1 E
Bayrūt 64 33 53N 35 31 E
Bayt Awlá 62 31 37N 35 2 E
Bayt Fajjār 62 31 38N 35 9 E
Bayt Fūrīk 62 32 11N 35 20 E
Bayt Ḥānūn 62 31 32N 34 32 E
Bayt Jālā 62 31 43N 35 11 E
Bayt Lahm 62 31 43N 35 12 E
Bayt Rīma 62 32 2N 35 6 E
Bayt Sāḥūr 62 31 42N 35 13 E
Bayt Ummar 62 31 38N 35 7 E
Bayt 'ūr al Taḥtā 62 31 54N 35 5 E
Baytīn 62 31 56N 35 14 E
Baytown 117 29 42N 94 57W
Baytūniyā 62 31 54N 35 10 E
Bayzo 85 13 52N 4 35 E
Baza 33 37 30N 2 47W
Bazar Dyuzi 57 41 12N 47 50 E
Bazarny Karabulak 55 52 15N 46 20 E
Bazarnyy Syzgan 55 53 45N 46 40 E
Bazartobe 57 49 26N 51 45 E
Bazaruto, I. do 93 21 40S 35 28 E
Bazas 20 44 27N 0 13W
Bazhong 77 31 52N 106 46 E
Beach 116 46 57N 103 58W
Beach City 112 40 38N 81 35W
Beachport 99 37 29S 140 0 E
Beachy Head 13 50 44N 0 16 E
Beacon 114 41 32N 73 58W
Beaconia 109 50 25N 96 31W
Beaconsfield 97 41 11S 146 48 E
Beagle, Canal 128 55 0S 68 30W
Bealanana 93 14 33N 48 44 E
Beamsville 112 43 12N 79 28W
Béar, C. 20 42 31N 3 8 E
Bear I. 15 51 38N 9 50W
Bear L., B.C., Can. 108 56 10N 126 52W
Bear L., Man., Can. 109 55 8N 96 0W
Bear L., U.S.A. 118 42 0N 111 20W
Bearcreek 118 45 11N 109 6W
Beardmore 106 49 36N 87 57W
Beardmore Glacier 5 84 30S 170 0 E
Beardstown 116 40 0N 90 25W
Béarn 20 43 8N 0 36W
Bearpaw Mt. 118 48 15N 109 30W
Bearskin Lake 106 53 58N 91 2W
Beas de Segura 33 38 15N 2 53W
Beasain 32 43 3N 2 11W
Beata, C. 121 17 40N 71 30W
Beatrice, U.S.A. 116 40 20N 96 40W
Beatrice, Zimb. 91 18 15S 30 55 E
Beatrice, C. 97 14 20S 136 55 E
Beatton → 108 56 15N 120 45W
Beatton River 108 57 26N 121 20W
Beatty 119 36 58N 116 46W
Beaucaire 21 43 48N 4 39 E
Beauce, Plaine de la 19 48 10N 1 45 E
Beauceville 107 46 13N 70 46W
Beaudesert 99 27 59S 153 0 E
Beaufort, Austral. 100 37 25S 143 25 E
Beaufort, Malay. 72 5 30N 115 40 E
Beaufort, N.C., U.S.A. 115 34 45N 76 40W
Beaufort, S.C., U.S.A. 115 32 25N 80 40W
Beaufort Sea 4 72 0N 140 0W
Beaufort West 92 32 18S 22 36 E
Beaugency 19 47 47N 1 38 E
Beauharnois 106 45 20N 73 52W
Beaujeu 21 46 10N 4 35 E
Beaulieu 20 44 59N 1 50 E
Beaulieu → 108 62 3N 113 11W
Beauly 14 57 29N 4 27W
Beauly → 14 57 26N 4 28W
Beaumaris 12 53 16N 4 7W
Beaumetz-les-Loges 19 50 15N 2 40 E
Beaumont, Dordogne, France 20 44 45N 0 46 E
Beaumont, Sarthe, France 18 48 13N 0 8 E
Beaumont, U.S.A. 117 30 5N 94 8W
Beaumont-de-Lomagne 20 43 53N 0 59 E
Beaumont-le-Roger 18 49 4N 0 47 E
Beaumont-sur-Oise 19 49 9N 2 17 E
Beaune 19 47 2N 4 50 E
Beaune-la-Rolande 19 48 4N 2 25 E
Beaupréau 18 47 12N 1 00W
Beauséjour 109 50 5N 96 35W
Beausset, Le 21 43 10N 5 46 E
Beauvais 19 49 25N 2 8 E
Beauval 109 55 9N 107 37W
Beauvoir 18 46 55N 2 1W
Beauvoir-sur-Niort 20 46 12N 0 30W
Beaver, Alaska, U.S.A. 104 66 20N 147 30W
Beaver, Okla., U.S.A. 117 36 52N 100 31W
Beaver, Pa., U.S.A. 112 40 40N 80 18W
Beaver, Utah, U.S.A. 119 38 20N 112 45W
Beaver →, B.C., Can. 108 59 52N 124 20W
Beaver →, Sask., Can. 109 55 26N 107 45W
Beaver City 116 40 13N 99 50W
Beaver Dam 116 43 28N 88 50W
Beaver Falls 114 40 44N 80 20W
Beaver I. 106 45 40N 85 31W
Beaver, R 106 55 55N 87 48W
Beaverhill L., Alta., Can. 108 53 27N 112 32W
Beaverhill L., Man., Can. 109 54 5N 94 50W
Beaverhill L., N.W.T., Can. 109 63 2N 104 22W
Beaverlodge 108 55 11N 119 29W
Beavermouth 108 51 32N 117 23W
Beaverstone → 106 54 59N 89 25W
Beaverton 112 44 26N 79 9W
Beawar 68 26 3N 74 18 E
Bebedouro 125 21 0S 48 25W
Beboa 93 17 22S 44 33 E
Bebra 24 50 59N 9 48 E
Beccles 13 52 27N 1 33 E
Bečej 42 45 36N 20 3 E
Beceni 46 45 23N 26 48 E
Becerreá 30 42 51N 7 10W
Béchar 82 31 38N 2 18W
Bechyně 26 49 17N 14 29 E
Beckley 114 37 50N 81 8W
Beckum 24 51 46N 8 3 E
Bécon 18 47 30N 0 50W
Bečva → 27 49 31N 17 40 E
Bédar 33 37 11N 1 59W
Bédarieux 20 43 37N 3 10 E
Bédarrides 21 44 2N 4 54 E
Beddouza, Ras 82 32 33N 9 9W
Bedele 87 8 31N 36 23 E
Bederkesa 24 53 37N 8 50 E
Bedeso 87 9 58N 40 52 E
Bedford, Can. 106 45 7N 72 59W
Bedford, S. Afr. 92 32 40S 26 10 E
Bedford, U.K. 13 52 8N 0 29W
Bedford, Ind., U.S.A. 114 38 50N 86 30W
Bedford, Iowa, U.S.A. 116 40 40N 94 41W
Bedford, Ohio, U.S.A. 114 41 23N 81 32W
Bedford, Pa., U.S.A. 112 40 1N 78 30W
Bedford, Va., U.S.A. 114 37 25N 79 30W
Bedford □ 13 52 4N 0 28W
Bedford, C. 97 15 14S 145 21 E
Będków 28 51 36N 19 44 E
Bednja → 39 46 12N 16 25 E
Bednodemyanovsk 55 53 55N 43 15 E
Bedónia 38 44 28N 9 36 E
Bedourie 97 24 30S 139 30 E
Bedous 20 43 0N 0 36W
Będzin 28 50 19N 19 7 E
Beech Grove 114 39 40N 86 2W
Beechworth 99 36 22S 146 43 E
Beechy 109 50 53N 107 24W
Beelitz 24 52 14N 12 58 E
Beenleigh 99 27 43S 153 10 E
Be'er Sheva' 62 31 15N 34 48 E
Be'er Sheva' → 62 31 12N 34 40 E
Be'er Toviyya 62 31 44N 34 42 E
Be'eri 62 31 25N 34 30 E
Be'erotayim 62 32 19N 34 59 E
Beersheba = Be'er Sheva' 62 31 15N 34 48 E
Beeskow 24 52 9N 14 14 E
Beeston 12 52 55N 1 11W
Beetzendorf 24 52 42N 11 6 E
Beeville 117 28 27N 97 44W
Befale 88 0 25N 20 45 E
Befotaka 93 23 49S 47 0 E
Bega 97 36 41S 149 51 E
Bega, Canalul 42 45 37N 20 46 E
Bégard 18 48 38N 3 18W
* Begemdir & Simen □ 87 12 55N 37 30 E
Bègles 20 44 45N 0 35W
Begna → 47 60 41N 10 0 E
Begonte 30 43 10N 7 40W
Begu-Sarai 69 25 24N 86 9 E
Behbehān 64 30 30N 50 15 E
Behror 68 27 51N 76 20 E
Behshahr 65 36 45N 53 35 E
Bei Jiang → 75 23 2N 112 58 E
Bei'an 75 48 10N 126 20 E
Beibei 75 29 47N 106 22 E
Beihai 75 21 28N 109 6 E
Beijing 76 39 55N 116 20 E
Beijing □ 76 39 55N 116 20 E
Beilen 16 52 52N 6 27 E
Beilngries 25 49 1N 11 27 E
Beilpajah 99 32 54S 143 52 E
Beilul 87 13 2N 42 20 E
Beira 91 19 50S 34 52 E
Beirut = Bayrūt 64 33 53N 35 31 E
Beit Lāhiyah 62 31 32N 34 30 E
Beitaolaizhao 76 44 58N 125 58 E
Beitbridge 91 22 12S 30 0 E
Beiuş 46 46 40N 22 21 E
Beizhen 76 37 20N 118 2 E
Beja 31 38 2N 7 53W
Béja 83 36 43N 9 12 E
Beja □ 31 37 55N 7 55W
Bejaia 83 36 42N 5 2 E
Béjar 30 40 23N 5 46W
Bejestān 65 34 30N 58 5 E
Bekasi 73 6 20S 107 0 E
Békés 27 46 47N 21 9 E
Békés □ 27 46 45N 21 0 E
Békéscsaba 27 46 40N 21 5 E
Bekily 93 24 13S 45 19 E
Bekoji 87 7 40N 39 17 E
Bekok 71 2 20N 103 7 E
Bekwai 85 6 30N 1 34W
Bela, India 69 25 50N 82 0 E
Bela, Pak. 66 26 12N 66 20 E
Bela Crkva 42 44 55N 21 27 E
Bela Palanka 42 43 13N 22 17 E
Bela Vista, Brazil 124 22 12S 56 20W
Bela Vista, Mozam. 93 26 10S 32 44 E
Bélâbre 20 46 34N 1 8 E
Belalcázar 31 38 35N 5 10W
Belanovica 42 44 15N 20 23 E
Belavenona 93 24 50S 47 4 E
Belawan 72 3 33N 98 32 E
Belaya → 52 56 0N 54 32 E
Belaya Glina 57 46 5N 40 48 E
Belaya Kalitva 57 48 13N 40 50 E
Belaya Kholunitsa 55 58 41N 50 13 E
Belaya, Mt. 87 11 25N 36 8 E
Belaya Tserkov 54 49 45N 30 10 E
Belceşti 46 47 19N 27 7 E
Bełchatów 28 51 21N 19 22 E
Belcher, C. 4 71 0N 161 0W
Belcher Is. 106 56 15N 78 45W
Belchite 32 41 18N 0 43W
Belebey 52 54 7N 54 7 E
Belém (Pará) 127 1 20S 48 30W
Belén, Argent. 124 27 40S 67 5W
Belén, Parag. 124 23 30S 57 6W
Belen 119 34 40N 106 50W
Belene 43 43 39N 25 10 E
Bélesta 20 42 55N 1 56 E
Belet Uen 63 4 30N 45 5 E
Belev 55 53 50N 36 5 E
Belfast, S. Afr. 93 25 42S 30 2 E
Belfast, U.K. 15 54 35N 5 56W
Belfast, Maine, U.S.A. 107 44 30N 69 0W
Belfast, N.Y., U.S.A. 112 42 21N 78 9W
Belfast □ 15 54 35N 5 56W
Belfast, L. 15 54 40N 5 50W
Belfield 116 46 54N 103 11W
Belfort 19 47 38N 6 50 E
Belfort □ 19 47 38N 6 52 E
Belfry 118 45 10N 109 2W
Belgaum 70 15 55N 74 35 E
Belgioioso 38 45 9N 9 21 E
Belgium ■ 16 50 30N 5 0 E
Belgorod 56 50 35N 36 35 E
Belgorod-Dnestrovskiy 56 46 11N 30 23 E
Belgrade 118 45 50N 111 10W
Belgrade = Beograd 42 44 50N 20 37 E
Belhaven 115 35 34N 76 35W
Beli Drim → 42 42 6N 20 25 E
Beli Manastir 42 45 45N 18 36 E
Beli Timok → 42 43 53N 22 14 E
Belice → 40 37 35N 12 55 E
Belin 20 44 30N 0 47W
Belinga 88 1 10N 13 2 E
Belingwe 91 20 29S 29 57 E
Belingwe, N. 91 20 37S 29 55 E
Belinskiy (Chembar) 55 53 0N 43 25 E
Belinţ 42 45 48N 21 54 E
Belinyu 72 1 35S 105 50 E
Belitung, P. 72 3 10S 107 50 E
Beliu 46 46 30N 22 0 E
Belize ■ 120 17 0N 88 30W
Belize City 120 17 25N 88 0W
Beljanica 42 44 08N 21 43 E
Belkovskiy, Ostrov 59 75 32N 135 44 E
Bell → 106 49 48N 77 38W
Bell Bay 99 41 6S 146 53 E
Bell I. 107 50 46N 55 35W
Bell-Irving → 108 56 12N 129 5W
Bell Peninsula 105 63 50N 82 0W
Bell Ville 124 32 40S 62 40W
Bella Bella 108 52 10N 128 10W
Bella Coola 108 52 25N 126 40W
Bella Unión 124 30 15S 57 40W
Bella Vista, Corrientes, Argent. 124 28 33S 59 0W
Bella Vista, Tucuman, Argent. 124 27 10S 65 25W
Bellac 20 46 7N 1 3 E
Bellágio 38 45 59N 9 15 E
Bellaire 114 40 1N 80 46W
Bellary 70 15 10N 76 56 E
Bellata 99 29 53S 149 46 E
Belle Fourche 116 44 43N 103 52W
Belle Fourche → 116 44 25N 102 19W
Belle Glade 115 26 43N 80 38W
Belle-Île 18 47 20N 3 10W
Belle Isle 107 51 57N 55 25W
Belle-Isle-en-Terre 18 48 33N 3 23W
Belle Isle, Str. of 107 51 30N 56 30W
Belle, La 115 26 45N 81 22W
Belle Plaine, Iowa, U.S.A. 116 41 51N 92 18W
Belle Plaine, Minn., U.S.A. 116 44 35N 93 48W
Belle Yella 84 7 24N 10 0W
Belledonne 21 45 30N 6 10 E
Belledune 107 47 55N 65 50W
Bellefontaine 114 40 20N 83 45W
Bellefonte 114 40 56N 77 45W
Bellegarde, Ain, France 21 46 4N 5 49 E
Bellegarde, Creuse, France 20 45 59N 2 18 E
Bellegarde, Loiret, France 19 48 0N 2 26 E
Bellême 18 48 22N 0 34 E
Belleoram 107 47 31N 55 25W
Belleville, Can. 106 44 10N 77 23W
Belleville, Rhône, France 21 46 7N 4 45 E
Belleville, Vendée, France 18 46 48N 1 28W
Belleville, Ill., U.S.A. 116 38 30N 90 0W
Belleville, Kans., U.S.A. 116 39 51N 97 38W
Belleville, N.Y., U.S.A. 113 43 46N 76 10W
Bellevue, Can. 108 49 35N 114 22W
Bellevue, Idaho, U.S.A. 118 43 25N 114 23W
Bellevue, Ohio, U.S.A. 112 41 20N 82 48W
Bellevue, Pa., U.S.A. 112 40 29N 80 3W
Belley 21 45 46N 5 41 E
Bellin (Payne Bay) 105 60 0N 70 0W
Bellingen 99 30 25S 152 50 E
Bellingham 118 48 45N 122 27W
Bellingshausen Sea 5 66 0S 80 0W
Bellinzona 25 46 11N 9 1 E
Bellona Reefs 97 21 26S 159 0 E
Bellows Falls 114 43 10N 72 30W
Bellpat 68 29 0N 68 5 E
Bellpuig 32 41 37N 1 1 E
Belluno 39 46 8N 12 13 E
Bellville 117 29 58N 96 18W
Bellwood 112 40 36N 78 21W
Belmar 113 40 10N 74 2W
Bélmez 31 38 17N 5 17W
Belmont, Austral. 99 33 4S 151 42 E
Belmont, Can. 112 42 53N 81 5W
Belmont, U.S.A. 112 42 14N 78 3W
Belmonte, Brazil 127 16 0S 39 0W
Belmonte, Port. 30 40 21N 7 20W
Belmonte, Spain 32 39 34N 2 43W
Belmopan 120 17 18N 88 30W
Belmullet 15 54 13N 9 58W
Belo Horizonte 127 19 55S 43 56W
Belo-sur-Mer 93 20 42S 44 0 E
Belo-Tsiribihina 93 19 40S 44 30 E
Belogorsk, R.S.F.S.R., U.S.S.R. 59 51 0N 128 20 E
Belogorsk, Ukraine S.S.R., U.S.S.R. 56 45 3N 34 35 E
Belogradchik 42 43 53N 22 15 E
Belogradets 43 43 22N 27 18 E
Beloha 93 25 10S 45 3 E
Beloit, Kans., U.S.A. 116 39 32N 98 9W
Beloit, Wis., U.S.A. 116 42 35N 89 0W
Belokorovichi 54 51 7N 28 2 E
Belomorsk 52 64 35N 34 30 E
Belonia 67 23 15N 91 30 E
Belopolye 54 51 14N 34 20 E
Beloretsk 52 53 58N 58 24 E
Belovo 58 54 30N 86 0 E
Beloye More 52 66 30N 38 0 E
Beloye, Oz. 52 60 10N 37 35 E
Beloye Ozero 57 45 15N 46 50 E
Belozem 43 42 12N 25 2 E
Belozersk 55 60 0N 37 30 E
Belpasso 41 37 37N 15 0 E
Belsito 40 37 50N 13 47 E
Beltana 99 30 48S 138 25 E
Belterra 127 2 45S 55 0W
Beltinci 39 46 37N 16 20 E
Belton, S.C., U.S.A. 115 34 31N 82 39W
Belton, Tex., U.S.A. 117 31 4N 97 30W
Belton Res. 117 31 8N 97 32W
Beltsy 56 47 48N 28 0 E
Belturbet 15 54 6N 7 28W
Belukha 58 49 50N 86 50 E
Beluran 72 5 48N 117 35 E
Beluša 27 49 5N 18 27 E
Belušić 42 43 50N 21 10 E
Belvedere Maríttimo 41 39 37N 15 52 E
Belvès 20 44 46N 1 0 E
Belvidere, Ill., U.S.A. 116 42 15N 88 55W
Belvidere, N.J., U.S.A. 113 40 48N 75 5W
Belvis de la Jara 31 39 45N 4 57W
Belyando → 97 21 38S 146 50 E
Belyy 54 55 48N 32 51 E
Belyy, Ostrov 58 73 30N 71 0 E
Belyy Yar 58 58 26N 84 39 E
Belzig 24 52 8N 12 36 E
Belzoni 117 33 12N 90 30W
Bełżyce 28 51 11N 22 17 E
Bemaraha, Lembalemban' i 93 18 40S 44 45 E
Bemarivo 93 21 45S 44 45 E
Bemarivo → 93 15 27S 47 40 E
Bemavo 93 21 33S 45 25 E
Bembéréke 85 10 11N 2 43 E
Bembesi 91 20 0S 28 58 E
Bembesi → 91 18 57S 27 47 E
Bembézar → 31 37 45N 5 13W
Bemidji 116 47 30N 94 50W
Ben 'Ammi 62 33 0N 35 7 E
Ben Cruachan 14 56 26N 5 8W
Ben Dearg 14 57 47N 4 58W
Ben Gardane 83 33 11N 11 11 E
Ben Hope 14 58 24N 4 36W
Ben Lawers 14 56 33N 4 13W
Ben Lomond, Austral. 97 41 38S 147 42 E
Ben Lomond, U.K. 14 56 12N 4 39W
Ben Macdhui 14 57 4N 3 40W
Ben Mhor 14 57 16N 7 21W
Ben More, Central, U.K. 14 56 23N 4 31W
Ben More, Strathclyde, U.K. 14 56 26N 6 2W
Ben More Assynt 14 58 7N 4 51W
Ben Nevis 14 56 48N 5 0W
Ben Slimane 82 33 38N 7 7W
Ben Vorlich 14 56 22N 4 15W
Ben Wyvis 14 57 40N 4 35W
Bena 85 11 20N 5 50 E
Bena Dibele 88 4 4S 22 50 E
Benagalbón 31 36 45N 4 15W
Benagerie 99 31 25S 140 22 E
Benahmed 82 33 4N 7 9W
Benalla 97 36 30S 146 0 E
Benambra, Mt. 100 36 31S 147 34 E
Benamejí 31 37 16N 4 33W
Benanee 99 34 31S 142 52 E
Benares = Varanasi 69 25 22N 83 8 E
Bénat, C. 21 43 5N 6 22 E
Benavente, Port. 31 38 59N 8 49W

* Renamed Gonder □

Benavente **Bilaspur**

Benavente, Spain 30 42 2N 5 43W
Benavides, Spain 30 42 30N 5 54W
Benavides, U.S.A. 117 27 35N 98 28W
Benbecula 14 57 26N 7 21W
Bencubbin 96 30 48S 117 52 E
Bend 118 44 2N 121 15W
Bendel □ 85 6 0N 6 0 E
Bender Beila 63 9 30N 50 48 E
Bendery 56 46 50N 29 30 E
Bendigo 97 36 40S 144 15 E
Bendorf 24 50 26N 7 34 E
Benē Beraq, Israel 62 32 6N 34 51 E
Benē Beraq, Israel 62 32 6N 34 51 E
Bénéna 84 13 9N 4 17W
Benenitra 93 23 27S 45 5 E
Benešov 26 49 46N 14 41 E
Bénestroff 19 48 54N 6 45 E
Benet 20 46 22N 0 35W
Benevento 41 41 7N 14 45 E
Benfeld 19 48 22N 7 34 E
Benga 91 16 11S 33 40 E
Bengal, Bay of 60 15 0N 90 0 E
Bengawan Solo → 73 7 5S 112 35 E
Bengbu 75 32 58N 117 20 E
Benghazi = Banghāzī 83 32 11N 20 3 E
Bengkalis 72 1 30N 102 10 E
Bengkulu 72 3 50S 102 12 E
Bengkulu □ 72 3 48S 102 16 E
Bengough 109 49 25N 105 10W
Benguela 89 12 37S 13 25 E
Benguerir 82 32 16N 7 56W
Benguérua, I. 93 21 58S 35 28 E
Benha 86 30 26N 31 8 E
Beni 90 0 30N 29 27 E
Beni → 126 10 23S 65 24W
Beni Abbès 82 30 5N 2 5W
Beni-Haoua 82 36 30N 1 30 E
Beni Mazâr 86 28 32N 30 44 E
Beni Mellal 82 32 21N 6 21W
Beni Ounif 82 32 0N 1 10W
Beni Saf 82 35 17N 1 15W
Beni Suef 86 29 5N 31 6 E
Beniah L. 108 63 23N 112 17W
Benicarló 32 40 23N 0 23 E
Benidorm 33 38 33N 0 9W
Benidorm, Islote de 33 38 31N 0 9W
Benin ■ 85 10 0N 2 0 E
Benin, Bight of 85 5 0N 3 0 E
Benin City 85 6 20N 5 31 E
Benisa 33 38 43N 0 03 E
Benjamin Aceval 124 24 58S 57 34W
Benjamin Constant 126 4 40S 70 15W
Benkelman 116 40 7N 101 32W
Benkovac 39 44 2N 15 37 E
Benlidi 98 24 35S 144 50 E
Bennett 108 59 56N 134 53W
Bennett, Ostrov 59 76 21N 148 56 E
Bennettsville 115 34 38N 79 39W
Bennington 114 42 52N 73 12W
Benoa 72 8 50S 115 20 E
Bénodet 18 47 53N 4 7W
Benoni 93 26 11S 28 18 E
Benoud 82 32 20N 0 16 E
Bensheim 25 49 40N 8 38 E
Benson 119 31 59N 110 19W
Bent 65 26 20N 59 31 E
Benteng 73 6 10S 120 30 E
Bentinck I. 97 17 3S 139 35 E
Bentiu 87 9 10N 29 55 E
Bento Gonçalves 125 29 10S 51 31W
Benton, Ark., U.S.A. 117 34 30N 92 35W
Benton, Ill., U.S.A. 116 38 0N 88 55W
Benton Harbor 114 42 10N 86 28W
Bentong 71 3 31N 101 55 E
Bentu Liben 87 8 32N 38 21 E
Benue □ 85 7 30N 7 30 E
Benue → 85 7 48N 6 46 E
Benxi 76 41 20N 123 48 E
Beo 73 4 25N 126 50 E
Beograd 42 44 50N 20 37 E
Beowawe 118 40 35N 116 30W
Beppu 74 33 15N 131 30 E
Berati 44 40 43N 19 59 E
Berau, Teluk 73 2 30S 132 30 E
Berber 86 18 0N 34 0 E
Berbera 63 10 30N 45 2 E
Berbérati 88 4 15N 15 40 E
Berberia, C. del 33 38 39N 1 24 E
Berbice → 126 6 20N 57 32W
Berceto 38 44 30N 10 0 E
Berchtesgaden 25 47 37N 12 58 E
Berck-sur-Mer 19 50 25N 1 36 E
Berdichev 56 49 57N 28 30 E
Berdsk 58 54 47N 83 2 E
Berdyansk 56 46 45N 36 50 E
Berea, Ky., U.S.A. 114 37 35N 84 18W
Berea, Ohio, U.S.A. 112 41 21N 81 50W
Berebere 73 2 25N 128 45 E
Bereda 63 11 45N 51 0 E
Berekum 84 7 29N 2 34W
Berenice 86 24 2N 35 25 E
Berens → 109 52 25N 97 2W
Berens I. 109 52 18N 97 18W
Berens River 109 52 25N 97 0W
Berestechko 54 50 22N 25 5 E
Bereşti 46 46 6N 27 50 E
Beretău → 46 46 59N 21 7 E
Berettyo → 27 46 59N 21 7 E
Berettyóújfalu 27 47 13N 21 33 E
Berevo, Majunga, Madag. 93 17 14S 44 17 E
Berevo, Tuléar, Madag. 93 19 44S 44 58 E
Bereza 54 52 31N 24 51 E
Berezhany 54 49 26N 24 58 E
Berezina → 54 52 33N 30 14 E
Berezna 55 51 35N 31 46 E
Berezniki 58 59 24N 56 46 E
Berezovka 56 47 14N 30 55 E
Berezovo 58 64 0N 65 0 E
Berg 47 59 10N 11 18 E
Berga, Spain 32 42 6N 1 48 E
Berga, Sweden 49 57 14N 16 3 E
Bergama 64 39 8N 27 15 E
Bérgamo 38 45 42N 9 40 E
Bergantiños 30 43 20N 8 40W
Bergedorf 24 53 28N 10 12 E
Bergen, Ger. 24 54 24N 13 26 E
Bergen, Neth. 16 52 40N 4 43 E
Bergen, Norway 47 60 23N 5 20 E
Bergen, U.S.A. 112 43 5N 77 56W
Bergen-op-Zoom 16 51 30N 4 18 E
Bergerac 20 44 51N 0 30 E
Bergheim 24 50 57N 6 38 E
Bergisch-Gladbach 24 50 59N 7 9 E
Bergkvara 49 56 23N 16 5 E
Bergsjö 48 61 59N 17 3 E
Bergues 19 50 58N 2 24 E
Bergum 16 53 13N 5 59 E
Bergvik 48 61 16N 16 50 E
Berhala, Selat 72 1 0S 104 15 E
Berhampore 69 24 2N 88 27 E
Berhampur 70 19 15N 84 54 E
Berheci → 46 46 7N 27 19 E
Bering Sea 94 58 0N 167 0 E
Bering Str. 104 66 0N 170 0W
Beringen 16 51 3N 5 14 E
Beringovskiy 59 63 3N 179 19 E
Berislav 56 46 50N 33 30 E
Berisso 124 34 56S 57 50W
Berja 33 36 50N 2 56W
Berkane 82 34 52N 2 20W
Berkeley 13 51 41N 2 28W
Berkeley Springs 114 39 38N 78 12W
Berkner I. 5 79 30S 50 0W
Berkovitsa 43 43 16N 23 8 E
Berkshire □ 13 51 30N 1 20W
Berland → 108 54 0N 116 50W
Berlanga 31 38 17N 5 50W
Berleburg 24 51 3N 8 22 E
Berlenga, Ilhas 31 39 25N 9 30W
Berlin, Ger. 24 52 32N 13 24 E
Berlin, Md., U.S.A. 114 38 19N 75 12W
Berlin, N.H., U.S.A. 114 44 29N 71 10W
Berlin, Wis., U.S.A. 114 43 58N 88 55W
Berlin, E. □ 24 52 30N 13 30 E
Berlin, W. □ 24 52 30N 13 20 E
Bermeja, Sierra 31 36 30N 5 11W
Bermejo →, Formosa, Argent. 124 26 51S 58 23W
Bermejo →, San Juan, Argent. 124 32 30S 67 30W
Bermeo 32 43 25N 2 47W
Bermillo de Sayago 30 41 22N 6 8W
Bermuda ■ 121 32 45N 65 0W
Bern (Berne) 25 46 57N 7 28 E
Bern (Berne) □ 25 46 45N 7 40 E
Bernado 119 34 30N 106 53W
Bernalda 41 40 24N 16 44 E
Bernalillo 119 35 17N 106 37W
Bernam → 71 3 45N 101 5 E
Bernardo de Irigoyen 125 26 15S 53 40W
Bernasconi 124 37 55S 63 44W
Bernau, Germ., E. 24 52 40N 13 35 E
Bernau, Germ., W. 25 47 45N 12 20 E
Bernay 18 49 5N 0 35 E
Bernburg 24 51 40N 11 42 E
Berndorf 26 47 59N 16 1 E
Berne = Bern 25 46 57N 7 28 E
Berneck 25 51 3N 11 40 E
Berner Alpen 25 46 27N 7 35 E
Bernese Oberland = Oberland 25 46 27N 7 35 E
Bernier I. 96 24 50S 113 12 E
Bernina, Piz 25 46 20N 9 54 E
Bernkastel-Kues 25 49 55N 7 04 E
Beror Hayil 62 31 34N 34 38 E
Béroubouay 85 10 34N 2 46 E
Beroun 26 49 57N 14 5 E
Berounka → 26 50 0N 13 47 E
Berovo 42 41 38N 22 51 E
Berrahal 83 36 54N 7 33 E
Berre, Étang de 21 43 27N 5 5 E
Berrechid 82 33 18N 7 36W
Berri 99 34 14S 140 35 E
Berriane 82 32 50N 3 46 E
Berrigan 100 35 38S 145 49 E
Berrouaghia 82 36 10N 2 53 E
Berry, Austral. 99 34 46S 150 43 E
Berry, France 19 47 0N 2 0 E
Berry Is. 121 25 40N 77 50W
Berryville 117 36 23N 93 35W
Bersenbrück 24 52 33N 7 56 E
Berthold 116 48 19N 101 45W
Berthoud 116 40 21N 105 5W
Bertincourt 19 50 5N 2 58 E
Bertoua 88 4 30N 13 45 E
Bertrand 116 40 35N 99 38W
Berufjörður 50 64 48N 14 29W
Berwick 114 41 4N 76 17W
Berwick-upon-Tweed 12 55 47N 2 0W
Berwyn Mts. 12 52 54N 3 26W
Berzasca 42 44 39N 21 58 E
Berzence 27 46 12N 17 11 E
Besalampy 93 16 43S 44 29 E
Besançon 19 47 15N 6 0 E
Besar 72 2 40S 116 0 E
Beserah 71 3 50N 103 21 E
Beshenkovichi 54 55 2N 29 29 E
Beška 42 45 8N 20 6 E
Beskydy 27 49 35N 18 40 E
Beslan 57 43 15N 44 28 E
Besna Kobila 42 42 31N 22 10 E
Besnard L. 109 55 25N 106 0W
Besni 64 37 41N 37 52 E
Besor, N. → 62 31 28N 34 22 E
Beşparmak Dağı 45 37 32N 27 30 E
Bessarabiya 46 47 0N 28 10 E
Bessarabka 56 46 21N 28 58 E
Bessèges 21 44 18N 4 8 E
Bessemer, Ala., U.S.A. 115 33 25N 86 57W
Bessemer, Mich., U.S.A. 116 46 27N 90 0W
Bessin 18 49 21N 1 0W
Bessines-sur-Gartempe 20 46 6N 1 22 E
Bet Alfa 62 32 31N 35 25 E
Bet Dagan 62 32 1N 34 49 E
Bet Guvrin 62 31 37N 34 54 E
Bet Ha'Emeq 62 32 58N 35 8 E
Bet Hashitta 62 32 31N 35 27 E
Bet Qeshet 62 32 41N 35 21 E
Bet She'an 62 32 30N 35 30 E
Bet Shemesh 62 31 44N 35 0 E
Bet Tadjine, Djebel 82 29 0N 3 30W
Bet Yosef 62 32 34N 35 33 E
Betafo 93 19 50S 46 51 E
Betanzos 30 43 15N 8 12W
Bétaré Oya 88 5 40N 14 5 E
Bétera 32 39 35N 0 28W
Bethal 93 26 27S 29 28 E
Bethanien 92 26 31S 17 8 E
Bethany, S. Afr. 92 29 34S 25 59 E
Bethany, U.S.A. 116 40 18N 94 0W
Bethany = Al Ayzarīyah 62 31 47N 35 15 E
Bethel, Alaska, U.S.A. 104 60 50N 161 50W
Bethel, Pa., U.S.A. 112 40 20N 80 2W
Bethel, Vt., U.S.A. 113 43 50N 72 37W
Bethlehem, S. Afr. 93 28 14S 28 18 E
Bethlehem, U.S.A. 114 40 39N 75 24W
Bethlehem = Bayt Lahm 62 31 43N 35 12 E
Bethulie 92 30 30S 25 59 E
Béthune 19 50 30N 2 38 E
Béthune → 18 49 53N 1 9 E
Betioky 93 23 48S 44 20 E
Beton Bazoches 19 48 42N 3 15 E
Betong, Malay. 72 1 24N 111 31 E
Betong, Thai. 71 5 45N 101 5 E
Betoota 99 25 45S 140 42 E
Betroka 93 23 16S 46 0 E
Betsiamites 107 48 56N 68 40W
Betsiamites → 107 48 56N 68 38W
Betsiboka → 93 16 3S 46 36 E
Betsjoeanaland 92 26 30S 22 30 E
Bettiah 69 26 48N 84 33 E
Bèttola 38 44 42N 9 32 E
Betul 68 21 58N 77 59 E
Betzdorf 24 50 47N 7 53 E
Beuca 46 44 14N 24 56 E
Beuil 21 44 6N 6 59 E
Beulah 116 47 18N 101 47W
Bevensen 24 53 5N 10 34 E
Beverley, Austral. 96 32 9S 116 56 E
Beverley, U.K. 12 53 52N 0 26W
Beverly, Mass., U.S.A. 113 42 32N 70 50W
Beverly, Wash., U.S.A. 118 46 55N 119 59W
Beverly Hills 119 34 4N 118 29W
Beverwijk 16 52 28N 4 38 E
Bex 25 46 15N 7 0 E
Beyin 84 5 1N 2 41W
Beykoz 43 41 8N 29 7 E
Beyla 84 8 30N 8 38W
Beynat 20 45 8N 1 44 E
Beyneu 58 45 10N 55 3 E
Beypazarı 64 40 10N 31 56 E
Beyşehir Gölü 64 37 40N 31 45 E
Bezdan 42 45 50N 18 57 E
Bezet 62 33 4N 35 8 E
Bezhetsk 55 57 47N 36 39 E
Bezhitsa 54 53 19N 34 17 E
Béziers 20 43 20N 3 12 E
Bezwada = Vijayawada 70 16 31N 80 39 E
Bhadra → 70 14 0N 75 20 E
Bhadrakh 69 21 10N 86 30 E
Bhadravati 70 13 49N 75 40 E
Bhagalpur 69 25 10N 87 0 E
Bhaisa 70 19 10N 77 58 E
Bhakkar 68 31 40N 71 5 E
Bhakra Dam 68 31 30N 76 45 E
Bhamo 67 24 15N 97 15 E
Bhamragarh 70 19 30N 80 40 E
Bhandara 69 21 5N 79 42 E
Bhanrer Ra. 68 23 40N 79 45 E
Bharatpur 68 27 15N 77 30 E
Bharuch 68 21 47N 73 0 E
Bhatghar L. 70 18 10N 73 48 E
Bhatiapara Ghat 69 23 13N 89 42 E
Bhatinda 68 30 15N 74 57 E
Bhatkal 70 13 58N 74 35 E
Bhatpara 69 22 50N 88 25 E
Bhattiprolu 70 16 7N 80 45 E
Bhaun 68 32 55N 72 40 E
Bhaunagar = Bhavnagar 68 21 45N 72 10 E
Bhavani 70 11 27N 77 43 E
Bhavani → 70 11 0N 78 15 E
Bhavnagar 68 21 45N 72 10 E
Bhawanipatna 70 19 55N 80 10 E
Bhera 68 32 29N 72 57 E
Bhilsa = Vidisha 68 23 28N 77 53 E
Bhilwara 68 25 25N 74 38 E
Bhima → 70 16 25N 77 17 E
Bhimavaram 70 16 30N 81 30 E
Bhind 68 26 30N 78 46 E
Bhir 70 19 4N 75 46 E
Bhiwandi 70 19 20N 73 0 E
Bhiwani 68 28 50N 76 9 E
Bhola 69 22 45N 90 35 E
Bhongir 70 17 30N 78 56 E
Bhopal 68 23 20N 77 30 E
Bhor 70 18 12N 73 53 E
Bhubaneswar 69 20 15N 85 50 E
Bhuj 68 23 15N 69 49 E
Bhumibol Dam 72 17 15N 98 58 E
Bhusaval 68 21 3N 75 46 E
Bhutan ■ 69 27 25N 90 30 E
Biafra, B. of = Bonny, Bight of 85 3 30N 9 20 E
Biak 73 1 10S 136 6 E
Biała 28 50 24N 17 40 E
Biała →, Białystok, Poland 28 53 11N 23 4 E
Biała →, Tarnów, Poland 27 50 3N 20 55 E
Biała Piska 28 53 37N 22 5 E
Biała Podlaska 28 52 4N 23 6 E
Biała Podlaska □ 28 52 0N 23 0 E
Biała Rawska 28 51 48N 20 29 E
Białobrzegi 28 52 27N 21 3 E
Białogard 28 54 2N 15 58 E
Białowieża 28 52 41N 23 49 E
Biały Bór 28 53 53N 16 51 E
Białystok 28 53 10N 23 10 E
Białystok □ 28 53 9N 23 10 E
Biancavilla 41 37 39N 14 50 E
Biaro 73 2 5N 125 26 E
Biarritz 20 43 29N 1 33W
Biasca 25 46 22N 8 58 E
Biba 86 28 55N 31 0 E
Bibala 89 14 44S 13 24 E
Bibane, Bahiret el 83 33 16N 11 13 E
Bibbiena 39 43 43N 11 50 E
Bibby I. 109 61 55N 93 0W
Biberach 25 48 5N 9 49 E
Bibey → 30 42 24N 7 13W
Bibiani 84 6 30N 2 8W
Bibile 70 7 10N 81 25 E
Biboohra 98 16 56S 145 25 E
Bibungwa 90 2 40S 28 15 E
Bic 107 48 20N 68 41W
Bicaj 44 42 0N 20 25 E
Bicaz 46 46 53N 26 5 E
Biccari 41 41 23N 15 12 E
Biche, La → 108 59 57N 123 50W
Bichena 87 10 28N 38 10 E
Bicknell, Ind., U.S.A. 114 38 50N 87 20W
Bicknell, Utah, U.S.A. 119 38 16N 111 35W
Bida 85 9 3N 5 58 E
Bidar 70 17 55N 77 35 E
Biddeford 107 43 30N 70 28W
Biddiyā 62 32 7N 35 4 E
Biddū 62 31 50N 35 8 E
Biddwara 87 5 11N 38 34 E
Bideford 13 51 1N 4 13W
Bidor 71 4 6N 101 15 E
Bié, Planalto de 89 12 0S 16 0 E
Bieber 118 41 4N 121 6W
Biebrza → 28 53 13N 22 25 E
Biecz 27 49 44N 21 15 E
Biel (Bienne) 25 47 8N 7 14 E
Bielawa 28 50 43N 16 37 E
Bielé Karpaty 27 49 5N 18 0 E
Bielefeld 24 52 2N 8 31 E
Bielersee 25 47 6N 7 5 E
Biella 38 45 33N 8 3 E
Bielsk Podlaski 28 52 47N 23 12 E
Bielsko-Biała 27 49 50N 19 2 E
Bielsko-Biała □ 27 49 45N 19 15 E
Bien Hoa 71 10 57N 106 49 E
Bienfait 109 49 10N 102 50W
Bienne = Biel 25 47 8N 7 14 E
Bienvenida 31 38 18N 6 12W
Bienville, L. 106 55 5N 72 40W
Biescas 32 42 37N 0 20W
Biese → 24 52 53N 11 46 E
Biesiesfontein 92 30 57S 17 58 E
Bietigheim 25 48 57N 9 8 E
Biferno → 41 41 59N 15 2 E
Big → 107 54 50N 58 55W
Big B. 107 55 43N 60 35W
Big Beaver 109 49 10N 105 10W
Big Belt Mts. 118 46 50N 111 30W
Big Bend 93 26 50S 32 2 E
Big Bend Nat. Park 117 29 15N 103 15W
Big Black → 117 32 0N 91 5W
Big Blue → 116 39 11N 96 40W
Big Cr. → 108 51 42N 122 41W
Big Cypress Swamp 115 26 12N 81 10W
Big Falls 116 48 11N 93 48W
Big Fork → 116 48 31N 93 43W
Big Horn 118 46 11N 107 25W
Big Horn Mts. = Bighorn Mts. 118 44 30N 107 30W
Big Lake 117 31 12N 101 25W
Big Moose 113 43 49N 74 58W
Big Muddy → 116 48 8N 104 36W
Big Pine 119 37 12N 118 17W
Big Piney 118 42 32N 110 3W
Big Quill L. 109 51 55N 104 50W
Big Rapids 114 43 42N 85 27W
Big River 109 53 50N 107 0W
Big Run 112 40 57N 78 55W
Big Sable Pt. 114 44 5N 86 30W
Big Sand L. 109 57 45N 99 45W
Big Sandy 118 48 12N 110 9W
Big Sandy Cr. → 116 38 6N 102 29W
Big Sioux → 116 42 30N 96 25W
Big Spring 117 32 10N 101 25W
Big Springs 116 41 4N 102 3W
Big Stone City 116 45 20N 96 30W
Big Stone Gap 115 36 52N 82 45W
Big Stone L. 116 45 30N 96 35W
Big Trout L. 106 53 40N 90 0W
Biganos 20 44 39N 0 59W
Bigfork 118 48 3N 114 2W
Biggar, Can. 109 52 4N 108 0W
Biggar, U.K. 14 55 38N 3 31W
Biggenden 99 25 31S 152 4 E
Bighorn → 118 46 9N 107 28W
Bighorn Mts. 118 44 30N 107 30W
Bignona 84 12 52N 16 14W
Bigorre 20 43 6N 0 5 E
Bigstone L. 109 53 42N 95 44W
Bigtimber 118 45 53N 110 0W
Bigwa 90 7 10S 39 10 E
Bihać 39 44 49N 15 57 E
Bihar 69 25 5N 85 40 E
Bihar □ 69 25 0N 86 0 E
Biharamulo 90 2 25S 31 25 E
Biharamulo □ 90 2 30S 31 20 E
Biharkeresztes 27 47 8N 21 44 E
Bihor □ 46 47 0N 22 10 E
Bihor, Munţii 46 46 29N 22 47 E
Bijagós, Arquipélago dos 84 11 15N 16 10W
Bijaipur 68 26 2N 77 20 E
Bijapur, Mad. P., India 70 18 50N 80 50 E
Bijapur, Mysore, India 70 16 50N 75 55 E
Bijār 64 35 52N 47 35 E
Bijeljina 42 44 46N 19 17 E
Bijelo Polje 42 43 1N 19 45 E
Bijie 77 27 20N 105 16 E
Bijnor 68 29 27N 78 11 E
Bikaner 68 28 2N 73 18 E
Bikapur 69 26 30N 82 7 E
Bikin 59 46 50N 134 20 E
Bikini Atoll 94 12 0N 167 30 E
Bikoué 85 3 55N 11 50 E
Bilād Banī Bū 'Alī 65 22 0N 59 20 E
Bilara 68 26 14N 73 53 E
Bilaspur, Mad. P., India 69 22 2N 82 15 E

Bilaspur Bogalusa

Bilaspur, Punjab, India 68 31 19N 76 50 E
Bilauk Taungdan 71 13 0N 99 0 E
Bilbao 32 43 16N 2 56W
Bilbeis 86 30 25N 31 34 E
Bilbor 46 47 6N 25 30 E
Bildudalur 50 65 41N 23 36W
Bileća 42 42 53N 18 27 E
Bilecik 64 40 5N 30 5 E
Biłgoraj 28 50 33N 22 42 E
Bilibino 59 68 3N 166 20 E
Bilibiza 91 12 30 S 40 20 E
Bilir 59 65 40N 131 20 E
Bilishti 44 40 37N 21 2 E
Bill 116 43 18N 105 18W
Billabong Creek 100 35 5 S 144 2 E
Billingham 12 54 36N 1 18W
Billings 118 45 43N 108 29W
Billingsfors 48 58 59N 12 15 E
Billiton Is = Belitung 72 3 10 S 107 50 E
Billom 20 45 43N 3 20 E
Bilma 81 18 50N 13 30 E
Bilo Gora 42 45 53N 17 15 E
Biloela 97 24 24 S 150 31 E
Biloxi 117 30 24N 88 53W
Bilpa Morea Claypan 99 25 0 S 140 0 E
Biltine 81 14 40N 20 50 E
Bilyana 98 18 5 S 145 50 E
Bilyarsk 55 54 58N 50 22 E
Bima 73 8 22 S 118 49 E
Bimban 86 24 24N 32 54 E
Bimberi Peak 100 35 44 S 148 51 E
Bimbila 85 8 54N 0 5 E
Bimbo 88 4 15N 18 33 E
Bimini Is. 121 25 42N 79 25W
Bin Xian 77 35 2N 108 4 E
Bina-Etawah 68 24 13N 78 14 E
Binalbagan 73 10 12N 122 50 E
Binalong 100 34 40 S 148 39 E
Binalud, Kuh-e 65 36 30N 58 30 E
Binatang 72 2 10N 111 40 E
Binche 16 50 26N 4 10 E
Binda 99 27 52 S 147 21 E
Bindle 99 27 40 S 148 45 E
Bindura 91 17 18 S 31 18 E
Bingara, N.S.W., Austral. 99 29 52 S 150 36 E
Bingara, Queens., Austral. 99 28 10 S 144 37 E
Bingen 25 49 57N 7 53 E
Bingerville 84 5 18N 3 49W
Bingham 107 45 5N 69 50W
Bingham Canyon 118 40 31N 112 10W
Binghamton 114 42 9N 75 54W
Bingöl 64 38 53N 40 29 E
Binh Dinh = An Nhon 71 13 55N 109 7 E
Binh Son 71 15 20N 108 40 E
Binjai 72 3 20N 98 30 E
Binnaway 99 31 28 S 149 24 E
Binongko 73 5 55 S 123 55 E
Binscarth 109 50 37N 101 17W
Bint Jubayl 62 33 8N 35 25 E
Bintan 72 1 0N 104 0 E
Bintulu 72 3 10N 113 0 E
Bintuni (Steenkool) 73 2 7 S 133 32 E
Binyamina 62 32 32N 34 56 E
Binyang 77 23 12N 108 47 E
Binz 24 54 23N 13 37 E
Binzert = Bizerte 83 37 15N 9 50 E
Bio Bio □ 124 37 35 S 72 0W
Biograd 39 43 56N 15 29 E
Biokovo 42 43 23N 17 0 E
Biougra 82 30 15N 9 14W
Biq'at Bet Netofa 62 32 49N 35 22 E
Bîr Abu Hashim 86 23 42N 34 6 E
Bîr Abu M'nqar 86 26 33N 27 33 E
Bîr Adal Deib 86 22 35N 36 10 E
Bi'r al Malfa 83 31 58N 15 18 E
Bir Aouine 83 32 25N 9 18 E
Bîr 'Asal 86 25 55N 34 20 E
Bir Autrun 81 18 15N 26 40 E
Bi'r Dhu'fān 83 31 59N 14 32 E
Bîr Diqnash 86 31 3N 25 23 E
Bir el Abbes 82 26 7N 6 9W
Bir el Ater 83 34 46N 8 3 E
Bîr el Basur 86 29 51N 25 49 E
Bîr el Gellaz 86 30 50N 26 40 E
Bîr el Shaqqa 86 30 54N 25 1 E
Bîr Fuad 86 30 35N 26 28 E
Bîr Haimur 86 22 45N 33 40 E
Bir Jdid 82 33 26N 8 0W
Bîr Kanayis 86 24 59N 33 15 E
Bîr Kerawein 86 27 10N 28 25 E
Bir Lahrache 83 32 1N 8 12 E
Bîr Maql 86 23 7N 33 40 E
Bîr Misaha 86 22 13N 27 59 E
Bir Mogrein 82 25 10N 11 25W
Bi'r Mubayrīk 64 23 22N 39 8 E
Bîr Murr 86 23 28N 30 10 E
Bi'r Nabālā 62 31 52N 35 12 E
Bîr Nakheila 86 24 1N 30 50 E
Bîr Qatrani 86 30 55N 26 10 E
Bîr Ranga 86 24 25N 35 15 E
Bir, Ras 87 12 0N 43 20 E
Bîr Sahara 86 22 54N 28 40 E
Bîr Seiyâla 86 26 10N 33 50 E
Bir Semguine 82 30 1N 5 39W
Bîr Shalatein 86 23 5N 35 25 E
Bîr Shebb 86 22 25N 29 40 E
Bîr Shût 86 23 50N 35 15 E
Bîr Terfawi 86 22 57N 28 55 E
Bîr Umm Qubûr 86 24 35N 34 2 E
Bîr Ungât 86 22 8N 33 48 E
Bîr Za'farâna 86 29 10N 32 40 E
Bîr Zāmūs 83 24 16N 15 6 E
Bi'r Zayt 62 31 59N 35 11 E
Bîr Zeidûn 86 25 45N 33 40 E
Bira 73 2 3 S 132 2 E
Bîra 46 47 2N 27 3 E
Birak Sulaymān 62 31 42N 35 7 E
Biramféro 84 11 40N 9 10W
Birao 81 10 20N 22 47 E
Birawa 90 2 20 S 28 48 E
Bîrca 46 43 59N 23 36 E
Birch Hills 109 52 59N 105 25W
Birch I. 109 52 26N 99 54W
Birch L., N.W.T., Can. 108 62 4N 116 33W
Birch L., Ont., Can. 106 51 23N 92 18W
Birch L., U.S.A. 106 47 48N 91 43W
Birch Mts. 108 57 30N 113 10W
Birch River 109 52 24N 101 6W
Birchip 99 35 56 S 142 55 E
Birchiş 46 45 58N 22 9 E
Bird 109 56 30N 94 13W
Bird City 116 39 48N 101 33W
Bird I., Austral. 97 22 10 S 155 28 E
Bird I., S. Afr. 92 32 3 S 18 17 E
Bird I. = Aves, I. de 121 12 0N 67 30W
Birdlip 13 51 50N 2 7W
Birdsville 97 25 51 S 139 20 E
Birdum 96 15 39 S 133 13 E
Birecik 64 37 0N 38 0 E
Bireuen 72 5 14N 96 39 E
Birifo 84 13 30N 14 0W
Birigui 125 21 18 S 50 16W
Birk 86 18 8N 41 30 E
Birka 86 22 11N 40 38 E
Birkenfeld 25 49 39N 7 11 E
Birkenhead 12 53 24N 3 1W
Birket Qârûn 86 29 30N 30 40 E
Birkfeld 26 47 21N 15 45 E
Birkhadem 82 36 43N 3 3 E
Bîrlad 46 46 15N 27 38 E
Birmingham, U.K. 13 52 30N 1 55W
Birmingham, U.S.A. 115 33 31N 86 50W
Birmitrapur 69 22 24N 84 46 E
Birni Ngaouré 85 13 5N 2 51 E
Birni Nkonni 85 13 55N 5 15 E
Birnin Gwari 85 11 0N 6 45 E
Birnin Kebbi 85 12 32N 4 12 E
Birnin Kudu 85 11 30N 9 29 E
Birobidzhan 59 48 50N 132 50 E
Birqîn 62 32 27N 35 15 E
Birr 15 53 7N 7 55W
Birrie → 99 29 43 S 146 37 E
Birsilpur 68 28 11N 72 15 E
Birsk 52 55 25N 55 30 E
Birtin 46 46 59N 22 31 E
Birtle 109 50 30N 101 5W
Biryuchiy 56 46 10N 35 0 E
Birzai 54 56 11N 24 45 E
Bîrzava 46 46 7N 21 59 E
Bisa 73 1 15 S 127 28 E
Bisáccia 41 41 0N 15 20 E
Bisacquino 40 37 42N 13 13 E
Bisalpur 69 28 14N 79 48 E
Bisbal, La 32 41 58N 3 2 E
Bisbee 119 31 30N 110 0W
Biscarrosse, Étang de 20 44 21N 1 10W
Biscay, B. of 6 45 0N 2 0W
Biscayne B. 115 25 40N 80 12W
Bisceglie 41 41 14N 16 30 E
Bischofshofen 26 47 26N 13 14 E
Bischofswerda 24 51 8N 14 11 E
Bischwiller 19 48 41N 7 50 E
Biscoe Bay 5 77 0 S 152 0W
Biscoe I. 5 66 0 S 67 0W
Biscostasing 106 47 18N 82 9W
Biševo 39 42 57N 16 3 E
Bisha 87 15 30N 37 31 E
Bisha, Wadi → 86 21 24N 43 26 E
Bishop, Calif., U.S.A. 119 37 20N 118 26W
Bishop, Tex., U.S.A. 117 27 35N 97 49W
Bishop Auckland 12 54 40N 1 40W
Bishop's Falls 107 49 2N 55 30W
Bishop's Stortford 13 51 52N 0 11 E
Bisignano 41 39 30N 16 17 E
Bisina, L. 90 1 38N 33 56 E
Biskra 83 34 50N 5 44 E
Biskupiec 28 53 53N 20 58 E
Bislig 73 8 15N 126 27 E
Bismarck 116 46 49N 100 49W
Bismarck Arch. 94 2 30 S 150 0 E
Bismarck Sea 98 4 10 S 146 50 E
Bismark 24 52 39N 11 31 E
Biso 90 1 44N 31 26 E
Bison 116 45 34N 102 28W
Bispfors 50 63 1N 16 37 E
Bispgården 48 63 2N 16 40 E
Bissagos = Bijagós, Arquipélago dos 84 11 15N 16 10W
Bissau 84 11 45N 15 45W
Bissett 109 51 2N 95 41W
Bissikrima 84 10 50N 10 58W
Bistcho L. 108 59 45N 118 50W
Bistreţu 46 43 54N 23 23 E
Bistrica = Ilirska-Bistrica 39 45 34N 14 14 E
Bistriţa 46 47 9N 24 35 E
Bistriţa → 46 46 30N 26 57 E
Bistriţa Năsăud □ 46 47 15N 24 30 E
Bistriţei, Munţii 46 47 15N 25 40 E
Biswan 69 27 29N 81 2 E
Bisztynek 28 54 8N 20 53 E
Bitam 88 2 5N 11 25 E
Bitburg 25 49 58N 6 32 E
Bitche 19 49 2N 7 25 E
Bitkine 81 11 59N 18 13 E
Bitlis 64 38 20N 42 3 E
Bitola (Bitolj) 42 41 5N 21 10 E
Bitonto 41 41 7N 16 40 E
Bitter Creek 118 41 39N 108 36W
Bitter L. = Buheirat-Murrat-el-Kubra 86 30 15N 32 40 E
Bitterfeld 24 51 36N 12 20 E
Bitterfontein 92 31 0 S 18 32 E
Bitterroot → 118 46 52N 114 6W
Bitterroot Range 118 46 0N 114 20W
Bitti 40 40 29N 9 20 E
Bittou 85 11 17N 0 18W
Biu 85 10 40N 12 3 E
Bivolari 46 47 31N 27 27 E
Bivolu 46 47 16N 25 58 E
Biwa-Ko 74 35 15N 136 10 E
Biwabik 116 47 33N 92 19W
Bixad 46 47 56N 23 28 E
Biyang 77 32 38N 113 21 E
Biysk 58 52 40N 85 0 E
Bizana 93 30 50 S 29 52 E
Bizerte (Binzert) 83 37 15N 9 50 E
Bjargtangar 50 65 30N 24 30W
Bjelasica 42 42 50N 19 40 E
Bjelašnica 42 43 43N 18 9 E
Bjelovar 42 45 56N 16 49 E
Bjerringbro 49 56 23N 9 39 E
Björbo 48 60 27N 14 44 E
Björneborg 48 59 14N 14 16 E
Bjørnøya 4 74 30N 19 0 E
Bjuv 49 56 5N 12 55 E
Blace 42 43 18N 21 17 E
Blachownia 28 50 49N 18 56 E
Black →, Can. 112 44 42N 79 19W
Black →, Ark., U.S.A. 117 35 38N 91 19W
Black →, N.Y., U.S.A. 113 43 59N 76 4W
Black →, Wis., U.S.A. 116 43 52N 91 22W
Black Diamond 108 50 45N 114 14W
Black Forest = Schwarzwald 25 48 0N 8 0 E
Black Hills 116 44 0N 103 50W
Black I. 109 51 12N 96 30W
Black L., Can. 109 59 12N 105 15W
Black L., U.S.A. 114 45 28N 84 15W
Black Mesa, Mt. 117 36 57N 102 55W
Black Mt. = Mynydd Du 13 51 45N 3 45W
Black Mts. 13 51 52N 3 5W
Black Range 119 33 30N 107 55W
Black River 121 18 0N 77 50W
Black River Falls 116 44 23N 90 52W
Black Sea 9 43 30N 35 0 E
Black Sugarloaf, Mt. 100 31 18 S 151 35 E
Black Volta → 84 8 41N 1 33W
Black Warrior → 115 32 32N 87 51W
Blackall 97 24 25 S 145 45 E
Blackball 101 42 22 S 171 26 E
Blackbull 98 17 55 S 141 45 E
Blackburn 12 53 44N 2 30W
Blackduck 116 47 43N 94 32W
Blackfoot 118 43 13N 112 12W
Blackfoot → 118 46 52N 113 53W
Blackfoot River Res. 118 43 0N 111 35W
Blackie 108 50 36N 113 37W
Blackpool 12 53 48N 3 3W
Blackriver 112 44 46N 83 17W
Blacks Harbour 107 45 3N 66 49W
Blacksburg 114 37 17N 80 23W
Blacksod B. 15 54 6N 10 0W
Blackstone 114 37 6N 78 0W
Blackstone → 108 61 5N 122 55W
Blackstone Ra. 96 26 00 S 129 00 E
Blackville 107 46 44N 65 50W
Blackwater 98 23 35 S 148 53 E
Blackwater →, Ireland 15 51 55N 7 50W
Blackwater →, U.K. 15 54 31N 6 35W
Blackwater Cr. → 99 25 56 S 144 30 E
Blackwell 117 36 55N 97 20W
Blaenau Ffestiniog 12 53 0N 3 57W
Blagaj 42 43 16N 17 55 E
Blagodarnoye 57 45 7N 43 37 E
Blagoevgrad (Gorna Dzhumayo) 42 42 2N 23 5 E
Blagoveshchensk 59 50 20N 127 30 E
Blain 18 47 29N 1 45W
Blaine 118 48 59N 122 43W
Blaine Lake 109 52 51N 106 52W
Blainville 19 48 33N 6 23 E
Blair 116 41 38N 96 10W
Blair Athol 97 22 42 S 147 31 E
Blair Atholl 14 56 46N 3 50W
Blairgowrie 14 56 36N 3 20W
Blairmore 108 49 40N 114 25W
Blairsville 112 40 27N 79 15W
Blaj 46 46 10N 23 57 E
Blake Pt. 116 48 12N 88 27W
Blakely 115 31 22N 85 0W
Blâmont 19 48 35N 6 50 E
Blanc, C. 83 37 15N 9 56 E
Blanc, Le 20 46 37N 1 3 E
Blanc, Mont 21 45 48N 6 50 E
Blanca, Bahía 128 39 10 S 61 30W
Blanca Peak 119 37 35N 105 29W
Blanchard 117 35 8N 97 40W
Blanche L., S. Austral., Austral. 97 29 15 S 139 40 E
Blanche L., W. Austral., Austral. 96 22 25 S 123 17 E
Blanco, S. Afr. 92 33 55 S 22 23 E
Blanco, U.S.A. 117 30 7N 98 30W
Blanco → 124 30 20 S 68 42W
Blanco, C., C. Rica 121 9 34N 85 8W
Blanco, C., Spain 33 39 21N 2 51 E
Blanco, C., U.S.A. 118 42 50N 124 40W
Blanda → 50 65 20N 19 40W
Blandford Forum 13 50 52N 2 10W
Blanding 119 37 35N 109 30W
Blanes 32 41 40N 2 48 E
Blanice → 26 49 10N 14 5 E
Blankenberge 16 51 20N 3 9 E
Blankenburg 24 51 46N 10 56 E
Blanquefort 20 44 55N 0 38W
Blanquillo 125 32 53 S 55 37W
Blansko 27 49 22N 16 40 E
Blantyre 91 15 45 S 35 0 E
Blarney 15 51 57N 8 35W
Błaski 28 51 38N 18 30 E
Blatná 26 49 25N 13 52 E
Blatnitsa 43 43 41N 28 32 E
Blato 39 42 56N 16 48 E
Blaubeuren 25 48 24N 9 47 E
Blaydon 12 54 56N 1 47W
Blaye 20 45 8N 0 40W
Blaye-les-Mines 20 44 1N 2 8 E
Blayney 99 33 32 S 149 14 E
Blaze, Pt. 96 12 56 S 130 11 E
Błażowa 27 49 53N 22 7 E
Bleckede 24 53 18N 10 43 E
Bled 39 46 27N 14 7 E
Blednaya, Gora 58 76 20N 65 0 E
Bleiburg 26 46 35N 14 49 E
Blejeşti 46 44 19N 25 27 E
Blekinge län □ 49 56 20N 15 20 E
Blenheim, Can. 112 42 20N 82 0W
Blenheim, N.Z. 101 41 38 S 173 57 E
Bléone → 21 44 5N 6 0 E
Bletchley 13 51 59N 0 44W
Bleymard, Le 20 44 30N 3 42 E
Blida 82 36 30N 2 49 E
Blidet Amor 83 32 59N 5 58 E
Blidö 48 59 37N 18 53 E
Blidsberg 49 57 56N 13 30 E
Bligh Sound 101 44 47 S 167 32 E
Blind River 106 46 10N 82 58W
Blinishti 44 41 52N 19 58 E
Blitar 73 8 5 S 112 11 E
Blitta 85 8 23N 1 6 E
Block I. 114 41 11N 71 35W
Block Island Sd. 113 41 17N 71 35W
Bloemfontein 92 29 6 S 26 14 E
Bloemhof 92 27 38 S 25 32 E
Blois 18 47 35N 1 20 E
Blomskog 48 59 16N 12 2 E
Blönduós 50 65 40N 20 12W
Błonie 28 52 12N 20 37 E
Bloodvein → 109 51 47N 96 43W
Bloody Foreland 15 55 10N 8 18W
Bloomer 116 45 8N 91 30W
Bloomfield, Can. 112 43 59N 77 14W
Bloomfield, Iowa, U.S.A. 116 40 44N 92 26W
Bloomfield, N. Mexico, U.S.A. 119 36 46N 107 59W
Bloomfield, Nebr., U.S.A. 116 42 38N 97 40W
Bloomfield River Mission 98 15 56 S 145 22 E
Bloomington, Ill., U.S.A. 116 40 27N 89 0W
Bloomington, Ind., U.S.A. 114 39 10N 86 30W
Bloomsburg 114 41 0N 76 30W
Blora 73 6 57 S 111 25 E
Blossburg 112 41 40N 77 4W
Blouberg 93 23 8 S 29 0 E
Blountstown 115 30 28N 85 5W
Bludenz 26 47 10N 9 50 E
Blue Island 114 41 40N 87 40W
Blue Lake 118 40 53N 124 0W
Blue Mesa Res. 119 38 30N 107 15W
Blue Mts., Austral. 97 33 40 S 150 0 E
Blue Mts., Ore., U.S.A. 118 45 15N 119 0W
Blue Mts., Pa., U.S.A. 114 40 30N 76 30W
Blue Mud B. 97 13 30 S 136 0 E
Blue Nile = An Nîl el Azraq □ 87 12 30N 34 30 E
Blue Nile = Nîl el Azraq → 87 15 38N 32 31 E
Blue Rapids 116 39 41N 96 39W
Blue Ridge Mts. 115 36 30N 80 15W
Blue Stack Mts. 15 54 46N 8 5W
Blueberry → 108 56 45N 120 49W
Bluefield 114 37 18N 81 14W
Bluefields 121 12 20N 83 50W
Bluff, Austral. 98 23 35 S 149 4 E
Bluff, N.Z. 101 46 37 S 168 20 E
Bluff, U.S.A. 119 37 17N 109 33W
Bluffton 114 40 43N 85 9W
Blumenau 125 27 0 S 49 0W
Blumenthal 24 53 5N 8 20 E
Blunt 116 44 32N 100 0W
Bly 118 42 23N 121 0W
Blyberg 48 61 9N 14 11 E
Blyth, Can. 112 43 44N 81 26W
Blyth, U.K. 12 55 8N 1 32W
Blythe 119 33 40N 114 33W
Blytheswood 112 42 8N 82 37W
Bø 47 59 25N 9 3 E
Bo 84 7 55N 11 50W
Bo Duc 71 11 58N 106 50 E
Bo Hai 76 39 0N 120 0 E
Bo Xian 77 33 50N 115 45 E
Boa Vista 126 2 48N 60 30W
Boaco 121 12 29N 85 35W
Boal 30 43 25N 6 49W
Boatman 99 27 16 S 146 55 E
Bobai 77 22 17N 109 59 E
Bobbili 70 18 35N 83 30 E
Bòbbio 38 44 47N 9 22 E
Bobcaygeon 106 44 33N 78 33W
Böblingen 25 48 41N 9 1 E
Bobo-Dioulasso 84 11 8N 4 13W
Boboc 43 45 13N 26 59 E
Bobolice 28 53 58N 16 37 E
Boboshevo 42 42 9N 23 0 E
Bobov Dol 42 42 20N 23 0 E
Bóbr → 28 52 4N 15 4 E
Bobraomby, Tanjon' i 93 12 40 S 49 10 E
Bobrinets 56 48 4N 32 5 E
Bobrov 55 51 5N 40 2 E
Bobruysk 54 53 10N 29 15 E
Bôca do Acre 126 8 50 S 67 27W
Boca, La 120 8 56N 79 30W
Boca Raton 115 26 21N 80 5W
Bocaiúva 127 17 7 S 43 49W
Bocanda 84 7 5N 4 31W
Bocaranga 88 7 0N 15 35 E
Bocas del Toro 121 9 15N 82 20W
Boceguillas 32 41 20N 3 39W
Bochnia 27 49 58N 20 27 E
Bocholt 24 51 50N 6 35 E
Bochov 26 50 9N 13 3 E
Bochum 24 51 28N 7 12 E
Bockenem 24 52 1N 10 8 E
Boćki 28 52 39N 23 3 E
Bocşa Montană 42 45 21N 21 47 E
Boda 88 4 19N 17 26 E
Böda 49 57 15N 17 3 E
Bodafors 49 57 48N 14 23 E
Bodaybo 59 57 50N 114 0 E
Boden 50 65 50N 21 42 E
Bodensee 25 47 35N 9 25 E
Bodenteich 24 52 49N 10 41 E
Bodhan 70 18 40N 77 44 E
Bodinayakkanur 70 10 2N 77 10 E
Bodinga 85 12 58N 5 10 E
Bodmin 13 50 28N 4 44W
Bodmin Moor 13 50 33N 4 36W
Bodrog → 27 48 15N 21 35 E
Bodrum 64 37 5N 27 30 E
Bódva → 27 48 19N 20 45 E
Boegoebergdam 92 29 7 S 22 9 E
Boën 21 45 44N 4 0 E
Boende 88 0 24 S 21 12 E
Boerne 117 29 48N 98 41W
Boffa 84 10 16N 14 3W
Bogalusa 117 30 50N 89 55W

Bogan **Brabant L.**

Bogan → 97 29 59 S 146 17 E
Bogan Gate 99 33 7 S 147 49 E
Bogantungan 98 23 41 S 147 17 E
Bogata 117 33 26N 95 10W
Bogatić 42 44 51N 19 30 E
Bogenfels 92 27 25 S 15 25 E
Bogense 49 55 34N 10 5 E
Boggabilla 99 28 36 S 150 24 E
Boggabri 99 30 45 S 150 0 E
Boggeragh Mts. 15 52 2N 8 55W
Bognor Regis 13 50 47N 0 40W
Bogø 49 54 55N 12 2 E
Bogo 73 11 3N 124 0 E
Bogodukhov 54 50 9N 35 33 E
Bogong, Mt. 97 36 47 S 147 17 E
Bogor 73 6 36 S 106 48 E
Bogoroditsk 55 53 47N 38 8 E
Bogorodsk 55 56 4N 43 30 E
Bogorodskoye 59 52 22N 140 30 E
Bogoso 84 5 38N 2 3W
Bogota 126 4 34N 74 0W
Bogotol 58 56 15N 89 50 E
Bogra 69 24 51N 89 22 E
Boguchany 59 58 40N 97 30 E
Boguchar 57 49 55N 40 32 E
Bogué 84 16 45N 14 10W
Boguslav 56 49 47N 30 53 E
Boguszów 28 50 45N 16 12 E
Bohain 19 49 59N 3 28 E
Bohemia 26 50 0N 14 0 E
Bohemian Forest = Böhmerwald 25 49 30N 12 40 E
Bohena Cr. → 99 30 17 S 149 42 E
Bohinjska Bistrica 39 46 17N 14 1 E
Böhmerwald 25 49 30N 12 40 E
Bohmte 24 52 24N 8 20 E
Bohol 73 9 50N 124 10 E
Bohotleh 63 8 20N 46 25 E
Boi 85 9 35N 9 27 E
Boi, Pta. de 125 23 55 S 45 15W
Boiano 41 41 28N 14 29 E
Boileau, C. 96 17 40 S 122 7 E
Boinitsa 42 43 58N 22 32 E
Boise 118 43 43N 116 9W
Boise City 117 36 45N 102 30W
Boissevain 109 49 15N 100 5W
Boite → 39 46 5N 12 5 E
Boitzenburg 24 53 16N 13 36 E
Boizenburg 24 53 22N 10 42 E
Bojador C. 80 26 0N 14 30W
Bojana → 42 41 52N 19 22 E
Bojanowo 28 51 43N 16 42 E
Bojnūrd 65 37 30N 57 20 E
Bojonegoro 73 7 11 S 111 54 E
Boju 85 7 22N 7 55 E
Boka 42 45 22N 20 52 E
Boka Kotorska 42 42 23N 18 32 E
Bokala 84 8 31N 4 33W
Boké 84 10 56N 14 17W
Bokhara → 99 29 55 S 146 42 E
Bokkos 85 9 17N 9 1 E
Boknafjorden 47 59 14N 5 40 E
Bokoro 81 12 25N 17 14 E
Bokote 88 0 12 S 21 8 E
Bokpyin 71 11 18N 98 42 E
Boksitogorsk 54 59 32N 33 56 E
Bokungu 88 0 35 S 22 50 E
Bol, Chad 81 13 30N 15 0 E
Bol, Yugo. 39 43 18N 16 38 E
Bolama 84 11 30N 15 30W
Bolan Pass 66 29 50N 67 20 E
Bolaños → 120 21 14N 104 8W
Bolbec 18 49 30N 0 30 E
Boldeşti 46 45 3N 26 2 E
Bole, China 75 45 11N 81 37 E
Bole, Ethiopia 87 6 36N 37 20 E
Bolekhov 54 49 0N 24 0 E
Bolesławiec 28 51 17N 15 37 E
Bolgatanga 85 10 44N 0 53W
Bolgrad 56 45 40N 28 32 E
Boli, China 76 45 46N 130 31 E
Boli, Sudan 87 6 2N 28 48 E
Bolinao C. 73 16 23N 119 55 E
Bolívar, Argent. 124 36 15 S 60 53W
Bolívar, Colomb. 126 2 0N 77 0W
Bolivar, Mo., U.S.A. 117 37 38N 93 22W
Bolivar, Tenn., U.S.A. 117 35 14N 89 0W
Bolivia ■ 126 17 6 S 64 0W
Boljevac 42 43 51N 21 58 E
Bolkhov 55 53 25N 36 0 E
Bollène 21 44 18N 4 45 E
Bollnäs 48 61 21N 16 24 E
Bollon 99 28 2 S 147 29 E
Bollstabruk 48 63 1N 17 40 E
Bollullos 31 37 19N 6 32W
Bolmen 49 56 55N 13 40 E
Bolobo 88 2 6 S 16 20 E
Bologna 39 44 30N 11 20 E
Bologne 19 48 10N 5 8 E
Bologoye 54 57 55N 34 0 E
Bolomba 88 0 35N 19 0 E
Bolong 73 7 6N 122 16 E
Boloven, Cao Nguyen 71 15 10N 106 30 E
Bolpur 69 23 40N 87 45 E
Bolsena 39 42 40N 11 58 E
Bolsena, L. di 39 42 35N 11 55 E
Bolshaya Glushitsa 55 52 24N 50 29 E
Bolshaya Martynovka 57 47 12N 41 46 E
Bolshaya Vradiyevka 56 47 50N 30 40 E
Bolshereche 58 56 4N 74 45 E
Bolshevik, Ostrov 59 78 30N 102 0 E
Bolshezemelskaya Tundra 52 67 0N 56 0 E
Bolshoi Kavkas 57 42 50N 44 0 E
Bolshoy Anyuy → 59 68 30N 160 49 E
Bolshoy Atlym 58 62 25N 66 50 E
Bolshoy Begichev, Ostrov 59 74 20N 112 30 E
Bolshoy Lyakhovskiy, Ostrov 59 73 35N 142 0 E
Bolshoy Tokmak 56 47 16N 35 42 E
Bol'shoy Tyuters, Ostrov 54 59 51N 27 13 E
Bolsward 16 53 3N 5 32 E
Boltaña 32 42 28N 0 4 E
Boltigen 25 46 38N 7 24 E
Bolton, Can. 112 43 54N 79 45W
Bolton, U.K. 12 53 35N 2 26W
Bolu 64 40 45N 31 35 E
Bolvadin 64 38 45N 31 4 E
Bolzano (Bozen) 39 46 30N 11 20 E
Bom Despacho 127 19 43 S 45 15W
Bom Jesus da Lapa 127 13 15 S 43 25W
Boma 88 5 50 S 13 4 E
Bomaderry 99 34 52 S 150 37 E
Bombala 97 36 56 S 149 15 E
Bombarral 31 39 15N 9 9W
Bombay 70 18 55N 72 50 E
Bomboma 88 2 25N 18 55 E
Bombombwa 90 1 40N 25 40 E
Bomi Hills 84 7 1N 10 38W
Bomili 90 1 45N 27 5 E
Bomokandi → 90 3 39N 26 8 E
Bomongo 88 1 27N 18 21 E
Bomu → 88 4 40N 23 30 E
Bon C. 83 37 1N 11 2 E
Bonaire 121 12 10N 68 15W
Bonang 99 37 11 S 148 41 E
Bonanza 121 13 54N 84 35W
Bonaparte Archipelago 96 14 0 S 124 30 E
Boñar 30 42 52N 5 19W
Bonaventure 107 48 5N 65 32W
Bonavista 107 48 40N 53 5W
Bonavista, C. 107 48 42N 53 5W
Bondeno 39 44 53N 11 22 E
Bondo 88 3 55N 23 53 E
Bondoukou 84 8 2N 2 47W
Bondowoso 73 7 56 S 113 49 E
Bone Rate 73 7 25 S 121 5 E
Bone Rate, Kepulauan 73 6 30 S 121 10 E
Bone, Teluk 73 4 10 S 120 50 E
Bonefro 41 41 42N 14 55 E
Bo'ness 14 56 0N 3 38W
Bong Son = Hoai Nhon 71 14 28N 109 1 E
Bongandanga 88 1 24N 21 3 E
Bongor 81 10 35N 15 20 E
Bongouanou 84 6 42N 4 15W
Bonham 117 33 30N 96 10W
Bonifacio 21 41 24N 9 10 E
Bonifacio, Bouches de 40 41 12N 9 15 E
Bonin Is. 94 27 0N 142 0 E
Bonke 87 6 5N 37 16 E
Bonn 24 50 43N 7 6 E
Bonnat 20 46 20N 1 54 E
Bonne Terre 117 37 57N 90 33W
Bonners Ferry 118 48 38N 116 21W
Bonnétable 18 48 11N 0 25 E
Bonneuil-Matours 18 46 41N 0 34 E
Bonneval 18 48 11N 1 24 E
Bonneville 21 46 5N 6 24 E
Bonney, L. 99 37 50 S 140 20 E
Bonnie Rock 96 30 29 S 118 22 E
Bonny, France 19 47 34N 2 50 E
Bonny, Nigeria 85 4 25N 7 13 E
Bonny → 85 4 20N 7 10 E
Bonny, Bight of 88 3 30N 9 20 E
Bonnyville 109 54 20N 110 45W
Bonoi 73 1 45 S 137 41 E
Bonorva 40 40 25N 8 47 E
Bontang 72 0 10N 117 30 E
Bonthain 73 5 34 S 119 56 E
Bonthe 84 7 30N 12 33W
Bontoc 73 17 7N 120 58 E
Bonyeri 84 5 1N 2 46W
Bonyhád 27 46 18N 18 32 E
Booker 117 36 29N 100 30W
Boolaboolka, L. 99 32 38 S 143 10 E
Booligal 99 33 58 S 144 53 E
Boom 16 51 6N 4 20 E
Boonah 99 27 58 S 152 41 E
Boone, Iowa, U.S.A. 116 42 5N 93 53W
Boone, N.C., U.S.A. 115 36 14N 81 43W
Booneville, Ark., U.S.A. 117 35 10N 93 54W
Booneville, Miss., U.S.A. 115 34 39N 88 34W
Boonville, Ind., U.S.A. 114 38 3N 87 13W
Boonville, Mo., U.S.A. 116 38 57N 92 45W
Boonville, N.Y., U.S.A. 114 43 31N 75 20W
Boorindal 99 30 22 S 146 11 E
Boorowa 99 34 28 S 148 44 E
Boothia, Gulf of 105 71 0N 90 0W
Boothia Pen. 104 71 0N 94 0W
Bootle, Cumb., U.K. 12 54 17N 3 24W
Bootle, Merseyside, U.K. 12 53 28N 3 1W
Booué 88 0 5 S 11 55 E
Bopeechee 99 29 36 S 137 22 E
Bophuthatswana □ 92 26 0 S 26 0 E
Boppard 25 50 13N 7 36 E
Boquete 121 8 49N 82 27W
Bor 26 49 41N 12 45 E
Bôr 87 6 10N 31 40 E
Bor, Sweden 49 57 9N 14 10 E
Bor, Yugo. 42 44 8N 22 7 E
Borah, Mt. 118 44 19N 113 46W
Borama 63 9 55N 43 7 E
Borang 87 4 50N 30 59 E
Borås 49 57 43N 12 56 E
Borāzjān 65 29 22N 51 10 E
Borba, Brazil 126 4 12 S 59 34W
Borba, Port. 31 38 50N 7 26W
Borçka 57 41 25N 41 41 E
Bordeaux 20 44 50N 0 36W
Borden 107 46 18N 63 47W
Borden I. 4 78 30N 111 30W
Borders □ 14 55 35N 2 50W
Bordertown 97 36 19 S 140 45 E
Borðeyri 50 65 12N 21 6W
Bordighera 38 43 47N 7 40 E
Bordj bou Arreridj 83 36 4N 4 45 E
Bordj Bourguiba 83 32 12N 10 2 E
Bordj el Hobra 83 32 9N 4 51 E
Bordj Fly Ste. Marie 82 27 19N 2 32W
Bordj-in-Eker 83 24 9N 5 3 E
Bordj Menaiel 83 36 46N 3 43 E
Bordj Messouda 83 30 12N 9 25 E
Bordj Nili 83 33 28N 3 2 E
Bordj Omar Driss 83 28 10N 6 40 E
Bordj Zelfana 83 32 27N 4 15 E
Borek Wielkopolski 28 51 54N 17 11 E
Borensberg 49 58 34N 15 17 E
Borgarnes 50 64 32N 21 55W
Børgefjellet 50 65 20N 13 45 E
Borger, Neth. 16 52 54N 6 44 E
Borger, U.S.A. 117 35 40N 101 20W
Borghamn 49 58 23N 14 41 E
Borgholm 49 56 52N 16 39 E
Bórgia 41 38 50N 16 30 E
Borgo San Dalmazzo 38 44 19N 7 29 E
Borgo San Lorenzo 39 43 57N 11 21 E
Borgo Valsugano 39 46 3N 11 27 E
Borgomanero 38 45 41N 8 28 E
Borgonovo Val Tidone 38 45 1N 9 28 E
Borgorose 39 42 12N 13 14 E
Borgosésia 38 45 43N 8 17 E
Borgvattnet 48 63 26N 15 48 E
Borislav 54 49 18N 23 28 E
Borisoglebsk 55 51 27N 42 5 E
Borisoglebskiy 55 56 28N 43 59 E
Borisov 54 54 17N 28 28 E
Borispol 54 50 21N 30 59 E
Borja, Peru 126 4 20 S 77 40W
Borja, Spain 32 41 48N 1 34W
Borjas Blancas 32 41 31N 0 52 E
Borken 24 51 51N 6 52 E
Borkou 81 18 15N 18 50 E
Borkum 24 53 36N 6 42 E
Borlänge 48 60 29N 15 26 E
Borley, C. 5 66 15 S 52 30 E
Bormida → 38 44 23N 8 13 E
Bórmio 38 46 28N 10 22 E
Borna 24 51 8N 12 31 E
Borneo 72 1 0N 115 0 E
Bornholm 49 55 10N 15 0 E
Bornholmsgattet 49 55 15N 14 20 E
Borno □ 85 12 30N 12 30 E
Bornos 31 36 48N 5 42W
Bornu Yassa 85 12 14N 12 25 E
Borobudur 73 7 36 S 110 13 E
Borodino 54 55 31N 35 40 E
Borogontsy 59 62 42N 131 8 E
Boromo 84 11 45N 2 58W
Borongan 73 11 37N 125 26 E
Bororen 98 24 13 S 151 33 E
Borotangba Mts. 87 6 30N 25 0 E
Borovan 43 43 27N 23 45 E
Borovichi 54 58 25N 33 55 E
Borovsk 55 55 12N 36 24 E
Borrby 49 55 27N 14 10 E
Borriol 32 40 4N 0 4W
Borroloola 97 16 4 S 136 17 E
Borşa 46 47 41N 24 50 E
Borsod-Abaúj-Zemplén □ 27 48 20N 21 0 E
Bort-les-Orgues 20 45 24N 2 29 E
Borth 13 52 29N 4 3W
Borujerd 64 33 55N 48 50 E
Borzhomi 57 41 48N 43 28 E
Borzna 54 51 18N 32 26 E
Borzya 59 50 24N 116 31 E
Bosa 40 40 17N 8 32 E
Bosanska Brod 42 45 10N 18 0 E
Bosanska Dubica 39 45 10N 16 50 E
Bosanska Gradiška 42 45 10N 17 15 E
Bosanska Kostajnica 39 45 11N 16 33 E
Bosanska Krupa 39 44 53N 16 10 E
Bosanski Novi 39 45 2N 16 22 E
Bosanski Samac 42 45 3N 18 29 E
Bosansko Grahovo 39 44 12N 16 26 E
Bosansko Petrovac 39 44 35N 16 21 E
Bosaso 63 11 12N 49 18 E
Boscastle 13 50 42N 4 42W
Boscotrecase 41 40 46N 14 28 E
Bose 77 23 53N 106 35 E
Boshan 76 36 28N 117 49 E
Boshoek 92 25 30 S 27 9 E
Boshof 92 28 31 S 25 13 E
Boshrūyeh 65 33 50N 57 30 E
Bosilegrad 42 42 30N 22 27 E
Boskovice 27 49 29N 16 40 E
Bosna → 42 45 4N 18 29 E
Bosna i Hercegovina □ 42 44 0N 18 0 E
Bosnia = Bosna □ 42 44 0N 18 0 E
Bosnik 73 1 5 S 136 10 E
Bōsō-Hantō 74 35 20N 140 20 E
Bosobolo 88 4 15N 19 50 E
Bosporus = Karadeniz Boğazı 64 41 10N 29 10 E
Bossangoa 88 6 35N 17 30 E
Bossekop 50 69 57N 23 15 E
Bossembélé 81 5 25N 17 40 E
Bossier City 117 32 28N 93 48W
Bosso 85 13 43N 13 19 E
Bossut C. 96 18 42 S 121 35 E
Bosten Hu 75 41 55N 87 40 E
Boston, U.K. 12 52 59N 0 2W
Boston, U.S.A. 114 42 20N 71 0W
Boston Bar 108 49 52N 121 30W
Bosut → 42 45 20N 19 0 E
Boswell, Can. 108 49 28N 116 45W
Boswell, Okla., U.S.A. 117 34 1N 95 50W
Boswell, Pa., U.S.A. 112 40 9N 79 2W
Botad 68 22 15N 71 40 E
Botevgrad 43 42 55N 23 47 E
Bothaville 92 27 23 S 26 34 E
Bothnia, G. of 50 63 0N 20 0 E
Bothwell, Austral. 99 42 20 S 147 1 E
Bothwell, Can. 112 42 38N 81 52W
Boticas 30 41 41N 7 40W
Botletle → 92 20 10 S 23 15 E
Botoroaga 46 44 8N 25 32 E
Botoşani 46 47 42N 26 41 E
Botoşani □ 46 47 50N 26 50 E
Botro 84 7 51N 5 19W
Botswana ■ 92 22 0 S 24 0 E
Bottineau 116 48 49N 100 25W
Bottrop 24 51 34N 6 59 E
Botucatu 125 22 55 S 48 30W
Botwood 107 49 6N 55 23W
Bou Alam 82 33 50N 1 26 E
Bou Ali 82 27 11N 0 4W
Bou Djébéha 84 18 25N 2 45W
Bou Guema 82 28 49N 0 19 E
Bou Ismael 82 36 38N 2 42 E
Bou Izakarn 82 29 12N 9 46W
Bou Saâda 83 35 11N 4 9 E
Bou Salem 83 36 45N 9 2 E
Bouaké 84 7 40N 5 2W
Bouar 88 6 0N 15 40 E
Bouârfa 82 32 32N 1 58 E
Bouca 88 6 45N 18 25 E
Boucau 20 43 32N 1 29W
Bouches-du-Rhône □ 21 43 37N 5 2 E
Bouda 82 27 50N 0 27W
Boudenib 82 31 59N 3 31W
Boufarik 82 36 34N 2 58 E
Bougainville C. 96 13 57 S 126 4 E
Bougaroun, C. 83 37 6N 6 30 E
Bougie = Bejaia 83 36 42N 5 2 E
Bougouni 84 11 30N 7 20W
Bouillon 16 49 44N 5 3 E
Bouïra 83 36 20N 3 59 E
Boulder, Austral. 96 30 46 S 121 30 E
Boulder, Colo., U.S.A. 116 40 3N 105 10W
Boulder, Mont., U.S.A. 118 46 14N 112 4W
Boulder City 119 36 0N 114 50W
Boulder Dam = Hoover Dam 119 36 0N 114 45W
Bouli 84 15 17N 12 18W
Boulia 97 22 52 S 139 51 E
Bouligny 19 49 17N 5 45 E
Boulogne → 18 47 12N 1 47W
Boulogne-sur-Gesse 20 43 18N 0 38 E
Boulogne-sur-Mer 19 50 42N 1 36 E
Bouloire 18 47 58N 0 33 E
Boulsa 85 12 39N 0 34W
Boultoum 85 14 45N 10 25 E
Boumalne 82 31 25N 6 0W
Bouna 84 9 10N 3 0W
Boundiali 84 9 30N 6 20W
Bountiful 118 40 57N 111 58W
Bounty I. 94 48 0 S 178 30 E
Bourbon-Lancy 20 46 37N 3 45 E
Bourbon-l'Archambault 20 46 36N 3 4 E
Bourbonnais 20 46 28N 3 0 E
Bourbonne-les-Bains 19 47 59N 5 45 E
Bourem 85 17 0N 0 24W
Bourg 20 45 3N 0 34W
Bourg-Argental 21 45 18N 4 32 E
Bourg-de-Péage 21 45 2N 5 3 E
Bourg-en-Bresse 21 46 13N 5 12 E
Bourg-St.-Andéol 21 44 23N 4 39 E
Bourg-St.-Maurice 21 45 35N 6 46 E
Bourganeuf 20 45 57N 1 45 E
Bourges 19 47 9N 2 25 E
Bourget 113 45 26N 75 9W
Bourget, L. du 21 45 44N 5 52 E
Bourgneuf, B. de 18 47 3N 2 10W
Bourgneuf-en-Retz 18 47 2N 1 58W
Bourgneuf-la-Fôret, Le 18 48 10N 0 59W
Bourgogne 19 47 0N 4 30 E
Bourgoin-Jallieu 21 45 36N 5 17 E
Bourgueil 18 47 17N 0 10 E
Bourke 97 30 8 S 145 55 E
Bournemouth 13 50 43N 1 53W
Bourriot-Bergonce 20 44 7N 0 14W
Bouscat, Le 20 44 53N 0 32W
Boussac 20 46 22N 2 13 E
Boussens 20 43 12N 0 58 E
Bousso 81 10 34N 16 52 E
Boutilimit 84 17 45N 14 40W
Boutonne → 20 45 55N 0 43 E
Bouvet I. = Bouvetøya 7 54 26 S 3 24 E
Bouvetøya 7 54 26 S 3 24 E
Bouznika 82 33 46N 7 6W
Bouzonville 19 49 17N 6 32 E
Bova Marina 41 37 59N 15 56 E
Bovalino Marina 41 38 9N 16 10 E
Bovec 39 46 20N 13 33 E
Bovigny 16 50 12N 5 55 E
Bovill 118 46 58N 116 27W
Bovino 41 41 15N 15 20 E
Bow Island 108 49 50N 111 23W
Bowbells 116 48 47N 102 19W
Bowdle 116 45 30N 99 40W
Bowen 97 20 0 S 148 16 E
Bowen → 98 20 24 S 147 20 E
Bowen Mts. 99 37 0 S 148 0 E
Bowie, Ariz., U.S.A. 119 32 15N 109 30W
Bowie, Tex., U.S.A. 117 33 33N 97 50W
Bowland, Forest of 12 54 0N 2 30W
Bowling Green, Ky., U.S.A. 114 37 0N 86 25W
Bowling Green, Ohio, U.S.A. 114 41 22N 83 40W
Bowling Green, C. 97 19 19 S 147 25 E
Bowman 116 46 12N 103 21W
Bowman I. 5 65 0 S 104 0 E
Bowmans 99 34 10 S 138 17 E
Bowmanville 106 43 55N 78 41W
Bowmore 14 55 45N 6 18W
Bowral 97 34 26 S 150 27 E
Bowraville 99 30 37 S 152 52 E
Bowron → 108 54 3N 121 50W
Bowser L. 108 56 30N 129 30W
Bowsman 109 52 14N 101 12W
Bowwood 91 17 5 S 26 20 E
Boxelder Cr. → 118 47 20N 108 30W
Boxholm 49 58 12N 15 3 E
Boxtel 16 51 36N 5 20 E
Boyabat 56 41 28N 34 42 E
Boyce 117 31 25N 92 39W
Boyer → 108 58 27N 115 57W
Boyle 15 53 58N 8 19W
Boyne → 15 53 43N 6 15W
Boyne City 114 45 13N 85 1W
Boyni Qara 65 36 20N 67 0 E
Boynton Beach 115 26 31N 80 3W
Bozburun 45 36 43N 28 8 E
Bozcaada 44 39 49N 26 3 E
Bozeman 118 45 40N 111 0W
Bozen = Bolzano 39 46 30N 11 20 E
Božepole Wielkopolski 28 54 33N 17 56 E
Boževac 42 44 32N 21 24 E
Bozouls 20 44 28N 2 43 E
Bozoum 88 6 25N 16 35 E
Bozovici 46 44 56N 22 1 E
Bra 38 44 41N 7 50 E
Brabant □ 16 50 46N 4 30 E
Brabant L. 109 55 58N 103 43W

Brabrand Bucharest

Brabrand 49 56 9N 10 7 E
Brač 39 43 20N 16 40 E
Bracadale, L. 14 57 20N 6 30W
Bracciano 39 42 6N 12 10 E
Bracciano, L. di 39 42 8N 12 11 E
Bracebridge 106 45 2N 79 19W
Brach 83 27 31N 14 20 E
Bracieux 19 47 30N 1 30 E
Bräcke 48 62 45N 15 26 E
Brackettville 117 29 21N 100 20W
Brački Kanal 39 43 24N 16 40 E
Brad 46 46 10N 22 50 E
Brádano → 41 40 23N 16 51 E
Braddock 112 40 24N 79 51W
Bradenton 115 27 25N 82 35W
Bradford, Can. 112 44 7N 79 34W
Bradford, U.K. 12 53 47N 1 45W
Bradford, Pa., U.S.A. 114 41 58N 78 41W
Bradford, Vt., U.S.A. 113 43 59N 72 9W
Brădiceni 46 45 3N 23 4 E
Bradley, Ark., U.S.A. 117 33 7N 93 39W
Bradley, S.D., U.S.A. 116 45 10N 97 40W
Bradley Institute 91 17 7 S 31 25 E
Bradore Bay 107 51 27N 57 18W
Bradshaw 97 15 21 S 130 16 E
Brady 117 31 8N 99 25W
Brædstrup 49 55 58N 9 37 E
Braeside 113 45 28N 76 24W
Braga 30 41 35N 8 25W
Braga □ 30 41 30N 8 30W
Bragado 124 35 2 S 60 27W
Bragança, Brazil 127 1 0 S 47 2W
Bragança, Port. 30 41 48N 6 50W
Bragança □ 30 41 30N 6 45W
Bragança Paulista 125 22 55 S 46 32W
Brahmanbaria 69 23 58N 91 15 E
Brahmani → 69 20 39N 86 46 E
Brahmaputra → 67 24 2N 90 59 E
Braich-y-pwll 12 52 47N 4 46W
Braidwood 99 35 27 S 149 49 E
Brăila 46 45 19N 27 59 E
Brăila □ 46 45 5N 27 30 E
Brainerd 116 46 20N 94 10W
Braintree, U.K. 13 51 53N 0 34 E
Braintree, U.S.A. 113 42 11N 71 0W
Brak → 92 29 35 S 22 55 E
Brake, Niedersachsen, Ger. 24 53 19N 8 30 E
Brake, Nordrhein, Ger. 24 51 43N 9 12 E
Bräkne-Hoby 49 56 14N 15 6 E
Brakwater 92 22 28 S 17 3 E
Brålanda 49 58 34N 12 21 E
Bralorne 108 50 50N 123 45W
Bramberg 25 50 6N 10 40 E
Bramminge 49 55 28N 8 42 E
Brämön 48 62 14N 17 40 E
Brampton 106 43 45N 79 45W
Bramsche 24 52 25N 7 58 E
Bramwell 98 12 8 S 142 37 E
Branco → 126 1 20 S 61 50W
Brande 49 55 57N 9 8 E
Brandenburg 24 52 24N 12 33 E
Brandfort 92 28 40 S 26 30 E
Brandon, Can. 109 49 50N 99 57W
Brandon, U.S.A. 113 43 48N 73 4W
Brandon B. 15 52 17N 10 8W
Brandon, Mt. 15 52 15N 10 15W
Brandsen 124 35 10 S 58 15W
Brandval 47 60 19N 12 1 E
Brandvlei 92 30 25 S 20 30 E
Brandýs 26 50 10N 14 40 E
Branford 113 41 15N 72 48W
Braniewo 28 54 25N 19 50 E
Bransfield Str. 5 63 0 S 59 0W
Brańsk 28 52 44N 22 51 E
Branson, Colo., U.S.A. 117 37 4N 103 53W
Branson, Mo., U.S.A. 117 36 40N 93 18W
Brantford 106 43 10N 80 15W
Brantôme 20 45 22N 0 39 E
Branxholme 99 37 52 S 141 49 E
Branzi 38 46 0N 9 46 E
Bras d'or, L. 107 45 50N 60 50W
Brasiléia 126 11 0 S 68 45W
Brasília 127 15 47 S 47 55 E
Braslav 54 55 38N 27 0 E
Braslovce 39 46 21N 15 3 E
Braşov 46 45 38N 25 35 E
Braşov □ 46 45 45N 25 15 E
Brass 85 4 35N 6 14 E
Brass → 85 4 15N 6 13 E
Brassac-les-Mines 20 45 24N 3 20 E
Brasschaat 16 51 19N 4 27 E
Brassey, Banjaran 72 5 0N 117 15 E
Brasstown Bald, Mt. 115 34 54N 83 45W
Bratislava 27 48 10N 17 7 E
Bratsigovo 43 42 1N 24 22 E
Bratsk 59 56 10N 101 30 E
Brattleboro 114 42 53N 72 37W
Braţul Chilia → 46 45 25N 29 20 E
Bratul Sfintu Gheorghe → 46 45 0N 29 20 E
Braţul Sulina → 46 45 10N 29 20 E
Bratunac 42 44 13N 19 21 E
Braunau 26 48 15N 13 3 E
Braunschweig 24 52 17N 10 28 E
Braunton 13 51 6N 4 9W
Brava 63 1 20N 44 8 E
Bråviken 48 58 38N 16 32 E
Bravo del Norte → 120 25 57N 97 9W
Brawley 119 32 58N 115 30W
Bray 15 53 12N 6 6W
Bray, Pays de 19 49 46N 1 26 E
Bray-sur-Seine 19 48 25N 3 14 E
Brazeau → 108 52 55N 115 14W
Brazil 114 39 32N 87 8W
Brazil ■ 127 10 0 S 50 0W
Brazilian Highlands = Brasil, Planalto 122 18 0 S 46 30W
Brazo Sur → 124 25 21 S 57 42W
Brazos → 117 28 53N 95 23W
Brazzaville 88 4 9 S 15 12 E
Brčko 42 44 54N 18 46 E
Brda → 28 53 8N 18 8 E
Breadalbane, Austral. 98 23 50 S 139 35 E
Breadalbane, U.K. 14 56 30N 4 15W
Breaksea Sd. 101 45 35 S 166 35 E
Bream Bay 101 35 56 S 174 28 E
Bream Head 101 35 51 S 174 36 E
Breas 124 25 29 S 70 24W
Brebes 73 6 52 S 109 3 E
Brechin, Can. 112 44 32N 79 10W
Brechin, U.K. 14 56 44N 2 40W
Breckenridge, Colo., U.S.A. 118 39 30N 106 2W
Breckenridge, Minn., U.S.A. 116 46 20N 96 36W
Breckenridge, Tex., U.S.A. 117 32 48N 98 55W
Břeclav 27 48 46N 16 53 E
Brecon 13 51 57N 3 23W
Brecon Beacons 13 51 53N 3 27W
Breda 16 51 35N 4 45 E
Bredaryd 49 57 10N 13 45 E
Bredasdorp 92 34 33 S 20 2 E
Bredbo 99 35 58 S 149 10 E
Bredstedt 24 54 37N 8 59 E
Bregalnica → 42 41 43N 22 9 E
Bregenz 26 47 30N 9 45 E
Bregovo 42 44 9N 22 39 E
Bréhal 18 48 53N 1 30W
Bréhat, I. de 18 48 51N 3 0W
Breiðafjörður 50 65 15N 23 15W
Breil 21 43 56N 7 31 E
Breisach 25 48 2N 7 37 E
Brejo 127 3 41 S 42 47W
Brekke 47 61 1N 5 26 E
Breloux-la-Crèche 20 46 23N 0 19W
Bremangerlandet 47 61 51N 5 0 E
Bremen 24 53 4N 8 47 E
Bremen □ 24 53 6N 8 46 E
Bremerhaven 24 53 34N 8 35 E
Bremerton 118 47 30N 122 38W
Bremervörde 24 53 28N 9 10 E
Bremnes 47 59 47N 5 8 E
Bremsnes 47 63 6N 7 40 E
Brenes 31 37 32N 5 54W
Brenham 117 30 5N 96 27W
Brenner Pass 26 47 0N 11 30 E
Breno 38 45 57N 10 20 E
Brent, Can. 106 46 2N 78 29W
Brent, U.K. 13 51 33N 0 18W
Brenta → 39 45 11N 12 18 E
Brentwood 13 51 37N 0 19 E
Bréscia 38 45 33N 10 13 E
Breskens 16 51 23N 3 33 E
Breslau = Wrocław 28 51 5N 17 5 E
Bresle → 18 50 4N 1 22 E
Bresles 19 49 25N 2 13 E
Bressanone 39 46 43N 11 40 E
Bressay I. 14 60 10N 1 5W
Bresse, La 19 48 0N 6 53 E
Bresse, Plaine de 19 46 50N 5 10 E
Bressuire 18 46 51N 0 30W
Brest, France 18 48 24N 4 31W
Brest, U.S.S.R. 54 52 10N 23 40 E
Bretagne 18 48 0N 3 0W
Bretçu 46 46 7N 26 18 E
Breteuil, Eur, France 18 48 50N 0 53 E
Breteuil, Oise, France 19 49 38N 2 18 E
Breton 108 53 7N 114 28W
Breton, Pertuis 20 46 17N 1 25W
Breton Sd. 117 29 40N 89 12W
Brett, C. 101 35 10 S 174 20 E
Bretten 25 49 2N 8 43 E
Brevard 115 35 19N 82 42W
Brevik 47 59 4N 9 42 E
Brewarrina 99 30 0 S 146 51 E
Brewer 107 44 43N 68 50W
Brewster, N.Y., U.S.A. 113 41 23N 73 37W
Brewster, Wash., U.S.A. 118 48 10N 119 51W
Brewster, Kap 4 70 7N 22 0W
Brewton 115 31 9N 87 2W
Breyten 93 26 16 S 30 0 E
Breytovo 55 58 18N 37 50 E
Brežice 39 45 54N 15 35 E
Brézina 82 33 4N 1 14 E
Březnice 26 49 32N 13 57 E
Breznik 42 42 44N 22 50 E
Brezno 27 48 50N 19 40 E
Brezovo 43 42 21N 25 5 E
Bria 88 6 30N 21 58 E
Briançon 21 44 54N 6 39 E
Briare 19 47 38N 2 45 E
Bribie I. 97 27 0 S 152 58 E
Bricon 19 48 5N 5 0 E
Bricquebec 18 49 28N 1 38W
Bridgehampton 113 40 56N 72 19W
Bridgend 13 51 30N 3 35W
Bridgeport, Calif., U.S.A. 119 38 14N 119 15W
Bridgeport, Conn., U.S.A. 114 41 12N 73 12W
Bridgeport, Nebr., U.S.A. 116 41 42N 103 10W
Bridgeport, Tex., U.S.A. 117 33 15N 97 45W
Bridger 118 45 20N 108 58W
Bridgeton 114 39 29N 75 10W
Bridgetown, Austral. 96 33 58 S 116 7 E
Bridgetown, Barbados 121 13 0N 59 30W
Bridgetown, Can. 107 44 55N 65 18W
Bridgewater, Can. 107 44 25N 64 31W
Bridgewater, Mass., U.S.A. 113 41 59N 70 56W
Bridgewater, S.D., U.S.A. 116 43 34N 97 29W
Bridgewater, C. 97 38 23 S 141 23 E
Bridgnorth 13 52 33N 2 25W
Bridgton 113 44 5N 70 41W
Bridgwater 13 51 7N 3 0W
Bridlington 12 54 6N 0 11W
Bridport, Austral. 99 40 59 S 147 23 E
Bridport, U.K. 13 50 43N 2 45W
Brie-Comte-Robert 19 48 40N 2 35 E
Brie, Plaine de la 19 48 35N 3 10 E
Briec 18 48 6N 4 0W
Brienne-le-Château 19 48 24N 4 30 E
Brienon 19 48 0N 3 35 E
Brienz 25 46 46N 8 2 E
Brienzersee 25 46 44N 7 53 E
Briey 19 49 14N 5 57 E
Brig 25 46 18N 7 59 E
Brigg 12 53 33N 0 30W
Briggsdale 116 40 40N 104 20W
Brigham City 118 41 30N 112 1W
Bright 99 36 42 S 146 56 E
Brighton, Austral. 99 35 5 S 138 30 E
Brighton, Can. 106 44 2N 77 44W
Brighton, U.K. 13 50 50N 0 9W
Brighton, U.S.A. 116 39 59N 104 50W
Brignogan-Plage 18 48 40N 4 20W
Brignoles 21 43 25N 6 5 E
Brihuega 32 40 45N 2 52W
Brikama 84 13 15N 16 45W
Brilliant, Can. 108 49 19N 117 38W
Brilliant, U.S.A. 112 40 15N 80 39W
Brilon 24 51 23N 8 32 E
Bríndisi 41 40 39N 17 55 E
Brinje 39 45 0N 15 9 E
Brinkley 117 34 55N 91 15W
Brinkworth 99 33 42 S 138 26 E
Brion, Î. 107 47 46N 61 26W
Brionne 18 49 11N 0 43 E
Brionski 39 44 55N 13 45 E
Brioude 20 45 18N 3 24 E
Briouze 18 48 42N 0 23W
Brisbane 97 27 25 S 153 2 E
Brisbane → 99 27 24 S 153 9 E
Brisighella 39 44 14N 11 46 E
Bristol, U.K. 13 51 26N 2 35W
Bristol, Conn., U.S.A. 114 41 44N 72 57W
Bristol, Pa., U.S.A. 113 40 6N 74 52W
Bristol, R.I., U.S.A. 113 41 40N 71 15W
Bristol, S.D., U.S.A. 116 45 25N 97 43W
Bristol, Tenn., U.S.A. 115 36 36N 82 11W
Bristol B. 104 58 0N 160 0W
Bristol Channel 13 51 18N 4 30W
Bristol I. 5 58 45 S 28 0W
Bristol L. 119 34 23N 116 50W
Bristow 117 35 55N 96 28W
British Antarctic Territory □ 5 66 0 S 45 0W
British Columbia □ 108 55 0N 125 15W
British Guiana = Guyana ■ 126 5 0N 59 0W
British Honduras = Belize ■ 120 17 0N 88 30W
British Isles 8 55 0N 4 0W
Brits 93 25 37 S 27 48 E
Britstown 92 30 37 S 23 30 E
Britt 106 45 46N 80 34W
Brittany = Bretagne 18 48 0N 3 0W
Britton 116 45 50N 97 47W
Brive-la-Gaillarde 20 45 10N 1 32 E
Briviesca 32 42 32N 3 19W
Brixton 98 23 32 S 144 57 E
Brlik 58 44 0N 74 5 E
Brno 27 49 10N 16 35 E
Bro 48 59 31N 17 38 E
Broach = Bharuch 68 21 47N 73 0 E
Broad → 115 33 59N 82 39W
Broad B. 14 58 14N 6 16W
Broad Haven 15 54 20N 9 55W
Broad Law 14 55 30N 3 22W
Broad Sd. 97 22 0 S 149 45 E
Broadford 100 37 14 S 145 4 E
Broads, The 12 52 45N 1 30 E
Broadsound Ra. 97 22 50 S 149 30 E
Broadus 116 45 28N 105 27W
Broadview 109 50 22N 102 35W
Broager 49 54 53N 9 40 E
Broaryd 49 57 7N 13 15 E
Brochet 109 57 53N 101 40W
Brochet, L. 109 58 36N 101 35W
Brock 109 51 26N 108 43W
Brocken 24 51 48N 10 40 E
Brockport 114 43 12N 77 56W
Brockton 113 42 8N 71 2W
Brockville 106 44 35N 75 41W
Brockway, Mont., U.S.A. 116 47 18N 105 46W
Brockway, Pa., U.S.A. 112 41 14N 78 48W
Brocton 112 42 25N 79 26W
Brod 42 41 35N 21 17 E
Brodarevo 42 43 14N 19 44 E
Brodeur Pen. 105 72 30N 88 10W
Brodick 14 55 34N 5 9W
Brodnica 28 53 15N 19 25 E
Brody 54 50 5N 25 10 E
Brogan 118 44 14N 117 32W
Broglie 18 49 0N 0 30 E
Brok 28 52 43N 21 52 E
Broken → 100 36 24 S 145 24 E
Broken Bay 100 33 30 S 151 15 E
Broken Bow, Nebr., U.S.A. 116 41 25N 99 35W
Broken Bow, Okla., U.S.A. 117 34 2N 94 43W
Broken Hill 97 31 58 S 141 29 E
Broken Hill = Kabwe 91 14 27 S 28 28 E
Brokind 49 58 13N 15 42 E
Bromfield 13 52 25N 2 45W
Bromley 13 51 20N 0 5 E
Bromölla 49 56 5N 14 28 E
Brønderslev 49 57 16N 9 57 E
Brong-Ahafo 84 7 50N 2 0W
Bronkhorstspruit 93 25 46 S 28 45 E
Bronnitsy 55 55 27N 38 10 E
Bronte, Italy 41 37 48N 14 49 E
Bronte, U.S.A. 117 31 54N 100 18W
Bronte Park 99 42 8 S 146 30 E
Brookfield 116 39 50N 93 4W
Brookhaven 117 31 40N 90 25W
Brookings, Oreg., U.S.A. 118 42 4N 124 10W
Brookings, S.D., U.S.A. 116 44 20N 96 45W
Brooklands 98 18 10 S 144 0 E
Brooklin 112 43 55N 78 55W
Brookmere 108 49 52N 120 53W
Brooks 108 50 35N 111 55W
Brooks B. 108 50 15N 127 55W
Brooks L. 109 61 55N 106 35W
Brooks Ra. 104 68 40N 147 0W
Brooksville 115 28 32N 82 21W
Brookton 96 32 22 S 117 1 E
Brookville 114 39 25N 85 0W
Brooloo 99 26 30 S 152 43 E
Broom, L. 14 57 55N 5 15W
Broome 96 18 0 S 122 15 E
Broons 18 48 20N 2 16W
Brora 14 58 0N 3 50W
Brora → 14 58 4N 3 52W
Brösarp 49 55 43N 14 6 E
Brosna → 15 53 8N 8 0W
Broşteni 46 47 14N 25 43 E
Brothers 118 43 56N 120 39W
Brøttum 47 61 2N 10 34 E
Brou 18 48 13N 1 11 E
Brouage 20 45 52N 1 4W
Broughton Island 105 67 33N 63 0W
Broughty Ferry 14 56 29N 2 50W
Broumov 27 50 35N 16 20 E
Brouwershaven 16 51 45N 3 55 E
Brovary 54 50 34N 30 48 E
Brovst 49 57 6N 9 31 E
Browerville 116 46 3N 94 50W
Brown Willy 13 50 35N 4 34W
Brownfield 117 33 10N 102 15W
Browning 118 48 35N 113 0W
Brownlee 109 50 43N 106 1W
Brownsville, Oreg., U.S.A. 118 44 29N 123 0W
Brownsville, Tenn., U.S.A. 117 35 35N 89 15W
Brownsville, Tex., U.S.A. 117 25 56N 97 25W
Brownwood 117 31 45N 99 0W
Brownwood, L. 117 31 51N 98 35W
Brozas 31 39 37N 6 47W
Bru 47 61 32N 5 11 E
Bruas 71 4 31N 100 46 E
Bruay-en-Artois 19 50 29N 2 33 E
Bruce, Mt. 96 22 37 S 118 8 E
Bruce Pen. 112 45 0N 81 30W
Bruche → 19 48 34N 7 43 E
Bruchsal 25 49 9N 8 39 E
Bruck an der Leitha 27 48 1N 16 47 E
Bruck an der Mur 26 47 24N 15 16 E
Brückenau 25 50 17N 9 48 E
Brue → 13 51 10N 2 59W
Bruges = Brugge 16 51 13N 3 13 E
Brugg 25 47 29N 8 11 E
Brugge 16 51 13N 3 13 E
Brühl 24 50 49N 6 51 E
Brûlé 108 53 15N 117 58W
Brûlon 18 47 58N 0 15W
Brumado 127 14 14 S 41 40W
Brumath 19 48 43N 7 40 E
Brumunddal 47 60 53N 10 56 E
Brundidge 115 31 43N 85 45W
Bruneau 118 42 57N 115 55W
Bruneau → 118 42 57N 115 58W
Brunei = Bandar Seri Begawan 72 4 52N 115 0 E
Brunei ■ 72 4 50N 115 0 E
Brunflo 48 63 5N 14 50 E
Brunico 39 46 50N 11 55 E
Brunkeberg 47 59 26N 8 28 E
Brunna 48 59 52N 17 25 E
Brunnen 25 46 59N 8 37 E
Brunner 101 42 27 S 171 20 E
Brunner, L. 101 42 37 S 171 27 E
Brunnsvik 48 60 12N 15 8 E
Bruno 109 52 20N 105 30W
Brunsbüttelkoog 24 53 52N 9 13 E
Brunswick, Ga., U.S.A. 115 31 10N 81 30W
Brunswick, Md., U.S.A. 114 39 20N 77 38W
Brunswick, Me., U.S.A. 107 43 53N 69 50W
Brunswick, Mo., U.S.A. 116 39 26N 93 10W
Brunswick, Ohio, U.S.A. 112 41 15N 81 50W
Brunswick = Braunschweig 24 52 17N 10 28 E
Brunswick B. 96 15 15 S 124 50 E
Brunswick, Pen. de 128 53 30 S 71 30W
Bruntál 27 50 0N 17 27 E
Bruny I. 97 43 20 S 147 15 E
Brusartsi 42 43 40N 23 5 E
Brush 116 40 17N 103 33W
Brushton 113 44 50N 74 62W
Brusio 25 46 14N 10 8 E
Brusque 125 27 5 S 49 0W
Brussel 16 50 51N 4 21 E
Brussels, Can. 112 43 45N 81 25W
Brussels, Ont., Can. 112 43 44N 81 15W
Brussels = Bruxelles 16 50 51N 4 21 E
Bruthen 99 37 42 S 147 50 E
Bruxelles 16 50 51N 4 21 E
Bruyères 19 48 10N 6 40 E
Brwinów 28 52 9N 20 40 E
Bryagovo 43 41 58N 25 8 E
Bryan, Ohio, U.S.A. 114 41 30N 84 30W
Bryan, Texas, U.S.A. 117 30 40N 96 27W
Bryan, Mt. 99 33 30 S 139 0 E
Bryanka 57 48 32N 38 45 E
Bryansk 54 53 13N 34 25 E
Bryanskoye 57 44 20N 47 10 E
Bryant 116 44 35N 97 28W
Bryne 47 58 44N 5 38 E
Bryson City 115 35 28N 83 25W
Brza Palanka 42 44 28N 22 27 E
Brzava → 42 45 21N 20 45 E
Brzeg 28 50 52N 17 30 E
Brzeg Din 28 51 16N 16 41 E
Brześć Kujawski 28 52 36N 18 55 E
Brzesko 27 49 59N 20 34 E
Brzeszcze 27 49 59N 19 10 E
Brzeziny 28 51 49N 19 42 E
Brzozów 27 49 41N 22 3 E
Bū Athlah 83 30 9N 15 39 E
Bu Craa 80 26 45N 12 50W
Bua Yai 71 15 33N 102 26 E
Buabuq 86 31 29N 25 29 E
Buapinang 73 4 40 S 121 30 E
Buayan 73 6 3N 125 6 E
Buba 84 11 40N 14 59W
Bubanza 90 3 6 S 29 23 E
Bucak 64 37 28N 30 36 E
Bucaramanga 126 7 0N 73 0W
Bucchiánico 39 42 20N 14 10 E
Bucecea 46 47 47N 26 28 E
Buchach 54 49 5N 25 25 E
Buchan 14 57 32N 2 8W
Buchan Ness 14 57 29N 1 48W
Buchanan, Can. 109 51 40N 102 45W
Buchanan, Liberia 84 5 57N 10 2W
Buchanan, L., Queens., Austral. 98 21 35 S 145 52 E
Buchanan, L., W. Australia, Austral. 96 25 33 S 123 2 E
Buchanan, L., U.S.A. 117 30 50N 98 25W
Buchans 107 48 50N 56 52W
Bucharest = Bucureşti 46 44 27N 26 10 E

Buchholz Caeté

Buchholz 24 53 19N 9 51 E
Buchloe 25 48 3N 10 45 E
Bückeburg 24 52 16N 9 2 E
Buckeye 119 33 28N 112 40W
Buckhannon 114 39 2N 80 10W
Buckhaven 14 56 10N 3 2W
Buckie 14 57 40N 2 58W
Buckingham, Can. 106 45 37N 75 24W
Buckingham, U.K. 13 52 0N 0 59W
Buckingham □ 13 51 50N 0 55W
Buckingham B. 97 12 10S 135 40 E
Buckingham Can. 70 14 0N 80 5 E
Buckinguy 99 31 3S 147 30 E
Buckland Newton 13 50 45N 2 25W
Buckley 118 47 10N 122 2W
Bucklin 117 37 37N 99 40W
Bucquoy 19 50 9N 2 43 E
Buctouche 107 46 30N 64 45W
Bucureşti 46 44 27N 26 10 E
Bucyrus 114 40 48N 83 0W
Budafok 27 47 26N 19 2 E
Budalin 67 22 20N 95 10 E
Budapest 27 47 29N 19 5 E
Budaun 68 28 5N 79 10 E
Budd Coast 5 68 0S 112 0 E
Buddusò 40 40 35N 9 18 E
Bude 13 50 49N 4 33W
Budeşti 46 44 13N 26 30 E
Budge Budge 69 22 30N 88 5 E
Búðareyri 50 65 2N 14 13W
Búðir 50 64 49N 23 23W
Budia 32 40 38N 2 46W
Budjala 88 2 50N 19 40 E
Búdrio 39 44 31N 11 31 E
Budva 42 42 17N 18 50 E
Budzyń 28 52 54N 16 59 E
Buea 85 4 10N 9 9 E
Buena Vista, Colo., U.S.A. 119 38 56N 106 6W
Buena Vista, Va., U.S.A. 114 37 47N 79 23W
Buena Vista L. 119 35 15N 119 21W
Buenaventura, Colomb. 126 3 53N 77 4W
Buenaventura, Mexico 120 29 50N 107 30W
Buendía, Pantano de 32 40 25N 2 43W
Buenos Aires 124 34 30S 58 20W
Buenos Aires □ 124 36 30S 60 0W
Buenos Aires, Lago 128 46 35S 72 30W
Buffalo, Mo., U.S.A. 117 37 40N 93 5W
Buffalo, N.Y., U.S.A. 114 42 55N 78 50W
Buffalo, Okla., U.S.A. 117 36 55N 99 42W
Buffalo, S.D., U.S.A. 116 45 39N 103 31W
Buffalo, Wyo., U.S.A. 118 44 25N 106 50W
Buffalo → 108 60 5N 115 5W
Buffalo Head Hills 108 57 25N 115 55W
Buffalo L. 108 52 27N 112 54W
Buffalo Narrows 109 55 51N 108 29W
Buffels → 92 29 36S 17 15 E
Buford 115 34 5N 84 0W
Bug →, Poland 28 52 31N 21 5 E
Bug →, U.S.S.R. 56 46 59N 31 58 E
Buga 126 4 0N 76 15W
Buganda □ 90 0 0N 31 30 E
Buganga 90 0 3S 32 0 E
Bugeat 20 45 36N 1 55 E
Bugel, Tanjung 72 6 26S 111 3 E
Bugojno 42 44 2N 17 25 E
Bugsuk 72 8 15N 117 15 E
Bugt 76 48 47N 121 56 E
Bugue, Le 20 44 55N 0 56 E
Bugulma 52 54 33N 52 48 E
Buguma 85 4 42N 6 55 E
Buguruslan 52 53 39N 52 26 E
Buhăeşti 46 46 47N 27 32 E
Buheirat-Murrat-el-Kubra 86 30 15N 32 40 E
Buhl, Idaho, U.S.A. 118 42 35N 114 54W
Buhl, Minn., U.S.A. 116 47 30N 92 46W
Buhuşi 46 46 41N 26 45 E
Buick 117 37 38N 91 2W
Builth Wells 13 52 10N 3 26W
Buinsk 55 55 0N 48 18 E
Buir Nur 75 47 50N 117 42 E
Buis-les-Baronnies 21 44 17N 5 16 E
Buitrago 30 41 0N 3 38W
Bujalance 31 37 54N 4 23W
Buján 30 42 59N 8 36W
Bujanovac 42 42 28N 21 44 E
Bujaraloz 32 41 29N 0 10W
Buje 39 45 24N 13 39 E
Bujumbura (Usumbura) 90 3 16S 29 18 E
Bük 27 47 22N 16 45 E
Buk 28 52 21N 16 30 E
Bukachacha 59 52 55N 116 50 E
Bukama 91 9 10S 25 50 E
Bukavu 90 2 20S 28 52 E
Bukene 90 4 15S 32 48 E
Bukhara 58 39 48N 64 25 E
Bukima 90 1 50S 33 25 E
Bukittinggi 72 0 20S 100 20 E
Bukkapatnam 70 14 14N 77 46 E
Bukoba 90 1 20S 31 49 E
Bukoba □ 90 1 30S 32 0 E
Bukowno 27 50 17N 19 35 E
Bukuru 85 9 42N 8 48 E
Bukuya 90 0 40N 31 52 E
Bula, Guin.-Biss. 84 12 7N 15 43W
Bula, Indon. 73 3 6S 130 30 E
Bulan 73 12 40N 123 52 E
Bulandshahr 68 28 28N 77 51 E
Bûlâq 86 25 10N 30 38 E
Bulawayo 91 20 7S 28 32 E
Buldana 68 20 30N 76 18 E
Bulgan 75 48 45N 103 34 E
Bulgaria ■ 43 42 35N 25 30 E
Bulgroo 99 25 47S 143 58 E
Bulhar 63 10 25N 44 30 E
Buli, Teluk 73 1 5N 128 25 E
Buliluyan, C. 72 8 20N 117 15 E
Bulki 87 6 11N 36 31 E
Bulkley → 108 55 15N 127 40W
Bull Shoals L. 117 36 40N 93 5W
Bullaque → 31 38 59N 4 17W
Bullas 33 38 2N 1 40W
Bulle 25 46 37N 7 3 E
Buller, Mt. 100 37 10S 146 28 E
Bullfinch 96 30 58S 119 3 E
Bulli 99 34 15S 150 57 E
Bullock Creek 98 17 43S 144 31 E
Bulloo → 97 28 43S 142 30 E
Bulloo Downs 99 28 31S 142 57 E
Bulloo L. 99 28 43S 142 25 E
Bulls 101 40 10S 175 24 E
Bully-les-Mines 19 50 27N 2 44 E
Bulnes 124 36 42S 72 19W
Bulo Burti 63 3 50N 45 33 E
Bulolo 98 7 10S 146 40 E
Bulqiza 44 41 30N 20 21 E
Bulsar 68 20 40N 72 58 E
Bultfontein 92 28 18S 26 10 E
Bulu Karakelong 73 4 35N 126 50 E
Bulukumba 73 5 33S 120 11 E
Bulun 59 70 37N 127 30 E
Bumba 88 2 13N 22 30 E
Bumbiri I. 90 1 40S 31 55 E
Bumble Bee 119 34 8N 112 18W
Bumhpa Bum 67 26 51N 97 14 E
Bumi → 91 17 0S 28 20 E
Buna, Kenya 90 2 58N 39 30 E
Buna, P.N.G. 98 8 42S 148 27 E
Bunazi 90 1 3S 31 23 E
Bunbah, Khalīj 81 32 20N 23 15 E
Bunbury 96 33 20S 115 35 E
Buncrana 15 55 8N 7 28W
Bundaberg 97 24 54S 152 22 E
Bünde 24 52 11N 8 33 E
Bundi 68 25 30N 75 35 E
Bundoran 15 54 24N 8 17W
Bundukia 87 5 14N 30 55 E
Bundure 100 35 10S 146 1 E
Bungendore 100 35 14S 149 30 E
Bungo-Suidō 74 33 0N 132 15 E
Bungoma 90 0 34N 34 34 E
Bungu 90 7 35S 39 0 E
Bungun Shara 75 49 0N 104 0 E
Bunia 90 1 35N 30 20 E
Bunji 69 35 45N 74 40 E
Bunju 72 3 35N 117 50 E
Bunkerville 119 36 47N 114 6W
Bunkie 117 31 1N 92 12W
Bunnell 115 29 28N 81 12W
Buñol 33 39 25N 0 47W
Buntok 72 1 40S 114 58 E
Bununu 85 9 51N 9 32 E
Bununu Dass 85 10 0N 9 31 E
Bunza 85 12 8N 4 0 E
Buol 73 1 15N 121 32 E
Buorkhaya, Mys 59 71 50N 132 40 E
Buqayq 64 26 0N 49 45 E
Buqei'a 62 32 58N 35 20 E
Bur Acaba 63 3 12N 44 20 E
Bûr Fuad 86 31 15N 32 20 E
Bûr Safâga 86 26 43N 33 57 E
Bûr Sa'îd 86 31 16N 32 18 E
Bûr Sûdân 86 19 32N 37 9 E
Bûr Taufiq 86 29 54N 32 32 E
Bura 90 1 4S 39 58 E
Buraimī, Al Wāhāt al 65 24 10N 55 43 E
Burao 63 9 32N 45 32 E
Buras 117 29 20N 89 33W
Buraydah 64 26 20N 44 8 E
Burbank 119 34 9N 118 23W
Burcher 99 33 30S 147 16 E
Burdekin → 98 19 38S 147 25 E
Burdett 108 49 50N 111 32W
Burdur 64 37 45N 30 22 E
Burdwan 69 23 14N 87 39 E
Bure 87 10 40N 37 4 E
Bure → 12 52 38N 1 45 E
Bureba, La 32 42 36N 3 24W
Büren 24 51 33N 8 34 E
Bureya → 59 49 27N 129 30 E
Burford 112 43 7N 80 27W
Burg, Magdeburg, Ger. 24 52 16N 11 50 E
Burg, Schleswig-Holstein, Ger. 24 54 25N 11 10 E
Burg el Arab 86 30 54N 29 32 E
Burg et Tuyur 86 20 55N 27 56 E
Burgas 43 42 33N 27 29 E
Burgaski Zaliv 43 42 30N 27 39 E
Burgdorf, Ger. 24 52 27N 10 0 E
Burgdorf, Switz. 25 47 3N 7 37 E
Burgenland □ 27 47 20N 16 20 E
Burgeo 107 47 37N 57 38W
Burgersdorp 92 31 0S 26 20 E
Burghausen 25 48 10N 12 50 E
Búrgio 40 37 35N 13 18 E
Burglengenfeld 25 49 11N 12 2 E
Burgo de Osma 32 41 35N 3 4W
Burgohondo 30 40 26N 4 47W
Burgos 32 42 21N 3 41W
Burgos □ 32 42 21N 3 42W
Burgstädt 24 50 55N 12 49 E
Burgsteinfurt 24 52 9N 7 23 E
Burgsvik 49 57 3N 18 19 E
Burguillos del Cerro 31 38 23N 6 35W
Burgundy = Bourgogne 19 47 0N 4 30 E
Burhanpur 68 21 18N 76 14 E
Burhou 18 49 45N 2 15W
Buri Pen. 87 15 25N 39 55 E
Burias 73 12 55N 123 5 E
Burica, Pta. 121 8 3N 82 51W
Burigi, L. 90 2 2S 31 22 E
Burin 107 47 1N 55 14W
Bûrîn 62 32 11N 35 15 E
Buriram 71 15 0N 103 0 E
Burji 87 5 29N 37 51 E
Burkburnett 117 34 7N 98 35W
Burke 118 47 31N 115 56W
Burke → 98 23 12S 139 33 E
Burketown 97 17 45S 139 33 E
Burk's Falls 106 45 37N 79 24W
Burley 118 42 37N 113 55W
Burlington, Can. 112 43 18N 79 45W
Burlington, Colo., U.S.A. 116 39 21N 102 18W
Burlington, Iowa, U.S.A. 116 40 50N 91 5W
Burlington, Kans., U.S.A. 116 38 15N 95 47W
Burlington, N.C., U.S.A. 115 36 7N 79 27W
Burlington, N.J., U.S.A. 114 40 5N 74 50W
Burlington, Vt., U.S.A. 114 44 27N 73 14W
Burlington, Wash., U.S.A. 118 48 29N 122 19W
Burlington, Wis., U.S.A. 114 42 41N 88 18W
Burlyu-Tyube 58 46 30N 79 10 E
Burma ■ 67 21 0N 96 30 E
Burnaby I. 108 52 25N 131 19W
Burnet 117 30 45N 98 11W
Burnett → 97 24 45S 152 23 E
Burney 118 40 56N 121 41W
Burnham 112 40 37N 77 34W
Burnie 97 41 4S 145 56 E
Burnley 12 53 47N 2 15W
Burns, Oreg., U.S.A. 118 43 40N 119 4W
Burns, Wyo., U.S.A. 116 41 13N 104 18W
Burns Lake 108 54 20N 125 45W
Burnside → 104 66 51N 108 4W
Burnt River 112 44 41N 78 42W
Burntwood → 109 56 8N 96 34W
Burntwood L. 109 55 22N 100 26W
Burqā 62 32 18N 35 11 E
Burqān 64 29 0N 47 57 E
Burqin 75 47 43N 87 0 E
Burra 97 33 40S 138 55 E
Burragorang, L. 100 33 52S 150 37 E
Burreli 44 41 36N 20 1 E
Burrendong, L. 100 32 45S 149 10 E
Burrewarra Pt. 100 35 50S 150 15 E
Burriana 32 39 50N 0 4W
Burrinjuck Dam 100 35 0S 148 34 E
Burrinjuck Res. 99 35 0S 148 36 E
Burro, Serranías del 120 29 0N 102 0W
Burruyacú 124 26 30S 64 40W
Burry Port 13 51 41N 4 17W
Bursa 64 40 15N 29 5 E
Burseryd 49 57 12N 13 17 E
Burstall 109 50 39N 109 54W
Burton L. 106 54 45N 78 20W
Burton-upon-Trent 12 52 48N 1 39W
Burtundy 99 33 45S 142 15 E
Buru 73 3 30S 126 30 E
Burullus, Bahra el 86 31 25N 31 0 E
Burundi ■ 90 3 15S 30 0 E
Burung 72 0 24N 103 33 E
Bururi 90 3 57S 29 37 E
Burutu 85 5 20N 5 29 E
Burwell 116 41 49N 99 8W
Bury 12 53 36N 2 19W
Bury St. Edmunds 13 52 15N 0 42 E
Buryat A.S.S.R. □ 59 53 0N 110 0 E
Buryn 54 51 13N 33 50 E
Burzenin 28 51 28N 18 47 E
Busalla 38 44 34N 8 58 E
Busango Swamp 91 14 15S 25 45 E
Buşayyah 64 30 0N 46 10 E
Busca 38 44 31N 7 29 E
Bushati 44 41 58N 19 34 E
Bushell 109 59 31N 108 45W
Bushenyi 90 0 35S 30 10 E
Bushnell, Ill., U.S.A. 116 40 32N 90 30W
Bushnell, Nebr., U.S.A. 116 41 18N 103 50W
Busia □ 90 0 25N 34 6 E
Busie 84 10 29N 2 22W
Businga 88 3 16N 20 59 E
Buskerud fylke □ 47 60 13N 9 0 E
Busko Zdrój 28 50 28N 20 42 E
Busoga □ 90 0 5N 33 30 E
Busovača 42 44 6N 17 53 E
Busra ash Shām 64 32 30N 36 25 E
Bussang 19 47 50N 6 50 E
Busselton 96 33 42S 115 15 E
Busseto 38 44 59N 10 2 E
Bussum 16 52 16N 5 10 E
Bustard Hd. 97 24 0S 151 48 E
Busto Arsizio 38 45 40N 8 50 E
Busto, C. 30 43 34N 6 28W
Busu-Djanoa 88 1 43N 21 23 E
Busuanga 73 12 10N 120 0 E
Büsum 24 54 7N 8 50 E
Buta 90 2 50N 24 53 E
Butare 90 2 31S 29 52 E
Bute 14 55 48N 5 2W
Bute Inlet 108 50 40N 124 53W
Butemba 90 1 9N 31 37 E
Butembo 90 0 9N 29 18 E
Butera 41 37 10N 14 10 E
Butha Qi 75 48 0N 122 32 E
Butiaba 90 1 50N 31 20 E
Butler, Mo., U.S.A. 116 38 17N 94 18W
Butler, Pa., U.S.A. 114 40 52N 79 52W
Butom Odrzánski 28 51 44N 15 48 E
Butte, Mont., U.S.A. 118 46 0N 112 31W
Butte, Nebr., U.S.A. 116 42 56N 98 54W
Butterworth 71 5 24N 100 23 E
Button B. 109 58 45N 94 23W
Butuan 73 8 57N 125 33 E
Butuku-Luba 85 3 29N 8 33 E
Butung 73 5 0S 122 45 E
Buturlinovka 55 50 50N 40 35 E
Butzbach 24 50 24N 8 40 E
Bützow 24 53 51N 11 59 E
Buxar 69 25 34N 83 58 E
Buxton, S. Afr. 92 27 38S 24 42 E
Buxton, U.K. 12 53 16N 1 54W
Buxy 19 46 44N 4 40 E
Buy 55 58 28N 41 28 E
Buyaga 59 59 50N 127 0 E
Buynaksk 57 42 48N 47 7 E
Büyük Çekmece 43 41 2N 28 35 E
Büyük Kemikli Burun 44 40 20N 26 15 E
Buzançais 18 46 54N 1 25 E
Buzău 46 45 10N 26 50 E
Buzău □ 46 45 20N 26 30 E
Buzău → 46 45 10N 27 20 E
Buzău, Pasul 46 45 35N 26 12 E
Buzaymah 81 24 50N 22 2 E
Buzen 74 33 35N 131 5 E
Buzet 39 45 24N 13 58 E
Buzi → 91 19 50S 34 43 E
Buziaş 42 45 38N 21 36 E
Buzuluk 52 52 48N 52 12 E
Buzuluk → 55 50 15N 42 7 E
Buzzards Bay 114 41 45N 70 38W
Bwana Mkubwe 91 13 8S 28 38 E
Byala, Ruse, Bulg. 43 43 28N 25 44 E
Byala, Varna, Bulg. 43 42 53N 27 55 E
Byala Slatina 43 43 26N 23 55 E
Byandovan, Mys 57 39 45N 49 28 E
Bychawa 28 51 1N 22 36 E
Byczyna 28 51 7N 18 12 E
Bydgoszcz 28 53 10N 18 0 E
Bydgoszcz □ 28 53 16N 17 33 E
Byelorussian S.S.R. □ 54 53 30N 27 0 E
Byers 116 39 46N 104 13W
Byesville 112 39 56N 81 32W
Bygland 47 58 50N 7 48 E
Byglandsfjord 47 58 40N 7 50 E
Byglandsfjorden 47 58 44N 7 50 E
Byhalia 117 34 53N 89 41W
Bykhov 54 53 31N 30 14 E
Bykle 47 59 20N 7 22 E
Bykovo 57 49 50N 45 25 E
Bylas 119 33 11N 110 9W
Bylderup 49 54 57N 9 6 E
Bylot I. 105 73 13N 78 34W
Byrd, C. 5 69 38S 76 7W
Byrd Land 5 79 30S 125 0W
Byrd Sub-Glacial Basin 5 82 0S 120 0W
Byrock 99 30 40S 146 27 E
Byron, C. 97 28 38S 153 40 E
Byrranga, Gory 59 75 0N 100 0 E
Byrum 49 57 16N 11 0 E
Byske 50 64 57N 21 11 E
Byske älv → 50 64 57N 21 13 E
Bystrzyca →, Lublin, Poland 28 51 21N 22 46 E
Bystrzyca →, Wrocław, Poland 28 51 12N 16 55 E
Bystrzyca Kłodzka 28 50 19N 16 39 E
Byten 54 52 50N 25 27 E
Bytom 28 50 25N 18 54 E
Bytów 28 54 10N 17 30 E
Byumba 90 1 35S 30 4 E
Bzenec 27 48 58N 17 18 E
Bzura → 28 52 25N 20 15 E

C

Ca Mau 71 9 7N 105 8 E
Ca Mau, Mui = Bai Bung 71 8 35N 104 42 E
Caacupé 124 25 23S 57 5W
Caála 89 12 46S 15 30 E
Caamano Sd. 108 52 55N 129 25W
Caazapá 124 26 8S 56 19W
Caazapá □ 125 26 10S 56 0W
Caballeria, C. de 32 40 5N 4 5 E
Cabañaquinta 30 43 10N 5 38W
Cabanatuan 73 15 30N 120 58 E
Cabanes 32 40 9N 0 2 E
Cabano 107 47 40N 68 56W
Čabar 39 45 36N 14 39 E
Cabedelo 127 7 0S 34 50W
Cabeza del Buey 31 38 44N 5 13W
Cabildo 124 32 30S 71 5W
Cabimas 126 10 23N 71 25W
Cabinda 88 5 33S 12 11 E
Cabinda □ 88 5 0S 12 30 E
Cabinet Mts. 118 48 0N 115 30W
Cabo Blanco 128 47 15S 65 47W
Cabo Frio 125 22 51S 42 3W
Cabo Pantoja 126 1 0S 75 10W
Cabonga, Réservoir 106 47 20N 76 40W
Cabool 117 37 10N 92 8W
Caboolture 99 27 5S 152 58 E
Cabora Bassa Dam 91 15 20S 32 50 E
Caborca (Heroica) 120 30 40N 112 10W
Cabot, Mt. 113 44 30N 71 25W
Cabot Strait 107 47 15N 59 40W
Cabra 31 37 30N 4 28W
Cabra del Santo Cristo 33 37 42N 3 16W
Cábras 40 39 57N 8 30 E
Cabrera, I. 33 39 8N 2 57 E
Cabrera, Sierra 30 42 12N 6 40W
Cabri 109 50 35N 108 25W
Cabriel → 33 39 14N 1 3W
Cacabelos 30 42 36N 6 44W
Čačak 42 43 54N 20 20 E
Cáceres, Brazil 126 16 5S 57 40W
Cáceres, Spain 31 39 26N 6 23W
Cáceres □ 31 39 45N 6 0W
Cache Bay 106 46 22N 80 0W
Cachepo 31 37 20N 7 49W
Cachéu 84 12 14N 16 8W
Cachi 124 25 5S 66 10W
Cachimbo, Serra do 127 9 30S 55 0W
Cachoeira 127 12 30S 39 0W
Cachoeira de Itapemirim 125 20 51S 41 7W
Cachoeira do Sul 125 30 3S 52 53W
Cachopo 31 37 20N 7 49W
Cacólo 88 10 9S 19 21 E
Caconda 89 13 48S 15 8 E
Cadarache, Barrage de 21 43 42N 5 47 E
Čadca 27 49 26N 18 45 E
Caddo 117 34 8N 96 18W
Cader Idris 12 52 43N 3 56W
Cadí, Sierra del 32 42 17N 1 42 E
Cadillac, Can. 106 48 14N 78 23W
Cadillac, France 20 44 38N 0 20W
Cadillac, U.S.A. 114 44 16N 85 25W
Cadiz 73 10 57N 123 15 E
Cádiz 31 36 30N 6 20W
Cadiz 112 40 13N 81 0W
Cádiz □ 31 36 36N 5 45W
Cádiz, G. de 31 36 40N 7 0W
Cadomin 108 53 2N 117 20W
Cadotte → 108 56 43N 117 10W
Cadours 20 43 44N 1 2 E
Caen 18 49 10N 0 22W
Caernarfon 12 53 8N 4 17W
Caernarfon B. 12 53 4N 4 40W
Caernarvon = Caernarfon 12 53 8N 4 17W
Caerphilly 13 51 34N 3 13W
Caesarea 62 32 30N 34 53 E
Caeté 127 19 55S 43 40W

Caetité Carbon

Caetité 127 13 50 S 42 32W
Cafayate 124 26 2 S 66 0W
Cafu 92 16 30 S 15 8 E
Cagayan 73 9 39N 121 16 E
Cagayan → 73 18 25N 121 42 E
Cagayan de Oro 73 8 30N 124 40 E
Cagli 39 43 32N 12 38 E
Cágliari 40 39 15N 9 6 E
Cágliari, G. di 40 39 8N 9 10 E
Cagnano Varano 41 41 49N 15 47 E
Cagnes-sur-Mer 21 43 40N 7 9 E
Caguas 121 18 14N 66 4W
Caha Mts. 15 51 45N 9 40W
Cahama 92 16 17 S 14 19 E
Caher 15 52 23N 7 56W
Cahersiveen 15 51 57N 10 13W
Cahore Pt. 15 52 34N 6 11W
Cahors 20 44 27N 1 27 E
Cahuapanas 126 5 15 S 77 0W
Caianda 91 11 2 S 23 31 E
Caibarién 121 22 30N 79 30W
Caicara 126 7 38N 66 10W
Caicó 127 6 20 S 37 0W
Caicos Is. 121 21 40N 71 40W
Caicos Passage 121 22 45N 72 45W
Cainsville 112 43 9N 80 15W
Caird Coast 5 75 0 S 25 0W
Cairn Gorm 14 57 7N 3 40W
Cairn Toul 14 57 3N 3 44W
Cairngorm Mts. 14 57 6N 3 42W
Cairns 97 16 57 S 145 45 E
Cairo, Ga., U.S.A. 115 30 52N 84 12W
Cairo, Illinois, U.S.A. 117 37 0N 89 10W
Cairo = El Qâhira 86 30 1N 31 14 E
Cairo Montenotte 38 44 23N 8 16 E
Caithness, Ord of 14 58 9N 3 37W
Caiundo 89 15 50 S 17 28 E
Caiza 126 20 2 S 65 40W
Cajamarca 126 7 5 S 78 28W
Cajarc 20 44 29N 1 50 E
Cajàzeiras 127 6 52 S 38 30W
Čajetina 42 43 47N 19 42 E
Čajniče 42 43 34N 19 5 E
Çakirgol 57 40 33N 39 40 E
Čakovec 39 46 23N 16 26 E
Cala 31 37 59N 6 21W
Cala → 31 37 38N 6 5W
Cala Cadolar, Punta de 33 38 38N 1 35 E
Calabar 85 4 57N 8 20 E
Calábria □ 41 39 24N 16 30 E
Calaburras, Pta. de 31 36 30N 4 38W
Calaceite 32 41 1N 0 11 E
Calafat 46 43 58N 22 59 E
Calafate 128 50 19 S 72 15W
Calahorra 32 42 18N 1 59W
Calais, France 19 50 57N 1 56 E
Calais, U.S.A. 107 45 11N 67 20W
Calais, Pas de 19 50 57N 1 20 E
Calalaste, Cord. de 124 25 0 S 67 0W
Calama, Brazil 126 8 0 S 62 50W
Calama, Chile 124 22 30 S 68 55W
Calamar, Bolívar, Colomb. 126 10 15N 74 55W
Calamar, Vaupés, Colomb. 126 1 58N 72 32W
Calamian Group 73 11 50N 119 55 E
Calamocha 32 40 50N 1 17W
Calañas 31 37 40N 6 53W
Calanda 32 40 56N 0 15W
Calang 72 4 37N 95 37 E
Calangiánus 40 40 56N 9 12 E
Calapan 73 13 25N 121 7 E
Călăraşi 46 44 12N 27 20 E
Calasparra 33 38 14N 1 41W
Calatafimi 40 37 56N 12 50 E
Calatayud 32 41 20N 1 40W
Calauag 73 13 55N 122 15 E
Calavà, C. 41 38 11N 14 55 E
Calavite, Cape 73 13 26N 120 20 E
Calbayog 73 12 4N 124 38 E
Calbe 24 51 57N 11 47 E
Calca 126 13 22 S 72 0W
Calcasieu L. 117 30 0N 93 17W
Calci 38 43 44N 10 31 E
Calcutta 69 22 36N 88 24 E
Caldaro 39 46 23N 11 15 E
Caldas da Rainha 31 39 24N 9 8W
Caldas de Reyes 30 42 36N 8 39W
Calder → 12 53 44N 1 21W
Caldera 124 27 5 S 70 55W
Caldwell, Idaho, U.S.A. 118 43 45N 116 42W
Caldwell, Kans., U.S.A. 117 37 5N 97 37W
Caldwell, Texas, U.S.A. 117 30 30N 96 42W
Caledon 92 34 14 S 19 26 E
Caledon → 92 30 31 S 26 5 E
Caledon B. 97 12 45 S 137 0 E
Caledonia, Can. 112 43 7N 79 58W
Caledonia, U.S.A. 112 42 57N 77 54W
Calella 32 41 37N 2 40 E
Calemba 92 16 0 S 15 44 E
Calera, La 124 32 50 S 71 10W
Calexico 119 32 40N 115 33W
Calf of Man 12 54 4N 4 48W
Calgary 108 51 0N 114 10W
Calhoun 115 34 30N 84 55W
Cali 126 3 25N 76 35W
Calicoan 73 10 59N 125 50 E
Calicut (Kozhikode) 70 11 15N 75 43 E
Caliente 119 37 36N 114 34W
California, Mo., U.S.A. 116 38 37N 92 30W
California, Pa., U.S.A. 112 40 5N 79 55W
California □ 119 37 25N 120 0W
California, Baja, T.N. □ 120 30 0N 115 0W
California, Baja, T.S. □ 120 25 50N 111 50W
California, Golfo de 120 27 0N 111 0W
California, Lr. = California, Baja 120 25 50N 111 50W
Călimăneşti 46 45 14N 24 20 E
Călimani, Munţii 46 47 12N 25 0 E
Călineşti 46 45 21N 24 18 E
Calingasta 124 31 15 S 69 30W
Calipatria 119 33 8N 115 30W
Calistoga 118 38 36N 122 32W
Calitri 41 40 54N 15 25 E
Callabonna, L. 97 29 40 S 140 5 E
Callac 18 48 25N 3 27W
Callan 15 52 33N 7 25W
Callander 14 56 15N 4 14W
Callao 126 12 0 S 77 0W
Callaway 116 41 20N 99 56W
Callide 98 24 18 S 150 28 E
Calling Lake 108 55 15N 113 12W
Callosa de Ensarriá. 33 38 40N 0 8W
Callosa de Segura 33 38 7N 0 53W
Calne 12 51 26N 2 0W
Calola 92 16 25 S 17 48 E
Calore → 41 41 11N 14 28 E
Caloundra 99 26 45 S 153 10 E
Calpe 33 38 39N 0 3 E
Calstock 106 49 47N 84 9W
Caltabellotta 40 37 36N 13 11 E
Caltagirone 41 37 13N 14 30 E
Caltanissetta 41 37 30N 14 3 E
Caluire-et-Cuire 21 45 49N 4 51 E
Calulo 88 10 1 S 14 56 E
Calumet 114 47 14N 88 27W
Calunda 89 12 7 S 23 36 E
Caluso 38 45 18N 7 52 E
Calvados □ 18 49 5N 0 15W
Calvert 117 30 59N 96 40W
Calvert I. 108 51 30N 128 0W
Calvinia 92 31 28 S 19 45 E
Calw 25 48 43N 8 44 E
Calzada Almuradiel 33 38 32N 3 28W
Calzada de Calatrava 31 38 42N 3 46W
Cam → 13 52 21N 0 16 E
Cam Lam 71 11 54N 109 10 E
Cam Ranh 71 11 54N 109 12 E
Camabatela 88 8 20 S 15 26 E
Camacupa 89 11 58 S 17 22 E
Camagüey 121 21 20N 78 0W
Camaiore 38 43 57N 10 18 E
Camaná 126 16 30 S 72 50W
Camaquã → 125 31 17 S 51 47W
Camarat, C. 21 43 12N 6 41 E
Camaret 18 48 16N 4 37W
Camargo 126 20 38 S 65 15 E
Camargue 21 43 34N 4 34 E
Camariñas 30 43 8N 9 12W
Camarón, C. 121 16 0N 85 0W
Camarones 128 44 50 S 65 40W
Camas 118 45 35N 122 24W
Camas Valley 118 43 0N 123 46W
Cambados 30 42 31N 8 49W
Cambará 125 23 2 S 50 5W
Cambay 68 22 23N 72 33 E
Cambay, G. of 68 20 45N 72 30 E
Cambil 33 37 40N 3 33W
Cambo-les-Bains 20 43 22N 1 23W
Cambodia ■ 71 12 15N 105 0 E
Camborne 13 50 13N 5 18W
Cambrai 19 50 11N 3 14 E
Cambria 119 35 39N 121 6W
Cambrian Mts. 13 52 25N 3 52W
Cambridge, Can. 106 43 23N 80 15W
Cambridge, N.Z. 101 37 54 S 175 29 E
Cambridge, U.K. 13 52 13N 0 8 E
Cambridge, Idaho, U.S.A. 118 44 36N 116 40W
Cambridge, Mass., U.S.A. 114 42 20N 71 8W
Cambridge, Md., U.S.A. 114 38 33N 76 2W
Cambridge, Minn., U.S.A. 116 45 34N 93 15W
Cambridge, N.Y., U.S.A. 113 43 2N 73 22W
Cambridge, Nebr., U.S.A. 116 40 20N 100 12W
Cambridge, Ohio, U.S.A. 114 40 1N 81 35W
Cambridge Bay 104 69 10N 105 0W
Cambridge Gulf 96 14 55 S 128 15 E
Cambridge Springs 112 41 47N 80 4W
Cambridgeshire □ 13 52 12N 0 7 E
Cambrils 32 41 8N 1 3 E
Cambuci 125 21 35 S 41 55W
Camden, Ala., U.S.A. 115 31 59N 87 15W
Camden, Ark., U.S.A. 117 33 40N 92 50W
Camden, Me., U.S.A. 107 44 14N 69 6W
Camden, N.J., U.S.A. 114 39 57N 75 7W
Camden, S.C., U.S.A. 115 34 17N 80 34W
Camdenton 117 38 0N 92 45W
Camembert 18 48 53N 0 10 E
Cámeri 38 45 30N 8 40 E
Camerino 39 43 10N 13 4 E
Cameron, Ariz., U.S.A. 119 35 55N 111 31W
Cameron, La., U.S.A. 117 29 50N 93 18W
Cameron, Mo., U.S.A. 116 39 42N 94 14W
Cameron, Tex., U.S.A. 117 30 53N 97 0W
Cameron Falls 106 49 8N 88 19W
Cameron Highlands 71 4 27N 101 22 E
Cameron Hills 108 59 48N 118 0W
Cameroon ■ 88 6 0N 12 30 E
Camerota 41 40 2N 15 21 E
Cameroun → 85 4 0N 9 35 E
Cameroun, Mt. 88 4 13N 9 10 E
Cametá 127 2 12 S 49 30W
Camiguin 73 8 55N 123 55 E
Caminha 30 41 50N 8 50W
Camino 118 38 47N 120 40W
Camira Creek 99 29 15 S 152 58 E
Cammal 112 41 24N 77 28W
Camocim 127 2 55 S 40 50W
Camogli 38 44 21N 9 9 E
Camooweal 97 19 56 S 138 7 E
Camopi → 127 3 10N 52 20W
Camp Crook 116 45 36N 103 59W
Camp Wood 117 29 41N 100 0W
Campagna 41 40 40N 15 5 E
Campana 124 34 10 S 58 55W
Campana, I. 128 48 20 S 75 20W
Campanario 31 38 52N 5 36W
Campania □ 41 40 50N 14 45 E
Campbell 112 41 5N 80 36W
Campbell I. 94 52 30 S 169 0 E
Campbell L. 109 63 14N 106 55W
Campbell River 108 50 5N 125 20W
Campbell Town 99 41 52 S 147 30 E
Campbellford 112 44 18N 77 48W
Campbellsville 114 37 23N 85 21W
Campbellton 107 47 57N 66 43W
Campbelltown 99 34 4 S 150 49 E
Campbeltown 14 55 25N 5 36W
Campeche 120 19 50N 90 32W
Campeche □ 120 19 50N 90 32W
Campeche, Bahía de 120 19 30N 93 0W
Camperdown 99 38 14 S 143 9 E
Camperville 109 51 59N 100 9W
Campi Salentina 41 40 22N 18 2 E
Campidano 40 39 30N 8 40 E
Campillo de Altobuey 32 39 36N 1 49W
Campillo de Llerena 31 38 30N 5 50W
Campillos 31 37 4N 4 51W
Campina Grande 127 7 20 S 35 47W
Campiña, La 31 37 45N 4 45W
Campinas 125 22 50 S 47 0W
Campli 39 42 44N 13 40 E
Campo, Camer. 88 2 22N 9 50 E
Campo, Spain 32 42 25N 0 24 E
Campo Belo 127 20 52 S 45 16W
Campo de Criptana 33 39 24N 3 7W
Campo de Gibraltar 31 36 15N 5 25W
Campo Formoso 127 10 30 S 40 20W
Campo Grande 127 20 25 S 54 40W
Campo Maíor 127 4 50 S 42 12W
Campo Maior 31 38 59N 7 7W
Campo Túres 39 46 53N 11 55 E
Campoalegre 126 2 41N 75 20W
Campobasso 41 41 34N 14 40 E
Campobello di Licata 40 37 16N 13 55 E
Campobello di Mazara 40 37 38N 12 45 E
Campofelice 40 37 54N 13 53 E
Camporeale 40 37 53N 13 3 E
Campos 125 21 50 S 41 20W
Campos Belos 127 13 10 S 47 3W
Campos del Puerto 33 39 26N 3 1 E
Campos Novos 125 27 21 S 51 50W
Camprodón 32 42 19N 2 23 E
Campuya → 126 1 40 S 73 30W
Camrose 108 53 0N 112 50W
Camsell Portage 109 59 37N 109 15W
Can Tho 71 10 2N 105 46 E
Canaan 113 42 1N 73 20W
Canada ■ 104 60 0N 100 0W
Cañada de Gómez 124 32 40 S 61 30W
Canadian 117 35 56N 100 25W
Canadian → 117 35 27N 95 3W
Canakkale 44 40 8N 26 30 E
Canakkale Boğazi 44 40 0N 26 0 E
Canal Flats 108 50 10N 115 48W
Canal latéral à la Garonne 20 44 25N 0 15 E
Canalejas 124 35 15 S 66 34W
Canals, Argent. 124 33 35 S 62 53W
Canals, Spain 33 38 58N 0 35W
Canandaigua 114 42 55N 77 18W
Cananea 120 31 0N 110 20W
Canarias, Islas 80 28 30N 16 0W
Canarreos, Arch. de los 121 21 35N 81 40W
Canary Is. = Canarias, Islas 80 29 30N 17 0W
Canaveral, C. 115 28 28N 80 31W
Cañaveras 32 40 27N 2 24W
Canavieiras 127 15 39 S 39 0W
Canbelego 99 31 32 S 146 18 E
Canberra 97 35 15 S 149 8 E
Canby, Calif., U.S.A. 118 41 26N 120 58W
Canby, Minn., U.S.A. 116 44 44N 96 15W
Canby, Ore., U.S.A. 118 45 16N 122 42W
Cancale 18 48 40N 1 50W
Canche → 19 50 31N 1 39 E
Candala 63 11 30N 49 58 E
Candas 30 43 35N 5 45W
Candé 18 47 34N 1 0W
Candela 41 41 8N 15 31 E
Candelaria 125 27 29 S 55 44W
Candelaria, Pta. de la 30 43 45N 8 0W
Candeleda 30 40 10N 5 14W
Candelo 99 36 47 S 149 43 E
Candia = Iráklion 45 35 20N 25 12 E
Candia, Sea of = Crete, Sea of 45 36 0N 25 0 E
Candle L. 109 53 50N 105 18W
Candlemas I. 5 57 3 S 26 40W
Cando 116 48 30N 99 14W
Canea = Khaniá 45 35 30N 24 4 E
Canelli 38 44 44N 8 18 E
Canelones 125 34 32 S 56 17W
Canet-Plage 20 42 41N 3 2 E
Cañete, Chile 124 37 50 S 73 30W
Cañete, Peru 126 13 8 S 76 30W
Cañete, Spain 32 40 3N 1 54W
Cañete de las Torres 31 37 53N 4 19W
Canfranc 32 42 42N 0 31W
Cangas 30 42 16N 8 47W
Cangas de Narcea 30 43 10N 6 32W
Cangas de Onís 30 43 21N 5 8W
Canguaretama 127 6 20 S 35 5W
Canguçu 125 31 22 S 52 43W
Cangxi 77 31 47N 105 59 E
Cangzhou 76 38 19N 116 52 E
Cani, I. 83 36 21N 10 5 E
Canicattì 40 37 21N 13 50 E
Canicattini 41 37 1N 15 3 E
Canim Lake 108 51 47N 120 54W
Canipaan 72 8 33N 117 15 E
Canisteo 112 42 17N 77 37W
Canisteo → 112 42 15N 77 30W
Cañiza, La 30 42 13N 8 16W
Cañizal 30 41 12N 5 22W
Canjáyar 33 37 1N 2 44W
Cankırı 64 40 40N 33 37 E
Cankuzo 90 3 10 S 30 31 E
Canmore 108 51 7N 115 18W
Cann River 99 37 35 S 149 7 E
Canna 14 57 3N 6 33W
Cannanore 70 11 53N 75 27 E
Cannes 21 43 32N 7 0 E
Canning Basin 96 19 50 S 124 0 E
Canning Town 69 22 23N 88 40 E
Cannington 112 44 20N 79 2W
Cannock 12 52 42N 2 2W
Cannon Ball → 116 46 20N 100 38W
Canoe L. 109 55 10N 108 15W
Canon City 116 38 27N 105 14W
Canora 109 51 40N 102 30W
Canosa di Púglia 41 41 13N 16 4 E
Canourgue, Le 20 44 26N 3 13 E
Canowindra 99 33 35 S 148 38 E
Canso 107 45 20N 61 0W
Cantabria, Sierra de 32 42 40N 2 30W
Cantabrian Mts. = Cantábrica, Cordillera 30 43 0N 5 10W
Cantábrica, Cordillera 30 43 0N 5 10W
Cantal □ 20 45 4N 2 45 E
Cantanhede 30 40 20N 8 36W
Cantavieja 32 40 31N 0 25W
Čantavir 42 45 55N 19 46 E
Canterbury, Austral. 99 25 23 S 141 53 E
Canterbury, U.K. 13 51 17N 1 5 E
Canterbury □ 101 43 45 S 171 19 E
Canterbury Bight 101 44 16 S 171 55 E
Canterbury Plains 101 43 55 S 171 22 E
Cantillana 31 37 36N 5 50W
Canton, Ga., U.S.A. 115 34 13N 84 29W
Canton, Ill., U.S.A. 116 40 32N 90 0W
Canton, Mass., U.S.A. 113 42 8N 71 8W
Canton, Miss., U.S.A. 117 32 40N 90 1W
Canton, Mo., U.S.A. 116 40 10N 91 33W
Canton, N.Y., U.S.A. 114 44 32N 75 3W
Canton, Ohio, U.S.A. 114 40 47N 81 22W
Canton, Okla., U.S.A. 117 36 5N 98 36W
Canton, S.D., U.S.A. 116 43 20N 96 35W
Canton = Guangzhou 75 23 5N 113 10 E
• Canton I. 94 2 50 S 171 40W
Canton L. 117 36 12N 98 40W
Cantù 38 45 44N 9 8 E
Canudos 126 7 13 S 58 5W
Canutama 126 6 30 S 64 20W
Canutillo 119 31 58N 106 36W
Canyon, Texas, U.S.A. 117 35 0N 101 57W
Canyon, Wyo., U.S.A. 118 44 43N 110 36W
Canyonlands Nat. Park 119 38 25N 109 30W
Canyonville 118 42 55N 123 14W
Canzo 38 45 54N 9 18 E
Cao Xian 77 34 50N 115 35 E
Cáorle 39 45 36N 12 51 E
Cap-aux-Meules 107 47 23N 61 52W
Cap-Chat 107 49 6N 66 40W
Cap-de-la-Madeleine 106 46 22N 72 31W
Cap-Haïtien 121 19 40N 72 20W
Capa Stilo 41 38 25N 16 35 E
Capáccio 41 40 26N 15 4 E
Capaia 88 8 27 S 20 13 E
Capanaparo → 126 7 1N 67 7W
Capbreton 20 43 39N 1 26W
Capdenac 20 44 34N 2 5 E
Cape → 98 20 49 S 146 51 E
Cape Barren I. 97 40 25 S 148 15 E
Cape Breton Highlands Nat. Park 107 46 50N 60 40W
Cape Breton I. 107 46 0N 60 30W
Cape Charles 114 37 15N 75 59W
Cape Coast 85 5 5N 1 15W
Cape Dorset 105 64 14N 76 32W
Cape Dyer 105 66 30N 61 22W
Cape Fear → 115 34 30N 78 25W
Cape Girardeau 117 37 20N 89 30W
Cape May 114 39 1N 74 53W
Cape Montague 107 46 5N 62 25W
Cape Palmas 84 4 25N 7 49W
Cape Province □ 92 32 0 S 23 0 E
Cape Tormentine 107 46 8N 63 47W
Cape Town (Kaapstad) 92 33 55 S 18 22 E
Cape Verde Is. ■ 6 17 10N 25 20W
Cape Vincent 113 44 9N 76 21W
Cape York Peninsula 97 12 0 S 142 30 E
Capela 127 10 30 S 37 0W
Capella 98 23 2 S 148 1 E
Capella, Mt. 98 5 4 S 141 8 E
Capelle, La 19 49 59N 3 50 E
Capendu 20 43 11N 2 31 E
Capernaum = Kefar Naḥum 62 32 54N 35 32 E
Capestang 20 43 20N 3 2 E
Capim → 127 1 40 S 47 47W
Capitan 119 33 33N 105 41W
Capizzi 41 37 50N 14 26 E
Čapljina 42 43 10N 17 43 E
Capoche → 91 15 35 S 33 0 E
Capraia 38 43 2N 9 50 E
Caprarola 39 42 21N 12 11 E
Capreol 106 46 43N 80 56W
Caprera 40 41 12N 9 28 E
Capri 41 40 34N 14 15 E
Capricorn, C. 97 23 30 S 151 13 E
Capricorn Group 98 23 30 S 151 55 E
Caprino Veronese 38 45 37N 10 47 E
Caprivi Strip 92 18 0 S 23 0 E
Captainganj 69 26 55N 83 45 E
Captain's Flat 99 35 35 S 149 27 E
Captieux 20 44 18N 0 16W
Cápua 41 41 7N 14 15 E
Capulin 117 36 48N 103 59W
Caquetá → 126 1 15 S 69 15W
Caracal 46 44 8N 24 22 E
Caracas 126 10 30N 66 55W
Caracol 127 9 15 S 43 22W
Caradoc 99 30 35 S 143 5 E
Caráglio 38 44 25N 7 25 E
Carajás, Serra dos 127 6 0 S 51 30W
Carangola 125 20 44 S 42 5W
Caransebeş 46 45 28N 22 18 E
Carantec 18 48 40N 3 55W
Carapelle → 41 41 3N 15 55 E
Caraş Severin □ 42 45 10N 22 10 E
Caraşova 42 45 11N 21 51 E
Caratasca, Laguna 121 15 20N 83 40W
Caratinga 127 19 50 S 42 10W
Caraúbas 127 5 43 S 37 33W
Caravaca 33 38 8N 1 52W
Caravággio 38 45 30N 9 39 E
Caravelas 127 17 45 S 39 15W
Caraveli 126 15 45 S 73 25W
Caràzinho 125 28 16 S 52 46W
Carballino 30 42 26N 8 5W
Carballo 30 43 13N 8 41W
Carberry 109 49 50N 99 25W
Carbia 30 42 48N 8 14W
Carbó 120 29 42N 110 58W
Carbon 108 51 30N 113 9W

• *Renamed Abariringa*

Carbonara, C. Cefalù

Carbonara, C. 40 39 8N 9 30 E
Carbondale, Colo, U.S.A. 118 39 30N 107 10W
Carbondale, Ill., U.S.A. 117 37 45N 89 10W
Carbondale, Pa., U.S.A. 114 41 37N 75 30W
Carbonear 107 47 42N 53 13W
Carboneras 33 37 0N 1 53W
Carboneras de Guadazaón 32 39 54N 1 50W
Carbonia 40 39 10N 8 30 E
Carcabuey 31 37 27N 4 17W
Carcagente 33 39 8N 0 28W
Carcajou 108 57 47N 117 6W
Carcans, Étang d' 20 45 6N 1 7W
Carcasse, C. 121 18 30N 74 28W
Carcassonne 20 43 13N 2 20 E
Carche 33 38 26N 1 9W
Carcross 104 60 13N 134 45W
Cardamom Hills 70 9 30N 77 15 E
Cárdenas, Cuba 121 23 0N 81 30W
Cárdenas, San Luis Potosí, Mexico 120 22 0N 99 41W
Cárdenas, Tabasco, Mexico 120 17 59N 93 21W
Cardenete 32 39 46N 1 41W
Cardiff 13 51 28N 3 11W
Cardigan 13 52 6N 4 41W
Cardigan B. 13 52 30N 4 30W
Cardinal 113 44 47N 75 23W
Cardona, Spain 32 41 56N 1 40 E
Cardona, Uruguay 124 33 53 S 57 18W
Cardoner → 32 41 41N 1 51 E
Cardross 109 49 50N 105 40W
Cardston 108 49 15N 113 20W
Cardwell 98 18 14 S 146 2 E
Careen L. 109 57 0N 108 11W
Carei 46 47 40N 22 29 E
Careme 73 6 55 S 108 27 E
Carentan 18 49 19N 1 15W
Carey, Idaho, U.S.A. 118 43 19N 113 58W
Carey, Ohio, U.S.A. 114 40 58N 83 22W
Carey, L. 96 29 0 S 122 15 E
Carey L. 109 62 12N 102 55W
Careysburg 84 6 34N 10 30W
Cargados Garajos 3 17 0 S 59 0 E
Cargèse 21 42 7N 8 35 E
Carhaix-Plouguer 18 48 18N 3 36W
Carhué 124 37 10 S 62 50W
Caribbean Sea 121 15 0N 75 0W
Cariboo Mts. 108 53 0N 121 0W
Caribou 107 46 55N 68 0W
Caribou →, Man., Can. 109 59 20N 94 44W
Caribou →, N.W.T., Can. 108 61 27N 125 45W
Caribou I. 106 47 22N 85 49W
Caribou Is. 108 61 55N 113 15W
Caribou L., Man., Can. 109 59 21N 96 10W
Caribou L., Ont., Can. 106 50 25N 89 5W
Caribou Mts. 108 59 12N 115 40W
Carignan 19 49 38N 5 10 E
Carignano 38 44 55N 7 40 E
Carinda 99 30 28 S 147 41 E
Cariñena 32 41 20N 1 13W
Carinhanha 127 14 15 S 44 46W
Carini 40 38 9N 13 10 E
Carinola 40 41 11N 13 58 E
Carinthia □ = Kärnten 26 46 52N 13 30 E
Caripito 126 10 8N 63 6W
Caritianas 126 9 20 S 63 6W
Carlbrod = Dimitrovgrad 42 43 0N 22 48 E
Carlentini 41 37 15N 15 2 E
Carleton Place 106 45 8N 76 9W
Carletonville 92 26 23 S 27 22 E
Carlin 118 40 44N 116 5W
Carlingford, L. 15 54 0N 6 5W
Carlinville 116 39 20N 89 55W
Carlisle, U.K. 12 54 54N 2 55W
Carlisle, U.S.A. 114 40 12N 77 10W
Carlitte, Pic 20 42 35N 1 55 E
Carloforte 40 39 10N 8 18 E
Carlos Casares 124 35 32 S 61 20W
Carlos Tejedor 124 35 25 S 62 25W
Carlota, La 124 33 30 S 63 20W
Carlow 15 52 50N 6 58W
Carlow □ 15 52 43N 6 50W
Carlsbad, Calif., U.S.A. 119 33 11N 117 25W
Carlsbad, N. Mex., U.S.A. 117 32 20N 104 14W
Carlyle, Can. 109 49 40N 102 20W
Carlyle, U.S.A. 116 38 38N 89 23W
Carmacks 104 62 5N 136 16W
Carmagnola 38 44 50N 7 42 E
Carman 109 49 30N 98 0W
Carmangay 108 50 10N 113 10W
Carmanville 107 49 23N 54 19W
Carmarthen 13 51 52N 4 20W
Carmarthen B. 13 51 40N 4 30W
Carmaux 20 44 3N 2 10 E
Carmel 113 41 25N 73 38W
Carmel-by-the-Sea 119 36 38N 121 55W
Carmel Mt. 62 32 45N 35 3 E
Carmelo 124 34 0 S 58 20W
Carmen, Colomb. 126 9 43N 75 8W
Carmen, Parag. 125 27 13 S 56 12W
Carmen de Patagones 128 40 50 S 63 0W
Carmen, I. 120 26 0N 111 20W
Cármenes 30 42 58N 5 34W
Carmensa 124 35 15 S 67 40W
Carmi 114 38 6N 88 10W
Carmila 98 21 55 S 149 24 E
Carmona 31 37 28N 5 42W
Carnarvon, Queens., Austral. 98 24 48 S 147 45 E
Carnarvon, W. Austral., Austral. 96 24 51 S 113 42 E
Carnarvon, S. Afr. 92 30 56 S 22 8 E
Carnarvon Ra. 99 25 15 S 148 30 E
Carnaxide 31 38 43N 9 14W
Carndonagh 15 55 15N 7 16W
Carnduff 109 49 10N 101 50W
Carnegie 112 40 24N 80 4W
Carnegie, L. 96 26 5 S 122 30 E
Carnic Alps = Karnische Alpen 26 46 36N 13 0 E
Carnot 88 4 59N 15 56 E
Carnot B. 96 17 20 S 121 30 E
Carnsore Pt. 15 52 10N 6 20W
Caro 114 43 29N 83 27W
Carol City 115 25 5N 80 16W
Carolina, Brazil 127 7 10 S 47 30W
Carolina, S. Afr. 93 26 5 S 30 6 E
Carolina, La 31 38 17N 3 38W
Caroline I. 95 9 15 S 150 3W
Caroline Is. 94 8 0N 150 0 E
Caron 109 50 30N 105 50W
Caroni → 126 8 21N 62 43W
Carovigno 41 40 42N 17 40 E
Carpathians 46 49 50N 21 0 E
Carpaţii Meridionali 46 45 30N 25 0 E
Carpenédolo 38 45 22N 10 25 E
Carpentaria Downs 98 18 44 S 144 20 E
Carpentaria, G. of 97 14 0 S 139 0 E
Carpentras 21 44 3N 5 2 E
Carpi 38 44 47N 10 52 E
Carpino 41 41 50N 15 51 E
Carpinteria 119 34 25N 119 31W
Carpio 30 41 13N 5 7W
Carrabelle 115 29 52N 84 40W
Carrara 38 44 5N 10 7 E
Carrascosa del Campo 32 40 2N 2 45W
Carrauntohill, Mt. 15 52 0N 9 49W
Carrick-on-Shannon 15 53 57N 8 7W
Carrick-on-Suir 15 52 22N 7 30W
Carrickfergus 15 54 43N 5 50W
Carrickfergus □ 15 54 43N 5 49W
Carrickmacross 15 54 0N 6 43W
Carrieton 99 32 25 S 138 31 E
Carrington 116 47 30N 99 7W
Carrión → 30 41 53N 4 32W
Carrión de los Condes 30 42 20N 4 37W
Carrizal Bajo 124 28 5 S 71 20W
Carrizalillo 124 29 5 S 71 30W
Carrizo Cr. 117 36 30N 103 40W
Carrizo Springs 117 28 28N 99 50W
Carrizozo 119 33 40N 105 57W
Carroll 116 42 2N 94 55W
Carrollton, Ga., U.S.A. 115 33 36N 85 5W
Carrollton, Ill., U.S.A. 116 39 20N 90 25W
Carrollton, Ky., U.S.A. 114 38 40N 85 10W
Carrollton, Mo., U.S.A. 116 39 19N 93 24W
Carrollton, Ohio, U.S.A. 112 40 31N 81 9W
Carron → 14 57 30N 5 30W
Carron, L. 14 57 22N 5 35W
Carrot → 109 53 50N 101 17W
Carrot River 109 53 17N 103 35W
Carrouges 18 48 34N 0 10W
Carruthers 109 52 52N 109 16W
Çarşamba 64 41 15N 36 45 E
Carse of Gowrie 14 56 30N 3 10W
Carsoli 39 42 7N 13 3 E
Carson 116 46 27N 101 29W
Carson City 118 39 12N 119 46W
Carson Sink 118 39 50N 118 40W
Carsonville 114 43 25N 82 39W
Carstairs 14 55 42N 3 41W
Cartagena, Colomb. 126 10 25N 75 33W
Cartagena, Spain 33 37 38N 0 59W
Cartago, Colomb. 126 4 45N 75 55W
Cartago, C. Rica 121 9 50N 85 52W
Cartaxo 31 39 10N 8 47W
Cartaya 31 37 16N 7 9W
Carteret 18 49 23N 1 47W
Cartersville 115 34 11N 84 48W
Carterton 101 41 2 S 175 31 E
Carthage, Ark., U.S.A. 117 34 4N 92 32W
Carthage, Ill., U.S.A. 116 40 25N 91 10W
Carthage, Mo., U.S.A. 117 37 10N 94 20W
Carthage, N.Y., U.S.A. 114 43 59N 75 37W
Carthage, S.D., U.S.A. 116 44 14N 97 38W
Carthage, Texas, U.S.A. 117 32 8N 94 20W
Cartier I. 96 12 31 S 123 29 E
Cartwright 107 53 41N 56 58W
Caruaru 127 8 15 S 35 55W
Carúpano 126 10 39N 63 15W
Caruthersville 117 36 10N 89 40W
Carvin 19 50 30N 2 57 E
Carvoeiro 126 1 30 S 61 59W
Carvoeiro, Cabo 31 39 21N 9 24W
Casa Branca 31 38 29N 8 12W
Casa Grande 119 32 53N 111 51W
Casa Nova 127 9 25 S 41 5W
Casablanca, Chile 124 33 20 S 71 25W
Casablanca, Moroc. 82 33 36N 7 36W
Casacalenda 41 41 45N 14 50 E
Casal di Principe 41 41 0N 14 8 E
Casalbordino 39 42 10N 14 34 E
Casale Monferrato 38 45 8N 8 28 E
Casalmaggiore 38 44 59N 10 25 E
Casalpusterlengo 38 45 10N 9 40 E
Casamance → 84 12 33N 16 46W
Casamássima 41 40 58N 16 55 E
Casarano 41 40 0N 18 10 E
Casares 31 36 27N 5 16W
Casas Grandes 120 30 22N 108 0W
Casas Ibañez 33 39 17N 1 30W
Casasimarro 33 39 22N 2 3W
Casatejada 30 39 54N 5 40W
Casavieja 30 40 17N 4 46W
Cascade, Idaho, U.S.A. 118 44 30N 116 2W
Cascade, Mont., U.S.A. 118 47 16N 111 46W
Cascade Locks 118 45 44N 121 54W
Cascade Ra. 102 47 0N 121 30W
Cascais 31 38 41N 9 25W
Cáscina 38 43 40N 10 32 E
Caselle Torinese 38 45 12N 7 39 E
Caserta 41 41 5N 14 20 E
Cashel 15 52 31N 7 53W
Cashmere 118 47 31N 120 30W
Casiguran 73 16 22N 122 7 E
Casilda 124 33 10 S 61 10W
Casimcea 46 44 45N 28 23 E
Casino 97 28 52 S 153 3 E
Casiquiare → 126 2 1N 67 7W
Caslan 108 54 38N 112 31W
Čáslav 26 49 54N 15 22 E
Casma 126 9 30 S 78 20W
Casola Valsenio 39 44 12N 11 40 E
Cásoli 39 42 7N 14 18 E
Caspe 32 41 14N 0 1W
Casper 118 42 52N 106 20W
Caspian Sea 53 43 0N 50 0 E
Casquets 18 49 46N 2 15W
Cass City 114 43 34N 83 24W
Cass Lake 116 47 23N 94 38W
Cassá de la Selva 32 41 53N 2 52 E
Cassano Iónio 41 39 47N 16 20 E
Cassel 19 50 48N 2 30 E
Casselman 113 45 19N 75 5W
Casselton 116 47 0N 97 15W
Cassiar 108 59 16N 129 40W
Cassiar Mts. 108 59 30N 130 30W
Cassino 40 41 30N 13 50 E
Cassis 21 43 14N 5 32 E
Cassville 117 36 45N 93 52W
Cástagneto Carducci 38 43 9N 10 36 E
Castéggio 38 45 1N 9 8 E
Castejón de Monegros 32 41 37N 0 15W
Castel di Sangro 39 41 47N 14 6 E
Castel San Giovanni 38 45 4N 9 25 E
Castel San Pietro 39 44 23N 11 30 E
Castelbuono 41 37 56N 14 4 E
Casteldelfino 38 44 35N 7 4 E
Castelfiorentino 38 43 36N 10 58 E
Castelfranco Emília 38 44 37N 11 2 E
Castelfranco Véneto 39 45 40N 11 56 E
Casteljaloux 20 44 19N 0 6 E
Castellabate 41 40 18N 14 55 E
Castellammare del Golfo 40 38 2N 12 53 E
Castellammare di Stábia 41 40 47N 14 29 E
Castellammare, G. di 40 38 5N 12 55 E
Castellamonte 38 45 23N 7 42 E
Castellana Grotte 41 40 53N 17 10 E
Castellane 21 43 50N 6 31 E
Castellaneta 41 40 40N 16 57 E
Castellar de Santisteban 33 38 16N 3 8W
Castelleone 38 45 19N 9 47 E
Castelli 124 36 7 S 57 47W
Castelló de Ampurias 32 42 15N 3 4 E
Castellón □ 32 40 15N 0 5W
Castellón de la Plana 32 39 58N 0 3W
Castellote 32 40 48N 0 15W
Castelltersol 32 41 45N 2 8 E
Castelmáuro 41 41 50N 14 40 E
Castelnau-de-Médoc 20 45 2N 0 48W
Castelnaudary 20 43 20N 1 58 E
Castelnovo ne' Monti 38 44 27N 10 26 E
Castelnuovo di Val di Cécina 38 43 12N 10 54 E
Castelo 125 20 33 S 41 14 E
Castelo Branco 30 39 50N 7 31W
Castelo Branco □ 30 39 52N 7 45W
Castelo de Paiva 30 41 2N 8 16W
Castelo de Vide 31 39 25N 7 27W
Castelsarrasin 20 44 2N 1 7 E
Casteltérmini 40 37 32N 13 38 E
Castelvetrano 40 37 40N 12 46 E
Casterton 99 37 30 S 141 30 E
Castets 20 43 52N 1 6W
Castiglione del Lago 39 43 7N 12 3 E
Castiglione della Pescáia 38 42 46N 10 53 E
Castiglione della Stiviere 38 45 23N 10 30 E
Castiglione Fiorentino 39 43 20N 11 55 E
Castilblanco 31 39 17N 5 5W
Castilla La Nueva 31 39 45N 3 20W
Castilla La Vieja 30 41 55N 4 0W
Castilla, Playa de 31 37 0N 6 33W
Castille = Castilla 30 40 0N 3 30W
Castillon, Barrage de 21 43 53N 6 33 E
Castillon-en-Couserans 20 42 56N 1 1 E
Castillon-la-Bataille 20 44 51N 0 2W
Castillonès 20 44 39N 0 37 E
Castillos 125 34 12 S 53 52W
Castle Dale 118 39 11N 111 1W
Castle Douglas 14 54 57N 3 57W
Castle Harbour 121 32 17N 64 44W
Castle Point 101 40 54 S 176 15 E
Castle Rock, Colo., U.S.A. 116 39 26N 104 50W
Castle Rock, Wash., U.S.A. 118 46 20N 122 58W
Castlebar 15 53 52N 9 17W
Castleblaney 15 54 7N 6 44W
Castlegar 108 49 20N 117 40W
Castlegate 118 39 45N 110 57W
Castlemaine 97 37 2 S 144 12 E
Castlereagh 15 53 47N 8 30W
Castlereagh □ 15 54 33N 5 53W
Castlereagh → 97 30 12 S 147 32 E
Castlereagh B. 96 12 10 S 135 10 E
Castletown 12 54 4N 4 40W
Castletown Bearhaven 15 51 40N 9 54W
Castlevale 98 24 30 S 146 48 E
Castor 108 52 15N 111 50W
Castres 20 43 37N 2 13 E
Castries 121 14 0N 60 50W
Castril 33 37 48N 2 46W
Castro, Brazil 125 24 45 S 50 0W
Castro, Chile 128 42 30 S 73 50W
Castro Alves 127 12 46 S 39 33W
Castro del Rio 31 37 41N 4 29W
Castro Marim 31 37 13N 7 26W
Castro Urdiales 32 43 23N 3 11W
Castro Verde 31 37 41N 8 4W
Castrojeriz 30 42 17N 4 9W
Castropol 30 43 32N 7 0W
Castroreale 41 38 5N 15 15 E
Castrovillari 41 39 49N 16 11 E
Castroville 117 29 20N 98 53W
Castuera 31 38 43N 5 37W
Casummit Lake 106 51 29N 92 22W
Cat I., Bahamas 121 24 30N 75 30W
Cat I., U.S.A. 117 30 15N 89 7W
Cat L. 106 51 40N 91 50W
Čata 27 47 58N 18 38 E
Catacáos 126 5 20 S 80 45W
Cataguases 125 21 23 S 42 39W
Catahoula L. 117 31 30N 92 5W
Catalão 127 18 10 S 47 57W
Catalina 107 48 31N 53 4W
Catalonia = Cataluña 32 41 40N 1 15 E
Cataluña 32 41 40N 1 15 E
Catamarca 124 28 30 S 65 50W
Catamarca □ 124 27 0 S 65 50W
Catanduanes 73 13 50N 124 20 E
Catanduva 125 21 5 S 48 58W
Catánia 41 37 31N 15 4 E
Catánia, G. di 41 37 25N 15 8 E
Catanzaro 41 38 54N 16 38 E
Catarman 73 12 28N 124 35 E
Catastrophe C. 96 34 59 S 136 0 E
Cateau, Le 19 50 6N 3 30 E
Cateel 73 7 47N 126 24 E
Cathcart 92 32 18 S 27 10 E
Cathlamet 118 46 12N 123 23W
Catio 84 11 17N 15 15W
Cativa 120 9 21N 79 49W
Catlettsburg 114 38 23N 82 38W
Cato I. 97 23 15 S 155 32 E
Catoche, C. 120 21 40N 87 8W
Catral 33 38 10N 0 47W
Catria, Mt. 39 43 28N 12 42 E
Catrimani 126 0 27N 61 41W
Catskill 114 42 14N 73 52W
Catskill Mts. 114 42 15N 74 15W
Cattaraugus 112 42 22N 78 52W
Cattólica 39 43 58N 12 43 E
Cattólica Eraclea 40 37 27N 13 24 E
Catuala 92 16 25 S 19 2 E
Catur 91 13 45 S 35 30 E
Cauca → 126 8 54N 74 28W
Caucaia 127 3 40 S 38 35W
Caucasus Mts. = Bolshoi Kavkas 57 42 50N 44 0 E
Caudebec-en-Caux 18 49 30N 0 42 E
Caudete 33 38 42N 1 2W
Caudry 19 50 7N 3 22 E
Caulnes 18 48 18N 2 10W
Caulónia 41 38 23N 16 25 E
Caúngula 88 8 26 S 18 38 E
Cauquenes 124 36 0 S 72 22W
Caura → 126 7 38N 64 53W
Cauresi → 91 17 8 S 33 0 E
Causapscal 107 48 19N 67 12W
Caussade 20 44 10N 1 33 E
Cauterets 20 42 52N 0 8W
Caux, Pays de 18 49 38N 0 35 E
Cava dei Tirreni 41 40 42N 14 42 E
Cávado → 30 41 32N 8 48W
Cavaillon 21 43 50N 5 2 E
Cavalaire-sur-Mer 21 43 10N 6 33 E
Cavalerie, La 20 44 0N 3 10 E
Cavalese 39 46 17N 11 29 E
Cavalier 116 48 50N 97 39W
Cavallo, Île de 21 41 22N 9 16 E
Cavally → 84 4 22N 7 32W
Cavan 15 54 0N 7 22W
Cavan □ 15 53 58N 7 10W
Cavárzere 39 45 8N 12 6 E
Cave City 114 37 13N 85 57W
Cavendish 99 37 31 S 142 2 E
Caviana, I. 127 0 10N 50 10W
Cavite 73 14 29N 120 55 E
Cavour 38 44 47N 7 22 E
Cavtat 42 42 35N 18 13 E
Cawndilla, L. 99 32 30 S 142 15 E
Cawnpore = Kanpur 69 26 28N 80 20 E
Caxias 127 4 55 S 43 20W
Caxias do Sul 125 29 10 S 51 10W
Caxine, C. 82 35 56N 0 27W
Caxito 88 8 30 S 13 30 E
Cay Sal Bank 121 23 45N 80 0W
Cayambe 126 0 3N 78 8W
Cayce 115 33 59N 81 10W
Cayenne 127 5 0N 52 18W
Cayes, Les 121 18 15N 73 46W
Cayeux-sur-Mer 19 50 10N 1 30 E
Caylus 20 44 15N 1 47 E
Cayman Is. 121 19 40N 80 30W
* Cayo 120 17 10N 89 0W
Cayo Romano 121 22 0N 78 0W
Cayuga, Can. 112 42 59N 79 50W
Cayuga, U.S.A. 113 42 54N 76 44W
Cayuga L. 114 42 45N 76 45W
Cazalla de la Sierra 31 37 56N 5 45W
Căzăneşti 46 44 36N 27 3 E
Cazaux et de Sanguinet, Étang de 20 44 29N 1 10W
Cazères 20 43 13N 1 5 E
Cazin 39 44 57N 15 57 E
Čazma 39 45 45N 16 39 E
Čazma → 39 45 35N 16 29 E
Cazombo 89 11 54 S 22 56 E
Cazorla 33 37 55N 3 2W
Cazorla, Sierra de 33 38 5N 2 55W
Cea → 30 42 0N 5 36W
Ceamurlia de Jos 43 44 43N 28 47 E
Ceanannus Mor 15 53 42N 6 53W
Ceará = Fortaleza 127 3 43 S 38 35W
Ceará □ 127 5 0 S 40 0W
Ceará Mirim 127 5 38 S 35 25W
Ceauru, L. 46 44 58N 23 11 E
Cebollar 124 29 10 S 66 35W
Cebollera, Sierra de 32 42 0N 2 30W
Cebreros 30 40 27N 4 28W
Cebu 73 10 18N 123 54 E
Ceccano 40 41 34N 13 18 E
Cece 27 46 46N 18 39 E
Cechi 84 6 15N 4 25W
Cecil Plains 99 27 30 S 151 11 E
Cécina 38 43 19N 10 33 E
Cécina → 38 43 19N 10 29 E
Ceclavin 30 39 50N 6 45W
Cedar → 116 41 17N 91 21W
Cedar City 119 37 41N 113 3W
Cedar Creek Res. 117 32 4N 96 5W
Cedar Falls 116 42 39N 92 29W
Cedar Key 115 29 9N 83 5W
Cedar L. 109 53 10N 100 0W
Cedar Rapids 116 42 0N 91 38W
Cedarburg 114 43 18N 87 55W
Cedartown 115 34 1N 85 15W
Cedarvale 108 55 1N 128 22W
Cedarville 118 41 37N 120 13W
Cedeira 30 43 39N 8 2W
Cedral 120 23 50N 100 42W
Cedrino → 40 40 23N 9 44 E
Cedro 127 6 34 S 39 3W
Cedros, I. de 120 28 10N 115 20W
Ceduna 96 32 7 S 133 46 E
Cedynia 28 52 53N 14 12 E
Cefalù 41 38 3N 14 1 E

¹ Renamed N'gage

* Renamed San Ignacio

Cega Chelmsford

Cega →	30	41 33N	4 46W
Cegléd	27	47 11N	19 47 E
Céglie Messápico	41	40 39N	17 31 E
Cehegín	33	38 6N	1 48W
Cehu-Silvaniei	46	47 24N	23 9 E
Ceiba, La	121	15 40N	86 50W
Ceica	46	46 53N	22 10 E
Ceira →	30	40 13N	8 16W
Cekhira	83	34 20N	10 5 E
Celano	39	42 6N	13 30 E
Celanova	30	42 9N	7 58W
Celaya	120	20 31N	100 37W
Celbridge	15	53 20N	6 33W
Celebes = Sulawesi	73	2 0S	120 0 E
Celebes Sea	73	3 0N	123 0 E
Čelić	42	44 43N	18 47 E
Celina	114	40 32N	84 31W
Celje	39	46 16N	15 18 E
Celldömölk	27	47 16N	17 10 E
Celle	24	52 37N	10 4 E
Celorico da Beira	30	40 38N	7 24W
Cement	117	34 56N	98 8W
Cengong	77	27 13N	108 44 E
Cenis, Col du Mt.	21	45 15N	6 55 E
Ceno →	38	44 4N	10 5 E
Cenon	20	44 50N	0 33W
Centallo	38	44 30N	7 35 E
Center, N.D., U.S.A.	116	47 9N	101 17W
Center, Texas, U.S.A.	117	31 50N	94 10W
Centerfield	119	39 9N	111 56W
Centerville, Ala., U.S.A.	115	32 55N	87 7W
Centerville, Iowa, U.S.A.	116	40 45N	92 57W
Centerville, Miss., U.S.A.	117	31 10N	91 3W
Centerville, Pa., U.S.A.	112	40 3N	79 59W
Centerville, S.D., U.S.A.	116	43 10N	96 58W
Centerville, Tenn., U.S.A.	115	35 46N	87 29W
Centerville, Tex., U.S.A.	117	31 15N	95 56W
Cento	39	44 43N	11 16 E
Central	119	32 46N	108 9W
Central □, Kenya	90	0 30S	37 30 E
Central □, Malawi	91	13 30S	33 30 E
Central □, U.K.	14	56 10N	4 30W
Central □, Zambia	91	14 25S	28 50 E
Central African Republic ■	88	7 0N	20 0 E
Central City, Ky., U.S.A.	114	37 20N	87 7W
Central City, Nebr., U.S.A.	116	41 8N	98 0W
Central, Cordillera, Colomb.	126	5 0N	75 0W
Central, Cordillera, C. Rica	121	10 10N	84 5W
Central I.	90	3 30N	36 0 E
Central Islip	113	40 49N	73 13W
Central Makran Range	65	26 30N	64 15 E
Central Patricia	106	51 30N	90 9W
Central Ra.	98	5 0S	143 0 E
Central Russian Uplands	9	54 0N	36 0 E
Central Siberian Plateau	59	65 0N	105 0 E
Centralia, Ill., U.S.A.	116	38 32N	89 5W
Centralia, Mo., U.S.A.	116	39 12N	92 6W
Centralia, Wash., U.S.A.	118	46 46N	122 59W
Centúripe	41	37 37N	14 41 E
Cephalonia = Kefallinía	45	38 15N	20 30 E
Cepin	42	45 32N	18 34 E
Ceprano	40	41 33N	13 30 E
Ceptura	46	45 1N	26 21 E
Cepu	73	7 12S	111 31 E
Ceram = Seram	73	3 10S	129 0 E
Ceram Sea = Seram Sea	73	2 30S	128 30 E
Cerbère	20	42 26N	3 10 E
Cerbicales, Îles	21	41 33N	9 22 E
Cerbu	46	44 46N	24 46 E
Cercal	31	37 48N	8 40W
Cercemaggiore	41	41 27N	14 43 E
Cerdaña	32	42 22N	1 35 E
Cerdedo	30	42 33N	8 23W
Cère →	20	44 55N	1 49 E
Cerea	39	45 12N	11 13 E
Ceres, Argent.	124	29 55S	61 55W
Ceres, Italy	38	45 19N	7 22 E
Ceres, S. Afr.	92	33 21S	19 18 E
Céret	20	42 30N	2 42 E
Cerignola	41	41 17N	15 53 E
Cerigo = Kíthira	45	36 15N	23 0 E
Cérilly	20	46 37N	2 50 E
Cerisiers	19	48 8N	3 30 E
Cerizay	18	46 50N	0 40W
Çerkeş	64	40 49N	32 52 E
Cerknica	39	45 48N	14 21 E
Cermerno	42	43 35N	20 25 E
Cerna	46	45 4N	28 17 E
Cerna →	46	44 45N	24 0 E
Cernavodă	46	44 22N	28 3 E
Cernay	19	47 44N	7 10 E
Cernik	42	45 17N	17 22 E
Cerralvo	120	24 20N	109 45 E
Cerreto Sannita	41	41 17N	14 34 E
Cerritos	120	22 27N	100 20W
Cerro	119	36 47N	105 36W
Certaldo	38	43 32N	11 2 E
Cervaro →	41	41 30N	15 52 E
Cervera	32	41 40N	1 16 E
Cervera de Pisuerga	30	42 51N	4 30W
Cervera del Río Alhama	32	42 2N	1 58W
Cérvia	39	44 15N	12 20 E
Cervignano del Friuli	39	45 49N	13 20 E
Cervinara	41	41 2N	14 36 E
Cervione	21	42 20N	9 29 E
Cervo	30	43 40N	7 24W
Cesaro	41	37 50N	14 38 E
Cesena	39	44 9N	12 14 E
Cesenático	39	44 12N	12 22 E
Cēsis	54	57 17N	25 28 E
Česká Lípa	26	50 45N	14 30 E
Česka Socialistická Republika □	26	49 30N	14 40 E
Česká Třebová	27	49 54N	16 27 E
České Budějovice	26	48 55N	14 25 E
České Velenice	26	48 45N	15 1 E
Ceskomoravská Vrchovina	26	49 30N	15 40 E
Český Brod	26	50 4N	14 52 E
Český Krumlov	26	48 43N	14 21 E
Český Těšin	27	49 45N	18 39 E
Çeşme	45	38 20N	26 23 E
Cessnock	97	32 50S	151 21 E
Cestas	20	44 44N	0 41W
Cestos →	84	5 40N	9 10W
Cetate	46	44 7N	23 2 E
Cétin Grad	39	45 9N	15 45 E
Cetina →	39	43 26N	16 42 E
Cetinje	42	42 23N	18 59 E
Cetraro	41	39 30N	15 56 E
Ceuta	82	35 52N	5 18W
Ceva	38	44 23N	8 3 E
Cévennes	20	44 10N	3 50 E
Ceyhan	64	37 4N	35 47 E
Ceylon = Sri Lanka ■	70	7 30N	80 50 E
Cèze →	21	44 13N	4 43 E
Cha Pa	71	22 20N	103 47 E
Chabeuil	21	44 54N	5 1 E
Chablais	21	46 20N	6 36 E
Chablis	19	47 47N	3 48 E
Chabounia	82	35 30N	2 38 E
Chacabuco	124	34 40S	60 27W
Chachapoyas	126	6 15S	77 50W
Chachro	68	25 5N	70 15 E
Chaco □	124	26 30S	61 0W
Chad ■	81	15 0N	17 15 E
Chad, L. = Tchad, L.	81	13 30N	14 30 E
Chadan	59	51 17N	91 35 E
Chadileuvú →	124	37 46S	66 0W
Chadiza	91	14 45S	32 27 E
Chadron	116	42 50N	103 0W
Chadyr-Lunga	56	46 3N	28 51 E
Chagda	59	58 45N	130 38 E
Chagny	19	46 57N	4 45 E
Chagoda	54	59 10N	35 15 E
Chagos Arch.	60	6 0S	72 0 E
Chágres →	120	9 10N	79 40W
Chāh Bahār	65	25 20N	60 40 E
Chāh Gay Hills	65	29 30N	64 0 E
Chaillé-les-Marais	20	46 25N	1 2W
Chaise-Dieu, La	20	45 20N	3 40 E
Chaize-le-Vicomte, La	18	46 40N	1 18W
Chaj Doab	68	32 15N	73 0 E
Chajari	124	30 42S	58 0W
Chake Chake	90	5 15S	39 45 E
Chakhansur	65	31 10N	62 0 E
Chakhansur □	65	30 0N	62 0 E
Chakonipau, L.	107	56 18N	68 30W
Chakradharpur	69	22 45N	85 40 E
Chakwal	68	32 56N	72 53 E
Chala	126	15 48S	74 20W
Chalais	20	45 16N	0 3 E
Chalakudi	70	10 18N	76 20 E
Chalcis = Khalkís	45	38 27N	23 42 E
Chaleur B.	107	47 55N	65 30W
Chalhuanca	126	14 15S	73 15W
Chalindrey	19	47 48N	5 26 E
Chaling	77	26 58N	113 30 E
Chalisgaon	70	20 30N	75 10 E
Chalkar	57	50 35N	51 52 E
Chalkar Oz.	57	50 33N	51 45 E
Chalky Inlet	101	46 3S	166 31 E
Challans	18	46 50N	1 52W
Challapata	126	18 53S	66 50W
Challerange	19	49 18N	4 46 E
Challis	118	44 32N	114 25W
Chalna	69	22 36N	89 35 E
Chalon-sur-Saône	19	46 48N	4 50 E
Chalonnes	18	47 20N	0 45W
Châlons-sur-Marne	19	48 58N	4 20 E
Châlus	20	45 39N	0 58 E
Cham	25	49 12N	12 40 E
Chama	119	36 54N	106 35W
Chaman	66	30 58N	66 25 E
Chamarajnagar-Ramasamudram	70	11 52N	76 52 E
Chamartín de la Rosa	30	40 28N	3 40W
Chamba	68	32 35N	76 10 E
Chambal →	69	26 29N	79 15 E
Chamberlain	116	43 50N	99 21W
Chambers	119	35 13N	109 30W
Chambersburg	114	39 53N	77 41W
Chambéry	21	45 34N	5 55 E
Chambly	113	45 27N	73 17W
Chambois	18	48 48N	0 6 E
Chambon-Feugerolles, Le	21	45 24N	4 18 E
Chambord	107	48 25N	72 6W
Chambri L.	98	4 15S	143 10 E
Chamical	124	30 22S	66 27W
Chamonix	21	45 55N	6 51 E
Champa	69	22 2N	82 43 E
Champagne, Can.	108	60 49N	136 30W
Champagne, France	19	49 0N	4 40 E
Champagne, Plaine de	19	49 0N	4 30 E
Champagnole	19	46 45N	5 55 E
Champaign	114	40 8N	88 14W
Champaubert	19	48 50N	3 45 E
Champdeniers	20	46 29N	0 25W
Champeix	20	45 37N	3 8 E
Champion B.	96	28 44S	114 36 E
Champlain, Can.	106	46 27N	72 24W
Champlain, U.S.A.	114	44 59N	73 27W
Champlain, L.	114	44 30N	73 20W
Champotón	120	19 20N	90 50W
Chamusca	31	39 21N	8 29W
Chañaral	124	26 23S	70 40W
Chanasma	68	23 44N	72 5 E
Chandalar	104	67 30N	148 35W
Chandannagar	69	22 52N	88 24 E
Chandausi	68	28 27N	78 49 E
Chandeleur Is.	117	29 48N	88 51W
Chandeleur Sd.	117	29 58N	88 40W
Chandigarh	68	30 43N	76 47 E
Chandler, Can.	107	48 18N	64 46W
Chandler, Ariz., U.S.A.	119	33 20N	111 56W
Chandler, Okla., U.S.A.	117	35 43N	96 53W
Chandmani	75	45 22N	98 2 E
Chandpur, Bangla.	69	23 8N	90 45 E
Chandpur, India	68	29 8N	78 19 E
Chandrapur	70	19 57N	79 25 E
Chang	68	26 59N	68 30 E
Chang Jiang →, Jiangsu, China	75	31 48N	121 10 E
Chang Jiang →, Shanghai, China	75	31 35N	121 15 E
Changanacheri	70	9 25N	76 31 E
Changbai	76	41 25N	128 5 E
Changbai Shan	76	42 20N	129 0 E
Changchiak'ou = Zhangjiakou	76	40 48N	114 55 E
Ch'angchou = Changzhou	75	31 47N	119 58 E
Changchun	76	43 57N	125 17 E
Changde	75	29 4N	111 35 E
Changfeng	77	32 28N	117 10 E
Changhai = Shanghai	75	31 15N	121 26 E
Changjiang	75	19 20N	108 55 E
Changjin-chŏsuji	76	40 30N	127 15 E
Changle	77	25 59N	119 27 E
Changli	76	39 40N	119 13 E
Changning	77	26 28N	112 22 E
Changping	76	40 14N	116 12 E
Changsha	75	28 12N	113 0 E
Changshou	77	29 51N	107 8 E
Changshu	77	31 38N	120 43 E
Changshun	77	26 3N	106 25 E
Changtai	77	24 35N	117 42 E
Changting	75	25 50N	116 22 E
Changyang	77	30 30N	111 10 E
Changzhi	76	36 10N	113 6 E
Changzhou	75	31 47N	119 58 E
Chanhanga	92	16 0S	14 8 E
Chanlar	57	40 25N	46 10 E
Channapatna	70	12 40N	77 15 E
Channel Is., U.K.	18	49 30N	2 40W
Channel Is., U.S.A.	119	33 55N	119 26W
Channel-Port aux Basques	107	47 30N	59 9W
Channing, Mich., U.S.A.	114	46 9N	88 1W
Channing, Tex., U.S.A.	117	35 45N	102 20W
Chantada	30	42 36N	7 46W
Chanthaburi	71	12 38N	102 12 E
Chantilly	19	49 12N	2 29 E
Chantonnay	18	46 40N	1 3W
Chantrey Inlet	104	67 48N	96 20W
Chanute	117	37 45N	95 25W
Chanza →	31	37 32N	7 30W
Chao Hu	77	31 30N	117 30 E
Chao Phraya →	71	13 32N	100 36 E
Chao'an	75	23 42N	116 32 E
Chaoyang, Guangdong, China	75	23 17N	116 30 E
Chaoyang, Liaoning, China	76	41 35N	120 22 E
Chapala	91	15 50S	37 35 E
Chapala, Lago de	120	20 10N	103 20W
Chapayevo	57	50 25N	51 10 E
Chapayevsk	55	53 0N	49 40 E
Chapecó	125	27 14S	52 41W
Chapel Hill	115	35 53N	79 3W
Chapelle-d'Angillon, La	19	47 21N	2 25 E
Chapelle-Glain, La	18	47 38N	1 11W
Chapleau	106	47 50N	83 24W
Chaplin	109	50 28N	106 40W
Chaplino	56	48 8N	36 15 E
Chaplygin	55	53 15N	40 0 E
Chapra	69	25 48N	84 44 E
Châr	80	21 32N	12 45 E
Chara	59	56 54N	118 20 E
Charadai	124	27 35S	60 0W
Charagua	126	19 45S	63 10W
Charaña	126	17 30S	69 25W
Charata	124	27 13S	61 14W
Charcas	120	23 10N	101 20W
Charcoal L.	109	58 49N	102 22W
Charcot I.	5	70 0S	75 0W
Chard	13	50 52N	2 59W
Chardara	58	41 16N	67 59 E
Chardon	112	41 34N	81 17W
Chardzhou	58	39 6N	63 34 E
Charente	20	45 40N	0 5 E
Charente □	20	45 50N	0 16 E
Charente →	20	45 57N	1 5W
Charente-Maritime □	20	45 30N	0 35W
Charentsavan	57	40 35N	44 41 E
Chārīkār	65	35 0N	69 10 E
Charité, La	19	47 10N	3 0 E
Chariton →	116	39 19N	92 58W
Charkhari	69	25 24N	79 45 E
Charkhi Dadri	68	28 37N	76 17 E
Charleroi	16	50 24N	4 27 E
Charlerol	112	40 8N	79 54W
Charles, C.	114	37 10N	75 59W
Charles City	116	43 2N	92 41W
Charles L.	109	59 50N	110 33W
Charles Town	114	39 20N	77 50W
Charleston, Ill., U.S.A.	114	39 30N	88 10W
Charleston, Miss., U.S.A.	117	34 2N	90 3W
Charleston, Mo., U.S.A.	117	36 52N	89 20W
Charleston, S.C., U.S.A.	115	32 47N	79 56W
Charleston, W. Va., U.S.A.	114	38 24N	81 36W
Charleston Harb.	115	32 46N	79 55W
Charlestown, S. Afr.	93	27 26S	29 53 E
Charlestown, U.S.A.	114	38 29N	85 40W
Charlesville	88	5 27S	20 59 E
Charleville	97	26 24S	146 15 E
Charleville = Rath Luirc	15	52 21N	8 40W
Charleville-Mézières	19	49 44N	4 40 E
Charlevoix	114	45 19N	85 14W
Charlieu	21	46 10N	4 10 E
Charlotte, Mich., U.S.A.	114	42 36N	84 48W
Charlotte, N.C., U.S.A.	115	35 16N	80 46W
Charlotte Amalie	121	18 22N	64 56W
Charlotte Harbor	115	26 58N	82 4W
Charlotte Waters	96	25 56S	134 54 E
Charlottenberg	48	59 54N	12 17 E
Charlottesville	114	38 1N	78 30W
Charlottetown	107	46 14N	63 8W
Charlton, Austral.	99	36 16S	143 24 E
Charlton, U.S.A.	116	40 59N	93 20W
Charlton I.	106	52 0N	79 20W
Charmes	19	48 22N	6 17 E
Charny	107	46 43N	71 15W
Charolles	21	46 27N	4 16 E
Charost	19	47 0N	2 7 E
Charouine	82	29 0N	0 15W
Charre	91	17 13S	35 10 E
Charroux	20	46 9N	0 25 E
Charters Towers	97	20 5S	146 13 E
Chartre, La	18	47 42N	0 34 E
Chartres	18	48 29N	1 30 E
Chascomús	124	35 30S	58 0W
Chasefu	91	11 55S	33 8 E
Chasovnya-Uchurskaya	59	57 15N	132 50 E
Chasseneuil-sur-Bonnieure	20	45 52N	0 29 E
Chata	68	27 42N	77 30 E
Châtaigneraie, La	18	46 38N	0 45W
Chatal Balkan = Udvoy Balkan	43	42 50N	26 50 E
Château-Chinon	19	47 4N	3 56 E
Château-du-Loir	18	47 40N	0 25 E
Château-Gontier	18	47 50N	0 48W
Château-la-Vallière	18	47 30N	0 20 E
Château-Landon	19	48 8N	2 40 E
Château, Le	20	45 52N	1 12W
Château-Porcien	19	49 31N	4 13 E
Château-Renault	18	47 36N	0 56 E
Château-Salins	19	48 50N	6 30 E
Château-Thierry	19	49 3N	3 20 E
Châteaubourg	18	48 7N	1 25W
Châteaubriant	18	47 43N	1 23W
Châteaudun	18	48 3N	1 20 E
Châteaugiron	18	48 3N	1 30W
Châteauguay	113	45 23N	73 45W
Châteaulin	18	48 11N	4 8W
Châteaumeillant	20	46 35N	2 12 E
Châteauneuf	18	48 35N	1 15 E
Châteauneuf-du-Faou	18	48 11N	3 50W
Châteauneuf-sur-Charente	20	45 36N	0 3W
Châteauneuf-sur-Cher	19	46 52N	2 18 E
Châteauneuf-sur-Loire	19	47 52N	2 13 E
Châteaurenard	21	43 53N	4 51 E
Châteauroux	19	46 50N	1 40 E
Châteaux-Arnoux	21	44 6N	6 0 E
Châtelaillon-Plage	20	46 5N	1 5W
Châtelaudren	18	48 33N	2 59W
Châtelet, Le, Cher, France	20	46 40N	2 20 E
Châtelet, Le, Seine-et-Marne, France	19	48 30N	2 47 E
Châtelguyon	20	45 55N	3 4 E
Châtellerault	18	46 50N	0 30 E
Châtelus-Malvaleix	20	46 18N	2 1 E
Chatfield	116	43 15N	91 58W
Chatham, N.B., Can.	107	47 2N	65 28W
Chatham, Ont., Can.	106	42 24N	82 11W
Chatham, U.K.	13	51 22N	0 32 E
Chatham, La., U.S.A.	117	32 22N	92 26W
Chatham, N.Y., U.S.A.	113	42 21N	73 32W
Chatham Is.	94	44 0S	176 40W
Chatham Str.	108	57 0N	134 40W
Châtillon, Loiret, France	19	47 36N	2 44 E
Châtillon, Marne, France	19	49 5N	3 43 E
Châtillon	38	45 45N	7 40 E
Châtillon-Coligny	19	47 50N	2 51 E
Châtillon-en-Bazois	19	47 3N	3 39 E
Châtillon-en-Diois	21	44 41N	5 29 E
Châtillon-sur-Indre	18	46 59N	1 10 E
Châtillon-sur-Seine	19	47 50N	4 33 E
Châtillon-sur-Sèvre	18	46 56N	0 45W
Chatmohar	69	24 15N	89 15 E
Chatra	69	24 12N	84 56 E
Chatrapur	69	19 22N	85 2 E
Châtre, La	20	46 35N	1 59 E
Chats, L. des	113	45 30N	76 20W
Chatsworth, Can.	112	44 27N	80 54W
Chatsworth, Zimb.	91	19 38S	31 13 E
Chattahoochee	115	30 43N	84 51W
Chattanooga	115	35 2N	85 17W
Chaudanne, Barrage de	21	43 51N	6 32 E
Chaudes-Aigues	20	44 51N	3 1 E
Chauffailles	21	46 13N	4 20 E
Chauk	67	20 53N	94 49 E
Chaukan La	67	27 0N	97 15 E
Chaulnes	19	49 48N	2 47 E
Chaumont, France	19	48 7N	5 8 E
Chaumont, U.S.A.	113	44 4N	76 9W
Chaumont-en-Vexin	19	49 16N	1 53 E
Chaumont-sur-Loire	18	47 29N	1 11 E
Chaunay	20	46 13N	0 9 E
Chauny	19	49 37N	3 12 E
Chausey, Îs.	18	48 52N	1 49W
Chaussin	19	46 59N	5 22 E
Chautauqua	112	42 17N	79 30W
Chauvigny	18	46 34N	0 39 E
Chauvin	109	52 45N	110 10W
Chaux-de-Fonds, La	25	47 7N	6 50 E
Chaves, Brazil	127	0 15S	49 55W
Chaves, Port.	30	41 45N	7 32W
Chavuma	89	13 4S	22 40 E
Chaykovskiy	52	56 47N	54 9 E
Chazelles-sur-Lyon	21	45 39N	4 22 E
Chazy	113	44 52N	73 28W
Cheb (Eger)	26	50 9N	12 28 E
Cheboksary	55	56 8N	47 12 E
Cheboygan	114	45 38N	84 29W
Chebsara	55	59 10N	38 59 E
Chech, Erg	82	25 0N	2 15W
Chechaouen	82	35 9N	5 15W
Chechen, Os.	57	43 59N	47 40 E
Checheno-Ingush A.S.S.R. □	57	43 30N	45 29 E
Chęciny	28	50 46N	20 28 E
Checleset B.	108	50 5N	127 35W
Checotah	117	35 31N	95 30W
Chedabucto B.	107	45 25N	61 8W
Cheduba I.	67	18 45N	93 40 E
Cheepie	99	26 33S	145 1 E
Chef-Boutonne	20	46 7N	0 4W
Chegdomyn	59	51 7N	133 1 E
Chegga	82	25 27N	5 40W
Chehalis	118	46 44N	122 59W
Cheiron	21	43 49N	6 58 E
Cheju Do	77	33 29N	126 34 E
Chekalin	55	54 10N	36 10 E
Chekiang = Zhejiang □	75	29 0N	120 0 E
Chela, Sa. da	92	16 20S	13 20 E
Chelan	118	47 49N	120 0W
Chelan, L.	108	48 5N	120 30W
Cheleken	53	39 26N	53 7 E
Chelforó	128	39 0S	66 33W
Chéliff, O. →	82	36 0N	0 8 E
Chelkar	58	47 48N	59 39 E
Chelkar Tengiz, Solonchak	58	48 0N	62 30 E
Chellala Dahrania	82	33 2N	0 1 E
Chelles	19	48 52N	2 33 E
Chełm	28	51 8N	23 30 E
Chełm □	28	51 15N	23 30 E
Chełmek	27	50 6N	19 16 E
Chełmno	28	53 20N	18 30 E
Chelmsford	13	51 44N	0 29 E

Chelmsford Dam Cilician Gates P.

Chelmsford Dam	93	27 55 S	29 59 E
Chelmźa	28	53 10N	18 39 E
Chelsea, Austral.	100	38 5 S	145 8 E
Chelsea, Can.	113	45 30N	75 47W
Chelsea, Okla., U.S.A.	117	36 35N	95 35W
Chelsea, Vt., U.S.A.	113	43 59N	72 27W
Cheltenham	13	51 55N	2 5W
Chelva	32	39 45N	1 0W
Chelyabinsk	58	55 10N	61 24 E
Chemainus	108	48 55N	123 42W
Chemillé	18	47 14N	0 45W
Chemnitz = Karl-Marx-Stadt	24	50 50N	12 55 E
Chemult	118	43 14N	121 47W
Chen, Gora	59	65 16N	141 50 E
Chen Xian	75	25 47N	113 1 E
Chenab →	68	30 23N	71 2 E
Chenachane, O. →	82	25 20N	3 20W
Chenango Forks	113	42 15N	75 51W
Chencha	87	6 15N	37 32 E
Chenchiang = Zhenjiang	75	32 12N	119 24 E
Cheney	118	47 29N	117 34W
Chengbu	77	26 18N	110 16 E
Chengcheng	77	35 8N	109 56 E
Chengde	76	40 59N	117 58 E
Chengdu	75	30 38N	104 2 E
Chenggu	77	33 10N	107 21 E
Chengjiang	75	24 39N	103 0 E
Ch'engtu = Chengdu	75	30 38N	104 2 E
Chengyang	76	36 18N	120 21 E
Chenxi	77	28 2N	110 12 E
Cheo Reo	71	13 25N	108 28 E
Cheom Ksan	71	14 13N	104 56 E
Chepelare	43	41 44N	24 40 E
Chepén	126	7 15 S	79 23W
Chepes	124	31 20 S	66 35W
Chepo	121	9 10N	79 6W
Cheptsa →	55	58 36N	50 4 E
Cheptulil, Mt.	90	1 25N	35 35 E
Chequamegon B.	116	46 40N	90 30W
Cher □	19	47 10N	2 30 E
Cher →	18	47 21N	0 29 E
Cheran	69	25 45N	90 44 E
Cherasco	38	44 39N	7 50 E
Cheraw	115	34 42N	79 54W
Cherbourg	18	49 39N	1 40W
Cherchell	82	36 35N	2 12 E
Cherdakly	55	54 25N	48 50 E
Cherdyn	52	60 24N	56 29 E
Cheremkhovo	59	53 8N	103 1 E
Cherepanovo	58	54 15N	83 30 E
Cherepovets	55	59 5N	37 55 E
Chergui, Chott ech	82	34 21N	0 25 E
Cherikov	54	53 32N	31 20 E
Cherkassy	56	49 27N	32 4 E
Cherkessk	57	44 15N	42 5 E
Cherlak	58	54 15N	74 55 E
Chernaya Kholunitsa	55	58 51N	51 52 E
Cherni	43	42 35N	23 18 E
Chernigov	54	51 28N	31 20 E
Chernikovsk	52	54 48N	56 8 E
Chernobyl	54	51 13N	30 15 E
Chernogorsk	59	53 49N	91 18 E
Chernomorskoye	56	45 31N	32 40 E
Chernovskoye	55	58 48N	47 20 E
Chernovtsy	56	48 15N	25 52 E
Chernoye	59	70 30N	89 10 E
Chernyakhovsk	54	54 36N	21 48 E
Chernyshkovskiy	57	48 30N	42 13 E
Chernyshovskiy	59	63 0N	112 30 E
Cherokee, Iowa, U.S.A.	116	42 40N	95 30W
Cherokee, Okla., U.S.A.	117	36 45N	98 25W
Cherokees, L. O'The	117	36 50N	95 12W
Cherquenco	128	38 35 S	72 0W
Cherrapunji	67	25 17N	91 47 E
Cherry Creek	118	39 50N	114 58W
Cherryvale	117	37 20N	95 33W
Cherskiy	59	68 45N	161 18 E
Cherskogo Khrebet	59	65 0N	143 0 E
Chertkovo	57	49 25N	40 19 E
Cherven	54	53 45N	28 28 E
Cherven-Bryag	43	43 17N	24 7 E
Chervonograd	54	50 25N	24 10 E
Cherwell →	13	51 46N	1 18W
Chesapeake	114	36 43N	76 15W
Chesapeake Bay	114	38 0N	76 12W
Cheshire □	12	53 14N	2 30W
Cheshskaya Guba	52	67 20N	47 0 E
Cheslatta L.	108	53 49N	125 20W
Chesley	112	44 17N	81 5W
Chesne, Le	19	49 30N	4 45 E
Cheste	33	39 30N	0 41W
Chester, U.K.	12	53 12N	2 53W
Chester, Calif., U.S.A.	118	40 22N	121 14W
Chester, Ill., U.S.A.	117	37 58N	89 50W
Chester, Mont., U.S.A.	118	48 31N	111 0W
Chester, N.Y., U.S.A.	113	41 22N	74 16W
Chester, Pa., U.S.A.	114	39 54N	75 20W
Chester, S.C., U.S.A.	115	34 44N	81 13W
Chesterfield	12	53 14N	1 26W
Chesterfield, Îles	94	19 52 S	158 15 E
Chesterfield In.	104	63 25N	90 45W
Chesterfield Inlet	104	63 30N	90 45W
Chesterton Range	99	25 30 S	147 27 E
Chesterville	113	45 6N	75 14W
Chesuncook L.	107	46 0N	69 10W
Chetaibi	83	37 1N	7 20 E
Chéticamp	107	46 37N	60 59W
Chetumal	120	18 30N	88 20W
Chetumal, Bahia de	120	18 40N	88 10W
Chetwynd	108	55 45N	121 36W
Chevanceaux	20	45 18N	0 14W
Cheviot Hills	12	55 20N	2 30W
Cheviot Ra.	99	25 20 S	143 45 E
Cheviot, The	12	55 29N	2 8W
Chew Bahir	87	4 40N	36 50 E
Chewelah	118	48 17N	117 43W
Cheyenne, Okla., U.S.A.	117	35 35N	99 40W
Cheyenne, Wyo., U.S.A.	116	41 9N	104 49W
Cheyenne →	116	44 40N	101 15W
Cheyenne Wells	116	38 51N	102 10W
Cheylard, Le	21	44 55N	4 25 E
Chhabra	68	24 40N	76 54 E
Chhatarpur	69	24 55N	79 35 E
Chhindwara	68	22 2N	78 59 E
Chhlong	71	12 15N	105 58 E
Chi →	71	15 11N	104 43 E
Chiamis	73	7 20 S	108 21 E
Chiamussu = Jiamusi	75	46 40N	130 26 E
Chiang Mai	71	18 47N	98 59 E
Chiange	89	15 35 S	13 40 E
Chiapa →	120	16 42N	93 0W
Chiapas □	120	17 0N	92 45W
Chiaramonte Gulfi	41	37 1N	14 41 E
Chiaravalle	39	43 38N	13 17 E
Chiaravalle Centrale	41	38 41N	16 25 E
Chiari	38	45 31N	9 55 E
Chiatura	57	42 15N	43 17 E
Chiávari	38	44 20N	9 20 E
Chiavenna	38	46 18N	9 23 E
Chiba	74	35 30N	140 7 E
Chiba □	74	35 30N	140 20 E
Chibabava	93	20 17 S	33 35 E
Chibatu	73	7 6 S	107 59 E
Chibemba, Angola	89	15 48 S	14 8 E
Chibemba, Angola	92	16 20 S	15 20 E
Chibia	89	15 10 S	13 42 E
Chibougamau	106	49 56N	74 24W
Chibougamau L.	106	49 50N	74 20W
Chibuk	85	10 52N	12 50 E
Chic-Chocs, Mts.	107	48 55N	66 0W
Chicacole = Srikakulam	70	18 14N	84 4 E
Chicago	114	41 53N	87 40W
Chicago Heights	114	41 29N	87 37W
Chichagof I.	108	58 0N	136 0W
Chichaoua	82	31 32N	8 44W
Chichén Itzá	120	20 40N	88 32W
Chichester	13	50 50N	0 47W
Chichibu	74	36 5N	139 10 E
Ch'ich'ihaerh = Qiqihar	75	47 26N	124 0 E
Chickasha	117	35 0N	98 0W
Chiclana de la Frontera	31	36 26N	6 9W
Chiclayo	126	6 42 S	79 50W
Chico	118	39 45N	121 54W
Chico →, Chubut, Argent.	128	44 0 S	67 0W
Chico →, Santa Cruz, Argent.	128	50 0 S	68 30W
Chicomo	93	24 31 S	34 6 E
Chicopee	114	42 6N	72 37W
Chicoutimi	107	48 28N	71 5W
Chidambaram	70	11 20N	79 45 E
Chidenguele	93	24 55 S	34 11 E
Chidley C.	105	60 23N	64 26W
Chiede	92	17 15 S	16 22 E
Chiefs Pt.	112	44 41N	81 18W
Chiemsee	25	47 53N	12 27 E
Chiengi	91	8 45 S	29 10 E
Chienti →	39	43 18N	13 45 E
Chieri	38	45 0N	7 50 E
Chiers →	19	49 39N	5 0 E
Chiese →	38	45 8N	10 25 E
Chieti	39	42 22N	14 10 E
Chifeng	76	42 18N	118 58 E
Chigirin	56	49 4N	32 38 E
Chignecto B.	107	45 30N	64 40W
Chiguana	124	21 0 S	67 58W
Chihli, G. of = Bo Hai	76	39 0N	120 0 E
Chihuahua	120	28 40N	106 3W
Chihuahua □	120	28 40N	106 3W
Chiili	58	44 20N	66 15 E
Chik Bollapur	70	13 25N	77 45 E
Chikhli	68	20 20N	76 18 E
Chikmagalur	70	13 15N	75 45 E
Chikodi	70	16 26N	74 38 E
Chikwawa	91	16 2 S	34 50 E
Chilako →	108	53 53N	122 57W
Chilanga	91	15 33 S	28 16 E
Chilapa	120	17 40N	99 11W
Chilas	69	35 25N	74 5 E
Chilcotin →	108	51 44N	122 23W
Childers	97	25 15 S	152 17 E
Childress	117	34 30N	100 15W
Chile ■	128	35 0 S	72 0W
Chile Rise	95	38 0 S	92 0W
Chilecito	124	29 10 S	67 30W
Chilete	126	7 10 S	78 50W
Chililabombwe	91	12 18 S	27 43 E
Chilin = Jilin	76	43 55N	126 30 E
Chilka L.	69	19 40N	85 25 E
Chilko →	108	52 0N	123 40W
Chilko, L.	108	51 20N	124 10W
Chillagoe	97	17 7 S	144 33 E
Chillán	124	36 40 S	72 10W
Chillicothe, Ill., U.S.A.	116	40 55N	89 32W
Chillicothe, Mo., U.S.A.	116	39 45N	93 30W
Chillicothe, Ohio, U.S.A.	114	39 20N	82 58W
Chilliwack	108	49 10N	121 54W
Chilo	68	27 25N	73 32 E
Chiloane, I.	93	20 40 S	34 55 E
Chiloé, I. de	128	42 30 S	73 50W
Chilpancingo	120	17 30N	99 30W
Chiltern Hills	13	51 44N	0 42W
Chilton	114	44 1N	88 12W
Chiluage	88	9 30 S	21 50 E
Chilubula	91	10 14 S	30 51 E
Chilumba	91	10 28 S	34 12 E
Chilwa, L.	91	15 15 S	35 40 E
Chimacum	118	48 1N	122 46W
Chimay	16	50 3N	4 20 E
Chimbay	58	42 57N	59 47 E
Chimborazo	126	1 29 S	78 55W
Chimbote	126	9 0 S	78 35W
Chimishliya	46	46 34N	28 44 E
Chimkent	58	42 18N	69 36 E
Chimoio	91	19 4 S	33 30 E
Chimpembe	91	9 31 S	29 33 E
Chin □	67	22 0N	93 0 E
Chin Ling Shan = Qinling Shandi	77	33 50N	108 10 E
China	120	25 40N	99 20W
China ■	75	30 0N	110 0 E
Chinan = Jinan	76	36 38N	117 1 E
Chinandega	121	12 35N	87 12W
Chinati Pk.	117	30 0N	104 25W
Chincha Alta	126	13 25 S	76 7W
Chinchilla	99	26 45 S	150 38 E
Chinchilla de Monte Aragón	33	38 53N	1 40W
Chinchón	32	40 9N	3 26W
Chinchorro, Banco	120	18 35N	87 20W
Chinchou = Jinzhou	76	41 5N	121 3 E
Chincoteague	114	37 58N	75 21W
Chinde	91	18 35 S	36 30 E
Chindwin →	67	21 26N	95 15 E
Chinga	91	15 13 S	38 35 E
Chingleput	70	12 42N	79 58 E
Chingola	91	12 31 S	27 53 E
Chingole	91	13 4 S	34 17 E
Ch'ingtao = Qingdao	76	36 5N	120 20 E
Chinguetti	80	20 25N	12 24W
Chingune	93	20 33 S	35 0 E
Chinhae	76	35 9N	128 47 E
Chinhanguanine	93	25 21 S	32 30 E
Chiniot	68	31 45N	73 0 E
Chinju	76	35 12N	128 2 E
Chinle	119	36 14N	109 38W
Chinnamanur	70	9 50N	77 24 E
Chinnampo	76	38 52N	125 10 E
Chinnur	70	18 57N	79 49 E
Chino Valley	119	34 54N	112 28W
Chinon	18	47 10N	0 15 E
Chinook, Can.	109	51 28N	110 59W
Chinook, U.S.A.	118	48 35N	109 19W
Chinsali	91	10 30 S	32 2 E
Chintamani	70	13 26N	78 3 E
Chióggia	39	45 13N	12 15 E
Chíos = Khíos	45	38 27N	26 9 E
* Chipai L.	106	52 56N	87 53W
Chipata	91	13 38 S	32 28 E
Chipatujah	73	7 45 S	108 0 E
Chipewyan L.	109	58 0N	98 27W
Chipinga	91	20 13 S	32 28 E
Chipiona	31	36 44N	6 26W
Chipley	115	30 45N	85 32W
Chiplun	70	17 31N	73 34 E
Chipman	107	46 6N	65 53W
Chipoka	91	13 57 S	34 28 E
Chippawa	112	43 5N	79 2W
Chippenham	13	51 27N	2 7W
Chippewa →	116	44 25N	92 10W
Chippewa Falls	116	44 55N	91 22W
Chiprovtsi	42	43 24N	22 52 E
Chiquián	126	10 10 S	77 0W
Chiquimula	120	14 51N	89 37W
Chiquinquira	126	5 37N	73 50W
Chir →	57	48 30N	43 0 E
Chirala	70	15 50N	80 26 E
Chiramba	91	16 55 S	34 39 E
Chirawa	68	28 14N	75 42 E
Chirayinkil	70	8 41N	76 49 E
Chirchik	58	41 29N	69 35 E
Chirfa	83	20 55N	12 22 E
Chiricahua Pk.	119	31 53N	109 14W
Chirikof I.	104	55 50N	155 40W
Chiriquí, Golfo de	121	8 0N	82 10W
Chiriquí, Lago de	121	9 10N	82 0W
† Chiriquí, Vol. de	121	8 55N	82 35W
Chirivira Falls	91	21 10 S	32 12 E
Chirnogi	46	44 7N	26 32 E
Chirpan	43	42 10N	25 19 E
Chirripó Grande, Cerro	121	9 29N	83 29W
Chisamba	91	14 55 S	28 20 E
Chisholm	108	54 55N	114 10W
Chishtian Mandi	68	29 50N	72 55 E
Chisimaio	79	0 22 S	42 32 E
Chisimba Falls	91	10 12 S	30 56 E
Chisineu Criş	42	46 32N	21 37 E
Chisone →	38	44 49N	7 25 E
Chisos Mts.	117	29 20N	103 15W
Chistopol	55	55 25N	50 38 E
Chita	59	52 0N	113 35 E
Chitapur	70	17 10N	77 5 E
Chitembo	89	13 30 S	16 50 E
Chitipa	91	9 41 S	33 19 E
Chitokoloki	89	13 50 S	23 13 E
Chitorgarh	68	24 52N	74 38 E
Chitrakot	70	19 10N	81 40 E
Chitral	66	35 50N	71 56 E
Chitravati →	70	14 45N	78 15 E
Chitré	121	7 59N	80 27W
Chittagong	67	22 19N	91 48 E
Chittagong □	67	24 5N	91 0 E
Chittoor	70	13 15N	79 5 E
Chittur	70	10 40N	76 45 E
Chiusa	39	46 38N	11 34 E
Chiusi	39	43 1N	11 58 E
Chiva	33	39 27N	0 41W
Chivasso	38	45 10N	7 52 E
Chivilcoy	124	34 55 S	60 0W
Chiwanda	91	11 23 S	34 55 E
Chizela	91	13 10 S	25 0 E
Chkalov = Orenburg	52	52 0N	55 5 E
Chkolovsk	55	56 50N	43 10 E
Chlumec	26	50 9N	15 29 E
Chmielnik	28	50 37N	20 43 E
Choba	90	2 30N	38 5 E
Chobe National Park	92	18 0 S	25 0 E
Chocianów	28	51 27N	15 55 E
Chociwel	28	53 29N	15 21 E
Chodaków	28	52 16N	20 18 E
Chodavaram	70	17 50N	82 57 E
Chodecz	28	52 24N	19 2 E
Chodziez	28	52 58N	16 58 E
Choele Choel	128	39 11 S	65 40W
Choisy-le-Roi	19	48 45N	2 24 E
Choix	120	26 40N	108 23W
Chojna	28	52 58N	14 25 E
Chojnice	28	53 42N	17 32 E
Chojnów	28	51 18N	15 58 E
Choke Mts.	87	11 18N	37 15 E
Chokurdakh	59	70 38N	147 55 E
Cholet	18	47 4N	0 52W
Choluteca	121	13 20N	87 14W
Choma	91	16 48 S	26 59 E
Chomen Swamp	87	9 20N	37 10 E
Chomu	68	27 15N	75 40 E
Chomutov	26	50 28N	13 23 E
Chon Buri	71	13 21N	101 1 E
Chonan	76	36 48N	127 9 E
Chone	126	0 40 S	80 0W
Chong'an	77	27 45N	118 0 E
Chongde	77	30 32N	120 26 E
Chongjin	76	41 47N	129 50 E
Chŏngju	76	39 40N	125 5 E
Chŏngju	76	36 39N	127 27 E
Chongli	76	40 58N	115 15 E
Chongqing	75	29 35N	106 25 E
Chongzuo	77	22 23N	107 20 E
Chŏnju	76	35 50N	127 4 E
Chonming Dao	77	31 40N	121 30 E
Chonos, Arch. de los	128	45 0 S	75 0W
Chopda	68	21 20N	75 15 E
Chopim →	125	25 35 S	53 5W
Chorley	12	53 39N	2 39W
Chorolque, Cerro	124	20 59 S	66 5W
Choroszcz	28	53 10N	22 59 E
Chorrera, La	120	8 50N	79 50W
Chortkov, U.S.S.R.	54	49 2N	25 46 E
Chortkov, U.S.S.R.	56	49 1N	25 42 E
Chŏrwŏn	76	38 15N	127 10 E
Chorzele	28	53 15N	20 55 E
Chorzów	28	50 18N	18 57 E
Chos-Malal	124	37 20 S	70 15W
Chosan	76	40 50N	125 47 E
Chōshi	74	35 45N	140 51 E
Choszczno	28	53 7N	15 25 E
Choteau	118	47 50N	112 10W
Chotila	68	22 23N	71 15 E
Chowchilla	119	37 11N	120 12W
Choybalsan	75	48 4N	114 30 E
Christchurch, N.Z.	101	43 33 S	172 47 E
Christchurch, U.K.	13	50 44N	1 33W
Christian I.	112	44 50N	80 12W
Christiana	92	27 52 S	25 8 E
Christiansfeld	49	55 21N	9 29 E
Christie B.	109	62 32N	111 10W
Christina →	109	56 40N	111 3W
Christmas I., Ind. Oc.	94	10 30 S	105 40 E
* Christmas I., Pac. Oc.	95	1 58N	157 27W
Chrudim	26	49 58N	15 43 E
Chrzanów	27	50 10N	19 21 E
Chtimba	91	10 30 S	34 13 E
Chu	58	43 36N	73 42 E
Chu →	71	19 53N	105 45 E
Chu Chua	108	51 22N	120 10W
Ch'uanchou = Quanzhou	75	24 55N	118 34 E
Chūbu □	74	36 45N	137 30 E
Chubut →	128	43 20 S	65 5W
Chuchi L.	108	55 12N	124 30W
Chudovo	54	59 10N	31 41 E
Chudskoye, Oz.	54	58 13N	27 30 E
Chūgoku □	74	35 0N	133 0 E
Chūgoku-Sanchi	74	35 0N	133 0 E
Chuguyev	56	49 55N	36 45 E
Chugwater	116	41 48N	104 47W
Chukai	71	4 13N	103 25 E
Chukhloma	55	58 45N	42 40 E
Chukotskiy Khrebet	59	68 0N	175 0 E
Chukotskoye More	59	68 0N	175 0W
Chula Vista	119	32 39N	117 8W
Chulman	59	56 52N	124 52 E
Chulucanas	126	5 8 S	80 10W
Chulym →	58	57 43N	83 51 E
Chumbicha	124	29 0 S	66 10W
Chumerna	43	42 45N	25 55 E
Chumikan	59	54 40N	135 10 E
Chumphon	71	10 35N	99 14 E
Chumuare	91	14 31 S	31 50 E
Chuna →	59	57 47N	94 37 E
Chun'an	77	29 35N	119 3 E
Chunchŏn	76	37 58N	127 44 E
Chunga	91	15 0 S	26 2 E
Chungking = Chongqing	75	29 35N	106 25 E
Chunian	68	30 57N	74 0 E
Chunya	91	8 30 S	33 27 E
Chunya □	90	7 48 S	33 0 E
Chuquibamba	126	15 47 S	72 44W
Chuquicamata	124	22 15 S	69 0W
Chuquisaca □	126	23 30 S	63 30W
Chur	25	46 52N	9 32 E
Churachandpur	67	24 20N	93 40 E
Churchill	109	58 47N	94 11W
Churchill →, Man., Can.	109	58 47N	94 12W
Churchill →, Newf., Can.	107	53 19N	60 10W
Churchill, C.	109	58 46N	93 12W
Churchill Falls	107	53 36N	64 19W
Churchill L.	109	55 55N	108 20W
Churchill Pk.	108	58 10N	125 10W
Churu	68	28 20N	74 50 E
Chushal	69	33 40N	78 40 E
Chusovoy	52	58 15N	57 40 E
Chuvash A.S.S.R. □	55	55 30N	47 0 E
Ci Xian	76	36 20N	114 25 E
Ciacova	42	45 35N	21 10 E
Cianjur	73	6 51 S	107 7 E
Cibadok	73	6 53 S	106 47 E
Cibatu	73	7 8 S	107 59 E
Cicero	114	41 48N	87 48W
Cidacos →	32	42 21N	1 38W
Cide	56	41 53N	33 1 E
Ciechanów	28	52 52N	20 38 E
Ciechanów □	28	53 0N	20 30 E
Ciechanowiec	28	52 40N	22 31 E
Ciechocinek	28	52 53N	18 45 E
Ciego de Avila	121	21 50N	78 50W
Ciénaga	126	11 1N	74 15W
Cienfuegos	121	22 10N	80 30W
Cieplice Śląskie Zdrój	28	50 50N	15 40 E
Cierp	20	42 55N	0 40 E
Cies, Islas	30	42 12N	8 55W
Cieszanów	28	50 14N	23 8 E
Cieszyn	27	49 45N	18 35 E
Cieza	33	38 17N	1 23W
Cifuentes	32	40 47N	2 37W
Cijara, Pantano de	31	39 18N	4 52W
Cijulang	73	7 42 S	108 27 E
Cikajang	73	7 25 S	107 48 E
Cikampek	73	6 23 S	107 28 E
Cilacap	73	7 43 S	109 0 E
Çıldır	57	41 10N	43 20 E
Cilician Gates P.	64	37 20N	34 52 E

* *Renamed Wapikopa, L.*

† *Renamed Barú, Vol.*

* *Renamed Kiritimati*

Cîlnicu Columbus

Name	Page	Lat.	Long.
Cîlnicu	46	44 54N	23 4 E
Cimahi	73	6 53 S	107 33 E
Cimarron, Kans., U.S.A.	117	37 50N	100 20W
Cimarron, N. Mex., U.S.A.	117	36 30N	104 52W
Cimarron →	117	36 10N	96 17W
Cimone, Mte.	38	44 10N	10 40 E
Cîmpic Turzii	46	46 34N	23 53 E
Cîmpina	46	45 10N	25 45 E
Cîmpulung, Argeş, Romania	46	45 17N	25 3 E
Cîmpulung, Moldovenesc, Romania	46	47 32N	25 30 E
Cîmpuri	43	46 0N	26 50 E
Cinca →	32	41 26N	0 21 E
Cincer	42	43 55N	17 5 E
Cincinnati	114	39 10N	84 26W
Cîndeşti	46	45 15N	26 42 E
Ciney	16	50 18N	5 5 E
Cingoli	39	43 23N	13 10 E
Cinigiano	39	42 53N	11 23 E
Cinto, Mt.	21	42 24N	8 54 E
Ciorani	46	44 45N	26 25 E
Ciotat, La	21	43 12N	5 36 E
Čiovo	39	43 30N	16 17 E
Circeo, Monte	40	41 14N	13 3 E
Circle, Alaska, U.S.A.	104	65 50N	144 10W
Circle, Montana, U.S.A.	116	47 26N	105 35W
Circleville, Ohio, U.S.A.	114	39 35N	82 57W
Circleville, Utah, U.S.A.	119	38 12N	112 24W
Cirebon	73	6 45 S	108 32 E
Cirencester	13	51 43N	1 59W
Cireşu	46	44 47N	22 31 E
Cirey-sur-Vezouze	19	48 35N	6 57 E
Ciriè	38	45 14N	7 35 E
Cirò	41	39 23N	17 3 E
Cisco	117	32 25N	99 0W
Cislău	46	45 14N	26 20 E
Cisna	27	49 12N	22 20 E
Cisnădie	46	45 42N	24 9 E
Cisterna di Latina	40	41 35N	12 50 E
Cisternino	41	40 45N	17 26 E
Citeli-Ckaro	57	41 33N	46 0 E
Citlaltépetl	120	19 0N	97 20W
Citrusdal	92	32 35 S	19 0 E
Città della Pieve	39	42 57N	12 0 E
Città di Castello	39	43 27N	12 14 E
Città Sant' Angelo	39	42 32N	14 5 E
Cittadella	39	45 39N	11 48 E
Cittaducale	39	42 24N	12 58 E
Cittanova	41	38 22N	16 5 E
Ciuc, Munţii	46	46 25N	26 5 E
Ciucaş	46	45 31N	25 56 E
Ciudad Acuña	120	29 20N	100 58W
Ciudad Altamirano	120	18 20N	100 40W
Ciudad Bolívar	126	8 5N	63 36W
Ciudad Camargo	120	27 41N	105 10W
Ciudad de Valles	120	22 0N	99 0W
Ciudad del Carmen	120	18 38N	91 50W
Ciudad Delicias = Delicias	120	28 10N	105 30W
Ciudad Guayana	126	8 0N	62 30W
Ciudad Guerrero	120	28 33N	107 28W
Ciudad Guzmán	120	19 40N	103 30W
Ciudad Juárez	120	31 40N	106 28W
Ciudad Madero	120	22 19N	97 50W
Ciudad Mante	120	22 50N	99 0W
Ciudad Obregón	120	27 28N	109 59W
Ciudad Real	31	38 59N	3 55W
Ciudad Real □	31	38 50N	4 0W
Ciudad Rodrigo	30	40 35N	6 32W
Ciudad Trujillo = Sto. Domingo	121	18 30N	70 0W
Ciudad Victoria	120	23 41N	99 9W
Ciudadela	32	40 0N	3 50 E
Ciulniţa	46	44 26N	27 22 E
Cividale del Friuli	39	46 6N	13 25 E
Civita Castellana	39	42 18N	12 24 E
Civitanova Marche	39	43 18N	13 41 E
Civitavécchia	39	42 6N	11 46 E
Civitella del Tronto	39	42 48N	13 40 E
Civray	20	46 10N	0 17 E
Çivril	64	38 20N	29 43 E
Cixerri →	40	39 20N	8 40 E
Cizre	64	37 19N	42 10 E
Clacton-on-Sea	13	51 47N	1 10 E
Clain →	18	46 47N	0 33 E
Claire, L.	108	58 35N	112 5W
Clairemont	117	33 9N	100 44W
Clairton	112	40 18N	79 54W
Clairvaux-les-Lacs	21	46 35N	5 45 E
Claise →	18	46 56N	0 42 E
Clamecy	19	47 28N	3 30 E
Clanton	115	32 48N	86 36W
Clanwilliam	92	32 11 S	18 52 E
Clara	15	53 20N	7 38W
Clare, Austral.	99	33 50 S	138 37 E
Clare, U.S.A.	114	43 47N	84 45W
Clare □	15	52 20N	9 0W
Clare →	15	53 22N	9 5W
Clare I.	15	53 48N	10 0W
Claremont	114	43 23N	72 20W
Claremont Pt.	98	14 1 S	143 41 E
Claremore	117	36 40N	95 37W
Claremorris	15	53 45N	9 0W
Clarence →, Austral.	97	29 25 S	153 22 E
Clarence →, N.Z.	101	42 10 S	173 56 E
Clarence I.	5	61 10 S	54 0W
Clarence, I.	128	54 0 S	72 0W
Clarence Str., Austral.	96	12 0 S	131 0 E
Clarence Str., U.S.A.	108	55 40N	132 10W
Clarendon, Ark., U.S.A.	117	34 41N	91 20W
Clarendon, Tex., U.S.A.	117	34 58N	100 54W
Clarenville	107	48 10N	54 1W
Claresholm	108	50 0N	113 33W
Clarie Coast	5	68 0 S	135 0 E
Clarinda	116	40 45N	95 0W
Clarion, Iowa, U.S.A.	116	42 41N	93 46W
Clarion, Pa., U.S.A.	112	41 12N	79 22W
Clarion →	112	41 9N	79 41W
Clarion Fracture Zone	95	20 0N	120 0W
Clark	116	44 55N	97 45W
Clark Fork	118	48 9N	116 9W
Clark Fork →	118	48 9N	116 15W
Clark Hill Res.	115	33 45N	82 20W
Clark, Pt.	112	44 4N	81 45W
Clarkdale	119	34 53N	112 3W
Clarke City	107	50 12N	66 38W
Clarke, I.	97	40 32 S	148 10 E
Clarke L.	109	54 24N	106 54W
Clarke Ra.	98	20 45 S	148 20 E
Clark's Fork →	118	45 39N	108 43W
Clark's Harbour	107	43 25N	65 38W
Clarks Summit	113	41 31N	75 44W
Clarksburg	114	39 18N	80 21W
Clarksdale	117	34 12N	90 33W
Clarkston	118	46 28N	117 2W
Clarksville, Ark., U.S.A.	117	35 29N	93 27W
Clarksville, Tenn., U.S.A.	115	36 32N	87 20W
Clarksville, Tex., U.S.A.	117	33 37N	94 59W
Clatskanie	118	46 9N	123 12W
Claude	117	35 8N	101 22W
Claveria	73	18 37N	121 4 E
Clay Center	116	39 27N	97 9W
Clayette, La	21	46 17N	4 19 E
Claypool	119	33 27N	110 55W
Claysville	112	40 5N	80 25W
Clayton, Idaho, U.S.A.	118	44 12N	114 31W
Clayton, N. Mex., U.S.A.	117	36 30N	103 10W
Cle Elum	118	47 15N	120 57W
Clear L.	118	39 5N	122 47W
Clear, C.	15	51 26N	9 30W
Clear I.	15	51 26N	9 30W
Clear Lake, S.D., U.S.A.	116	44 48N	96 41W
Clear Lake, Wash., U.S.A.	118	48 27N	122 15W
Clear Lake Res.	118	41 55N	121 10W
Clearfield, Pa., U.S.A.	114	41 0N	78 27W
Clearfield, Utah, U.S.A.	118	41 10N	112 0W
Clearmont	118	44 43N	106 29W
Clearwater, Can.	108	51 38N	120 2W
Clearwater, U.S.A.	115	27 58N	82 45W
Clearwater →, Alta., Can.	108	52 22N	114 57W
Clearwater →, Alta., Can.	109	56 44N	111 23W
Clearwater Cr.	108	61 36N	125 30W
Clearwater, Mts.	118	46 20N	115 30W
Clearwater Prov. Park	109	54 0N	101 0W
Cleburne	117	32 18N	97 25W
Clécy	18	48 55N	0 29W
Cleethorpes	12	53 33N	0 2W
Cleeve Cloud	13	51 56N	2 0W
Clelles	21	44 50N	5 38 E
Clerks Rocks	5	56 0 S	34 30W
Clermont, Austral.	97	22 49 S	147 39 E
Clermont, France	19	49 23N	2 24 E
Clermont-en-Argonne	19	49 5N	5 4 E
Clermont-Ferrand	20	45 46N	3 4 E
Clermont-l'Hérault	20	43 38N	3 26 E
Clerval	19	47 25N	6 30 E
Clervaux	16	50 4N	6 2 E
Cléry-Saint-André	19	47 50N	1 46 E
Cles	38	46 21N	11 4 E
Cleveland, Austral.	99	27 30 S	153 15 E
Cleveland, Miss., U.S.A.	117	33 43N	90 43W
Cleveland, Ohio, U.S.A.	114	41 28N	81 43W
Cleveland, Okla., U.S.A.	117	36 21N	96 33W
Cleveland, Tenn., U.S.A.	115	35 9N	84 52W
Cleveland, Tex., U.S.A.	117	30 18N	95 0W
Cleveland □	12	54 35N	1 8 E
Cleveland, C.	97	19 11 S	147 1 E
Cleveland Heights	112	41 32N	81 30W
Clevelândia	125	26 24 S	52 23W
Clew B.	15	53 54N	9 50W
Clewiston	115	26 44N	80 50W
Clifden, Ireland	15	53 30N	10 2W
Clifden, N.Z.	101	46 1 S	167 42 E
Cliff	119	33 0N	108 36W
Clifton, Austral.	99	27 59 S	151 53 E
Clifton, Ariz., U.S.A.	119	33 8N	109 23W
Clifton, Tex., U.S.A.	117	31 46N	97 35W
Clifton Forge	114	37 49N	79 51W
Climax	109	49 10N	108 20W
Clinch →	115	36 0N	84 29W
Clingmans Dome	115	35 35N	83 30W
Clint	119	31 37N	106 11W
Clinton, B.C., Can.	108	51 6N	121 35W
Clinton, Ont., Can.	106	43 37N	81 32W
Clinton, N.Z.	101	46 12 S	169 23 E
Clinton, Ark., U.S.A.	117	35 37N	92 30W
Clinton, Ill., U.S.A.	116	40 8N	89 0W
Clinton, Ind., U.S.A.	114	39 40N	87 22W
Clinton, Iowa, U.S.A.	116	41 50N	90 12W
Clinton, Mass., U.S.A.	114	42 26N	71 40W
Clinton, Mo., U.S.A.	116	38 20N	93 46W
Clinton, N.C., U.S.A.	115	35 5N	78 15W
Clinton, Okla., U.S.A.	117	35 30N	99 0W
Clinton, S.C., U.S.A.	115	34 30N	81 54W
Clinton, Tenn., U.S.A.	115	36 6N	84 10W
Clinton C.	98	22 30 S	150 45 E
Clinton Colden L.	104	63 58N	107 27W
Clintonville	116	44 35N	88 46W
Clipperton Fracture Zone	95	19 0N	122 0W
Clipperton, I.	95	10 18N	109 13W
Clisson	18	47 5N	1 16W
Clive L.	108	63 13N	118 54W
Cloates, Pt.	96	22 43 S	113 40 E
Clocolan	93	28 55 S	27 34 E
Clodomira	124	27 35 S	64 14W
Clonakilty	15	51 37N	8 53W
Clonakilty B.	15	51 33N	8 50W
Cloncurry	97	20 40 S	140 28 E
Cloncurry →	98	18 37 S	140 40 E
Clones	15	54 10N	7 13W
Clonmel	15	52 22N	7 42W
Cloppenburg	24	52 50N	8 3 E
Cloquet	116	46 40N	92 30W
Clorinda	124	25 16 S	57 45W
Cloud Peak	118	44 23N	107 10W
Cloudcroft	119	33 0N	105 48W
Cloverdale	118	38 49N	123 0W
Clovis, Calif., U.S.A.	119	36 47N	119 45W
Clovis, N. Mex., U.S.A.	117	34 20N	103 10W
Cloyes	18	48 0N	1 14 E
Cluj-Napoca	46	46 47N	23 38 E
Cluj □	46	46 45N	23 30 E
Clunes	99	37 20 S	143 45 E
Cluny	21	46 26N	4 38 E
Cluses	21	46 5N	6 35 E
Clusone	38	45 54N	9 58 E
Clutha →	101	46 20 S	169 49 E
Clwyd □	12	53 5N	3 20W
Clwyd →	12	53 20N	3 30W
Clyde, Can.	105	70 30N	68 30W
Clyde, N.Z.	101	45 12 S	169 20 E
Clyde, U.S.A.	112	43 8N	76 52W
Clyde →	14	55 56N	4 29W
Clyde, Firth of	14	55 20N	5 0W
Clydebank	14	55 54N	4 25W
Clymer	112	42 3N	79 39W
Côa →	30	41 5N	7 6W
Coachella	119	33 44N	116 13W
Coahoma	117	32 17N	101 20W
Coahuayana →	120	18 41N	103 45W
Coahuila de Zaragoza □	120	27 0N	103 0W
Coal →	108	59 39N	126 57W
Coalane	91	17 48 S	37 2 E
Coalcomán	120	18 40N	103 10W
Coaldale	108	49 45N	112 35W
Coalgate	117	34 35N	96 13W
Coalinga	119	36 10N	120 21W
Coalville, U.K.	12	52 43N	1 21W
Coalville, U.S.A.	118	40 58N	111 24W
Coari	126	4 8 S	63 7W
Coast □	90	2 40 S	39 45 E
Coast Mts.	108	55 0N	129 0W
Coast Ranges	102	41 0N	123 0W
Coastal Plains Basin	96	30 10 S	115 30 E
Coatbridge	14	55 52N	4 2W
Coatepeque	120	14 46N	91 55W
Coatesville	114	39 59N	75 55W
Coaticook	107	45 10N	71 46W
Coats I.	105	62 30N	83 0W
Coats Land	5	77 0 S	25 0W
Coatzacoalcos	120	18 7N	94 25W
Cobadin	46	44 5N	28 13 E
Cobalt	106	47 25N	79 42W
Cobán	120	15 30N	90 21W
Cobar	97	31 27 S	145 48 E
Cóbh	15	51 50N	8 18W
Cobija	126	11 0 S	68 50W
Cobleskill	114	42 40N	74 30W
Coboconk	112	44 39N	78 48W
Cobourg	106	43 58N	78 10W
Cobourg Pen.	96	11 20 S	132 15 E
Cobram	99	35 54 S	145 40 E
Cobre	118	41 6N	114 25W
Coburg	25	50 15N	10 58 E
Coca	30	41 13N	4 32W
Cocanada = Kakinada	70	16 50N	82 11 E
Cocentaina	33	38 45N	0 27W
Cocha, La	124	27 50 S	65 40W
Cochabamba	126	17 26 S	66 10W
Cochem	25	50 8N	7 7 E
Cochemane	91	17 0 S	32 54 E
Cochin	70	9 59N	76 22 E
Cochin China = Nam-Phan	71	10 30N	106 0 E
Cochise	119	32 6N	109 58W
Cochran	115	32 25N	83 23W
Cochrane, Alta., Can.	108	51 11N	114 30W
Cochrane, Ont., Can.	106	49 0N	81 0W
Cochrane →	109	59 0N	103 40W
Cochrane, L.	128	47 10 S	72 0W
Cockatoo I.	96	16 6 S	123 37 E
Cockburn	99	32 5 S	141 0 E
Cockburn, Canal	128	54 30 S	72 0W
Cockburn I.	106	45 55N	83 22W
Coco →	121	15 0N	83 8W
Coco Chan.	71	13 50N	93 25 E
Coco Solo	120	9 22N	79 53W
Cocoa	115	28 22N	80 40W
Cocobeach	88	0 59N	9 34 E
Cocora	46	44 45N	27 3 E
Cocos I.	95	5 25N	87 55W
Cocos Is.	94	12 10 S	96 55 E
Cod, C.	111	42 8N	70 10W
Codajás	126	3 55 S	62 0W
Coderre	109	50 11N	106 31W
Codigoro	39	44 50N	12 5 E
Codó	127	4 30 S	43 55W
Codogno	38	45 10N	9 42 E
Codróipo	39	45 57N	13 0 E
Codru, Munţii	46	46 30N	22 15 E
Cody	118	44 35N	109 0W
Coe Hill	106	44 52N	77 50W
Coelemu	124	36 30 S	72 48W
Coen	97	13 52 S	143 12 E
Coesfeld	24	51 56N	7 10 E
Coeur d'Alene	118	47 45N	116 51W
Cœur d'Alene L.	118	47 32N	116 48W
Coevorden	16	52 40N	6 44 E
Coffeyville	117	37 0N	95 40W
Coffs Harbour	97	30 16 S	153 5 E
Cofrentes	33	39 13N	1 5W
Cogealac	46	44 36N	28 36 E
Coghinas →	40	40 55N	8 48 E
Coghinas, L. di	40	40 46N	9 3 E
Cognac	20	45 41N	0 20W
Cogne	38	45 37N	7 21 E
Cogolludo	32	40 59N	3 10W
Cohagen	118	47 2N	106 36W
Cohoes	114	42 47N	73 42W
Cohuna	99	35 45 S	144 15 E
Coiba, I.	121	7 30N	81 40W
Coig →	128	51 0 S	69 10W
Coihaique	128	45 30 S	71 45W
Coimbatore	70	11 2N	76 59 E
Coimbra, Brazil	126	19 55 S	57 48W
Coimbra, Port.	30	40 15N	8 27W
Coimbra □	30	40 12N	8 25W
Coín	31	36 40N	4 48W
Cojimies	126	0 20N	80 0W
Cojocna	46	46 45N	23 50 E
Cojutepequé	120	13 41N	88 54W
Čoka	42	45 57N	20 12 E
Cokeville	118	42 4N	111 0W
Col di Tenda	38	44 7N	7 36 E
Colaba Pt.	70	18 54N	72 47 E
Colac	97	38 21 S	143 35 E
Colachel	70	8 10N	77 15 E
Colares	31	38 48N	9 30W
Colbeck, C.	5	77 6 S	157 48W
Colbinabbin	99	36 38 S	144 48 E
Colborne	112	44 0N	77 53W
Colby	116	39 27N	101 2W
Colchagua □	124	34 30 S	71 0W
Colchester	13	51 54N	0 55 E
Coldstream	14	55 39N	2 14W
Coldwater, Can.	112	44 42N	79 40W
Coldwater, U.S.A.	117	37 18N	99 24W
Colebrook, Austral.	99	42 31 S	147 21 E
Colebrook, U.S.A.	114	44 54N	71 29W
Coleman, Can.	108	49 40N	114 30W
Coleman, U.S.A.	117	31 52N	99 30W
Coleman →	97	15 6 S	141 38 E
Colenso	93	28 44 S	29 50 E
Coleraine, Austral.	99	37 36 S	141 40 E
Coleraine, U.K.	15	55 8N	6 40 E
Coleraine □	15	55 8N	6 40 E
Coleridge, L.	101	43 17 S	171 30 E
Coleroon →	70	11 25N	79 50 E
Colesberg	92	30 45 S	25 5 E
Colfax, La., U.S.A.	117	31 35N	92 39W
Colfax, Wash., U.S.A.	118	46 57N	117 28W
Colhué Huapi, L.	128	45 30 S	69 0W
Cólico	38	46 8N	9 22 E
Coligny	93	26 17 S	26 15 E
Colima	120	19 10N	103 40W
Colima □	120	19 10N	103 40W
Colima, Nevado de	120	19 35N	103 45W
Colina	124	33 13 S	70 45W
Colina do Norte	84	12 28N	15 0W
Colinas	127	6 0 S	44 10W
Colinton	100	35 50 S	149 10 E
Coll	14	56 40N	6 35W
Collaguasi	124	21 5 S	68 45W
Collarada, Peña	32	42 43N	0 29W
Collarenebri	99	29 33 S	148 34 E
Collbran	119	39 16N	107 58W
Colle di Val d'Elsa	39	43 25N	11 7 E
Colle Salvetti	38	43 34N	10 27 E
Colle Sannita	41	41 22N	14 48 E
Collécchio	38	44 45N	10 10 E
Colleen Bawn	91	21 0 S	29 12 E
College Park	115	33 42N	84 27W
Collette	107	46 40N	65 30W
Collie	96	33 22 S	116 8 E
Collier B.	96	16 10 S	124 15 E
Colline Metallifere	38	43 10N	11 0 E
Collingwood, Austral.	98	22 20 S	142 31 E
Collingwood, Can.	106	44 29N	80 13W
Collingwood, N.Z.	101	40 41 S	172 40 E
Collins	106	50 17N	89 27W
Collinsville	97	20 30 S	147 56 E
Collipulli	124	37 55 S	72 30W
Collo	83	36 58N	6 37 E
Collonges	21	46 9N	5 52 E
Collooney	15	54 11N	8 28W
Colmar	19	48 5N	7 20 E
Colmars	21	44 11N	6 39 E
Colmenar	31	36 54N	4 20W
Colmenar de Oreja	32	40 6N	3 25W
Colmenar Viejo	30	40 39N	3 47W
Colne	12	53 51N	2 11W
Colo →	99	33 25 S	150 52 E
Cologna Véneta	39	45 19N	11 21 E
Cologne = Köln	24	50 56N	9 58 E
Colomb-Béchar = Béchar	82	31 38N	2 18W
Colombey-les-Belles	19	48 32N	5 54 E
Colombey-les-Deux-Églises	19	48 13N	4 50 E
Colômbia	127	20 10 S	48 40W
Colombia ■	126	3 45N	73 0W
Colombo	70	6 56N	79 58 E
Colombus	119	31 54N	107 43W
Colome	116	43 20N	99 44W
Colón, Argent.	124	32 12 S	58 10W
Colón, Cuba	121	22 42N	80 54W
Colón, Panama	120	9 20N	79 54W
Colonella	39	42 52N	13 50 E
Colonia	124	34 25 S	57 50W
Colonia Dora	124	28 34 S	62 59W
Colonial Hts.	114	37 19N	77 25W
Colonne, C. delle	41	39 2N	17 11 E
Colonsay, Can.	109	51 59N	105 52W
Colonsay, U.K.	14	56 4N	6 12W
Colorado □	110	37 40N	106 0W
Colorado →, Argent.	128	39 50 S	62 8W
Colorado →, Calif., U.S.A.	119	34 45N	114 40W
Colorado →, Tex., U.S.A.	117	28 36N	95 58W
Colorado City	117	32 25N	100 50W
Colorado Desert	110	34 20N	116 0W
Colorado, I.	120	9 12N	79 50W
Colorado Plateau	119	36 40N	110 30W
Colorado R. Aqueduct	119	34 17N	114 10W
Colorado Springs	116	38 55N	104 50W
Colorno	38	44 55N	10 21 E
Colton, N.Y., U.S.A.	113	44 34N	74 58W
Colton, Wash., U.S.A.	118	46 41N	117 6W
Columbia, La., U.S.A.	117	32 7N	92 5W
Columbia, Miss., U.S.A.	117	31 16N	89 50W
Columbia, Mo., U.S.A.	116	38 58N	92 20W
Columbia, Pa., U.S.A.	114	40 2N	76 30W
Columbia, S.C., U.S.A.	115	34 0N	81 0W
Columbia, Tenn., U.S.A.	115	35 40N	87 0W
Columbia →	118	46 15N	124 5W
Columbia Basin	118	47 30N	118 30W
Columbia, C.	4	83 0N	70 0W
Columbia City	114	41 8N	85 30W
Columbia, District of □	114	38 55N	77 0W
Columbia Falls	118	48 25N	114 16W
Columbia Heights	116	45 5N	93 10W
Columbia, Mt.	108	52 8N	117 20W
Columbiana	112	40 53N	80 40W
Columbretes, Is.	32	39 50N	0 50 E
Columbus, Ga., U.S.A.	115	32 30N	84 58W
Columbus, Ind., U.S.A.	114	39 14N	85 55W
Columbus, Kans., U.S.A.	117	37 15N	94 30W
Columbus, Miss., U.S.A.	115	33 30N	88 26W
Columbus, Mont., U.S.A.	118	45 38N	109 14W
Columbus, N.D., U.S.A.	116	48 52N	102 48W
Columbus, Nebr., U.S.A.	116	41 30N	97 25W
Columbus, Ohio, U.S.A.	114	39 57N	83 1W
Columbus, Tex., U.S.A.	117	29 42N	96 33W
Columbus, Wis., U.S.A.	116	43 20N	89 2W

Colunga Cradock

Colunga **30** 43 29N 5 16W
Colusa **118** 39 15N 122 1W
Colville **118** 48 33N 117 54W
Colville → **104** 70 25N 151 0W
Colville, C. **101** 36 29S 175 21 E
Colwyn Bay **12** 53 17N 3 44W
Coma **87** 8 29N 36 53 E
Comácchio **39** 44 41N 12 10 E
Comallo **128** 41 0S 70 5W
Comana **46** 44 10N 26 10 E
Comanche, Okla., U.S.A. **117** 34 27N 97 58W
Comanche, Tex., U.S.A. **117** 31 55N 98 35W
Comănești **46** 46 25N 26 26 E
Combahee → **115** 32 30N 80 31W
Combeaufontaine **19** 47 38N 5 54 E
Comber **112** 42 14N 82 33W
Comblain-au-Pont **16** 50 29N 5 35 E
Combles **19** 50 0N 2 50 E
Combourg **18** 48 25N 1 46W
Combronde **20** 45 58N 3 5 E
Comeragh Mts. **15** 52 17N 7 35W
Comet **98** 23 36S 148 38 E
Comilla **69** 23 28N 91 10 E
Comino, C. **40** 40 28N 9 47 E
Comino I. **36** 36 0N 14 20 E
Cómiso **41** 36 57N 14 35 E
Comitán **120** 16 18N 92 9W
Commentry **20** 46 20N 2 46 E
Commerce, Ga., U.S.A. **115** 34 10N 83 25W
Commerce, Tex., U.S.A. **117** 33 15N 95 50W
Commercy **19** 48 46N 5 34 E
Committee B. **105** 68 30N 86 30W
Commonwealth B. **5** 67 0S 144 0 E
Commoron Cr. → **99** 28 22S 150 8 E
Communism Pk. = Kommunisma, Pic **65** 38 40N 72 0 E
Como **38** 45 48N 9 5 E
Como, L. di **38** 46 5N 9 17 E
Comodoro Rivadavia **128** 45 50S 67 40W
Comorin, C. **70** 8 3N 77 40 E
Comoriște **42** 45 10N 21 35 E
Comoro Is. **3** 12 10S 44 15 E
Comox **108** 49 42N 124 55W
Compiègne **19** 49 24N 2 50 E
Compíglia Maríttima **38** 43 4N 10 37 E
Comporta **31** 38 22N 8 46W
Comprida, I. **125** 24 50S 47 42W
Compton Downs **99** 30 28S 146 30 E
Côn Dao **71** 8 45N 106 45 E
Conakry **84** 9 29N 13 49W
Conara Junction **99** 41 50S 147 26 E
Concarneau **18** 47 52N 3 56W
Conceição **91** 18 47S 36 7 E
Conceição da Barra **127** 18 35S 39 45W
Conceição do Araguaia **127** 8 0S 49 2W
Concepción, Argent. **124** 27 20S 65 35W
Concepción, Boliv. **126** 16 15S 62 8W
Concepción, Chile **124** 36 50S 73 0W
Concepción, Parag. **124** 23 22S 57 26W
Concepción □ **124** 37 0S 72 30W
Concepción → **120** 30 32N 113 2W
Concepción del Oro **120** 24 40N 101 30W
Concepción del Uruguay **124** 32 35S 58 20W
Concepción, L. **126** 17 20S 61 20W
Concepción, La = Ri-Aba **85** 3 28N 8 40 E
Concepcion, Pt. **119** 34 27N 120 27W
Concepción, Punta **120** 26 55N 111 59W
Conception B. **92** 23 55S 14 22 E
Conception I. **121** 23 52N 75 9W
Conception, Pt. **119** 34 30N 120 34W
Concession **91** 17 27S 30 56 E
Conchas Dam **117** 35 25N 104 10W
Conche **107** 50 55N 55 58W
Conches **18** 48 51N 2 43 E
Concho **119** 34 32N 109 43W
Concho → **117** 31 30N 99 45W
Conchos → **120** 29 32N 104 25W
Concord, N.C., U.S.A. **115** 35 28N 80 35W
Concord, N.H., U.S.A. **114** 43 12N 71 30W
Concordia **124** 31 20S 58 2W
Concórdia **126** 4 36S 66 36W
Concordia **116** 39 35N 97 40W
Concordia, La **120** 16 8N 92 38W
Concots **20** 44 26N 1 40 E
Concrete **118** 48 35N 121 49W
Condamine → **97** 27 7S 149 48 E
Condat **20** 45 21N 2 46 E
Condé **19** 50 26N 3 34 E
Conde **116** 45 13N 98 5W
Condé-sur-Noireau **18** 48 51N 0 33W
Condeúba **127** 14 52S 42 0W
Condobolin **99** 33 4S 147 6 E
Condom **20** 43 57N 0 22 E
Condon **118** 45 15N 120 8W
Condove **38** 45 8N 7 19 E
Conegliano **39** 45 53N 12 18 E
Conejera, I. **33** 39 11N 2 58 E
Conflans-en-Jarnisy **19** 49 10N 5 52 E
Confolens **20** 46 2N 0 40 E
Confuso → **124** 25 9S 57 34W
Congleton **12** 53 10N 2 12W
Congo = Zaïre → **88** 1 30N 28 0 E
Congo ■ **88** 1 0S 16 0 E
Congo Basin **78** 0 10S 24 30 E
Congonhas **125** 20 30S 43 52W
Congress **119** 34 11N 112 56W
Conil **31** 36 17N 6 10W
Coniston **106** 46 29N 80 51W
Conjeevaram = Kanchipuram **70** 12 52N 79 45 E
Conjuboy **98** 18 35S 144 35 E
Conklin **109** 55 38N 111 5W
Conlea **99** 30 7S 144 35 E
Conn, L. **15** 54 3N 9 15W
Connacht **15** 53 23N 8 40W
Conneaut **114** 41 55N 80 32W
Connecticut □ **114** 41 40N 72 40W
Connecticut → **114** 41 17N 72 21W
Connell **118** 46 36N 118 51W
Connellsville **114** 40 3N 79 32W
Connemara **15** 53 29N 9 45W
Connemaugh → **112** 40 38N 79 42W
Conner, La **118** 48 22N 122 27W
Connerré **18** 48 3N 0 30 E
Connersville **114** 39 40N 85 10W
Connors Ra. **98** 21 40S 149 10 E
Conoble **99** 32 55S 144 33 E
Conon → **14** 57 33N 4 28W
Cononaco → **126** 1 32S 75 35W
Cononbridge **14** 57 32N 4 30W
Conquest **109** 51 32N 107 14W
Conquet, Le **18** 48 21N 4 46W
Conrad **118** 48 11N 112 0W
Conran, C. **99** 37 49S 148 44 E
Conroe **117** 30 15N 95 28W
Conselheiro Lafaiete **125** 20 40S 43 48W
Conshohocken **113** 40 5N 75 18W
Consort **109** 52 1N 110 46W
Constance = Konstanz **25** 47 39N 9 10 E
Constance, L. = Bodensee **25** 47 35N 9 25 E
Constanța **46** 44 14N 28 38 E
Constanța □ **46** 44 15N 28 15 E
Constantina **31** 37 51N 5 40W
Constantine **83** 36 25N 6 42 E
Constitución, Chile **124** 35 20S 72 30W
Constitución, Uruguay **124** 42 0S 57 50W
Consuegra **31** 39 28N 3 36W
Consul **109** 49 20N 109 30W
Contact **118** 41 50N 114 56W
Contai **69** 21 54N 87 46 E
Contamana **126** 7 19S 74 55W
Contarina **39** 45 2N 12 13 E
Contas → **127** 14 17S 39 1W
Contes **21** 43 49N 7 19 E
Contoocook **113** 43 13N 71 45W
Contra Costa **93** 25 9S 33 30 E
Contres **18** 47 24N 1 26 E
Contrexéville **19** 48 6N 5 53 E
Conversano **41** 40 57N 17 8 E
Conway, Ark., U.S.A. **117** 35 5N 92 30W
Conway, N.H., U.S.A. **114** 43 58N 71 8W
Conway, S.C., U.S.A. **115** 33 49N 79 2W
Conway = Conwy **12** 53 17N 3 50W
Conwy **12** 53 17N 3 50W
Conwy → **12** 53 18N 3 50W
Coober Pedy **96** 29 1S 134 43 E
Cooch Behar **69** 26 22N 89 29 E
Cook **116** 47 49N 92 39W
Cook, Bahía **128** 55 10S 70 0W
Cook Inlet **104** 59 0N 151 0W
Cook Is. **95** 17 0S 160 0W
Cook, Mt. **101** 43 36S 170 9 E
Cook Strait **101** 41 15S 174 29 E
Cookeville **115** 36 12N 85 30W
Cookhouse **92** 32 44S 25 47 E
Cookshire **113** 45 25N 71 38W
Cookstown **15** 54 40N 6 43W
Cookstown □ **15** 54 40N 6 43W
Cooksville **112** 43 36N 79 35W
Cooktown **97** 15 30S 145 16 E
Coolabah **99** 31 1S 146 43 E
Cooladdi **99** 26 37S 145 23 E
Coolah **99** 31 48S 149 41 E
Coolamon **99** 34 46S 147 8 E
Coolangatta **99** 28 11S 153 29 E
Coolgardie **96** 30 55S 121 8 E
Coolidge **119** 33 1N 111 35W
Coolidge Dam **119** 33 10N 110 30W
Cooma **97** 36 12S 149 8 E
Coonabarabran **99** 31 14S 149 18 E
Coonamble **97** 30 56S 148 27 E
Coondapoor **70** 13 42N 74 40 E
Coongie **99** 27 9S 140 8 E
Coongoola **99** 27 43S 145 51 E
Cooninie, L. **99** 26 4S 139 59 E
Coonoor **70** 11 21N 76 45 E
Cooper **117** 33 20N 95 40W
Cooper → **115** 33 0N 79 55W
Coopers Cr. → **97** 28 29S 137 46 E
Cooperstown, N.D., U.S.A. **116** 47 30N 98 6W
Cooperstown, N.Y., U.S.A. **114** 42 42N 74 57W
Coorabulka **98** 23 41S 140 20 E
Coorong, The **97** 35 50S 139 20 E
Cooroy **99** 26 22S 152 54 E
Coos Bay **118** 43 26N 124 7W
Cootamundra **99** 34 36S 148 1 E
Cootehill **15** 54 5N 7 5W
Cooyar **99** 26 59S 151 51 E
Cooyeana **98** 24 29S 138 45 E
Copahue Paso **124** 37 49S 71 8W
Copainalá **120** 17 8N 93 11W
Cope **116** 39 44N 102 50W
Cope, Cabo **33** 37 26N 1 28W
Copenhagen = København **49** 55 41N 12 34 E
Copertino **41** 40 17N 18 2 E
Copiapó **124** 27 30S 70 20W
Copiapó → **124** 27 19S 70 56W
Copley **99** 30 36S 138 26 E
Copp L. **108** 60 14N 114 40W
Copparo **39** 44 52N 11 49 E
Copper Center **104** 62 10N 145 25W
Copper Cliff **106** 46 28N 81 4W
Copper Harbor **114** 47 31N 87 55W
Copper Queen **91** 17 29S 29 18 E
Copperbelt □ **91** 13 15S 27 30 E
Coppermine **104** 67 50N 115 5W
Coppermine → **104** 67 49N 116 4W
Coquet → **12** 55 18N 1 45W
Coquilhatville = Mbandaka **88** 0 1N 18 18 E
Coquille **118** 43 15N 124 12W
Coquimbo **124** 30 0S 71 20W
Coquimbo □ **124** 31 0S 71 0W
Corabia **46** 43 48N 24 30 E
Coracora **126** 15 5S 73 45W
Coradi, Is. **41** 40 27N 17 10 E
Coral Gables **115** 25 45N 80 16W
Coral Harbour **105** 64 8N 83 10W
Coral Sea **94** 15 0S 150 0 E
Coral Sea Islands Terr. **97** 20 0S 155 0 E
Corangamite, L. **100** 38 0S 143 30 E
Coraopolis **112** 40 30N 80 10W
Corato **41** 41 12N 16 22 E
Corbeil-Essonnes **19** 48 36N 2 26 E
Corbie **19** 49 54N 2 30 E
Corbières **20** 42 55N 2 35 E
Corbigny **19** 47 16N 3 40 E
Corbin **114** 37 0N 84 3W
Corbones → **31** 37 36N 5 39W
Corby **13** 52 49N 0 31W
Corcoles → **33** 39 40N 3 18W
Corcoran **119** 36 6N 119 35W
Corcubión **30** 42 56N 9 12W
Cordele **115** 31 55N 83 49W
Cordell **117** 35 18N 99 0W
Cordenons **39** 45 59N 12 42 E
Cordes **20** 44 5N 1 57 E
Córdoba, Argent. **124** 31 20S 64 10W
Córdoba, Mexico **120** 18 50N 97 0W
Córdoba, Spain **31** 37 50N 4 50W
Córdoba □, Argent. **124** 31 22S 64 15W
Córdoba □, Spain **31** 38 5N 5 0W
Córdoba, Sierra de **124** 31 10S 64 25W
Cordon **73** 16 42N 121 32 E
Cordova, Ala., U.S.A. **115** 33 45N 87 12W
Cordova, Alaska, U.S.A. **104** 60 36N 145 45W
Corella **32** 42 7N 1 48W
Corella → **98** 19 34S 140 47 E
Corfield **98** 21 40S 143 21 E
Corfu = Kérkira **44** 39 38N 19 50 E
Corgo **30** 42 56N 7 25W
Cori **40** 41 39N 12 53 E
Coria **30** 40 0N 6 33W
Coricudgy, Mt. **100** 32 51S 150 24 E
Corigliano Cálabro **41** 39 36N 16 31 E
Corinna **99** 41 35S 145 10 E
Corinth, Miss., U.S.A. **115** 34 54N 88 30W
Corinth, N.Y., U.S.A. **113** 43 15N 73 50W
Corinth = Kórinthos **45** 38 19N 22 24 E
Corinth Canal **45** 37 58N 23 0 E
Corinth, G. of = Korinthiakós **45** 38 16N 22 30 E
Corinto, Brazil **127** 18 20S 44 30W
Corinto, Nic. **121** 12 30N 87 10W
Corj □ **46** 45 5N 23 25 E
Cork **15** 51 54N 8 30W
Cork □ **15** 51 50N 8 50W
Cork Harbour **15** 51 46N 8 16W
Corlay **18** 48 20N 3 5W
Corleone **40** 37 48N 13 16 E
Corleto Perticara **41** 40 23N 16 2 E
Çorlu **43** 41 11N 27 49 E
Cormack L. **108** 60 56N 121 37W
Cormòns **39** 45 58N 13 29 E
Cormorant **109** 54 14N 100 35W
Cormorant L. **109** 54 15N 100 50W
Corn Is. = Maiz, Is. del **121** 12 0N 83 0W
Cornélio Procópio **125** 23 7S 50 40W
Cornell **116** 45 10N 91 8W
Corner Brook **107** 48 57N 57 58W
Corner Inlet **97** 38 45S 146 20 E
Corníglio **38** 44 29N 10 5 E
Corning, Ark., U.S.A. **117** 36 27N 90 34W
Corning, Calif., U.S.A. **118** 39 56N 122 9W
Corning, Iowa, U.S.A. **116** 40 57N 94 40W
Corning, N.Y., U.S.A. **114** 42 10N 77 3W
Corno, Monte **39** 42 28N 13 34 E
Cornwall, Austral. **99** 41 33S 148 7 E
Cornwall, Can. **106** 45 2N 74 44W
Cornwall □ **13** 50 26N 4 40W
Cornwallis I. **4** 75 8N 95 0W
Corny Pt. **99** 34 55S 137 0 E
Coro **126** 11 25N 69 41W
Coroatá **127** 4 8S 44 0W
Corocoro **126** 17 15S 68 28W
Coroico **126** 16 0S 67 50W
Coromandel **101** 36 45S 175 31 E
Coromandel Coast **70** 12 30N 81 0 E
Corona, Austral. **99** 31 16S 141 24 E
Corona, Calif., U.S.A. **119** 33 49N 117 36W
Corona, N. Mex., U.S.A. **119** 34 15N 105 32W
Coronada **119** 32 45N 117 9W
Coronado, Bahía de **121** 9 0N 83 40W
Coronation **108** 52 5N 111 27W
Coronation Gulf **104** 68 25N 110 0W
Coronation I., Antarct. **5** 60 45S 46 0W
Coronation I., U.S.A. **108** 55 52N 134 20W
Coronda **124** 31 58S 60 56W
Coronel **124** 37 0S 73 10W
Coronel Bogado **124** 27 11S 56 18W
Coronel Dorrego **124** 38 40S 61 10W
Coronel Oviedo **124** 25 24S 56 30W
Coronel Pringles **124** 38 0S 61 30W
Coronel Suárez **124** 37 30S 61 52W
Coronel Vidal **124** 37 28S 57 45W
Çorovoda **44** 40 31N 20 14 E
Corowa **99** 35 58S 146 21 E
Corozal, Belize **120** 18 23N 88 23W
Corozal, Panama **120** 8 59N 79 34W
Corps **21** 44 50N 5 56 E
Corpus **125** 27 10S 55 30W
Corpus Christi **117** 27 50N 97 28W
Corpus Christi L. **117** 28 5N 97 54W
Corque **126** 18 20S 67 41W
Corral de Almaguer **32** 39 45N 3 10W
Corréggio **38** 44 46N 10 47 E
Correntes, C. das **93** 24 6S 35 34 E
Corrèze □ **20** 45 20N 1 45 E
Correze → **20** 45 10N 1 28 E
Corrib, L. **15** 53 5N 9 10W
Corrientes **124** 27 30S 58 45W
Corrientes □ **124** 28 0S 57 0W
Corrientes →, Argent. **124** 30 42S 59 38W
Corrientes →, Peru **126** 3 43S 74 35W
Corrientes, C., Colomb. **126** 5 30N 77 34W
Corrientes, C., Cuba **121** 21 43N 84 30W
Corrientes, C., Mexico **120** 20 25N 105 42W
Corrigan **117** 31 0N 94 48W
Corry **114** 41 55N 79 39W
Corse **21** 42 0N 9 0 E
Corse, C. **21** 43 1N 9 25 E
Corse-du-Sud □ **21** 41 45N 9 0 E
Corsica = Corse **21** 42 0N 9 0 E
Corsicana **117** 32 5N 96 30W
Corté **21** 42 19N 9 11 E
Corte do Pinto **31** 37 42N 7 29W
Cortegana **31** 37 52N 6 49W
Cortez **119** 37 24N 108 35W
Cortina d'Ampezzo **39** 46 32N 12 9 E
Cortland **114** 42 35N 76 11W
Cortona **39** 43 16N 12 0 E
Coruche **31** 38 57N 8 30W
Çorum **64** 40 30N 34 57 E
Corumbá **126** 19 0S 57 30W
Corumbá de Goiás **127** 16 0S 48 50W
Coruña, La **30** 43 20N 8 25W
Coruña, La □ **30** 43 10N 8 30W
Corund **46** 46 30N 25 13 E
Corunna = La Coruña **30** 43 20N 8 25W
Corvallis **118** 44 36N 123 15W
Corvette, L. de la **106** 53 25N 74 3W
Corydon **116** 40 42N 93 22W
Cosalá **120** 24 28N 106 40W
Cosamaloapan **120** 18 23N 95 50W
Cosenza **41** 39 17N 16 14 E
Coșereni **46** 44 38N 26 35 E
Coshocton **114** 40 17N 81 51W
Cosne-sur-Loire **19** 47 24N 2 54 E
Cospeito **30** 43 12N 7 34W
Cosquín **124** 31 15S 64 30W
Cossato **38** 45 34N 8 10 E
Cossé-le-Vivien **18** 47 57N 0 54W
Cosson → **19** 47 30N 1 15 E
Costa Blanca **33** 38 25N 0 10W
Costa Brava **32** 41 30N 3 0 E
Costa del Sol **31** 36 30N 4 30W
Costa Dorada **32** 40 45N 1 15 E
Costa Rica ■ **121** 10 0N 84 0W
Costa Smeralda **40** 41 5N 9 35 E
Costigliole d'Asti **38** 44 48N 8 11 E
Costilla **119** 37 0N 105 30W
Coștiui **46** 47 53N 24 2 E
Coswig **24** 51 52N 12 31 E
Cotabato **73** 7 14N 124 15 E
Cotagaita **124** 20 45S 65 40W
Côte d'Azur **21** 43 25N 6 50 E
Côte d'Or **19** 47 10N 4 50 E
Côte-d'Or □ **19** 47 30N 4 50 E
Côte-St.-André, La **21** 45 24N 5 15 E
Coteau des Prairies **116** 44 30N 97 0W
Coteau du Missouri, Plat. du **116** 47 0N 101 0W
Coteau Landing **113** 45 15N 74 13W
Cotentin **18** 49 30N 1 30W
Côtes de Meuse **19** 49 15N 5 22 E
Côtes-du-Nord □ **18** 48 25N 2 40W
Cotiella **32** 42 31N 0 19 E
Cotina → **42** 43 36N 18 50 E
Cotonou **85** 6 20N 2 25 E
Cotopaxi, Vol. **126** 0 40S 78 30W
Cotronei **41** 39 9N 16 45 E
Cotswold Hills **13** 51 42N 2 10W
Cottage Grove **118** 43 48N 123 2W
Cottbus **24** 51 44N 14 20 E
Cottbus □ **24** 51 43N 13 30 E
Cottonwood **119** 34 48N 112 1W
Cotulla **117** 28 26N 99 14W
Coubre, Pte. de la **20** 45 42N 1 15W
Couches **19** 46 53N 4 30 E
Couço **31** 38 59N 8 17W
Coudersport **114** 41 45N 77 40W
Couëron **18** 47 13N 1 44W
Couesnon → **18** 48 38N 1 32W
Couhé-Vérac **20** 46 18N 0 12 E
Coulanges **19** 47 30N 3 30 E
Coulee City **118** 47 36N 119 18W
Coulman I. **5** 73 35S 170 0 E
Coulommiers **19** 48 50N 3 3 E
Coulon → **21** 43 51N 5 0 E
Coulonge → **106** 45 52N 76 46W
Coulonges **20** 46 28N 0 35W
Council, Alaska, U.S.A. **104** 64 55N 163 45W
Council, Idaho, U.S.A. **118** 44 44N 116 26W
Council Bluffs **116** 41 20N 95 50W
Council Grove **116** 38 41N 96 30W
Courantyne → **126** 5 55N 57 5W
Courçon **20** 46 15N 0 50W
Couronne, C. **21** 43 19N 5 3 E
Cours **21** 46 7N 4 19 E
Coursan **20** 43 14N 3 4 E
Courseulles **18** 49 20N 0 29W
Courtenay **108** 49 45N 125 0W
Courtine, La **20** 45 43N 2 16 E
Courtrai = Kortrijk **16** 50 50N 3 17 E
Courtright **112** 42 49N 82 28W
Courville **18** 48 28N 1 15 E
Coushatta **117** 32 0N 93 21W
Coutances **18** 49 3N 1 28W
Couterne **18** 48 30N 0 25W
Coutras **20** 45 3N 0 8W
Coutts **108** 49 0N 111 57W
Covarrubias **32** 42 4N 3 31W
Covasna **46** 45 50N 26 10 E
Covasna □ **46** 45 50N 26 0 E
Coventry **13** 52 25N 1 31W
Coventry L. **109** 61 15N 106 15W
Covilhã **30** 40 17N 7 31W
Covington, Ga., U.S.A. **115** 33 36N 83 50W
Covington, Ky., U.S.A. **114** 39 5N 84 30W
Covington, Okla., U.S.A. **117** 36 21N 97 36W
Covington, Tenn., U.S.A. **117** 35 34N 89 39W
Cowal, L. **97** 33 40S 147 25 E
Cowan **109** 52 5N 100 45W
Cowan, L. **96** 31 45S 121 45 E
Cowan L. **109** 54 0N 107 15W
Cowangie **99** 35 12S 141 26 E
Cowansville **113** 45 14N 72 46W
Cowarie **99** 27 45S 138 15 E
Cowdenbeath **14** 56 7N 3 20W
Cowes **13** 50 45N 1 18W
Cowra **97** 33 49S 148 42 E
Coxim **127** 18 30S 54 55W
Cox's Bazar **67** 21 26N 91 59 E
Cox's Cove **107** 49 7N 58 5W
Coyuca de Benítez **120** 17 1N 100 8W
Coyuca de Catalan **120** 18 18N 100 41W
Cozad **116** 40 55N 99 57W
Cozumel, Isla de **120** 20 30N 86 40W
Craboon **99** 32 3S 149 30 E
Cracow **99** 25 17S 150 17 E
Cracow = Kraków **27** 50 4N 19 57 E
Cradock **92** 32 8S 25 36 E

Craig
Damba

Craig, Alaska, U.S.A. **108** 55 30N 133 5W
Craig, Colo., U.S.A. **118** 40 32N 107 33W
Craigavon = Lurgan **15** 54 28N 6 20W
Craigmore **91** 20 28 S 32 50 E
Crailsheim **25** 49 7N 10 5 E
Craiova **46** 44 21N 23 48 E
Cramsie **98** 23 20 S 144 15 E
Cranberry Portage **109** 54 35N 101 23W
Cranbrook, Austral. **99** 42 0 S 148 5 E
Cranbrook, Can. **108** 49 30N 115 46W
Crandon **116** 45 32N 88 52W
Crane, Oregon, U.S.A. **118** 43 21N 118 39W
Crane, Texas, U.S.A. **117** 31 26N 102 27W
Cranston **113** 41 47N 71 27W
Craon **18** 47 50N 0 58W
Craonne **19** 49 27N 3 46 E
Craponne **20** 45 20N 3 51 E
Crasna **46** 46 32N 27 51 E
Crasna → **46** 47 44N 22 35 E
Crasnei, Munţii **46** 47 0N 23 20 E
Crater, L. **118** 42 55N 122 3W
Crater Pt. **98** 5 25 S 152 9 E
Crateús **127** 5 10 S 40 39W
Crati → **41** 39 41N 16 30 E
Crato, Brazil **127** 7 10 S 39 25W
Crato, Port. **31** 39 16N 7 39W
Crau **21** 43 32N 4 40 E
Crawford **116** 42 40N 103 25W
Crawfordsville **114** 40 2N 86 51W
Crawley **13** 51 7N 0 10W
Crazy Mts. **118** 46 14N 110 30W
Crean L. **109** 54 5N 106 9W
Crécy-en-Brie **19** 48 50N 2 53 E
Crécy-en-Ponthieu **19** 50 15N 1 53 E
Crediton **112** 43 17N 81 33W
Cree →, Can. **109** 58 57N 105 47W
Cree →, U.K. **14** 54 51N 4 24W
Cree L. **109** 57 30N 106 30W
Creede **119** 37 56N 106 59W
Creel **120** 27 45N 107 38W
Creighton **116** 42 30N 97 52W
Creil **19** 49 15N 2 34 E
Crema **38** 45 21N 9 40 E
Cremona **38** 45 8N 10 2 E
Crepaja **42** 45 1N 20 38 E
Crépy **19** 49 37N 3 32 E
Crépy-en-Valois **19** 49 14N 2 54 E
Cres **39** 44 58N 14 25 E
Cresbard **116** 45 13N 98 57W
Crescent, Okla., U.S.A. **117** 35 58N 97 36W
Crescent, Oreg., U.S.A. **118** 43 30N 121 37W
Crescent City **118** 41 45N 124 12W
Crescentino **38** 45 11N 8 7 E
Crespino **39** 44 59N 11 51 E
Crespo **124** 32 2 S 60 19W
Cressy **99** 38 2 S 143 40 E
Crest **21** 44 44N 5 2 E
Crested Butte **119** 38 57N 107 0W
Crestline **112** 40 46N 82 45W
Creston, Can. **108** 49 10N 116 31W
Creston, Iowa, U.S.A. **116** 41 0N 94 20W
Creston, Wash., U.S.A. **118** 47 47N 118 36W
Creston, Wyo., U.S.A. **118** 41 46N 107 50W
Crestview **115** 30 45N 86 35W
Creswick **100** 37 25 S 143 58 E
Crete **116** 40 38N 96 58W
Crete = Kríti **45** 35 15N 25 0 E
Crete, La **108** 58 11N 116 24W
Crete, Sea of **45** 36 0N 25 0 E
Cretin, C. **98** 6 40 S 147 53 E
Creus, C. **32** 42 20N 3 19 E
Creuse □ **20** 46 0N 2 0 E
Creuse → **20** 47 0N 0 34 E
Creusot, Le **19** 46 50N 4 24 E
Creuzburg **24** 51 3N 10 15 E
Crevalcore **39** 44 41N 11 10 E
Crèvecœur-le-Grand **19** 49 37N 2 5 E
Crevillente **33** 38 12N 0 48W
Crewe **12** 53 6N 2 28W
Crib Point **99** 38 22 S 145 13 E
Criciúma **125** 28 40 S 49 23W
Crieff **14** 56 22N 3 50W
Crikvenica **39** 45 11N 14 40 E
Crimea = Krymskaya **56** 45 0N 34 0 E
Crimmitschau **24** 50 48N 12 23 E
Crinan **14** 56 6N 5 34W
Cristeşti **46** 47 15N 26 33 E
Cristóbal **120** 9 19N 79 54W
Crişul Alb → **42** 46 42N 21 17 E
Crişul Negru → **46** 46 38N 22 26 E
Crişul Repede → **46** 46 55N 20 59 E
Crivitz **24** 53 35N 11 39 E
Crna Gora **42** 42 10N 21 30 E
Crna Gora □ **42** 42 40N 19 20 E
Crna Reka → **42** 41 33N 21 59 E
Crna Trava **42** 42 49N 22 19 E
Crni Drim → **42** 41 17N 20 40 E
Crni Timok → **42** 43 53N 22 15 E
Crnoljeva Planina **42** 42 20N 21 0 E
Črnomelj **39** 45 33N 15 10 E
Croaghpatrick **15** 53 46N 9 40W
Croatia = Hrvatska □ **39** 45 20N 16 0 E
Crocker, Barisan **72** 5 40N 116 30 E
Crocker I. **96** 11 12 S 132 32 E
Crockett **117** 31 20N 95 30W
Crocodile = Krokodil → **93** 25 26 S 32 0 E
Crocodile Is. **96** 12 3 S 134 58 E
Crocq **20** 45 52N 2 21 E
Croisette, C. **21** 43 13N 5 20 E
Croisic, Le **18** 47 18N 2 30W
Croisic, Pte. du **18** 47 19N 2 31W
Croix, La, L. **106** 48 20N 92 15W
Cromarty, Can. **109** 58 3N 94 9W
Cromarty, U.K. **14** 57 40N 4 2W
Cromer **12** 52 56N 1 18 E
Cromwell **101** 45 3 S 169 14 E
Cronat **19** 46 43N 3 40 E
Cronulla **100** 34 3 S 151 8 E
Crooked →, Can. **108** 54 50N 122 54W
Crooked →, U.S.A. **118** 44 30N 121 16W
Crooked I. **121** 22 50N 74 10W
Crookston, Minn., U.S.A. **116** 47 50N 96 40W
Crookston, Nebr., U.S.A. **116** 42 56N 100 45W
Crooksville **114** 39 45N 82 8W
Crookwell **99** 34 28 S 149 24 E
Crosby, Minn., U.S.A. **116** 46 28N 93 57W
Crosby, N.D., U.S.A. **109** 48 55N 103 18W
Crosby, Pa., U.S.A. **112** 41 45N 78 23W
Crosbyton **117** 33 37N 101 12W
Cross → **85** 4 42N 8 21 E
Cross City **115** 29 35N 83 5W
Cross Fell **12** 54 44N 2 29W
Cross L. **109** 54 45N 97 30W
Cross Plains **117** 32 8N 99 7W
Cross River □ **85** 6 0N 8 0 E
Cross Sound **104** 58 20N 136 30W
Crosse, La, Kans., U.S.A. **116** 38 33N 99 20W
Crosse, La, Wis., U.S.A. **116** 43 48N 91 13W
Crossett **117** 33 10N 91 57W
Crossfield **108** 51 25N 114 0W
Crosshaven **15** 51 48N 8 19W
Croton-on-Hudson **113** 41 12N 73 55W
Crotone **41** 39 5N 17 6 E
Crow → **108** 59 41N 124 20W
Crow Agency **118** 45 40N 107 30W
Crow Hd. **15** 51 34N 10 9W
Crowell **117** 33 59N 99 45W
Crowley **117** 30 15N 92 20W
Crown Point **114** 41 24N 87 23W
Crows Nest **99** 27 16 S 152 4 E
Crowsnest Pass **108** 49 40N 114 40W
Croydon, Austral. **97** 18 13 S 142 14 E
Croydon, U.K. **13** 51 18N 0 5W
Crozet Is. **3** 46 27 S 52 0 E
Crozon **18** 48 15N 4 30W
Cruz Alta **125** 28 45 S 53 40W
Cruz, C. **121** 19 50N 77 50W
Cruz del Eje **124** 30 45 S 64 50W
Cruz, La **120** 23 55N 106 54W
Cruzeiro **125** 22 33 S 45 0W
Cruzeiro do Oeste **125** 23 46 S 53 4W
Cruzeiro do Sul **126** 7 35 S 72 35W
Cry L. **108** 58 45N 129 0W
Crystal Brook **99** 33 21 S 138 12 E
Crystal City, Mo., U.S.A. **116** 38 15N 90 23W
Crystal City, Tex., U.S.A. **117** 28 40N 99 50W
Crystal Falls **114** 46 9N 88 11W
Crystal River **115** 28 54N 82 35W
Crystal Springs **117** 31 59N 90 25W
Csongrád **27** 46 43N 20 12 E
Csongrád □ **27** 46 32N 20 15 E
Csorna **27** 47 38N 17 18 E
Csurgo **27** 46 16N 17 9 E
Cu Lao Hon **71** 10 54N 108 18 E
Cuácua → **91** 17 54 S 37 0 E
Cuamato **92** 17 2 S 15 7 E
Cuamba **91** 14 45 S 36 22 E
Cuando → **89** 14 0 S 19 30 E
Cuando Cubango □ **92** 16 25 S 20 0 E
Cuangar **92** 17 36 S 18 39 E
Cuarto → **124** 33 25 S 63 2W
Cuba, Port. **31** 38 10N 7 54W
Cuba, N. Mex., U.S.A. **119** 36 0N 107 0W
Cuba, N.Y., U.S.A. **112** 42 12N 78 18W
Cuba ■ **121** 22 0N 79 0W
Cubango → **92** 18 50 S 22 25 E
Cuchi **89** 14 37 S 16 58 E
Cúcuta **126** 7 54N 72 31W
Cudahy **114** 42 54N 87 50W
Cudalbi **46** 45 46N 27 41 E
Cuddalore **70** 11 46N 79 45 E
Cuddapah **70** 14 30N 78 47 E
Cuddapan, L. **99** 25 45 S 141 26 E
Cudgewa **99** 36 10 S 147 42 E
Cudillero **30** 43 33N 6 9W
Cue **96** 27 25 S 117 54 E
Cuéllar **30** 41 23N 4 21W
Cuenca, Ecuador **126** 2 50 S 79 9W
Cuenca, Spain **32** 40 5N 2 10W
Cuenca □ **32** 40 0N 2 0W
Cuenca, Serranía de **32** 39 55N 1 50W
Cuerda del Pozo, Pantano de la **32** 41 51N 2 44W
Cuernavaca **120** 18 50N 99 20W
Cuero **117** 29 5N 97 17W
Cuers **21** 43 14N 6 5 E
Cuervo **117** 35 5N 104 25W
Cuevas del Almanzora **33** 37 18N 1 58W
Cuevo **126** 20 15 S 63 30W
Cugir **46** 45 48N 23 25 E
Cuiabá **127** 15 30 S 56 0W
Cuiabá → **127** 17 5 S 56 36W
Cuillin Hills **14** 57 14N 6 15W
Cuillin Sd. **14** 57 4N 6 20W
Cuiluan **76** 47 51N 128 32 E
Cuima **89** 13 25 S 15 45 E
Cuiseaux **21** 46 30N 5 22 E
Cuito → **92** 18 1 S 20 48 E
Cuitzeo, L. de **120** 19 55N 101 5W
Cujmir **46** 44 13N 22 57 E
Culan **20** 46 34N 2 20 E
Culbertson **116** 48 9N 104 30W
Culcairn **99** 35 41 S 147 3 E
Culebra, Sierra de la **30** 41 55N 6 20W
Culgoa → **99** 29 56 S 146 20 E
Culiacán **120** 24 50N 107 23W
Culion **73** 11 54N 120 1 E
Cúllar de Baza **33** 37 35N 2 34W
Cullarin Range **99** 34 30 S 149 30 E
Cullen **14** 57 45N 2 50W
Cullen Pt. **98** 11 57 S 141 54 E
Cullera **33** 39 9N 0 17W
Cullman **115** 34 13N 86 50W
Culloden Moor **14** 57 29N 4 7W
Culoz **21** 45 47N 5 46 E
Culpeper **114** 38 29N 77 59W
Culuene → **127** 12 56 S 52 51W
Culver, Pt. **96** 32 54 S 124 43 E
Culverden **101** 42 47 S 172 49 E
Cumali **45** 36 42N 27 28 E
Cumaná **126** 10 30N 64 5W
Cumberland, B.C., Can. **108** 49 40N 125 0W
Cumberland, Qué., Can. **113** 45 30N 75 24W
Cumberland, Md., U.S.A. **114** 39 40N 78 43W
Cumberland, Wis., U.S.A. **116** 45 32N 92 3W
Cumberland → **115** 36 15N 87 0W
Cumberland I. **115** 30 52N 81 30W
Cumberland Is. **97** 20 35 S 149 10 E
Cumberland L. **109** 54 3N 102 18W
Cumberland Pen. **105** 67 0N 64 0W
Cumberland Plat. **115** 36 0N 84 30W
Cumberland Sd. **105** 65 30N 66 0W
Cumborah **99** 29 40 S 147 45 E
Cumbres Mayores **31** 38 4N 6 39W
Cumbria □ **12** 54 35N 2 55W
Cumbrian Mts. **12** 54 30N 3 0W
Cumbum **70** 15 40N 79 10 E
Cumnock, Austral. **99** 32 59 S 148 46 E
Cumnock, U.K. **14** 55 27N 4 18W
Cuncumén **124** 31 53 S 70 38W
Cunene → **92** 17 20 S 11 50 E
Cúneo **38** 44 23N 7 31 E
Cunillera, I. **33** 38 59N 1 13 E
Cunlhat **20** 45 38N 3 32 E
Cunnamulla **97** 28 2 S 145 38 E
Cuorgnè **38** 45 23N 7 39 E
Cupar, Can. **109** 50 57N 104 10W
Cupar, U.K. **14** 56 20N 3 0W
Cupica, Golfo de **126** 6 25N 77 30W
Ćuprija **42** 43 57N 21 26 E
Curaçao **121** 12 10N 69 0W
Curanilahue **124** 37 29 S 73 28W
Curaray → **126** 2 20 S 74 5W
Cure → **19** 47 40N 3 41 E
Curepto **124** 35 8 S 72 1W
Curiapo **126** 8 33N 61 5W
Curicó **124** 34 55 S 71 20W
Curicó □ **124** 34 50 S 71 15W
Curitiba **125** 25 20 S 49 10W
Currabubula **99** 31 16 S 150 44 E
Currais Novos **127** 6 13 S 36 30W
Curralinho **127** 1 45 S 49 46W
Currant **118** 38 51N 115 32W
Curraweena **99** 30 47 S 145 54 E
Currawilla **99** 25 10 S 141 20 E
Current → **117** 37 15N 91 10W
Currie, Austral. **99** 39 56 S 143 53 E
Currie, U.S.A. **118** 40 16N 114 45W
Currie, Mt. **93** 30 29 S 29 21 E
Currituck Sd. **115** 36 20N 75 50W
Currockbilly Mt. **100** 35 25 S 150 0 E
Curtea de Argeş **46** 45 12N 24 42 E
Curtis, Spain **30** 43 7N 8 4W
Curtis, U.S.A. **116** 40 41N 100 32W
Curtis I. **97** 23 35 S 151 10 E
Curuápanema → **127** 2 25 S 55 2W
Curuçá **127** 0 43 S 47 50W
Curuguaty **125** 24 31 S 55 42W
Çürüksu Çayi → **53** 37 27N 27 11 E
Curundu **120** 8 59N 79 38W
Curup **72** 4 26 S 102 13 E
Cururupu **127** 1 50 S 44 50W
Curuzú Cuatiá **124** 29 50 S 58 5W
Curvelo **127** 18 45 S 44 27W
Cushing **117** 35 59N 96 46W
Cushing, Mt. **108** 57 35N 126 57W
Cusihuiriáchic **120** 28 10N 106 50W
Cusna, Monte **38** 44 13N 10 25 E
Cusset **20** 46 8N 3 28 E
Custer **116** 43 45N 103 38W
Cut Bank **118** 48 40N 112 15W
Cuthbert **115** 31 47N 84 47W
Cutro **41** 39 1N 16 58 E
Cuttaburra → **99** 29 43 S 144 22 E
Cuttack **69** 20 25N 85 57 E
Cuvier, C. **96** 23 14 S 113 22 E
Cuvier I. **101** 36 27 S 175 50 E
Cuxhaven **24** 53 51N 8 41 E
Cuyahoga Falls **114** 41 8N 81 30W
Cuyo **73** 10 50N 121 5 E
Cuzco, Boliv. **126** 20 0 S 66 50W
Cuzco, Peru **126** 13 32 S 72 0W
Čvrsnica **42** 43 36N 17 35 E
Cwmbran **13** 51 39N 3 0W
Cyangugu **90** 2 29 S 28 54 E
Cybinka **28** 52 12N 14 46 E
Cyclades = Kikladhes **45** 37 20N 24 30 E
Cygnet **99** 43 8 S 147 1 E
Cynthiana **114** 38 23N 84 10W
Cypress Hills **109** 49 40N 109 30W
Cyprus ■ **64** 35 0N 33 0 E
Cyrenaica **81** 27 0N 23 0 E
Cyrene = Shaḥḥāt **81** 32 40N 21 35 E
Czaplinek **28** 53 34N 16 14 E
Czar **109** 52 27N 110 50W
Czarna →, Piotrkow Trybunalski, Poland **28** 51 18N 19 55 E
Czarna →, Tarnobrzeg, Poland **28** 50 3N 21 21 E
Czarna Woda **28** 53 51N 18 6 E
Czarne **28** 53 42N 16 58 E
Czarnków **28** 52 55N 16 38 E
Czechoslovakia ■ **27** 49 0N 17 0 E
Czechowice-Dziedzice **27** 49 54N 18 59 E
Czeladz **28** 50 16N 19 2 E
Czempiń **28** 52 9N 16 33 E
Czeremcha **28** 52 31N 23 21 E
Czersk **28** 53 46N 17 58 E
Czerwieńsk **28** 52 1N 15 13 E
Czerwionka **27** 50 7N 18 37 E
Częstochowa **28** 50 49N 19 7 E
Częstochowa □ **28** 50 45N 19 0 E
Człopa **28** 53 6N 16 6 E
Człuchów **28** 53 41N 17 22 E
Czyzew **28** 52 48N 22 19 E

D

Da → **71** 21 15N 105 20 E
Da Hinggan Ling **75** 48 0N 121 0 E
Da Lat **71** 11 56N 108 25 E
Da Nang **71** 16 4N 108 13 E
Da Qaidam **75** 37 50N 95 15 E
Da Yunhe, Jiangsu, China **77** 34 25N 120 5 E
Da Yunhe, Zhejiang, China **77** 30 45N 120 35 E
Da'an **76** 45 30N 124 7 E
Dab'a, Râs el **86** 31 3N 28 31 E
Daba Shan **75** 32 0N 109 0 E
Dabai **85** 11 25N 5 15 E
Dabakala **84** 8 15N 4 20W
Dabbūrīya **62** 32 42N 35 22 E
Dabhoi **68** 22 10N 73 20 E
Dąbie, Poland **28** 53 27N 14 45 E
Dąbie, Poland **28** 52 5N 18 50 E
Dabo **72** 0 30 S 104 33 E
Dabola **84** 10 50N 11 5W
Dabou **84** 5 20N 4 23W
Daboya **85** 9 30N 1 20W
Dabrowa Górnicza **28** 50 15N 19 10 E
Dabrowa Tarnówska **27** 50 10N 20 59 E
Dąbrówno **28** 53 27N 20 2 E
Dabus → **87** 10 48N 35 10 E
Dacato → **87** 7 25N 42 40 E
*Dacca **69** 23 43N 90 26 E
*Dacca □ **69** 24 25N 90 25 E
Dachau **25** 48 16N 11 27 E
Dadanawa **126** 2 50N 59 30W
Daday **56** 41 28N 33 27 E
Dade City **115** 28 20N 82 12W
Dades, Oued → **82** 30 58N 6 44W
Dadiya **85** 9 35N 11 24 E
Dadra and Nagar Haveli □ **68** 20 5N 73 0 E
Dadri = Charkhi Dadri **68** 28 37N 76 17 E
Dadu **68** 26 45N 67 45 E
Dāeni **46** 44 51N 28 10 E
Daet **73** 14 2N 122 55 E
Dafang **77** 27 9N 105 39 E
Dagana **84** 16 30N 15 35W
Dagash **86** 19 19N 33 25 E
Dagestan A.S.S.R. □ **57** 42 30N 47 0 E
Dagestanskiye Ogni **57** 42 6N 48 12 E
Daghfeli **86** 19 18N 32 40 E
Dagö = Hiiumaa **54** 58 50N 22 45 E
Dagupan **73** 16 3N 120 20 E
Dahab **86** 28 30N 34 31 E
Dahlak Kebir **87** 15 50N 40 10 E
Dahlenburg **24** 53 11N 10 43 E
Dahlonega **115** 34 35N 83 59W
Dahme, Germ., E. **24** 51 51N 13 25 E
Dahme, Germ., W. **24** 54 13N 11 5 E
Dahomey = Benin ■ **85** 10 0N 2 0 E
Dahra **84** 15 22N 15 30W
Dahra, Massif de **82** 36 7N 1 21 E
Dai Shan **77** 30 25N 122 10 E
Dai Xian **76** 39 4N 112 58 E
Daimiel **33** 39 5N 3 35W
Daingean **15** 53 18N 7 15W
Daintree **98** 16 20 S 145 20 E
Daiō-Misaki **74** 34 15N 136 45 E
Dairût **86** 27 34N 30 43 E
Daitari **69** 21 10N 85 46 E
Dajarra **97** 21 42 S 139 30 E
Dakar **84** 14 34N 17 29W
Dakhla **80** 23 50N 15 53W
Dakhla, El Wâhât el- **86** 25 30N 28 50 E
Dakhovskaya **57** 44 13N 40 13 E
Dakingari **85** 11 37N 4 1 E
Dakor **68** 22 45N 73 11 E
Dakoro **85** 14 31N 6 46 E
Dakota City **116** 42 27N 96 28W
Đakovica **42** 42 22N 20 26 E
Đakovo **42** 45 19N 18 24 E
Dalaba **84** 10 42N 12 15W
Dalachi **76** 36 48N 105 0 E
Dalai Nur **76** 43 20N 116 45 E
Dalandzadgad **75** 43 27N 104 30 E
Dalbandin **65** 29 0N 64 23 E
Dalbeattie **14** 54 55N 3 50W
Dalbosjön **49** 58 40N 12 45 E
Dalby, Austral. **97** 27 10 S 151 17 E
Dalby, Sweden **49** 55 40N 13 22 E
Dale **47** 61 22N 5 23 E
Dalen **47** 59 26N 8 0 E
Dalga **86** 27 39N 30 41 E
Dalhart **117** 36 10N 102 30W
Dalhousie, Can. **107** 48 5N 66 26W
Dalhousie, India **68** 32 38N 76 0 E
Dali, Shaanxi, China **77** 34 48N 109 58 E
Dali, Yunnan, China **75** 25 40N 100 10 E
Daliang Shan **75** 28 0N 102 45 E
Dalias **33** 36 49N 2 52W
Dāliyat el Karmel **62** 32 43N 35 2 E
Dalj **42** 45 29N 18 59 E
Dalkeith **14** 55 54N 3 5W
Dall I. **108** 54 59N 133 25W
Dallarnil **99** 25 19 S 152 2 E
Dallas, Oregon, U.S.A. **118** 45 0N 123 15W
Dallas, Texas, U.S.A. **117** 32 50N 96 50W
Dallol **87** 14 14N 40 17 E
Dalmacija □ **42** 43 20N 17 0 E
Dalmatia = Dalmacija □ **42** 43 20N 17 0 E
Dalmellington **14** 55 20N 4 25W
Dalneretchensk **59** 45 50N 133 40 E
Daloa **84** 7 0N 6 30W
Dalrymple, Mt. **97** 21 1 S 148 39 E
Dalsjöfors **49** 57 46N 13 5 E
Dalskog **49** 58 44N 12 18 E
Dalton, Can. **106** 48 11N 84 1W
Dalton, Ga., U.S.A. **115** 34 47N 84 58W
Dalton, Mass., U.S.A. **113** 42 28N 73 11W
Dalton, Nebr., U.S.A. **116** 41 27N 103 0W
Dalton Iceberg Tongue **5** 66 15 S 121 30 E
Daltonganj **69** 24 0N 84 4 E
Dalvík **50** 65 58N 18 32W
Daly → **96** 13 35 S 130 19 E
Daly L. **109** 56 32N 105 39W
Daly Waters **96** 16 15 S 133 24 E
Dama, Wadi → **86** 27 12N 35 50 E
Daman **68** 20 25N 72 57 E
Daman □ **68** 20 25N 72 58 E
Damanhûr **86** 31 0N 30 30 E
Damar **73** 7 7 S 128 40 E
Damaraland **92** 21 0 S 17 0 E
Damascus = Dimashq **64** 33 30N 36 18 E
Damaturu **85** 11 45N 11 55 E
Damāvand **65** 35 47N 52 0 E
Damāvand, Qolleh-ye **65** 35 56N 52 10 E
Damba **88** 6 44 S 15 20 E

*Renamed Dhaka

Dāmghān Dessye

Dāmghān 65 36 10N 54 17 E
Dāmienesti 46 46 44N 27 1 E
Damietta = Dumyât 86 31 24N 31 48 E
Daming 76 36 15N 115 6 E
Dāmīya 62 32 6N 35 34 E
Dammarie 19 48 20N 1 30 E
Dammartin 19 49 3N 2 41 E
Damme 24 52 32N 8 12 E
Damodar → 69 23 17N 87 35 E
Damoh 69 23 50N 79 28 E
Damous 82 36 31N 1 42 E
Dampier 96 20 41 S 116 42 E
Dampier Arch. 96 20 38 S 116 32 E
Dampier Downs 96 18 24 S 123 5 E
Dampier, Selat 73 0 40 S 131 0 E
Dampier Str. 98 5 50 S 148 0 E
Damville 18 48 51N 1 5 E
Damvillers 19 49 20N 5 21 E
Dan-Gulbi 85 11 40N 6 15 E
Dan Xian 77 19 31N 109 33 E
Dana 73 11 0 S 122 52 E
Dana, Lac 106 50 53N 77 20W
Danakil Depression 87 12 45N 41 0 E
Danao 73 10 31N 124 1 E
Danbury 114 41 23N 73 29W
Danby L. 119 34 17N 115 0W
Dandeldhura 69 29 20N 80 35 E
Dandenong 99 38 0 S 145 15 E
Dandong 76 40 10N 124 20 E
Danforth 107 45 39N 67 57W
* Danger Is. 95 10 53 S 165 49W
Danger Pt. 92 34 40 S 19 17 E
Dangla 87 11 18N 36 56 E
Dangora 85 11 30N 8 7 E
Dangshan 77 34 27N 116 22 E
Dangtu 77 31 32N 118 25 E
Dangyang 77 30 52N 111 44 E
Daniel 118 42 56N 110 2W
Daniel's Harbour 107 50 13N 57 35W
Danielskull 92 28 11 S 23 33 E
Danielson 113 41 50N 71 52W
Danilov 55 58 16N 40 13 E
Danilovgrad 42 42 38N 19 9 E
Danilovka 55 50 25N 44 12 E
Danissa 90 3 15N 40 58 E
Danja 85 11 21N 7 30 E
Dankalwa 85 11 52N 12 12 E
Dankama 85 13 20N 7 44 E
Dankov 55 53 20N 39 5 E
Danlí 121 14 4N 86 35W
Dannemora, Sweden 48 60 12N 17 51 E
Dannemora, U.S.A. 114 44 41N 73 44W
Dannenberg 24 53 7N 11 4 E
Dannevirke 101 40 12 S 176 8 E
Dannhauser 93 28 0 S 30 3 E
Danshui 77 25 12N 121 25 E
Dansville 114 42 32N 77 41W
Dantan 69 21 57N 87 20 E
Dante 63 10 25N 51 26 E
Danube → 43 45 20N 29 40 E
Danukandi 69 23 32N 90 43 E
Danvers 113 42 34N 70 55W
Danville, Ill., U.S.A. 114 40 10N 87 40W
Danville, Ky., U.S.A. 114 37 40N 84 45W
Danville, Va., U.S.A. 115 36 40N 79 20W
Danzhai 77 26 11N 107 48 E
Danzig = Gdańsk 28 54 22N 18 40 E
Dao 73 10 30N 121 57 E
Dão → 30 40 20N 8 11W
Dao Xian 77 25 36N 111 31 E
Daosa 68 26 52N 76 20 E
Daoud = Aïn Beida 83 35 44N 7 22 E
Daoulas 18 48 22N 4 17W
Dapong 85 10 55N 0 16 E
Daqing Shan 76 40 40N 111 0 E
Daqu Shan 77 30 25N 122 20 E
Dar al Hamrā, Ad 64 27 22N 37 43 E
Dar es Salaam 90 6 50 S 39 12 E
Dar'ā 62 32 36N 36 7 E
Dārāb 65 28 50N 54 30 E
Darabani 46 48 10N 26 39 E
Daraj 83 30 10N 10 28 E
Daravica 42 42 32N 20 8 E
Daraw 86 24 22N 32 51 E
Darazo 85 11 1N 10 24 E
Darband 66 34 20N 72 50 E
Darbhanga 69 26 15N 85 55 E
Darby 118 46 2N 114 7W
Darda 42 45 40N 18 41 E
Dardanelle 117 35 12N 93 9W
Dardanelles = Canakkale Boğazi 44 40 0N 26 0 E
Darfo 38 45 52N 10 11 E
Dargai 66 34 25N 71 55 E
Dargan Ata 58 40 29N 62 10 E
Dargaville 101 35 57 S 173 52 E
Darhan Muminggan Lianheqi 76 41 40N 110 28 E
Dari 87 5 48N 30 26 E
Darien 120 9 7N 79 46W
Darién, G. del 126 9 0N 77 0W
Darjeeling 69 27 3N 88 18 E
Dark Cove 107 48 47N 54 13W
Darling → 97 34 4 S 141 54 E
Darling Downs 99 27 30 S 150 30 E
Darling Ra. 96 32 30 S 116 0 E
Darlington, U.K. 12 54 33N 1 33W
Darlington, S.C., U.S.A. 115 34 18N 79 50W
Darlington, Wis., U.S.A. 116 42 43N 90 7W
Darlington Point 100 34 37 S 146 1 E
Darłowo 28 54 25N 16 25 E
Dărmăneşti 46 46 21N 26 33 E
Darmstadt 25 49 51N 8 40 E
Darnah 81 32 40N 22 35 E
Darnall 93 29 23 S 31 18 E
Darnétal 18 49 25N 1 10 E
Darney 19 48 5N 6 0 E
Darnick 100 32 48 S 143 38 E
Darnley B. 104 69 30N 123 30W
Darnley, C. 5 68 0 S 69 0 E
Daroca 32 41 9N 1 25W
Darr 98 23 13 S 144 7 E
Darr → 98 23 39 S 143 50 E
Darrington 118 48 14N 121 37W
* Renamed Pakapuka

Darror → 63 10 30N 50 0 E
Darsana 69 23 35N 88 48 E
Darsi 70 15 46N 79 44 E
Darsser Ort 24 54 29N 12 31 E
Dart → 13 50 24N 3 36W
Dart, C. 5 73 6 S 126 20W
Dartmoor 13 50 36N 4 0W
Dartmouth, Austral. 98 23 31 S 144 44 E
Dartmouth, Can. 107 44 40N 63 30W
Dartmouth, U.K. 13 50 21N 3 35W
Dartmouth, L. 99 26 4 S 145 18 E
Dartuch, C. 32 39 55N 3 49 E
Daru 98 9 3 S 143 13 E
Daruvar 42 45 35N 17 14 E
Darvaza 58 40 11N 58 24 E
Darwha 68 20 15N 77 45 E
Darwin 96 12 25 S 130 51 E
Darwin Glacier 5 79 53 S 159 0 E
Daryacheh-ye-Sistan 65 31 0N 61 0 E
Daryapur 68 20 55N 77 20 E
Das 65 25 20N 53 30 E
Dashkesan 57 40 40N 46 0 E
Dasht → 65 25 10N 61 40 E
Dasht-e Kavīr 65 34 30N 55 0 E
Dasht-e Lūt 65 31 30N 58 0 E
Dasht-e Mārgow 65 30 40N 62 30 E
Daska 68 32 20N 74 20 E
Dassa-Zoume 85 7 46N 2 14 E
Dasseneiland 92 33 25 S 18 3 E
Datça 45 36 46N 27 40 E
Datia 68 25 39N 78 27 E
Datian 77 25 40N 117 50 E
Datong, Anhui, China 77 30 48N 117 44 E
Datong, Shanxi, China 76 40 6N 113 18 E
Dattapur 68 20 45N 78 15 E
Datu Piang 73 7 2N 124 30 E
Datu, Tanjung 72 2 5N 109 39 E
Daugava → 54 57 4N 24 3 E
Daugavpils 54 55 53N 26 32 E
Daulatabad 70 19 57N 75 15 E
Daun 25 50 10N 6 53 E
Dauphin 109 51 9N 100 5W
Dauphin I. 115 30 16N 88 10W
Dauphin L. 109 51 20N 99 45W
Dauphiné 21 45 15N 5 25 E
Dauqa 86 19 30N 41 0 E
Daura, Borno, Nigeria 85 11 31N 11 24 E
Daura, Kaduna, Nigeria 85 13 2N 8 21 E
Davangere 70 14 25N 75 55 E
Davao 73 7 0N 125 40 E
Davao, G. of 73 6 30N 125 48 E
Dāvar Panāh 65 27 25N 62 15 E
Davenport, Iowa, U.S.A. 116 41 30N 90 40W
Davenport, Wash., U.S.A. 118 47 40N 118 5W
Davenport Downs 98 24 8 S 141 7 E
Davenport Ra. 96 20 28 S 134 0 E
David 121 8 30N 82 30W
David City 116 41 18N 97 10W
David Gorodok 54 52 4N 27 8 E
Davidson 109 51 16N 105 59W
Davis, Antarct. 5 68 34 S 17 55 E
Davis, U.S.A. 118 38 33N 121 44W
Davis Dam 119 35 11N 114 35W
Davis Inlet 107 55 50N 60 59W
Davis Mts. 117 30 42N 104 15W
Davis Sea 5 66 0 S 92 0 E
Davis Str. 105 65 0N 58 0W
Davos 25 46 48N 9 49 E
Davy L. 109 58 53N 108 18W
Dawa → 87 4 11N 42 6 E
Dawaki, Bauchi, Nigeria 85 9 25N 9 33 E
Dawaki, Kano, Nigeria 85 12 5N 8 23 E
Dawes Ra. 98 24 40 S 150 40 E
Dawson, Can. 104 64 10N 139 30W
Dawson, Ga., U.S.A. 115 31 45N 84 28W
Dawson, N.D., U.S.A. 116 46 56N 99 45W
Dawson → 97 23 25 S 149 45 E
Dawson Creek 108 55 45N 120 15W
Dawson, I. 128 53 50 S 70 50W
Dawson Inlet 109 61 50N 93 25W
Dawson Range 98 24 30 S 149 48 E
Dax 20 43 44N 1 3W
Daxian 75 31 15N 107 23 E
Daxin 77 22 50N 107 11 E
Daxue Shan 75 30 30N 101 30 E
Daye 77 30 6N 114 58 E
Daylesford 100 37 21 S 144 9 E
Dayong 77 29 11N 110 30 E
Dayr Abū Sa'īd 62 32 30N 35 42 E
Dayr al-Ghuşūn 62 32 21N 35 4 E
Dayr az Zawr 64 35 20N 40 5 E
Dayr Dirwān 62 31 55N 35 15 E
Daysland 108 52 50N 112 20W
Dayton, Ohio, U.S.A. 114 39 45N 84 10W
Dayton, Pa., U.S.A. 112 40 54N 79 18W
Dayton, Tenn., U.S.A. 115 35 30N 85 1W
Dayton, Wash., U.S.A. 118 46 20N 118 10W
Daytona Beach 115 29 14N 81 0W
Dayu 77 25 24N 114 22 E
Dayville 118 44 33N 119 37W
Dazhu 77 30 41N 107 15 E
Dazu 77 29 40N 105 42 E
De Aar 92 30 39 S 24 0 E
De Funiak Springs 115 30 42N 86 10W
De Grey 96 20 12 S 119 12 E
De Land 115 29 1N 81 19W
De Leon 117 32 9N 98 35W
De Pere 114 44 28N 88 1W
De Queen 117 34 3N 94 24W
De Quincy 117 30 30N 93 27W
De Ridder 117 30 48N 93 15W
De Smet 116 44 25N 97 35W
De Soto 116 38 7N 90 33W
De Tour 114 45 59N 83 56W
De Witt 117 34 19N 91 20W
Dead Sea = Miyet, Bahr el 64 31 30N 35 30 E
Deadwood 116 44 23N 103 44W
Deadwood L. 108 59 10N 128 30W
Deakin 96 30 46 S 128 0 E
Deal 13 51 13N 1 25 E
Dealesville 92 28 41 S 25 44 E
Dean, Forest of 13 51 50N 2 35W

Deán Funes 124 30 20 S 64 20W
Dearborn 106 42 18N 83 15W
Dease → 108 59 56N 128 32W
Dease L. 108 58 40N 130 5W
Dease Lake 108 58 25N 130 6W
Death Valley 119 36 19N 116 52W
Death Valley Junc. 119 36 21N 116 30W
Death Valley Nat. Monument 119 36 30N 117 0W
Deauville 18 49 23N 0 2 E
Deba Habe 85 10 14N 11 20 E
Debaltsevo 56 48 22N 38 26 E
Debao 77 23 21N 106 46 E
Debar 42 41 31N 20 30 E
Debden 109 53 30N 106 50W
Debdou 82 33 59N 3 0W
Dębica 27 50 2N 21 25 E
Dęblin 28 51 34N 21 50 E
Debno 28 52 44N 14 41 E
Débo, L. 84 15 14N 4 15W
Debolt 108 55 12N 118 1W
Debrc 42 44 38N 19 53 E
Debre Birhan 87 9 41N 39 31 E
Debre Markos 87 10 20N 37 40 E
Debre May 87 11 20N 37 25 E
Debre Sina 87 9 51N 39 50 E
Debre Tabor 87 11 50N 38 26 E
Debre Zebit 87 11 48N 38 30 E
Debrecen 27 47 33N 21 42 E
Dečani 42 42 30N 20 10 E
Decatur, Ala., U.S.A. 115 34 35N 87 0W
Decatur, Ga., U.S.A. 115 33 47N 84 17W
Decatur, Ill., U.S.A. 116 39 50N 89 0W
Decatur, Ind., U.S.A. 114 40 50N 84 56W
Decatur, Texas, U.S.A. 117 33 15N 97 35W
Decazeville 20 44 34N 2 15 E
Deccan 70 18 0N 79 0 E
Deception I. 5 63 0 S 60 15W
Deception L. 109 56 33N 104 13W
Děčín 26 50 47N 14 12 E
Decize 19 46 50N 3 28 E
Deckerville 112 43 33N 82 46W
Decollatura 41 39 2N 16 21 E
Decorah 116 43 20N 91 50W
Deda 46 46 56N 24 50 E
Dedéagach = Alexandroúpolis 44 40 50N 25 54 E
Dedham 113 42 14N 71 10W
Dedilovo 55 53 59N 37 50 E
Dédougou 84 12 30N 3 25W
Dedurú Oya 70 7 32N 79 50 E
Dedza 91 14 20 S 34 20 E
Dee →, Scot., U.K. 14 57 4N 2 7W
Dee →, Wales, U.K. 12 53 15N 3 7W
Deep B. 108 61 15N 116 35W
Deepdale 96 21 42 S 116 10 E
Deepwater 99 29 25 S 151 51 E
Deer → 109 58 23N 94 13W
Deer Lake, Newf., Can. 107 49 11N 57 27W
Deer Lake, Ontario, Can. 109 52 36N 94 20W
Deer Lodge 118 46 25N 112 40W
Deer Park 118 47 55N 117 21W
Deer River 116 47 21N 93 44W
Deeral 98 17 14 S 145 55 E
Deerdepoort 92 24 37 S 26 27 E
Deesa 68 24 18N 72 10 E
Deferiet 113 44 2N 75 41W
Defiance 114 41 20N 84 20W
Deganya 62 32 43N 35 34 E
Degebe → 31 38 13N 7 29W
Degeh Bur 63 8 11N 43 31 E
Degema 85 4 50N 6 48 E
Deggendorf 25 48 49N 12 59 E
Degloor 70 18 34N 77 33 E
Deh Bīd 65 30 39N 53 11 E
Deh Kheyr 65 28 45N 54 40 E
Dehibat 83 32 0N 10 47 E
Dehiwala 70 6 50N 79 51 E
Dehkareqan 64 37 43N 45 55 E
Dehra Dun 68 30 20N 78 4 E
Dehri 69 24 50N 84 15 E
Dehui 76 44 30N 125 40 E
Deinze 16 50 59N 3 32 E
Dej 46 47 10N 23 52 E
Deje 48 59 35N 13 29 E
Dekalb 116 41 55N 88 45W
Dekemhare 87 15 6N 39 0 E
Dekese 88 3 24 S 21 24 E
Del Norte 119 37 40N 106 27W
Del Rio 117 29 23N 100 50W
Delagua 117 37 21N 104 35W
Delai 86 17 21N 36 6 E
Delano 119 35 48N 119 13W
Delareyville 92 26 41 S 25 26 E
Delavan 116 42 40N 88 39W
Delaware 114 40 20N 83 0W
Delaware □ 114 39 0N 75 40W
Delaware → 114 39 20N 75 25W
Delčevo 42 41 58N 22 46 E
Delegate 99 37 4 S 148 56 E
Delémont 25 47 22N 7 20 E
Delft 16 52 1N 4 22 E
Delft I. 70 9 30N 79 40 E
Delfzijl 16 53 20N 6 55 E
Delgado, C. 91 10 45 S 40 40 E
Delgo 86 20 6N 30 40 E
Delhi, Can. 112 42 51N 80 30W
Delhi, India 68 28 38N 77 17 E
Delhi, U.S.A. 113 42 17N 74 56W
Deli Jovan 42 44 13N 22 9 E
Delia 108 51 38N 112 23W
Delice → 64 39 45N 34 15 E
Delicias 120 28 10N 105 30W
Delitzsch 24 51 32N 12 22 E
Dell City 119 31 58N 105 19W
Dell Rapids 116 43 53N 96 44W
Delle 19 47 30N 7 2 E
Dellys 83 36 57N 3 57 E
Delmar 113 42 37N 73 47W
Delmenhorst 24 53 3N 8 37 E
Delmiro Gouveia 127 9 24 S 38 6W
Delnice 39 45 23N 14 50 E
Delong, Ostrova 59 76 40N 149 20 E
Deloraine, Austral. 99 41 30 S 146 40 E

Deloraine, Can. 109 49 15N 100 29W
Delorme, L. 107 54 31N 69 52W
Delphi, Greece 45 38 28N 22 30 E
Delphi, U.S.A. 114 40 37N 86 40W
Delphos 114 40 51N 84 17W
Delportshoop 92 28 22 S 24 20 E
Delray Beach 115 26 27N 80 4W
Delsbo 48 61 48N 16 32 E
Delta, Colo., U.S.A. 119 38 44N 108 5W
Delta, Utah, U.S.A. 118 39 21N 112 29W
Delungra 99 29 39 S 150 51 E
Delvina 44 39 59N 20 4 E
Delvinákion 44 39 57N 20 32 E
Demanda, Sierra de la 32 42 15N 3 0W
Demba 88 5 28 S 22 15 E
Dembecha 87 10 32N 37 30 E
Dembi 87 8 5N 36 25 E
Dembia 90 3 33N 25 48 E
Dembidolo 87 8 34N 34 50 E
Demer → 16 50 57N 4 42 E
Demetrias 44 39 22N 23 1 E
Demidov 54 55 16N 31 30 E
Deming 119 32 10N 107 50W
Demini → 126 0 46 S 62 56W
Demmin 24 53 54N 13 2 E
Demnate 82 31 44N 6 59W
Demonte 38 44 18N 7 18 E
Demopolis 115 32 30N 87 48W
Dempo, Mt. 72 4 2 S 103 15 E
Demyansk 54 57 40N 32 27 E
Den Burg 16 53 3N 4 47 E
Den Haag = 's Gravenhage 16 52 7N 4 17 E
Den Helder 16 52 57N 4 45 E
Den Oever 16 52 56N 5 2 E
Denain 19 50 20N 3 22 E
Denau 58 38 16N 67 54 E
Denbigh 12 53 12N 3 26W
Dendang 72 3 7 S 107 56 E
Dendermonde 16 51 2N 4 5 E
Deneba 87 9 47N 39 10 E
Deng Xian 77 32 34N 112 4 E
Denge 85 12 52N 5 21 E
Dengi 85 9 25N 9 55 E
Denham 96 25 56 S 113 31 E
Denham Ra. 97 21 55 S 147 46 E
Denia 33 38 49N 0 8 E
Deniliquin 97 35 30 S 144 58 E
Denison, Iowa, U.S.A. 116 42 0N 95 18W
Denison, Texas, U.S.A. 117 33 50N 96 40W
Denison Range 97 28 30 S 136 5 E
Denizli 64 37 42N 29 2 E
Denman Glacier 5 66 45 S 99 25 E
Denmark 96 34 59 S 117 25 E
Denmark ■ 49 55 30N 9 0 E
Denmark Str. 6 66 0N 30 0W
Dennison 112 40 21N 81 21W
Denpasar 72 8 45 S 115 14 E
Denton, Mont., U.S.A. 118 47 25N 109 56W
Denton, Texas, U.S.A. 117 33 12N 97 10W
D'Entrecasteaux Is. 98 9 0 S 151 0 E
D'Entrecasteaux Pt. 96 34 50 S 115 57 E
Denu 85 6 4N 1 8 E
Denver 116 39 45N 105 0W
Denver City 117 32 58N 102 48W
Deoband 68 29 42N 77 43 E
Deobhog 70 19 53N 82 44 E
Deogarh 69 21 32N 84 45 E
Deoghar 69 24 30N 86 42 E
Deolali 70 19 58N 73 50 E
Deoli 68 25 50N 75 20 E
Deoria 69 26 31N 83 48 E
Deosai Mts. 69 35 40N 75 0 E
Depew 112 42 55N 78 43W
Deping 76 37 25N 116 58 E
Deposit 113 42 5N 75 23W
Deputatskiy 59 69 18N 139 54 E
Dêqên 75 28 34N 98 51 E
Deqing 77 23 8N 111 42 E
Dera Ghazi Khan 68 30 5N 70 43 E
Dera Ismail Khan 68 31 50N 70 50 E
* Dera Ismail Khan □ 68 32 30N 70 0 E
Derbent 56 42 5N 48 4 E
Derby, Austral. 96 17 18 S 123 38 E
Derby, U.K. 12 52 55N 1 28W
Derby, Conn., U.S.A. 113 41 20N 73 5W
Derby, N.Y., U.S.A. 112 42 40N 78 59W
Derby □ 12 52 55N 1 28W
Derecske 27 47 20N 21 33 E
Derg → 15 54 42N 7 26W
Derg, L. 15 53 0N 8 20W
Dergachi 55 50 9N 36 11 E
Dergaon 67 26 45N 94 0 E
Dermantsi 43 43 8N 24 17 E
Dernieres Isles 117 29 0N 90 45W
Derryveagh Mts. 15 55 0N 8 40W
Derudub 86 17 31N 36 7 E
Derval 18 47 40N 1 41W
Dervéni 45 38 8N 22 25 E
Derventa 42 44 59N 17 55 E
Derwent 109 53 41N 110 58W
Derwent →, Derby, U.K. 12 52 53N 1 17W
Derwent →, N. Yorks., U.K. 12 53 45N 0 57W
Derwentwater, L. 12 54 35N 3 9W
Des Moines, Iowa, U.S.A. 116 41 35N 93 37W
Des Moines, N. Mex., U.S.A. 117 36 50N 103 51W
Des Moines → 116 40 23N 91 25W
Desaguadero →, Argent. 124 34 30 S 66 46W
Desaguadero →, Boliv. 126 18 24 S 67 5W
Deschaillons 107 46 32N 72 7W
Descharme → 109 56 51N 109 13W
Deschutes → 118 45 30N 121 0W
Dese 87 11 5N 39 40 E
Desenzano del Gardo 38 45 28N 10 32 E
Desert Center 119 33 45N 115 27W
Deskenatlata L. 108 60 55N 112 3W
Desna → 54 50 33N 30 32 E
Desnătui → 46 44 15N 23 27 E
Desolación, I. 128 53 0 S 74 0W
Despeñaperros, Paso 33 38 24N 3 30W
Despotovac 42 44 6N 21 30 E
Dessau 24 51 49N 12 15 E
Dessye = Dese 87 11 5N 39 40 E
* Now part of North West Frontier □

D'Estrees B. Donja Stubica

D'Estrees B. **99** 35 55 S 137 45 E
Desuri **68** 25 18N 73 35 E
Desvrès **19** 50 40N 1 48 E
Deta **42** 45 24N 21 13 E
Detinja → **42** 43 51N 19 45 E
Detmold **24** 51 55N 8 50 E
Detour Pt. **114** 45 37N 86 35W
Detroit, Mich., U.S.A. **106** 42 23N 83 5W
Detroit, Tex., U.S.A. **117** 33 40N 95 10W
Detroit Lakes **116** 46 50N 95 50W
Dett **91** 18 38 S 26 50 E
Deurne, Belg. **16** 51 12N 4 24 E
Deurne, Neth. **16** 51 27N 5 49 E
Deutsche Bucht **24** 54 10N 7 51 E
Deutschlandsberg **26** 46 49N 15 14 E
Deux-Sèvres □ **18** 46 35N 0 20W
Deva **46** 45 53N 22 55 E
Devakottai **70** 9 55N 78 45 E
Devaprayag **68** 30 13N 78 35 E
Dévaványa **27** 47 2N 20 59 E
Deveci Daği **56** 40 10N 36 0 E
Devecser **27** 47 6N 17 26 E
Deventer **16** 52 15N 6 10 E
Deveron → **14** 57 40N 2 31W
Devesel **46** 44 28N 22 41 E
Devgad Baria **68** 22 40N 73 55 E
Devgad, I. **70** 14 48N 74 5 E
Devils Lake **116** 48 5N 98 50W
Devils Paw **108** 58 47N 134 0W
Devil's Pt. **70** 9 26N 80 6 E
Devin **43** 41 44N 24 24 E
Devizes **13** 51 21N 2 0W
Devnya **43** 43 13N 27 33 E
Devolii → **44** 40 57N 20 15 E
Devon **108** 53 24N 113 44W
Devon I. **4** 75 10N 85 0W
Devonport, Austral. **97** 41 10 S 146 22 E
Devonport, N.Z. **101** 36 49 S 174 49 E
Devonport, U.K. **13** 50 23N 4 11W
Devonshire □ **13** 50 50N 3 40W
Dewas **68** 22 59N 76 3 E
Dewetsdorp **92** 29 33 S 26 39 E
Dewsbury **12** 53 42N 1 38W
Dexter, Mo., U.S.A. **117** 36 50N 90 0W
Dexter, N. Mex., U.S.A. **117** 33 15N 104 25W
Deyhūk **65** 33 15N 57 30 E
Deyyer **65** 27 55N 51 55 E
Dezadeash L. **108** 60 28N 136 58W
Dezfūl **64** 32 20N 48 30 E
Dezh Shāhpūr **64** 35 30N 46 25 E
Dezhneva, Mys **59** 66 5N 169 40W
Dezhou **76** 37 26N 116 18 E
Dháfni **45** 37 48N 22 1 E
Dhafra **65** 23 20N 54 0 E
Dhahaban **86** 21 58N 39 3 E
Dhahira **65** 23 40N 57 0 E
Dhahiriya = Az Zāhirīyah **62** 31 25N 34 58 E
Dhahran = Az Zahrān **64** 26 18N 50 10 E
Dhamar **63** 14 30N 44 20 E
Dhamási **44** 39 43N 22 11 E
Dhampur **68** 29 19N 78 33 E
Dhamtari **69** 20 42N 81 35 E
Dhanbad **69** 23 50N 86 30 E
Dhankuta **69** 26 55N 87 40 E
Dhanora **69** 20 20N 80 22 E
Dhar **68** 22 35N 75 26 E
Dharampur, Gujarat, India **70** 20 32N 73 17 E
Dharampur, Mad. P., India **68** 22 13N 75 18 E
Dharapuram **70** 10 45N 77 34 E
Dharmapuri **70** 12 10N 78 10 E
Dharmavaram **70** 14 29N 77 44 E
Dharmsala (Dharamsala) **68** 32 16N 76 23 E
Dhaulagiri **69** 28 39N 83 28 E
Dhebar, L. **68** 24 10N 74 0 E
Dhenkanal **69** 20 45N 85 35 E
Dhenoúsa **45** 37 8N 25 48 E
Dheskáti **44** 39 55N 21 49 E
Dhespotikó **45** 36 57N 24 58 E
Dhestina **45** 38 25N 22 31 E
Dhidhimótikhon **44** 41 22N 26 29 E
Dhikti **45** 35 8N 25 22 E
Dhilianáta **45** 38 15N 20 34 E
Dhílos **45** 37 23N 25 15 E
Dhimitsána **45** 37 36N 22 3 E
Dhírfis **45** 38 40N 23 54 E
Dhodhekánisos **45** 36 35N 27 0 E
Dhokós **45** 37 20N 23 20 E
Dholiana **44** 39 54N 20 32 E
Dholka **68** 22 44N 72 29 E
Dholpur **68** 26 45N 77 59 E
Dhomokós **45** 39 10N 22 18 E
Dhond **70** 18 26N 74 40 E
Dhoraji **68** 21 45N 70 37 E
Dhoxáton **44** 41 9N 24 16 E
Dhragonísi **45** 37 27N 25 29 E
Dhrangadhra **68** 22 59N 71 31 E
Dhriopís **45** 37 25N 24 35 E
Dhrol **68** 22 33N 70 25 E
Dhubaibah **65** 23 25N 54 35 E
Dhubri **69** 26 2N 89 59 E
Dhula **63** 15 10N 47 30 E
Dhulia **68** 20 58N 74 50 E
Dhurm → **86** 20 18N 42 53 E
Di Linh, Cao Nguyen **71** 11 30N 108 0 E
Día **45** 35 26N 25 13 E
Diablo Heights **120** 8 58N 79 34W
Diafarabé **84** 14 9N 4 57W
Diala **84** 14 10N 10 0W
Dialakoro **84** 12 18N 7 54W
Diallassagou **84** 13 47N 3 41W
Diamante **124** 32 5 S 60 40W
Diamante → **124** 34 30 S 66 46W
Diamantina **127** 18 17 S 43 40W
Diamantina → **97** 26 45 S 139 10 E
Diamantino **127** 14 30 S 56 30W
Diamond Harbour **69** 22 11N 88 14 E
Diamond Mts. **118** 40 0N 115 58W
Diamondville **118** 41 51N 110 30W
Diancheng **77** 21 30N 111 4 E
Diano Marina **38** 43 55N 8 3 E
Dianra **84** 8 45N 6 14W
Diapaga **85** 12 5N 1 46 E
Diapangou **85** 12 5N 0 10 E
Diariguila **84** 10 35N 10 2W
Dibaya **88** 6 30 S 22 57 E
Dibaya-Lubue **88** 4 12 S 19 54 E
Dibbi **87** 4 10N 41 52 E
Dibble Glacier Tongue **5** 66 8 S 134 32 E
Dibete **92** 23 45 S 26 32 E
Dibrugarh **67** 27 29N 94 55 E
Dickinson **116** 46 50N 102 48W
Dickson **115** 36 5N 87 22W
Dickson City **113** 41 29N 75 40W
Dickson (Dikson) **58** 73 40N 80 5 E
Dicomano **39** 43 53N 11 30 E
Didesa, W. → **87** 10 2N 35 32 E
Didiéni **84** 13 53N 8 6W
Didsbury **108** 51 35N 114 10W
Didwana **68** 27 23N 17 36 E
Die **21** 44 47N 5 22 E
Diébougou **84** 11 0N 3 15W
Diefenbaker L. **109** 51 0N 106 55W
Diego Garcia **3** 7 50 S 72 50 E
Diekirch **16** 49 52N 6 10 E
Diélette **18** 49 33N 1 52W
Diéma **84** 14 32N 9 12W
Diémbéring **84** 12 29N 16 47W
Dien Bien **71** 21 20N 103 0 E
Diepholz **24** 52 37N 8 22 E
Dieppe **18** 49 54N 1 4 E
Dieren **16** 52 3N 6 6 E
Dierks **117** 34 9N 94 0W
Diest **16** 50 58N 5 4 E
Dieulefit **21** 44 32N 5 4 E
Dieuze **19** 48 49N 6 43 E
Differdange **16** 49 31N 5 54 E
Dig **68** 27 28N 77 20 E
Digba **90** 4 25N 25 48 E
Digby **107** 44 38N 65 50W
Digges **109** 58 40N 94 0W
Digges Is. **105** 62 40N 77 50W
Dighinala **67** 23 15N 92 5 E
Dighton **116** 38 30N 100 26W
Digne **21** 44 5N 6 12 E
Digoin **20** 46 29N 3 58 E
Digos **73** 6 45N 125 20 E
Digranes **50** 66 4N 14 44 E
Digras **70** 20 6N 77 45 E
Digul → **73** 7 7 S 138 42 E
Dihang → **67** 27 48N 95 30 E
Dijlah, Nahr → **64** 31 0N 47 25 E
Dijon **19** 47 20N 5 0 E
Dikala **87** 4 45N 31 28 E
Dikkil **87** 11 8N 42 20 E
Dikomu di Kai **92** 24 58 S 24 36 E
Diksmuide **16** 51 2N 2 52 E
Dikwa **85** 12 4N 13 30 E
Dila **87** 6 21N 38 22 E
Dili **73** 8 39 S 125 34 E
Dilizhan **57** 40 46N 44 57 E
Dilj **42** 45 29N 18 1 E
Dillenburg **24** 50 44N 8 17 E
Dilley **117** 28 40N 99 12W
Dilling **87** 12 3N 29 35 E
Dillingen **25** 48 32N 10 29 E
Dillon, Can. **109** 55 56N 108 35W
Dillon, Mont., U.S.A. **118** 45 9N 112 36W
Dillon, S.C., U.S.A. **115** 34 26N 79 20W
Dillon → **109** 55 56N 108 56W
Dilston **99** 41 22 S 147 10 E
Dimashq **64** 33 30N 36 18 E
Dimbokro **84** 6 45N 4 46W
Dimboola **99** 36 28 S 142 7 E
Dîmboviţa □ **46** 45 0N 25 30 E
Dîmboviţa → **46** 44 14N 26 13 E
Dîmbovnic → **46** 44 28N 25 18 E
Dimbulah **98** 17 8 S 145 4 E
Dimitrovgrad, Bulg. **43** 42 5N 25 35 E
Dimitrovgrad, U.S.S.R. **55** 54 14N 49 39 E
Dimitrovgrad, Yugo. **42** 43 0N 22 48 E
Dimitrovo = Pernik **42** 42 35N 23 2 E
Dimmitt **117** 34 36N 102 16W
Dimo **87** 5 19N 29 10 E
Dimona **62** 31 2N 35 1 E
Dimovo **42** 43 43N 22 50 E
Dinagat **73** 10 10N 125 40 E
Dinajpur **69** 25 33N 88 43 E
Dinan **18** 48 28N 2 2W
Dinant **16** 50 16N 4 55 E
Dinapur **69** 25 38N 85 5 E
Dinar **64** 38 5N 30 15 E
Dinara Planina **39** 43 50N 16 35 E
Dinard **18** 48 38N 2 6W
Dinaric Alps = Dinara Planina **9** 43 50N 16 35 E
Dinder, Nahr ed → **87** 14 6N 33 40 E
Dindi → **70** 16 24N 78 15 E
Dindigul **70** 10 25N 78 0 E
Ding Xian **76** 38 30N 114 59 E
Dingbian **76** 37 35N 107 32 E
Dingelstädt **24** 51 19N 10 19 E
Dinghai **77** 30 1N 122 6 E
Dingle **15** 52 9N 10 17W
Dingle B. **15** 52 3N 10 20W
Dingmans Ferry **113** 41 13N 74 55W
Dingnan **77** 24 45N 115 0 E
Dingo **98** 23 38 S 149 19 E
Dingolfing **25** 48 38N 12 30 E
Dingtao **77** 35 5N 115 35 E
Dinguiraye **84** 11 18N 10 49W
Dingwall **14** 57 36N 4 26W
Dingxi **76** 35 30N 104 33 E
Dingxiang **76** 38 30N 112 58 E
Dinokwe (Palla Road) **92** 23 29 S 26 37 E
Dinosaur National Monument **118** 40 30N 108 58W
Dinuba **119** 36 31N 119 22W
Dio **49** 56 37N 14 15 E
Diósgyör **27** 48 7N 20 43 E
Diosig **46** 47 18N 22 2 E
Diourbel **84** 14 39N 16 12W
Diplo **68** 24 35N 69 35 E
Dipolog **73** 8 36N 123 20 E
Dipşa **46** 46 58N 24 27 E
Dir **66** 35 08N 71 59 E
Diré **84** 16 20N 3 25W
Dire Dawa **87** 9 35N 41 45 E
Direction, C. **97** 12 51 S 143 32 E
Diriamba **121** 11 51N 86 19W
Dirk Hartog I. **96** 25 50 S 113 5 E
Dirranbandi **97** 28 33 S 148 17 E
Disa **87** 12 5N 34 15 E
Disappointment, C. **118** 46 20N 124 0W
Disappointment L. **96** 23 20 S 122 40 E
Disaster B. **97** 37 15 S 150 0 E
Discovery B. **97** 38 10 S 140 40 E
Disentis **25** 46 42N 8 50 E
Dishna **86** 26 9N 32 32 E
Disina **85** 11 35N 9 50 E
Disko **4** 69 45N 53 30W
Disko Bugt **4** 69 10N 52 0W
Disna **54** 55 32N 28 11 E
Disna → **54** 55 34N 28 12 E
Distrito Federal □ **127** 15 45 S 47 45W
Disûq **86** 31 8N 30 35 E
Diu **68** 20 45N 70 58 E
Dives → **18** 49 18N 0 7W
Dives-sur-Mer **18** 49 18N 0 8W
Divi Pt. **70** 15 59N 81 9 E
Divichi **57** 41 15N 48 57 E
Divide **118** 45 48N 112 47W
Divinópolis **127** 20 10 S 44 54W
Divnoye **57** 45 55N 43 21 E
Divo **84** 5 48N 5 15W
Diwal Kol **66** 34 23N 67 52 E
Dixie **118** 45 37N 115 27W
Dixon, Ill., U.S.A. **116** 41 50N 89 30W
Dixon, Mont., U.S.A. **118** 47 19N 114 25W
Dixon, N. Mex., U.S.A. **119** 36 15N 105 57W
Dixon Entrance **108** 54 30N 132 0W
Dixonville **108** 56 32N 117 40W
Diyarbakir **64** 37 55N 40 18 E
Diz Chah **65** 35 30N 55 30 E
Djado **83** 21 4N 12 14 E
Djado, Plateau du **83** 21 29N 12 21 E
Djakarta = Jakarta **73** 6 9 S 106 49 E
Djamâa **83** 33 32N 5 59 E
Djamba **92** 16 45 S 13 58 E
Djambala **88** 2 32 S 14 30 E
Djanet **83** 24 35N 9 32 E
Djaul I. **98** 2 58 S 150 57 E
Djawa = Jawa **73** 7 0 S 110 0 E
Djebiniana **83** 35 1N 11 0 E
Djelfa **82** 34 40N 3 15 E
Djema **90** 6 3N 25 15 E
Djendel **82** 36 15N 2 25 E
Djeneïene **83** 31 45N 10 9 E
Djenné **84** 14 0N 4 30W
Djenoun, Garet el **83** 25 4N 5 31 E
Djerba **83** 33 52N 10 51 E
Djerba, Île de **83** 33 56N 11 0 E
Djerid, Chott **83** 33 42N 8 30 E
Djibo **85** 14 9N 1 35W
Djibouti **87** 11 30N 43 5 E
Djibouti ■ **63** 12 0N 43 0 E
Djolu **88** 0 35N 22 5 E
Djorong **72** 3 58 S 114 56 E
Djougou **85** 9 40N 1 45 E
Djoum **88** 2 41N 12 35 E
Djourab **81** 16 40N 18 50 E
Djugu **90** 1 55N 30 35 E
Djúpivogur **50** 64 39N 14 17W
Djursholm **48** 59 25N 18 6 E
Djursland **49** 56 27N 10 45 E
Dmitriev-Lgovskiy **54** 52 10N 35 0 E
Dmitriya Lapteva, Proliv **59** 73 0N 140 0 E
Dmitrov **55** 56 25N 37 32 E
Dmitrovsk-Orlovskiy **54** 52 29N 35 10 E
Dneiper = Dnepr → **56** 46 30N 32 18 E
Dnepr → **56** 46 30N 32 18 E
Dneprodzerzhinsk **56** 48 32N 34 37 E
Dneprodzerzhinskoye Vdkhr. **56** 49 0N 34 0 E
Dnepropetrovsk **56** 48 30N 35 0 E
Dneprorudnoye **56** 47 21N 34 58 E
Dnestr → **56** 46 18N 30 17 E
Dnestrovski = Belgorod **56** 50 35N 36 35 E
Dniester = Dnestr → **56** 46 18N 30 17 E
Dno **54** 57 50N 29 58 E
Doba **81** 8 40N 16 50 E
Dobbiaco **39** 46 44N 12 13 E
Dobbyn **97** 19 44 S 139 59 E
Dobczyce **27** 49 52N 20 25 E
Döbeln **24** 51 7N 13 10 E
Doberai, Jazirah **73** 1 25 S 133 0 E
Dobiegniew **28** 52 59N 15 45 E
Doblas **124** 37 5 S 64 0W
Dobo **73** 5 45 S 134 15 E
Doboj **42** 44 46N 18 6 E
Dobra, Konin, Poland **28** 51 55N 18 37 E
Dobra, Szczecin, Poland **28** 53 34N 15 20 E
Dobra, Dîmbovita, Romania **43** 44 52N 25 40 E
Dobra, Hunedoara, Romania **46** 45 54N 22 36 E
Dobre Miasto **28** 53 58N 20 26 E
Dobrinishta **43** 41 49N 23 34 E
Dobřiš **26** 49 46N 14 10 E
Dobrodzień **28** 50 45N 18 25 E
Dobropole **56** 48 25N 37 2 E
Dobruja **46** 44 30N 28 15 E
Dobrush **55** 52 28N 30 19 E
Dobrzyń nad Wisłą **28** 52 39N 19 22 E
Dobtong **87** 6 25N 31 40 E
Dodecanese = Dhodhekánisos **45** 36 35N 27 0 E
Dodge Center **116** 44 1N 92 50W
Dodge City **117** 37 42N 100 0W
Dodge L. **109** 59 50N 105 36W
Dodgeville **116** 42 55N 90 8W
Dodo **87** 5 10N 29 57 E
Dodola **87** 6 59N 39 11 E
Dodoma **90** 6 8 S 35 45 E
Dodoma □ **90** 6 0 S 36 0 E
Dodona **44** 39 40N 20 46 E
Dodsland **109** 51 50N 108 45W
Dodson **118** 48 23N 108 16W
Doetinchem **16** 51 59N 6 18 E
Doftana **46** 45 11N 25 45 E
Dog Creek **108** 51 35N 122 14W
Dog L., Man., Can. **109** 51 2N 98 31W
Dog L., Ont., Can. **106** 48 18N 89 30W
Doğanbey **45** 37 40N 27 10 E
Dogliani **38** 44 35N 7 55 E
Dogondoutchi **85** 13 38N 4 2 E
Dogran **68** 31 48N 73 35 E
Doguéraoua **85** 14 0N 5 31 E
Dohad **68** 22 50N 74 15 E
Dohazari **67** 22 10N 92 5 E
Doi **73** 2 14N 127 49 E
Doi Luang **71** 18 30N 101 0 E
Doig → **108** 56 25N 120 40W
Dois Irmãos, Sa. **127** 9 0 S 42 30W
Dojransko Jezero **42** 41 13N 22 44 E
Dokka **47** 60 49N 10 7 E
Dokka → **47** 61 7N 10 0 E
Dokkum **16** 53 20N 5 59 E
Dokri **68** 27 25N 68 7 E
Dol-de-Bretagne **18** 48 34N 1 47W
Doland **116** 44 55N 98 5W
Dolbeau **107** 48 53N 72 18W
Dole **19** 47 7N 5 31 E
Doleib, Wadi → **87** 12 10N 33 15 E
Dolgellau **12** 52 44N 3 53W
Dolgelley = Dolgellau **12** 52 44N 3 53W
Dolginovo **54** 54 39N 27 29 E
Dolianova **40** 39 23N 9 11 E
Dolinskaya **56** 48 6N 32 46 E
Dolj □ **46** 44 10N 23 30 E
Dollart **16** 53 20N 7 10 E
Dolna Banya **43** 42 18N 23 44 E
Dolni Dŭbnik **43** 43 24N 24 26 E
Dolo, Ethiopia **87** 4 11N 42 3 E
Dolo, Italy **39** 45 25N 12 4 E
Dolomites = Dolomiti **39** 46 30N 11 40 E
Dolomiti **39** 46 30N 11 40 E
Dolores, Argent. **124** 36 20 S 57 40W
Dolores, Uruguay **124** 33 34 S 58 15W
Dolores, Colo., U.S.A. **119** 37 30N 108 30W
Dolores, Tex., U.S.A. **117** 27 40N 99 38W
Dolores → **119** 38 49N 108 17W
Đolovo **42** 44 55N 20 52 E
Dolphin and Union Str. **104** 69 5N 114 45W
Dolphin C. **128** 51 10 S 59 0W
Dolsk **28** 51 59N 17 3 E
Dom Pedrito **125** 31 0 S 54 40W
Doma **85** 8 25N 8 18 E
Domasi **91** 15 15 S 35 22 E
Domazlice **26** 49 28N 13 0 E
Dombarovskiy **58** 50 46N 59 32 E
Dombasle **19** 48 38N 6 21 E
Dombes **21** 46 3N 5 0 E
Dombóvár **27** 46 21N 18 9 E
Dombrád **27** 48 13N 21 54 E
Domburg **16** 51 34N 3 30 E
Domel I. = Letsok-aw Kyun **71** 11 30N 98 25 E
Domérat **20** 46 21N 2 32 E
Domeyko **124** 29 0 S 71 0W
Domeyko, Cordillera **124** 24 30 S 69 0W
Domfront **18** 48 37N 0 40W
Dominador **124** 24 21 S 69 20W
Dominica ■ **121** 15 20N 61 20W
Dominican Rep. ■ **121** 19 0N 70 30W
Dömitz **24** 53 9N 11 13 E
Domme **20** 44 48N 1 12 E
Domo **63** 7 50N 47 10 E
Domodóssola **38** 46 6N 8 19 E
Dompaire **19** 48 14N 6 14 E
Dompierre-sur-Besbre **20** 46 31N 3 41 E
Dompim **84** 5 10N 2 5W
Domrémy **19** 48 26N 5 40 E
Domsjö **48** 63 16N 18 41 E
Domville, Mt. **99** 28 1 S 151 15 E
Domvraina **45** 38 15N 22 59 E
Domžale **39** 46 9N 14 35 E
Don →, India **70** 16 20N 76 15 E
Don →, Eng., U.K. **12** 53 41N 0 51W
Don →, Scot., U.K. **14** 57 14N 2 5W
Don →, U.S.S.R. **57** 47 4N 39 18 E
Don Benito **31** 38 53N 5 51W
Don Martín, Presa de **120** 27 30N 100 50W
Dona Ana **91** 17 25 S 35 5 E
Donaghadee **15** 54 38N 5 32W
Donald **99** 36 23 S 143 0 E
Donalda **108** 52 35N 112 34W
Donaldsonville **117** 30 2N 91 0W
Donalsonville **115** 31 3N 84 52W
Donau → **23** 48 10N 17 0 E
Donaueschingen **25** 47 57N 8 30 E
Donauwörth **25** 48 42N 10 47 E
Donawitz **26** 47 22N 15 4 E
Doncaster **12** 53 31N 1 9W
Dondo, Angola **88** 9 45 S 14 25 E
Dondo, Mozam. **91** 19 33 S 34 46 E
Dondo, Teluk **73** 0 29N 120 30 E
Dondra Head **70** 5 55N 80 40 E
Donegal **15** 54 39N 8 8W
Donegal □ **15** 54 53N 8 0W
Donegal B. **15** 54 30N 8 35W
Donets → **57** 47 33N 40 55 E
Donetsk **56** 48 0N 37 45 E
Donga **85** 7 45N 10 2 E
Dongara **96** 29 14 S 114 57 E
Dongargarh **69** 21 10N 80 40 E
Donges **18** 47 18N 2 4W
Dongfang **77** 18 50N 108 33 E
Donggala **73** 0 30 S 119 40 E
Donggou **76** 39 52N 124 10 E
Dongguan **77** 22 58N 113 44 E
Dongguang **76** 37 50N 116 30 E
Dongjingcheng **76** 44 0N 129 10 E
Donglan **77** 24 30N 107 21 E
Dongliu **77** 30 13N 116 55 E
Dongola **86** 19 9N 30 22 E
Dongou **88** 2 0N 18 5 E
Dongping **76** 35 55N 116 20 E
Dongshan **77** 23 43N 117 30 E
Dongsheng **76** 39 50N 110 0 E
Dongtai **77** 32 51N 120 21 E
Dongting Hu **75** 29 18N 112 45 E
Dongxing **75** 21 34N 108 0 E
Dongyang **77** 29 13N 120 15 E
Doniphan **117** 36 40N 90 50W
Donja Stubica **39** 45 59N 16 0 E

Donji Dušnik Dzhelinde

Donji Dušnik 42 43 12N 22 5 E
Donji Miholjac 42 45 45N 18 10 E
Donji Milanovac 42 44 28N 22 6 E
Donji Vakuf 42 44 8N 17 24 E
Donjon, Le 20 46 22N 3 48 E
Dønna 50 66 6N 12 30 E
Donna 117 26 12N 98 2W
Donnaconna 107 46 41N 71 41W
Donnelly's Crossing 101 35 42 S 173 38 E
Donora 112 40 11N 79 50W
Donor's Hills 98 18 42 S 140 33 E
Donskoy 55 53 55N 38 15 E
Donya Lendava 39 46 35N 16 25 E
Donzère-Mondragon 21 44 28N 4 43 E
Donzère-Mondragon, Barrage de 21 44 13N 4 42 E
Donzy 19 47 20N 3 6 E
Doon → 14 55 26N 4 41W
Dor (Tantūra) 62 32 37N 34 55 E
Dora Báltea → 38 45 11N 8 5 E
Dora, L. 96 22 0 S 123 0 E
Dora Riparia → 38 45 5N 7 44 E
Dorada, La 126 5 30N 74 40W
Doran L. 109 61 13N 108 6W
Dorat, Le 20 46 14N 1 5 E
Dorchester 13 50 42N 2 28W
Dorchester, C. 105 65 27N 77 27W
Dordogne □ 20 45 5N 0 40 E
Dordogne → 20 45 2N 0 36W
Dordrecht, Neth. 16 51 48N 4 39 E
Dordrecht, S. Afr. 92 31 20 S 27 3 E
Dore → 20 45 50N 3 35 E
Doré L. 109 54 46N 107 17W
Doré Lake 109 54 38N 107 36W
Dore, Mt. 20 45 32N 2 50 E
Dorfen 25 48 16N 12 10 E
Dorgali 40 40 18N 9 35 E
Dori 85 14 3N 0 2W
Doring → 92 31 54 S 18 39 E
Dorion 106 45 23N 74 3W
Dormaa-Ahenkro 84 7 15N 2 52W
Dormo, Ras 87 13 14N 42 35 E
Dornberg 39 55 45N 13 50 E
Dornbirn 26 47 25N 9 45 E
Dornes 19 46 48N 3 18 E
Dornoch 14 57 52N 4 0W
Dornoch Firth 14 57 52N 4 0W
Doro 85 16 9N 0 51W
Dorog 27 47 42N 18 45 E
Dorogobuzh 54 54 50N 33 18 E
Dorohoi 46 47 56N 26 30 E
Döröö Nuur 75 48 0N 93 0 E
Dorre I. 96 25 13 S 113 12 E
Dorrigo 99 30 20 S 152 44 E
Dorris 118 41 59N 121 58W
Dorset, Can. 112 45 14N 78 54W
Dorset, U.S.A. 112 41 4N 80 40W
Dorset □ 13 50 48N 2 25W
Dorsten 24 51 40N 6 55 E
Dortmund 24 51 32N 7 28 E
Dörtyol 64 36 52N 36 12 E
Dorum 24 53 40N 8 33 E
Doruma 90 4 42N 27 33 E
Dos Bahías, C. 128 44 58 S 65 32W
Dos Cabezas 119 32 10N 109 37W
Dos Hermanas 31 37 16N 5 55W
Dosso 85 13 0N 3 13 E
Dothan 115 31 10N 85 25W
Douai 19 50 21N 3 4 E
Douala 88 4 0N 9 45 E
Douaouir 82 20 45N 3 0W
Douarnenez 18 48 6N 4 21W
Douăzeci Şi Trei August 46 43 55N 28 40 E
Double Island Pt. 99 25 56 S 153 11 E
Doubrava → 26 49 40N 15 30 E
Doubs □ 19 47 10N 6 20 E
Doubs → 19 46 53N 5 1 E
Doubtful B. 96 34 15 S 119 28 E
Doubtful Sd. 101 45 20 S 166 49 E
Doubtless B. 101 34 55 S 173 26 E
Doudeville 18 49 43N 0 47 E
Doué 18 47 11N 0 20W
Douentza 84 14 58N 2 48W
Douglas, S. Afr. 92 29 4 S 23 46 E
Douglas, U.K. 12 54 9N 4 29W
Douglas, Alaska, U.S.A. 108 58 23N 134 24W
Douglas, Ariz., U.S.A. 119 31 21N 109 30W
Douglas, Ga., U.S.A. 115 31 32N 82 52W
Douglas, Wyo., U.S.A. 116 42 45N 105 20W
Douglastown 107 48 46N 64 24W
Douglasville 115 33 46N 84 43W
Douirat 82 33 2N 4 11W
Doukáton, Ákra 45 38 34N 20 30 E
Doulevant 19 48 22N 4 53 E
Doullens 19 50 10N 2 20 E
Doumé 88 4 15N 13 25 E
Douna 84 13 13N 6 0W
Dounreay 14 58 34N 3 44W
Dourados 125 22 9 S 54 50W
Dourados → 125 21 58 S 54 18W
Dourdan 19 48 30N 2 0 E
Douro → 30 41 8N 8 40W
Douvaine 21 46 19N 6 16 E
Douz 83 33 25N 9 0 E
Douze → 20 43 54N 0 30W
Dove → 12 52 51N 1 36W
Dove Creek 119 37 46N 108 59W
Dover, Austral. 99 43 18 S 147 2 E
Dover, U.K. 13 51 7N 1 19 E
Dover, Del., U.S.A. 114 39 10N 75 31W
Dover, N.H., U.S.A. 114 43 12N 70 51W
Dover, N.J., U.S.A. 113 40 53N 74 34W
Dover, Ohio, U.S.A. 114 40 32N 81 30W
Dover-Foxcroft 107 45 14N 69 14W
Dover Plains 113 41 43N 73 35W
Dover, Pt. 96 32 32 S 125 32 E
Dover, Str. of 18 51 0N 1 30 E
Dovey → 13 52 32N 4 0W
Dovrefjell 47 62 15N 9 33 E
Dowa 91 13 38 S 33 58 E
Dowagiac 114 42 0N 86 8W
Dowlat Yār 65 34 30N 65 45 E
Dowlatabad 65 28 20N 56 40W
Down □ 15 54 20N 6 0W
Downey 118 42 29N 112 3W
Downham Market 13 52 36N 0 22 E
Downieville 118 39 34N 120 50W
Downpatrick 15 54 20N 5 43W
Downpatrick Hd. 15 54 20N 9 21W
Dowshī 65 35 35N 68 43 E
Doylestown 113 40 21N 75 10W
Draa, C. 82 28 47N 11 0W
Draa, Oued → 82 30 29N 6 1W
Drac → 21 45 13N 5 41 E
Drachten 16 53 7N 6 5 E
Drăgăneşti 46 44 9N 24 32 E
Drăgăneşti-Viaşca 46 44 5N 25 33 E
Dragaš 42 42 5N 20 35 E
Drăgăsani 46 44 39N 24 17 E
Dragina 42 44 30N 19 25 E
Dragocvet 42 44 0N 21 15 E
Dragoman, Prokhod 42 43 0N 22 53 E
Dragonera, I. 32 39 35N 2 19 E
Dragovishtitsa (Perivol) 42 42 22N 22 39 E
Draguignan 21 43 30N 6 27 E
Drain 118 43 45N 123 17W
Drake, Austral. 99 28 55 S 152 25 E
Drake, U.S.A. 116 47 56N 100 21W
Drake Passage 5 58 0 S 68 0W
Drakensberg 93 31 0 S 28 0 E
Dráma 44 41 9N 24 10 E
Dráma □ 44 41 20N 24 0 E
Drammen 47 59 42N 10 12 E
Drangajökull 50 66 9N 22 15W
Drangedal 47 59 6N 9 3 E
Dranov, Ostrov 46 44 55N 29 30 E
Drau = Drava → 26 46 32N 14 58 E
Drava → 42 45 33N 18 55 E
Draveil 19 48 41N 2 25 E
Dravograd 39 46 36N 15 5 E
Drawa → 28 52 52N 15 59 E
Drawno 28 53 13N 15 46 E
Drawsko Pomorskie 28 53 35N 15 50 E
Drayton Valley 108 53 12N 114 58W
Dren 42 43 8N 20 44 E
Drenthe □ 16 52 52N 6 40 E
Dresden, Can. 112 42 35N 82 11W
Dresden, Ger. 24 51 2N 13 45 E
Dresden □ 24 51 12N 14 0 E
Dreux 18 48 44N 1 23 E
Drezdenko 28 52 50N 15 49 E
Driffield 12 54 0N 0 25W
Driftwood 112 41 22N 78 9W
Driggs 118 43 50N 111 8W
Drin i zi → 44 41 37N 20 28 E
Drina → 42 44 53N 19 21 E
Drincea → 46 44 20N 22 55 E
Drînceni 46 46 49N 28 10 E
Drini → 44 42 20N 20 0 E
Drinjača → 42 44 15N 19 8 E
Driva → 47 62 33N 9 38 E
Drivstua 47 62 26N 9 47 E
Drniš 39 43 51N 16 10 E
Drøbak 47 59 39N 10 39 E
Drobin 28 52 42N 19 58 E
Drogheda 15 53 45N 6 20W
Drogichin 54 52 15N 25 8 E
Drogobych 54 49 20N 23 30 E
Drohiczyn 28 52 24N 22 39 E
Droichead Nua 15 53 11N 6 50W
Droitwich 13 52 16N 2 10W
Drôme □ 21 44 38N 5 15 E
Drôme → 21 44 46N 4 46 E
Dromedary, C. 99 36 17 S 150 10 E
Dronero 38 44 29N 7 22 E
Dronfield 98 21 12 S 140 3 E
Dronne → 20 45 2N 0 9W
Dronning Maud Land 5 72 30 S 12 0 E
Dronninglund 49 57 10N 10 19 E
Dropt → 20 44 35N 0 6W
Drosendorf 26 48 52N 15 37 E
Drouzhba 43 43 15N 28 0 E
Drumbo 112 43 16N 80 35W
Drumheller 108 51 25N 112 40W
Drummond 118 46 40N 113 4W
Drummond I. 106 46 0N 83 40W
Drummond Ra. 97 23 45 S 147 10 E
Drummondville 106 45 55N 72 25W
Drumright 117 35 59N 96 38W
Druskininkai 54 54 3N 23 58 E
Drut → 54 53 3N 30 42 E
Druya 54 55 45N 27 28 E
Druzhina 59 68 14N 145 18 E
Drvar 39 44 21N 16 23 E
Drvenik 39 43 27N 16 3 E
Drwęca → 28 53 0N 18 42 E
Dry Tortugas 121 24 38N 82 55W
Dryanovo 43 42 59N 25 28 E
Dryden, Can. 109 49 47N 92 50W
Dryden, U.S.A. 117 30 3N 102 3W
Drygalski I. 5 66 0 S 92 0 E
Drysdale → 96 13 59 S 126 51 E
Drzewiczka → 28 51 36N 20 36 E
Dschang 85 5 32N 10 3 E
Du Bois 114 41 8N 78 46W
Du Quoin 116 38 0N 89 10W
Duanesburg 113 42 45N 74 11W
Duaringa 98 23 42 S 149 42 E
Ḍubā 64 27 10N 35 40 E
Dubai = Dubayy 65 25 18N 55 20 E
Dubawnt → 109 64 33N 100 6W
Dubawnt, L. 109 63 4N 101 42W
Dubayy 65 25 18N 55 20 E
Dubbo 97 32 11 S 148 35 E
Dubele 90 2 56N 29 35 E
Dubica 39 45 11N 16 48 E
Dublin, Ireland 15 53 20N 6 18W
Dublin, Ga., U.S.A. 115 32 30N 82 34W
Dublin, Tex., U.S.A. 117 32 0N 98 20W
Dublin □ 15 53 24N 6 20W
Dublin B. 15 53 18N 6 5W
Dubna, U.S.S.R. 55 54 8N 36 59 E
Dubna, U.S.S.R. 55 56 44N 37 10 E
Dubno 54 50 25N 25 45 E
Dubois 118 44 7N 112 9W
Dubossary 56 47 15N 29 10 E
Dubossasy Vdkhr. 56 47 30N 29 0 E
Dubovka 57 49 5N 44 50 E
Dubovskoye 57 47 28N 42 46 E
Dubrajpur 69 23 48N 87 25 E
Dubréka 84 9 46N 13 31W
Dubrovitsa 54 51 31N 26 35 E
Dubrovnik 42 42 39N 18 6 E
Dubrovskoye 59 58 55N 111 10 E
Dubuque 116 42 30N 90 41W
Duchang 77 29 18N 116 12 E
Duchesne 118 40 14N 110 22W
Duchess 97 21 20 S 139 50 E
Ducie I. 95 24 40 S 124 48W
Duck Lake 109 52 50N 106 16W
Duck Mt. Prov. Parks 109 51 45N 101 0W
Duderstadt 24 51 30N 10 15 E
Dudinka 59 69 30N 86 13 E
Dudley 13 52 30N 2 5W
Dudna → 70 19 17N 76 54 E
Dueñas 30 41 52N 4 33W
Dueodde 49 54 59N 15 4 E
Duero → 30 41 8N 8 40W
Duff Is. 94 9 53 S 167 8 E
Dufftown 14 57 26N 3 9W
Dugi 39 44 0N 15 0 E
Dugo Selo 39 45 51N 16 18 E
Duifken Pt. 97 12 33 S 141 38 E
Duisburg 24 51 27N 6 42 E
Duiwelskloof 93 23 42 S 30 10 E
Dukati 44 40 16N 19 32 E
Duke I. 108 54 50N 131 20W
Dukelsky průsmyk 27 49 25N 21 42 E
Dukhān 65 25 25N 50 50 E
Dukhovshchina 54 55 15N 32 27 E
Dukla 27 49 30N 21 35 E
Duku, Bauchi, Nigeria 85 10 43N 10 43 E
Duku, Sokoto, Nigeria 85 11 11N 4 55 E
Dulce → 124 30 32 S 62 33W
Dulce, Golfo 121 8 40N 83 20W
Dŭlgopol 43 43 3N 27 22 E
Dullewala 68 31 50N 71 25 E
Dülmen 24 51 49N 7 18 E
Dulovo 43 43 48N 27 9 E
Dululu 98 23 48 S 150 15 E
Duluth 116 46 48N 92 10W
Dum Dum 69 22 39N 88 33 E
Dum Duma 67 27 40N 95 40 E
Dum Hadjer 81 13 18N 19 41 E
Dumaguete 73 9 17N 123 15 E
Dumai 72 1 35N 101 28 E
Dumaran 73 10 33N 119 50 E
Dumaring 73 1 46N 118 10 E
Dumas, Ark., U.S.A. 117 33 52N 91 30W
Dumas, Tex., U.S.A. 117 35 50N 101 58W
Dumbarton 14 55 58N 4 35W
Dumbrăveni 46 46 14N 24 34 E
Dumfries 14 55 4N 3 37W
Dumfries & Galloway □ 14 55 0N 4 0W
Dumka 69 24 12N 87 15 E
Dümmersee 24 52 30N 8 21 E
Dumoine → 106 46 13N 77 51W
Dumoine L. 106 46 55N 77 55W
Dumraon 69 25 33N 84 8 E
Dumyât 86 31 24N 31 48 E
Dumyât, Masabb 86 31 28N 31 51 E
Dun Laoghaire 15 53 17N 6 9W
Dun-le-Palestel 20 46 18N 1 39 E
Dun-sur-Auron 19 46 53N 2 33 E
Duna → 27 45 51N 18 48 E
Dunaföldvár 27 46 50N 18 57 E
Dunaj → 27 48 5N 17 10 E
Dunajec → 27 50 15N 20 44 E
Dunajska Streda 27 48 0N 17 37 E
Dunapatai 27 46 39N 19 4 E
Dunărea → 46 45 30N 8 15 E
Dunaszekcsö 27 46 6N 18 45 E
Dunaújváros 27 47 0N 18 57 E
Dunav → 42 44 47N 21 20 E
Dunavtsi 42 43 57N 22 53 E
Dunback 101 45 23 S 170 36 E
Dunbar, Austral. 98 16 0 S 142 22 E
Dunbar, U.K. 14 56 0N 2 32W
Dunblane 14 56 10N 3 58W
Duncan, Can. 108 48 45N 123 40W
Duncan, Ariz., U.S.A. 119 32 46N 109 6W
Duncan, Okla., U.S.A. 117 34 25N 98 0W
Duncan L. 108 62 51N 113 58W
Duncan, L. 106 53 29N 77 58W
Duncan Pass. 71 11 0N 92 30 E
Duncan Town 121 22 15N 75 45W
Duncannon 112 40 23N 77 2W
Dundalk, Can. 112 44 10N 80 24W
Dundalk, Ireland 15 54 1N 6 25W
Dundalk Bay 15 53 55N 6 15W
Dundas 106 43 17N 79 59W
Dundas I. 108 54 30N 130 50W
Dundas, L. 96 32 35 S 121 50 E
Dundas Str. 96 11 15 S 131 35 E
Dundee, S. Afr. 93 28 11 S 30 15 E
Dundee, U.K. 14 56 29N 3 0W
Dundoo 99 27 40 S 144 37 E
Dundrum 15 54 17N 5 50W
Dundrum B. 15 54 12N 5 40W
Dundwara 68 27 48N 79 9 E
Dunedin, N.Z. 101 45 50 S 170 33 E
Dunedin, U.S.A. 115 28 1N 82 45W
Dunedin → 108 59 30N 124 5W
Dunfermline 14 56 5N 3 28W
Dungannon, Can. 112 43 51N 81 36W
Dungannon, U.K. 15 54 30N 6 47W
Dungannon □ 15 54 30N 6 55W
Dungarpur 68 23 52N 73 45 E
Dungarvan 15 52 6N 7 40W
Dungarvan Bay 15 52 5N 7 35W
Dungeness 13 50 54N 0 59 E
Dungo, L. do 92 17 15 S 19 0 E
Dungog 99 32 22 S 151 46 E
Dungu 90 3 40N 28 32 E
Dungunâb 86 21 10N 37 9 E
Dungunâb, Khalij 86 21 5N 37 12 E
Dunhinda Falls 70 7 5N 81 6 E
Dunhua 76 43 20N 128 14 E
Dunhuang 75 40 8N 94 36 E
Dunières 21 45 13N 4 20 E
Dunk I. 98 17 59 S 146 29 E
Dunkeld 14 56 34N 3 36W
Dunkerque 19 51 2N 2 20 E
Dunkery Beacon 13 51 15N 3 37W
Dunkirk 114 42 30N 79 18W
Dunkirk = Dunkerque 19 51 2N 2 20 E
Dunkuj 87 12 50N 32 49 E
Dunkwa, Central, Ghana 84 6 0N 1 47W
Dunkwa, Central, Ghana 85 5 30N 1 0W
Dunlap 116 41 50N 95 36W
Dunmanus B. 15 51 31N 9 50W
Dunmore 114 41 27N 75 38W
Dunmore Hd. 15 52 10N 10 35W
Dunn 115 35 18N 78 36W
Dunnellon 115 29 4N 82 28W
Dunnet Hd. 14 58 38N 3 22W
Dunning 116 41 52N 100 4W
Dunnville 112 42 54N 79 36W
Dunolly 99 36 51 S 143 44 E
Dunoon 14 55 57N 4 56W
Dunqul 86 23 26N 31 37 E
Duns 14 55 47N 2 20W
Dunseith 116 48 49N 100 2W
Dunsmuir 118 41 10N 122 18W
Dunstable 13 51 53N 0 31W
Dunstan Mts. 101 44 53 S 169 35 E
Dunster 108 53 8N 119 50W
Dunvegan L. 109 60 8N 107 10W
Duolun 76 42 12N 116 28 E
Dupree 116 45 4N 101 35W
Dupuyer 118 48 11N 112 31W
Duque de Caxias 125 22 45 S 43 19W
Duquesne 112 40 22N 79 55W
Dūrā 62 31 31N 35 1 E
Durack Range 96 16 50 S 127 40 E
Durance → 21 43 55N 4 45 E
Durand 114 42 54N 83 58W
Durango, Mexico 120 24 3N 104 39W
Durango, Spain 32 43 13N 2 40W
Durango, U.S.A. 119 37 16N 107 50W
Durango □ 120 25 0N 105 0W
Durant 117 34 0N 96 25W
Duratón → 30 41 37N 4 7W
Durazno 124 33 25 S 56 31W
Durazzo = Durrësi 44 41 19N 19 28 E
Durban, France 20 43 0N 2 49 E
Durban, S. Afr. 93 29 49 S 31 1 E
Dúrcal 31 37 0N 3 34W
Đurđevac 42 46 2N 17 3 E
Düren 24 50 48N 6 30 E
Durg 69 21 15N 81 22 E
Durgapur 69 23 30N 87 20 E
Durham, Can. 106 44 10N 80 49W
Durham, U.K. 12 54 47N 1 34W
Durham, U.S.A. 115 36 0N 78 55W
Durham □ 12 54 42N 1 45W
Durmitor 34 43 10N 19 0 E
Durness 14 58 34N 4 45W
Durrës 44 41 19N 19 28 E
Durrësi 44 41 19N 19 28 E
Durrie 99 25 40 S 140 15 E
Durtal 18 47 40N 0 18W
Duru 90 4 14N 28 50 E
D'Urville I. 101 40 50 S 173 55 E
D'Urville, Tanjung 73 1 28 S 137 54 E
Duryea 113 41 20N 75 45W
Dusa Mareb 63 5 30N 46 15 E
Dûsh 86 24 35N 30 41 E
Dushak 58 37 13N 60 1 E
Dushan 77 25 48N 107 30 E
Dushanbe 58 38 33N 68 48 E
Dusheti 57 42 10N 44 42 E
Dusky Sd. 101 45 47 S 166 30 E
Düsseldorf 24 51 15N 6 46 E
Duszniki-Zdrój 28 50 24N 16 24 E
Dutch Harbor 104 53 54N 166 35W
Dutlhe 92 23 58 S 23 46 E
Dutsan Wai 85 10 50N 8 10 E
Dutton 112 42 39N 81 30W
Dutton → 98 20 44 S 143 10 E
Duved 48 63 24N 12 55 E
Duvno 42 43 42N 17 13 E
Duwādimi 64 24 35N 44 15 E
Duyun 77 26 18N 107 29 E
Duzce 64 40 50N 31 10 E
Duzdab = Zāhedān 65 29 30N 60 50 E
Dve Mogili 43 43 35N 25 55 E
Dvina, Sev. 52 64 32N 40 30 E
Dvinsk = Daugavpils 54 55 53N 26 32 E
Dvinskaya Guba 52 65 0N 39 0 E
Dvor 39 45 4N 16 22 E
Dvorce 27 49 50N 17 34 E
Dvur Králové 26 50 27N 15 50 E
Dwarka 68 22 18N 69 8 E
Dwight, Can. 112 45 20N 79 1W
Dwight, U.S.A. 114 41 5N 88 25W
Dyakovskoya 55 60 5N 41 12 E
Dyatkovo 54 53 40N 34 27 E
Dyatlovo 54 53 28N 25 28 E
Dyer, C. 105 66 40N 61 0W
Dyer Plateau 5 70 45 S 65 30W
Dyersburg 117 36 2N 89 20W
Dyfed □ 13 52 0N 4 30W
Dyje → 27 48 37N 16 56 E
Dynevor Downs 99 28 10 S 144 20 E
Dynów 27 49 50N 22 11 E
Dysart 109 50 57N 104 2W
Dzamin Üüd 75 43 50N 111 58 E
Dzerzhinsk, Byelorussian S.S.R., U.S.S.R. 54 53 40N 27 1 E
Dzerzhinsk, R.S.F.S.R., U.S.S.R. 55 56 14N 43 30 E
Dzhalal-Abad 58 40 56N 73 0 E
Dzhalinda 59 53 26N 124 0 E
Dzhambeyty 57 50 15N 52 30 E
Dzhambul 58 42 54N 71 22 E
Dzhankoi 56 45 40N 34 20 E
Dzhanybek 57 49 25N 46 50 E
Dzhardzhan 59 68 10N 124 10 E
Dzhelinde 59 70 0N 114 20 E

Dzhetygara Elbow

Dzhetygara 58 52 11N 61 12 E
Dzhezkazgan 58 47 44N 67 40 E
Dzhikimde 59 59 1N 121 47 E
Dzhizak 58 40 6N 67 50 E
Dzhugdzur, Khrebet 59 57 30N 138 0 E
Dzhungarskiye Vorota 58 45 0N 82 0 E
Dzhvari 57 42 42N 42 4 E
Działdowo 28 53 15N 20 15 E
Działoszyce 28 50 22N 20 20 E
Działoszyn 28 51 6N 18 50 E
Dzierzgoń 28 53 58N 19 20 E
Dzierżoniów 28 50 45N 16 39 E
Dzioua 83 33 14N 5 14 E
Dziwnów 28 54 2N 14 45 E
Dzungarian Gate = Alataw Shankou 75 45 5N 81 57 E
Dzuumod 75 47 45N 106 58 E

E

Eabamet, L. 106 51 30N 87 46W
Eads 116 38 30N 102 46W
Eagle, Alaska, U.S.A. 104 64 44N 141 7W
Eagle, Colo., U.S.A. 118 39 39N 106 55W
Eagle → 107 53 36N 57 26W
Eagle Butt 116 45 1N 101 12W
Eagle Grove 116 42 37N 93 53W
Eagle L., Calif., U.S.A. 118 40 35N 120 50W
Eagle L., Me., U.S.A. 107 46 23N 69 22W
Eagle Lake 117 29 35N 96 21W
Eagle Nest 119 36 33N 105 13W
Eagle Pass 117 28 45N 100 35W
Eagle River 116 45 55N 89 17W
Eaglehawk 99 36 39 S 144 16 E
Ealing 13 51 30N 0 19W
Earl Grey 109 50 57N 104 43W
Earle 117 35 18N 90 26W
Earlimart 119 35 53N 119 16W
Earn → 14 56 20N 3 19W
Earn, L. 14 56 23N 4 14W
Earnslaw, Mt. 101 44 32 S 168 27 E
Earth 117 34 18N 102 30W
Easley 115 34 52N 82 35W
East Angus 107 45 30N 71 40W
East Aurora 112 42 46N 78 38W
East B. 117 29 2N 89 16W
East Bengal 67 24 0N 90 0 E
East Beskids = Vychodné Beskydy 27 49 30N 22 0 E
East Brady 112 40 59N 79 36W
East C. 101 37 42 S 178 35 E
East Chicago 114 41 40N 87 30W
East China Sea 75 30 5N 126 0 E
East Coulee 108 51 23N 112 27W
East Falkland 128 51 30 S 58 30W
East Grand Forks 116 47 55N 97 5W
East Greenwich 113 41 39N 71 27W
East Hartford 113 41 45N 72 39W
East Helena 118 46 37N 111 58W
East Indies 72 0 0 120 0 E
East Jordan 114 45 10N 85 7W
East Kilbride 14 55 46N 4 10W
East Lansing 114 42 44N 84 29W
East Liverpool 114 40 39N 80 35W
East London 93 33 0 S 27 55 E
East Orange 114 40 46N 74 13W
East Pacific Ridge 95 15 0 S 110 0W
East Pakistan = Bangladesh ■ 67 24 0N 90 0 E
East Palestine 112 40 50N 80 32W
East Pine 108 55 48N 120 12W
East Pt. 107 46 27N 61 58W
East Point 115 33 40N 84 28W
East Providence 113 41 48N 71 22W
East Retford 12 53 19N 0 55W
East St. Louis 116 38 37N 90 4W
East Schelde → = Oosterschelde 16 51 38N 3 40 E
East Siberian Sea 59 73 0N 160 0 E
East Stroudsburg 113 41 1N 75 11W
East Sussex □ 13 51 0N 0 20 E
East Tawas 114 44 17N 83 31W
Eastbourne, N.Z. 101 41 19 S 174 55 E
Eastbourne, U.K. 13 50 46N 0 18 E
Eastend 109 49 32N 108 50W
Easter I. 95 27 8 S 109 23W
Easter Islands 95 27 0 S 109 0W
Eastern □, Kenya 90 0 0 S 38 30 E
Eastern □, Uganda 90 1 50N 33 45 E
Eastern Cr. → 98 20 40 S 141 35 E
Eastern Ghats 70 14 0N 78 50 E
Eastern Province □ 84 8 15N 11 0W
Easterville 109 53 8N 99 49W
Easthampton 113 42 15N 72 41W
Eastland 117 32 26N 98 45W
Eastleigh 13 50 58N 1 21W
Eastmain → 106 52 27N 78 26W
Eastmain (East Main) 106 52 10N 78 30W
Eastman, Can. 113 45 18N 72 19W
Eastman, U.S.A. 115 32 13N 83 20W
Easton, Md., U.S.A. 114 38 47N 76 7W
Easton, Pa., U.S.A. 114 40 41N 75 15W
Easton, Wash., U.S.A. 118 47 14N 121 8W
Eastport 107 44 57N 67 0W
Eaton 116 40 35N 104 42W
Eatonia 109 51 13N 109 25W
Eatonton 115 33 22N 83 24W
Eatontown 113 40 18N 74 7W
Eau Claire, S.C., U.S.A. 115 34 5N 81 2W
Eau Claire, Wis., U.S.A. 116 44 46N 91 30W
Eauze 20 43 53N 0 7 E
Ebagoola 98 14 15 S 143 12 E
Eban 85 9 40N 4 50 E
Ebbw Vale 13 51 47N 3 12W
Ebeggui 83 26 2N 6 0 E
Ebensburg 112 40 29N 78 43W
Ebensee 26 47 48N 13 46 E
Eberbach 25 49 27N 8 59 E
Eberswalde 24 52 49N 13 50 E
Ebingen 25 48 13N 9 1 E
Eboli 41 40 39N 15 2 E
Ebolowa 88 2 55N 11 10 E
Ebrach 25 49 50N 10 30 E
Ébrié, Lagune 84 5 12N 4 26W
Ebro → 32 40 43N 0 54 E
Ebro, Pantano del 30 43 0N 3 58W
Ebstorf 24 53 2N 10 23 E
Eceabat 44 40 11N 26 21 E
Éceuillé 18 47 10N 1 19 E
Echelles, Les 21 45 27N 5 45 E
Echmiadzin 57 40 12N 44 19 E
Echo Bay 106 46 29N 84 4W
Echo Bay (Port Radium) 104 66 05N 117 55W
Echoing → 109 55 51N 92 5W
Echternach 16 49 49N 6 25 E
Echuca 100 36 10 S 144 20 E
Ecija 31 37 30N 5 10W
Eckernförde 24 54 26N 9 50 E
Écommoy 18 47 50N 0 17 E
Écos 19 49 9N 1 35 E
Écouché 18 48 42N 0 10W
Ecuador ■ 126 2 0 S 78 0W
Ed 49 58 55N 11 55 E
Ed Dabbura 86 17 40N 34 15 E
Ed Dâmer 86 17 27N 34 0 E
Ed Debba 86 18 0N 30 51 E
Ed-Déffa 86 30 40N 26 30 E
Ed Deim 87 10 10N 28 20 E
Ed Dueim 87 14 0N 32 10 E
Edam, Can. 109 53 11N 108 46W
Edam, Neth. 16 52 31N 5 3 E
Edapally 70 11 19N 78 3 E
Eday 14 59 11N 2 47W
Edd 87 14 0N 41 38 E
Eddrachillis B. 14 58 16N 5 10W
Eddystone 13 50 11N 4 16W
Eddystone Pt. 99 40 59 S 148 20 E
Ede, Neth. 16 52 4N 5 40 E
Ede, Nigeria 85 7 45N 4 29 E
Édea 88 3 51N 10 9 E
Edehon L. 109 60 25N 97 15W
Edekel, Adrar 83 23 56N 6 47 E
Eden, Austral. 99 37 3 S 149 55 E
Eden, N.C., U.S.A. 115 36 29N 79 53W
Eden, N.Y., U.S.A. 112 42 39N 78 55W
Eden, Tex., U.S.A. 117 31 16N 99 50W
Eden, Wyo., U.S.A. 118 42 2N 109 27W
Eden → 12 54 57N 3 2W
Eden L. 109 56 38N 100 15W
Edenburg 92 29 43 S 25 58 E
Edenderry 15 53 21N 7 3W
Edenton 115 36 5N 76 36W
Edenville 93 27 37 S 27 34 E
Eder → 24 51 15N 9 25 E
Ederstausee 24 51 11N 9 0 E
Edgar 116 40 25N 98 0W
Edgartown 113 41 22N 70 28W
Edge Hill 13 52 7N 1 28W
Edgefield 115 33 50N 81 59W
Edgeley 116 46 27N 98 41W
Edgemont 116 43 15N 103 53W
Edgeøya 4 77 45N 22 30 E
Edhessa 44 40 48N 22 5 E
Edievale 101 45 49 S 169 22 E
Edina, Liberia 84 6 0N 10 10W
Edina, U.S.A. 116 40 6N 92 10W
Edinburg 117 26 22N 98 10W
Edinburgh 14 55 57N 3 12W
Edirne 43 41 40N 26 34 E
Edithburgh 99 35 5 S 137 43 E
Edjeleh 83 28 38N 9 50 E
Edmeston 113 42 42N 75 15W
Edmond 117 35 37N 97 30W
Edmonds 118 47 47N 122 22W
Edmonton, Austral. 98 17 2 S 145 46 E
Edmonton, Can. 108 53 30N 113 30W
Edmund L. 109 54 45N 93 17W
Edmundston 107 47 23N 68 20W
Edna 117 29 0N 96 40W
Edna Bay 108 55 55N 133 40W
Edolo 38 46 10N 10 21 E
Edremit 64 39 34N 27 0 E
Edsbyn 48 61 23N 15 49 E
Edsel Ford Ra. 5 77 0 S 143 0W
Edsele 48 63 25N 16 32 E
Edson 108 53 35N 116 28W
Eduardo Castex 124 35 50 S 64 18W
Edward → 99 35 0 S 143 30 E
Edward I. 106 48 22N 88 37W
Edward, L. 90 0 25 S 29 40 E
Edward VII Pen. 5 80 0 S 150 0W
Edwards Plat. 117 30 30N 101 5W
Edwardsville 113 41 15N 75 56W
Edzo 108 62 49N 116 4W
Eekloo 16 51 11N 3 33 E
Ef'e, Nahal 62 31 9N 35 13 E
Eferding 26 48 18N 14 1 E
Eferi 83 24 30N 9 28 E
Effingham 114 39 8N 88 30W
Eforie Sud 46 44 1N 28 37 E
Ega → 32 42 19N 1 55W
Égadi, Ísole 40 37 55N 12 16 E
Eganville 106 45 32N 77 5W
Egeland 116 48 42N 99 6W
Egenolf L. 109 59 3N 100 0W
Eger 27 47 53N 20 27 E
Eger → 27 47 38N 20 50 E
Egersund 47 58 26N 6 1 E
Egerton, Mt. 96 24 42 S 117 44 E
Egg L. 109 55 5N 105 30W
Eggenburg 26 48 38N 15 50 E
Eggenfelden 25 48 24N 12 46 E
Égletons 20 45 24N 2 3 E
Egmont, C. 101 39 16 S 173 45 E
Egmont, Mt. 101 39 17 S 174 5 E
Eğridir 64 37 52N 30 51 E
Eğridir Gölü 64 37 53N 30 50 E
Egtved 49 55 38N 9 18 E
Egume 85 7 30N 7 14 E
Éguzon 20 46 27N 1 33 E
Egvekinot 59 66 19N 179 50W
Egyek 27 47 39N 20 52 E
Egypt ■ 86 28 0N 31 0 E
Eha Amufu 85 6 30N 7 46 E
Ehime □ 74 33 30N 132 40 E
Ehingen 25 48 16N 9 43 E
Ehrwald 26 47 24N 10 56 E
Eibar 32 43 11N 2 28W
Eichstatt 25 48 53N 11 12 E
Eida 47 60 32N 6 43 E
Eider → 24 54 19N 8 58 E
Eidsvold 99 25 25 S 151 12 E
Eifel 25 50 10N 6 45 E
Eiffel Flats 91 18 20 S 30 0 E
Eigg 14 56 54N 6 10W
Eighty Mile Beach 96 19 30 S 120 40 E
Eil 63 8 0N 49 50 E
Eil, L. 14 56 50N 5 15W
Eildon, L. 99 37 10 S 146 0 E
Eileen L. 109 62 16N 107 37W
Eilenburg 24 51 28N 12 38 E
Ein el Luweiqa 87 14 5N 33 50 E
Einasleigh 97 18 32 S 144 5 E
Einasleigh → 98 17 30 S 142 17 E
Einbeck 24 51 48N 9 50 E
Eindhoven 16 51 26N 5 30 E
Einsiedeln 25 47 7N 8 46 E
Eiríksjökull 50 64 46N 20 24W
Eirunepé 126 6 35 S 69 53W
Eisenach 24 50 58N 10 18 E
Eisenberg 24 50 59N 11 50 E
Eisenerz 26 47 32N 14 54 E
Eisenhüttenstadt 24 52 9N 14 41 E
Eisenkappel 26 46 29N 14 36 E
Eisenstadt 27 47 51N 16 31 E
Eiserfeld 24 50 50N 7 59 E
Eisfeld 24 50 25N 10 54 E
Eisleben 24 51 31N 11 31 E
Ejby 49 55 25N 9 56 E
Eje, Sierra del 30 42 24N 6 54W
Ejea de los Caballeros 32 42 7N 1 9W
Ekalaka 116 45 55N 104 30W
Eket 85 4 38N 7 56 E
Eketahuna 101 40 38 S 175 43 E
Ekhinos 44 41 16N 25 1 E
Ekibastuz 58 51 50N 75 10 E
Ekimchan 59 53 0N 133 0W
Ekoli 90 0 23 S 24 13 E
Eksjö 49 57 40N 14 58W
Ekwan → 106 53 12N 82 15W
Ekwan Pt. 106 53 16N 82 7W
El Aaiún 80 27 9N 13 12W
El Aat 62 32 50N 35 45 E
El Abiodh-Sidi-Cheikh 82 32 53N 0 31 E
El Aïoun 82 34 33N 2 30W
El 'Aiyat 86 29 36N 31 15 E
El Alamein 86 30 48N 28 58 E
El 'Arag 86 28 40N 26 20 E
El Arahal 31 37 15N 5 33W
El Arba 82 36 37N 3 12 E
El Aricha 82 34 13N 1 10W
El Arîhã 62 31 52N 35 27 E
El Arish 98 17 35 S 146 1 E
El 'Arîsh 86 31 8N 33 50 E
El Arrouch 83 36 37N 6 53 E
* El Asnam 82 36 10N 1 20 E
El Astillero 30 43 24N 3 49W
El Badâri 86 27 4N 31 25 E
El Bahrein 86 28 30N 26 25 E
El Ballâs 86 26 2N 32 43 E
El Balyana 86 26 10N 32 3 E
El Baqeir 86 18 40N 33 40 E
El Barco de Ávila 30 40 21N 5 31W
El Barco de Valdeorras 30 42 23N 7 0W
El Bauga 86 18 18N 33 52 E
El Bawiti 86 28 25N 28 45 E
El Bayadh 82 33 40N 1 1 E
El Bierzo 30 42 45N 6 30W
El Bluff 121 11 59N 83 40W
El Bonillo 33 38 57N 2 35W
El Cajon 119 32 49N 117 0W
El Callao 126 7 18N 61 50W
El Camp 32 41 5N 1 10 E
El Campo 117 29 10N 96 20W
El Castillo 31 37 41N 6 19W
El Centro 119 32 50N 115 40W
El Cerro, Boliv. 126 17 30 S 61 40W
El Cerro, Spain 31 37 45N 6 57W
El Coronil 31 37 5N 5 38W
El Cuy 128 39 55 S 68 25W
El Cuyo 120 21 30N 87 40W
El Dab'a 86 31 0N 28 27 E
El Deir 86 25 25N 32 20 E
El Dere 63 3 50N 47 8 E
El Dias 120 20 40N 87 20W
El Dilingat 86 30 50N 30 31 E
El Diviso 126 1 22N 78 14W
El Djem 83 35 18N 10 42 E
El Djouf 84 20 0N 11 30 E
El Dorado, Ark., U.S.A. 117 33 10N 92 40W
El Dorado, Kans., U.S.A. 117 37 55N 96 56W
El Dorado, Venez. 126 6 55N 61 37W
El Dorado Springs 117 37 54N 93 59W
El Eglab 82 26 20N 4 30W
El Escorial 30 40 35N 4 7W
El Eulma 83 36 9N 5 42 E
El Faiyûm 86 29 19N 30 50 E
El Fâsher 87 13 33N 25 26 E
El Fashn 86 28 50N 30 54 E
El Ferrol 30 43 29N 8 15W
El Fifi 87 10 4N 25 0 E
El Fuerte 120 26 30N 108 40W
El Gal 63 10 58N 50 20 E
El Gebir 87 13 40N 29 40 E
El Gedida 86 25 40N 28 30 E
El Geteina 87 14 50N 32 27 E
El Gezira □ 87 15 0N 33 0 E
El Gîza 86 30 0N 31 10 E
El Goléa 82 30 30N 2 50 E
El Guettar 83 34 5N 4 38 E
El Hadjira 83 32 36N 5 30 E
El Hagiz 87 15 15N 35 50 E
El Hajeb 82 33 43N 5 13W
El Hammam 86 30 52N 29 25 E
El Hank 82 24 30N 7 0W
El Harrache 80 36 45N 3 5 E
El Hawata 87 13 25N 34 42 E
El Heiz 86 27 50N 28 40 E
El 'Idisât 86 25 30N 32 35 E
El Iskandarîya 86 31 0N 30 0 E
El Istwâ'ya □ 87 5 0N 30 0 E
El Jadida 80 33 11N 8 17W
El Jebelein 81 12 40N 32 55 E
El Kab 86 19 27N 32 46 E
El Kala 83 36 50N 8 30 E
El Kalâa 82 32 4N 7 27W
El Kamlin 87 15 3N 33 11 E
El Kantara, Alg. 83 35 14N 5 45 E
El Kantara, Tunisia 83 33 45N 10 58 E
El Karaba 86 18 32N 33 41 E
El Kef 83 36 12N 8 47 E
El Khandaq 86 18 30N 30 30 E
El Khârga 86 25 30N 30 33 E
El Khartûm 87 15 31N 32 35 E
El Khartûm □ 87 16 0N 33 0 E
El Khartûm Bahrî 87 15 40N 32 31 E
El-Khroubs 83 36 10N 6 55 E
El Khureiba 86 28 3N 35 10 E
El Kseur 83 36 46N 4 49 E
El Ksiba 82 32 45N 6 1W
El Kuntilla 86 30 1N 34 45 E
El Laqâwa 81 11 25N 29 1 E
El Laqeita 86 25 50N 33 15 E
El Leiya 87 16 15N 35 28 E
El Mafâza 87 13 38N 34 30 E
El Mahalla el Kubra 86 31 0N 31 0 E
El Mahârîq 86 25 35N 30 35 E
El Mahmûdîya 86 31 10N 30 32 E
El Maiz 82 28 19N 0 9W
El-Maks el-Bahari 86 24 30N 30 40 E
El Manshâh 86 26 26N 31 50 E
El Mansour 82 27 47N 0 14W
El Mansûra 86 31 0N 31 19 E
El Manzala 86 31 10N 31 50 E
El Marâgha 86 26 35N 31 10 E
El Masid 87 15 15N 33 0 E
El Matariya 86 31 15N 32 0 E
El Meghaier 83 33 55N 5 58 E
El Meraguen 82 28 0N 0 7W
El Metemma 87 16 50N 33 10 E
El Milagro 124 30 59 S 65 59W
El Milia 83 36 51N 6 13 E
El Minyâ 86 28 7N 30 33 E
El Molar 32 40 42N 3 45W
El Mreyye 84 18 0N 6 0W
El Obeid 87 13 8N 30 10 E
El Odaiya 81 12 8N 28 12 E
El Oro 120 19 48N 100 8W
El Oro = Sta. María del Oro 120 25 50N 105 20W
El Oued 83 33 20N 6 58 E
El Palmito, Presa 120 25 40N 105 30W
El Panadés 32 41 10N 1 30 E
El Pardo 30 40 31N 3 47W
El Paso 119 31 50N 106 30W
El Pedernoso 33 39 29N 2 45W
El Pedroso 31 37 51N 5 45W
El Pobo de Dueñas 32 40 46N 1 39W
El Portal 119 37 44N 119 49W
El Prat de Llobregat 32 41 18N 2 3 E
El Progreso 120 15 26N 87 51W
El Provencío 33 39 23N 2 35W
El Pueblito 120 29 3N 105 4W
El Qâhira 86 30 1N 31 14 E
El Qantara 86 30 51N 32 20 E
El Qasr 86 25 44N 28 42 E
El Quseima 86 30 40N 34 15 E
El Qusîya 86 27 29N 30 44 E
El Râshda 86 25 36N 28 57 E
El Reno 117 35 30N 98 0W
El Ribero 30 42 30N 8 30W
El Rîdisiya 86 24 56N 32 51 E
El Ronquillo 31 37 44N 6 10W
El Rubio 31 37 22N 5 0W
El Saff 86 29 34N 31 16 E
El Salvador ■ 120 13 50N 89 0W
El Sancejo 31 37 4N 5 6W
El Sauce 121 13 0N 86 40W
El Shallal 86 24 0N 32 53 E
El Simbillawein 86 30 48N 31 13 E
El Suweis 86 29 58N 32 31 E
El Thamad 86 29 40N 34 28 E
El Tigre 126 8 44N 64 15W
El Tocuyo 126 9 47N 69 48W
El Tofo 124 29 22 S 71 18W
El Tránsito 124 28 52 S 70 17W
El Tûr 86 28 14N 33 36 E
El Turbio 128 51 45 S 72 5W
El Uqsur 86 25 41N 32 38 E
El Vado 32 41 2N 3 18W
El Vallés 32 41 35N 2 20 E
El Vigía 126 8 38N 71 39W
El Wak 90 2 49N 40 56 E
El Waqf 86 25 45N 32 15 E
El Wâsta 86 29 19N 31 12 E
El Weguet 87 5 28N 42 17 E
El Wuz 81 15 0N 30 7 E
Elafónisos 45 36 29N 22 56 E
Elamanchili = Yellamanchilli 70 17 26N 82 50 E
Elandsvlei 92 32 19 S 19 31 E
Élassa 45 35 18N 26 21 E
Elassón 44 39 53N 22 12 E
Elat 62 29 30N 34 56 E
Eláthia 45 38 37N 22 46 E
Elâzığ 64 38 37N 39 14 E
Elba, Italy 38 42 48N 10 15 E
Elba, U.S.A. 115 31 27N 86 4W
Elbasani 44 41 9N 20 9 E
Elbasani-Berati □ 44 40 58N 20 0 E
Elbe → 24 53 50N 9 0 E
Elbert, Mt. 119 39 5N 106 27W
Elberta 114 44 35N 86 14W
Elberton 115 34 7N 82 51W
Elbeuf 18 49 17N 1 2 E
Elbidtan 64 38 13N 37 12 E
Elbing = Elbląg 28 54 10N 19 25 E
Elbląg 28 54 10N 19 25 E
Elbląg □ 28 54 15N 19 30 E
Elbow 109 51 7N 106 35W

* *Renamed Ech Cheliff*

Elbrus Estevan

Elbrus 57 43 21N 42 30 E
Elburg 16 52 26N 5 50 E
Elburz Mts. = Alborz 65 36 0N 52 0 E
Elche 33 38 15N 0 42 W
Elche de la Sierra 33 38 27N 2 3W
Elcho I. 97 11 55 S 135 45 E
Elda 33 38 29N 0 47W
Eldon 116 38 20N 92 38W
Eldora 116 42 20N 93 5W
Eldorado, Argent. 125 26 28 S 54 43W
Eldorado, Can. 109 59 35N 108 30W
Eldorado, Mexico 120 24 20N 107 22W
Eldorado, Ill., U.S.A. 114 37 50N 88 25W
Eldorado, Tex., U.S.A. 117 30 52N 100 35W
Eldoret 90 0 30N 35 17 E
Eldred 112 41 57N 78 24W
Electra 117 34 0N 99 0W
Elefantes → 93 24 10 S 32 40 E
Elektrogorsk 55 55 56N 38 50 E
Elektrostal 55 55 41N 38 32 E
Elele 85 5 5N 6 50 E
Elena 43 42 55N 25 53 E
Elephant Butte Res. 119 33 45N 107 30W
Elephant I. 5 61 0 S 55 0W
Elephant Pass 70 9 35N 80 25 E
Eleshnitsa 43 41 52N 23 36 E
Eleuthera 121 25 0N 76 20W
Elevsís 45 38 4N 23 26 E
Elevtheroúpolis 44 40 52N 24 20 E
Elgepiggen 47 62 10N 11 21 E
Elgeyo-Marakwet □ 90 0 45N 35 30 E
Elgin, N.B., Can. 107 45 48N 65 10W
Elgin, Ont., Can. 113 44 36N 76 13W
Elgin, U.K. 14 57 39N 3 20W
Elgin, Ill., U.S.A. 114 42 0N 88 20W
Elgin, N.D., U.S.A. 116 46 24N 101 46W
Elgin, Nebr., U.S.A. 116 41 58N 98 3W
Elgin, Nev., U.S.A. 119 37 21N 114 20W
Elgin, Oreg., U.S.A. 118 45 37N 118 0W
Elgin, Texas, U.S.A. 117 30 21N 97 22W
Elgon, Mt. 90 1 10N 34 30 E
Eliase 73 8 21 S 130 48 E
Elida 117 33 56N 103 41W
Elikón, Mt. 45 38 18N 22 45 E
Elin Pelin 43 42 40N 23 36 E
Elisabethville = Lubumbashi 91 11 40 S 27 28 E
Elista 57 46 16N 44 14 E
Elizabeth, Austral. 97 34 42 S 138 41 E
Elizabeth, U.S.A. 114 40 37N 74 12W
Elizabeth City 115 36 18N 76 16W
Elizabethton 115 36 20N 82 13W
Elizabethtown, Ky., U.S.A. 114 37 40N 85 54W
Elizabethtown, N.Y., U.S.A. 113 44 13N 73 36W
Elizabethtown, Pa., U.S.A. 113 40 8N 76 36W
Elizondo 32 43 12N 1 30W
Ełk 28 53 50N 22 21 E
Ełk → 28 53 41N 22 28 E
Elk City 117 35 25N 99 25W
Elk Island Nat. Park 108 53 35N 112 59W
Elk Lake 106 47 40N 80 25W
Elk Point 109 53 54N 110 55W
Elk River, Idaho, U.S.A. 118 46 50N 116 8W
Elk River, Minn., U.S.A. 116 45 17N 93 34W
Elkhart, Ind., U.S.A. 114 41 42N 85 55W
Elkhart, Kans., U.S.A. 117 37 3N 101 54W
Elkhorn 109 49 59N 101 14W
Elkhorn → 116 41 7N 98 15W
Elkhotovo 57 43 19N 44 15 E
Elkhovo 43 42 10N 26 40 E
Elkin 115 36 17N 80 50W
Elkins 114 38 53N 79 53W
Elko, Can. 108 49 20N 115 10W
Elko, U.S.A. 118 40 50N 115 50W
Ellef Ringnes I. 4 78 30N 102 2W
Ellen, Mt. 119 38 4N 110 56W
Ellendale 116 46 3N 98 30W
Ellensburg 118 47 0N 120 30W
Ellenville 114 41 42N 74 23W
Ellery, Mt. 99 37 28 S 148 47 E
Ellesmere I. 4 79 30N 80 0W
Ellesworth Land 5 76 0 S 89 0W
Ellice Is. = Tuvalu ■ 94 8 0 S 176 0 E
Ellinwood 116 38 27N 98 37W
Elliot 93 31 22 S 27 48 E
Elliot Lake 106 46 25N 82 35W
Ellis 116 39 0N 99 39W
Ellisville 117 31 38N 89 12W
Ellon 14 57 21N 2 5W
Ellore = Eluru 70 16 48N 81 8 E
Ells → 108 57 18N 111 40W
Ellsworth 116 38 47N 98 15W
Ellsworth Land 5 76 0 S 89 0W
Ellsworth Mts. 5 78 30 S 85 0W
Ellwangen 25 48 57N 10 9 E
Ellwood City 114 40 52N 80 19W
Elm 25 46 54N 9 10 E
Elma, Can. 109 49 52N 95 55W
Elma, U.S.A. 118 47 0N 123 30 E
Elmalı 64 36 44N 29 56 E
Elmhurst 114 41 52N 87 58W
Elmina 85 5 5N 1 21W
Elmira, Can. 112 43 36N 80 33W
Elmira, U.S.A. 114 42 8N 76 49W
Elmore 99 36 30 S 144 37 E
Elmshorn 24 53 44N 9 40 E
Elmvale 112 44 35N 79 52W
Elne 20 42 36N 2 58 E
Elora 112 43 41N 80 26W
Elos 45 36 46N 22 43 E
Eloy 119 32 46N 111 33W
Éloyes 19 48 6N 6 36 E
Elrose 109 51 12N 108 0W
Elsas 106 48 32N 82 55W
Elsinore, Cal., U.S.A. 119 33 40N 117 15W
Elsinore, Utah, U.S.A. 119 38 40N 112 2W
Elspe 24 51 10N 8 1 E
Elster → 24 51 25N 11 57 E
Elsterwerda 24 51 27N 13 32 E
Eltham 101 39 26 S 174 19 E
Elton 57 49 5N 46 52 E
Eluru 70 16 48N 81 8 E
Elvas 31 38 50N 7 10W
Elven 18 47 44N 2 36W
Elverum 47 60 53N 11 34 E
Elvo → 38 45 23N 8 21 E
Elvran 47 63 24N 11 3 E
Elwood, Ind., U.S.A. 114 40 20N 85 50W
Elwood, Nebr., U.S.A. 116 40 38N 99 51W
Ely, U.K. 13 52 24N 0 16 E
Ely, Minn., U.S.A. 116 47 54N 91 52W
Ely, Nev., U.S.A. 118 39 10N 114 50W
Elyashiv 62 32 23N 34 55 E
Elyria 114 41 22N 82 8W
Elyrus 45 35 15N 23 45 E
Elz → 25 48 21N 7 45 E
Emådalen 48 61 20N 14 44 E
Emba 58 48 50N 58 8 E
Emba → 58 45 25N 52 30 E
Embarcación 124 23 10 S 64 0W
Embarras Portage 109 58 27N 111 28W
Embóna 45 36 13N 27 51 E
Embrun 21 44 34N 6 30 E
Embu 90 0 32 S 37 38 E
Embu □ 90 0 30 S 37 35 E
Emden 24 53 22N 7 12 E
'Emeq Yizre'el 62 32 35N 35 12 E
Emerald 97 23 32 S 148 10 E
Emerson 109 49 0N 97 10W
Emery 119 38 59N 111 17W
Emery Park 119 32 10N 110 59W
Emi Koussi 83 20 0N 18 55 E
Emilia-Romagna □ 38 44 33N 10 40 E
Emilius, Mte. 38 45 41N 7 23 E
Eminabad 68 32 2N 74 8 E
Emine, Nos 43 42 40N 27 56 E
Emlenton 112 41 11N 79 41W
Emlichheim 24 52 37N 6 51 E
Emmaboda 49 56 37N 15 32 E
Emme → 25 47 0N 7 42 E
Emmeloord 16 52 44N 5 46 E
Emmen 16 52 48N 6 57 E
Emmendingen 25 48 7N 7 51 E
Emmental 25 47 0N 7 35 E
Emmerich 24 51 50N 6 12 E
Emmet 98 24 45 S 144 30 E
Emmetsburg 116 43 3N 94 40W
Emmett 118 43 51N 116 33W
Emöd 27 47 57N 20 47 E
Emona 43 42 43N 27 53 E
Empalme 120 28 1N 110 49W
Empangeni 93 28 50 S 31 52 E
Empedrado 124 28 0 S 58 46W
Emperor Seamount Chain 94 40 0N 170 0 E
Empoli 38 43 43N 10 57 E
Emporia, Kans., U.S.A. 116 38 25N 96 10W
Emporia, Va., U.S.A. 115 36 41N 77 32W
Emporium 114 41 30N 78 17W
Empress 109 50 57N 110 0W
Ems → 24 52 37N 9 26 E
Emsdale 112 45 32N 79 19W
Emsdetten 24 52 11N 7 31 E
Emu 76 43 40N 128 6 E
Emu Park 98 23 13 S 150 50 E
En Gedi 62 31 28N 35 25 E
En Gev 62 32 47N 35 38 E
En Harod 62 32 33N 35 22 E
'En Kerem 62 31 47N 35 6 E
En Nahud 87 12 45N 28 25 E
Enafors 48 63 17N 12 20 E
Enana 92 17 30 S 16 23 E
Enånger 48 61 30N 17 9 E
Enaratoli 73 3 55 S 136 21 E
Enard B. 14 58 5N 5 20W
Encantadas, Serra 125 30 40 S 53 0W
Encanto, C. 73 15 45N 121 38 E
Encarnación 125 27 15 S 55 50W
Encarnación de Diaz 120 21 30N 102 13W
Enchi 84 5 53N 2 48W
Encinal 117 28 3N 99 25W
Encino 119 34 38N 105 40W
Encounter B. 97 35 45 S 138 45 E
Endau 71 2 40N 103 38 E
Endau → 71 2 30N 103 30 E
Ende 73 8 45 S 121 40 E
Endeavour 109 52 10N 102 39W
Endeavour Str. 97 10 45 S 142 0 E
Endelave 49 55 46N 10 18 E
Enderbury I. 94 3 8 S 171 5W
Enderby 108 50 35N 119 10W
Enderby Land 5 66 0 S 53 0 E
Enderlin 116 46 37N 97 41W
Endicott, N.Y., U.S.A. 114 42 6N 76 2W
Endicott, Wash., U.S.A. 118 47 0N 117 45W
Endröd 27 46 55N 20 47 E
Enez 44 40 45N 26 5 E
Enfida 83 36 6N 10 28 E
Enfield 13 51 39N 0 4W
Engadin = Engiadina 25 46 51N 10 18 E
Engaño, C., Dom. Rep. 121 18 30N 68 20W
Engaño, C., Phil. 73 18 35N 122 23 E
Engelberg 25 46 48N 8 26 E
Engels 55 51 28N 46 6 E
Engemann L. 109 58 0N 106 55W
Enger 47 60 35N 10 20 E
Enggano 72 5 20 S 102 40 E
Enghien 16 50 37N 4 2 E
Engiadina 25 46 51N 10 18 E
Engil 82 33 12N 4 32W
Engkilili 72 1 3N 111 42 E
England 117 34 30N 91 58W
England □ 11 53 0N 2 0W
Englee 107 50 45N 56 5W
Englehart 106 47 49N 79 52W
Engler L. 109 59 8N 106 52W
Englewood, Colo., U.S.A. 116 39 40N 105 0W
Englewood, Kans., U.S.A. 117 37 7N 99 59W
Englewood, N.J., U.S.A. 113 40 54N 73 59W
English → 109 50 35N 93 30W
English Bazar 69 24 58N 88 10 E
English Channel 18 50 0N 2 0W
English River 106 49 14N 91 0W
Enid 117 36 26N 97 52W
Enipévs → 44 39 22N 22 17 E
Eniwetok 94 11 30N 162 15 E
Enkeldoorn 91 19 2 S 30 52 E
Enkhuizen 16 52 42N 5 17 E
Enköping 48 59 37N 17 4 E
Enna 41 37 34N 14 15 E
Ennadai 109 61 8N 100 53W
Ennadai L. 109 61 0N 101 0W
Ennedi 81 17 15N 22 0 E
Enngonia 99 29 21 S 145 50 E
Ennis, Ireland 15 52 51N 8 59W
Ennis, Mont., U.S.A. 118 45 20N 111 42W
Ennis, Texas, U.S.A. 117 32 15N 96 40W
Enniscorthy 15 52 30N 6 35W
Enniskillen 15 54 20N 7 40W
Ennistimon 15 52 56N 9 18W
Enns 26 48 12N 14 28 E
Enns → 26 48 14N 14 32 E
Enontekiö 50 68 23N 23 37 E
Enping 77 22 16N 112 21 E
Enriquillo, L. 121 18 20N 72 5W
Enschede 16 52 13N 6 53 E
Ensenada, Argent. 124 34 55 S 57 55W
Ensenada, Mexico 120 31 50N 116 50W
Enshi 77 30 18N 109 29 E
Ensisheim 19 47 50N 7 20 E
Entebbe 90 0 4N 32 28 E
Enterprise, Can. 108 60 47N 115 45W
Enterprise, Oreg., U.S.A. 118 45 30N 117 18W
Enterprise, Utah, U.S.A. 119 37 37N 113 36W
Entre Ríos, Boliv. 124 21 30 S 64 25W
Entre Ríos, Mozam. 91 14 57 S 37 20 E
Entre Rios □ 124 30 30 S 58 30W
Entrecasteaux, Pt. d' 96 34 50 S 115 56 E
Entrepeñas, Pantano de 32 40 34N 2 42W
Enugu 85 6 20N 7 30 E
Enugu Ezike 85 7 0N 7 29 E
Enumclaw 118 47 12N 122 0W
Envermeières 18 49 54N 1 16 E
Envermeu 18 49 53N 1 15 E
Enz → 25 49 1N 9 6 E
Enza → 38 44 54N 10 31 E
Eólie, I. 41 38 30N 14 50 E
Epanomí 44 40 25N 22 59 E
Epe, Neth. 16 52 21N 5 59 E
Epe, Nigeria 85 6 36N 3 59 E
Épernay 19 49 3N 3 56 E
Épernon 19 48 35N 1 40 E
Ephesus, Turkey 45 37 50N 27 33 E
Ephesus, Turkey 64 38 0N 27 19 E
Ephraim 118 39 21N 111 37W
Ephrata 118 47 20N 119 32W
Epidaurus Limera 45 36 46N 23 0 E
Epila 32 41 36N 1 17W
Épinac-les-Mines 19 46 59N 4 31 E
Épinal 19 48 10N 6 27 E
Episcopia Bihorulu 46 47 12N 21 55 E
Epitálion 45 37 37N 21 30 E
Epping 13 51 42N 0 8 E
Epukiro 92 21 40 S 19 9 E
Equatorial Guinea ■ 88 2 0 S 8 0 E
Er Rahad 87 12 45N 30 32 E
Er Rif 82 35 1N 4 1W
Er Roseires 87 11 55N 34 30 E
Er Yébigué 83 22 30N 17 30 E
Erandol 68 20 56N 75 20 E
Erāwadī Myit = Irrawaddy → 67 15 50N 95 6 E
Erba, Italy 38 45 49N 9 12 E
Erba, Sudan 86 19 5N 36 51 E
Ercha 59 69 45N 147 20 E
Erciyaş Dağı 64 38 30N 35 30 E
Erdao Jiang → 76 43 0N 127 0 E
Erding 25 48 18N 11 55 E
Erdre → 18 47 13N 1 32W
Erebus, Mt. 5 77 35 S 167 0 E
Erechim 125 27 35 S 52 15W
Ereğli, Turkey 64 41 15N 31 30 E
Ereğli, Turkey 64 37 31N 34 4 E
Erei, Monti 41 37 20N 14 20 E
Erenhot 76 43 48N 111 59 E
Eresma → 30 41 26N 40 45W
Eressós 45 39 11N 25 57 E
Erfenis Dam 92 28 30 S 26 50 E
Erfjord 47 59 20N 6 14 E
Erfoud 82 31 30N 4 15W
Erft → 24 51 11N 6 44 E
Erfurt 24 50 58N 11 2 E
Erfurt □ 24 51 10N 10 30 E
Ergani 64 38 17N 39 49 E
Ergene → 43 41 1N 26 22 E
Ergeni Vozyshennost 57 47 0N 44 0 E
Ergli 54 56 54N 25 38 E
Ergun Zuoqi 76 50 47N 121 31 E
Eria → 30 42 3N 5 44W
Eriba 87 16 40N 36 10 E
Eriboll, L. 14 58 28N 4 41W
Érice 40 38 4N 12 34 E
Erie 114 42 10N 80 7W
Erie Canal 112 43 15N 78 0W
Erie, L. 112 42 15N 81 0W
Erieau 112 42 16N 81 57W
Erigavo 63 10 35N 47 20 E
Erikoúsa 44 39 55N 19 14 E
Eriksdale 109 50 52N 98 7W
Erikslund 48 62 31N 15 54 E
Erímanthos 45 37 57N 21 50 E
Erimo-misaki 74 41 50N 143 15 E
Erithraí 45 38 13N 23 20 E
Eritrea □ 87 14 0N 41 0 E
Erjas → 31 39 40N 7 1W
Erlangen 25 49 35N 11 0 E
Ermelo, Neth. 16 52 18N 5 35 E
Ermelo, S. Afr. 93 26 31 S 29 59 E
Ermenak 64 36 38N 33 0 E
Ermióni 45 37 23N 23 15 E
Ermoúpolis = Síros 45 37 28N 24 57 E
Ernakulam = Cochin 70 9 59N 76 22 E
Erne → 15 54 30N 8 16W
Erne, Lough 15 54 26N 7 46W
Ernée 18 48 18N 0 56W
Ernstberg 25 50 14N 6 46 E
Erode 70 11 24N 77 45 E
Eromanga 99 26 40 S 143 11 E
Erongo 92 21 39 S 15 58 E
Erquy 18 48 38N 2 29W
Erquy, Cap d' 18 48 39N 2 29W
Erramala Hills 70 15 30N 78 15 E
Errer → 87 7 32N 42 35 E
Errigal, Mt. 15 55 2N 8 8W
Erris Hd. 15 54 19N 10 0W
Erseka 44 40 22N 20 40 E
Erskine 116 47 37N 96 0W
Erstein 19 48 25N 7 38 E
Ertil 55 51 55N 40 50 E
Ertvågøy 47 63 13N 8 26 E
Eruwa 85 7 33N 3 26 E
Ervy-le-Châtel 19 48 2N 3 55 E
Erwin 115 36 10N 82 28W
Erzgebirge 24 50 25N 13 0 E
Erzin 59 50 15N 95 10 E
Erzincan 64 39 46N 39 30 E
Erzurum 64 39 57N 41 15 E
Es Sahrâ' Esh Sharqîya 86 26 0N 33 30 E
Es Sînâ' 86 29 0N 34 0 E
Es Sûkî 87 13 20N 33 58 E
Esambo 90 3 48 S 23 30 E
Esan-Misaki 74 41 40N 141 10 E
Esbjerg 49 55 29N 8 29 E
Escalante 119 37 47N 111 37W
Escalante → 119 37 17N 110 53W
Escalón 120 26 46N 104 20W
Escalona 30 40 9N 4 29W
Escambia → 115 30 32N 87 15W
Escanaba 114 45 44N 87 5W
Esch-sur-Alzette 16 49 32N 6 0 E
Eschallens 25 46 39N 6 38 E
Eschede 24 52 44N 10 13 E
Eschwege 24 51 10N 10 3 E
Eschweiler 24 50 49N 6 14 E
Escobal 120 9 6N 80 1W
Escondido 119 33 9N 117 4W
Escuinapa 120 22 50N 105 50W
Escuintla 120 14 20N 90 48W
Eséka 85 3 41N 10 44 E
Esens 24 53 40N 7 35 E
Esera → 32 42 6N 0 15 E
Eşfahān 65 33 0N 53 0 E
Esgueva → 30 41 40N 4 43W
Esh Sham = Dimashq 64 33 30N 36 18 E
Esh Shamâlîya □ 86 19 0N 29 0 E
Eshowe 93 28 50 S 31 30 E
Eshta' ol 62 31 47N 35 0 E
Esiama 84 4 56N 2 25W
Esino → 39 43 39N 13 22 E
Esk →, Dumfries, U.K. 14 54 58N 3 4W
Esk →, N. Yorks., U.K. 12 54 27N 0 36W
Eskifjörður 50 65 3N 13 55W
Eskilstuna 48 59 22N 16 32 E
Eskimo Pt. 109 61 10N 94 15W
Eskişehir 64 39 50N 30 35 E
Esla → 30 41 29N 6 3W
Esla, Pantano del 30 41 29N 6 3W
Eslöv 49 55 50N 13 20 E
Esmeralda, La 124 22 16 S 62 33W
Esmeraldas 126 1 0N 79 40W
Espalion 20 44 32N 2 47 E
Espalmador, I. 33 38 47N 1 26 E
Espanola 106 46 15N 81 46W
Espardell, I. del 33 38 48N 1 29 E
Esparraguera 32 41 33N 1 52 E
Espejo 31 37 40N 4 34W
Esperance 96 33 45 S 121 55 E
Esperance B. 96 33 48 S 121 55 E
Esperanza 124 31 29 S 61 3W
Espéraza 20 42 56N 2 14 E
Espevær 47 59 35N 5 7 E
Espichel, C. 31 38 22N 9 16W
Espiel 31 38 11N 5 1W
Espigão, Serra do 125 26 35 S 50 30W
Espinal 126 4 9N 74 53W
Espinhaço, Serra do 127 17 30 S 43 30W
Espinho 30 41 1N 8 38W
Espinilho, Serra do 125 28 30 S 55 0W
Espinosa de los Monteros 30 43 5N 3 34W
Espírito Santo □ 127 20 0 S 40 45W
Espíritu Santo, B. del 120 19 15N 87 0W
Espíritu Santo, I. 120 24 30N 110 23W
Espluga de Francolí 32 41 24N 1 7 E
Espuña, Sierra 33 37 51N 1 35W
Espungabera 93 20 29 S 32 45 E
Esquel 128 42 55 S 71 20W
Esquina 124 30 0 S 59 30W
Essaouira (Mogador) 82 31 32N 9 48W
Essarts, Les 18 46 47N 1 12W
Essebie 90 2 58N 30 40 E
Essen, Belg. 16 51 28N 4 28 E
Essen, Ger. 24 51 28N 6 59 E
Essequibo → 126 6 50N 58 30W
Essex, Can. 112 42 10N 82 49W
Essex, U.S.A. 113 44 17N 73 21W
Essex □ 13 51 48N 0 30 E
Esslingen 25 48 43N 9 19 E
Essonne □ 19 48 30N 2 20 E
Essvik 48 62 18N 17 24 E
Estaca, Pta. del 30 43 46N 7 42W
Estadilla 32 42 4N 0 16 E
Estados, I. de Los 128 54 40 S 64 30W
Estagel 20 42 47N 2 40 E
Estância 127 11 16 S 37 26W
Estancia 119 34 50N 106 1W
Estarreja 30 40 45N 8 35W
Estats, Pic d' 32 42 40N 1 24 E
Estcourt 93 28 58 S 29 53 E
Este 39 45 12N 11 40 E
Esteban 30 43 33N 6 5W
Estelí 121 13 9N 86 22W
Estella 32 42 40N 2 0W
Estelline, S.D., U.S.A. 116 44 39N 96 52W
Estelline, Texas, U.S.A. 117 34 35N 100 27W
Estena → 31 39 23N 4 44W
Estepa 31 37 17N 4 52W
Estepona 31 36 24N 5 7W
Esterhazy 109 50 37N 102 5W
Esternay 19 48 44N 3 33 E
Esterri de Aneu 32 42 38N 1 5 E
Estevan 109 49 10N 102 59W

Estevan Group Ferland

Estevan Group 108 53 3N 129 38W
Estherville 116 43 25N 94 50W
Estissac 19 48 16N 3 48 E
Eston 109 51 8N 108 40W
Estonian S.S.R. □ 54 58 30N 25 30 E
Estoril 31 38 42N 9 23W
Estouk 85 18 14N 1 2 E
Estrada, La 30 42 43N 8 27W
Estrêla, Serra da 30 40 10N 7 45W
Estrella 33 38 25N 3 35W
Estremoz 31 38 51N 7 39W
Estrondo, Serra do 127 7 20 S 48 0W
Esztergom 27 47 47N 18 44 E
Et Tîdra 84 19 45N 16 20W
Eţ Ţîra 62 32 14N 34 56 E
Étables-sur-Mer 18 48 38N 2 51W
Etah 68 27 35N 78 40 E
Étain 19 49 13N 5 38 E
Etamamu 107 50 18N 59 59W
Étampes 19 48 26N 2 10 E
Étang 19 46 52N 4 10 E
Etanga 92 17 55 S 13 00 E
Étaples 19 50 30N 1 39 E
Etawah 68 26 48N 79 6 E
Etawah → 115 34 20N 84 15W
Etawney L. 109 57 50N 96 50W
Eteh 85 7 2N 7 28 E
Ethel, Oued el → 82 28 31N 3 37W
Ethelbert 109 51 32N 100 25W
Ethiopia ■ 63 8 0N 40 0 E
Ethiopian Highlands 78 10 0N 37 0 E
Etive, L. 14 56 30N 5 12W
Etna, Mt. 41 37 45N 15 0 E
Etne 47 59 40N 5 56 E
Etoile 91 11 33 S 27 30 E
Etolin I. 108 56 5N 132 20W
Etosha Pan 92 18 40 S 16 30 E
Etowah 115 35 20N 84 30W
Étrépagny 18 49 18N 1 36 E
Étretat 18 49 42N 0 12 E
Étroits, Les 107 47 24N 68 54W
Etropole 43 42 50N 24 0 E
Ettlingen 25 48 58N 8 25 E
Ettrick Water 14 55 31N 2 55W
Etuku 90 3 42 S 25 45 E
Etzatlán 120 20 48N 104 5W
Eu 18 50 3N 1 26 E
Euabalong West 100 33 3 S 146 23 E
Euboea = Évvoia 45 38 40N 23 40 E
Eucla Basin 96 31 19 S 126 9 E
Euclid 114 41 32N 81 31W
Eucumbene, L. 99 36 2 S 148 40 E
Eudora 117 33 5N 91 17W
Eufaula, Ala., U.S.A. 115 31 55N 85 11W
Eufaula, Okla., U.S.A. 117 35 20N 95 33W
Eufaula, L. 117 35 15N 95 28W
Eugene 118 44 0N 123 8W
Eugenia, Punta 120 27 50N 115 5W
Eugowra 99 33 22 S 148 24 E
Eulo 99 28 10 S 145 3 E
Eunice, La., U.S.A. 117 30 35N 92 28W
Eunice, N. Mex., U.S.A. 117 32 30N 103 10W
Eupen 16 50 37N 6 3 E
Euphrates = Furāt, Nahr al → 64 31 0N 47 25 E
Eure □ 18 49 6N 1 0 E
Eure → 18 49 18N 1 12 E
Eure-et-Loir □ 18 48 22N 1 30 E
Eureka, Can. 4 80 0N 85 56W
Eureka, Calif., U.S.A. 118 40 50N 124 0W
Eureka, Kans., U.S.A. 117 37 50N 96 20W
Eureka, Mont., U.S.A. 118 48 53N 115 6W
Eureka, Nev., U.S.A. 118 39 32N 116 2W
Eureka, S.D., U.S.A. 116 45 49N 99 38W
Eureka, Utah, U.S.A. 118 40 0N 112 9W
Euroa 99 36 44 S 145 35 E
Europa, Picos de 30 43 10N 4 49W
Europa Pt. = Europa, Pta. de 31 36 3N 5 21W
Europa, Pta. de 31 36 3N 5 21W
Europe 8 50 0N 20 0 E
Europoort 16 51 57N 4 10 E
Euskirchen 24 50 40N 6 45 E
Eustis 115 28 54N 81 36W
Eutin 24 54 7N 10 38 E
Eutsuk L. 108 53 20N 126 45W
Eval 62 32 15N 35 15 E
Evale 92 16 33 S 15 44 E
Evanger 47 60 39N 6 7 E
Evans 116 40 25N 104 43W
Evans Head 99 29 7 S 153 27 E
Evans L. 106 50 50N 77 0W
Evans Mills 113 44 6N 75 48W
Evans Pass 116 41 0N 105 35W
Evanston, Ill., U.S.A. 114 42 0N 87 40W
Evanston, Wyo., U.S.A. 118 41 10N 111 0W
Evansville, Ind., U.S.A. 114 38 0N 87 35W
Evansville, Wis., U.S.A. 116 42 47N 89 18W
Évaux-les-Bains 20 46 12N 2 29 E
Eveleth 116 47 29N 92 46W
Even Yahuda 62 32 16N 34 53 E
Evensk 59 62 12N 159 30 E
Evenstad 47 61 25N 11 7 E
Everard, L. 96 31 30 S 135 0 E
Everard Ras. 96 27 5 S 132 28 E
Everest, Mt. 69 28 5N 86 58 E
Everett, Pa., U.S.A. 112 40 2N 78 24W
Everett, Wash., U.S.A. 118 48 0N 122 10W
Everglades, Fla., U.S.A. 115 26 0N 80 30W
Everglades, Fla., U.S.A. 115 25 52N 81 23W
Everglades Nat. Park. 115 25 27N 80 53W
Evergreen 115 31 28N 86 55W
Everson 118 48 57N 122 22W
Evesham 13 52 6N 1 57W
Evian-les-Bains 21 46 24N 6 35 E
Evinayong 88 1 26N 10 35 E
Évinos → 45 38 27N 21 40 E
Evisa 21 42 15N 8 48 E
Evje 47 58 36N 7 51 E
Évora 31 38 33N 7 57W
Évora □ 31 38 33N 7 50W
Évreux 18 49 0N 1 8 E
Evritania □ 45 39 5N 21 30 E
Évron 18 48 10N 0 24W
Évros □ 44 41 10N 26 0 E
Evrótas → 45 36 50N 22 40 E
Évvoia 45 38 30N 24 0 E
Évvoia □ 45 38 40N 23 40 E
Ewe, L. 14 57 49N 5 38W
Ewing 116 42 18N 98 22W
Ewo 88 0 48 S 14 45 E
Exaltación 126 13 10 S 65 20W
Excelsior Springs 116 39 20N 94 10W
Excideuil 20 45 20N 1 4 E
Exe → 13 50 38N 3 27W
Exeter, Can. 112 43 21N 81 29W
Exeter, U.K. 13 50 43N 3 31W
Exeter, Calif., U.S.A. 119 36 17N 119 9W
Exeter, N.H., U.S.A. 113 43 0N 70 58W
Exeter, Nebr., U.S.A. 116 40 43N 97 30W
Exmes 18 48 45N 0 10 E
Exmoor 13 51 10N 3 59W
Exmouth, Austral. 96 21 54 S 114 10 E
Exmouth, U.K. 13 50 37N 3 26W
Exmouth G. 96 22 15 S 114 15 E
Expedition Range 97 24 30 S 149 12 E
Extremadura 31 39 30N 6 5W
Exuma Sound 121 24 30N 76 20W
Eyasi, L. 90 3 30 S 35 0 E
Eyeberry L. 109 63 8N 104 43W
Eyemouth 14 55 53N 2 5W
Eygurande 20 45 40N 2 26 E
Eyjafjörður 50 66 15N 18 30W
Eymet 20 44 40N 0 25 E
Eymoutiers 20 45 40N 1 45 E
Eyrarbakki 50 63 52N 21 9W
Eyre 96 32 15 S 126 18 E
Eyre Cr. → 97 26 40 S 139 0 E
Eyre, L. 97 29 30 S 137 26 E
Eyre Mts. 101 45 25 S 168 25 E
Eyre (North), L. 97 28 30 S 137 20 E
Eyre Pen. 96 33 30 S 137 17 E
Eyre (South), L. 99 29 18 S 137 25 E
Eyzies, Les 20 44 56N 1 1 E
Ez Zeidab 86 17 25N 33 55 E
Ezcaray 32 42 19N 3 0W
Ezine 44 39 48N 26 12 E

F

Fabens 119 31 30N 106 8W
Fåborg 49 55 6N 10 15 E
Fabriano 39 43 20N 12 52 E
Făcăeni 46 44 32N 27 53 E
Facatativá 126 4 49N 74 22W
Fachi 80 18 6N 11 34 E
Facture 20 44 39N 0 58W
Fada 81 17 13N 21 34 E
Fada-n-Gourma 85 12 10N 0 30 E
Fadd 27 46 28N 18 49 E
Faddeyevskiy, Ostrov 59 76 0N 150 0 E
Fâḍilī 64 26 55N 49 10 E
Fadlab 86 17 42N 34 2 E
Faenza 39 44 17N 11 53 E
Fafa 85 15 22N 0 48 E
Fafe 30 41 27N 8 11W
Fagam 85 11 1N 10 1 E
Făgăras 46 45 48N 24 58 E
Făgăras, Munţii 46 45 40N 24 40 E
Fågelsjö 48 61 50N 14 35 E
Fagerhult 49 57 8N 15 40 E
Fagersta 48 60 1N 15 46 E
Făget 46 45 52N 22 10 E
Făget, Munţii 46 47 40N 23 10 E
Fagnano Castello 41 39 31N 16 4 E
Fagnano, L. 128 54 30 S 68 0W
Fagnières 19 48 58N 4 20 E
Fahraj 65 29 0N 59 0 E
Fahūd 65 22 18N 56 28 E
Fair Hd. 15 55 14N 6 10W
Fair Isle 11 59 30N 1 40W
Fairbank 119 31 44N 110 12W
Fairbanks 104 64 50N 147 50W
Fairbury 116 40 5N 97 5W
Fairfax 117 36 37N 96 45W
Fairfield, Austral. 100 33 53 S 150 57 E
Fairfield, Ala., U.S.A. 115 33 30N 87 0W
Fairfield, Calif., U.S.A. 118 38 14N 122 1W
Fairfield, Conn., U.S.A. 113 41 8N 73 16W
Fairfield, Idaho, U.S.A. 118 43 21N 114 46W
Fairfield, Ill., U.S.A. 114 38 20N 88 20W
Fairfield, Iowa, U.S.A. 116 41 0N 91 58W
Fairfield, Mont., U.S.A. 118 47 40N 112 0W
Fairfield, Texas, U.S.A. 117 31 40N 96 0W
Fairford 109 51 37N 98 38W
Fairhope 115 30 35N 87 50W
Fairlie 101 44 5 S 170 49 E
Fairmont, Minn., U.S.A. 116 43 37N 94 30W
Fairmont, W. Va., U.S.A. 114 39 29N 80 10W
Fairmont Hot Springs 108 50 20N 115 56W
Fairplay 119 39 9N 105 40W
Fairport, N.Y., U.S.A. 114 43 8N 77 29W
Fairport, Ohio, U.S.A. 112 41 45N 81 17W
Fairview, Austral. 98 15 31 S 144 17 E
Fairview, Can. 108 56 5N 118 25W
Fairview, N. Dak., U.S.A. 116 47 49N 104 7W
Fairview, Okla., U.S.A. 117 36 19N 98 30W
Fairview, Utah, U.S.A. 118 39 50N 111 0W
Fairweather, Mt. 104 58 55N 137 45W
Faith 116 45 2N 102 4W
Faizabad 69 26 45N 82 10 E
Faizpur 68 21 14N 75 49 E
Fajardo 121 18 20N 65 39W
Fakfak 73 3 0 S 132 15 E
Fakiya 43 42 10N 27 6 E
Fakobli 84 7 23N 7 23W
Fakse 49 55 15N 12 8 E
Fakse B. 49 55 11N 12 15 E
Fakse Ladeplads 49 55 11N 12 9 E
Faku 76 42 32N 123 21 E
Falaise 18 48 54N 0 12W
Falakrón Óros 44 41 15N 23 58 E
Falam 67 23 0N 93 45 E
Falces 32 42 24N 1 48W
Fălciu 46 46 17N 28 7 E
Falcon, C. 82 35 50N 0 50W
Falcon Dam 117 26 50N 99 20W
Falconara Marittima 39 43 37N 13 23 E
Falconer 112 42 7N 79 13W
Faléa 84 12 16N 11 17W
Falenki 55 58 22N 51 35 E
Faleshty 56 47 32N 27 44 E
Falfurrias 117 27 14N 98 8W
Falher 108 55 44N 117 15W
Falkenberg, Ger. 24 51 34N 13 13 E
Falkenberg, Sweden 49 56 54N 12 30 E
Falkensee 24 52 35N 13 6 E
Falkenstein 24 50 27N 12 24 E
Falkirk 14 56 0N 3 47W
Falkland Is. 128 51 30 S 59 0W
Falkland Is. Dependency □ 5 57 0 S 40 0W
Falkland Sd. 128 52 0 S 60 0W
Falkonéra 45 36 50N 23 52 E
Falköping 49 58 12N 13 33 E
Fall Brook 119 33 25N 117 12W
Fall River 114 41 45N 71 5W
Fall River Mills 118 41 1N 121 30W
Fallon, Mont., U.S.A. 116 46 52N 105 8W
Fallon, Nev., U.S.A. 118 39 31N 118 51W
Falls City, Nebr., U.S.A. 116 40 0N 95 40W
Falls City, Oreg., U.S.A. 118 44 54N 123 29W
Falls Creek 112 41 8N 78 49W
Falmouth, Jamaica 121 18 30N 77 40W
Falmouth, U.K. 13 50 9N 5 5W
Falmouth, U.S.A. 114 38 40N 84 20W
False Divi Pt. 70 15 43N 80 50 E
Falset 32 41 7N 0 50 E
Falso, C. 121 15 12N 83 21W
Falster 49 54 45N 11 55 E
Falsterbo 49 55 23N 12 50 E
Fălticeni 46 47 21N 26 20 E
Falun 48 60 37N 15 37 E
Famagusta 64 35 8N 33 55 E
Famatina, Sierra, de 124 27 30 S 68 0W
Family L. 109 51 54N 95 27W
Fan Xian 76 35 55N 115 38 E
Fana, Mali 84 13 0N 6 56W
Fana, Norway 47 60 16N 5 20 E
Fanárion 44 39 24N 21 47 E
Fandriana 93 20 14 S 47 21 E
Fang Xian 77 32 3N 110 40 E
Fangchang 77 31 5N 118 4 E
Fangcheng 77 33 18N 112 59 E
Fangliao 77 22 22N 120 38 E
Fangzheng 76 49 50N 128 48 E
Fani i Madh → 44 41 56N 20 16 E
Fanjiatun 76 43 40N 125 0 E
Fannich, L. 14 57 40N 5 0W
* Fanning I. 95 3 51N 159 22W
Fanny Bay 108 49 27N 124 48W
Fanø 49 55 25N 8 25 E
Fano 39 43 50N 13 0 E
Fanshaw 108 57 11N 133 30W
Fao (Al Fāw) 64 30 0N 48 30 E
Faqirwali 68 29 27N 73 0 E
Fara in Sabina 39 42 13N 12 44 E
Faradje 90 3 50N 29 45 E
Faradofay 93 25 2 S 47 0 E
Farafangana 93 22 49 S 47 50 E
Farâfra, El Wâhât el- 86 27 15N 28 20 E
Farāh 65 32 20N 62 7 E
Farāh □ 65 32 25N 62 10 E
Farahalana 93 14 26 S 50 10 E
Faraid, Gebel 86 23 33N 35 19 E
Faramana 84 11 56N 4 45W
Faranah 84 10 3N 10 45W
Farasān, Jazā'ir 63 16 45N 41 55 E
Faratsiho 93 19 24 S 46 57 E
Fardes → 33 37 35N 3 0W
Fareham 13 50 52N 1 11W
Farewell, C. 101 40 29 S 172 43 E
Farewell C. = Farvel, K. 4 59 48N 43 55W
Fargo 116 46 52N 96 40W
Fari'a → 62 32 12N 35 27 E
Faribault 116 44 15N 93 19W
Faridkot 68 30 44N 74 45 E
Faridpur 69 23 15N 89 55 E
Färila 48 61 48N 15 50 E
Farim 84 12 27N 15 9W
Farīmān 65 35 40N 59 49 E
Farina 99 30 3 S 138 15 E
Faringe 48 59 55N 18 7 E
Fâriskûr 86 31 20N 31 43 E
Farmakonisi 45 37 17N 27 8 E
Farmerville 117 32 48N 92 23W
Farmington, N. Mex., U.S.A. 119 36 45N 108 28W
Farmington, N.H., U.S.A. 113 43 25N 71 7W
Farmington, Utah, U.S.A. 118 41 0N 111 12W
Farmington → 113 41 51N 72 38W
Farmville 114 37 19N 78 22W
Farnborough 13 51 17N 0 46W
Farne Is. 12 55 38N 1 37W
Farnham 113 45 17N 72 59W
Faro, Brazil 127 2 10 S 56 39W
Faro, Port. 31 37 2N 7 55W
Faro □ 31 37 12N 8 10W
Faroe Is. 8 62 0N 7 0W
Farquhar, C. 96 23 50 S 113 36 E
Farrar → 14 57 30N 4 30W
Farrars, Cr. → 98 25 35 S 140 43 E
Farrāshband 65 28 57N 52 5 E
Farrell 114 41 13N 80 29W
Farrell Flat 99 33 48 S 138 48 E
Farrukhabad-cum-Fatehgarh 69 27 30N 79 32 E
Fars □ 65 29 30N 55 0 E
Fársala 44 39 17N 22 23 E
Farsø 49 56 46N 9 19 E
Farsund 47 58 5N 6 55 E
Fartak, Râs 64 28 5N 34 34 E
Fartura, Serra da 125 26 21 S 52 52W
Faru 85 12 48N 6 12 E
Farum 49 55 49N 12 21 E
Farvel, Kap 4 59 48N 43 55W
Farwell 117 34 25N 103 0W
Faryab □ 65 36 0N 65 0 E
Fasā 65 29 0N 53 39 E
Fasano 41 40 50N 17 20 E
Fashoda 87 9 50N 32 2 E
Fastnet Rock 15 51 22N 9 37W
Fastov 54 50 7N 29 57 E
Fatagar, Tanjung 73 2 46 S 131 57 E
Fatehgarh 69 27 25N 79 35 E
Fatehpur, Raj., India 68 28 0N 74 40 E
Fatehpur, Ut. P., India 69 25 56N 81 13 E
Fatesh 55 52 8N 35 57 E
Fatick 84 14 19N 16 27W
Fatima 107 47 24N 61 53W
Fátima 31 39 37N 8 39W
Fatoya 84 11 37N 9 10W
Faucille, Col de la 21 46 22N 6 2 E
Faucilles, Monts 19 48 5N 5 50 E
Faulkton 116 45 4N 99 8W
Faulquemont 19 49 3N 6 36 E
Fauquembergues 19 50 36N 2 5 E
Făurei 46 45 6N 27 19 E
Fauresmith 92 29 44 S 25 17 E
Fauske 50 67 17N 15 25 E
Fåvang 47 61 27N 10 11 E
Favara 40 37 19N 13 39 E
Favignana 40 37 56N 12 18 E
Favignana, I. 40 37 56N 12 18 E
Favone 21 41 47N 9 26 E
Favourable Lake 106 52 50N 93 39W
Fawn → 106 52 22N 88 20W
Faxaflói 50 64 29N 23 0W
Faya-Largeau 81 17 58N 19 6 E
Fayd 64 27 1N 42 52 E
Fayence 21 43 38N 6 42 E
Fayette, Ala., U.S.A. 115 33 40N 87 50W
Fayette, Mo., U.S.A. 116 39 10N 92 40W
Fayette, La 114 40 22N 86 52W
Fayetteville, Ark., U.S.A. 117 36 0N 94 5W
Fayetteville, N.C., U.S.A. 115 35 0N 78 58W
Fayetteville, Tenn., U.S.A. 115 35 8N 86 30W
Fayón 32 41 15N 0 20 E
Fazilka 68 30 27N 74 2 E
Fazilpur 68 29 18N 70 29 E
Fdérik 80 22 40N 12 45W
Feale → 15 52 26N 9 40W
Fear, C. 115 33 51N 78 0W
Feather → 118 38 47N 121 36W
Featherston 101 41 6 S 175 20 E
Featherstone 91 18 42 S 30 55 E
Fécamp 18 49 45N 0 22 E
Fedala = Mohammedia 82 33 44N 7 21W
Federación 124 31 0 S 57 55W
Fedjadj, Chott el 83 33 52N 9 14 E
Fedje 47 60 47N 4 43 E
Fehérgyarmat 27 48 0N 22 30 E
Fehmarn 24 54 26N 11 10 E
Fei Xian 77 35 18N 117 59 E
Feilding 101 40 13 S 175 35 E
Feira de Santana 127 12 15 S 38 57W
Fejér □ 27 47 9N 18 30 E
Fejø 49 54 55N 11 30 E
Fekete → 27 45 47N 18 15 E
Felanitx 33 39 28N 3 9 E
Feldbach 26 46 57N 15 52 E
Feldberg, Germ., E. 24 53 20N 13 26 E
Feldberg, Germ., W. 25 47 51N 7 58 E
Feldkirch 26 47 15N 9 37 E
Feldkirchen 26 46 44N 14 6 E
Felipe Carrillo Puerto 120 19 38N 88 3W
Felixstowe 13 51 58N 1 22 E
Felletin 20 45 53N 2 11 E
Feltre 39 46 1N 11 55 E
Femø 49 54 58N 11 53 E
Femunden 47 62 10N 11 53 E
Fen He → 76 35 36N 110 42 E
Fenelon Falls 112 44 32N 78 45W
Feneroa 87 13 5N 39 3 E
Feng Xian, Jiangsu, China 77 34 43N 116 35 E
Feng Xian, Shaanxi, China 77 33 54N 106 40 E
Fengári 44 40 25N 25 32 E
Fengcheng, Jiangxi, China 77 28 12N 115 48 E
Fengcheng, Liaoning, China 76 40 28N 124 5 E
Fengdu 77 29 55N 107 41 E
Fengfeng 76 36 28N 114 8 E
Fenghua 77 29 40N 121 25 E
Fenghuang 77 27 57N 109 29 E
Fengjie 75 31 5N 109 36 E
Fengkai 77 23 24N 111 30 E
Fengle 77 31 29N 112 29 E
Fengning 76 41 10N 116 33 E
Fengtai 76 39 50N 116 18 E
Fengxian 77 30 55N 121 26 E
Fengxiang 77 34 29N 107 25 E
Fengxin 77 28 41N 115 18 E
Fengyang 77 32 51N 117 29 E
Fengzhen 76 40 25N 113 2 E
Feni Is. 98 4 0 S 153 40 E
Fenit 15 52 17N 9 51W
Fennimore 116 42 58N 90 41W
Fenny 69 22 55N 91 32 E
Feno, C. de 21 41 58N 8 33 E
Fenoarivo Afovoany 93 18 26 S 46 34 E
Fenoarivo Atsinanana 93 17 22 S 49 25 E
Fens, The 12 52 45N 0 2 E
Fenton 114 42 47N 83 44W
Fenyang 76 37 18N 111 48 E
Feodosiya 56 45 2N 35 28 E
Fer, C. de 83 37 3N 7 10 E
Ferdow 65 33 58N 58 2 E
Fère-Champenoise 19 48 45N 4 0 E
Fère-en-Tardenois 19 49 10N 3 30 E
Fère, La 19 49 40N 3 20 E
Ferentino 40 41 42N 13 14 E
Ferfer 63 5 4N 45 9 E
Fergana 58 40 23N 71 19 E
Fergus 106 43 43N 80 24W
Fergus Falls 116 46 18N 96 7W
Fergusson I. 98 9 30 S 150 45 E
Fériana 83 34 59N 8 33 E
Feričanci 42 45 32N 18 0 E
Ferkane 83 34 37N 7 26 E
Ferkéssédougou 84 9 35N 5 6W
Ferlach 26 46 26N 14 18 E
Ferland 106 50 19N 88 27W

* *Renamed Tabuaeran*

Fortune B. Galley Hd.

Fortune B. 107 47 30N 55 22W
Forūr 65 26 20N 54 30 E
Fos 21 43 26N 4 56 E
Foshan 75 23 4N 113 5 E
Fossacesia 39 42 15N 14 30 E
Fossano 38 44 33N 7 40 E
Fossil 118 45 0N 120 9W
Fossilbrook P.O. 98 17 47 S 144 29 E
Fossombrone 39 43 41N 12 49 E
Fosston 116 47 33N 95 39W
Foster 113 45 17N 72 30W
Foster → 109 55 47N 105 49W
Fostoria 114 41 8N 83 25W
Fougamou 88 1 16 S 10 30 E
Fougères 18 48 21N 1 14W
Foul Pt. 70 8 35N 81 18 E
Foulness I. 13 51 36N 0 55 E
Foulness Pt. 13 51 36N 0 59 E
Foulpointe 93 17 41 S 49 31 E
Foum Assaka 82 29 8N 10 24W
Foum Zguid 82 30 2N 6 59W
Foumban 85 5 45N 10 50 E
Foundiougne 84 14 5N 16 32W
Fountain, Colo., U.S.A. 116 38 42N 104 40W
Fountain, Utah, U.S.A. 118 39 41N 111 37W
Fourchambault 19 47 0N 3 3 E
Fourchu 107 45 43N 60 17W
Fourmies 19 50 1N 4 2 E
Fournás 45 39 3N 21 52 E
Foúrnoi, Greece 45 37 36N 26 32 E
Foúrnoi, Greece 45 37 36N 26 28 E
Fours 19 46 50N 3 42 E
Fouta Djalon 84 11 20N 12 10W
Foux, Cap-à- 121 19 43N 73 27W
Foveaux Str. 101 46 42 S 168 10 E
Fowey 13 50 20N 4 39W
Fowler, Calif., U.S.A. 119 36 41N 119 41W
Fowler, Colo., U.S.A. 116 38 10N 104 0W
Fowler, Kans., U.S.A. 117 37 28N 100 7W
Fowlerton 117 28 26N 98 50W
Fownhope 13 52 0N 2 37W
Fox → 109 56 3N 93 18W
Fox Valley 109 50 30N 109 25W
Foxe Basin 105 68 30N 77 0W
Foxe Channel 105 66 0N 80 0W
Foxe Pen. 105 65 0N 76 0W
Foxen, L. 48 59 25N 11 55 E
Foxpark 118 41 4N 106 6W
Foxton 101 40 29 S 175 18 E
Foyle, Lough 15 55 6N 7 8W
Foynes 15 52 37N 9 5W
Foz 30 43 33N 7 20W
Fôz do Cunene 92 17 15 S 11 48 E
Foz do Gregório 126 6 47 S 70 44W
Foz do Iguaçu 125 25 30 S 54 30W
Frackville 113 40 46N 76 15W
Fraga 32 41 32N 0 21 E
Framingham 113 42 18N 71 26W
Frampol 28 50 41N 22 40 E
Franca 127 20 33 S 47 30W
Francavilla al Mare 39 42 25N 14 16 E
Francavilla Fontana 41 40 32N 17 35 E
France ■ 17 47 0N 3 0 E
Frances 99 36 41 S 140 55 E
Frances → 108 60 16N 129 10W
Frances L. 108 61 23N 129 30W
Franceville 88 1 40 S 13 32 E
Franche-Comté 19 46 30N 5 50 E
Francisco I. Madero, Coahuila, Mexico 120 25 48N 103 18W
Francisco I. Madero, Durango, Mexico 120 24 32N 104 22W
Francofonte 41 37 13N 14 50 E
François, Can. 107 47 35N 56 45W
François, Mart. 121 14 38N 60 57W
François L. 108 54 0N 125 30W
Franeker 16 53 12N 5 33 E
Frankado 87 12 30N 43 12 E
Frankenberg 24 51 3N 8 47 E
Frankenthal 25 49 32N 8 21 E
Frankenwald 25 50 18N 11 36 E
Frankfort, Madag. 93 27 17 S 28 30 E
Frankfort, Ind., U.S.A. 114 40 20N 86 33W
Frankfort, Kans., U.S.A. 116 39 42N 96 26W
Frankfort, Ky., U.S.A. 114 38 12N 84 52W
Frankfort, Mich., U.S.A. 114 44 38N 86 14W
Frankfurt □ 24 52 30N 14 0 E
Frankfurt am Main 25 50 7N 8 40 E
Frankfurt an der Oder 24 52 50N 14 31 E
Fränkische Alb 25 49 20N 11 30 E
Fränkische Rezal → 25 49 11N 11 1 E
Fränkische Saale → 25 50 30N 9 42 E
Fränkische Schweiz 25 49 45N 11 10 E
Franklin, Ky., U.S.A. 115 36 40N 86 30W
Franklin, La., U.S.A. 117 29 45N 91 30W
Franklin, Mass., U.S.A. 113 42 4N 71 23W
Franklin, N.H., U.S.A. 114 43 28N 71 39W
Franklin, N.J., U.S.A. 113 41 9N 74 38W
Franklin, Nebr., U.S.A. 116 40 9N 98 55W
Franklin, Pa., U.S.A. 114 41 22N 79 45W
Franklin, Tenn., U.S.A. 115 35 54N 86 53W
Franklin, Va., U.S.A. 115 36 40N 76 58W
Franklin, W. Va., U.S.A. 114 38 38N 79 21W
• Franklin □ 105 71 0N 99 0W
Franklin B. 104 69 45N 126 0W
Franklin D. Roosevelt L. 118 48 30N 118 16W
Franklin I. 5 76 10 S 168 30 E
Franklin, L. 118 40 20N 115 26W
Franklin Mts. 104 65 0N 125 0W
Franklin Str. 104 72 0N 96 0W
Franklinton 117 30 53N 90 10W
Franklinville 112 42 21N 78 28W
Franks Peak 118 43 50N 109 5W
Frankston 99 38 8 S 145 8 E
Fränsta 48 62 30N 16 11 E
Frantsa Josifa, Zemlya 58 82 0N 55 0 E
Franz 106 48 25N 84 30W
Franz Josef Land = Frantsa Josifa 58 79 0N 62 0 E
Franzburg 24 54 9N 12 52 E
Frascati 40 41 48N 12 41 E
Fraser →, B.C., Can. 108 49 7N 123 11W
Fraser →, Newf., Can. 107 56 39N 62 10W
Fraser I. 97 25 15 S 153 10 E
Fraser Lake 108 54 0N 124 50W
Fraserburg 92 31 55 S 21 30 E
Fraserburgh 14 57 41N 2 0W
Fraserdale 106 49 55N 81 37W
Frashëri 44 40 23N 20 26 E
Frasne 19 46 50N 6 10 E
Frauenfeld 25 47 34N 8 54 E
Fray Bentos 124 33 10 S 58 15W
Frechilla 30 42 8N 4 50W
Fredericia 49 55 34N 9 45 E
Frederick, Md., U.S.A. 114 39 25N 77 23W
Frederick, Okla., U.S.A. 117 34 22N 99 0W
Frederick, S.D., U.S.A. 116 45 55N 98 29W
Frederick Reef 97 20 58 S 154 23 E
Frederick Sd. 108 57 10N 134 0W
Fredericksburg, Tex., U.S.A. 117 30 17N 98 55W
Fredericksburg, Va., U.S.A. 114 38 16N 77 29W
Frederickstown 117 37 35N 90 15W
Fredericton 107 45 57N 66 40W
Fredericton Junc. 107 45 41N 66 40W
Frederikshavn 49 57 28N 10 31 E
Frederikssund 49 55 50N 12 3 E
Fredonia, Ariz., U.S.A. 119 36 59N 112 36W
Fredonia, Kans., U.S.A. 117 37 34N 95 50W
Fredonia, N.Y., U.S.A. 114 42 26N 79 20W
Fredrikstad 47 59 13N 10 57 E
Freehold 113 40 15N 74 18W
Freeland 113 41 3N 75 48W
Freeling, Mt. 96 22 35 S 133 06 E
Freels, C. 107 49 15N 53 30W
Freeman 116 43 25N 97 20W
Freeport, Bahamas 121 26 30N 78 47W
Freeport, Can. 107 44 15N 66 20W
Freeport, Ill., U.S.A. 116 42 18N 89 40W
Freeport, N.Y., U.S.A. 114 40 39N 73 35W
Freeport, Tex., U.S.A. 117 28 55N 95 22W
Freetown 84 8 30N 13 17W
Frégate, L. 106 53 15N 74 45W
Fregenal de la Sierra 31 38 10N 6 39W
Fregene 40 41 50N 12 12 E
Fregeneda, La 30 40 58N 6 54W
Fréhel, C. 18 48 40N 2 20W
Frei 47 63 4N 7 48 E
Freiberg 24 50 55N 13 20 E
Freibourg = Fribourg 25 46 49N 7 9 E
Freiburg, Baden, Ger. 25 48 0N 7 52 E
Freiburg, Niedersachsen, Ger. 24 53 49N 9 17 E
Freire 128 38 54 S 72 38W
Freirina 124 28 30 S 71 10W
Freising 25 48 24N 11 47 E
Freistadt 26 48 30N 14 30 E
Freital 24 51 0N 13 40 E
Fréjus 21 43 25N 6 44 E
Fremantle 96 32 7 S 115 47 E
Fremont, Mich., U.S.A. 114 43 29N 85 59W
Fremont, Nebr., U.S.A. 116 41 30N 96 30W
Fremont, Ohio, U.S.A. 114 41 20N 83 5W
Fremont → 119 38 15N 110 20W
Fremont, L. 118 43 0N 109 50W
French → 114 41 30N 80 2W
French Guiana ■ 127 4 0N 53 0W
French I. 100 38 20 S 145 22 E
French Terr. of Afars & Issas = Djibouti ■ 87 11 30N 42 15 E
Frenchglen 118 42 48N 119 0W
Frenchman → 118 48 24N 107 5W
Frenchman Butte 109 53 35N 109 38W
Frenchman Creek → 116 40 13N 100 50W
Frenda 82 35 2N 1 1 E
Fresco → 127 7 15 S 51 30W
Freshfield, C. 5 68 25 S 151 10 E
Fresnay 18 48 17N 0 1 E
Fresnillo 120 23 10N 103 0W
Fresno 119 36 47N 119 50W
Fresno Alhandiga 30 40 42N 5 37W
Fresno Res. 118 48 40N 110 0W
Freudenstadt 25 48 27N 8 25 E
Frévent 19 50 15N 2 17 E
Freycinet Pen. 97 42 10 S 148 25 E
Freyung 25 48 48N 13 33 E
Fria 84 10 27N 13 38W
Fria, C. 92 18 0 S 12 0 E
Frias 124 28 40 S 65 5W
Fribourg 25 46 49N 7 9 E
Fribourg □ 25 46 40N 7 0 E
Fridafors 49 56 25N 14 39 E
Friedberg, Bayern, Ger. 25 48 21N 10 59 E
Friedberg, Hessen, Ger. 25 50 21N 8 46 E
Friedland 24 53 40N 13 33 E
Friedrichshafen 25 47 39N 9 29 E
Friedrichskoog 24 54 1N 8 52 E
Friedrichsort 24 54 24N 10 11 E
Friedrichstadt 24 54 23N 9 6 E
Friendly (Tonga) Is. 101 22 0 S 173 0W
Friesach 26 46 57N 14 24 E
Friesack 24 52 43N 12 35 E
Friesland □ 16 53 5N 5 50 E
Friesoythe 24 53 1N 7 51 E
Frijoles 120 9 11N 79 48W
Frillesås 49 57 20N 12 12 E
Frinnaryd 49 57 55N 14 50 E
Frio → 117 28 30N 98 10W
Friona 117 34 40N 102 42W
Frisian Is. 24 53 30N 6 0 E
Fristad 49 57 50N 13 0 E
Fritch 117 35 40N 101 35W
Fritsla 49 57 33N 12 47 E
Fritzlar 24 51 8N 9 19 E
Friuli-Venezia Giulia □ 39 46 0N 13 0 E
Friville-Escarbotin 19 50 5N 1 33 E
Frobisher B. 105 62 30N 66 0W
Frobisher Bay 105 63 44N 68 31W
Frobisher L. 109 56 20N 108 15W
Frohavet 50 63 50N 9 35 E
Froid 116 48 20N 104 29W
Frolovo 57 49 45N 43 40 E
Fromberg 118 42 25N 108 58W
Frombork 28 54 21N 19 41 E
Frome 13 51 16N 2 17W
Frome, L. 97 30 45 S 139 45 E
Fromentine 18 46 53N 2 9W
Frómista 30 42 16N 4 25W
Front Range 118 40 0N 105 40W
Front Royal 114 38 55N 78 10W
Fronteira 31 39 3N 7 39W
Frontera 120 18 30N 92 40W
Frontignan 20 43 27N 3 45 E
Frosinone 40 41 38N 13 20 E
Frosolone 41 41 34N 14 27 E
Frostburg 114 39 43N 78 57W
Frostisen 50 68 14N 17 10 E
Frouard 19 48 47N 6 8 E
Frövi 48 59 28N 15 24 E
Frøya 47 63 43N 8 40 E
Fruges 19 50 30N 2 8 E
Frumoasa 46 46 28N 25 48 E
Frunze 58 42 54N 74 46 E
Fruška Gora 42 45 7N 19 30 E
Frutal 127 20 0 S 49 0W
Frutigen 25 46 35N 7 38 E
Frýdek-Místek 27 49 40N 18 20 E
Frýdlant, Severočeský, Czech. 26 50 56N 15 9 E
Frýdlant, Severomoravsky, Czech. 27 49 35N 18 20 E
Fryvaldov = Jeseník 27 50 0N 17 8 E
Fthiótis □ 45 38 50N 22 25 E
Fu Xian, Liaoning, China 76 39 38N 121 58 E
Fu Xian, Shaanxi, China 76 36 0N 109 20 E
Fucécchio 38 43 44N 10 51 E
Fucheng 76 37 50N 116 10 E
Fuchou = Fuzhou 75 26 5N 119 16 E
Fuchuan 77 24 50N 111 5 E
Fuchun Jiang → 77 30 5N 120 5 E
Fúcino, Conca del 39 42 1N 13 31 E
Fuding 77 27 20N 120 12 E
Fuencaliente 31 38 25N 4 18W
Fuengirola 31 36 32N 4 41W
Fuente Álamo 33 38 44N 1 24W
Fuente Álamo 33 37 42N 1 6W
Fuente de Cantos 31 38 15N 6 18W
Fuente de San Esteban, La 30 40 49N 6 15W
Fuente del Maestre 31 38 31N 6 28W
Fuente el Fresno 31 39 14N 3 46W
Fuente Ovejuna 31 38 15N 5 25W
Fuentes de Andalucía 31 37 28N 5 20W
Fuentes de Ebro 32 41 31N 0 38W
Fuentes de León 31 38 5N 6 32W
Fuentes de Oñoro 30 40 33N 6 52W
Fuentesaúco 30 41 15N 5 30W
Fuerte → 120 25 50N 109 25W
Fuerte Olimpo 124 21 0 S 57 51W
Fuerteventura 80 28 30N 14 0W
Fŭget, Munţii 46 45 50N 22 9 E
Fugløysund 50 70 15N 20 20 E
Fugou 77 34 3N 114 25 E
Fuhai 75 47 2N 87 25 E
Fuji-no-miya 74 35 10N 138 40 E
Fuji-San 74 35 22N 138 44 E
Fujian □ 75 26 0N 118 0 E
Fujin 76 47 16N 132 1 E
Fujisawa 74 35 22N 139 29 E
Fukien = Fujian □ 75 26 0N 118 0 E
Fukuchiyama 74 35 19N 135 9 E
Fukui 74 36 0N 136 10 E
Fukui □ 74 36 0N 136 12 E
Fukuoka 74 33 39N 130 21 E
Fukuoka □ 74 33 30N 131 0 E
Fukushima 74 37 44N 140 28 E
Fukushima □ 74 37 30N 140 15 E
Fukuyama 74 34 35N 133 20 E
Fulda 24 50 32N 9 41 E
Fulda → 24 51 27N 9 40 E
Fuling 77 29 40N 107 20 E
Fullerton, Calif., U.S.A. 119 33 52N 117 58W
Fullerton, Nebr., U.S.A. 116 41 25N 98 0W
Fulton, Mo., U.S.A. 116 38 50N 91 55W
Fulton, N.Y., U.S.A. 114 43 20N 76 22W
Fulton, Tenn., U.S.A. 115 36 31N 88 53W
Fuluälven 48 61 18N 13 4 E
Fulufjället 48 61 32N 12 41 E
Fumay 19 50 0N 4 40 E
Fumel 20 44 30N 0 58 E
Funabashi 74 35 45N 140 0 E
Funafuti 94 8 30 S 179 0 E
Funchal 80 32 38N 16 54W
Fundación 126 10 31N 74 11W
Fundão 30 40 8N 7 30W
Fundy, B. of 107 45 0N 66 0W
Funing, Jiangsu, China 77 33 45N 119 50 E
Funing, Yunnan, China 77 23 35N 105 45 E
Funiu Shan 77 33 30N 112 20 E
Funsi 84 10 21N 1 54W
Funtua 85 11 30N 7 18 E
Fuping 76 38 48N 114 12 E
Fuqing 77 25 41N 119 21 E
Fur 49 56 50N 9 0 E
Furāt, Nahr al → 64 31 0N 47 25 E
Furmanov 55 57 10N 41 9 E
Furmanovo 57 49 42N 49 25 E
Furnas, Reprêsa de 125 20 50 S 45 0W
Furneaux Group 97 40 10 S 147 50 E
Furness, Pen. 12 54 12N 3 10W
Fürstenau 24 52 32N 7 40 E
Fürstenberg 24 53 11N 13 9 E
Fürstenfeld 26 47 3N 16 3 E
Fürstenfeldbruck 25 48 10N 11 15 E
Fürstenwalde 24 52 20N 14 3 E
Fürth 25 49 29N 11 0 E
Furth im Wald 25 49 19N 12 51 E
Furtwangen 25 48 3N 8 14 E
Furudal 48 61 10N 15 11 E
Furusund 48 59 40N 18 55 E
Fury and Hecla Str. 105 69 56N 84 0W
Fusa 47 60 12N 5 37 E
Fusagasuga 126 4 21N 74 22W
Fuscaldo 41 39 25N 16 1 E
Fushan 76 37 30N 121 15 E
Fushë Arrëzi 44 42 4N 20 2 E
Fushun 76 41 50N 123 56 E
Fusong 76 42 20N 127 15 E
Füssen 25 47 35N 10 43 E
Fusui 77 22 40N 107 56 E
Futuna 94 14 25 S 178 20 E
Fuwa 86 31 12N 30 33 E
Fuxin 76 42 5N 121 48 E
Fuyang, Anhui, China 77 33 0N 115 48 E
Fuyang, Zhejiang, China 77 30 5N 119 57 E
Fuyu 76 45 12N 124 43 E
Fuyuan 75 48 20N 134 5 E
Füzesgyarmat 27 47 6N 21 14 E
Fuzhou, Fujian, China 75 26 5N 119 16 E
Fuzhou, Jiangxi, China 75 28 0N 116 25 E
Fylde 12 53 50N 2 58W
Fyn 49 55 20N 10 30 E
Fyne, L. 14 56 0N 5 20W
Fyns Amtskommune □ 49 55 15N 10 30 E
Fyresvatn 47 59 6N 8 10 E

G

Gaanda 85 10 10N 12 27 E
Gabarin 85 11 8N 10 27 E
Gabas → 20 43 46N 0 42W
Gabela 88 11 0 S 14 24 E
Gabès 83 33 53N 10 2 E
Gabès, Golfe de 83 34 0N 10 30 E
Gabgaba, W. 86 22 10N 33 5 E
Gabin 28 52 23N 19 41 E
Gabon ■ 88 0 10 S 10 0 E
Gaborone 92 24 45 S 25 57 E
Gabriels 113 44 26N 74 12W
Gabrovo 43 42 52N 25 19 E
Gacé 18 48 49N 0 20 E
Gach Sārān 65 30 15N 50 45 E
Gacko 42 43 10N 18 33 E
Gadag-Batgeri 70 15 30N 75 45 E
Gadamai 87 17 11N 36 10 E
Gadap 68 25 5N 67 28 E
Gadarwara 68 22 50N 78 50 E
Gadebusch 24 53 41N 11 6 E
Gadein 87 8 10N 28 45 E
Gadhada 68 22 0N 71 35 E
Gádor, Sierra de 33 36 57N 2 45W
Gadsden, Ala., U.S.A. 115 34 1N 86 0W
Gadsden, Ariz., U.S.A. 119 32 35N 114 47W
Gadwal 70 16 10N 77 50 E
Gadyach 54 50 21N 34 0 E
Găeşti 46 44 48N 25 19 E
Gaeta 40 41 12N 13 35 E
Gaeta, G. di 40 41 0N 13 25 E
Gaffney 115 35 3N 81 40W
Gafsa 83 32 24N 8 43 E
Gagarin (Gzhatsk) 54 55 38N 35 0 E
Gagetown 107 45 46N 66 10W
Gagino 55 55 15N 45 1 E
Gagliano del Capo 41 39 50N 18 23 E
Gagnef 48 60 36N 15 5 E
Gagnoa 84 6 56N 5 16W
Gagnon 107 51 50N 68 5W
Gagnon, L. 109 62 3N 110 27W
Gagra 57 43 20N 40 10 E
Gahini 90 1 50 S 30 30 E
Gahmar 69 25 27N 83 49 E
Gai Xian 76 40 22N 122 20 E
Gaibanda 69 25 20N 89 36 E
Gaïdhouronisi 45 34 53N 25 41 E
Gail 117 32 48N 101 25W
Gail → 26 46 36N 13 53 E
Gaillac 20 43 54N 1 54 E
Gaillon 18 49 10N 1 20 E
Gaines 112 41 46N 77 35W
Gainesville, Fla., U.S.A. 115 29 38N 82 20W
Gainesville, Ga., U.S.A. 115 34 17N 83 47W
Gainesville, Mo., U.S.A. 117 36 35N 92 26W
Gainesville, Tex., U.S.A. 117 33 40N 97 10W
Gainsborough 12 53 23N 0 46W
Gairdner L. 96 31 30 S 136 0 E
Gairloch, L. 14 57 43N 5 45W
Gaj 42 45 28N 17 3 E
Gal Oya Res. 70 7 5N 81 30 E
Galachipa 69 22 8N 90 26 E
Galán, Cerro 124 25 55 S 66 52W
Galana → 90 3 9 S 40 8 E
Galangue 89 13 42 S 16 9 E
Galanta 27 48 11N 17 45 E
Galápagos 95 0 0 89 0W
Galas → 71 4 55N 101 57 E
Galashiels 14 55 37N 2 50W
Galatás 45 37 30N 23 26 E
Galaţi 46 45 27N 28 2 E
Galaţi □ 46 45 45N 27 30 E
Galatina 41 40 10N 18 10 E
Galátone 41 40 8N 18 3 E
Galax 115 36 42N 80 57W
Galaxidhion 45 38 22N 22 23 E
Galbraith 98 16 25 S 141 30 E
Galcaio 63 6 30N 47 30 E
Galdhøpiggen 47 61 38N 8 18 E
Galela 73 1 50N 127 49 E
Galera 33 37 45N 2 33W
Galesburg 116 40 57N 90 23W
Galeton 112 41 43N 77 40W
Gali 57 42 37N 41 46 E
Galicea Mare 46 44 4N 23 19 E
Galich 55 58 23N 42 12 E
Galiche 43 43 34N 23 50 E
Galicia 30 42 43N 7 45W
Galilee = Hagalil 62 32 53N 35 18 E
Galilee, L. 98 22 20 S 145 50 E
Galion 112 40 43N 82 48W
Galite, Is. de la 83 37 30N 8 59 E
Galiuro Mts. 119 32 40N 110 30W
Gallabat 81 12 58N 36 11 E
Gallarate 38 45 40N 8 48 E
Gallardon 19 48 32N 1 47 E
Gallatin 115 36 24N 86 27W
Galle 70 6 5N 80 10 E
Gállego → 32 41 39N 0 51W
Gallegos → 128 51 35 S 69 0W
Galley Hd. 15 51 32N 8 56W

• *Now part of Central Arctic and Baffin* □

Galliate	38	45 27N	8 44 E
Gallinas, Pta.	126	12 28N	71 40W
Gallipoli	41	40 8N	18 0 E
Gallipoli = Gelibolu	44	40 28N	26 43 E
Gallipolis	114	38 50N	82 10W
Gällivare	50	67 9N	20 40 E
Gallo, C.	40	38 13N	13 19 E
Gallocanta, Laguna de	32	40 58N	1 30W
Galloway	14	55 0N	4 25W
Galloway, Mull of	14	54 38N	4 50W
Gallup	119	35 30N	108 45W
Gallur	32	41 52N	1 19W
Gal'on	62	31 38N	34 51 E
Galong	99	34 37 S	148 34 E
Galtström	48	62 10N	17 30 E
Galtür	26	46 58N	10 11 E
Galty Mts.	15	52 22N	8 10W
Galtymore	15	52 22N	8 12W
Galva	116	41 10N	90 0W
Galve de Sorbe	32	41 13N	3 10W
Galveston	117	29 15N	94 48W
Galveston B.	117	29 30N	94 50W
Gálvez, Argent.	124	32 0 S	61 14W
Gálvez, Spain	31	39 42N	4 16W
Galway	15	53 16N	9 4W
Galway □	15	53 16N	9 3W
Galway B.	15	53 10N	9 20W
Gamari, L.	87	11 32N	41 40 E
Gamawa	85	12 10N	10 31 E
Gambaga	85	10 30N	0 28W
Gambat	68	27 17N	68 26 E
Gambela	87	8 14N	34 38 E
Gambia ■	84	13 25N	16 0W
Gambia →	84	13 28N	16 34W
Gamboa	120	9 8N	79 42W
Gamboli	68	29 53N	68 24 E
* Gambos	89	14 37 S	14 40 E
Gamerco	119	35 33N	108 56W
Gammon →	109	51 24N	95 44W
Gammouda	83	35 3N	9 39 E
Gan	20	43 12N	0 27W
Gan Goriama, Mts.	85	7 44N	12 45 E
Gan Jiang →	75	29 15N	116 0 E
Gan Shemu'el	62	32 28N	34 56 E
Gan Yavne	62	31 48N	34 42 E
Ganado, Ariz., U.S.A.	119	35 46N	109 41W
Ganado, Tex., U.S.A.	117	29 4N	96 31W
Gananoque	106	44 20N	76 10W
Ganaveh	65	29 35N	50 35 E
Gancheng	77	18 51N	108 37 E
Gand = Gent	16	51 2N	3 42 E
Ganda	89	13 3 S	14 35 E
Gandak →	69	25 39N	85 13 E
Gandava	68	28 32N	67 32 E
Gander	107	48 58N	54 35W
Gander L.	107	48 58N	54 35W
Ganderowe Falls	91	17 20 S	29 10 E
Gandesa	32	41 3N	0 26 E
Gandhi Sagar	68	24 40N	75 40 E
Gandi	85	12 55N	5 49 E
Gandia	33	38 58N	0 9W
Gandino	38	45 50N	9 52 E
Gandole	85	8 28N	11 35 E
Ganedidalem = Gani	73	0 48 S	128 14 E
Ganetti	86	18 0N	31 10 E
Ganga →	69	23 20N	90 30 E
Ganga, Mouths of the	69	21 30N	90 0 E
Ganganagar	68	29 56N	73 56 E
Gangapur	68	26 32N	76 49 E
Gangara	85	14 35N	8 29 E
Gangavati	70	15 30N	76 36 E
Gangaw	67	22 5N	94 5 E
Gangdisê Shan	67	31 20N	81 0 E
Ganges	20	43 56N	3 42 E
Ganges = Ganga →	69	23 20N	90 30 E
Gangoh	68	29 46N	77 18 E
Gangtok	69	27 20N	88 37 E
Gani	73	0 48 S	128 14 E
Ganj	68	27 45N	78 57 E
Gannat	20	46 7N	3 11 E
Gannett Pk.	118	43 15N	109 38W
Gannvalley	116	44 3N	98 57W
Ganquan	76	36 20N	109 20 E
Gänserdorf	27	48 20N	16 43 E
Gansu □	75	36 0N	104 0 E
Ganta (Gompa)	84	7 15N	8 59W
Gantheaume B.	96	27 40 S	114 10 E
Gantheaume, C.	99	36 4 S	137 32 E
Gantsevichi	54	52 49N	26 30 E
Ganyu	77	34 50N	119 8 E
Ganyushkino	57	46 35N	49 20 E
Ganzhou	75	25 51N	114 56 E
Gao □	85	18 0N	1 0 E
Gao Bang	71	22 37N	106 18 E
Gao'an	77	28 26N	115 17 E
Gaomi	76	36 20N	119 42 E
Gaoping	76	35 45N	112 55 E
Gaoua	84	10 20N	3 8W
Gaoual	84	11 45N	13 25W
Gaoxiong	75	22 38N	120 18 E
Gaoyou	77	32 47N	119 26 E
Gaoyou Hu	77	32 45N	119 20 E
Gaoyuan	76	37 8N	117 58 E
Gap	21	44 33N	6 5 E
Gar	75	32 10N	79 58 E
Garachiné	121	8 0N	78 12W
Garanhuns	127	8 50 S	36 30W
Garawe	84	4 35N	8 0W
Garba Tula	90	0 30N	38 32 E
Garber	117	36 30N	97 36W
Garberville	118	40 11N	123 50W
Gard	63	9 30N	49 6 E
Gard □	21	44 2N	4 10 E
Gard →	21	43 51N	4 37 E
Garda, L. di	38	45 40N	10 40 E
Gardala	81	5 40N	37 25 E
Gardanne	21	43 27N	5 27 E
Garde L.	109	62 50N	106 13W
Gardelegen	24	52 32N	11 21 E
Garden City, Kans., U.S.A.	117	38 0N	100 45W
Garden City, Tex., U.S.A.	117	31 52N	101 28W
Gardez	66	33 37N	69 9 E

* *Renamed Kipungo*

Gardhíki	45	38 50N	21 55 E
Gardiner	118	45 3N	110 42W
Gardiners I.	113	41 4N	72 5W
Gardner	114	42 35N	72 0W
Gardner Canal	108	53 27N	128 8W
Gardnerville	118	38 59N	119 47W
Gardno, Jezioro	28	54 40N	17 7 E
Garešnica	42	45 36N	16 56 E
Garéssio	38	44 12N	8 1 E
Garfield	118	47 3N	117 8W
Gargaliánoi	45	37 4N	21 38 E
Gargano, Mte.	41	41 43N	15 43 E
Gargans, Mt.	20	45 37N	1 39 E
Gargouna	85	15 56N	0 13 E
Garhshankar	68	31 13N	76 11 E
Garibaldi Prov. Park	108	49 50N	122 40W
Garies	92	30 32 S	17 59 E
Garigliano →	40	41 13N	13 44 E
Garissa	90	0 25 S	39 40 E
Garissa □	90	0 20 S	40 0 E
Garkida	85	10 27N	12 36 E
Garko	85	11 45N	8 53 E
Garland	118	41 47N	112 10W
Garlasco	38	45 11N	8 55 E
Garm	58	39 0N	70 20 E
Garmisch-Partenkirchen	25	47 30N	11 5 E
Garmsâr	65	35 20N	52 25 E
Garner	116	43 4N	93 37W
Garnett	116	38 18N	95 12W
Garo Hills	69	25 30N	90 30 E
Garob	92	26 37 S	16 0 E
Garoe	63	8 25N	48 33 E
Garonne →	20	45 2N	0 36W
Garoua (Garwa)	85	9 19N	13 21 E
Garrel	24	52 58N	7 59 E
Garrigues	20	43 40N	3 30 E
Garrison, Mont., U.S.A.	118	46 30N	112 56W
Garrison, N.D., U.S.A.	116	47 39N	101 27W
Garrison, Tex., U.S.A.	117	31 50N	94 28W
Garrison Res.	116	47 30N	102 0W
Garrovillas	31	39 40N	6 33W
Garrucha	33	37 11N	1 49W
Garry →	14	56 47N	3 47W
Garry L.	104	65 58N	100 18W
Garsen	90	2 20 S	40 5 E
Garson →	109	56 20N	110 1W
Garson L.	109	56 19N	110 2W
Gartempe →	20	46 47N	0 49 E
Gartz	24	53 12N	14 23 E
Garu	85	10 55N	0 11W
Garut	73	7 14 S	107 53 E
Garvão	31	37 42N	8 21W
Garvie Mts.	101	45 30 S	168 50 E
Garwa	69	24 11N	83 47 E
Garwolin	28	51 55N	21 38 E
Gary	114	41 35N	87 20W
Garz	24	54 17N	13 21 E
Garzê	75	31 39N	99 58 E
Garzón	126	2 10N	75 40W
Gasan Kuli	58	37 40N	54 20 E
Gascogne	20	43 45N	0 20 E
Gascogne, G. de	32	44 0N	2 0W
Gascony = Gascogne	20	43 45N	0 20 E
Gascoyne →	96	24 52 S	113 37 E
Gascueña	32	40 18N	2 31W
Gash, Wadi →	87	16 48N	35 51 E
Gashaka	85	7 20N	11 29 E
Gashua	85	12 54N	11 0 E
Gaspé	107	48 52N	64 30W
Gaspé, C.	107	48 48N	64 7W
Gaspé, Pén. de	107	48 45N	65 40W
Gaspésie, Parc Prov. de la	107	48 55N	65 50W
Gassaway	114	38 42N	80 43W
Gássino Torinese	38	45 8N	7 50 E
Gassol	85	8 34N	10 25 E
Gastonia	115	35 17N	81 10W
Gastoúni	45	37 51N	21 15 E
Gastoúri	44	39 34N	19 54 E
Gastre	128	42 20 S	69 15W
Gata, C. de	33	36 41N	2 13W
Gata, Sierra de	30	40 20N	6 45W
Gataga →	108	58 35N	126 59W
Gătaia	42	45 26N	21 30 E
Gatchina	54	59 35N	30 9 E
Gateshead	12	54 57N	1 37W
Gatesville	117	31 29N	97 45W
Gaths	91	20 2 S	30 32 E
Gatico	124	22 29 S	70 20W
Gâtinais	19	48 5N	2 40 E
Gâtine, Hauteurs de	20	46 35N	0 45W
Gatineau	113	45 29N	75 39W
Gatineau →	106	45 27N	75 42W
Gatineau, Parc de la	106	45 40N	76 0W
* Gatooma	91	18 20 S	29 52 E
Gattinara	38	45 37N	8 22 E
Gatun	120	9 16N	79 55W
Gatun Dam	120	9 16N	79 55W
Gatun, L.	120	9 7N	79 56W
Gatun Locks	120	9 16N	79 55W
Gaucín	31	36 31N	5 19W
Gauer L.	109	57 0N	97 50W
Gauhati	67	26 10N	91 45 E
Gauja →	54	57 10N	24 16 E
Gaula →	47	63 21N	10 14 E
Gaussberg	5	66 45 S	89 0 E
Gausta	47	59 50N	8 37 E
Gavá	32	41 18N	2 0 E
Gavarnie	20	42 44N	0 3W
Gavăter	65	25 10N	61 31 E
Gavdhopoúla	45	34 56N	24 0 E
Gávdhos	45	34 50N	24 5 E
Gavião	31	39 28N	7 56W
Gävle	48	60 40N	17 9 E
Gävleborgs län □	48	61 30N	16 15 E
Gavorrano	38	42 55N	10 49 E
Gavray	18	48 55N	1 20W
Gavrilov Yam	55	57 18N	39 49 E
Gávrion	45	37 54N	24 44 E
Gawachab	92	27 4 S	17 55 E
Gawilgarh Hills	68	21 15N	76 45 E
Gawler	97	34 30 S	138 42 E
Gawler Ranges	96	32 30 S	135 45 E

* *Renamed Kadoma*

Gaxun Nur	75	42 22N	100 30 E
Gay	52	51 27N	58 27 E
Gaya, India	69	24 47N	85 4 E
Gaya, Niger	85	11 52N	3 28 E
Gaya, Nigeria	85	11 57N	9 0 E
Gaylord	114	45 1N	84 41W
Gayndah	97	25 35 S	151 32 E
Gaysin	56	48 57N	28 25 E
Gayvoron	56	48 22N	29 52 E
Gaza	62	31 30N	34 28 E
Gaza □	93	23 10 S	32 45 E
Gaza Strip	62	31 29N	34 25 E
Gazaoua	85	13 32N	7 55 E
Gazelle Pen.	98	4 40 S	152 0 E
Gazi	90	1 3N	24 30 E
Gaziantep	64	37 6N	37 23 E
Gazli	58	40 14N	63 24 E
Gbarnga	84	7 19N	9 13W
Gbekebo	85	6 20N	4 56 E
Gboko	85	7 17N	9 4 E
Gbongan	85	7 28N	4 20 E
Gcuwa	93	32 20 S	28 11 E
Gdańsk	28	54 22N	18 40 E
Gdańsk □	28	54 10N	18 30 E
Gdańska, Zatoka	28	54 30N	19 20 E
Gdov	54	58 48N	27 55 E
Gdynia	28	54 35N	18 33 E
Ge'a	62	31 38N	34 37 E
Gebe	73	0 5N	129 25 E
Gebeit Mine	86	21 3N	36 29 E
Gebel Mûsa	86	28 32N	33 59 E
Gecha	87	7 30N	35 18 E
Gedaref	87	14 2N	35 28 E
Gede, Tanjung	72	6 46 S	105 12 E
Gedera	62	31 49N	34 46 E
Gedo	87	9 2N	37 25 E
Gèdre	20	42 47N	0 2 E
Gedser	49	54 35N	11 55 E
Gedser Odde	49	54 30N	11 58 E
Geelong	97	38 10 S	144 22 E
Geestenseth	24	53 31N	8 51 E
Geesthacht	24	53 25N	10 20 E
Geidam	85	12 57N	11 57 E
Geikie →	109	57 45N	103 52W
Geili	87	16 1N	32 37 E
Geilo	47	60 32N	8 14 E
Geinica	27	48 51N	20 55 E
Geisingen	25	47 55N	8 37 E
Geislingen	25	48 37N	9 51 E
Geita	90	2 48 S	32 12 E
Geita □	90	2 50 S	32 10 E
Gejiu	75	23 20N	103 10 E
Gel →	87	7 5N	29 10 E
Gel River	87	7 5N	29 10 E
Gela	41	37 6N	14 18 E
Gela, Golfo di	41	37 0N	14 8 E
Geladi	63	6 59N	46 30 E
Gelderland □	16	52 5N	6 10 E
Geldermalsen	16	51 53N	5 17 E
Geldern	24	51 32N	6 18 E
Geldrop	16	51 25N	5 32 E
Geleen	16	50 57N	5 49 E
Gelehun	84	8 20N	11 40W
Gelendzhik	56	44 33N	38 10 E
Gelibolu	44	40 28N	26 43 E
Gelnhausen	25	50 12N	9 12 E
Gelsenkirchen	24	51 30N	7 5 E
Gelting	24	54 43N	9 53 E
Gemas	71	2 37N	102 36 E
Gembloux	16	50 34N	4 43 E
Gemena	88	3 13N	19 48 E
Gemerek	64	39 15N	36 10 E
Gemona del Friuli	39	46 16N	13 7 E
Gemsa	86	27 39N	33 35 E
Gemu-Gofa □	87	5 40N	36 40 E
Gemünden	25	50 3N	9 43 E
Gen He →	76	50 16N	119 32 E
Genale	87	6 0N	39 30 E
Gençay	20	46 23N	0 23 E
Gendringen	16	51 52N	6 21 E
Geneina, Gebel	86	29 2N	33 55 E
General Acha	124	37 20 S	64 38W
General Alvear, Buenos Aires, Argent.	124	36 0 S	60 0W
General Alvear, Mendoza, Argent.	124	35 0 S	67 40W
General Artigas	124	26 52 S	56 16W
General Belgrano	124	36 35 S	58 47W
General Cabrera	124	32 53 S	63 52W
General Guido	124	36 40 S	57 50W
General Juan Madariaga	124	37 0 S	57 0W
General La Madrid	124	37 17 S	61 20W
General MacArthur	73	11 18N	125 28 E
General Martin Miguel de Güemes	124	24 35 S	65 0W
General Paz	124	27 45 S	57 36W
General Pico	124	35 45 S	63 50W
General Pinedo	124	27 15 S	61 20W
General Pinto	124	34 45 S	61 50W
General Santos	73	6 5N	125 14 E
General Toshevo	43	43 42N	28 6 E
General Trías	120	28 21N	106 22W
General Viamonte	124	35 1 S	61 3W
General Villegas	124	35 0 S	63 0W
Genesee, Idaho, U.S.A.	118	46 31N	116 59W
Genesee, Pa., U.S.A.	112	42 0N	77 54W
Genesee →	114	42 35N	78 0W
Geneseo, Ill., U.S.A.	116	41 25N	90 10W
Geneseo, Kans., U.S.A.	116	38 32N	98 8W
Geneseo, N.Y., U.S.A.	112	42 49N	77 49W
Geneva, Ala., U.S.A.	115	31 2N	85 52W
Geneva, N.Y., U.S.A.	114	42 53N	77 0W
Geneva, Nebr., U.S.A.	116	40 35N	97 35W
Geneva, Ohio, U.S.A.	114	41 49N	80 58W
Geneva = Genève	25	46 12N	6 9 E
Geneva, L.	114	42 38N	88 30W
Geneva, L. = Léman, Lac	25	46 26N	6 30 E
Genève	25	46 12N	6 9 E
Genève □	25	46 10N	6 10 E
Gengenbach	25	48 25N	8 0 E
Genichesk	56	46 12N	34 50 E
Genil →	31	37 42N	5 19W

Génissiat, Barrage de	21	46 1N	5 48 E
Genjem	73	2 46 S	140 12 E
Genk	16	50 58N	5 32 E
Genlis	19	47 15N	5 12 E
Gennargentu, Mti. del	40	40 0N	9 10 E
Gennep	16	51 41N	5 59 E
Gennes	18	47 20N	0 17W
Genoa, Austral.	99	37 29 S	149 35 E
Genoa, N.Y., U.S.A.	113	42 40N	76 32W
Genoa, Nebr., U.S.A.	116	41 31N	97 44W
Genoa = Génova	38	44 24N	8 57 E
Génova	38	44 24N	8 56 E
Génova, Golfo di	38	44 0N	9 0 E
Gent	16	51 2N	3 42 E
Genthin	24	52 24N	12 10 E
Geographe B.	96	33 30 S	115 15 E
Geographe Chan.	96	24 30 S	113 0 E
Geokchay	57	40 42N	47 43 E
Georga, Zemlya	58	80 30N	49 0 E
George	92	33 58 S	22 29 E
George →	107	58 49N	66 10W
George, L., N.S.W., Austral.	99	35 10 S	149 25 E
George, L., S. Austral., Austral.	99	37 25 S	140 0 E
George, L., Uganda	90	0 5N	30 10 E
George, L., Fla., U.S.A.	115	29 15N	81 35W
George, L., N.Y., U.S.A.	113	43 30N	73 30W
George River = Port Nouveau	105	58 30N	65 50W
George Sound	101	44 52 S	167 25 E
George Town, Austral.	99	41 5 S	146 49 E
George Town, Bahamas	121	23 33N	75 47W
George Town, Malay.	71	5 25N	100 15 E
George V Coast	5	69 0 S	148 0 E
George VI Sound	5	71 0 S	68 0W
George West	117	28 18N	98 5W
Georgetown, Austral.	97	18 17 S	143 33 E
Georgetown, Ont., Can.	106	43 40N	79 56W
Georgetown, P.E.I., Can.	107	46 13N	62 24W
Georgetown, Gambia	84	13 30N	14 47W
Georgetown, Guyana	126	6 50N	58 12W
Georgetown, Colo., U.S.A.	118	39 46N	105 49W
Georgetown, Ky., U.S.A.	114	38 13N	84 33W
Georgetown, Ohio, U.S.A.	114	38 50N	83 50W
Georgetown, S.C., U.S.A.	115	33 22N	79 15W
Georgetown, Tex., U.S.A.	117	30 40N	97 45W
Georgi Dimitrov	43	42 15N	23 54 E
Georgi Dimitrov, Yazovir	43	42 37N	25 18 E
Georgia □	115	32 0N	82 0W
Georgia, Str. of	108	49 25N	124 0W
Georgian B.	106	45 15N	81 0W
Georgian S.S.R. □	57	42 0N	43 0 E
Georgievsk	57	44 12N	43 28 E
Georgina →	97	23 30 S	139 47 E
Georgiu-Dezh	55	51 3N	39 30 E
Gera	24	50 53N	12 11 E
Gera □	24	50 45N	11 45 E
Geraardsbergen	16	50 45N	3 53 E
Geral de Goiás, Serra	127	12 0 S	46 0W
Geral, Serra	125	26 25 S	50 0W
Geraldine	118	47 36N	110 18W
Geraldton, Austral.	96	28 48 S	114 32 E
Geraldton, Can.	106	49 44N	86 59W
Gérardmer	19	48 3N	6 50 E
Gerede	56	40 45N	32 10 E
Gereshk	65	31 47N	64 35 E
Gérgal	33	37 7N	2 31W
Gerik	71	5 25N	101 0 E
Gering	116	41 51N	103 30W
Gerizim	62	32 13N	35 15 E
Gerlach	118	40 43N	119 27W
Gerlachovka	27	49 11N	20 7 E
Gerlogubi	63	6 53N	45 3 E
German Planina	42	42 20N	22 0 E
Germansen Landing	108	55 43N	124 40W
Germany, East ■	24	52 0N	12 0 E
Germany, West ■	24	52 0N	9 0 E
Germersheim	25	49 13N	8 20 E
Germiston	93	26 15 S	28 10 E
Gernsheim	25	49 44N	8 29 E
Gerolstein	25	50 12N	6 40 E
Gerolzhofen	25	49 54N	10 21 E
Gerona	32	41 58N	2 46 E
Gerona □	32	42 11N	2 30 E
Gerrard	108	50 30N	117 17W
Gers □	20	43 35N	0 38 E
Gers →	20	44 9N	0 39 E
Gersfeld	24	50 27N	9 57 E
Gersoppa Falls	70	14 12N	74 46 E
Gerufa	92	19 17 S	26 0 E
Geseke	24	51 38N	8 29 E
Geser	73	3 50 S	130 54 E
Gesso →	38	44 24N	7 33 E
Gestro, Wabi →	87	4 12N	42 2 E
Getafe	30	40 18N	3 44W
Gethsémani	107	50 13N	60 40W
Gettysburg, Pa., U.S.A.	114	39 47N	77 18W
Gettysburg, S.D., U.S.A.	116	45 3N	99 56W
Getz Ice Shelf	5	75 0 S	130 0W
Gévaudan	20	44 40N	3 40 E
Gevgelija	42	41 9N	22 30 E
Gévora →	31	38 53N	6 57W
Gex	21	46 21N	6 3 E
Geyikli	44	39 50N	26 12 E
Geyser	118	47 17N	110 30W
Geysir	50	64 19N	20 18W
Ghaghara →	69	25 45N	84 40 E
Ghalla, Wadi el →	87	10 25N	27 32 E
Ghana ■	85	6 0N	1 0W
Ghansor	69	22 39N	80 1 E
Ghanzi	92	21 50 S	21 34 E
Ghanzi □	92	21 50 S	21 45 E
Gharbîya, Es Sahrâ el	86	27 40N	26 30 E
Ghard Abû Muharik	86	26 50N	30 0 E
Ghardaïa	82	32 20N	3 37 E
Ghârib, G.	86	28 6N	32 54 E
Ghârib, Râs	86	28 6N	33 18 E
Gharyān	83	32 10N	13 0 E
Gharyān □	83	30 35N	12 0 E
Ghat	83	24 59N	10 11 E
Ghatal	69	22 40N	87 46 E
Ghatampur	69	26 8N	80 13 E
Ghatprabha →	70	16 15N	75 20 E
Ghayl	64	21 40N	46 20 E

Ghazal, Bahr el Gorki

Ghazal, Bahr el → **81** 15 0N 17 0 E
Ghazâl, Bahr el → **87** 9 31N 30 25 E
Ghazaouet **82** 35 8N 1 50W
Ghaziabad **68** 28 42N 77 26 E
Ghazipur **69** 25 38N 83 35 E
Ghazni **66** 33 30N 68 28 E
Ghaznī □ **65** 33 0N 68 0 E
Ghedi **38** 45 24N 10 16 E
Ghelari **46** 45 38N 22 45 E
Ghèlinsor **63** 6 28N 46 39 E
Ghent = Gand **16** 51 2N 3 42 E
Gheorghe Gheorghiu-Dej **46** 46 17N 26 47 E
Gheorgheni **46** 46 43N 25 41 E
Ghergani **46** 44 37N 25 37 E
Gherla **46** 47 0N 23 57 E
Ghilarza **40** 40 8N 8 50 E
Ghisonaccia **21** 42 1N 9 26 E
Ghod → **70** 18 30N 74 35 E
Ghot Ogrein **86** 31 10N 25 20 E
Ghotaru **68** 27 20N 70 1 E
Ghotki **68** 28 5N 69 21 E
Ghowr □ **65** 34 0N 64 20 E
Ghudāmis **83** 30 11N 9 29 E
Ghugri **69** 22 39N 80 41 E
Ghugus **70** 19 58N 79 12 E
Ghulam Mohammad Barrage **68** 25 30N 68 20 E
Ghūriān **65** 34 17N 61 25 E
Gia Nghia **71** 12 0N 107 42 E
Gian **73** 5 45N 125 20 E
Giannutri **38** 42 16N 11 5 E
Giant Mts. = Krkonoše **26** 50 50N 16 10 E
Giant's Causeway **15** 55 15N 6 30W
Giarre **41** 37 44N 15 10 E
Giaveno **38** 45 3N 7 20 E
Gibara **121** 21 9N 76 11W
Gibbon **116** 40 49N 98 45W
Gibe → **87** 7 20N 37 36 E
Gibellina **40** 37 48N 13 0 E
Gibeon **92** 25 7 S 17 45 E
Gibraléon **31** 37 23N 6 58W
Gibraltar **31** 36 7N 5 22W
Gibraltar, Str. of **31** 35 55N 5 40W
Gibson Des. **96** 24 0 S 126 0 E
Gibsons **108** 49 24N 123 32W
Giddalur **70** 15 20N 78 57 E
Giddings **117** 30 11N 96 58W
Gidole **87** 5 40N 37 25 E
Gien **19** 47 40N 2 36 E
Giessen **24** 50 34N 8 40 E
Gifatin, Geziret **86** 27 10N 33 50 E
Gifhorn **24** 52 29N 10 32 E
Gifu **74** 35 30N 136 45 E
Gifu □ **74** 35 40N 137 0 E
Gigant **57** 46 28N 41 20 E
Giganta, Sa. de la **120** 25 30N 111 30W
Gigen **43** 43 40N 24 28 E
Gigha **14** 55 42N 5 45W
Giglio **38** 42 20N 10 52 E
Gignac **20** 43 39N 3 32 E
Gigüela → **33** 39 8N 3 44W
Gijón **30** 43 32N 5 42W
Gil I. **108** 53 12N 129 15W
Gila → **119** 32 43N 114 33W
Gila Bend **119** 33 0N 112 46W
Gila Bend Mts. **119** 33 15N 113 0W
Gilan □ **64** 37 0N 48 0 E
Gilău **46** 46 45N 23 23 E
Gilbert → **97** 16 35 S 141 15 E
Gilbert Is. **94** 1 0N 176 0 E
Gilbert Plains **109** 51 9N 100 28W
Gilbert River **98** 18 9 S 142 52 E
Gilberton **98** 19 16 S 143 35 E
Gilf el Kebîr, Hadabat el **86** 23 50N 25 50 E
Gilford I. **108** 50 40N 126 30W
Gilgandra **97** 31 43 S 148 39 E
Gilgil **90** 0 30 S 36 20 E
Gilgit **69** 35 50N 74 15 E
Giljeva Planina **42** 43 9N 20 0 E
Gillam **109** 56 20N 94 40W
Gilleleje **49** 56 8N 12 19 E
Gillette **116** 44 20N 105 30W
Gilliat **98** 20 40 S 141 28 E
Gillingham **13** 51 23N 0 34 E
Gilmer **117** 32 44N 94 55W
Gilmore **99** 35 20 S 148 12 E
Gilmour **106** 44 48N 77 37W
Gilo → **87** 8 10N 33 15 E
Gilort → **46** 44 38N 23 32 E
Gilroy **119** 37 1N 121 37W
Gimbi **87** 9 3N 35 42 E
Gimigliano **41** 38 58N 16 32 E
Gimli **109** 50 40N 97 0W
Gimo **48** 60 11N 18 12 E
Gimone → **20** 44 0N 1 6 E
Gimont **20** 43 38N 0 52 E
Gimzo **62** 31 56N 34 56 E
Gin → **70** 6 5N 80 7 E
Gin Gin **99** 25 0 S 151 58 E
Ginâh **86** 25 21N 30 30 E
Gindie **98** 23 44 S 148 8 E
Gineta, La **33** 39 8N 2 1W
Gingiova **46** 43 54N 23 50 E
Ginir **87** 7 6N 40 40 E
Ginosa **41** 40 35N 16 45 E
Ginzo de Limia **30** 42 3N 7 47W
Giohar **63** 2 48N 45 30 E
Gióia del Colle **41** 40 49N 16 55 E
Gióia, G. di **41** 38 30N 15 50 E
Gióia Táuro **41** 38 26N 15 53 E
Gioiosa Iónica **41** 38 20N 16 19 E
Gióna, Óros **45** 38 38N 22 14 E
Giong, Teluk **73** 4 50N 118 20 E
Giovi, Passo dei **38** 44 33N 8 57 E
Giovinazzo **41** 41 10N 16 40 E
Gippsland **97** 37 45 S 147 15 E
Gir Hills **68** 21 0N 71 0 E
Girab **68** 26 2N 70 38 E
Giraltovce **27** 49 7N 21 32 E
Girard, Kans., U.S.A. **117** 37 30N 94 50W
Girard, Ohio, U.S.A. **112** 41 10N 80 42W
Girard, Pa., U.S.A. **112** 42 1N 80 21W
Girardot **126** 4 18N 74 48W
Girdle Ness **14** 57 9N 2 2W
Giresun **64** 40 55N 38 30 E
Girga **86** 26 17N 31 55 E
Giridih **69** 24 10N 86 21 E
Girifalco **41** 38 49N 16 25 E
Girilambone **99** 31 16 S 146 57 E
Giro **85** 11 7N 4 42 E
Giromagny **19** 47 44N 6 50 E
Gironde □ **20** 44 45N 0 30W
Gironde → **20** 45 32N 1 7W
Gironella **32** 42 2N 1 53 E
Giru **98** 19 30 S 147 5 E
Girvan **14** 55 15N 4 50W
Gisborne **101** 38 39 S 178 5 E
Gisenyi **90** 1 41 S 29 15 E
Giske **47** 62 30N 6 3 E
Gislaved **49** 57 19N 13 32 E
Gisors **19** 49 15N 1 47 E
Gitega (Kitega) **90** 3 26 S 29 56 E
Giuba → **63** 1 30N 42 35 E
Giugliano in Campania **41** 40 55N 14 12 E
Giulianova **39** 42 45N 13 58 E
Giurgeni **46** 44 45N 27 48 E
Giurgiu **46** 43 52N 25 57 E
Giv'at Brenner **62** 31 52N 34 47 E
Giv'atayim **62** 32 4N 34 49 E
Give **49** 55 51N 9 13 E
Givet **19** 50 8N 4 49 E
Givors **21** 45 35N 4 45 E
Givry **19** 46 41N 4 46 E
Giyon **87** 8 33N 38 1 E
Giza = El Gîza **86** 30 1N 31 11 E
Gizhiga **59** 62 3N 160 30 E
Gizhiginskaya, Guba **59** 61 0N 158 0 E
Giżycko **28** 54 2N 21 48 E
Gizzeria **41** 38 57N 16 10 E
Gjegjan **44** 41 58N 20 3 E
Gjerstad **47** 58 54N 9 0 E
Gjirokastra **44** 40 7N 20 10 E
Gjoa Haven **104** 68 20N 96 8W
Gjøl **49** 57 4N 9 42 E
Gjøvik **47** 60 47N 10 43 E
Glace Bay **107** 46 11N 59 58W
Glacier B. **108** 58 30N 136 10W
Glacier Nat. Park, Can. **108** 51 15N 117 30W
Glacier Nat. Park, U.S.A. **118** 48 35N 113 40W
Glacier Park **118** 48 30N 113 18W
Glacier Peak Mt. **118** 48 7N 121 7W
Gladewater **117** 32 30N 94 58W
Gladstone, Austral. **99** 33 15 S 138 22 E
Gladstone, Can. **109** 50 13N 98 57W
Gladstone, U.S.A. **114** 45 52N 87 1W
Gladwin **114** 43 59N 84 29W
Gladys L. **108** 59 50N 133 0W
Glafsfjorden **48** 59 30N 12 37 E
Głagów Małapolski **27** 50 10N 21 56 E
Gláma **50** 65 48N 23 0W
Glåma → **47** 59 12N 10 57 E
Glamoč **39** 44 3N 16 51 E
Glan **49** 58 37N 16 0 E
Glarus **25** 47 3N 9 4 E
Glasco, Kans., U.S.A. **116** 39 25N 97 50W
Glasco, N.Y., U.S.A. **113** 42 3N 73 57W
Glasgow, U.K. **14** 55 52N 4 14W
Glasgow, Ky., U.S.A. **114** 37 2N 85 55W
Glasgow, Mont., U.S.A. **118** 48 12N 106 35W
Glastonbury, U.K. **13** 51 9N 2 42W
Glastonbury, U.S.A. **113** 41 42N 72 27W
Glauchau **24** 50 50N 12 33 E
Glazov **55** 58 9N 52 40 E
Gleisdorf **26** 47 6N 15 44 E
Gleiwitz = Gliwice **28** 50 22N 18 41 E
Glen **113** 44 7N 71 10W
Glen Affric **14** 57 15N 5 0W
Glen Canyon Dam **119** 37 0N 111 25W
Glen Canyon Nat. Recreation Area **119** 37 30N 111 0W
Glen Coe **12** 56 40N 5 0W
Glen Cove **113** 40 51N 73 37W
Glen Garry **14** 57 3N 5 7W
Glen Innes **97** 29 44 S 151 44 E
Glen Lyon **113** 41 10N 76 7W
Glen Mor **14** 57 12N 4 37 E
Glen Moriston **14** 57 10N 4 58W
Glen Orchy **14** 56 27N 4 52W
Glen Spean **14** 56 53N 4 40W
Glen Ullin **116** 46 48N 101 46W
Glénans, Îles. de **18** 47 42N 4 0W
Glenburnie **100** 37 51 S 140 50 E
Glencoe, Can. **112** 42 45N 81 43W
Glencoe, S. Afr. **93** 28 11 S 30 11 E
Glencoe, U.S.A. **116** 44 45N 94 10W
Glendale, Ariz., U.S.A. **119** 33 40N 112 8W
Glendale, Calif., U.S.A. **119** 34 7N 118 18W
Glendale, Oreg., U.S.A. **118** 42 44N 123 29W
Glendale, Zimb. **91** 17 22 S 31 5 E
Glendive **116** 47 7N 104 40W
Glendo **116** 42 30N 105 0W
Glenelg **99** 34 58 S 138 31 E
Glenelg → **99** 38 4 S 140 59 E
Glengarriff **15** 51 45N 9 33W
Glengyle **98** 24 48 S 139 37 E
Glenmora **117** 31 1N 92 34W
Glenmorgan **99** 27 14 S 149 42 E
Glenns Ferry **118** 43 0N 115 15W
Glenorchy **99** 42 49 S 147 18 E
Glenore **98** 17 50 S 141 12 E
Glenormiston **98** 22 55 S 138 50 E
Glenreagh **99** 30 2 S 153 1 E
Glenrock **118** 42 53N 105 55W
Glenrothes **14** 56 12N 3 11W
Glens Falls **114** 43 20N 73 40W
Glenties **15** 54 48N 8 18W
Glenville **114** 38 56N 80 50W
Glenwood, Alta., Can. **108** 49 21N 113 31W
Glenwood, Newf., Can. **107** 49 0N 54 58W
Glenwood, Ark., U.S.A. **117** 34 20N 93 30W
Glenwood, Hawaii, U.S.A. **110** 19 29N 155 10W
Glenwood, Iowa, U.S.A. **116** 41 7N 95 41W
Glenwood, Minn., U.S.A. **116** 45 38N 95 21W
Glenwood Sprs. **118** 39 39N 107 21W
Glina **39** 45 20N 16 6 E
Glinojeck **28** 52 49N 20 21 E
Glittertind **47** 61 40N 8 32 E
Gliwice **28** 50 22N 18 41 E
Globe **119** 33 25N 110 53W
Glodeanu Siliştea **46** 44 50N 26 48 E
Glödnitz **26** 46 53N 14 7 E
Glodyany **46** 47 45N 27 31 E
Gloggnitz **26** 47 41N 15 56 E
Głogów **28** 51 37N 16 5 E
Głogowek **28** 50 21N 17 53 E
Glorieuses, Îles **93** 11 30 S 47 20 E
Glossop **12** 53 27N 1 56W
Gloucester, Austral. **99** 32 0 S 151 59 E
Gloucester, U.K. **13** 51 52N 2 15W
Gloucester, U.S.A. **113** 42 38N 70 39W
Gloucester, C. **98** 5 26 S 148 21 E
Gloucester I. **98** 20 0 S 148 30 E
Gloucestershire □ **13** 51 44N 2 10W
Gloversville **114** 43 5N 74 18W
Glovertown **107** 48 40N 54 03W
Główno **28** 51 59N 19 42 E
Głubczyce **27** 50 13N 17 52 E
Glubokiy **57** 48 35N 40 25 E
Glubokoye **54** 55 10N 27 45 E
Glūbovo **43** 42 8N 25 55 E
Głuchołazy **28** 50 19N 17 24 E
Glücksburg **24** 54 48N 9 34 E
Glückstadt **24** 53 46N 9 28 E
Glukhov **54** 51 40N 33 58 E
Glussk **54** 52 53N 28 41 E
Glyngøre **49** 56 46N 8 52 E
Gmünd, Kärnten, Austria **26** 46 54N 13 31 E
Gmünd, Niederösterreich, Austria **26** 48 45N 15 0 E
Gmunden **26** 47 55N 13 48 E
Gnarp **48** 62 3N 17 16 E
Gnesta **48** 59 3N 17 17 E
Gniew **28** 53 50N 18 50 E
Gniewkowo **28** 52 54N 18 25 E
Gniezno **28** 52 30N 17 35 E
Gnjilane **42** 42 28N 21 29 E
Gnoien **24** 53 58N 12 41 E
Gnosjö **49** 57 22N 13 43 E
Gnowangerup **96** 33 58 S 117 59 E
Go Cong **71** 10 22N 106 40 E
Goa **70** 15 33N 73 59 E
Goa □ **70** 15 33N 73 59 E
Goageb **92** 26 49 S 17 15 E
Goalen Hd. **99** 36 33 S 150 4 E
Goalpara **69** 26 10N 90 40 E
Goalundo Ghat **69** 23 50N 89 47 E
Goaso **84** 6 48N 2 30W
Goat Fell **14** 55 37N 5 11W
Goba **87** 7 1N 39 59 E
Gobabis **92** 22 30 S 19 0 E
Gobi **75** 44 0N 111 0 E
Gobichettipalayam **70** 11 31N 77 21 E
Gobo **87** 5 40N 31 10 E
Goch **24** 51 40N 6 9 E
Gochas **92** 24 59 S 18 55 E
Godavari → **70** 16 25N 82 18 E
Godavari Point **70** 17 0N 82 20 E
Godbout **107** 49 20N 67 38W
Godda **69** 24 50N 87 13 E
Goddua **83** 26 26N 14 19 E
Godech **42** 43 1N 23 4 E
Godegård **49** 58 43N 15 8 E
Goderich **106** 43 45N 81 41W
Goderville **18** 49 38N 0 22 E
Godhavn **4** 69 15N 53 38W
Godhra **68** 22 49N 73 40 E
Gödöllö **27** 47 38N 19 25 E
Godoy Cruz **124** 32 56 S 68 52W
Gods → **109** 56 22N 92 51W
Gods L. **109** 54 40N 94 15W
Godthåb **4** 64 10N 51 35W
Godwin Austen (K2) **69** 36 0N 77 0 E
Goeie Hoop, Kaap die **92** 34 24 S 18 30 E
Goéland, L. au **106** 49 50N 76 48W
Goeree **16** 51 50N 4 0 E
Goes **16** 51 30N 3 55 E
Gogama **106** 47 35N 81 43W
Gogango **98** 23 40 S 150 2 E
Gogebic, L. **116** 46 20N 89 34W
Gogha **68** 21 40N 72 20 E
Gogolin **28** 50 30N 18 0 E
Gogra = Ghaghara → **67** 26 0N 84 20 E
Gogriâl **87** 8 30N 28 8 E
Goiânia **127** 16 43 S 49 20W
Goiás **127** 15 55 S 50 10W
Goiás □ **127** 12 10 S 48 0W
Góis **30** 40 10N 8 6W
Goisern **26** 47 38N 13 38 E
Gojam □ **87** 10 55N 36 30 E
Gojeb, Wabi → **87** 7 12N 36 40 E
Gojra **68** 31 10N 72 40 E
Gokak **70** 16 11N 74 52 E
Gokarannath **69** 27 57N 80 39 E
Gokarn **70** 14 33N 74 17 E
Gökçeada **44** 40 10N 25 50 E
Gokteik **67** 22 26N 97 0 E
Gokurt **68** 29 40N 67 26 E
Gola **69** 28 3N 80 32 E
Golakganj **69** 26 8N 89 52 E
Golaya Pristen **56** 46 29N 32 32 E
Golchikha **4** 71 45N 83 30 E
Golconda **118** 40 58N 117 32W
Gold Beach **118** 42 25N 124 25W
Gold Coast, Austral. **99** 28 0 S 153 25 E
Gold Coast, W. Afr. **85** 4 0N 1 40W
Gold Hill **118** 42 28N 123 2W
Gold River **108** 49 46N 126 3 E
Gołdap **28** 54 19N 22 18 E
Goldberg **24** 53 34N 12 6 E
Golden, Can. **108** 51 20N 117 59W
Golden, U.S.A. **116** 39 42N 105 15W
Golden Bay **101** 40 40 S 172 50 E
Golden Gate **118** 37 54N 122 30W
Golden Hinde **108** 49 40N 125 44W
Golden Lake **112** 45 34N 77 21W
Golden Prairie **109** 50 13N 109 37W
Golden Rock **70** 10 45N 78 48 E
Golden Vale **15** 52 33N 8 17W
Goldendale **118** 45 53N 120 48W
Goldfield **119** 37 45N 117 13W
Goldfields **109** 59 28N 108 29W
Goldsand L. **109** 57 2N 101 8W
Goldsboro **115** 35 24N 77 59W
Goldsmith **117** 32 0N 102 40W
Goldthwaite **117** 31 25N 98 32W
Golegã **31** 39 24N 8 29W
Golęniów **28** 53 35N 14 50 E
Golfito **121** 8 41N 83 5W
Golfo Aranci **40** 41 0N 9 35 E
Goliad **117** 28 40N 97 22W
Golija, Crna Gora, Yugo. **42** 43 5N 18 45 E
Golija, Srbija, Yugo. **42** 43 22N 20 15 E
Golina **28** 52 15N 18 4 E
Göllersdorf **27** 48 29N 16 7 E
Golo → **21** 42 31N 9 32 E
Golovanevsk **56** 48 25N 30 30 E
Golspie **14** 57 58N 3 58W
Golub Dobrzyń **28** 53 7N 19 2 E
Golubac **42** 44 38N 21 38 E
Golyam Perelik **43** 41 36N 24 33 E
Golyama Kamchiya → **43** 43 10N 27 55 E
Goma, Rwanda **90** 2 11 S 29 18 E
Goma, Zaïre **90** 1 37 S 29 10 E
Gomare **92** 19 25 S 22 8 E
Gomati → **69** 25 32N 83 11 E
Gombari **90** 2 45N 29 3 E
Gombe **85** 10 19N 11 2 E
Gombe → **90** 4 38 S 31 40 E
Gombi **85** 10 12N 12 30 E
Gomel **54** 52 28N 31 0 E
Gomera **80** 28 7N 17 14W
Gómez Palacio **120** 25 40N 104 0W
Gommern **24** 52 5N 11 47 E
Gomogomo **73** 6 39 S 134 43 E
Gomotartsi **42** 44 6N 22 57 E
Gomphoi **44** 39 31N 21 27 E
Gonābād **65** 34 15N 58 45 E
Gonaïves **121** 19 20N 72 42W
Gonâve, G. de la **121** 19 29N 72 42W
Gonbab-e Kāvūs **65** 37 20N 55 25 E
Gönc **27** 48 28N 21 14 E
Gonda **69** 27 9N 81 58 E
Gondal **68** 21 58N 70 52 E
Gonder **87** 12 39N 37 30 E
Gondia **69** 21 23N 80 10 E
Gondola **91** 19 10 S 33 37 E
Gondomar, Port. **30** 41 10N 8 35W
Gondomar, Spain **30** 42 7N 8 45W
Gondrecourt-le-Château **19** 48 26N 5 30 E
Gonghe **75** 36 18N 100 32 E
Gongola □ **85** 8 0N 12 0 E
Gongola → **85** 9 30N 12 4 E
Goniadz **28** 53 30N 22 44 E
Goniri **85** 11 30N 12 15 E
Gonnesa **40** 39 17N 8 27 E
Gónnos **44** 39 52N 22 29 E
Gonnosfanadiga **40** 39 30N 8 39 E
Gonzales, Calif., U.S.A. **119** 36 35N 121 30W
Gonzales, Tex., U.S.A. **117** 29 30N 97 30W
González Chaves **124** 38 02 S 60 05W
Good Hope, C. of = Goeie Hoop, K. die **92** 34 24 S 18 30 E
Goodenough I. **98** 9 20 S 150 15 E
Gooderham **106** 44 54N 78 21W
Goodeve **109** 51 4N 103 10W
Gooding **118** 43 0N 114 44W
Goodland **116** 39 22N 101 44W
Goodnight **117** 35 4N 101 13W
Goodooga **99** 29 3 S 147 28 E
Goodsoil **109** 54 24N 109 13W
Goodsprings **119** 35 51N 115 30W
Goole **12** 53 42N 0 52W
Goolgowi **99** 33 58 S 145 41 E
Goombalie **99** 29 59 S 145 26 E
Goonda **91** 19 48 S 33 57 E
Goondiwindi **97** 28 30 S 150 21 E
Goor **16** 52 13N 6 33 E
Gooray **99** 28 25 S 150 2 E
Goose → **107** 53 20N 60 35W
Goose Bay **107** 53 15N 60 20W
Goose L. **118** 42 0N 120 30W
Gooty **70** 15 7N 77 41 E
Gopalganj, Bangla. **69** 23 1N 89 50 E
Gopalganj, India **69** 26 28N 84 30 E
Göppingen **25** 48 42N 9 40 E
Gor **33** 37 23N 2 58W
Góra, Leszno, Poland **28** 51 40N 16 31 E
Góra, Płock, Poland **28** 52 39N 20 6 E
Góra Kalwaria **28** 51 59N 21 14 E
Gorakhpur **69** 26 47N 83 23 E
Goražde **42** 43 38N 18 58 E
Gorbatov **55** 56 12N 43 2 E
Gorbea, Peña **32** 43 1N 2 50W
Gorda, Punta **121** 14 20N 83 10W
Gordon, Austral. **99** 32 7 S 138 20 E
Gordon, U.S.A. **116** 42 49N 102 12W
Gordon → **99** 42 27 S 145 30 E
Gordon Downs **96** 18 48 S 128 33 E
Gordon L., Alta., Can. **109** 56 30N 110 25W
Gordon L., N.W.T., Can. **108** 63 5N 113 11W
Gordonia **92** 28 13 S 21 10 E
Gordonvale **98** 17 5 S 145 50 E
Gore **99** 28 17 S 151 30 E
Goré **81** 7 59N 16 31 E
Gore, Ethiopia **87** 8 12N 35 32 E
Gore, N.Z. **101** 46 5 S 168 58 E
Gore Bay **106** 45 57N 82 28W
Gorey **15** 52 41N 6 18W
Gorgān **65** 36 55N 54 30 E
Gorgona **38** 43 27N 9 52 E
Gorgona, I. **126** 3 0N 78 10W
Gorgora **87** 12 15N 37 17 E
Gorham **113** 44 23N 71 10W
Gori **57** 42 0N 44 7 E
Gorinchem **16** 51 50N 4 59 E
Goritsy **55** 57 4N 36 43 E
Gorizia **39** 45 56N 13 37 E
Górka **28** 51 39N 16 58 E
Gorki **54** 54 17N 30 59 E

Gorki Grindsted

Gorki = Gorkiy 55 56 20N 44 0 E
Gorkiy 55 56 20N 44 0 E
Gorkovskoye Vdkhr. 55 57 2N 43 4 E
Gørlev 49 55 30N 11 15 E
Gorlice 27 49 35N 21 11 E
Görlitz 24 51 10N 14 59 E
Gorlovka 56 48 19N 38 5 E
Gorman 117 32 15N 98 43W
Gorna Oryakhovitsa 43 43 7N 25 40 E
Gornja Radgona 39 46 40N 16 2 E
Gornja Tuzla 42 44 35N 18 46 E
Gornji Grad 39 46 20N 14 52 E
Gornji Milanovac 42 44 00N 20 29 E
Gornji Vakuf 42 43 57N 17 34 E
Gorno Ablanovo 43 43 37N 25 43 E
Gorno-Altaysk 58 51 50N 86 5 E
Gorno Slinkino 58 60 5N 70 0 E
Gornyatski 52 67 32N 64 3 E
Gornyy 55 51 50N 48 30 E
Gorodenka 56 48 41N 25 29 E
Gorodets 55 56 38N 43 28 E
Gorodische 55 53 13N 45 40 E
Gorodishche 56 49 17N 31 27 E
Gorodnitsa 54 50 46N 27 19 E
Gorodnya 54 51 55N 31 33 E
Gorodok, Byelorussia, U.S.S.R. 54 55 30N 30 3 E
Gorodok, Ukraine, U.S.S.R. 54 49 46N 23 32 E
Goroka 98 6 7 S 145 25 E
Gorokhov 54 50 30N 24 45 E
Gorokhovets 55 56 13N 42 39 E
Gorom Gorom 85 14 26N 0 14W
Goromonzi 91 17 52 S 31 22 E
Gorong, Kepulauan 73 4 5 S 131 25 E
Gorongosa, Sa. da 91 18 27 S 34 2 E
Gorongose → 93 20 30 S 34 40 E
Gorontalo 73 0 35N 123 5 E
Goronyo 85 13 29N 5 39 E
Górowo Iławeckie 28 54 17N 20 30 E
Gorron 18 48 25N 0 50W
Gort 15 53 4N 8 50W
Gorumahisani 69 22 20N 86 24 E
Gorzkowice 28 51 13N 19 36 E
Gorzno 28 53 12N 19 38 E
Gorzów Śląski 28 51 3N 18 22 E
Gorzów Wielkopolski 28 52 43N 15 15 E
Gorzów Wielkopolski □ 28 52 45N 15 30 E
Gosford 99 33 23 S 151 18 E
Goshen, S. Afr. 92 25 50 S 25 0 E
Goshen, Ind., U.S.A. 114 41 36N 85 46W
Goshen, N.Y., U.S.A. 113 41 23N 74 21W
Goslar 24 51 55N 10 23 E
Gospič 39 44 35N 15 23 E
Gosport 13 50 48N 1 8W
Gostivar 42 41 48N 20 57 E
Gostyń 28 51 50N 17 3 E
Gostynin 28 52 26N 19 29 E
Göta älv → 49 57 42N 11 54 E
Göteborg 49 57 43N 11 59 E
Götene 49 58 32N 13 30 E
Gotha 24 50 56N 10 42 E
Gothenburg 116 40 58N 100 8W
Gotland 49 57 30N 18 33 E
Gotō-Rettō 74 32 55N 129 5 E
Gotse Delchev (Nevrokop) 43 41 43N 23 46 E
Göttingen 24 51 31N 9 55 E
Gottwaldov (Zlin) 27 49 14N 17 40 E
Goubangzi 76 41 20N 121 52 E
Gouda 16 52 1N 4 42 E
Goudiry 84 14 15N 12 45W
Gough I. 7 40 10 S 9 45W
Gouin Rés. 106 48 35N 74 40W
Gouitafla 84 7 30N 5 53W
Goula Touila 82 21 50N 1 57W
Goulburn 97 34 44 S 149 44 E
Goulburn → 100 36 6 S 144 55 E
Goulburn Is. 96 11 40 S 133 20 E
Goulia 84 10 1N 7 11W
Goulimine 82 28 56N 10 0W
Goulmina 82 31 41N 4 57W
Gouménissa 44 40 56N 22 37 E
Gounou-Gaya 81 9 38N 15 31 E
Goúra 45 37 56N 22 20 E
Gourara 82 29 0N 0 30 E
Gouraya 82 36 31N 1 56 E
Gourdon 20 44 44N 1 23 E
Gouré 85 14 0N 10 10 E
Gouri 81 19 36N 19 36 E
Gourits → 92 34 21 S 21 52 E
Gourma Rharous 85 16 55N 1 50W
Gournay-en-Bray 19 49 29N 1 44 E
Gourock Ra. 99 36 0 S 149 25 E
Goursi 84 12 42N 2 37W
Gouverneur 113 44 18N 75 30W
Gouzon 20 46 12N 2 14 E
Govan 109 51 20N 105 0W
Gove 97 12 25 S 136 55 E
Governador Valadares 127 18 15 S 41 57W
Gowan Ra. 98 25 0 S 145 0 E
Gowanda 114 42 29N 78 58W
Gowd-e Zirreh 65 29 45N 62 0 E
Gower, The 13 51 35N 4 10W
Gowna, L. 15 53 52N 7 35W
Gowrie, Carse of 14 56 30N 3 10W
Goya 124 29 10 S 59 10W
Goyllarisquisga 126 10 31 S 76 24W
Goz Beïda 81 12 10N 21 20 E
Goz Regeb 87 16 3N 35 33 E
Gozdnica 28 51 28N 15 4 E
Gozo (Ghawdex) 36 36 0N 14 13 E
Graaff-Reinet 92 32 13 S 24 32 E
Grabow 24 53 17N 11 31 E
Grabów 28 51 31N 18 7 E
Gračac 39 44 18N 15 57 E
Gračanica 42 44 43N 18 18 E
Graçay 19 47 10N 1 50 E
Grace 118 42 38N 111 46W
Graceville 116 45 36N 96 23W
Gracias a Dios, C. 121 15 0N 83 10W
Gradačac 42 44 52N 18 26 E
Gradeška Planina 42 41 30N 22 15 E
Gradets 43 42 46N 26 30 E
Grado, Italy 39 45 40N 13 20 E
Grado, Spain 30 43 23N 6 4W
Gradule 99 28 32 S 149 15 E
Grady 117 34 52N 103 15W
Graeca, Lacul 46 44 5N 26 10 E
Graénalon, L. 50 64 10N 17 20W
Grafenau 25 48 51N 13 24 E
Gräfenberg 25 49 39N 11 15 E
Grafton, Austral. 97 29 38 S 152 58 E
Grafton, U.S.A. 116 48 30N 97 25W
Grafton, C. 97 16 51 S 146 0 E
Gragnano 41 40 42N 14 30 E
Graham, Can. 106 49 20N 90 30W
Graham, N.C., U.S.A. 115 36 5N 79 22W
Graham, Tex., U.S.A. 117 33 7N 98 38W
Graham → 108 56 31N 122 17W
Graham Bell, Os. 58 80 5N 70 0 E
Graham I. 108 53 40N 132 30W
Graham Land 5 65 0 S 64 0W
Graham Mt. 119 32 46N 109 58W
Grahamdale 109 51 23N 98 30W
Grahamstown 92 33 19 S 26 31 E
Grahovo 42 42 40N 18 40 E
Graïba 83 34 30N 10 13 E
Graie, Alpi 38 45 30N 7 10 E
Grain Coast 84 4 20N 10 0W
Grajaú 127 5 50 S 46 4W
Grajaú → 127 3 41 S 44 48W
Grajewo 28 53 39N 22 30 E
Gral. Martin Miguel de Gäemes 124 24 50 S 65 0W
Gramada 42 43 49N 22 39 E
Gramat 20 44 48N 1 43 E
Grammichele 41 37 12N 14 37 E
Grámmos, Óros 44 40 18N 20 47 E
Grampian □ 14 57 0N 3 0W
Grampian Mts. 14 56 50N 4 0W
Grampians, Mts. 99 37 0 S 142 20 E
Gran Canaria 80 27 55N 15 35W
Gran Chaco 124 25 0 S 61 0W
Gran Paradiso 38 45 33N 7 17 E
Gran Sasso d'Italia 39 42 25N 13 30 E
Granada, Nic. 121 11 58N 86 0W
Granada, Spain 33 37 10N 3 35W
Granada, U.S.A. 117 38 5N 102 20W
Granada □ 31 37 18N 3 0W
Granard 15 53 47N 7 30W
Granbury 117 32 28N 97 48W
Granby 106 45 25N 72 45W
Grand →, Mo., U.S.A. 116 39 23N 93 6W
Grand →, Mo., U.S.A. 116 39 23N 93 6W
Grand →, S.D., U.S.A. 116 45 40N 100 32W
Grand Bahama 121 26 40N 78 30W
Grand Bank 107 47 6N 55 48W
Grand Bassam 84 5 10N 3 49W
Grand Béréby 84 4 38N 6 55W
Grand-Bourge 121 15 53N 61 19W
Grand Canyon 119 36 3N 112 9W
Grand Canyon National Park 119 36 15N 112 20W
Grand Cayman 121 19 20N 81 20W
Grand Cess 84 4 40N 8 12W
Grand-Combe, La 21 44 13N 4 2 E
Grand Coulee 118 47 48N 119 1W
Grand Coulee Dam 118 48 0N 118 50W
Grand Erg Occidental 82 30 20N 1 0 E
Grand Erg Oriental 83 30 0N 6 30 E
Grand Falls 107 48 56N 55 40W
Grand Forks, Can. 108 49 0N 118 30W
Grand Forks, U.S.A. 116 48 0N 97 3W
Grand-Fougeray 18 47 44N 1 43W
Grand Haven 114 43 3N 86 13W
Grand I. 106 46 30N 86 40W
Grand Island 116 40 59N 98 25W
Grand Isle 117 29 15N 89 58W
Grand Junction 119 39 0N 108 30W
Grand L., N.B., Can. 107 45 57N 66 7W
Grand L., Newf., Can. 107 53 40N 60 30W
Grand L., Newf., Can. 107 49 0N 57 30W
Grand L., U.S.A. 117 29 55N 92 45W
Grand Lac Victoria 106 47 35N 77 35W
Grand Lahou 84 5 10N 5 0W
Grand Lake 118 40 20N 105 54W
Grand-Lieu, Lac de 18 47 6N 1 40W
Grand-Luce, Le 18 47 52N 0 28 E
Grand Manan I. 107 44 45N 66 52W
Grand Marais, Can. 116 47 45N 90 25W
Grand Marais, U.S.A. 114 46 39N 85 59W
Grand Mère 106 46 36N 72 40W
Grand Popo 85 6 15N 1 57 E
Grand Portage 106 47 58N 89 41W
Grand-Pressigny, Le 18 46 55N 0 48 E
Grand Rapids, Can. 109 53 12N 99 19W
Grand Rapids, Mich., U.S.A. 114 42 57N 86 40W
Grand Rapids, Minn., U.S.A. 116 47 15N 93 29W
Grand St.-Bernard, Col. du 25 45 53N 7 11 E
Grand Teton 118 43 54N 111 50W
Grand Valley 118 39 30N 108 2W
Grand View 109 51 10N 100 42W
Grandas de Salime 30 43 13N 6 53W
Grande →, Jujuy, Argent. 124 24 20 S 65 2W
Grande →, Mendoza, Argent. 124 36 52 S 69 45W
Grande →, Boliv. 126 15 51 S 64 39W
Grande →, Bahia, Brazil 127 11 30 S 44 30W
Grande →, Minas Gerais, Brazil 127 20 6 S 51 4W
Grande →, Spain 33 39 6N 0 48W
Grande →, U.S.A. 117 25 57N 97 9W
Grande, B. 128 50 30 S 68 20W
Grande Baie 107 48 19N 70 52W
Grande Baleine → 106 55 20N 77 50W
Grande Cache 108 53 53N 119 8W
Grande, Coxilha 125 28 18 S 51 30W
Grande de Santiago → 120 21 20N 105 50W
Grande-Entrée 107 47 30N 61 40W
Grande, La 118 45 15N 118 0W
Grande-Motte, La 21 43 23N 4 3 E
Grande Prairie 108 55 10N 118 50W
Grande-Rivière 107 48 26N 64 30W
Grande-Saulde → 19 47 22N 1 55 E
Grande-Vallée 107 49 14N 65 8W
Grandes-Bergeronnes 107 48 16N 69 35W
Grandfalls 117 31 21N 102 51W
Grandoe Mines 108 56 29N 129 54W
Grândola 31 38 12N 8 35W
Grandpré 19 49 20N 4 50 E
Grandview 118 46 13N 119 58W
Grandvilliers 19 49 40N 1 57 E
Graneros 124 34 5 S 70 45W
Grange, La, Ga., U.S.A. 115 33 4N 85 0W
Grange, La, Ky., U.S.A. 114 38 20N 85 20W
Grange, La, Tex., U.S.A. 117 29 54N 96 52W
Grangemouth 14 56 1N 3 43W
Granger, U.S.A. 118 46 25N 120 5W
Granger, Wyo., U.S.A. 118 41 35N 109 58W
Grängesberg 48 60 6N 15 1 E
Grangeville 118 45 57N 116 4W
Granite City 116 38 45N 90 3W
Granite Falls 116 44 45N 95 35W
Granite Pk. 118 45 8N 109 52W
Granity 101 41 39 S 171 51 E
Granja 127 3 7 S 40 50W
Granja de Moreruela 30 41 48N 5 44W
Granja de Torrehermosa 31 38 19N 5 35W
Gränna 49 58 1N 14 28 E
Granollers 32 41 39N 2 18 E
Gransee 24 53 0N 13 10 E
Grant 116 40 53N 101 42W
Grant City 116 40 30N 94 25W
Grant, Mt. 118 38 34N 118 48W
Grant, Pt. 100 38 32 S 145 6 E
Grant Range Mts. 119 38 30N 115 30W
Grantham 12 52 55N 0 39W
Grantown-on-Spey 14 57 19N 3 36W
Grants 119 35 14N 107 51W
Grants Pass 118 42 30N 123 22W
Grantsburg 116 45 46N 92 44W
Grantsville 118 40 35N 112 32W
Granville, France 18 48 50N 1 35W
Granville, N.D., U.S.A. 116 48 18N 100 48W
Granville, N.Y., U.S.A. 114 43 24N 73 16W
Granville L. 109 56 18N 100 30W
Grao de Gandia 33 39 0N 0 7W
Grapeland 117 31 30N 95 31W
Gras, L. de 104 64 30N 110 30W
Graskop 93 24 56 S 30 49 E
Gräsö 48 60 28N 18 35 E
Grass → 109 56 3N 96 33W
Grass Range 118 47 0N 109 0W
Grass River Prov. Park 109 54 40N 100 50W
Grass Valley, Calif., U.S.A. 118 39 18N 121 0W
Grass Valley, Oreg., U.S.A. 118 45 22N 120 48W
Grassano 41 40 38N 16 17 E
Grasse 21 43 38N 6 56 E
Graubünden (Grisons) □ 25 46 45N 9 30 E
Graulhet 20 43 45N 1 58 E
Graus 32 42 11N 0 20 E
Grave, Pte. de 20 45 34N 1 4W
Gravelbourg 109 49 50N 106 35W
Gravelines 19 51 0N 2 10 E
's-Gravenhage 16 52 7N 4 17 E
Gravenhurst 112 44 52N 79 20W
Gravesend, Austral. 99 29 35 S 150 20 E
Gravesend, U.K. 13 51 25N 0 22 E
Gravina di Púglia 41 40 48N 16 25 E
Gravois, Pointe-à- 121 16 15N 73 56W
Gravone → 21 41 58N 8 45 E
Gray 19 47 27N 5 35 E
Grayling 114 44 40N 84 42W
Grayling → 108 59 21N 125 0W
Grays Harbor 118 46 55N 124 8W
Grays L. 118 43 8N 111 30W
Grayson 109 50 45N 102 40W
Graz 26 47 4N 15 27 E
Grazalema 31 36 46N 5 23W
Grdelica 42 42 55N 22 3 E
Greasy L. 108 62 55N 122 12W
Great Abaco I. 121 26 25N 77 10W
Great Australia Basin 97 26 0 S 140 0 E
Great Australian Bight 96 33 30 S 130 0 E
Great Bahama Bank 121 23 15N 78 0W
Great Barrier I. 101 36 11 S 175 25 E
Great Barrier Reef 97 18 0 S 146 50 E
Great Barrington 113 42 11N 73 22W
Great Basin 118 40 0N 116 30W
Great Bear → 104 65 0N 124 0W
Great Bear L. 104 65 30N 120 0W
Great Bena 113 41 57N 75 45W
Great Bend 116 38 25N 98 55W
Great Blasket I. 15 52 5N 10 30W
Great Britain 8 54 0N 2 15W
Great Bushman Land 92 29 20 S 19 20 E
Great Central 108 49 20N 125 10W
Great Divide, The 100 35 0 S 149 17 E
Great Dividing Ra. 97 23 0 S 146 0 E
Great Exuma I. 121 23 30N 75 50W
Great Falls, Can. 109 50 27N 96 1W
Great Falls, U.S.A. 118 47 27N 111 12W
Great Fish →, C. Prov., S. Afr. 92 31 30 S 20 16 E
Great Fish →, C. Prov., S. Afr. 92 33 28 S 27 5 E
Great Guana Cay 121 24 0N 76 20W
Great Harbour Deep 107 50 25N 56 32W
Great I. 109 58 53N 96 35W
Great Inagua I. 121 21 0N 73 20W
Great Indian Desert = Thar Desert 68 28 0N 72 0 E
Great Lake 97 41 50 S 146 40 E
Great Orme's Head 12 53 20N 3 52W
Great Ouse → 12 52 47N 0 22 E
Great Palm I. 98 18 45 S 146 40 E
Great Plains 102 47 0N 105 0W
Great Ruaha → 90 7 56 S 37 52 E
Great Salt Lake 102 41 0N 112 30W
Great Salt Lake Desert 118 40 20N 113 50W
Great Salt Plains Res. 117 36 40N 98 15W
Great Sandy Desert 96 21 0 S 124 0 E
Great Scarcies → 84 9 0N 13 0W
Great Slave L. 108 61 23N 115 38W
Great Smoky Mt. Nat. Park 115 35 39N 83 30W
Great Stour → 13 51 15N 1 20 E
Great Victoria Des. 96 29 30 S 126 30 E
Great Wall 76 38 30N 109 30 E
Great Whernside 12 54 9N 1 59W
Great Winterhoek 92 33 07 S 19 10 E
Great Yarmouth 12 52 40N 1 45 E
Greater Antilles 121 17 40N 74 0W
Greater London □ 13 51 30N 0 5W
Greater Manchester □ 12 53 30N 2 15W
Greater Sunda Is. 72 7 0 S 112 0 E
Grebbestad 49 58 42N 11 15 E
Grebenka 54 50 9N 32 22 E
Greco, Mte. 40 41 48N 14 0 E
Gredos, Sierra de 30 40 20N 5 0W
Greece ■ 44 40 0N 23 0 E
Greeley, Colo., U.S.A. 116 40 30N 104 40W
Greeley, Nebr., U.S.A. 116 41 36N 98 32W
Green →, Ky., U.S.A. 114 37 54N 87 30W
Green →, Utah, U.S.A. 119 38 11N 109 53W
Green B. 114 45 0N 87 30W
Green Bay 114 44 30N 88 0W
Green C. 99 37 13 S 150 1 E
Green Cove Springs 115 29 59N 81 40W
Green Is. 98 4 35 S 154 10 E
Green Island 101 45 55 S 170 26 E
Green River 119 38 59N 110 10W
Greenbush, Mich., U.S.A. 112 44 35N 83 19W
Greenbush, Minn., U.S.A. 116 48 46N 96 10W
Greencastle 114 39 40N 86 48W
Greene 113 42 20N 75 45W
Greenfield, Ind., U.S.A. 114 39 47N 85 51W
Greenfield, Iowa, U.S.A. 116 41 18N 94 28W
Greenfield, Mass., U.S.A. 114 42 38N 72 38W
Greenfield, Miss., U.S.A. 117 37 28N 93 50W
Greenfield Park 113 45 29N 73 29W
Greenland □ 4 66 0N 45 0W
Greenland Sea 4 73 0N 10 0W
Greenock 14 55 57N 4 46W
Greenore 15 54 2N 6 8W
Greenore Pt. 15 52 15N 6 20W
Greenport 113 41 5N 72 23W
Greensboro, Ga., U.S.A. 115 33 34N 83 12W
Greensboro, N.C., U.S.A. 115 36 7N 79 46W
Greensburg, Ind., U.S.A. 114 39 20N 85 30W
Greensburg, Kans., U.S.A. 117 37 38N 99 20W
Greensburg, Pa., U.S.A. 114 40 18N 79 31W
Greenville, Liberia 84 5 1N 9 6W
Greenville, Ala., U.S.A. 115 31 50N 86 37W
Greenville, Calif., U.S.A. 118 40 8N 121 0W
Greenville, Ill., U.S.A. 116 38 53N 89 22W
Greenville, Me., U.S.A. 107 45 30N 69 32W
Greenville, Mich., U.S.A. 114 43 12N 85 14W
Greenville, Miss., U.S.A. 117 33 25N 91 0W
Greenville, N.C., U.S.A. 115 35 37N 77 26W
Greenville, Ohio, U.S.A. 114 40 5N 84 38W
Greenville, Pa., U.S.A. 114 41 23N 80 22W
Greenville, S.C., U.S.A. 115 34 54N 82 24W
Greenville, Tenn., U.S.A. 115 36 13N 82 51W
Greenville, Tex., U.S.A. 117 33 5N 96 5W
Greenwater Lake Prov. Park 109 52 32N 103 30W
Greenwich, U.K. 13 51 28N 0 0
Greenwich, Conn., U.S.A. 113 41 1N 73 38W
Greenwich, N.Y., U.S.A. 113 43 2N 73 36W
Greenwich, Ohio, U.S.A. 112 41 1N 82 32W
Greenwood, Can. 108 49 10N 118 40W
Greenwood, Miss., U.S.A. 117 33 30N 90 4W
Greenwood, S.C., U.S.A. 115 34 13N 82 13W
Gregory 116 43 14N 99 20W
Gregory → 98 17 53 S 139 17 E
Gregory Downs 98 18 35 S 138 45 E
Gregory, L. 97 28 55 S 139 0 E
Gregory Lake 96 20 10 S 127 30 E
Gregory Ra. 97 19 30 S 143 40 E
Greiffenberg 24 53 6N 13 57 E
Greifswald 24 54 6N 13 23 E
Greifswalder Bodden 24 54 12N 13 35 E
Greifswalder Oie 24 54 15N 13 55 E
Grein 26 48 14N 14 51 E
Greiner Wald 26 48 30N 15 0 E
Greiz 24 50 39N 12 12 E
Gremikha 52 67 50N 39 40 E
Grenå 49 56 25N 10 53 E
Grenada 117 33 45N 89 50W
Grenada ■ 121 12 10N 61 40W
Grenade 20 43 47N 1 17 E
Grenadines 121 12 40N 61 20W
Grenen 49 57 44N 10 40 E
Grenfell, Austral. 99 33 52 S 148 8 E
Grenfell, Can. 109 50 30N 102 56W
Grenoble 21 45 12N 5 42 E
Grenora 116 48 38N 103 54W
Grenville, C. 97 12 0 S 143 13 E
Grenville Chan. 108 53 40N 129 46W
Gréoux-les-Bains 21 43 45N 5 52 E
Gresham 118 45 30N 122 25W
Gresik 73 7 13 S 112 38 E
Grëssoney St. Jean 38 45 49N 7 47 E
Gretna Green 14 55 0N 3 3W
Greven 24 52 7N 7 36 E
Grevená 44 40 4N 21 25 E
Grevená □ 44 40 2N 21 25 E
Grevenbroich 24 51 6N 6 32 E
Grevenmacher 16 49 41N 6 26 E
Grevesmühlen 24 53 51N 11 10 E
Grevie 49 56 22N 12 46 E
Grey → 101 42 27 S 171 12 E
Grey, C. 97 13 0 S 136 35 E
Grey Range 97 27 0 S 143 30 E
Grey Res. 107 48 20N 56 30W
Greybull 118 44 30N 108 3W
Greytown, N.Z. 101 41 5 S 175 29 E
Greytown, S. Afr. 93 29 1 S 30 36 E
Gribanovskiy 55 51 28N 41 50 E
Gribbell I. 108 53 23N 129 0W
Gridley 118 39 27N 121 47W
Griekwastad 92 28 49 S 23 15 E
Griffin 115 33 17N 84 14W
Griffith 97 34 18 S 146 2 E
Grillby 48 59 38N 17 15 E
Grim, C. 97 40 45 S 144 45 E
Grimari 88 5 43N 20 6 E
Grimaylov 54 49 20N 26 5 E
Grimma 24 51 14N 12 44 E
Grimmen 24 54 6N 13 2 E
Grimsby 112 43 12N 79 34W
Grimsby, Greater 12 53 35N 0 5W
Grimsey 50 66 33N 18 0W
Grimshaw 108 56 10N 117 40W
Grimstad 47 58 22N 8 35 E
Grindelwald 25 46 38N 8 2 E
Grindsted 49 55 46N 8 55 E

Grindu Haifeng

Grindu 46 44 44N 26 50 E
Grinnell 116 41 45N 92 43W
Griñón 30 40 13N 3 51W
Grintavec 39 46 22N 14 32 E
Grip 47 63 16N 7 37 E
Griqualand East 93 30 30 S 29 0 E
Griqualand West 92 28 40 S 23 30 E
Grisolles 20 43 49N 1 19 E
Grisslehamn 48 60 5N 18 49 E
Griz Nez, C. 19 50 50N 1 35 E
Grmeč Planina 39 44 43N 16 16 E
Groais I. 107 50 55N 55 35W
Groblersdal 93 25 15 S 29 25 E
Grobming 26 47 27N 13 54 E
Grocka 42 44 40N 20 42 E
Gródek 28 53 6N 23 40 E
Grodkow 28 50 43N 17 21 E
Grodno 54 53 42N 23 52 E
Grodzisk Mázowiecki 28 52 7N 20 37 E
Grodzisk Wielkopolski 28 52 15N 16 22 E
Grodzyanka 54 53 31N 28 42 E
Groesbeck 117 31 32N 96 34W
Groix 18 47 38N 3 29W
Groix, I. de 18 47 38N 3 28W
Grójec 28 51 50N 20 58 E
Gronau, Niedersachsen, Ger. 24 52 5N 9 47 E
Gronau, Nordrhein-Westfalen, Ger. 24 52 13N 7 2 E
Grong 50 64 25N 12 8 E
Groningen 16 53 15N 6 35 E
Groningen □ 16 53 16N 6 40 E
Grönskåra 49 57 5N 15 43 E
Groom 117 35 12N 100 59W
Groot → 92 33 45 S 24 36 E
Groot Berg → 92 32 47 S 18 8 E
Groot-Brakrivier 92 34 2 S 22 18 E
Groot Karoo 92 32 35 S 23 0 E
Groote Eylandt 97 14 0 S 136 40 E
Grootfontein 92 19 31 S 18 6 E
Grootlaagte → 92 20 55 S 21 27 E
Gros C. 108 61 59N 113 32W
Grosa, P. 33 39 6N 1 36 E
Grósio 38 46 18N 10 17 E
Grosne → 21 46 42N 4 56 E
Gross Glockner 26 47 5N 12 40 E
Gross Ottersleben 24 52 5N 11 33 E
Grossenbrode 24 54 21N 11 4 E
Grossenhain 24 51 17N 13 32 E
Grosseto 38 42 45N 11 7 E
Grossgerungs 26 48 34N 14 57 E
Groswater B. 107 54 20N 57 40W
Groton, Conn., U.S.A. 113 41 22N 72 12W
Groton, S.D., U.S.A. 116 45 27N 98 6W
Grottáglie 41 40 32N 17 25 E
Grottaminarda 41 41 5N 15 4 E
Grottammare 39 42 59N 13 52 E
Grouard Mission 108 55 33N 116 9W
Grouin, Pointe du 18 48 43N 1 51W
Groundhog → 106 48 45N 82 58W
Grouse Creek 118 41 44N 113 57W
Grove City 112 41 10N 80 5W
Groveton, N.H., U.S.A. 114 44 34N 71 30W
Groveton, Tex., U.S.A. 117 31 5N 95 4W
Groznjan 39 45 22N 13 43 E
Groznyy 57 43 20N 45 45 E
Grubišno Polje 42 45 44N 17 12 E
Grudovo 43 42 21N 27 10 E
Grudusk 28 53 3N 20 38 E
Grudziądz 28 53 30N 18 47 E
Gruissan 20 43 8N 3 7 E
Grumo Áppula 41 41 2N 16 43 E
Grums 48 59 22N 13 5 E
Grünberg 24 50 37N 8 55 E
Grundy Center 116 42 22N 92 45W
Grungedal 47 59 44N 7 43 E
Gruver 117 36 19N 101 20W
Gruyères 25 46 35N 7 4 E
Gruža 42 43 54N 20 46 E
Gryazi 55 52 30N 39 58 E
Gryazovets 55 58 50N 40 10 E
Grybów 27 49 36N 20 55 E
Grycksbo 48 60 40N 15 29 E
Gryfice 28 53 55N 15 13 E
Gryfino 28 53 16N 14 29 E
Gryfow Sl. 28 51 2N 15 24 E
Grythyttan 48 59 41N 14 32 E
Grytviken 5 53 50 S 37 10W
Gstaad 25 46 28N 7 18 E
Guacanayabo, G. de 121 20 40N 77 20W
Guachípas → 124 25 40 S 65 30W
Guadajoz → 31 37 50N 4 51W
Guadalajara, Mexico 120 20 40N 103 20W
Guadalajara, Spain 32 40 37N 3 12W
Guadalajara □ 32 40 47N 3 0W
Guadalcanal, Solomon Is. 94 9 32 S 160 12 E
Guadalcanal, Spain 31 38 5N 5 52W
Guadalén → 31 38 5N 3 32W
Guadales 124 34 30 S 67 55W
Guadalete → 31 36 35N 6 13W
Guadalhorce → 31 36 41N 4 27W
Guadalimar → 33 38 5N 3 28W
Guadalmena → 33 38 19N 2 56W
Guadalmez → 31 38 46N 5 4W
Guadalope → 32 41 15N 0 3W
Guadalquivir → 31 36 47N 6 22W
Guadalupe, Spain 31 39 27N 5 17W
Guadalupe, U.S.A. 119 34 59N 120 33W
Guadalupe → 117 28 30N 96 53W
Guadalupe Bravos 120 31 20N 106 10W
Guadalupe I. 95 21 20N 118 50W
Guadalupe Pk. 119 31 50N 105 30W
Guadalupe, Sierra de 31 39 28N 5 30W
Guadarrama, Sierra de 30 41 0N 4 0W
Guadeloupe 121 16 20N 61 40W
Guadeloupe Passage 121 16 50N 62 15W
Guadiamar → 31 36 55N 6 24W
Guadiana → 31 37 14N 7 22W
Guadiana Menor → 33 37 56N 3 15W
Guadiaro → 31 36 17N 5 17W
Guadiato → 31 37 48N 5 5W
Guadiela → 32 40 22N 2 49W
Guadix 33 37 18N 3 11W
Guafo, Boca del 128 43 35 S 74 0W
Guaíra 125 24 5 S 54 10W
Guaira, La 126 10 36N 66 56W
Guaitecas, Islas 128 44 0 S 74 30W
Guajará-Mirim 126 10 50 S 65 20W
Guajira, Pen. de la 126 12 0N 72 0W
Gualdo Tadino 39 43 14N 12 46 E
Gualeguay 124 33 10 S 59 14W
Gualeguaychú 124 33 3 S 59 31W
Guam 94 13 27N 144 45 E
Guaminí 124 37 1 S 62 28W
Guamúchil 120 25 25N 108 3W
Guan Xian 75 31 2N 103 38 E
Guanabacoa 121 23 8N 82 18W
Guanacaste, Cordillera del 121 10 40N 85 4W
Guanaceví 120 25 40N 106 0W
Guanahani = San Salvador, I. 121 24 0N 74 40W
Guanajay 121 22 56N 82 42W
Guanajuato 120 21 0N 101 20W
Guanajuato □ 120 20 40N 101 20W
Guanare 126 8 42N 69 12W
Guandacol 124 29 30 S 68 40W
Guane 121 22 10N 84 7W
Guang'an 77 30 28N 106 35 E
Guangde 77 30 54N 119 25 E
Guangdong □ 75 23 0N 113 0 E
Guanghua 75 32 22N 111 38 E
Guangshun 77 26 8N 106 21 E
Guangxi Zhuangzu Zizhiqu □ 75 24 0N 109 0 E
Guangyuan 77 32 26N 105 51 E
Guangze 77 27 30N 117 12 E
Guangzhou 75 23 5N 113 10 E
Guanipa → 126 9 56N 62 26W
Guantánamo 121 20 10N 75 14W
Guantao 76 36 42N 115 25 E
Guanyun 77 34 20N 119 18 E
Guápiles 121 10 10N 83 46W
Guaporé → 126 11 55 S 65 4W
Guaqui 126 16 41 S 68 54W
Guara, Sierra de 32 42 19N 0 15W
Guarapari 125 20 40 S 40 30W
Guarapuava 125 25 20 S 51 30W
Guaratinguetá 125 22 49 S 45 9W
Guaratuba 125 25 53 S 48 38W
Guarda 30 40 32N 7 20W
Guarda □ 30 40 40N 7 20W
Guardafui, C. = Asir, Ras 63 11 55N 51 16 E
Guardamar del Segura 33 38 5N 0 39W
Guardavalle 41 38 31N 16 30 E
Guardia, La 30 41 56N 8 52W
Guardiagrele 39 42 11N 14 11 E
Guardo 30 42 47N 4 50W
Guareña 31 38 51N 6 6W
Guareña → 30 41 29N 5 23W
Guaria □ 124 25 45 S 56 30W
Guarujá 125 24 2 S 46 25W
Guarus 125 21 44 S 41 20W
Guasdualito 126 7 15N 70 44W
Guasipati 126 7 28N 61 54W
Guastalla 38 44 55N 10 40 E
Guatemala 120 14 40N 90 22W
Guatemala ■ 120 15 40N 90 30W
Guatire 126 10 28N 66 32W
Guaviare → 126 4 3N 67 44W
Guaxupé 125 21 10 S 47 5W
Guayama 121 17 59N 66 7W
Guayaquil 126 2 15 S 79 52W
Guayaquil, G. de 126 3 10 S 81 0W
Guaymas 120 27 59N 110 54W
Guazhou 77 32 17N 119 21 E
Guba 91 10 38 S 26 27 E
Gûbâl 86 27 30N 34 0 E
Gúbbio 39 43 20N 12 34 E
Gubin 28 51 57N 14 43 E
Gubio 85 12 30N 12 42 E
Gubkin 55 51 17N 37 32 E
Guča 42 43 46N 20 15 E
Guchil 71 5 35N 102 10 E
Gudalur 70 11 30N 76 29 E
Gudata 57 43 7N 40 10 E
Gudenå 49 56 27N 9 40 E
Gudermes 57 43 24N 46 5 E
Gudhjem 49 55 12N 14 58 E
Gudiña, La 30 42 4N 7 8W
Gudivada 70 16 30N 81 3 E
Gudiyatam 70 12 57N 78 55 E
Gudur 70 14 12N 79 55 E
Guebwiller 19 47 55N 7 12 E
Guecho 32 43 21N 2 59W
Guékédou 84 8 40N 10 5W
Guelma 83 36 25N 7 29 E
Guelph 106 43 35N 80 20W
Guelt es Stel 82 35 12N 3 1 E
Guelttara 82 29 23N 2 10W
Guemar 83 33 30N 6 49 E
Guéméné-Penfao 18 47 38N 1 50W
Guéméné-sur-Scorff 18 48 4N 3 13W
Guéné 85 11 44N 3 16 E
Guer 18 47 54N 2 8W
Güera, La 80 20 51N 17 0W
Guérande 18 47 20N 2 26W
Guerche, La 18 47 57N 1 16W
Guerche-sur-l'Aubois, La 19 46 58N 2 56 E
Guercif 82 34 14N 3 21W
Guéréda 81 14 31N 22 5 E
Guéret 20 46 11N 1 51 E
Guérigny 19 47 6N 3 10 E
Guernica 32 43 19N 2 40W
Guernsey, Chan. Is. 18 49 30N 2 35W
Guernsey, U.S.A. 116 42 19N 104 45W
Guerrara, Oasis, Alg. 83 32 51N 4 22 E
Guerrara, Saoura, Alg. 82 28 5N 0 8W
Guerrero □ 120 17 30N 100 0W
Guerzim 82 29 39N 1 40W
Guest I. 5 76 18 S 148 0W
Gueugnon 21 46 36N 4 2 E
Gueydan 117 30 3N 92 30W
Guglionesi 41 41 55N 14 54 E
Gui Jiang → 77 23 30N 111 15 E
Gui Xian 77 23 8N 109 35 E
Guia Lopes da Laguna 125 21 26 S 56 7W
Guichi 77 30 39N 117 27 E
Guider 85 9 56N 13 57 E
Guidimouni 85 13 42N 9 31 E
Guidong 77 26 7N 113 57 E
Guiglo 84 6 45N 7 30W
Guijo de Coria 30 40 6N 6 28W
Guildford 13 51 14N 0 34W
Guilford 107 45 12N 69 25W
Guilin 75 25 18N 110 15 E
Guillaumes 21 44 5N 6 52 E
Guillestre 21 44 39N 6 40 E
Guilvinec 18 47 48N 4 17W
Guimarães, Braz. 127 2 9 S 44 42W
Guimarães, Port. 30 41 28N 8 24W
Guimaras 73 10 35N 122 37 E
Guinea ■ 84 10 20N 10 0W
Guinea-Bissau ■ 84 12 0N 15 0W
Guinea, Gulf of 85 3 0N 2 30 E
Güines 121 22 50N 82 0W
Guingamp 18 48 34N 3 10W
Guipavas 18 48 26N 4 29W
Guiping 75 23 21N 110 2 E
Guipúzcoa □ 32 43 12N 2 15W
Guir, O. → 82 31 29N 2 17W
Güiria 126 10 32N 62 18W
Guiscard 19 49 40N 3 0 E
Guise 19 49 52N 3 35 E
Guitiriz 30 43 11N 7 50W
Guiuan 73 11 5N 125 55 E
Guixi 77 28 16N 117 15 E
Guiyang, Guizhou, China 75 26 32N 106 40 E
Guiyang, Hunan, China 77 25 46N 112 42 E
Guizhou □ 75 27 0N 107 0 E
Gujan-Mestras 20 44 38N 1 4W
Gujarat □ 68 23 20N 71 0 E
Gujranwala 68 32 10N 74 12 E
Gujrat 68 32 40N 74 2 E
Gukovo 57 48 1N 39 58 E
Gulargambone 100 31 20 S 148 30 E
Gulbarga 70 17 20N 76 50 E
Gulbene 54 57 8N 26 52 E
Guledgud 70 16 3N 75 48 E
Gulf Basin 96 15 20 S 129 0 E
Gulfport 117 30 21N 89 3W
Gulgong 99 32 20 S 149 49 E
Gulistan 68 30 30N 66 35 E
Gull Lake 109 50 10N 108 29W
Gullringen 49 57 48N 15 44 E
Gulma 85 12 40N 4 23 E
Gülpinar 44 39 32N 26 10 E
Gulshad 58 46 45N 74 25 E
Gulsvik 47 60 24N 9 38 E
Gulu 90 2 48N 32 17 E
Gulwe 90 6 30 S 36 25 E
Gulyaypole 56 47 45N 36 21 E
Gum Lake 99 32 42 S 143 9 E
Gumal → 68 31 40N 71 50 E
Gumbaz 68 30 2N 69 0 E
Gumel 85 12 39N 9 22 E
Gumiel de Hizán 32 41 46N 3 41W
Gumlu 98 19 53 S 147 41 E
Gumma □ 74 36 30N 138 20 E
Gummersbach 24 51 2N 7 32 E
Gummi 85 12 4N 5 9 E
Gümüsane 64 40 30N 39 30 E
Gümüşhaciköy 56 40 50N 35 18 E
Gumzai 73 5 28 S 134 42 E
Guna 68 24 40N 77 19 E
Guna Mt. 87 11 50N 37 40 E
Gundagai 99 35 3 S 148 6 E
Gundelfingen 25 48 33N 10 22 E
Gundih 73 7 10 S 110 56 E
Gundlakamma → 70 15 30N 80 15 E
Gungu 88 5 43 S 19 20 E
Gunisao → 109 53 56N 97 53W
Gunisao L. 109 53 33N 96 15W
Gunnedah 97 30 59 S 150 15 E
Gunning 100 34 47 S 149 14 E
Gunnison, Colo., U.S.A. 119 38 32N 106 56W
Gunnison, Utah, U.S.A. 118 39 11N 111 48W
Gunnison → 119 39 3N 108 30W
Guntakal 70 15 11N 77 27 E
Guntersville 115 34 18N 86 16W
Guntur 70 16 23N 80 30 E
Gunung-Sitoli 72 1 15N 97 30 E
Gunungapi 73 6 45 S 126 30 E
Gunupur 70 19 5N 83 50 E
Günz → 25 48 27N 10 16 E
Gunza 88 10 50 S 13 50 E
Günzburg 25 48 27N 10 16 E
Gunzenhausen 25 49 6N 10 45 E
Guo He → 77 32 59N 117 10 E
Guoyang 77 33 32N 116 12 E
Gupis 69 36 15N 73 20 E
Gura 68 25 12N 71 39 E
Gura Humorului 46 47 35N 25 53 E
Gura-Teghii 46 45 30N 26 25 E
Gurag 87 8 20N 38 20 E
Gürchan 64 34 55N 49 25 E
Gurdaspur 68 32 5N 75 31 E
Gurdon 117 33 55N 93 10W
Gurdzhaani 57 41 43N 45 52 E
Gurgaon 68 28 27N 77 1 E
Gurghiu, Munţii 46 46 41N 25 15 E
Gurk → 26 46 35N 14 31 E
Gurkha 69 28 5N 84 40 E
Gurley 99 29 45 S 149 48 E
Gurun 71 5 49N 100 27 E
Gurupá 127 1 25 S 51 35W
Gurupá, I. Grande de 127 1 25 S 51 45W
Gurupi → 127 1 13 S 46 6W
Guryev 57 47 5N 52 0 E
Gus-Khrustalnyy 55 55 42N 40 44 E
Gusau 85 12 12N 6 40 E
Gusev 54 54 35N 22 10 E
Gushan 76 39 50N 123 35 E
Gushi 77 32 11N 115 41 E
Gushiago 85 9 55N 0 15W
Gusinje 42 42 35N 19 50 E
Gúspini 40 39 32N 8 38 E
Gusselby 48 59 38N 15 14 E
Güssing 27 47 3N 16 20 E
Gustanj 39 46 36N 14 49 E
Gustine 119 37 14N 121 0 E
Güstrow 24 53 47N 12 12 E
Gusum 49 58 16N 16 30 E
Guta = Kalárovo 27 47 54N 18 0 E
Gütersloh 24 51 54N 8 25 E
Guthalongra 98 19 52 S 147 50 E
Guthega Dam 100 36 20 S 148 27 E
Guthrie 117 35 55N 97 30W
Guttenberg 116 42 46N 91 10W
Guyana ■ 126 5 0N 59 0W
Guyang 76 41 0N 110 5 E
Guyenne 20 44 30N 0 40 E
Guymon 117 36 45N 101 30W
Guyra 99 30 15 S 151 40 E
Guyuan 76 36 0N 106 20 E
Guzhen 77 33 22N 117 18 E
Guzmán, Laguna de 120 31 25N 107 25W
Gwa 67 17 36N 94 34 E
Gwaai 91 19 15 S 27 45 E
Gwabegar 99 30 31 S 149 0 E
Gwadabawa 85 13 28N 5 15 E
Gwādar 66 25 10N 62 18 E
Gwagwada 85 10 15N 7 15 E
Gwalior 68 26 12N 78 10 E
Gwanda 91 20 55 S 29 0 E
Gwandu 85 12 30N 4 41 E
Gwane 90 4 45N 25 48 E
Gwaram 85 10 15N 10 25 E
Gwarzo 85 12 20N 8 55 E
Gwda → 28 53 3N 16 44 E
Gweebarra B. 15 54 52N 8 21W
Gweedore 15 55 4N 8 15W
* Gwelo 91 19 28 S 29 45 E
Gwent □ 13 51 45N 2 55W
Gwi 85 9 0N 7 10 E
Gwinn 114 46 15N 87 29W
Gwio Kura 85 12 40N 11 2 E
Gwol 84 10 58N 1 59W
Gwoza 85 11 5N 13 40 E
Gwydir → 97 29 27 S 149 48 E
Gwynedd □ 12 53 0N 4 0W
Gyaring Hu 75 34 50N 97 40 E
Gydanskiy P-ov. 58 70 0N 78 0 E
Gyland 47 58 24N 6 45 E
Gympie 97 26 11 S 152 38 E
Gyoda 74 36 10N 139 30 E
Gyoma 27 46 56N 20 50 E
Gyöngyös 27 47 48N 20 0 E
Györ 27 47 41N 17 40 E
Györ-Sopron □ 27 47 40N 17 20 E
Gypsum Pt. 108 61 53N 114 35W
Gypsumville 109 51 45N 98 40W
Gyttorp 48 59 31N 14 58 E
Gyula 27 46 38N 21 17 E
Gzhatsk = Gagarin 54 55 30N 35 0 E

H

Ha 'Arava 62 30 50N 35 20 E
Haag 25 48 11N 12 12 E
Haapamäki 50 62 18N 24 28 E
Haapsalu 54 58 56N 23 30 E
Haarlem 16 52 23N 4 39 E
Haast → 101 43 50 S 169 2 E
Hab Nadi Chauki 66 25 0N 66 50 E
Habana, La 121 23 8N 82 22W
Habaswein 90 1 2N 39 30 E
Habay 108 58 50N 118 44W
Habiganj 69 24 24N 91 30 E
Hablingbo 49 57 12N 18 16 E
Habo 49 57 55N 14 6 E
Hachenburg 24 50 40N 7 49 E
Hachijō-Jima 74 33 5N 139 45 E
Hachinohe 74 40 30N 141 29 E
Hachiōji 74 35 40N 139 20 E
Hadali 68 32 16N 72 11 E
Hadarba, Ras 86 22 4N 36 51 E
Hadd, Ras al 65 22 35N 59 50 E
Haddington 14 55 57N 2 48W
Hadejia 85 12 30N 10 5 E
Hadejia → 85 12 50N 10 51 E
Haden 99 27 13 S 151 54 E
Hadera 62 32 27N 34 55 E
Hadera, N. → 62 32 28N 34 52 E
Haderslev 49 55 15N 9 30 E
Hadhra 86 20 10N 41 5 E
Hadhramaut = Haḑramawt 63 15 30N 49 30 E
Hadibu 63 12 35N 54 2 E
Hadjeb El Aïoun 83 35 21N 9 32 E
Haḑramawt 63 15 30N 49 30 E
Hadrians Wall 12 55 0N 2 30W
Hadsten 49 56 19N 10 3 E
Hadsund 49 56 44N 10 8 E
Haeju 76 38 3N 125 45 E
Haerhpin = Harbin 76 45 48N 126 40 E
Ḩafar al Baţin 64 28 25N 46 0 E
Hafizabad 68 32 5N 73 40 E
Haflong 67 25 10N 93 5 E
Hafnarfjörður 50 64 4N 21 57W
Haft-Gel 64 31 30N 49 32 E
Hafun, Ras 63 10 29N 51 30 E
Hagalil 62 32 53N 35 18 E
Hagari → 70 15 40N 77 0 E
Hagen 24 51 21N 7 29 E
Hagenow 24 53 25N 11 10 E
Hagerman 117 33 5N 104 22W
Hagerstown 114 39 39N 77 46W
Hagetmau 20 43 39N 0 37W
Hagfors 48 60 3N 13 45 E
Häggenås 48 63 24N 14 55 E
Hagi, Iceland 50 65 28N 23 25W
Hagi, Japan 74 34 30N 131 22 E
Hagolan 62 33 0N 35 45 E
Hags Hd. 15 52 57N 9 30W
Hague, C. de la 18 49 44N 1 56W
Hague, The = s'-Gravenhage 16 52 7N 4 17 E
Haguenau 19 48 49N 7 47 E
Hai □ 90 3 10 S 37 10 E
Haicheng 76 40 50N 122 45 E
Haifeng 77 22 58N 115 10 E

* *Renamed Gweru*

Haiger Håverud

Haiger **24** 50 44N 8 12 E
Haikang **77** 20 52N 110 8 E
Haikou **75** 20 1N 110 16 E
Ḩā'il **64** 27 28N 41 45 E
Hailar **75** 49 10N 119 38 E
Hailar He → **76** 49 30N 117 50 E
Hailey **118** 43 30N 114 15W
Haileybury **106** 47 30N 79 38W
Hailin **76** 44 37N 129 30 E
Hailing Dao **77** 21 35N 111 47 E
Hailong **76** 42 32N 125 40 E
Hailun **75** 47 28N 126 50 E
Hailuoto **50** 65 3N 24 45 E
Haimen **77** 31 52N 121 10 E
Hainan **77** 19 0N 110 0 E
Hainan Dao **75** 19 0N 109 30 E
Hainaut □ **16** 50 30N 4 0 E
Hainburg **27** 48 9N 16 56 E
Haines **118** 44 51N 117 59W
Haines City **115** 28 6N 81 35W
Haines Junction **108** 60 45N 137 30W
Hainfeld **26** 48 3N 15 48 E
Haining **77** 30 28N 120 40 E
Haiphong **71** 20 47N 106 41 E
Haiti ■ **121** 19 0N 72 30W
Haiya Junction **86** 18 20N 36 21 E
Haiyan **77** 30 28N 120 58 E
Haiyang **76** 36 47N 121 9 E
Haiyuan **76** 36 35N 105 52 E
Haja **73** 3 19 S 129 37 E
Hajar Bangar **81** 10 40N 22 45 E
Hajar, Jabal **64** 26 5N 39 10 E
Hajdú-Bihar □ **27** 47 30N 21 30 E
Hajdúböszörmény **27** 47 40N 21 30 E
Hajdúdurog **27** 47 48N 21 30 E
Hajdúhadház **27** 47 40N 21 40 E
Hajdúnánás **27** 47 50N 21 26 E
Hajdúsámson **27** 47 37N 21 42 E
Hajdúszobaszló **27** 47 27N 21 22 E
Hajipur **69** 25 45N 85 13 E
Hajówka **28** 52 47N 23 35 E
Hajr **65** 24 0N 56 34 E
Hakansson, Mts. **91** 8 40 S 25 45 E
Håkantorp **49** 58 18N 12 55 E
Hakken-Zan **74** 34 10N 135 54 E
Hakodate **74** 41 45N 140 44 E
Ḩalab = Aleppo **64** 36 10N 37 15 E
Ḩalabjah **64** 35 10N 45 58 E
Halaib **86** 22 12N 36 30 E
Halbe **86** 19 40N 42 15 E
Halberstadt **24** 51 53N 11 2 E
Halcombe **101** 40 8 S 175 30 E
Halcyon, Mt. **73** 13 0N 121 30 E
Halden **47** 59 9N 11 23 E
Haldensleben **24** 52 17N 11 30 E
Haldia **67** 22 5N 88 3 E
Haldwani-cum-Kathgodam **69** 29 31N 79 30 E
Haleakala Crater **110** 20 43N 156 12W
Haleyville **115** 34 15N 87 40W
Half Assini **84** 5 1N 2 50W
Halfway **118** 44 56N 117 8W
Halfway → **108** 56 12N 121 32W
Ḩalḩul **62** 31 35N 35 7 E
Hali, Si. Arab. **86** 18 40N 41 15 E
Hali, Yemen **63** 18 30N 41 30 E
Haliburton **106** 45 3N 78 30W
Halicarnassus **45** 37 3N 27 30 E
Halifax, Austral. **98** 18 32 S 146 22 E
Halifax, Can. **107** 44 38N 63 35W
Halifax, U.K. **12** 53 43N 1 51W
Halifax B. **97** 18 50 S 147 0 E
Halifax I. **92** 26 38 S 15 4 E
Halīl Rūd → **65** 27 40N 58 30 E
Hall **26** 47 17N 11 30 E
Hall Beach **105** 68 46N 81 12W
Hallabro **49** 56 22N 15 5 E
Hallands län □ **49** 56 50N 12 50 E
Hallands Väderö **49** 56 27N 12 34 E
Hallandsås **49** 56 22N 13 0 E
Halle, Belg. **16** 50 44N 4 13 E
Halle, Halle, Ger. **24** 51 29N 12 0 E
Halle, Nordrhein-Westfalen, Ger. **24** 52 4N 8 20 E
Halle □ **24** 51 28N 11 58 E
Hällefors **48** 59 47N 14 31 E
Hallefors **49** 59 46N 14 30 E
Hallein **26** 47 40N 13 5 E
Hällekis **49** 58 38N 13 27 E
Hallett **99** 33 25 S 138 55 E
Hallettsville **117** 29 28N 96 57W
Hällevadsholm **49** 58 35N 11 33 E
Halley Bay **5** 75 31 S 26 36W
Hallia → **70** 16 55N 79 20 E
Halliday **116** 47 20N 102 25W
Halliday L. **109** 61 21N 108 56W
Hallingskeid **47** 60 40N 7 17 E
Hällnäs **50** 64 19N 19 36 E
Hallock **109** 48 47N 97 0W
Halls Creek **96** 18 16 S 127 38 E
Hallsberg **48** 59 5N 15 7 E
Hallstahammar **48** 59 38N 16 15 E
Hallstatt **26** 47 33N 13 38 E
Hallstavik **48** 60 5N 18 37 E
Hallstead **113** 41 56N 75 45W
Halmahera **73** 0 40N 128 0 E
Halmeu **46** 47 57N 23 2 E
Halmstad **49** 56 41N 12 52 E
Halq el Oued **83** 36 53N 10 18 E
Hals **49** 56 59N 10 18 E
Halsa **47** 63 3N 8 14 E
Halsafjorden **47** 63 5N 8 10 E
Hälsingborg = Helsingborg **49** 56 3N 12 42 E
Halstad **116** 47 21N 96 50W
Haltdalen **47** 62 56N 11 8 E
Haltern **24** 51 44N 7 10 E
Halul **65** 25 40N 52 40 E
Ham **19** 49 45N 3 4 E
Hamab **92** 28 7 S 19 16 E
Hamad **87** 15 20N 33 32 E
Hamada **74** 34 56N 132 4 E
Hamadān **64** 34 52N 48 32 E
Hamadān □ **64** 35 0N 49 0 E
Hamadia **82** 35 28N 1 57 E
Hamāh **64** 35 5N 36 40 E
Hamamatsu **74** 34 45N 137 45 E
Hamar **47** 60 48N 11 7 E
Hamarøy **50** 68 5N 15 38 E
Hamâta, Gebel **86** 24 17N 35 0 E
Hamber Prov. Park **108** 52 20N 118 0W
Hamburg, Ger. **24** 53 32N 9 59 E
Hamburg, Ark., U.S.A. **117** 33 15N 91 47W
Hamburg, Iowa, U.S.A. **116** 40 37N 95 38W
Hamburg, N.Y., U.S.A. **112** 42 44N 78 50W
Hamburg, Pa., U.S.A. **113** 40 33N 76 0W
Hamburg □ **24** 53 30N 10 0 E
Hamden **113** 41 21N 72 56W
Hamdh, W. → **86** 24 55N 36 20 E
Hämeen lääni □ **51** 61 24N 24 10 E
Hämeenlinna **50** 61 0N 24 28 E
Hamélé **84** 10 56N 2 45W
Hameln **24** 52 7N 9 24 E
Hamer Koke **87** 5 15N 36 45 E
Hamersley Ra. **96** 22 0 S 117 45 E
Hamhung **76** 39 54N 127 30 E
Hami **75** 42 55N 93 25 E
Hamilton, Austral. **97** 37 45 S 142 2 E
Hamilton, Berm. **121** 32 15N 64 45W
Hamilton, Can. **106** 43 15N 79 50W
Hamilton, N.Z. **101** 37 47 S 175 19 E
Hamilton, U.K. **14** 55 47N 4 2W
Hamilton, Mo., U.S.A. **116** 39 45N 93 59W
Hamilton, Mont., U.S.A. **118** 46 20N 114 6W
Hamilton, N.Y., U.S.A. **114** 42 49N 75 31W
Hamilton, Ohio, U.S.A. **114** 39 20N 84 35W
Hamilton, Tex., U.S.A. **117** 31 40N 98 5W
Hamilton → **98** 23 30 S 139 47 E
Hamilton Hotel **98** 22 45 S 140 40 E
Hamilton Inlet **107** 54 0N 57 30W
Hamiota **109** 50 11N 100 38W
Hamlet **115** 34 56N 79 40W
Hamley Bridge **99** 34 17 S 138 35 E
Hamlin, N.Y., U.S.A. **112** 43 17N 77 55W
Hamlin, Tex., U.S.A. **117** 32 58N 100 8W
Hamm **24** 51 40N 7 49 E
Hammam Bouhadjar **82** 35 23N 0 58W
Hammamet **83** 36 24N 10 38 E
Hammamet, G. de **83** 36 10N 10 48 E
Hammarstrand **48** 63 7N 16 20 E
Hammel **49** 56 16N 9 52 E
Hammelburg **25** 50 7N 9 54 E
Hammeren **49** 55 18N 14 47 E
Hammerfest **50** 70 39N 23 41 E
Hammond, Ind., U.S.A. **114** 41 40N 87 30W
Hammond, La., U.S.A. **117** 30 32N 90 30W
Hammonton **114** 39 40N 74 47W
Hamneda **49** 56 41N 13 51 E
Hamoyet, Jebel **86** 17 33N 38 2 E
Hampden **101** 45 18 S 170 50 E
Hampshire □ **13** 51 3N 1 20W
Hampshire Downs **13** 51 10N 1 10W
Hampton, Ark., U.S.A. **117** 33 35N 92 29W
Hampton, Iowa, U.S.A. **116** 42 42N 93 12W
Hampton, N.H., U.S.A. **113** 42 56N 70 48W
Hampton, S.C., U.S.A. **115** 32 52N 81 2W
Hampton, Va., U.S.A. **114** 37 4N 76 18W
Hampton Harbour **96** 20 30 S 116 30 E
Hampton Tableland **96** 32 0 S 127 0 E
Hamrat esh Sheykh **87** 14 38N 27 55 E
Han Jiang → **77** 23 25N 116 40 E
Han Shui → **77** 30 35N 114 18 E
Hana **110** 20 45N 155 59W
Hanak **86** 25 32N 37 0 E
Hanang **90** 4 30 S 35 25 E
Hanau **25** 50 8N 8 56 E
Hancheng **76** 35 31N 110 25 E
Hancock, Mich., U.S.A. **116** 47 10N 88 40W
Hancock, Minn., U.S.A. **116** 45 26N 95 46W
Hancock, Pa., U.S.A. **113** 41 57N 75 19W
Handa, Japan **74** 34 53N 137 0 E
Handa, Somalia **63** 10 37N 51 2 E
Handan **76** 36 35N 114 28 E
Handen **48** 59 12N 18 12 E
Handeni **90** 5 25 S 38 2 E
Handeni □ **90** 5 30 S 38 0 E
Handlová **27** 48 45N 18 35 E
Handub **86** 19 15N 37 16 E
Hanegev **62** 30 50N 35 0 E
Haney **108** 49 12N 122 40W
Hanford **119** 36 23N 119 39W
Hangang → **76** 37 50N 126 30 E
Hangayn Nuruu **75** 47 30N 100 0 E
Hangchou = Hangzhou **75** 30 18N 120 11 E
Hanggin Houqi **76** 40 58N 107 4 E
Hangklip, K. **92** 34 26 S 18 48 E
Hangö **51** 59 50N 22 57 E
Hangu **76** 39 18N 117 53 E
Hangzhou **75** 30 18N 120 11 E
Hangzhou Wan **75** 30 15N 120 45 E
Ḩanīsh J. **63** 13 45N 42 46 E
Haniska **27** 48 37N 21 15 E
Hanita **62** 33 5N 35 10 E
Hankinson **116** 46 9N 96 58W
Hanko **51** 59 59N 22 57 E
Hankou **77** 30 35N 114 30 E
Hanksville **119** 38 19N 110 45W
Hanmer **101** 42 32 S 172 50 E
Hann, Mt. **96** 16 0 S 126 0 E
Hanna **108** 51 40N 111 54W
Hannaford **116** 47 23N 98 11W
Hannah **116** 48 58N 98 42W
Hannah B. **106** 51 40N 80 0W
Hannibal **116** 39 42N 91 22W
Hannik **86** 18 12N 32 20 E
Hannover **24** 52 23N 9 43 E
Hanö **49** 56 2N 14 50 E
Hanöbukten **49** 55 35N 14 30 E
Hanoi **71** 21 5N 105 55 E
Hanover, Can. **112** 44 9N 81 2W
Hanover, S. Afr. **92** 31 4 S 24 29 E
Hanover, N.H., U.S.A. **114** 43 43N 72 17W
Hanover, Ohio, U.S.A. **112** 40 5N 82 17W
Hanover, Pa., U.S.A. **114** 39 46N 76 59W
Hanover = Hannover **24** 52 23N 9 43 E
Hanover, I. **128** 51 0 S 74 50W
Hansi **68** 29 10N 75 57 E
Hansjö **48** 61 10N 14 40 E
Hanson Range **96** 27 0 S 136 30 E
Hanwood **100** 34 22 S 146 2 E
Hanyang **77** 30 35N 114 2 E
Hanyin **77** 32 54N 108 28 E
Hanzhong **75** 33 10N 107 1 E
Hanzhuang **77** 34 33N 117 23 E
Haparanda **50** 65 52N 24 8 E
Happy **117** 34 47N 101 50W
Happy Camp **118** 41 52N 123 22W
Happy Valley **107** 53 15N 60 20W
Hapur **68** 28 45N 77 45 E
Ḩaql **86** 29 10N 35 0 E
Har **73** 5 16 S 133 14 E
Har Hu **75** 38 20N 97 38 E
Har Us Nuur **75** 48 0N 92 0 E
Har Yehuda **62** 31 35N 34 57 E
Ḩaraḑ **64** 24 22N 49 0 E
Haraisan Plateau **64** 23 0N 47 40 E
Haramsøya **47** 62 39N 6 12 E
Harardera **63** 4 33N 47 38 E
Harat **87** 16 5N 39 26 E
Harazé, Chad **81** 14 20N 19 12 E
Harazé, Chad **81** 9 57N 20 48 E
Harbin **76** 45 48N 126 40 E
Harboør **49** 56 38N 8 10 E
Harbor Beach **114** 43 50N 82 38W
Harbor Springs **114** 45 28N 85 0W
Harbour Breton **107** 47 29N 55 50W
Harbour Grace **107** 47 40N 53 22W
Harburg **24** 53 27N 9 58 E
Hårby **49** 55 13N 10 7 E
Harcourt **98** 24 17 S 149 55 E
Harda **68** 22 27N 77 5 E
Hardangerfjorden **47** 60 15N 6 0 E
Hardangerjøkulen **47** 60 30N 7 0 E
Hardangervidda **47** 60 20N 7 20 E
Hardap Dam **92** 24 32 S 17 50 E
Hardenberg **16** 52 34N 6 37 E
Harderwijk **16** 52 21N 5 38 E
Hardin **118** 45 44N 107 35W
Harding **93** 30 35 S 29 55 E
Hardisty **108** 52 40N 111 18W
Hardman **118** 45 12N 119 40W
Hardoi **69** 27 26N 80 6 E
Hardwar **68** 29 58N 78 9 E
Hardwick **113** 44 30N 72 20W
Hardy **117** 36 20N 91 30W
Hardy, Pen. **128** 55 30 S 68 20W
Hare B. **107** 51 15N 55 45W
Hare Gilboa **62** 32 31N 35 25 E
Hare Meron **62** 32 59N 35 24 E
Haren **24** 52 47N 7 18 E
Harer **87** 9 20N 42 8 E
Harer □ **87** 7 12N 42 0 E
Hareto **87** 9 23N 37 6 E
Harfleur **18** 49 30N 0 10 E
Hargeisa **63** 9 30N 44 2 E
Harghita □ **46** 46 30N 25 30 E
Harghita, Mţii **46** 46 25N 25 35 E
Hargshamn **48** 60 12N 18 30 E
Hari → **72** 1 16 S 104 5 E
Haricha, Hamada el **82** 22 40N 3 15W
Harihar **70** 14 32N 75 44 E
Haringhata → **69** 22 0N 89 58 E
Haripad **70** 9 14N 76 28 E
Harīrūd **65** 35 0N 61 0 E
Harīrūd → **65** 34 20N 62 30 E
Harkat **86** 20 25N 39 40 E
Harlan, Iowa, U.S.A. **116** 41 37N 95 20W
Harlan, Tenn., U.S.A. **115** 36 50N 83 20W
Harlech **12** 52 52N 4 7W
Harlem **118** 48 29N 108 47W
Harlingen, Neth. **16** 53 11N 5 25 E
Harlingen, U.S.A. **117** 26 20N 97 50W
Harlowton **118** 46 30N 109 54W
Harmånger **48** 61 55N 17 20 E
Harmil **87** 16 30N 40 10 E
Harney Basin **118** 43 30N 119 0W
Harney L. **118** 43 0N 119 0W
Harney Pk. **116** 43 52N 103 33W
Härnön **48** 62 36N 18 0 E
Härnösand **48** 62 38N 18 0 E
Haro **32** 42 35N 2 55W
Haro, C. **120** 27 50N 110 55W
Harp L. **107** 55 5N 61 50W
Harpanahalli **70** 14 47N 76 2 E
Harpe, La **116** 40 30N 91 0W
Harper **84** 4 25N 7 43W
Harplinge **49** 56 45N 12 45 E
Harrand **68** 29 28N 70 3 E
Ḩarrat al Kishb **64** 22 30N 40 15 E
Harrat al 'Uwairidh **64** 26 50N 38 0 E
Harrat Khaibar **86** 25 45N 40 0 E
Harrat Nawāsīf **86** 21 30N 42 0 E
Harriman **115** 36 0N 84 35W
Harrington Harbour **107** 50 31N 59 30W
Harris **14** 57 50N 6 55W
Harris L. **96** 31 10 S 135 10 E
Harris, Sd. of **14** 57 44N 7 6W
Harrisburg, Ill., U.S.A. **117** 37 42N 88 30W
Harrisburg, Nebr., U.S.A. **116** 41 36N 103 46W
Harrisburg, Oreg., U.S.A. **118** 44 16N 123 10W
Harrisburg, Pa., U.S.A. **114** 40 18N 76 52W
Harrismith **93** 28 15 S 29 8 E
Harrison, Ark., U.S.A. **117** 36 10N 93 4W
Harrison, Idaho, U.S.A. **118** 47 30N 116 51W
Harrison, Nebr., U.S.A. **116** 42 42N 103 52W
Harrison B. **104** 70 25N 151 30W
Harrison, C. **107** 54 55N 57 55W
Harrison L. **108** 49 33N 121 50W
Harrisonburg **114** 38 28N 78 52W
Harrisonville **116** 38 39N 94 21W
Harriston **106** 43 57N 80 53W
Harrisville **106** 44 40N 83 19W
Harrogate **12** 53 59N 1 32W
Harrow, Can. **112** 42 2N 82 55W
Harrow, U.K. **13** 51 35N 0 15W
Harsefeld **24** 53 26N 9 31 E
Harstad **50** 68 48N 16 30 E
Hart **114** 43 42N 86 21W
Hartbees → **92** 28 45 S 20 32 E
Hartberg **26** 47 17N 15 58 E
Hartford, Conn., U.S.A. **114** 41 47N 72 41W
Hartford, Ky., U.S.A. **114** 37 26N 86 50W
Hartford, S.D., U.S.A. **116** 43 40N 96 58W
Hartford, Wis., U.S.A. **116** 43 18N 88 25W
Hartford City **114** 40 22N 85 20W
Hartland **107** 46 20N 67 32W
Hartland Pt. **13** 51 2N 4 32W
Hartlepool **12** 54 42N 1 11W
Hartley **91** 18 10 S 30 14 E
Hartley Bay **108** 53 25N 129 15W
Hartmannberge **92** 17 0 S 13 0 E
Hartney **109** 49 30N 100 35W
Hartselle **115** 34 25N 86 55W
Hartshorne **117** 34 51N 95 30W
Hartsville **115** 34 23N 80 2W
Hartwell **115** 34 21N 82 52W
Harunabad **68** 29 35N 73 8 E
Harur **70** 12 3N 78 29 E
Harvey, Ill., U.S.A. **114** 41 40N 87 40W
Harvey, N.D., U.S.A. **116** 47 50N 99 58W
Harwich **13** 51 56N 1 18 E
Haryana □ **68** 29 0N 76 10 E
Harz **24** 51 40N 10 40 E
Harzgerode **24** 51 38N 11 8 E
Hasa **64** 26 0N 49 0 E
Hasaheisa **87** 14 44N 33 20 E
Hasani **86** 25 0N 37 8 E
Hasanpur **68** 28 43N 78 17 E
Haselünne **24** 52 40N 7 30 E
Hasharon **62** 32 12N 34 49 E
Hashefela **62** 31 30N 34 43 E
Håsjö **48** 63 1N 16 5 E
Haskell, Okla., U.S.A. **117** 35 51N 95 40W
Haskell, Tex., U.S.A. **117** 33 10N 99 45W
Haslach **25** 48 16N 8 7 E
Hasle **49** 55 11N 14 44 E
Haslev **49** 55 18N 11 57 E
Hasparren **20** 43 24N 1 18W
Hasselt **16** 50 56N 5 21 E
Hassene, Ad. **82** 21 0N 4 0 E
Hassfurt **25** 50 2N 10 30 E
Hassi Berrekrem **83** 33 45N 5 16 E
Hassi bou Khelala **82** 30 17N 0 18W
Hassi Daoula **83** 33 4N 5 38 E
Hassi Djafou **82** 30 55N 3 35 E
Hassi el Abiod **82** 31 47N 3 37 E
Hassi el Biod **83** 28 30N 6 0 E
Hassi el Gassi **83** 30 52N 6 5 E
Hassi el Hadjar **83** 31 28N 4 45 E
Hassi er Rmel **82** 32 56N 3 17 E
Hassi Imoulaye **83** 29 54N 9 10 E
Hassi Inifel **82** 29 50N 3 41 E
Hassi Marroket **82** 30 10N 3 0 E
Hassi Messaoud **83** 31 43N 6 8 E
Hassi Rhénami **83** 31 50N 5 58 E
Hassi Tartrat **83** 30 5N 6 28 E
Hassi Zerzour **82** 30 51N 3 56W
Hastings, Can. **112** 44 18N 77 57W
Hastings, N.Z. **101** 39 39 S 176 52 E
Hastings, U.K. **13** 50 51N 0 36 E
Hastings, Mich., U.S.A. **114** 42 40N 85 20W
Hastings, Minn., U.S.A. **116** 44 41N 92 51W
Hastings, Nebr., U.S.A. **116** 40 34N 98 22W
Hastings Ra. **99** 31 15 S 152 14 E
Hästveda **49** 56 17N 13 55 E
Hat Nhao **71** 14 46N 106 32 E
Hatch **119** 32 45N 107 8W
Hatches Creek **96** 20 56 S 135 12 E
Hatchet L. **109** 58 36N 103 40W
Haţeg **46** 45 36N 22 55 E
Haţeg, Mţii. **46** 45 25N 23 0 E
Hatfield P.O. **99** 33 54 S 143 49 E
Hatgal **75** 50 26N 100 9 E
Hathras **68** 27 36N 78 6 E
Hattah **99** 34 48 S 142 17 E
Hatteras, C. **115** 35 10N 75 30W
Hattiesburg **117** 31 20N 89 20W
Hatvan **27** 47 40N 19 45 E
Hau Bon = Cheo Reo **71** 13 25N 108 28 E
Haug **47** 60 23N 10 26 E
Haugastøl **47** 60 30N 7 50 E
Haugesund **47** 59 23N 5 13 E
Haultain → **109** 55 51N 106 46W
Hauraki Gulf **101** 36 35 S 175 5 E
Hauran **62** 32 50N 36 15 E
Hausruck **26** 48 6N 13 30 E
Haut Atlas **82** 32 30N 5 0W
Haut-Rhin □ **19** 48 0N 7 15 E
Haut Zaïre □ **90** 2 20N 26 0 E
Hautah, Wahāt al **64** 23 40N 47 0 E
Haute-Corse □ **21** 42 30N 9 30 E
Haute-Garonne □ **20** 43 28N 1 30 E
Haute-Loire □ **20** 45 5N 3 50 E
Haute-Marne □ **19** 48 10N 5 20 E
Haute-Saône □ **19** 47 45N 6 10 E
Haute-Savoie □ **21** 46 0N 6 20 E
Haute-Vienne □ **20** 45 50N 1 10 E
Hauterive **107** 49 10N 68 16W
Hautes-Alpes □ **21** 44 42N 6 20 E
Hautes-Pyrénées □ **20** 43 0N 0 10 E
Hauteville **21** 45 58N 5 36 E
Hautmont **19** 50 15N 3 55 E
Hauts-de-Seine □ **19** 48 52N 2 15 E
Hauts Plateaux **82** 34 14N 1 0 E
Hauzenberg **25** 48 39N 13 38 E
Havana **116** 40 19N 90 3W
Havana = La Habana **121** 23 8N 82 22W
Havasu, L. **119** 34 18N 114 28W
Havdhem **49** 57 10N 18 20 E
Havelange **16** 50 23N 5 15 E
Havelock, N.B., Can. **107** 46 2N 65 24W
Havelock, Ont., Can. **106** 44 26N 77 53W
Havelock, N.Z. **101** 41 17 S 173 48 E
Havelock I. **71** 11 55N 93 2 E
Haverfordwest **13** 51 48N 4 59W
Haverhill **114** 42 50N 71 2W
Haveri **70** 14 53N 75 24 E
Havering **13** 51 33N 0 20 E
Haverstraw **113** 41 12N 73 58W
Håverud **49** 58 50N 12 28 E

Havîrna Hogansville

Havîrna 46 48 4N 26 43 E
Havlíčkův Brod 26 49 36N 15 33 E
Havneby 49 55 5N 8 34 E
Havre 118 48 34N 109 40W
Havre-St.-Pierre 107 50 18N 63 33W
Havre-Aubert 107 47 12N 61 56W
Havre, Le 18 49 30N 0 5 E
Havza 64 41 0N 35 35 E
Haw → 115 35 36N 79 3W
Hawaii □ 110 20 30N 157 0W
Hawaii 110 20 0N 155 0W
Hawaiian Is. 110 20 30N 156 0W
Hawaiian Ridge 95 24 0N 165 0W
Hawarden, Can. 109 51 25N 106 36W
Hawarden, U.S.A. 116 43 2N 96 28W
Hawea Lake 101 44 28 S 169 19 E
Hawera 101 39 35 S 174 19 E
Hawick 14 55 25N 2 48W
Hawk Junction 106 48 5N 84 38W
Hawke B. 101 39 25 S 177 20 E
Hawke, C. 100 32 13 S 152 34 E
Hawker 97 31 59 S 138 22 E
Hawke's Bay □ 101 39 45 S 176 35 E
Hawkesbury 106 45 37N 74 37W
Hawkesbury → 97 33 30 S 151 10 E
Hawkesbury I. 108 53 37N 129 3W
Hawkinsville 115 32 17N 83 30W
Hawkwood 99 25 45 S 150 50 E
Hawley 116 46 58N 96 20W
Hawrân 62 32 45N 36 15 E
Hawthorne 118 38 31N 118 37W
Hawzen 87 13 58N 39 28 E
Haxtun 116 40 40N 102 39W
Hay, Austral. 97 34 30 S 144 51 E
Hay, U.K. 13 52 4N 3 9W
Hay →, Austral. 97 25 14 S 138 0 E
Hay →, Can. 108 60 50N 116 26W
Hay L. 108 58 50N 118 50W
Hay Lakes 108 53 12N 113 2W
Hay River 108 60 51N 115 44W
Hay Springs 116 42 40N 102 38W
Hayange 19 49 20N 6 2 E
Hayden, Ariz., U.S.A. 119 33 2N 110 48W
Hayden, Colo., U.S.A. 118 40 30N 107 22W
Haydon 98 18 0 S 141 30 E
Haye-Descartes, La 18 46 58N 0 42 E
Haye-du-Puits, La 18 49 17N 1 33W
Hayes 116 44 22N 101 1W
Hayes → 109 57 3N 92 12W
Haynesville 117 33 0N 93 7W
Hays, Can. 108 50 6N 111 48W
Hays, U.S.A. 116 38 55N 99 25W
Hayward 116 46 2N 91 30W
Hayward's Heath 13 51 0N 0 5W
Hazard 114 37 18N 83 10W
Hazaribagh 69 23 58N 85 26 E
Hazaribagh Road 69 24 12N 85 57 E
Hazebrouck 19 50 42N 2 31 E
Hazelton, Can. 108 55 20N 127 42W
Hazelton, U.S.A. 116 46 30N 100 15W
Hazen, N.D., U.S.A. 116 47 18N 101 38W
Hazen, Nev., U.S.A. 118 39 37N 119 2W
Hazlehurst, Ga., U.S.A. 115 31 50N 82 35W
Hazlehurst, Miss., U.S.A. 117 31 52N 90 24W
Hazleton 114 40 58N 76 0W
Ḥazor 62 33 2N 35 32 E
He Xian 77 24 27N 111 30 E
Head of Bight 96 31 30 S 131 25 E
Headlands 91 18 15 S 32 2 E
Healdsburg 118 38 33N 122 51W
Healdton 117 34 16N 97 31W
Healesville 99 37 35 S 145 30 E
Heanor 12 53 1N 1 20W
Heard I. 3 53 0 S 74 0 E
Hearne 117 30 54N 96 35W
Hearne B. 109 60 10N 99 10W
Hearne L. 108 62 20N 113 10W
Hearst 106 49 40N 83 41W
Heart → 116 46 40N 100 51W
Heart's Content 107 47 54N 53 27W
Heath Pt. 107 49 8N 61 40W
Heath Steele 107 47 17N 66 5W
Heavener 117 34 54N 94 36W
Hebbronville 117 27 20N 98 40W
Hebei □ 76 39 0N 116 0 E
Hebel 99 28 58 S 147 47 E
Heber Springs 117 35 29N 91 59W
Hebert 109 50 30N 107 10W
Hebgen, L. 118 44 50N 111 15W
Hebi 76 35 57N 114 7 E
Hebrides 14 57 30N 7 0W
Hebrides, Inner Is. 14 57 20N 6 40W
Hebrides, Outer Is. 14 57 30N 7 40W
Hebron, Can. 105 58 5N 62 30W
Hebron, N.D., U.S.A. 116 46 56N 102 2W
Hebron, Nebr., U.S.A. 116 40 15N 97 33W
Hebron = Al Khalil 62 31 32N 35 6 E
Heby 48 59 56N 16 53 E
Hecate Str. 108 53 10N 130 30W
Hechi 75 24 40N 108 2 E
Hechingen 25 48 20N 8 58 E
Hechuan 75 30 2N 106 12 E
Hecla 116 45 56N 98 8W
Hecla I. 109 51 10N 96 43W
Heddal 47 59 36N 9 9 E
Hédé 18 48 18N 1 49W
Hede 48 62 23N 13 30 E
Hedemora 48 60 18N 15 58 E
Hedley 117 34 53N 100 39W
Hedmark fylke □ 47 61 17N 11 40 E
Hedrum 47 59 7N 10 5 E
Heemstede 16 52 22N 4 37 E
Heerde 16 52 24N 6 2 E
Heerenveen 16 52 57N 5 55 E
Heerlen 16 50 55N 6 0 E
Ḥefa 62 32 46N 35 0 E
Hefei 75 31 52N 117 18 E
Hegang 75 47 20N 130 19 E
Hegyalja 27 48 25N 21 25 E
Heide 24 54 10N 9 7 E
Heidelberg, Ger. 25 49 23N 8 41 E
Heidelberg, C. Prov., S. Afr. 92 34 6 S 20 59 E
Heidelberg, Trans., S. Afr. 93 26 30 S 28 23 E
Heidenheim 25 48 40N 10 10 E
Heilbron 93 27 16 S 27 59 E
Heilbronn 25 49 8N 9 13 E
Heiligenblut 26 47 2N 12 51 E
Heiligenhafen 24 54 21N 10 58 E
Heiligenstadt 24 51 22N 10 9 E
Heilongjiang □ 75 48 0N 126 0 E
Heilunkiang = Heilongjiang □ 75 48 0N 126 0 E
Heim 47 63 26N 9 5 E
Heinola 51 61 13N 26 2 E
Heinze Is. 71 14 25N 97 45 E
Hejaz = Ḥijāz 64 26 0N 37 30 E
Hejian 76 38 25N 116 5 E
Hejiang 77 28 43N 105 46 E
Hekimhan 64 38 50N 38 0 E
Hekla 50 63 56N 19 35W
Hekou 75 22 30N 103 59 E
Hel 28 54 37N 18 47 E
Helagsfjället 48 62 54N 12 25 E
Helan Shan 76 39 0N 105 55 E
Helechosa 31 39 22N 4 53W
Helena, Ark., U.S.A. 117 34 30N 90 35W
Helena, Mont., U.S.A. 118 46 40N 112 0W
Helensburgh, Austral. 100 34 11 S 151 1 E
Helensburgh, U.K. 14 56 0N 4 44W
Helensville 101 36 41 S 174 29 E
Ḥelez 62 31 36N 34 39 E
Helgasjön 49 57 0N 14 50 E
Helgeroa 47 59 0N 9 45 E
Helgoland 24 54 10N 7 51 E
Heligoland = Helgoland 24 54 10N 7 51 E
Heliopolis 86 30 6N 31 17 E
Hell-Ville 93 13 25 S 48 16 E
Hellebæk 49 56 4N 12 32 E
Helleland 47 58 33N 6 7 E
Hellendoorn 16 52 24N 6 27 E
Hellevoetsluis 16 51 50N 4 8 E
Hellín 33 38 31N 1 40W
Helmand □ 65 31 20N 64 0 E
Helmand → 66 31 12N 61 34 E
Helmand, Hamun 65 31 15N 61 15 E
Helme → 24 51 40N 11 20 E
Helmond 16 51 29N 5 41 E
Helmsdale 14 58 7N 3 40W
Helmstedt 24 52 16N 11 0 E
Helnæs 49 55 9N 10 0 E
Helper 118 39 44N 110 56W
Helsingborg 49 56 3N 12 42 E
Helsinge 49 56 2N 12 12 E
Helsingfors 51 60 15N 25 3 E
Helsingør 49 56 2N 12 35 E
Helsinki 51 60 15N 25 3 E
Helska, Mierzeja 28 54 45N 18 40 E
Helston 13 50 7N 5 17W
Helvellyn 12 54 31N 3 1W
Helwân 86 29 50N 31 20 E
Hemavati → 70 12 30N 76 20 E
Hemet 119 33 45N 116 59W
Hemingford 116 42 21N 103 4W
Hemphill 117 31 21N 93 49W
Hempstead 117 30 5N 96 5W
Hemse 49 57 15N 18 22 E
Hemsö 48 62 43N 18 5 E
Henan □ 75 34 0N 114 0 E
Henares → 32 40 24N 3 30W
Hendaye 20 43 23N 1 47W
Henderson, Argent. 124 36 18 S 61 43W
Henderson, Ky., U.S.A. 114 37 50N 87 38W
Henderson, N.C., U.S.A. 115 36 20N 78 25W
Henderson, Nev., U.S.A. 119 36 2N 115 0W
Henderson, Pa., U.S.A. 115 35 25N 88 40W
Henderson, Tex., U.S.A. 117 32 5N 94 49W
Hendersonville 115 35 21N 82 28W
Hendon 99 28 5 S 151 50 E
Hendorf 46 46 4N 24 55 E
Heng Xian 77 22 40N 109 17 E
Hengdaohezi 76 44 52N 129 0 E
Hengelo 16 52 3N 6 19 E
Hengshan, Hunan, China 77 27 16N 112 45 E
Hengshan, Shaanxi, China 76 37 58N 109 5 E
Hengshui 76 37 41N 115 40 E
Hengyang 75 26 52N 112 33 E
Hénin-Beaumont 19 50 25N 2 58 E
Henlopen, C. 114 38 48N 75 5W
Hennan, L. 48 62 3N 55 46 E
Hennebont 18 47 49N 3 19W
Hennenman 92 27 59 S 27 1 E
Hennessy 117 36 8N 97 53W
Hennigsdorf 24 52 38N 13 13 E
Henrichemont 19 47 20N 2 30 E
Henrietta 117 33 50N 98 15W
Henrietta Maria C. 106 55 9N 82 20W
Henrietta, Ostrov 59 77 6N 156 30 E
Henry 116 41 5N 89 20W
Henryetta 117 35 30N 96 0W
Hensall 112 43 26N 81 30W
Hentiyn Nuruu 75 48 30N 108 30 E
Henty 99 35 30 S 147 0 E
Henzada 67 17 38N 95 26 E
Hephaestia 44 39 55N 25 14 E
Heping 77 24 29N 115 0 E
Heppner 118 45 21N 119 34W
Hepu 77 21 40N 109 12 E
Hepworth 112 44 37N 81 9W
Herad 47 58 8N 6 47 E
Héraðsflói 50 65 42N 14 12W
Héraðsvötn → 50 65 45N 19 25W
Herāt 65 34 20N 62 7 E
Herāt □ 65 35 0N 62 0 E
Hérault □ 20 43 34N 3 15 E
Hérault → 20 43 17N 3 26 E
Herbault 18 47 36N 1 8 E
Herbert → 98 18 31 S 146 17 E
Herbert Downs 98 23 7 S 139 9 E
Herberton 98 17 20 S 145 25 E
Herbiers, Les 18 46 52N 1 0W
Herbignac 18 47 27N 2 18W
Herborn 24 50 40N 8 19 E
Herby 28 50 45N 18 50 E
Hercegnovi 42 42 30N 18 33 E
Herðubreið 50 65 11N 16 21W
Hereford, U.K. 13 52 4N 2 42W
Hereford, U.S.A. 117 34 50N 102 28W
Hereford and Worcester □ 13 52 10N 2 30W
Herefoss 47 58 32N 8 23 E
Herentals 16 51 12N 4 51 E
Herfølge 49 55 26N 12 9 E
Herford 24 52 7N 8 40 E
Héricourt 19 47 32N 6 45 E
Herington 116 38 43N 97 0W
Herisau 25 47 22N 9 17 E
Hérisson 20 46 32N 2 42 E
Herkimer 114 43 0N 74 59W
Herm 18 49 30N 2 28W
Hermagor 26 46 38N 13 23 E
Herman 116 45 51N 96 8W
Hermann 116 38 40N 91 25W
Hermannsburg 24 52 49N 10 6 E
Hermanus 92 34 27 S 19 12 E
Herment 20 45 45N 2 24 E
Hermidale 99 31 30 S 146 42 E
Hermiston 118 45 50N 119 16W
Hermitage 101 43 44 S 170 5 E
Hermite, I. 128 55 50 S 68 0W
Hermon, Mt. = Ash Shaykh, J. 64 33 20N 35 51 E
Hermosillo 120 29 10N 111 0W
Hernad → 27 47 56N 21 8 E
Hernandarias 125 25 20 S 54 40W
Hernando, Argent. 124 32 28 S 63 40W
Hernando, U.S.A. 117 34 50N 89 59W
Herne 24 51 33N 7 12 E
Herne Bay 13 51 22N 1 8 E
Herning 49 56 8N 8 58 E
Heroica Nogales = Nogales 120 31 20N 110 56W
Heron Bay 106 48 40N 86 25W
Herowābād 64 38 37N 48 32 E
Herreid 116 45 53N 100 5W
Herrera 31 37 26N 4 55W
Herrera de Alcántar 31 39 39N 7 25W
Herrera de Pisuerga 30 42 35N 4 20W
Herrera del Duque 31 39 10N 5 3W
Herrick 99 41 5 S 147 55 E
Herrin 117 37 50N 89 0W
Herrljunga 49 58 5N 13 1 E
Hersbruck 25 49 30N 11 25 E
Herstal 16 50 40N 5 38 E
Hersvik 47 61 10N 4 53 E
Hertford 13 51 47N 0 4W
Hertford □ 13 51 51N 0 5W
's-Hertogenbosch 16 51 42N 5 17 E
Hertzogville 92 28 9 S 25 30 E
Hervás 30 40 16N 5 52W
Hervey B. 97 25 0 S 152 52 E
* Hervey Is. 95 19 30 S 159 0W
Herzberg, Cottbus, Ger. 24 51 40N 13 13 E
Herzberg, Niedersachsen, Ger. 24 51 38N 10 20 E
Herzliyya 62 32 10N 34 50 E
Herzogenburg 26 48 17N 15 41 E
Hesdin 19 50 21N 2 0 E
Hesel 24 53 18N 7 36 E
Heskestad 47 58 28N 6 22 E
Hespeler 112 43 26N 80 19W
Hesse = Hessen 24 50 40N 9 20 E
Hessen □ 24 50 40N 9 20 E
Hettinger 116 46 0N 102 38W
Hettstedt 24 51 39N 11 30 E
Hève, C. de la 18 49 30N 0 5 E
Heves □ 27 47 50N 20 0 E
Hevron → 62 31 12N 34 42 E
Hewett, C. 105 70 16N 67 45W
Hex River 92 33 30 S 19 35 E
Hexham 12 54 58N 2 7W
Hexigten Qi 76 43 18N 117 30 E
Heyfield 100 37 59 S 146 47 E
Heysham 12 54 5N 2 53W
Heywood 99 38 8 S 141 37 E
Hi-no-Misaki 74 35 26N 132 38 E
Hialeach 115 25 49N 80 17W
Hiawatha, Kans., U.S.A. 116 39 55N 95 33W
Hiawatha, Utah, U.S.A. 118 39 29N 111 1W
Hibbing 116 47 30N 93 0W
Hickman 117 36 35N 89 8W
Hickory 115 35 46N 81 17W
Hicks Pt. 97 37 49 S 149 17 E
Hicksville 113 40 46N 73 30W
Hida 46 47 10N 23 19 E
Hida-Sammyaku 74 36 30N 137 40 E
Hidalgo 120 24 15N 99 26W
Hidalgo del Parral 120 26 58N 105 40W
Hidalgo, Presa M. 120 26 30N 108 35W
Hiddensee 24 54 30N 13 6 E
Hieflau 26 47 36N 14 46 E
Hiendelaencina 32 41 5N 3 0W
Hierro 80 27 44N 18 0 E
Higashiōsaka 74 34 40N 135 37 E
Higgins 117 36 9N 100 1W
High Atlas = Haut Atlas 82 32 30N 5 0W
High I. 107 56 40N 61 10W
High Island 117 29 32N 94 22W
High Level 108 58 31N 117 8W
High Point 115 35 57N 79 58W
High Prairie 108 55 30N 116 30W
High River 108 50 30N 113 50W
High Springs 115 29 50N 82 40W
High Tatra 27 49 30N 20 00 E
High Wycombe 13 51 37N 0 45W
Highbury 98 16 25 S 143 9 E
Highland □ 14 57 30N 5 0W
Highland Park 114 42 10N 87 50W
Highmore 116 44 35N 99 26W
Highrock L. 109 57 5N 105 32W
Higley 119 33 27N 111 46W
Hihya 86 30 40N 31 36 E
Hiiumaa 54 58 50N 22 45 E
Hijar 32 41 10N 0 27W
Ḥijārah, Ṣaḥrā' al 64 30 25N 44 30 E
Hiko 119 37 30N 115 13W
Hikone 74 35 15N 136 10 E
Hildburghhausen 25 50 24N 10 43 E
Hildesheim 24 52 9N 9 55 E
Hill City, Idaho, U.S.A. 118 43 20N 115 2W
Hill City, Kans., U.S.A. 116 39 25N 99 51W
Hill City, Minn., U.S.A. 116 46 57N 93 35W

* Renamed Manuae

Hill City, S.D., U.S.A. 116 43 58N 103 35W
Hill Island L. 109 60 30N 109 50W
Hillared 49 57 37N 13 10 E
Hillegom 16 52 18N 4 35 E
Hillerød 49 55 56N 12 19 E
Hillerstorp 49 57 20N 13 52 E
Hillingdon 13 51 33N 0 29W
Hillman 114 45 5N 83 52W
Hillmond 109 53 26N 109 41W
Hillsboro, Kans., U.S.A. 116 38 22N 97 10W
Hillsboro, N. Mex., U.S.A. 119 33 0N 107 35W
Hillsboro, N.D., U.S.A. 116 47 23N 97 9W
Hillsboro, N.H., U.S.A. 114 43 8N 71 56W
Hillsboro, Oreg., U.S.A. 118 45 31N 123 0W
Hillsboro, Tex., U.S.A. 117 32 0N 97 10W
Hillsdale, Mich., U.S.A. 114 41 55N 84 40W
Hillsdale, N.Y., U.S.A. 113 42 11N 73 30W
Hillsport 106 49 27N 85 34W
Hillston 97 33 30 S 145 31 E
Hilo 110 19 44N 155 5W
Hilonghilong 73 9 10N 125 45 E
Hilton 112 43 16N 77 48W
Hilversum 16 52 14N 5 10 E
Himachal Pradesh □ 68 31 30N 77 0 E
Himalaya 67 29 0N 84 0 E
Himara 44 40 8N 19 43 E
Himeji 74 34 50N 134 40 E
Himi 74 36 50N 137 0 E
Himmerland 49 56 45N 9 30 E
Ḥimş 64 34 40N 36 45 E
Hinako, Kepulauan 72 0 50N 97 20 E
Hinchinbrook I. 97 18 20 S 146 15 E
Hinckley, U.K. 13 52 33N 1 21W
Hinckley, U.S.A. 118 39 18N 112 41W
Hindås 49 57 42N 12 27 E
Hindaun 68 26 44N 77 5 E
Hindmarsh L. 99 36 5 S 141 55 E
Hindol 69 20 40N 85 10 E
Hindsholm 49 55 30N 10 40 E
Hindu Bagh 68 30 56N 67 50 E
Hindu Kush 65 36 0N 71 0 E
Hindupur 70 13 49N 77 32 E
Hines Creek 108 56 20N 118 40W
Hinganghat 68 20 30N 78 52 E
Hingham 118 48 34N 110 29W
Hingoli 70 19 41N 77 15 E
Hinlopenstretet 4 79 35N 18 40 E
Hinna 85 10 25N 11 35 E
Hinojosa del Duque 31 38 30N 5 9W
Hinsdale 118 48 26N 107 2W
Hinterrhein → 25 46 40N 9 25 E
Hinton, Can. 108 53 26N 117 34W
Hinton, U.S.A. 114 37 40N 80 51W
Hippolytushoef 16 52 54N 4 58 E
Hirakud 69 21 32N 83 51 E
Hirakud Dam 69 21 32N 83 45 E
Hiratsuka 74 35 19N 139 21 E
Hirhafok 83 23 49N 5 45 E
Hîrlău 46 47 23N 27 0 E
Hirosaki 74 40 34N 140 28 E
Hiroshima 74 34 24N 132 30 E
Hiroshima □ 74 34 50N 133 0 E
Hirsoholmene 49 57 30N 10 36 E
Hirson 19 49 55N 4 4 E
Hîrşova 46 44 40N 27 59 E
Hirtshals 49 57 36N 9 57 E
Ḥiṣn Dibā 65 25 45N 56 16 E
Hispaniola 121 19 0N 71 0W
Hissar 68 29 12N 75 45 E
Hita 74 33 20N 130 58 E
Hitachi 74 36 36N 140 39 E
Hitchin 13 51 57N 0 16W
Hitoyoshi 74 32 13N 130 45 E
Hitra 47 63 30N 8 45 E
Hitzacker 24 53 9N 11 1 E
Ḥiyyon, N. → 62 30 25N 35 10 E
Hjalmar L. 109 61 33N 109 25W
Hjälmare kanal 48 59 20N 15 59 E
Hjälmaren 48 59 18N 15 40 E
Hjartdal 47 59 37N 8 41 E
Hjerkinn 47 62 13N 9 33 E
Hjørring 49 57 29N 9 59 E
Hjorted 49 57 37N 16 19 E
Hjortkvarn 49 58 54N 15 26 E
Hlinsko 26 49 45N 15 54 E
Hlohovec 27 48 26N 17 49 E
Hṅak 4 70 40N 52 10W
Ho 85 6 37N 0 27 E
Ho Chi Minh, Phanh Bho 71 10 58N 106 40 E
Hoa Binh 71 20 50N 105 20 E
Hoai Nhon (Bon Son) 71 14 28N 109 1 E
Hoare B. 105 65 17N 62 30W
Hobart, Austral. 97 42 50 S 147 21 E
Hobart, U.S.A. 117 35 0N 99 5W
Hobbs 117 32 40N 103 3W
Hobbs Coast 5 74 50 S 131 0W
Hoboken, Belg. 16 51 11N 4 21 E
Hoboken, U.S.A. 113 40 45N 74 4W
Hobro 49 56 39N 9 46 E
Hoburgen 49 56 55N 18 7 E
Hochatown 117 34 11N 94 39W
Hochschwab 26 47 35N 15 0 E
Höchst 25 50 6N 8 33 E
Höchstadt 25 49 42N 10 48 E
Hockenheim 25 49 18N 8 33 E
Hodgson 109 51 13N 97 36W
Hódmezövásárhely 27 46 28N 20 22 E
Hodna, Chott el 83 35 30N 5 0 E
Hodna, Monts du 83 35 52N 4 42 E
Hodonín 27 48 50N 17 10 E
Hoëdic 18 47 21N 2 52W
Hoek van Holland 16 52 0N 4 7 E
Hoëveld 93 26 30 S 30 0 E
Hof, Ger. 25 50 18N 11 55 E
Hof, Iceland 50 64 33N 14 40W
Höfðakaupstaður 50 65 50N 20 19W
Hofgeismar 24 51 29N 9 23 E
Hofors 48 60 31N 16 15 E
Hofsjökull 50 64 49N 18 48W
Hofsós 50 65 53N 19 26W
Hōfu 74 34 3N 131 34 E
Hogansville 115 33 14N 84 50W

Hogeland Hunterville

Hogeland 118 48 51N 108 40W
Hogenakai Falls 70 12 6N 77 50 E
Högfors 48 59 58N 15 3 E
Högsäter 49 58 38N 12 5 E
Högsby 49 57 10N 16 1 E
Högsjö 48 59 4N 15 44 E
Hoh Xil Shan 75 35 0N 89 0 E
Hohe Rhön 25 50 24N 9 58 E
Hohe Tauern 26 47 11N 12 40 E
Hohe Venn 16 50 30N 6 5 E
Hohenau 27 48 36N 16 55 E
Hohenems 26 47 22N 9 42 E
Hohenstein Ernstthal 24 50 48N 12 43 E
Hohenwald 115 35 35N 87 30W
Hohenwestedt 24 54 6N 9 30 E
Hohhot 76 40 52N 111 40 E
Hohoe 85 7 8N 0 32 E
Hoi An 71 15 30N 108 19 E
Hoi Xuan 71 20 25N 105 9 E
Hoisington 116 38 33N 98 50W
Højer 49 54 58N 8 42 E
Hok 49 57 31N 14 16 E
Hökensås 49 58 0N 14 5 E
Hökerum 49 57 51N 13 16 E
Hokianga Harbour 101 35 31 S 173 22 E
Hokitika 101 42 42 S 171 0 E
Hokkaidō □ 74 43 30N 143 0 E
Hokksund 47 59 44N 9 59 E
Hol-Hol 87 11 20N 42 50 E
Holbæk 49 55 43N 11 43 E
Holbrook, Austral. 99 35 42 S 147 18 E
Holbrook, U.S.A. 119 35 54N 110 10W
Holden, Can. 108 53 13N 112 11W
Holden, U.S.A. 118 39 0N 112 26W
Holdenville 117 35 5N 96 25W
Holderness 12 53 45N 0 5W
Holdfast 109 50 58N 105 25W
Holdrege 116 40 26N 99 22W
Hole 47 60 6N 10 12 E
Hole-Narsipur 70 12 48N 76 16 E
Holešov 27 49 20N 17 35 E
Holguín 121 20 50N 76 20W
Holič 27 48 49N 17 10 E
Hollabrunn 26 48 34N 16 5 E
Hollams Bird I. 92 24 40 S 14 30 E
Holland 114 42 47N 86 7W
Hollandia = Jayapura 73 2 28 S 140 38 E
Höllen 47 58 6N 7 49 E
Hollfeld 25 49 56N 11 18 E
Hollick Kenyon Plateau 5 82 0 S 110 0W
Hollidaysburg 114 40 26N 78 25W
Hollis 117 34 45N 99 55W
Hollister, Calif., U.S.A. 119 36 51N 121 24W
Hollister, Idaho, U.S.A. 118 42 21N 114 40W
Holly 116 38 7N 102 7W
Holly Hill 115 29 15N 81 3W
Holly Springs 117 34 45N 89 25W
Hollywood, Calif., U.S.A. 110 34 7N 118 25W
Hollywood, Fla., U.S.A. 115 26 0N 80 9W
Holm 48 62 40N 16 40 E
Holman Island 104 70 42N 117 41W
Hólmavík 50 65 42N 21 40W
Holmedal 47 61 22N 5 11 E
Holmegil 48 59 10N 11 44 E
Holmestrand 47 59 31N 10 14 E
Holmsbu 47 59 32N 10 27 E
Holmsjön 48 62 26N 15 20 E
Holmsland Klit 49 56 0N 8 5 E
Holmsund 50 63 41N 20 20 E
Holod 46 46 49N 22 8 E
Holon 62 32 2N 34 47 E
Holroyd → 97 14 10 S 141 36 E
Holstebro 49 56 22N 8 37 E
Holsworthy 13 50 48N 4 21W
Holt 50 63 33N 19 48W
Holte 49 55 50N 12 29 E
Holton, Can. 107 54 31N 57 12W
Holton, U.S.A. 116 39 28N 95 44W
Holtville 119 32 50N 115 27W
Holum 47 58 6N 7 32 E
Holwerd 16 53 22N 5 54 E
Holy Cross 104 62 10N 159 52W
Holy I., England, U.K. 12 55 42N 1 48W
Holy I., Wales, U.K. 12 53 17N 4 37W
Holyhead 12 53 18N 4 38W
Holyoke, Colo., U.S.A. 116 40 39N 102 18W
Holyoke, Mass., U.S.A. 114 42 14N 72 37W
Holyrood 107 47 27N 53 8W
Holzkirchen 25 47 53N 11 42 E
Holzminden 24 51 49N 9 31 E
Homa Bay 90 0 36 S 34 30 E
* Homa Bay □ 90 0 50 S 34 30 E
Homalin 67 24 55N 95 0 E
Homberg 24 51 2N 9 20 E
Hombori 85 15 20N 1 38W
Homburg 25 49 19N 7 21 E
Home B. 105 68 40N 67 10W
Home Hill 97 19 43 S 147 25 E
Homedale 118 43 42N 116 59W
Homer, Alaska, U.S.A. 104 59 40N 151 35W
Homer, La., U.S.A. 117 32 50N 93 4W
Homestead, Austral. 98 20 20 S 145 40 E
Homestead, Fla., U.S.A. 115 25 29N 80 27W
Homestead, Oreg., U.S.A. 118 45 5N 116 57W
Hominy 117 36 26N 96 24W
Homnabad 70 17 45N 77 11 E
Homoine 93 23 55 S 35 8 E
Homoljske Planina 42 44 10N 21 45 E
Homorod 46 46 5N 25 15 E
Homs = Ḩimş 64 34 40N 36 45 E
Hon Chong 71 10 25N 104 30 E
Honan = Henan □ 75 34 0N 114 0 E
Honda 126 5 12N 74 45W
Hondeklipbaai 92 30 19 S 17 17 E
Hondo 117 29 22N 99 6W
Hondo → 120 18 25N 88 21W
Honduras ■ 121 14 40N 86 30W
Honduras, Golfo de 120 16 50N 87 0W
Honesdale 113 41 34N 75 17W
Honey L. 118 40 13N 120 14W
Honfleur 18 49 25N 0 13 E
Hong Kong ■ 75 22 11N 114 14 E
Hong'an 77 31 20N 114 40 E
Hongha → 71 22 0N 104 0 E
Honghai Wan 77 22 40N 115 0 E
Honghu 77 29 50N 113 30 E
Hongjiang 75 27 7N 109 59 E
Hongshui He → 75 23 48N 109 30 E
Hongtong 76 36 16N 111 40 E
Honguedo, Détroit d' 107 49 15N 64 0W
Hongze Hu 75 33 15N 118 35 E
Honiara 94 9 27 S 159 57 E
Honiton 13 50 48N 3 11W
Honkorâb, Ras 86 24 35N 35 10 E
Honolulu 110 21 19N 157 52W
Honshū 74 36 0N 138 0 E
Hontoria del Pinar 32 41 50N 3 10W
Hood Mt. 118 45 24N 121 41W
Hood, Pt. 96 34 23 S 119 34 E
Hood River 118 45 45N 121 31W
Hoodsport 118 47 24N 123 7W
Hooge 24 54 31N 8 36 E
Hoogeveen 16 52 44N 6 30 E
Hoogezand 16 53 11N 6 45 E
Hooghly → 69 21 56N 88 4 E
Hooghly-Chinsura 69 22 53N 88 27 E
Hook Hd. 15 52 8N 6 57W
Hook I. 98 20 4 S 149 0 E
Hook of Holland = Hoek van Holland 16 52 0N 4 7 E
Hooker 117 36 55N 101 10W
Hoopeston 114 40 30N 87 40W
Hoopstad 92 27 50 S 25 55 E
Hoorn 16 52 38N 5 4 E
Hoover Dam 119 36 0N 114 45W
Hooversville 112 40 8N 78 57W
Hop Bottom 113 41 41N 75 47W
Hopà 57 41 28N 41 30 E
Hope, Can. 108 49 25N 121 25 E
Hope, Ark., U.S.A. 117 33 40N 93 36W
Hope, N.D., U.S.A. 116 47 21N 97 42W
Hope Bay 5 65 0 S 55 0W
Hope, L. 99 28 24 S 139 18 E
Hope Pt. 104 68 20N 166 50W
Hope Town 121 26 35N 76 57W
Hopedale 107 55 28N 60 13W
Hopefield 92 33 3 S 18 22 E
Hopei = Hebei □ 76 39 0N 116 0 E
Hopelchén 120 19 46N 89 50W
Hopen 47 63 27N 8 2 E
Hopetoun, Vic., Austral. 99 35 42 S 142 22 E
Hopetoun, W. Australia, Austral. 100 33 57 S 120 7 E
Hopetown 92 29 34 S 24 3 E
Hopkins 116 40 31N 94 45W
Hopkins → 100 38 25 S 142 30 E
Hopkinsville 115 36 52N 87 26W
Hopland 118 39 0N 123 7W
Hoptrup 49 55 11N 9 28 E
Hoquiam 118 46 50N 123 55W
Horazdovice 26 49 19N 13 42 E
Horcajo de Santiago 32 39 50N 3 1W
Hordaland fylke □ 47 60 25N 6 15 E
Horden Hills 96 20 40 S 130 20 E
Horezu 46 45 6N 24 0 E
Horgen 25 47 15N 8 35 E
Horgoš 42 46 10N 20 0 E
Horice 26 50 21N 15 39 E
Horlick Mts. 5 84 0 S 102 0W
Hormoz 65 27 35N 55 0 E
Hormoz, Jaz. ye 65 27 8N 56 28 E
Hormuz Str. 65 26 30N 56 30 E
Horn, Austria 26 48 39N 15 40 E
Horn, Ísafjarðarsýsla, Iceland 50 66 28N 22 28W
Horn, Suður-Múlasýsla, Iceland 50 65 10N 13 31W
Horn → 108 61 30N 118 1W
Horn, Cape = Hornos, Cabo de 128 55 50 S 67 30W
Horn Head 15 55 13N 8 0W
Horn, I. 115 30 17N 88 40W
Horn Mts. 108 62 15N 119 15W
Hornachuelos 31 37 50N 5 14W
Hornavan 50 66 15N 17 30 E
Hornbæk 49 56 5N 12 26 E
Hornbeck 117 31 22N 93 20W
Hornbrook 118 41 58N 122 37W
Hornburg 24 52 2N 10 36 E
Horncastle 12 53 13N 0 8W
Horndal 48 60 18N 16 23 E
Hornell 114 42 23N 77 41W
Hornell L. 108 62 20N 119 25W
Hornepayne 106 49 14N 84 48W
Hornindal 47 61 58N 6 30 E
Hornnes 47 58 34N 7 45 E
Hornos, Cabo de 128 55 50 S 67 30W
Hornoy 19 49 50N 1 54 E
Hornsby 99 33 42 S 151 2 E
Hornsea 12 53 55N 0 10W
Hornslandet 48 61 35N 17 37 E
Hornslet 49 56 18N 10 19 E
Hörnum 24 54 44N 8 18 E
Horovice 26 49 48N 13 53 E
Horqin Youyi Qianqi 75 46 5N 122 3 E
Horqueta 124 23 15 S 56 55W
Horra, La 30 41 44N 3 53W
Horred 49 57 22N 12 28 E
Horse Cr. → 116 41 57N 103 58W
Horse Is. 107 50 15N 55 50W
Horsefly L. 108 52 25N 121 0W
Horsens 49 55 52N 9 51 E
Horsens Fjord 49 55 50N 10 0 E
Horseshoe Dam 119 33 45N 111 35W
Horsham, Austral. 97 36 44 S 142 13 E
Horsham, U.K. 13 51 4N 0 20W
Horšovský Týn 26 49 31N 12 58 E
Horten 47 59 25N 10 32 E
Hortobágy → 27 47 30N 21 6 E
Horton 116 39 42N 95 30W
Horton → 104 69 56N 126 52W
Hörvik 49 56 2N 14 45 E
Horwood, L. 106 48 5N 82 20W
Hosaina 87 7 30N 37 47 E
Hosdurga 70 13 49N 76 17 E
Hose, Pegunungan 72 2 5N 114 6 E
Hoshangabad 68 22 45N 77 45 E
Hoshiarpur 68 31 30N 75 58 E
Hosmer 116 45 36N 99 29W
Hospet 70 15 15N 76 20 E
Hospitalet de Llobregat 32 41 21N 2 6 E
Hospitalet, L' 20 42 36N 1 47 E
Hoste, I. 128 55 0 S 69 0W
Hostens 20 44 30N 0 40W
Hot 71 18 8N 98 29 E
Hot Creek Ra. 118 39 0N 116 0W
Hot Springs, Ari., U.S.A. 117 34 30N 93 0W
Hot Springs, S.D., U.S.A. 116 43 25N 103 30W
Hotagen 50 63 50N 14 30 E
Hotan 75 37 25N 79 55 E
Hotazel 92 27 17 S 23 00 E
Hotchkiss 119 38 47N 107 47W
Hoting 50 64 8N 16 15 E
Hotolishti 44 41 10N 20 25 E
Hottentotsbaai 92 26 8 S 14 59 E
Houat 18 47 24N 2 58W
Houck 119 35 15N 109 15W
Houdan 19 48 48N 1 35 E
Houffalize 16 50 8N 5 48 E
Houghton 116 47 9N 88 39W
Houghton L. 114 44 20N 84 40W
Houghton-le-Spring 12 54 51N 1 28W
Houhora 101 34 49 S 173 9 E
Houlton 107 46 5N 67 50W
Houma 117 29 35N 90 44W
Houndé 84 11 34N 3 31W
Hourtin 20 45 11N 1 4W
Hourtin, Étang d' 20 45 10N 1 6W
Houston, Can. 108 54 25N 126 39W
Houston, Mo., U.S.A. 117 37 20N 92 0W
Houston, Tex., U.S.A. 117 29 50N 95 20W
Houtman Abrolhos 96 28 43 S 113 48 E
Hov 49 55 55N 10 15 E
Hova 49 58 53N 14 14 E
Høvåg 47 58 10N 8 16 E
Hovd (Jargalant) 75 48 2N 91 37 E
Hovden 47 59 33N 7 22 E
Hove 13 50 50N 0 10W
Hovmantorp 49 56 47N 15 7 E
Hövsgöl Nuur 75 51 0N 100 30 E
Hovsta 48 59 22N 15 15 E
Howakil 87 15 10N 40 16 E
Howar, Wadi → 87 17 30N 27 8 E
Howard, Austral. 99 25 16 S 152 32 E
Howard, Kans., U.S.A. 117 37 30N 96 16W
Howard, Pa., U.S.A. 112 41 0N 77 40W
Howard, S.D., U.S.A. 116 44 2N 97 30W
Howard L. 109 62 15N 105 57W
Howe 118 43 48N 113 0W
Howe, C. 97 37 30 S 150 0 E
Howell 114 42 38N 83 56W
Howick, Can. 113 45 11N 73 51W
Howick, S. Afr. 93 29 28 S 30 14 E
Howick Group 98 14 20 S 145 30 E
Howitt, L. 99 27 40 S 138 40 E
Howley 107 49 12N 57 2W
Howrah 69 22 37N 88 20 E
Howth Hd. 15 53 21N 6 0W
Höxter 24 51 45N 9 26 E
Hoy I. 14 58 50N 3 15W
Hoya 24 52 47N 9 10 E
Hoyerswerda 24 51 26N 14 14 E
Hoyos 30 40 9N 6 45W
Hpungan Pass 67 27 30N 96 55 E
Hrádec Králové 26 50 15N 15 50 E
Hrádek 27 48 46N 16 16 E
Hranice 27 49 34N 17 45 E
Hron → 27 47 49N 18 45 E
Hrubieszów 28 50 49N 23 51 E
Hrubý Nizký Jeseník 27 50 7N 17 10 E
Hrvatska 39 45 20N 16 0 E
Hrvatska □ 42 45 20N 18 0 E
Hsenwi 67 23 22N 97 55 E
Hsiamen = Xiamen 75 24 25N 118 4 E
Hsian = Xi'an 77 34 15N 109 0 E
Hsinhailien = Lianyungang 77 34 40N 119 11 E
Hsüchou = Xuzhou 77 34 18N 117 18 E
Hua Hin 71 12 34N 99 58 E
Hua Xian, Henan, China 77 35 30N 114 30 E
Hua Xian, Shaanxi, China 77 34 30N 109 48 E
Huacheng 77 24 4N 115 37 E
Huacho 126 11 10 S 77 35W
Huachón 126 10 35 S 76 0W
Huachuan 76 46 50N 130 21 E
Huade 76 41 55N 113 59 E
Huadian 76 43 0N 126 40 E
Huai He → 75 33 0N 118 30 E
Huai'an 77 33 30N 119 10 E
Huaide 76 43 30N 124 40 E
Huainan 75 32 38N 116 58 E
Huaiyang 77 33 40N 114 52 E
Huaiyuan 77 24 31N 108 22 E
Huajianzi 76 41 23N 125 20 E
Huajuapan de Leon 120 17 50N 97 48W
Hualian 77 23 59N 121 37 E
Huallaga → 126 5 0 S 75 30W
Hualpai Pk. 119 35 8N 113 58W
Huambo 89 12 42 S 15 54 E
Huan Jiang → 76 34 28N 109 0 E
Huan Xian 76 36 33N 107 7 E
Huancabamba 126 5 10 S 79 15W
Huancane 126 15 10 S 69 44W
Huancapi 126 13 40 S 74 0W
Huancavelica 126 12 50 S 75 5W
Huancayo 126 12 5 S 75 12W
Huang He 75 37 55N 118 50 E
Huangchuan 77 32 15N 115 10 E
Huangliu 75 18 20N 108 50 E
Huanglong 76 35 30N 109 59 E
Huangshi 75 30 10N 115 3 E
Huangyan 77 28 38N 121 19 E
Huánuco 126 9 55 S 76 15W
Huaraz 126 9 30 S 77 32W
Huarmey 126 10 5 S 78 5W
Huascarán 126 9 8 S 77 36W
Huasco 124 28 30 S 71 15W
Huasco → 124 28 27 S 71 13W
Huatabampo 120 26 50N 109 50W
Huay Namota 120 21 56N 104 30W
Huayllay 126 11 03 S 76 21W
Hubbard 117 31 50N 96 50W
Hubbart Pt. 109 59 21N 94 41W
Hubei □ 75 31 0N 112 0 E
Hubli 70 15 22N 75 15 E
Hückelhoven-Ratheim 24 51 6N 6 13 E
Huczwa → 28 50 49N 23 58 E
Huddersfield 12 53 38N 1 49W
Hudi 86 17 43N 34 18 E
Hudiksvall 48 61 43N 17 10 E
Hudson, Can. 109 50 6N 92 09W
Hudson, Mass., U.S.A. 113 42 23N 71 35W
Hudson, Mich., U.S.A. 114 41 50N 84 20W
Hudson, N.Y., U.S.A. 114 42 15N 73 46W
Hudson, Wis., U.S.A. 116 44 57N 92 45W
Hudson, Wyo., U.S.A. 118 42 54N 108 37W
Hudson → 114 40 42N 74 2W
Hudson Bay, Can. 105 60 0N 86 0W
Hudson Bay, Sask., Can. 109 52 51N 102 23W
Hudson Falls 114 43 18N 73 34W
Hudson Hope 108 56 0N 121 54W
Hudson Mts. 5 74 32 S 99 20W
Hudson Str. 105 62 0N 70 0W
Hue 71 16 30N 107 35 E
Huebra → 30 41 2N 6 48W
Huedin 46 46 52N 23 2 E
Huelgoat 18 48 22N 3 46W
Huelma 33 37 39N 3 28W
Huelva 31 37 18N 6 57W
Huelva □ 31 37 40N 7 0W
Huelva → 31 37 27N 6 0W
Huentelauquén 124 31 38 S 71 33W
Huércal Overa 33 37 23N 1 57W
Huerta, Sa. de la 124 31 10 S 67 30W
Huertas, C. de las 33 38 21N 0 24W
Huerva → 32 41 39N 0 52W
Huesca 32 42 8N 0 25W
Huesca □ 32 42 20N 0 1 E
Huéscar 33 37 44N 2 35W
Huetamo 120 18 36N 100 54W
Huete 32 40 10N 2 43W
Hugh → 96 25 1 S 134 1 E
Hughenden 97 20 52 S 144 10 E
Hughes 104 66 0N 154 20W
Hugo 116 39 12N 103 27W
Hugoton 117 37 11N 101 22W
Hui Xian 76 35 27N 113 12 E
Hui'an 77 25 1N 118 43 E
Huichang 77 25 32N 115 45 E
Huichapán 120 20 24N 99 40W
Huihe 76 48 12N 119 17 E
Huila, Nevado del 126 3 0N 76 0W
Huilai 77 23 0N 116 18 E
Huimin 76 37 27N 117 28 E
Huinan 76 42 40N 126 2 E
Huinca Renancó 124 34 51 S 64 22W
Huining 76 35 38N 105 0 E
Huinong 76 39 5N 106 35 E
Huisne → 18 47 59N 0 11 E
Huize 75 26 24N 103 15 E
Huizhou 77 23 0N 114 23 E
Hukawng Valley 67 26 30N 96 30 E
Hukou 77 29 45N 116 21 E
Hukuntsi 92 23 58 S 21 45 E
Hula 87 6 33N 38 30 E
Hulan 75 46 1N 126 37 E
Ḩulayfā' 64 25 58N 40 45 E
Huld 75 45 5N 105 30 E
Hulda 62 31 50N 34 51 E
Hulin 76 45 48N 132 59 E
Hull, Can. 106 45 25N 75 44W
Hull, U.K. 12 53 45N 0 20W
Hull → 12 53 43N 0 25W
Hulst 16 51 17N 4 2 E
Hultsfred 49 57 30N 15 52 E
Hulun Nur 75 49 0N 117 30 E
Huma 76 51 43N 126 38 E
Huma He → 76 51 42N 126 42 E
Humahuaca 124 23 10 S 65 25W
Humaitá, Brazil 126 7 35 S 63 1W
Humaitá, Parag. 124 27 2 S 58 31W
Humansdorp 92 34 2 S 24 46 E
Humbe 92 16 40 S 14 55 E
Humber → 12 53 40N 0 10W
Humberside □ 12 53 50N 0 30W
Humble 117 29 59N 93 18W
Humboldt, Can. 109 52 15N 105 9W
Humboldt, Iowa, U.S.A. 116 42 42N 94 15W
Humboldt, Tenn., U.S.A. 117 35 50N 88 55W
Humboldt → 118 40 2N 118 31W
Humboldt Gletscher 4 79 30N 62 0W
Hume, L. 97 36 0 S 147 0 E
Humenné 27 48 55N 21 50 E
Humphreys Pk. 119 35 24N 111 38W
Humpolec 26 49 31N 15 20 E
Hūn 83 29 2N 16 0 E
Húnaflói 50 65 50N 20 50W
Hunan □ 75 27 30N 112 0 E
Hunchun 76 42 52N 130 28 E
Hundested 49 55 58N 11 52 E
Hundred Mile House 108 51 38N 121 18W
Hunedoara 46 45 40N 22 50 E
Hunedoara □ 46 45 50N 22 54 E
Hünfeld 24 50 40N 9 47 E
Hungary ■ 27 47 20N 19 20 E
Hungary, Plain of 9 47 0N 20 0 E
Hungerford 99 28 58 S 144 24 E
Hŭngnam 76 39 49N 127 45 E
Huni Valley 84 5 33N 1 56W
Hunsberge 92 27 45 S 17 12 E
Hunsrück 25 49 30N 7 0 E
Hunstanton 12 52 57N 0 30 E
Hunsur 70 12 16N 76 16 E
Hunte → 24 52 30N 8 19 E
Hunter, N.D., U.S.A. 116 47 12N 97 17W
Hunter, N.Y., U.S.A. 113 42 13N 74 13W
Hunter → 100 32 52 S 151 46 E
Hunter I., Austral. 97 40 30 S 144 45 E
Hunter I., Can. 108 51 55N 128 0W
Hunter Ra. 99 32 45 S 150 15 E
Hunters Road 91 19 9 S 29 49 E
Hunterton 99 26 12 S 148 30 E
Hunterville 101 39 56 S 175 35 E

* *Renamed South Nyanza*

Huntingburg
Inthanon, Doi

Huntingburg 114 38 20N 86 58W
Huntingdon, Can. 106 45 6N 74 10W
Huntingdon, U.K. 13 52 20N 0 11W
Huntingdon, U.S.A. 114 40 28N 78 1W
Huntington, Ind., U.S.A. 114 40 52N 85 30W
Huntington, N.Y., U.S.A. 113 40 52N 73 25W
Huntington, Oreg., U.S.A. 118 44 22N 117 21W
Huntington, Ut., U.S.A. 118 39 24N 111 1W
Huntington, W. Va., U.S.A. 114 38 20N 82 30W
Huntington Beach 119 33 40N 118 0W
Huntington Park 119 33 58N 118 15W
Huntly, N.Z. 101 37 34S 175 11 E
Huntly, U.K. 14 57 27N 2 48W
Huntsville, Can. 106 45 20N 79 14W
Huntsville, Ala., U.S.A. 115 34 45N 86 35W
Huntsville, Tex., U.S.A. 117 30 45N 95 35W
Hunyani → 91 15 57S 30 39 E
Huo Xian 76 36 36N 111 42 E
Huon, G. 98 7 0S 147 30 E
Huonville 97 43 0S 147 5 E
Huoqiu 77 32 20N 116 12 E
Huoshao Dao 77 22 40N 121 30 E
Hupeh □ = Hubei □ 75 31 0N 112 0 E
Hurbanovo 27 47 51N 18 11 E
Hure Qi 76 42 45N 121 45 E
Hurezani 46 44 49N 23 40 E
Hurghada 86 27 15N 33 50 E
Hurley, N. Mex., U.S.A. 119 32 45N 108 7W
Hurley, Wis., U.S.A. 116 46 26N 90 10W
Huron, Ohio, U.S.A. 112 41 22N 82 34W
Huron, S.D., U.S.A. 116 44 22N 98 12W
Huron, L. 112 45 0N 83 0W
Hurricane 119 37 10N 113 12W
Hurso 87 9 35N 41 33 E
Hurum, Buskerud, Norway 47 59 36N 10 23 E
Hurum, Oppland, Norway 47 61 9N 8 46 E
Hurunui → 101 42 54S 173 18 E
Hurup 49 56 46N 8 25 E
Húsavík 50 66 3N 17 21W
Huşi 46 46 41N 28 7 E
Huskvarna 49 57 47N 14 15 E
Husøy 47 61 3N 4 44 E
Hussar 108 51 3N 112 41W
Hustopéce 27 48 57N 16 43 E
Husum, Ger. 24 54 27N 9 3 E
Husum, Sweden 48 63 21N 19 12 E
Hutchinson, Kans., U.S.A. 117 38 3N 97 59W
Hutchinson, Minn., U.S.A. 116 44 50N 94 22W
Hutou 76 45 58N 133 38 E
Huttenberg 26 46 56N 14 33 E
Hüttental 24 50 52N 8 1 E
Huttig 117 33 5N 92 10W
Hutton, Mt. 99 25 51S 148 20 E
Huwun 87 4 23N 40 6 E
Ḩuwwārah 62 32 9N 35 15 E
Huy 16 50 31N 5 15 E
Hvaler 47 59 4N 11 1 E
Hvammur 50 65 13N 21 49W
Hvar 39 43 11N 16 28 E
Hvarski Kanal 39 43 15N 16 35 E
Hvitá 50 64 40N 21 5W
Hvitá → 50 64 0N 20 58W
Hvitárvatn 50 64 37N 19 50W
Hvitsten 47 59 35N 10 42 E
Hwang Ho = Huang He → 76 37 50N 118 50 E
Hyannis 116 42 0N 101 45W
Hyargas Nuur 75 49 0N 93 0 E
Hyatts 114 38 59N 76 55W
Hybo 48 61 49N 16 15 E
Hyderabad, India 70 17 22N 78 29 E
Hyderabad, Pak. 68 25 23N 68 24 E
* Hyderabad □ 68 25 3N 68 24 E
Hyères 21 43 8N 6 9 E
Hyères, Îles d' 21 43 0N 6 28 E
Hyesan 76 41 20N 128 10 E
Hyland → 108 59 52N 128 12W
Hylestad 47 59 6N 7 29 E
Hyltebruk 49 56 59N 13 15 E
Hyndman Pk. 118 43 50N 114 10W
Hyōgo □ 74 35 15N 135 0 E
Hyrum 118 41 35N 111 56W
Hysham 118 46 21N 107 11W
Hythe 13 51 4N 1 5 E
Hyvinkää 51 60 38N 24 50 E

I

I-n-Azaoua 83 20 45N 7 31 E
I-n-Échaï 82 20 10N 2 5W
I-n-Gall 85 16 51N 7 1 E
I-n-Tabedog 82 19 48N 1 11 E
Iabès, Erg 82 27 30N 2 2W
Iaco → 126 9 3S 68 34W
Iacobeni 46 47 25N 25 20 E
Iakora 93 23 6S 46 40 E
Ialomiţa □ 46 44 30N 27 30 E
Ialomiţa → 46 44 42N 27 51 E
Ianca 46 45 6N 27 29 E
Iara 46 46 31N 23 35 E
Iaşi 46 47 20N 27 0 E
Iba 73 15 22N 120 0 E
Ibadan 85 7 22N 3 58 E
Ibagué 126 4 20N 75 20W
Iballja 44 42 12N 20 0 E
Ibăneşti 46 46 45N 24 50 E
Ibar → 42 43 43N 20 45 E
Ibaraki □ 74 36 10N 140 10 E
Ibarra 126 0 21N 78 7W
Ibba 87 4 49N 29 2 E
Ibba, Bahr el 87 5 30N 28 55 E
Ibbenbüren 24 52 16N 7 41 E
Ibembo 90 2 35N 23 35 E
Ibera, Laguna 124 28 30S 57 9W
Iberian Peninsula 8 40 0N 5 0W
Iberville 106 45 19N 73 17W
Iberville, Lac d' 106 55 55N 73 15W
Ibi 85 8 15N 9 44 E
Ibiá 127 19 30S 46 30W
Ibicuy 124 33 55S 59 10W
Ibioapaba, Sa. da 127 4 0S 41 30W
Ibiza 33 38 54N 1 26 E
Íblei, Monti 41 37 15N 14 45 E
Ibo 91 12 22S 40 40 E
Ibonma 73 3 29S 133 31 E
Ibotirama 127 12 13S 43 12W
Ibriktepe 44 41 2N 26 33 E
Ibshawâi 86 29 21N 30 40 E
Ibu 73 1 35N 127 33 E
Iburg 24 52 10N 8 3 E
Icá 126 14 0S 75 48W
Iça → 126 2 55S 67 58W
Içana 126 0 21N 67 19W
Iceland ■ 50 65 0N 19 0W
Icha 59 55 30N 156 0 E
Ich'ang = Yichang 75 30 40N 111 20 E
Ichchapuram 70 19 10N 84 40 E
Ichihara 74 35 28N 140 5 E
Ichihawa 74 35 44N 139 55 E
Ichilo → 126 15 57S 64 50W
Ichinomiya 74 35 18N 136 48 E
Ichnya 54 50 52N 32 24 E
Icht 82 29 6N 8 54W
Icy Str. 108 58 20N 135 30W
Ida Grove 116 42 20N 95 25W
Idabel 117 33 53N 94 50W
Idaga Hamus 87 14 13N 39 48 E
Idah 85 7 5N 6 40 E
Idaho □ 118 44 10N 114 0W
Idaho City 118 43 50N 115 52W
Idaho Falls 118 43 30N 112 1W
Idaho Springs 118 39 49N 105 30W
Idanha-a-Nova 30 39 50N 7 15W
Idar-Oberstein 25 49 43N 7 19 E
Idd el Ghanam 81 11 30N 24 19 E
Iddan 63 6 10N 48 55 E
Idehan 83 27 10N 11 30 E
Idehan Marzūq 83 24 50N 13 51 E
Idelès 83 23 50N 5 53 E
Idfû 86 25 0N 32 49 E
Ídhi Óros 45 35 15N 24 45 E
Ídhra 45 37 20N 23 28 E
Idi 72 5 2N 97 37 E
Idi Amin Dada, L. = Edward, L. 90 0 25S 29 40 E
Idiofa 88 4 55S 19 42 E
Idkerberget 48 60 22N 15 15 E
Idku, Bahra el 86 31 18N 30 18 E
Idlip 64 35 55N 36 38 E
Idna 62 31 34N 34 58 E
Idrija 39 46 0N 14 5 E
Idritsa 54 56 25N 28 30 E
Idstein 25 50 13N 8 17 E
Idutywa 93 32 8S 28 18 E
Ieper 16 50 51N 2 53 E
Ierápetra 45 35 0N 25 44 E
Ierissós 44 40 22N 23 52 E
Ierissóu Kólpos 44 40 27N 23 57 E
Ierzu 40 39 48N 9 32 E
Iesi 39 43 32N 13 12 E
Ifach, Punta 33 38 38N 0 5 E
Ifanadiana 93 21 19S 47 39 E
Ife 85 7 30N 4 31 E
Iférouâne 85 19 5N 8 24 E
Iffley 98 18 53S 141 12 E
Ifni 82 29 29N 10 12W
Ifon 85 6 58N 5 40 E
Iforas, Adrar des 85 19 40N 1 40 E
Ifrane 82 33 33N 5 7W
Iganga 90 0 37N 33 28 E
Igarapava 127 20 3S 47 47W
Igarapé Açu 127 1 4S 47 33W
Igarka 59 67 30N 86 33 E
Igatimi 125 24 5S 55 40W
Igatpuri 70 19 40N 73 35 E
Igbetti 85 8 44N 4 8 E
Igbo-Ora 85 7 29N 3 15 E
Igboho 85 8 53N 3 50 E
Iggesund 48 61 39N 17 10 E
Ighil Izane 82 35 44N 0 31 E
Iglene 82 22 57N 4 58 E
Iglésias 40 39 19N 8 27 E
Igli 82 30 25N 2 19W
Igloolik 105 69 20N 81 49W
Igma 82 29 9N 6 24W
Igma, Gebel el 86 28 55N 34 0 E
Ignace 106 49 30N 91 40W
Igoshevo 55 59 25N 42 35 E
Igoumenítsa 44 39 32N 20 18 E
Iguaçu → 125 25 36S 54 36W
Iguaçu, Cat. del 125 25 41S 54 26W
Iguala 120 18 20N 99 40W
Igualada 32 41 37N 1 37 E
Iguassu = Iguaçu 125 25 41N 54 26W
Iguatu 127 6 20S 39 18W
Iguéla 88 2 0S 9 16 E
Igunga □ 90 4 20S 33 45 E
Ihiala 85 5 51N 6 55 E
Ihosy 93 22 24S 46 8 E
Ihotry, L. 93 21 56S 43 41 E
Ii 50 65 19N 25 22 E
Iida 74 35 35N 137 50 E
Iijoki → 50 65 20N 25 20 E
Iisalmi 50 63 32N 27 10 E
Iizuka 74 33 38N 130 42 E
Ijebu-Igbo 85 6 56N 4 1 E
Ijebu-Ode 85 6 47N 3 58 E
IJmuiden 16 52 28N 4 35 E
IJssel → 16 52 35N 5 50 E
IJsselmeer 16 52 45N 5 20 E
Ijuí → 125 27 58S 55 20W
Ikale 85 7 40N 5 37 E
Ikare 85 7 32N 5 40 E
Ikaría 45 37 35N 26 10 E
Ikast 49 56 8N 9 10 E
Ikeja 85 6 36N 3 23 E
Ikela 88 1 6S 23 6 E
Ikerre-Ekiti 85 7 25N 5 19 E
Ikhtiman 43 42 27N 23 48 E
Iki 74 33 45N 129 42 E
Ikimba L. 90 1 30S 31 20 E
Ikire 85 7 23N 4 15 E
Ikom 85 6 0N 8 42 E
Ikopa → 93 16 45S 46 40 E
Ikot Ekpene 85 5 12N 7 40 E
Ikungu 90 1 33S 33 42 E
Ikurun 85 7 54N 4 40 E
Ila 85 8 0N 4 39 E
Ilagan 73 17 7N 121 53 E
Ilam 69 26 58N 87 58 E
Ilanskiy 59 56 14N 96 3 E
Ilaro 85 6 53N 3 3 E
Iława 28 53 36N 19 34 E
Ilayangudi 70 9 34N 78 37 E
Ilbilbie 98 21 45S 149 20 E
Île-à-la Crosse 109 55 27N 107 53W
Île-à-la-Crosse, Lac 109 55 40N 107 45W
Île-Bouchard, L' 18 47 7N 0 26 E
Île-de-France 19 49 0N 2 20 E
Île-sur-le-Doubs, L' 19 47 26N 6 34 E
Ilebo 88 4 17S 20 55 E
Ileje □ 91 9 30S 33 25 E
Ilek 58 51 32N 53 21 E
Ilek → 52 51 30N 53 22 E
Ilero 85 8 0N 3 20 E
Ilesha, Oyo, Nigeria 85 7 37N 4 40 E
Ilesha, Oyo, Nigeria 85 8 57N 3 28 E
Ilford 109 56 4N 95 35W
Ilfov □ 46 44 20N 26 0 E
Ilfracombe, Austral. 97 23 30S 144 30 E
Ilfracombe, U.K. 13 51 13N 4 8W
Ílhavo 30 40 33N 8 43W
Ilhéus 127 14 49S 39 2W
Ilia 46 45 57N 22 40 E
Ilia □ 45 37 45N 21 35 E
Ilich 58 40 50N 68 27 E
Iliff 116 40 50N 103 3W
Iligan 73 8 12N 124 13 E
Ilikí, L. 45 38 24N 23 15 E
Iliodhrómia 44 39 12N 23 50 E
Ilion 114 43 0N 75 3W
Ilirska-Bistrica 39 45 34N 14 14 E
Ilkal 70 15 57N 76 8 E
Ilkeston 12 52 59N 1 19W
Illana B. 73 7 35N 123 45 E
Illapel 124 32 0S 71 10W
'Illār 62 32 23N 35 7 E
Ille 20 42 40N 2 37 E
Ille-et-Vilaine □ 18 48 10N 1 30W
Iller → 25 48 23N 9 58 E
Illescas 30 40 8N 3 51W
Illiers 18 48 18N 1 15 E
Illimani 126 16 30S 67 50W
Illinois □ 111 40 15N 89 30W
Illinois → 111 38 55N 90 28W
Illium = Troy 44 39 57N 26 12 E
Illizi 83 26 31N 8 32 E
Illora 31 37 17N 3 53W
Ilm → 24 51 7N 11 45 E
Ilmen, Oz. 54 58 15N 31 10 E
Ilmenau 24 50 41N 10 55 E
Ilo 126 17 40S 71 20W
Ilobu 85 7 45N 4 25 E
Iloilo 73 10 45N 122 33 E
Ilok 42 45 15N 19 20 E
Ilora 85 7 45N 3 50 E
Ilorin 85 8 30N 4 35 E
Iloulya 57 49 15N 44 2 E
Ilovatka 55 50 30N 45 50 E
Ilovlya → 57 49 14N 43 54 E
Iłowa 28 51 30N 15 10 E
Ilubabor □ 87 7 25N 35 0 E
Ilukste 54 55 55N 26 20 E
Ilva Mică 46 47 17N 24 40 E
Ilwaki 73 7 55S 126 30 E
Ilyichevsk 56 46 10N 30 35 E
Iłża 28 51 10N 21 15 E
Iłżanka → 28 51 14N 21 48 E
Imabari 74 34 4N 133 0 E
Imaloto → 93 23 27S 45 13 E
Imandra, Oz. 52 67 30N 33 0 E
Imari 74 33 15N 129 52 E
Imasa 86 18 0N 36 12 E
Imathía □ 44 40 30N 22 15 E
Imbâbah 86 30 5N 31 12 E
Imbler 118 45 31N 118 0W
Imdahane 82 32 8N 7 0W
imeni 26 Bakinskikh Komissarov (Neft-chala) 53 39 19N 49 12 E
imeni 26 Bakinskikh Komissarov (Vyshzha) 53 39 22N 54 10 E
Imeni Poliny Osipenko 59 52 30N 136 29 E
Imeri, Serra 126 0 50N 65 25W
Imerimandroso 93 17 26S 48 35 E
Imi (Hinna) 87 6 28N 42 10 E
Imishly 57 39 49N 48 4 E
Imitek 82 29 43N 8 10W
Imlay 118 40 45N 118 9W
Imlay City 112 43 0N 83 2W
Immenstadt 25 47 34N 10 13 E
Immingham 12 53 37N 0 12W
Immokalee 115 26 25N 81 26W
Imo □ 85 5 15N 7 20 E
Imola 39 44 20N 11 42 E
Imotski 42 43 27N 17 12 E
Imperatriz 127 5 30S 47 29W
Impéria 38 43 52N 8 0 E
Imperial, Can. 109 51 21N 105 28W
Imperial, Calif., U.S.A. 119 32 52N 115 34W
Imperial, Nebr., U.S.A. 116 40 38N 101 39W
Imperial Dam 119 32 50N 114 30W
Impfondo 88 1 40N 18 0 E
Imphal 67 24 48N 93 56 E
Imphy 19 46 56N 3 15 E
İmroz = Gökçeada 44 40 10N 25 50 E
Imst 26 47 15N 10 44 E
Imuruan B. 73 10 40N 119 10 E
In Belbel 82 27 55N 1 12 E
In Delimane 85 15 52N 1 31 E
In Rhar 82 27 10N 1 59 E
In Salah 82 27 10N 2 32 E
In Tallak 85 16 19N 3 15 E
Ina 74 35 50N 138 0 E
Ina-Bonchi 74 35 45N 137 58 E
Inangahua Junc. 101 41 52S 171 59 E
Inanwatan 73 2 10S 132 14 E
Iñapari 126 11 0S 69 40W
Inari 50 68 54N 27 5 E
Inarijärvi 50 69 0N 28 0 E
Inawashiro-Ko 74 37 29N 140 6 E
Inca 32 39 43N 2 54 E
Incaguasi 124 29 12S 71 5W
İnce-Burnu 64 42 7N 34 56 E
Inchon 76 37 27N 126 40 E
Incio 30 42 39N 7 21W
Incomáti → 93 25 46S 32 43 E
Incudine, L' 21 41 50N 9 12 E
Inda Silase 87 14 10N 38 15 E
Indalsälven → 48 62 36N 17 30 E
Indaw 67 24 15N 96 5 E
Indbir 87 8 7N 37 52 E
Independence, Calif., U.S.A. 119 36 51N 118 14W
Independence, Iowa, U.S.A. 116 42 27N 91 52W
Independence, Kans., U.S.A. 117 37 10N 95 43W
Independence, Mo., U.S.A. 116 39 3N 94 25W
Independence, Oreg., U.S.A. 118 44 53N 123 12W
Independence Fjord 4 82 10N 29 0W
Independence Mts. 118 41 30N 116 2W
Independenţa 46 45 25N 27 42 E
Inderborskiy 57 48 30N 51 42 E
India ■ 3 20 0N 78 0 E
Indian → 115 27 59N 80 34W
Indian-Antarctic Ridge 94 49 0S 120 0 E
Indian Cabins 108 59 52N 117 40W
Indian Harbour 107 54 27N 57 13W
Indian Head 109 50 30N 103 41W
Indian Ocean 3 5 0S 75 0 E
Indiana 114 40 38N 79 9W
Indiana □ 114 40 0N 86 0W
Indianapolis 114 39 42N 86 10W
Indianola, Iowa, U.S.A. 116 41 20N 93 32W
Indianola, Miss., U.S.A. 117 33 27N 90 40W
Indiga 52 67 50N 48 50 E
Indigirka → 59 70 48N 148 54 E
Indija 42 45 6N 20 7 E
Indio 119 33 46N 116 15W
Indonesia ■ 72 5 0S 115 0 E
Indore 68 22 42N 75 53 E
Indramayu 73 6 21S 108 20 E
Indramayu, Tg. 73 6 20S 108 20 E
Indravati → 70 19 20N 80 20 E
Indre □ 19 46 50N 1 39 E
Indre → 18 47 16N 0 19 E
Indre-et-Loire □ 18 47 12N 0 40 E
Indus → 68 24 20N 67 47 E
Indus, Mouth of the 68 24 00N 68 00 E
İnebolu 64 41 55N 33 40 E
İnegöl 64 40 5N 29 31 E
Ineu 42 46 26N 21 51 E
Inezgane 82 30 25N 9 29W
Infante, Kaap 92 34 27S 20 51 E
Infantes 33 38 43N 3 1W
Infiernillo, Presa del 120 18 9N 102 0W
Infiesto 30 43 21N 5 21W
Ingende 88 0 12S 18 57 E
Ingenio Santa Ana 124 27 25S 65 40W
Ingersoll 112 43 4N 80 55W
Ingham 97 18 43S 146 10 E
Ingleborough 12 54 11N 2 23W
Inglewood, Queensland, Austral. 99 28 25S 151 2 E
Inglewood, Vic., Austral. 99 36 29S 143 53 E
Inglewood, N.Z. 101 39 9S 174 14 E
Inglewood, U.S.A. 119 33 58N 118 21W
Ingólfshöfði 50 63 48N 16 39W
Ingolstadt 25 48 45N 11 26 E
Ingomar 118 46 35N 107 21W
Ingonish 107 46 42N 60 18W
Ingore 84 12 24N 15 48W
Ingrid Christensen Coast 5 69 30S 76 00 E
Ingul → 56 46 50N 32 15 E
Ingulec 56 47 42N 33 14 E
Ingulets → 56 46 41N 32 48 E
Inguri →, U.S.S.R. 57 42 38N 41 35 E
Inguri →, U.S.S.R. 57 42 15N 41 48 E
Inhaca, I. 93 26 1S 32 57 E
Inhafenga 93 20 36S 33 53 E
Inhambane 93 23 54S 35 30 E
Inhambane □ 93 22 30S 34 20 E
Inhaminga 91 18 26S 35 0 E
Inharrime 93 24 30S 35 0 E
Inharrime → 93 24 30S 35 0 E
Iniesta 33 39 27N 1 45W
Ining = Yining 75 43 58N 81 10 E
Inírida → 126 3 55N 67 52W
Inishbofin 15 53 35N 10 12W
Inishmore 15 53 8N 9 45W
Inishowen 15 55 14N 7 15W
Injune 97 25 53S 148 32 E
Inklin 108 58 56N 133 5W
Inklin → 108 58 50N 133 10W
Inkom 118 42 51N 112 15W
Inle L. 67 20 30N 96 58 E
Inn → 25 48 35N 13 28 E
Innamincka 99 27 44S 140 46 E
Inner Hebrides 14 57 0N 6 30W
Inner Mongolia = Nei Monggol Zizhiqu □ 76 42 0N 112 0 E
Inner Sound 14 57 30N 5 55W
Innerkip 112 43 13N 80 42W
Innerste → 24 52 45N 9 40 E
Innetalling I. 106 56 0N 79 0W
Innisfail, Austral. 97 17 33S 146 5 E
Innisfail, Can. 108 52 0N 113 57W
Innsbruck 26 47 16N 11 23 E
Inny → 15 53 30N 7 50W
Inongo 88 1 55S 18 30 E
Inoucdjouac (Port Harrison) 105 58 25N 78 15W
Inowrocław 28 52 50N 18 12 E
Inquisivi 126 16 50S 67 10W
Insein 67 16 50N 96 5 E
Însurăţei 46 44 50N 27 40 E
Inta 52 66 5N 60 8 E
Intendente Alvear 124 35 12S 63 32W
Interior 116 43 46N 101 59W
Interlaken 25 46 41N 7 50 E
International Falls 116 48 36N 93 25W
Interview I. 71 12 55N 92 42 E
Inthanon, Doi 71 18 35N 98 29 E

* Now part of Sind □

Intiyaco Janikowo

Intiyaco 124 28 43 S 60 5W
Inútil, B. 128 53 30 S 70 15W
Inuvik 104 68 16N 133 40W
Inveraray 14 56 13N 5 5W
Inverbervie 14 56 50N 2 17W
Invercargill 101 46 24 S 168 24 E
Inverell 97 29 45 S 151 8 E
Invergordon 14 57 41N 4 10W
Invermere 108 50 30N 116 2W
Inverness, Can. 107 46 15N 61 19W
Inverness, U.K. 14 57 29N 4 12W
Inverness, U.S.A. 115 28 50N 82 20W
Inverurie 14 57 15N 2 21W
Investigator Group 96 34 45 S 134 20 E
Investigator Str. 97 35 30 S 137 0 E
Invona 112 40 46N 78 35W
Inya 58 50 28N 86 37 E
Inyanga 91 18 12 S 32 40 E
Inyangani 91 18 5 S 32 50 E
Inyantue 91 18 30 S 26 40 E
Inyazura 91 18 40 S 32 16 E
Inyo Range 119 37 0N 118 0W
Inyokern 119 35 38N 117 48W
Inza 55 53 55N 46 25 E
Inzhavino 55 52 22N 42 30 E
Ioánnina 44 39 42N 20 47 E
Ioánnina (Janinà) □ 44 39 39N 20 57 E
Iola 117 38 0N 95 20W
Ion Corvin 46 44 7N 27 50 E
Iona 14 56 20N 6 25W
Ione, Calif., U.S.A. 118 38 20N 120 56W
Ione, Wash., U.S.A. 118 48 44N 117 29W
Ionia 114 42 59N 85 7W
Ionian Is. = Iónioi Nísoi 45 38 40N 20 0 E
Ionian Sea 35 37 30N 17 30 E
Iónioi Nísoi 45 38 40N 20 0 E
Iori → 57 41 3N 46 17 E
Íos 45 36 41N 25 20 E
Iowa □ 116 42 18N 93 30W
Iowa City 116 41 40N 91 35W
Iowa Falls 116 42 30N 93 15W
Ipala 90 4 30 S 32 52 E
Ipameri 127 17 44 S 48 9W
Ipáti 45 38 52N 22 14 E
Ipatovo 57 45 45N 42 50 E
Ipel → 27 48 10N 19 35 E
Ipiales 126 0 50N 77 37W
Ipin = Yibin 75 28 45N 104 32 E
Ípiros □ 44 39 30N 20 30 E
Ipixuna 126 7 0 S 71 40W
Ipoh 71 4 35N 101 5 E
Ippy 88 6 5N 21 7 E
Ípsala 44 40 55N 26 23 E
Ipsárion Óros 44 40 40N 24 40 E
Ipswich, Austral. 97 27 35 S 152 40 E
Ipswich, U.K. 13 52 4N 1 9 E
Ipswich, Mass., U.S.A. 113 42 40N 70 50W
Ipswich, S.D., U.S.A. 116 45 28N 99 1W
Ipu 127 4 23 S 40 44W
Iput → 54 52 26N 31 2 E
Iquique 126 20 19 S 70 5W
Iquitos 126 3 45 S 73 10W
Iracoubo 127 5 30N 53 10W
Iráklia 45 36 50N 25 28 E
Iráklion 45 35 20N 25 12 E
Iráklion □ 45 35 10N 25 10 E
Irala 125 25 55 S 54 35W
Iramba □ 90 4 30 S 34 30 E
Iran ■ 65 33 0N 53 0 E
Iran, Pegunungan 72 2 20N 114 50 E
Iranamadu Tank 70 9 23N 80 29 E
Īrānshahr 65 27 15N 60 40 E
Irapuato 120 20 40N 101 30W
Iraq ■ 64 33 0N 44 0 E
Irarrar, O. → 82 20 0N 1 30 E
Irati 125 25 25 S 50 38W
Irbid 62 32 35N 35 48 E
Irebu 88 0 40 S 17 46 E
Iregua → 32 42 27N 2 24 E
Ireland ■ 15 53 0N 8 0W
Ireland I. 121 32 16N 64 50W
Ireland's Eye 15 53 25N 6 4W
Irele 85 7 40N 5 40 E
Iret 59 60 3N 154 20 E
Irgiz, Bol. 55 52 10N 49 10 E
Irhârharene 83 27 37N 7 30 E
Irharrhar, O. → 83 28 3N 6 15 E
Irherm 82 30 7N 8 18W
Irhil Mgoun 82 31 30N 6 28W
Irian Jaya □ 73 4 0 S 137 0 E
Irié 84 8 15N 9 10W
Iringa 90 7 48 S 35 43 E
Iringa □ 90 7 48 S 35 43 E
Irinjalakuda 70 10 21N 76 14 E
Iriri → 127 3 52 S 52 37W
Irish Sea 12 54 0N 5 0W
Irkineyeva 59 58 30N 96 49 E
Irkutsk 59 52 18N 104 20 E
Irma 109 52 55N 111 14W
Iroise, Mer d' 18 48 15N 4 45W
Iron Baron 99 32 58 S 137 11 E
Iron Gate = Portile de Fier 46 44 42N 22 30 E
Iron Knob 97 32 46 S 137 8 E
Iron Mountain 114 45 49N 88 4W
Iron River 116 46 6N 88 40W
Ironbridge 13 52 38N 2 29W
Ironstone Kopje 92 25 17 S 24 5 E
Ironton, Mo., U.S.A. 117 37 40N 90 40W
Ironton, Ohio, U.S.A. 114 38 35N 82 40W
Ironwood 116 46 30N 90 10W
Iroquois Falls 106 48 46N 80 41W
Irpen 54 50 30N 30 15 E
Irrara Cr. → 99 29 35 S 145 31 E
Irrawaddy □ 67 17 0N 95 0 E
Irrawaddy → 67 15 50N 95 6 E
Irsina 41 40 45N 16 15 E
Irtysh → 58 61 4N 68 52 E
Irumu 90 1 32N 29 53 E
Irún 32 43 20N 1 52W
Irurzun 32 42 55N 1 50W
Irvine, Can. 109 49 57N 110 16W
Irvine, U.K. 14 55 37N 4 40W
Irvine, U.S.A. 114 37 42N 83 58W
Irvinestown 15 54 28N 7 38W
Irymple 99 34 14 S 142 8 E
Is-sur-Tille 19 47 30N 5 10 E
Isa 85 13 14N 6 24 E
Isaac → 97 22 55 S 149 20 E
Isabel 116 45 27N 101 22W
Isabela, I. 120 21 51N 105 55W
Isabella, Cord. 121 13 30N 85 25W
Ísafjarðardjúp 50 66 10N 23 0W
Ísafjörður 50 66 5N 23 9W
Isagarh 68 24 48N 77 51 E
Isaka 90 3 56 S 32 59 E
Isangi 88 0 52N 24 10 E
Isar → 25 48 49N 12 58 E
Isarco → 39 46 57N 11 18 E
Ísari 45 37 22N 22 0 E
Isbergues 19 50 36N 2 24 E
Isbiceni 46 43 45N 24 40 E
Íschia 40 40 45N 13 51 E
Ise 74 34 25N 136 45 E
Ise-Wan 74 34 43N 136 43 E
Isefjord 49 55 53N 11 50 E
Iseo 38 45 40N 10 3 E
Iseo, L. d' 38 45 45N 10 3 E
Iseramagazi 90 4 37 S 32 10 E
Isère □ 21 45 15N 5 40 E
Isère → 21 44 59N 4 51 E
Iserlohn 24 51 22N 7 40 E
Isérnia 41 41 35N 14 12 E
Iseyin 85 8 0N 3 36 E
Ishikari-Wan (Otaru-Wan) 74 43 25N 141 1 E
Ishikawa □ 74 36 30N 136 30 E
Ishim 58 56 10N 69 30 E
Ishim → 58 57 45N 71 10 E
Ishinomaki 74 38 32N 141 20 E
Ishmi 44 41 33N 19 34 E
Ishpeming 114 46 30N 87 40W
Isigny-sur-Mer 18 49 19N 1 6W
Isil Kul 58 54 55N 71 16 E
Isiolo 90 0 24N 37 33 E
Isiolo □ 90 0 30N 37 30 E
Isipingo Beach 93 30 00 S 30 57 E
Isiro 90 2 53N 27 40 E
Isisford 98 24 15 S 144 21 E
İskenderun 64 36 32N 36 10 E
İskilip 56 40 50N 34 20 E
Iskůr → 43 43 45N 24 25 E
Iskůr, Yazovir 43 42 23N 23 30 E
Iskut → 108 56 45N 131 49W
Isla → 14 56 32N 3 20W
Isla Cristina 31 37 13N 7 17W
Islamabad 66 33 40N 73 10 E
Islamkot 68 24 42N 70 13 E
Islampur 70 17 2N 74 20 E
Island → 108 60 25N 121 12W
Island Falls, Can. 106 49 35N 81 20W
Island Falls, U.S.A. 107 46 0N 68 16W
Island L. 109 53 47N 94 25W
Island Pond 114 44 50N 71 50W
Islands, B. of, Can. 107 49 11N 58 15W
Islands, B. of, N.Z. 101 35 20 S 174 20 E
Islay 14 55 46N 6 10W
Isle → 20 44 55N 0 15W
Isle-Adam, L' 19 49 6N 2 14 E
Isle aux Morts 107 47 35N 59 0W
Isle-Jourdain, L', Gers, France 20 43 36N 1 5 E
Isle-Jourdain, L', Vienne, France 20 46 13N 0 31 E
Isle of Wight □ 13 50 40N 1 20W
Isle Royale 116 48 0N 88 50W
Isleta 119 34 58N 106 46W
Ismail 56 45 22N 28 46 E
Ismâ'ilîya 86 30 37N 32 18 E
Ismaning 25 48 14N 11 41 E
Ismay 116 46 33N 104 44W
Isna 86 25 17N 32 30 E
Isola del Gran Sasso d'Italia 39 42 30N 13 40 E
Ísola del Liri 40 41 39N 13 32 E
Ísola della Scala 38 45 16N 11 0 E
Ísola di Capo Rizzuto 41 38 56N 17 5 E
Isparta 64 37 47N 30 30 E
Isperikh 43 43 43N 26 50 E
Íspica 41 36 47N 14 53 E
İspir 57 40 40N 40 50 E
Israel ■ 62 32 0N 34 50 E
Issia 84 6 33N 6 33W
Issoire 20 45 32N 3 15 E
Issoudun 19 46 57N 2 0 E
Issyk-Kul, Ozero 58 42 25N 77 15 E
Ist 39 44 17N 14 47 E
İstanbul 64 41 0N 29 0 E
Istiaía 45 38 57N 23 9 E
Istok 42 42 45N 20 24 E
Istokpoga, L. 115 27 22N 81 14W
Istra, U.S.S.R. 55 55 55N 36 50 E
Istra, Yugo. 39 45 10N 14 0 E
Istranca Dağları 43 41 48N 27 30 E
Istres 21 43 31N 4 59 E
Istria = Istra 39 45 10N 14 0 E
Itá 124 25 29 S 57 21W
Itabaiana 127 7 18 S 35 19W
Itaberaba 127 12 32 S 40 18W
Itabira 127 19 37 S 43 13W
Itabirito 125 20 15 S 43 48W
Itabuna 127 14 48 S 39 16W
Itaituba 127 4 10 S 55 50W
Itajaí 125 27 50 S 48 39W
Itajubá 125 22 24 S 45 30W
Itaka 91 8 50 S 32 49 E
Italy ■ 36 42 0N 13 0 E
Itampolo 93 24 41 S 43 57 E
Itapecuru-Mirim 127 3 24 S 44 20W
Itaperuna 127 21 10 S 41 54W
Itapetininga 125 23 36 S 48 7W
Itapeva 125 23 59 S 48 59W
Itapicuru →, Bahia, Brazil 127 11 47 S 37 32W
Itapicuru →, Maranhão, Brazil 127 2 52 S 44 12W
Itapuá □ 125 26 40 S 55 40W
Itaquari 125 20 20 S 40 25W
Itaquatiara 126 2 58 S 58 30W
Itaquí 124 29 8 S 56 30W
Itararé 125 24 6 S 49 23W
Itarsi 68 22 36N 77 51 E
Itatí 124 27 16 S 58 15W
Itatuba 126 5 46 S 63 20W
Itchen → 13 50 57N 1 20W
Itéa 45 38 25N 22 25 E
Ithaca 114 42 25N 76 30W
Ithaca = Itháki 45 38 25N 20 43 E
Itháki 45 38 25N 20 40 E
Ito 74 34 58N 139 5 E
Itoman 77 26 7N 127 40 E
Iton → 18 49 9N 1 12 E
Itonamas → 126 12 28 S 64 24W
Itsa 86 29 15N 30 47 E
Íttiri 40 40 38N 8 32 E
Itu, Brazil 125 23 17 S 47 15W
Itu, Nigeria 85 5 10N 7 58 E
Ituaçu 127 13 50 S 41 18W
Ituiutaba 127 19 0 S 49 25W
Itumbiara 127 18 20 S 49 10W
Ituna 109 51 10N 103 24W
Itunge Port 91 9 40 S 33 55 E
Iturbe 124 23 0 S 65 25W
Ituri → 90 1 40N 27 1 E
Iturup, Ostrov 59 45 0N 148 0 E
Ituyuro → 124 22 40 S 63 50W
Itzehoe 24 53 56N 9 31 E
Ivaí → 125 23 18 S 53 42W
Ivalo 50 68 38N 27 35 E
Ivalojoki → 50 68 40N 27 40 E
Ivangorod 54 59 37N 28 40 E
Ivangrad 42 42 51N 19 52 E
Ivanhoe 97 32 56 S 144 20 E
Ivanhoe L. 109 60 25N 106 30W
Ivanić Grad 39 45 41N 16 25 E
Ivanjica 42 43 35N 20 12 E
Ivanjšcice 39 46 12N 16 13 E
Ivankoyskoye Vdkhr. 55 56 37N 36 32 E
Ivano-Frankovsk 56 48 56N 24 43 E
Ivano-Frankovsk (Stanislav) 54 48 40N 24 40 E
Ivanovo, Byelorussia, U.S.S.R. 54 52 7N 25 29 E
Ivanovo, R.S.F.S.R., U.S.S.R. 55 57 5N 41 0 E
Ivato 93 20 37 S 47 10 E
Ivaylovgrad 43 41 32N 26 8 E
Ivdel 52 60 42N 60 24 E
Ivinheima → 125 23 14 S 53 42W
Iviza = Ibiza 33 39 0N 1 30 E
Ivohibe 93 22 31 S 46 57 E
Ivory Coast ■ 84 7 30N 5 0W
Ivösjön 49 56 8N 14 25 E
Ivrea 38 45 30N 7 52 E
Ivugivik, (N.D. d'Ivugivic) 105 62 24N 77 55W
Iwahig 72 8 35N 117 32 E
Iwaki 74 37 3N 140 55 E
Iwakuni 74 34 15N 132 8 E
Iwata 74 34 42N 137 51 E
Iwate □ 74 39 30N 141 30 E
Iwate-San 74 39 51N 141 0 E
Iwo 85 7 39N 4 9 E
IwoniczZdrój 27 49 37N 21 47 E
Ixiamas 126 13 50 S 68 5W
Ixopo 93 30 11 S 30 5 E
Ixtepec 120 16 32N 95 10W
Ixtlán de Juárez 120 17 23N 96 28W
Ixtlán del Río 120 21 5N 104 21W
Izabel, L. de 120 15 30N 89 10W
Izamal 120 20 56N 89 1W
Izberbash 57 42 35N 47 52 E
Izbica 28 50 53N 23 10 E
Izbica Kujawska 28 52 25N 18 30 E
Izegem 16 50 55N 3 12 E
Izgrev 43 43 36N 26 58 E
*Izhevsk 52 56 51N 53 14 E
İzmir (Smyrna) 53 38 25N 27 8 E
İzmit 64 40 45N 29 50 E
Iznajar 31 37 15N 4 19W
Iznalloz 33 37 24N 3 30W
Izobil'nyy 57 45 25N 41 44 E
Izola 39 45 32N 13 39 E
Izra 62 32 51N 36 15 E
Izra' 62 32 52N 36 5 E
Iztochni Rodopi 43 41 45N 25 30 E
Izumi-sano 74 34 23N 135 18 E
Izumo 74 35 20N 132 46 E
Izyaslav 54 50 5N 26 50 E
Izyum 56 49 12N 37 19 E

J

Jaba 87 6 20N 35 7 E
Jaba' 62 32 20N 35 13 E
Jabal el Awlîya 87 15 10N 32 31 E
Jabalón → 31 38 53N 4 5W
Jabalpur 69 23 9N 79 58 E
Jabālyah 62 31 32N 34 27 E
Jablah 64 35 20N 36 0 E
Jablanac 39 44 42N 14 56 E
Jablonec 26 50 43N 15 10 E
Jablonica 27 48 37N 17 26 E
Jabłonowo 28 53 23N 19 10 E
Jaboticabal 125 21 15 S 48 17W
Jabukovac 42 44 22N 22 21 E
Jaburu 126 5 30 S 64 0W
Jaca 32 42 35N 0 33W
Jacareí 125 23 20 S 46 0W
Jacarèzinho 125 23 5 S 50 0W
Jáchymov 26 50 22N 12 55 E
Jackman 107 45 35N 70 17W
Jacksboro 117 33 14N 98 15W
Jackson, Austral. 99 26 39 S 149 39 E
Jackson, Ala., U.S.A. 115 31 32N 87 53W
Jackson, Calif., U.S.A. 118 38 19N 120 47W
Jackson, Ky., U.S.A. 114 37 35N 83 22W
Jackson, Mich., U.S.A. 114 42 18N 84 25W
Jackson, Minn., U.S.A. 116 43 35N 95 0W
Jackson, Miss., U.S.A. 117 32 20N 90 10W
Jackson, Mo., U.S.A. 117 37 25N 89 42W
Jackson, Ohio, U.S.A. 114 39 0N 82 40W
Jackson, Tenn., U.S.A. 115 35 40N 88 50W
Jackson, Wyo., U.S.A. 118 43 30N 110 49W
Jackson Bay 101 43 58 S 168 42 E
Jackson, L. 118 43 55N 110 40W
Jacksons 101 42 46 S 171 32 E
Jacksonville, Ala., U.S.A. 115 33 49N 85 45W
Jacksonville, Fla., U.S.A. 115 30 15N 81 38W
Jacksonville, Ill., U.S.A. 116 39 42N 90 15W
Jacksonville, N.C., U.S.A. 115 34 50N 77 29W
Jacksonville, Oreg., U.S.A. 118 42 19N 122 56W
Jacksonville, Tex., U.S.A. 117 31 58N 95 19W
Jacksonville Beach 115 30 19N 81 26W
Jacmel 121 18 14N 72 32W
Jacob Lake 119 36 45N 112 12W
Jacobabad 68 28 20N 68 29 E
Jacobina 127 11 11 S 40 30W
Jacob's Well 62 32 13N 35 13 E
Jacques-Cartier, Mt. 107 48 57N 66 0W
Jacqueville 84 5 12N 4 25W
Jacuí → 125 30 2 S 51 15W
Jacundá → 127 1 57 S 50 26W
Jade 24 53 22N 8 14 E
Jadebusen 24 53 30N 8 15 E
Jadotville = Likasi 91 10 55 S 26 48 E
Jadovnik 42 43 20N 19 45 E
Jadów 28 52 28N 21 38 E
Jadraque 32 40 55N 2 55W
Jādū 83 32 0N 12 0 E
Jaén, Peru 126 5 25 S 78 40W
Jaén, Spain 31 37 44N 3 43W
Jaén □ 31 37 50N 3 30W
Jaerens Rev 47 58 45N 5 45 E
Jafène 82 20 35N 5 30W
Jaffa = Tel Aviv-Yafo 62 32 4N 34 48 E
Jaffa, C. 99 36 58 S 139 40 E
Jaffna 70 9 45N 80 2 E
Jagadhri 68 30 10N 77 20 E
Jagadishpur 69 25 30N 84 21 E
Jagdalpur 70 19 3N 82 0 E
Jagersfontein 92 29 44 S 25 27 E
Jagst → 25 49 14N 9 11 E
Jagtial 70 18 50N 79 0 E
Jaguariaíva 125 24 10 S 49 50W
Jaguaribe → 127 4 25 S 37 45W
Jagüey Grande 121 22 35N 81 7W
Jahangirabad 68 28 19N 78 4 E
Jahrom 65 28 30N 53 31 E
Jailolo 73 1 5N 127 30 E
Jailolo, Selat 73 0 5N 129 5 E
Jainti 69 26 45N 89 40 E
Jaipur 68 27 0N 75 50 E
Jajce 42 44 19N 17 17 E
Jajpur 69 20 53N 86 22 E
Jakarta 73 6 9 S 106 49 E
Jakobstad (Pietarsaari) 50 63 40N 22 43 E
Jakupica 42 41 45N 21 22 E
Jal 117 32 8N 103 8W
Jalai Nur 76 49 27N 117 42 E
Jalalabad, Afghan. 66 34 30N 70 29 E
Jalalabad, India 69 27 41N 79 42 E
Jalalpur Jattan 68 32 38N 74 11 E
Jalapa, Guat. 120 14 39N 89 59W
Jalapa, Mexico 120 19 30N 96 56W
Jalas, Jabal al 64 27 30N 36 30 E
Jalaun 69 26 8N 79 25 E
Jaleswar 69 26 38N 85 48 E
Jalgaon, Maharashtra, India 68 21 0N 75 42 E
Jalgaon, Maharashtra, India 68 21 2N 76 31 E
Jalingo 85 8 55N 11 25 E
Jalisco □ 120 20 0N 104 0W
Jallas → 30 42 54N 9 8W
Jalna 70 19 48N 75 38 E
Jalón → 32 41 47N 1 4W
Jalpa 120 21 38N 102 58W
Jalpaiguri 69 26 32N 88 46 E
Jalq 65 27 35N 62 46 E
Jaluit I. 94 6 0N 169 30 E
Jamaari 85 11 44N 9 53 E
Jamaica ■ 121 18 10N 77 30W
Jamalpur, Bangla. 69 24 52N 89 56 E
Jamalpur, India 69 25 18N 86 28 E
Jamalpurganj 69 23 2N 88 1 E
Jamanxim → 127 4 43 S 56 18W
Jambe 73 1 15 S 132 10 E
Jambi 72 1 38 S 103 30 E
Jambi □ 72 1 30 S 102 30 E
Jambusar 68 22 3N 72 51 E
James → 116 42 52N 97 18W
James B. 106 51 30N 80 0W
James Range 96 24 10 S 132 30 E
James Ross I. 5 63 58 S 57 50W
Jamestown, Austral. 97 33 10 S 138 32 E
Jamestown, S. Afr. 92 31 6 S 26 45 E
Jamestown, Ky., U.S.A. 114 37 0N 85 5W
Jamestown, N.D., U.S.A. 116 46 54N 98 42W
Jamestown, N.Y., U.S.A. 114 42 5N 79 18W
Jamestown, Pa., U.S.A. 112 41 32N 80 27W
Jamestown, Tenn., U.S.A. 115 36 25N 85 0W
Jamkhandi 70 16 30N 75 15 E
Jammā'īn 62 32 8N 35 12 E
Jammalamadugu 70 14 51N 78 25 E
Jammerbugt 49 57 15N 9 20 E
Jammu 68 32 43N 74 54 E
Jammu & Kashmir □ 66 34 25N 77 0 E
Jamnagar 68 22 30N 70 6 E
Jamner 68 20 45N 75 52 E
Jampur 68 29 39N 70 40 E
Jamrud Fort 66 33 59N 71 24 E
Jamshedpur 69 22 44N 86 12 E
Jamtara 69 23 59N 86 49 E
Jämtlands län □ 48 62 40N 13 50 E
Jan Kemp 92 27 55 S 24 51 E
Jan L. 109 54 56N 102 55W
Jan Mayen Is. 4 71 0N 9 0W
Jand 66 33 30N 72 6 E
Janda, Laguna de la 31 36 15N 5 45W
Jandaq 65 34 3N 54 22 E
Jandola 68 32 20N 70 9 E
Jandowae 99 26 45 S 151 7 E
Jándula → 31 38 3N 4 6W
Janesville 116 42 39N 89 1W
Janga 85 10 5N 1 0W
Jangaon 70 17 44N 79 5 E
Jangeru 72 2 20 S 116 29 E
Janikowo 28 52 45N 18 7 E

*Renamed Ustinov

Janīn Jyväskylä

Janīn **62** 32 28N 35 18 E
Janja **42** 44 40N 19 17 E
Janjevo **42** 42 35N 21 19 E
Janjina **42** 42 58N 17 25 E
Jánoshalma **27** 46 18N 19 21 E
Jánosháza **27** 47 8N 17 12 E
Jánossomorja **27** 47 47N 17 11 E
Janów **28** 50 44N 19 27 E
Janów Lubelski **28** 50 48N 22 23 E
Janów Podlaski **28** 52 11N 23 11 E
Janowiec Wielkopolski **28** 52 45N 17 30 E
Januária **127** 15 25 S 44 25W
Janub Dârfûr □ **87** 11 0N 25 0 E
Janub Kordofân □ **87** 12 0N 30 0 E
Janville **19** 48 10N 1 50 E
Janzé **18** 47 55N 1 28W
Jaora **68** 23 40N 75 10 E
Japan ■ **74** 36 0N 136 0 E
Japan, Sea of **74** 40 0N 135 0 E
Japan Trench **94** 32 0N 142 0 E
Japara **73** 6 30 S 110 40 E
Japen = Yapen **73** 1 50 S 136 0 E
Japurá → **126** 3 8 S 64 46W
Jaque **126** 7 27N 78 8W
Jara, La **119** 37 16N 106 0W
Jaraicejo **31** 39 40N 5 49W
Jaraiz **30** 40 4N 5 45W
Jarales **119** 34 39N 106 51W
Jarama → **32** 40 2N 3 39W
Jarandilla **30** 40 8N 5 39W
Jaranwala **68** 31 15N 73 26 E
Jarash **62** 32 17N 35 54 E
Jarbidge **118** 41 56N 115 27W
Jardim **124** 21 28 S 56 2W
Jardín → **33** 38 50N 2 10W
Jardines de la Reina, Is. **121** 20 50N 78 50W
Jargalant (Kobdo) **75** 48 2N 91 37 E
Jargeau **19** 47 50N 2 1 E
Jarmen **24** 53 56N 13 20 E
Jarnac **20** 45 40N 0 11W
Jarny **19** 49 9N 5 53 E
Jarocin **28** 51 59N 17 29 E
Jaroměr **26** 50 22N 15 52 E
Jarosław **27** 50 2N 22 42 E
Järpås **49** 58 23N 12 57 E
Järpen **48** 63 21N 13 26 E
Jarso **87** 5 15N 37 30 E
Jarvis **112** 42 53N 80 6W
Jarvis I. **95** 0 15 S 159 55W
Jarvornik **27** 50 23N 17 2 E
Jarwa **69** 27 38N 82 30 E
Jaša Tomić **42** 45 26N 20 50 E
Jasien **28** 51 46N 15 0 E
Jasin **71** 2 20N 102 26 E
Jāsk **65** 25 38N 57 45 E
Jasło **27** 49 45N 21 30 E
Jasper, Alta., Can. **108** 52 55N 118 5W
Jasper, Ont., Can. **113** 44 52N 75 57W
Jasper, Ala., U.S.A. **115** 33 48N 87 16W
Jasper, Fla., U.S.A. **115** 30 31N 82 58W
Jasper, Minn., U.S.A. **116** 43 52N 96 22W
Jasper, Tex., U.S.A. **117** 30 59N 93 58W
Jasper Nat. Park **108** 52 50N 118 8W
Jassy = Iaşi **46** 47 10N 27 40 E
Jastrebarsko **39** 45 41N 15 39 E
Jastrowie **28** 53 26N 16 49 E
Jastrzębie Zdrój **27** 49 57N 18 35 E
Jászapáti **27** 47 32N 20 10 E
Jászárokszállás **27** 47 39N 20 1 E
Jászberény **27** 47 30N 19 55 E
Jászkiser **27** 47 27N 20 20 E
Jászladány **27** 47 23N 20 10 E
Jataí **127** 17 58 S 51 48W
Jati **68** 24 20N 68 19 E
Jatibarang **73** 6 28 S 108 18 E
Jatinegara **73** 6 13 S 106 52 E
Játiva **33** 39 0N 0 32W
Jatobal **127** 4 35 S 49 33W
Jatt **62** 32 24N 35 2 E
Jaú **125** 22 10 S 48 30W
Jauja **126** 11 45 S 75 15W
Jaunjelgava **54** 56 35N 25 0 E
Jaunpur **69** 25 46N 82 44 E
Java = Jawa **73** 7 0 S 110 0 E
Java Sea **72** 4 35 S 107 15 E
Java Trench **94** 10 0 S 110 0W
Javadi Hills **70** 12 40N 78 40 E
Jávea **33** 38 48N 0 10 E
Javhlant = Ulyasutay **75** 47 56N 97 28 E
Javla **70** 17 18N 75 9 E
Javron **18** 48 25N 0 25W
Jawa **73** 7 0 S 110 0 E
Jawor **28** 51 4N 16 11 E
Jaworzno **27** 50 13N 19 11 E
Jay **117** 36 25N 94 46W
Jaya, Puncak **73** 3 57 S 137 17 E
Jayapura **73** 2 28 S 140 38 E
Jayawijaya, Pegunungan **73** 5 0 S 139 0 E
Jayton **117** 33 17N 100 35W
Jean **119** 35 47N 115 20W
Jean Marie River **104** 61 32N 120 38W
Jean Rabel **121** 19 50N 73 5W
Jeanerette **117** 29 52N 91 38W
Jeanette, Ostrov **59** 76 43N 158 0 E
Jeannette **112** 40 20N 79 36W
Jebba, Moroc. **82** 35 11N 4 43W
Jebba, Nigeria **85** 9 9N 4 48 E
Jebel, Bahr el → **81** 15 38N 32 31 E
Jebel Qerri **87** 16 16N 32 50 E
Jedburgh **14** 55 28N 2 33W
Jedlicze **27** 49 43N 21 40 E
Jedlnia-Letnisko **28** 51 25N 21 19 E
Jędrzejów **28** 50 35N 20 15 E
Jedwabne **28** 53 17N 22 18 E
Jedway **108** 52 17N 131 14W
Jeetze → **24** 53 9N 11 6 E
Jefferson, Iowa, U.S.A. **116** 42 3N 94 25W
Jefferson, Ohio, U.S.A. **112** 41 40N 80 46W
Jefferson, Tex., U.S.A. **117** 32 45N 94 23W
Jefferson, Wis., U.S.A. **116** 43 0N 88 49W
Jefferson City, Mo., U.S.A. **116** 38 34N 92 10W
Jefferson City, Tenn., U.S.A. **115** 36 8N 83 30W
Jefferson, Mt., Nev., U.S.A. **118** 38 51N 117 0W
Jefferson, Mt., Oreg., U.S.A. **118** 44 45N 121 50W
Jeffersonville **114** 38 20N 85 42W
Jega **85** 12 15N 4 23 E
Jekabpils **54** 56 29N 25 57 E
Jelenia Góra **28** 50 50N 15 45 E
Jelenia Góra □ **28** 51 0N 15 30 E
Jelgava **54** 56 41N 23 49 E
Jelica **42** 43 50N 20 17 E
Jelli **87** 5 25N 31 45 E
Jellicoe **106** 49 40N 87 30W
Jelšava **27** 48 37N 20 15 E
Jemaja **72** 3 5N 105 45 E
Jember **73** 8 11 S 113 41 E
Jembongan **72** 6 45N 117 20 E
Jemeppe **16** 50 37N 5 30 E
Jemnice **26** 49 1N 15 34 E
Jena, Ger. **24** 50 56N 11 33 E
Jena, U.S.A. **117** 31 41N 92 7W
Jenbach **26** 47 24N 11 47 E
Jendouba **83** 36 29N 8 47 E
Jenkins **114** 37 13N 82 41W
Jennings **117** 30 10N 92 45W
Jennings → **108** 59 38N 132 5W
Jenny **49** 57 47N 16 35 E
Jeparit **99** 36 8 S 142 1 E
Jequié **127** 13 51 S 40 5W
Jequitinhonha **127** 16 30 S 41 0W
Jequitinhonha → **127** 15 51 S 38 53W
Jerada **82** 34 17N 2 10W
Jerantut **71** 3 56N 102 22 E
Jérémie **121** 18 40N 74 10W
Jerez de García Salinas **120** 22 39N 103 0W
Jerez de la Frontera **31** 36 41N 6 7W
Jerez de los Caballeros **31** 38 20N 6 45W
Jerez, Punta **120** 22 58N 97 40W
Jericho **98** 23 38 S 146 6 E
Jericho = El Arīhā **62** 31 52N 35 27 E
Jerichow **24** 52 30N 12 2 E
Jerilderie **99** 35 20 S 145 41 E
Jermyn **113** 41 31N 75 31W
Jerome **119** 34 50N 112 0W
Jerrobert **109** 51 56N 109 8W
Jersey City **114** 40 41N 74 8W
Jersey, I. **18** 49 13N 2 7W
Jersey Shore **114** 41 17N 77 18W
Jerseyville **116** 39 5N 90 20W
Jerusalem **62** 31 47N 35 10 E
Jervis B. **97** 35 8 S 150 46 E
Jesenice **39** 46 28N 14 3 E
Jeseník **27** 50 0N 17 8 E
Jesenske **27** 48 20N 20 10 E
Jesselton = Kota Kinabalu **72** 6 0N 116 4 E
Jessnitz **24** 51 42N 12 19 E
Jessore **69** 23 10N 89 10 E
Jesup **115** 31 36N 81 54W
Jesús María **124** 30 59 S 64 5W
Jetmore **117** 38 10N 99 57W
Jetpur **68** 21 45N 70 10 E
Jevnaker **47** 60 15N 10 26 E
Jewett, Ohio, U.S.A. **112** 40 22N 81 2W
Jewett, Tex., U.S.A. **117** 31 20N 96 8W
Jewett City **113** 41 36N 72 0W
Jeypore **70** 18 50N 82 38 E
Jeziorak, Jezioro **28** 53 40N 19 35 E
Jeziorany **28** 53 58N 20 46 E
Jeziorka → **28** 51 59N 20 57 E
Jhajjar **68** 28 37N 76 42 E
Jhal Jhao **66** 26 20N 65 35 E
Jhalawar **68** 24 40N 76 10 E
Jhang Maghiana **68** 31 15N 72 22 E
Jhansi **68** 25 30N 78 36 E
Jharia **69** 23 45N 86 26 E
Jharsuguda **69** 21 56N 84 5 E
Jhelum **68** 33 0N 73 45 E
Jhelum → **68** 31 20N 72 10 E
Jhunjhunu **68** 28 10N 75 30 E
Ji Xian **76** 36 7N 110 40 E
Jia Xian **76** 38 12N 110 28 E
Jiamusi **75** 46 40N 130 26 E
Ji'an **75** 27 6N 114 59 E
Jianchuan **75** 26 38N 99 55 E
Jiande **77** 29 23N 119 15 E
Jiangbei **77** 29 40N 106 34 E
Jiange **77** 32 4N 105 32 E
Jiangjin **77** 29 14N 106 14 E
Jiangling **75** 30 25N 112 12 E
Jiangmen **75** 22 32N 113 0 E
Jiangshan **77** 28 40N 118 37 E
Jiangsu □ **75** 33 0N 120 0 E
Jiangxi □ **75** 27 30N 116 0 E
Jiangyin **77** 31 54N 120 17 E
Jiangyong **77** 25 20N 111 22 E
Jiangyou **77** 31 44N 104 43 E
Jianning **77** 26 50N 116 50 E
Jian'ou **75** 27 3N 118 17 E
Jianshi **77** 30 37N 109 38 E
Jianshui **75** 23 36N 102 43 E
Jianyang **77** 27 20N 118 5 E
Jiao Xian **76** 36 18N 120 1 E
Jiaohe **76** 38 2N 116 20 E
Jiaozhou Wan **76** 36 5N 120 10 E
Jiaozuo **77** 35 16N 113 12 E
Jiawang **77** 34 28N 117 26 E
Jiaxing **75** 30 49N 120 45 E
Jiayi **75** 23 30N 120 24 E
Jibāl **63** 22 10N 56 8 E
Jibiya **85** 13 5N 7 12 E
Jibou **46** 47 15N 23 17 E
Jibuti = Djibouti ■ **63** 12 0N 43 0 E
Jičín **26** 50 25N 15 28 E
Jiddah **64** 21 29N 39 10 E
Jido **67** 29 2N 94 58 E
Jifnā **62** 31 58N 35 13 E
Jihlava **26** 49 28N 15 35 E
Jihlava → **26** 48 55N 16 36 E
Jihočeský □ **26** 49 8N 14 35 E
Jihomoravský □ **27** 49 5N 16 30 E
Jijel **83** 36 52N 5 50 E
Jijiga **63** 9 20N 42 50 E
Jijona **33** 38 34N 0 30W
Jikamshi **85** 12 12N 7 45 E
Jilin **76** 43 44N 126 30 E
Jilin □ **76** 44 0N 124 0 E
Jiloca → **32** 41 21N 1 39W
Jilong **75** 25 8N 121 42 E
Jílové **26** 49 52N 14 29 E
Jima **87** 7 40N 36 47 E
Jimbolia **42** 45 47N 20 43 E
Jimena de la Frontera **31** 36 27N 5 24W
Jiménez **120** 27 10N 104 54W
Jimo **76** 36 23N 120 30 E
Jin Xian **76** 38 55N 121 42 E
Jinan **76** 36 38N 117 1 E
Jincheng **76** 35 29N 112 50 E
Jind **68** 29 19N 76 22 E
Jindabyne **99** 36 25 S 148 35 E
Jindabyne L. **100** 36 20 S 148 38 E
Jindrichuv Hradeç **26** 49 10N 15 2 E
Jing He → **77** 34 27N 109 4 E
Jing Xian **77** 26 33N 109 40 E
Jingchuan **76** 35 20N 107 20 E
Jingdezhen **75** 29 20N 117 11 E
Jinggu **75** 23 35N 100 41 E
Jinghai **76** 38 55N 116 55 E
Jingle **76** 38 20N 111 55 E
Jingmen **77** 31 0N 112 10 E
Jingning **76** 35 30N 105 43 E
Jingshan **77** 31 1N 113 7 E
Jingtai **76** 37 10N 104 6 E
Jingxi **75** 23 8N 106 27 E
Jingyu **76** 42 25N 126 45 E
Jingyuan **76** 36 30N 104 40 E
Jingziguan **77** 33 15N 111 0 E
Jinhe **76** 51 18N 121 32 E
Jinhua **75** 29 8N 119 38 E
Jining, Nei Mongol Zizhiqu, China **76** 41 5N 113 0 E
Jining, Shandong, China **77** 35 22N 116 34 E
Jinja **90** 0 25N 33 12 E
Jinjini **84** 7 26N 3 42W
Jinmen Dao **77** 24 25N 118 25 E
Jinnah Barrage **65** 32 58N 71 33 E
Jinotega **121** 13 6N 85 59W
Jinotepe **121** 11 50N 86 10W
Jinshi **75** 29 40N 111 50 E
Jinxiang **77** 35 5N 116 22 E
Jinzhou **76** 41 5N 121 3 E
Jiparaná (Machado) → **126** 8 3 S 62 52W
Jipijapa **126** 1 0 S 80 40W
Jiquilpan **120** 19 57N 102 42W
Jishou **77** 28 21N 109 43 E
Jisr al Ḩusayn (Allenby) Br. **62** 31 53N 35 33 E
Jisr ash Shughūr **64** 35 49N 36 18 E
Jitra **71** 6 16N 100 25 E
Jiu → **46** 44 40N 23 25 E
Jiudengkou **76** 39 56N 106 40 E
Jiujiang **75** 29 42N 115 58 E
Jiuling Shan **77** 28 40N 114 40 E
Jiuquan **75** 39 50N 98 20 E
Jixi **76** 45 20N 130 50 E
Jizera → **26** 50 10N 14 43 E
Jizl Wadi **64** 25 30N 38 30 E
Joaçaba **125** 27 5 S 51 31W
João Pessoa **127** 7 10 S 34 52W
Joaquín V. González **124** 25 10 S 64 0W
Jobourg, Nez de **18** 49 41N 1 57W
Jódar **33** 37 50N 3 21W
Jodhpur **68** 26 23N 73 8 E
Joensuu **52** 62 37N 29 49 E
Jœuf **19** 49 12N 6 1 E
Joggins **107** 45 42N 64 27W
Jogjakarta = Yogyakarta **73** 7 49 S 110 22 E
Johannesburg **93** 26 10 S 28 2 E
Johansfors **49** 56 42N 15 32 E
John Day **118** 44 25N 118 57W
John Day → **118** 45 44N 120 39W
John H. Kerr Res. **115** 36 20N 78 30W
John o' Groats **14** 58 39N 3 3W
Johnson **117** 37 35N 101 48W
Johnson City, N.Y., U.S.A. **114** 42 7N 75 57W
Johnson City, Tenn., U.S.A. **115** 36 18N 82 21W
Johnson City, Tex., U.S.A. **117** 30 15N 98 24W
Johnsonburg **112** 41 30N 78 40W
Johnson's Crossing **108** 60 29N 133 18W
Johnston Falls = Mambilima Falls **91** 10 31 S 28 45 E
Johnston I. **95** 17 10N 169 8W
Johnstone Str. **108** 50 28N 126 0W
Johnstown, N.Y., U.S.A. **114** 43 1N 74 20W
Johnstown, Pa., U.S.A. **114** 40 19N 78 53W
Johor □ **71** 2 5N 103 20 E
Joigny **19** 48 0N 3 20 E
Joinvile **125** 26 15 S 48 55 E
Joinville **19** 48 27N 5 10 E
Joinville I. **5** 65 0 S 55 30W
Jokkmokk **50** 66 35N 19 50 E
Jökulsá á Brú → **50** 65 40N 14 16W
Jökulsá Fjöllum → **50** 66 10N 16 30W
Joliet **114** 41 30N 88 0W
Joliette **106** 46 3N 73 24W
Jolo **73** 6 0N 121 0 E
Jombang **73** 7 33 S 112 14 E
Jome **73** 1 16 S 127 30 E
Jomfruland **49** 58 52N 9 36 E
Jönåker **49** 58 44N 16 40 E
Jonava **54** 55 8N 24 12 E
Jones Sound **4** 76 0N 85 0W
Jonesboro, Ark., U.S.A. **117** 35 50N 90 45W
Jonesboro, Ill., U.S.A. **117** 37 26N 89 18W
Jonesboro, La., U.S.A. **117** 32 15N 92 41W
Jonesport **107** 44 32N 67 38W
Jonglei **87** 6 25N 30 50 E
Joniskis **54** 56 13N 23 35 E
Jönköping **49** 57 45N 14 10 E
Jönköpings län □ **49** 57 30N 14 30 E
Jonquière **107** 48 27N 71 14W
Jonsberg **49** 58 30N 16 48 E
Jonsered **49** 57 45N 12 10 E
Jonzac **20** 45 27N 0 28W
Joplin **117** 37 0N 94 31W
Jordan, Phil. **73** 10 41N 122 38 E
Jordan, U.S.A. **118** 47 25N 106 58W
Jordan ■ **64** 31 0N 36 0 E
Jordan → **62** 31 48N 35 32 E
Jordan Valley **118** 43 0N 117 2W
Jordanów **27** 49 41N 19 49 E
Jorhat **67** 26 45N 94 12 E
Jorm **65** 36 50N 70 52 E
Jörn **50** 65 4N 20 1 E
Jørpeland **47** 59 3N 6 1 E
Jorquera → **124** 28 3 S 69 58W
Jos **85** 9 53N 8 51 E
Jošanička Banja **42** 43 24N 20 47 E
José Batlle y Ordóñez **125** 33 20 S 55 10W
Joseni **46** 46 42N 25 29 E
Joseph **118** 45 27N 117 13W
Joseph Bonaparte G. **96** 14 35 S 128 50 E
Joseph City **119** 35 0N 110 16W
Joseph, L., Newf., Can. **107** 52 45N 65 18W
Joseph, L., Ont., Can. **112** 45 10N 79 44W
Josselin **18** 47 57N 2 33W
Jostedal **47** 61 35N 7 15 E
Jotunheimen **47** 61 35N 8 25 E
Jourdanton **117** 28 54N 98 32W
Joussard **108** 55 22N 115 50W
Jovellanos **121** 22 40N 81 10W
Jowzjān □ **65** 36 10N 66 0 E
Joyeuse **21** 44 29N 4 16 E
Józefów **28** 52 10N 21 11 E
Ju Xian **77** 36 35N 118 20 E
Juan Aldama **120** 24 20N 103 23W
Juan Bautista **119** 36 55N 121 33W
Juan Bautista Alberdi **124** 34 26 S 61 48W
Juan de Fuca Str. **118** 48 15N 124 0W
Juan de Nova **93** 17 3 S 43 45 E
Juan Fernández, Arch. de **95** 33 50 S 80 0W
Juan José Castelli **124** 25 27 S 60 57W
Juan L. Lacaze **124** 34 26 S 57 25W
Juárez **124** 37 40 S 59 43W
Juárez, Sierra de **120** 32 0N 116 0W
Juàzeiro **127** 9 30 S 40 30W
Juàzeiro do Norte **127** 7 10 S 39 18W
Jubbulpore = Jabalpur **69** 23 9N 79 58 E
Jübek **24** 54 31N 9 24 E
Jubga **57** 44 19N 38 48 E
Juby, C. **80** 28 0N 12 59W
Júcar → **33** 39 5N 0 10W
Juchitán **120** 16 27N 95 5W
Judaea = Yehuda **62** 31 35N 34 57 E
Judenburg **26** 47 12N 14 38 E
Judith → **118** 47 44N 109 38W
Judith Gap **118** 46 40N 109 46W
Judith Pt. **113** 41 20N 71 30W
Jugoslavia = Yugoslavia ■ **37** 44 0N 20 0 E
Juigalpa **121** 12 6N 85 26W
Juillac **20** 45 20N 1 19 E
Juist **24** 53 40N 7 0 E
Juiz de Fora **127** 21 43 S 43 19W
Jujuy □ **124** 23 20 S 65 40W
Julesberg **116** 41 0N 102 20W
Juli **126** 16 10 S 69 25W
Julia Cr. → **98** 20 0 S 141 11 E
Julia Creek **97** 20 39 S 141 44 E
Juliaca **126** 15 25 S 70 10W
Julian **119** 33 4N 116 38W
Julian Alps = Julijske Alpe **39** 46 15N 14 1 E
Julianehåb **4** 60 43N 46 0W
Jülich **24** 50 55N 6 20 E
Julijske Alpe **39** 46 15N 14 1 E
Jullundur **68** 31 20N 75 40 E
Julu **76** 37 15N 115 2 E
Jumbo **91** 17 30 S 30 58 E
Jumentos Cays **121** 23 0N 75 40 E
Jumet **16** 50 27N 4 25 E
Jumilla **33** 38 28N 1 19W
Jumla **69** 29 15N 82 13 E
Jumna = Yamuna → **68** 25 30N 81 53 E
Junagadh **68** 21 30N 70 30 E
Junction, Tex., U.S.A. **117** 30 29N 99 48W
Junction, Utah, U.S.A. **119** 38 10N 112 15W
Junction B. **96** 11 52 S 133 55 E
Junction City, Kans., U.S.A. **116** 39 4N 96 55W
Junction City, Oreg., U.S.A. **118** 44 14N 123 12W
Jundah **97** 24 46 S 143 2 E
Jundiaí **125** 24 30 S 47 0W
Juneau **104** 58 20N 134 20W
Junee **97** 34 53 S 147 35 E
Jungfrau **25** 46 32N 7 58 E
Junggar Pendi **75** 44 30N 86 0 E
Jungshahi **68** 24 52N 67 44 E
Juniata → **112** 40 30N 77 40W
Junín **124** 34 33 S 60 57W
Junín de los Andes **128** 39 45 S 71 0W
Jūniyah **64** 33 59N 35 38 E
Junnar **70** 19 12N 73 58 E
Junquera, La **32** 42 25N 2 53 E
Junta, La **117** 38 0N 103 30W
Juntura **118** 43 44N 118 4W
Jupiter → **107** 49 29N 63 37W
Jur, Nahr el → **87** 8 45N 29 15 E
Jura, France **19** 46 35N 6 5 E
Jura, U.K. **14** 56 0N 5 50W
Jura □ **19** 46 47N 5 45 E
Jura, Sd. of **14** 55 57N 5 45W
Jura Suisse **25** 47 10N 7 0 E
Jurado **126** 7 7N 77 46W
Jurien B. **96** 30 17 S 115 0 E
Jurilovca **46** 44 46N 28 52 E
Juruá → **126** 2 37 S 65 44W
Juruena → **126** 7 20 S 58 3W
Juruti **127** 2 9 S 56 4W
Jussey **19** 47 50N 5 55 E
Justo Daract **124** 33 52 S 65 12W
Jüterbog **24** 52 0N 13 6 E
Juticalpa **121** 14 40N 86 12W
Jutland = Jylland **8** 56 25N 9 30 E
Juvigny-sous-Andaine **18** 48 32N 0 30W
Juvisy **19** 48 43N 2 23 E
Juwain **65** 31 45N 61 30 E
Juzennecourt **19** 48 10N 4 48 E
Jylland **8** 56 25N 9 30 E
Jyväskylä **72** 62 14N 25 50 E

K2 Kaputir

K

K2 66 35 58N 76 32 E
Kaalasin 71 16 26N 103 30 E
Kaap die Goeie Hoop 92 34 24S 18 30 E
Kaap Plato 92 28 30S 24 0 E
Kaapkruis 92 21 43S 14 0 E
Kaapstad = Cape Town 92 33 55S 18 22 E
Kabaena 73 5 15S 122 0 E
Kabala 84 9 38N 11 37W
Kabale 90 1 15S 30 0 E
Kabalo 90 6 0S 27 0 E
Kabambare 90 4 41S 27 39 E
Kabango 91 8 35S 28 30 E
Kabanjahe 72 3 6N 98 30 E
Kabara 84 16 40N 2 50W
Kabardinka 56 44 40N 37 57 E
Kabardino-Balkar-A.S.S.R. □ 57 43 30N 43 30 E
Kabare 73 0 4S 130 58 E
Kabarega Falls 90 2 15N 31 30 E
Kabasalan 73 7 47N 122 44 E
Kabba 85 7 50N 6 3 E
Kabi 85 13 30N 12 35 E
Kabinakagami L. 106 48 54N 84 25W
Kabīr Kūh 64 33 0N 47 30 E
Kabīr, Zab al 64 36 0N 43 0 E
Kabkabīyah 81 13 50N 24 0 E
Kabna 86 19 6N 32 40 E
Kabompo 91 13 36S 24 14 E
Kabompo → 89 14 10S 23 11 E
Kabondo 91 8 58S 25 40 E
Kabongo 90 7 22S 25 33 E
Kabou 85 9 28N 0 55 E
Kaboudia, Rass 83 35 13N 11 10 E
Kabra 98 23 25S 150 25 E
Kabūd Gonbad 65 37 5N 59 45 E
Kabul 66 34 28N 69 11 E
Kabúl □ 65 34 30N 69 0 E
Kabul → 66 33 55N 72 14 E
Kabunga 90 1 38S 28 3 E
Kaburuang 73 3 50N 126 30 E
Kabushiya 87 16 54N 33 41 E
Kabwe 91 14 30S 28 29 E
Kačanik 42 42 13N 21 12 E
Kachanovo 54 57 25N 27 38 E
Kachebera 91 13 50S 32 50 E
Kachin □ 67 26 0N 97 30 E
Kachira, L. 90 0 40S 31 7 E
Kachiry 58 53 10N 75 50 E
Kachisi 87 9 40N 37 50 E
Kackar 57 40 45N 41 10 E
Kadan Kyun 72 12 30N 98 20 E
Kadarkút 27 46 13N 17 39 E
Kadayanallur 70 9 3N 77 22 E
Kade 85 6 7N 0 56W
Kadi 68 23 18N 72 23 E
Kadina 97 34 0S 137 43 E
Kadiri 70 14 12N 78 13 E
Kadirli 64 37 23N 36 5 E
Kadiyevka 57 48 35N 38 40 E
Kadoka 116 43 50N 101 31W
Kadom 55 54 37N 42 30 E
Kâdugli 81 11 0N 29 45 E
Kaduna 85 10 30N 7 21 E
Kaduna □ 85 11 0N 7 30 E
Kaédi 84 16 9N 13 28W
Kaelé 85 10 7N 14 27 E
Kaesŏng 76 37 58N 126 35 E
Kāf 64 31 25N 37 29 E
Kafakumba 88 9 38S 23 46 E
Kafan 53 39 18N 46 15 E
Kafanchan 85 9 40N 8 20 E
Kafareti 85 10 25N 11 12 E
Kaffrine 84 14 8N 15 36W
Kafia Kingi 81 9 20N 24 25 E
Kafinda 91 12 32S 30 20 E
Kafirévs, Ákra 45 38 9N 24 38 E
Kafr 'Ayn 62 32 3N 35 7 E
Kafr el Dauwâr 86 31 8N 30 8 E
Kafr el Sheikh 86 31 15N 30 50 E
Kafr Kammā 62 32 44N 35 26 E
Kafr Kannā 62 32 45N 35 20 E
Kafr Mālik 62 32 0N 35 18 E
Kafr Mandā 62 32 49N 35 15 E
Kafr Quaddūm 62 32 14N 35 7 E
Kafr Rā'ī 62 32 23N 35 9 E
Kafr Şīr 62 33 19N 35 23 E
Kafr Yāsīf 62 32 58N 35 10 E
Kafue 91 15 46S 28 9 E
Kafue Flats 91 15 40S 27 25 E
Kafulwe 91 9 0S 29 1 E
Kaga Bandoro 88 7 0N 19 10 E
Kagan 58 39 43N 64 33 E
Kagawa □ 74 34 15N 134 0 E
Kagera → 90 0 57S 31 47 E
Kağizman 64 40 5N 43 10 E
Kagoshima 74 31 35N 130 33 E
Kagoshima □ 74 31 30N 130 30 E
Kagoshima-Wan 74 31 25N 130 40 E
Kagul 56 45 50N 28 15 E
Kahajan → 72 3 40S 114 0 E
Kahama 90 4 8S 32 30 E
Kahama □ 90 3 50S 32 0 E
Kahe 90 3 30S 37 25 E
Kahemba 88 7 18S 18 55 E
Kahil, Djebel bou 83 34 26N 4 0 E
Kahniah → 108 58 15N 120 55W
Kahnūj 65 27 55N 57 40 E
Kahoka 116 40 25N 91 42W
Kahoolawe 110 20 33N 156 35W
Kai Besar 73 5 35S 133 0 E
Kai Kai 92 19 52S 21 15 E
Kai, Kepulauan 73 5 55S 132 45W
Kai-Ketjil 73 5 45S 132 40 E
Kaiama 85 9 36N 4 1 E
Kaiapoi 101 42 24S 172 40 E
Kaieteur Falls 126 5 1N 59 10W
Kaifeng 77 34 48N 114 21 E
Kaihua 77 29 12N 118 20 E
Kaiingveld 92 30 0S 22 0 E
Kaikohe 101 35 25S 173 49 E
Kaikoura 101 42 25S 173 43 E
Kaikoura Pen. 101 42 25S 173 43 E
Kaikoura Ra. 101 41 59S 173 41 E
Kailahun 84 8 18N 10 39W
Kaili 77 26 33N 107 59 E
Kailu 76 43 38N 121 18 E
Kailua 110 19 39N 156 0W
Kaimana 73 3 39S 133 45 E
Kaimanawa Mts. 101 39 15S 175 56 E
Kaimganj 69 27 33N 79 24 E
Kaimur Hill 69 24 30N 82 0 E
Kainantu 98 6 18S 145 52 E
Kaingaroa Forest 101 38 24S 176 30 E
Kainji Res. 85 10 1N 4 40 E
Kaipara Harbour 101 36 25S 174 14 E
Kaiping 77 22 23N 112 42 E
Kaipokok B. 107 54 54N 59 47W
Kairana 68 29 24N 77 15 E
Kaironi 73 0 47S 133 40 E
Kairouan 83 35 45N 10 5 E
Kairuku 98 8 51S 146 35 E
Kaiserslautern 25 49 30N 7 43 E
Kaitaia 101 35 8S 173 17 E
Kaitangata 101 46 17S 169 51 E
Kaithal 68 29 48N 76 26 E
Kaiwi Channel 110 21 13N 157 30W
Kaiyuan 76 42 28N 124 1 E
Kajaani 50 64 17N 27 46 E
Kajabbi 97 20 0S 140 1 E
Kajan → 72 2 55N 117 35 E
Kajang 71 2 59N 101 48 E
Kajiado 90 1 53S 36 48 E
Kajiado □ 90 2 0S 36 30 E
Kajo Kaji 87 3 58N 31 40 E
Kajoa 73 0 1N 127 28 E
Kaka 81 10 38N 32 10 E
Kakabeka Falls 106 48 24N 89 37W
Kakamega 90 0 20N 34 46 E
Kakamega □ 90 0 20N 34 46 E
Kakanj 42 44 9N 18 7 E
Kakanui Mts. 101 45 10S 170 30 E
Kakegawa 74 34 45N 138 1 E
Kakhib 57 42 28N 46 34 E
Kakhovka 56 46 40N 33 15 E
Kakhovskoye Vdkhr. 56 47 5N 34 16 E
Kakinada (Cocanada) 70 16 57N 82 11 E
Kakisa → 108 61 3N 118 10W
Kakisa L. 108 60 56N 117 43W
Kakwa → 108 54 37N 118 28W
Kala 85 12 2N 14 40 E
Kala Oya → 70 8 20N 79 45 E
Kalaa-Kebira 83 35 59N 10 32 E
Kalabagh 68 33 0N 71 28 E
Kalabahi 73 8 13S 124 31 E
Kalabáka 44 39 42N 21 39 E
Kalabo 89 14 58S 22 40 E
Kalach 55 50 22N 41 0 E
Kalach na Donu 57 48 43N 43 32 E
Kaladan → 67 20 20N 93 5 E
Kaladar 112 44 37N 77 5W
Kalahari 92 24 0S 21 30 E
Kalahari Gemsbok Nat. Park 92 25 30S 20 30 E
Kalahasti 70 13 45N 79 44 E
Kalakamati 93 20 40S 27 25 E
Kalakan 59 55 15N 116 45 E
Kalama, U.S.A. 118 46 0N 122 55W
Kalama, Zaïre 90 2 52S 28 35 E
Kalamariá 44 40 33N 22 55 E
Kalamata 45 37 3N 22 10 E
Kalamazoo 114 42 20N 85 35W
Kalamazoo → 114 42 40N 86 12W
Kalamb 70 18 3N 74 48 E
Kalambo Falls 91 8 37S 31 35 E
Kálamos, Greece 45 38 37N 20 55 E
Kálamos, Greece 45 38 17N 23 52 E
Kalamoti 45 38 15N 26 4 E
Kalan 64 39 7N 39 32 E
Kalao 73 7 21S 121 0 E
Kalaotoa 73 7 20S 121 50 E
Kälarne 48 62 59N 16 8 E
Kalárovo 27 47 54N 18 0 E
Kalasin 71 16 26N 103 30 E
Kalat 66 29 8N 66 31 E
* Kalat □ 68 27 30N 66 0 E
Kálathos (Calato) 45 36 9N 28 8 E
Kalaus → 57 45 40N 44 7 E
Kalávrita 45 38 3N 22 8 E
Kalecik 56 40 4N 33 26 E
Kalegauk Kyun 67 15 33N 97 35 E
Kalehe 90 2 6S 28 50 E
Kalema 90 1 12S 31 55 E
Kalemie 90 5 55S 29 9 E
Kalety 28 50 35N 18 52 E
Kalewa 67 23 10N 94 15 E
Kálfafellsstaður 50 64 11N 15 53W
Kalgan = Zhangjiakou 76 40 48N 114 55 E
Kalgoorlie 96 30 40S 121 22 E
Kaliakra, Nos 43 43 21N 28 30 E
Kalianda 72 5 50S 105 45 E
Kalibo 73 11 43N 122 22 E
Kaliganj Town 69 22 25N 89 8 E
Kalima 90 2 33S 26 32 E
Kalimantan Barat □ 72 0 0 110 30 E
Kalimantan Selatan □ 72 2 30S 115 30 E
Kalimantan Tengah □ 72 2 0S 113 30 E
Kalimantan Timur □ 72 1 30N 116 30 E
Kálimnos 45 37 0N 27 0 E
Kalimpong 69 27 4N 88 35 E
Kalinadi → 70 14 50N 74 7 E
Kalinin 55 56 55N 35 55 E
Kaliningrad 54 54 42N 20 32 E
Kalinkovichi 54 52 12N 29 20 E
Kalinovik 42 43 31N 18 29 E
Kalipetrovo (Stančevo) 43 44 5N 27 14 E
Kaliro 90 0 56N 33 30 E
Kalirrákhi 44 40 40N 24 35 E
Kalispell 118 48 10N 114 22W
Kalisz 28 51 45N 18 8 E
Kalisz □ 28 51 30N 18 0 E
Kalisz Pomorski 28 53 17N 15 55 E
Kaliua 90 5 5S 31 48 E
Kaliveli Tank 70 12 5N 79 50 E
Kalix → 50 65 50N 23 11 E
Kalka 68 30 46N 76 57 E
Kalkaska 106 44 44N 85 11W
Kalkfeld 92 20 57S 16 14 E
Kalkfontein 92 22 4S 20 57 E
Kalkrand 92 24 1S 17 35 E
Kallakurichi 70 11 44N 79 1 E
Kållandsö 49 58 40N 13 5 E
Kallia 62 31 46N 35 30 E
Kallidaikurichi 70 8 38N 77 31 E
Kallinge 49 56 15N 15 18 E
Kallithéa 45 37 55N 23 41 E
Kallmeti 44 41 51N 19 41 E
Kallonís, Kólpos 45 39 10N 26 10 E
Kallsjön 50 63 38N 13 0 E
Kalmalo 85 13 40N 5 20 E
Kalmar 49 56 40N 16 20 E
Kalmar län □ 49 57 25N 16 0 E
Kalmar sund 49 56 40N 16 25 E
Kalmyk A.S.S.R. □ 57 46 5N 46 1 E
Kalmykovo 57 49 0N 51 47 E
Kalna 69 23 13N 88 25 E
Kalo 98 10 1S 147 48 E
Kalocsa 27 46 32N 19 0 E
Kalofer 43 42 37N 24 59 E
Kaloko 90 6 47S 25 48 E
Kalol, Gujarat, India 68 23 15N 72 33 E
Kalol, Gujarat, India 68 22 37N 73 31 E
Kalolímnos 45 37 4N 27 8 E
Kalomo 91 17 0S 26 30 E
Kaloneròn 45 37 20N 21 38 E
Kalpi 69 26 8N 79 47 E
Kalrayan Hills 70 11 45N 78 40 E
Kalsubai 70 19 35N 73 45 E
Kaltungo 85 9 48N 11 19 E
Kalu 68 25 5N 67 39 E
Kaluga 55 54 35N 36 10 E
Kalulushi 91 12 50S 28 3 E
Kalundborg 49 55 41N 11 5 E
Kalush 54 49 3N 24 23 E
Kałuszyn 28 52 13N 21 52 E
Kalutara 70 6 35N 80 0 E
Kalwaria 27 49 53N 19 41 E
Kalya 52 60 15N 59 59 E
Kalyan 68 20 30N 74 3 E
Kalyazin 55 57 15N 37 55 E
Kam Keut 71 18 20N 104 48 E
Kama 90 3 30S 27 5 E
Kama → 52 55 45N 52 0 E
Kamachumu 90 1 37S 31 37 E
Kamaishi 74 39 20N 142 0 E
Kamalia 68 30 44N 72 42 E
Kamandorskiye Ostrava 59 55 0N 167 0 E
Kamapanda 91 12 5S 24 0 E
Kamaran 63 15 21N 42 35 E
Kamativi 91 18 15S 27 27 E
Kamba 85 11 50N 3 45 E
Kambam 70 9 45N 77 16 E
Kambar 68 27 37N 68 1 E
Kambarka 52 56 15N 54 11 E
Kambia 84 9 3N 12 53W
Kambolé 91 8 47S 30 48 E
Kambove 91 10 51S 26 33 E
Kamchatka, P-ov. 59 57 0N 160 0 E
Kamen 58 53 50N 81 30 E
Kamen Kashirskiy 54 51 39N 24 56 E
Kamenica, Srbija, Yugo. 42 44 25N 19 40 E
Kamenica, Srbija, Yugo. 42 43 27N 22 27 E
Kamenice 26 49 18N 15 2 E
Kamenjak, Rt 39 44 47N 13 55 E
Kamenka, R.S.F.S.R., U.S.S.R. 52 65 58N 44 0 E
Kamenka, R.S.F.S.R., U.S.S.R. 55 50 47N 39 20 E
Kamenka, R.S.F.S.R., U.S.S.R. 55 53 10N 44 5 E
Kamenka, Ukraine S.S.R., U.S.S.R. 56 49 3N 32 6 E
Kamenka Bugskaya 54 50 8N 24 16 E
Kamenka Dneprovskaya 56 47 29N 34 14 E
Kameno 43 42 34N 27 18 E
Kamenolomini 57 47 40N 40 14 E
Kamensk-Shakhtinskiy 57 48 23N 40 20 E
Kamensk Uralskiy 58 56 25N 62 2 E
Kamenskiy, R.S.F.S.R., U.S.S.R. 55 50 48N 45 25 E
Kamenskiy, R.S.F.S.R., U.S.S.R. 57 49 20N 41 15 E
Kamenskoye 59 62 45N 165 30 E
Kamenyak 43 43 24N 26 57 E
Kamenz 24 51 17N 14 7 E
Kami 44 42 17N 20 18 E
Kamiah 118 46 12N 116 2W
Kamień Krajeński 28 53 32N 17 32 E
Kamień Pomorski 28 53 57N 14 43 E
Kamienna → 28 51 6N 21 47 E
Kamienna Góra 28 50 47N 16 2 E
Kamiensk 28 51 12N 19 29 E
Kamilukuak, L. 109 62 22N 101 40W
Kamina 91 8 45S 25 0 E
Kaminak L. 109 62 10N 95 0W
Kamituga 90 3 2S 28 10 E
Kamloops 108 50 40N 120 20W
Kamloops L. 108 50 45N 120 40W
Kamnik 39 46 14N 14 37 E
Kamo 57 40 21N 45 7 E
Kamoke 68 32 4N 74 4 E
Kamp → 26 48 23N 15 42 E
Kampala 90 0 20N 32 30 E
Kampar 71 4 18N 101 9 E
Kampar → 72 0 30N 103 8 E
Kampen 16 52 33N 5 53 E
Kampolombo, L. 91 11 37S 29 42 E
Kampot 71 10 36N 104 10 E
Kamptee 68 21 9N 79 19 E
Kampti 84 10 7N 3 25W
Kampuchea = Cambodia ■ 71 13 0N 105 0 E
Kampung → 73 5 44S 138 24 E
Kampungbaru = Tolitoli 73 1 5N 120 50 E
Kamrau, Teluk 73 3 30S 133 36 E
Kamsack 109 51 34N 101 54W
Kamskoye Ustye 55 55 10N 49 20 E
Kamskoye Vdkhr. 52 58 0N 56 0 E
Kamuchawie L. 109 56 18N 101 59W
Kamyshin 55 50 10N 45 24 E
Kamyzyak 57 46 4N 48 10 E
Kanaaupscow 106 54 2N 76 30W
Kanab 119 37 3N 112 29W
Kanab Creek 119 37 0N 112 40W
Kanagawa □ 74 35 20N 139 20 E
Kanairiktok → 107 55 2N 60 18W
Kanakapura 70 12 33N 77 28 E
Kanália 44 39 30N 22 53 E
Kananga 88 5 55S 22 18 E
Kanarraville 119 37 34N 113 12W
Kanash 55 55 30N 47 32 E
Kanastraíon, Ákra 44 39 57N 23 45 E
Kanawha → 114 38 50N 82 8W
Kanazawa 74 36 30N 136 38 E
Kanchanaburi 71 14 2N 99 31 E
Kanchenjunga 69 27 50N 88 10 E
Kanchipuram (Conjeeveram) 70 12 52N 79 45 E
Kańczuga 27 49 59N 22 25 E
Kanda Kanda 88 6 52S 23 48 E
Kandahar 65 31 32N 65 30 E
Kandalaksha 52 67 9N 32 30 E
Kandalakshkiy Zaliv 52 66 0N 35 0 E
Kandangan 72 2 50S 115 20 E
Kandanos 45 35 19N 23 44 E
Kandhíla 45 37 46N 22 22 E
Kandhkot 68 28 16N 69 8 E
Kandhla 68 29 18N 77 19 E
Kandi, Benin 85 11 7N 2 55 E
Kandi, India 69 23 58N 88 5 E
Kandla 68 23 0N 70 10 E
Kandos 99 32 45S 149 58 E
Kandukur 70 15 12N 79 57 E
Kandy 70 7 18N 80 43 E
Kane 114 41 39N 78 53W
Kane Bassin 4 79 30N 68 0W
Kanevskaya 57 46 3N 39 3 E
Kanfanar 39 45 7N 13 50 E
Kangaba 84 11 56N 8 25W
Kangar 71 6 27N 100 12 E
Kangaroo I. 97 35 45S 137 0 E
Kangaroo Mts. 98 23 25S 142 0 E
Kangavar 64 34 40N 48 0 E
Kangean, Kepulauan 72 6 55S 115 23 E
Kangerdlugsuak 4 68 10N 32 20W
Kanggyee 76 41 0N 126 35 E
Kangnūng 76 37 45N 128 54 E
Kango 88 0 11N 10 5 E
Kangto 67 27 50N 92 35 E
Kanhangad 70 12 21N 74 58 E
Kanheri 70 19 13N 72 50 E
Kani 84 8 29N 6 36W
Kaniama 90 7 30S 24 12 E
Kaniapiskau → 107 56 40N 69 30W
Kaniapiskau L. 107 54 10N 69 55W
Kanin Nos, Mys 52 68 45N 43 20 E
Kanin, P-ov. 52 68 0N 45 0 E
Kanina 44 40 23N 19 30 E
Kaniva 99 36 22S 141 18 E
Kanjiža 42 46 3N 20 4 E
Kankakee 114 41 6N 87 50W
Kankakee → 114 41 23N 88 16W
Kankan 84 10 23N 9 15W
Kanker 70 20 10N 81 40 E
Kankunskiy 59 57 37N 126 8 E
Kannapolis 115 35 32N 80 37W
Kannauj 69 27 3N 79 56 E
Kano 85 12 2N 8 30 E
Kano □ 85 11 45N 9 0 E
Kanoroba 84 9 7N 6 8W
Kanowit 72 2 14N 112 20 E
Kanowna 96 30 32S 121 31 E
Kanoya 74 31 25N 130 50 E
Kanpetlet 67 21 10N 93 59 E
Kanpur 69 26 28N 80 20 E
Kansas □ 116 38 40N 98 0W
Kansas → 116 39 7N 94 36W
Kansas City, Kans., U.S.A. 116 39 0N 94 40W
Kansas City, Mo., U.S.A. 116 39 3N 94 30W
Kansenia 91 10 20S 26 0 E
Kansk 59 56 20N 95 37 E
Kansu = Gansu □ 75 37 0N 103 0 E
Kantang 71 7 25N 99 31 E
Kantché 85 13 31N 8 30 E
Kanté 85 9 57N 1 3 E
Kantemirovka 57 49 43N 39 55 E
Kanturk 15 52 10N 8 55W
Kanuma 74 36 34N 139 42 E
Kanus 92 27 50S 18 39 E
Kanye 92 25 0S 25 28 E
Kanyu 92 20 7S 24 37 E
Kanzenze 91 10 30S 25 12 E
Kanzi, Ras 90 7 1S 39 33 E
Kaohsiung = Gaoxiong 75 22 38N 120 18 E
Kaokoveld 92 18 20S 13 37 E
Kaolack 84 14 5N 16 8W
Kapadvanj 68 23 5N 73 0 E
Kapanga 88 8 30S 22 40 E
Kapchagai 58 43 50N 77 10 E
Kapéllo, Ákra 45 36 9N 23 3 E
Kapema 91 10 45S 28 22 E
Kapfenberg 26 47 26N 15 18 E
Kapiri Mposhi 91 13 59S 28 43 E
Kapisa □ 65 35 0N 69 20 E
Kapiskau → 106 52 47N 81 55W
Kapit 72 2 0N 112 55 E
Kapiti I. 101 40 50S 174 56 E
Kaplice 26 48 42N 14 30 E
Kapoeta 87 4 50N 33 35 E
Kápolnásnyék 27 47 16N 18 41 E
Kapos → 27 46 44N 18 30 E
Kaposvár 27 46 25N 17 47 E
Kappeln 24 54 37N 9 56 E
Kapps 92 22 32S 17 18 E
Kaprije 39 43 42N 15 43 E
Kapsukas 54 54 33N 23 19 E
Kapuas → 72 0 25S 109 20 E
Kapuas Hulu, Pegunungan 72 1 30N 113 30 E
Kapulo 91 8 18S 29 15 E
Kapunda 99 34 20S 138 56 E
Kapurthala 68 31 23N 75 25 E
Kapuskasing 106 49 25N 82 30W
Kapuskasing → 106 49 49N 82 0W
Kapustin Yar 57 48 37N 45 40 E
Kaputir 90 2 5N 35 28 E

* Now part of Baluchistan □

Kapuvár Kent

Place	Page	Lat.	Long.
Kapuvár	**27**	47 36N	17 1 E
Kara, Turkey	**45**	36 58N	27 30 E
Kara, U.S.S.R.	**58**	69 10N	65 0 E
Kara Bogaz Gol, Zaliv	**53**	41 0N	53 30 E
Kara Burun	**45**	38 41N	26 28 E
Kara Kalpak A.S.S.R. □	**58**	43 0N	60 0 E
Kara Sea	**58**	75 0N	70 0 E
Kara, Wadi	**86**	20 0N	41 25 E
Karabük	**64**	41 12N	32 37 E
Karaburuni	**44**	40 25N	19 20 E
Karabutak	**58**	49 59N	60 14 E
Karachala	**57**	39 45N	48 53 E
Karachayevsk	**57**	43 50N	42 0 E
Karachev	**54**	53 10N	35 5 E
Karachi	**68**	24 53N	67 0 E
Karachi □	**68**	25 30N	67 0 E
Karád	**27**	46 41N	17 51 E
Karad	**70**	17 15N	74 10 E
Karadeniz Boğazı	**64**	41 10N	29 10 E
Karaga	**85**	9 58N	0 28W
Karaganda	**58**	49 50N	73 10 E
Karagayly	**58**	49 26N	76 0 E
Karaginskiy, Ostrov	**59**	58 45N	164 0 E
Karagiye Depression	**53**	43 27N	51 45 E
Karagwe □	**90**	2 0 S	31 0 E
Karaikkudi	**70**	10 0N	78 45 E
Karaitivu I.	**70**	9 45N	79 52 E
Karaitivu, I.	**70**	8 22N	79 47 E
Karaj	**65**	35 48N	51 0 E
Karakas	**58**	48 20N	83 30 E
Karakitang	**73**	3 14N	125 28 E
Karakoram Pass	**66**	35 33N	77 50 E
Karakoram Ra.	**66**	35 30N	77 0 E
Karakum, Peski	**58**	39 30N	60 0 E
Karalon	**59**	57 5N	115 50 E
Karaman	**64**	37 14N	33 13 E
Karamay	**75**	45 30N	84 58 E
Karambu	**72**	3 53 S	116 6 E
Karamea Bight	**101**	41 22 S	171 40 E
Karamoja □	**90**	3 0N	34 15 E
Karamsad	**68**	22 35N	72 50 E
Karanganjar	**73**	7 38 S	109 37 E
Karanja	**68**	20 29N	77 31 E
Karasburg	**92**	28 0 S	18 44 E
Karasino	**58**	66 50N	86 50 E
Karasjok	**50**	69 27N	25 30 E
Karasuk	**58**	53 44N	78 2 E
Karatau	**58**	43 10N	70 28 E
Karatau, Khrebet	**58**	43 30N	69 30 E
Karauli	**68**	26 30N	77 4 E
Karávi	**45**	36 49N	23 37 E
Karawanken	**26**	46 30N	14 40 E
Karazhal	**58**	48 2N	70 49 E
Karbalā	**64**	32 36N	44 3 E
Kårböle	**48**	61 59N	15 22 E
Karcag	**27**	47 19N	20 57 E
Karda	**59**	55 0N	103 16 E
Kardhámila	**45**	38 35N	26 5 E
Kardhítsa	**44**	39 23N	21 54 E
Kardhítsa □	**44**	39 15N	21 50 E
Kärdla	**54**	58 50N	22 40 E
Kareeberge	**92**	30 50 S	22 0 E
Kareima	**86**	18 30N	31 49 E
Karelian A.S.S.R. □	**52**	65 30N	32 30 E
Karen	**71**	12 49N	92 53 E
Kargānrūd	**64**	37 55N	49 0 E
Kargasok	**58**	59 3N	80 53 E
Kargat	**58**	55 10N	80 15 E
Kargı	**56**	41 11N	34 30 E
Kargil	**69**	34 32N	76 12 E
Kargopol	**52**	61 30N	38 58 E
Kargowa	**28**	52 5N	15 51 E
Karguéri	**85**	13 27N	10 30 E
Karia ba Mohammed	**82**	34 22N	5 12W
Kariaí	**44**	40 14N	24 19 E
Kariba	**91**	16 28 S	28 50 E
Kariba Gorge	**91**	16 30 S	28 50 E
Kariba Lake	**91**	16 40 S	28 25 E
Karibib	**92**	21 0 S	15 56 E
Karikal	**70**	10 59N	79 50 E
Karimata, Kepulauan	**72**	1 25 S	109 0 E
Karimata, Selat	**72**	2 0 S	108 40 E
Karimnagar	**70**	18 26N	79 10 E
Karimunjawa, Kepulauan	**72**	5 50 S	110 30 E
Karin	**63**	10 50N	45 52 E
Káristos	**45**	38 1N	24 29 E
Kariya	**74**	34 58N	137 1 E
Karkal	**70**	13 15N	74 56 E
Karkar I.	**98**	4 40 S	146 0 E
Karkaralinsk	**58**	49 26N	75 30 E
Karkinitskiy Zaliv	**56**	45 56N	33 0 E
Karkur	**62**	32 29N	34 57 E
Karkur Tohl	**86**	22 5N	25 5 E
Karl Libknekht	**54**	51 40N	35 35 E
Karl-Marx-Stadt	**24**	50 50N	12 55 E
Karl-Marx-Stadt □	**24**	50 45N	13 0 E
Karla, L. = Voiviïs, L.	**44**	39 30N	22 45 E
Karlino	**28**	54 3N	15 53 E
Karlobag	**39**	44 32N	15 5 E
Karlovac	**39**	45 31N	15 36 E
Karlovka	**56**	49 29N	35 8 E
Karlovy Vary	**26**	50 13N	12 51 E
Karlsborg	**49**	58 33N	14 33 E
Karlshamn	**49**	56 10N	14 51 E
Karlskoga	**48**	59 22N	14 33 E
Karlskrona	**49**	56 10N	15 35 E
Karlsruhe	**25**	49 3N	8 23 E
Karlstad, Sweden	**48**	59 23N	13 30 E
Karlstad, U.S.A.	**116**	48 38N	96 30W
Karlstadt	**25**	49 57N	9 46 E
Karmøy	**47**	59 15N	5 15 E
Karnal	**68**	29 42N	77 2 E
Karnali →	**69**	29 0N	83 20 E
Karnaphuli Res.	**67**	22 40N	92 20 E
Karnataka □	**70**	14 15N	76 0 E
Karnes City	**117**	28 53N	97 53W
Karnische Alpen	**26**	46 36N	13 0 E
Kärnten □	**26**	46 52N	13 30 E
Karo	**84**	12 16N	3 18W
Karoi	**91**	16 48 S	29 45 E
Karonga	**91**	9 57 S	33 55 E
Karoonda	**99**	35 1 S	139 59 E
Káros	**45**	36 54N	25 40 E
Karousádhes	**44**	39 47N	19 45 E
Kárpathos	**45**	35 37N	27 10 E
Karpáthos, Stenón	**45**	36 0N	27 30 E
Karpinsk	**52**	59 45N	60 1 E
Karpogory	**52**	63 59N	44 27 E
Karrebæk	**49**	55 12N	11 39 E
Kars, Turkey	**64**	40 40N	43 5 E
Kars, U.S.S.R.	**56**	40 36N	43 5 E
Karsakpay	**58**	47 55N	66 40 E
Karsha	**57**	49 45N	51 35 E
Karshi	**58**	38 53N	65 48 E
Karst	**39**	45 35N	14 0 E
Karsun	**55**	54 14N	46 57 E
Kartál Óros	**44**	41 15N	25 13 E
Kartaly	**58**	53 3N	60 40 E
Kartapur	**68**	31 27N	75 32 E
Karthaus	**112**	41 8N	78 9W
Kartuzy	**28**	54 22N	18 10 E
Karufa	**73**	3 50 S	133 20 E
Karumba	**98**	17 31 S	140 50 E
Karumo	**90**	2 25 S	32 50 E
Karumwa	**90**	3 12 S	32 38 E
Karungu	**90**	0 50 S	34 10 E
Karup	**49**	56 19N	9 10 E
Karur	**70**	10 59N	78 2 E
Karviná	**27**	49 53N	18 25 E
Karwi	**69**	25 12N	80 57 E
Kas Kong	**71**	11 27N	102 12 E
Kasache	**91**	13 25 S	34 20 E
Kasai →	**88**	3 30 S	16 10 E
Kasai Oriental □	**90**	5 0 S	24 30 E
Kasaji	**91**	10 25 S	23 27 E
Kasama	**91**	10 16 S	31 9 E
Kasane	**92**	17 34 S	24 50 E
Kasanga	**91**	8 30 S	31 10 E
Kasangulu	**88**	4 33 S	15 15 E
Kasaragod	**70**	12 30N	74 58 E
Kasba L.	**109**	60 20N	102 10W
Kasba Tadla	**82**	32 36N	6 17W
Kasempa	**91**	13 30 S	25 44 E
Kasenga	**91**	10 20 S	28 45 E
Kasese	**90**	0 13N	30 3 E
Kasewa	**91**	14 28 S	28 53 E
Kasganj	**68**	27 48N	78 42 E
Kashabowie	**106**	48 40N	90 26W
Kāshān	**65**	34 5N	51 30 E
Kashi	**75**	39 30N	76 2 E
Kashimbo	**91**	11 12 S	26 19 E
Kashin	**55**	57 20N	37 36 E
Kashipur, Orissa, India	**70**	19 16N	83 3 E
Kashipur, Ut. P., India	**68**	29 15N	79 0 E
Kashira	**55**	54 45N	38 10 E
Kāshmar	**65**	35 16N	58 26 E
Kashmir	**69**	34 0N	76 0 E
Kashmor	**68**	28 28N	69 32 E
Kashpirovka	**55**	53 0N	48 30 E
Kashun Noerh = Gaxun Nur	**75**	42 22N	100 30 E
Kasimov	**55**	54 55N	41 20 E
Kasinge	**90**	6 15 S	26 58 E
Kasiruta	**73**	0 25 S	127 12 E
Kaskaskia →	**116**	37 58N	89 57W
Kaskattama →	**109**	57 3N	90 4W
Kaskinen	**50**	62 22N	21 15 E
Kaskö	**50**	62 22N	21 15 E
Kaslo	**108**	49 55N	116 55W
Kasmere L.	**109**	59 34N	101 10W
Kasongo	**90**	4 30 S	26 33 E
Kasongo Lunda	**88**	6 35 S	16 49 E
Kásos	**45**	35 20N	26 55 E
Kasos, Stenón	**45**	35 30N	26 30 E
Kaspi	**57**	41 54N	44 17 E
Kaspichan	**43**	43 18N	27 11 E
Kaspiysk	**57**	42 52N	47 40 E
Kaspiyskiy	**57**	45 22N	47 23 E
Kassab ed Doleib	**87**	13 30N	33 35 E
Kassaba	**86**	22 40N	29 55 E
Kassala	**87**	16 0N	36 0 E
Kassalâ □	**87**	15 20N	36 26 E
Kassándra	**44**	40 0N	23 30 E
Kassel	**24**	51 19N	9 32 E
Kassinga	**89**	15 5 S	16 4 E
Kassinger	**86**	18 46N	31 51 E
Kassue	**73**	6 58 S	139 21 E
Kastamonu	**64**	41 25N	33 43 E
Kastav	**39**	45 22N	14 20 E
Kastélli	**45**	35 29N	23 38 E
Kastéllion	**45**	35 12N	25 20 E
Kastellorizon = Megiste	**35**	36 8N	29 34 E
Kastellou, Ákra	**45**	35 30N	27 15 E
Kastlösa	**49**	56 26N	16 25 E
Kastóri	**45**	37 10N	22 17 E
Kastoría	**44**	40 30N	21 19 E
Kastoría □	**44**	40 30N	21 15 E
Kastorías, L.	**44**	40 30N	21 20 E
Kastornoye	**55**	51 55N	38 2 E
Kastós	**45**	38 35N	20 55 E
Kástron	**44**	39 50N	25 2 E
Kastrosikiá	**45**	39 6N	20 36 E
Kasulu	**90**	4 37 S	30 5 E
Kasulu □	**90**	4 37 S	30 5 E
Kasumkent	**57**	41 47N	48 15 E
Kasungu	**91**	13 0 S	33 29 E
Kasur	**68**	31 5N	74 25 E
Kata	**59**	58 46N	102 40 E
Kataba	**91**	16 5 S	25 10 E
Katako Kombe	**90**	3 25 S	24 20 E
Katákolon	**45**	37 38N	21 19 E
Katale	**90**	4 52 S	31 7 E
Katamatite	**99**	36 6 S	145 41 E
Katanda, Zaïre	**90**	0 55 S	29 21 E
Katanda, Zaïre	**90**	7 52 S	24 13 E
Katangi	**69**	21 56N	79 50 E
Katangli	**59**	51 42N	143 14 E
Katanning	**96**	33 40 S	117 33 E
Katastári	**45**	37 50N	20 45 E
Katavi Swamp	**90**	6 50 S	31 10 E
Kateríni	**44**	40 18N	22 37 E
Katha	**67**	24 10N	96 30 E
Katherîna, Gebel	**86**	28 30N	33 57 E
Katherine	**96**	14 27 S	132 20 E
Kathiawar	**68**	22 20N	71 0 E
Kati	**84**	12 41N	8 4W
Katiet	**72**	2 21 S	99 54 E
Katihar	**69**	25 34N	87 36 E
Katima Mulilo	**92**	17 28 S	24 13 E
Katimbira	**91**	12 40 S	34 0 E
Katiola	**84**	8 10N	5 10W
Katkopberg	**92**	30 0 S	20 0 E
Katlanovo	**42**	41 52N	21 40 E
Katmandu	**69**	27 45N	85 20 E
Kato Akhaïa	**45**	38 8N	21 33 E
Káto Stavros	**44**	40 39N	23 43 E
Katol	**68**	21 17N	78 38 E
Katompe	**90**	6 2 S	26 23 E
Katonga →	**90**	0 34N	31 50 E
Katoomba	**97**	33 41 S	150 19 E
Katowice	**28**	50 17N	19 5 E
Katowice □	**28**	50 10N	19 0 E
Katrine, L.	**14**	56 15N	4 30W
Katrineholm	**48**	59 9N	16 12 E
Katsepe	**93**	15 45 S	46 15 E
Katsina Ala →	**85**	7 10N	9 20 E
Katsuura	**74**	35 10N	140 20 E
Kattawaz-Urgun □	**65**	32 10N	68 20 E
Kattegatt	**49**	57 0N	11 20 E
Katumba	**90**	7 40 S	25 17 E
Katungu	**90**	2 55 S	40 3 E
Katwa	**69**	23 30N	88 5 E
Katwijk-aan-Zee	**16**	52 12N	4 24 E
Katy	**28**	51 2N	16 45 E
Kauai	**110**	22 0N	159 30W
Kauai Chan.	**110**	21 45N	158 50W
Kaub	**25**	50 5N	7 46 E
Kaufbeuren	**25**	47 50N	10 37 E
Kaufman	**117**	32 35N	96 20W
Kaukauna	**114**	44 20N	88 13W
Kaukauveld	**92**	20 0 S	20 15 E
Kaukonen	**50**	67 31N	24 53 E
Kauliranta	**50**	66 27N	23 41 E
Kaunas	**54**	54 54N	23 54 E
Kaura Namoda	**85**	12 37N	6 33 E
Kautokeino	**50**	69 0N	23 4 E
Kavacha	**59**	60 16N	169 51 E
Kavadarci	**42**	41 26N	22 3 E
Kavaja	**44**	41 11N	19 33 E
Kavali	**70**	14 55N	80 1 E
Kavála	**44**	40 57N	24 28 E
Kavála □	**44**	41 5N	24 30 E
Kavála Kólpos	**44**	40 50N	24 25 E
Kavarna	**43**	43 26N	28 22 E
Kavieng	**98**	2 36 S	150 51 E
Kavkaz, Bolshoi	**57**	42 50N	44 0 E
Kavoúsi	**45**	35 7N	25 51 E
Kaw = Caux	**127**	4 30N	52 15W
Kawa	**87**	13 42N	32 34 E
Kawagama L.	**112**	45 18N	78 45W
Kawagoe	**74**	35 55N	139 29 E
Kawaguchi	**74**	35 52N	139 45 E
Kawaihae	**110**	20 3N	155 50W
Kawambwa	**91**	9 48 S	29 3 E
Kawardha	**69**	22 0N	81 17 E
Kawasaki	**74**	35 35N	139 42 E
Kawene	**106**	48 45N	91 15W
Kawerau	**101**	38 7 S	176 42 E
Kawhia Harbour	**101**	38 5 S	174 51 E
Kawio, Kepulauan	**73**	4 30N	125 30 E
Kawnro	**67**	22 48N	99 8 E
Kawthaung	**71**	10 5N	98 36 E
Kawthoolei □ = Kawthule	**67**	18 0N	97 30 E
Kawthule □	**67**	18 0N	97 30 E
Kaya	**85**	13 4N	1 10W
Kayah □	**67**	19 15N	97 15 E
Kayangulam	**70**	9 10N	76 33 E
Kaycee	**118**	43 45N	106 46W
Kayeli	**73**	3 20 S	127 10 E
Kayenta	**119**	36 46N	110 15W
Kayes	**84**	14 25N	11 30W
Kayima	**84**	8 54N	11 15W
Kayomba	**91**	13 11 S	24 2 E
Kayoro	**85**	11 0N	1 28W
Kayrunnera	**99**	30 40 S	142 30 E
Kaysatskoye	**57**	49 47N	46 49 E
Kayseri	**64**	38 45N	35 30 E
Kaysville	**118**	41 2N	111 58W
Kayuagung	**72**	3 24 S	104 50 E
Kazachinskoye	**59**	56 16N	107 36 E
Kazachye	**59**	70 52N	135 58 E
Kazakh S.S.R. □	**58**	50 0N	70 0 E
Kazan	**55**	55 48N	49 3 E
Kazanlúk	**43**	42 38N	25 20 E
Kazanskaya	**57**	49 50N	41 10 E
Kazatin	**56**	49 45N	28 50 E
Kazbek	**57**	42 42N	44 30 E
Kāzerūn	**65**	29 38N	51 40 E
Kazi Magomed	**57**	40 3N	49 0 E
Kazimierz Dolny	**28**	51 19N	21 57 E
Kazimierza Wielka	**28**	50 15N	20 30 E
Kazincbarcika	**27**	48 17N	20 36 E
Kaztalovka	**57**	49 47N	48 43 E
Kazumba	**88**	6 25 S	22 5 E
Kazym →	**58**	63 54N	65 50 E
Kcynia	**28**	53 0N	17 30 E
Ké-Macina	**84**	13 58N	5 22W
Kéa	**45**	37 35N	24 22 E
Kea	**45**	37 30N	24 22 E
Keams Canyon	**119**	35 53N	110 9W
Kearney	**116**	40 45N	99 3W
Keban	**64**	38 50N	38 50 E
Kébi	**84**	9 18N	6 37W
Kebili	**83**	33 47N	9 0 E
Kebnekaise	**50**	67 53N	18 33 E
Kebri Dehar	**63**	6 45N	44 17 E
Kebumen	**73**	7 42 S	109 40 E
Kecel	**27**	46 31N	19 16 E
Kechika →	**108**	59 41N	127 12W
Kecskemét	**27**	46 57N	19 42 E
Kedada	**87**	5 25N	35 58 E
Kedah □	**71**	5 50N	100 40 E
Kedainiai	**54**	55 15N	24 2 E
Kedgwick	**107**	47 40N	67 20W
Kedia Hill	**92**	21 28 S	24 37 E
Kediri	**73**	7 51 S	112 1 E
Kédougou	**84**	12 35N	12 10W
Kedzierzyn	**28**	50 20N	18 12 E
Keefers	**108**	50 0N	121 40W
Keeley L.	**109**	54 54N	108 8W
Keeling Is. = Cocos Is.	**94**	12 12 S	96 55 E
Keene	**114**	42 57N	72 17W
Keeper Hill	**15**	52 46N	8 17W
Keer-Weer, C.	**97**	14 0 S	141 32 E
Keeseville	**113**	44 29N	73 30W
Keetmanshoop	**92**	26 35 S	18 8 E
Keewatin	**116**	47 23N	93 0W
Keewatin □	**109**	63 20N	95 0W
Keewatin →	**109**	56 29N	100 46W
Kefa □	**87**	6 55N	36 30 E
Kefallinia	**45**	38 20N	20 30 E
Kefamenanu*	**73**	9 28 S	124 29 E
Kefar 'Eqron	**62**	31 52N	34 49 E
Kefar Hasīdim	**62**	32 47N	35 5 E
Kefar Nahum	**62**	32 54N	35 34 E
Kefar Sava	**62**	32 11N	34 54 E
Kefar Szold	**62**	33 11N	35 39 E
Kefar Vitkin	**62**	32 22N	34 53 E
Kefar Yehezqel	**62**	32 34N	35 22 E
Kefar Yona	**62**	32 20N	34 54 E
Kefar Zekharya	**62**	31 43N	34 57 E
Kefar Zetim	**62**	32 48N	35 27 E
Keffi	**85**	8 55N	7 43 E
Keflavík	**50**	64 2N	22 35W
Keg River	**108**	57 54N	117 55W
Kegahka	**107**	50 9N	61 18W
Kegalla	**70**	7 15N	80 21 E
Kehl	**25**	48 34N	7 50 E
Keighley	**12**	53 52N	1 54W
Keimoes	**92**	28 41 S	21 0 E
Keita	**85**	14 46N	5 56 E
Keith, Austral.	**99**	36 6 S	140 20 E
Keith, U.K.	**14**	57 33N	2 58W
Keith Arm	**104**	64 20N	122 15W
Kekri	**68**	26 0N	75 10 E
Kël	**59**	69 30N	124 10 E
Kelamet	**87**	16 0N	38 30 E
Kelan	**76**	38 43N	111 31 E
Kelang	**71**	3 2N	101 26 E
Kelani Ganga →	**70**	6 58N	79 50 E
Kelantan □	**71**	5 10N	102 0 E
Kelantan →	**71**	6 13N	102 14 E
Këlcyra	**44**	40 22N	20 12 E
Kelheim	**25**	48 58N	11 57 E
Kelibia	**83**	36 50N	11 3 E
Kellé	**88**	0 8 S	14 38 E
Keller	**118**	48 2N	118 44W
Kellerberrin	**96**	31 36 S	117 38 E
Kellett C.	**4**	72 0N	126 0W
Kelleys I.	**112**	41 35N	82 42W
Kellogg	**118**	47 30N	116 5W
Kelloselkä	**50**	66 56N	28 53 E
Kells = Ceanannus Mor	**15**	53 42N	6 53W
Kélo	**81**	9 10N	15 45 E
Kelowna	**108**	49 50N	119 25W
Kelsey Bay	**108**	50 25N	126 0W
Kelso, N.Z.	**101**	45 54 S	169 15 E
Kelso, U.K.	**14**	55 36N	2 27W
Kelso, U.S.A.	**118**	46 10N	122 57W
Keluang	**71**	2 3N	103 18 E
Kelvington	**109**	52 10N	103 30W
Kem	**52**	65 0N	34 38 E
Kem →	**52**	64 57N	34 41 E
Kem-Kem	**82**	30 40N	4 30W
Kema	**73**	1 22N	125 8 E
Kemah	**64**	39 32N	39 5 E
Kemano	**108**	53 35N	128 0W
Kembolcha	**87**	11 2N	39 42 E
Kemenets-Podolskiy	**56**	48 40N	26 40 E
Kemerovo	**58**	55 20N	86 5 E
Kemi	**50**	65 44N	24 34 E
Kemi älv = Kemijoki →	**50**	65 47N	24 32 E
Kemijärvi	**50**	66 43N	27 22 E
Kemijoki →	**50**	65 47N	24 32 E
Kemmerer	**118**	41 52N	110 30W
Kemp Coast	**5**	69 0 S	55 0 E
Kemp L.	**117**	33 45N	99 15W
Kempsey	**97**	31 1 S	152 50 E
Kempt, L.	**106**	47 25N	74 22W
Kempten	**25**	47 42N	10 18 E
Kemptville	**106**	45 0N	75 38W
Kenadsa	**82**	31 48N	2 26W
Kendal, Indon.	**72**	6 56 S	110 14 E
Kendal, U.K.	**12**	54 19N	2 44W
Kendall	**99**	31 35 S	152 44 E
Kendall →	**98**	14 4 S	141 35 E
Kendallville	**114**	41 25N	85 15W
Kendari	**73**	3 50 S	122 30 E
Kendawangan	**72**	2 32 S	110 17 E
Kende	**85**	11 30N	4 12 E
Kendervicës, m. e.	**44**	40 15N	19 52 E
Kendrapara	**69**	20 35N	86 30 E
Kendrick	**118**	46 43N	116 41W
Kenedy	**117**	28 49N	97 51W
Kenema	**84**	7 50N	11 14W
Keng Tung	**67**	21 0N	99 30 E
Kenge	**88**	4 50 S	17 4 E
Kengeja	**90**	5 26 S	39 45 E
Kenhardt	**92**	29 19 S	21 12 E
Kénitra (Port Lyautey)	**82**	34 15N	6 40W
Kenmare, Ireland	**15**	51 52N	9 35W
Kenmare, U.S.A.	**116**	48 40N	102 4W
Kenmare →	**15**	51 40N	10 0W
Kenmore	**100**	34 44 S	149 45 E
Kenn Reef	**97**	21 12 S	155 46 E
Kennebec	**116**	43 56N	99 54W
Kennedy	**91**	18 52 S	27 10 E
Kennedy Taungdeik	**67**	23 15N	93 45 E
Kennet →	**13**	51 24N	0 58W
Kennett	**117**	36 7N	90 0W
Kennewick	**118**	46 11N	119 2W
Kénogami	**107**	48 25N	71 15W
Kenogami →	**106**	51 6N	84 28W
Kenora	**109**	49 47N	94 29W
Kenosha	**114**	42 33N	87 48W
Kensington, Can.	**107**	46 28N	63 34W
Kensington, U.S.A.	**116**	39 48N	99 2W
Kensington Downs	**98**	22 31 S	144 19 E
Kent, Ohio, U.S.A.	**114**	41 8N	81 20W

Kent Kiparissía

Kent, Oreg., U.S.A. **118** 45 11N 120 45W
Kent, Tex., U.S.A. **117** 31 5N 104 12W
Kent □ **13** 51 12N 0 40 E
Kent Group **99** 39 30 S 147 20 E
Kent Pen. **104** 68 30N 107 0W
Kentau **58** 43 32N 68 36 E
Kentland **114** 40 45N 87 25W
Kenton **114** 40 40N 83 35W
Kentucky □ **114** 37 20N 85 0W
Kentucky → **114** 38 41N 85 11W
Kentucky Dam **114** 37 2N 88 15W
Kentucky L. **115** 36 25N 88 0W
Kentville **107** 45 6N 64 29W
Kentwood **117** 31 0N 90 30W
Kenya ■ **90** 1 0N 38 0 E
Kenya, Mt. **90** 0 10 S 37 18 E
Keokuk **116** 40 25N 91 24W
Kep-i-Gjuhës **44** 40 28N 19 15 E
Kepi **73** 6 32 S 139 19 E
Kepice **28** 54 16N 16 51 E
Kępno **28** 51 18N 17 58 E
Keppel B. **97** 23 21 S 150 55 E
Kepsut **64** 39 40N 28 9 E
Kerala □ **70** 11 0N 76 15 E
Kerang **97** 35 40 S 143 55 E
Keratéa **45** 37 48N 23 58 E
Keraudren, C. **99** 19 58 S 119 45 E
Keray **65** 26 15N 57 30 E
Kerch **56** 45 20N 36 20 E
Kerchenskiy Proliv **56** 45 10N 36 30 E
Kerchoual **85** 17 12N 0 20 E
Kerem Maharal **62** 32 39N 34 59 E
Kerema **98** 7 58 S 145 50 E
Keren **87** 15 45N 38 28 E
Kerewan **84** 13 29N 16 10W
Kerguelen **3** 48 15 S 69 10 E
Keri **45** 37 40N 20 49 E
Keri Kera **87** 12 21N 32 42 E
Kericho **90** 0 22 S 35 15 E
Kericho □ **90** 0 30 S 35 15 E
Kerinci **72** 1 40 S 101 15 E
Kerkenna, Iles **83** 34 48N 11 11 E
Kerki **58** 37 50N 65 12 E
Kerkinitis, Límni **44** 41 12N 23 10 E
Kérkira **44** 39 38N 19 50 E
Kerkrade **16** 50 53N 6 4 E
Kerma **86** 19 33N 30 32 E
Kermadec Is. **94** 30 0 S 178 15W
Kermadec Trench **94** 30 30 S 176 0W
Kermān **65** 30 15N 57 1 E
Kermān □ **65** 30 0N 57 0 E
** Kermānshāh **64** 34 23N 47 0 E
Kermānshāhān □ **64** 34 0N 46 30 E
Kerme Körfezi **45** 36 55N 27 50 E
Kermen **43** 42 30N 26 16 E
Kermit **117** 31 56N 103 3W
Kern → **119** 35 16N 119 18W
Kerrobert **109** 52 0N 109 11W
Kerrville **117** 30 1N 99 8W
Kerry □ **15** 52 7N 9 35W
Kerry Hd. **15** 52 26N 9 56W
Kersa **87** 9 28N 41 48 E
Kerteminde **49** 55 28N 10 39 E
Kertosono **73** 7 38 S 112 9 E
Kerulen → **75** 48 48N 117 0 E
Kerzaz **82** 29 29N 1 37W
Kesagami → **106** 51 40N 79 45W
Kesagami L. **106** 50 23N 80 15W
Keşan **44** 40 49N 26 38 E
Keski-Suomen lääni □ **50** 62 0N 25 30 E
Kestell **93** 28 17 S 28 42 E
Kestenga **52** 66 0N 31 50 E
Keswick **12** 54 35N 3 9W
Keszthely **27** 46 50N 17 15 E
Ket → **58** 58 55N 81 32 E
Keta **85** 5 49N 1 0 E
Ketapang **72** 1 55 S 110 0 E
Ketchikan **104** 55 25N 131 40W
Ketchum **118** 43 41N 114 27W
Kete Krachi **85** 7 46N 0 1W
Ketef, Khalîg Umm el **86** 23 40N 35 35 E
Keti Bandar **68** 24 8N 67 27 E
Ketri **68** 28 1N 75 50 E
Kętrzyn **28** 54 7N 21 22 E
Kettering **13** 52 24N 0 44W
Kettle → **109** 56 40N 89 34W
Kettle Falls **118** 48 41N 118 2W
Kety **27** 49 51N 19 16 E
Kevin **118** 48 45N 111 58W
Kewanee **116** 41 18N 89 55W
Kewaunee **114** 44 27N 87 30W
Keweenaw B. **114** 46 56N 88 23W
Keweenaw Pen. **114** 47 30N 88 0W
Keweenaw Pt. **114** 47 26N 87 40W
Key Harbour **106** 45 50N 80 45W
Key West **121** 24 33N 82 0W
Keyport **113** 40 26N 74 12W
Keyser **114** 39 26N 79 0W
Keystone, S.D., U.S.A. **116** 43 54N 103 27W
Keystone, W. Va., U.S.A. **114** 37 30N 81 30W
Kezhma **59** 58 59N 101 9 E
Kežmarok **27** 49 10N 20 28 E
Khabarovo **58** 69 30N 60 30 E
Khabarovsk **59** 48 30N 135 5 E
Khābūr → **64** 35 0N 40 30 E
Khachmas **57** 41 31N 48 42 E
Khachraud **68** 23 25N 75 20 E
Khadari, W. el → **87** 10 29N 27 15 E
Khadro **68** 26 11N 68 50 E
Khadyzhensk **57** 44 26N 39 32 E
Khagaria **69** 25 30N 86 32 E
Khaibar **86** 25 49N 39 16 E
Khaipur, Bahawalpur, Pak. **68** 29 34N 72 17 E
Khaipur, Hyderabad, Pak. **68** 27 32N 68 49 E
Khair **68** 27 57N 77 46 E
Khairabad **69** 27 33N 80 47 E
Khairagarh Raj **69** 21 27N 81 2 E
* Khairpur □ **68** 27 20N 69 8 E
Khakhea **92** 24 48 S 23 22 E
Khalfallah **82** 34 20N 0 16 E
Khalij-e-Fars □ **65** 28 20N 51 45 E
Khalilabad **69** 26 48N 83 5 E
Khálki **44** 39 36N 22 30 E
Khalkidhikí □ **44** 40 25N 23 20 E
Khalkís **45** 38 27N 23 42 E
Khalmer-Sede = Tazovskiy **58** 67 30N 78 30 E
Khalmer Yu **58** 67 58N 65 1 E
Khalturin **55** 58 40N 48 50 E
Khamaria **69** 23 10N 80 52 E
Khamas Country **92** 21 45 S 26 30 E
Khambhalia **68** 22 14N 69 41 E
Khamgaon **68** 20 42N 76 37 E
Khamilonísion **45** 35 50N 26 15 E
Khamir **63** 16 0N 44 0 E
Khammam **70** 17 11N 80 6 E
Khān Yūnis **62** 31 21N 34 18 E
Khānābād **65** 36 45N 69 5 E
Khānaqīn **64** 34 23N 45 25 E
Khandrá **45** 35 3N 26 8 E
Khandwa **68** 21 49N 76 22 E
Khandyga **59** 62 42N 135 35 E
Khanewal **68** 30 20N 71 55 E
* Khanh Hung **71** 9 37N 105 50 E
Khaniá **45** 35 30N 24 4 E
Khaniá □ **45** 35 30N 24 0 E
Khanion Kólpos **45** 35 33N 23 55 E
Khanka, Oz. **59** 45 0N 132 30 E
Khanna **68** 30 42N 76 16 E
Khanpur **68** 28 42N 70 35 E
Khanty-Mansiysk **58** 61 0N 69 0 E
Khapcheranga **59** 49 42N 112 24 E
Kharagpur **69** 22 20N 87 25 E
Kharaij **86** 21 25N 41 0 E
Kharan Kalat **66** 28 34N 65 21 E
Kharānaq **65** 32 20N 54 45 E
Kharda **70** 18 40N 75 34 E
Khârga, El Wâhât el **86** 25 10N 30 35 E
Khargon **68** 21 45N 75 40 E
Kharit, Wadi el → **86** 24 26N 33 3 E
Khārk, Jazireh **64** 29 15N 50 28 E
Kharkov **56** 49 58N 36 20 E
Kharmanli **43** 41 55N 25 55 E
Kharovsk **55** 59 56N 40 13 E
Kharsānīya **64** 27 10N 49 10 E
Khartoum = El Khartûm **87** 15 31N 32 35 E
Khasab **65** 26 14N 56 15 E
Khasavyurt **57** 43 16N 46 40 E
Khasebake **92** 20 42 S 24 29 E
Khāsh **65** 28 15N 61 15 E
Khashm el Girba **87** 14 59N 35 58 E
Khashuri **57** 41 58N 43 35 E
Khasi Hills **69** 25 30N 91 30 E
Khaskovo **43** 41 56N 25 30 E
Khatanga **59** 72 0N 102 20 E
Khatanga → **59** 72 55N 106 0 E
Khatangskiy, Saliv **4** 66 0N 112 0 E
Khatauli **68** 29 17N 77 43 E
Khatyrka **59** 62 3N 175 15 E
Khavār □ **64** 37 20N 47 0 E
Khaybar, Harrat **64** 25 45N 40 0 E
Khazzân Jabal el Awliyâ **87** 15 24N 32 20 E
Khed, Maharashtra, India **70** 17 43N 73 27 E
Khed, Maharashtra, India **70** 18 51N 73 56 E
Khekra **68** 28 52N 77 20 E
Khemelnik **56** 49 33N 27 58 E
Khemis Miliana **82** 36 11N 2 14 E
Khemissèt **82** 33 50N 6 1W
Khemmarat **71** 16 10N 105 15 E
Khenchela **83** 35 28N 7 11 E
Khenifra **82** 32 58N 5 46W
Kherrata **83** 36 27N 5 13 E
Khérson **44** 41 5N 22 47 E
Kherson **56** 46 35N 32 35 E
Khersónisos Akrotíri **45** 35 30N 24 10 E
Kheta → **59** 71 54N 102 6 E
Khiliomódhion **45** 37 48N 22 51 E
Khilok **59** 51 30N 110 45 E
Khimki **55** 55 50N 37 20 E
Khíos **45** 38 27N 26 9 E
Khisar-Momina Banya **43** 42 30N 24 44 E
Khiuma = Hiiumaa **54** 58 50N 22 45 E
Khiva **58** 41 30N 60 18 E
Khīyāv **64** 38 30N 47 45 E
Khlebarovo **43** 43 37N 26 15 E
Khlong → **71** 15 30N 98 50 E
Khmelnitskiy **56** 49 23N 27 0 E
Khmer Rep. = Cambodia ■ **71** 12 15N 105 0 E
Khojak P. **65** 30 55N 66 30 E
Khokholskiy **55** 51 35N 38 40 E
Kholm, Afghan. **65** 36 45N 67 40 E
Kholm, U.S.S.R. **54** 57 10N 31 15 E
Kholmsk **59** 47 40N 142 5 E
Khomas Hochland **92** 22 40 S 16 0 E
Khomeyn **64** 33 40N 50 7 E
Khomo **92** 21 7 S 24 35 E
Khon Kaen **71** 16 30N 102 47 E
Khong **71** 14 5N 105 56 E
Khong → **71** 15 0N 106 50 E
Khonu **59** 66 30N 143 12 E
Khoper → **55** 49 30N 42 20 E
Khor el 'Atash **87** 13 20N 34 15 E
Khóra **45** 37 3N 21 42 E
Khóra Sfakion **45** 35 15N 24 9 E
Khorāsān □ **65** 34 0N 58 0 E
Khorat = Nakhon Ratchasima **71** 14 59N 102 12 E
Khorat, Cao Nguyen **71** 15 30N 102 50 E
Khorb el Ethel **82** 28 30N 6 17W
Khorixas **92** 20 16 S 14 59 E
Khorog **58** 37 30N 71 36 E
Khorol **56** 49 48N 33 15 E
Khorramābād **64** 33 30N 48 25 E
Khorramshahr **64** 30 29N 48 15 E
Khotin **56** 48 31N 26 27 E
Khouribga **82** 32 58N 6 57W
Khowai **67** 24 5N 91 40 E
Khoyniki **54** 51 54N 29 55 E
Khrami → **57** 41 30N 45 0 E
Khrenovoye **55** 51 4N 40 16 E
Khristianá **45** 36 14N 25 13 E
Khtapodhiá **45** 37 24N 25 34 E
Khu Khan **71** 14 42N 104 12 E
Khulna **69** 22 45N 89 34 E
Khulo **57** 41 33N 42 19 E
Khumago **92** 20 26 S 24 32 E
Khunzakh **57** 42 35N 46 42 E
Khūr **65** 32 55N 58 18 E
Khurai **68** 24 3N 78 23 E
Khurayş **64** 24 55N 48 5 E
Khurja **68** 28 15N 77 58 E
Khūryān Mūryān, Jazā 'ir **63** 17 30N 55 58 E
Khushab **68** 32 20N 72 20 E
Khuzdar **66** 27 52N 66 30 E
Khūzetān □ **64** 31 0N 50 0 E
Khvalynsk **55** 52 30N 48 2 E
Khvatovka **55** 52 24N 46 32 E
Khvor **65** 33 45N 55 0 E
Khvormūj **65** 28 40N 51 30 E
Khvoy **64** 38 35N 45 0 E
Khvoynaya **54** 58 58N 34 28 E
Khyber Pass **66** 34 10N 71 8 E
Kiabukwa **91** 8 40 S 24 48 E
Kiadho → **70** 19 37N 77 40 E
Kiama **99** 34 40 S 150 50 E
Kiamba **73** 6 2N 124 46 E
Kiambi **90** 7 15 S 28 0 E
Kiambu **90** 1 8 S 36 50 E
Kiangsi = Jiangxi □ **75** 27 30N 116 0 E
Kiangsu = Jiangsu □ **75** 33 0N 120 0 E
Kiáton **45** 38 2N 22 43 E
Kibæk **49** 56 2N 8 51 E
Kibanga Port **90** 0 10N 32 58 E
Kibangou **88** 3 26 S 12 22 E
Kibara **90** 2 8 S 33 30 E
Kibare, Mts. **90** 8 25 S 27 10 E
Kibombo **90** 3 57 S 25 53 E
Kibondo **90** 3 35 S 30 45 E
Kibondo □ **90** 4 0 S 30 55 E
Kibumbu **90** 3 32 S 29 45 E
Kibungu **90** 2 10 S 30 32 E
Kibuye, Burundi **90** 3 39 S 29 59 E
Kibuye, Rwanda **90** 2 3 S 29 21 E
Kibwesa **90** 6 30 S 29 58 E
Kibwezi **90** 2 27 S 37 57 E
Kičevo **42** 41 34N 20 59 E
Kichiga **59** 59 50N 163 5 E
Kicking Horse Pass **108** 51 28N 116 16W
Kidal **85** 18 26N 1 22 E
Kidderminster **13** 52 24N 2 13W
Kidete **90** 6 25 S 37 17 E
Kidira **84** 14 28N 12 13W
Kidnappers, C. **101** 39 38 S 177 5 E
Kidston **98** 18 52 S 144 8 E
Kidugallo **90** 6 49 S 38 15 E
Kiel **24** 54 16N 10 8 E
Kiel Kanal = Nord-Ostee-Kanal **24** 54 15N 9 40 E
Kielce **28** 50 52N 20 42 E
Kielce □ **28** 50 40N 20 40 E
Kieler Bucht **24** 54 30N 10 30 E
Kienge **91** 10 30 S 27 30 E
Kiessé **85** 13 29N 4 1 E
Kiev = Kiyev **54** 50 30N 30 28 E
Kifār 'Aşyūn **62** 31 39N 35 7 E
Kiffa **84** 16 37N 11 24W
Kifisiá **45** 38 4N 23 49 E
Kifissós → **45** 38 35N 23 20 E
Kifrī **64** 34 45N 45 0 E
Kigali **90** 1 59 S 30 4 E
Kigarama **90** 1 1 S 31 50 E
Kigoma □ **90** 5 0 S 30 0 E
Kigoma-Ujiji **90** 4 55 S 29 36 E
Kigomasha, Ras **90** 4 58 S 38 58 E
Kihee **99** 27 23 S 142 37 E
Kii-Suidō **74** 33 40N 135 0 E
Kikinda **42** 45 50N 20 30 E
Kikládhes **45** 37 20N 24 30 E
Kikládhes □ **45** 37 0N 25 0 E
Kikori **98** 7 25 S 144 15 E
Kikori → **98** 7 38 S 144 20 E
Kikwit **88** 5 5 S 18 45 E
Kilafors **48** 61 14N 16 36 E
Kilakarai **70** 9 12N 78 47 E
Kilalki **45** 36 15N 27 35 E
Kilauea Crater **110** 19 24N 155 17W
Kilcoy **99** 26 59 S 152 30 E
Kildare **15** 53 10N 6 50W
Kildare □ **15** 53 10N 6 50W
Kilgore **117** 32 22N 94 55W
Kilifi **90** 3 40 S 39 48 E
Kilifi □ **90** 3 30 S 39 40 E
Kilimanjaro **90** 3 7 S 37 20 E
Kilimanjaro □ **90** 4 0 S 38 0 E
Kilindini **90** 4 4 S 39 40 E
Kilis **64** 36 50N 37 10 E
Kiliya **56** 45 28N 29 16 E
Kilju **76** 40 57N 129 25 E
Kilkee **15** 52 41N 9 40W
Kilkenny **15** 52 40N 7 17W
Kilkenny □ **15** 52 35N 7 15W
Kilkieran B. **15** 53 18N 9 45W
Kilkís **44** 40 58N 22 57 E
Kilkís □ **44** 41 5N 22 50 E
Killala **15** 54 13N 9 12W
Killala B. **15** 54 20N 9 12W
Killaloe **15** 52 48N 8 28W
Killaloe Sta. **112** 45 33N 77 25W
Killam **108** 52 47N 111 51W
Killarney, Can. **106** 45 55N 81 30W
Killarney, Ireland **15** 52 2N 9 30W
Killarney, Lakes of **15** 52 0N 9 30W
Killary Harbour **15** 53 38N 9 52W
Killdeer, Can. **109** 49 6N 106 22W
Killdeer, U.S.A. **116** 47 26N 102 48W
Killeen **117** 31 7N 97 45W
Killiecrankie, Pass of **14** 56 44N 3 46W
Killin **14** 56 28N 4 20W
Killíni, Ilía, Greece **45** 37 55N 21 8 E
Killíni, Korinthía, Greece **45** 37 54N 22 25 E
Killybegs **15** 54 38N 8 26W
Kilmarnock **14** 55 36N 4 30W
Kilmez **55** 56 58N 50 55 E
Kilmez → **55** 56 58N 50 28 E
Kilmore **99** 37 25 S 144 53 E
Kilondo **91** 9 45 S 34 20 E
Kilosa **90** 6 48 S 37 0 E
Kilosa □ **90** 6 48 S 37 0 E
Kilrush **15** 52 39N 9 30W
Kilsmo **48** 59 6N 15 35 E
Kilwa □ **91** 9 0 S 39 0 E
Kilwa Kisiwani **91** 8 58 S 39 32 E
Kilwa Kivinje **91** 8 45 S 39 25 E
Kilwa Masoko **91** 8 55 S 39 30 E
Kim **117** 37 18N 103 20W
Kimaam **73** 7 58 S 138 53 E
Kimamba **90** 6 45 S 37 10 E
Kimba **97** 33 8 S 136 23 E
Kimball, Nebr., U.S.A. **116** 41 17N 103 40W
Kimball, S.D., U.S.A. **116** 43 47N 98 57W
Kimbe **98** 5 33 S 150 11 E
Kimbe B. **98** 5 15 S 150 30 E
Kimberley, Austral. **96** 16 20 S 127 0 E
Kimberley, Can. **108** 49 40N 115 59W
Kimberley, S. Afr. **92** 28 43 S 24 46 E
Kimberly **118** 42 33N 114 25W
Kimchaek **76** 40 40N 129 10 E
Kimchŏn **76** 36 11N 128 4 E
Kími **45** 38 38N 24 6 E
Kímolos **45** 36 48N 24 37 E
Kimovsk **55** 54 0N 38 29 E
Kimparana **84** 12 48N 5 0W
Kimry **55** 56 55N 37 15 E
Kimsquit **108** 52 45N 126 57W
Kimstad **49** 58 35N 15 58 E
Kinabalu **72** 6 0N 116 0 E
Kínaros **45** 36 59N 26 15 E
Kinaskan L. **108** 57 38N 130 8W
Kincaid **109** 49 40N 107 0W
Kincardine **106** 44 10N 81 40W
Kinda **91** 9 18 S 25 4 E
Kindersley **109** 51 30N 109 10W
Kindia **84** 10 0N 12 52W
Kindu **90** 2 55 S 25 50 E
Kinel **55** 53 15N 50 40 E
Kineshma **55** 57 30N 42 5 E
Kinesi **90** 1 25 S 33 50 E
King City **119** 36 11N 121 8W
King Cr. → **98** 24 35 S 139 30 E
King Frederick VI Land = Kong Frederik VI.s. Kyst **4** 63 0N 43 0W
King George B. **128** 51 30 S 60 30W
King George I. **5** 60 0 S 60 0W
King George Is. **105** 57 20N 80 30W
King George Sd. **96** 35 5 S 118 0 E
King I., Austral. **97** 39 50 S 144 0 E
King I., Can. **108** 52 10N 127 40W
King I. = Kadah Kyun **71** 12 30N 98 20 E
King Leopold Ranges **96** 17 30 S 125 45 E
King, Mt. **99** 25 10 S 147 30 E
King Sd. **96** 16 50 S 123 20 E
King William I. **104** 69 10N 97 25W
King William's Town **92** 32 51 S 27 22 E
Kingaroy **97** 26 32 S 151 51 E
Kingfisher **117** 35 50N 97 55W
Kingisepp **54** 59 25N 28 40 E
Kingisepp (Kuressaare) **54** 58 15N 22 30 E
Kingman, Ariz., U.S.A. **119** 35 12N 114 2W
Kingman, Kans., U.S.A. **117** 37 41N 98 9W
Kings → **119** 36 10N 119 50W
Kings Canyon National Park **119** 37 0N 118 35W
King's Lynn **12** 52 45N 0 25 E
Kings Mountain **115** 35 13N 81 20W
King's Peak **118** 40 46N 110 27W
Kingsbridge **13** 50 17N 3 46W
Kingsburg **119** 36 35N 119 36W
Kingscote **99** 35 40 S 137 38 E
Kingscourt **15** 53 55N 6 48W
Kingsley **116** 42 37N 95 58W
Kingsley Dam **116** 41 20N 101 40W
Kingsport **115** 36 33N 82 36W
Kingston, Can. **106** 44 14N 76 30W
Kingston, Jamaica **121** 18 0N 76 50W
Kingston, N.Z. **101** 45 20 S 168 43 E
Kingston, N.Y., U.S.A. **114** 41 55N 74 0W
Kingston, Pa., U.S.A. **114** 41 19N 75 58W
Kingston, R.I., U.S.A. **113** 41 29N 71 30W
Kingston South East **97** 36 51 S 139 55 E
Kingston-upon-Thames **13** 51 23N 0 20W
Kingstown **121** 13 10N 61 10W
Kingstree **115** 33 40N 79 48W
Kingsville, Can. **106** 42 2N 82 45W
Kingsville, U.S.A. **117** 27 30N 97 53W
Kingussie **14** 57 5N 4 2W
Kinistino **109** 52 57N 105 2W
Kinkala **88** 4 18 S 14 49 E
Kinleith **101** 38 20 S 175 56 E
Kinmount **112** 44 48N 78 45W
Kinn **47** 61 34N 4 45 E
Kinna **49** 57 32N 12 42 E
Kinnaird **108** 49 17N 117 39W
Kinnairds Hd. **14** 57 40N 2 0W
Kinnared **49** 57 2N 13 7 E
Kinneret **62** 32 44N 35 34 E
Kinneret, Yam **62** 32 45N 35 35 E
Kinoje → **106** 52 8N 81 25W
Kinoni **90** 0 41 S 30 28 E
Kinross **14** 56 13N 3 25W
Kinsale **15** 51 42N 8 31W
Kinsale, Old Hd. of **15** 51 37N 8 32W
Kinsarvik **47** 60 22N 6 43 E
Kinshasa **88** 4 20 S 15 15 E
Kinsley **117** 37 57N 99 30W
Kinston **115** 35 18N 77 35W
Kintampo **85** 8 5N 1 41W
Kintap **72** 3 51 S 115 13 E
Kintyre **14** 55 30N 5 35W
Kintyre, Mull of **14** 55 17N 5 55W
Kinushseo → **106** 55 15N 83 45W
Kinuso **108** 55 20N 115 25W
Kinyangiri **90** 4 25 S 34 37 E
Kinzig → **25** 48 37N 7 49 E
Kinzua **112** 41 52N 78 58W
Kinzua Dam **112** 41 53N 79 0W
Kióni **45** 38 27N 20 41 E
Kiosk **106** 46 6N 78 53W
Kiowa, Kans., U.S.A. **117** 37 3N 98 30W
Kiowa, Okla., U.S.A. **117** 34 45N 95 50W
Kipahigan L. **109** 55 20N 101 55W
Kipanga **90** 6 15 S 35 20 E
Kiparissía **45** 37 15N 21 40 E

* *Now part of Sind* □
** *Renamed Bakhtāran*
* *Renamed Soc Trang*

Kiparissiakós Kólpos Kopliku

Kiparissiakós Kólpos	45	37 25N	21 25 E
Kipembawe	90	7 38 S	33 27 E
Kipengere Ra.	91	9 12 S	34 15 E
Kipili	90	7 28 S	30 32 E
Kipini	90	2 30 S	40 32 E
Kipling	109	50 6N	102 38W
Kippure	15	53 11N	6 23W
Kipushi	91	11 48 S	27 12 E
Kirandul	70	18 33N	81 10 E
Kiratpur	68	29 32N	78 12 E
Kirchhain	24	50 49N	8 54 E
Kirchheim	25	48 38N	9 20 E
Kirchheim-Bolanden	25	49 40N	8 0 E
Kirchschlag	27	47 30N	16 19 E
Kirensk	59	57 50N	107 55 E
Kirgiz S.S.R. □	58	42 0N	75 0 E
Kirgiziya Steppe	53	50 0N	55 0 E
Kiri	88	1 29 S	19 0 E
Kiribati ■	94	1 0N	176 0 E
Kiriburu	69	22 0N	85 0 E
Kırıkkale	64	39 51N	33 32 E
Kirillov	55	59 51N	38 14 E
Kirin = Jilin	76	43 55N	126 30 E
Kirin = Jilin □	76	44 0N	126 0 E
Kirindi →	70	6 15N	81 20 E
Kirishi	54	59 28N	31 59 E
Kirkcaldy	14	56 7N	3 10W
Kirkcudbright	14	54 50N	4 3W
Kirkee	70	18 34N	73 56 E
Kirkenær	47	60 27N	12 3 E
Kirkenes	50	69 40N	30 5 E
Kirkintilloch	14	55 57N	4 10W
Kirkjubæjarklaustur	50	63 47N	18 4W
Kirkland	119	34 29N	112 46W
Kirkland Lake	106	48 9N	80 2W
Kırklareli	43	41 44N	27 15 E
Kirksville	116	40 8N	92 35W
Kirkūk	64	35 30N	44 21 E
Kirkwall	14	58 59N	2 59W
Kirkwood	92	33 22 S	25 15 E
Kirlampudi	70	17 12N	82 12 E
Kirn	25	49 46N	7 29 E
Kirov, R.S.F.S.R., U.S.S.R.	54	54 3N	34 20 E
Kirov, R.S.F.S.R., U.S.S.R.	58	58 35N	49 40 E
Kirovabad	57	40 45N	46 20 E
Kirovakan	57	40 48N	44 30 E
Kirovo-Chepetsk	55	58 28N	50 0 E
Kirovograd	56	48 35N	32 20 E
Kirovsk, R.S.F.S.R., U.S.S.R.	52	67 48N	33 50 E
Kirovsk, Turkmen S.S.R., U.S.S.R.	58	37 42N	60 23 E
Kirovsk, Ukraine S.S.R., U.S.S.R.	57	48 35N	38 30 E
Kirovski	57	45 51N	48 11 E
Kirovskiy	59	54 27N	155 42 E
Kirriemuir, Can.	109	51 56N	110 20W
Kirriemuir, U.K.	14	56 41N	3 0W
Kirsanov	55	52 35N	42 40 E
Kırşehir	64	39 14N	34 5 E
Kirstonia	92	25 30 S	23 45 E
Kirtachi	85	12 52N	2 30 E
Kirteh	65	32 15N	63 0 E
Kirthar Range	68	27 0N	67 0 E
Kiruna	50	67 52N	20 15 E
Kirundu	90	0 50 S	25 35 E
Kirya	55	55 5N	46 45 E
Kiryū	74	36 24N	139 20 E
Kisa	49	58 0N	15 39 E
Kisaga	90	4 30 S	34 23 E
Kisámou, Kólpos	45	35 30N	23 38 E
Kisanga	90	2 30N	26 35 E
Kisangani	90	0 35N	25 15 E
Kisar	73	8 5 S	127 10 E
Kisaran	72	3 0N	99 37 E
Kisarawe	90	6 53 S	39 0 E
Kisarawe □	90	7 3 S	39 0 E
Kisarazu	74	35 23N	139 55 E
Kisbér	27	47 30N	18 0 E
Kiselevsk	58	54 5N	86 39 E
Kishanganj	69	26 3N	88 14 E
Kishangarh	68	27 50N	70 30 E
Kishi	85	9 1N	3 52 E
Kishinev	56	47 0N	28 50 E
Kishiwada	74	34 28N	135 22 E
Kishon	62	32 49N	35 2 E
Kishorganj	69	24 26N	90 40 E
Kishtwar	69	33 20N	75 48 E
Kisii	90	0 40 S	34 45 E
Kisii □	90	0 40 S	34 45 E
Kisiju	90	7 23 S	39 19 E
Kısır, Dağ	57	41 0N	43 5 E
Kisizi	90	1 0 S	29 58 E
Kiska I.	104	52 0N	177 30 E
Kiskatinaw →	108	56 8N	120 10W
Kiskittogisu L.	109	54 13N	98 20W
Kiskomárom = Zalakomár	27	46 33N	17 10 E
Kiskörös	27	46 37N	19 20 E
Kiskundorozsma	27	46 16N	20 5 E
Kiskunfélegyháza	27	46 42N	19 53 E
Kiskunhalas	27	46 28N	19 37 E
Kiskunmajsa	27	46 30N	19 48 E
Kislovodsk	57	43 50N	42 45 E
Kiso-Sammyaku	74	35 45N	137 45 E
Kisoro	90	1 17 S	29 48 E
Kispest	27	47 27N	19 9 E
Kissidougou	84	9 5N	10 0W
Kissimmee	115	28 18N	81 22W
Kissimmee →	115	27 20N	80 55W
Kississing L.	109	55 10N	101 20W
Kistanje	39	43 58N	15 55 E
Kisterenye	27	48 3N	19 50 E
Kisújszállás	27	47 12N	20 50 E
Kisumu	90	0 3 S	34 45 E
Kisvárda	27	48 14N	22 4 E
Kiswani	90	4 5 S	37 57 E
Kiswere	91	9 27 S	39 30 E
Kit Carson	116	38 48N	102 45W
Kita	84	13 5N	9 25W
Kitab	58	39 7N	66 52 E
Kitaibaraki	74	36 50N	140 45 E
Kitakami-Gawa →	74	38 25N	141 19 E
Kitakyūshū	74	33 50N	130 50 E
Kitale	90	1 0N	35 0 E
Kitangiri, L.	90	4 5 S	34 20 E
Kitaya	91	10 38 S	40 8 E
Kitchener	106	43 27N	80 29W
Kitega = Citega	90	3 30 S	29 58 E
Kitengo	90	7 26 S	24 8 E
Kiteto □	90	5 0 S	37 0 E
Kitgum	90	3 17N	32 52 E
Kíthira	45	36 9N	23 0 E
Kíthnos	45	37 26N	24 27 E
Kitimat	108	54 3N	128 38W
Kitinen →	50	67 34N	26 40 E
Kitiyab	87	17 13N	33 35 E
Kítros	44	40 22N	22 34 E
Kittakittaooloo, L.	99	28 3 S	138 14 E
Kittanning	114	40 49N	79 30W
Kittatinny Mts.	113	41 0N	75 0W
Kittery	114	43 7N	70 42W
Kitui	90	1 17 S	38 0 E
Kitui □	90	1 30 S	38 25 E
Kitwe	91	12 54 S	28 13 E
Kitzbühel	26	47 27N	12 24 E
Kitzingen	25	49 44N	10 9 E
Kivalo	50	66 18N	26 0 E
Kivarli	68	24 33N	72 46 E
Kivotós	44	40 13N	21 26 E
Kivu □	90	3 10 S	27 0 E
Kivu, L.	90	1 48 S	29 0 E
Kiyev	54	50 30N	30 28 E
Kiyevskoye Vdkhr.	54	51 0N	30 0 E
Kizel	52	59 3N	57 40 E
Kiziguru	90	1 46 S	30 23 E
Kızıl Irmak →	56	39 15N	36 0 E
Kizil Yurt	57	43 13N	46 54 E
Kızılcahamam	56	40 30N	32 30 E
Kizimkazi	90	6 28 S	39 30 E
Kizlyar	57	43 51N	46 40 E
Kizyl-Arvat	58	38 58N	56 15 E
Kjellerup	49	56 17N	9 25 E
Kladanj	42	44 14N	18 42 E
Kladnica	42	43 23N	20 2 E
Kladno	26	50 10N	14 7 E
Kladovo	42	44 36N	22 33 E
Klagenfurt	26	46 38N	14 20 E
Klagshamn	49	55 32N	12 53 E
Klagstorp	49	55 22N	13 23 E
Klaipeda	54	55 43N	21 10 E
Klamath →	118	41 40N	124 4W
Klamath Falls	118	42 20N	121 50W
Klamath Mts.	118	41 20N	123 0W
Klanjec	39	46 3N	15 45 E
Klappan →	108	58 0N	129 43W
Klaten	73	7 43 S	110 36 E
Klatovy	26	49 23N	13 18 E
Klawak	108	55 35N	133 0W
Klawer	92	31 44 S	18 36 E
Kłecko	28	52 38N	17 25 E
Kleczew	28	52 22N	18 9 E
Kleena Kleene	108	52 0N	124 59W
Klein	118	46 26N	108 31W
Klein-Karas	92	27 33 S	18 7 E
Klein Karoo	92	33 45 S	21 30 E
Klekovača	39	44 25N	16 32 E
Klemtu	108	52 35N	128 55W
Klenovec, Czech.	27	48 36N	19 54 E
Klenovec, Yugo.	42	41 32N	20 49 E
Klerksdorp	92	26 51 S	26 38 E
Kleszczele	28	52 35N	23 19 E
Kletnya	54	53 23N	33 12 E
Kletsk	54	53 5N	26 45 E
Kletskiy	57	49 20N	43 0 E
Kleve	24	51 46N	6 10 E
Klickitat	118	45 50N	121 10W
Klimovichi	54	53 36N	32 0 E
Klin	55	56 20N	36 48 E
Klinaklini →	108	51 21N	125 40W
Klintsey	54	52 50N	32 10 E
Klipplaat	92	33 0 S	24 22 E
Klisura	43	42 40N	24 28 E
Klitmøller	49	57 3N	8 30 E
Kljajićevo	42	45 45N	19 17 E
Kljuć	39	44 32N	16 48 E
Kłobuck	28	50 55N	18 55 E
Kłodawa	28	52 15N	18 55 E
Kłodzko	28	50 28N	16 38 E
Klondike	104	64 0N	139 26W
Klosi	44	41 28N	20 10 E
Klosterneuburg	27	48 18N	16 19 E
Klosters	25	46 52N	9 52 E
Klötze	24	52 38N	11 9 E
Klouto	85	6 57N	0 44 E
Kluane L.	104	61 15N	138 40W
Kluczbork	28	50 58N	18 12 E
Klyuchevskaya, Guba	59	55 50N	160 30 E
Knaresborough	12	54 1N	1 29W
Knee L., Man., Can.	109	55 3N	94 45W
Knee L., Sask., Can.	109	55 51N	107 0W
Kneïss, I.	83	34 22N	10 18 E
Knezha	43	43 30N	24 5 E
Knić	42	43 53N	20 45 E
Knight Inlet	108	50 45N	125 40W
Knighton	13	52 21N	3 2W
Knight's Landing	118	38 50N	121 43W
Knin	39	44 1N	16 17 E
Knittelfeld	26	47 13N	14 51 E
Knjaževac	42	43 35N	22 18 E
Knob, C.	96	34 32 S	119 16 E
Knockmealdown Mts.	15	52 16N	8 0W
Knokke	16	51 20N	3 17 E
Knossos	45	35 16N	25 10 E
Knox	114	41 18N	86 36W
Knox, C.	108	54 11N	133 5W
Knox City	117	33 26N	99 49W
Knox Coast	5	66 30 S	108 0 E
Knoxville, Iowa, U.S.A.	116	41 20N	93 5W
Knoxville, Tenn., U.S.A.	115	35 58N	83 57W
Knurów	27	50 13N	18 38 E
Knutshø	47	62 18N	9 41 E
Knysna	92	34 2 S	23 2 E
Knyszyn	28	53 20N	22 56 E
Ko Chang	71	12 0N	102 20 E
Ko Kut	71	11 40N	102 32 E
Ko Phra Thong	71	9 6N	98 15 E
Ko Tao	71	10 6N	99 48 E
Koartac (Notre Dame de Koartac)	105	60 55N	69 40W
Koba, Aru, Indon.	73	6 37 S	134 37 E
Koba, Bangka, Indon.	72	2 26 S	106 14 E
Kobarid	39	46 15N	13 30 E
Kobayashi	74	31 56N	130 59 E
Kobdo = Hovd	75	48 2N	91 37 E
Kōbe	74	34 45N	135 10 E
Kobelyaki	56	49 11N	34 9 E
København	49	55 41N	12 34 E
Koblenz	25	50 21N	7 36 E
Kobo	87	12 2N	39 56 E
Kobrin	54	52 15N	24 22 E
Kobroor, Kepulauan	73	6 10 S	134 30 E
Kobuleti	57	41 55N	41 45 E
Kobylin	28	51 43N	17 12 E
Kobyłka	28	52 21N	21 10 E
Kobylkino	55	54 8N	43 56 E
Kobylnik	54	54 58N	26 39 E
Kočane	42	43 12N	21 52 E
Kočani	42	41 55N	22 25 E
Koçarlı	45	37 45N	27 43 E
Koceljevo	42	44 28N	19 50 E
Kočevje	39	45 39N	14 50 E
Kochas	69	25 15N	83 56 E
Kocher →	25	49 14N	9 12 E
Kocheya	59	52 32N	120 42 E
Kōchi	74	33 30N	133 35 E
Kōchi □	74	33 40N	133 30 E
Kochiu = Gejiu	75	23 20N	103 10 E
Kock	28	51 38N	22 27 E
Koddiyar Bay	70	8 33N	81 15 E
Kodiak	104	57 30N	152 45W
Kodiak I.	104	57 30N	152 45W
Kodiang	71	6 21N	100 18 E
Kodinar	68	20 46N	70 46 E
Kodori →	57	42 47N	41 10 E
Koes	92	26 0 S	19 15 E
Kofiau	73	1 11 S	129 50 E
Köflach	26	47 4N	15 5 E
Koforidua	85	6 3N	0 17W
Kōfu	74	35 40N	138 30 E
Kogaluk →	107	56 12N	61 44W
Kogin Baba	85	7 55N	11 35 E
Koh-i-Bābā	65	34 30N	67 0 E
Kohat	66	33 40N	71 29 E
Kohima	67	25 35N	94 10 E
Kohler Ra.	5	77 0 S	110 0W
Kohtla Järve	54	59 20N	27 20 E
Kojetin	27	49 21N	17 20 E
Koka	86	20 5N	30 35 E
Kokand	58	40 30N	70 57 E
Kokanee Glacier Prov. Park	108	49 47N	117 10W
Kokas	73	2 42 S	132 26 E
Kokava	27	48 35N	19 50 E
Kokchetav	58	53 20N	69 25 E
Kokemäenjoki →	51	61 32N	21 44 E
Kokhma	55	56 55N	41 18 E
Kokkola (Gamlakarleby)	50	63 50N	23 8 E
Koko	85	11 28N	4 29 E
Koko Kyunzu	71	14 10N	93 25 E
Kokoda	98	8 54 S	147 47 E
Kokolopozo	84	5 8N	6 5W
Kokomo	114	40 30N	86 6W
Kokonau	73	4 43 S	136 26 E
Kokopo	98	4 22 S	152 19 E
Kokoro	85	14 12N	0 55 E
Koksoak →	105	58 30N	68 10W
Kokstad	93	30 32 S	29 29 E
Kokuora	59	71 35N	144 50 E
Kola, Indon.	73	5 35 S	134 30 E
Kola, U.S.S.R.	52	68 45N	33 8 E
Kola Pen. = Kolskiy P-ov.	52	67 30N	38 0 E
Kolahun	84	8 15N	10 4W
Kolaka	73	4 3 S	121 46 E
Kolar	70	13 12N	78 15 E
Kolar Gold Fields	70	12 58N	78 16 E
Kolari	50	67 20N	23 48 E
Kolarovgrad	43	43 18N	26 55 E
Kolašin	42	42 50N	19 31 E
Kolby Kås	49	55 48N	10 32 E
Kolchugino	55	56 17N	39 22 E
Kolda	84	12 55N	14 57W
Kolding	49	55 30N	9 29 E
Kole	88	3 16 S	22 42 E
Koléa	82	36 38N	2 46 E
* Kolepom, Pulau	73	8 0 S	138 30 E
Kolguyev, Ostrov	52	69 20N	48 30 E
Kolhapur	70	16 43N	74 15 E
Kolia	84	9 46N	6 28W
Kolín	26	50 2N	15 9 E
Kolind	49	56 21N	10 34 E
Kölleda	24	51 11N	11 14 E
Kollegal	70	12 9N	77 9 E
Kolleru L.	70	16 40N	81 10 E
Kolmanskop	92	26 45 S	15 14 E
Köln	24	50 56N	6 58 E
Kolno	28	53 25N	21 56 E
Koło	28	52 14N	18 40 E
Kołobrzeg	28	54 10N	15 35 E
Kologriv	55	58 48N	44 25 E
Kolokani	84	13 35N	7 45W
Kolomna	55	55 8N	38 45 E
Kolomyya	56	48 31N	25 2 E
Kolondiéba	84	11 5N	6 54W
Kolonodale	73	2 3 S	121 25 E
Kolosib	67	24 15N	92 45 E
Kolpashevo	58	58 20N	83 5 E
Kolpino	54	59 44N	30 39 E
Kolpny	55	52 12N	37 10 E
Kolskiy Poluostrov	52	67 30N	38 0 E
Kolskiy Zaliv	52	69 23N	34 0 E
Kolubara →	42	44 35N	20 15 E
Kolumna	28	51 36N	19 14 E
Koluszki	28	51 45N	19 46 E
Kolwezi	91	10 40 S	25 25 E
Kolyberovo	55	55 15N	38 40 E
Kolyma →	59	69 30N	161 0 E
Kolymskoye, Okhotsko	59	63 0N	157 0 E
Kôm Ombo	86	24 25N	32 52 E
Komárno	27	47 49N	18 5 E
Komárom	27	47 43N	18 7 E
Komárom □	27	47 35N	18 20 E
Komarovo	54	58 38N	33 40 E
Komatipoort	93	25 25 S	31 55 E
Kombissiri	85	12 4N	1 20W
Kombori	84	13 26N	3 56W
Kombóti	45	39 6N	21 5 E
Komen	39	45 49N	13 45 E
Komenda	85	5 4N	1 28W
Komi A.S.S.R. □	52	64 0N	55 0 E
Komiža	39	43 3N	16 11 E
Komló	27	46 15N	18 16 E
Kommamur Canal	70	16 0N	80 25 E
Kommunarsk	57	48 30N	38 45 E
Kommunizma, Pik	58	39 0N	72 2 E
Komnes	47	59 30N	9 55 E
Komodo	73	8 37 S	119 20 E
Komoé	84	5 12N	3 44W
Komono	88	3 10 S	13 20 E
Komoran, Pulau	73	8 18 S	138 45 E
Komotini	44	41 9N	25 26 E
Komovi	42	42 41N	19 39 E
Kompong Cham	71	12 0N	105 30 E
Kompong Chhnang	71	12 20N	104 35 E
Kompong Speu	71	11 26N	104 32 E
Kompong Thom	71	12 35N	104 51 E
Komrat	56	46 18N	28 40 E
Komsberge	92	32 40 S	20 45 E
Komsomolets, Ostrov	59	80 30N	95 0 E
Komsomolsk, R.S.F.S.R., U.S.S.R.	55	57 2N	40 20 E
Komsomolsk, R.S.F.S.R., U.S.S.R.	59	50 30N	137 0 E
Komsomolskaya	5	66 33 S	93 1 E
Komsomolskiy	55	53 30N	49 30 E
Konakovo	55	56 52N	36 45 E
Konarhá □	65	35 30N	71 3 E
Konawa	117	34 59N	96 46W
Kondagaon	70	19 35N	81 35 E
Kondakovo	59	69 36N	152 0 E
Konde	90	4 57 S	39 45 E
Kondiá	44	39 49N	25 10 E
Kondoa	90	4 55 S	35 50 E
Kondoa □	90	5 0 S	36 0 E
Kondopaga	52	62 12N	34 17 E
Kondratyevo	59	57 22N	98 15 E
Konduga	85	11 35N	13 26 E
Konevo	52	62 8N	39 20 E
Kong	84	8 54N	4 36W
Kong Christian IX.s Land	4	68 0N	36 0W
Kong Christian X.s Land	4	74 0N	29 0W
Kong Franz Joseph Fd.	4	73 20N	24 30W
Kong Frederik IX.s Land	4	67 0N	52 0W
Kong Frederik VI.s Kyst	4	63 0N	43 0W
Kong Frederik VIII.s Land	4	78 30N	26 0W
Kong, Koh	71	11 20N	103 0 E
Kong Oscar Fjord	4	72 20N	24 0W
Konga	49	56 30N	15 6 E
Kongeå	49	55 24N	9 39 E
Kongju	76	36 30N	127 0 E
Konglu	67	27 13N	97 57 E
Kongolo, Kasai Or., Zaïre	90	5 26 S	24 49 E
Kongolo, Shaba, Zaïre	90	5 22 S	27 0 E
Kongor	81	7 1N	31 27 E
Kongoussi	85	13 19N	1 32W
Kongsberg	47	59 39N	9 39 E
Kongsvinger	47	60 12N	12 2 E
Kongwa	90	6 11 S	36 26 E
Koni	91	10 40 S	27 11 E
Koni, Mts.	91	10 36 S	27 10 E
Koniecpol	28	50 46N	19 40 E
Königsberg = Kaliningrad	54	54 42N	20 32 E
Königshofen	25	50 18N	10 29 E
Königslutter	24	52 14N	10 50 E
Königswusterhausen	24	52 19N	13 38 E
Konin	28	52 12N	18 15 E
Konin □	28	52 15N	18 30 E
Konispoli	44	39 42N	20 10 E
Kónitsa	44	40 5N	20 48 E
Konjic	42	43 42N	17 58 E
Konjice	39	46 20N	15 28 E
Konkouré →	84	9 50N	13 42W
Könnern	24	51 40N	11 45 E
Konnur	70	16 14N	74 49 E
Kono	84	8 30N	11 5W
Konongo	85	6 40N	1 15W
Konosha	52	61 0N	40 5 E
Konotop	54	51 12N	33 7 E
Konqi He →	75	40 45N	90 10 E
Końskie	28	51 15N	20 23 E
Konsmo	47	58 16N	7 23 E
Konstantinovka	56	48 32N	37 39 E
Konstantinovski	57	47 33N	41 10 E
Konstantynów Łódźki	28	51 45N	19 20 E
Konstanz	25	47 39N	9 10 E
Kontagora	85	10 23N	5 27 E
Kontum	71	14 24N	108 0 E
Konya	64	37 52N	32 35 E
Konya Ovasi	64	38 30N	33 0 E
Konz	25	49 41N	6 36 E
Konza	90	1 45 S	37 7 E
Koo-wee-rup	100	38 13 S	145 28 E
Koolan I.	96	16 0 S	123 45 E
Kooloonong	99	34 48 S	143 10 E
Koondrook	99	35 33 S	144 8 E
Koorawatha	99	34 2 S	148 33 E
Kooskia	118	46 9N	115 59W
Koostatak	109	51 26N	97 26W
Kootenai →	118	49 15N	117 39W
Kootenay L.	108	49 45N	116 50W
Kootenay Nat. Park	108	51 0N	116 0W
Kopanovka	57	47 28N	46 50 E
Kopaonik Planina	42	43 10N	21 50 E
Kopargaon	70	19 51N	74 28 E
Kópavogur	50	64 6N	21 55W
Koper	39	45 31N	13 44 E
Kopervik	47	59 17N	5 17 E
Kopeysk	58	55 7N	61 37 E
Köping	48	59 31N	16 3 E
Kopiste	39	42 48N	16 42 E
Kopliku	44	42 15N	19 25 E

* *Renamed Yos Sudarso, P.*

Köpmanholmen	**48**	63 10N	18 35 E
Koppal	**70**	15 23N	76 5 E
Koppang	**47**	61 34N	11 3 E
Kopparbergs län □	**48**	61 20N	14 15 E
Koppeh Dāgh	**65**	38 0N	58 0 E
Kopperå	**47**	63 24N	11 50 E
Koppom	**48**	59 43N	12 10 E
Koprivlen	**43**	41 36N	23 53 E
Koprivnica	**39**	46 12N	16 45 E
Koprivshtitsa	**43**	42 40N	24 19 E
Kopychintsy	**54**	49 7N	25 58 E
Kopys	**54**	54 20N	30 17 E
Korab	**42**	41 44N	20 40 E
Korakiána	**44**	39 42N	19 45 E
Koraput	**70**	18 50N	82 40 E
Korba	**69**	22 20N	82 45 E
Korbach	**24**	51 17N	8 50 E
Korça	**44**	40 37N	20 50 E
Korça □	**44**	40 40N	20 50 E
Korčula	**39**	42 57N	17 8 E
Korčulanski Kanal	**39**	43 3N	16 40 E
Kordestan	**64**	35 30N	42 0 E
Kordestān □	**64**	36 0N	47 0 E
Korea Bay	**76**	39 0N	124 0 E
Koregaon	**70**	17 40N	74 10 E
Korenevo	**54**	51 27N	34 55 E
Korenovsk	**57**	45 30N	39 22 E
Korets	**54**	50 40N	27 5 E
Korgus	**86**	19 16N	33 29 E
Korhogo	**84**	9 29N	5 28W
Koribundu	**84**	7 41N	11 46W
Korim	**73**	0 58 S	136 10 E
Korinthía □	**45**	37 50N	22 35 E
Korinthiakós Kólpos	**45**	38 16N	22 30 E
Kórinthos	**45**	37 56N	22 55 E
Korioumé	**84**	16 35N	3 0W
Kōriyama	**74**	37 24N	140 23 E
Körmend	**27**	47 5N	16 35 E
Kornat	**39**	43 50N	15 20 E
Korneshty	**56**	47 21N	28 1 E
Korneuburg	**27**	48 20N	16 20 E
Kornsjø	**47**	58 57N	11 39 E
Kornstad	**47**	62 59N	7 27 E
Koro, Fiji	**101**	17 19 S	179 23 E
Koro, Ivory C.	**84**	8 32N	7 30W
Koro, Mali	**84**	14 1N	2 58W
Koro Sea	**101**	17 30 S	179 45W
Korocha	**55**	50 55N	37 30 E
Korogwe	**90**	5 5 S	38 25 E
Korogwe □	**90**	5 0 S	38 20 E
Koroit	**99**	38 18 S	142 24 E
Koróni	**45**	36 48N	21 57 E
Korónia, Límni	**44**	40 47N	23 37 E
Koronís	**45**	37 12N	25 35 E
Koronowo	**28**	53 19N	17 55 E
Koror	**73**	7 20N	134 28 E
Körös →	**27**	46 43N	20 12 E
Köröstarcsa	**27**	46 53N	21 3 E
Korosten	**54**	50 57N	28 25 E
Korotoyak	**55**	51 1N	39 2 E
Korraraika, Helodranon' i	**93**	17 45 S	43 57 E
Korsakov	**59**	46 36N	142 42 E
Korshunovo	**59**	58 37N	110 10 E
Korsun Shevchenkovskiy	**56**	49 26N	31 16 E
Korsze	**28**	54 11N	21 9 E
Korti	**86**	18 6N	31 33 E
Kortrijk	**16**	50 50N	3 17 E
Korwai	**68**	24 7N	78 5 E
Koryakskiy Khrebet	**59**	61 0N	171 0 E
Kos	**45**	36 50N	27 15 E
Kosa	**87**	7 50N	36 50 E
Kosaya Gora	**55**	54 10N	37 30 E
Koschagyl	**53**	46 40N	54 0 E
Kościan	**28**	52 5N	16 40 E
Kościerzyna	**28**	54 8N	17 59 E
Kosciusko	**117**	33 3N	89 34W
Kosciusko I.	**108**	56 0N	133 40W
Kosciusko, Mt.	**97**	36 27 S	148 16 E
Kösély →	**27**	47 25N	21 5 E
Kosgi	**70**	16 58N	77 43 E
Kosha	**86**	20 50N	30 30 E
K'oshih = Kashi	**75**	39 30N	76 2 E
Koshk-e Kohneh	**65**	34 55N	62 30 E
Kosi	**68**	27 48N	77 29 E
Kosi-meer	**93**	27 0 S	32 50 E
Košice	**27**	48 42N	21 15 E
Kosjerić	**42**	44 0N	19 55 E
Koslan	**52**	63 28N	48 52 E
Kosŏng	**76**	38 40N	128 22 E
Kosovo, Pokrajina	**42**	42 40N	21 5 E
Kosovo, Soc. Aut. Pokrajina □	**42**	42 30N	21 0 E
Kosovska-Mitrovica	**42**	42 54N	20 52 E
Kostajnica	**39**	45 17N	16 30 E
Kostamuksa	**52**	62 34N	32 44 E
Kostanjevica	**39**	45 51N	15 27 E
Kostelec	**27**	50 14N	16 35 E
Kostenets	**43**	42 15N	23 52 E
Koster	**92**	25 52 S	26 54 E
Kôstî	**87**	13 8N	32 43 E
Kostolac	**42**	44 37N	21 15 E
Kostopol	**54**	50 51N	26 22 E
Kostroma	**55**	57 50N	40 58 E
Kostromskoye Vdkhr.	**55**	57 52N	40 49 E
Kostrzyn, Poland	**28**	52 24N	17 14 E
Kostrzyn, Poland	**28**	52 35N	14 39 E
Kostyukovichi	**54**	53 20N	32 4 E
Koszalin	**28**	53 50N	16 8 E
Koszalin □	**28**	53 40N	16 10 E
Köszeg	**27**	47 23N	16 33 E
Kot Adu	**68**	30 30N	71 0 E
Kot Moman	**68**	32 13N	73 0 E
Kota	**68**	25 14N	75 49 E
Kota Baharu	**71**	6 7N	102 14 E
Kota Belud	**72**	6 21N	116 26 E
Kota Kinabalu	**72**	6 0N	116 4 E
Kota Tinggi	**71**	1 44N	103 53 E
Kotaagung	**72**	5 38 S	104 29 E
Kotabaru	**72**	3 20 S	116 20 E
Kotabumi	**72**	4 49 S	104 54 E
Kotagede	**73**	7 54 S	110 26 E
Kotamobagu	**73**	0 57N	124 31 E
Kotaneelee →	**108**	60 11N	123 42W
Kotawaringin	**72**	2 28 S	111 27 E
Kotcho L.	**108**	59 7N	121 12W
Kotel	**43**	42 52N	26 26 E
Kotelnich	**55**	58 20N	48 10 E
Kotelnikovo	**57**	47 38N	43 8 E
Kotelnyy, Ostrov	**59**	75 10N	139 0 E
Kothagudam	**70**	17 30N	80 40 E
Kothapet	**70**	19 21N	79 28 E
Köthen	**24**	51 44N	11 59 E
Kothi	**69**	24 45N	80 40 E
Kotiro	**68**	26 17N	67 13 E
Kotka	**51**	60 28N	26 58 E
Kotlas	**52**	61 15N	47 0 E
Kotlenska Planina	**43**	42 56N	26 30 E
Kotli	**66**	33 30N	73 55 E
Kotonkoro	**85**	11 3N	5 58 E
Kotor	**42**	42 25N	18 47 E
Kotor Varoš	**42**	44 38N	17 22 E
Kotoriba	**39**	46 23N	16 48 E
Kotovo	**55**	50 22N	44 45 E
Kotovsk	**56**	47 45N	29 35 E
Kotputli	**68**	27 43N	76 12 E
Kotri	**68**	25 22N	68 22 E
Kotri →	**70**	19 15N	80 35 E
Kótronas	**45**	36 38N	22 29 E
Kötschach-Mauthen	**26**	46 41N	13 1 E
Kottayam	**70**	9 35N	76 33 E
Kottur	**70**	10 34N	76 56 E
Kotuy →	**59**	71 54N	102 6 E
Kotzebue	**104**	66 50N	162 40W
Kouango	**88**	5 0N	20 10 E
Koudougou	**84**	12 10N	2 20W
Koufonisi	**45**	34 56N	26 8 E
Koufonísia	**45**	36 57N	25 35 E
Kougaberge	**92**	33 48 S	23 50 E
Kouibli	**84**	7 15N	7 14W
Kouilou →	**88**	4 10 S	12 5 E
Kouki	**88**	7 22N	17 3 E
Koula Moutou	**88**	1 15 S	12 25 E
Koulen	**71**	13 50N	104 40 E
Koulikoro	**84**	12 40N	7 50W
Koumala	**98**	21 38 S	149 15 E
Koumankou	**84**	11 58N	6 6W
Koumbia, Guin.	**84**	11 48N	13 29W
Koumbia, Upp. Vol.	**84**	11 10N	3 50W
Koumboum	**84**	10 25N	13 0W
Koumpenntoum	**84**	13 59N	14 34W
Koumra	**81**	8 50N	17 35 E
Koundara	**84**	12 29N	13 18W
Kounradskiy	**58**	46 59N	75 0 E
Kountze	**117**	30 20N	94 22W
Koupéla	**85**	12 11N	0 21W
Kourizo, Passe de	**83**	22 28N	15 27 E
Kouroussa	**84**	10 45N	9 45W
Koussané	**84**	14 53N	11 14W
Kousseri	**81**	12 0N	14 55 E
Koutiala	**84**	12 25N	5 23W
Kouto	**84**	9 53N	6 25W
Kouvé	**85**	6 25N	1 25 E
Kovačica	**42**	45 5N	20 38 E
Kovdor	**52**	67 34N	30 24 E
Kovel	**54**	51 10N	24 20 E
Kovilpatti	**70**	9 10N	77 50 E
Kovin	**42**	44 44N	20 59 E
Kovrov	**55**	56 25N	41 25 E
Kovur, Andhra Pradesh, India	**70**	17 3N	81 39 E
Kovur, Andhra Pradesh, India	**70**	14 30N	80 1 E
Kowal	**28**	52 32N	19 7 E
Kowalewo Pomorskie	**28**	53 10N	18 52 E
Kowkash	**106**	50 20N	87 12W
Kowloon	**75**	22 20N	114 15 E
Koyabuti	**73**	2 36 S	140 37 E
Koyan, Pegunungan	**72**	3 15N	114 30 E
Koyuk	**104**	64 55N	161 20W
Koyukuk →	**104**	64 56N	157 30W
Koyulhisar	**56**	40 20N	37 52 E
Koza	**77**	26 19N	127 46 E
Kozan	**64**	37 35N	35 50 E
Kozáni	**44**	40 19N	21 47 E
Kozáni □	**44**	40 18N	21 45 E
Kozara	**39**	45 0N	17 0 E
Kozarac	**39**	44 58N	16 48 E
Kozelsk	**54**	54 2N	35 48 E
Kozhikode = Calicut	**70**	11 15N	75 43 E
Kozhva	**52**	65 10N	57 0 E
Koziegłowy	**28**	50 37N	19 8 E
Kozienice	**28**	51 35N	21 34 E
Kozje	**39**	46 5N	15 35 E
Kozle	**28**	50 20N	18 8 E
Kozloduy	**43**	43 45N	23 42 E
Kozlovets	**43**	43 30N	25 20 E
Koźmin	**28**	51 48N	17 27 E
Kozmodemyansk	**55**	56 20N	46 36 E
Kozuchów	**28**	51 45N	15 31 E
Kpabia	**85**	9 10N	0 20W
Kpalimé	**85**	6 57N	0 44 E
Kpandae	**85**	8 30N	0 2W
Kpessi	**85**	8 4N	1 16 E
Kra Buri	**71**	10 22N	98 46 E
Kra, Isthmus of = Kra, Kho Khot	**71**	10 15N	99 30 E
Kra, Kho Khot	**71**	10 15N	99 30 E
Kragan	**73**	6 43 S	111 38 E
Kragerø	**47**	58 52N	9 25 E
Kragujevac	**42**	44 2N	20 56 E
Krajenka	**28**	53 18N	16 59 E
Krakatau = Rakata, Pulau	**72**	6 10 S	105 20 E
Kraków	**27**	50 4N	19 57 E
Kraków □	**27**	50 0N	20 0 E
Kraksaan	**73**	7 43 S	113 23 E
Kråkstad	**47**	59 39N	10 55 E
Králiky	**27**	50 6N	16 45 E
Kraljevo	**42**	43 44N	20 41 E
Kralovice	**26**	49 59N	13 29 E
Královský Chlmec	**27**	48 27N	22 0 E
Kralupy	**26**	50 13N	14 20 E
Kramatorsk	**56**	48 50N	37 30 E
Kramer	**119**	35 0N	117 38W
Kramfors	**48**	62 55N	17 48 E
Kramis, C.	**82**	36 26N	0 45 E
Krångede	**48**	63 9N	16 10 E
Kraniá	**44**	39 53N	21 18 E
Kranidhion	**45**	37 20N	23 10 E
Kranj	**39**	46 16N	14 22 E
Kranjska Gora	**39**	46 29N	13 48 E
Krapina	**39**	46 10N	15 52 E
Krapina →	**39**	45 50N	15 50 E
Krapivna	**55**	53 58N	37 10 E
Krapkowice	**28**	50 29N	17 56 E
Krasavino	**52**	60 58N	46 29 E
Kraskino	**59**	42 44N	130 48 E
Kraslice	**26**	50 19N	12 31 E
Krasnaya Gorbatka	**55**	55 52N	41 45 E
Krasnaya Polyana	**57**	43 40N	40 13 E
Kraśnik	**28**	50 55N	22 5 E
Kraśnik Fabryczny	**28**	50 58N	22 11 E
Krasnoarmeisk	**56**	48 18N	37 11 E
Krasnoarmeysk, R.S.F.S.R., U.S.S.R.	**55**	51 0N	45 42 E
Krasnoarmeysk, R.S.F.S.R., U.S.S.R.	**57**	48 30N	44 25 E
Krasnodar	**57**	45 5N	39 0 E
Krasnodon	**57**	48 17N	39 44 E
Krasnodonetskaya	**57**	48 5N	40 50 E
Krasnogorskiy	**55**	56 10N	48 28 E
Krasnograd	**56**	49 27N	35 27 E
Krasnogvardeyskoye	**57**	45 52N	41 33 E
Krasnogvardyesk	**56**	45 32N	34 16 E
Krasnokamsk	**52**	58 4N	55 48 E
Krasnokutsk	**54**	50 10N	34 50 E
Krasnoperekopsk	**56**	46 0N	33 54 E
Krasnoselkupsk	**58**	65 20N	82 10 E
Krasnoslobodsk, R.S.F.S.R., U.S.S.R.	**55**	54 25N	43 45 E
Krasnoslobodsk, R.S.F.S.R., U.S.S.R.	**57**	48 42N	44 33 E
Krasnoturinsk	**58**	59 46N	60 12 E
Krasnoufimsk	**52**	56 57N	57 46 E
Krasnouralsk	**52**	58 21N	60 3 E
Krasnovishersk	**52**	60 23N	57 3 E
Krasnovodsk	**53**	40 0N	52 52 E
Krasnoyarsk	**59**	56 8N	93 0 E
Krasnoye, Kalmyk A.S.S.R., U.S.S.R.	**57**	46 16N	45 0 E
Krasnoye, R.S.F.S.R., U.S.S.R.	**55**	59 15N	47 40 E
Krasnoye = Krasnyy	**54**	54 25N	31 30 E
Krasnozavodsk	**55**	56 27N	38 25 E
Krasny Liman	**56**	48 58N	37 50 E
Krasny Sulin	**57**	47 52N	40 8 E
Krasnystaw	**28**	50 57N	23 5 E
Krasnyy	**54**	54 25N	31 30 E
Krasnyy Kholm	**55**	58 10N	37 10 E
Krasnyy Kut	**55**	50 50N	47 0 E
Krasnyy Luch	**57**	48 13N	39 0 E
Krasnyy Profintern	**55**	57 45N	40 27 E
Krasnyy Yar, Kalmyk A.S.S.R., U.S.S.R.	**57**	46 43N	48 23 E
Krasnyy Yar, R.S.F.S.R., U.S.S.R.	**55**	53 30N	50 22 E
Krasnyy Yar, R.S.F.S.R., U.S.S.R.	**55**	50 42N	44 45 E
Krasnyye Baki	**55**	57 8N	45 10 E
Krasnyyoskolskoye Vdkhr.	**56**	49 30N	37 30 E
Kraszna →	**27**	48 0N	22 20 E
Kratie	**71**	12 32N	106 10 E
Kratovo	**42**	42 6N	22 10 E
Krau	**73**	3 19 S	140 5 E
Kravanh, Chuor Phnum	**71**	12 0N	103 32 E
Krawang	**73**	6 19N	107 18 E
Krefeld	**24**	51 20N	6 32 E
Krémaston, Límni	**45**	38 52N	21 30 E
Kremenchug	**56**	49 5N	33 25 E
Kremenchugskoye Vdkhr.	**56**	49 20N	32 30 E
Kremenets	**56**	50 8N	25 43 E
Kremenica	**42**	40 55N	21 25 E
Kremennaya	**56**	49 1N	38 10 E
Kremges = Svetlovodsk	**56**	49 5N	33 15 E
Kremikovtsi	**43**	42 46N	23 28 E
Kremmen	**24**	52 45N	13 1 E
Kremmling	**118**	40 10N	106 30W
Kremnica	**27**	48 45N	18 50 E
Krems	**26**	48 25N	15 36 E
Kremsmünster	**26**	48 3N	14 8 E
Kretinga	**54**	55 53N	21 15 E
Krettamia	**82**	28 47N	3 27W
Krettsy	**54**	58 15N	32 30 E
Kreuzberg	**25**	50 22N	9 58 E
Kribi	**88**	2 57N	9 56 E
Krichem	**43**	42 8N	24 28 E
Krichev	**54**	53 45N	31 50 E
Krim	**39**	45 53N	14 30 E
Krionéri	**45**	38 20N	21 35 E
Krishna →	**70**	15 57N	80 59 E
Krishnagiri	**70**	12 32N	78 16 E
Krishnanagar	**69**	23 24N	88 33 E
Krishnaraja Sagara	**70**	12 20N	76 30 E
Kristiansand	**47**	58 9N	8 1 E
Kristianstad	**49**	56 2N	14 9 E
Kristiansund	**47**	63 7N	7 45 E
Kristiinankaupunki	**50**	62 16N	21 21 E
Kristinehamn	**48**	59 18N	14 13 E
Kristinestad	**50**	62 16N	21 21 E
Kríti	**45**	35 15N	25 0 E
Kritsá	**45**	35 10N	25 41 E
Kriva →	**42**	42 5N	21 47 E
Kriva Palanka	**42**	42 11N	22 19 E
Krivaja →	**42**	44 27N	18 9 E
Krivelj	**42**	44 8N	22 5 E
Krivoy Rog	**56**	47 51N	33 20 E
Križevci	**39**	46 3N	16 32 E
Krk	**39**	45 8N	14 40 E
Krka →	**39**	45 50N	15 30 E
Krkonoše	**26**	50 50N	15 35 E
Krnov	**27**	50 5N	17 40 E
Krobia	**28**	51 47N	16 59 E
Kročehlavy	**26**	50 8N	14 9 E
Krøderen	**47**	60 9N	9 49 E
Krokawo	**28**	54 47N	18 9 E
Krokeaí	**45**	36 53N	22 32 E
Krokom	**48**	63 20N	14 30 E
Krolevets	**54**	51 35N	33 20 E
Kroměříž	**27**	49 18N	17 21 E
Krompachy	**27**	48 54N	20 52 E
Kromy	**54**	52 40N	35 48 E
Kronach	**25**	50 14N	11 19 E
Kronobergs län □	**49**	56 45N	14 30 E
Kronprins Olav Kyst	**5**	69 0 S	42 0 E
Kronprinsesse Märtha Kyst	**5**	73 30 S	10 0 E
Kronshtadt	**54**	60 5N	29 45 E
Kroonstad	**92**	27 43 S	27 19 E
Kröpelin	**24**	54 4N	11 48 E
Kropotkin, R.S.F.S.R., U.S.S.R.	**57**	45 28N	40 28 E
Kropotkin, R.S.F.S.R., U.S.S.R.	**59**	59 0N	115 30 E
Kropp	**24**	54 24N	9 32 E
Krościenko	**27**	49 29N	20 25 E
Krośniewice	**28**	52 15N	19 11 E
Krosno	**27**	49 42N	21 46 E
Krosno □	**27**	49 35N	22 0 E
Krosno Odrzańskie	**28**	52 3N	15 7 E
Krotoszyn	**28**	51 42N	17 23 E
Krraba	**44**	41 13N	20 0 E
Krško	**39**	45 57N	15 30 E
Krstača	**42**	42 57N	20 8 E
Kruger Nat. Park	**93**	24 0 S	31 40 E
Krugersdorp	**93**	26 5 S	27 46 E
Kruis, Kaap	**92**	21 55 S	13 57 E
Kruja	**44**	41 32N	19 46 E
Krulevshchina	**54**	55 5N	27 45 E
Kruma	**44**	42 14N	20 28 E
Krumbach	**25**	48 15N	10 22 E
Krumovgrad	**43**	41 29N	25 38 E
Krung Thep	**71**	13 45N	100 35 E
Krupanj	**42**	44 25N	19 22 E
Krupina	**27**	48 22N	19 5 E
Krupinica →	**27**	48 15N	18 52 E
Kruševac	**42**	43 35N	21 28 E
Kruševo	**42**	41 23N	21 19 E
Kruszwica	**28**	52 40N	18 20 E
Kruzof I.	**108**	57 10N	135 40W
Krylbo	**48**	60 7N	16 15 E
Krymsk Abinsk	**56**	44 50N	38 0 E
Krymskiy P-ov.	**56**	45 0N	34 0 E
Krynica	**27**	49 25N	20 57 E
Krynica Morska	**28**	54 23N	19 28 E
Krynki	**28**	53 17N	23 43 E
Krzepice	**28**	50 58N	18 50 E
Krzeszów	**28**	50 24N	22 21 E
Krzeszowice	**27**	50 8N	19 37 E
Krzna →	**28**	51 59N	22 47 E
Krzywiń	**28**	51 58N	16 50 E
Krzyz	**28**	52 52N	16 0 E
Ksabi	**82**	32 51N	4 13W
Ksar Chellala	**82**	35 13N	2 19 E
Ksar el Boukhari	**82**	35 51N	2 52 E
Ksar el Kebir	**82**	35 0N	6 0W
Ksar es Souk = Ar Rachidiya	**82**	31 58N	4 20W
Ksar Rhilane	**83**	33 0N	9 39 E
Ksiba, El	**82**	32 46N	6 0W
Ksour, Mts. des	**82**	32 45N	0 30W
Kstovo	**55**	56 12N	44 13 E
Kuala	**72**	2 55N	105 47 E
Kuala Kangsar	**71**	4 46N	100 56 E
Kuala Kerai	**71**	5 30N	102 12 E
Kuala Kubu Baharu	**71**	3 34N	101 39 E
Kuala Lipis	**71**	4 10N	102 '3 E
Kuala Lumpur	**71**	3 9N	101 41 E
Kuala Sedili Besar	**71**	1 55N	104 5 E
Kuala Terengganu	**72**	5 20N	103 8 E
Kualakapuas	**72**	2 55 S	114 20 E
Kualakurun	**72**	1 10 S	113 50 E
Kualapembuang	**72**	3 14 S	112 38 E
Kualasimpang	**72**	4 17N	98 3 E
Kuandang	**73**	0 56N	123 1 E
Kuandian	**76**	40 45N	124 45 E
Kuangchou = Guangzhou	**75**	23 5N	113 10 E
Kuantan	**71**	3 49N	103 20 E
Kuba	**57**	41 21N	48 32 E
Kubak	**66**	27 10N	63 10 E
Kuban →	**56**	45 20N	37 30 E
Kubenskoye, Oz.	**55**	59 40N	39 25 E
Kuberle	**57**	47 0N	42 20 E
Kubrat	**43**	43 49N	26 31 E
Kučevo	**42**	44 30N	21 40 E
Kuchaman	**68**	27 13N	74 47 E
Kuchenspitze	**26**	47 7N	10 12 E
Kuching	**72**	1 33N	110 25 E
Kuçove = Qytet Stalin	**44**	40 47N	19 57 E
Kücük Kuyu	**44**	39 35N	26 27 E
Kudalier →	**70**	18 35N	79 48 E
Kudat	**72**	6 55N	116 55 E
Kudremukh, Mt.	**70**	13 15N	75 20 E
Kudus	**73**	6 48 S	110 51 E
Kudymkar	**58**	59 1N	54 39 E
Kueiyang = Guiyang	**75**	26 32N	106 40 E
Kufrinjah	**62**	32 20N	35 41 E
Kufstein	**26**	47 35N	12 11 E
Kugong I.	**106**	56 18N	79 50W
Kūh-e 'Alijūq	**65**	31 30N	51 41 E
Kūh-e Dīnār	**65**	30 40N	51 0 E
Kūh-e-Hazārān	**65**	29 35N	57 20 E
Kūh-e-Jebāl Bārez	**65**	29 0N	58 0 E
Kūh-e Sorkh	**65**	35 30N	58 45 E
Kūh-e Taftān	**65**	28 40N	61 0 E
Kūhak	**65**	27 12N	63 10 E
Kūhhā-ye-Bashākerd	**65**	26 45N	59 0 E
Kūhhā-ye Sabalān	**64**	38 15N	47 45 E
Kuhnsdorf	**26**	46 37N	14 38 E
Kūhpāyeh	**65**	32 44N	52 20 E
Kuile He →	**76**	49 32N	124 42 E
Kuito	**89**	12 22 S	16 55 E
Kukavica	**42**	42 48N	21 57 E
Kukawa	**85**	12 58N	13 27 E
Kukësi	**44**	42 5N	20 20 E
Kukësi □	**44**	42 25N	20 15 E
Kukmor	**55**	56 11N	50 54 E
Kukvidze	**55**	50 40N	43 15 E
Kula, Bulg.	**42**	43 52N	22 36 E
Kula, Yugo.	**42**	45 37N	19 32 E
Kulai	**71**	1 44N	103 35 E
Kulal, Mt.	**90**	2 42N	36 57 E
Kulaly, O.	**57**	45 0N	50 0 E
Kulasekharapattanam	**70**	8 20N	78 0 E
Kuldiga	**54**	56 58N	21 59 E
Kuldja = Yining	**75**	43 58N	81 10 E
Kuldu	**87**	12 50N	28 30 E
Kulebaki	**55**	55 22N	42 25 E
Kulen Vakuf	**39**	44 35N	16 2 E

Kuli Lampang

Kuli 57 42 2N 47 12 E
Küllük 45 37 12N 27 36 E
Kulm 116 46 22N 98 58W
Kulmbach 25 50 6N 11 27 E
Kulsary 58 46 59N 54 1 E
Kultay 57 45 5N 51 40 E
Kulti 69 23 43N 86 50 E
Kulunda 58 52 35N 78 57 E
Kulwin 99 35 0S 142 42 E
Kulyab 58 37 55N 69 50 E
Kum Tekei 58 43 10N 79 30 E
Kuma → 57 44 55N 47 0 E
Kumaganum 85 13 8N 10 38 E
Kumagaya 74 36 9N 139 22 E
Kumai 72 2 44S 111 43 E
Kumamba, Kepulauan 73 1 36S 138 45 E
Kumamoto 74 32 45N 130 45 E
Kumamoto □ 74 32 55N 130 55 E
Kumanovo 42 42 9N 21 42 E
Kumara 101 42 37S 171 12 E
Kumasi 84 6 41N 1 38W
Kumba 88 4 36N 9 24 E
Kumbakonam 70 10 58N 79 25 E
Kumbarilla 99 27 15S 150 55 E
Kumbo 85 6 15N 10 36 E
Kumbukkan Oya → 70 6 35N 81 40 E
Kumeny 55 58 10N 49 47 E
Kumertau 52 52 46N 55 47 E
Kumi 90 1 30N 33 58 E
Kumkale 44 40 0N 26 13 E
Kumla 48 59 8N 15 10 E
Kummerower See 24 53 47N 12 52 E
Kumo 85 10 1N 11 12 E
Kumon Bum 67 26 30N 97 15 E
Kumta 70 14 29N 74 25 E
Kumtorkala 57 43 2N 46 50 E
Kumylzhenskaya 57 49 51N 42 38 E
Kunágota 27 46 26N 21 3 E
Kunama 99 35 35S 148 4 E
Kunashir, Ostrov 59 44 0N 146 0 E
Kunch 68 26 0N 79 10 E
Kunda 54 59 30N 26 34 E
Kundiawa 98 6 2S 145 1 E
Kundla 68 21 21N 71 25 E
Kungala 99 29 58S 153 7 E
Kungälv 49 57 53N 11 59 E
Kunghit I. 108 52 6N 131 3W
Kungrad 58 43 6N 58 54 E
Kungsbacka 49 57 30N 12 5 E
Kungur 52 57 25N 56 57 E
Kungurri 98 21 3S 148 46 E
Kunhegyes 27 47 22N 20 36 E
Kuningan 73 6 59S 108 29 E
Kunlong 67 23 20N 98 50 E
Kunlun Shan 75 36 0N 85 0 E
Kunmadaras 27 47 28N 20 45 E
Kunming 75 25 1N 102 41 E
Kunnamkulam 70 10 38N 76 7 E
Kunsan 76 35 59N 126 45 E
Kunshan 77 31 22N 120 58 E
Kunszentmárton 27 46 50N 20 20 E
Kununurra 96 15 40S 128 50 E
Kunwarara 98 22 55S 150 9 E
Kunya-Urgenoh 58 42 19N 59 10 E
Künzelsau 25 49 17N 9 41 E
Kuopio 50 62 53N 27 35 E
Kuopion lääni □ 50 63 25N 27 10 E
Kupa → 39 45 28N 16 24 E
Kupang 73 10 19S 123 39 E
Kupres 42 44 1N 17 15 E
Kupyansk 56 49 52N 37 35 E
Kupyansk-Uzlovoi 56 49 45N 37 34 E
Kuqa 75 41 35N 82 30 E
Kura → 57 39 50N 49 20 E
Kuranda 98 16 48S 145 35 E
Kurashiki 74 34 40N 133 50 E
Kurayoshi 74 35 26N 133 50 E
Kurduvadi 70 18 8N 75 29 E
Kürdzhali 43 41 38N 25 21 E
Kure 74 34 14N 132 32 E
Kuressaare = Kingisepp 54 58 15N 22 15 E
Kurgaldzhino 58 50 35N 70 20 E
Kurgan 58 55 26N 65 18 E
Kurganinsk 57 44 54N 40 34 E
Kurgannaya = Kurganinsk 57 44 54N 40 34 E
Kuria Maria I. = Khūryān Mūryān, Jazā 'ir 63 17 30N 55 58 E
Kurichchi 70 11 36N 77 35 E
Kuridala P.O 98 21 16S 140 29 E
Kuril Is. = Kurilskiye Os. 59 45 0N 150 0 E
Kuril Trench 94 44 0N 153 0 E
Kurilsk 59 45 14N 147 53 E
Kurilskiye Ostrova 59 45 0N 150 0 E
Kuring Kuru 92 17 42S 18 32 E
Kurkur 86 23 50N 32 0 E
Kurkūrah 83 31 30N 20 1 E
Kurla 70 19 5N 72 52 E
Kurlovskiy 55 55 25N 40 40 E
Kurmuk 87 10 33N 34 21 E
Kurnool 70 15 45N 78 0 E
Kurovskoye 55 55 35N 38 55 E
Kurow 101 44 44S 170 29 E
Kurów 28 51 23N 22 12 E
Kurrajong 99 33 33S 150 42 E
Kurri Kurri 99 32 50S 151 28 E
Kursavka 57 44 29N 42 32 E
Kuršenai 54 56 1N 23 3 E
Kurseong 69 26 56N 88 18 E
Kursk 55 51 42N 36 11 E
Kuršumlija 42 43 9N 21 19 E
Kuršumlijska Banja 42 43 3N 21 11 E
Kuru (Chel), Bahr el 87 8 10N 26 50 E
Kuruktag 75 41 0N 89 0 E
Kuruman 92 27 28S 23 28 E
Kurume 74 33 15N 130 30 E
Kurunegala 70 7 30N 80 23 E
Kurya 59 61 15N 108 10 E
Kuşada Körfezı 45 37 56N 27 0 E
Kuşadası 45 37 52N 27 15 E
Kusawa L. 108 60 20N 136 13W
Kusel 25 49 31N 7 25 E
Kushchevskaya 57 46 33N 39 35 E
Kushiro 74 43 0N 144 25 E
Kushiro → 74 42 59N 144 23 E
Kushka 58 35 20N 62 18 E
Kushtia 69 23 55N 89 5 E
Kushum → 57 49 0N 50 20 E
Kushva 52 58 18N 59 45 E
Kuskokwim → 104 60 17N 162 27W
Kuskokwim Bay 104 59 50N 162 56W
Kussharo-Ko 74 43 38N 144 21 E
Kustanay 58 53 10N 63 35 E
Kütahya 64 39 30N 30 2 E
Kutaisi 57 42 19N 42 40 E
Kutaraja = Banda Aceh 72 5 35N 95 20 E
Kutch, G. of 68 22 50N 69 15 E
Kutch, Rann of 68 24 0N 70 0 E
Kutina 39 45 29N 16 48 E
Kutiyana 68 21 36N 70 2 E
Kutjevo 42 45 23N 17 55 E
Kutkashen 57 40 58N 47 47 E
Kutná Hora 26 49 57N 15 16 E
Kutno 28 52 15N 19 23 E
Kuttabul 98 21 5S 148 48 E
Kutu 88 2 40S 18 11 E
Kutum 87 14 10N 24 40 E
Kúty 27 48 40N 17 3 E
Kuvshinovo 54 57 2N 34 11 E
Kuwait = Al Kuwayt 64 29 30N 47 30 E
Kuwait ■ 64 29 30N 47 30 E
Kuwana 74 35 0N 136 43 E
Kuybyshev 58 55 27N 78 19 E
Kuybyshev 58 53 8N 50 6 E
Kuybyshevskoye Vdkhr. 55 55 2N 49 30 E
Küysanjaq 64 36 5N 44 38 E
Kuyto, Oz. 52 64 40N 31 0 E
Kuyumba 59 60 58N 96 59 E
Kuzey Anadolu Dağlari 64 41 30N 35 0 E
Kuzhithura 70 8 18N 77 11 E
Kuzmin 42 45 2N 19 25 E
Kuznetsk 55 53 12N 46 40 E
Kuzomen 52 66 22N 36 50 E
Kvænangen 50 70 5N 21 15 E
Kvam 47 61 40N 9 42 E
Kvamsøy 47 61 7N 6 28 E
Kvareli 57 41 27N 45 47 E
Kvarner 39 44 50N 14 10 E
Kvarnerič 39 44 43N 14 37 E
Kvernes 47 63 1N 7 44 E
Kvillsfors 49 57 24N 15 29 E
Kvine → 47 58 17N 6 56 E
Kvinesdal 47 58 19N 6 57 E
Kviteseid 47 59 24N 8 29 E
Kwabhaga 93 30 51S 29 0 E
Kwadacha → 108 57 28N 125 38W
Kwakhanai 92 21 39S 21 16 E
Kwakoegron 127 5 12N 55 25W
Kwale, Kenya 90 4 15S 39 31 E
Kwale, Nigeria 85 5 46N 6 26 E
Kwale □ 90 4 15S 39 10 E
Kwamouth 88 3 9S 16 12 E
Kwando → 92 18 27S 23 32 E
Kwangsi-Chuang = Guangxi Zhuangzu □ 75 24 0N 109 0 E
Kwangtung = Guangdong □ 75 23 0N 113 0 E
Kwara □ 85 8 0N 5 0 E
Kwataboahegan → 106 51 9N 80 50W
Kwatisore 73 3 18S 134 50 E
Kweichow = Guizhou □ 75 27 0N 107 0 E
Kwidzyn 28 53 44N 18 55 E
Kwiguk 104 63 45N 164 35W
Kwimba □ 90 3 0S 33 0 E
Kwinana 96 32 15S 115 47 E
Kwisa → 28 51 34N 15 24 E
Kwoka 73 0 31S 132 27 E
Kyabé 81 9 30N 19 0 E
Kyabra Cr. → 99 25 36S 142 55 E
Kyabram 99 36 19S 145 4 E
Kyaikto 71 17 20N 97 3 E
Kyakhta 59 50 30N 106 25 E
Kyangin 67 18 20N 95 20 E
Kyaukpadaung 67 20 52N 95 8 E
Kyaukpyu 67 19 28N 93 30 E
Kyaukse 67 21 36N 96 10 E
Kyenjojo 90 0 40N 30 37 E
Kyle Dam 91 20 15S 31 0 E
Kyle of Lochalsh 14 57 17N 5 43W
Kyll → 25 49 48N 6 42 E
Kyllburg 25 50 2N 6 35 E
Kyneton 99 37 10S 144 29 E
Kynuna 98 21 37S 141 55 E
Kyō-ga-Saki 74 35 45N 135 15 E
Kyoga, L. 90 1 35N 33 0 E
Kyogle 99 28 40S 153 0 E
Kyongju 76 35 51N 129 14 E
Kyongpyaw 67 17 12N 95 10 E
Kyōto 74 35 0N 135 45 E
Kyōto □ 74 35 15N 135 45 E
Kyren 59 51 45N 101 45 E
Kyrenia 64 35 20N 33 20 E
Kyritz 24 52 57N 12 25 E
Kystatyam 59 67 20N 123 10 E
Kytal Ktakh 59 65 30N 123 40 E
Kyulyunken 59 64 10N 137 5 E
Kyunhla 67 23 25N 95 15 E
Kyuquot 108 50 3N 127 25W
Kyurdamir 57 40 25N 48 3 E
Kyūshū 74 33 0N 131 0 E
Kyūshū-Sanchi 74 32 35N 131 17 E
Kyustendil 42 42 16N 22 41 E
Kyusyur 59 70 39N 127 15 E
Kywong 99 34 58S 146 44 E
Kyzyl 59 51 50N 94 30 E
Kyzyl-Kiya 58 40 16N 72 8 E
Kyzylkum, Peski 58 42 30N 65 0 E
Kzyl-Orda 58 44 48N 65 28 E

L

Laa 27 48 43N 16 23 E
Laaber → 25 49 0N 12 3 E
Laage 24 53 55N 12 21 E
Laasphe 24 50 56N 8 23 E
Laba → 57 45 11N 39 42 E
Labastide 20 43 28N 2 39 E
Labastide-Murat 20 44 39N 1 33 E
Labbézenga 85 15 2N 0 48 E
Labdah = Leptis Magna 83 32 40N 14 12 E
Labé 84 11 24N 12 16W
Labe = Elbe → 26 50 50N 14 12 E
Laberec → 27 48 37N 21 58 E
Laberge, L. 108 61 11N 135 12W
Labin 39 45 5N 14 8 E
Labinsk 57 44 40N 40 48 E
Labis 71 2 22N 103 2 E
Labiszyn 28 52 57N 17 54 E
Laboe 24 54 25N 10 13 E
Labouheyre 20 44 13N 0 55W
Laboulaye 124 34 10S 63 30W
Labra, Peña 30 43 3N 4 26W
Labrador City 107 52 57N 66 55W
Labrador, Coast of □ 105 53 20N 61 0W
Lábrea 126 7 15S 64 51W
Labrède 20 44 41N 0 32W
Labuan 72 5 21N 115 13 E
Labuha 73 0 30S 127 30 E
Labuhan 73 6 26S 105 50 E
Labuhanbajo 73 8 28S 120 1 E
Labuk, Telok 72 6 10N 117 50 E
Labytnangi 58 66 39N 66 21 E
Łabżenica 28 53 18N 17 15 E
Lac Allard 107 50 33N 63 24W
Lac Bouchette 107 48 16N 72 11W
Lac du Flambeau 116 46 1N 89 51W
Lac Édouard 106 47 40N 72 16W
Lac la Biche 108 54 45N 111 58W
Lac la Martre 104 63 8N 117 16W
Lac-Mégantic 107 45 35N 70 53W
Lac Seul 109 50 28N 92 0W
Lacanau, Étang de 20 44 58N 1 7W
Lacanau-Médoc 20 44 59N 1 5W
Lacantúm → 120 16 36N 90 40W
Lacara → 31 38 55N 6 25W
Lacaune 20 43 43N 2 40 E
Lacaune, Mts. de 20 43 43N 2 50 E
Laccadive Is. = Lakshadweep Is. 60 10 0N 72 30 E
Lacepede B. 99 36 40S 139 40 E
Lacepede Is. 96 16 55S 122 0 E
Lacerdónia 91 18 3S 35 35 E
Lachine 106 45 30N 73 40W
Lachlan → 97 34 22S 143 55 E
Lachmangarh 68 27 50N 75 4 E
Lachute 106 45 39N 74 21W
Lackawanna 114 42 49N 78 50W
Lacolle 113 45 5N 73 22W
Lacombe 108 52 30N 113 44W
Lacona 113 43 37N 76 5W
Láconi 40 39 54N 9 4 E
Laconia 114 43 32N 71 30W
Lacq 20 43 25N 0 35W
Lacrosse 118 46 51N 117 58W
Ladakh Ra. 69 34 0N 78 0 E
Lądekzdrój 28 50 21N 16 53 E
Ládhon → 45 37 40N 21 50 E
Ladik 56 40 57N 35 58 E
Ladismith 92 33 28S 21 15 E
Lādīz 65 28 55N 61 15 E
Ladnun 68 27 38N 74 25 E
Ladoga, L. = Ladozhskoye Oz. 52 61 15N 30 30 E
Ladon 19 48 0N 2 30 E
Ladozhskoye Ozero 52 61 15N 30 30 E
Lady Grey 92 30 43S 27 13 E
Ladybrand 92 29 9S 27 29 E
Ladysmith, Can. 108 49 0N 123 49W
Ladysmith, S. Afr. 93 28 32S 29 46 E
Ladysmith, U.S.A. 116 45 27N 91 4W
Lae 94 6 40S 147 2 E
Læsø 49 57 15N 10 53 E
Læsø Rende 49 57 20N 10 45 E
Lafayette, Colo., U.S.A. 116 40 0N 105 2W
Lafayette, Ga., U.S.A. 115 34 44N 85 15W
Lafayette, La., U.S.A. 117 30 18N 92 0W
Lafayette, Tenn., U.S.A. 115 36 35N 86 0W
Laferte → 108 61 53N 117 44W
Lafia 85 8 30N 8 34 E
Lafiagi 85 8 52N 5 20 E
Lafleche 109 49 45N 106 40W
Lafon 87 5 5N 32 29 E
Laforsen 48 61 56N 15 3 E
Lagan →, Sweden 49 56 56N 13 58 E
Lagan →, U.K. 15 54 35N 5 55W
Lagarfljót → 50 65 40N 14 18W
Lage, Ger. 24 52 0N 8 47 E
Lage, Spain 30 43 13N 9 0W
Lågen →, Oppland, Norway 47 61 8N 10 25 E
Lågen →, Vestfold, Norway 47 59 3N 10 5 E
Lägerdorf 24 53 53N 9 35 E
Laggers Pt. 99 30 52S 153 4 E
Laghân □ 65 34 20N 70 0 E
Laghouat 82 33 50N 2 59 E
Lagnieu 21 45 55N 5 20 E
Lagny 19 48 52N 2 40 E
Lago 41 39 9N 16 8 E
Lagôa 31 37 8N 8 27W
Lagoaça 30 41 11N 6 44W
Lagodekhi 57 41 50N 46 22 E
Lagónegro 41 40 8N 15 45 E
Lagonoy Gulf 73 13 50N 123 50 E
Lagos, Nigeria 85 6 25N 3 27 E
Lagos, Port. 31 37 5N 8 41W
Lagos de Moreno 120 21 21N 101 55W
Lagrange 96 18 45S 121 43 E
Laguardia 32 42 33N 2 35W
Laguépie 20 44 8N 1 57 E
Laguna, Brazil 125 28 30S 48 50W
Laguna, U.S.A. 119 35 3N 107 28W
Laguna Beach 119 33 31N 117 52W
Laguna Dam 119 32 55N 114 30W
Laguna de la Janda 31 36 15N 5 45W
Laguna Limpia 124 26 32S 59 45W
Laguna Madre 120 27 0N 97 20W
Lagunas, Chile 124 21 0S 69 45W
Lagunas, Peru 126 5 10S 75 35W
Laha 76 48 12N 124 35 E
Lahad Datu 73 5 0N 118 20 E
Laharpur 69 27 43N 80 56 E
Lahat 72 3 45S 103 30 E
Lahewa 72 1 22N 97 12 E
Lahijan 64 37 10N 50 6 E
Lahn → 25 50 52N 8 35 E
Laholm 49 56 30N 13 2 E
Laholmsbukten 49 56 30N 12 45 E
Lahontan Res. 118 39 28N 118 58W
Lahore 68 31 32N 74 22 E
Lahore □ 68 31 55N 74 5 E
* Lahr 25 48 20N 7 52 E
Lahti 51 60 58N 25 40 E
Laï 81 9 25N 16 18 E
Lai Chau 71 22 5N 103 3 E
Laibin 75 23 42N 109 14 E
Laidley 99 27 39S 152 20 E
Laifeng 77 29 27N 109 20 E
Laignes 19 47 50N 4 20 E
Laikipia □ 90 0 30N 36 30 E
Laingsburg 92 33 9S 20 52 E
Lairg 14 58 1N 4 24W
Lais 72 3 35S 102 0 E
Laiyang 76 36 59N 120 45 E
Laizhou Wan 76 37 30N 119 30 E
Laja → 120 20 55N 100 46W
Lajere 85 11 58N 11 25 E
Lajes 125 27 48S 50 20W
Lajkovac 42 44 27N 20 14 E
Lajosmizse 27 47 3N 19 32 E
Lakaband 68 31 2N 69 15 E
Lakar 73 8 15S 128 17 E
Lake Andes 116 43 10N 98 32W
Lake Anse 114 46 42N 88 25W
Lake Arthur 117 30 8N 92 40W
Lake Cargelligo 97 33 15S 146 22 E
Lake Charles 117 30 15N 93 10W
Lake City, Colo, U.S.A. 119 38 3N 107 27W
Lake City, Fla., U.S.A. 115 30 10N 82 40W
Lake City, Iowa, U.S.A. 116 42 12N 94 42W
Lake City, Mich., U.S.A. 114 44 20N 85 10W
Lake City, Minn., U.S.A. 116 44 28N 92 21W
Lake City, Pa., U.S.A. 112 42 2N 80 20W
Lake City, S.C., U.S.A. 115 33 51N 79 44W
Lake George 113 43 25N 73 43W
Lake Harbour 105 62 50N 69 50W
Lake Havasu City 119 34 25N 114 29W
Lake Lenore 109 52 24N 104 59W
Lake Louise 108 51 30N 116 10W
Lake Mead Nat. Rec. Area 119 36 0N 114 30W
Lake Mills 116 43 23N 93 33W
Lake Nash 98 20 57S 138 0 E
Lake Providence 117 32 49N 91 12W
Lake River 106 54 30N 82 31W
Lake Superior Prov. Park 106 47 45N 84 45W
Lake Village 117 33 20N 91 19W
Lake Wales 115 27 55N 81 32W
Lake Worth 115 26 36N 80 3W
Lakefield 106 44 25N 78 16W
Lakeland 115 28 0N 82 0W
Lakemba 101 18 13S 178 47W
Lakes Entrance 99 37 50S 148 0 E
Lakeside, Ariz., U.S.A. 119 34 12N 109 59W
Lakeside, Nebr., U.S.A. 116 42 5N 102 24W
Lakeview 118 42 15N 120 22W
Lakewood, N.J., U.S.A. 114 40 5N 74 13W
Lakewood, Ohio, U.S.A. 114 41 28N 81 50W
Lakhaniá 45 35 58N 27 54 E
Lákhi 45 35 24N 23 57 E
Lakhpat 68 23 48N 68 47 E
Laki 50 64 4N 18 14W
Lakin 117 37 58N 101 18W
Lakitusaki → 106 54 21N 82 25W
Lakonía □ 45 36 55N 22 30 E
Lakonikós Kólpos 45 36 40N 22 40 E
Lakota, Ivory C. 84 5 50N 5 30W
Lakota, U.S.A. 116 48 0N 98 22W
Laksefjorden 50 70 45N 26 50 E
Lakselv 50 70 2N 24 56 E
Lakshmi Kantapur 69 22 5N 88 20 E
Lala Ghat 67 24 30N 92 40 E
Lala Musa 68 32 40N 73 57 E
Lalago 90 3 28S 33 58 E
Lalapanzi 91 19 20S 30 15 E
Lalganj 69 25 52N 85 13 E
Lalibela 87 12 2N 39 2 E
Lalin 76 45 12N 127 0 E
Lalín 30 42 40N 8 5W
Lalinde 20 44 50N 0 44 E
Lalitpur 68 24 42N 78 28 E
Lama Kara 85 9 30N 1 15 E
Lamaing 67 15 25N 97 53 E
Lamar, Colo., U.S.A. 116 38 9N 102 35W
Lamar, Mo., U.S.A. 117 37 30N 94 20W
Lamas 126 6 28S 76 31W
Lamastre 21 44 59N 4 35 E
Lambach 26 48 6N 13 51 E
Lamballe 18 48 29N 2 31W
Lambaréné 88 0 41S 10 12 E
Lambasa 101 16 30S 179 10 E
Lambay I. 15 53 30N 6 0W
Lambert 116 47 44N 104 39W
Lambert Glacier 5 71 0S 70 0 E
Lambesc 21 43 39N 5 16 E
Lambi Kyun (Sullivan I.) 71 10 50N 98 20 E
Lámbia 45 37 52N 21 53 E
Lambro → 38 45 8N 9 32 E
Lame 85 45 35N 106 40W
Lame Deer 118 45 45N 106 40W
Lamego 30 41 5N 7 52W
Lamèque 107 47 45N 64 38W
Lameroo 99 35 19S 140 33 E
Lamesa 117 32 45N 101 57W
Lamía 45 38 55N 22 26 E
† Lamitan 73 6 40N 122 10 E
Lammermuir Hills 14 55 50N 2 40W
Lamoille 118 40 47N 115 31W
Lamon Bay 73 14 30N 122 20 E
Lamont 108 53 46N 112 50W
Lampa 126 15 22S 70 22W
Lampang, Thai. 71 18 18N 99 31 E
Lampang, Thai. 71 18 16N 99 32 E

* *Now part of Punjab □*
† *Renamed Isabela*

Lampasas Lenora

Lampasas **117** 31 5N 98 10W
Lampaul **18** 48 28N 5 7W
Lampazos de Naranjo **120** 27 2N 100 32W
Lampedusa **36** 35 36N 12 40 E
Lampeter **13** 52 6N 4 6W
Lampione **83** 35 33N 12 20 E
Lampman **109** 49 25N 102 50W
Lamprechtshausen **26** 48 0N 12 58 E
Lamprey **109** 58 33N 94 8W
Lampung □ **72** 5 30S 104 30 E
Lamu **90** 2 16S 40 55 E
Lamu □ **90** 2 0S 40 45 E
Lamut, Tg. **72** 3 50S 105 58 E
Lamy **119** 35 30N 105 58W
Lan Xian **76** 38 15N 111 35 E
Lan Yu **77** 22 5N 121 35 E
Lanai I. **110** 20 50N 156 55W
Lanak La **69** 34 27N 79 32 E
Lanak'o Shank'ou = Lanak La **69** 34 27N 79 32 E
Lanao, L. **73** 7 52N 124 15 E
Lanark, Can. **113** 45 1N 76 22W
Lanark, U.K. **14** 55 40N 3 48W
Lancashire □ **12** 53 40N 2 30W
Lancaster, Can. **113** 45 10N 74 30W
Lancaster, U.K. **12** 54 3N 2 48W
Lancaster, Calif., U.S.A. **119** 34 47N 118 8W
Lancaster, Ky., U.S.A. **114** 37 40N 84 40W
Lancaster, N.H., U.S.A. **114** 44 27N 71 33W
Lancaster, N.Y., U.S.A. **112** 42 53N 78 43W
Lancaster, Pa., U.S.A. **114** 40 4N 76 19W
Lancaster, S.C., U.S.A. **115** 34 45N 80 47W
Lancaster, Wis., U.S.A. **116** 42 48N 90 43W
Lancaster Sd. **4** 74 13N 84 0W
Lancer **109** 50 48N 108 53W
Lanchow = Lanzhou **76** 36 1N 103 52 E
Lanciano **39** 42 15N 14 22 E
Łancut **27** 50 10N 22 13 E
Lándana **88** 5 11S 12 5 E
Landau, Bayern, Ger. **25** 48 41N 12 41 E
Landau, Rhld-Pfz., Ger. **25** 49 12N 8 7 E
Landeck **26** 47 9N 10 34 E
Landen **16** 50 45N 5 5 E
Lander **118** 42 50N 108 49W
Landerneau **18** 48 28N 4 17W
Landeryd **49** 57 7N 13 15 E
Landes □ **20** 43 57N 0 48W
Landes, Les **20** 44 20N 1 0W
Landete **32** 39 56N 1 25W
Landi Kotal **66** 34 7N 71 6 E
Landivisiau **18** 48 31N 4 6W
Landquart **25** 46 58N 9 32 E
Landrecies **19** 50 7N 3 40 E
Land's End **13** 50 4N 5 43W
Landsberg **25** 48 3N 10 52 E
Landsborough Cr. → **98** 22 28S 144 35 E
Landsbro **49** 57 24N 14 56 E
Landshut **25** 48 31N 12 10 E
Landskrona **49** 55 53N 12 50 E
Landstuhl **25** 49 25N 7 34 E
Landvetter **49** 57 41N 12 17 E
Lanesboro **113** 41 57N 75 34W
Lanett **115** 33 0N 85 15W
Lang Bay **108** 49 45N 124 21W
Lang Shan **76** 41 0N 106 30 E
Lang Son **71** 21 52N 106 42 E
La'nga Co **67** 30 45N 81 15 E
Lángadhás **44** 40 46N 23 2 E
Langádhia **45** 37 43N 22 1 E
Långan → **48** 63 19N 14 44 E
Langara I. **108** 54 14N 133 1W
Langdon **116** 48 47N 98 24W
Langeac **20** 45 7N 3 29 E
Langeais **18** 47 20N 0 24 E
Langeb Baraka → **86** 17 28N 36 50 E
Langeberge, C. Prov., S. Afr. **92** 33 55S 21 40 E
Langeberge, C. Prov., S. Afr. **92** 28 15S 22 33 E
Langeland **49** 54 56N 10 48 E
Langen **25** 49 59N 8 40 E
Langenburg **109** 50 51N 101 43W
Langeness **24** 54 34N 8 35 E
Langenlois **26** 48 29N 15 40 E
Langeoog **24** 53 44N 7 33 E
Langeskov **49** 55 22N 10 35 E
Langesund **47** 59 0N 9 45 E
Länghem **49** 57 36N 13 14 E
Langhirano **38** 44 39N 10 16 E
Langholm **14** 55 9N 2 59W
Langjökull **50** 64 39N 20 12W
Langkawi, P. **71** 6 25N 99 45 E
Langkon **72** 6 30N 116 40 E
Langlade **107** 46 50N 56 20W
Langlois **118** 42 54N 124 26W
Langnau **25** 46 56N 7 47 E
Langogne **20** 44 43N 3 50 E
Langon **20** 44 33N 0 16W
Langøya **50** 68 45N 14 50 E
Langpran, Gunong **72** 1 0N 114 23 E
Langres **19** 47 52N 5 20 E
Langres, Plateau de **19** 47 45N 5 3 E
Langsa **72** 4 30N 97 57 E
Långsele **48** 63 12N 17 4 E
Långshyttan **48** 60 27N 16 2 E
Langtry **117** 29 50N 101 33W
Languedoc **20** 43 58N 4 0 E
Langxiangzhen **76** 39 43N 116 8 E
Langzhong **75** 31 38N 105 58 E
Lanigan **109** 51 51N 105 2W
Lankao **77** 34 48N 114 50 E
Lannemezan **20** 43 8N 0 23 E
Lannilis **18** 48 35N 4 32W
Lannion **18** 48 46N 3 29W
Lanouaille **20** 45 24N 1 9 E
Lansdale **113** 40 14N 75 18W
Lansdowne, Austral. **99** 31 48S 152 30 E
Lansdowne, Can. **113** 44 24N 76 1W
Lansdowne House **106** 52 14N 87 53W
Lansford **113** 40 48N 75 55W
Lansing **114** 42 47N 84 40W
Lanslebourg **21** 45 17N 6 52 E
Lant, Pulau **72** 4 10S 116 0 E
Lanus **124** 34 44S 58 27W
Lanusei **40** 39 53N 9 31 E
Lanxi **77** 29 13N 119 28 E
Lanzarote **80** 29 0N 13 40W
Lanzhou **76** 36 1N 103 52 E
Lanzo Torinese **38** 45 16N 7 29 E
Lao → **41** 39 45N 15 45 E
Lao Cai **71** 22 30N 103 57 E
Laoag **73** 18 7N 120 34 E
Laoang **73** 12 32N 125 8 E
Laoha He → **76** 43 25N 120 35 E
Laois □ **15** 53 0N 7 20W
Laon **19** 49 33N 3 35 E
Laona **114** 45 32N 88 41W
Laos ■ **71** 17 45N 105 0 E
Lapa **125** 25 46S 49 44W
Lapalisse **20** 46 15N 3 38 E
Laparan Cap **73** 6 0N 120 0 E
Lapeer **114** 43 3N 83 20W
Lapi □ **50** 67 0N 27 0 E
Lapland = Lappland **50** 68 7N 24 0 E
Laporte **113** 41 27N 76 30W
Lapovo **42** 44 10N 21 2 E
Lappland **50** 68 7N 24 0 E
Laprairie **113** 45 20N 73 30W
Laprida **124** 37 34S 60 45W
Laptev Sea **59** 76 0N 125 0 E
Lapuş, Munţii **46** 47 20N 23 50 E
Lapush **118** 47 56N 124 33W
Lăpusul → **46** 47 25N 23 40 E
Łapy **28** 52 59N 22 52 E
Lār **65** 27 40N 54 14 E
Larabanga **84** 9 16N 1 56W
Laracha **30** 43 15N 8 35W
Larache **82** 35 10N 6 5W
Laragne-Monteglin **21** 44 18N 5 49 E
Laramie **116** 41 20N 105 38W
Laramie Mts. **116** 42 0N 105 30W
Laranjeiras do Sul **125** 25 23S 52 23W
Larantuka **73** 8 21S 122 55 E
Larap **73** 14 18N 122 39 E
Larat **73** 7 0S 132 0 E
Lårdal **47** 59 25N 8 10 E
Larde **91** 16 28S 39 43 E
Larder Lake **106** 48 5N 79 40W
Lárdhos, Ákra **45** 36 4N 28 10 E
Laredo, Spain **32** 43 26N 3 28W
Laredo, U.S.A. **117** 27 34N 99 29W
Laredo Sd. **108** 52 30N 128 53W
Largentière **21** 44 34N 4 18 E
Largs **14** 55 48N 4 51W
Lari **38** 43 34N 10 35 E
Lariang **73** 1 26S 119 17 E
Larimore **116** 47 55N 97 35W
Larino **41** 41 48N 14 54 E
Lárisa **44** 39 49N 22 28 E
Lárisa □ **44** 39 39N 22 24 E
Larkana **68** 27 32N 68 18 E
Larkollen **47** 59 20N 10 41 E
Larnaca **64** 35 0N 33 35 E
Larne **15** 54 52N 5 50W
Larned **116** 38 15N 99 10W
Larrimah **96** 15 35S 133 12 E
Larsen Ice Shelf **5** 67 0S 62 0W
Larvik **47** 59 4N 10 0 E
Laryak **58** 61 15N 80 0 E
Larzac, Causse du **20** 44 0N 3 17 E
Las Animas **117** 38 8N 103 18W
Las Anod **63** 8 26N 47 19 E
Las Blancos **33** 37 38N 0 49W
Las Brenãs **124** 27 5S 61 7W
Las Cabezas de San Juan **31** 37 0N 5 58W
Las Cascadas **120** 9 5N 79 41W
Las Cruces **119** 32 18N 106 50W
Las Flores **124** 36 10S 59 7W
Las Heras **124** 32 51S 68 49W
Las Khoreh **63** 11 10N 48 20 E
Las Lajas **128** 38 30S 70 25W
Las Lomitas **124** 24 43S 60 35W
Las Marismas **31** 37 5N 6 20W
Las Navas de la Concepción **31** 37 56N 5 30W
Las Navas de Tolosa **31** 38 18N 3 38W
Las Palmas, Argent. **124** 27 8S 58 45W
Las Palmas, Canary Is. **80** 28 7N 15 26W
Las Palmas □ **80** 28 10N 15 28W
Las Piedras **125** 34 44S 56 14W
Las Pipinas **124** 35 30S 57 19W
Las Plumas **128** 43 40S 67 15W
Las Rosas **124** 32 30S 61 35W
Las Tablas **121** 7 49N 80 14W
Las Termas **124** 27 29S 64 52W
Las Varillas **124** 31 50S 62 50W
Las Vegas, N. Mex., U.S.A. **119** 35 35N 105 10W
Las Vegas, Nev., U.S.A. **119** 36 10N 115 5W
Lascano **125** 33 35S 54 12W
Lascaux **20** 45 5N 1 10 E
Lashburn **109** 53 10N 109 40W
Lashio **67** 22 56N 97 45 E
Lashkar **68** 26 10N 78 10 E
Łasin **28** 53 30N 19 2 E
Lasíthi □ **45** 35 5N 25 50 E
Lask **28** 51 34N 19 8 E
Łaskarzew **28** 51 48N 21 36 E
Laško **39** 46 10N 15 16 E
Lassay **18** 48 27N 0 30W
Lassen Pk. **118** 40 29N 121 31W
Last Mountain L. **109** 51 5N 105 14W
Lastoursville **88** 0 55S 12 38 E
Lastovo **39** 42 46N 16 55 E
Lastovski Kanal **39** 42 50N 17 0 E
Latacunga **126** 0 50S 78 35W
Latakia = Al Lādhiqīyah **64** 35 30N 35 45 E
Latchford **106** 47 20N 79 50W
Laterza **41** 40 38N 16 47 E
Lathen **24** 52 51N 7 21 E
Latiano **41** 40 33N 17 43 E
Latina **40** 41 26N 12 53 E
Latisana **39** 45 47N 13 1 E
Latium = Lazio **39** 42 10N 12 30 E
Latorica → **27** 48 28N 21 50 E
Latouche Treville, C. **96** 18 27S 121 49 E
Latrobe **112** 40 19N 79 21W
Latrónico **41** 40 5N 16 0 E
Latrun **62** 31 50N 34 58 E
Latur **70** 18 25N 76 40 E
Latvian S.S.R. □ **54** 56 50N 24 0 E
Lau (Eastern) Group **101** 17 0S 178 30W
Lauchhammer **24** 51 35N 13 48 E
Laudal **47** 58 15N 7 30 E
Lauenburg **24** 53 23N 10 33 E
Lauffen **25** 49 4N 9 9 E
Laugarbakki **50** 65 20N 20 55W
Laujar **33** 37 0N 2 54W
Launceston, Austral. **97** 41 24S 147 8 E
Launceston, U.K. **13** 50 38N 4 21W
Laune → **15** 52 5N 9 40W
Launglon Bok **71** 13 50N 97 54 E
Laupheim **25** 48 13N 9 53 E
Laura **97** 15 32S 144 32 E
Laureana di Borrello **41** 38 28N 16 5 E
Laurel, Miss., U.S.A. **117** 31 41N 89 9W
Laurel, Mont., U.S.A. **118** 45 46N 108 49W
Laurencekirk **14** 56 50N 2 30W
Laurens **115** 34 32N 82 2W
Laurentian Plat. **107** 52 0N 70 0W
Laurentides, Parc Prov. des **107** 47 45N 71 15W
Lauria **41** 40 3N 15 50 E
Laurie I. **5** 60 44S 44 37W
Laurie L. **109** 56 35N 101 57W
Laurinburg **115** 34 50N 79 25W
Laurium **114** 47 14N 88 26W
Lausanne **25** 46 32N 6 38 E
Laut, Kepulauan **72** 4 45N 108 0 E
Laut Ketil, Kepulauan **72** 4 45S 115 40 E
Lauterbach **24** 50 39N 9 23 E
Lauterecken **25** 49 38N 7 35 E
Lautoka **101** 17 37S 177 27 E
Lauzon **107** 46 48N 71 10W
Lava Hot Springs **118** 42 38N 112 1W
Lavadores **30** 42 14N 8 41W
Lavagna **38** 44 18N 9 22 E
Laval **18** 48 4N 0 48W
Lavalle **124** 28 15S 65 15W
Lavandou, Le **21** 43 8N 6 22 E
Lávara **44** 41 19N 26 22 E
Lavardac **20** 44 12N 0 20 E
Lavaur **20** 43 30N 1 49 E
Lavaveix **20** 46 5N 2 8 E
Lavelanet **20** 42 57N 1 51 E
Lavello **41** 41 4N 15 47 E
Laverendrye Prov. Park **106** 46 15N 17 15W
Laverne **117** 36 43N 99 58W
Laverton **96** 28 44S 122 29 E
Lavi **62** 32 47N 35 25 E
Lavik **47** 61 6N 5 25 E
Lávkos **45** 39 9N 23 14 E
Lavos **30** 40 6N 8 49W
Lavras **125** 21 20S 45 0W
Lavre **31** 38 46N 8 22W
Lavrentiya **59** 65 35N 171 0W
Lávrion **45** 37 40N 24 4 E
Lavumisa **93** 27 20S 31 55 E
Lawas **72** 4 55N 115 25 E
Lawele **73** 5 16S 123 3 E
Lawn Hill **98** 18 36S 138 33 E
Lawng Pit **67** 25 30N 97 25 E
Lawra **84** 10 39N 2 51W
Lawrence, Kans., U.S.A. **116** 39 0N 95 10W
Lawrence, Mass., U.S.A. **114** 42 40N 71 9W
Lawrenceburg, Ind., U.S.A. **114** 39 5N 84 50W
Lawrenceburg, Tenn., U.S.A. **115** 35 12N 87 19W
Lawrenceville **115** 33 55N 83 59W
Lawton **117** 34 33N 98 25W
Lawu **73** 7 40S 111 13 E
Laxford, L. **14** 58 25N 5 10W
Laxmeshwar **70** 15 9N 75 28 E
Laylá **64** 22 10N 46 40 E
Layon → **18** 47 20N 0 45W
Laysan I. **95** 25 30N 167 0W
Laytonville **118** 39 44N 123 29W
Lazarevac **42** 44 23N 20 17 E
Lazio □ **39** 42 10N 12 30 E
Łazy **28** 50 27N 19 24 E
Lea → **13** 51 30N 0 10W
Lead **116** 44 20N 103 40W
Leader **109** 50 50N 109 30W
Leadhills **14** 55 25N 3 47W
Leadville **119** 39 17N 106 23W
Leaf → **117** 31 0N 88 45W
Leakey **117** 29 45N 99 45W
Leamington, Can. **106** 42 3N 82 36W
Leamington, U.K. **13** 52 18N 1 32W
Leamington, U.S.A. **118** 39 37N 112 17W
Leandro Norte Alem **125** 27 34S 55 15W
Learmonth **96** 22 13S 114 10 E
Leask **109** 53 5N 106 45W
Leavenworth, Mo., U.S.A. **116** 39 25N 95 0W
Leavenworth, Wash., U.S.A. **118** 47 44N 120 37W
Łeba **28** 54 45N 17 32 E
Łeba → **28** 54 46N 17 33 E
Lebak **73** 6 32N 124 5 E
Lebane **42** 42 56N 21 44 E
Lebanon, Ind., U.S.A. **114** 40 3N 86 28W
Lebanon, Kans., U.S.A. **116** 39 50N 98 35W
Lebanon, Ky., U.S.A. **114** 37 35N 85 15W
Lebanon, Mo., U.S.A. **117** 37 40N 92 40W
Lebanon, Oreg., U.S.A. **118** 44 31N 122 57W
Lebanon, Pa., U.S.A. **114** 40 20N 76 28W
Lebanon, Tenn., U.S.A. **115** 36 15N 86 20W
Lebanon ■ **64** 34 0N 36 0 E
Lebec **119** 34 50N 118 59W
Lebedin **54** 50 35N 34 30 E
Lebedyan **55** 53 0N 39 10 E
Lebombo-berge **93** 24 30S 32 0 E
Lębork **28** 54 33N 17 46 E
Lebrija **31** 36 53N 6 5W
Łebsko, Jezioro **28** 54 40N 17 25 E
Lebu **124** 37 40S 73 47W
Lecce **41** 40 20N 18 10 E
Lecco **38** 45 50N 9 27 E
Lecco, L. di. **38** 45 51N 9 22 E
Lécera **32** 41 13N 0 43W
Lech **26** 47 13N 10 9 E
Lech → **25** 48 44N 10 56 E
Lechang **77** 25 10N 113 20 E
Lechtaler Alpen **26** 47 15N 10 30 E
Lectoure **20** 43 56N 0 38 E
Łeczna **28** 51 18N 22 53 E
Łeczyca **28** 52 5N 19 15 E
Ledbury **13** 52 3N 2 25W
Ledeč **26** 49 41N 15 18 E
Ledesma **30** 41 6N 5 59W
Ledong **77** 18 41N 109 5 E
Leduc **108** 53 15N 113 30W
Ledyczek **28** 53 33N 16 59 E
Lee, Mass., U.S.A. **113** 42 17N 73 18W
Lee, Nev., U.S.A. **118** 40 35N 115 36W
Lee → **15** 51 50N 8 30W
Leech L. **116** 47 9N 94 23W
Leedey **117** 35 53N 99 24W
Leeds, U.K. **12** 53 48N 1 34W
Leeds, U.S.A. **115** 33 32N 86 30W
Leek **12** 53 7N 2 2W
Leer **24** 53 13N 7 29 E
Leesburg **115** 28 47N 81 52W
Leesville **117** 31 12N 93 15W
Leeton **97** 34 33S 146 23 E
Leetonia **112** 40 53N 80 45W
Leeuwarden **16** 53 15N 5 48 E
Leeuwin, C. **96** 34 20S 115 9 E
Leeward Is., Atl. Oc. **121** 16 30N 63 30W
Leeward Is., Pac. Oc. **95** 16 0S 147 0W
Lefors **117** 35 30N 100 50W
Lefroy, L. **96** 31 21S 121 40 E
Łeg → **28** 50 42N 21 50 E
Legal **108** 53 55N 113 35W
Legazpi **73** 13 10N 123 45 E
Leghorn = Livorno **38** 43 32N 10 18 E
Legion **91** 21 25S 28 30 E
Legionowo **28** 52 25N 20 50 E
Legnago **39** 45 10N 11 19 E
Legnano **38** 45 35N 8 55 E
Legnica **28** 51 12N 16 10 E
Legnica □ **28** 51 30N 16 0 E
Legrad **39** 46 17N 16 51 E
Legume **99** 28 20S 152 19 E
Leh **69** 34 9N 77 35 E
Lehi **118** 40 20N 111 51W
Lehighton **113** 40 50N 75 44W
Lehliu **46** 44 29N 26 20 E
Lehrte **24** 52 22N 9 58 E
Lehututu **92** 23 54S 21 55 E
Leiah **68** 30 58N 70 58 E
Leibnitz **26** 46 47N 15 34 E
Leicester **13** 52 39N 1 9W
Leicester □ **13** 52 40N 1 10W
Leichhardt → **97** 17 35S 139 48 E
Leichhardt Ra. **98** 20 46S 147 40 E
Leiden **16** 52 9N 4 30 E
Leie → **16** 51 2N 3 45 E
Leigh Creek **97** 30 28S 138 24 E
Leikanger **47** 61 10N 6 52 E
Leine → **24** 52 20N 9 50 E
Leinster □ **15** 53 0N 7 10W
Leinster, Mt. **15** 52 38N 6 47W
Leipzig **24** 51 20N 12 23 E
Leipzig □ **24** 51 20N 12 30 E
Leiria **31** 39 46N 8 53W
Leiria □ **31** 39 46N 8 53W
Leith **14** 55 59N 3 10W
Leith Hill **13** 51 10N 0 23W
Leitha → **27** 48 0N 16 35 E
Leitrim **15** 54 0N 8 5W
Leitrim □ **15** 54 8N 8 0W
Leiyang **77** 26 27N 112 45 E
Leiza **32** 43 5N 1 55W
Leizhou Bandao **77** 21 0N 110 0 E
Leizhou Wan **77** 20 50N 110 20 E
Lek → **16** 52 0N 6 0 E
Lekáni **44** 41 10N 24 35 E
Lekhainá **45** 37 57N 21 16 E
Leksula **73** 3 46S 126 31 E
Leland **117** 33 25N 90 52W
Leland Lakes **109** 60 0N 110 59W
Leleque **128** 42 28S 71 0W
Lelystad **16** 52 30N 5 25 E
Lema **85** 12 58N 4 13 E
Léman, Lac **25** 46 26N 6 30 E
Lemera **90** 3 0S 28 55 E
Lemery **73** 13 51N 120 56 E
Lemgo **24** 52 2N 8 52 E
Lemhi Ra. **118** 44 30N 113 30W
Lemmer **16** 52 51N 5 43 E
Lemmon **116** 45 59N 102 10W
Lemoore **119** 36 23N 119 46W
Lempdes **20** 45 22N 3 17 E
Lemvig **49** 56 33N 8 20 E
Lena → **59** 72 52N 126 40 E
Lenartovce **27** 48 18N 20 19 E
Lencloître **18** 46 50N 0 20 E
Lendinara **39** 45 4N 11 37 E
Lengau de Vaca, Pta. **124** 30 14S 71 38W
Lengerich **24** 52 12N 7 50 E
Lenggong **71** 5 6N 100 58 E
Lenggries **25** 47 41N 11 34 E
Lengyeltóti **27** 46 40N 17 40 E
Lenhovda **49** 57 0N 15 16 E
Lenin **57** 48 20N 40 56 E
Leninabad **58** 40 17N 69 37 E
Leninakan **57** 40 47N 43 50 E
Leningrad **54** 59 55N 30 20 E
Lenino **56** 45 17N 35 46 E
Leninogorsk **58** 50 20N 83 30 E
Leninsk, R.S.F.S.R., U.S.S.R. **57** 48 40N 45 15 E
Leninsk, R.S.F.S.R., U.S.S.R. **58** 46 10N 43 46 E
Leninsk-Kuznetskiy **58** 54 44N 86 10 E
Leninskaya Sloboda **55** 56 7N 44 29 E
Leninskoye, R.S.F.S.R., U.S.S.R. **55** 58 23N 47 3 E
Leninskoye, R.S.F.S.R., U.S.S.R. **59** 47 56N 132 38 E
Lenk **25** 46 27N 7 28 E
Lenkoran **53** 39 45N 48 50 E
Lenmalu **73** 1 45S 130 15 E
Lenne → **24** 51 25N 7 30 E
Lennoxville **113** 45 22N 71 51W
Leno **38** 45 24N 10 14 E
Lenoir **115** 35 55N 81 36W
Lenoir City **115** 35 40N 84 20W
Lenora **116** 39 39N 100 1W

Lithgow Low Rocky Pt.

Lithgow 97 33 25 S 150 8 E
Lithinon, Ákra 45 34 55N 24 44 E
Lithuanian S.S.R. □ 54 55 30N 24 0 E
Litija 39 46 3N 14 50 E
Litókhoron 44 40 8N 22 34 E
Litoměřice 26 50 33N 14 10 E
Litomysl 27 49 52N 16 20 E
Litschau 26 48 58N 15 4 E
Little Abaco I. 121 26 50N 77 30W
Little America 5 79 0 S 160 0W
Little Andaman I. 71 10 40N 92 15 E
Little Barrier I. 101 36 12 S 175 8 E
Little Belt Mts. 118 46 50N 111 0W
Little Blue → 116 39 41N 96 40W
Little Bushman Land 92 29 10 S 18 10 E
Little Cadotte → 108 56 41N 117 6W
Little Churchill → 109 57 30N 95 22W
Little Colorado → 119 36 11N 111 48W
Little Current 106 45 55N 82 0W
Little Current → 106 50 57N 84 36W
Little Falls, Minn., U.S.A. 116 45 58N 94 19W
Little Falls, N.Y., U.S.A. 114 43 3N 74 50W
Little Fork → 116 48 31N 93 35W
Little Grand Rapids 109 52 0N 95 29W
Little Humboldt → 118 41 0N 117 43W
Little Inagua I. 121 21 40N 73 50W
Little Lake 119 35 58N 117 58W
Little Marais 116 47 24N 91 8W
Little Minch 14 57 35N 6 45W
Little Missouri → 116 47 30N 102 25W
Little Namaqualand 92 29 0 S 17 9 E
Little Ouse → 13 52 25N 0 50 E
Little Rann of Kutch 68 23 25N 71 25 E
Little Red → 117 35 11N 91 27W
Little River 101 43 45 S 172 49 E
Little Rock 117 34 41N 92 10W
Little Ruaha → 90 7 57 S 37 53 E
Little Sable Pt. 114 43 40N 86 32W
Little Sioux → 116 41 49N 96 4W
Little Smoky → 108 54 44N 117 11W
Little Snake → 118 40 27N 108 26W
Little Valley 112 42 15N 78 48W
Little Wabash → 114 37 54N 88 5W
Littlefield 117 33 57N 102 17W
Littlefork 116 48 24N 93 35W
Littlehampton 13 50 48N 0 32W
Littleton 114 44 19N 71 47W
Liuba 77 33 38N 106 55 E
Liucheng 77 24 38N 109 14 E
Liukang Tenggaja 73 6 45 S 118 50 E
Liuli 91 11 3 S 34 38 E
Liuwa Plain 89 14 20 S 22 30 E
Liuyang 77 28 10N 113 37 E
Liuzhou 75 24 22N 109 22 E
Livada 46 47 52N 23 5 E
Livadherón 44 40 2N 21 57 E
Livarot 18 49 0N 0 9 E
Live Oak 115 30 17N 83 0W
Livermore, Mt. 117 30 45N 104 8W
Liverpool, Austral. 97 33 54 S 150 58 E
Liverpool, Can. 107 44 5N 64 41W
Liverpool, U.K. 12 53 25N 3 0W
Liverpool Plains 97 31 15 S 150 15 E
Liverpool Ra. 97 31 50 S 150 30 E
Livingston, Guat. 120 15 50N 88 50W
Livingston, U.S.A. 118 45 40N 110 40W
Livingstone, U.S.A. 117 30 44N 94 54W
Livingstone, Zambia 91 17 46 S 25 52 E
Livingstone I. 5 63 0 S 60 15W
Livingstone Memorial 91 12 20 S 30 18 E
Livingstone Mts. 91 9 40 S 34 20 E
Livingstonia 91 10 38 S 34 5 E
Livno 42 43 50N 17 0 E
Livny 55 52 30N 37 30 E
Livorno 38 43 32N 10 18 E
Livramento 125 30 55 S 55 30W
Livron-sur-Drôme 21 44 46N 4 51 E
Liwale 91 9 48 S 37 58 E
Liwale □ 91 9 0 S 38 0 E
Liwiec → 28 52 36N 21 34 E
Lixoúrion 45 38 14N 20 24 E
Lizard I. 98 14 42 S 145 30 E
Lizard Pt. 13 49 57N 5 11W
Lizzano 41 40 23N 17 25 E
Ljig 42 44 13N 20 18 E
Ljubija 39 44 55N 16 35 E
Ljubinje 42 42 58N 18 5 E
Ljubljana 39 46 4N 14 33 E
Ljubno 39 46 25N 14 46 E
Ljubovija 42 44 11N 19 22 E
Ljubuški 42 43 12N 17 34 E
Ljung 49 58 1N 13 3 E
Ljungan → 48 62 18N 17 23 E
Ljungaverk 48 62 30N 16 5 E
Ljungby 49 56 49N 13 55 E
Ljusdal 48 61 46N 16 3 E
Ljusnan → 48 61 12N 17 8 E
Ljusne 48 61 13N 17 7 E
Ljutomer 39 46 31N 16 11 E
Llagostera 32 41 50N 2 54 E
Llancanelo, Salina 124 35 40 S 69 8W
Llandeilo 13 51 53N 4 0W
Llandovery 13 51 59N 3 49W
Llandrindod Wells 13 52 15N 3 23W
Llandudno 12 53 19N 3 51W
Llanelli 13 51 41N 4 11W
Llanes 30 43 25N 4 50W
Llangollen 12 52 58N 3 10W
Llanidloes 13 52 28N 3 31W
Llano 117 30 45N 98 41W
Llano → 117 30 50N 98 25W
Llano Estacado 117 34 0N 103 0W
Llanos 126 5 0N 71 35W
Llera 120 23 19N 99 1W
Llerena 31 38 17N 6 0W
Llico 124 34 46 S 72 5W
Llobregat → 32 41 19N 2 9 E
Lloret de Mar 32 41 41N 2 53 E
Lloyd B. 98 12 45 S 143 27 E
Lloyd L. 109 57 22N 108 57W
Lloydminster 109 53 17N 110 0W
Lluchmayor 33 39 29N 2 53 E
Llullaillaco, volcán 124 24 43 S 68 30W
Loa 119 38 18N 111 40W
Loa → 124 21 26 S 70 41W
Loano 38 44 8N 8 14 E
Lobatse 92 25 12 S 25 40 E
Löbau 24 51 5N 14 42 E
Lobenstein 24 50 25N 11 39 E
Lobería 124 38 10 S 58 40W
Łobez 28 53 38N 15 39 E
Lobito 89 12 18 S 13 35 E
Lobón, Canal de 31 38 50N 6 55W
Lobos 124 35 10 S 59 0W
Lobos, I. 120 27 15N 110 30W
Lobos, Is. 122 6 57 S 80 45W
Lobstick L. 107 54 0N 65 0W
Loc Binh 71 21 46N 106 54 E
Loc Ninh 71 11 50N 106 34 E
Locarno 25 46 10N 8 47 E
Lochaber 14 56 55N 5 0W
Lochcarron 14 57 25N 5 30W
Loche, La 109 56 29N 109 26W
Lochem 16 52 9N 6 26 E
Loches 18 47 7N 1 0 E
Lochgelly 14 56 7N 3 18W
Lochgilphead 14 56 2N 5 37W
Lochinver 14 58 9N 5 15W
Lochnagar, Austral. 98 23 33 S 145 38 E
Lochnagar, U.K. 14 56 57N 3 14W
Łochów 28 52 33N 21 42 E
Lochy → 14 56 52N 5 3W
Lock 99 33 34 S 135 46 E
Lock Haven 114 41 7N 77 31W
Lockeport 107 43 47N 65 4W
Lockerbie 14 55 7N 3 21W
Lockhart, Austral. 99 35 14 S 146 40 E
Lockhart, U.S.A. 117 29 55N 97 40W
Lockney 117 34 7N 101 27W
Lockport 114 43 12N 78 42W
Locle, Le 25 47 3N 6 44 E
Locminé 18 47 54N 2 51W
Locri 41 38 14N 16 14 E
Locronan 18 48 7N 4 15W
Loctudy 18 47 50N 4 12W
Lod 62 31 57N 34 54 E
Lodalskåpa 47 61 47N 7 13 E
Loddon → 100 35 31 S 143 51 E
Lodeinoye Pole 52 60 44N 33 33 E
Lodève 20 43 44N 3 19 E
Lodge Grass 118 45 21N 107 20W
Lodgepole 116 41 12N 102 40W
Lodgepole Cr. → 116 41 20N 104 30W
Lodhran 68 29 32N 71 30 E
Lodi, Italy 38 45 19N 9 30 E
Lodi, U.S.A. 118 38 12N 121 16W
Lodja 90 3 30 S 23 23 E
Lodosa 32 42 25N 2 4W
Lödöse 49 58 2N 12 9 E
Lodwar 90 3 10N 35 40 E
Łódź 28 51 45N 19 27 E
Łódź □ 28 51 45N 19 27 E
Loengo 90 4 48 S 26 30 E
Lofer 26 47 35N 12 41 E
Lofoten 50 68 30N 15 0 E
Lofsdalen 48 62 10N 13 20 E
Lofsen → 48 62 7N 13 57 E
Loftahammar 49 57 54N 16 41 E
Logan, Kans., U.S.A. 116 39 40N 99 35W
Logan, Ohio, U.S.A. 114 39 25N 82 22W
Logan, Utah, U.S.A. 118 41 45N 111 50W
Logan, W. Va., U.S.A. 114 37 51N 81 59W
Logan, Mt. 104 60 31N 140 22W
Logan Pass 108 48 41N 113 44W
Logansport, Ind., U.S.A. 114 40 45N 86 21W
Logansport, La., U.S.A. 117 31 58N 93 58W
Logar □ 65 34 0N 69 0 E
Logo 87 5 20N 30 18 E
Logroño 32 42 28N 2 27W
* Logroño □ 32 42 28N 2 27W
Logrosán 31 39 20N 5 32W
Løgstør 49 56 58N 9 14 E
Lohardaga 69 23 27N 84 45 E
Lohja 51 60 12N 24 5 E
Lohr 25 50 0N 9 35 E
Loi-kaw 67 19 40N 97 17 E
Loimaa 51 60 50N 23 5 E
Loir → 18 47 33N 0 32W
Loir-et-Cher □ 18 47 40N 1 20 E
Loire □ 21 45 40N 4 5 E
Loire → 18 47 16N 2 10W
Loire-Atlantique □ 18 47 25N 1 40W
Loiret □ 19 47 58N 2 10 E
Loitz 24 53 58N 13 8 E
Loja, Ecuador 126 3 59 S 79 16W
Loja, Spain 31 37 10N 4 10W
Loji 73 1 38 S 127 28 E
Loka 87 4 13N 31 0 E
Lokandu 90 2 30 S 25 45 E
Løken 47 59 48N 11 29 E
Lokeren 16 51 6N 3 59 E
Lokhvitsa 54 50 25N 33 18 E
Lokichokio 90 4 19N 34 13 E
Lokitaung 90 4 12N 35 48 E
Lokka 50 67 49N 27 45 E
Løkken 49 57 22N 9 41 E
Løkkenverk 47 63 8N 9 45 E
Loknya 54 56 49N 30 4 E
Lokoja 85 7 47N 6 45 E
Lokolama 88 2 35 S 19 50 E
Lokwei 77 19 5N 110 31 E
Lol → 87 9 13N 26 30 E
Lola 84 7 52N 8 29W
Lolibai, Gebel 87 3 50N 33 0 E
Lolimi 87 4 35N 34 0 E
Loliondo 90 2 2 S 35 39 E
Lolland 49 54 45N 11 30 E
Lollar 24 50 39N 8 43 E
Lolo 118 46 50N 114 8W
Lolodorf 85 3 16N 10 49 E
Lom 43 43 48N 23 12 E
Lom → 42 43 45N 23 15 E
Loma 118 47 59N 110 29W
Lomami → 90 0 46N 24 16 E
Lomas de Zamóra 124 34 45 S 58 25W
Lombard 118 46 7N 111 28W
Lombardia □ 38 45 35N 9 45 E
Lombardy = Lombardia 38 45 35N 9 45 E
Lombez 20 43 29N 0 55 E
Lomblen 73 8 30 S 123 32 E
Lombok 72 8 45 S 116 30 E
Lomé 85 6 9N 1 20 E
Lomela 88 2 19 S 23 15 E
Lomela → 88 1 30 S 22 50 E
Lomello 38 45 5N 8 46 E
Lometa 117 31 15N 98 25W
Lomié 88 3 13N 13 38 E
Lomma 49 55 43N 13 6 E
Lomond 108 50 24N 112 36W
Lomond, L. 14 56 8N 4 38W
Lomonosov 54 59 57N 29 53 E
Lompobatang 73 5 24 S 119 56 E
Lompoc 119 34 41N 120 32W
Lomsegga 47 61 49N 8 21 E
Łomża 28 53 10N 22 2 E
Łomża □ 28 53 0N 22 30 E
Lonavla 70 18 46N 73 29 E
Loncoche 128 39 20 S 72 50W
Londa 70 15 30N 74 30 E
Londe, La 21 43 8N 6 14 E
Londiani 90 0 10 S 35 33 E
Londinières 18 49 50N 1 25 E
London, Can. 106 42 59N 81 15W
London, U.K. 13 51 30N 0 5W
London, Ky., U.S.A. 114 37 11N 84 5W
London, Ohio, U.S.A. 114 39 54N 83 28W
London, Greater □ 13 51 30N 0 5W
Londonderry 15 55 0N 7 20W
Londonderry □ 15 55 0N 7 20W
Londonderry, C. 96 13 45 S 126 55 E
Londonderry, I. 128 55 0 S 71 0W
Londrina 125 23 18 S 51 10W
Lone Pine 119 36 35N 118 2W
Long Beach, Calif., U.S.A. 119 33 46N 118 12W
Long Beach, N.Y., U.S.A. 113 40 35N 73 40W
Long Beach, Wash., U.S.A. 118 46 20N 124 1W
Long Branch 114 40 19N 74 0W
Long Creek 118 44 43N 119 6W
Long Eaton 12 52 54N 1 16W
Long I., Austral. 98 22 8 S 149 53 E
Long I., Bahamas 121 23 20N 75 10W
Long I., P.N.G. 98 5 20 S 147 5 E
Long I., U.S.A. 114 40 50N 73 20W
Long I. Sd. 113 41 10N 73 0W
Long L. 106 49 30N 86 50W
Long Lake 113 43 57N 74 25W
Long Pine 116 42 33N 99 41W
Long Pt., Newf., Can. 107 48 47N 58 46W
Long Pt., Ont., Can. 112 42 35N 80 2W
Long Point B. 112 42 40N 80 10W
Long Range Mts. 107 49 30N 57 30W
Long Str. 4 70 0N 175 0 E
Long Xian 77 34 55N 106 55 E
Long Xuyen 71 10 19N 105 28 E
Longá 45 36 53N 21 55 E
Long'an 77 23 10N 107 40 E
Longarone 39 46 15N 12 18 E
Longchuan 77 24 5N 115 17 E
Longde 76 35 30N 106 20 E
Longeau 19 47 47N 5 20 E
Longford, Austral. 99 41 32 S 147 3 E
Longford, Ireland 15 53 43N 7 50W
Longford □ 15 53 42N 7 45W
Longhua 76 41 18N 117 45 E
Longido 90 2 43 S 36 42 E
Longiram 72 0 5 S 115 45 E
Longjiang 76 47 20N 123 12 E
Longkou 76 37 40N 120 18 E
Longlac 106 49 45N 86 25W
Longlin 77 24 47N 105 20 E
Longmen 77 23 40N 114 18 E
Longmont 116 40 10N 105 4W
Longnan 77 24 55N 114 47 E
Longnawan 72 1 51N 114 55 E
Longobucco 41 39 27N 16 37 E
Longone → 81 10 0N 15 40 E
Longquan 77 28 7N 119 10 E
Longreach 97 23 28 S 144 14 E
Longs Peak 118 40 20N 105 37W
Longshan 77 29 29N 109 25 E
Longsheng 77 25 48N 110 0 E
Longton 98 20 58 S 145 55 E
Longtown 13 51 58N 2 59W
Longué 18 47 22N 0 8W
Longueau 19 49 52N 2 21 E
Longueuil 113 45 32N 73 28W
Longuyon 19 49 27N 5 35 E
Longview, Can. 108 50 32N 114 10W
Longview, Tex., U.S.A. 117 32 30N 94 45W
Longview, Wash., U.S.A. 118 46 9N 122 58W
Longwy 19 49 30N 5 45 E
Longxi 76 34 53N 104 40 E
Longzhou 77 22 22N 106 50 E
Lonigo 39 45 23N 11 22 E
Löningen 24 52 43N 7 44 E
Lonja → 39 45 30N 16 40 E
Lonoke 117 34 48N 91 57W
Lons-le-Saunier 19 46 40N 5 31 E
Lønstrup 49 57 29N 9 47 E
Looc 73 12 20N 112 5 E
Lookout, C., Can. 106 55 18N 83 56W
Lookout, C., U.S.A. 115 34 30N 76 30W
Loolmalasin 90 3 0 S 35 53 E
Loon →, Alta., Can. 108 57 8N 115 3W
Loon →, Man., Can. 109 55 53N 101 59W
Loon Lake 109 54 2N 109 10W
Loop Hd. 15 52 34N 9 55W
Lop Nor = Lop Nur 75 40 20N 90 10 E
Lop Nur 75 40 20N 90 10 E
Lopare 42 44 39N 18 46 E
Lopatin 57 43 50N 47 35 E
Lopatina, G. 59 50 47N 143 10 E
Lopaye 87 6 37N 33 40 E
Lopera 31 37 56N 4 14W
Lopez, C. 88 0 47 S 8 40 E
Lopphavet 50 70 27N 21 15 E
Lora →, Afghan. 65 32 0N 67 15 E
Lora →, Norway 47 62 8N 8 42 E
Lora del Rio 31 37 39N 5 33W
Lora, Hamun-i- 66 29 38N 64 58 E
Lora, La 30 42 45N 4 0W
Lorain 114 41 28N 82 55W
Loralai 68 30 20N 68 41 E
Lorca 33 37 41N 1 42W
Lord Howe I. 94 31 33 S 159 6 E
Lord Howe Ridge 94 30 0 S 162 30 E
Lordsburg 119 32 22N 108 45W
Lorengau 98 2 1 S 147 15 E
Loreto, Brazil 127 7 5 S 45 10W
Loreto, Italy 39 43 26N 13 36 E
Loreto Aprutina 39 42 24N 13 59 E
Lorgues 21 43 28N 6 22 E
Lorient 18 47 45N 3 23W
Loristān □ 64 33 20N 47 0 E
Lorn 14 56 26N 5 10W
Lorn, Firth of 14 56 20N 5 40W
Lorne 99 38 33 S 143 59 E
Lörrach 25 47 36N 7 38 E
Lorraine 19 49 0N 6 0 E
Lorrainville 106 47 21N 79 23W
Los Alamos 119 35 57N 106 17W
Los Andes 124 32 50 S 70 40W
Los Angeles, Chile 124 37 28 S 72 23W
Los Angeles, U.S.A. 119 34 0N 118 10W
Los Angeles Aqueduct 119 35 25N 118 0W
Los Banos 119 37 8N 120 56W
Los Barrios 31 36 11N 5 30W
Los Blancos 124 23 40 S 62 30W
Los Gatos 119 37 15N 121 59W
Los Hermanos 126 11 45N 84 25W
Los, Îles de 84 9 30N 13 50W
Los Lamentos 120 30 36N 105 50W
Los Lunas 119 34 48N 106 47W
Los Mochis 120 25 45N 109 5W
Los Monegros 32 41 29N 0 13W
Los Olivos 119 34 40N 120 7W
Los Palacios y Villafranca 31 37 10N 5 55W
Los Roques 126 11 50N 66 45W
Los Santos de Maimona 31 38 27N 6 22W
Los Testigos 126 11 23N 63 6W
Los Vilos 124 32 10 S 71 30W
Los Yébenes 31 39 36N 3 55W
Loshkalakh 59 62 45N 147 20 E
Łosice 28 52 13N 22 43 E
Lošinj 39 44 30N 14 30 E
Lossiemouth 14 57 43N 3 17W
Losuia 98 8 30 S 151 4 E
Lot □ 20 44 39N 1 40 E
Lot → 20 44 18N 0 20 E
Lot-et-Garonne □ 20 44 22N 0 30 E
Lota 124 37 5 S 73 10W
Løten 47 60 51N 11 21 E
Lothian □ 14 55 50N 3 0W
Lothiers 19 46 42N 1 33 E
Lotschbergtunnel 25 46 26N 7 43 E
Lottefors 48 61 25N 16 24 E
Loubomo 88 4 9 S 12 47 E
Loudéac 18 48 11N 2 47W
Loudon 115 35 35N 84 22W
Loudonville 112 40 40N 82 15W
Loudun 18 47 0N 0 5 E
Loué 18 47 59N 0 9W
Loue → 19 47 1N 5 27 E
Louga 84 15 45N 16 5W
Loughborough 12 52 46N 1 11W
Loughrea 15 53 11N 8 33W
Loughros More B. 15 54 48N 8 30W
Louhans 21 46 38N 5 12 E
Louis Trichardt 93 23 0 S 29 43 E
Louis XIV, Pte. 106 54 37N 79 45W
Louisa 114 38 5N 82 40W
Louisbourg 107 45 55N 60 0W
Louise I. 108 52 55N 131 50W
Louiseville 106 46 20N 72 56W
Louisiade Arch. 94 11 10 S 153 0 E
Louisiana 116 39 25N 91 0W
Louisiana □ 117 30 50N 92 0W
Louisville, Ky., U.S.A. 114 38 15N 85 45W
Louisville, Miss., U.S.A. 117 33 7N 89 3W
Loulay 20 46 3N 0 30W
Loulé 31 37 9N 8 0W
Lount L. 109 50 10N 94 20W
Louny 26 50 20N 13 48 E
Loup City 116 41 19N 98 57W
Loupe, La 18 48 29N 1 1 E
Lourdes 20 43 6N 0 3W
Lourdes-du-Blanc-Sablon 107 51 24N 57 12W
Lourenço-Marques = Maputo 93 25 58 S 32 32 E
Loures 31 38 50N 9 9W
Lourinhã 31 39 14N 9 17W
Louroux-Béconnais, Le 18 47 30N 0 55W
Lousã 30 40 7N 8 14W
Louth, Austral. 99 30 30 S 145 8 E
Louth, Ireland 15 53 47N 6 33W
Louth, U.K. 12 53 23N 0 0W
Louth □ 15 53 55N 6 30W
Loutrá Aidhipsoú 45 38 54N 23 2 E
Loutráki 45 38 0N 22 57 E
Louvière, La 16 50 27N 4 10 E
Louviers 18 49 12N 1 10 E
Lovat → 54 58 14N 30 28 E
Lovćen 42 42 23N 18 51 E
Love 109 53 29N 104 10W
Lovech 43 43 8N 24 42 E
Loveland 116 40 27N 105 4W
Lovell 118 44 51N 108 20W
Lovelock 118 40 17N 118 25W
Lóvere 38 45 50N 10 4 E
Loviisa 51 60 28N 26 12 E
Loving 117 32 17N 104 4W
Lovington 117 33 0N 103 20W
Lovios 30 41 55N 8 4W
Lovisa 51 60 28N 26 12 E
Lovosice 26 50 30N 14 2 E
Lovran 39 45 18N 14 15 E
Lovrin 42 45 58N 20 48 E
Lövstabukten 48 60 35N 17 45 E
Low Rocky Pt. 97 42 59 S 145 29 E

* *Renamed La Rioja* □

Lowa McLure

Lowa	90	1 25S	25 47 E
Lowa →	90	1 24S	25 51 E
Lowell	114	42 38N	71 19W
Lower Arrow L.	108	49 40N	118 5W
Lower Austria = Niederösterreich □	26	48 25N	15 40 E
Lower Hutt	101	41 10S	174 55 E
Lower L.	118	41 17N	120 3W
Lower Lake	118	38 56N	122 36W
Lower Neguac	107	47 20N	65 10W
Lower Post	108	59 58N	128 30W
Lower Red L.	116	47 58N	95 0W
Lower Saxony = Niedersachsen □	24	52 45N	9 0 E
Lowestoft	13	52 29N	1 44 E
Łowicz	28	52 6N	19 55 E
Lowville	114	43 48N	75 30W
Loxton	97	34 28S	140 31 E
Loyalty Is. = Loyauté, Is.	94	21 0S	167 30 E
Loyang = Luoyang	77	34 40N	112 26 E
Loyev, U.S.S.R.	54	51 55N	30 40 E
Loyev, U.S.S.R.	54	51 56N	30 46 E
Loyoro	90	3 22N	34 14 E
Lož	39	45 43N	30 14 E
Lozère □	20	44 35N	3 30 E
Loznica	42	44 32N	19 14 E
Lozovaya	56	49 0N	36 20 E
Luachimo	88	7 23S	20 48 E
Luacono	88	11 15S	21 37 E
Lualaba →	90	0 26N	25 20 E
Luampa	91	15 4S	24 20 E
Lu'an	77	31 45N	116 29 E
Luan Chau	71	21 38N	103 24 E
Luan Xian	76	39 40N	118 40 E
Luanda	88	8 50S	13 15 E
Luang Prabang	71	19 52N	102 10 E
Luangwa Valley	91	13 30S	31 30 E
Luanping	76	40 53N	117 23 E
Luanshya	91	13 3S	28 28 E
Luapula □	91	11 0S	29 0 E
Luapula →	91	9 26S	28 33 E
Luarca	30	43 32N	6 32W
Luashi	91	10 50S	23 36 E
Luau	88	10 40S	22 10 E
Lubaczów	28	50 10N	23 8 E
Lubalo	88	9 10S	19 15 E
Lubań	28	51 5N	15 15 E
Lubana, Ozero	54	56 45N	27 0 E
Lubang Is.	73	13 50N	120 12 E
Lubartów	28	51 28N	22 42 E
Lubawa	28	53 30N	19 48 E
Lübben	24	51 56N	13 54 E
Lübbenau	24	51 49N	13 59 E
Lubbock	117	33 40N	101 53W
Lübeck	24	53 52N	10 41 E
Lübecker Bucht	24	54 3N	11 0 E
Lubefu	90	4 47S	24 27 E
Lubefu →	90	4 10S	23 0 E
Lubero = Luofu	90	0 1S	29 15 E
Lubicon L.	108	56 23N	115 56W
Lubień Kujawski	28	52 23N	19 9 E
Lubin	28	51 24N	16 11 E
Lublin	28	51 12N	22 38 E
Lublin □	28	51 5N	22 30 E
Lubliniec	28	50 43N	18 45 E
Lubny	54	50 3N	32 58 E
Lubok Antu	72	1 3N	111 50 E
Lubon	28	52 21N	16 51 E
Lubongola	90	2 35S	27 50 E
Lubotin	27	49 17N	20 53 E
Lubran	64	34 0N	36 0 E
Lubraniec	28	52 33N	18 50 E
Lubsko	28	51 45N	14 57 E
Lübtheen	24	53 18N	11 4 E
Lubuagan	73	17 21N	121 10 E
Lubudi →	91	9 0S	25 35 E
Lubuklinggau	72	3 15S	102 55 E
Lubuksikaping	72	0 10N	100 15 E
Lubumbashi	91	11 40S	27 28 E
Lubunda	90	5 12S	26 41 E
Lubungu	91	14 35S	26 24 E
Lubutu	90	0 45S	26 30 E
Luc-en-Diois	21	44 36N	5 28 E
Luc, Le	21	43 23N	6 21 E
Lucan	112	43 11N	81 24W
Lucca	38	43 50N	10 30 E
Luce Bay	14	54 45N	4 48W
Lucea	121	18 25N	78 10W
Lucedale	115	30 55N	88 34W
Lucena, Phil.	73	13 56N	121 37 E
Lucena, Spain	31	37 27N	4 31W
Lucena del Cid	32	40 9N	0 17W
Lučenec	27	48 18N	19 42 E
Lucera	41	41 30N	15 20 E
Lucerne = Luzern	25	47 3N	8 18 E
Luchena →	33	37 44N	1 50W
Lucheringo →	91	11 43S	36 17 E
Lüchow	24	52 58N	11 8 E
Lucira	89	14 0S	12 35 E
Luckau	24	51 50N	13 43 E
Luckenwalde	24	52 5N	13 11 E
Lucknow	69	26 50N	81 0 E
Luçon	20	46 28N	1 10W
Lüda	76	38 50N	121 40 E
Luda Kamchiya →	43	43 3N	27 29 E
Ludbreg	39	46 15N	16 38 E
Lüdenscheid	24	51 13N	7 37 E
Lüderitz	92	26 41S	15 8 E
Ludewe □	91	10 0S	34 50 E
Ludhiana	68	30 57N	75 56 E
Lüdinghausen	24	51 46N	7 28 E
Ludington	114	43 58N	86 27W
Ludlow, U.K.	13	52 23N	2 42W
Ludlow, Calif., U.S.A.	119	34 43N	116 10W
Ludlow, Vt., U.S.A.	113	43 25N	72 40W
Ludus	46	46 29N	24 5 E
Ludvika	48	60 8N	15 14 E
Ludwigsburg	25	48 53N	9 11 E
Ludwigshafen	25	49 27N	8 27 E
Ludwigslust	24	53 19N	11 28 E
Ludza	54	56 32N	27 43 E
Luebo	88	5 21S	21 23 E
Lueki	90	3 20S	25 48 E
Luena, Zaïre	91	9 28S	25 43 E
Luena, Zambia	91	10 40S	30 25 E
Lüeyang	77	33 22N	106 10 E
Lufeng	77	22 57N	115 38 E
Lufkin	117	31 25N	94 40W
Lufupa	91	10 37S	24 56 E
Luga	54	58 40N	29 55 E
Luga →	54	59 40N	28 18 E
Lugang	77	24 4N	120 23 E
Lugano	25	46 0N	8 57 E
Lugano, L. di	25	46 0N	9 0 E
Lugansk = Voroshilovgrad	57	48 35N	39 20 E
Lugard's Falls	90	3 6S	38 41 E
Lugela	91	16 25S	36 43 E
Lugenda →	91	11 25S	38 33 E
Lugh Ganana	63	3 48N	42 34 E
Lugnaquilla	15	52 58N	6 28W
Lugnvik	48	62 56N	17 55 E
Lugo, Italy	39	44 25N	11 53 E
Lugo, Spain	30	43 2N	7 35W
Lugo □	30	43 0N	7 30W
Lugoj	42	45 42N	21 57 E
Lugones	30	43 26N	5 50W
Lugovoy	58	42 54N	72 45 E
Luhe →	24	53 18N	10 11 E
Luiana	92	17 25S	22 59 E
Luino	38	46 0N	8 42 E
Luis Correia	127	3 0S	41 35W
Luitpold Coast	5	78 30S	32 0W
Luize	88	7 40S	22 30 E
Luizi	90	6 0S	27 25 E
Luján	124	34 45S	59 5W
Lukanga Swamps	91	14 30S	27 40 E
Lukenie →	88	3 0S	18 50 E
Lukhisaral	69	25 11N	86 5 E
Lūki	43	41 50N	24 43 E
Lukolela, Equateur, Zaïre	88	1 10S	17 12 E
Lukolela, Kasai Or., Zaïre	90	5 23S	24 32 E
Lukosi	91	18 30S	26 30 E
Lukovit	43	43 13N	24 11 E
Łuków	28	51 55N	22 23 E
Lukoyanov	55	55 2N	44 29 E
Lule älv →	50	65 35N	22 10 E
Luleå	50	65 35N	22 10 E
Lüleburgaz	43	41 23N	27 22 E
Luling	117	29 45N	97 40W
Lulong	76	39 53N	118 51 E
Lulonga →	88	1 0N	19 0 E
Lulua →	88	6 30S	22 50 E
Luluabourg = Kananga	88	5 55S	22 26 E
Lumai	89	13 13S	21 25 E
Lumajang	73	8 8S	113 16 E
Lumbala	89	14 18S	21 18 E
Lumberton, Miss., U.S.A.	117	31 4N	89 28W
Lumberton, N. Mex., U.S.A.	119	36 58N	106 57W
Lumberton, N.C., U.S.A.	115	34 37N	78 59W
Lumbres	19	50 40N	2 5 E
Lumbwa	90	0 12S	35 28 E
Lumby	108	50 10N	118 50W
Lumsden	101	45 44S	168 27 E
Lumut	71	4 13N	100 37 E
Lunavada	68	23 8N	73 37 E
Lunca	46	47 22N	25 1 E
Lund, Sweden	49	55 44N	13 12 E
Lund, U.S.A.	118	38 53N	115 0W
Lundazi	91	12 20S	33 7 E
Lunde	47	59 17N	9 5 E
Lunderskov	49	55 29N	9 19 E
Lundi →	91	21 43S	32 34 E
Lundu	72	1 40N	109 50 E
Lundy	13	51 10N	4 41W
Lune →	12	54 0N	2 51W
Lüneburg	24	53 15N	10 23 E
Lüneburg Heath = Lüneburger Heide	24	53 0N	10 0 E
Lüneburger Heide	24	53 0N	10 0 E
Lunel	21	43 39N	4 9 E
Lünen	24	51 36N	7 31 E
Lunenburg	107	44 22N	64 18W
Lunéville	19	48 36N	6 30 E
Lunga →	91	14 34S	26 25 E
Lungi Airport	84	8 40N	13 17W
Lungleh	67	22 55N	92 45 E
Luni	68	26 0N	73 6 E
Luni →	68	24 41N	71 14 E
Luninets	54	52 15N	26 50 E
Luning	118	38 30N	118 10W
Lunino	55	53 35N	45 6 E
Lunner	47	60 19N	10 35 E
Lunsemfwa →	91	14 54S	30 12 E
Lunsemfwa Falls	91	14 30S	29 6 E
Luo He →	77	34 35N	110 20 E
Luobei	76	47 35N	130 50 E
Luocheng	77	24 48N	108 53 E
Luochuan	76	35 45N	109 26 E
Luoding	77	22 45N	111 40 E
Luodong	77	24 41N	121 46 E
Luofu	90	0 10S	29 15 E
Luoning	77	34 35N	111 40 E
Luoyang	77	34 40N	112 26 E
Luoyuan	77	26 28N	119 30 E
Luozi	88	4 54S	14 0 E
Lupeni	46	45 21N	23 13 E
Łupków	27	49 15N	22 4 E
Luque, Parag.	124	25 19S	57 25W
Luque, Spain	31	37 35N	4 16W
Luray	114	38 39N	78 26W
Lure	19	47 40N	6 30 E
Luremo	88	8 30S	17 50 E
Lurgan	15	54 28N	6 20W
Lusaka	91	15 28S	28 16 E
Lusambo	90	4 58S	23 28 E
Lusangaye	90	4 54S	26 0 E
Luseland	109	52 5N	109 24W
Lushan	77	33 45N	112 55 E
Lushih	77	34 3N	111 3 E
Lushnja	44	40 55N	19 41 E
Lushoto	90	4 47S	38 20 E
Lushoto □	90	4 45S	38 20 E
Lüshun	76	38 45N	121 15 E
Lusignan	20	46 26N	0 8 E
Lusigny-sur-Barse	19	48 16N	4 15 E
Lusk	116	42 47N	104 27W
Lussac-les-Châteaux	20	46 24N	0 43 E
Luta = Lüda	76	38 50N	121 40 E
Luton	13	51 53N	0 24W
Lutong	72	4 30N	114 0 E
Lutsk	54	50 50N	25 15 E
Lützow Holmbukta	5	69 10S	37 30 E
Luverne	116	43 35N	96 12W
Luvua	91	8 48S	25 17 E
Luwegu →	91	8 31S	37 23 E
Luwuk	73	0 56S	122 47 E
Luxembourg	16	49 37N	6 9 E
Luxembourg ■	16	50 0N	6 0 E
Luxembourg □	16	49 58N	5 30 E
Luxeuil-les-Bains	19	47 49N	6 24 E
Luxi	77	28 20N	110 7 E
Luxor = El Uqsur	86	25 41N	32 38 E
Luy →	20	43 39N	1 9W
Luy-de-Béarn →	20	43 39N	0 48W
Luy-de-France →	20	43 39N	0 48W
Luz-St-Sauveur	20	42 53N	0 1 E
Luza	52	60 39N	47 10 E
Luzern	25	47 3N	8 18 E
Luzern □	25	47 2N	7 55 E
Luzhai	77	24 29N	109 42 E
Luzhou	75	28 52N	105 20 E
Luziânia	127	16 20S	48 0W
Luzon	73	16 0N	121 0 E
Luzy	19	46 47N	3 58 E
Luzzi	41	39 28N	16 17 E
Lvov	54	49 50N	24 0 E
Lwówek	28	52 28N	16 10 E
Lwówek Śląski	28	51 7N	15 38 E
Lyakhovichi	54	53 2N	26 32 E
Lyakhovskiye, Ostrova	59	73 40N	141 0 E
Lyaki	57	40 34N	47 22 E
Lyallpur = Faisalabad	68	31 30N	73 5 E
Lyaskovets	43	43 6N	25 44 E
Lychen	24	53 13N	13 20 E
Lyckeby	49	56 12N	15 37 E
Lycksele	50	64 38N	18 40 E
Lycosura	45	37 20N	22 3 E
Lydda = Lod	62	31 57N	34 54 E
Lydenburg	93	25 10S	30 29 E
Lyell	101	41 48S	172 4 E
Lyell I.	108	52 40N	131 35W
Lyell Range	101	41 38S	172 20 E
Lygnern	49	57 30N	12 15 E
Lykling	47	59 42N	5 12 E
Lyman	118	41 24N	110 15W
Lyme Regis	13	50 44N	2 57W
Lymington	13	50 46N	1 32W
Łyńa →	28	54 37N	21 14 E
Lynchburg	114	37 23N	79 10W
Lynd →	98	16 28S	143 18 E
Lynd Ra.	99	25 30S	149 20 E
Lynden, Can.	112	43 14N	80 9W
Lynden, U.S.A.	118	48 56N	122 32W
Lyndhurst	99	30 15S	138 18 E
Lyndonville, N.Y., U.S.A.	112	43 19N	78 25W
Lyndonville, Vt., U.S.A.	113	44 32N	72 1W
Lyngdal, Aust-Agder, Norway	47	58 8N	7 7 E
Lyngdal, Buskerud, Norway	47	59 54N	9 32 E
Lynn	114	42 28N	70 57W
Lynn Canal	108	58 50N	135 20W
Lynn Lake	109	56 51N	101 3W
Lynton	13	51 14N	3 50W
Lyntupy	54	55 4N	26 23 E
Lynx L.	109	62 25N	106 15W
Lyø	49	55 3N	10 9 E
Lyon	21	45 46N	4 50 E
Lyonnais	21	45 45N	4 15 E
Lyons, Colo., U.S.A.	116	40 17N	105 15W
Lyons, Ga., U.S.A.	115	32 10N	82 15W
Lyons, Kans., U.S.A.	116	38 24N	98 13W
Lyons, N.Y., U.S.A.	114	43 3N	77 0W
Lyons = Lyon	21	45 46N	4 50 E
Lyrestad	49	58 48N	14 4 E
Lys →	19	50 39N	2 24 E
Lysá	26	50 11N	14 51 E
Lysekil	49	58 17N	11 26 E
Lyskovo	55	56 0N	45 3 E
Lysva	52	58 07N	57 49 E
Lysvik	48	60 1N	13 9 E
Lytle	117	29 14N	98 46W
Lyttelton	101	43 35S	172 44 E
Lytton	108	50 13N	121 31W
Lyuban	54	59 16N	31 18 E
Lyubcha	54	53 46N	26 1 E
Lyubertsy	55	55 39N	37 50 E
Lyubim	55	58 20N	40 39 E
Lyubimets	43	41 50N	26 5 E
Lyuboml, U.S.S.R.	54	51 10N	24 2 E
Lyuboml, U.S.S.R.	54	51 11N	24 4 E
Lyubotin	56	50 0N	36 0 E
Lyubytino	54	58 50N	33 16 E
Lyudinovo	54	53 52N	34 28 E

M

Mā'ad	62	32 37N	35 36 E
Ma'alah	64	26 31N	47 20 E
Maamba	92	17 17S	26 28 E
Ma'ânn	64	30 12N	35 44 E
Ma'anshan	77	31 44N	118 29 E
Ma'arrat un Nu'man	64	35 38N	36 40 E
Maas →	16	51 45N	4 32 E
Maaseik	16	51 6N	5 45 E
Maassluis	16	51 56N	4 16 E
Maastricht	16	50 50N	5 40 E
Maave	93	21 4S	34 47 E
Mabel L.	108	50 35N	118 43W
Mabenge	90	4 15N	24 12 E
Mablethorpe	12	53 21N	0 14 E
Maboma	90	2 30N	28 10 E
Mabrouk	85	19 29N	1 15W
Mabton	118	46 15N	120 12W
Mac Nutt	109	51 5N	101 36W
Mac Tier	112	45 9N	79 46W
Macachín	124	37 10S	63 43W
Macaé	125	22 20S	41 43W
McAlester	117	34 57N	95 46W
McAllen	117	26 12N	98 15W
Macallister →	100	38 2S	146 59 E
Macamic	106	48 45N	79 0W
Macão	31	39 35N	7 59W
Macao = Macau ■	75	22 16N	113 35 E
Macapá	127	0 5N	51 4W
McArthur →	97	15 54S	136 40 E
McArthur River	97	16 27S	136 7 E
Macau	127	5 0S	36 40W
Macau ■	75	22 16N	113 35 E
McBride	108	53 20N	120 19W
McCall	118	44 55N	116 6W
McCamey	117	31 8N	102 15W
McCammon	118	42 41N	112 11W
McCauley I.	108	53 40N	130 15W
Macclesfield	12	53 16N	2 9W
McClintock	109	57 50N	94 10W
McCloud	118	41 14N	122 5W
McClure	112	40 42N	77 20W
McClure Str.	4	75 0N	119 0W
McClusky	116	47 30N	100 31W
McComb	117	31 13N	90 30W
McCook	116	40 15N	100 35W
McCusker →	109	55 32N	108 39W
McDame	108	59 44N	128 59W
McDermitt	118	42 0N	117 45W
Macdonald →	100	33 22S	151 0 E
McDonald Is.	3	54 0S	73 0 E
Macdonald L.	96	23 30S	129 0 E
Macdonnell Ranges	96	23 40S	133 0 E
Macdougall L.	104	66 0N	98 27W
MacDowell L.	106	52 15N	92 45W
Macduff	14	57 40N	2 30W
Maceda	30	42 16N	7 39W
* Macedo de Cavaleiros	88	11 25S	16 45 E
Macedonia = Makedhonía	44	40 39N	22 0 E
Macedonia = Makedonija	42	41 53N	21 40 E
Maceió	127	9 40S	35 41W
Maceira	31	39 41N	8 55W
Macenta	84	8 35N	9 32W
Macerata	39	43 19N	13 28 E
McFarlane →	109	59 12N	107 58W
Macfarlane, L.	97	32 0S	136 40 E
McGehee	117	33 40N	91 25W
McGill	118	39 27N	114 50W
Macgillycuddy's Reeks	15	52 2N	9 45W
MacGregor	109	49 57N	98 48W
McGregor, Iowa, U.S.A.	116	42 58N	91 15W
McGregor, Minn., U.S.A.	116	46 37N	93 17W
McGregor →	108	55 10N	122 0W
McGregor Ra.	99	27 0S	142 45 E
Mach	66	29 50N	67 20 E
Machado = Jiparana →	126	8 3S	62 52W
Machagai	124	26 56S	60 2W
Machakos	90	1 30S	37 15 E
Machakos □	90	1 30S	37 15 E
Machala	126	3 20S	79 57W
Machanga	93	20 59S	35 0 E
Machattie, L.	97	24 50S	139 48 E
Machava	93	25 54S	32 28 E
Machece	91	19 15S	35 32 E
Machecoul	18	47 0N	1 49W
Macheng	77	31 12N	115 2 E
Machevna	59	61 20N	172 20 E
Machezo	31	39 21N	4 20W
Machias	107	44 40N	67 28W
Machichaco, Cabo	32	43 28N	2 47W
Machichi →	109	57 3N	92 6W
Machilipatnam	70	16 12N	81 8 E
Machine, La	19	46 54N	3 27 E
Machiques	126	10 4N	72 34W
Machupicchu	126	13 8S	72 30W
Machynlleth	13	52 36N	3 51W
** Macias Nguema Biyoga	85	3 30N	8 40 E
Maciejowice	28	51 36N	21 26 E
McIlwraith Ra.	97	13 50S	143 20 E
Măcin	46	45 16N	28 8 E
Macina	84	14 50N	5 0W
McIntosh	116	45 57N	101 20W
McIntosh L.	109	55 45N	105 0W
Macintyre →	97	28 37S	150 47 E
Macizo Galaico	30	42 30N	7 30W
Mackay, Austral.	97	21 8S	149 11 E
Mackay, U.S.A.	118	43 58N	113 37W
Mackay →	108	57 10N	111 38W
Mackay, L.	96	22 30S	129 0 E
McKees Rock	112	40 27N	80 3W
McKeesport	114	40 21N	79 50W
Mackenzie	108	55 20N	123 05W
McKenzie	115	36 10N	88 31W
† Mackenzie □	104	61 30N	115 0W
Mackenzie →, Austral.	97	23 38S	149 46 E
Mackenzie →, Can.	104	69 10N	134 20W
McKenzie →	118	44 2N	123 6W
Mackenzie City = Linden	126	6 0N	58 10W
Mackenzie Highway	108	58 0N	117 15W
Mackenzie Mts.	104	64 0N	130 0W
Mackinaw City	114	45 47N	84 44W
McKinlay	98	21 16S	141 18 E
McKinlay →	98	20 50S	141 28 E
McKinley, Mt.	104	63 2N	151 0W
McKinley Sea	4	84 0N	10 0W
McKinney	117	33 10N	96 40W
Mackinnon Road	90	3 40S	39 1 E
McKittrick	119	35 18N	119 39W
Macksville	99	30 40S	152 56 E
McLaughlin	116	45 50N	100 50W
Maclean	97	29 26S	153 16 E
McLean	117	35 15N	100 35W
McLeansboro	116	38 5N	88 30W
Maclear	93	31 2S	28 23 E
Macleay →	97	30 56S	153 0 E
McLennan	108	55 42N	116 50W
MacLeod, B.	109	62 53N	110 0W
McLeod L.	96	24 9S	113 47 E
MacLeod Lake	108	54 58N	123 0W
M'Clintock Chan.	104	72 0N	102 0W
McLoughlin, Mt.	118	42 10N	122 19W
McLure	108	51 2N	120 13W

* *Renamed Andulo*
** *Renamed Bioko*
† *Now part of Fort Smith and Inuvik* □

McMechen Mamahatun

McMechen 112 39 57N 80 44W
McMillan L. 117 32 40N 104 20W
McMinnville, Oreg., U.S.A. 118 45 16N 123 11W
McMinnville, Tenn., U.S.A. 115 35 43N 85 45W
McMorran 109 51 19N 108 42W
McMurdo Sd. 5 77 0S 170 0E
McMurray = Fort McMurray 108 56 45N 111 27W
McNary 119 34 4N 109 53W
McNaughton L. 108 52 0N 118 10W
Macodoene 93 23 32S 35 5E
Macomb 116 40 25N 90 40W
Macomer 40 40 16N 8 48E
Mâcon 21 46 19N 4 50E
Macon, Ga., U.S.A. 115 32 50N 83 37W
Macon, Miss., U.S.A. 115 33 7N 88 31W
Macon, Mo., U.S.A. 116 39 40N 92 26W
Macondo 89 12 37S 23 46E
Macossa 91 17 55S 33 56E
Macoun L. 109 56 32N 103 40W
Macovane 93 21 30S 35 0E
McPherson 116 38 25N 97 40W
Macpherson Ra. 99 28 15S 153 15E
Macquarie → 97 30 5S 147 30E
Macquarie Harbour 97 42 15S 145 23E
Macquarie Is. 94 54 36S 158 55E
Macquarie, L. 100 33 4S 151 36E
MacRobertson Coast 5 68 30S 63 0E
Macroom 15 51 54N 8 57W
Macubela 91 16 53S 37 49E
Macugnaga 38 45 57N 7 58E
Macuiza 91 18 7S 34 29E
Macuse 91 17 45S 37 10E
Macuspana 120 17 46N 92 36W
Macusse 92 17 48S 20 23E
Mácuzari, Presa 120 27 10N 109 10W
McVille 116 47 46N 98 11W
Madā 'in Salih 86 26 51N 37 58E
Madagali 85 10 56N 13 33E
Madagascar ■ 93 20 0S 47 0E
Madā'in Sālih 64 26 46N 37 57E
Madama 83 22 0N 13 40E
Madame I. 107 45 30N 60 58W
Madan 43 41 30N 24 57E
Madanapalle 70 13 33N 78 28E
Madang 94 5 12S 145 49E
Madaoua 85 14 5N 6 27E
Madara 85 11 45N 10 35E
Madaripur 69 23 19N 90 15E
Madauk 67 17 56N 96 52E
Madawaska 112 45 30N 77 55W
Madawaska → 106 45 27N 76 21W
Madaya 67 22 12N 96 10E
Madbar 87 6 17N 30 45E
Maddalena 40 41 15N 9 23E
Maddalena, La 40 41 13N 9 25E
Maddaloni 41 41 4N 14 23E
Madden Dam 120 9 13N 79 37W
Madden Lake 120 9 20N 79 37W
Madeira 80 32 50N 17 0W
Madeira → 126 3 22S 58 45W
Madeleine, Îs. de la 107 47 30N 61 40W
Madera 119 37 0N 120 1W
Madha 70 18 0N 75 30E
Madhubani 69 26 21N 86 7E
Madhya Pradesh □ 68 21 50N 81 0E
Madill 117 34 5N 96 49W
Madimba 88 5 0S 15 0E
Madīnat ash Sha'b 63 12 50N 45 0E
Madingou 88 4 10S 13 33E
Madirovalo 93 16 26S 46 32E
Madison, Fla., U.S.A. 115 30 29N 83 39W
Madison, Ind., U.S.A. 114 38 42N 85 20W
Madison, Nebr., U.S.A. 116 41 53N 97 25W
Madison, Ohio, U.S.A. 112 41 45N 81 4W
Madison, S.D., U.S.A. 116 44 0N 97 8W
Madison, Wis., U.S.A. 116 43 5N 89 25W
Madison → 118 45 56N 111 30W
Madison Junc. 118 44 42N 110 56W
Madisonville, Ky., U.S.A. 114 37 20N 87 30W
Madisonville, Tex., U.S.A. 117 30 57N 95 55W
Madista 92 21 15S 25 6E
Madiun 73 7 38S 111 32E
Madley 13 52 3N 2 51W
Madol 87 9 3N 27 45E
Madon → 19 48 36N 6 6E
Madona 54 56 53N 26 5E
Madonie, Le 40 37 50N 13 50E
Madras, India 70 13 8N 80 19E
Madras, U.S.A. 118 44 40N 121 10W
Madras = Tamil Nadu □ 70 11 0N 77 0E
Madre de Dios → 126 10 59S 66 8W
Madre de Dios, I. 128 50 20S 75 10W
Madre del Sur, Sierra 120 17 30N 100 0W
Madre, Laguna, Mexico 120 25 0N 97 30W
Madre, Laguna, U.S.A. 117 25 0N 97 40W
Madre Occidental, Sierra 120 27 0N 107 0W
Madre Oriental, Sierra 120 25 0N 100 0W
Madre, Sierra, Mexico 120 16 0N 93 0W
Madre, Sierra, Phil. 73 17 0N 122 0E
Madri 68 24 16N 73 32E
Madrid 30 40 25N 3 45W
Madrid □ 30 40 30N 3 45W
Madridejos 31 39 28N 3 33W
Madrigal de las Altas Torres 30 41 5N 5 0W
Madrona, Sierra 31 38 27N 4 16W
Madroñera 31 39 26N 5 42W
Madu 87 14 37N 26 4E
Madura, Selat 73 7 30S 113 20E
Madurai 70 9 55N 78 10E
Madurantakam 70 12 30N 79 50E
Madzhalis 57 42 9N 47 47E
Mae Hong Son 71 19 16N 98 1E
Mae Sot 71 16 43N 98 34E
Maebashi 74 36 24N 139 4E
Maella 32 41 8N 0 7E
Măeruş 46 45 53N 25 31E
Maesteg 13 51 36N 3 40W
Maestra, Sierra 121 20 15N 77 0W
Maestrazgo, Mts. del 32 40 30N 0 25W
Maevatanana 93 16 56N 46 49E
Ma'fan 83 25 56N 14 29E
Mafeking, Can. 109 52 40N 101 10W
* Mafeking, S. Afr. 92 25 50S 25 38E
Maféré 84 5 30N 3 2W
Mafeteng 92 29 51S 27 15E
Maffra 99 37 53S 146 58E
Mafia 90 7 45S 39 50E
Mafra, Brazil 125 26 10S 50 0W
Mafra, Port. 31 38 55N 9 20W
Mafungabusi Plateau 91 18 30S 29 8E
Magadan 59 59 38N 150 50E
Magadi 90 1 54S 36 19E
Magadi, L. 90 1 54S 36 19E
Magaliesburg 93 26 1S 27 32E
Magallanes, Estrecho de 128 52 30S 75 0W
Magangué 126 9 14N 74 45W
Magaria 85 13 4N 9 5E
Magburaka 84 8 47N 12 0W
Magdalena, Argent. 124 35 5S 57 30W
Magdalena, Boliv. 126 13 13S 63 57W
Magdalena, Malay. 72 4 25N 117 55E
Magdalena, Mexico 120 30 50N 112 0W
Magdalena, U.S.A. 119 34 10N 107 20W
Magdalena →, Colomb. 126 11 6N 74 51W
Magdalena →, Mexico 120 30 40N 112 25W
Magdalena, B. 120 24 30N 112 10W
Magdalena, I. 120 24 40N 112 15W
Magdalena, Llano de la 120 25 0N 111 30W
Magdeburg 24 52 8N 11 36E
Magdeburg □ 24 52 20N 11 30E
Magdi'el 62 32 10N 34 54E
Magdub 87 13 42N 25 5E
Magee 117 31 53N 89 45W
Magee, I. 15 54 48N 5 44W
Magelang 73 7 29S 110 13E
Magellan's Str. = Magallanes, Est. de 128 52 30S 75 0W
Magenta 38 45 28N 8 53E
Maggia → 25 46 18N 8 36E
Maggiorasca, Mte. 38 44 33N 9 29E
Maggiore, L. 38 46 0N 8 35E
Maghama 84 15 32N 12 57W
Maghâr 62 32 54N 35 24E
Magherafelt 15 54 44N 6 37W
Maghnia 82 34 50N 1 43W
Magione 39 43 10N 12 12E
Maglaj 42 44 33N 18 7E
Magliano in Toscana 39 42 36N 11 18E
Máglie 41 40 8N 18 17E
Magnac-Laval 20 46 13N 1 11E
Magnetic Pole, 1976 (North) 4 76 12N 100 12W
Magnetic Pole, 1976 (South) 5 68 48S 139 30E
Magnisía □ 44 39 15N 22 45E
Magnitogorsk 52 53 27N 59 4E
Magnolia, Ark., U.S.A. 117 33 18N 93 12W
Magnolia, Miss., U.S.A. 117 31 8N 90 28W
Magnor 47 59 56N 12 15E
Magny-en-Vexin 19 49 9N 1 47E
Magog 107 45 18N 72 9W
Magoro 90 1 45N 34 12E
Magosa = Famagusta 64 35 8N 33 55E
Magoye 91 16 1S 27 30E
Magpie L. 107 51 0N 64 41W
Magrath 108 49 25N 112 50W
Magro → 33 39 11N 0 25W
Magrur, Wadi → 87 16 5N 26 30E
Magu □ 90 2 31S 33 28E
Maguarinho, C. 127 0 15S 48 30W
Maguse L. 109 61 40N 95 10W
Maguse Pt. 109 61 20N 93 50W
Magwe 67 20 10N 95 0E
Mahābād 64 36 50N 45 45E
Mahabaleshwar 70 17 58N 73 43E
Mahabharat Lekh 69 28 30N 82 0E
Mahabo 93 20 23S 44 40E
Mahad 70 18 6N 73 29E
Mahadeo Hills 68 22 20N 78 30E
Mahadeopur 70 18 48N 80 0E
Mahagi 90 2 20N 31 0E
Mahajamba → 93 15 33S 47 8E
Mahajamba, Helodranon' i 93 15 24S 47 5E
Mahajan 68 28 48N 73 56E
Mahajanga □ 93 17 0S 47 0E
Mahajilo → 93 19 42S 45 22E
Mahakam → 72 0 35S 117 17E
Mahalapye 92 23 1S 26 51E
Maḩallāt 65 33 55N 50 30E
Mahanadi → 69 20 20N 86 25E
Mahanoro 93 19 54S 48 48E
Mahanoy City 113 40 48N 76 10W
Maharashtra □ 70 20 30N 75 30E
Maharès 83 34 32N 10 29E
Mahari Mts. 90 6 20S 30 0E
Mahasolo 93 19 7S 46 22E
Mahaweli → Ganga 70 8 30N 81 15E
Mahboobabad 70 17 42N 80 2E
Mahbubnagar 70 16 45N 77 59E
Mahdia 83 35 28N 11 0E
Mahé 70 11 42N 75 34E
Mahendra Giri 70 8 20N 77 30E
Mahenge 91 8 45S 36 41E
Maheno 101 45 10S 170 50E
Mahia Pen. 101 39 9S 177 55E
Mahirija 82 34 0N 3 16W
Mahmiya 87 17 12N 33 43E
Mahmud Kot 68 30 16N 71 0E
Mahmudia 46 45 5N 29 5E
Mahnomen 116 47 22N 95 57W
Mahoba 69 25 15N 79 55E
Mahón 32 39 53N 4 16E
Mahone Bay 107 44 30N 64 20W
Mahuta 85 11 32N 4 58E
Mai-Ndombe, L. 88 2 0S 18 20E
Maîche 19 47 16N 6 48E
Maicurú → 127 2 14S 54 17W
Máida 41 38 51N 16 21E
Maidenhead 13 51 31N 0 42W
Maidi 87 16 20N 42 45E
Maidstone, Can. 109 53 5N 109 20W
Maidstone, U.K. 13 51 16N 0 31E
Maiduguri 85 12 0N 13 20E
Maignelay 19 49 32N 2 30E
Maigudo 87 7 30N 37 8E
Maijdi 69 22 48N 91 10E
Maikala Ra. 69 22 0N 81 0E
Mailly-le-Camp 19 48 41N 4 12E
Mailsi 68 29 48N 72 15E
Main →, Ger. 25 50 0N 8 18E
Main →, U.K. 15 54 49N 6 20W
Main Centre 109 50 35N 107 21W
Mainburg 25 48 37N 11 49E
Maine 18 48 0N 0 0E
Maine □ 107 45 20N 69 0W
Maine → 15 52 10N 9 40W
Maine-et-Loire □ 18 47 31N 0 30W
Maïne-Soroa 85 13 13N 12 2E
Maingkwan 67 26 15N 96 37E
Mainit, L. 73 9 31N 125 30E
Mainland, Orkney, U.K. 14 59 0N 3 10W
Mainland, Shetland, U.K. 14 60 15N 1 22W
Mainpuri 68 27 18N 79 4E
Maintenon 19 48 35N 1 35E
Maintirano 93 18 3S 44 1E
Mainz 25 50 0N 8 17E
Maipú 124 36 52S 57 50W
Maiquetía 126 10 36N 66 57W
Maira → 38 44 49N 7 38E
Mairabari 67 26 30N 92 22E
Maisi, Pta. de 121 20 10N 74 10W
Maisse 19 48 24N 2 21E
Maitland, N.S.W., Austral. 97 32 33S 151 36E
Maitland, S. Australia, Austral. 99 34 23S 137 40E
Maitland → 112 43 45N 81 33W
Maiyema 85 12 5N 4 25E
Maizuru 74 35 25N 135 22E
Majalengka 73 6 55S 108 14E
Majd el Kurūm 62 32 56N 35 15E
Majene 73 3 38S 118 57E
Majevica Planina 42 44 45N 18 50E
Maji 87 6 12N 35 30E
Major 109 51 52N 109 37W
Majorca, I. = Mallorca 32 39 30N 3 0E
Maka 84 13 40N 14 10W
Makak 85 3 36N 11 0E
Makale 73 3 6S 119 51E
Makamba 90 4 8S 29 49E
Makari 88 12 35N 14 28E
Makarikari = Makgadikgadi Salt Pans 92 20 40S 25 45E
Makarovo 59 57 40N 107 45E
Makarska 42 43 20N 17 2E
Makaryev 55 57 52N 43 50E
Makasar = Ujung Pandang 73 5 10S 119 20E
Makasar, Selat 73 1 0S 118 20E
Makat 58 47 39N 53 19E
Makedhonía □ 44 40 39N 22 0E
Makedonija □ 42 41 53N 21 40E
Makena 110 20 39N 156 27W
Makeni 84 8 55N 12 5W
Makeyevka 56 48 0N 38 0E
Makgadikgadi Salt Pans 92 20 40S 25 45E
Makhachkala 57 43 0N 47 30E
Makhambet, U.S.S.R. 57 47 43N 51 40E
Makhambet, U.S.S.R. 57 47 40N 51 35E
Makharadze 57 41 55N 42 2E
Makian 73 0 20N 127 20E
** Makin 94 3 30N 174 0E
Makindu 90 2 18S 37 50E
Makinsk 58 52 37N 70 26E
Makkah 86 21 30N 39 54E
Makkovik 107 55 10N 59 10W
† Maklakovo 59 58 16N 92 29E
Makó 27 46 14N 20 33E
Makokou 88 0 40N 12 50E
Makongo 90 3 25N 26 17E
Makoro 90 3 10N 29 59E
Makoua 88 0 5S 15 50E
Maków Mazowiecki 28 52 52N 21 6E
Maków Podhal 27 49 43N 19 45E
Makrá 45 36 15N 25 54E
Makran 65 26 13N 61 30E
Makran Coast Range 66 25 40N 64 0E
Makrana 68 27 2N 74 46E
Mákri 44 40 52N 25 40E
Maksimkin Yar 58 58 42N 86 50E
Maktar 83 35 48N 9 12E
Mākū 64 39 15N 44 31E
Makumbi 88 5 50S 20 43E
Makunda 92 22 30S 20 7E
Makurazaki 74 31 15N 130 20E
Makurdi 85 7 43N 8 35E
Makwassie 92 27 17S 26 0E
Mal B. 15 52 50N 9 30W
Mal i Gjalicës së Lumës 44 42 2N 20 25E
Mal i Gribës 44 40 17N 19 45E
Mal i Nemërçkës 44 40 15N 20 15E
Mal i Tomorit 44 40 42N 20 11E
Mala Kapela 39 44 45N 15 30E
Mala, Pta. 121 7 28N 80 2W
Malabang 73 7 36N 124 3E
Malabar Coast 70 11 0N 75 0E
Malacca, Str. of 71 3 0N 101 0E
Malacky 27 48 27N 17 0E
Malad City 118 42 10N 112 20E
Málaga 31 36 43N 4 23W
Malaga 117 32 12N 104 2W
Málaga □ 31 36 38N 4 58W
Malagarasi 90 5 5S 30 50E
Malagarasi → 90 5 12S 29 47E
Malagón 31 39 11N 3 52W
Malagón → 31 37 35N 7 29W
Malaimbandy 93 20 20S 45 36E
Malakâl 87 9 33N 31 40E
Malakand 66 34 40N 71 55E
Malakoff 117 32 10N 95 55W
Malamyzh 59 50 0N 136 50E
Malang 73 7 59S 112 45E
Malanje 88 9 36S 16 17E
Mälaren 48 59 30N 17 10E
Malargüe 124 35 32S 69 30W
Malartic 106 48 9N 78 9W
Malatya 64 38 25N 38 20E
Malawi ■ 91 13 0S 34 0E
Malawi, L. 91 12 30S 34 30E
Malay Pen. 71 7 25N 100 0E
Malaya □ 71 4 0N 102 0E
Malaya Belozërka 56 47 12N 34 56E
Malaya Vishera 54 58 55N 32 25E
Malaya Viska 56 48 39N 31 36E
Malaybalay 73 8 5N 125 7E
Malāyer 64 34 19N 48 51E
Malaysia ■ 72 5 0N 110 0E
Malazgirt 64 39 10N 42 33E
Malbaie, La 107 47 40N 70 10W
Malbon 98 21 5S 140 17E
Malbork 28 54 3N 19 1E
Malcésine 38 45 46N 10 48E
Malchin 24 53 43N 12 44E
Malchow 24 53 29N 12 25E
Malcolm 96 28 51S 121 25E
Malczyce 28 51 14N 16 29E
Maldegem 16 51 14N 3 26E
Malden, Mass., U.S.A. 113 42 26N 71 5W
Malden, Mo., U.S.A. 117 36 35N 90 0W
Malden I. 95 4 3S 155 1W
Maldives ■ 60 7 0N 73 0E
Maldonado 125 35 0S 55 0W
Maldonado, Punta 120 16 19N 98 35W
Malé 38 46 20N 10 55E
Malé Karpaty 27 48 30N 17 20E
Maléa, Ákra 45 36 28N 23 7E
Malegaon 68 20 30N 74 38E
Malei 91 17 12S 36 58E
Malela 90 4 22S 26 8E
Målerås 49 56 54N 15 34E
Malerkotla 68 30 32N 75 58E
Máles 45 35 6N 25 35E
Malesherbes 19 48 15N 2 24E
Maleshevska Planina 42 41 38N 23 7E
Malestroit 18 47 49N 2 25W
Malfa 41 38 35N 14 50E
Malgobek 57 43 30N 44 34E
Malgomaj 50 64 40N 16 30E
Malgrat 32 41 39N 2 46E
Malha 81 15 8N 25 10E
Malheur → 118 44 3N 116 59W
Malheur L. 118 43 19N 118 42W
Mali 84 12 10N 12 20W
Mali ■ 85 15 0N 2 0W
Mali → 67 25 40N 97 40E
Mali Kanal 42 45 36N 19 24E
Mali Kyun 71 13 0N 98 20E
Malih → 62 32 20N 35 34E
Malik 73 0 39S 123 16E
Malili 73 2 42S 121 6E
Malimba, Mts. 90 7 30S 29 30E
Malin 54 50 46N 29 3E
Malin Hd. 15 55 18N 7 24W
Malinau 72 3 35N 116 40E
Malindi 90 3 12S 40 5E
Maling 73 1 0N 121 0E
Malingping 73 6 45S 106 2E
Malinyi 91 8 56S 36 0E
Maliqi 44 40 45N 20 48E
Malita 73 6 19N 125 39E
Maljenik 42 43 59N 21 55E
Malkapur, Maharashtra, India 68 20 53N 73 58E
Malkapur, Maharashtra, India 70 16 57N 73 58E
Małkinia Górna 28 52 42N 22 5E
Malko Tŭrnovo 43 41 59N 27 31E
Mallacoota 100 37 40S 149 40E
Mallacoota Inlet 97 37 34S 149 40E
Mallaig 14 57 0N 5 50W
Mallawan 69 27 4N 80 12E
Mallawi 86 27 44N 30 44E
Mallemort 21 43 44N 5 11E
Málles Venosta 38 46 42N 10 32E
Mállia 45 35 17N 25 27E
Mallorca 32 39 30N 3 0E
Mallorytown 113 44 29N 75 53W
Mallow 15 52 8N 8 40W
Malmbäck 49 57 34N 14 28E
Malmberget 50 67 11N 20 40E
Malmédy 16 50 25N 6 2E
Malmesbury 92 33 28S 18 41E
Malmö 49 55 36N 12 59E
Malmöhus län □ 49 55 45N 13 30E
Malmslätt 49 58 27N 15 33E
Malmyzh 55 56 35N 50 41E
Malnaş 46 46 2N 25 49E
Malo Konare 43 42 12N 24 24E
Maloarkhangelsk 55 52 28N 36 30E
Malolos 73 14 50N 120 49E
Malombe L. 91 14 40S 35 15E
Malomir 43 42 16N 26 30E
Malone 114 44 50N 74 19W
Malorad 43 43 28N 23 41E
Malorita 54 51 50N 24 3E
Maloyaroslovets 55 55 2N 36 20E
Malozemelskaya Tundra 52 67 0N 50 0E
Malpartida 31 39 26N 6 30W
Malpelo 126 4 3N 81 35W
Malpica 30 43 19N 8 50W
Malprabha → 70 16 20N 76 5E
Malta, Idaho, U.S.A. 118 42 15N 113 30W
Malta, Mont., U.S.A. 118 48 20N 107 55W
Malta ■ 36 35 50N 14 30E
Malta Channel 40 36 40N 14 0E
Malton, Can. 112 43 42N 79 38W
Malton, U.K. 12 54 9N 0 48W
Maluku 73 1 0S 127 0E
Maluku □ 73 3 0S 128 0E
Maluku, Kepulauan 73 3 0S 128 0E
Malumfashi 85 11 48N 7 39E
Malung 48 60 42N 13 44E
Malvalli 70 12 28N 77 8E
Malvan 70 16 2N 73 30E
Malvern, U.K. 13 52 7N 2 19W
Malvern, U.S.A. 117 34 22N 92 50W
Malvern Hills 13 52 0N 2 19W
Malvérnia 93 22 6S 31 42E
Malvik 47 63 25N 10 40E
Malvinas, Is. = Falkland Is. 128 51 30S 59 0W
Malya 90 3 5S 33 38E
Malyy Lyakhovskiy, Ostrov 59 74 7N 140 36E
Mama 59 58 18N 112 54E
Mamadysh 55 55 44N 51 23E
Mamahatun 64 39 50N 40 23E

* Renamed Mafikeng

* Renamed Peninsular Malaysia

† Renamed Lesosibirsk

** Renamed Butaritari

Mamaia Market Harborough

Mamaia	46	44 18N	28 37 E
Mamanguape	127	6 50S	35 4W
Mamasa	73	2 55S	119 20 E
Mambasa	90	1 22N	29 3 E
Mamberamo →	73	2 0S	137 50 E
Mambilima	91	10 31S	28 45 E
Mambirima	91	11 25S	27 33 E
Mambo	90	4 52S	38 22 E
Mambrui	90	3 5S	40 5 E
Mamburao	73	13 13N	120 39 E
Mameigwess L.	106	52 35N	87 50W
Mamers	18	48 21N	0 22 E
Mamfe	85	5 50N	9 15 E
Mámmola	41	38 23N	16 13 E
Mammoth	119	32 46N	110 43W
Mamoré →	126	10 23S	65 53W
Mamou	84	10 15N	12 0W
Mampatá	84	11 54N	14 53W
Mampawah	72	0 30N	109 5 E
Mampong	85	7 6N	1 26W
Mamry, Jezioro	28	54 5N	21 50 E
Mamuju	73	2 41S	118 50 E
Man	84	7 30N	7 40W
Man →	70	17 31N	75 32 E
Man, I. of	12	54 15N	4 30W
Man Na	67	23 27N	97 19 E
Mana	127	5 45N	53 55W
Måna →	47	59 55N	8 50 E
Manaar, Gulf of	70	8 30N	79 0 E
Manacapuru	126	3 16S	60 37W
Manacor	32	39 34N	3 13 E
Manado	73	1 29N	124 51 E
Managua	121	12 6N	86 20W
Managua, L.	121	12 20N	86 30W
Manakara	93	22 8S	48 1 E
Manam I.	98	4 5S	145 0 E
Manamāh, Al	65	26 11N	50 35 E
Manambao →	93	17 35S	44 0 E
Manambato	93	13 43S	49 7 E
Manambolo →	93	19 18S	44 22 E
Manambolosy	93	16 2S	49 40 E
Mananara	93	16 10S	49 46 E
Mananara →	93	23 21S	47 42 E
Mananjary	93	21 13S	48 20 E
Manantenina	93	24 17S	47 19 E
Manaos = Manaus	126	3 0S	60 0W
Manapouri	101	45 34S	167 39 E
Manapouri, L.	101	45 32S	167 32 E
Manar →	70	18 50N	77 20 E
Manas	75	44 17N	85 56 E
Manasir	65	24 30N	51 10 E
Manaslu, Mt.	69	28 33N	84 33 E
Manasquan	113	40 7N	74 3W
Manassa	119	37 12N	105 58W
Manaung	67	18 45N	93 40 E
Manaus	126	3 0S	60 0W
Manawan L.	109	55 24N	103 14W
Manay	73	7 17N	126 33 E
Mancelona	114	44 54N	85 5W
Mancha, La	33	39 10N	2 54W
Mancha Real	31	37 48N	3 39W
Manche □	18	49 10N	1 20W
Manchegorsk	52	67 40N	32 40 E
Manchester, U.K.	12	53 30N	2 15W
Manchester, Conn., U.S.A.	114	41 47N	72 30W
Manchester, Ga., U.S.A.	115	32 53N	84 32W
Manchester, Iowa, U.S.A.	116	42 28N	91 27W
Manchester, Ky., U.S.A.	114	37 9N	83 45W
Manchester, N.H., U.S.A.	114	42 58N	71 29W
Manchester, N.Y., U.S.A.	112	42 56N	77 16W
Manchester, Vt., U.S.A.	113	43 10N	73 5W
Manchester L.	109	61 28N	107 29W
Manciano	39	42 35N	11 30 E
Mancifa	87	6 53N	41 50 E
Mand →	65	28 20N	52 30 E
Manda, Chunya, Tanz.	90	6 51S	32 29 E
Manda, Ludewe, Tanz.	91	10 30S	34 40 E
Mandaguari	125	23 32S	51 42W
Mandal	47	58 2N	7 25 E
Mandalay	67	22 0N	96 4 E
Mandale = Mandalay	67	22 0N	96 4 E
Mandalī	64	33 43N	45 28 E
Mandalya Körfezi	45	37 15N	27 20 E
Mandan	116	46 50N	101 0W
Mandapeta	70	16 47N	81 56 E
Mandar, Teluk	73	3 35S	119 15 E
Mandas	40	39 40N	9 8 E
Mandasaur	68	24 3N	75 8 E
Mandasor = Mandasaur	68	24 3N	75 8 E
Mandawai (Katingan) →	72	3 30S	113 0 E
Mandelieu-la-Napoule	21	43 34N	6 57 E
Mandera	90	3 55N	41 53 E
Mandera □	90	3 30N	41 0 E
Mandi	68	31 39N	76 58 E
Mandioli	73	0 40S	127 20 E
Mandla	69	22 39N	80 30 E
Mandø	49	55 18N	8 33 E
Mandoto	93	19 34S	46 17 E
Mandoúdhion	45	38 48N	23 29 E
Mandráki	45	36 36N	27 11 E
Mandrare →	93	25 10S	46 30 E
Mandritsara	93	15 50S	48 49 E
Mandúria	41	40 25N	17 38 E
Mandvi	68	22 51N	69 22 E
Mandya	70	12 30N	77 0 E
Mandzai	68	30 55N	67 6 E
Mané	85	12 59N	1 21W
Manengouba, Mts.	85	5 0N	9 50 E
Maner →	70	18 30N	79 40 E
Maneroo	98	23 22S	143 53 E
Maneroo Cr. →	98	23 21S	143 53 E
Manfalût	86	27 20N	30 52 E
Manfred	99	33 19S	143 45 E
Manfredónia	41	41 40N	15 55 E
Manfredónia, G. di	41	41 30N	16 10 E
Manga, Niger	85	15 0N	14 0 E
Manga, Upp. Vol.	85	11 40N	1 4W
Mangaia	101	21 55S	157 55W
Mangalagiri	70	16 26N	80 36 E
Mangalia	46	43 50N	28 35 E
Mangalore	70	12 55N	74 47 E
Manganeses	30	41 45N	5 43W
Mangaon	70	18 15N	73 20 E
Manger	47	60 38N	5 3 E
Manggar	72	2 50S	108 10 E
Manggawitu	73	4 8S	133 32 E
Mangkalihat, Tanjung	73	1 2N	118 59 E
Manglaur	68	29 44N	77 49 E
Mangnai	75	37 52N	91 43 E
Mango	85	10 20N	0 30 E
Mangoky →	93	21 29S	43 41 E
Mangole	73	1 50S	125 55 E
Mangombe	90	1 20S	26 48 E
Mangonui	101	35 1S	173 32 E
Mangualde	30	40 38N	7 48W
Mangueigne	81	10 30N	21 15 E
Mangueira, Lagoa da	125	33 0S	52 50W
Manguéni, Hamada	83	22 35N	12 40 E
Mangum	117	34 50N	99 30W
Mangyshlak P-ov.	57	44 30N	52 30 E
Mangyshlakskiy Zaliv	57	44 40N	50 50 E
Manhattan, Kans., U.S.A.	116	39 10N	96 40W
Manhattan, Nev., U.S.A.	119	38 31N	117 3W
Manhiça	93	25 23S	32 49 E
Manhuaçu	127	20 15S	42 2W
Mania →	93	19 42S	45 22 E
Maniago	39	46 11N	12 40 E
Manica e Sofala □	93	19 10S	33 45 E
Manicaland □	91	19 0S	32 30 E
Manicoré	126	5 48S	61 16W
Manicouagan →	107	49 30N	68 30W
Manicouagan L.	107	51 25N	68 15W
Manīfah	64	27 44N	49 0 E
Manigotagan	109	51 6N	96 18W
Manigotagan L.	109	50 52N	95 37W
Manihiki	95	10 24S	161 1W
Manika, Plat. de la	91	10 0S	25 5 E
Manila, Phil.	73	14 40N	121 3 E
Manila, U.S.A.	118	41 0N	109 44W
Manila B.	73	14 0N	120 0 E
Manilla	99	30 45S	150 43 E
Manimpé	84	14 11N	5 28W
Manipur □	67	25 0N	94 0 E
Manipur →	67	23 45N	94 20 E
Manisa	64	38 38N	27 30 E
Manistee	114	44 15N	86 20W
Manistee →	114	44 15N	86 21W
Manistique	114	45 59N	86 18W
Manito L.	109	52 43N	109 43W
Manitoba □	109	55 30N	97 0W
Manitoba, L.	109	51 0N	98 45W
Manitou	109	49 15N	98 32W
Manitou I.	106	47 22N	87 30W
Manitou Is.	114	45 8N	86 0W
Manitou L., Ont., Can.	109	49 15N	93 0W
Manitou L., Qué., Can.	107	50 55N	65 17W
Manitou Springs	116	38 52N	104 55W
Manitoulin I.	106	45 40N	82 30W
Manitowaning	106	45 46N	81 49W
Manitowoc	114	44 8N	87 40W
Manizales	126	5 5N	75 32W
Manja	93	21 26S	44 20 E
Manjakandriana	93	18 55S	47 47 E
Manjeri	70	11 7N	76 11 E
Manjhand	68	25 50N	68 10 E
Manjil	64	36 46N	49 30 E
Manjimup	96	34 15S	116 6 E
Manjra →	70	18 49N	77 52 E
Mankato, Kans., U.S.A.	116	39 49N	98 11W
Mankato, Minn., U.S.A.	116	44 8N	93 59W
Mankayana	93	26 38S	31 6 E
Mankono	84	8 1N	6 10W
Mankota	109	49 25N	107 5W
Manlleu	32	42 2N	2 17 E
Manly	99	33 48S	151 17 E
Manmad	70	20 18N	74 28 E
Manna	72	4 25S	102 55 E
Mannahill	99	32 25S	140 0 E
Mannar	70	9 1N	79 54 E
Mannar, G. of	70	8 30N	79 0 E
Mannar I.	70	9 5N	79 45 E
Mannargudi	70	10 45N	79 51 E
Mannheim	25	49 28N	8 29 E
Manning, Can.	108	56 53N	117 39W
Manning, U.S.A.	115	33 40N	80 9W
Manning →	100	31 52S	152 43 E
Manning Prov. Park	108	49 5N	120 45W
Mannington	114	39 35N	80 25W
Mannu →	40	39 15N	9 32 E
Mannu, C.	40	40 2N	8 24 E
Mannum	99	34 50S	139 20 E
Mano	84	8 3N	12 2W
Manokwari	73	0 54S	134 0 E
Manolás	45	38 4N	21 21 E
Manombo	93	22 57S	43 28 E
Manono	90	7 15S	27 25 E
Manosque	21	43 49N	5 47 E
Manouane L.	107	50 45N	70 45W
Manresa	32	41 48N	1 50 E
Mans, Le	18	48 0N	0 10 E
Mansa, Gujarat, India	68	23 27N	72 45 E
Mansa, Punjab, India	68	30 0N	75 27 E
Mansa, Zambia	91	11 13S	28 55 E
Mansel I.	105	62 0N	80 0W
Mansfield, Austral.	100	37 4S	146 6 E
Mansfield, U.K.	12	53 8N	1 12W
Mansfield, La., U.S.A.	117	32 2N	93 40W
Mansfield, Mass., U.S.A.	113	42 2N	71 12W
Mansfield, Ohio, U.S.A.	114	40 45N	82 30W
Mansfield, Pa., U.S.A.	112	41 48N	77 4W
Mansfield, Wash., U.S.A.	118	47 51N	119 44W
Mansilla de las Mulas	30	42 30N	5 25W
Mansle	20	45 52N	0 9 E
Mansoa	84	12 0N	15 20W
Manson Creek	108	55 37N	124 32W
Mansoura	83	36 1N	4 31 E
Manta	126	1 0S	80 40W
Mantalingajan, Mt.	72	8 55N	117 45 E
Mantare	90	2 42S	33 13 E
Manteca	119	37 50N	121 12W
Manteo	115	35 55N	75 41W
Mantes-la-Jolie	19	49 0N	1 41 E
Manthani	70	18 40N	79 35 E
Manthelan	18	47 9N	0 47 E
Manti	118	39 23N	111 32W
Mantiqueira, Serra da	125	22 0S	44 0W
Manton	114	44 23N	85 25W
Mantorp	49	58 21N	15 20 E
Mántova	38	45 20N	10 42 E
Mänttä	50	62 0N	24 40 E
Mantua = Mántova	38	45 20N	10 42 E
Manturovo	55	58 30N	44 30 E
Manu	126	12 10S	70 51W
Manua Is.	101	14 13S	169 35W
Manuel Alves →	127	11 19S	48 28W
Manui	73	3 35S	123 5 E
Manukan	73	8 14N	123 3 E
Manus I.	98	2 0S	147 0 E
Manvi	70	15 57N	76 59 E
Manville	116	42 48N	104 36W
Manwath	70	19 19N	76 32 E
Many	117	31 36N	93 28W
Manyane	92	23 21S	21 42 E
Manyara, L.	90	3 40S	35 50 E
Manych →	57	47 15N	40 0 E
Manych-Gudilo, Oz.	57	46 24N	42 38 E
Manyonga →	90	4 10S	34 15 E
Manyoni	90	5 45S	34 55 E
Manyoni □	90	6 30S	34 30 E
Manzai	68	32 12N	70 15 E
Manzala, Bahra el	86	31 10N	31 56 E
Manzanares	33	39 0N	3 22W
Manzaneda, Cabeza de	30	42 12N	7 15W
Manzanillo, Cuba	121	20 20N	77 31W
Manzanillo, Mexico	120	19 0N	104 20W
Manzanillo, Pta.	121	9 30N	79 40W
Manzano Mts.	119	34 30N	106 45W
Manzhouli	75	49 35N	117 25 E
Manzini	93	26 30S	31 25 E
Mao	81	14 4N	15 19 E
Maoke, Pegunungan	73	3 40S	137 30 E
Maoming	75	21 50N	110 54 E
Mapam Yumco	75	30 45N	81 28 E
Mapia, Kepulauan	73	0 50N	134 20 E
Mapimí	120	25 50N	103 50W
Mapimí, Bolsón de	120	27 30N	104 15W
Mapinga	90	6 40S	39 12 E
Mapinhane	93	22 20S	35 0 E
Maple Creek	109	49 55N	109 29W
Mapleton	118	44 4N	123 58W
Maplewood	116	38 33N	90 18W
Maprik	98	3 44S	143 3 E
Mapuca	70	15 36N	73 46 E
Mapuera →	126	1 5S	57 2W
Maputo	93	25 58S	32 32 E
Maputo, B. de	93	25 50S	32 45 E
Maqnā	64	28 25N	34 50 E
Maquela do Zombo	88	6 0S	15 15 E
Maquinchao	128	41 15S	68 50W
Maquoketa	116	42 4N	90 40W
Mår →	47	59 59N	8 46 E
Mar Chiquita, L.	124	30 40S	62 50W
Mar del Plata	124	38 0S	57 30W
Mar Menor, L.	33	37 40N	0 45W
Mar, Serra do	125	25 30S	49 0W
Mara	90	1 30S	34 32 E
Mara □	90	1 45S	34 20 E
Maraã	126	1 52S	65 25W
Marabá	127	5 20S	49 5W
Maracá, I. de	127	2 10N	50 30W
Maracaibo	126	10 40N	71 37W
Maracaibo, Lago de	126	9 40N	71 30W
Maracaju	125	21 38S	55 9W
Maracay	126	10 15N	67 28W
Marādah	83	29 15N	19 15 E
Maradi	85	13 29N	8 10 E
Maradun	85	12 35N	6 18 E
Marāgheh	64	37 30N	46 12 E
Marāh	64	25 0N	45 35 E
Marajó, Ilha de	127	1 0S	49 30W
Maralal	90	1 0N	36 38 E
Maralinga	96	30 13S	131 32 E
Marama	99	35 10S	140 10 E
Marampa	84	8 45N	12 28W
Maramureș □	46	47 45N	24 0 E
Marana	119	32 30N	111 9W
Maranchón	32	41 6N	2 15W
Marand	64	38 30N	45 45 E
Marandellas	91	18 5S	31 42 E
Maranguape	127	3 55S	38 50W
Maranhão = São Luis	127	2 39S	44 15W
Maranhão □	127	5 0S	46 0W
Marano, L. di	39	45 42N	13 13 E
Maranoa →	97	27 50S	148 37 E
Marañón →	126	4 30S	73 35W
Maraş	64	37 37N	36 53 E
Mărășești	46	45 52N	27 14 E
Maratea	41	39 59N	15 43 E
Marateca	31	38 34N	8 40W
Marathókambos	45	37 43N	26 42 E
Marathon, Austral.	98	20 51S	143 32 E
Marathon, Can.	106	48 44N	86 23W
Marathón	45	38 11N	23 58 E
Marathon, N.Y., U.S.A.	113	42 25N	76 3W
Marathon, Tex., U.S.A.	117	30 15N	103 15W
Maratua	73	2 10N	118 35 E
Marbella	31	36 30N	4 57W
Marble Bar	96	21 9S	119 44 E
Marble Falls	117	30 30N	98 15W
Marblehead	113	42 29N	70 51W
Marburg	24	50 49N	8 36 E
Marby	48	63 7N	14 18 E
Marcal →	27	47 41N	17 32 E
Marcali	27	46 35N	17 25 E
Marcaria	38	45 7N	10 34 E
March	13	52 33N	0 5 E
Marchand = Rommani	82	33 20N	6 40W
Marché	20	46 0N	1 20 E
Marche □	39	43 22N	13 10 E
Marche-en-Famenne	16	50 14N	5 19 E
Marchena	31	37 18N	5 23W
Marches = Marche	39	43 22N	13 10 E
Marciana Marina	38	42 44N	10 12 E
Marcianise	41	41 3N	14 16 E
Marcigny	21	46 17N	4 2 E
Marcillac-Vallon	20	44 29N	2 27 E
Marcillat	20	46 12N	2 38 E
Marck	19	50 57N	1 57 E
Marckolsheim	19	48 10N	7 30 E
Marcos Juárez	124	32 42S	62 5W
Marcus	94	24 0N	153 45 E
Marcus Necker Ridge	94	20 0N	175 0 E
Marcy Mt.	113	44 7N	73 55W
Mardin	64	37 20N	40 43 E
Maree L.	14	57 40N	5 30W
Mareeba	97	16 59S	145 28 E
Marek	73	4 41S	120 24 E
Marek = Stanke Dimitrov	42	42 17N	23 9 E
Maremma	38	42 45N	11 15 E
Marëna	84	14 0N	7 20W
Marenberg	39	46 38N	15 13 E
Marengo	116	41 42N	92 5W
Marennes	20	45 49N	1 7W
Marenyi	90	4 22S	39 8 E
Marerano	93	21 23S	44 52 E
Maréttimo	40	37 58N	12 5 E
Mareuil-sur-Lay	20	46 32N	1 14W
Marfa	117	30 15N	104 0W
Marganets	56	47 40N	34 40 E
Margao	70	15 12N	73 58 E
Margaret Bay	108	51 20N	126 35W
Margaret L.	108	58 56N	115 25W
Margarita	120	9 20N	79 55W
Margarita, Isla de	126	11 0N	64 0W
Margarítion	44	39 22N	20 26 E
Margate, S. Afr.	93	30 50S	30 20 E
Margate, U.K.	13	51 23N	1 24 E
Margeride, Mts. de la	20	44 43N	3 38 E
Margherita di Savola	41	41 25N	16 5 E
Marghita	46	47 22N	22 22 E
Margonin	28	52 58N	17 5 E
Marguerite	108	52 30N	122 25W
Marhoum	82	34 27N	0 11W
Mari, A.S.S.R. □	55	56 30N	48 0 E
María Elena	124	22 18S	69 40W
María Grande	124	31 45S	59 55W
Maria I.	96	14 52S	135 45 E
Maria van Diemen, C.	101	34 29S	172 40 E
Mariager	49	56 40N	10 0 E
Mariager Fjord	49	56 42N	10 19 E
Mariakani	90	3 50S	39 27 E
Marian L.	108	63 0N	116 15W
Mariana Is.	94	17 0N	145 0 E
Mariana Trench	94	13 0N	145 0 E
Marianao	121	23 8N	82 24W
Marianna, Ark., U.S.A.	117	34 48N	90 48W
Marianna, Fla., U.S.A.	115	30 45N	85 15W
Mariannelund	49	57 37N	15 35 E
Mariánské Lázně	26	49 48N	12 41 E
Marias →	118	47 56N	110 30W
Mariato, Punta	121	7 12N	80 52W
Mariazell	26	47 47N	15 19 E
Ma'rib	63	15 25N	45 30 E
Maribo	49	54 48N	11 30 E
Maribor	39	46 36N	15 40 E
Marico →	92	23 35S	26 57 E
Maricopa, Ariz., U.S.A.	119	33 5N	112 2W
Maricopa, Calif., U.S.A.	119	35 7N	119 27W
Marîdî	87	4 55N	29 25 E
Maridi, Wadi →	87	6 15N	29 21 E
Marie-Galante	121	15 56N	61 16W
Mariecourt	105	61 30N	72 0W
Mariefred	48	59 15N	17 12 E
Mariehamn	51	60 5N	19 55 E
Marienberg, Ger.	24	50 40N	13 10 E
Marienberg, Neth.	16	52 30N	6 35 E
Marienbourg	16	50 6N	4 31 E
Mariental	92	24 36S	18 0 E
Marienville	112	41 27N	79 8W
Mariestad	49	58 43N	13 50 E
Marietta, Ga., U.S.A.	115	34 0N	84 30W
Marietta, Ohio, U.S.A.	114	39 27N	81 27W
Marieville	113	45 26N	73 10W
Marignane	21	43 25N	5 13 E
Mariinsk	58	56 10N	87 20 E
Mariinskiy Posad	55	56 10N	47 45 E
Marília	125	22 13S	50 0W
Marín	30	42 23N	8 42W
Marina di Cirò	41	39 22N	17 8 E
Mariña, La	30	43 30N	7 40W
Marina Plains	98	14 37S	143 57 E
Marinduque	73	13 25N	122 0 E
Marine City	114	42 45N	82 29W
Marinel, Le	91	10 25S	25 17 E
Marineo	40	37 57N	13 23 E
Marinette, Ariz., U.S.A.	119	33 41N	112 16W
Marinette, Wis., U.S.A.	114	45 4N	87 40W
Maringá	125	23 26S	52 2W
Marinha Grande	31	39 45N	8 56W
Marion, Ala., U.S.A.	115	32 33N	87 20W
Marion, Ill., U.S.A.	117	37 45N	88 55W
Marion, Ind., U.S.A.	114	40 35N	85 40W
Marion, Iowa, U.S.A.	116	42 2N	91 36W
Marion, Kans., U.S.A.	116	38 25N	97 2W
Marion, Mich., U.S.A.	114	44 7N	85 8W
Marion, N.C., U.S.A.	115	35 42N	82 0W
Marion, Ohio, U.S.A.	114	40 38N	83 8W
Marion, S.C., U.S.A.	115	34 11N	79 22W
Marion, Va., U.S.A.	115	36 51N	81 29W
Marion, L.	115	33 30N	80 15W
Marion Reef	97	19 10S	152 17 E
Mariposa	119	37 31N	119 59W
Mariscal Estigarribia	124	22 3S	60 40W
Maritime Alps = Alpes Maritimes	38	44 10N	7 10 E
Maritsa	43	42 1N	25 50 E
Maritsá	45	36 22N	28 10 E
Maritsa →	43	42 15N	24 0 E
Mariyampole = Kapsukas	54	54 33N	23 19 E
Marka	86	18 14N	41 19 E
Markapur	70	15 44N	79 19 E
Markaryd	49	56 28N	13 35 E
Markdale	112	44 19N	80 39W
Marked Tree	117	35 35N	90 24W
Markelsdorfer Huk	24	54 33N	11 0 E
Marken	16	52 26N	5 12 E
Market Drayton	12	52 55N	2 30W
Market Harborough	13	52 29N	0 55W

Markham Mbulu

Markham 112 43 52N 79 16W
Markham → 98 6 41 S 147 2 E
Markham I. 4 84 0N 0 45W
Markham L. 109 62 30N 102 35W
Markham Mt. 5 83 0S 164 0 E
Marki 28 52 20N 21 2 E
Markoupoulon 45 37 53N 23 57 E
Markovac 42 44 14N 21 7 E
Markovo 59 64 40N 169 40 E
Markoye 85 14 39N 0 2 E
Marks 55 51 45N 46 50 E
Marksville 117 31 10N 92 2W
Markt Schwaben 25 48 14N 11 49 E
Marktredwitz 25 50 1N 12 2 E
Marlboro 113 42 19N 71 33W
Marlborough 98 22 46 S 149 52 E
Marlborough □ 101 41 45 S 173 33 E
Marlborough Downs 13 51 25N 1 55W
Marle 19 49 43N 3 47 E
Marlin 117 31 25N 96 50W
Marlow, Ger. 24 54 8N 12 34 E
Marlow, U.S.A. 117 34 40N 97 58W
Marmagao 70 15 25N 73 56 E
Marmande 20 44 30N 0 10 E
Marmara 56 40 35N 27 38 E
Marmara Denizi 64 40 45N 28 15 E
Marmara, Sea of = Marmara Denizi 64 40 45N 28 15 E
Marmaris 64 36 50N 28 14 E
Marmarth 116 46 21N 103 52W
Marmion L. 106 48 55N 91 20W
Marmolada, Mte. 39 46 25N 11 55 E
Marmolejo 31 38 3N 4 13W
Marmora 106 44 28N 77 41W
Marnay 19 47 20N 5 48 E
Marne 24 53 57N 9 1 E
Marne □ 19 49 0N 4 10 E
Marne → 19 8 23N 18 36 E
Marnoo 100 36 40 S 142 54 E
Marnueli 57 41 30N 44 48 E
Maroala 93 15 23 S 47 59 E
Maroantsetra 93 15 26 S 49 44 E
Maromandia 93 14 13 S 48 5 E
Maroni → 127 4 0N 52 0W
Marónia 44 40 53N 25 24 E
Maroochydore 99 26 29 S 153 5 E
Maroona 99 37 27 S 142 54 E
Maros → 27 46 15N 20 13 E
Marosakoa 93 15 26 S 46 38 E
Marostica 39 45 44N 11 40 E
Maroua 85 10 40N 14 20 E
Marovoay 93 16 6 S 46 39 E
Marquard 92 28 40 S 27 28 E
Marqueira 31 38 41N 9 9W
Marquesas Is. 95 9 30 S 140 0W
Marquette 114 46 30N 87 21W
Marquise 19 50 50N 1 40 E
Marra, Gebel 87 7 20N 27 35 E
Marradi 39 44 5N 11 37 E
Marrakech 82 31 9N 8 0W
Marrawah 99 40 55 S 144 42 E
Marree 97 29 39 S 138 1 E
Marrimane 93 22 58 S 33 34 E
Marronne → 20 45 4N 1 56 E
Marroquí, Punta 31 36 0N 5 37W
Marrowie Creek 99 33 23 S 145 40 E
Marrubane 91 18 0 S 37 0 E
Marrupa 91 13 8 S 37 30 E
Mars, Le 116 43 0N 96 0W
Marsa Brega 83 30 24N 19 37 E
Marsá Susah 81 32 52N 21 59 E
Marsabit 90 2 18N 38 0 E
Marsabit □ 90 2 45N 37 45 E
Marsala 40 37 48N 12 25 E
Marsaxlokk (Medport) 36 35 47N 14 32 E
Marsciano 39 42 54N 12 20 E
Marsden 99 33 47 S 147 32 E
Marseillan 20 43 23N 3 31 E
Marseille 21 43 18N 5 23 E
Marseilles = Marseille 21 43 18N 5 23 E
Marsh I. 117 29 35N 91 50W
Marsh L. 116 45 5N 96 0W
Marshall, Liberia 84 6 8N 10 22W
Marshall, Ark., U.S.A. 117 35 58N 92 40W
Marshall, Mich., U.S.A. 114 42 17N 84 59W
Marshall, Minn., U.S.A. 116 44 25N 95 45W
Marshall, Mo., U.S.A. 116 39 8N 93 15W
Marshall, Tex., U.S.A. 117 32 29N 94 20W
Marshall Is. 94 9 0N 171 0 E
Marshalltown 116 42 5N 92 56W
Marshfield, Mo., U.S.A. 117 37 20N 92 58W
Marshfield, Wis., U.S.A. 116 44 42N 90 10W
Mársico Nuovo 41 40 26N 15 43 E
Märsta 48 59 37N 17 52 E
Marstal 49 54 51N 10 30 E
Marstrand 49 57 53N 11 35 E
Mart 117 31 34N 96 51W
Marta → 39 42 14N 11 42 E
Martaban 67 16 30N 97 35 E
Martaban, G. of 67 16 5N 96 30 E
Martagne 18 46 59N 0 57W
Martano 41 40 14N 18 18 E
Martapura, Kalimantan, Indon. 72 3 22 S 114 47 E
Martapura, Sumatera, Indon. 72 4 19 S 104 22 E
Marte 85 12 23N 13 46 E
Martel 20 44 57N 1 37 E
Martelange 16 49 49N 5 43 E
Martés, Sierra 33 39 20N 1 0W
Marthaguy Creek → 99 30 16 S 147 35 E
Martha's Vineyard 114 41 25N 70 35W
Martigné-Ferchaud 18 47 50N 1 20W
Martigny 25 46 6N 7 3 E
Martigues 21 43 24N 5 4 E
Martil 82 35 36N 5 15W
Martin, Czech. 27 49 6N 18 48 E
Martin, S.D., U.S.A. 116 43 11N 101 45W
Martin, Tenn., U.S.A. 117 36 23N 88 51W
Martín → 32 41 18N 0 19W
Martin, L. 115 32 45N 85 50W
Martina Franca 41 40 42N 17 20 E
Martinborough 101 41 14 S 175 29 E
Martinique 121 14 40N 61 0W
Martinique Passage 121 15 15N 61 0W
Martinon 45 38 35N 23 15 E
Martinópolis 125 22 11 S 51 12W
Martins Ferry 113 40 5N 80 46W
Martinsberg 26 48 22N 15 9 E
Martinsburg, Pa., U.S.A. 112 40 18N 78 21W
Martinsburg, W. Va., U.S.A. 114 39 30N 77 57W
Martinsville, Ind., U.S.A. 114 39 29N 86 23W
Martinsville, Va., U.S.A. 115 36 41N 79 52W
Marton 101 40 4 S 175 23 E
Martorell 32 41 28N 1 56 E
Martos 31 37 44N 3 58W
Martuni 57 40 9N 45 10 E
Maru 85 12 22N 6 22 E
Marudi 72 4 10N 114 19 E
Ma'ruf 65 31 30N 67 6 E
Marugame 74 34 15N 133 40 E
Marúggio 41 40 20N 17 33 E
Marulan 99 34 43 S 150 3 E
Marunga 92 17 28 S 20 2 E
Marungu, Mts. 90 7 30 S 30 0 E
Mårvatn 47 60 8N 8 14 E
Marvejols 20 44 33N 3 19 E
Marwar 68 25 43N 73 45 E
Mary 58 37 40N 61 50 E
Mary Frances L. 109 63 19N 106 13W
Mary Kathleen 97 20 44 S 139 48 E
Maryborough, Queens., Austral. 97 25 31 S 152 37 E
Maryborough, Vic., Austral. 97 37 0 S 143 44 E
Maryfield 109 49 50N 101 35W
Maryland □ 114 39 10N 76 40W
Maryland Jc. 91 17 45 S 30 31 E
Maryport 12 54 43N 3 30W
Mary's Harbour 107 52 18N 55 51W
Marystown 107 47 10N 55 10W
Marysvale 119 38 25N 112 17W
Marysville, Can. 108 49 35N 116 0W
Marysville, Calif., U.S.A. 118 39 14N 121 40W
Marysville, Kans., U.S.A. 116 39 50N 96 49W
Marysville, Mich., U.S.A. 112 42 55N 82 29W
Marysville, Ohio, U.S.A. 114 40 15N 83 20W
Maryvale 99 28 4 S 152 12 E
Maryville 115 35 50N 84 0W
Marzūq 83 25 53N 13 57 E
Masada = Mesada 62 31 20N 35 19 E
Masahunga 90 2 6 S 33 18 E
Masai Steppe 90 4 30 S 36 30 E
Masaka 90 0 21 S 31 45 E
Masalembo, Kepulauan 72 5 35 S 114 30 E
Masalima, Kepulauan 72 5 4 S 117 5 E
Masamba 73 2 30 S 120 15 E
Masan 76 35 11N 128 32 E
Masanasa 33 39 25N 0 25W
Masandam, Ras 65 26 30N 56 30 E
Masasi 91 10 45 S 38 52 E
Masasi □ 91 10 45 S 38 50 E
Masaya 121 12 0N 86 7W
Masba 85 10 35N 13 1 E
Masbate 73 12 21N 123 36 E
Mascara 82 35 26N 0 6 E
Mascota 120 20 30N 104 50W
Masela 73 8 9 S 129 51 E
Maseru 92 29 18 S 27 30 E
Mashaba 91 20 2 S 30 29 E
Mashābih 64 25 35N 36 30 E
Mashan 77 23 40N 108 11 E
Mashhad 65 36 20N 59 35 E
Mashi 85 13 0N 7 54 E
Mashike 74 43 31N 141 30 E
Mashkel, Hamun-i- 66 28 30N 63 0 E
Mashki Chah 66 29 5N 62 30 E
Mashtaga 57 40 35N 50 0 E
Masi 50 69 26N 23 40 E
Masi Manimba 88 4 40 S 17 54 E
Masindi 90 1 40N 31 43 E
Masindi Port 90 1 43N 32 2 E
Masisea 126 8 35 S 74 22W
Masisi 90 1 23 S 28 49 E
Masjed Soleyman 64 31 55N 49 18 E
Mask, L. 15 53 36N 9 24W
Maski 70 15 56N 76 46 E
Maslen Nos 43 42 18N 27 48 E
Maslinica 39 43 24N 16 13 E
Masnou 32 41 28N 2 20 E
Masoala, Tanjon' i 93 15 59 S 50 13 E
Masoarivo 93 19 3 S 44 19 E
Masohi 73 3 2 S 128 15 E
Masomeloka 93 20 17 S 48 37 E
Mason, S.D., U.S.A. 116 45 12N 103 27W
Mason, Tex., U.S.A. 117 30 45N 99 15W
Mason City, Iowa, U.S.A. 116 43 9N 93 12W
Mason City, Wash., U.S.A. 118 48 0N 119 0W
Masqat 65 23 37N 58 36 E
Massa 38 44 2N 10 7 E
Massa Maríttima 38 43 3N 10 52 E
Massa, O. → 82 30 2N 9 40W
Massachusetts □ 114 42 25N 72 0W
Massachusetts B. 113 42 30N 70 0W
Massada 62 33 41N 35 36 E
Massafra 41 40 35N 17 8 E
Massaguet 81 12 28N 15 26 E
Massakory 81 13 0N 15 49 E
Massangena 93 21 34 S 33 0 E
Massarosa 38 43 53N 10 17 E
Massat 20 42 53N 1 21 E
Massawa = Mitsiwa 87 15 35N 39 25 E
Massena 114 44 52N 74 55W
Massénya 81 11 21N 16 9 E
Masset 108 54 2N 132 10W
Massiac 20 45 15N 3 11 E
Massif Central 20 45 30N 2 21 E
Massillon 114 40 47N 81 30W
Massinga 93 23 46 S 32 4 E
Masson 113 45 32N 75 25W
Masson I. 5 66 10 S 93 20 E
Mastaba 86 20 52N 39 30 E
Mastanli = Momchilgrad 43 41 33N 25 23 E
Masterton 101 40 56 S 175 39 E
Mástikho, Ákra 45 38 10N 26 2 E
Mastuj 69 36 20N 72 36 E
Mastung 66 29 50N 66 56 E
Mastura 86 23 7N 38 52 E
Masuda 74 34 40N 131 51 E
Maswa □ 90 3 30 S 34 0 E
Matabeleland North □ 91 19 0 S 28 0 E
Matabeleland South □ 91 21 0 S 29 0 E
Mataboor 73 1 41 S 138 3 E
Matachel → 31 38 50N 6 17W
Matachewan 106 47 56N 80 39W
Matad 75 47 11N 115 27 E
Matadi 88 5 52 S 13 31 E
Matagalpa 121 13 0N 85 58W
Matagami 106 49 45N 77 34W
Matagami, L. 106 49 50N 77 40W
Matagorda 117 28 43N 96 0W
Matagorda B. 117 28 30N 96 15W
Matagorda I. 117 28 10N 96 40W
Matak, P. 72 3 18N 106 16 E
Matakana 99 32 59 S 145 54 E
Matale 70 7 30N 80 37 E
Matam 84 15 34N 13 17W
Matameye 85 13 26N 8 28 E
Matamoros, Coahuila, Mexico 120 25 33N 103 15W
Matamoros, Puebla, Mexico 120 18 2N 98 17W
Matamoros, Tamaulipas, Mexico 120 25 50N 97 30W
Ma'ṭan as Sarra 81 21 45N 22 0 E
Matandu → 91 8 45 S 34 19 E
Matane 107 48 50N 67 33W
Matankari 85 13 46N 4 1 E
Matanuska 104 61 39N 149 19W
Matanzas 121 23 0N 81 40W
Matapan, C. = Taínaron, Akra 45 36 22N 22 27 E
Matapédia 107 48 0N 66 59W
Matara 70 5 58N 80 30 E
Mataram 72 8 41 S 116 10 E
Matarani 126 77 0 S 72 10W
Mataranka 96 14 55 S 133 4 E
Mataró 32 41 32N 2 29 E
Matarraña → 32 41 14N 0 22 E
Mataruška Banja 42 43 40N 20 45 E
Matatiele 93 30 20 S 28 49 E
Mataura 101 46 11 S 168 51 E
Matehuala 120 23 40N 100 40W
Mateke Hills 91 21 48 S 31 0 E
Matélica 39 43 15N 13 0 E
Matera 41 40 40N 16 37 E
Mátészalka 27 47 58N 22 20 E
Matetsi 91 18 12 S 26 0 E
Mateur 83 37 0N 9 40 E
Matfors 48 62 21N 17 2 E
Matha 20 45 52N 0 20W
Matheson Island 109 51 45N 96 56W
Mathis 117 28 4N 97 48W
Mathura 68 27 30N 77 40 E
Mati 73 6 55N 126 15 E
Mati → 44 41 40N 20 0 E
Matías Romero 120 16 53N 95 2W
Matibane 91 14 49 S 40 45 E
Matima 92 20 15 S 24 26 E
Matlock 12 53 8N 1 32W
Matmata 83 33 37N 9 59 E
Matna 87 13 49N 35 10 E
Mato Grosso □ 127 14 0 S 55 0W
Mato Grosso, Planalto do 127 15 0 S 59 57W
Matochkin Shar 58 73 10N 56 40 E
Matopo Hills 91 20 36 S 28 20 E
Matopos 91 20 20 S 28 29 E
Matosinhos 30 41 11N 8 42W
Matour 21 46 19N 4 29 E
Matrah 65 23 37N 58 30 E
Matrûh 86 31 19N 27 9 E
Matsena 85 13 5N 10 5 E
Matsesta 57 43 34N 39 51 E
Matsue 74 35 25N 133 10 E
Matsumoto 74 36 15N 138 0 E
Matsuyama 74 33 45N 132 45 E
Mattagami → 106 50 43N 81 29W
Mattancheri 70 9 50N 76 15 E
Mattawa 106 46 20N 78 45W
Mattawamkeag 107 45 30N 68 21W
Matterhorn 25 45 58N 7 39 E
Mattersburg 27 47 44N 16 24 E
Matthew Town 121 20 57N 73 40W
Matthew's Ridge 126 7 37N 60 10W
Mattice 106 49 40N 83 20W
Mattituck 113 40 58N 72 32W
Mattmar 48 63 18N 13 45 E
Matua 72 2 58 S 110 46 E
Matuba 93 24 28 S 32 49 E
Matucana 126 11 55 S 76 25W
Matun 66 33 22N 69 58 E
Maturín 126 9 45N 63 11W
Matveyev Kurgan 57 47 35N 38 47 E
Mau-é-ele 93 24 18 S 34 2 E
Mau Escarpment 90 0 40 S 36 0 E
Mau Ranipur 68 25 16N 79 8 E
Maubeuge 19 50 17N 3 57 E
Maubourguet 20 43 29N 0 1 E
Maude 99 34 29 S 144 18 E
Maudheim 5 71 5 S 11 0W
Maudin Sun 67 16 0N 94 30 E
Maués 126 3 20 S 57 45W
Maui 110 20 45N 156 20 E
Mauke 101 20 09 S 157 20W
Maule □ 124 36 5 S 72 30W
Mauléon-Licharre 20 43 14N 0 54W
Maumee 114 41 35N 83 40W
Maumee → 114 41 42N 83 28W
Maumere 73 8 38 S 122 13 E
Maun 92 20 0 S 23 26 E
Mauna Kea 110 19 50N 155 28W
Mauna Loa 110 21 8N 157 10W
Maunath Bhanjan 69 25 56N 83 33 E
Maungmagan Kyunzu 71 14 0N 97 48 E
Maupin 118 45 12N 121 9W
Maure-de-Bretagne 18 47 53N 2 0W
Maurepas L. 117 30 18N 90 35W
Maures 21 43 15N 6 15 E
Mauriac 20 45 13N 2 19 E
Maurice L. 96 29 30 S 131 0 E
Mauritania ■ 80 20 50N 10 0W
Mauritius ■ 3 20 0 S 57 0 E
Mauron 18 48 9N 2 18W
Maurs 20 44 43N 2 12 E
Mauston 116 43 48N 90 5W
Mauterndorf 26 47 9N 13 40 E
Mauvezin 20 43 44N 0 53 E
Mauzé-sur-le-Mignon 20 46 12N 0 41W
Mavelikara 70 9 14N 76 32 E
Mavinga 89 15 50 S 20 21 E
Mavli 68 24 45N 73 55 E
Mavqi'im 62 31 38N 34 32 E
Mavrova 44 40 26N 19 32 E
Mavuradonha Mts. 91 16 30 S 31 30 E
Mawa 90 2 45N 26 40 E
Mawana 68 29 6N 77 58 E
Mawand 68 29 33N 68 38 E
Mawk Mai 67 20 14N 97 37 E
Mawson Base 5 67 30 S 62 53 E
Max 116 47 50N 101 20W
Maxcanú 120 20 40N 92 0W
Maxhamish L. 108 59 50N 123 17W
Maxixe 93 23 54 S 35 17 E
Maxville 113 45 17N 74 51W
Maxwelton 98 20 43 S 142 41 E
May Downs 98 22 38 S 148 55 E
May Glacier Tongue 5 66 08 S 130 35 E
May Pen 121 17 58N 77 15W
Maya 32 43 12N 1 29W
Maya → 59 54 31N 134 41 E
Maya Mts. 120 16 30N 89 0W
Mayaguana 121 22 30N 72 44W
Mayagüez 121 18 12N 67 9W
Mayahi 85 13 58N 7 40 E
Mayals 32 41 22N 0 30 E
Mayarí 121 20 40N 75 41W
Mayavaram = Mayuram 70 11 3N 79 42 E
Maybell 118 40 30N 108 4W
Maychew 87 12 50N 39 31 E
Maydena 99 42 45 S 146 30 E
Maydos 44 40 13N 26 20 E
Mayen 25 50 18N 7 10 E
Mayenne 18 48 20N 0 38W
Mayenne □ 18 48 10N 0 40W
Mayenne → 18 47 30N 0 32W
Mayer 119 34 28N 112 17W
Mayerthorpe 108 53 57N 115 8W
Mayfield 115 36 45N 88 40W
Mayhill 119 32 58N 105 30W
Maykop 57 44 35N 40 25 E
Maymyo 71 22 2N 96 28 E
Maynooth 15 53 22N 6 38W
Mayo 104 63 38N 135 57W
Mayo □ 15 53 47N 9 7W
Mayo → 120 26 45N 109 47W
Mayo L. 104 63 45N 135 0W
Mayon, Mt. 73 13 15N 123 42 E
Mayor I. 101 37 16 S 176 17 E
Mayorga 30 42 10N 5 16W
Mayskiy 57 43 47N 44 2 E
Mayson L. 109 57 55N 107 10W
Maysville 114 38 39N 83 46W
Maythalūn 62 32 21N 35 16 E
Mayu 73 1 30N 126 30 E
Mayuram 70 11 3N 79 42 E
Mayville, N.D., U.S.A. 116 47 30N 97 23W
Mayville, N.Y., U.S.A. 112 42 14N 79 31W
Mayya 59 61 44N 130 18 E
Mazabuka 91 15 52 S 27 44 E
Mazagán = El Jadida 82 33 11N 8 17W
Mazagão 127 0 7 S 51 16W
Mazamet 20 43 30N 2 20 E
Mazán 126 3 30 S 73 0W
Mazan Deran □ 65 36 30N 52 0 E
Mazar-e Sharīf 65 36 41N 67 0 E
Mazar, O. → 82 31 50N 1 36 E
Mazara del Vallo 40 37 40N 12 34 E
Mazarredo 128 47 10 S 66 50W
Mazarrón 33 37 38N 1 19W
Mazarrón, Golfo de 33 37 27N 1 19W
Mazaruni → 126 6 25N 58 35W
Mazatenango 120 14 35N 91 30W
Mazatlán 120 23 10N 106 30W
Mažeikiai 54 56 20N 22 20 E
Māzhān 65 32 30N 59 0 E
Mazīnān 65 36 19N 56 56 E
Mazoe, Mozam. 91 16 42 S 33 7 E
Mazoe, Zimb. 91 17 28 S 30 58 E
Mazrūb 87 14 0N 29 20 E
Mazu Dao 77 26 10N 119 55 E
Mazurian Lakes = Mazurski, Pojezierze 28 53 50N 21 0 E
Mazurski, Pojezierze 28 53 50N 21 0 E
Mazzarino 41 37 19N 14 12 E
Mbaba 84 14 59N 16 44W
Mbabane 93 26 18 S 31 6 E
Mbagne 84 16 6N 14 47W
M'bahiakro 84 7 33N 4 19W
Mbaïki 88 3 53N 18 1 E
Mbala 91 8 46 S 31 24 E
Mbale 90 1 8N 34 12 E
Mbalmayo 88 3 33N 11 33 E
Mbamba Bay 91 11 13 S 34 49 E
Mbandaka 88 0 1N 18 18 E
Mbanga 85 4 30N 9 33 E
Mbanza Congo 88 6 18 S 14 16 E
Mbanza Ngungu 88 5 12 S 14 53 E
Mbarara 90 0 35 S 30 40 E
Mbatto 84 6 28N 4 22W
Mbenkuru → 91 9 25 S 39 50 E
Mberubu 85 6 10N 7 38 E
Mbesuma 91 10 0 S 32 2 E
Mbeya 91 8 54 S 33 29 E
Mbeya □ 90 8 15 S 33 30 E
Mbinga 91 10 50 S 35 0 E
Mbinga □ 91 10 50 S 35 0 E
Mbini = Rio Muni □ 88 1 30N 10 0 E
Mboki 87 5 19N 25 58 E
Mboro 84 15 9N 16 54W
Mboune 84 14 42N 13 34W
Mbour 84 14 22N 16 54W
Mbout 84 16 1N 12 38W
Mbozi □ 91 9 0 S 32 50 E
Mbuji-Mayi 90 6 9 S 23 40 E
Mbulu 90 3 45 S 35 30 E
Mbulu □ 90 3 52 S 35 33 E

Mburucuyá Miarinarivo

Mburucuyá 124 28 1 S 58 14W
Mcherrah 82 27 0N 4 30W
Mchinja 91 9 44 S 39 45 E
Mchinji 91 13 47 S 32 58 E
Mdennah 82 24 37N 6 0W
Mdina 36 35 51N 14 25 E
Mead, L. 119 36 1N 114 44W
Meade 117 37 18N 100 25W
Meadow Lake 109 54 10N 108 26W
Meadow Lake Prov. Park 109 54 27N 109 0W
Meadow Valley Wash → 119 36 39N 114 35W
Meadville 114 41 39N 80 9W
Meaford 106 44 36N 80 35W
Mealhada 30 40 22N 8 27W
Mealy Mts. 107 53 10N 58 0W
Meander River 108 59 2N 117 42W
Meares, C. 118 45 37N 124 0W
Mearim → 127 3 4 S 44 35W
Meath □ 15 53 32N 6 40W
Meath Park 109 53 27N 105 22W
Meaulne 20 46 36N 2 36 E
Meaux 19 48 58N 2 50 E
Mecanhelas 91 15 12 S 35 54 E
Mecca 119 33 37N 116 3W
Mecca = Makkah 86 21 30N 39 54 E
Mechanicsburg 112 40 12N 77 0W
Mechanicville 113 42 54N 73 41W
Mechara 87 8 36N 40 20 E
Mechelen 16 51 2N 4 29 E
Mecheria 82 33 35N 0 18W
Mechernich 24 50 35N 6 39 E
Mechetinskaya 57 46 45N 40 32 E
Mechra Benâbbou 82 32 39N 7 48W
Mecidiye 44 40 38N 26 32 E
Mecitözü 56 40 32N 35 17 E
Meconta 91 14 59 S 39 50 E
Meda 30 40 57N 7 18W
Meda → 96 17 20 S 123 50 E
Medak 70 18 1N 78 15 E
Medan 72 3 40N 98 38 E
Medanosa, Pta. 128 48 8 S 66 0W
Medawachchiya 70 8 30N 80 30 E
Medéa 82 36 12N 2 50 E
Mededa 42 43 44N 19 15 E
Medellín 126 6 15N 75 35W
Medemblik 16 52 46N 5 8 E
Médenine 83 33 21N 10 30 E
Mederdra 84 17 0N 15 38W
Medford, Oreg., U.S.A. 118 42 20N 122 52W
Medford, Wis., U.S.A. 116 45 9N 90 21W
Medgidia 46 44 15N 28 19 E
Medi 87 5 4N 30 42 E
Media Agua 124 31 58 S 68 25W
Media Luna 124 34 45 S 66 44W
Mediaş 46 46 9N 24 22 E
Medical Lake 118 47 35N 117 42W
Medicina 39 44 29N 11 38 E
Medicine Bow 118 41 56N 106 11W
Medicine Bow Pk. 118 41 21N 106 19W
Medicine Bow Ra. 118 41 10N 106 25W
Medicine Hat 109 50 0N 110 45W
Medicine Lake 116 48 30N 104 30W
Medicine Lodge 117 37 20N 98 37W
Medina, N.D., U.S.A. 116 46 57N 99 20W
Medina, N.Y., U.S.A. 114 43 15N 78 27W
Medina, Ohio, U.S.A. 114 41 9N 81 50W
Medina = Al Madīnah 64 24 35N 39 35 E
Medina → 117 29 10N 98 20W
Medina de Ríoseco 30 41 53N 5 3W
Medina del Campo 30 41 18N 4 55W
Medina L. 117 29 35N 98 58W
Medina-Sidonia 31 36 28N 5 57W
Medinaceli 32 41 12N 2 30W
Mediterranean Sea 34 35 0N 15 0 E
Medjerda, O. → 83 37 7N 10 13 E
Medley 109 54 25N 110 16W
Médoc 20 45 10N 0 56W
Medstead 109 53 19N 108 5W
Medulin 39 44 49N 13 55 E
Medveda 42 42 50N 21 32 E
Medveditsa →, R.S.F.S.R., U.S.S.R. 55 49 35N 42 41 E
Medveditsa →, R.S.F.S.R., U.S.S.R. 55 57 5N 37 30 E
Medvedok 55 57 20N 50 1 E
Medvezhi, Ostrava 59 71 0N 161 0 E
Medvezhyegorsk 52 63 0N 34 25 E
Medway → 13 51 28N 0 45 E
Medyn 55 54 58N 35 52 E
Medzev 27 48 43N 20 55 E
Medzilaborce 27 49 17N 21 52 E
Meekatharra 96 26 32 S 118 29 E
Meeker 118 40 1N 107 58W
Meerane 24 50 51N 12 30 E
Meersburg 25 47 42N 9 16 E
Meerut 68 29 1N 77 42 E
Meeteetse 118 44 10N 108 56W
Mega 87 3 57N 38 19 E
Megálo Khorío 45 36 27N 27 24 E
Megálo Petalí 45 38 0N 24 15 E
Megalópolis 45 37 25N 22 7 E
Meganísi 45 38 39N 20 48 E
Mégara 45 37 58N 23 22 E
Megarine 83 33 14N 6 2 E
Megdhova → 45 39 10N 21 45 E
Mégève 21 45 51N 6 37 E
Meghezez, Mt. 87 9 18N 39 26 E
Meghna → 69 22 50N 90 50 E
Megiddo 62 32 36N 35 11 E
Mégiscane, L. 106 48 35N 75 55W
Megiste 35 36 8N 29 34 E
Mehadia 46 44 56N 22 23 E
Mehaïguene, O. → 82 32 15N 2 59 E
Meharry, Mt. 96 22 59 S 118 35 E
Mehedinţi □ 46 44 40N 22 45 E
Meheisa 86 19 38N 32 57 E
Mehndawal 69 26 58N 83 5 E
Mehsana 68 23 39N 72 26 E
Mehun-sur-Yèvre 19 47 10N 2 13 E
Mei Jiang → 77 24 25N 116 35 E
Mei Xian 75 24 16N 116 6 E
Meiganga 88 6 30N 14 25 E
Meiktila 67 20 53N 95 54 E
Meiningen 24 50 32N 10 25 E
Me'ir Shefeya 62 32 35N 34 58 E
Meira, Sierra de 30 43 15N 7 15W
Meiringen 25 46 43N 8 12 E
Meissen 24 51 10N 13 29 E
Meissner 24 51 13N 9 51 E
Meitan 77 27 45N 107 29 E
Méjean, Causse 20 44 15N 3 30 E
Mejillones 124 23 10 S 70 30W
Mékambo 88 1 2N 13 50 E
Mekdela 87 11 24N 39 10 E
Mekele 87 13 33N 39 30 E
Meklong = Samut Songkhram 71 13 24N 100 1 E
Meknès 82 33 57N 5 33W
Meko 85 7 27N 2 52 E
Mekong → 71 9 30N 106 15 E
Mekongga 73 3 39 S 121 15 E
Melagiri Hills 70 12 20N 77 30 E
Melah, Sebkhet el 82 29 20N 1 30W
Melaka 71 2 15N 102 15 E
Melaka □ 71 2 20N 102 15 E
Melalap 72 5 10N 116 5 E
Mélambes 45 35 8N 24 40 E
Melanesia 94 4 0 S 155 0 E
Melapalaiyam 70 8 39N 77 44 E
Melbourne, Austral. 97 37 50 S 145 0 E
Melbourne, U.S.A. 115 28 4N 80 35W
Melchor Múzquiz 120 27 50N 101 30W
Melchor Ocampo (San Pedro Ocampo) 120 24 52N 101 40W
Méldola 39 44 7N 12 3 E
Meldorf 24 54 5N 9 5 E
Mêle-sur-Sarthe, Le 18 48 31N 0 22 E
Melegnano 38 45 21N 9 20 E
Melenci 42 45 32N 20 20 E
Melenki 55 55 20N 41 37 E
Mélèzes → 105 57 30N 71 0W
Melfi, Chad 81 11 0N 17 59 E
Melfi, Italy 41 41 0N 15 33 E
Melfort, Can. 109 52 50N 104 37W
Melfort, Zimb. 91 18 0 S 31 25 E
Melgaço 30 42 7N 8 15W
Melgar de Fernamental 30 42 27N 4 17W
Melhus 47 63 17N 10 18 E
Meligalá 45 37 15N 21 59 E
Melilla 82 35 21N 2 57W
Melilot 62 31 22N 34 37 E
Melipilla 124 33 42 S 71 15W
Mélissa Óros 45 37 32N 26 4 E
Melita 109 49 15N 101 0W
Mélito di Porto Salvo 41 37 55N 15 47 E
Melitopol 56 46 50N 35 22 E
Melk 26 48 13N 15 20 E
Mellan-Fryken 48 59 45N 13 10 E
Mellansel 50 63 25N 18 17 E
Melle, France 20 46 14N 0 10W
Melle, Ger. 24 52 12N 8 20 E
Mellégue, O. → 83 36 32N 8 51 E
Mellen 116 46 19N 90 36W
Mellerud 49 58 41N 12 28 E
Mellette 116 45 11N 98 29W
Mellid 30 42 55N 8 1W
Mellish Reef 97 17 25 S 155 50 E
Mellit 87 14 7N 25 34 E
Mellrichstadt 25 50 26N 10 19 E
Melnik 43 41 30N 23 25 E
Mělník 26 50 22N 14 23 E
Melo 125 32 20 S 54 10W
Melolo 73 9 53 S 120 40 E
Melovoye 57 49 25N 40 5 E
Melrhir, Chott 83 34 25N 6 24 E
Melrose, Austral. 99 32 42 S 146 57 E
Melrose, U.K. 14 53 35N 2 44W
Melrose, U.S.A. 117 34 27N 103 33W
Melstone 118 46 36N 107 50W
Melsungen 24 51 8N 9 34 E
Melton Mowbray 12 52 46N 0 52W
Melun 19 48 32N 2 39 E
Melur 70 10 2N 78 23 E
Melut 87 10 30N 32 13 E
Melville 109 50 55N 102 50W
Melville B. 97 12 0 S 136 45 E
Melville, C. 97 14 11 S 144 30 E
Melville I., Austral. 96 11 30 S 131 0 E
Melville I., Can. 4 75 30N 112 0W
Melville, L. 107 53 30N 60 0W
Melville Pen. 105 68 0N 84 0W
Melvin → 108 59 11N 117 31W
Mélykút 27 46 11N 19 25 E
Memaliaj 44 40 25N 19 58 E
Memba 91 14 11 S 40 30 E
Memboro 73 9 30 S 119 30 E
Membrilla 33 38 59N 3 21W
Memel 93 27 38 S 29 36 E
Memel = Klaipeda 54 55 43N 21 10 E
Memmingen 25 47 59N 10 12 E
Memphis, Tenn., U.S.A. 117 35 7N 90 0W
Memphis, Tex., U.S.A. 117 34 45N 100 30W
Mena 117 34 40N 94 15W
Mena → 87 5 40N 40 50 E
Menai Strait 12 53 14N 4 10W
Ménaka 85 15 59N 2 18 E
Menan = Chao Phraya → 71 13 32N 100 36 E
Menarandra → 93 25 17 S 44 30 E
Menard 117 30 57N 99 48W
Menasha 114 44 13N 88 27W
Menate 72 0 12 S 113 3 E
Mendawai → 72 3 17 S 113 21 E
Mende 20 44 31N 3 30 E
Mendebo Mts. 87 7 0N 39 22 E
Menderes → 64 37 25N 28 45 E
Mendi, Ethiopia 87 9 47N 35 4 E
Mendi, P.N.G. 98 6 11 S 143 39 E
Mendip Hills 13 51 17N 2 40W
Mendocino 118 39 26N 123 50W
Mendocino Seascarp 95 41 0N 140 0W
Mendota, Calif., U.S.A. 119 36 46N 120 24W
Mendota, Ill., U.S.A. 116 41 35N 89 5W
Mendoza 124 32 50 S 68 52W
Mendoza □ 124 33 0 S 69 0W
Mene Grande 126 9 49N 70 56W
Menemen 64 38 34N 27 3 E
Menen 16 50 47N 3 7 E
Menfi 40 37 36N 12 57 E
Mengcheng 77 33 18N 116 31 E
Mengeš 39 46 24N 14 35 E
Menggala 72 4 30 S 105 15 E
Mengibar 31 37 58N 3 48W
Mengoub 82 29 49N 5 26W
Mengshan 77 24 14N 110 55 E
Mengzi 75 23 20N 103 22 E
Menihek L. 107 54 0N 67 0W
Menin = Menen 16 50 47N 3 7 E
Menindee 97 32 20 S 142 25 E
Menindee, L. 99 32 20 S 142 25 E
Meningie 99 35 35 S 139 0 E
Menominee 114 45 9N 87 39W
Menominee → 114 45 5N 87 36W
Menomonie 116 44 50N 91 54W
Menongue 89 14 48 S 17 52 E
Menorca 32 40 0N 4 0 E
Mentawai, Kepulauan 72 2 0 S 99 0 E
Menton 21 43 50N 7 29 E
Mentor 112 41 40N 81 21W
Menzel-Bourguiba 83 39 9N 9 49 E
Menzel Chaker 83 35 0N 10 26 E
Menzel-Temime 83 36 46N 11 0 E
Menzelinsk 52 55 53N 53 1 E
Menzies 96 29 40 S 120 58 E
Me'ona (Tarshiha) 62 33 1N 35 15 E
Mepaco 91 15 57 S 30 48 E
Meppel 16 52 42N 6 12 E
Meppen 24 52 41N 7 20 E
Mequinenza 32 41 22N 0 17 E
Mer Rouge 117 32 47N 91 48W
Merabéllou, Kólpos 45 35 10N 25 50 E
Merak 73 5 56 S 106 0 E
Meran = Merano 39 46 40N 11 10 E
Merano 39 46 40N 11 10 E
Merate 38 45 42N 9 23 E
Merauke 73 8 29 S 140 24 E
Merbabu 73 7 30 S 110 40 E
Merbein 99 34 10 S 142 2 E
Merca 63 1 48N 44 50 E
Mercadal 32 39 59N 4 5 E
Mercara 70 12 30N 75 45 E
Mercato Saraceno 39 43 57N 12 11 E
Merced 119 37 18N 120 30W
Mercedes, Buenos Aires, Argent. 124 34 40 S 59 30W
Mercedes, Corrientes, Argent. 124 29 10 S 58 5W
Mercedes, San Luis, Argent. 124 33 40 S 65 21W
Mercedes, Uruguay 124 33 12 S 58 0W
Merceditas 124 28 20 S 70 35W
Mercer, N.Z. 101 37 16 S 175 5 E
Mercer, U.S.A. 112 41 14N 80 13W
Mercy C. 105 65 0N 63 30W
Merdrignac 18 48 11N 2 27W
Meredith C. 128 52 15 S 60 40W
Meredith, L. 117 35 30N 101 35W
Merei 46 45 7N 26 43 E
Méréville 19 48 20N 2 5 E
Mergenevsky 57 49 59N 51 15 E
Mergui Arch. = Myeik Kyunzu 71 11 30N 97 30 E
Mérida, Mexico 120 20 9N 89 40W
Mérida, Spain 31 38 55N 6 25W
Mérida, Venez. 126 8 24N 71 8W
Meriden 114 41 33N 72 47W
Meridian, Idaho, U.S.A. 118 43 41N 116 25W
Meridian, Miss., U.S.A. 115 32 20N 88 42W
Meridian, Tex., U.S.A. 117 31 55N 97 37W
Mering 25 48 15N 11 0 E
Meringur 100 34 20 S 141 19 E
Meriruma 127 1 15N 54 50W
Merkel 117 32 30N 100 0W
Merksem 16 51 16N 4 25 E
Merlebach 19 49 5N 6 52 E
Merlerault, Le 18 48 41N 0 16 E
Mern 49 55 3N 12 3 E
Merowe 86 18 29N 31 46 E
Merredin 96 31 28 S 118 18 E
Merrick 14 55 8N 4 30W
Merrickville 113 44 55N 75 50W
Merrill, Oregon, U.S.A. 118 42 2N 121 37W
Merrill, Wis., U.S.A. 116 45 11N 89 41W
Merriman 116 42 55N 101 42W
Merritt 108 50 10N 120 45W
Merriwa 99 32 6 S 150 22 E
Merriwagga 99 33 47 S 145 43 E
Merry I. 106 55 29N 77 31W
Merrygoen 99 31 51 S 149 12 E
Merryville 117 30 47N 93 31W
Mersa Fatma 87 14 57N 40 17 E
Mersch 16 49 44N 6 7 E
Merseburg 24 51 20N 12 0 E
Mersey → 12 53 20N 2 56W
Merseyside □ 12 53 25N 2 55W
Mersin 64 36 51N 34 36 E
Mersing 71 2 25N 103 50 E
Merta 68 26 39N 74 4 E
Merthyr Tydfil 13 51 45N 3 23W
Mértola 31 37 40N 7 40 E
Mertzon 117 31 17N 100 48W
Méru 19 49 13N 2 8 E
Meru, Kenya 90 0 3N 37 40 E
Meru, Tanz. 90 3 15 S 36 46 E
Meru □ 90 0 3N 37 46 E
Merville 19 50 38N 2 38 E
Méry-sur-Seine 19 48 31N 3 54 E
Merzifon 56 40 53N 35 32 E
Merzig 25 49 26N 6 37 E
Merzouga, Erg Tin 83 24 0N 11 4 E
Mesa 119 33 20N 111 56W
Mesa, La, Calif., U.S.A. 119 32 48N 117 5W
Mesa, La, N. Mex., U.S.A. 119 32 6N 106 48W
Mesach Mellet 83 24 30N 11 30 E
Mesada 62 31 20N 35 19 E
Mesagne 41 40 34N 17 48 E
Mesaras, Kólpos 45 35 6N 24 47 E
Meschede 24 51 20N 8 17 E
Mesfinto 87 13 20N 37 22 E
Mesgouez, L. 106 51 20N 75 0W
Meshchovsk 54 54 22N 35 17 E
Meshed = Mashhad 65 36 20N 59 35 E
Meshoppen 113 41 36N 76 3W
Meshra er Req 81 8 25N 29 18 E
Mesick 114 44 24N 85 42W
Mesilinka → 108 56 6N 124 30W
Mesilla 119 32 20N 106 50W
Meslay-du-Maine 18 47 58N 0 33W
Mesocco 25 46 23N 9 12 E
Mesolóngion 45 38 21N 21 28 E
Mesopotamia = Al Jazirah 64 33 30N 44 0 E
Mesoraca 41 39 5N 16 47 E
Mésou Volímais 45 37 53N 20 35 E
Mess Cr. → 108 57 55N 131 14W
Messac 18 47 49N 1 50W
Messad 82 34 8N 3 30 E
Messalo → 91 12 25 S 39 15 E
Méssaména 85 3 48N 12 49 E
Messeix 20 45 37N 2 33 E
Messeue 45 37 12N 21 58 E
Messina, Italy 41 38 10N 15 32 E
Messina, S. Afr. 93 22 20 S 30 0 E
Messina, Str. di 41 38 5N 15 35 E
Messíni 45 37 4N 22 1 E
Messínia □ 45 37 10N 22 0 E
Messiniakós, Kólpos 45 36 45N 22 5 E
Messkirch 25 47 59N 9 7 E
Mesta → 43 41 30N 24 0 E
Mestá, Ákra 45 38 16N 25 53 E
Mestanza 31 38 35N 4 4W
Město Teplá 26 49 59N 12 52 E
Mestre 39 45 30N 12 13 E
Městys Zelezná Ruda 26 49 8N 13 15 E
Meta → 126 6 12N 67 28W
Metairie 117 29 59N 90 9W
Metalici, Munţii 42 46 15N 22 50 E
Metaline Falls 118 48 52N 117 22W
Metán 124 25 30 S 65 0W
Metauro → 39 43 50N 13 3 E
Metema 87 12 56N 36 13 E
Metengobalame 91 14 49 S 34 30 E
Méthana 45 37 35N 23 23 E
Methóni 45 36 49N 21 42 E
Methven 101 43 38 S 171 40 E
Methy L. 109 56 28N 109 30W
Metkovets 43 43 37N 23 10 E
Metković 42 43 6N 17 39 E
Metlakatla 108 55 10N 131 33W
Metlaoui 83 34 24N 8 24 E
Metlika 39 45 40N 15 20 E
Metropolis 117 37 10N 88 47W
Métsovon 44 39 48N 21 12 E
Mettuppalaiyam 70 11 18N 76 59 E
Mettur 70 11 48N 77 47 E
Mettur Dam 70 11 45N 77 45 E
Metulla 62 33 17N 35 34 E
Metz 19 49 8N 6 10 E
Meulaboh 72 4 11N 96 3 E
Meulan 19 49 0N 1 52 E
Meung-sur-Loire 19 47 50N 1 40 E
Meureudu 72 5 19N 96 10 E
Meurthe → 19 48 47N 6 9 E
Meurthe-et-Moselle □ 19 48 52N 6 0 E
Meuse □ 19 49 8N 5 25 E
Meuse → 16 50 45N 5 41 E
Meuselwitz 24 51 3N 12 18 E
Mexborough 12 53 29N 1 18W
Mexia 117 31 38N 96 32W
Mexiana, I. 127 0 0 49 30W
Mexicali 120 32 40N 115 30W
México 120 19 20N 99 10W
Mexico, Me., U.S.A. 113 44 35N 70 30W
Mexico, Mo., U.S.A. 116 39 10N 91 55W
Mexico ■ 120 20 0N 100 0W
México □ 120 19 20N 99 10W
Mexico, G. of 120 25 0N 90 0W
Meyenburg 24 53 19N 12 15 E
Meymac 20 45 32N 2 10 E
Meymaneh 65 35 53N 64 38 E
Meyrargues 21 43 38N 5 32 E
Meyrueis 20 44 12N 3 27 E
Meyssac 20 45 3N 1 40 E
Mezdra 43 43 12N 23 42 E
Mèze 20 43 27N 3 36 E
Mezen 52 65 50N 44 20 E
Mézenc 21 44 55N 4 11 E
Mezeş, Munţii 46 47 5N 23 5 E
Mezha → 54 55 50N 31 45 E
Mézidon 18 49 5N 0 1W
Mézilhac 21 44 49N 4 21 E
Mézin 20 44 4N 0 16 E
Mezőberény 27 46 49N 21 3 E
Mezőfalva 27 46 55N 18 49 E
Mezőhegyes 27 46 19N 20 49 E
Mezőkövácsháza 27 46 25N 20 57 E
Mezőkövesd 27 47 49N 20 35 E
Mézos 20 44 5N 1 10W
Mezőtúr 27 47 0N 20 41 E
Mezquital 120 23 29N 104 23W
Mezzolombardo 38 46 13N 11 5 E
Mgeta 91 8 22 S 36 6 E
Mglin 54 53 2N 32 50 E
Mhlaba Hills 91 18 30 S 30 30 E
Mhow 68 22 33N 75 50 E
Miahuatlán 120 16 21N 96 36W
Miajadas 31 39 9N 5 54W
Mialar 68 26 15N 70 20 E
Miallo 98 16 28 S 145 22 E
Miami, Ariz., U.S.A. 119 33 25N 110 54W
Miami, Fla., U.S.A. 115 25 45N 80 15W
Miami, Tex., U.S.A. 117 35 44N 100 38W
Miami → 114 39 20N 84 40W
Miami Beach 115 25 49N 80 6W
Miamisburg 114 39 40N 84 11W
Mian Xian 77 33 10N 106 32 E
Mianchi 77 34 48N 111 48 E
Mīāndow āb 64 37 0N 46 5 E
Miandrivazo 93 19 31 S 45 29 E
Mīāneh 64 37 30N 47 40 E
Mianwali 68 32 38N 71 28 E
Mianyang, Hubei, China 77 30 25N 113 25 E
Mianyang, Sichuan, China 77 31 22N 104 47 E
Miaoli 75 24 37N 120 49 E
Miarinarivo 93 18 57 S 46 55 E

Miass Mobutu Sese Seko, L.

Miass 52 54 59N 60 6 E
Miasteczko Kraj 28 53 7N 17 1 E
Miastko 28 54 0N 16 58 E
Micăsasa 46 46 7N 24 7 E
Michalovce 27 48 47N 21 58 E
Michelstadt 25 49 40N 9 0 E
Michigan □ 111 44 40N 85 40W
Michigan City 114 41 42N 86 56W
Michigan, L. 114 44 0N 87 0W
Michipicoten 106 47 55N 84 55W
Michipicoten I. 106 47 40N 85 40W
Michoacan □ 120 19 0N 102 0W
Michurin 43 42 9N 27 51 E
Michurinsk 55 52 58N 40 27 E
Miclere 98 22 34S 147 32 E
Mico, Pta. 121 12 0N 83 30W
Micronesia 94 11 0N 160 0 E
Mid Glamorgan □ 13 51 40N 3 25W
Mid-Indian Ridge 94 40 0S 75 0 E
Mid-Oceanic Ridge 94 42 0S 90 0 E
Midai, P. 72 3 0N 107 47 E
Midale 109 49 25N 103 20W
Midas 118 41 14N 116 48W
Middagsfjället 48 63 27N 12 19 E
Middelburg, Neth. 16 51 30N 3 36 E
Middelburg, C. Prov., S. Afr. 92 31 30S 25 0 E
Middelburg, Trans., S. Afr. 93 25 49S 29 28 E
Middelfart 49 55 30N 9 43 E
Middle Alkali L. 118 41 30N 120 3W
Middle Andaman I. 71 12 30N 92 30 E
Middle Loup → 116 41 17N 98 23W
Middleboro 113 41 56N 70 52W
Middleburg, N.Y., U.S.A. 113 42 36N 74 19W
Middleburg, Pa., U.S.A. 112 40 46N 77 5W
Middlebury 113 44 0N 73 9W
Middleport 114 39 0N 82 5W
Middlesboro 115 36 36N 83 43W
Middlesbrough 12 54 35N 1 14W
Middlesex 113 40 36N 74 30W
Middleton 107 44 57N 65 4W
Middleton Cr. → 98 22 35S 141 51 E
Middleton P.O. 98 22 22S 141 32 E
Middletown, Conn., U.S.A. 114 41 37N 72 40W
Middletown, N.Y., U.S.A. 114 41 28N 74 28W
Middletown, Ohio, U.S.A. 114 39 29N 84 25W
Middletown, Pa., U.S.A. 113 40 12N 76 44W
Midelt 82 32 46N 4 44W
Midi, Canal du 20 43 45N 1 21 E
Midi d'Ossau 32 42 50N 0 25W
Midland, Austral. 96 31 54S 115 59 E
Midland, Can. 106 44 45N 79 50W
Midland, Mich., U.S.A. 114 43 37N 84 17W
Midland, Pa., U.S.A. 112 40 39N 80 27W
Midland, Tex., U.S.A. 117 32 0N 102 3W
Midlands □ 91 19 40S 29 0 E
Midleton 15 51 52N 8 12W
Midlothian 117 32 30N 97 0W
Midnapore 69 22 25N 87 21 E
Midongy Atsimo 93 23 35S 47 1 E
Midongy, Tangorombohitr' i 93 23 30S 47 0 E
Midour → 20 43 54N 0 30W
Midouze → 20 43 48N 0 51W
Midvale 118 40 39N 111 58W
Midway Is. 94 28 13N 177 22W
Midwest 118 43 27N 106 19W
Midyat 64 37 25N 41 23 E
Midzur 42 43 24N 22 40 E
Mie □ 74 34 30N 136 10 E
Miechów 28 50 21N 20 5 E
Miedwie, Jezioro 28 53 17N 14 54 E
Międzybód 28 51 25N 17 34 E
Międzychód 28 52 35N 15 53 E
Międzylesie 28 50 8N 16 40 E
Międzyrzec Podlaski 28 51 58N 22 45 E
Międzyrzecz 28 52 26N 15 35 E
Międzyzdroje 28 53 56N 14 26 E
Miejska 28 51 39N 16 58 E
Miélan 20 43 27N 0 19 E
Mielec 28 50 15N 21 25 E
Mienga 92 17 12S 19 48 E
Miercurea Ciuc 46 46 21N 25 48 E
Mieres 30 43 18N 5 48W
Mieroszów 28 50 40N 16 11 E
Mieso 87 9 15N 40 43 E
Mieszkowice 28 52 47N 14 30 E
Migdāl 62 32 51N 35 30 E
Migdal Afeq 62 32 5N 34 58 E
Migennes 19 47 58N 3 31 E
Migliarino 39 44 45N 11 56 E
Miguel Alemán, Presa 120 18 15N 96 40W
Miguel Alves 127 4 11S 42 55W
Mihara 74 34 24N 133 5 E
Mijares → 32 39 55N 0 1W
Mijas 31 36 36N 4 40W
Mikese 90 6 48S 37 55 E
Mikha-Tskhakaya 57 42 15N 42 7 E
Mikhailovka 56 47 36N 35 16 E
Mikhaylov 55 54 14N 39 0 E
Mikhaylovgrad 43 43 27N 23 16 E
Mikhaylovka, Azerbaijan, U.S.S.R. 57 41 31N 48 52 E
Mikhaylovka, R.S.F.S.R., U.S.S.R. 55 50 3N 43 5 E
Mikhnevo 55 55 4N 37 59 E
Mikinai 45 37 43N 22 46 E
Mikindani 91 10 15S 40 2 E
Mikkeli 51 61 43N 27 15 E
Mikkeli □ 50 62 0N 28 0 E
Mikkwa → 108 58 25N 114 46W
Mikniya 87 17 0N 33 45 E
Mikołajki 28 53 49N 21 37 E
Mikołów 27 50 10N 18 50 E
Míkonos 45 37 30N 25 25 E
Mikrí Préspa, Límni 44 40 47N 21 3 E
Mikrón Dhérion 44 41 19N 26 6 E
Mikstat 28 51 32N 17 59 E
Mikulov 27 48 48N 16 39 E
Mikumi 90 7 26S 37 0 E
Mikun 52 62 20N 50 0 E
Mikura-Jima 74 33 52N 139 36 E
Milaca 116 45 45N 93 40W
Milagro 126 2 11S 79 36W
Milan, Mo., U.S.A. 116 40 10N 93 5W
Milan, Tenn., U.S.A. 115 35 55N 88 45W
Milan = Milano 38 45 28N 9 10 E
Milange 91 16 3S 35 45 E
Milano 38 45 28N 9 10 E
Milâs 64 37 20N 27 50 E
Milazzo 41 38 13N 15 13 E
Milbank 116 45 17N 96 38W
Milden 109 51 29N 107 32W
Mildmay 112 44 3N 81 7W
Mildura 97 34 13S 142 9 E
Miléai 44 39 20N 23 9 E
Miles, Austral. 97 26 40S 150 9 E
Miles, U.S.A. 117 31 39N 100 11W
Miles City 116 46 24N 105 50W
Milestone 109 49 59N 104 31W
Mileto 41 38 37N 16 3 E
Miletto, Mte. 41 41 26N 14 23 E
Miletus 45 37 20N 27 33 E
Milevsko 26 49 27N 14 21 E
Milford, Conn., U.S.A. 113 41 13N 73 4W
Milford, Del., U.S.A. 114 38 52N 75 27W
Milford, Mass., U.S.A. 113 42 8N 71 30W
Milford, Pa., U.S.A. 113 41 20N 74 47W
Milford, Utah, U.S.A. 119 38 20N 113 0W
Milford Haven 13 51 43N 5 2W
Milford Haven, B. 13 51 40N 5 10W
Milford Sd. 101 44 41S 167 47 E
Milḥ, Baḥr al 64 32 40N 43 35 E
Milḥ, Ras al 81 31 54N 25 6 E
Miliana, Aïn Salah, Alg. 82 27 20N 2 32 E
Miliana, Médéa, Alg. 82 36 20N 2 15 E
Milicz 28 51 31N 17 19 E
Militello in Val di Catánia 41 37 16N 14 46 E
Milk → 118 48 5N 106 15W
Milk River 108 49 10N 112 5W
Milk, Wadi el → 86 17 55N 30 20 E
Mill City 118 44 45N 122 28W
Mill I. 5 66 0S 101 30 E
Millau 20 44 8N 3 4 E
Millbridge 112 44 41N 77 36W
Millbrook 112 44 10N 78 29W
Mille 115 33 7N 83 15W
Mille Lacs, L. 116 46 10N 93 30W
Mille Lacs, L. des 106 48 45N 90 35W
Millen 115 32 50N 81 57W
Miller 116 44 35N 98 59W
Millerovo 57 48 57N 40 28 E
Millersburg, Ohio, U.S.A. 112 40 32N 81 52W
Millersburg, Pa., U.S.A. 112 40 32N 76 58W
Millerton 113 41 57N 73 32W
Millevaches, Plateau de 20 45 45N 2 0 E
Millicent 97 37 34S 140 21 E
Millinocket 107 45 45N 68 45W
Millmerran 99 27 53S 151 16 E
Mills L. 108 61 30N 118 20W
Millsboro 112 40 0N 80 0W
Milltown Malbay 15 52 51N 9 25W
Millville 114 39 22N 75 0W
Millwood Res. 117 33 45N 94 0W
Milly 19 48 24N 2 28 E
Milna 39 43 20N 16 28 E
Milne Inlet 105 72 30N 80 0W
Milnor 116 46 19N 97 29W
Milo 108 50 34N 112 53W
Mílos 45 36 44N 24 25 E
Miloševo 42 45 42N 20 20 E
Miłosław 28 52 12N 17 32 E
Milparinka P.O. 99 29 46S 141 57 E
Miltenberg 25 49 41N 9 13 E
Milton, Can. 112 43 33N 79 53W
Milton, N.Z. 101 46 7S 169 59 E
Milton, U.K. 14 57 18N 4 32W
Milton, Fla., U.S.A. 115 30 38N 87 0W
Milton, Pa., U.S.A. 114 41 0N 76 53W
Milton-Freewater 118 45 57N 118 24W
Milton Keynes 13 52 3N 0 42W
Miltou 81 10 14N 17 26 E
Milverton 112 43 34N 80 55W
Milwaukee 114 43 9N 87 58W
Milwaukie 118 45 27N 122 39W
Mim 84 6 57N 2 33W
Mimizan 20 44 12N 1 13W
Mimon 26 50 38N 14 43 E
Min Jiang →, Fujian, China 75 26 0N 119 35 E
Min Jiang →, Sichuan, China 75 28 45N 104 40 E
Min Xian 77 34 25N 104 0 E
Mina 119 38 21N 118 9W
Mina Pirquitas 124 22 40S 66 30W
Mīnā Su'ud 64 28 45N 48 28 E
Mīnā'al Aḥmadī 64 29 5N 48 10 E
Mīnāb 65 27 10N 57 1 E
Minago → 109 54 33N 98 59W
Minaki 109 49 59N 94 40W
Minamata 74 32 10N 130 30 E
Minas 125 34 20S 55 10W
Minas Basin 107 45 20N 64 12W
Minas de Rio Tinto 31 37 42N 6 35W
Minas de San Quintín 31 38 49N 4 23W
Minas Gerais □ 127 18 50S 46 0W
Minas, Sierra de las 120 15 9N 89 31W
Minatitlán 120 17 58N 94 35W
Minbu 67 20 10N 94 52 E
Mincio → 38 45 4N 10 59 E
Mindanao 73 8 0N 125 0 E
* Mindanao Sea 73 9 0N 124 0 E
Mindanao Trench 73 8 0N 128 0 E
Mindel → 25 48 31N 10 23 E
Mindelheim 25 48 4N 10 30 E
Minden, Can. 112 44 55N 78 43W
Minden, Ger. 24 52 18N 8 45 E
Minden, U.S.A. 117 32 40N 93 20W
Mindiptana 73 5 55S 140 22 E
Mindona, L. 100 33 6S 142 6 E
Mindoro 73 13 0N 121 0 E
Mindoro Strait 73 12 30N 120 30 E
Mindouli 88 4 12S 14 28 E
Minehead 13 51 12N 3 29W
Mineola 117 32 40N 95 30W
Mineral Wells 117 32 50N 98 5W
Mineralnyye Vody 57 44 2N 43 8 E

* Renamed Bohol Sea

Minersville, Pa., U.S.A. 113 40 11N 76 17W
Minersville, Utah, U.S.A. 119 38 14N 112 58W
Minerva 112 40 43N 81 8W
Minervino Murge 41 41 6N 16 4 E
Minetto 113 43 24N 76 28W
Mingan 107 50 20N 64 0W
Mingechaur 57 40 45N 47 0 E
Mingechaurskoye Vdkhr. 57 40 56N 47 20 E
Mingela 98 19 52S 146 38 E
Mingera Cr. → 98 20 38S 138 10 E
Minggang 77 32 24N 114 3 E
Mingin 67 22 50N 94 30 E
Minglanilla 32 39 34N 1 38W
Mingorria 30 40 45N 4 40W
Mingxi 77 26 18N 117 12 E
Minićevo 42 43 42N 22 18 E
Minidoka 118 42 47N 113 34W
Minigwal L. 96 29 31S 123 14 E
Minipi, L. 107 52 25N 60 45W
Mink L. 108 61 54N 117 40W
Minna 85 9 37N 6 30 E
Minneapolis, Kans., U.S.A. 116 39 11N 97 40W
Minneapolis, Minn., U.S.A. 116 44 58N 93 20W
Minnedosa 109 50 14N 99 50W
Minnesota □ 116 46 40N 94 0W
Minnesund 47 60 23N 11 14 E
Minnitaki L. 106 49 57N 92 10W
Miño → 30 41 52N 8 40W
Minoa 45 35 6N 25 45 E
Minorca = Menorca 32 40 0N 4 0 E
Minore 99 32 14S 148 27 E
Minot 116 48 10N 101 15W
Minqing 77 26 15N 118 50 E
Minquiers, Les 18 48 58N 2 8W
Minsen 24 53 43N 7 58 E
Minsk 54 53 52N 27 30 E
Mińsk Mazowiecki 28 52 10N 21 33 E
Mintaka Pass 69 37 0N 74 58 E
Minto 104 64 55N 149 20W
Minton 109 49 10N 104 35W
Minturn 118 39 35N 106 25W
Minturno 40 41 15N 13 43 E
Minûf 86 30 26N 30 52 E
Minusinsk 59 53 50N 91 20 E
Minutang 67 28 15N 96 30 E
Minvoul 88 2 9N 12 8 E
Minya el Qamh 86 30 31N 31 21 E
Mionica 42 44 14N 20 6 E
Mir 85 14 5N 11 59 E
Mir-Bashir 57 40 20N 46 58 E
Mira, Italy 39 45 26N 12 9 E
Mira, Port. 30 40 26N 8 44W
Mira → 31 37 43N 8 47W
Mirabella Eclano 41 41 3N 14 59 E
Miraflores Locks 120 8 59N 79 36W
Miraj 70 16 50N 74 45 E
Miram 98 21 15S 148 55 E
Miramar, Argent. 124 38 15S 57 50W
Miramar, Mozam. 93 23 50S 35 35 E
Miramas 21 43 33N 4 59 E
Mirambeau 20 45 23N 0 35W
Miramichi B. 107 47 15N 65 0W
Miramont-de-Guyenne 20 44 37N 0 21 E
Miranda 127 20 10S 56 15W
Miranda de Ebro 32 42 41N 2 57W
Miranda do Corvo 30 40 6N 8 20W
Miranda do Douro 30 41 30N 6 16W
Mirande 20 43 31N 0 25 E
Mirandela 30 41 32N 7 10W
Mirando City 117 27 28N 98 59W
Mirandola 38 44 53N 11 2 E
Mirandópolis 125 21 9S 51 6W
Mirango 91 13 32S 34 58 E
Mirano 39 45 29N 12 6 E
Mirassol 125 20 46S 49 28W
Mirbāṭ 63 17 0N 54 45 E
Mirear 86 23 15N 35 41 E
Mirebeau, Côte-d'or, France 19 47 25N 5 20 E
Mirebeau, Vienne, France 18 46 49N 0 10 E
Mirecourt 19 48 20N 6 10 E
Mirgorod 54 49 58N 33 37 E
Miri 72 4 18N 114 0 E
Miriam Vale 98 24 20S 151 33 E
Mirim, Lagoa 125 32 45S 52 50W
Mirnyy, Antarct. 5 66 33S 93 1 E
Mirnyy, U.S.S.R. 59 62 33N 113 53 E
Miroč 42 44 32N 22 16 E
Mirond L. 109 55 6N 102 47W
Mirosławiec 28 53 20N 16 5 E
Mirpur Bibiwari 68 28 33N 67 44 E
Mirpur Khas 68 25 30N 69 0 E
Mirpur Sakro 68 24 33N 67 41 E
Mirria 85 13 43N 9 7 E
Mirror 108 52 30N 113 7W
Mîrşani 46 44 1N 23 59 E
Mirsk 28 50 58N 15 23 E
Miryang 76 35 31N 128 44 E
Mirzaani 57 41 24N 46 5 E
Mirzapur-cum-Vindhyachal 69 25 10N 82 34 E
Miscou I. 107 47 57N 64 31W
Mish'āb, Ra'as al 64 28 15N 48 43 E
Mishan 75 45 37N 131 48 E
Mishawaka 114 41 40N 86 8W
Mishbih, Gebel 86 22 38N 34 44 E
Mishima 74 35 10N 138 52 E
Mishmar Ayyalon 62 31 52N 34 57 E
Mishmar Ha' Emeq 62 32 37N 35 7 E
Mishmar Ha Negev 62 31 22N 34 48 E
Mishmar Ha Yarden 62 33 0N 35 36 E
Misilmeri 40 38 2N 13 25 E
Misima I. 98 10 40S 152 45 E
Misiones □, Argent. 125 27 0S 55 0W
Misiones □, Parag. 124 27 0S 56 0W
Miskīn 65 23 44N 56 52 E
Miskitos, Cayos 121 14 26N 82 50W
Miskolc 27 48 7N 20 50 E
Misoke 90 0 42S 28 2 E
Misool 73 1 52S 130 10 E
Misrātah 83 32 24N 15 3 E
Misrātah □ 83 29 0N 16 0 E
Misriç 64 37 55N 41 40 E
Missanabie 106 48 20N 84 6W
Missinaibi → 106 50 43N 81 29W
Missinaibi L. 106 48 23N 83 40W
Mission, S.D., U.S.A. 116 43 21N 100 36W
Mission, Tex., U.S.A. 117 26 15N 98 20W
Mission City 108 49 10N 122 15W
Missisa L. 106 52 20N 85 7W
Mississagi → 106 46 15N 83 9W
Mississippi → 117 29 0N 89 15W
Mississippi, Delta of the 117 29 15N 90 30W
Mississippi L. 113 45 5N 76 10W
Mississippi □ 117 33 25N 89 0W
Missoula 118 46 52N 114 0W
Missouri □ 116 38 25N 92 30W
Missouri → 116 38 50N 90 8W
Missouri Valley 116 41 33N 95 53W
Mistake B. 109 62 8N 93 0W
Mistassini → 107 48 42N 72 20W
Mistassini L. 106 51 0N 73 30W
Mistastin L. 107 55 57N 63 20W
Mistatim 109 52 52N 103 22W
Mistelbach 27 48 34N 16 34 E
Misterbianco 41 37 32N 15 0 E
Mistretta 41 37 56N 14 20 E
Misty L. 109 58 53N 101 40W
Mît Ghamr 86 30 42N 31 12 E
Mitatib 87 15 59N 36 12 E
Mitchell, Austral. 97 26 29S 147 58 E
Mitchell, Can. 112 43 28N 81 12W
Mitchell, Ind., U.S.A. 114 38 42N 86 25W
Mitchell, Nebr., U.S.A. 116 41 58N 103 45W
Mitchell, Oreg., U.S.A. 118 44 31N 120 8W
Mitchell, S.D., U.S.A. 116 43 40N 98 0W
Mitchell → 97 15 12S 141 35 E
Mitchell, Mt. 115 35 40N 82 20W
Mitchelstown 15 52 16N 8 18W
Mitha Tiwana 68 32 13N 72 6 E
Míthimna 44 39 20N 26 12 E
Mitiaro, I. 101 19 49S 157 43W
Mitilíni 45 39 6N 26 35 E
Mitilinoí 45 37 42N 26 56 E
Mitla 120 16 55N 96 24W
Mito 74 36 20N 140 30 E
Mitsinjo 93 16 1S 45 52 E
Mitsiwa 87 15 35N 39 25 E
Mitsiwa Channel 87 15 30N 40 0 E
Mitta Mitta → 100 36 14S 147 10 E
Mittagong 99 34 28S 150 29 E
Mittelland Kanal 24 52 23N 7 45 E
Mittenwalde 24 52 16N 13 33 E
Mitterteich 25 49 57N 12 15 E
Mittweida 24 50 59N 13 0 E
Mitú 126 1 8N 70 3W
Mitumba 90 7 8S 31 2 E
Mitumba, Chaîne des 90 6 0S 29 0 E
Mitwaba 91 8 2S 27 17 E
Mityana 90 0 23N 32 2 E
Mitzic 88 0 45N 11 40 E
Mixteco → 120 18 11N 98 30W
Miyagi □ 74 38 15N 140 45 E
Miyâh, W. el → 86 25 0N 33 23 E
Miyake-Jima 74 34 0N 139 30 E
Miyako 74 39 40N 141 59 E
Miyakonojō 74 31 40N 131 5 E
Miyazaki 74 31 56N 131 30 E
Miyazaki □ 74 32 30N 131 30 E
Miyazu 74 35 35N 135 10 E
Miyet, Bahr el 64 31 30N 35 30 E
Miyun 76 40 28N 116 50 E
Mizal 64 23 59N 45 11 E
Mizamis = Ozamiz 73 8 15N 123 50 E
Mizdah 83 31 30N 13 0 E
Mizen Hd., Cork, Ireland 15 51 27N 9 50W
Mizen Hd., Wicklow, Ireland 15 52 52N 6 4W
Mizhi 76 37 47N 110 12 E
Mizil 46 44 59N 26 29 E
Mizoram □ 67 23 30N 92 40 E
Mizpe Ramon 62 30 34N 34 49 E
Mjöbäck 49 57 28N 12 53 E
Mjölby 49 58 20N 15 10 E
Mjømna 47 60 55N 4 55 E
Mjörn 49 57 55N 12 25 E
Mjøsa 47 60 48N 11 0 E
Mkata 90 5 45S 38 20 E
Mkokotoni 90 5 55S 39 15 E
Mkomazi 90 4 40S 38 7 E
Mkulwe 91 8 37S 32 20 E
Mkumbi, Ras 90 7 38S 39 55 E
Mkushi 91 14 25S 29 15 E
Mkushi River 91 13 32S 29 45 E
Mkuze → 93 27 45S 32 30 E
Mladá Boleslav 26 50 27N 14 53 E
Mladenovac 42 44 28N 20 44 E
Mlala Hills 90 6 50S 31 40 E
Mlange 91 16 2S 35 33 E
Mlava → 42 44 45N 21 13 E
Mława 28 53 9N 20 25 E
Mlinište 39 44 15N 16 50 E
Mljet 42 42 43N 17 30 E
Mljetski Kanal 42 42 48N 17 35 E
Młynąry 28 54 12N 19 46 E
Młynary 28 54 12N 19 43 E
Mme 85 6 18N 10 14 E
Mo 47 59 28N 7 50 E
Mo i Rana 50 66 15N 14 7 E
Moa 73 8 0S 128 0 E
Moa → 84 6 59N 11 36 E
Moab 119 38 40N 109 35W
Moabi 88 2 24S 10 59 E
Moala 101 18 36S 179 53 E
Moalie Park 99 29 42S 143 3 E
Moaña 30 42 18N 8 43W
Moapa 119 36 45N 114 37W
Moba 90 7 0S 29 48 E
Mobaye 88 4 25N 21 5 E
Mobayi 88 4 15N 21 8 E
Moberley 116 39 25N 92 25W
Moberly → 108 56 12N 120 55W
Mobile 115 30 41N 88 3W
Mobile B. 115 30 30N 88 0W
Mobile, Pt. 115 30 15N 88 0W
Mobridge 116 45 31N 100 28W
Mobutu Sese Seko, L. 90 1 30N 31 0 E

Mocabe Kasari | Moosup

Mocabe Kasari	91	9 58 S	26 12 E
Moçambique	91	15 3 S	40 42 E
Moçambique □	91	14 45 S	38 30 E
* Moçâmedes	89	15 7 S	12 11 E
* Moçâmedes □	92	16 35 S	12 30 E
Mochudi	92	24 27 S	26 7 E
Mocimboa da Praia	91	11 25 S	40 20 E
Mociu	46	46 46N	24 3 E
Möckeln	49	56 40N	14 15 E
Moclips	118	47 14N	124 10W
Mocoa	126	1 7N	76 35W
Mococa	125	21 28 S	47 0W
Mocorito	120	25 30N	107 53W
Moctezuma	120	29 50N	109 0W
Moctezuma →	120	21 59N	98 34W
Mocuba	91	16 54 S	36 57 E
Modalen	47	60 49N	5 48 E
Modane	21	45 12N	6 40 E
Modasa	68	23 30N	73 21 E
Modder →	92	29 2 S	24 37 E
Modderrivier	92	29 2 S	24 38 E
Módena	38	44 39N	10 55 E
Modena	119	37 55N	113 56W
Modesto	119	37 43N	121 0W
Módica	41	36 52N	14 45 E
Modigliana	39	44 9N	11 48 E
Modlin	28	52 24N	20 41 E
Mödling	27	48 5N	16 17 E
Modo	87	5 31N	30 33 E
Modra	27	48 19N	17 20 E
Modriča	42	44 57N	18 17 E
Moe	97	38 12 S	146 19 E
Moebase	91	17 3 S	38 41 E
Moei →	71	17 25N	98 10 E
Moëlan-sur-Mer	18	47 49N	3 38W
Moengo	127	5 45N	54 20W
Moffat	14	55 20N	3 27W
Moga	68	30 48N	75 8 E
Mogadishu = Muqdisho	63	2 2N	45 25 E
Mogador = Essaouira	82	31 32N	9 48W
Mogadouro	30	41 22N	6 47W
Mogami →	74	38 45N	140 0 E
Mogaung	67	25 20N	97 0 E
Møgeltønder	49	54 57N	8 48 E
Mogente	33	38 52N	0 45W
Mogho	87	4 54N	40 16 E
Mogi das Cruzes	125	23 31 S	46 11W
Mogi-Guaçu →	125	20 53 S	48 10W
Mogi-Mirim	125	22 29 S	47 0W
Mogielnica	28	51 42N	20 41 E
Mogilev	54	53 55N	30 18 E
Mogilev-Podolskiy	56	48 20N	27 40 E
Mogilno	28	52 39N	17 55 E
Mogincual	91	15 35 S	40 25 E
Mogliano Véneto	39	45 33N	12 15 E
Mogocha	59	53 40N	119 50 E
Mogoi	73	1 55 S	133 10 E
Mogok	67	23 0N	96 40 E
Mogollon	119	33 25N	108 48W
Mogollon Mesa	119	35 0N	111 0W
Moguer	31	37 15N	6 52W
Mohács	27	45 58N	18 41 E
Mohall	116	48 46N	101 30W
Moḩammadābād	65	37 52N	59 5 E
Mohammadia	82	35 33N	0 3 E
Mohammedia	82	33 44N	7 21W
Mohawk	119	32 45N	113 50W
Mohawk →	113	42 47N	73 42W
Mohe	76	53 28N	122 17 E
Moheda	49	57 1N	14 35 E
Möhne →	24	51 29N	7 57 E
Moholm	49	58 37N	14 5 E
Mohon	19	49 45N	4 44 E
Mohoro	90	8 6 S	39 8 E
Moia	87	5 3N	28 2 E
Moidart, L.	14	56 47N	5 40W
Moinabad	70	17 44N	77 16 E
Moineşti	46	46 28N	26 31 E
Mointy	58	47 10N	73 18 E
Moirans	21	45 20N	5 33 E
Moirans-en-Montagne	21	46 26N	5 43 E
Moíres	45	35 4N	24 56 E
Moisakula	54	58 3N	25 12 E
Moisie	107	50 12N	66 1W
Moisie →	107	50 14N	66 5W
Moissac	20	44 7N	1 5 E
Moïssala	81	8 21N	17 46 E
Moita	31	38 38N	8 58W
Mojácar	33	37 6N	1 55W
Mojados	30	41 26N	4 40W
Mojave	119	35 8N	118 8W
Mojave Desert	119	35 0N	116 30W
Mojo, Boliv.	124	21 48 S	65 33W
Mojo, Ethiopia	87	8 35N	39 5 E
Mojo, Indon.	72	8 10 S	117 40 E
Mojokerto	73	7 29 S	112 25 E
Mokai	101	38 32 S	175 56 E
Mokambo	91	12 25 S	28 20 E
Mokameh	69	25 24N	85 55 E
Mokhós	45	35 16N	25 27 E
Mokhotlong	93	29 22 S	29 2 E
Moknine	83	35 35N	10 58 E
Mokokchung	67	26 15N	94 30 E
Mokra Gora	42	42 50N	20 30 E
Mokronog	39	45 57N	15 9 E
Moksha →	55	54 45N	41 53 E
Mokshan	55	53 25N	44 35 E
Mol	16	51 11N	5 5 E
Mola, C. de la	32	39 40N	4 20 E
Mola di Bari	41	41 3N	17 5 E
Moláoi	45	36 49N	22 56 E
Molat	39	44 15N	14 50 E
Molchanovo	58	57 40N	83 50 E
Mold	12	53 10N	3 10W
Moldava nad Bodvou	27	48 38N	21 0 E
Moldavia = Moldova	46	46 30N	27 0 E
Moldavian S.S.R. □	56	47 0N	28 0 E
Molde	47	62 45N	7 9 E
Moldova	46	46 30N	27 0 E
Moldova Nouă	42	44 45N	21 41 E
Moldoveanu	43	45 36N	24 45 E
Molepolole	92	24 28 S	25 28 E
Molfetta	41	41 12N	16 35 E
Molina de Aragón	32	40 46N	1 52W
Moline	116	41 30N	90 30W
Molinella	39	44 38N	11 40 E
Molinos	124	25 28 S	66 15W
Moliro	90	8 12 S	30 30 E
Molise □	39	41 45N	14 30 E
Moliterno	41	40 14N	15 50 E
Mollahat	69	22 56N	89 48 E
Mölle	49	56 17N	12 31 E
Molledo	30	43 8N	4 6W
Mollendo	126	17 0 S	72 0W
Mollerusa	32	41 37N	0 54 E
Mollina	31	37 8N	4 38W
Mölln	24	53 37N	10 41 E
Mölltorp	49	58 30N	14 26 E
Mölndal	49	57 40N	12 3 E
Molochansk	56	47 15N	35 35 E
Molochnaya →	56	47 0N	35 30 E
Molodechno	54	54 20N	26 50 E
Molokai	110	21 8N	157 0W
Moloma →	55	58 20N	48 15 E
Molong	99	33 5 S	148 54 E
Molopo →	92	28 30 S	20 13 E
Mólos	45	38 47N	22 37 E
Moloundou	88	2 8N	15 15 E
Molsheim	19	48 33N	7 29 E
Molson L.	109	54 22N	96 40W
Molteno	92	31 22 S	26 22 E
Molu	73	6 45 S	131 40 E
Molucca Sea	73	4 0 S	124 0 E
Moluccas = Maluku	73	1 0 S	127 0 E
Molusi	92	20 21 S	24 29 E
Moma, Mozam.	91	16 47 S	39 4 E
Moma, Zaïre	90	1 35 S	23 52 E
Momanga	92	18 7 S	21 41 E
Mombasa	90	4 2 S	39 43 E
Mombuey	30	42 3N	6 20W
Momchilgrad	43	41 33N	25 23 E
Momi	90	1 42 S	27 0 E
Mompós	126	9 14N	74 26W
Møn	49	54 57N	12 15 E
Mon →	67	20 25N	94 30 E
Mona, Canal de la	121	18 30N	67 45W
Mona, I.	121	18 5N	67 54W
Mona, Pta.	121	9 37N	82 36W
Mona, Punta	31	36 43N	3 45W
Monach Is.	14	57 32N	7 40W
Monaco ■	21	43 46N	7 23 E
Monadhliath Mts.	14	57 10N	4 4W
Monaghan	15	54 15N	6 58W
Monaghan □	15	54 10N	7 0W
Monahans	117	31 35N	102 50W
Monapo	91	14 56 S	40 19 E
Monarch Mt.	108	51 55N	125 57W
Monastier-sur-Gazeille, Le	20	44 57N	3 59 E
Monastir	83	35 50N	10 49 E
Monastyriska	54	49 8N	25 14 E
Moncada	32	39 30N	0 24W
Moncalieri	38	45 0N	7 40 E
Moncalvo	38	45 3N	8 15 E
Moncão	30	42 4N	8 27W
Moncarapacho	31	37 5N	7 46W
Moncayo, Sierra del	32	41 48N	1 50W
Mönchengladbach	24	51 12N	6 23 E
Monchique	31	37 19N	8 38W
Monclova	120	26 50N	101 30W
Moncontour	18	48 22N	2 38W
Moncoutant	18	46 43N	0 35W
Moncton	107	46 7N	64 51W
Mondego →	30	40 9N	8 52W
Mondego, Cabo	30	40 11N	8 54W
Mondeodo	73	3 34 S	122 9 E
Mondolfo	39	43 45N	13 8 E
Mondoñedo	30	43 25N	7 23W
Mondovì	38	44 23N	7 49 E
Mondovi	116	44 37N	91 40W
Mondragon	21	44 13N	4 44 E
Mondragone	40	41 8N	13 52 E
Monduli □	90	3 0 S	36 0 E
Monemvasia	45	36 41N	23 3 E
Monessen	114	40 9N	79 50W
Monesterio	31	38 6N	6 15W
Monestier-de-Clermont	21	44 55N	5 38 E
Monêtier-les-Bains, Le	21	44 58N	6 30 E
Monett	117	36 55N	93 56W
Monfalcone	39	45 49N	13 32 E
Monflanquin	20	44 32N	0 47 E
Monforte	31	39 6N	7 25W
Monforte de Lemos	30	42 31N	7 33W
Mong Cai	71	21 27N	107 54 E
Mong Hsu	67	21 54N	98 30 E
Mong Kung	67	21 35N	97 35 E
Mong Lang	71	21 29N	97 52 E
Mong Nai	67	20 32N	97 46 E
Mong Pawk	67	22 4N	99 16 E
Mong Ton	67	20 17N	98 45 E
Mong Wa	67	21 26N	100 27 E
Mong Yai	67	22 21N	98 3 E
Mongalla	87	5 8N	31 42 E
Mongers, L.	96	29 25 S	117 5 E
Monghyr	69	25 23N	86 30 E
Mongla	69	22 8N	89 35 E
Mongo	81	12 14N	18 43 E
Mongolia ■	75	47 0N	103 0 E
Mongonu	85	12 40N	13 32 E
Mongororo	81	12 3N	22 26 E
Mongu	89	15 16 S	23 12 E
Môngua	92	16 43 S	15 20 E
Monistrol	20	45 57N	3 38 E
Monistrol-St-Loire	21	45 17N	4 11 E
Monkey Bay	91	14 7 S	35 1 E
Mońki	28	53 23N	22 48 E
Monkira	98	24 46 S	140 30 E
Monkoto	88	1 38 S	20 35 E
Monmouth, U.K.	13	51 48N	2 43W
Monmouth, U.S.A.	116	40 50N	90 40W
Mono, L.	119	38 0N	119 9W
Monongahela	112	40 12N	79 56W
Monópoli	41	40 57N	17 18 E
Monor	27	47 21N	19 27 E
Monóvar	33	38 28N	0 53W
Monqoumba	88	3 33N	18 40 E
Monreal del Campo	32	40 47N	1 20W
Monreale	40	38 6N	13 16 E
Monroe, Ga., U.S.A.	115	33 47N	83 43W
Monroe, La., U.S.A.	117	32 32N	92 4W
Monroe, Mich., U.S.A.	114	41 55N	83 26W
Monroe, N.C., U.S.A.	115	35 2N	80 37W
Monroe, N.Y., U.S.A.	113	41 19N	74 11W
Monroe, Utah, U.S.A.	119	38 45N	112 5W
Monroe, Wis., U.S.A.	116	42 38N	89 40W
Monroe City	116	39 40N	91 40W
Monroeville	115	31 33N	87 15W
Monrovia, Liberia	84	6 18N	10 47W
Monrovia, U.S.A.	119	34 7N	118 1W
Mons	16	50 27N	3 58 E
Monsaraz	31	38 28N	7 22W
Monse	73	4 0 S	123 10 E
Monségur	20	44 38N	0 4 E
Monsélice	39	45 16N	11 46 E
Mont-de-Marsan	20	43 54N	0 31W
Mont d'Or, Tunnel	19	46 45N	6 18 E
Mont-Dore, Le	20	45 35N	2 50 E
Mont-Joli	107	48 37N	68 10W
Mont Laurier	106	46 35N	75 30W
Mont-sous-Vaudrey	19	46 58N	5 36 E
Mont-St-Michel, Le	18	48 40N	1 30W
Mont Tremblant Prov. Park	106	46 30N	74 30W
Montabaur	24	50 26N	7 49 E
Montagnac	20	43 29N	3 28 E
Montagnana	39	45 13N	11 29 E
Montagu	92	33 45 S	20 8 E
Montagu I.	5	58 25 S	26 20W
Montague, Can.	107	46 10N	62 39W
Montague, Calif., U.S.A.	118	41 47N	122 30W
Montague, Mass., U.S.A.	113	42 31N	72 33W
Montague, I.	120	31 40N	114 56W
Montague I.	104	60 0N	147 0W
Montague Sd.	96	14 28 S	125 20 E
Montaigu	18	46 59N	1 18W
Montalbán	32	40 50N	0 45W
Montalbano di Elicona	41	38 1N	15 0 E
Montalbano Iónico	41	40 17N	16 33 E
Montalbo	32	39 53N	2 42W
Montalcino	39	43 4N	11 30 E
Montalegre	30	41 49N	7 47W
Montalto di Castro	39	42 20N	11 36 E
Montalto Uffugo	41	39 25N	16 9 E
Montamarta	30	41 39N	5 49W
Montaña	126	6 0 S	73 0W
Montana □	110	47 0N	110 0W
Montánchez	31	39 15N	6 8W
Montargis	19	48 0N	2 43 E
Montauban	20	44 0N	1 21 E
Montauk	114	41 3N	71 57W
Montauk Pt.	113	41 4N	71 52W
Montbard	19	47 38N	4 20 E
Montbéliard	19	47 31N	6 48 E
Montblanch	32	41 23N	1 4 E
Montbrison	21	45 36N	4 3 E
Montcalm, Pic de	20	42 40N	1 25 E
Montceau-les-Mines	19	46 40N	4 23 E
Montchanin	38	46 47N	4 30 E
Montclair	113	40 53N	74 13W
Montcornet	19	49 40N	4 0 E
Montcuq	20	44 21N	1 13 E
Montdidier	19	49 38N	2 35 E
Monte Alegre	127	2 0 S	54 0W
Monte Azul	127	15 9 S	42 53W
Monte Bello Is.	96	20 30 S	115 45 E
Monte-Carlo	21	43 46N	7 23 E
Monte Caseros	124	30 10 S	57 50W
Monte Comán	124	34 40 S	67 53W
Monte Lindo →	124	23 56 S	57 12W
Monte Quemado	124	25 53 S	62 41W
Monte Redondo	30	39 53N	8 50W
Monte San Giovanni	40	41 39N	13 33 E
Monte San Savino	39	43 20N	11 42 E
Monte Sant' Ángelo	41	41 42N	15 59 E
Monte Santu, C. di	40	40 5N	9 42 E
Monte Vista	119	37 40N	106 8W
Monteagudo	125	27 14 S	54 8W
Montealegre	33	38 48N	1 17W
Montebello	106	45 40N	74 55W
Montebelluna	39	45 47N	12 3 E
Montebourg	18	49 30N	1 20W
Montecastrilli	39	42 40N	12 30 E
Montecatini Terme	38	43 55N	10 48 E
Montecristi	126	1 0 S	80 40W
Montecristo	38	42 20N	10 20 E
Montefalco	39	42 53N	12 38 E
Montefiascone	39	42 31N	12 2 E
Montefrío	31	37 20N	4 0W
Montego Bay	121	18 30N	78 0W
Montegranaro	39	43 13N	13 38 E
Montehanin	19	46 46N	4 44 E
Montejicar	33	37 33N	3 30W
Montélimar	21	44 33N	4 45 E
Montella	41	40 50N	15 0 E
Montellano	31	36 59N	5 36W
Montello	116	43 49N	89 21W
Montelupo Fiorentino	38	43 44N	11 2 E
Montemor-o-Novo	31	38 40N	8 12W
Montemor-o-Velho	30	40 11N	8 40W
Montemorelos	120	25 11N	99 42W
Montendre	20	45 16N	0 26W
Montenegro	125	29 39 S	51 29W
Montenegro = Crna Gora □	42	42 40N	19 20 E
Montenero di Bisaccia	39	42 0N	14 47 E
Montepuez	91	13 8 S	38 59 E
Montepuez →	91	12 32 S	40 27 E
Montepulciano	39	43 5N	11 46 E
Montereale	39	42 31N	13 13 E
Montereau	19	48 22N	2 57 E
Monterey	119	36 35N	121 57W
Montería	126	8 46N	75 53W
Monteros	124	27 11 S	65 30W
Monterotondo	39	42 3N	12 36 E
Monterrey	120	25 40N	100 30W
Montes Claros	127	16 30 S	43 50W
Montesano	118	47 0N	123 39W
Montesárchio	41	41 5N	14 37 E
Montescaglioso	41	40 34N	16 40 E
Montesilvano	39	42 30N	14 8 E
Montevarchi	39	43 30N	11 32 E
Montevideo	125	34 50 S	56 11W
Montezuma	116	41 32N	92 35W
Montfaucon, Haute-Loire, France	21	45 11N	4 20 E
Montfaucon, Meuse, France	19	49 16N	5 8 E
Montfort-l'Amaury	19	48 47N	1 49 E
Montfort-sur-Meu	18	48 8N	1 58W
Montgenèvre	21	44 56N	6 42 E
Montgomery, U.K.	13	52 34N	3 9W
Montgomery, Ala., U.S.A.	115	32 20N	86 20W
Montgomery, W. Va., U.S.A.	114	38 9N	81 21W
Montgomery = Sahiwal	68	30 45N	73 8 E
Montguyon	20	45 12N	0 12W
Monthey	25	46 15N	6 56 E
Monticelli d'Ongina	38	45 3N	9 56 E
Monticello, Ark., U.S.A.	117	33 40N	91 48W
Monticello, Fla., U.S.A.	115	30 35N	83 50W
Monticello, Ind., U.S.A.	114	40 40N	86 45W
Monticello, Iowa, U.S.A.	116	42 18N	91 12W
Monticello, Ky., U.S.A.	115	36 52N	84 50W
Monticello, Minn., U.S.A.	116	45 17N	93 52W
Monticello, Miss., U.S.A.	117	31 35N	90 8W
Monticello, N.Y., U.S.A.	113	41 37N	74 42W
Monticello, Utah, U.S.A.	119	37 55N	109 27W
Montichiari	38	45 28N	10 29 E
Montier	19	48 30N	4 45 E
Montignac	20	45 4N	1 10 E
Montigny-les-Metz	19	49 7N	6 10 E
Montigny-sur-Aube	19	47 57N	4 45 E
Montijo	31	38 52N	6 39W
Montijo, Presa de	31	38 55N	6 26W
Montilla	31	37 36N	4 40W
Montivideo	116	44 55N	95 40W
Montlhéry	19	48 39N	2 15 E
Montluçon	20	46 22N	2 36 E
Montmagny	107	46 58N	70 34W
Montmarault	20	46 19N	2 57 E
Montmartre	109	50 14N	103 27W
Montmédy	19	49 30N	5 20 E
Montmélian	21	45 30N	6 4 E
Montmirail	19	48 51N	3 30 E
Montmoreau-St-Cybard	20	45 23N	0 8 E
Montmorency	107	46 53N	71 11W
Montmorillon	20	46 26N	0 50 E
Montmort	19	48 55N	3 49 E
Monto	97	24 52 S	151 6 E
Montoire	18	47 45N	0 52 E
Montório al Vomano	39	42 35N	13 38 E
Montoro	31	38 1N	4 27W
Montour Falls	112	42 20N	76 51W
Montpelier, Idaho, U.S.A.	118	42 15N	111 20W
Montpelier, Ohio, U.S.A.	114	41 34N	84 40W
Montpelier, Vt., U.S.A.	114	44 15N	72 38W
Montpellier	20	43 37N	3 52 E
Montpezat-de-Quercy	20	44 15N	1 30 E
Montpon	20	45 2N	0 11 E
Montréal, Can.	106	45 31N	73 34W
Montréal, France	20	43 13N	2 8 E
Montreal L.	109	54 20N	105 45W
Montreal Lake	109	54 3N	105 46W
Montredon-Labessonniè	20	43 45N	2 18 E
Montréjeau	20	43 6N	0 35 E
Montrésor	18	47 10N	1 10 E
Montreuil	19	50 27N	1 45 E
Montreuil-Bellay	18	47 8N	0 9W
Montreux	25	46 26N	6 55 E
Montrevault	18	47 17N	1 2W
Montrevel-en-Bresse	21	46 21N	5 8 E
Montrichard	18	47 20N	1 10 E
Montrose, U.K.	14	56 43N	2 28W
Montrose, Col., U.S.A.	119	38 30N	107 52W
Montrose, Pa., U.S.A.	113	41 50N	75 55W
Monts, Pte des	107	49 20N	67 12W
Monts-sur-Guesnes	18	46 55N	0 13 E
Montsalvy	20	44 41N	2 30 E
Montsant, Sierra de	32	41 17N	1 0 E
Montsauche	19	47 13N	4 0 E
Montsech, Sierra del	32	42 0N	0 45 E
Montseny	32	41 55N	2 25W
Montserrat, Spain	32	41 36N	1 49 E
Montserrat, W. Indies	121	16 40N	62 10W
Montuenga	30	41 3N	4 38W
Montuiri	32	39 34N	2 59 E
Monveda	88	2 52N	21 30 E
Monywa	67	22 7N	95 11 E
Monza	38	45 35N	9 15 E
Monze	91	16 17 S	27 29 E
Monze, C.	66	24 47N	66 37 E
Monzón	32	41 52N	0 10 E
Moolawatana	99	29 55 S	139 45 E
Moonah →	98	22 3 S	138 33 E
Moonbeam	106	49 20N	82 10W
Moonie	99	27 46 S	150 20 E
Moonie →	97	29 19 S	148 43 E
Moonta	99	34 6 S	137 32 E
Mooraberree	99	25 13 S	140 54 E
Moorcroft	116	44 17N	104 58W
Moore, L.	96	29 50 S	117 35 E
Moorefield	114	39 5N	78 59W
Moores Res.	113	44 45N	71 50W
Mooresville	115	35 36N	80 45W
Moorfoot Hills	14	55 44N	3 8W
Moorhead	116	46 51N	96 44W
Mooroopna	99	36 25 S	145 22 E
Moorreesburg	92	33 6 S	18 38 E
Moosburg	25	48 28N	11 57 E
Moose →	106	51 20N	80 25W
Moose Factory	106	51 16N	80 32W
Moose I.	109	51 42N	97 10W
Moose Jaw	109	50 24N	105 30W
Moose Jaw Cr. →	109	50 34N	105 18W
Moose Lake, Can.	109	53 43N	100 20W
Moose Lake, U.S.A.	116	46 27N	92 48W
Moose Mountain Cr. →	109	49 13N	102 12W
Moose Mountain Prov. Park	109	49 48N	102 25W
Moose River	106	50 48N	81 17W
Moosehead L.	107	45 34N	69 40W
Moosomin	109	50 9N	101 40W
Moosonee	106	51 17N	80 39W
Moosup	113	41 44N	71 52W

* *Renamed Namibe*

Mopipi Mullsjö

Mopipi	92	21 6 S	24 55 E
Mopoi	90	5 6N	26 54 E
Mopti	84	14 30N	4 0W
Moqatta	87	14 38N	35 50 E
Moquegua	126	17 15 S	70 46W
Mór	27	47 25N	18 12 E
Móra	31	38 55N	8 10W
Mora, Sweden	48	61 2N	14 38 E
Mora, Minn., U.S.A.	116	45 52N	93 19W
Mora, N. Mex., U.S.A.	119	35 58N	105 21W
Mora de Ebro	32	41 6N	0 38 E
Mora de Rubielos	32	40 15N	0 45W
Mora la Nueva	32	41 7N	0 39 E
Morača →	42	42 20N	19 9 E
Moradabad	68	28 50N	78 50 E
Morafenobe	93	17 50 S	44 53 E
Morąg	28	53 55N	19 56 E
Moral de Calatrava	33	38 51N	3 33W
Moraleja	30	40 6N	6 43W
Moran, Kans., U.S.A.	117	37 53N	94 35W
Moran, Wyo., U.S.A.	118	43 53N	110 37W
Morano Cálabro	41	39 51N	16 8 E
Morant Cays	121	17 22N	76 0W
Morant Pt.	121	17 55N	76 12W
Morar L.	14	56 57N	5 40W
Moratalla	33	38 14N	1 49W
Moratuwa	70	6 45N	79 55 E
Morava →	27	48 10N	16 59 E
Moravia	116	40 50N	92 50W
Moravian Hts. = Ceskemoravská V.	26	49 30N	15 40 E
Moravica →	42	43 52N	20 8 E
Moravice →	27	49 50N	17 43 E
Moravița	42	45 17N	21 14 E
Moravská Třebová	27	49 45N	16 40 E
Moravské Budějovice	26	49 4N	15 49 E
Morawhanna	126	8 30N	59 40W
Moray Firth	14	57 50N	3 30W
Morbach	25	49 48N	7 7 E
Morbegno	38	46 8N	9 34 E
Morbihan □	18	47 55N	2 50W
Morcenx	20	44 0N	0 55W
Mordelles	18	48 5N	1 52W
Morden	109	49 15N	98 10W
Mordialloc	100	38 1 S	145 6 E
Mordovian A.S.S.R. □	55	54 20N	44 30 E
Mordovo	55	52 6N	40 50 E
Mordy	28	52 13N	22 31 E
Møre og Romsdal fylke □	47	62 30N	8 0 E
Morea	9	37 45N	22 10 E
Moreau →	116	45 15N	100 43W
Morecambe	12	54 5N	2 52W
Morecambe B.	12	54 7N	3 0W
Moree	97	29 28 S	149 54 E
Morehead	114	38 12N	83 22W
Morehead City	115	34 46N	76 44W
Morelia	120	19 40N	101 11W
Morella, Austral.	98	23 0 S	143 52 E
Morella, Spain	32	40 35N	0 5W
Morelos □	120	18 40N	99 10W
Morena, Sierra	31	38 20N	4 0W
Morenci	119	33 7N	109 20W
Moreni	46	44 59N	25 36 E
Moresby I.	108	52 30N	131 40W
Morestel	21	45 40N	5 28 E
Moret	19	48 22N	2 58 E
Moreton	98	12 22 S	142 30 E
Moreton B.	97	27 10 S	153 10 E
Moreton I.	97	27 10 S	153 25 E
Moreuil	19	49 46N	2 30 E
Morez	21	46 31N	6 2 E
Morgan, Austral.	99	34 0 S	139 35 E
Morgan, U.S.A.	118	41 3N	111 44W
Morgan City	117	29 40N	91 15W
Morganfield	114	37 40N	87 55W
Morganton	115	35 46N	81 48W
Morgantown	114	39 39N	79 58W
Morganville	99	25 10 S	151 50 E
Morgat	18	48 15N	4 32W
Morgenzon	93	26 45 S	29 36 E
Morges	25	46 31N	6 29 E
Morhange	19	48 55N	6 38 E
Mori	38	45 51N	10 59 E
Moriarty	119	35 3N	106 2W
Morice L.	108	53 50N	127 40W
Moriki	85	12 52N	6 30 E
Morinville	108	53 49N	113 41W
Morioka	74	39 45N	141 8 E
Morkalla	99	34 23 S	141 10 E
Morlaàs	20	43 21N	0 18W
Morlaix	18	48 36N	3 52W
Mormanno	41	39 53N	15 59 E
Mormant	19	48 37N	2 52 E
Mornington	99	38 15 S	145 5 E
Mornington I.	97	16 30 S	139 30 E
Mornington, I.	128	49 50 S	75 30W
Mórnos →	45	38 30N	22 0 E
Moro	87	10 50N	30 9 E
Moro G.	73	6 30N	123 0 E
Morobe	98	7 49 S	147 38 E
Morocco ■	82	32 0N	5 50W
Morococha	126	11 40 S	76 5W
Morogoro	90	6 50 S	37 40 E
Morogoro □	90	8 0 S	37 0 E
Moroleón	120	20 8N	101 32W
Morombe	93	21 45 S	43 22 E
Moron	124	34 39 S	58 37W
Morón	121	22 8N	78 39W
Mörön →	75	47 14N	110 37 E
Morón de Almazán	32	41 29N	2 27W
Morón de la Frontera	31	37 6N	5 28W
Morondava	93	20 17 S	44 17 E
Morondo	84	8 57N	6 47W
Moronou	84	6 16N	4 59W
Morotai	73	2 10N	128 30 E
Moroto	90	2 28N	34 42 E
Moroto Summit	90	2 30N	34 43 E
Morozov (Bratan)	43	42 30N	25 10 E
Morozovsk	57	48 25N	41 50 E
Morpeth	12	55 11N	1 41W
Morphou	64	35 12N	32 59 E
Morrilton	117	35 10N	92 45W
Morrinhos	127	17 45 S	49 10W
Morrinsville	101	37 40 S	175 32 E
Morris, Can.	109	49 25N	97 22W
Morris, Ill., U.S.A.	114	41 20N	88 20W
Morris, Minn., U.S.A.	116	45 33N	95 56W
Morrisburg	106	44 55N	75 7W
Morrison	116	41 47N	90 0W
Morristown, Ariz., U.S.A.	119	33 54N	112 35W
Morristown, N.J., U.S.A.	113	40 48N	74 30W
Morristown, S.D., U.S.A.	116	45 57N	101 44W
Morristown, Tenn., U.S.A.	115	36 18N	83 20W
Morro Bay	119	35 27N	120 54W
Morro, Pta.	124	27 6 S	71 0W
Morrosquillo, Golfo de	121	9 35N	75 40W
Mörrum	49	56 12N	14 45 E
Mors	49	56 50N	8 45 E
Morshansk	55	53 28N	41 50 E
Mörsil	48	63 19N	13 40 E
Mortagne	20	45 28N	0 49W
Mortagne →	19	48 33N	6 27 E
Mortagne-au-Perche	18	48 31N	0 33 E
Mortain	18	48 40N	0 57W
Mortara	38	45 15N	8 43 E
Morteau	19	47 3N	6 35 E
Morteros	124	30 50 S	62 0W
Mortes, R. das →	127	11 45 S	50 44W
Mortlake	99	38 5 S	142 50 E
Morton, Tex., U.S.A.	117	33 39N	102 49W
Morton, Wash., U.S.A.	118	46 33N	122 17W
Morundah	99	34 57 S	146 19 E
Moruya	99	35 58 S	150 3 E
Morvan, Mts. du	19	47 5N	4 0 E
Morven	99	26 22 S	147 5 E
Morvern	14	56 38N	5 44W
Morvi	68	22 50N	70 42 E
Morwell	97	38 10 S	146 22 E
Moryn	28	52 51N	14 22 E
Morzhovets, Ostrov	52	66 44N	42 35 E
Mosalsk	54	54 30N	34 55 E
Mosbach	25	49 21N	9 9 E
Mošćenice	39	45 17N	14 16 E
Mosciano Sant' Ángelo	39	42 42N	13 52 E
Moscos Is.	72	14 0N	97 30 E
Moscow	118	46 45N	116 59W
Moscow = Moskva	55	55 45N	37 35 E
Mosel →	16	50 22N	7 36 E
Moselle = Mosel →	16	50 22N	7 36 E
Moselle □	19	48 59N	6 33 E
Moses Lake	118	47 9N	119 17W
Mosgiel	101	45 53 S	170 21 E
Moshi	90	3 22 S	37 18 E
Moshi □	90	3 22 S	37 18 E
Moshupa	92	24 46 S	25 29 E
Mošina	28	52 15N	16 50 E
Mosjøen	50	65 51N	13 12 E
Moskenesøya	50	67 58N	13 0 E
Moskenstraumen	50	67 47N	12 45 E
Moskva	55	55 45N	37 35 E
Moskva →	55	55 5N	38 51 E
Moslavačka Gora	39	45 40N	16 37 E
Mosomane (Artesia)	92	24 2 S	26 19 E
Mosonmagyaróvár	27	47 52N	17 18 E
Mošorin	42	45 19N	20 4 E
Mospino	56	47 52N	38 0 E
Mosquera	126	2 35N	78 24W
Mosquero	117	35 48N	103 57W
Mosqueruela	32	40 21N	0 27W
Mosquitos, Golfo de los	121	9 15N	81 10W
Moss	47	59 27N	10 40 E
Moss Vale	99	34 32 S	150 25 E
Mossaka	88	1 15 S	16 45 E
Mossbank	109	49 56N	105 56W
Mossburn	101	45 41 S	168 15 E
Mosselbaai	92	34 11 S	22 8 E
Mossendjo	88	2 55 S	12 42 E
Mossgiel	99	33 15 S	144 5 E
Mossman	97	16 21 S	145 15 E
Mossoró	127	5 10 S	37 15W
Mosstrand	47	59 51N	8 4 E
Mossuril	91	14 58 S	40 42 E
Mossy →	109	54 5N	102 58W
Most	26	50 31N	13 38 E
Mostaganem	82	35 54N	0 5 E
Mostar	42	43 22N	17 50 E
Mostardas	125	31 2 S	50 51W
Mostefa, Rass	83	36 55N	11 3 E
Mosterøy	47	59 5N	5 37 E
Mostiska	54	49 48N	23 4 E
Mosty	54	53 27N	24 38 E
Mosul = Al Mawşil	64	36 20N	43 5 E
Mosvatn	47	59 52N	8 5 E
Mota del Cuervo	32	39 30N	2 52W
Mota del Marqués	30	41 38N	5 11W
Motagua →	120	15 44N	88 14W
Motala	49	58 32N	15 1 E
Mothe-Achard, La	18	46 37N	1 40W
Motherwell	14	55 48N	4 0W
Motihari	69	26 30N	84 55 E
Motilla del Palancar	32	39 34N	1 55W
Motnik	39	46 14N	14 54 E
Motovun	39	45 20N	13 50 E
Motozintla de Mendoza	120	15 21N	92 14W
Motril	33	36 31N	3 37W
Motru →	46	44 44N	22 59 E
Mott	116	46 25N	102 29W
Motte-Chalançon, La	21	44 30N	5 21 E
Motte, La	21	44 20N	6 3 E
Móttola	41	40 38N	17 0 E
Motueka	101	41 7 S	173 1 E
Motul	120	21 0N	89 20W
Mouanda	88	1 28 S	13 7 E
Mouchalagane →	107	50 56N	68 41W
Moucontant	18	46 43N	0 36W
Moúdhros	44	39 50N	25 18 E
Moudjeria	84	17 50N	12 28W
Moudon	25	46 40N	6 49 E
Mouila	88	1 50 S	11 0 E
Moulamein	99	35 3 S	144 1 E
Moule	121	16 20N	61 22W
Moulins	20	46 35N	3 19 E
Moulmein	67	16 30N	97 40 E
Moulouya, O. →	82	35 5N	2 25W
Moulton	117	29 35N	97 8W
Moultrie	115	31 11N	83 47W
Moultrie, L.	115	33 25N	80 10W
Mound City, Mo., U.S.A.	116	40 2N	95 25W
Mound City, S.D., U.S.A.	116	45 46N	100 3W
Moúnda, Ákra	45	38 5N	20 45 E
Moundou	81	8 40N	16 10 E
Moundsville	114	39 53N	80 43W
Mount Airy	115	36 31N	80 37W
Mount Albert	112	44 8N	79 19W
Mount Angel	118	45 4N	122 46W
Mount Barker, S.A., Austral.	99	35 5 S	138 52 E
Mount Barker, W.A., Austral.	96	34 38 S	117 40 E
Mount Carmel, Ill., U.S.A.	114	38 20N	87 48W
Mount Carmel, Pa., U.S.A.	114	40 46N	76 25W
Mount Clemens	106	42 35N	82 50W
Mount Coolon	98	21 25 S	147 25 E
Mount Darwin	91	16 45 S	31 33 E
Mount Desert I.	107	44 15N	68 25W
Mount Dora	115	28 49N	81 32W
Mount Douglas	98	21 35 S	146 50 E
Mount Edgecumbe	108	57 8N	135 22W
Mount Enid	96	21 42 S	116 26 E
Mount Forest	106	43 59N	80 43W
Mount Gambier	97	37 50 S	140 46 E
Mount Garnet	98	17 37 S	145 6 E
Mount Hope	114	37 52N	81 9W
Mount Horeb	116	43 0N	89 42W
Mount Howitt	99	26 31 S	142 16 E
Mount Isa	97	20 42 S	139 26 E
Mount Larcom	98	23 48 S	150 59 E
Mount Lofty Ra.	97	34 35 S	139 5 E
Mount McKinley Nat. Park	104	64 0N	150 0W
Mount Magnet	96	28 2 S	117 47 E
Mount Margaret	99	26 54 S	143 21 E
Mount Maunganui	101	37 40 S	176 14 E
Mount Morgan	97	23 40 S	150 25 E
Mount Morris	114	42 43N	77 50W
Mount Mulligan	98	16 45 S	144 47 E
Mount Nicholas	96	22 54 S	120 27 E
Mount Oxide Mine	98	19 30 S	139 29 E
Mount Pearl	107	47 31N	52 47W
Mount Perry	99	25 13 S	151 42 E
Mount Pleasant, Iowa, U.S.A.	116	41 0N	91 35W
Mount Pleasant, Mich., U.S.A.	114	43 35N	84 47W
Mount Pleasant, Pa., U.S.A.	112	40 9N	79 31W
Mount Pleasant, S.C., U.S.A.	115	32 45N	79 48W
Mount Pleasant, Tenn., U.S.A.	115	35 31N	87 11W
Mount Pleasant, Tex., U.S.A.	117	33 5N	95 0W
Mount Pleasant, Ut., U.S.A.	118	39 40N	111 29W
Mount Pocono	113	41 8N	75 21W
Mount Rainier Nat. Park.	118	46 50N	121 43W
Mount Revelstoke Nat. Park	108	51 5N	118 30W
Mount Robson	108	52 56N	119 15W
Mount Robson Prov. Park	108	53 0N	119 0W
Mount Shasta	118	41 20N	122 18W
Mount Sterling, Ill., U.S.A.	116	40 0N	90 40W
Mount Sterling, Ky., U.S.A.	114	38 0N	84 0W
Mount Surprise	98	18 10 S	144 17 E
Mount Union	112	40 22N	77 51W
Mount Vernon, Ind., U.S.A.	116	38 17N	88 57W
Mount Vernon, N.Y., U.S.A.	114	40 57N	73 49W
Mount Vernon, Ohio, U.S.A.	114	40 20N	82 30W
Mount Vernon, Wash., U.S.A.	108	48 25N	122 20W
Mount Whaleback	96	23 18 S	119 44 E
Mountain City, Nev., U.S.A.	118	41 54N	116 0W
Mountain City, Tenn., U.S.A.	115	36 30N	81 50W
Mountain Grove	117	37 5N	92 20W
Mountain Home, Ark., U.S.A.	117	36 20N	92 25W
Mountain Home, Idaho, U.S.A.	118	43 11N	115 45W
Mountain Iron	116	47 30N	92 37W
Mountain Park.	108	52 50N	117 15W
Mountain View, Ark., U.S.A.	117	35 52N	92 10W
Mountain View, Calif., U.S.A.	119	37 26N	122 5W
Mountainair	119	34 35N	106 15W
Mountmellick	15	53 7N	7 20W
Moura, Austral.	98	24 35 S	149 58 E
Moura, Brazil	126	1 32 S	61 38W
Moura, Port.	31	38 7N	7 30W
Mourão	31	38 22N	7 22W
Mourdi Depression	81	18 10N	23 0 E
Mourdiah	84	14 35N	7 25W
Moure, La	116	46 27N	98 17W
Mourenx	20	43 23N	0 36W
Mouri	85	5 6N	1 14W
Mourilyan	98	17 35 S	146 3 E
Mourmelon-le-Grand	19	49 8N	4 22 E
Mourne →	15	54 45N	7 39W
Mourne Mts.	15	54 10N	6 0W
Mouscron	16	50 45N	3 12 E
Moussoro	81	13 41N	16 35 E
Mouthe	19	46 44N	6 12 E
Moutier	25	47 16N	7 21 E
Moûtiers	21	45 29N	6 31 E
Moutong	73	0 28N	121 13 E
Mouy	19	49 18N	2 20 E
Mouzáki	44	39 25N	21 37 E
Moville	15	55 11N	7 3W
Moy →	15	54 5N	8 50W
Moyale, Ethiopia	87	3 34N	39 4 E
Moyale, Kenya	90	3 30N	39 0 E
Moyamba	84	8 4N	12 30W
Moyen Atlas	80	32 0N	5 0W
Moyle □	15	55 10N	6 15W
Moyobamba	126	6 0 S	77 0W
Moyyero →	59	68 44N	103 42 E
Mozambique = Moçambique	91	15 3 S	40 42 E
Mozambique ■	91	19 0 S	35 0 E
Mozambique Chan.	93	20 0 S	39 0 E
Mozdok	57	43 45N	44 48 E
Mozhaysk	55	55 30N	36 2 E
Mozhga	55	56 26N	52 15 E
Mozirje	39	46 22N	14 58 E
Mozyr	54	52 0N	29 15 E
Mpanda	90	6 23 S	31 1 E
Mpanda □	90	6 23 S	31 40 E
Mpésoba	84	12 31N	5 39W
Mpika	91	11 51 S	31 25 E
Mpulungu	91	8 51 S	31 5 E
Mpwapwa	90	6 23 S	36 30 E
Mpwapwa □	90	6 30 S	36 20 E
Mrągowo	28	53 52N	21 18 E
Mramor	42	43 20N	21 45 E
Mrimina	82	29 50N	7 9W
Mrkonjić Grad	42	44 26N	17 4 E
Mrkopalj	39	45 21N	14 52 E
Mrocza	28	53 16N	17 35 E
Msab, Oued en →	83	32 25N	5 20 E
Msaken	83	35 49N	10 33 E
Msambansovu	91	15 50 S	30 3 E
M'sila	83	35 46N	4 30 E
Msta →	54	58 25N	31 20 E
Mstislavl	54	54 0N	31 50 E
Mszana Dolna	27	49 41N	20 5 E
Mszczonów	28	51 58N	20 33 E
Mtama	91	10 17 S	39 21 E
Mtilikwe →	91	21 9 S	31 30 E
Mtsensk	55	53 25N	36 30 E
Mtskheta	57	41 52N	44 45 E
Mtwara-Mikindani	91	10 20 S	40 20 E
Mu Us Shamo	76	39 0N	109 0 E
Muaná	127	1 25 S	49 15W
Muang Chiang Rai	71	19 52N	99 50 E
Muang Lamphun	71	18 40N	99 2 E
Muang Phichit	71	16 29N	100 21 E
Muar	71	2 3N	102 34 E
Muar →	71	2 15N	102 48 E
Muarabungo	72	1 28 S	102 52 E
Muaradjuloi	72	0 12 S	114 3 E
Muaraenim	72	3 40 S	103 50 E
Muarakaman	72	0 2 S	116 45 E
Muaratebo	72	1 30 S	102 26 E
Muaratembesi	72	1 42 S	103 8 E
Muaratewe	72	0 58 S	114 52 E
Mubarakpur	69	26 6N	83 18 E
Mubende	90	0 33N	31 22 E
Mubi	85	10 18N	13 16 E
Mücheln	24	51 18N	11 49 E
Muchinga Mts.	91	11 30 S	31 30 E
Muchkapskiy	55	51 52N	42 28 E
Muck	14	56 50N	6 15W
Muckadilla	99	26 35 S	148 23 E
Mucuri	127	18 0 S	39 36W
Mucusso	92	18 1 S	21 25 E
Mudanjiang	76	44 38N	129 30 E
Mudanya	56	40 25N	28 50 E
Muddy →	119	38 0N	110 22W
Mudgee	97	32 32 S	149 31 E
Mudjatik →	109	56 1N	107 36W
Muecate	91	14 55 S	39 40 E
Muêda	91	11 36 S	39 28 E
Muela, La	32	41 36N	1 7W
Muerto, Mar	120	16 10N	94 10W
Muertos, Punta de los	33	36 57N	1 54W
Mufindi □	91	8 30 S	35 20 E
Mufulira	91	12 32 S	28 15 E
Mufumbiro Range	90	1 25 S	29 30 E
Mugardos	30	43 27N	8 15W
Muge	31	39 3N	8 40W
Muge →	31	39 8N	8 44W
Múggia	39	45 36N	13 47 E
Mugia	30	43 3N	9 10W
Mugila, Mts.	90	7 0 S	28 50 E
Muğla	64	37 15N	28 22 E
Müglizh	43	42 37N	25 32 E
Mugshin	63	19 35N	54 40 E
Mugu	69	29 45N	82 30 E
Muhammad Qol	86	20 53N	37 9 E
Muhammad Râs	86	27 42N	34 13 E
Muhammadabad	69	26 4N	83 25 E
Muharraqa = Sa'ad	62	31 28N	34 33 E
Muhesi →	90	7 0 S	35 20 E
Muheza □	90	5 0 S	39 0 E
Mühldorf	25	48 14N	12 33 E
Mühlhausen	24	51 12N	10 29 E
Mühlig Hofmann fjella	5	72 30 S	5 0 E
Muhutwe	90	1 35 S	31 45 E
Mui Bai Bung	71	8 35N	104 42 E
Mui Ron	71	18 7N	106 27 E
Muikamachi	74	37 15N	138 50 E
Muine Bheag	15	52 42N	6 57W
Muiños	30	41 58N	7 59W
Mukachevo	54	48 27N	22 45 E
Mukah	72	2 55N	112 5 E
Mukawwa, Geziret	86	23 55N	35 53 E
Mukden = Shenyang	76	41 48N	123 27 E
Mukhtolovo	55	55 29N	43 15 E
Mukishi	91	8 30 S	24 44 E
Mukomuko	72	2 30 S	101 10 E
Mukomwenze	90	6 49 S	27 15 E
Muktsar	68	30 30N	74 30 E
Mukur	66	32 50N	67 42 E
Mukutawa →	109	53 10N	97 24W
Mukwela	91	17 0 S	26 40 E
Mula	33	38 3N	1 33W
Mula →	70	18 34N	74 21 E
Mulange	90	3 40 S	27 10 E
* Mulatas, Arch. de las	121	9 50N	78 31W
Mulchén	124	37 45 S	72 20W
Mulde →	24	51 10N	12 48 E
Mule Creek	116	43 19N	104 8W
Muleba	90	1 50 S	31 37 E
Muleba □	90	2 0 S	31 30 E
Muleshoe	117	34 17N	102 42W
Mulgrave	107	45 38N	61 31W
Mulgrave I.	98	10 5 S	142 10 E
Mulhacén	33	37 4N	3 20W
Mülheim	24	51 26N	6 53 E
Mulhouse	19	47 40N	7 20 E
Muling He →	76	45 53N	133 30 E
Mull	14	56 27N	6 0W
Mullaittvu	70	9 15N	80 49 E
Mullen	116	42 5N	101 0W
Mullengudgery	99	31 43 S	147 23 E
Mullens	114	37 34N	81 22W
Muller, Pegunungan	72	0 30N	113 30 E
Mullet Pen.	15	54 10N	10 2W
Mullewa	96	28 29 S	115 30 E
Müllheim	25	47 48N	7 37 E
Mulligan →	98	26 40 S	139 0 E
Mullin	117	31 33N	98 38W
Mullingar	15	53 31N	7 20W
Mullins	115	34 12N	79 15W
Mullsjö	49	57 56N	13 55 E

* *Renamed San Blas, Arch. de*

Mullumbimby Nanjeko

Name	Page	Lat.	Long.
Mullumbimby	99	28 30 S	153 30 E
Mulobezi	91	16 45 S	25 7 E
Mulshi L.	70	18 30 N	73 48 E
Multai	68	21 50 N	78 21 E
Multan	68	30 15 N	71 36 E
* Multan □	68	30 29 N	72 29 E
Multrå	48	63 10 N	17 24 E
Mulumbe, Mts.	91	8 40 S	27 30 E
Mulungushi Dam	91	14 48 S	28 48 E
Mulvane	117	37 30 N	97 15 W
Mulwad	86	18 45 N	30 39 E
Mulwala	100	35 59 S	146 0 E
Mumra	57	45 45 N	47 41 E
Mun →	71	15 17 N	103 0 E
Muna	73	5 0 S	122 30 E
Munamagi	54	57 43 N	27 4 E
Münchberg	25	50 11 N	11 48 E
Muncheberg	24	52 30 N	14 9 E
München	25	48 8 N	11 33 E
Munchen-Gladbach = Mönchengladbach	24	51 12 N	6 23 E
Muncho Lake	108	59 0 N	125 50 W
Muncie	114	40 10 N	85 20 W
Mundakayam	70	9 30 N	76 50 E
Mundala, Puncak	73	4 30 S	141 0 E
Mundare	108	53 35 N	112 20 W
Munday	117	33 26 N	99 39 W
Münden	24	51 25 N	9 42 E
Mundo →	33	38 30 N	2 15 W
Mundo Novo	127	11 55 S	40 29 W
Mundra	68	22 54 N	69 48 E
Munera	33	39 2 N	2 29 W
Muneru →	70	16 45 N	80 3 E
Mungallala	99	26 28 S	147 34 E
Mungallala Cr. →	99	28 53 S	147 5 E
Mungana	98	17 8 S	144 27 E
Mungaoli	68	24 24 N	78 7 E
Mungari	91	17 12 S	33 30 E
Mungbere	90	2 36 N	28 28 E
Mungindi	97	28 58 S	149 1 E
Munhango	89	12 10 S	18 38 E
Munich = München	25	48 8 N	11 33 E
Munising	114	46 25 N	86 39 W
Munjiye	86	18 47 N	41 20 E
Munka-Ljungby	49	56 16 N	12 58 E
Munkedal	49	58 28 N	11 40 E
Munkfors	48	59 50 N	13 30 E
Munku-Sardyk	59	51 45 N	100 20 E
Münnerstadt	25	50 15 N	10 11 E
Muñoz Gamero, Pen.	128	52 30 S	73 5 E
Munroe L.	109	59 13 N	98 35 W
Munster, France	19	48 2 N	7 8 E
Munster, Ger.	24	52 59 N	10 5 E
Münster	24	51 58 N	7 37 E
Munster □	15	52 20 N	8 40 W
Muntele Mare	46	46 30 N	23 12 E
Muntok	72	2 5 S	105 10 E
Munyak	58	43 30 N	59 15 E
Munyama	91	16 5 S	28 31 E
Muon Pak Beng	71	19 51 N	101 4 E
Muonio	50	67 57 N	23 40 E
Mupa	89	16 5 S	15 50 E
Muping	76	37 22 N	121 36 E
Muqaddam, Wadi →	86	18 4 N	31 30 E
Muqdisho	63	2 2 N	45 25 E
Mur →	26	46 18 N	16 53 E
Mur-de-Bretagne	18	48 12 N	3 0 W
Mura →	39	46 18 N	16 53 E
Murallón, Cuerro	128	49 48 S	73 30 W
Muranda	90	1 52 S	29 20 E
Murang'a	90	0 45 S	37 9 E
Murashi	55	59 30 N	49 0 E
Murat	20	45 7 N	2 53 E
Murau	26	47 6 N	14 10 E
Muravera	40	39 25 N	9 35 E
Murça	30	41 24 N	7 28 W
Murchison →	96	27 45 S	114 0 E
Murchison Falls = Kabarega Falls	90	2 15 N	31 38 E
Murchison Ra.	96	20 0 S	134 10 E
Murchison Rapids	91	15 55 S	34 35 E
Murcia	33	38 20 N	1 10 W
Murcia □	33	37 50 N	1 30 W
Murdo	116	43 56 N	100 43 W
Murdoch Pt.	98	14 37 S	144 55 E
Mure, La	21	44 55 N	5 48 E
Mureş □	46	46 45 N	24 40 E
Mureş (Mureşul) →	46	46 15 N	20 13 E
Muret	20	43 30 N	1 20 E
Murfatlar	46	44 10 N	28 26 E
Murfreesboro	115	35 50 N	86 21 W
Murg →	25	48 55 N	8 10 E
Murgab	58	38 10 N	74 2 E
Murgeni	46	46 12 N	28 1 E
Murgon	97	26 15 S	151 54 E
Muriaé	125	21 8 S	42 23 W
Murias de Paredes	30	42 52 N	6 11 W
Muriel Mine	91	17 14 S	30 40 E
Müritz see	24	53 25 N	12 40 E
Murka	90	3 27 S	38 0 E
Murmansk	52	68 57 N	33 10 E
Murnau	25	47 40 N	11 11 E
Muro, France	21	42 34 N	8 54 E
Muro, Spain	32	39 44 N	3 3 E
Muro, C. de	21	41 44 N	8 37 E
Muro Lucano	41	40 45 N	15 30 E
Murom	55	55 35 N	42 3 E
Muroran	74	42 25 N	141 0 E
Muros	30	42 45 N	9 5 W
Muros y de Noya, Ría de	30	42 45 N	9 0 W
Muroto-Misaki	74	33 15 N	134 10 E
Murowana Goślina	28	52 35 N	17 0 E
Murphy	118	43 11 N	116 33 W
Murphysboro	117	37 50 N	89 20 W
Murrat	86	18 51 N	29 33 E
Murray, Ky., U.S.A.	115	36 40 N	88 20 W
Murray, Utah, U.S.A.	118	40 41 N	111 58 W
Murray →, Austral.	97	35 20 S	139 22 E
Murray →, Can.	108	56 11 N	120 45 W
Murray Bridge	97	35 6 S	139 14 E
Murray Harbour	107	46 0 N	62 28 W
Murray, L., P.N.G.	98	7 0 S	141 35 E
Murray, L., U.S.A.	115	34 8 N	81 30 W
Murray Seascarp	95	30 0 N	135 0 W
Murraysburg	92	31 58 S	23 47 E
Murrayville	100	35 16 S	141 11 E
Murree	66	33 56 N	73 28 E
Murrumbidgee →	97	34 43 S	143 12 E
Murrumburrah	99	34 32 S	148 22 E
Murrurundi	99	31 42 S	150 51 E
Mursala	72	1 41 N	98 28 E
Murshid	86	21 40 N	31 10 E
Murshidabad	69	24 11 N	88 19 E
Murska Sobota	39	46 39 N	16 12 E
Murtazapur	68	20 40 N	77 25 E
Murtle L.	108	52 8 N	119 38 W
Murtoa	99	36 35 S	142 28 E
Murtosa	30	40 44 N	8 40 W
Murungu	90	4 12 S	31 10 E
Murwara	69	23 46 N	80 28 E
Murwillumbah	97	28 18 S	153 27 E
Muryo	73	6 36 S	110 53 E
Mürz →	26	47 30 N	15 25 E
Mürzzuschlag	26	47 36 N	15 41 E
Muş	64	38 45 N	41 30 E
Musa Khel Bazar	68	30 59 N	69 52 E
Mūsá Qal'eh	65	32 20 N	64 50 E
Musairik, Wadi →	86	19 30 N	43 10 E
Musala	43	42 13 N	23 37 E
Musan, Kor., N.	76	42 12 N	129 12 E
Musan, Kor., N.	76	42 12 N	129 12 E
Musangu	91	10 28 S	23 55 E
Musasa	90	3 25 S	31 30 E
Musay'īd	65	25 0 N	51 33 E
Muscat = Masqat	65	23 37 N	58 36 E
Muscat & Oman = Oman ■	63	23 0 N	58 0 E
Muscatine	116	41 25 N	91 5 W
Musel	30	43 34 N	5 42 W
Musgrave Ras.	96	26 0 S	132 0 E
Mushie	88	2 56 S	16 55 E
Mushin	85	6 32 N	3 21 E
Musi →, India	70	16 41 N	79 40 E
Musi →, Indon.	72	2 20 S	104 56 E
Muskeg →	108	60 20 N	123 20 W
Muskegon	114	43 15 N	86 17 W
Muskegon →	114	43 25 N	86 0 W
Muskegon Hts.	114	43 12 N	86 17 W
Muskogee	117	35 50 N	95 25 W
Muskwa →	108	58 47 N	122 48 W
Musmar	86	18 13 N	35 40 E
Musofu	91	13 30 S	29 0 E
Musoma	90	1 30 S	33 48 E
Musoma □	90	1 50 S	34 30 E
Musquaro, L.	107	50 38 N	61 5 W
Musquodoboit Harbour	107	44 50 N	63 9 W
Musselburgh	14	55 57 N	3 3 W
Musselshell →	118	47 21 N	107 58 W
Mussidan	20	45 2 N	0 22 E
Mussomeli	40	37 35 N	13 43 E
Mussooree	68	30 27 N	78 6 E
Mussuco	92	17 2 S	19 3 E
Mustang	69	29 10 N	83 55 E
Musters, L.	128	45 20 S	69 25 W
Muswellbrook	97	32 16 S	150 56 E
Muszyna	27	49 22 N	20 55 E
Mût	86	25 28 N	28 58 E
Mut	64	36 40 N	33 28 E
Mutanda, Mozam.	93	21 0 S	33 34 E
Mutanda, Zambia	91	12 24 S	26 13 E
Mutaray	59	60 56 N	101 0 E
Muting	73	7 23 S	140 20 E
Mutshatsha	91	10 35 S	24 20 E
Muttaburra	97	22 38 S	144 29 E
Mutuáli	91	14 55 S	37 0 E
Muvatupusha	70	9 53 N	76 35 E
Muxima	88	9 33 S	13 58 E
Muy, Le	21	43 28 N	6 34 E
Muya	59	56 27 N	115 50 E
Muyinga	90	3 14 S	30 33 E
Muzaffarabad	69	34 25 N	73 30 E
Muzaffargarh	68	30 5 N	71 14 E
Muzaffarnagar	68	29 26 N	77 40 E
Muzaffarpur	69	26 7 N	85 23 E
Muzhi	58	65 25 N	64 40 E
Muzillac	18	47 35 N	2 30 W
Muzon C.	108	54 40 N	132 40 W
Muztag	75	36 20 N	87 28 E
Mvôlô	87	6 2 N	29 53 E
Mwadui	90	3 26 S	33 32 E
Mwambo	91	10 30 S	40 22 E
Mwandi	91	17 30 S	24 51 E
Mwanza, Tanz.	90	2 30 S	32 58 E
Mwanza, Zaïre	90	7 55 S	26 43 E
Mwanza, Zambia	91	16 58 S	24 28 E
Mwanza □	90	2 0 S	33 0 E
Mwaya	91	9 32 S	33 55 E
Mweelrea	15	53 37 N	9 48 W
Mweka	88	4 50 S	21 34 E
Mwenga	90	3 1 S	28 28 E
Mweru, L.	91	9 0 S	28 40 E
Mweza Range	91	21 0 S	30 0 E
Mwilambwe	90	8 7 S	25 0 E
Mwimbi	91	8 38 S	31 39 E
Mwinilunga	91	11 43 S	24 25 E
My Tho	71	10 29 N	106 23 E
Mya, O. →	83	30 46 N	4 54 E
Myall →	100	32 30 S	152 15 E
Myanaung	67	18 18 N	95 22 E
Myaungmya	67	16 30 N	94 40 E
Mycenae = Mikínai	45	37 43 N	22 46 E
Myeik Kyunzu	71	11 30 N	97 30 E
Myerstown	113	40 22 N	76 18 W
Myitkyina	67	25 24 N	97 26 E
Myjava	27	48 41 N	17 37 E
Mymensingh	69	24 45 N	90 24 E
Myndus	45	37 3 N	27 14 E
Mynydd ddu	13	51 45 N	3 45 W
Myrdal	47	60 43 N	7 10 E
Mýrdalsjökull	50	63 40 N	19 6 W
Myrtle Beach	115	33 43 N	78 50 W
Myrtle Creek	118	43 0 N	123 9 W
Myrtle Point	118	43 0 N	124 4 W
Myrtleford	100	36 34 S	146 44 E
Mysen	47	59 33 N	11 20 E
Myslenice	27	49 51 N	19 57 E
Myślibórz	28	52 55 N	14 50 E
Mysłowice	27	50 15 N	19 12 E
Mysore	70	12 17 N	76 41 E
Mysore □ = Karnataka	70	13 15 N	77 0 E
Mystic	113	41 21 N	71 58 W
Mystishchi	55	55 50 N	37 50 E
Myszków	28	50 45 N	19 22 E
Myszyniec	28	53 23 N	21 21 E
Myton	118	40 10 N	110 2 W
Mývatn	50	65 36 N	17 0 W
Mze →	26	49 46 N	13 24 E
Mzimba	91	11 55 S	33 39 E
Mzimvubu →	93	31 38 S	29 33 E
Mzuzu	91	11 30 S	33 55 E

N

Name	Page	Lat.	Long.
N' Dioum	84	16 31 N	14 39 W
Naab →	25	49 1 N	12 2 E
Na'am	87	9 42 N	28 27 E
Na'an	62	31 53 N	34 52 E
Naantali	51	60 29 N	22 2 E
Naas	15	53 12 N	6 40 W
Nababiep	92	29 36 S	17 46 E
Nabadwip	69	23 34 N	88 20 E
Nabas	73	11 47 N	122 6 E
Nabburg	25	49 27 N	12 11 E
* Nabereznyje Celny	58	55 42 N	52 19 E
Nabeul	83	36 30 N	10 44 E
Nabha	68	30 26 N	76 14 E
Nabire	73	3 15 S	135 26 E
Nabisar	68	25 8 N	69 40 E
Nabisipi →	107	50 14 N	62 13 W
Nabiswera	90	1 27 N	32 15 E
Nablus = Nābulus	62	32 14 N	35 15 E
Naboomspruit	93	24 32 S	28 40 E
Nābulus	62	32 14 N	35 15 E
Nacala-Velha	91	14 32 S	40 34 E
Nacaroa	91	14 22 S	39 56 E
Naches	118	46 48 N	120 42 W
Nachingwea	91	10 23 S	38 49 E
Nachingwea □	91	10 30 S	38 30 E
Nachna	68	27 34 N	71 41 E
Náchod	27	50 25 N	16 8 E
Nacka	48	59 17 N	18 12 E
Nackara	99	32 48 S	139 12 E
Naco	119	31 24 N	109 58 W
Nacogdoches	117	31 33 N	94 39 W
Nacozari	120	30 24 N	109 39 W
Nadi	86	18 40 N	33 41 E
Nadiad	68	22 41 N	72 56 E
Nădlac	42	46 10 N	20 50 E
Nador	82	35 14 N	2 58 W
Nadūshan	65	32 2 N	53 35 E
Nadvoitsy	52	63 52 N	34 14 E
Nadvornaya	56	48 37 N	24 30 E
Nadym	58	65 35 N	72 42 E
Nadym →	58	66 12 N	72 0 E
Nærbø	47	58 40 N	5 39 E
Næstved	49	55 13 N	11 44 E
Nafada	85	11 8 N	11 20 E
Naft-e Shāh	64	34 0 N	45 30 E
Nafūd ad Dahy	64	22 0 N	45 0 E
Nafūsah, Jabal	83	32 12 N	12 30 E
Nag Hammâdi	86	26 2 N	32 18 E
Naga	73	13 38 N	123 15 E
Naga, Kreb en	82	24 12 N	6 0 W
Nagagami →	106	49 40 N	84 40 W
Nagaland □	67	26 0 N	94 30 E
Nagano	74	36 40 N	138 10 E
Nagano □	74	36 15 N	138 0 E
Nagaoka	74	37 27 N	138 50 E
Nagappattinam	70	10 46 N	79 51 E
Nagar Parkar	68	24 28 N	70 46 E
Nagari Hills	70	13 3 N	79 45 E
Nagarjuna Sagar	70	16 35 N	79 17 E
Nagasaki	74	32 47 N	129 50 E
Nagasaki □	74	32 50 N	129 40 E
Nagaur	68	27 15 N	73 45 E
Nagbhil	70	20 34 N	79 55 E
Nagercoil	70	8 12 N	77 26 E
Nagina	68	29 30 N	78 30 E
Nagīneh	65	34 20 N	57 15 E
Nago	77	26 36 N	128 0 E
Nagold	25	34 14 N	57 2 E
Nagold →	25	48 52 N	8 42 E
Nagoorin	98	24 17 S	151 15 E
Nagornyy	59	55 58 N	124 57 E
Nagorsk	55	59 18 N	50 48 E
Nagoya	74	35 10 N	136 50 E
Nagpur	68	21 8 N	79 10 E
Nagyatád	27	46 14 N	17 22 E
Nagyecsed	27	47 53 N	22 24 E
Nagykanizsa	27	46 28 N	17 0 E
Nagykörös	27	47 5 N	19 48 E
Nagyléta	27	47 23 N	21 55 E
Naha	77	26 13 N	127 42 E
Nahalal	62	32 41 N	35 12 E
Nahanni Butte	108	61 2 N	123 31 W
Nahanni Nat. Park	108	61 15 N	125 0 W
Nahariyya	62	33 1 N	35 5 E
Nahāvand	64	34 10 N	48 22 E
Nahe →	25	49 58 N	7 57 E
Nahf	62	32 56 N	35 18 E
Nahīya, Wadi →	86	28 55 N	31 0 E
Nahlin	108	58 55 N	131 38 W
Nahud	86	18 12 N	41 40 E
Naicam	109	52 30 N	104 30 W
Nā'ifah	63	19 59 N	50 46 E
Naila	25	50 19 N	11 43 E
Nain	107	56 34 N	61 40 W
Nā'īn	65	32 54 N	53 0 E
Naini Tal	69	29 30 N	79 30 E
Naintré	18	46 46 N	0 29 E
Naipu	46	44 12 N	25 47 E
Naira	73	4 28 S	130 0 E
Nairn	14	57 35 N	3 54 W
Nairobi	90	1 17 S	36 48 E
Naivasha	90	0 40 S	36 30 E
Naivasha L.	90	0 48 S	36 20 E
Najac	20	44 14 N	1 58 E
Najafābād	65	32 40 N	51 15 E
Najd	64	26 30 N	42 0 E
Nájera	32	42 26 N	2 48 W
Najerilla →	32	42 32 N	2 48 W
Najibabad	68	29 40 N	78 20 E
Najin	76	42 12 N	130 15 E
Nakalagba	90	2 50 N	27 58 E
Nakamura	74	33 0 N	133 0 E
Nakfa	87	16 40 N	38 32 E
Nakhichevan A.S.S.R. □	53	39 14 N	45 30 E
Nakhl	86	29 55 N	33 43 E
Nakhodka	59	42 53 N	132 54 E
Nakhon Phanom	71	17 23 N	104 43 E
Nakhon Ratchasima (Khorat)	71	14 59 N	102 12 E
Nakhon Sawan	71	15 35 N	100 10 E
Nakhon Si Thammarat	71	8 29 N	100 0 E
Nakina, B.C., Can.	108	59 12 N	132 52 W
Nakina, Ont., Can.	106	50 10 N	86 40 W
Nakło nad Notecią	28	53 9 N	17 38 E
Nakodar	68	31 8 N	75 31 E
Nakskov	49	54 50 N	11 8 E
Näkten	48	62 48 N	14 38 E
Naktong →	76	35 7 N	128 57 E
Nakuru	90	0 15 S	36 4 E
Nakuru □	90	0 15 S	35 5 E
Nakuru, L.	90	0 23 S	36 5 E
Nakusp	108	50 20 N	117 45 W
Nal →	66	25 20 N	65 30 E
Nalchik	57	43 30 N	43 33 E
Nälden	48	63 21 N	14 14 E
Näldsjön	48	63 25 N	14 15 E
Nalerigu	85	10 35 N	0 25 W
Nalgonda	70	17 6 N	79 15 E
Nalhati	69	24 17 N	87 52 E
Nallamalai Hills	70	15 30 N	78 50 E
Nalón →	30	43 32 N	6 4 W
Nālūt	83	31 54 N	11 0 E
Nam Co	75	30 30 N	90 45 E
Nam Dinh	71	20 25 N	106 5 E
Nam-Phan	72	10 30 N	106 0 E
Nam Phong	71	16 42 N	102 52 E
Nam Tha	71	20 58 N	101 30 E
Nama unde	92	17 18 S	15 50 E
Namak, Daryácheh-ye	65	34 30 N	52 0 E
Namak, Kavir-e	65	34 30 N	57 30 E
Namakkal	70	11 13 N	78 13 E
Namaland	92	24 30 S	17 0 E
Namangan	58	41 0 N	71 40 E
Namapa	91	13 43 S	39 50 E
Namaqualand	92	30 0 S	18 0 E
Namasagali	90	1 2 N	33 0 E
Namatanai	98	3 40 S	152 29 E
Namber	73	1 2 S	134 49 E
Nambour	97	26 32 S	152 58 E
Nambucca Heads	99	30 37 S	153 0 E
Namche Bazar	69	27 51 N	86 47 E
Namecunda	91	14 54 S	37 37 E
Nameh	72	2 34 N	116 21 E
Nameponda	91	15 50 S	39 50 E
Náměšť nad Oslavou	27	49 12 N	16 10 E
Námestovo	27	49 24 N	19 25 E
Nametil	91	15 40 S	39 21 E
Namew L.	109	54 14 N	101 56 W
Namib Desert = Namib Woestyn	92	22 30 S	15 0 E
Namib-Woestyn	92	22 30 S	15 0 E
Namibia ■	92	22 0 S	18 9 E
Namlea	73	3 18 S	127 5 E
Namoi →	99	30 12 S	149 30 E
Namous, O. en →	82	31 0 N	0 15 W
Nampa	118	43 34 N	116 34 W
Nampula	91	15 6 N	39 15 E
Namrole	73	3 46 S	126 46 E
Namse Shankou	67	30 0 N	82 25 E
Namsen →	50	64 27 N	11 42 E
Namsos	50	64 29 N	11 30 E
Namtay	59	62 43 N	129 37 E
Namtu	67	23 5 N	97 28 E
Namtumbo	91	10 30 S	36 4 E
Namu	108	51 52 N	127 50 W
Namucha Shank'ou	69	30 0 N	82 28 E
Namur	16	50 27 N	4 52 E
Namur □	16	50 17 N	5 0 E
Namutoni	92	18 49 S	16 55 E
Namwala	91	15 44 S	26 30 E
Namysłów	28	51 6 N	17 42 E
Nan	71	18 52 N	100 42 E
Nana	46	44 17 N	26 34 E
Nanaimo	108	49 10 N	124 0 W
Nanam	76	41 44 N	129 40 E
Nanan	77	24 59 N	118 21 E
Nanango	97	26 40 S	152 0 E
Nan'ao	77	23 28 N	117 5 E
Nanao	74	37 0 N	137 0 E
Nanbu	77	31 18 N	106 3 E
Nanchang	75	28 42 N	115 55 E
Nancheng	77	27 33 N	116 35 E
Nanching = Nanjing	75	32 2 N	118 47 E
Nanchong	75	30 43 N	106 2 E
Nanchuan	77	29 9 N	107 6 E
Nancy	19	48 42 N	6 12 E
Nanda Devi	69	30 23 N	79 59 E
Nandan	77	24 58 N	107 29 E
Nander	70	19 10 N	77 20 E
Nandewar Ra.	99	30 15 S	150 35 E
Nandi	101	17 42 S	177 20 E
Nandi □	90	0 15 N	35 0 E
Nandikotkur	70	15 52 N	78 18 E
Nandura	68	20 52 N	76 25 E
Nandurbar	68	21 20 N	74 15 E
Nandyal	70	15 30 N	78 30 E
Nanga-Eboko	88	4 41 N	12 22 E
Nanga Parbat	69	35 10 N	74 35 E
Nangade	91	11 5 S	39 36 E
Nangapinoh	72	0 20 S	111 44 E
Nangarhár □	65	34 20 N	70 0 E
Nangatayap	72	1 32 S	110 34 E
Nangeya Mts.	90	3 30 N	33 30 E
Nangis	19	48 33 N	3 0 E
Nanjangud	70	12 6 N	76 43 E
Nanjeko	91	15 31 S	23 30 E

* *Now part of Punjab* □

* *Renamed Brezhnev*

Nanjiang Nevis

Nanjiang 77 32 28N 106 51 E
Nanjing 75 32 2N 118 47 E
Nanjirinji 91 9 41 S 39 5 E
Nankana Sahib 68 31 27N 73 38 E
Nankang 77 25 40N 114 45 E
Nanking = Nanjing 75 32 2N 118 47 E
Nannine 96 26 51 S 118 18 E
Nanning 75 22 48N 108 20 E
Nanpara 69 27 52N 81 33 E
Nanpi 76 38 2N 116 45 E
Nanping 75 26 38N 118 10 E
Nanripe 91 13 52 S 38 52 E
Nansei-Shotō 74 26 0N 128 0 E
Nansen Sd. 4 81 0N 91 0W
Nansio 90 2 3 S 33 4 E
Nant 20 44 1N 3 18 E
Nantes 18 47 12N 1 33W
Nanteuil-le-Haudouin 19 49 9N 2 48 E
Nantiat 20 46 1N 1 11 E
Nanticoke 114 41 12N 76 1W
Nanton 108 50 21N 113 46W
Nantong 77 32 1N 120 52 E
Nantua 21 46 10N 5 35 E
Nantucket I. 102 41 16N 70 3W
Nanuque 127 17 50 S 40 21W
Nanxiong 77 25 6N 114 15 E
Nanyang 75 33 11N 112 30 E
Nanyuan 76 39 44N 116 22 E
Nanyuki 90 0 2N 37 4 E
Nanzhang 77 31 45N 111 50 E
Náo, C. de la 33 38 44N 0 14 E
Naococane L. 107 52 50N 70 45W
Naoetsu 74 37 12N 138 10 E
Naogaon 69 24 52N 88 52 E
Naoli He → 76 47 18N 134 9 E
Náousa 44 40 42N 22 9 E
Napa 118 38 18N 122 17W
Napanee 106 44 15N 77 0W
Napanoch 113 41 44N 74 22W
Napier 101 39 30 S 176 56 E
Naples 115 26 10N 81 45W
Naples = Nápoli 41 40 50N 14 17 E
Napo → 126 3 20 S 72 40W
Napoleon, N. Dak., U.S.A. 116 46 32N 99 49W
Napoleon, Ohio, U.S.A. 114 41 24N 84 7W
Nápoli 41 40 50N 14 17 E
Nápoli, G. di 41 40 40N 14 10 E
Napopo 90 4 15N 28 0 E
Nappa Merrie 99 27 36 S 141 7 E
Naqâda 86 25 53N 32 42 E
Nara, Japan 74 34 40N 135 49 E
Nara, Mali 84 15 10N 7 20W
Nara □ 74 34 30N 136 0 E
Nara, Canal 68 24 30N 69 20 E
Nara Visa 117 35 39N 103 10W
Naracoorte 97 36 58 S 140 45 E
Naradhan 99 33 34 S 146 17 E
Narasapur 70 16 26N 81 40 E
Narasaropet 70 16 14N 80 4 E
Narathiwat 71 6 30N 101 48 E
Narayanganj 69 23 40N 90 33 E
Narayanpet 70 16 45N 77 30 E
Narbonne 20 43 11N 3 0 E
Narcea → 30 43 33N 6 44W
Nardò 41 40 10N 18 0 E
Narew 28 52 55N 23 31 E
Narew → 28 52 26N 20 41 E
Nari → 68 29 40N 68 0 E
Narindra, Helodranon' i 93 14 55 S 47 30 E
Narmada → 68 21 38N 72 36 E
Narnaul 68 28 5N 76 11 E
Narni 39 42 30N 12 30 E
Naro, Ghana 84 10 22N 2 27W
Naro, Italy 40 37 18N 13 48 E
Naro Fominsk 55 55 23N 36 43 E
Narodnaya, G. 52 65 5N 60 0 E
Narok 90 1 55 S 33 52 E
Narok □ 90 1 20 S 36 30 E
Narón 30 43 32N 8 9W
Narooma 99 36 14 S 150 4 E
Narowal 68 32 6N 74 52 E
Narrabri 97 30 19 S 149 46 E
Narran → 99 28 37 S 148 12 E
Narrandera 97 34 42 S 146 31 E
Narraway → 108 55 44N 119 55W
Narrogin 96 32 58 S 117 14 E
Narromine 97 32 12 S 148 12 E
Narsampet 70 17 57N 79 58 E
Narsimhapur 68 22 54N 79 14 E
Nartkala 57 43 33N 43 51 E
Narva 54 59 23N 28 12 E
Narva → 54 59 27N 28 2 E
Narvik 50 68 28N 17 26 E
Narvskoye Vdkhr. 54 59 18N 28 14 E
Narwana 68 29 39N 76 6 E
Naryan-Mar 52 68 0N 53 0 E
Naryilco 99 28 37 S 141 53 E
Narym 58 59 0N 81 30 E
Narymskoye 58 49 10N 84 15 E
Naryn 58 41 26N 75 58 E
Nasa 50 66 29N 15 23 E
Nasarawa 85 8 32N 7 41 E
Năsăud 46 47 19N 24 29 E
Naseby 101 45 1 S 170 10 E
Naser, Buheirat en 86 23 0N 32 30 E
Nashua, Iowa, U.S.A. 116 42 55N 92 34W
Nashua, Mont., U.S.A. 118 48 10N 106 25W
Nashua, N.H., U.S.A. 114 42 50N 71 25W
Nashville, Ark., U.S.A. 117 33 56N 93 50W
Nashville, Ga., U.S.A. 115 31 3N 83 15W
Nashville, Tenn., U.S.A. 115 36 12N 86 46W
Našice 42 45 32N 18 4 E
Nasielsk 28 52 35N 20 50 E
Nasik 70 19 58N 73 50 E
Nasirabad 68 26 15N 74 45 E
Naskaupi → 107 53 47N 60 51W
Naso 41 38 8N 14 46 E
Nass → 108 55 0N 129 40W
Nassau, Bahamas 121 25 0N 77 20W
Nassau, U.S.A. 113 42 30N 73 34W
Nassau, Bahía 128 55 20 S 68 0W
Nasser City = Kôm Ombo 86 24 25N 32 52 E
Nasser, L. = Naser, Buheiret en 86 23 0N 32 30 E
Nassian 84 8 28N 3 28W
Nässjö 49 57 39N 14 42 E
Nastopoka Is. 106 57 0N 77 0W
Näsum 49 56 10N 14 29 E
Näsviken 48 61 46N 16 52 E
Nat Kyizin 71 14 57N 97 59 E
Nata 92 20 12 S 26 12 E
Natagaima 126 3 37N 75 6W
Natal, Brazil 127 5 47 S 35 13W
Natal, Can. 108 49 43N 114 51W
Natal, Indon. 72 0 35N 99 7 E
Natal □ 93 28 30 S 30 30 E
Natalinci 42 44 15N 20 49 E
Naṭanz 65 33 30N 51 55 E
Natashquan 107 50 14N 61 46W
Natashquan → 107 50 7N 61 50W
Natchez 117 31 35N 91 25W
Natchitoches 117 31 47N 93 4W
Nathalia 99 36 1 S 145 13 E
Nathdwara 68 24 55N 73 50 E
Natick 113 42 16N 71 19W
Natih 65 22 25N 56 30 E
Natimuk 99 36 42 S 142 0 E
Nation → 108 55 30N 123 32W
National City 119 32 39N 117 7W
Natitingou 85 10 20N 1 26 E
Natividad, I. 120 27 50N 115 10W
Natoma 116 39 14N 99 0W
Natron, L. 90 2 20 S 36 0 E
Natrona 112 40 39N 79 43W
Natrûn, W. el. → 86 30 25N 30 13 E
Natuna Besar, Kepulauan 72 4 0N 108 15 E
Natuna Selatan, Kepulauan 72 2 45N 109 0 E
Natural Bridge 113 44 5N 75 30W
Naturaliste, C. 96 33 32 S 115 0 E
Naturaliste C. 99 40 50 S 148 15 E
Naturaliste Channel 96 25 20 S 113 0 E
Naubinway 106 46 7N 85 27W
Naucelle 20 44 13N 2 20 E
Nauders 26 46 54N 10 30 E
Nauen 24 52 36N 12 52 E
Naugatuck 113 41 28N 73 4W
Naujoji Vilnia 54 54 48N 25 27 E
Naumburg 24 51 10N 11 48 E
Nauru 94 1 0 S 166 0 E
Nauru Is. 94 0 32 S 166 55 E
Nauta 126 4 31 S 73 35W
Nautla 120 20 20N 96 50W
Nava del Rey 30 41 22N 5 6W
Navacerrada, Puerto de 30 40 47N 4 0W
Navahermosa 31 39 41N 4 28W
Navajo Res. 119 36 55N 107 30W
Navalcarnero 30 40 17N 4 5W
Navalmoral de la Mata 30 39 52N 5 33W
Navalvillar de Pela 31 39 9N 5 24W
Navan = An Uaimh 15 53 39N 6 40W
Navare 20 43 20N 1 20W
Navarino, I. 128 55 0 S 67 40W
Navarra □ 32 42 40N 1 40W
Navarre, France 20 43 15N 1 20W
Navarre, U.S.A. 112 40 43N 81 31W
Navarrenx 20 43 20N 0 45W
Navas del Marqués, Las 30 40 36N 4 20W
Navasota 117 30 20N 96 5W
Navassa 121 18 30N 75 0W
Nave 38 45 35N 10 17 E
Naver → 14 58 34N 4 15W
Navia 30 43 35N 6 42W
Navia → 30 43 15N 6 50W
Navia de Suarna 30 42 58N 6 59W
Navidad 124 33 57 S 71 50W
Navlya 54 52 53N 34 30 E
Navoi 58 40 9N 65 22 E
Navojoa 120 27 0N 109 30W
Navolok 52 62 33N 39 57 E
Návpaktos 45 38 23N 21 50 E
Návplion 45 37 33N 22 50 E
Navrongo 85 10 51N 1 3W
Navsari 68 20 57N 72 59 E
Nawa Kot 68 28 21N 71 24 E
Nawabganj, Bangla. 69 24 35N 88 14 E
Nawabganj, India 69 26 56N 81 14 E
Nawabganj, Bareilly 69 28 32N 79 40 E
Nawabshah 68 26 15N 68 25 E
Nawada 69 24 50N 85 33 E
Nawakot 69 27 55N 85 10 E
Nawalgarh 68 27 50N 75 15 E
Nawapara 69 20 46N 82 33 E
Nawāsīf, Harrat 64 21 20N 42 10 E
Nawi 86 18 32N 30 50 E
Náxos 45 37 8N 25 25 E
Nay 20 43 10N 0 18W
Nāy Band 65 27 20N 52 40 E
Nayakhan 59 61 56N 159 0 E
Nayarit □ 120 22 0N 105 0W
Nayé 84 14 28N 12 12W
Nazaré 31 39 36N 9 4W
Nazas 120 25 10N 104 6W
Nazas → 120 25 35N 103 25W
Naze, The 13 51 53N 1 19 E
Nazerat 62 32 42N 35 17 E
Nazir Hat 67 22 35N 91 49 E
Nazko 108 53 1N 123 37W
Nazko → 108 53 7N 123 34W
Nzret 87 8 32N 39 22 E
Nchanga 91 12 30 S 27 49 E
Ncheu 91 14 50 S 34 47 E
Ndala 90 4 45 S 33 15 E
Ndalatando 88 9 12 S 14 48 E
Ndali 85 9 50N 2 46 E
Ndareda 90 4 12 S 35 30 E
Ndélé 88 8 25N 20 36 E
Ndendé 88 2 22 S 11 23 E
Ndjamena 81 12 10N 14 59 E
Ndjolé 88 0 10 S 10 45 E
Ndola 91 13 0 S 28 34 E
Ndoto Mts. 90 2 0N 37 0 E
Nduguti 90 4 18 S 34 41 E
Nea → 47 63 15N 11 0 E
Néa Epídhavros 45 37 40N 23 7 E
Néa Flippiás 44 39 12N 20 53 E
Néa Kallikrátia 44 40 21N 23 1 E
Néa Víssi 44 41 34N 26 33 E
Neagh, Lough 15 54 35N 6 25W
Neah Bay 118 48 25N 124 40W
Neamţ □ 46 47 0N 26 20 E
Neápolis, Kozan, Greece 44 40 20N 21 24 E
Neápolis, Lakonia, Greece 45 36 27N 23 8 E
Near Is. 104 53 0N 172 0 E
Neath 13 51 39N 3 49W
Nebbou 85 11 9N 1 51W
Nebine Cr. → 99 29 27 S 146 56 E
Nebit Dag 58 39 30N 54 22 E
Nebolchy, U.S.S.R. 54 59 12N 32 58 E
Nebolchy, U.S.S.R. 54 59 8N 33 18 E
Nebraska □ 116 41 30N 100 0W
Nebraska City 116 40 40N 95 52W
Nébrodi, Monti 40 37 55N 14 50 E
Necedah 116 44 2N 90 7W
Nechako → 108 53 30N 122 44W
Neches → 117 29 55N 93 52W
Neckar → 25 49 31N 8 26 E
Necochea 124 38 30 S 58 50W
Nedelišće 39 46 23N 16 22 E
Nédha → 45 37 25N 21 45 E
Nedroma 82 35 1N 1 45W
Nedstrand 47 59 21N 5 49 E
Needles 119 34 50N 114 35W
Needles, The 13 50 39N 1 35W
Ñeembucú □ 124 27 0 S 58 0W
Neemuch (Nimach) 68 24 30N 74 56 E
Neenah 114 44 10N 88 30W
Neepawa 109 50 15N 99 30W
Nefta 83 33 53N 7 50 E
Neftah Sidi Boubekeur 82 35 1N 0 4 E
Neftegorsk 57 44 25N 39 45 E
Neftyannyye Kamni 53 40 20N 50 55 E
Negapatam = Nagappattinam 70 10 46N 79 50 E
Negaunee 114 46 30N 87 36W
Negba 62 31 40N 34 41 E
Negele 87 5 20N 39 36 E
Negeri Sembilan □ 71 2 50N 102 10 E
Negev = Hanegev 62 30 50N 35 0 E
Negoiu 46 45 35N 24 32 E
Negombo 70 7 12N 79 50 E
Negotin 42 44 16N 22 37 E
Negotino 42 41 29N 22 9 E
Negra, La 124 23 46 S 70 18W
Negra, Peña 30 42 11N 6 30W
Negra Pt. 73 18 40N 120 50 E
Negreira 30 42 54N 8 45W
Negreşti 46 46 50N 27 30 E
Négrine 83 34 30N 7 30 E
Negro →, Argent. 128 41 2 S 62 47W
Negro →, Brazil 126 3 0 S 60 0W
Negro →, Uruguay 125 33 24 S 58 22W
Negros 73 10 0N 123 0 E
Negru Vodă 46 43 47N 28 21 E
Nehbandān 65 31 35N 60 5 E
Neheim-Hüsten 24 51 27N 7 58 E
Nehoiaşu 46 45 24N 26 20 E
Nei Monggol Zizhiqu □ 76 42 0N 112 0 E
Neidpath 109 50 12N 107 20W
Neihart 118 47 0N 110 44W
Neijiang 75 29 35N 104 55 E
Neilton 118 17 24N 123 52W
Neira de Jusá 30 42 53N 7 14W
Neisse → 24 52 4N 14 46 E
Neiva 126 2 56N 75 18W
Neixiang 77 33 10N 111 52 E
Nejanilini L. 109 59 33N 97 48W
Nejo 87 9 30N 35 28 E
Nekemte 87 9 4N 36 30 E
Nêkheb 86 25 10N 32 48 E
Neksø 49 55 4N 15 8 E
Nelas 30 40 32N 7 52W
Nelaug 47 58 39N 8 40 E
Nelia 98 20 39 S 142 12 E
Nelidovo 54 56 13N 32 49 E
Neligh 116 42 11N 98 2W
Nelkan 59 57 40N 136 4 E
Nellikuppam 70 11 46N 79 43 E
Nellore 70 14 27N 79 59 E
Nelma 59 47 39N 139 0 E
Nelson, Austral. 100 38 3 S 141 2 E
Nelson, Can. 108 49 30N 117 20W
Nelson, N.Z. 101 41 18 S 173 16 E
Nelson, U.K. 12 53 50N 2 14W
Nelson, Ariz., U.S.A. 119 35 35N 113 16W
Nelson, Nev., U.S.A. 119 35 46N 114 48W
Nelson □ 101 42 11 S 172 15 E
Nelson → 109 54 33N 98 2W
Nelson, C., Austral. 99 38 26 S 141 32 E
Nelson, C., P.N.G. 98 9 0 S 149 20 E
Nelson, Estrecho 128 51 30 S 75 0W
Nelson Forks 108 59 30N 124 0W
Nelson House 109 55 47N 98 51W
Nelson L. 109 55 48N 100 7W
Nelspruit 93 25 29 S 30 59 E
Néma 84 16 40N 7 15W
Neman (Nemunas) → 54 55 25N 21 10 E
Neméa 45 37 49N 22 40 E
Nemeiben L. 109 55 20N 105 20W
Nemira 46 46 17N 26 19 E
Nemours 19 48 16N 2 40 E
Nemunas = Neman → 54 55 25N 21 10 E
Nemuro 74 43 20N 145 35 E
Nemuro-Kaikyō 74 43 30N 145 30 E
Nemuy 59 55 40N 136 9 E
Nen Jiang → 76 45 28N 124 30 E
Nenagh 15 52 52N 8 11W
Nenana 104 64 30N 149 20W
Nene → 12 52 38N 0 13 E
Nenjiang 75 49 10N 125 10 E
Neno 91 15 25 S 34 40 E
Nenusa, Kepulauan 73 4 45N 127 1 E
Neodesha 117 37 30N 95 37W
Néon Petritsi 44 41 16N 23 15 E
Neosho 117 36 56N 94 28W
Neosho → 117 35 59N 95 10W
Nepal ■ 69 28 0N 84 30 E
Nepalganj 69 28 5N 81 40 E
Nephi 118 39 43N 111 52W
Nephin 15 54 1N 9 21W
Nepomuk 26 49 29N 13 35 E
Neptune City 113 40 13N 74 4W
Néra → 42 44 48N 21 25 E
Nérac 20 44 8N 0 21 E
Nerchinsk 59 52 0N 116 39 E
Nerchinskiy Zavod 59 51 20N 119 40 E
Nereju 46 45 43N 26 43 E
Nerekhta 55 57 26N 40 38 E
Néret L. 107 54 45N 70 44W
Neretva → 42 43 1N 17 27 E
Neretvanski Kanal 42 43 7N 17 10 E
Neringa 54 55 30N 21 5 E
Nerja 31 36 43N 3 55W
Nerl → 55 56 11N 40 34 E
Nerokoúrou 45 35 29N 24 3 E
Nerpio 33 38 11N 2 16W
Nerva 31 37 42N 6 30W
Nes 50 65 53N 17 24W
Nes Ziyyona 62 31 56N 34 48W
Nesbyen 47 60 34N 9 35 E
Nesebûr 43 42 41N 27 46 E
Nesflaten 47 59 38N 6 48 E
Neskaupstaður 50 65 9N 13 42W
Nesland 47 59 31N 7 59 E
Neslandsvatn 47 58 57N 9 10 E
Nesle 19 49 45N 2 53 E
Nesodden 47 59 48N 10 40 E
Nesque → 21 43 59N 4 59 E
Ness, Loch 14 57 15N 4 30W
Nestórion Óros 44 40 24N 21 5 E
Néstos → 44 41 20N 24 35 E
Nesttun 47 60 19N 5 21 E
Nesvizh 54 53 14N 26 38 E
Netanya 62 32 20N 34 51 E
Nète → 16 51 7N 4 14 E
Nether Stowey 13 51 0N 3 10W
Netherbury 13 50 46N 2 45W
Netherdale 97 21 10 S 148 33 E
Netherlands ■ 16 52 0N 5 30 E
Netherlands Antilles □ 121 12 30N 68 0W
Netherlands Guiana = Surinam ■ 127 4 0N 56 0W
Neto → 41 39 13N 17 8 E
Netrakona 69 24 53N 90 47 E
Nettancourt 19 48 51N 4 57 E
Nettilling L. 105 66 30N 71 0W
Nettuno 40 41 29N 12 40 E
Netzahualcoyotl, Presa 120 17 10N 93 30W
Neu-Isenburg 25 50 3N 8 42 E
Neu-Ulm 25 48 23N 10 2 E
Neubrandenburg 24 53 33N 13 17 E
Neubrandenburg □ 24 53 30N 13 20 E
Neubukow 24 54 1N 11 40 E
Neuburg 25 48 43N 11 11 E
Neuchâtel 25 47 0N 6 55 E
Neuchâtel □ 25 47 0N 6 55 E
Neuchâtel, Lac de 25 46 53N 6 50 E
Neudau 26 47 11N 16 6 E
Neuenhaus 24 52 30N 6 55 E
Neuf-Brisach 19 48 0N 7 30 E
Neufahrn 25 48 44N 12 11 E
Neufchâteau, Belg. 16 49 50N 5 25 E
Neufchâteau, France 19 48 21N 5 40 E
Neufchâtel 19 49 43N 1 30 E
Neufchâtel-sur-Aisne 19 49 26N 4 0 E
Neuhaus 24 53 16N 10 54 E
Neuillé-Pont-Pierre 18 47 33N 0 33 E
Neuilly-St-Front 19 49 10N 3 15 E
Neukalen 24 53 49N 12 48 E
Neumarkt 25 49 16N 11 28 E
Neumarkt-Sankt Veit 25 48 22N 12 30 E
Neumünster 24 54 4N 9 58 E
Neung-sur-Beuvron 19 47 30N 1 50 E
Neunkirchen, Austria 26 47 43N 16 4 E
Neunkirchen, Ger. 25 49 23N 7 12 E
Neuquén 128 38 55 S 68 0 E
Neuquén □ 124 38 0 S 69 50W
Neuruppin 24 52 56N 12 48 E
Neuse → 115 35 5N 76 30W
Neusiedl 27 47 57N 16 50 E
Neusiedler See 27 47 50N 16 47 E
Neuss 24 51 12N 6 39 E
Neussargues-Moissac 20 45 9N 3 1 E
Neustadt, Baden-W., Ger. 25 47 54N 8 13 E
Neustadt, Bayern, Ger. 25 50 23N 11 0 E
Neustadt, Bayern, Ger. 25 49 42N 12 10 E
Neustadt, Bayern, Ger. 25 48 48N 11 47 E
Neustadt, Bayern, Ger. 25 49 34N 10 37 E
Neustadt, Gera, Ger. 24 50 45N 11 43 E
Neustadt, Hessen, Ger. 24 50 51N 9 9 E
Neustadt, Niedersachsen, Ger. 24 52 30N 9 30 E
Neustadt, Potsdam, Ger. 24 52 50N 12 27 E
Neustadt, Rhld-Pfz., Ger. 25 49 21N 8 10 E
Neustadt, Schleswig-Holstein, Ger. 24 54 6N 10 49 E
Neustrelitz 24 53 22N 13 4 E
Neuvic 20 45 23N 2 16 E
Neuville, Rhône, France 21 45 52N 4 51 E
Neuville, Vienne, France 18 46 41N 0 15 E
Neuville-aux-Bois 19 48 4N 2 3 E
Neuvy-le-Roi 18 47 36N 0 36 E
Neuvy-St-Sépulchure 20 46 35N 1 48 E
Neuvy-sur-Barangeon 19 47 20N 2 15 E
Neuwerk 24 53 55N 8 30 E
Neuwied 24 50 26N 7 29 E
Neva → 54 59 50N 30 30 E
Nevada 117 37 51N 94 22W
Nevada □ 118 39 20N 117 0W
Nevada City 118 39 20N 121 0W
Nevada de Sta. Marta, Sa. 126 10 55N 73 50W
Nevada, Sierra, Spain 33 37 3N 3 15W
Nevada, Sierra, U.S.A. 118 39 0N 120 30W
Nevado, Cerro 124 35 30 S 68 32W
Nevanka 59 56 31N 98 55 E
Nevasa 70 19 34N 75 0 E
Nevel 54 56 0N 29 55 E
Nevers 19 47 0N 3 9 E
Nevertire 99 31 50 S 147 44 E
Nevesinje 42 43 14N 18 6 E
Neville 109 49 58N 107 39W
Nevinnomyssk 57 44 40N 42 0 E
Nevis 121 17 0N 62 30W

Nevlunghavn Nootka I.

Nevlunghavn **47** 55 58N 9 52 E
Nevrokop = Gotse Delchev **43** 41 33N 23 46 E
Nevşehir **64** 38 33N 34 40 E
Nevyansk **52** 57 30N 60 13 E
New Albany, Ind., U.S.A. **114** 38 20N 85 50W
New Albany, Miss., U.S.A. **117** 34 30N 89 0W
New Albany, Pa., U.S.A. **113** 41 35N 76 28W
New Amsterdam **126** 6 15N 57 36W
New Bedford **114** 41 40N 70 52W
New Bern **115** 35 8N 77 3W
New Bethlehem **112** 41 0N 79 22W
New Bloomfield **112** 40 24N 77 12W
New Boston **117** 33 27N 94 21W
New Braunfels **117** 29 43N 98 9W
New Brighton, N.Z. **101** 43 29 S 172 43 E
New Brighton, U.S.A. **112** 40 42N 80 19W
New Britain, P.N.G. **94** 5 50 S 150 20 E
New Britain, U.S.A. **114** 41 41N 72 47W
New Brunswick **114** 40 30N 74 28W
New Brunswick □ **107** 46 50N 66 30W
New Bussa **85** 9 53N 4 31 E
New Byrd **5** 80 0 S 120 0W
New Caledonia = Nouvelle-Calédonie **94** 21 0 S 165 0 E
New Castile = Castilla La Neuva **31** 39 45N 3 20W
New Castle, Ind., U.S.A. **114** 39 55N 85 23W
New Castle, Pa., U.S.A. **114** 41 0N 80 20W
New City **113** 41 8N 74 0W
New Cristóbal **120** 9 22N 79 40W
New Cumberland **112** 40 30N 80 36W
New Delhi **68** 28 37N 77 13 E
New Denver **108** 50 0N 117 25W
New England **116** 46 36N 102 47W
New England Ra. **97** 30 20 S 151 45 E
New Forest **13** 50 53N 1 40W
New Glasgow **107** 45 35N 62 36W
New Guinea **94** 4 0 S 136 0 E
New Hamburg **112** 43 23N 80 42W
New Hampshire □ **114** 43 40N 71 40W
New Hampton **116** 43 2N 92 20W
New Hanover, P.N.G. **98** 2 30 S 150 10 E
New Hanover, S. Afr. **93** 29 22 S 30 31 E
New Haven, Conn., U.S.A. **114** 41 20N 72 54W
New Haven, Mich., U.S.A. **112** 42 44N 82 46W
New Hazelton **108** 55 20N 127 30W
* New Hebrides **94** 15 0 S 168 0 E
New Iberia **117** 30 2N 91 54W
New Ireland **94** 3 20 S 151 50 E
New Jersey □ **114** 40 30N 74 10W
New Kensington **114** 40 36N 79 43W
New Lexington **114** 39 40N 82 15W
New Liskeard **106** 47 31N 79 41W
New London, Conn., U.S.A. **114** 41 23N 72 8W
New London, Minn., U.S.A. **116** 45 17N 94 55W
New London, Ohio, U.S.A. **112** 41 4N 82 25W
New London, Wis., U.S.A. **116** 44 23N 88 43W
New Madrid **117** 36 40N 89 30W
New Meadows **118** 45 0N 116 32W
New Mexico □ **110** 34 30N 106 0W
New Milford, Conn., U.S.A. **113** 41 35N 73 25W
New Milford, Pa., U.S.A. **113** 41 50N 75 45W
New Norfolk **97** 42 46 S 147 2 E
New Orleans **117** 30 0N 90 5W
New Philadelphia **114** 40 29N 81 25W
New Plymouth, N.Z. **101** 39 4 S 174 5 E
New Plymouth, U.S.A. **118** 43 58N 116 49W
New Providence **121** 25 25N 78 35W
New Radnor **13** 52 15N 3 10W
New Richmond **116** 45 6N 92 34W
New Roads **117** 30 43N 91 30W
New Rochelle **113** 40 55N 73 46W
New Rockford **116** 47 44N 99 7W
New Ross **15** 52 24N 6 58W
New Salem **116** 46 51N 101 25W
New Siberian Is. = Novosibirskiye Os. **59** 75 0N 142 0 E
New Smyrna Beach **115** 29 0N 80 50W
New South Wales □ **97** 33 0 S 146 0 E
New Town **116** 47 59N 102 30W
New Ulm **116** 44 15N 94 30W
New Waterford **107** 46 13N 60 4W
New Westminster **108** 49 13N 122 55W
New York □ **114** 42 40N 76 0W
New York City **114** 40 45N 74 0W
New Zealand ■ **94** 40 0 S 176 0 E
Newala **91** 10 58 S 39 18 E
Newala □ **91** 10 46 S 39 20 E
Newark, Del., U.S.A. **114** 39 42N 75 45W
Newark, N.J., U.S.A. **114** 40 41N 74 12W
Newark, N.Y., U.S.A. **114** 43 2N 77 10W
Newark, Ohio, U.S.A. **114** 40 5N 82 24W
Newark-on-Trent **12** 53 6N 0 48W
Newaygo **114** 43 25N 85 48W
Newberg **118** 45 22N 123 0W
Newberry, Mich., U.S.A. **114** 46 20N 85 32W
Newberry, S.C., U.S.A. **115** 34 17N 81 37W
Newbrook **108** 54 24N 112 57W
Newburgh **114** 41 30N 74 1W
Newbury, U.K. **13** 51 24N 1 19W
Newbury, U.S.A. **113** 44 7N 72 6W
Newburyport **114** 42 48N 70 50W
Newcastle, Austral. **97** 33 0 S 151 46 E
Newcastle, Can. **107** 47 1N 65 38W
Newcastle, S. Afr. **93** 27 45 S 29 58 E
Newcastle, U.K. **15** 54 13N 5 54W
Newcastle, U.S.A. **116** 43 50N 104 12W
Newcastle Emlyn **13** 52 2N 4 29W
Newcastle Ra. **97** 15 45 S 130 15 E
Newcastle-under-Lyme **12** 53 2N 2 15W
Newcastle-upon-Tyne **12** 54 59N 1 37W
Newcastle Waters **96** 17 30 S 133 28 E
Newdegate **96** 33 6 S 119 0 E
Newe Etan **62** 32 30N 35 32 E
Newe Sha'anan **62** 32 47N 34 59 E
Newe Zohar **62** 31 9N 35 21 E
Newell **116** 44 48N 103 25W
Newenham, C. **104** 58 40N 162 15W
Newfoundland **107** 48 30N 56 0W
Newfoundland □ **107** 53 0N 58 0W
Newhalem **108** 48 41N 121 16W
Newham **13** 51 31N 0 2 E
Newhaven **13** 50 47N 0 4 E
Newkirk **117** 36 52N 97 3W
Newman, Mt. **96** 23 20 S 119 34 E
Newmarket, Can. **112** 44 3N 79 28W
Newmarket, Ireland **15** 52 13N 9 0W
Newmarket, U.K. **13** 52 15N 0 23 E
Newmarket, U.S.A. **113** 43 4N 70 57W
Newnan **115** 33 22N 84 48W
Newnes **99** 33 9 S 150 16 E
Newport, Gwent, U.K. **13** 51 35N 3 0W
Newport, I. of W., U.K. **13** 50 42N 1 18W
Newport, Salop, U.K. **13** 52 47N 2 22W
Newport, Ark., U.S.A. **117** 35 38N 91 15W
Newport, Ky., U.S.A. **114** 39 5N 84 23W
Newport, N.H., U.S.A. **114** 43 23N 72 8W
Newport, Oreg., U.S.A. **118** 44 41N 124 2W
Newport, Pa., U.S.A. **112** 40 28N 77 8W
Newport, R.I., U.S.A. **114** 41 13N 71 19W
Newport, Tenn., U.S.A. **115** 35 59N 83 12W
Newport, Vt., U.S.A. **114** 44 57N 72 17W
Newport, Wash., U.S.A. **118** 48 11N 117 2W
Newport Beach **119** 33 40N 117 58W
Newport News **114** 37 2N 76 30W
Newquay **13** 50 24N 5 6W
Newry **15** 54 10N 6 20W
Newry & Mourne □ **15** 54 10N 6 15W
Newton, Iowa, U.S.A. **116** 41 40N 93 3W
Newton, Mass., U.S.A. **114** 42 21N 71 10W
Newton, Miss., U.S.A. **117** 32 19N 89 10W
Newton, N.C., U.S.A. **115** 35 42N 81 10W
Newton, N.J., U.S.A. **114** 41 3N 74 46W
Newton, Texas, U.S.A. **117** 30 54N 93 42W
Newton Abbot **13** 50 32N 3 37W
Newton Boyd **99** 29 45 S 152 16 E
Newton Stewart **14** 54 57N 4 30W
Newtonmore **14** 57 4N 4 7W
Newtown **13** 52 31N 3 19W
Newtownabbey **15** 54 40N 5 55W
Newtownabbey □ **15** 54 45N 6 0W
Newtownards **15** 54 37N 5 40W
Newville **112** 40 10N 77 24W
Nexon **20** 45 41N 1 11 E
Neya **55** 58 21N 43 49 E
Neyrīz **65** 29 15N 54 19 E
Neyshābūr **65** 36 10N 58 50 E
Neyyattinkara **70** 8 26N 77 5 E
Nezhin **54** 51 5N 31 55 E
Nezperce **118** 46 13N 116 15W
Ngabang **72** 0 23N 109 55 E
Ngabordamlu, Tanjung **73** 6 56 S 134 11 E
Ngambé **88** 5 48N 11 29 E
Ngami Depression **92** 20 30 S 22 46 E
Ngamo **91** 19 3 S 27 32 E
Nganglong Kangri **67** 33 0N 81 0 E
Nganjuk **73** 7 32 S 111 55 E
Ngaoundéré **88** 7 15N 13 35 E
Ngapara **101** 44 57 S 170 46 E
Ngara **90** 2 29 S 30 40 E
Ngara □ **90** 2 29 S 30 40 E
Ngau **101** 18 2 S 179 18 E
Ngawi **73** 7 24 S 111 26 E
Ngha Lo **71** 21 33N 104 28 E
Ngiva **92** 16 48 S 15 50 E
Ngoma **91** 13 8 S 33 45 E
Ngomahura **91** 20 26 S 30 43 E
Ngomba **91** 8 20 S 32 53 E
Ngop **87** 6 17N 30 9 E
Ngoring Hu **75** 34 55N 97 5 E
Ngorkou **84** 15 40N 3 41W
Ngorongoro **90** 3 11 S 35 32 E
Ngozi **90** 2 54 S 29 50 E
Ngudu **90** 2 58 S 33 25 E
Nguigmi **81** 14 20N 13 20 E
Ngunga **90** 3 37 S 33 37 E
Ngunza **88** 11 10 S 13 48 E
Nguru **85** 12 56N 10 29 E
Nguru Mts. **90** 6 0 S 37 30 E
Nha Trang **71** 12 16N 109 10 E
Nhacoongo **93** 24 18 S 35 14 E
Nhangutazi, L. **93** 24 0 S 34 30 E
Nhill **99** 36 18 S 141 40 E
Nia-nia **90** 1 30N 27 40 E
Niafounké **84** 16 0N 4 5W
Niagara **114** 45 45N 88 0W
Niagara Falls, Can. **106** 43 7N 79 5W
Niagara Falls, U.S.A. **114** 43 5N 79 0W
Niagara-on-the-Lake **112** 43 15N 79 4W
Niah **72** 3 58N 113 46 E
Nialia, L. **100** 33 20 S 141 42 E
Niamey **85** 13 27N 2 6 E
Nianforando **84** 9 37N 10 36W
Nianfors **48** 61 36N 16 46 E
Niangara **90** 3 42N 27 50 E
Nianzishan **76** 47 31N 122 53 E
Nias **72** 1 0N 97 30 E
Niassa □ **91** 13 30 S 36 0 E
Nibbiano **38** 44 54N 9 20 E
Nibe **49** 56 59N 9 38 E
Nibong Tebal **71** 5 10N 100 29 E
Nicaragua ■ **121** 11 40N 85 30W
Nicaragua, Lago de **121** 12 0N 85 30W
Nicastro **41** 39 0N 16 18 E
Nice **21** 43 42N 7 14 E
Niceville **115** 30 30N 86 30W
Nichinan **74** 31 38N 131 23 E
Nicholás, Canal **121** 23 30N 80 5W
Nicholasville **114** 37 54N 84 31W
Nichols **113** 42 1N 76 22W
Nicholson **113** 41 37N 75 47W
Nicobar Is. **60** 9 0N 93 0 E
Nicola **108** 50 12N 120 40W
Nicolet **106** 46 17N 72 35W
Nicolls Town **121** 25 8N 78 0W
Nicopolis **45** 39 2N 20 37 E
Nicosia, Cyprus **64** 35 10N 33 25 E
Nicosia, Italy **41** 37 45N 14 22 E
Nicótera **41** 38 33N 15 57 E
Nicoya, G. de **121** 10 0N 85 0W
Nicoya, Pen. de **121** 9 45N 85 40W
Nidd → **12** 54 1N 1 32W
Nidda **24** 50 24N 9 2 E
Nidda → **25** 50 6N 8 34 E
Nidzica **28** 53 25N 20 28 E
Niebüll **24** 54 47N 8 49 E
Nied → **19** 49 23N 6 40 E
Niederaula **24** 50 48N 9 37 E
Niederbronn **19** 48 57N 7 39 E
Niedere Tauern **26** 47 20N 14 0 E
Niedermarsberg **24** 51 28N 8 52 E
Niederösterreich □ **26** 48 25N 15 40 E
Niedersachsen □ **24** 52 45N 9 0 E
Niellé **84** 10 5N 5 38W
Niemba **90** 5 58 S 28 24 E
Niemcza **28** 50 42N 16 47 E
Niemodlin **28** 50 38N 17 38 E
Niemur **100** 35 17 S 144 9 E
Nienburg **24** 52 38N 9 15 E
Niepołomice **27** 50 3N 20 13 E
Niers → **24** 51 45N 5 58 E
Niesky **24** 51 18N 14 48 E
Nieszawa **28** 52 52N 18 50 E
Nieuw Amsterdam **127** 5 53N 55 5W
Nieuw Nickerie **127** 6 0N 56 59W
Nieuwpoort **16** 51 8N 2 45 E
Nieves **30** 42 7N 8 26W
Nièvre □ **19** 47 10N 3 40 E
Niğde **64** 38 0N 34 40 E
Nigel **93** 26 27 S 28 25 E
Niger ■ **85** 13 30N 10 0 E
Niger □ **85** 10 0N 5 0 E
Niger → **85** 5 33N 6 33 E
Nigeria ■ **85** 8 30N 8 0 E
Nightcaps **101** 45 57 S 168 2 E
Nigríta **44** 40 56N 23 29 E
Nihtaur **69** 29 20N 78 23 E
Nii-Jima **74** 34 20N 139 15 E
Niigata **74** 37 58N 139 0 E
Niigata □ **74** 37 15N 138 45 E
Niihama **74** 33 55N 133 16 E
Niihau **110** 21 55N 160 10W
Nijar **33** 36 53N 2 15W
Nijkerk **16** 52 13N 5 30 E
Nijmegen **16** 51 50N 5 52 E
Nijverdal **16** 52 22N 6 28 E
Nike **85** 6 26N 7 29 E
Nikel **50** 69 24N 30 12 E
Nikiniki **73** 9 49 S 124 30 E
Nikitas **44** 40 13N 23 34 E
Nikki **85** 9 58N 3 12 E
Nikkō **74** 36 45N 139 35 E
Nikolayev **56** 46 58N 32 0 E
Nikolayevsk **55** 50 0N 45 35 E
Nikolayevsk-na-Amur **59** 53 8N 140 44 E
Nikolsk **55** 59 30N 45 28 E
Nikolskoye **59** 55 12N 166 0 E
Nikopol, Bulg. **43** 43 43N 24 54 E
Nikopol, U.S.S.R. **56** 47 35N 34 25 E
Niksar **56** 40 31N 37 2 E
Nīkshahr **65** 26 15N 60 10 E
Nikšić **42** 42 50N 18 57 E
Nîl el Abyad → **87** 15 38N 32 31 E
Nîl el Azraq → **87** 15 38N 32 31 E
Nîl, Nahr en → **86** 30 10N 31 6 E
Niland **119** 33 16N 115 30W
Nile = Nîl, Nahr en → **86** 30 10N 31 6 E
Nile □ **90** 2 0N 31 30 E
Nile Delta **86** 31 40N 31 0 E
Niles **114** 41 8N 80 40W
Nilgiri Hills **70** 11 30N 76 30 E
Nimach = Neemuch **68** 24 30N 74 56 E
Nimbahera **68** 24 37N 74 45 E
Nîmes **21** 43 50N 4 23 E
Nimfaíon, Ákra- **44** 40 5N 24 20 E
Nimingarra **96** 20 31 S 119 55 E
Nimmitabel **99** 36 29 S 149 15 E
Nimneryskiy **59** 57 50N 125 10 E
Nimrod Glacier **5** 82 27 S 161 0 E
Nimule **87** 3 32N 32 3 E
Nin **39** 44 16N 15 12 E
Nindigully **99** 28 21 S 148 50 E
Ninemile **108** 56 0N 130 7W
Ninety Mile Beach, The **97** 38 15 S 147 24 E
Nineveh = Nīnawá **64** 36 25N 43 10 E
Ning'an **76** 44 22N 129 20 E
Ningbo **75** 29 51N 121 28 E
Ningde **75** 26 38N 119 23 E
Ningdu **77** 26 25N 115 59 E
Ningjin **76** 37 35N 114 57 E
Ningming **77** 22 8N 107 4 E
Ningpo = Ningbo **75** 29 51N 121 28 E
Ningqiang **77** 32 47N 106 15 E
Ningshan **77** 33 21N 108 21 E
Ningsia Hui A.R. = Ningxia Huizu Zizhiqu □ **76** 38 0N 106 0 E
Ningwu **76** 39 0N 112 18 E
Ningxia Huizu Zizhiqu □ **76** 38 0N 106 0 E
Ningxiang **77** 28 15N 112 30 E
Ningyuan **77** 25 37N 111 57 E
Ninh Binh **71** 20 15N 105 55 E
Ninove **16** 50 51N 4 2 E
Nioaque **125** 21 5 S 55 50W
Niobrara **116** 42 48N 97 59W
Niobrara → **116** 42 45N 98 0W
Niono **84** 14 15N 6 0W
Nioro du Rip **84** 13 40N 15 50W
Nioro du Sahel **84** 15 15N 9 30W
Niort **20** 46 19N 0 29W
Nipani **70** 16 20N 74 25 E
Nipawin **109** 53 20N 104 0W
Nipawin Prov. Park **109** 54 0N 104 37W
Nipigon **106** 49 0N 88 17W
Nipigon, L. **106** 49 50N 88 30W
Nipin → **109** 55 46N 108 35W
Nipishish L. **107** 54 12N 60 45W
Nipissing L. **106** 46 20N 80 0W
Nipomo **119** 35 4N 120 29W
Niquelândia **127** 14 33 S 48 23W
Nira → **70** 17 58N 75 8 E
Nirmal **70** 19 3N 78 20 E
Nirmali **69** 26 20N 86 35 E
Niš **42** 43 19N 21 58 E
Nisa **31** 39 30N 7 41W
Nişāb **63** 14 25N 46 29 E
Nišava → **42** 43 20N 21 46 E
Niscemi **41** 37 8N 14 21 E
Nishinomiya **74** 34 45N 135 20 E
Nísíros **45** 36 35N 27 12 E
Niskibi → **106** 56 29N 88 9W
Nisko **28** 50 35N 22 7 E
Nisporeny **46** 47 4N 28 10 E
Nissafors **49** 57 25N 13 37 E
Nissan → **49** 56 40N 12 51 E
Nissedal **47** 59 10N 8 30 E
Nisser **47** 59 7N 8 28 E
Nissum Fjord **49** 56 20N 8 11 E
Nisutlin → **108** 60 14N 132 34W
Niţā' **64** 27 15N 48 35 E
Nitchequon **107** 53 10N 70 58W
Niterói **125** 22 52 S 43 0W
Nith → **14** 55 20N 3 5W
Nitra **27** 48 19N 18 4 E
Nitra → **27** 47 46N 18 10 E
Nittedal **47** 60 1N 10 57 E
Nittendau **25** 49 12N 12 16 E
Niuafo'ou **101** 15 30 S 175 58W
Niue I. (Savage I.) **95** 19 2 S 169 54W
Niut **72** 0 55N 110 6 E
Nivelles **16** 50 35N 4 20 E
Nivernais **19** 47 0N 3 40 E
Nixon, Nev., U.S.A. **118** 39 54N 119 22W
Nixon, Tex., U.S.A. **117** 29 17N 97 45W
Nizam Sagar **70** 18 10N 77 58 E
Nizamabad **70** 18 45N 78 7 E
Nizamghat **67** 28 20N 95 45 E
Nizhne Kolymsk **59** 68 34N 160 55 E
Nizhne-Vartovskoye **58** 60 56N 76 38 E
Nizhneangarsk **59** 55 47N 109 30 E
Nizhnegorskiy **56** 45 27N 34 38 E
Nizhneudinsk **59** 54 54N 99 3 E
Nizhneyansk **59** 71 26N 136 4 E
Nizhniy Lomov **55** 53 34N 43 38 E
Nizhniy Novgorod = Gorkiy **55** 56 20N 44 0 E
Nizhniy Tagil **52** 57 55N 59 57 E
Nizhnyaya Tunguska → **59** 64 20N 93 0 E
Nizip **64** 37 5N 37 50 E
Nízké Tatry **27** 48 55N 20 0 E
Nizza Monferrato **38** 44 46N 8 22 E
Njakwa **91** 11 1 S 33 56 E
Njanji **91** 14 25 S 31 46 E
Njinjo **91** 8 48 S 38 54 E
Njombe **91** 9 20 S 34 50 E
Njombe □ **91** 9 20 S 34 49 E
Njombe → **90** 6 56 S 35 6 E
Nkambe **85** 6 35N 10 40 E
Nkana **91** 12 50 S 28 8 E
Nkawkaw **85** 6 36N 0 49W
Nkhota Kota **91** 12 56 S 34 15 E
Nkongsamba **88** 4 55N 9 55 E
Nkwanta **84** 6 10N 2 10W
Noatak **104** 67 32N 162 59W
Nobel **112** 45 25N 80 6W
Nobeoka **74** 32 36N 131 41 E
Noblejas **32** 39 58N 3 26W
Noblesville **114** 40 1N 85 59W
Noce → **38** 46 9N 11 4 E
Nocera Inferiore **41** 40 45N 14 37 E
Nocera Terinese **41** 39 2N 16 9 E
Nocera Umbra **39** 43 8N 12 47 E
Noci **41** 40 47N 17 7 E
Nockatunga **99** 27 42 S 142 42 E
Nocona **117** 33 48N 97 45W
Nocrich **46** 45 55N 24 26 E
Noel **117** 36 36N 94 29W
Nogales, Mexico **120** 31 20N 110 56W
Nogales, U.S.A. **119** 31 33N 110 56W
Nogat → **28** 54 17N 19 17 E
Nōgata **74** 33 48N 130 44 E
Nogent-en-Bassigny **19** 48 0N 5 20 E
Nogent-le-Rotrou **18** 48 20N 0 50 E
Nogent-sur-Seine **19** 48 30N 3 30 E
Noginsk, Moskva, U.S.S.R. **55** 55 50N 38 25 E
Noginsk, Sib., U.S.S.R. **59** 64 30N 90 50 E
Nogoa → **97** 23 40 S 147 55 E
Nogoyá **124** 32 24 S 59 48W
Nógrád □ **27** 48 0N 19 30 E
Nogueira de Ramuin **30** 42 21N 7 43W
Noguera Pallaresa → **32** 42 15N 1 0 E
Noguera Ribagorzana → **32** 41 40N 0 43 E
Nohar **68** 29 11N 74 49 E
Noi → **71** 14 50N 100 15 E
Noire, Mt. **18** 48 11N 3 40W
Noirétable **20** 45 48N 3 46 E
Noirmoutier **18** 47 0N 2 15W
Noirmoutier, Î. de **18** 46 58N 2 10W
Nojane **92** 23 15 S 20 14 E
Nok Kundi **66** 28 50N 62 45 E
Nokaneng **92** 19 40 S 22 17 E
Nokhtuysk **59** 60 0N 117 45 E
Nokomis **109** 51 35N 105 0W
Nokomis L. **109** 57 0N 103 0W
Nol **49** 57 56N 12 5 E
Nola, C. Afr. Rep. **88** 3 35N 16 4 E
Nola, Italy **41** 40 54N 14 29 E
Nolay **19** 46 58N 4 35 E
Noli, C. di **38** 44 12N 8 26 E
Nolinsk **55** 57 28N 49 57 E
Noma Omuramba → **92** 18 52 S 20 53 E
Noman L. **109** 62 15N 108 55W
Nome **104** 64 30N 165 24W
Nonacho L. **109** 61 42N 109 40W
Nonancourt **18** 48 47N 1 11 E
Nonant-le-Pin **18** 48 42N 0 12 E
Nonda **98** 20 40 S 142 28 E
Nong Khae **71** 14 29N 100 53 E
Nong Khai **71** 17 50N 102 46 E
Nong'an **76** 44 25N 125 5 E
Nonoava **120** 27 28N 106 44W
Nontron **20** 45 31N 0 40 E
Noonan **116** 48 51N 102 59W
Noondoo **99** 28 35 S 148 30 E
Noord Brabant □ **16** 51 40N 5 0 E
Noord Holland □ **16** 52 30N 4 45 E
Noordbeveland **16** 51 35N 3 50 E
Noordoostpolder **16** 52 45N 5 45 E
Noordwijk aan Zee **16** 52 14N 4 26 E
Nootka **108** 49 38N 126 38W
Nootka I. **108** 49 32N 126 42W

* *Renamed Vanuatu* ■

Nóqui Nyköping

Nóqui 88 5 55S 13 30 E
Nora, Ethiopia 87 16 6N 40 4 E
Nora, Sweden 48 59 32N 15 2 E
Noranda 106 48 20N 79 0W
Norberg 48 60 4N 15 56 E
Nórcia 39 42 50N 13 5 E
Nord □ 19 50 15N 3 30 E
Nord-Ostee Kanal 24 54 15N 9 40 E
Nord-Süd Kanal 24 53 0N 10 32 E
Nord-Trøndelag fylke □ 50 64 20N 12 0 E
Nordagutu 47 59 25N 9 20 E
Nordaustlandet 4 79 14N 23 0 E
Nordborg 49 55 5N 9 50 E
Nordby, Arhus, Denmark 49 55 58N 10 32 E
Nordby, Ribe, Denmark 49 55 27N 8 24 E
Norddal 47 62 15N 7 14 E
Norddalsfjord 47 61 39N 5 23 E
Norddeich 24 53 37N 7 10 E
Nordegg 108 52 29N 116 5W
Norden 24 53 35N 7 12 E
Nordenham 24 53 29N 8 28 E
Norderhov 47 60 7N 10 17 E
Norderney 24 53 42N 7 15 E
Nordfjord 47 61 55N 5 30 E
Nordfriesische Inseln 24 54 40N 8 20 E
Nordhausen 24 51 29N 10 47 E
Nordhorn 24 52 27N 7 4 E
Nordjyllands Amtskommune □ 49 57 0N 10 0 E
Nordkapp, Norway 50 71 10N 25 44 E
Nordkapp, Svalb. 4 80 31N 20 0 E
Nordkinn 9 71 8N 27 40 E
Nordland fylke □ 50 65 40N 13 0 E
Nördlingen 25 48 50N 10 30 E
Nordrhein-Westfalen □ 24 51 45N 7 30 E
Nordstrand 24 54 27N 8 50 E
Nordvik 59 74 2N 111 32 E
Nore 47 60 10N 9 0 E
Nore → 15 52 40N 7 20W
Norefjell 47 60 16N 9 29 E
Norembega 106 48 59N 80 43W
Noresund 47 60 11N 9 37 E
Norfolk, Nebr., U.S.A. 116 42 3N 97 25W
Norfolk, Va., U.S.A. 114 36 40N 76 15W
Norfolk □ 12 52 39N 1 0 E
Norfolk Broads 12 52 30N 1 15 E
Norfolk I. 94 28 58S 168 3 E
Norfork Res. 117 36 13N 92 15W
Norilsk 59 69 20N 88 6 E
Norley 99 27 45S 143 48 E
Norma, Mt. 98 20 55S 140 42 E
Normal 116 40 30N 89 0W
Norman 117 35 12N 97 30W
Norman → 97 17 28S 140 49 E
Norman Wells 104 65 17N 126 51W
Normanby → 97 14 23S 144 10 E
Normanby I. 98 10 55S 151 5 E
Normandie 18 48 45N 0 10 E
Normandie, Collines de 18 48 55N 0 45W
Normandin 106 48 49N 72 31W
Normandy = Normandie 18 48 45N 0 10 E
Normanton 97 17 40S 141 10 E
Norquay 109 51 53N 102 5W
Norquinco 128 41 51S 70 55W
Norrahammar 49 57 43N 14 7 E
Norrbotten □ 50 66 30N 22 30 E
Norrby 50 64 55N 18 15 E
Nørre Åby 49 55 27N 9 52 E
Nørre Nebel 49 55 47N 8 17 E
Nørresundby 49 57 5N 9 52 E
Norris 118 45 40N 111 40W
Norristown 114 40 9N 75 21W
Norrköping 49 58 37N 16 11 E
Norrland □ 50 66 50N 18 0 E
Norrtälje 48 59 46N 18 42 E
Norsholm 49 58 31N 15 59 E
Norsk 59 52 30N 130 0 E
North Adams 114 42 42N 73 6W
North America 102 40 0N 100 0W
North Andaman I. 71 13 15N 92 40 E
North Atlantic Ocean 6 30 0N 50 0W
North Battleford 109 52 50N 108 17W
North Bay 106 46 20N 79 30W
North Belcher Is. 106 56 50N 79 50W
North Bend, Can. 108 49 50N 121 27W
North Bend, Oreg., U.S.A. 118 43 28N 124 14W
North Bend, Pa., U.S.A. 112 41 20N 77 42W
North Berwick, U.K. 14 56 4N 2 44W
North Berwick, U.S.A. 113 43 18N 70 43W
North Buganda □ 90 1 0N 32 0 E
North Canadian → 117 35 17N 95 31W
North C., Antarct. 5 71 0S 166 0 E
North C., Can. 107 47 2N 60 20W
North C., N.Z. 101 34 23S 173 4 E
North Caribou L. 106 52 50N 90 40W
North Carolina □ 115 35 30N 80 0W
North Channel, Br. Is. 14 55 0N 5 30W
North Channel, Can. 106 46 0N 83 0W
North Chicago 114 42 19N 87 50W
North Dakota □ 116 47 30N 100 0W
North Down □ 15 54 40N 5 45W
North Downs 13 51 17N 0 30 E
North East 112 42 17N 79 50W
North East Frontier Agency = Arunachal Pradesh □ 67 28 0N 95 0 E
North East Providence Chan. 121 26 0N 76 0W
North Eastern □ 90 1 30N 40 0 E
North Esk → 14 56 44N 2 25W
North European Plain 9 55 0N 20 0 E
North Foreland 13 51 22N 1 28 E
North Frisian Is. = Nordfr'sche Inseln 24 54 50N 8 20 E
North Henik L. 109 61 45N 97 40W
North Horr 90 3 20N 37 8 E
North I., Kenya 90 4 5N 36 5 E
North I., N.Z. 101 38 0S 175 0 E
North Kingsville 112 41 53N 80 42W
North Knife → 109 58 53N 94 45W
North Koel → 69 24 45N 83 50 E
North Korea ■ 76 40 0N 127 0 E
North Lakhimpur 67 27 14N 94 7 E
North Las Vegas 119 36 15N 115 6W
North Loup → 116 41 17N 98 23W
North Mashonaland □ 91 16 30S 30 0 E
North Minch 14 58 5N 5 55W
North Nahanni → 108 62 15N 123 20W
North Ossetian A.S.S.R. □ 57 43 30N 44 30 E
North Palisade 119 37 6N 118 32W
North Platte 116 41 10N 100 50W
North Platte → 116 41 15N 100 45W
North Pt. 107 47 5N 64 0W
North Pole 4 90 0N 0 0 E
North Portal 109 49 0N 102 33W
North Powder 118 45 2N 117 59W
North Ronaldsay 14 59 20N 2 30W
North Sea 8 56 0N 4 0 E
North Sentinel I. 71 11 35N 92 15 E
North Sporades = Voriai Sporádhes 45 39 15N 23 30 E
North Stradbroke I. 97 27 35S 153 28 E
North Sydney 107 46 12N 60 15W
North Thompson → 108 50 40N 120 20W
North Tonawanda 114 43 5N 78 50W
North Troy 113 44 59N 72 24W
North Truchas Pk. 119 36 0N 105 30W
North Twin I. 106 53 20N 80 0W
North Tyne → 12 54 59N 2 7W
North Uist 14 57 40N 7 15W
North Vancouver 108 49 25N 123 3W
North Vernon 114 39 0N 85 35W
North Village 121 32 15N 64 45W
North Wabiskaw L. 108 56 0N 113 55W
North Walsham 12 52 49N 1 22 E
North West Basin 96 25 45S 115 0 E
North West C. 96 21 45S 114 9 E
North West Christmas I. Ridge 95 6 30N 165 0W
North West Highlands 14 57 35N 5 2W
North West Providence Channel 121 26 0N 78 0W
North West River 107 53 30N 60 10W
North Western □ 91 13 30S 25 30 E
North York Moors 12 54 25N 0 50W
North Yorkshire □ 12 54 15N 1 25W
Northallerton 12 54 20N 1 26W
Northam 96 31 35S 116 42 E
Northampton, Austral. 96 28 27S 114 33 E
Northampton, U.K. 13 52 14N 0 54W
Northampton, Mass., U.S.A. 114 42 22N 72 31W
Northampton, Pa., U.S.A. 113 40 38N 75 24W
Northampton □ 13 52 16N 0 55W
Northampton Downs 98 24 35S 145 48 E
Northbridge 113 42 12N 71 40W
Northeim 24 51 42N 10 0 E
Northern □, Malawi 91 11 0S 34 0 E
Northern □, Uganda 90 3 5N 32 30 E
Northern □, Zambia 91 10 30S 31 0 E
Northern Circars 70 17 30N 82 30 E
Northern Group 101 10 00S 160 00W
Northern Indian L. 109 57 20N 97 20W
Northern Ireland □ 15 54 45N 7 0W
Northern Light, L. 106 48 15N 90 39W
Northern Province □ 84 9 15N 11 30W
Northern Territory □ 96 16 0S 133 0 E
Northfield 116 44 30N 93 10W
Northome 116 47 53N 94 15W
Northport, Ala., U.S.A. 115 33 15N 87 35W
Northport, Mich., U.S.A. 114 45 8N 85 39W
Northport, Wash., U.S.A. 118 48 55N 117 48W
Northumberland □ 12 55 12N 2 0W
Northumberland, C. 97 38 5S 140 40 E
Northumberland Is. 98 21 30S 149 50 E
Northumberland Str. 107 46 20N 64 0W
Northwest Territories □ 104 65 0N 100 0W
Northwich 12 53 16N 2 30W
Northwood, Iowa, U.S.A. 116 43 27N 93 0W
Northwood, N.D., U.S.A. 116 47 44N 97 30W
Norton, U.S.A. 116 39 50N 99 53W
Norton, Zimb. 91 17 52S 30 40 E
Norton Sd. 104 64 0N 164 0W
Nortorf 24 54 14N 9 47 E
Norwalk, Conn., U.S.A. 114 41 9N 73 25W
Norwalk, Ohio, U.S.A. 114 41 13N 82 38W
Norway 114 45 46N 87 57W
Norway House 109 53 59N 97 50W
Norwegian Dependency 5 66 0S 15 0 E
Norwegian Sea 6 66 0N 1 0 E
Norwich, Can. 112 42 59N 80 36W
Norwich, U.K. 12 52 38N 1 17 E
Norwich, Conn., U.S.A. 113 41 33N 72 5W
Norwich, N.Y., U.S.A. 114 42 32N 75 30W
Norwood, Can. 112 44 23N 77 59W
Norwood, U.S.A. 113 42 10N 71 10W
Nosok 58 70 10N 82 20 E
Nosovka 54 50 50N 31 37 E
Noşratābād 65 29 55N 60 0 E
Noss Hd. 14 58 29N 3 4W
Nossebro 49 58 12N 12 43 E
Nossob → 92 26 55S 20 37 E
Nosy Boraha 93 16 50S 49 55 E
Nosy Varika 93 20 35S 48 32 E
Noteć → 28 52 44N 15 26 E
Notigi Dam 109 56 40N 99 10W
Notikewin → 108 57 2N 117 38W
Notios Evvoïkos Kólpos 45 38 20N 24 0 E
Noto 41 36 52N 15 4 E
Noto, G. di 41 36 50N 15 10 E
Noto-Hanto 74 37 0N 137 0 E
Notodden 47 59 35N 9 17 E
Notre-Dame 107 46 18N 64 46W
Notre Dame B. 107 49 45N 55 30W
Notre Dame de Koartac 105 60 55N 69 40W
Notsé 85 7 0N 1 17 E
Nottaway → 106 51 22N 78 55W
Nøtterøy 47 59 14N 10 24 E
Nottingham 12 52 57N 1 10W
Nottingham □ 12 53 10N 1 0W
Nottoway → 114 36 33N 76 55W
Notwani → 92 23 35S 26 58 E
Nouâdhibou 80 20 54N 17 0W
Nouâdhibou, Ras 80 20 50N 17 0W
Nouakchott 84 18 9N 15 58W
Noumea 94 22 17S 166 30 E
Noupoort 92 31 10S 24 57 E
Nouveau Comptoir (Paint Hills) 106 53 0N 78 49W
Nouvelle Calédonie 94 21 0S 165 0 E
Nouzonville 19 49 48N 4 44 E
Nová Baňa 27 48 28N 18 39 E
Nová Bystřice 26 49 2N 15 8 E
† Nova Chaves 88 10 31S 21 15 E
Nova Cruz 127 6 28S 35 25W
Nova Esperança 125 23 8S 52 24W
Nova Friburgo 125 22 16S 42 30W
Nova Gaia 88 10 10S 17 35 E
Nova Gradiška 42 45 17N 17 28 E
Nova Iguaçu 125 22 45S 43 28W
Nova Iorque 127 7 0S 44 5W
Nova Lamego 84 12 19N 14 11W
Nova Lima 125 19 59S 43 51W
Nova Lisboa = Huambo 89 12 42S 15 44 E
Nova Lusitânia 91 19 50S 34 34 E
Nova Mambone 93 21 0S 35 3 E
Nova Mesto 39 45 47N 15 12 E
Nova Paka 26 50 29N 15 30 E
Nova Scotia □ 107 45 10N 63 0W
Nova Sofala 93 20 7S 34 42 E
Nova Varoš 42 43 29N 19 48 E
Nova Venécia 127 18 45S 40 24W
Nova Zagora 43 42 32N 25 59 E
Novaci, Romania 46 45 10N 23 42 E
Novaci, Yugo. 42 41 5N 21 29 E
Noval Iorque 127 6 48S 44 0W
Novaleksandrovskaya 57 45 29N 41 17 E
Novannenskiy 55 50 32N 42 39 E
Novara 38 45 27N 8 36 E
Novaya Kakhovka 56 46 42N 33 27 E
Novaya Ladoga 52 60 7N 32 16 E
Novaya Lyalya 58 59 10N 60 35 E
Novaya Sibir, O. 59 75 10N 150 0 E
Novaya Zemlya 58 75 0N 56 0 E
Nové Město 27 48 45N 17 50 E
Nové Zámky 27 48 0N 18 8 E
Novelda 33 38 24N 0 45W
Novellara 38 44 50N 10 43 E
Noventa Vicentina 39 45 18N 11 30 E
Novgorod 54 58 30N 31 25 E
Novgorod-Severskiy 54 52 2N 33 10 E
Novi Bečej 42 45 36N 20 10 E
Novi Grad 39 45 19N 13 33 E
Novi Kneževa 42 46 4N 20 8 E
* Novi Krichim 43 42 8N 24 31 E
Novi Lígure 38 44 45N 8 47 E
Novi Pazar, Bulg. 43 43 25N 27 15 E
Novi Pazar, Yugo. 42 43 12N 20 28 E
Novi Sad 42 45 18N 19 52 E
Novi Vinodolski 39 45 10N 14 48 E
Novigrad 39 44 10N 15 32 E
Nôvo Hamburgo 125 29 37S 51 7W
Novo-Zavidovskiy 55 56 32N 36 29 E
Novoakrainka 56 48 25N 31 30 E
Novoaltaysk 58 53 30N 84 0 E
Novoazovsk 56 47 15N 38 4 E
Novobelitsa 54 52 27N 31 2 E
Novobogatinskoye 57 47 20N 51 11 E
Novocherkassk 57 47 27N 40 5 E
Novodevichye 55 53 37N 48 50 E
Novograd-Volynskiy 54 50 34N 27 35 E
Novogrudok 54 53 40N 25 50 E
Novokayakent 57 42 30N 47 52 E
Novokazalinsk 58 45 48N 62 6 E
Novokhopersk 55 51 5N 41 39 E
Novokuybyshevsk 55 53 7N 49 58 E
Novokuznetsk 58 53 45N 87 10 E
Novomirgorod 56 48 45N 31 33 E
Novomoskovsk, R.S.F.S.R., U.S.S.R. 55 54 5N 38 15 E
Novomoskovsk, Ukraine, U.S.S.R. 56 48 33N 35 17 E
Novopolotsk 54 55 32N 28 37 E
Novorossiysk 56 44 43N 37 46 E
Novorybnoye 59 72 50N 105 50 E
Novorzhev 54 57 3N 29 25 E
Novoselitsa 56 48 14N 26 15 E
Novoshakhtinsk 57 47 46N 39 58 E
Novosibirsk 58 55 0N 83 5 E
Novosibirskiye Ostrava 59 75 0N 142 0 E
Novosil 55 52 58N 36 58 E
Novosokolniki 54 56 33N 30 5 E
Novotroitsk 52 51 10N 58 15 E
Novotulskiy 55 54 10N 37 43 E
Novouzensk 55 50 32N 48 17 E
Novovolynsk 54 50 45N 24 4 E
Novovyatsk 55 58 29N 49 44 E
Novozybkov 54 52 30N 32 0 E
Novska 42 45 19N 17 0 E
Novvy Port 58 67 40N 72 30 E
Novy Bug 56 47 34N 32 29 E
Nový Bydzov 26 50 14N 15 29 E
Novy Dwór Mazowiecki 28 52 26N 20 44 E
Nový Jičín 27 49 30N 18 0 E
Novyy Afon 57 43 7N 40 50 E
Novyy Oskol 55 50 44N 37 55 E
Now Shahr 65 36 40N 51 40 E
Nowa Deba 28 50 26N 21 41 E
Nowa Huta 27 50 5N 20 30 E
Nowa Ruda 28 50 35N 16 30 E
Nowa Skalmierzyce 28 51 43N 18 0 E
Nowa Sól 28 51 48N 15 44 E
Nowe 28 53 41N 18 44 E
Nowe Miasteczko 28 51 42N 15 42 E
Nowe Miasto 28 51 38N 20 34 E
Nowe Miasto Lubawskie 28 53 27N 19 33 E
Nowe Warpno 28 53 42N 14 18 E
Nowgong 67 26 20N 92 50 E
Nowingi 100 34 33S 142 15 E
Nowogard 28 53 41N 15 10 E
Nowogród 28 53 14N 21 53 E
Nowra 97 34 53S 150 35 E
Nowy Dwór, Białystok, Poland 28 53 40N 23 30 E
Nowy Dwór, Gdansk, Poland 28 54 13N 19 7 E
Nowy Korczyn 28 50 19N 20 48 E
Nowy Sącz 27 49 40N 20 41 E
Nowy Sącz □ 27 49 30N 20 30 E
Nowy Staw 28 54 13N 19 2 E
Nowy Tomyśl 28 52 19N 16 10 E
Noxen 113 41 25N 76 4W
Noxon 118 48 0N 115 43W
Noya 30 42 48N 8 53W
Noyant 18 47 30N 0 6 E
Noyers 19 47 40N 4 0 E
Noyes I. 108 55 30N 133 40W
Noyon 19 49 34N 3 0 E
Nozay 18 47 34N 1 38W
Nsa, O. en → 83 32 28N 5 24 E
Nsanje 91 16 55S 35 12 E
Nsawam 85 5 50N 0 24W
Nsomba 91 10 45S 29 51 E
Nsukka 85 6 51N 7 29 E
Nuanetsi → 91 22 40S 31 50 E
Nuba Mts. = Nubah, Jibalan 87 12 0N 31 0 E
Nubah, Jibalan 87 12 0N 31 0 E
Nûbîya, Es Sahrâ En 86 21 30N 33 30 E
Ñuble □ 124 37 0S 72 0W
Nuboai 73 2 10S 136 30 E
Nueces → 117 27 50N 97 30W
Nueima → 62 31 54N 35 25 E
Nueltin L. 109 60 30N 99 30W
Nueva Gerona 121 21 53N 82 49W
Nueva Imperial 128 38 45S 72 58W
Nueva Palmira 124 33 52S 58 20W
Nueva Rosita 120 28 0N 101 11W
Nueva San Salvador 120 13 40N 89 18W
Nuéve de Julio 124 35 30S 61 0W
Nuevitas 121 21 30N 77 20W
Nuevo, Golfo 128 43 0S 64 30W
Nuevo Laredo 120 27 30N 99 30W
Nuevo León □ 120 25 0N 100 0W
Nugget Pt. 101 46 27S 169 50 E
Nugrus, Gebel 86 24 47N 34 35 E
Nuhaka 101 39 3S 177 45 E
Nuits 19 47 44N 4 12 E
Nuits-St-Georges 19 47 10N 4 56 E
Nukheila (Merga) 86 19 1N 26 21 E
Nuku'alofa 101 21 10S 174 0W
Nukus 58 42 20N 59 7 E
Nulato 104 64 40N 158 10W
Nules 32 39 51N 0 9W
Nullagine 96 21 53S 120 6 E
Nullarbor Plain 96 30 45S 129 0 E
Numalla, L. 99 28 43S 144 20 E
Numan 85 9 29N 12 3 E
Numata 74 36 45N 139 4 E
Numatinna → 87 7 38N 27 20 E
Numazu 74 35 7N 138 51 E
Numfoor 73 1 0S 134 50 E
Numurkah 99 36 5S 145 26 E
Nunaksaluk I. 107 55 49N 60 20W
Nuneaton 13 52 32N 1 29W
Nungo 91 13 23S 37 43 E
Nungwe 90 2 48S 32 2 E
Nunivak 104 60 0N 166 0W
Nunkun 69 33 57N 76 2 E
Nunspeet 16 52 21N 5 45 E
Nuomin He → 76 46 45N 126 55 E
Nuoro 40 40 20N 9 20 E
Nuqayy, Jabal 83 23 11N 19 30 E
Nure → 38 45 3N 9 49 E
Nuremburg = Nürnberg 25 49 26N 11 5 E
Nuriootpa 99 34 27S 139 0 E
Nurlat 55 54 29N 50 45 E
Nürnberg 25 49 26N 11 5 E
Nurran, L. = Terewah, L. 99 29 52S 147 35 E
Nurri 40 39 43N 9 13 E
Nurzec → 28 52 37N 22 25 E
Nusa Barung 73 8 22S 113 20 E
Nusa Kambangan 73 7 47S 109 0 E
Nusa Tenggara Barat □ 72 8 50S 117 30 E
Nusa Tenggara Timur □ 73 9 30S 122 0 E
Nushki 66 29 35N 66 0 E
Nutak 105 57 28N 61 59W
Nuwakot 69 28 10N 83 55 E
Nuwara Eliya 70 6 58N 80 48 E
Nuweiba' 86 28 58N 34 40 E
Nuweveldberge 92 32 10S 21 45 E
Nuyts Arch. 96 32 35S 133 20 E
Nuyts, Pt. 96 35 4S 116 38 E
Nuzvid 70 16 47N 80 53 E
Nxau-Nxau 92 18 57S 21 4 E
Nyaake (Webo) 84 4 52N 7 37W
Nyabing 96 33 30S 118 7 E
Nyack 113 41 5N 73 57W
Nyadal 48 62 48N 17 59 E
Nyah West 100 35 16S 143 21 E
Nyahanga 90 2 20S 33 37 E
Nyahua 90 5 25S 33 23 E
Nyahururu 90 0 2N 36 27 E
Nyainqentanglha Shan 75 30 0N 90 0 E
Nyakanazi 90 3 2S 31 10 E
Nyakrom 85 5 40N 0 50W
Nyâlâ 87 12 2N 24 58 E
Nyamandhlovu 91 19 55S 28 16 E
Nyambiti 90 2 48S 33 27 E
Nyamwaga 90 1 27S 34 33 E
Nyandekwa 90 3 57S 32 32 E
Nyanding →, 87 8 40N 32 41 E
Nyandoma 52 61 40N 40 12 E
Nyangana 92 18 0S 20 40 E
Nyanguge 90 2 30S 33 12 E
Nyankpala 85 9 21N 0 58W
Nyanza, Burundi 90 4 21S 29 36 E
Nyanza, Rwanda 90 2 20S 29 42 E
Nyanza □ 90 0 10S 34 15 E
Nyarling → 108 60 41N 113 23W
Nyasa, L. = Malawi, L. 91 12 0S 34 30 E
Nyazepetrovsk 52 56 3N 59 36 E
Nyazwidzi → 91 20 0S 31 17 E
Nyborg 49 55 18N 10 47 E
Nybro 49 56 44N 15 55 E
Nyda 58 66 40N 72 58 E
Nyeri 90 0 23S 36 56 E
Nyerol 87 8 41N 32 1 E
Nyhem 48 62 54N 15 37 E
Nyiel 87 6 9N 31 13 E
Nyinahin 84 6 43N 2 3W
Nyírbátor 27 47 49N 22 9 E
Nyíregyháza 27 47 58N 21 47 E
Nykarleby 50 63 22N 22 31 E
Nykøbing, Sjælland, Denmark 49 55 55N 11 40 E
Nykøbing, Storstrøm, Denmark 49 54 56N 11 52 E
Nykøbing, Viborg, Denmark 49 56 48N 8 51 E
Nyköping 49 58 45N 17 0 E

* Renamed Stamboliyski

† Renamed Muconda

Nykroppa Onehunga

Nykroppa 48 59 37N 14 18 E
Nykvarn 48 59 11N 17 25 E
Nyland 48 63 1N 17 45 E
Nylstroom 93 24 42 S 28 22 E
Nymagee 99 32 7 S 146 20 E
Nymburk 26 50 10N 15 1 E
Nynäshamn 48 58 54N 17 57 E
Nyngan 99 31 30 S 147 8 E
Nyon 25 46 23N 6 14 E
Nyong → 85 3 17N 9 54 E
Nyons 21 44 22N 5 10 E
Nyord 49 55 4N 12 13 E
Nyou 85 12 42N 2 1W
Nysa 28 50 30N 17 22 E
Nysa →, Poland/Poland 28 52 4N 14 46 E
Nysa →, Poland 28 50 49N 17 40 E
Nyssa 118 43 56N 117 2W
Nysted 49 54 40N 11 44 E
Nyunzu 90 5 57 S 27 58 E
Nyurba 59 63 17N 118 28 E
Nzega 90 4 10 S 33 12 E
Nzega □ 90 4 10 S 33 10 E
N'Zérékoré 84 7 49N 8 48W
Nzeto 88 7 10 S 12 52 E
Nzilo, Chutes de 91 10 18 S 25 27 E
Nzubuka 90 4 45 S 32 50 E

O

Oacoma 116 43 50N 99 26W
Oahe 116 44 33N 100 29W
Oahe Dam 116 44 28N 100 25W
Oahe Res. 116 45 30N 100 25W
Oahu 110 21 30N 158 0W
Oak Creek 118 40 15N 106 59W
Oak Harb. 118 48 20N 122 38W
Oak Hill 114 38 0N 81 7W
Oak Park 114 41 55N 87 45W
Oak Ridge 115 36 1N 84 12W
Oakbank 99 33 4 S 140 33 E
Oakdale, Calif., U.S.A. 119 46 14N 98 4W
Oakdale, La., U.S.A. 117 30 50N 92 38W
Oakengates 12 52 42N 2 29W
Oakes 116 46 14N 98 4W
Oakesdale 118 47 11N 117 15W
Oakey 99 27 25 S 151 43 E
Oakham 12 52 40N 0 43W
Oakland, Calif., U.S.A. 119 37 50N 122 18W
Oakland, Oreg., U.S.A. 118 43 23N 123 18W
Oakland City 114 38 20N 87 20W
Oakleigh 100 37 54 S 145 6 E
Oakley, Id., U.S.A. 118 42 14N 113 55W
Oakley, Kans., U.S.A. 116 39 8N 100 51W
Oakridge 118 43 47N 122 31W
Oakwood 117 31 35N 94 45W
Oamaru 101 45 5 S 170 59 E
Oates Coast 5 69 0 S 160 0 E
Oatman 119 35 1N 114 19W
Oaxaca 120 17 2N 96 40W
Oaxaca □ 120 17 0N 97 0W
Ob → 58 66 45N 69 30 E
Oba 106 49 4N 84 7W
Obala 85 4 9N 11 32 E
Oban, N.Z. 101 46 55 S 168 10 E
Oban, U.K. 14 56 25N 5 30W
Obbia 63 5 25N 48 30 E
Obed 108 53 30N 117 10W
Obera 125 27 21 S 55 2W
Oberammergau 25 47 35N 11 3 E
Oberdrauburg 26 46 44N 12 58 E
Oberengadin 25 46 35N 9 55 E
Oberhausen 24 51 28N 6 50 E
Oberkirch 25 48 31N 8 5 E
Oberlin, Kans., U.S.A. 116 39 52N 100 31W
Oberlin, La., U.S.A. 117 30 42N 92 42W
Oberlin, Ohio, U.S.A. 112 41 15N 82 10W
Obernai 19 48 28N 7 30 E
Oberndorf 25 48 17N 8 35 E
Oberon 99 33 45 S 149 52 E
Oberösterreich □ 26 48 10N 14 0 E
Oberpfälzer Wald 25 49 30N 12 25 E
Oberstdorf 25 47 25N 10 16 E
Obi, Kepulauan 73 1 23 S 127 45 E
Obiaruku 85 5 51N 6 9 E
Óbidos, Brazil 127 1 50 S 55 30W
Óbidos, Port. 31 39 19N 9 10W
Obihiro 74 42 56N 143 12 E
Obilatu 73 1 25 S 127 20 E
Obilnoye 57 47 32N 44 30 E
Obing 25 48 0N 12 25 E
Obisfelde 24 52 27N 10 57 E
Objat 20 45 16N 1 24 E
Obluchye 59 49 1N 131 4 E
Obninsk 55 55 8N 36 37 E
Obo, C. Afr. Rep. 90 5 20N 26 32 E
Obo, Ethiopia 87 3 46N 38 52 E
Oboa, Mt. 90 1 45N 34 45 E
Obock 87 12 0N 43 20 E
Oborniki 28 52 39N 16 50 E
Oborniki Śląskie 28 51 17N 16 53 E
Oboyan 55 51 13N 36 37 E
Obrenovac 42 44 40N 20 11 E
Obrovac 39 44 11N 15 41 E
Observatory Inlet 108 55 10N 129 54W
Obshchi Syrt 9 52 0N 53 0 E
Obskaya Guba 58 69 0N 73 0 E
Obuasi 85 6 17N 1 40W
Obubra 85 6 8N 8 20 E
Obzor 43 42 50N 27 52 E
Ocala 115 29 11N 82 5W
Ocampo 120 28 9N 108 24W
Ocaña 32 39 55N 3 30W
Ocanomowoc 116 43 7N 88 30W
Ocate 117 36 12N 104 59W
Occidental, Cordillera 126 5 0N 76 0W
Ocean City 114 39 18N 74 34W
Ocean, I. = Banaba 94 0 52 S 169 35 E
Ocean Park 118 46 30N 124 2W
Oceanlake 118 45 0N 124 0W
Oceanport 113 40 20N 74 3W
Oceanside 119 33 13N 117 26W
Ochagavia 32 42 55N 1 5W
Ochamchire 57 42 46N 41 32 E
Ochil Hills 14 56 14N 3 40W
Ochre River 109 51 4N 99 47W
Ochsenfurt 25 49 38N 10 3 E
Ochsenhausen 25 48 4N 9 57 E
Ocilla 115 31 35N 83 12W
Ockelbo 48 60 54N 16 45 E
Ocmulgee → 115 31 58N 82 32W
Ocna Mureş 46 46 23N 23 55 E
Ocna Sibiului 46 45 52N 24 2 E
Ocnele Mari 46 45 8N 24 18 E
Oconee → 115 31 58N 82 32W
Oconto 114 44 52N 87 53W
Oconto Falls 114 44 52N 88 10W
Ocotal 121 13 41N 86 31W
Ocotlán 120 20 21N 102 42W
Ocreza → 31 39 32N 7 50W
Ócsa 27 47 17N 19 15 E
Octave 119 34 10N 112 43W
Octeville 18 49 38N 1 40W
Ocumare del Tuy 126 10 7N 66 46W
Ocussi 73 9 20 S 124 23 E
Oda 85 5 50N 0 51W
Oda, Jebel 86 20 21N 36 39 E
Ódáðahraun 50 65 5N 17 0W
Ödåkra 49 56 7N 12 45 E
Odawara 74 35 20N 139 6 E
Odda 47 60 3N 6 35 E
Odder 49 55 58N 10 10 E
Oddur 63 4 11N 43 52 E
Ödeborg 49 58 32N 11 58 E
Odei → 109 56 6N 96 54W
Odemira 31 37 35N 8 40W
Ödemiş 64 38 15N 28 0 E
Odendaalsrus 92 27 48 S 26 45 E
Odense 49 55 22N 10 23 E
Odenwald 25 49 40N 9 0 E
Oder → 24 53 33N 14 38 E
Oderzo 39 45 47N 12 29 E
Odessa, Can. 113 44 17N 76 43W
Odessa, Tex., U.S.A. 117 31 51N 102 23W
Odessa, Wash., U.S.A. 118 47 19N 118 35W
Odessa, U.S.S.R. 56 46 30N 30 45 E
Odiakwe 92 20 12 S 25 17 E
Odiel → 31 37 10N 6 55W
Odienné 84 9 30N 7 34W
Odobeşti 46 45 43N 27 4 E
Odolanów 28 51 34N 17 40 E
O'Donnell 117 33 0N 101 48W
Odorheiul Secuiesc 46 46 21N 25 21 E
Odoyevo 55 53 56N 36 42 E
Odra →, Poland 28 53 33N 14 38 E
Odra →, Spain 30 42 14N 4 17W
Odžaci 42 45 30N 19 17 E
Odžak 42 45 3N 18 18 E
Oeiras, Brazil 127 7 0 S 42 8W
Oeiras, Port. 31 38 41N 9 18W
Oelrichs 116 43 11N 103 14W
Oelsnitz 24 50 24N 12 11 E
Oelwein 116 42 41N 91 55W
Ofanto → 41 41 22N 16 13 E
Offa 85 8 13N 4 42 E
Offaly □ 15 53 15N 7 30W
Offenbach 25 50 6N 8 46 E
Offenburg 25 48 29N 7 56 E
Offerdal 48 63 28N 14 0 E
Offida 39 42 56N 13 40 E
Offranville 18 49 52N 1 0 E
Ofidhousa 45 36 33N 26 8 E
Ofotfjorden 50 68 27N 16 40 E
Oga-Hantō 74 39 58N 139 47 E
Ogahalla 106 50 6N 85 51W
Ōgaki 74 35 21N 136 37 E
Ogallala 116 41 12N 101 40W
Ogbomosho 85 8 1N 4 11 E
Ogden, Iowa, U.S.A. 116 42 3N 94 0W
Ogden, Utah, U.S.A. 118 41 13N 112 1W
Ogdensburg 114 44 40N 75 27W
Ogeechee → 115 31 51N 81 6W
Oglio → 38 45 2N 10 39 E
Ogmore 98 22 37 S 149 35 E
Ogna 47 58 31N 5 48 E
Ognon → 19 47 16N 5 28 E
Ogoja 85 6 38N 8 39 E
Ogoki → 106 51 38N 85 57W
Ogoki L. 106 50 50N 87 10W
Ogoki Res. 106 50 45N 88 15W
Ogooué → 88 1 0 S 10 0 E
Ogosta → 43 43 48N 23 55 E
Ogowe = Ogooué → 88 1 0 S 10 0 E
Ograźden 42 41 30N 22 50 E
Ogrein 86 17 55N 34 50 E
Ogulin 39 45 16N 15 16 E
Ogun □ 85 7 0N 3 0 E
Oguta 85 5 44N 6 44 E
Ogwashi-Uku 85 6 15N 6 30 E
Ogwe 85 5 0N 7 14 E
Ohai 101 44 55 S 168 0 E
Ohakune 101 39 24 S 175 24 E
Ohau, L. 101 44 15 S 169 53 E
Ohey 16 50 26N 5 8 E
O'Higgins □ 124 34 15 S 70 45W
Ohio □ 114 40 20N 14 10 E
Ohio → 114 38 0N 86 0W
Ohre →, Czech. 26 50 30N 14 10 E
Ohre →, Ger. 24 52 18N 11 47 E
Ohrid 42 41 8N 20 52 E
Ohridsko, Jezero 42 41 8N 20 52 E
Ohrigstad 93 24 19 S 30 36 E
Öhringen 25 49 11N 9 31 E
Oil City 114 41 26N 79 40W
Oinousa 45 38 33N 26 14 E
Oise □ 19 49 28N 2 30 E
Oise → 19 49 0N 2 4 E
Ōita 74 33 14N 131 36 E
Ōita □ 74 33 15N 131 30 E
Oiticica 127 5 3 S 41 5W
Ojai 119 34 28N 119 16W
Ojinaga 120 29 34N 104 25W
Ojos del Salado, Cerro 124 27 0 S 68 40W
Oka → 55 56 20N 43 59 E
Okaba 73 8 6 S 139 42 E
Okahandja 92 22 0 S 16 59 E
Okahukura 94 38 48 S 175 14 E
Okanagan L. 108 50 0N 119 30W
Okandja 88 0 35 S 13 45 E
Okanogan 118 48 6N 119 43W
Okanogan → 118 48 6N 119 43W
Okány 27 46 52N 21 21 E
Okaputa 92 20 5 S 17 0 E
Okara 68 30 50N 73 31 E
Okarito 101 43 15 S 170 9 E
Okavango Swamps 92 18 45 S 22 45 E
Okaya 74 36 0N 138 10 E
Okayama 74 34 40N 133 54 E
Okayama □ 74 35 0N 133 50 E
Okazaki 74 34 57N 137 10 E
Oke-Iho 85 8 1N 3 18 E
Okeechobee 115 27 16N 80 46W
Okeechobee L. 115 27 0N 80 50W
Okefenokee Swamp 115 30 50N 82 15W
Okehampton 13 50 44N 4 1W
Okene 85 7 32N 6 11 E
Oker → 24 52 30N 10 22 E
Okha 59 53 40N 143 0 E
Ókhi Óros 45 38 5N 24 25 E
Okhotsk 59 59 20N 143 10 E
Okhotsk, Sea of 59 55 0N 145 0 E
Okhotskiy Perevoz 59 61 52N 135 35 E
Okhotsko Kolymskoye 59 63 0N 157 0 E
Oki-Shotō 74 36 5N 133 15 E
Okiep 92 29 39 S 17 53 E
Okigwi 85 5 52N 7 20 E
Okija 85 5 54N 6 55 E
Okinawa □ 77 26 40N 128 0 E
Okitipupa 85 6 31N 4 50 E
Oklahoma □ 117 35 20N 97 30W
Oklahoma City 117 35 25N 97 30W
Okmulgee 117 35 38N 96 0W
Oknitsa 56 48 25N 27 30 E
Okolo 90 2 37N 31 8 E
Okolona 117 34 0N 88 45W
Okondeka 92 21 38 S 15 37 E
Okonek 28 53 32N 16 51 E
Okrika 85 4 40N 7 10 E
Oktabrsk 58 49 28N 57 25 E
Oktyabrsk 55 53 11N 48 40 E
Oktyabrskiy, Byelorussia, U.S.S.R. 54 52 38N 28 53 E
Oktyabrskiy, R.S.F.S.R., U.S.S.R. 52 54 28N 53 28 E
Oktyabrskoy Revolyutsii, Os. 59 79 30N 97 0 E
Oktyabrskoye 58 62 28N 66 3 E
Oktyabrskoye = Zhovtnevoye 56 47 54N 32 2 E
Okulovka 54 58 25N 33 19 E
Okuru 101 43 55 S 168 55 E
Okushiri-Tō 74 42 15N 139 30 E
Okuta 85 9 14N 3 12 E
Okwa → 92 22 30 S 23 0 E
Ola 117 35 2N 93 10W
Ólafsfjörður 50 66 4N 18 39W
Ólafsvík 50 64 53N 23 43W
Olancha 119 36 15N 118 1W
Olanchito 121 15 30N 86 30W
Öland 49 56 45N 16 38 E
Olargues 20 43 34N 2 53 E
Olary 99 32 18 S 140 19 E
Olascoaga 124 35 15 S 60 39W
Olathe 116 38 50N 94 50W
Olavarría 124 36 55 S 60 20W
Oława 28 50 57N 17 20 E
Ólbia 40 40 55N 9 30 E
Ólbia, G. di 40 40 55N 9 35 E
Old Bahama Chan. = Bahama, Canal Viejo de 121 22 10N 77 30W
Old Castile = Castilla la Vieja □ 30 41 55N 4 0W
Old Castle 15 53 46N 7 10W
Old Cork 98 22 57 S 141 52 E
Old Crow 104 67 30N 140 5 E
Old Dongola 86 18 11N 30 44 E
Old Forge, N.Y., U.S.A. 113 43 43N 74 58W
Old Forge, Pa., U.S.A. 113 41 20N 75 46W
Old Fort → 109 58 36N 110 24W
Old Shinyanga 90 3 33 S 33 27 E
Old Speckle, Mt. 113 44 35N 70 57W
Old Town 107 45 0N 68 41W
Old Wives L. 109 50 5N 106 0W
Oldbury 13 51 38N 2 30W
Oldeani 90 3 22 S 35 35 E
Oldenburg, Niedersachsen, Ger. 24 53 10N 8 10 E
Oldenburg, Schleswig-Holstein, Ger. 24 54 16N 10 53 E
Oldenzaal 16 52 19N 6 53 E
Oldham 12 53 33N 2 8W
Oldman → 108 49 57N 111 42W
Olds 108 51 50N 114 10W
Olean 114 42 8N 78 25W
Olecko 28 54 2N 22 31 E
Oléggio 38 45 36N 8 38 E
Oleiros 30 39 56N 7 56W
Olekma → 59 60 22N 120 42 E
Olekminsk 59 60 25N 120 30 E
Olenegorsk 52 68 9N 33 18 E
Olenek 59 68 28N 112 18 E
Olenek → 59 73 0N 120 10 E
Olenino 54 56 15N 33 30 E
Oléron, Île d' 20 45 55N 1 15W
Oleśnica 28 51 13N 17 22 E
Olesno 28 50 51N 18 26 E
Olevsk 54 51 12N 27 39 E
Olga 59 43 50N 135 14 E
Olga, L. 106 49 47N 77 15W
Olga, Mt. 96 25 20 S 130 50 E
Olgastretet 4 78 35N 25 0 E
Ølgod 49 55 49N 8 36 E
Olhão 31 37 3N 7 48W
Olib 39 44 23N 14 44 E
Olib, I. 39 44 23N 14 44 E
Oliena 40 40 18N 9 22 E
Oliete 32 41 1N 0 41W
Olifants → 93 24 5 S 31 20 E
Olifantshoek 92 27 57 S 22 42 E
Ólimbos 45 35 44N 27 11 E
Ólimbos, Óros 44 40 6N 22 23 E
Olímpia 125 20 44 S 48 54W
Olimpo □ 124 20 30 S 58 45W
Olite 32 42 29N 1 40W
Oliva, Argent. 124 32 0 S 63 38W
Oliva, Spain 33 38 58N 0 9W
Oliva de la Frontera 31 38 17N 6 54W
Oliva, Punta del 30 43 37N 5 28W
Olivares 32 39 46N 2 20W
Oliveira 127 20 39 S 44 50W
Oliveira de Azemeis 30 40 49N 8 29W
Olivença 91 11 47 S 35 13 E
Olivenza 31 38 41N 7 9W
Oliver 108 49 13N 119 37W
Oliver L. 109 56 56N 103 22W
Olkhovka 57 49 48N 44 32 E
Olkusz 28 50 18N 19 33 E
Ollagüe 124 21 15 S 68 10W
Olmedo 30 41 20N 4 43W
Olney, Ill., U.S.A. 114 38 40N 88 0W
Olney, Tex., U.S.A. 117 33 25N 98 45W
Olofström 49 56 17N 14 32 E
Oloma 85 3 29N 11 19 E
Olomane → 107 50 14N 60 37W
Olomouc 27 49 38N 17 12 E
Olonets 52 61 10N 33 0 E
Olongapo 73 14 50N 120 18 E
Oloron, Gave d' 20 43 33N 1 5W
Oloron-Ste-Marie 20 43 11N 0 38W
Olot 32 42 11N 2 30 E
Olovo 42 44 8N 18 35 E
Olovyannaya 59 50 58N 115 35 E
Oloy → 59 66 29N 159 29 E
Olpe 24 51 2N 7 50 E
Olshanka 56 48 16N 30 58 E
Olshany 56 50 3N 35 53 E
Olsztyn 28 53 48N 20 29 E
Olsztyn □ 28 54 0N 21 0 E
Olsztynek 28 53 34N 20 19 E
Olt □ 46 44 20N 24 30 E
Olt → 46 43 50N 24 40 E
Olten 25 47 21N 7 53 E
Olteniţa 46 44 7N 26 42 E
Olton 117 34 16N 102 7W
Oltu 64 40 35N 41 58 E
Olvega 32 41 47N 2 0W
Olvera 31 36 55N 5 18W
Olympia, Greece 45 37 39N 21 39 E
Olympia, U.S.A. 118 47 0N 122 58W
Olympic Mts. 118 47 50N 123 45W
Olympic Nat. Park 118 47 48N 123 30W
Olympus, Mt. 118 47 52N 123 40W
Olympus, Mt. = Ólimbos, Óros 44 40 6N 22 23 E
Olyphant 113 41 27N 75 36W
Om → 58 54 59N 73 22 E
Om Hajer 87 14 20N 36 41 E
Ōmachi 74 36 30N 137 50 E
Omagh 15 54 36N 7 20W
Omagh □ 15 54 35N 7 15W
Omaha 116 41 15N 96 0W
Omak 118 48 24N 119 31W
Oman ■ 63 23 0N 58 0 E
Oman, G. of 65 24 30N 58 30 E
Omaruru 92 21 26 S 16 0 E
Omaruru → 92 22 7 S 14 15 E
Omate 126 16 45 S 71 0W
Ombai, Selat 73 8 30 S 124 50 E
Ombo 47 59 18N 6 0 E
Omboué 88 1 35 S 9 15 E
Ombrone → 38 42 39N 11 0 E
Omchi 83 21 22N 17 53 E
Omdurmân 87 15 40N 32 28 E
Omegna 38 45 52N 8 23 E
Omeonga 90 3 40 S 24 22 E
Ometepe, Isla de 121 11 32N 85 35W
Ometepec 120 16 39N 98 23W
Omez 62 32 22N 35 0 E
Omineca → 108 56 3N 124 16W
Omiš 39 43 28N 16 40 E
Omišalj 39 45 13N 14 32 E
Omitara 92 22 16 S 18 2 E
Ōmiya 74 35 54N 139 38 E
Omme Å → 49 55 56N 8 32 E
Ommen 16 52 31N 6 26 E
Omo → 81 6 25N 36 10 E
Omolon → 59 68 42N 158 36 E
Omsk 58 55 0N 73 12 E
Omsukchan 59 62 32N 155 48 E
Omul, Vf. 46 45 27N 25 29 E
Omulew → 28 53 5N 21 33 E
Ōmura 74 32 56N 130 0 E
Omurtag 43 43 8N 26 26 E
Ōmuta 74 33 0N 130 26 E
Omutninsk 55 58 45N 52 4 E
Oña 32 42 43N 3 25W
Onaga 116 39 32N 96 12W
Onalaska 116 43 53N 91 14W
Onamia 116 46 4N 93 38W
Onancock 114 37 42N 75 49W
Onang 73 3 2 S 118 49 E
Onaping L. 106 47 3N 81 30W
Onarheim 47 59 57N 5 35 E
Oñate 32 43 3N 2 25W
Onavas 120 28 28N 109 30W
Onawa 116 42 2N 96 2W
Onaway 114 45 21N 84 11W
Oncesti 46 43 56N 25 52 E
Oncócua 92 16 30 S 13 25 E
Onda 32 39 55N 0 17W
Ondangua 92 17 57 S 16 4 E
Ondárroa 32 43 19N 2 25W
Ondava → 27 48 27N 21 48 E
Ondo 85 7 4N 4 47 E
Ondo □ 85 7 0N 5 0 E
Öndörhaan 75 47 19N 110 39 E
Öndverðarnes 50 64 52N 24 0W
Onega 52 64 0N 38 10 E
Onega → 52 63 58N 37 55 E
Onega, G. of = Onezhskaya G. 52 64 30N 37 0 E
Onega, L. = Onezhskoye Oz. 52 62 0N 35 30 E
Onehunga 101 36 55 S 174 48 E

Oneida Ouesso

Oneida 114 43 5N 75 40W
Oneida L. 114 43 12N 76 0W
O'Neill 116 42 30N 98 38W
Onekotan, Ostrov 59 49 25N 154 45 E
Onema 90 4 35 S 24 30 E
Oneonta, Ala., U.S.A. 115 33 58N 86 29W
Oneonta, N.Y., U.S.A. 114 42 26N 75 5W
Onezhskaya Guba 52 64 30N 37 0 E
Onezhskoye Ozero 52 62 0N 35 30 E
Ongarue 101 38 42 S 175 19 E
Ongniud Qi 76 43 0N 118 38 E
Ongoka 90 1 20 S 26 0 E
Ongole 70 15 33N 80 2 E
Onguren 59 53 38N 107 36 E
Oni 57 42 33N 43 26 E
Onida 116 44 42N 100 5W
Onilahy → 93 23 34 S 43 45 E
Onitsha 85 6 6N 6 42 E
Onoda 74 34 2N 131 25 E
Ons, Islas d' 30 42 23N 8 55W
Onsala 49 57 26N 12 0 E
Onslow 96 21 40 S 115 12 E
Onslow B. 115 34 20N 77 20W
Onstwedde 16 53 2N 7 4 E
Ontake-San 74 35 53N 137 29 E
Ontaneda 30 43 12N 3 57W
Ontario, Calif., U.S.A. 119 34 2N 117 40W
Ontario, Oreg., U.S.A. 118 44 1N 117 1W
Ontario □ 106 52 0N 88 10W
Ontario, L. 106 43 40N 78 0W
Onteniente 33 38 50N 0 35W
Ontonagon 116 46 52N 89 19W
Ontur 33 38 38N 1 29W
Oodnadatta 96 27 33 S 135 30 E
Ooldea 96 30 27 S 131 50 E
Oona River 108 53 57N 130 16W
Oorindi 98 20 40 S 141 1 E
Oost-Vlaanderen □ 16 51 5N 3 50 E
Oostende 16 51 15N 2 50 E
Oosterhout 16 51 39N 4 47 E
Oosterschelde 16 51 33N 4 0 E
Ootacamund 70 11 30N 76 44 E
Ootsa L. 108 53 50N 126 2W
Ootsi 92 25 2 S 25 45 E
Opaka 43 43 28N 26 10 E
Opala, U.S.S.R. 59 51 58N 156 30 E
Opala, Zaïre 88 0 40 S 24 20 E
Opalenica 28 52 18N 16 24 E
Opan 43 42 13N 25 41 E
Opanake 70 6 35N 80 40 E
Opasatika 106 49 30N 82 50W
Opasquia 109 53 16N 93 34W
Opatija 39 45 21N 14 17 E
Opatów 28 50 50N 21 27 E
Opava 27 49 57N 17 58 E
Opelousas 117 30 35N 92 7W
Opémisca L. 106 50 0N 75 0W
Opheim 118 48 52N 106 30W
Ophir 104 63 10N 156 40W
Ophthalmia Ra. 96 23 15 S 119 30 E
Opi 85 6 36N 7 28 E
Opinaca → 106 52 15N 78 2W
Opinaca L. 106 52 39N 76 20W
Opiskotish, L. 107 53 10N 67 50W
Opobo 85 4 35N 7 34 E
Opochka 54 56 42N 28 45 E
Opoczno 28 51 22N 20 18 E
Opole 28 50 42N 17 58 E
Opole □ 28 50 40N 17 56 E
Oporto = Porto 30 41 8N 8 40W
Opotiki 101 38 1 S 177 19 E
Opp 115 31 19N 86 13W
Oppegård 47 59 48N 10 48 E
Oppenheim 25 49 50N 8 22 E
Óppido Mamertina 41 38 16N 15 59 E
Oppland fylke □ 47 61 15N 9 40 E
Oppstad 47 60 17N 11 40 E
Oprtalj 39 45 23N 13 50 E
Opua 101 35 19 S 174 9 E
Opunake 101 39 26 S 173 52 E
Opuzen 42 43 1N 17 34 E
Or Yehuda 62 32 2N 34 50 E
Ora, Israel 62 30 55N 35 1 E
Ora, Italy 39 46 20N 11 19 E
Oracle 119 32 36N 110 46W
Oradea 46 47 2N 21 58 E
Öræfajökull 50 64 2N 16 39W
Orahovac 42 42 24N 20 40 E
Orahovica 42 45 35N 17 52 E
Orai 69 25 58N 79 30 E
Oraison 21 43 55N 5 55 E
Oran, Alg. 82 35 45N 0 39W
Oran, Argent. 124 23 10 S 64 20W
Orange, Austral. 97 33 15 S 149 7 E
Orange, France 21 44 8N 4 47 E
Orange, Mass., U.S.A. 113 42 35N 72 15W
Orange, Tex., U.S.A. 117 30 10N 93 50W
Orange, Va., U.S.A. 114 38 17N 78 5W
Orange, C. 127 4 20N 51 30W
Orange Free State = Oranje Vrystaat □ 92 28 30 S 27 0 E
Orange Grove 117 27 57N 97 57W
Orange Walk 120 18 6N 88 33W
Orangeburg 115 33 35N 80 53W
Orangeville 106 43 55N 80 5W
Oranienburg 24 52 45N 13 15 E
Oranje → 92 28 41 S 16 28 E
Oranje Vrystaat □ 92 28 30 S 27 0 E
Oranjemund 92 28 38 S 16 29 E
Or'Aquiva 62 32 30N 34 54 E
Oras 73 12 9N 125 28 E
Orašje 42 45 1N 18 42 E
Orăştie 46 45 50N 23 10 E
Oraşul Stalin = Braşov 46 45 38N 25 35 E
Orava → 27 49 24N 19 20 E
Oravita 42 45 2N 21 43 E
Orb → 20 43 17N 3 17 E
Orba → 38 44 53N 8 37 E
Ørbæk 49 55 17N 10 39 E
Orbe 25 46 43N 6 32 E
Orbec 18 49 1N 0 23 E
Orbetello 39 42 26N 11 11 E
Órbigo → 30 42 5N 5 42W
Orbost 97 37 40 S 148 29 E
Örbyhus 48 60 15N 17 43 E
Orce 33 37 44N 2 28W
Orce → 33 37 44N 2 28W
Orchies 19 50 28N 3 14 E
Orchila, Isla 126 11 48N 66 10W
Orco → 38 45 10N 7 52 E
Ord → 96 15 33 S 138 15 E
Ord, Mt. 96 17 20 S 125 34 E
Ordenes 30 43 5N 8 29W
Orderville 119 37 18N 112 43W
Ordos = Mu Us Shamo 76 39 0N 109 0 E
Ordu 64 40 55N 37 53 E
Orduña, Álava, Spain 32 42 58N 2 58 E
Orduña, Granada, Spain 33 37 20N 3 30W
Ordway 116 38 15N 103 42W
Ordzhonikidze, R.S.F.S.R., U.S.S.R. 57 43 0N 44 43 E
Ordzhonikidze, Ukraine S.S.R., U.S.S.R. 56 47 39N 34 3 E
Ore, Sweden 48 61 8N 15 10 E
Ore, Zaïre 90 3 17N 29 30 E
Ore Mts. = Erzgebirge 24 50 25N 13 0 E
Orebić 42 43 0N 17 11 E
Örebro 48 59 20N 15 18 E
Örebro län □ 48 59 27N 15 0 E
Oregon 116 42 1N 89 20W
Oregon □ 118 44 0N 121 0W
Oregon City 118 45 21N 122 35W
Öregrund 48 60 21N 18 30 E
Öregrundsgrepen 48 60 25N 18 15 E
Orekhov 56 47 30N 35 48 E
Orekhovo-Zuyevo 55 55 50N 38 55 E
Orel 55 52 57N 36 3 E
Orel → 56 48 30N 34 54 E
Orellana, Canal de 31 39 2N 6 0W
Orellana la Vieja 31 39 1N 5 32W
Orellana, Pantano de 31 39 5N 5 10W
Orem 118 40 20N 111 45W
Oren 45 37 3N 27 57 E
Orenburg 52 51 45N 55 6 E
Orense 30 42 19N 7 55W
Orense □ 30 42 15N 7 51W
Orepuki 101 46 19 S 167 46 E
Orestiás 44 41 30N 26 33 E
Øresund 49 55 45N 12 45 E
Orford Ness 13 52 6N 1 31 E
Orgaña 32 42 13N 1 20 E
Orgaz 31 39 39N 3 53W
Orgeyev 56 47 24N 28 50 E
Orgon 21 43 47N 5 3 E
Orgūn 65 32 55N 69 12 E
Orhon Gol → 75 49 30N 106 0 E
Ória 41 40 30N 17 38 E
Orient 96 28 7 S 142 50 E
Oriental, Cordillera 126 6 0N 73 0W
Oriente 124 38 44 S 60 37W
Origny-Ste-Benoîte 19 49 50N 3 30 E
Orihuela 33 38 7N 0 55W
Orihuela del Tremedal 32 40 33N 1 39W
Oriku 44 40 20N 19 30 E
Orinoco → 126 9 15N 61 30W
Orissa □ 69 20 0N 84 0 E
Oristano 40 39 54N 8 35 E
Oristano, Golfo di 40 39 50N 8 22 E
Orizaba 120 18 50N 97 10W
Orizare 43 42 44N 27 39 E
Ørje 47 59 29N 11 39 E
Orjen 42 42 35N 18 34 E
Orjiva 33 36 53N 3 24W
Orkanger 47 63 18N 9 52 E
Orkelljunga 49 56 17N 13 17 E
Örkény 27 47 9N 19 26 E
Orkla → 47 63 18N 9 51 E
Orkney 92 26 58 S 26 40 E
Orkney □ 14 59 0N 3 0W
Orkney Is. 14 59 0N 3 0W
Orla 28 52 42N 23 20 E
Orland 118 39 46N 122 12W
Orlando 115 28 30N 81 25W
Orlando, C. d' 41 38 10N 14 43 E
Orléanais 19 48 0N 2 0 E
Orléans 19 47 54N 1 52 E
Orleans 113 44 49N 72 10W
Orléans, Î. d' 107 46 54N 70 58W
Orlice → 26 50 5N 16 10 E
Orlické Hory 27 50 15N 16 30 E
Orlik 59 52 30N 99 55 E
Orlov 27 49 17N 20 51 E
Orlov Gay 55 50 56N 48 19 E
Orlovat 42 45 14N 20 33 E
Ormara 66 25 16N 64 33 E
Ormea 38 44 9N 7 54 E
Ormília 44 40 16N 23 39 E
Ormoc 73 11 0N 124 37 E
Ormond, N.Z. 101 38 33 S 177 56 E
Ormond, U.S.A. 115 29 13N 81 5W
Ormož 39 46 25N 16 10 E
Ormstown 113 45 8N 74 0W
Ornans 19 47 7N 6 10 E
Orne □ 18 48 40N 0 5 E
Orne → 18 49 18N 0 15W
Orneta 28 54 8N 20 9 E
Ørnhøj 49 56 13N 8 34 E
Ornö 48 59 4N 18 24 E
Örnsköldsvik 48 63 17N 18 40 E
Oro → 120 25 35N 105 2W
Orocué 126 4 48N 71 20W
Orodo 85 5 34N 7 4 E
Orogrande 119 32 20N 106 4W
Orol 30 43 34N 7 39W
Oromocto 107 45 54N 66 29W
Oron 85 4 48N 8 14 E
Orono 112 43 59N 78 37W
Oropesa 30 39 57N 5 10W
Oroqen Zizhiqi 76 50 34N 123 43 E
Oroquieta 73 8 32N 123 44 E
Orós 127 6 15 S 38 55W
Orosei, G. di 40 40 15N 9 40 E
Orosháza 27 46 32N 20 42 E
Orotukan 59 62 16N 151 42 E
Oroville, Calif., U.S.A. 118 39 31N 121 30W
Oroville, Wash., U.S.A. 118 48 58N 119 30W
Orrefors 49 56 50N 15 45 E
Orroroo 99 32 43 S 138 38 E
Orrville 112 40 50N 81 46W
Orsa 48 61 7N 14 37 E
Orsara di Púglia 41 41 17N 15 16 E
Orsasjön 48 61 7N 14 37 E
Orsha 54 54 30N 30 25 E
Orsk 52 51 12N 58 34 E
Ørslev 49 55 3N 11 56 E
Orsogna 39 42 13N 14 17 E
Orşova 46 44 41N 22 25 E
Ørsted 49 56 30N 10 20 E
Orta, L. d' 38 45 48N 8 21 E
Orta Nova 41 41 20N 15 40 E
Orte 39 42 28N 12 23 E
Ortegal, C. 30 43 43N 7 52W
Orthez 20 43 29N 0 48W
Ortigueira 30 43 40N 7 50W
Ortles 38 46 31N 10 33 E
Ortón → 126 10 50 S 67 0W
Ortona 39 42 21N 14 24 E
Orune 40 40 25N 9 20 E
Oruro 126 18 0 S 67 9W
Orust 49 58 10N 11 40 E
Orūzgān □ 65 33 30N 66 0 E
Orvault 18 47 17N 1 38W
Orvieto 39 42 43N 12 8 E
Orwell 112 41 32N 80 52W
Orwell → 13 52 2N 1 12 E
Oryakhovo 43 43 40N 23 57 E
Orzinuovi 38 45 24N 9 55 E
Orzyc → 28 52 46N 21 14 E
Orzysz 28 53 50N 21 58 E
Os 47 60 9N 5 30 E
Osa 52 57 17N 55 26 E
Osa → 28 53 33N 18 46 E
Osa, Pen. de 121 8 0N 84 0W
Osage, Iowa, U.S.A. 116 43 15N 92 50W
Osage, Wyo., U.S.A. 116 43 59N 104 25W
Osage → 116 38 35N 91 57W
Osage City 116 38 43N 95 51W
Ōsaka 74 34 40N 135 30 E
Ōsaka □ 74 34 30N 135 30 E
Osawatomie 116 38 30N 94 55W
Osborne 116 39 30N 98 45W
Osby 49 56 23N 13 59 E
Osceola, Ark., U.S.A. 117 35 40N 90 0W
Osceola, Iowa, U.S.A. 116 41 0N 93 20W
Oschatz 24 51 17N 13 8 E
Oschersleben 24 52 2N 11 13 E
Öschiri 40 40 43N 9 7 E
Oscoda 114 44 26N 83 20W
Oscoda-Au-Sable 112 44 26N 83 20W
Osečina 42 44 23N 19 34 E
Ösel = Saaremaa 54 58 30N 22 30W
Osëry 55 54 52N 38 28 E
Osh 58 40 37N 72 49 E
Oshawa 106 43 50N 78 50W
Ōshima 74 34 44N 139 24 E
Oshkosh, Nebr., U.S.A. 116 41 27N 102 20W
Oshkosh, Wis., U.S.A. 116 44 3N 88 35W
Oshmyany 54 54 26N 25 52 E
Oshogbo 85 7 48N 4 37 E
Oshwe 88 3 25 S 19 28 E
Osica de Jos 46 44 14N 24 20 E
Osieczna 28 51 55N 16 40 E
Osijek 42 45 34N 18 41 E
Ósilo 40 40 45N 8 41 E
Osimo 39 43 28N 13 30 E
Osintorf 54 54 40N 30 39 E
Osipenko = Berdyansk 56 46 45N 36 50 E
Osipovichi 54 53 19N 28 33 E
Oskaloosa 116 41 18N 92 40W
Oskarshamn 49 57 15N 16 27 E
Oskélanéo 106 48 5N 75 15W
Oskol → 55 49 6N 37 25 E
Oslo 47 59 55N 10 45 E
Oslob 73 9 31N 123 26 E
Oslofjorden 47 59 20N 10 35 E
Osmanabad 70 18 5N 76 10 E
Osmancık 56 40 45N 34 47 E
Osmaniye 64 37 5N 36 10 E
Ösmo 48 58 58N 17 55 E
Osnabrück 24 52 16N 8 2 E
Ośno Lubuskie 28 52 28N 14 51 E
Osobláha 27 50 17N 17 44 E
Osogovska Planina 42 42 10N 22 30 E
Osor 38 44 42N 14 24 E
Osorio 125 29 53 S 50 17W
Osorno, Chile 128 40 25 S 73 0W
Osorno, Spain 30 42 24N 4 22W
Osoyoos 108 49 0N 119 30W
Ospika → 108 56 20N 124 0W
Osprey Reef 97 13 52 S 146 36 E
Oss 16 51 46N 5 32 E
Ossa de Montiel 33 38 58N 2 45W
Ossa, Mt. 97 41 52 S 146 3 E
Óssa, Oros 44 39 47N 22 42 E
Ossabaw I. 115 31 45N 81 8W
Osse → 20 44 7N 0 17 E
Ossining 114 41 9N 73 50W
Ossipee 113 43 41N 71 9W
Ossokmanuan L. 107 53 25N 65 0W
Ossora 59 59 20N 163 13 E
Ostashkov 54 57 4N 33 2 E
Oste → 24 53 30N 9 12 E
Ostend = Oostende 16 51 15N 2 50 E
Oster 54 50 57N 30 53 E
Osterburg 24 52 47N 11 44 E
Osterburken 25 49 26N 9 25 E
Österbybruk 48 60 13N 17 55 E
Österbymo 49 57 49N 15 15 E
Östergötlands län □ 49 58 35N 15 45 E
Osterholz-Scharmbeck 24 53 14N 8 48 E
Østerild 49 57 2N 8 51 E
Österkorsberga 49 57 18N 15 6 E
Osterøya 47 60 32N 5 30 E
Östersund 48 63 10N 14 38 E
Østfold fylke □ 47 59 25N 11 25 E
Ostfreisland 24 53 20N 7 30 E
Ostfriesische Inseln 24 53 45N 7 15 E
Óstia, Lido di (Lido di Roma) 40 41 43N 12 17 E
Ostíglia 39 45 4N 11 9 E
Ostra 39 43 40N 13 5 E
Ostrava 27 49 51N 18 18 E
Ostróda 28 53 42N 19 58 E
Ostrog 54 50 20N 26 30 E
Ostrogozhsk 55 50 55N 39 7 E
Ostrogróg Szamotuły 28 52 37N 16 33 E
Ostrołeka 28 53 4N 21 32 E
Ostrołeka □ 28 53 0N 21 30 E
Ostrov, Bulg. 43 43 40N 24 9 E
Ostrov, Romania 46 44 6N 27 24 E
Ostrov, U.S.S.R. 54 57 25N 28 20 E
Ostrów Lubelski 28 51 29N 22 51 E
Ostrów Mazowiecka 28 52 50N 21 51 E
Ostrów Wielkopolski 28 51 36N 17 44 E
Ostrowiec-Świętokrzyski 28 50 55N 21 22 E
Ostrozac 42 43 43N 17 49 E
Ostrzeszów 28 51 25N 17 52 E
Ostseebad-Kühlungsborn 24 54 10N 11 40 E
Ostuni 41 40 44N 17 34 E
Osum → 43 43 40N 24 50 E
Osumi → 44 40 40N 20 10 E
Ōsumi-Kaikyō 74 30 55N 131 0 E
Osuna 31 37 14N 5 8W
Oswego 114 43 29N 76 30W
Oswestry 12 52 52N 3 3W
Oświęcim 27 50 2N 19 11 E
Otago □ 101 44 44 S 169 10 E
Otago Harb. 101 45 47 S 170 42 E
Ōtake 74 34 12N 132 13 E
Otaki 101 40 45 S 175 10 E
Otaru 74 43 10N 141 0 E
Otava → 26 49 26N 14 12 E
Otavalo 126 0 13N 78 20W
Otavi 92 19 40 S 17 24 E
Otchinjau 92 16 30 S 13 56 E
Otelec 42 45 36N 20 50 E
Otero de Rey 30 43 6N 7 36W
Othello 118 46 53N 119 8W
Othonoí 44 39 52N 19 22 E
Óthris, Óros 45 39 4N 22 42 E
Otira Gorge 101 42 53 S 171 33 E
Otis 116 40 12N 102 58W
Otjiwarongo 92 20 30 S 16 33 E
Otmuchów 28 50 28N 17 10 E
Otočac 39 44 53N 15 12 E
Otorohanga 101 38 12 S 175 14 E
Otoskwin → 106 52 13N 88 6W
Otosquen 109 53 17N 102 1W
Otra → 47 58 8N 8 1 E
Otranto 41 40 9N 18 28 E
Otranto, C. d' 41 40 7N 18 30 E
Otranto, Str. of 41 40 15N 18 40 E
Ōtsu 74 35 0N 135 50 E
Otta 47 61 46N 9 32 E
Otta → 47 61 46N 9 31 E
Ottapalam 70 10 46N 76 23 E
Ottawa, Can. 106 45 27N 75 42W
Ottawa, Ill., U.S.A. 116 41 20N 88 55W
Ottawa, Kans., U.S.A. 116 38 40N 95 6W
Ottawa = Outaouais → 106 45 27N 74 8W
Ottawa Is. 105 59 35N 80 10W
Ottélé 85 3 38N 11 19 E
Ottenby 49 56 15N 16 24 E
Otter L. 109 55 35N 104 39W
Otter Rapids, Ont., Can. 106 50 11N 81 39W
Otter Rapids, Sask., Can. 109 55 38N 104 44W
Otterberg 25 49 30N 7 46 E
Otterndorf 24 53 47N 8 52 E
Ottersheim 26 48 21N 14 12 E
Otterup 49 55 30N 10 22 E
Otterville 112 42 55N 80 36W
Otto Beit Bridge 91 15 59 S 28 56 E
Ottosdal 92 26 46 S 25 59 E
Ottoshoop 92 25 45 S 25 58 E
Ottsjö 48 63 13N 13 2 E
Ottumwa 116 41 0N 92 25W
Otu 85 8 14N 3 22 E
Otukpa (Al Owuho) 85 7 9N 7 41 E
Oturkpo 85 7 16N 8 8 E
Otway, Bahía 128 53 30 S 74 0W
Otway, C. 97 38 52 S 143 30 E
Otwock 28 52 5N 21 20 E
Ötz 26 47 13N 10 53 E
Ötz → 26 47 14N 10 50 E
Ötztaler Alpen 26 46 45N 11 0 E
Ou → 71 20 4N 102 13 E
Ou-Sammyaku 74 39 20N 140 35 E
Ouachita → 117 31 38N 91 49W
Ouachita, L. 117 34 40N 93 25W
Ouachita Mts. 117 34 50N 94 30W
Ouadâne 80 20 50N 11 40W
Ouadda 88 8 15N 22 20 E
Ouagadougou 85 12 25N 1 30W
Ouahigouya 84 13 31N 2 25W
Ouahila 82 27 50N 5 0W
Ouahran = Oran 82 35 49N 0 39W
Oualâta 84 17 20N 6 55W
Ouallene 82 24 41N 1 11 E
Ouanda Djallé 88 8 55N 22 53 E
Ouango 88 4 19N 22 30 E
Ouargla 83 31 59N 5 16 E
Ouarkziz, Djebel 82 28 50N 8 0W
Ouarzazate 82 30 55N 6 50W
Ouatagouna 85 15 11N 0 43 E
Oubangi → 88 1 0N 17 50 E
Oubarakai, O. → 83 27 20N 9 0 E
Ouche → 19 47 6N 5 16 E
Ouddorp 16 51 50N 3 57 E
Oude Rijn → 16 52 12N 4 24 E
Oudenaarde 16 50 50N 3 37 E
Oudon 18 47 22N 1 19W
Oudon → 18 47 38N 1 18 E
Oudtshoorn 92 33 35 S 22 14 E
Oued Zem 82 32 52N 6 34W
Ouellé 84 7 26N 4 1W
Ouenza 83 35 57N 8 4 E
Ouessa 84 11 4N 2 47W
Ouessant, Île d' 18 48 28N 5 6W
Ouesso 88 1 37N 16 5 E

Ouest, Pte. Papua New Guinea

Ouest, Pte.	**107**	49 52N	64 40W
Ouezzane	**82**	34 51N	5 35W
Ouidah	**85**	6 25N	2 0 E
Ouistreham	**18**	49 17N	0 18W
Oujda	**82**	34 41N	1 55W
Oujeft	**80**	20 2N	13 0W
Ould Yenjé	**84**	15 38N	12 16W
Ouled Djellal	**83**	34 28N	5 2 E
Ouled Naïl, Mts. des	**82**	34 30N	3 30 E
Oulmès	**82**	33 17N	6 0W
Oulu	**50**	65 1N	25 29 E
Oulu □	**50**	65 10N	27 20 E
Oulujärvi	**50**	64 25N	27 15 E
Oulujoki →	**50**	65 1N	25 30 E
Oulx	**38**	45 2N	6 49 E
Oum Chalouba	**81**	15 48N	20 46 E
Oum-el-Bouaghi	**83**	35 55N	7 6 E
Oum el Ksi	**82**	29 4N	6 59W
Oum-er-Rbia, O. →	**82**	33 19N	8 21W
Oumè	**84**	6 21N	5 27W
Ounane, Dj.	**83**	25 4N	7 19 E
Ounguati	**92**	21 54 S	15 46 E
Ounianga-Kébir	**81**	19 4N	20 29 E
Ounianga Sérir	**81**	18 54N	19 51 E
Our →	**16**	49 55N	6 5 E
Ouray	**119**	38 3N	107 40W
Ourcq →	**19**	49 1N	3 1 E
Oureg, Oued el →	**82**	32 34N	2 10 E
Ouricuri	**127**	7 53 S	40 5W
Ourinhos	**125**	23 0 S	49 54W
Ourique	**31**	37 38N	8 16W
Ouro Fino	**125**	22 16 S	46 25W
Ouro Prêto	**125**	20 20 S	43 30W
Ouro Sogui	**84**	15 36N	13 19W
Oursi	**85**	14 41N	0 27W
Ourthe →	**16**	50 29N	5 35 E
Ouse	**99**	42 38 S	146 42 E
Ouse →, Sussex, U.K.	**13**	50 43N	0 3 E
Ouse →, Yorks., U.K.	**12**	54 3N	0 7 E
Oust	**20**	42 52N	1 13 E
Oust →	**18**	47 35N	2 6W
Outaouais →	**106**	45 27N	74 8W
Outardes →	**107**	49 24N	69 30W
Outat Oulad el Haj	**82**	33 22N	3 42W
Outer Hebrides	**14**	57 30N	7 40W
Outer I.	**107**	51 10N	58 35W
Outes	**30**	42 52N	8 55W
Outjo	**92**	20 5 S	16 7 E
Outlook, Can.	**109**	51 30N	107 0W
Outlook, U.S.A.	**116**	48 53N	104 46W
Outreau	**19**	50 40N	1 36 E
Ouvèze →	**21**	43 59N	4 51 E
Ouyen	**97**	35 1 S	142 22 E
Ouzouer-le-Marché	**18**	47 54N	1 32 E
Ovada	**38**	44 39N	8 40 E
Ovalau	**101**	17 40 S	178 48 E
Ovalle	**124**	30 33 S	71 18W
Ovar	**30**	40 51N	8 40W
Ovens →	**100**	36 2 S	146 12 E
Over Flakkee	**16**	51 45N	4 5 E
Overijssel □	**16**	52 25N	6 35 E
Overpelt	**16**	51 12N	5 20 E
Overton	**119**	36 32N	114 31W
Övertorneå	**50**	66 23N	23 38 E
Overum	**49**	58 0N	16 20 E
Ovid	**116**	41 0N	102 17W
Ovidiopol	**56**	46 15N	30 30 E
Oviedo	**30**	43 25N	5 50W
Oviedo □	**30**	43 20N	6 0W
Oviken	**48**	63 0N	14 23 E
Oviksfjällen	**48**	63 0N	13 49 E
Ovoro	**85**	5 26N	7 16 E
Övre Sirdal	**47**	58 48N	6 43 E
Ovruch	**54**	51 25N	28 45 E
Owaka	**101**	46 27 S	169 40 E
Owambo	**92**	17 20 S	16 30 E
Owase	**74**	34 7N	136 12 E
Owatonna	**116**	44 3N	93 10W
Owbeh	**65**	34 28N	63 10 E
Owego	**114**	42 6N	76 17W
Owen Falls	**90**	0 30N	33 5 E
Owen Sound	**106**	44 35N	80 55W
Owen Stanley Range	**98**	8 30 S	147 0 E
Owendo	**88**	0 17N	9 30 E
Owens L.	**119**	36 20N	118 0W
Owensboro	**114**	37 40N	87 5W
Owensville	**116**	38 20N	91 30W
Owerri	**85**	5 29N	7 0 E
Owl →	**109**	57 51N	92 44W
Owo	**85**	7 10N	5 39 E
Owosso	**114**	43 0N	84 10W
Owyhee	**118**	42 0N	116 3W
Owyhee →	**118**	43 46N	117 2W
Owyhee Res.	**118**	43 40N	117 16W
Ox Mts.	**15**	54 6N	9 0W
Oxberg	**48**	61 7N	14 11 E
Oxelösund	**49**	58 43N	17 15 E
Oxford, N.Z.	**101**	43 18 S	172 11 E
Oxford, U.K.	**13**	51 45N	1 15W
Oxford, Miss., U.S.A.	**117**	34 22N	89 30W
Oxford, N.C., U.S.A.	**115**	36 19N	78 36W
Oxford, Ohio, U.S.A.	**114**	39 30N	84 40W
Oxford □	**13**	51 45N	1 15W
Oxford L.	**109**	54 51N	95 37W
Oxía	**45**	38 16N	21 5 E
Oxílithos	**45**	38 35N	24 7 E
Oxley	**99**	34 11 S	144 6 E
Oxnard	**119**	34 10N	119 14W
Oya	**72**	2 55N	111 55 E
Oyem	**88**	1 34N	11 31 E
Oyen	**109**	51 22N	110 28W
Öyeren	**47**	59 50N	11 15 E
Oykel →	**14**	57 55N	4 26W
Oymyakon	**59**	63 25N	142 44 E
Oyo	**85**	7 46N	3 56 E
Oyo □	**85**	8 0N	3 30 E
Oyonnax	**21**	46 16N	5 40 E
Oyster B.	**113**	40 52N	73 32W
Øystese	**47**	60 22N	6 9 E
Ozamis (Mizamis)	**73**	8 15N	123 50 E
Ozark, Ala., U.S.A.	**115**	31 29N	85 39W
Ozark, Ark., U.S.A.	**117**	35 30N	93 50W
Ozark, Mo., U.S.A.	**117**	37 0N	93 15W
Ozark Plateau	**117**	37 20N	91 40W
Ozarks, L. of	**116**	38 10N	92 40W
Ózd	**27**	48 14N	20 15 E
Ozieri	**40**	40 35N	9 0 E
Ozimek	**28**	50 41N	18 11 E
Ozona	**117**	30 43N	101 11W
Ozorków	**28**	51 57N	19 16 E
Ozren	**42**	43 55N	18 29 E
Ozuluama	**120**	21 40N	97 50W
Ozun	**46**	45 47N	25 50 E

P

Pa	**84**	11 33N	3 19W
Pa-an	**67**	16 51N	97 40 E
Pa Sak →	**71**	15 30N	101 0 E
Paar →	**25**	48 13N	10 59 E
Paarl	**92**	33 45 S	18 56 E
Paatsi →	**50**	68 55N	29 0 E
Paauilo	**110**	20 3N	155 22W
Pab Hills	**66**	26 30N	66 45 E
Pabianice	**28**	51 40N	19 20 E
Pabna	**69**	24 1N	89 18 E
Pabo	**90**	3 1N	32 10 E
Pacaja →	**127**	1 56 S	50 50W
Pacaraima, Sierra	**126**	4 0N	62 30W
Pacasmayo	**126**	7 20 S	79 35W
Pacaudière, La	**20**	46 11N	3 52 E
Paceco	**40**	37 59N	12 32 E
Pachhar	**68**	24 40N	77 42 E
Pachino	**41**	36 43N	15 4 E
Pachora	**68**	20 38N	75 29 E
Pachuca	**120**	20 10N	98 40W
Pacific	**108**	54 48N	128 28W
Pacific-Antarctic Basin	**95**	46 0 S	95 0W
Pacific-Antarctic Ridge	**95**	43 0 S	115 0W
Pacific Grove	**119**	36 38N	121 58W
Pacific Ocean	**94**	10 0N	140 0W
Pacitan	**73**	8 12 S	111 7 E
Pacofi	**108**	53 0N	132 30W
Pacov	**26**	49 27N	15 0 E
Pacsa	**27**	46 44N	17 2 E
Paczków	**28**	50 28N	17 0 E
Padaido, Kepulauan	**73**	1 5 S	138 0 E
Padalarang	**73**	7 50 S	107 30 E
Padang	**72**	1 0 S	100 20 E
Padangpanjang	**72**	0 40 S	100 20 E
Padangsidempuan	**72**	1 30N	99 15 E
Padborg	**49**	54 49N	9 21 E
Paddockwood	**109**	53 30N	105 30W
Paderborn	**24**	51 42N	8 44 E
Padeşul	**46**	45 40N	22 22 E
Padina	**46**	44 50N	27 8 E
Padloping Island	**105**	67 0N	62 50W
Padmanabhapuram	**70**	8 16N	77 17 E
Pádova	**39**	45 24N	11 52 E
Padra	**68**	22 15N	73 7 E
Padrauna	**69**	26 54N	83 59 E
Padre I.	**117**	27 0N	97 20W
Padrón	**30**	42 41N	8 39W
Padstow	**12**	50 33N	4 57W
Padua = Pádova	**39**	45 24N	11 52 E
Paducah, Ky., U.S.A.	**114**	37 0N	88 40W
Paducah, Tex., U.S.A.	**117**	34 3N	100 16W
Padul	**31**	37 1N	3 38W
Padula	**41**	40 20N	15 40 E
Padwa	**70**	18 27N	82 47 E
Paeroa	**101**	37 23 S	175 41 E
Paesana	**38**	44 40N	7 18 E
Pag	**39**	44 30N	14 50 E
Paga	**85**	11 1N	1 8W
Pagadian	**73**	7 55N	123 30 E
Pagai Selatan	**72**	3 0 S	100 15W
Pagai Utara	**72**	2 35 S	100 0 E
Pagalu = Annobón	**79**	1 25 S	5 36 E
Pagastikós Kólpos	**44**	39 15N	23 0 E
Pagatan	**72**	3 33 S	115 59 E
Page, Ariz., U.S.A.	**119**	36 57N	111 27W
Page, N.D., U.S.A.	**116**	47 11N	97 37W
Paglieta	**39**	42 10N	14 30 E
Pagny-sur-Moselle	**19**	48 59N	6 2 E
Pago Pago	**101**	14 16 S	170 43W
Pagosa Springs	**119**	37 16N	107 4W
Pagwa River	**106**	50 2N	85 14W
Pahala	**110**	19 12N	155 25W
Pahang □	**71**	3 40N	102 20 E
Pahang →	**71**	3 30N	103 9 E
Pahiatua	**101**	40 27 S	175 50 E
Pahokee	**115**	26 50N	80 40W
Pahrump	**119**	36 15N	116 0W
Paia	**110**	20 54N	156 22W
Paide	**54**	58 57N	25 31 E
Paignton	**13**	50 26N	3 33W
Päijänne, L.	**51**	61 30N	25 30 E
Pailin	**71**	12 46N	102 36 E
Paimbœuf	**18**	47 17N	2 0W
Paimpol	**18**	48 48N	3 4W
Painan	**72**	1 21 S	100 34 E
Painesville	**114**	41 42N	81 18W
Paint I.	**109**	55 28N	97 57W
Paint Rock	**117**	31 30N	99 56W
Painted Desert	**119**	36 0N	111 30W
Paintsville	**114**	37 50N	82 50W
Paisley, Can.	**112**	44 18N	81 16W
Paisley, U.K.	**14**	55 51N	4 27W
Paisley, U.S.A.	**118**	42 43N	120 40W
Paita	**126**	5 11 S	81 9W
Paiva →	**30**	41 4N	8 16W
Pajares	**30**	43 1N	5 46W
Pajares, Puerto de	**30**	43 0N	5 46W
Pajeczno	**28**	51 10N	19 0 E
Pak Lay	**71**	18 15N	101 27 E
Pakala	**70**	13 29N	79 8 E
Pakanbaru	**72**	0 30N	101 15 E
Pakaraima Mts.	**126**	6 0N	60 0W
Pakistan ■	**66**	30 0N	70 0 E
Pakistan, East = Bangladesh ■	**67**	24 0N	90 0 E
Pakokku	**67**	21 20N	95 0 E
Pakosc	**28**	52 48N	18 6 E
Pakpattan	**68**	30 25N	73 27 E
Pakrac	**42**	45 27N	17 12 E
Paks	**27**	46 38N	18 55 E
Pakse	**71**	15 5N	105 52 E
Paktīā □	**65**	33 0N	69 15 E
Pakwach	**90**	2 28N	31 27 E
Pala, Chad	**81**	9 25N	15 5 E
Pala, Zaïre	**90**	6 45 S	29 30 E
Palabek	**90**	3 22N	32 33 E
Palacios	**117**	28 44N	96 12W
Palafrugell	**32**	41 55N	3 10 E
Palagiano	**41**	40 35N	17 0 E
Palagonía	**41**	37 20N	14 43 E
Palagruža	**39**	42 24N	16 15 E
Palaiokastron	**45**	35 12N	26 18 E
Palaiokhóra	**45**	35 16N	23 39 E
Pálairos	**45**	38 45N	20 51 E
Palais, Le	**18**	47 20N	3 10W
Palakol	**70**	16 31N	81 46 E
Palam	**70**	19 0N	77 0 E
Palamás	**44**	39 26N	22 4 E
Palamós	**32**	41 50N	3 10 E
Palampur	**68**	32 10N	76 30 E
Palana, Austral.	**99**	39 45 S	147 55 E
Palana, U.S.S.R.	**59**	59 10N	159 59 E
Palanan	**73**	17 8N	122 29 E
Palanan Pt.	**73**	17 17N	122 30 E
Palangkaraya	**72**	2 16 S	113 56 E
Palanpur	**68**	24 10N	72 25 E
Palapye	**92**	22 30 S	27 7 E
Palar →	**70**	12 27N	80 13 E
Palatka, U.S.A.	**115**	29 40N	81 40W
Palatka, U.S.S.R.	**59**	60 6N	150 54 E
* Palau Is.	**94**	7 30N	134 30 E
Palauig	**73**	15 26N	119 54 E
Palauk	**71**	13 10N	98 40 E
Palavas	**20**	43 32N	3 56 E
Palawan	**72**	9 30N	118 30 E
Palayancottai	**70**	8 45N	77 45 E
Palazzo San Gervásio	**41**	40 53N	15 58 E
Palazzolo Acreide	**41**	37 4N	14 54 E
Paldiski	**54**	59 23N	24 9 E
Pale	**42**	43 50N	18 38 E
Paleleh	**73**	1 10N	121 50 E
Palembang	**72**	3 0 S	104 50 E
Palencia	**30**	42 1N	4 34W
Palencia □	**30**	42 31N	4 33W
Palermo, Italy	**40**	38 8N	13 20 E
Palermo, U.S.A.	**118**	39 30N	121 37W
Palestine, Asia	**62**	32 0N	35 0 E
Palestine, U.S.A.	**117**	31 42N	95 35W
Palestrina	**40**	41 50N	12 52 E
Paletwa	**67**	21 10N	92 50 E
Palghat	**70**	10 46N	76 42 E
Pali	**68**	25 50N	73 20 E
Palinuro, C.	**41**	40 1N	15 14 E
Palisade	**116**	40 21N	101 10W
Palitana	**68**	21 32N	71 49 E
Palizada	**120**	18 18N	92 8W
Palizzi	**41**	37 58N	15 59 E
Palk Bay	**70**	9 30N	79 15 E
Palk Strait	**70**	10 0N	79 45 E
Palkonda	**70**	18 36N	83 48 E
Palkonda Ra.	**70**	13 50N	79 20 E
Pallanza = Verbánia	**38**	45 50N	8 55 E
Pallasovka	**55**	50 4N	47 0 E
Palleru →	**70**	16 45N	80 2 E
Pallisa	**90**	1 12N	33 43 E
Pallu	**68**	28 59N	74 14 E
Palm Beach	**115**	26 46N	80 0W
Palm Is.	**97**	18 40 S	146 35 E
Palm Springs	**119**	33 51N	116 35W
Palma, Canary Is.	**8**	28 40N	17 50W
Palma, Mozam.	**91**	10 46 S	40 29 E
Palma →	**127**	12 33 S	47 52W
Palma, B. de	**33**	39 30N	2 39 E
Palma de Mallorca	**32**	39 35N	2 39 E
Palma del Río	**31**	37 43N	5 17W
Palma di Montechiaro	**40**	37 12N	13 46 E
Palma, La, Canary Is.	**80**	28 40N	17 50W
Palma, La, Panama	**121**	8 15N	78 0W
Palma, La, Spain	**31**	37 21N	6 38W
Palma Soriano	**121**	20 15N	76 0W
Palmahim	**62**	31 56N	34 44 E
Palmanova	**39**	45 54N	13 18 E
Palmares	**127**	8 41 S	35 28W
Palmarola	**40**	40 57N	12 50 E
Palmas	**125**	26 29 S	52 0W
Palmas, C.	**84**	4 27N	7 46W
Pálmas, G. di	**40**	39 0N	8 30 E
Palmdale	**119**	34 36N	118 7W
Palmeira dos Índios	**127**	9 25 S	36 37W
Palmeirinhas, Pta. das	**88**	9 2 S	12 57 E
Palmela	**31**	38 32N	8 57W
Palmer, Alaska, U.S.A.	**104**	61 35N	149 10W
Palmer, Mass., U.S.A.	**113**	42 9N	72 21W
Palmer →, N. Terr., Austral.	**96**	24 46 S	133 25 E
Palmer →, Queens., Austral.	**98**	15 34 S	142 26 E
Palmer Arch	**5**	64 15 S	65 0W
Palmer Lake	**116**	39 10N	104 52W
Palmer Land	**5**	73 0 S	60 0W
Palmerston	**112**	43 50N	80 51W
Palmerston, C.	**97**	21 32 S	149 29 E
Palmerston North	**101**	40 21 S	175 39 E
Palmerton	**113**	40 47N	75 36W
Palmetto	**115**	27 33N	82 33W
Palmi	**41**	38 21N	15 51 E
Palmira, Argent.	**124**	32 59 S	68 34W
Palmira, Colomb.	**126**	3 32N	76 16W
Palms	**112**	43 37N	82 47W
Palmyra, Mo., U.S.A.	**116**	39 45N	91 30W
Palmyra, N.Y., U.S.A.	**112**	42 5N	77 18W
Palmyra = Tudmur	**64**	34 30N	37 17 E
Palmyra Is.	**95**	5 52N	162 6W
Palni	**70**	10 30N	77 30 E
Palni Hills	**70**	10 14N	77 33 E
Palo Alto	**119**	37 25N	122 8W
Palo del Colle	**41**	41 4N	16 43 E
Paloma, La	**124**	30 35 S	71 0W
Palombara Sabina	**39**	42 4N	12 45 E
Palopo	**73**	3 0 S	120 16 E
Palos, Cabo de	**33**	37 38N	0 40W
Palouse	**118**	46 59N	117 5W
Palparara	**98**	24 47 S	141 28 E
Pålsboda	**49**	59 3N	15 22 E
Palu, Indon.	**73**	1 0 S	119 52 E
Palu, Turkey	**64**	38 45N	40 0 E
Paluan	**73**	13 26N	120 29 E
Palwal	**68**	28 8N	77 19 E
Pama	**85**	11 19N	0 44 E
Pamamaroo, L.	**100**	32 17 S	142 28 E
Pamanukan	**73**	6 16 S	107 49 E
Pamban I.	**70**	9 15N	79 20 E
Pamekasan	**73**	7 10 S	113 29 E
Pameungpeuk	**73**	7 38 S	107 44 E
Pamiers	**20**	43 7N	1 39 E
Pamir	**58**	37 40N	73 0 E
Pamlico →	**115**	35 25N	76 30W
Pamlico Sd.	**115**	35 20N	76 0W
Pampa	**117**	35 35N	100 58W
Pampa de las Salinas	**124**	32 1 S	66 58W
Pampa, La □	**124**	36 50 S	66 0W
Pampanua	**73**	4 16 S	120 8 E
Pamparato	**38**	44 16N	7 54 E
Pampas, Argent.	**124**	35 0 S	63 0W
Pampas, Peru	**126**	12 20 S	74 50W
Pamplona, Colomb.	**126**	7 23N	72 39W
Pamplona, Spain	**32**	42 48N	1 38W
Pampoenpoort	**92**	31 3 S	22 40 E
Pana	**116**	39 25N	89 10W
Panaca	**119**	37 51N	114 23W
Panagyurishte	**43**	42 30N	24 15 E
Panaitan	**73**	6 35 S	105 10 E
Panaji (Panjim)	**70**	15 25N	73 50 E
Panamá	**121**	9 0N	79 25W
Panama ■	**121**	8 48N	79 55W
Panama Canal	**121**	9 10N	79 37W
Panama City	**115**	30 10N	85 41W
Panamá, Golfo de	**121**	8 4N	79 20W
Panamint Mts.	**119**	36 30N	117 20W
Panão	**126**	9 55 S	75 55W
Panarea	**41**	38 38N	15 3 E
Panaro →	**38**	44 55N	11 25 E
Panarukan	**73**	7 40 S	113 52 E
Panay	**73**	11 10N	122 30 E
Panay, G.	**73**	11 0N	122 30 E
Pancake Ra.	**119**	38 30N	116 0W
Pančevo	**42**	44 52N	20 41 E
Panciu	**46**	45 54N	27 8 E
Panco	**73**	8 42 S	118 40 E
Pancorbo, Paso	**32**	42 32N	3 5W
Pandan	**73**	11 45N	122 10 E
Pandeglang	**73**	6 25 S	106 0 E
Pandharpur	**70**	17 41N	75 20 E
Pandhurna	**68**	21 36N	78 35 E
Pandilla	**32**	41 32N	3 43W
Pando	**125**	34 44 S	56 0W
Pando, L. = Hope L.	**99**	28 24 S	139 18 E
Panevezys	**54**	55 42N	24 25 E
Panfilov	**58**	44 10N	80 0 E
Panfilovo	**55**	50 25N	42 46 E
Pang-Long	**67**	23 11N	98 45 E
Pang-Yang	**67**	22 7N	98 48 E
Panga	**90**	1 52N	26 18 E
Pangaion Óros	**44**	40 50N	24 0 E
Pangalanes, Canal des	**93**	22 48 S	47 50 E
Pangani	**90**	5 25 S	38 58 E
Pangani □	**90**	5 25 S	39 0 E
Pangani →	**90**	5 26 S	38 58 E
Pangfou = Bengbu	**77**	32 56N	117 20 E
Pangil	**90**	3 10 S	26 35 E
Pangkah, Tanjung	**73**	6 51 S	112 33 E
Pangkalanberandan	**72**	4 1N	98 20 E
Pangkalanbuun	**72**	2 41 S	111 37 E
Pangkalansusu	**72**	4 2N	98 13 E
Pangkoh	**72**	3 5 S	114 8 E
Pangnirtung	**105**	66 8N	65 54W
Pangrango	**73**	6 46 S	107 1 E
Panguitch	**119**	37 52N	112 30W
Pangutaran Group	**73**	6 18N	120 34 E
Panhandle	**117**	35 23N	101 23W
Pani Mines	**68**	22 29N	73 50 E
Pania-Mutombo	**90**	5 11 S	23 51 E
Panipat	**68**	29 25N	77 2 E
Panjal Range	**68**	32 30N	76 50 E
Panjgur	**66**	27 0N	64 5 E
Panjim = Panaji	**70**	15 25N	73 50 E
Panjinad Barrage	**65**	29 22N	71 15 E
Pankajene	**73**	4 46 S	119 34 E
Pankalpinang	**72**	2 0 S	106 0 E
Pankshin	**85**	9 16N	9 25 E
Panna	**69**	24 40N	80 15 E
Panna Hills	**69**	24 40N	81 15 E
Pannuru	**70**	16 5N	80 34 E
Panorama	**125**	21 21 S	51 51W
Panruti	**70**	11 46N	79 35 E
Panshan	**76**	41 3N	122 2 E
Panshi	**76**	42 58N	126 5 E
Pantano	**119**	32 0N	110 32W
Pantar	**73**	8 28 S	124 10 E
Pantelleria	**40**	36 52N	12 0 E
Pantón	**30**	42 31N	7 37W
Pánuco	**120**	22 0N	98 15W
Panyam	**85**	9 27N	9 8 E
Panyu	**77**	22 51N	113 20 E
Páola	**41**	39 21N	16 2 E
Paola	**116**	38 36N	94 50W
Paonia	**119**	38 56N	107 37W
Paoting = Baoding	**76**	38 50N	115 28 E
Paot'ou = Baotou	**76**	40 32N	110 2 E
Paoua	**88**	7 9N	16 20 E
Papá	**27**	47 22N	17 30 E
Papagayo →	**120**	16 36N	99 43W
Papagayo, Golfo de	**121**	10 30N	85 50W
Papagni →	**70**	15 35N	77 45 E
Papakura	**101**	37 4 S	174 59 E
Papantla	**120**	20 30N	97 30W
Papar	**72**	5 45N	116 0 E
Pápas, Ákra	**45**	38 13N	21 20 E
Papenburg	**24**	53 7N	7 25 E
Papigochic →	**120**	29 9N	109 40W
Paposo	**124**	25 0 S	70 30W
Papua, Gulf of	**98**	9 0 S	144 50 E
Papua New Guinea ■	**94**	8 0 S	145 0 E

* *Renamed Belau*

Papuča Penne

Papuča	39	44 22N	15 30 E
Papudo	124	32 29S	71 27W
Papuk	42	45 30N	17 30 E
Papun	67	18 0N	97 30 E
Pará = Belém	127	1 20S	48 30W
Pará □	127	3 20S	52 0W
Parábita	41	40 3N	18 8 E
Paraburdoo	96	23 14S	117 32 E
Paracatu	127	17 10S	46 50W
Parachilna	99	31 10S	138 21 E
Parachinar	66	33 55N	70 5 E
Paraćin	42	43 54N	21 27 E
Paradas	31	37 18N	5 29W
Paradela	30	42 44N	7 37W
Paradip	69	20 15N	86 35 E
Paradise	118	47 27N	114 17W
Paradise ~→	107	53 27N	57 19W
Paradise Valley	118	41 30N	117 28W
Parado	73	8 42S	118 30 E
Paradyż	28	51 19N	20 2 E
Paragould	117	36 5N	90 30W
Paragua ~→	126	6 55N	62 55W
Paragua, La	126	6 50N	63 20W
Paraguaçu ~→	127	12 45S	38 54W
Paraguaçu Paulista	125	22 22S	50 35W
Paraguaná, Pen. de	126	12 0N	70 0W
Paraguarí	124	25 36S	57 0W
Paraguarí □	124	26 0S	57 10W
Paraguay ■	124	23 0S	57 0W
Paraguay ~→	124	27 18S	58 38W
Paraíba = João Pessoa	127	7 10S	35 0W
Paraíba □	127	7 0S	36 0W
Paraíba do Sul ~→	125	21 37S	41 3W
Parainen	51	60 18N	22 18 E
Parakhino Paddubye	54	58 26N	33 10 E
Parakou	85	9 25N	2 40 E
Parálion-Astrous	45	37 25N	22 45 E
Paramagudi	70	9 31N	78 39 E
Paramaribo	127	5 50N	55 10W
Paramithiá	44	39 30N	20 35 E
Paramushir, Ostrov	59	50 24N	156 0 E
Paran ~→	62	30 20N	35 10 E
Paraná	124	31 45S	60 30W
Paranã	127	12 30S	47 48W
Paraná □	125	24 30S	51 0W
Paraná ~→	124	33 43S	59 15W
Paranaguá	125	25 30S	48 30W
Paranaíba ~→	127	20 6S	51 4W
Paranapanema ~→	125	22 40S	53 9W
Paranapiacaba, Serra do	125	24 31S	48 35W
Paranavaí	125	23 4S	52 56W
Parang, Jolo, Phil.	73	5 55N	120 54 E
Parang, Mindanao, Phil.	73	7 23N	124 16 E
Parapóla	45	36 55N	23 27 E
Paraspóri, Ákra	45	35 55N	27 15 E
Paratinga	127	12 40S	43 10W
Paratoo	99	32 42S	139 40 E
Parattah	99	42 22S	147 23 E
Paray-le-Monial	21	46 27N	4 7 E
Parbati ~→	68	25 50N	76 30 E
Parbhani	68	19 8N	76 52 E
Parchim	24	53 25N	11 50 E
Parczew	28	51 40N	22 52 E
Pardes Hanna	62	32 28N	34 57 E
Pardilla	30	41 33N	3 43W
Pardo ~→, Bahia, Brazil	127	15 40S	39 0W
Pardo ~→, Mato Grosso, Brazil	125	21 46S	52 9W
Pardo ~→, São Paulo, Brazil	127	20 10S	48 38W
Pardubice	26	50 3N	15 45 E
Pare	73	7 43S	112 12 E
Pare □	90	4 10S	38 0 E
Pare Mts.	90	4 0S	37 45 E
Parecis, Serra dos	126	13 0S	60 0W
Paredes de Nava	30	42 9N	4 42W
Paren	59	62 30N	163 15 E
Parent	106	47 55N	74 35W
Parent, Lac.	106	48 31N	77 1W
Parentis-en-Born	20	44 21N	1 4W
Parepare	73	4 0S	119 40 E
Parfino	54	57 59N	31 34 E
Parfuri	93	22 28S	31 17 E
Parguba	52	62 20N	34 27 E
Parham	113	44 39N	76 43W
Pariaguán	126	8 51N	64 34W
Pariaman	72	0 47S	100 11 E
Paricutín, Cerro	120	19 28N	102 15W
Parigi, Java, Indon.	73	7 42S	108 29 E
Parigi, Sulawesi, Indon.	73	0 50S	120 5 E
Parika	126	6 50N	58 20W
Parima, Serra	126	2 30N	64 0W
Parinari	126	4 35S	74 25W
Parincea	46	46 27N	27 9 E
Parîng	46	45 20N	23 37 E
Parintins	127	2 40S	56 50W
Pariparit Kyun	67	14 55S	93 45 E
Paris, Can.	106	43 12N	80 25W
Paris, France	19	48 50N	2 20 E
Paris, Idaho, U.S.A.	118	42 13N	111 30W
Paris, Ky., U.S.A.	114	38 12N	84 12W
Paris, Tenn., U.S.A.	115	36 20N	88 20W
Paris, Tex., U.S.A.	117	33 40N	95 30W
Paris, Ville de □	19	48 50N	2 20 E
Parish	113	43 24N	76 9W
Pariti	73	10 15S	123 45 E
Park City	118	40 42N	111 35W
Park Falls	116	45 58N	90 27W
Park Range	118	40 0N	106 30W
Park Rapids	116	46 56N	95 0W
Park River	116	48 25N	97 43W
Park Rynie	93	30 25S	30 45 E
Park View	119	36 45N	106 37W
Parker, Ariz., U.S.A.	119	34 8N	114 16W
Parker, S.D., U.S.A.	116	43 25N	97 7W
Parker Dam	119	34 13N	114 5W
Parkersburg	114	39 18N	81 31W
Parkerview	109	51 21N	103 18W
Parkes, A.C.T., Austral.	97	35 18S	149 8 E
Parkes, N.S.W., Austral.	97	33 9S	148 11 E
Parkside	109	53 10N	106 33W
Parkston	116	43 25N	98 0W
Parksville	108	49 20N	124 21W
Parlakimedi	70	18 45N	84 5 E
Parma, Italy	38	44 50N	10 20 E
Parma, Idaho, U.S.A.	118	43 49N	116 59W
Parma, Ohio, U.S.A.	112	41 25N	81 42W
Parma ~→	38	44 56N	10 26 E
Parnaguá	127	10 10S	44 38W
Parnaíba, Piauí, Brazil	127	2 54S	41 47W
Parnaíba, São Paulo, Brazil	127	19 34S	51 14W
Parnaíba ~→	127	3 0S	41 50W
Parnassós	45	38 35N	22 30 E
Párnis	45	38 14N	23 45 E
Párnon Óros	45	37 15N	22 45 E
Pärnu	54	58 28N	24 33 E
Parola	68	20 47N	75 7 E
Paroo ~→	97	31 28S	143 32 E
Paroo Chan.	97	30 50S	143 35 E
Páros, Greece	45	37 5N	25 9 E
Páros, Greece	45	37 5N	25 12 E
Parowan	119	37 54N	112 56W
Parpaillon	21	44 30N	6 40 E
Parral	124	36 10S	71 52W
Parramatta	99	33 48S	151 1 E
Parras	120	25 30N	102 20W
Parrett ~→	13	51 7N	2 58W
Parris I.	115	32 20N	80 30W
Parrsboro	107	45 30N	64 25W
Parry Is.	4	77 0N	110 0W
Parry Sound	106	45 20N	80 0W
Parsberg	25	49 10N	11 43 E
Parseta ~→	28	54 11N	15 34 E
Parshall	116	47 56N	102 11W
Parsnip ~→	108	55 10N	123 2W
Parsons	117	37 20N	95 17W
Partabpur	70	20 0N	80 42 E
Partanna	40	37 43N	12 51 E
Partapgarh	68	24 2N	74 40 E
Parthenay	18	46 38N	0 16W
Partinico	40	38 3N	13 6 E
Partur	70	19 40N	76 14 E
Paru ~→	127	1 33S	52 38W
Parur	70	10 13N	76 14 E
Paruro	126	13 45S	71 50W
Parván □	65	35 0N	69 0 E
Parvatipuram	70	18 50N	83 25 E
Parys	92	26 52S	27 29 E
Pas-de-Calais □	19	50 30N	2 30 E
Pasadena, Calif., U.S.A.	119	34 5N	118 9W
Pasadena, Tex., U.S.A.	117	29 45N	95 14W
Pasaje	126	3 23S	79 50W
Pasaje ~→	124	25 39S	63 56W
Pascagoula	117	30 21N	88 30W
Pascagoula ~→	117	30 21N	88 35W
Paşcani	46	47 14N	26 45 E
Pasco	118	46 10N	119 0W
Pasco, Cerro de	126	10 45S	76 10W
Pasewalk	24	53 30N	14 0 E
Pasfield L.	109	58 24N	105 20W
Pasha ~→	54	60 29N	32 55 E
Pashmakli = Smolyan	43	41 36N	24 38 E
Pasing	25	48 9N	11 27 E
Pasir Mas	71	6 2N	102 8 E
Pasir Puteh	71	5 50N	102 24 E
Pasirian	73	8 13S	113 8 E
Pasłęka ~→	28	54 26N	19 46 E
Pasley, C.	96	33 52S	123 35 E
Pašman	39	43 58N	15 20 E
Pasni	66	25 15N	63 27 E
Paso de Indios	128	43 55S	69 0W
Paso de los Libres	124	29 44S	57 10W
Paso de los Toros	124	32 45S	56 30W
Paso Robles	119	35 40N	120 45W
Paspébiac	107	48 3N	65 17W
Pasrur	68	32 16N	74 43 E
Passage West	15	51 52N	8 20W
Passaic	113	40 50N	74 8W
Passau	25	48 34N	13 27 E
Passero, C.	41	36 42N	15 8 E
Passo Fundo	125	28 10S	52 20W
Passos	127	20 45S	46 37W
Passow	24	53 13N	14 10 E
Passy	21	45 55N	6 41 E
Pastaza ~→	126	4 50S	76 52W
Pastęk	28	54 3N	19 41 E
Pasto	126	1 13N	77 17W
Pastrana	32	40 27N	2 53W
Pasuruan	73	7 40S	112 44 E
Pasym	28	53 48N	20 49 E
Pásztó	27	47 52N	19 43 E
Patagonia, Argent.	128	45 0S	69 0W
Patagonia, U.S.A.	119	31 35N	110 45W
Patan, Gujarat, India	70	17 22N	73 57 E
Patan, Maharashtra, India	68	23 54N	72 14 E
Patani	73	0 20N	128 50 E
Pataudi	68	28 18N	76 48 E
Patay	19	48 2N	1 40 E
Patchewollock	99	35 22S	142 12 E
Patchogue	114	40 46N	73 1W
Patea	101	39 45S	174 30 E
Pategi	85	8 50N	5 45 E
Patensie	92	33 46S	24 49 E
Paternò	41	37 34N	14 53 E
Paternoster, Kepulauan	72	7 5S	118 15 E
Pateros	118	48 4N	119 58W
Paterson, Austral.	100	32 37S	151 39 E
Paterson, U.S.A.	114	40 55N	74 10W
Pathankot	68	32 18N	75 45 E
Pathfinder Res.	118	42 30N	107 0W
Pati	73	6 45S	111 3 E
Patiala	68	30 23N	76 26 E
Patine Kouka	84	12 45N	13 45W
Patkai Bum	67	27 0N	95 30 E
Pátmos	45	37 21N	26 36 E
Patna	69	25 35N	85 12 E
Patonga	90	2 45N	33 15 E
Patos de Minas	127	18 35S	46 32W
Patos, Lag. dos	125	31 20S	51 0 E
Patosi	44	40 42N	19 38 E
Patquia	124	25 30N	102 11W
Pátrai	45	38 14N	21 47 E
Pátraikós, Kólpos	45	38 17N	21 30 E
Patrocínio	127	18 57S	47 0W
Patta	90	2 10S	41 0 E
Pattada	40	40 35N	9 7 E
Pattanapuram	70	9 6N	76 50 E
Pattani	71	6 48N	101 15 E
Patten	107	45 59N	68 28W
Patterson, Calif., U.S.A.	119	37 30N	121 9W
Patterson, La., U.S.A.	117	29 44N	91 20W
Patti, India	68	31 17N	74 54 E
Patti, Italy	41	38 8N	14 57 E
Pattoki	68	31 5N	73 52 E
Patton	112	40 38N	78 40W
Pattukkottai	70	10 25N	79 20 E
Patuakhali	69	22 20N	90 25 E
Patuca ~→	121	15 50N	84 18W
Patuca, Punta	121	15 49N	84 14W
Pátzcuaro	120	19 30N	101 40W
Pau	20	43 19N	0 25W
Pau, Gave de	20	43 33N	1 12W
Pauillac	20	45 11N	0 46W
Pauini ~→	126	1 42S	62 50W
Pauk	67	21 27N	94 30 E
Paul I.	107	56 30N	61 20W
Paulhan	20	43 33N	3 28 E
Paulis = Isiro	90	2 47N	27 37 E
Paulistana	127	8 9S	41 9W
Paullina	116	42 55N	95 40W
Paulo Afonso	127	9 21S	38 15W
Paulpietersburg	93	27 23S	30 50 E
Pauls Valley	117	34 40N	97 17W
Pauni	69	20 48N	79 40 E
Pavelets	55	53 49N	39 14 E
Pavia	38	45 10N	9 10 E
Pavlikeni	43	43 14N	25 20 E
Pavlodar	58	52 33N	77 0 E
Pavlograd	56	48 30N	35 52 E
Pavlovo, Gorkiy, U.S.S.R.	55	55 58N	43 5 E
Pavlovo, Yakut A.S.S.R., U.S.S.R.	59	63 5N	115 25 E
Pavlovsk	55	50 26N	40 5 E
Pavlovskaya	57	46 17N	39 47 E
Pavlovskiy-Posad	55	55 47N	38 42 E
Pavullo nel Frignano	38	44 20N	10 50 E
Pawhuska	117	36 40N	96 25W
Pawling	113	41 35N	73 37W
Pawnee	117	36 24N	96 50W
Pawnee City	116	40 8N	96 10W
Pawtucket	114	41 51N	71 22W
Paximádhia	45	35 0N	24 35 E
Paxoí	44	39 14N	20 12 E
Paxton, Ill., U.S.A.	114	40 25N	88 7W
Paxton, Nebr., U.S.A.	116	41 12N	101 27W
Paya Bakri	71	2 3N	102 44 E
Payakumbah	72	0 20S	100 35 E
Payerne	25	46 49N	6 56 E
Payette	118	44 0N	117 0W
Paymogo	31	37 44N	7 21W
Payne L.	105	59 30N	74 30W
Paynesville, Liberia	84	6 20N	10 45W
Paynesville, U.S.A.	116	45 21N	94 44W
Pays Basque	20	43 15N	1 0W
Paysandú	124	32 19S	58 8W
Payson, Ariz., U.S.A.	119	34 17N	111 15W
Payson, Utah, U.S.A.	118	40 8N	111 41W
Paz ~→	120	13 44N	90 10W
Paz, Bahía de la	120	24 15N	110 25W
Paz, La, Entre Ríos, Argent.	124	30 50S	59 45W
Paz, La, San Luis, Argent.	124	33 30S	67 20W
Paz, La, Boliv.	126	16 20S	68 10W
Paz, La, Hond.	120	14 20N	87 47W
Paz, La, Mexico	120	24 10N	110 20W
Pazar	64	41 10N	40 50 E
Pazardzhik	43	42 12N	24 20 E
Pazin	39	45 14N	13 56 E
Pčinja ~→	42	41 50N	21 45 E
Pe Ell	118	46 30N	123 18W
Peabody	113	42 31N	70 56W
Peace ~→	108	59 0N	111 25W
Peace Point	108	59 7N	112 27W
Peace River	108	56 15N	117 18W
Peach Springs	119	35 36N	113 30W
Peak Downs	98	22 14S	148 0 E
Peak Hill	99	32 47S	148 11 E
Peak Range	97	22 50S	148 20 E
Peak, The	12	53 24N	1 53W
Peake	99	35 25S	140 0 E
Peake Mt.	119	38 25N	109 12W
Pearce	119	31 57N	109 56W
Pearl ~→	117	30 23N	89 45W
Pearl Banks	70	8 45N	79 45 E
Pearl City	110	21 24N	158 0W
Pearsall	117	28 55N	99 8W
Pearse I.	108	54 52N	130 14W
Peary Land	4	82 40N	33 0W
Pease ~→	117	34 12N	99 7W
Pebane	91	17 10S	38 8 E
Pebas	126	3 10S	71 46W
Peć	42	42 40N	20 17 E
Péccioli	38	43 32N	10 43 E
Pechea	46	45 36N	27 49 E
Pechenezhin	56	48 30N	24 48 E
Pechenga	52	69 30N	31 25 E
Pechnezhskoye Vdkhr.	55	50 0N	37 10 E
Pechora ~→	52	68 13N	54 15 E
Pechorskaya Guba	52	68 40N	54 0 E
Pechory	54	57 48N	27 40 E
Pecica	42	46 10N	21 3 E
Pečka	42	44 18N	19 33 E
Pécora, C.	40	39 28N	8 23 E
Pecos	117	31 25N	103 35W
Pecos ~→	117	29 42N	102 30W
Pécs	27	46 5N	18 15 E
Peddapalli	70	18 40N	79 24 E
Peddapuram	70	17 6N	8 13 E
Pedra Azul	127	16 2S	41 17W
Pedreiras	127	4 32S	44 40W
Pedrera, La	126	1 18S	69 43W
Pedro Afonso	127	9 0S	48 10W
Pedro Cays	121	17 5N	77 48W
Pedro de Valdivia	124	22 55S	69 38W
Pedro Juan Caballero	125	22 30S	55 40W
Pedro Miguel Locks	120	9 1N	79 36W
Pedro Muñoz	33	39 25N	2 56W
Pedrógão Grande	30	39 55N	8 9W
Peduyim	62	31 20N	34 37 E
Peebinga	99	34 52S	140 57 E
Peebles	14	55 40N	3 12W
Peekskill	114	41 18N	73 57W
Peel	12	54 14N	4 40W
Peel ~→, Austral.	99	30 50S	150 29 E
Peel ~→, Can.	104	67 0N	135 0W
Peene ~→	24	54 9N	13 46 E
Peera Peera Poolanna L.	99	26 30S	138 0 E
Peers	108	53 40N	116 0W
Pegasus Bay	101	43 20S	173 10 E
Peggau	26	47 12N	15 21 E
Pegnitz	25	49 45N	11 33 E
Pegnitz ~→	25	49 29N	10 59 E
Pego	33	38 51N	0 8W
Pegu Yoma	67	19 0N	96 0 E
Pehčevo	42	41 41N	22 55 E
Pehuajó	124	35 45S	62 0W
Peine, Chile	124	23 45S	68 8W
Peine, Ger.	24	52 19N	10 12 E
Peip'ing = Beijing	76	39 55N	116 20 E
Peiss	25	47 58N	11 47 E
Peissenberg	25	47 48N	11 4 E
Peitz	24	51 50N	14 23 E
Peixe	127	12 0S	48 40W
Pek ~→	42	44 45N	21 29 E
Pekalongan	73	6 53S	109 40 E
Pekan	71	3 30N	103 25 E
Pekin	116	40 35N	89 40W
Peking = Beijing	76	39 55N	116 20 E
Pelabuhan Ratu, Teluk	73	7 5S	106 30 E
Pelabuhanratu	73	7 0S	106 32 E
Pélagos	44	39 17N	24 4 E
Pelaihari	72	3 55S	114 45 E
Pelat, Mont	21	44 16N	6 42 E
Pełczyce	28	53 3N	15 16 E
Peleaga	46	45 22N	22 55 E
Pelee I.	106	41 47N	82 40W
Pelée, Mt.	121	14 48N	61 0W
Pelee, Pt.	106	41 54N	82 31W
Pelekech, mt.	90	3 52N	35 8 E
Peleng	73	1 20S	123 30 E
Pelham	115	31 5N	84 6W
Pelhřimov	26	49 24N	15 12 E
Pelican L.	109	52 28N	100 20W
Pelican Narrows	109	55 10N	102 56W
Pelican Portage	108	55 51N	112 35W
Pelican Rapids	109	52 45N	100 42W
Peljesac	42	42 55N	17 25 E
Pelkosenniemi	50	67 6N	27 28 E
Pella, Greece	44	40 46N	22 23 E
Pella, U.S.A.	116	41 30N	93 0W
Pélla □	44	40 52N	22 0 E
Péllaro	41	38 1N	15 40 E
Pellworm	24	54 30N	8 40 E
Pelly ~→	104	62 47N	137 19W
Pelly Bay	105	68 38N	89 50W
Pelly L.	104	66 0N	102 0W
Peloponnes = Pelóponnisos □	45	37 10N	22 0 E
Pelopónnisos □	45	37 10N	22 0 E
Peloritani, Monti	41	38 2N	15 25 E
Peloro, C.	41	38 15N	15 40 E
Pelorus Sound	101	40 59S	173 59 E
Pelotas	125	31 42S	52 23W
Pelôvo	43	43 26N	24 17 E
Pelvoux, Massif de	21	44 52N	6 20 E
Pemalang	73	6 53S	109 23 E
Pematang	72	0 12S	102 4 E
Pematangsiantar	72	2 57N	99 5 E
Pemba, Mozam.	91	12 58S	40 30 E
Pemba, Tanz.	90	5 0S	39 45 E
Pemba, Zambia	91	16 30S	27 28 E
Pemba Channel	90	5 0S	39 37 E
Pemberton, Austral.	96	34 30S	116 0 E
Pemberton, Can.	108	50 25N	122 50W
Pembina	109	48 58N	97 15W
Pembina ~→	109	49 0N	98 12W
Pembine	114	45 38N	87 59W
Pembino	116	48 58N	97 15W
Pembroke, Can.	106	45 50N	77 7W
Pembroke, U.K.	13	51 41N	4 57W
Pembroke, U.S.A.	115	32 5N	81 32W
Pen-y-Ghent	12	54 10N	2 15W
Peña de Francia, Sierra de	30	40 32N	6 10W
Peña, Sierra de la	32	42 32N	0 45W
Penafiel	30	41 12N	8 17W
Peñafiel	30	41 35N	4 7W
Peñaflor	31	37 43N	5 21W
Peñalara, Pico	30	40 51N	3 57W
Penamacôr	30	40 10N	7 10W
Penang = Pinang	71	5 25N	100 15 E
Penápolis	125	21 30S	50 0W
Peñaranda de Bracamonte	30	40 53N	5 13W
Peñarroya-Pueblonuevo	31	38 19N	5 16W
Peñas, C. de	30	43 42N	5 52W
Peñas de San Pedro	33	38 44N	2 0W
Penas, G. de	128	47 0S	75 0W
Peñausende	30	41 17N	5 52W
Pench'i = Benxi	76	41 20N	123 48 E
Pend Oreille ~→	118	49 4N	117 37W
Pend Oreille, L.	118	48 0N	116 30W
Pendálofon	44	40 14N	21 12 E
Pendelikón	45	38 10N	23 53 E
Pendembu	84	9 7N	12 14W
Pendleton	118	45 35N	118 50W
Penedo	127	10 15S	36 36W
Penetanguishene	106	44 50N	79 55W
Pengalengan	73	7 9S	107 30 E
Penge, Kasai Oriental, Congo	90	5 30S	24 33 E
Penge, Kivu, Congo	90	4 27S	28 25 E
Penglai	76	37 48N	120 42 E
Pengshui	77	29 17N	108 12 E
Penguin	99	41 8S	146 6 E
Penhalonga	91	18 52S	32 40 E
Peniche	31	39 19N	9 22W
Penicuik	14	55 50N	3 14W
Penida	72	8 45S	115 30 E
Peñíscola	32	40 22N	0 24 E
Penmarch	18	47 49N	4 21W
Penmarch, Pte. de	18	47 48N	4 22W
Pennabilli	39	43 50N	12 17 E
Pennant	109	50 32N	108 14W
Penne	39	42 28N	13 56 E

Pennel Glacier Piorini, L.

Pennel Glacier **5** 69 20 S 157 27 E
Penner → **70** 14 35N 80 10 E
Pennine, Alpi **38** 46 4N 7 30 E
Pennines **12** 54 50N 2 20W
Pennino, Mte. **39** 43 6N 12 54 E
Pennsylvania □ **114** 40 50N 78 0W
Penny **108** 53 51N 121 20W
Pennyan **114** 42 39N 77 7W
Peno **54** 57 2N 32 49 E
Penola **97** 37 25 S 140 21 E
Penong **96** 31 59 S 133 5 E
Penonomé **121** 8 31N 80 21W
Penrhyn Is. **95** 9 0 S 158 30W
Penrith, Austral. **97** 33 43 S 150 38 E
Penrith, U.K. **12** 54 40N 2 45W
Pensacola **115** 30 30N 87 10W
Pensacola Mts. **5** 84 0 S 40 0W
Pense **109** 50 25N 104 59W
Penshurst **99** 37 49 S 142 20 E
Penticton **108** 49 30N 119 38W
Pentland **97** 20 32 S 145 25 E
Pentland Firth **14** 58 43N 3 10W
Pentland Hills **14** 55 48N 3 25W
Penukonda **70** 14 5N 77 38 E
Penylan L. **109** 61 50N 106 20W
Penza **55** 53 15N 45 5 E
Penzance **13** 50 7N 5 32W
Penzberg **25** 47 46N 11 23 E
Penzhino **59** 63 30N 167 55 E
Penzhinskaya Guba **59** 61 30N 163 0 E
Penzlin **24** 53 32N 13 6 E
Peoria, Ariz., U.S.A. **119** 33 40N 112 15W
Peoria, Ill., U.S.A. **116** 40 40N 89 40W
Pepperwood **118** 40 23N 124 0W
Peqini **44** 41 4N 19 44 E
Pera Hd. **98** 12 55 S 141 37 E
Perabumiiih **72** 3 27 S 104 15 E
Perak → **71** 5 10N 101 4 E
Perakhóra **45** 38 2N 22 56 E
Perales de Alfambra **32** 40 38N 1 0W
Perales del Puerto **30** 40 10N 6 40W
Peralta **32** 42 21N 1 49W
Pérama **45** 35 20N 24 40 E
Perast **42** 42 31N 18 47 E
Percé **107** 48 31N 64 13W
Perche **18** 48 31N 1 1 E
Perche, Collines du **18** 48 30N 0 40 E
Percy **18** 48 55N 1 11W
Percy Is. **98** 21 39 S 150 16 E
Pereira **126** 4 49N 75 43W
Perekerten **99** 34 55 S 143 40 E
Perekop **56** 46 10N 33 42 E
Pereslavi-Zalesskiy **55** 56 45N 38 50 E
Pereyaslav Khmelnitskiy **54** 50 3N 31 28 E
Pérez, I. **120** 22 24N 89 42W
Perg **26** 48 15N 14 38 E
Pergamino **124** 33 52 S 60 30W
Pérgine Valsugano **39** 46 4N 11 15 E
Pérgola **39** 43 35N 12 50 E
Perham **116** 46 36N 95 36W
Perhentian, Kepulauan **71** 5 54N 102 42 E
Periam **42** 46 2N 20 59 E
Péribonca → **107** 48 45N 72 5W
Péribonca, L. **107** 50 1N 71 10W
Perico **124** 24 20 S 65 5W
Pericos **120** 25 3N 107 42W
Périers **18** 49 11N 1 25W
Périgord **20** 45 0N 0 40 E
Périgueux **20** 45 10N 0 42 E
Perijá, Sierra de **126** 9 30N 73 3W
Peristéra **45** 39 15N 23 58 E
Periyakulam **70** 10 5N 77 30 E
Periyar → **70** 10 15N 76 10 E
Periyar, L. **70** 9 25N 77 10 E
Perkam, Tg. **73** 1 35 S 137 50 E
Perković **39** 43 41N 16 10 E
Perlas, Arch. de las **121** 8 41N 79 7W
Perlas, Punta de **121** 12 30N 83 30W
Perleberg **24** 53 5N 11 50 E
Perlevka **55** 51 48N 38 57 E
Perlez **42** 45 11N 20 22 E
Perlis □ **71** 6 30N 100 15 E
Perm (Molotov) **52** 58 0N 57 10 E
Përmeti **44** 40 15N 20 21 E
Pernambuco = Recife **127** 8 0 S 35 0W
Pernambuco □ **127** 8 0 S 37 0W
Pernik **42** 42 35N 23 2 E
Péronne **19** 49 55N 2 57 E
Perosa Argentina **38** 44 57N 7 11 E
Perow **108** 54 35N 126 10W
Perpendicular Pt. **99** 31 37 S 152 52 E
Perpignan **20** 42 42N 2 53 E
Perros-Guirec **18** 48 49N 3 28W
Perry, Fla., U.S.A. **115** 30 9N 83 40W
Perry, Ga., U.S.A. **115** 32 25N 83 41W
Perry, Iowa, U.S.A. **116** 41 48N 94 5W
Perry, Maine, U.S.A. **115** 44 59N 67 20W
Perry, Okla., U.S.A. **117** 36 20N 97 20W
Perryton **117** 36 28N 100 48W
Perryville **117** 37 42N 89 50W
Persberg **48** 59 47N 14 15 E
Persepolis **65** 29 55N 52 50 E
Persia = Iran ■ **65** 35 0N 50 0 E
Persian Gulf **65** 27 0N 50 0 E
Perstorp **49** 56 10N 13 25 E
Perth, Austral. **96** 31 57 S 115 52 E
Perth, Can. **106** 44 55N 76 15W
Perth, U.K. **14** 56 24N 3 27W
Perth Amboy **114** 40 31N 74 16W
Perthus, Le **20** 42 30N 2 53 E
Pertuis **21** 43 42N 5 30 E
Peru, Ill., U.S.A. **116** 41 18N 89 12W
Peru, Ind., U.S.A. **114** 40 42N 86 0W
Peru ■ **126** 8 0 S 75 0W
Peru-Chile Trench **95** 20 0 S 72 0W
Perúgia **39** 43 6N 12 24 E
Perušić **39** 44 40N 15 22 E
Pervomaysk, R.S.F.S.R., U.S.S.R. **55** 54 56N 43 58 E
Pervomaysk, Ukraine S.S.R., U.S.S.R. **56** 48 10N 30 46 E
Pervouralsk **52** 56 55N 60 0 E
Pésaro **39** 43 55N 12 53 E
Pescara **39** 42 28N 14 13 E
Pescara → **39** 42 28N 14 13 E
Peschanokopskoye **57** 46 14N 41 4 E
Péscia **38** 43 54N 10 40 E
Pescina **39** 42 0N 13 39 E
Peshawar **66** 34 2N 71 37 E
* Peshawar □ **66** 33 30N 71 20 E
Peshkopia **44** 41 41N 20 25 E
Peshtera **43** 42 2N 24 18 E
Peshtigo **114** 45 4N 87 46W
Peski **55** 51 14N 42 29 E
Peskovka **55** 59 23N 52 20 E
Pêso da Régua **30** 41 10N 7 47W
Pesqueira **127** 8 20 S 36 42W
Pesqueria → **120** 25 54N 99 11W
Pessac **20** 44 48N 0 37W
Pest □ **27** 47 29N 19 5 E
Pestovo **54** 58 33N 35 42 E
Pestravka **55** 52 28N 49 57 E
Péta **45** 39 10N 21 2 E
Petah Tiqwa **62** 32 6N 34 53 E
Petalidhion **45** 36 57N 21 55 E
Petaling Jaya **71** 3 4N 101 42 E
Petaluma **118** 38 13N 122 39W
Petange **16** 49 33N 5 55 E
Petatlán **120** 17 31N 101 16W
Petauke **91** 14 14 S 31 20 E
Petawawa **106** 45 54N 77 17W
Petén Itzá, Lago **120** 16 58N 89 50W
Peter 1st, I. **5** 69 0 S 91 0W
Peter Pond L. **109** 55 55N 108 44W
Peterbell **106** 48 36N 83 21W
Peterborough, Austral. **97** 32 58 S 138 51 E
Peterborough, Can. **112** 44 20N 78 20W
Peterborough, U.K. **13** 52 35N 0 14W
Peterborough, U.S.A. **113** 42 55N 71 59W
Peterhead **14** 57 30N 1 49W
Petersburg, Alas., U.S.A. **108** 56 50N 133 0W
Petersburg, Ind., U.S.A. **114** 38 30N 87 15W
Petersburg, Va., U.S.A. **114** 37 17N 77 26W
Petersburg, W. Va., U.S.A. **114** 38 59N 79 10W
Petford **98** 17 20 S 144 58 E
Petília Policastro **41** 39 7N 16 48 E
Petit Bois I. **115** 30 16N 88 25W
Petit-Cap **107** 48 3N 64 30W
Petit Goâve **121** 18 27N 72 51W
Petit-Quevilly, Le **18** 49 26N 1 0 E
Petit Saint Bernard, Col du **38** 45 40N 6 52 E
Petitcodiac **107** 45 57N 65 11W
Petite Baleine → **106** 55 50N 77 0W
Petite Saguenay **107** 48 15N 70 4W
Petitsikapau, L. **107** 54 37N 66 25W
Petlad **68** 22 30N 72 45 E
Peto **120** 20 10N 88 53W
Petone **101** 41 13 S 174 53 E
Petoskey **106** 45 22N 84 57W
Petra, Jordan **62** 30 20N 35 22 E
Petra, Spain **32** 39 37N 3 6 E
Petra, Ostrova **4** 76 15N 118 30 E
Petralia **41** 37 49N 14 4 E
Petrel **33** 38 30N 0 46W
Petrich **43** 41 24N 23 13 E
Petrijanec **39** 46 23N 16 17 E
Petrikov **54** 52 11N 28 29 E
Petrila **46** 45 29N 23 29 E
Petrinja **39** 45 28N 16 18 E
Petrolândia **127** 9 5 S 38 20W
Petrolia **106** 42 54N 82 9W
Petrolina **127** 9 24 S 40 30W
Petromagoúla **45** 38 31N 23 0 E
Petropavlovsk **58** 54 53N 69 13 E
Petropavlovsk-Kamchatskiy **59** 53 3N 158 43 E
Petrópolis **125** 22 33 S 43 9W
Petroşeni **46** 45 28N 23 20 E
Petroskey **114** 45 22N 84 57W
Petrova Gora **39** 45 15N 15 45 E
Petrovac, Crna Gora, Yugo. **42** 42 13N 18 57 E
Petrovac, Srbija, Yugo. **42** 44 22N 21 26 E
Petrovaradin **42** 45 16N 19 55 E
Petrovsk **55** 52 22N 45 19 E
Petrovsk-Zabaykalskiy **59** 51 20N 108 55 E
Petrovskoye = Svetlograd **57** 45 25N 42 58 E
Petrozavodsk **52** 61 41N 34 20 E
Petrus Steyn **93** 27 38 S 28 8 E
Petrusburg **92** 29 4 S 25 26 E
Petukhovka **54** 53 42N 30 54 E
Peumo **124** 34 21 S 71 12W
Peureulak **72** 4 48N 97 45 E
Pevek **59** 69 41N 171 19 E
Peveragno **38** 44 20N 7 37 E
Peyrehorade **20** 43 34N 1 7W
Peyruis **21** 44 1N 5 56 E
Pézenas **20** 43 28N 3 24 E
Pezinok **27** 48 17N 17 17 E
Pfaffenhofen **25** 48 31N 11 31 E
Pfarrkirchen **25** 48 25N 12 57 E
Pfeffenhausen **25** 48 40N 11 58 E
Pforzheim **25** 48 53N 8 43 E
Pfullendorf **25** 47 55N 9 15 E
Pfungstadt **25** 49 47N 8 36 E
Phala **92** 23 45 S 26 50 E
Phalodi **68** 27 12N 72 24 E
Phalsbourg **19** 48 46N 7 15 E
Phan Rang **71** 11 34N 109 0 E
Phan Thiet **71** 11 1N 108 9 E
Phanae **45** 38 8N 25 87 E
Phangan, Ko **71** 9 45N 100 0 E
Phangnga **71** 8 28N 98 30 E
Phanh Bho Ho Chi Minh **71** 10 58N 106 40 E
Pharenda **69** 27 5N 83 17 E
Phatthalung **71** 7 39N 100 6 E
Phelps, N.Y., U.S.A. **112** 42 57N 77 5W
Phelps, Wis., U.S.A. **116** 46 2N 89 2W
Phelps L. **109** 59 15N 103 15W
Phenix City **115** 32 30N 85 0W
Phetchabun **71** 16 25N 101 8 E
Phetchabun, Thiu Khao **71** 16 0N 101 20 E
Phetchaburi **71** 13 1N 99 55 E
Phichai **71** 17 22N 100 10 E
Philadelphia, Miss., U.S.A. **117** 32 47N 89 5W
Philadelphia, N.Y., U.S.A. **113** 44 9N 75 40W
Philadelphia, Pa., U.S.A. **114** 40 0N 75 10W
Philip **116** 44 4N 101 42W
Philippeville **16** 50 12N 4 33 E
Philippi **44** 41 1N 24 16 E
Philippi L. **98** 24 20 S 138 55 E
Philippines ■ **73** 12 0N 123 0 E
Philippolis **92** 30 15 S 25 16 E
Philippopolis = Plovdiv **43** 42 8N 24 44 E
Philipsburg, Mont., U.S.A. **118** 46 20N 113 21W
Philipsburg, Pa., U.S.A. **112** 40 53N 78 10W
Philipstown **92** 30 28 S 24 30 E
Phillip **97** 38 30 S 145 12 E
Phillips, Texas, U.S.A. **117** 35 48N 101 17W
Phillips, Wis., U.S.A. **116** 45 41N 90 22W
Phillipsburg, Kans., U.S.A. **116** 39 48N 99 20W
Phillipsburg, Pa., U.S.A. **113** 40 43N 75 12W
Phillott **99** 27 53 S 145 50 E
Philmont **113** 42 14N 73 37W
Philomath **118** 44 28N 123 21W
Phitsanulok **71** 16 50N 100 12 E
Phnom Dangrek **71** 14 20N 104 0 E
Phnom Penh **71** 11 33N 104 55 E
Phnom Thbeng **71** 13 50N 104 56 E
Phoenix, Ariz., U.S.A. **119** 33 30N 112 10W
Phoenix, N.Y., U.S.A. **113** 43 13N 76 18W
Phoenix Is. **94** 3 30 S 172 0W
Phoenixville **113** 40 12N 75 29W
Phong Saly **71** 21 42N 102 9 E
Phra Chedi Sam Ong **71** 15 16N 98 23 E
Phra Nakhon Si Ayutthaya **71** 14 25N 100 30 E
Phrae **71** 18 7N 100 9 E
Phrao **71** 19 23N 99 15 E
Phu Doan **71** 21 40N 105 10 E
Phu Loi **71** 20 14N 103 14 E
Phu Ly **71** 20 35N 105 50 E
Phu Qui **71** 19 20N 105 20 E
Phuket **71** 7 52N 98 22 E
Phulera (Phalera) **68** 26 52N 75 16 E
† Phuoc Le **71** 10 30N 107 10 E
Piacenza **38** 45 2N 9 42 E
Piádena **38** 45 8N 10 22 E
Pialba **97** 25 20 S 152 45 E
Pian Cr. → **99** 30 2 S 148 12 E
Piana **21** 42 15N 8 34 E
Pianella **39** 42 24N 14 5 E
Pianoro **39** 44 20N 11 20 E
Pianosa, Puglia, Italy **39** 42 12N 15 44 E
Pianosa, Toscana, Italy **38** 42 36N 10 4 E
Piapot **109** 49 59N 109 8W
Piare → **39** 45 32N 12 44 E
Pias **31** 38 1N 7 29W
Piaseczno **28** 52 5N 21 2 E
Piaski **28** 51 8N 22 52 E
Piastów **28** 52 12N 20 48 E
Piatra **46** 43 51N 25 9 E
Piatra Neamţ **46** 46 56N 26 21 E
Piatra Olt **46** 44 22N 24 16 E
Piauí □ **127** 7 0 S 43 0W
Piave → **39** 45 32N 12 44 E
Piazza Ármerina **41** 37 21N 14 20 E
Pibor → **87** 7 35N 33 0 E
Pibor Post **87** 6 47N 33 3 E
Pica **126** 20 35 S 69 25W
Picardie **19** 50 0N 2 15 E
Picardie, Plaine de **19** 50 0N 2 0 E
Picardy = Picardie **19** 50 0N 2 15 E
Picayune **117** 30 31N 89 40W
Picerno **41** 40 40N 15 37 E
Pichilemu **124** 34 22 S 72 0W
Pickerel L. **106** 48 40N 91 25W
Pickle Lake **106** 51 30N 90 12W
Pico **8** 38 28N 28 18W
Pico Truncado **128** 46 40 S 68 0W
Picos Ancares, Sierra de **30** 42 51N 6 52W
Picquigny **19** 49 56N 2 10 E
Picton, Austral. **99** 34 12 S 150 34 E
Picton, Can. **106** 44 1N 77 9W
Picton, N.Z. **101** 41 18 S 174 3 E
Pictou **107** 45 41N 62 42W
Picture Butte **108** 49 55N 112 45W
Picún Leufú **128** 39 30 S 69 5W
Pidurutalagala **70** 7 10N 80 50 E
Piedad, La **120** 20 20N 102 1W
Piedicavallo **38** 45 41N 7 57 E
Piedmont **115** 33 55N 85 39W
Piedmont = Piemonte **38** 45 0N 7 30 E
Piedmont Plat. **115** 34 0N 81 30W
Piedmonte d'Alife **41** 41 22N 14 22 E
Piedra → **32** 41 18N 1 47W
Piedrabuena **31** 39 0N 4 10W
Piedrahita **30** 40 28N 5 23W
Piedras Blancas Pt. **119** 35 45N 121 18W
Piedras Negras **120** 28 35N 100 35W
Piedras, R. de las → **126** 12 30 S 69 15W
Piemonte □ **38** 45 0N 7 30 E
Piensk **28** 51 16N 15 2 E
Pierce **118** 46 29N 115 53W
Piercefield **113** 44 13N 74 35W
Piería □ **44** 40 13N 22 25 E
Pierre, France **19** 46 54N 5 13 E
Pierre, U.S.A. **116** 44 23N 100 20W
Pierre Benite, Barrage **21** 45 42N 4 49 E
Pierrefeu **21** 43 8N 6 9 E
Pierrefonds **19** 49 20N 3 0 E
Pierrefontaine **19** 47 14N 6 32 E
Pierrefort **20** 44 55N 2 50 E
Pierrelatte **21** 44 23N 4 43 E
Pieštany **27** 48 38N 17 55 E
Piesting → **27** 48 6N 16 40 E
Pieszyce **28** 50 43N 16 33 E
Piet Retief **93** 27 1 S 30 50 E
Pietarsaari **50** 63 40N 22 43 E
Pietermaritzburg **93** 29 35 S 30 25 E
Pietersburg **93** 23 54 S 29 25 E
Pietraperzia **41** 37 26N 14 8 E
Pietrasanta **38** 43 57N 10 12 E
Pietrosu **46** 47 12N 25 8 E
Pietrosul **46** 47 35N 24 43 E
Pieve di Cadore **39** 46 25N 12 22 E
Pieve di Teco **38** 44 3N 7 54 E
Pievepélago **38** 44 12N 10 35 E
Pigádhia **45** 35 30N 27 12 E
Pigadhítsa **44** 39 59N 21 23 E
Pigeon **114** 43 50N 83 17W
Pigeon I. **70** 14 2N 74 20 E
Piggott **117** 36 20N 90 10W
Pigna **38** 43 57N 7 40 E
Pigüe **124** 37 36 S 62 25W
Pihani **69** 27 36N 80 15 E
Pikalevo **54** 59 37N 34 0 E
Pikes Peak **116** 38 50N 105 10W
Piketberg **92** 32 55 S 18 40 E
Pikeville **114** 37 30N 82 30W
Pikwitonei **109** 55 35N 97 9W
Piła **28** 53 10N 16 48 E
Pila **33** 38 16N 1 11W
Piła □ **28** 53 0N 17 0 E
Pilaía **44** 40 32N 22 59 E
Pilani **68** 28 22N 75 33 E
Pilar, Brazil **127** 9 36 S 35 56W
Pilar, Parag. **124** 26 50 S 58 20W
Pilas **73** 6 39N 121 37 E
Pilawa **28** 51 57N 21 32 E
Pilbara **96** 21 15 S 118 16 E
Pilcomayo → **124** 25 21 S 57 42W
Pili **45** 36 50N 27 15 E
Pilibhit **69** 28 40N 79 50 E
Pilica → **28** 51 52N 21 17 E
Pilion **44** 39 27N 23 7 E
Pilis **27** 47 17N 19 35 E
Pilisvörösvár **27** 47 38N 18 56 E
Pilkhawa **68** 28 43N 77 42 E
Pilos **45** 36 55N 21 42 E
Pilot Mound **109** 49 15N 98 54W
Pilot Point **117** 33 26N 97 0W
Pilot Rock **118** 45 30N 118 50W
Pilsen = Plzen **26** 49 45N 13 22 E
Pilštanj **39** 46 8N 15 39 E
Pilzno **27** 50 0N 21 16 E
Pima **119** 32 54N 109 50W
Pimba **97** 31 18 S 136 46 E
Pimenta Bueno **126** 11 35 S 61 10W
Pimentel **126** 6 45 S 79 55W
Pina **32** 41 29N 0 33W
Pinang **71** 5 25N 100 15 E
Pinar del Río **121** 22 26N 83 40W
Pinaroo **97** 35 17 S 140 53 E
Pincehely **27** 46 41N 18 27 E
Pincher Creek **108** 49 30N 113 57W
Pinchi L. **108** 54 38N 124 30W
Pinckneyville **116** 38 5N 89 20W
Pincota **42** 46 20N 21 45 E
Pińczów **28** 50 32N 20 32 E
Pind Dadan Khan **68** 32 36N 73 7 E
Pindiga **85** 9 58N 10 53 E
Pindos Óros **44** 40 0N 21 0 E
Pindus Mts. = Pindos Óros **44** 40 0N 21 0 E
Pine **119** 34 27N 111 30W
Pine → **109** 58 50N 105 38W
Pine Bluff **117** 34 10N 92 0W
Pine, C. **107** 46 37N 53 32W
Pine City **116** 45 46N 93 0W
Pine Creek **96** 13 50 S 132 10 E
Pine Falls **109** 50 34N 96 11W
Pine, La **118** 43 40N 121 30W
Pine Pass **108** 55 25N 122 42W
Pine Point **108** 60 50N 114 28W
Pine Ridge **116** 43 0N 102 35W
Pine River, Can. **109** 51 45N 100 30W
Pine River, U.S.A. **116** 46 43N 94 24W
Pinedale **119** 34 23N 110 16W
Pinega → **52** 64 8N 46 54 E
Pinehill **98** 23 38 S 146 57 E
Pinerolo **38** 44 47N 7 21 E
Pineto **39** 42 36N 14 4 E
Pinetop **119** 34 10N 109 57W
Pinetown **93** 29 48 S 30 54 E
Pinetree **118** 43 42N 105 52W
Pineville, Ky., U.S.A. **115** 36 42N 83 42W
Pineville, La., U.S.A. **117** 31 22N 92 30W
Piney **19** 48 22N 4 21 E
Ping → **71** 15 42N 100 9 E
Pingding **76** 37 47N 113 38 E
Pingdingshan **77** 33 43N 113 27 E
Pingdong **75** 22 39N 120 30 E
Pingdu **76** 36 42N 119 59 E
Pingguo **77** 23 19N 107 36 E
Pinghe **77** 24 17N 117 21 E
Pingjiang **77** 28 45N 113 36 E
Pingle **77** 24 40N 110 40 E
Pingliang **76** 35 35N 106 31 E
Pingluo **76** 38 52N 106 30 E
Pingnan **77** 23 33N 110 22 E
Pingtan Dao **77** 25 29N 119 47 E
Pingwu **75** 32 25N 104 30 E
Pingxiang, Guangxi Zhuangzu, China **75** 22 6N 106 46 E
Pingxiang, Jiangxi, China **77** 27 43N 113 48 E
Pingyao **76** 37 12N 112 10 E
Pinhal **125** 22 10 S 46 46W
Pinhel **30** 40 50N 7 1W
Pini **72** 0 10N 98 40 E
Piniós →, Ilia, Greece **45** 37 48N 21 20 E
Piniós →, Trikkala, Greece **44** 39 55N 22 10 E
Pinjarra **96** 32 37 S 115 52 E
Pink → **109** 56 50N 103 50W
Pinkafeld **27** 47 22N 16 9 E
Pinneberg **24** 53 39N 9 48 E
Pinos **120** 22 20N 101 40W
Pinos, I. de **121** 21 40N 82 40W
Pinos Pt. **119** 36 38N 121 57W
Pinos Puente **31** 37 15N 3 45W
Pinrang **73** 3 46 S 119 41 E
Pinsk **54** 52 10N 26 1 E
Pintados **126** 20 35 S 69 40W
Pinyang **77** 27 42N 120 31 E
Pinyug **52** 60 5N 48 0 E
Pinzolo **38** 46 9N 10 45 E
Pioche **119** 38 0N 114 35W
Piombino **38** 42 54N 10 30 E
Piombino, Canale di **38** 42 50N 10 25 E
Pioner, Os. **59** 79 50N 92 0 E
Pionki **28** 51 29N 21 28 E
Piorini, L. **126** 3 15 S 62 35W

* *Now part of North West Frontier* □

† *Renamed Ba Ria*

Piotrków Trybunalski — Porreras

Piotrków Trybunalski 28 51 23N 19 43 E
Piotrków Trybunalski □ 28 51 30N 19 45 E
Piove di Sacco 39 45 18N 12 1 E
Pīp 65 26 45N 60 10 E
Pipar 68 26 25N 73 31 E
Pipariya 68 22 45N 78 23 E
Pipéri 44 39 20N 24 19 E
Pipestone 116 44 0N 96 20W
Pipestone → 106 52 53N 89 23W
Pipestone Cr. → 109 49 42N 100 45W
Pipmuacan, Rés. 107 49 45N 70 30W
Pipriac 18 47 49N 1 58W
Piqua 114 40 10N 84 10W
Piquiri → 125 24 3 S 54 14W
Piracicaba 125 22 45 S 47 40W
Piracuruca 127 3 50 S 41 50W
Piræus = Piraiévs 45 37 57N 23 42 E
Piraiévs 45 37 57N 23 42 E
Piraiévs □ 45 37 0N 23 30 E
Piráino 41 38 10N 14 52 E
Pirajuí 125 21 59 S 49 29W
Piran (Pirano) 39 45 31N 13 33 E
Pirané 124 25 42 S 59 6W
Pirapora 127 17 20 S 44 56W
Pirdop 43 42 40N 24 10 E
Pirganj 69 25 51N 88 24 E
Pírgos, Ilia, Greece 45 37 40N 21 27 E
Pírgos, Messinia, Greece 45 36 50N 22 16 E
Pirgovo 43 43 44N 25 43 E
Piriac-sur-Mer 18 47 22N 2 33W
Piribebuy 124 25 26 S 57 2W
Pirin Planina 43 41 40N 23 30 E
Pirineos 32 42 40N 1 0 E
Piripiri 127 4 15 S 41 46W
Pirmasens 25 49 12N 7 30 E
Pirna 24 50 57N 13 57 E
Pirojpur 69 22 35N 90 1 E
Pirot 42 43 9N 22 39 E
Pirtleville 119 31 25N 109 35W
Piru 73 3 4 S 128 12 E
Piryatin 54 50 15N 32 25 E
Piryí 45 38 13N 25 59 E
Pisa 38 43 43N 10 23 E
Pisa → 28 53 14N 21 52 E
Pisagua 126 19 40 S 70 15W
Pisarovina 39 45 35N 15 50 E
Pisciotta 41 40 7N 15 12 E
Pisco 126 13 50 S 76 12W
Piscu 46 45 30N 27 43 E
Písek 26 49 19N 14 10 E
Pishan 75 37 30N 78 33 E
Pising 73 5 8 S 121 53 E
Pissos 20 44 19N 0 49W
Pisticci 41 40 24N 16 33 E
Pistóia 38 43 57N 10 53 E
Pistol B. 109 62 25N 92 37W
Pisuerga → 30 41 33N 4 52W
Pisz 28 53 38N 21 49 E
Pitarpunga, L. 99 34 24 S 143 30 E
Pitcairn I. 95 25 5 S 130 5W
Pite älv → 50 65 20N 21 25 E
Piteå 50 65 20N 21 25 E
Piterka 55 50 41N 47 29 E
Piteşti 46 44 52N 24 54 E
Pithapuram 70 17 10N 82 15 E
Pithion 44 41 24N 26 40 E
Pithiviers 19 48 10N 2 13 E
Pitigliano 39 42 38N 11 40 E
Pitlochry 14 56 43N 3 43W
Pitt I. 108 53 30N 129 50W
Pittsburg, Calif., U.S.A. 118 38 1N 121 50W
Pittsburg, Kans., U.S.A. 117 37 21N 94 43W
Pittsburg, Tex., U.S.A. 117 32 59N 94 58W
Pittsburgh 114 40 25N 79 55W
Pittsfield, Ill., U.S.A. 116 39 35N 90 46W
Pittsfield, Mass., U.S.A. 114 42 28N 73 17W
Pittsfield, N.H., U.S.A. 113 43 17N 71 18W
Pittston 114 41 19N 75 50W
Pittsworth 99 27 41 S 151 37 E
Pituri → 98 22 35 S 138 30 E
Piura 126 5 15 S 80 38W
Piva → 42 43 20N 18 50 E
Piwniczna 27 49 27N 20 42 E
Piyai 44 39 17N 21 25 E
Pizzo 41 38 44N 16 10 E
Placentia 107 47 20N 54 0W
Placentia B. 107 47 0N 54 40W
Placerville 118 38 47N 120 51W
Placetas 121 22 15N 79 44W
Plačkovica 42 41 45N 22 30 E
Plain Dealing 117 32 56N 93 41W
Plainfield 114 40 37N 74 28W
Plains, Kans., U.S.A. 117 37 20N 100 35W
Plains, Mont., U.S.A. 118 47 27N 114 57W
Plains, Tex., U.S.A. 117 33 11N 102 50W
Plainview, Nebr., U.S.A. 116 42 25N 97 48W
Plainview, Tex., U.S.A. 117 34 10N 101 40W
Plainville 116 39 18N 99 19W
Plainwell 114 42 28N 85 40W
Plaisance 20 43 36N 0 3 E
Pláka 44 40 0N 25 24 E
Plakenska Planina 42 41 14N 21 2 E
Plakhino 58 67 45N 86 5 E
Planá 26 49 50N 12 44 E
Plancoët 18 48 32N 2 13W
Plandište 42 45 16N 21 10 E
Planina, Slovenija, Yugo. 39 46 10N 15 20 E
Planina, Slovenija, Yugo. 39 45 47N 14 19 E
Plankinton 116 43 45N 98 27W
Plano 117 33 0N 96 45W
Plant City 115 28 0N 82 8W
Plant, La 116 45 11N 100 40W
Plaquemine 117 30 20N 91 15W
Plasencia 30 40 3N 6 8W
Plaški 39 45 4N 15 22 E
Plassen 48 61 9N 12 30 E
Plaster Rock 107 46 53N 67 22W
Plata, La 124 35 0 S 57 55W
Plata, Río de la 124 34 45 S 57 30W
Platani → 40 37 23N 13 16 E
Plateau 5 79 55 S 40 0 E
Plateau □ 85 8 0N 8 30 E
Plateau du Coteau du Missouri 116 47 9N 101 5W
Platí, Ákra- 44 40 27N 24 0 E
Plato 126 9 47N 74 47W
Platte 116 43 28N 98 50W
Platte → 116 39 16N 94 50W
Platteville 116 40 18N 104 47W
Plattling 25 48 46N 12 53 E
Plattsburg 114 44 41N 73 30W
Plattsmouth 116 41 0N 95 50W
Plau 24 53 27N 12 16 E
Plauen 24 50 29N 12 9 E
Plav 42 42 38N 19 57 E
Plavinas 54 56 35N 25 46 E
Plavnica 42 42 20N 19 13 E
Plavsk 55 53 40N 37 18 E
Playgreen L. 109 54 0N 98 15W
Pleasant Bay 107 46 51N 60 48W
Pleasant Hill 116 38 48N 94 14W
Pleasanton 117 29 0N 98 30W
Pleasantville 114 39 25N 74 30W
Pléaux 20 45 8N 2 13 E
Pleiku (Gia Lai) 71 13 57N 108 0 E
Plélan-le-Grand 18 48 0N 2 7W
Plémet 18 48 11N 2 36W
Pléneuf-Val-André 18 48 35N 2 32W
Pleniţa 46 44 14N 23 10 E
Plenty, Bay of 101 37 45 S 177 0 E
Plentywood 116 48 45N 104 35W
Plesetsk 52 62 40N 40 10 E
Plessisville 107 46 14N 71 47W
Plestin-les-Grèves 18 48 40N 3 39W
Pleszew 28 51 53N 17 47 E
Pleternica 42 45 17N 17 48 E
Pletipi L. 107 51 44N 70 6W
Pleven 43 43 26N 24 37 E
Plevlja 42 43 21N 19 21 E
Ploče 42 43 4N 17 26 E
Płock 28 52 32N 19 40 E
Płock □ 28 52 30N 19 45 E
Plöcken Passo 39 46 37N 12 57 E
Ploëmeur 18 47 44N 3 26W
Ploërmel 18 47 55N 2 26W
Ploieşti 46 44 57N 26 5 E
Plomárion 45 38 58N 26 24 E
Plomb du Cantal 20 45 2N 2 48 E
Plombières 19 47 59N 6 27 E
Plomin 39 45 8N 14 10 E
Plön 24 54 8N 10 22 E
Plöner See 24 45 10N 10 22 E
Plonge, Lac La 109 55 8N 107 20W
Płońsk 28 52 37N 20 21 E
Płoty 28 53 48N 15 18 E
Plouaret 18 48 37N 3 28W
Plouay 18 47 55N 3 21W
Ploučnice → 26 50 46N 14 13 E
Ploudalmézeau 18 48 34N 4 41W
Plougasnou 18 48 42N 3 49W
Plouha 18 48 41N 2 57W
Plouhinec 18 48 0N 4 29W
Plovdiv 43 42 8N 24 44 E
Plum I. 113 41 10N 72 12W
Plummer 118 47 21N 116 59W
Plumtree 91 20 27 S 27 55 E
Plunge 54 55 53N 21 59 E
Pluvigner 18 47 46N 3 1W
Plymouth, U.K. 13 50 23N 4 9W
Plymouth, Ind., U.S.A. 114 41 20N 86 19W
Plymouth, Mass., U.S.A. 113 41 58N 70 40W
Plymouth, N.C., U.S.A. 115 35 54N 76 46W
Plymouth, N.H., U.S.A. 113 43 44N 71 41W
Plymouth, Pa., U.S.A. 113 41 17N 76 0W
Plymouth, Wis., U.S.A. 114 43 42N 87 58W
Plymouth Sd. 13 50 20N 4 10W
Plynlimon = Pumlumon Fawr 13 52 29N 3 47W
Plyussa 54 58 40N 29 20 E
Plyussa → 54 58 40N 29 0 E
Plzen 26 49 45N 13 22 E
Pniewy 28 52 31N 16 16 E
Pô 85 11 14N 1 5W
Po → 38 44 57N 12 4 E
Po, Foci del 39 44 55N 12 30 E
Po Hai = Bo Hai 76 39 0N 120 0 E
Pobé 85 7 0N 2 56 E
Pobeda 59 65 12N 146 12 E
Pobedino 59 49 51N 142 49 E
Pobedy Pik 58 40 45N 79 58 E
Pobiedziska 28 52 29N 17 11 E
Pobla de Lillet, La 32 42 16N 1 59 E
Pobla de Segur 32 42 15N 0 58 E
Pobladura de Valle 30 42 6N 5 44W
Pocahontas, Arkansas, U.S.A. 117 36 18N 91 0W
Pocahontas, Iowa, U.S.A. 116 42 41N 94 42W
Pocatello 118 42 50N 112 25W
Počátky 26 49 15N 15 14 E
Pochep 54 52 58N 33 29 E
Pochinki 55 54 41N 44 59 E
Pochinok 54 54 28N 32 29 E
Pöchlarn 26 48 12N 15 12 E
Pochontas 108 53 10N 117 51W
Pochutla 120 15 50N 96 31W
Pocomoke City 114 38 4N 75 32W
Poços de Caldas 125 21 50 S 46 33W
Poddebice 28 51 54N 18 58 E
Poděbrady 26 50 9N 15 8 E
Podensac 20 44 40N 0 22W
Podgorač 42 45 27N 18 13 E
Podgorica = Titograd 42 42 30N 19 19 E
Podkamennaya Tunguska → 59 61 50N 90 13 E
Podlapac 39 44 37N 15 47 E
Podmokly 26 50 48N 14 10 E
Podoleni 46 46 46N 26 39 E
Podolínec 27 49 16N 20 31 E
Podolsk 55 55 25N 37 30 E
Podor 84 16 40N 15 2W
Podporozhy 52 60 55N 34 2 E
Podravska Slatina 42 45 42N 17 45 E
Podu Turcului 46 46 11N 27 25 E
Podujevo 42 42 54N 21 10 E
Poel 24 54 0N 11 25 E
Pofadder 92 29 10 S 19 22 E
Pogamasing 106 46 55N 81 50W
Poggiardo 41 40 3N 18 21 E
Poggibonsi 39 43 27N 11 8 E
Pogoanele 46 44 55N 27 0 E
Pogorzela 28 51 50N 17 12 E
Pogradeci 44 40 57N 20 37 E
Poh 73 0 46 S 122 51 E
Pohang 76 36 1N 129 23 E
Pohorelá 27 48 50N 20 2 E
Pohořelice 27 48 59N 16 31 E
Pohorje 39 46 30N 15 20 E
Poiana Mare 46 43 57N 23 5 E
Poiana Ruscăi, Munţii 46 45 45N 22 25 E
Poinsett, C. 5 65 42 S 113 18 E
Point Edward 106 43 0N 82 30W
Point Pedro 70 9 50N 80 15 E
Point Pleasant, U.S.A. 113 40 5N 74 4W
Point Pleasant, W. Va., U.S.A. 114 38 50N 82 7W
Pointe-à-la Hache 117 29 35N 89 55W
Pointe-à-Pitre 121 16 10N 61 30W
Pointe Noire 88 4 48 S 11 53 E
Poirino 38 44 55N 7 50 E
Poissy 19 48 55N 2 0 E
Poitiers 18 46 35N 0 20 E
Poitou, Plaines et Seuil du 20 46 30N 0 1W
Poix 19 49 47N 2 0 E
Poix-Terron 19 49 38N 4 38 E
Pojoaque 119 35 55N 106 0W
Pokataroo 99 29 30 S 148 36 E
Poko, Sudan 87 5 41N 31 55 E
Poko, Zaïre 90 3 7N 26 52 E
Pokrov 55 55 55N 39 7 E
Pokrovsk 59 61 29N 126 12 E
Pol 30 43 9N 7 20W
Pola de Allande 30 43 16N 6 37W
Pola de Gordón, La 30 42 51N 5 41W
Pola de Lena 30 43 10N 5 49W
Pola de Siero 30 43 24N 5 39W
Pola de Somiedo 30 43 5N 6 15W
Polacca 119 35 52N 110 25W
Polan 65 25 30N 61 10 E
Poland ■ 28 52 0N 20 0 E
Polanów 28 54 7N 16 41 E
Polar Sub-Glacial Basin 5 85 0 S 110 0 E
Polcura 124 37 17 S 71 43W
Połczyn Zdrój 28 53 47N 16 5 E
Polden Hills 13 51 7N 2 50W
Polessk 54 54 50N 21 8 E
Polevskoy 52 56 26N 60 11 E
Polewali, Sulawesi, Indon. 73 4 8 S 119 43 E
Polewali, Sulawesi, Indon. 73 3 21 S 119 23 E
Polgar 27 47 54N 21 6 E
Poli 88 8 34N 13 15 E
Poliaigos 45 36 45N 24 38 E
Policastro, Golfo di 41 39 55N 15 35 E
Police 28 53 33N 14 33 E
Polička 27 49 43N 16 15 E
Polignano a Mare 41 41 0N 17 12 E
Poligny 19 46 50N 5 42 E
Políkhnitas 45 39 4N 26 10 E
Polillo Is. 73 14 56N 122 0 E
Polístena 41 38 25N 16 4 E
Políyiros 44 40 23N 23 25 E
Polk 112 41 22N 79 57W
Polkowice 28 51 29N 16 3 E
Polla 41 40 31N 15 27 E
Pollachi 70 10 35N 77 0 E
Pollensa 32 39 54N 3 1 E
Pollensa, B. de 32 39 53N 3 8 E
Póllica 41 40 13N 15 3 E
Pollino, Mte. 41 39 54N 16 13 E
Pollock 116 45 58N 100 18W
Polna 54 58 31N 28 0 E
Polnovat 58 63 50N 65 54 E
Polo 116 42 0N 89 38W
Pologi 56 47 29N 36 15 E
Polonnoye 54 50 6N 27 30 E
Polotsk 54 55 30N 28 50 E
Polski Trŭmbesh 43 43 20N 25 38 E
Polsko Kosovo 43 43 23N 25 38 E
Polson 118 47 45N 114 12W
Poltava 56 49 35N 34 35 E
Polunochnoye 52 60 52N 60 25 E
Polur 70 12 32N 79 11 E
Polyanovgrad 43 42 39N 26 59 E
Polyarny 52 69 8N 33 20 E
Polynesia 95 10 0 S 162 0W
Pomarance 38 43 18N 10 51 E
Pomarico 41 40 31N 16 33 E
Pombal, Brazil 127 6 45 S 37 50W
Pombal, Port. 30 39 55N 8 40W
Pómbia 45 35 0N 24 51 E
Pomeroy, Ohio, U.S.A. 114 39 0N 82 0W
Pomeroy, Wash., U.S.A. 118 46 30N 117 33W
Pomona 119 34 2N 117 49W
Pomorie 43 42 32N 27 41 E
Pomoshnaya 56 48 13N 31 36 E
Pompano Beach 115 26 12N 80 6W
Pompei 41 40 45N 14 30 E
Pompey 19 48 50N 6 2 E
Pompeys Pillar 118 46 0N 108 0W
Ponape 94 6 55N 158 10 E
Ponask, L. 106 54 0N 92 41W
Ponass L. 109 52 16N 103 58W
Ponca 116 42 38N 96 41W
Ponca City 117 36 40N 97 5W
Ponce 121 18 1N 66 37W
Ponchatoula 117 30 27N 90 25W
Poncheville, L. 106 50 10N 76 55W
Poncin 21 46 6N 5 25 E
Pond Inlet 105 72 40N 77 0W
Pondicherry 70 11 59N 79 50 E
Pondoland 93 31 10 S 29 30 E
Ponds, I. of 107 53 27N 55 52W
Ponferrada 30 42 32N 6 35W
Pongo, Wadi → 87 8 42N 27 40 E
Poniatowa 28 51 11N 22 3 E
Poniec 28 51 48N 16 50 E
Ponikva 39 46 16N 15 26 E
Ponnaiyar → 70 11 50N 79 45 E
Ponnani 70 10 45N 75 59 E
Ponneri 70 13 20N 80 15 E
Ponnyadaung 67 22 0N 94 10 E
Ponoi 52 67 0N 41 0 E
Ponoi → 52 66 59N 41 17 E
Ponoka 108 52 42N 113 40W
Ponorogo 73 7 52 S 111 29 E
Pons, France 20 45 35N 0 34W
Pons, Spain 32 41 55N 1 12 E
Ponsul → 31 39 40N 7 31W
Pont-à-Mousson 19 48 54N 6 1 E
Pont-Audemer 18 49 21N 0 30 E
Pont-Aven 18 47 51N 3 47W
Pont Canavese 38 45 24N 7 33 E
Pont-de-Roide 19 47 23N 6 45 E
Pont-de-Salars 20 44 18N 2 44 E
Pont-de-Vaux 19 46 26N 4 56 E
Pont-de-Veyle 21 46 17N 4 53 E
Pont-l'Abbé 18 47 52N 4 15W
Pont-l'Évêque 18 49 18N 0 11 E
Pont-St-Esprit 21 44 16N 4 40 E
Pont-sur-Yonne 19 48 18N 3 10 E
Ponta Grossa 125 25 7 S 50 10W
Ponta Pora 125 22 20 S 55 35W
Pontacq 20 43 11N 0 8W
Pontailler 19 47 18N 5 24 E
Pontarlier 19 46 54N 6 20 E
Pontassieve 39 43 47N 11 25 E
Pontaubault 18 48 40N 1 20W
Pontaumur 20 45 52N 2 40 E
Pontcharra 21 45 26N 6 1 E
Pontchartrain, L. 117 30 12N 90 0W
Pontchâteau 18 47 25N 2 5W
Ponte da Barca 30 41 48N 8 25W
Ponte de Sor 31 39 17N 7 57W
Ponte dell' Olio 38 44 52N 9 39 E
Ponte di Legno 38 46 15N 10 30 E
Ponte do Lima 30 41 46N 8 35W
Ponte do Pungué 91 19 30 S 34 33 E
Ponte Leccia 21 42 28N 9 13 E
Ponte Macassar 73 9 30 S 123 58 E
Ponte nell' Alpi 39 46 10N 12 18 E
Ponte Nova 125 20 25 S 42 54W
Ponte San Martino 38 45 36N 7 47 E
Ponte San Pietro 38 45 42N 9 35 E
Pontebba 39 46 30N 13 17 E
Pontecorvo 40 41 28N 13 40 E
Pontedera 38 43 40N 10 37 E
Pontefract 12 53 42N 1 19W
Ponteix 109 49 46N 107 29W
Pontelandolfo 41 41 17N 14 41 E
Pontevedra 30 42 26N 8 40W
Pontevedra □ 30 42 25N 8 39W
Pontevedra, R. de → 30 42 22N 8 45W
Pontevico 38 45 16N 10 6 E
Pontiac, Ill., U.S.A. 116 40 50N 88 40W
Pontiac, Mich., U.S.A. 114 42 40N 83 20W
Pontian Kechil 71 1 29N 103 23 E
Pontianak 72 0 3 S 109 15 E
Pontine Is. = Ponziane, Isole 40 40 55N 13 0 E
Pontine Mts. = Karadeniz D. 64 41 30N 35 0 E
Pontínia 40 41 25N 13 2 E
Pontivy 18 48 5N 3 0W
Pontoise 19 49 3N 2 5 E
Ponton → 108 58 27N 116 11W
Pontorson 18 48 34N 1 30W
Pontrémoli 38 44 22N 9 52 E
Pontrieux 18 48 42N 3 10W
Ponts-de-Cé, Les 18 47 25N 0 30W
Pontypool, Can. 112 44 6N 78 38W
Pontypool, U.K. 13 51 42N 3 1W
Pontypridd 13 51 36N 3 21W
Ponza 40 40 55N 12 57 E
Ponziane, Isole 40 40 55N 13 0 E
Poole 13 50 42N 1 58W
Pooley I. 108 52 45N 128 15W
Poona = Pune 70 18 29N 73 57 E
Poonamallee 70 13 3N 80 10 E
Pooncarie 99 33 22 S 142 31 E
Poopelloe, L. 99 31 40 S 144 0 E
Poopó, Lago de 126 18 30 S 67 35W
Popayán 126 2 27N 76 36W
Poperinge 16 50 51N 2 42 E
Popigay 59 72 1N 110 39 E
Popilta, L. 99 33 10 S 141 42 E
Popina 43 44 7N 26 57 E
Popio, L. 99 33 10 S 141 52 E
Poplar 116 48 3N 105 9W
Poplar →, Man., Can. 109 53 0N 97 19W
Poplar →, N.W.T., Can. 108 61 22N 121 52W
Poplar Bluff 117 36 45N 90 22W
Poplarville 117 30 55N 89 30W
Popocatepetl 120 19 10N 98 40W
Popokabaka 88 5 41 S 16 40 E
Pópoli 39 42 12N 13 50 E
Popondetta 98 8 48 S 148 17 E
Popovača 39 45 30N 16 41 E
Popovo 43 43 21N 26 18 E
Poprád 27 49 3N 20 18 E
Poprád → 27 49 38N 20 42 E
Porbandar 68 21 44N 69 43 E
Porcher I. 108 53 50N 130 30W
Porcuna 31 37 52N 4 11W
Porcupine →, Can. 109 59 11N 104 46W
Porcupine →, U.S.A. 104 66 35N 145 15W
Pordenone 39 45 58N 12 40 E
Pordim 43 43 23N 24 51 E
Poreč 39 45 14N 13 36 E
Poretskoye 55 55 9N 46 21 E
Pori 51 61 29N 21 48 E
Pori 45 35 58N 23 13 E
Porjus 50 66 57N 19 50 E
Porkhov 54 57 45N 29 38 E
Porkkala 51 59 59N 24 26 E
Porlamar 126 10 57N 63 51W
Porlezza 38 46 2N 9 8 E
Porma → 30 42 49N 5 28W
Pornic 18 47 7N 2 5W
Poronaysk 59 49 13N 143 0 E
Póros 45 37 30N 23 30 E
Poroshiri-Dake 74 42 41N 142 52 E
Poroszló 27 47 39N 20 40 E
Poroto Mts. 91 9 0 S 33 30 E
Porquerolles, Îles de 21 43 0N 6 13 E
Porrentruy 25 47 25N 7 6 E
Porreras 32 39 31N 3 2 E

Porretta, Passo di | Pripet Marshes

Porretta, Passo di **38** 44 2N 10 56 E
Porsangen **50** 70 40N 25 40 E
Porsgrunn **47** 59 10N 9 40 E
Port **19** 47 43N 6 4 E
Port Adelaide **99** 34 46 S 138 30 E
Port Alberni **108** 49 40N 124 50W
Port Albert **100** 38 42 S 146 42 E
Port Albert Victor **68** 21 0N 71 30 E
Port Alfred, Can. **107** 48 18N 70 53W
Port Alfred, S. Afr. **92** 33 36 S 26 55 E
Port Alice **108** 50 20N 127 25W
Port Allegany **114** 41 49N 78 17W
Port Allen **117** 30 30N 91 15W
Port Alma **98** 23 38 S 150 53 E
Port Angeles **118** 48 7N 123 30W
Port Antonio **121** 18 10N 76 30W
Port Aransas **117** 27 49N 97 4W
Port Arthur, Austral. **97** 43 7 S 147 50 E
Port Arthur, U.S.A. **117** 30 0N 94 0W
Port au Port B. **107** 48 40N 58 50W
Port-au-Prince **121** 18 40N 72 20W
Port Augusta **97** 32 30 S 137 50 E
Port Augusta West **97** 32 29 S 137 29 E
Port Austin **106** 44 3N 82 59W
Port Bell **90** 0 18N 32 35 E
Port Bergé Vaovao **93** 15 33 S 47 40 E
Port Blair **71** 11 40N 92 30 E
Port Blandford **107** 48 20N 54 10W
Port Bolivar **117** 29 20N 94 40W
Port Bou **32** 42 25N 3 9 E
Port Bouët **84** 5 16N 3 57W
Port Bradshaw **97** 12 30 S 137 20 E
Port Broughton **99** 33 37 S 137 56 E
Port Burwell **106** 42 40N 80 48W
Port-Cartier **107** 50 2N 66 50W
Port Chalmers **101** 45 49 S 170 30 E
Port Chester **114** 41 0N 73 41W
Port Clements **108** 53 40N 132 10W
Port Clinton **114** 41 30N 82 58W
Port Colborne **106** 42 50N 79 10W
Port Coquitlam **108** 49 15N 122 45W
Port Credit **112** 43 33N 79 35W
Port Dalhousie **112** 43 13N 79 16W
Port Darwin, Austral. **96** 12 24 S 130 45 E
Port Darwin, Falk. Is. **128** 51 50 S 59 0W
Port Davey **97** 43 16 S 145 55 E
Port-de-Bouc **21** 43 24N 4 59 E
Port-de-Paix **121** 19 50N 72 50W
Port Dickson **71** 2 30N 101 49 E
Port Douglas **98** 16 30 S 145 30 E
Port Dover **112** 42 47N 80 12W
Port Edward **108** 54 12N 130 10W
Port Elgin **106** 44 25N 81 25W
Port Elizabeth **92** 33 58 S 25 40 E
Port Ellen **14** 55 38N 6 10W
Port-en-Bessin **18** 49 21N 0 45W
Port Erin **12** 54 5N 4 45W
Port Etienne = Nouâdhibou **80** 20 54N 17 0W
Port Fairy **97** 38 22 S 142 12 E
Port Fouâd = Bûr Fuad **86** 31 15N 32 20 E
Port-Gentil **88** 0 40 S 8 50 E
Port Gibson **117** 31 57N 91 0W
Port Glasgow **14** 55 57N 4 40W
Port Harcourt **85** 4 40N 7 10 E
Port Hardy **108** 50 41N 127 30W
Port Harrison **105** 58 25N 78 15W
Port Hawkesbury **107** 45 36N 61 22W
Port Hedland **96** 20 25 S 118 35 E
Port Henry **114** 44 0N 73 30W
Port Hood **107** 46 0N 61 32W
Port Hope **106** 43 56N 78 20W
Port Huron **114** 43 0N 82 28W
Port Isabel **117** 26 4N 97 9W
Port Jackson **97** 33 50 S 151 18 E
Port Jefferson **114** 40 58N 73 5W
Port Jervis **113** 41 22N 74 42W
Port-Joinville **18** 46 45N 2 23W
Port Katon **57** 46 52N 38 46 E
Port Kelang **71** 3 0N 101 23 E
Port Kembla **99** 34 52 S 150 49 E
Port-la-Nouvelle **20** 43 1N 3 3 E
Port Laoise **15** 53 2N 7 20W
Port Lavaca **117** 28 38N 96 38W
Port-Leucate-Barcarès **20** 42 53N 3 3 E
Port Lincoln **96** 34 42 S 135 52 E
Port Loko **84** 8 48N 12 46W
Port Louis **18** 47 42N 3 22W
Port Lyautey = Kenitra **82** 34 15N 6 40W
Port Macdonnell **99** 38 0 S 140 48 E
Port Macquarie **97** 31 25 S 152 25 E
Port Maria **121** 18 25N 77 5W
Port Mellon **108** 49 32N 123 31W
Port-Menier **107** 49 51N 64 15W
Port Moresby **94** 9 24 S 147 8 E
Port Mouton **107** 43 58N 64 50W
Port Musgrave **97** 11 55 S 141 50 E
Port-Navalo **18** 47 34N 2 54W
Port Nelson **109** 57 3N 92 36W
Port Nolloth **92** 29 17 S 16 52 E
Port Nouveau-Québec (George River) **105** 58 30N 65 59W
Port O'Connor **117** 28 26N 96 24W
Port of Spain **121** 10 40N 61 31W
Port Orchard **118** 47 31N 122 38W
Port Oxford **118** 42 45N 124 28W
Port Pegasus **101** 47 12 S 167 41 E
Port Perry **106** 44 6N 78 56W
Port Phillip B. **97** 38 10 S 144 50 E
Port Pirie **97** 33 10 S 138 1 E
Port Pólnocny **28** 54 25N 18 42 E
Port Radium = Echo Bay **104** 66 10N 117 40W
Port Renfrew **108** 48 30N 124 20W
Port Rowan **106** 42 40N 80 30W
Port Safaga = Bûr Safâga **86** 26 43N 33 57 E
Port Said = Bûr Sa'îd **86** 31 16N 32 18 E
Port St. Joe **115** 29 49N 85 20W
Port St. Louis **93** 13 7 S 48 48 E
Port-St-Louis-du-Rhône **21** 43 23N 4 49 E
Port Sanilac **106** 43 26N 82 33W
Port Saunders **107** 50 40N 57 18W
Port Severn **112** 44 48N 79 43W
Port Shepstone **93** 30 44 S 30 28 E
Port Simpson **108** 54 30N 130 20W
Port Stanley **106** 42 40N 81 10W
Port Stephens **97** 32 38 S 152 12 E
Port Sudan = Bûr Sûdân **86** 19 32N 37 9 E
Port Talbot **13** 51 35N 3 48W
Port Taufiq = Bûr Taufiq **86** 29 54N 32 32 E
Port Townsend **118** 48 7N 122 50W
Port-Vendres **20** 42 32N 3 8 E
Port Vladimir **52** 69 25N 33 6 E
Port Washington **114** 43 25N 87 52W
Port Weld **71** 4 50N 100 38 E
Portachuelo **126** 17 10 S 63 20W
Portadown **15** 54 27N 6 26W
Portage **116** 43 31N 89 25W
Portage La Prairie **109** 49 58N 98 18W
Portageville **117** 36 25N 89 40W
Portalegre **31** 39 19N 7 25W
Portalegre □ **31** 39 20N 7 40W
Portales **117** 34 12N 103 25W
Portarlington **15** 53 10N 7 10W
Porte, La **114** 41 36N 86 43W
Portel **31** 38 19N 7 41W
Porter L., N.W.T., Can. **109** 61 41N 108 5W
Porter L., Sask., Can. **109** 56 20N 107 20W
Porterville, S. Afr. **92** 33 0 S 18 57 E
Porterville, U.S.A. **119** 36 5N 119 0W
Porthcawl **13** 51 28N 3 42W
Porthill **118** 49 0N 116 30W
Portile de Fier **46** 44 42N 22 30 E
Portimão **31** 37 8N 8 32W
Portland, N.S.W., Austral. **99** 33 20 S 150 0 E
Portland, Victoria, Austral. **97** 38 20 S 141 35 E
Portland, Can. **113** 44 42N 76 12W
Portland, Conn., U.S.A. **113** 41 34N 72 39W
Portland, Me., U.S.A. **107** 43 40N 70 15W
Portland, Mich., U.S.A. **114** 42 52N 84 58W
Portland, Oreg., U.S.A. **118** 45 35N 122 40W
Portland B. **99** 38 15 S 141 45 E
Portland, Bill of **13** 50 31N 2 27W
Portland, C. **97** 40 46 S 148 0 E
Portland, I. of **13** 50 32N 2 25W
Portland Prom. **105** 58 40N 78 33W
Portneuf **107** 46 43N 71 55W
Porto **30** 41 8N 8 40W
Porto □ **30** 41 8N 8 20W
Pôrto Alegre **125** 30 5 S 51 10W
Porto Alexandre **92** 15 55 S 11 55 E
Porto Amboim = Gunza **88** 10 50 S 13 50 E
Porto Argentera **38** 44 15N 7 27 E
Porto Azzurro **38** 42 46N 10 24 E
Porto Botte **40** 39 3N 8 33 E
Porto Civitanova **39** 43 19N 13 44 E
Pôrto de Móz **127** 1 41 S 52 13W
Porto Empédocle **40** 37 18N 13 30 E
Pôrto Esperança **126** 19 37 S 57 29W
Pôrto Franco **127** 6 20 S 47 24W
Porto Garibaldi **39** 44 41N 12 14 E
Porto, G. de **21** 42 17N 8 34 E
Pórto Lágo **44** 40 58N 25 6 E
Porto Mendes **125** 24 30 S 54 15W
Pôrto Murtinho **126** 21 45 S 57 55W
Pôrto Nacional **127** 10 40 S 48 30W
Porto Novo, Benin **85** 6 23N 2 42 E
Porto Novo, India **70** 11 30N 79 38 E
Porto Recanati **39** 43 26N 13 40 E
Porto San Giórgio **39** 43 11N 13 49 E
Porto Santo **80** 33 45N 16 25W
Porto Santo Stefano **38** 42 26N 11 7 E
Pôrto São José **125** 22 43 S 53 10W
Pôrto Seguro **127** 16 26 S 39 5W
Porto Tolle **39** 44 57N 12 20 E
Porto Tórres **40** 40 50N 8 23 E
Pôrto União **125** 26 10 S 51 10W
Pôrto Válter **126** 8 15 S 72 40W
Porto-Vecchio **21** 41 35N 9 16 E
Pôrto Velho **126** 8 46 S 63 54W
Portoferráio **38** 42 50N 10 20 E
Portogruaro **39** 45 47N 12 50 E
Portola **118** 39 49N 120 28W
Portomaggiore **39** 44 41N 11 47 E
Portoscuso **40** 39 12N 8 22 E
Portovénere **38** 44 2N 9 50 E
Portoviejo **126** 1 7 S 80 28W
Portpatrick **14** 54 50N 5 7W
Portree **14** 57 25N 6 11W
Portrush **15** 55 13N 6 40W
Portsall **18** 48 37N 4 45W
Portsmouth, Domin. **121** 15 34N 61 27W
Portsmouth, U.K. **13** 50 48N 1 6W
Portsmouth, N.H., U.S.A. **114** 43 5N 70 45W
Portsmouth, Ohio, U.S.A. **114** 38 45N 83 0W
Portsmouth, R.I., U.S.A. **113** 41 35N 71 15W
Portsmouth, Va., U.S.A. **114** 36 50N 76 20W
Portsoy **14** 57 41N 2 41W
Porttipahta **50** 68 5N 26 40 E
Portugal ■ **30** 40 0N 7 0W
Portugalete **32** 43 19N 3 4W
Portuguese-Guinea = Guinea-Bissau ■ **84** 12 0N 15 0W
Portuguese Timor □ = Timor **73** 8 0 S 126 30 E
Portumna **15** 53 5N 8 12W
Portville **112** 42 3N 78 21W
Porvenir **128** 53 10 S 70 16W
Porvoo **51** 60 24N 25 40 E
Porzuna **31** 39 9N 4 9W
Posada → **40** 40 40N 9 45 E
Posadas, Argent. **125** 27 30 S 55 50W
Posadas, Spain **31** 37 47N 5 11W
Poschiavo **25** 46 19N 10 4 E
Posets **32** 42 39N 0 25 E
Poshan = Boshan **76** 36 28N 117 49 E
Posidhion, Ákra **44** 39 57N 23 30 E
Posidium **45** 35 30N 27 10 E
Poso **73** 1 20 S 120 55 E
Posse **127** 14 4 S 46 18W
Possel **88** 5 5N 19 10 E
Possession I. **5** 72 4 S 172 0 E
Pössneck **24** 50 42N 11 34 E
Post **117** 33 13N 101 21W
Post Falls **118** 47 46N 116 59W
Postavy **54** 55 4N 26 50 E
Poste Maurice Cortier (Bidon 5) **82** 22 14N 1 2 E
Postmasburg **92** 28 18 S 23 5 E
Postojna **39** 45 46N 14 12 E
Potamós, Andikíthira, Greece **45** 36 18N 22 58 E
Potamós, Kíthira, Greece **45** 36 15N 22 58 E
Potchefstroom **92** 26 41 S 27 7 E
Potcoava **46** 44 30N 24 39 E
Poteau **117** 35 5N 94 37W
Poteet **117** 29 4N 98 35W
Potelu, Lacul **46** 43 44N 24 20 E
Potenza **41** 40 40N 15 50 E
Potenza → **39** 43 27N 13 38 E
Potenza Picena **39** 43 22N 13 37 E
Poteriteri, L. **101** 46 5 S 167 10 E
Potes **30** 43 15N 4 42W
Potgietersrus **93** 24 10 S 28 55 E
Poti **57** 42 10N 41 38 E
Potiskum **85** 11 39N 11 2 E
Potlogi **46** 44 34N 25 34 E
Potomac → **114** 38 0N 76 23W
Potosí **126** 19 38 S 65 50W
Pototan **73** 10 54N 122 38 E
Potrerillos **124** 26 30 S 69 30W
Potsdam, Ger. **24** 52 23N 13 4 E
Potsdam, U.S.A. **114** 44 40N 74 59W
Potsdam □ **24** 52 40N 12 50 E
Pottenstein **25** 49 46N 11 25 E
Potter **116** 41 15N 103 20W
Pottery Hill = Abu Ballas **86** 24 26N 27 36 E
Pottstown **114** 40 17N 75 40W
Pottsville **114** 40 39N 76 12W
Pouancé **18** 47 44N 1 10W
Pouce Coupé **108** 55 40N 120 10W
Poughkeepsie **114** 41 40N 73 57W
Pouilly **19** 47 18N 2 57 E
Poulaphouca Res. **15** 53 8N 6 30W
Pouldu, Le **18** 47 41N 3 36W
Poulsbo **118** 47 45N 122 39W
Pourri, Mont **21** 45 32N 6 52 E
Pouso Alegre, Mato Grosso, Brazil **127** 11 46 S 57 16W
Pouso Alegre, Minas Gerais, Brazil **125** 22 14 S 45 57W
Pouzages **20** 46 40N 0 50W
Pouzauges **18** 46 47N 0 50W
Povenets **52** 62 50N 34 50 E
Poverty Bay **101** 38 43 S 178 2 E
Povlen **42** 44 9N 19 44 E
Póvoa de Lanhosa **30** 41 33N 8 15W
Póvoa de Varzim **30** 41 25N 8 46W
Povorino **55** 51 12N 42 5 E
Powassan **106** 46 5N 79 25W
Powder → **116** 46 47N 105 12W
Powder River **118** 43 5N 107 0W
Powell **118** 44 45N 108 45W
Powell Creek **96** 18 6 S 133 46 E
Powell, L. **119** 37 25N 110 45W
Powell River **108** 49 50N 124 35W
Powers, Mich., U.S.A. **114** 45 40N 87 32W
Powers, Oreg., U.S.A. **118** 42 53N 124 2W
Powers Lake **116** 48 37N 102 38W
Powys □ **13** 52 20N 3 20W
Poyang Hu **75** 29 5N 116 20 E
Poyarkovo **59** 49 36N 128 41 E
Poysdorf **27** 48 40N 16 37 E
Poza de la Sal **32** 42 35N 3 31W
Poza Rica **120** 20 33N 97 27W
Požarevac **42** 44 35N 21 18 E
Požega **42** 43 53N 20 2 E
Poznań **28** 52 25N 16 55 E
Poznań □ **28** 52 50N 17 0 E
Pozo Alcón **33** 37 42N 2 56W
Pozo Almonte **126** 20 10 S 69 50W
Pozo Colorado **124** 23 30 S 58 45W
Pozoblanco **31** 38 23N 4 51W
Pozzallo **41** 36 44N 14 52 E
Pozzuoli **41** 40 46N 14 6 E
Pra → **85** 5 1N 1 37W
Prabuty **28** 53 47N 19 15 E
Prača **42** 43 47N 18 43 E
Prachatice **26** 49 1N 14 0 E
Prachin Buri **71** 14 0N 101 25 E
Prachuap Khiri Khan **71** 11 49N 99 48 E
Pradelles **20** 44 46N 3 52 E
Prades **20** 42 38N 2 23 E
Prado **127** 17 20 S 39 13W
Prado del Rey **31** 36 48N 5 33W
Præstø **49** 55 8N 12 2 E
Pragersko **39** 46 27N 15 42 E
Prague = Praha **26** 50 5N 14 22 E
Praha **26** 50 5N 14 22 E
Prahecq **20** 46 19N 0 26W
Prahita → **70** 19 0N 79 55 E
Prahova □ **46** 45 10N 26 0 E
Prahova → **46** 44 50N 25 50 E
Prahovo **42** 44 18N 22 39 E
Praid **46** 46 32N 25 10 E
Prainha, Amazonas, Brazil **126** 7 10 S 60 30W
Prainha, Pará, Brazil **127** 1 45 S 53 30W
Prairie **98** 20 50 S 144 35 E
Prairie → **117** 34 30N 99 23W
Prairie City **118** 44 27N 118 44W
Prairie du Chien **116** 43 1N 91 9W
Praja **72** 8 39 S 116 17 E
Pramánda **44** 39 32N 21 8 E
Prang **85** 8 1N 0 56W
Prapat **72** 2 41N 98 58 E
Praszka **28** 51 5N 18 31 E
Prata **127** 19 25 S 48 54W
Prática di Mare **40** 41 40N 12 26 E
Prato **38** 43 53N 11 5 E
Prátola Peligna **39** 42 7N 13 51 E
Pratovécchio **39** 43 44N 11 43 E
Prats-de-Mollo **20** 42 25N 2 27 E
Pratt **117** 37 40N 98 45W
Prattville **115** 32 30N 86 28W
Pravara → **70** 19 35N 74 45 E
Pravdinsk **55** 56 29N 43 28 E
Pravia **30** 43 30N 6 12W
Pré-en-Pail **18** 48 28N 0 10W
Pré St. Didier **38** 45 45N 7 0 E
Precordillera **124** 30 0 S 69 1W
Predáppio **39** 44 7N 11 58 E
Predazzo **39** 46 19N 11 37 E
Predejane **42** 42 51N 22 9 E
Preeceville **109** 51 57N 102 40W
Préfailles **18** 47 9N 2 11W
Pregrada **39** 46 11N 15 45 E
Preko **39** 44 7N 15 14 E
Prelate **109** 50 51N 109 24W
Prelog **39** 46 18N 16 32 E
Premier **108** 56 4N 129 56W
Premier Downs **96** 30 30 S 126 30 E
Premont **117** 27 19N 98 8W
Premuda **39** 44 20N 14 36 E
Prenj **42** 43 33N 17 53 E
Prenjasi **44** 41 6N 20 32 E
Prentice **116** 45 31N 90 19W
Prenzlau **24** 53 19N 13 51 E
Prepansko Jezero **44** 40 55N 21 0 E
Preparis North Channel **71** 15 12N 93 40 E
Preparis South Channel **71** 14 36N 93 40 E
Přerov **27** 49 28N 17 27 E
Presanella **38** 46 13N 10 40 E
Prescott, Can. **106** 44 45N 75 30W
Prescott, Ariz., U.S.A. **119** 34 35N 112 30W
Prescott, Ark., U.S.A. **117** 33 49N 93 22W
Preservation Inlet **101** 46 8 S 166 35 E
Preševo **42** 42 19N 21 39 E
Presho **116** 43 56N 100 4W
Presicce **41** 39 53N 18 13 E
Presidencia de la Plaza **124** 27 0 S 29 50W
Presidencia Roque Saenz Peña **124** 26 45 S 60 30W
Presidente Epitácio **127** 21 56 S 52 6W
Presidente Hayes □ **124** 24 0 S 59 0W
Presidente Hermes **126** 11 17 S 61 55W
Presidente Prudente **125** 22 5 S 51 25W
Presidio **117** 29 30N 104 20W
Preslav **43** 43 10N 26 52 E
Preslavska Planina **43** 43 10N 26 45 E
Prešov **27** 49 0N 21 15 E
Prespa **43** 41 44N 24 55 E
Prespa, L. = Prepansko Jezero **44** 40 55N 21 0 E
Presque Isle **107** 46 40N 68 0W
Presseger See **26** 46 37N 13 26 E
Prestbury **13** 51 54N 2 2W
Prestea **84** 5 22N 2 7W
Presteigne **13** 52 17N 3 0W
Přeštice **26** 49 34N 13 20 E
Preston, Can. **112** 43 23N 80 21W
Preston, U.K. **12** 53 46N 2 42W
Preston, Idaho, U.S.A. **118** 42 10N 111 55W
Preston, Minn., U.S.A. **116** 43 39N 92 3W
Preston, Nev., U.S.A. **118** 38 59N 115 2W
Preston, C. **96** 20 51 S 116 12 E
Prestonpans **14** 55 58N 3 0W
Prestwick **14** 55 30N 4 38W
Pretoria **93** 25 44 S 28 12 E
Preuilly-sur-Claise **18** 46 51N 0 56 E
Préveza **45** 38 57N 20 47 E
Préveza □ **44** 39 20N 20 40 E
Prey-Veng **71** 11 35N 105 29 E
Priazovskoye **56** 46 44N 35 40 E
Pribilof Is. **4** 56 0N 170 0W
Priboj **42** 43 35N 19 32 E
Pribram **26** 49 41N 14 2 E
Price **118** 39 40N 110 48W
Price I. **108** 52 23N 128 41W
Prichalnaya **57** 48 57N 44 33 E
Priego **32** 40 26N 2 21W
Priego de Córdoba **31** 37 27N 4 12W
Priekule **54** 57 27N 21 45 E
Prien **25** 47 52N 12 20 E
Prieska **92** 29 40 S 22 42 E
Priest L. **118** 48 30N 116 55W
Priest River **118** 48 11N 116 55W
Priestly **108** 54 8N 125 20W
Prievidza **27** 48 46N 18 36 E
Prijedor **39** 44 58N 16 41 E
Prijepolje **42** 43 27N 19 40 E
Prikaspiyskaya Nizmennost **57** 47 0N 48 0 E
Prikumsk **56** 44 30N 44 10 E
Prilep **42** 41 21N 21 37 E
Priluki **54** 50 30N 32 24 E
Primorsko **43** 42 15N 27 44 E
Primorsko-Akhtarsk **56** 46 2N 38 10 E
Primorskoye **56** 47 10N 37 38 E
Primrose L. **109** 54 55N 109 45W
Prince Albert **109** 53 15N 105 50W
Prince Albert Mts. **5** 76 0 S 161 30 E
Prince Albert Nat. Park **109** 54 0N 106 25W
Prince Albert Pen. **104** 72 30N 116 0W
Prince Albert Sd. **104** 70 25N 115 0W
Prince Alfred C. **4** 74 20N 124 40W
Prince Charles I. **105** 67 47N 76 12W
Prince Charles Mts. **5** 72 0 S 67 0 E
Prince Edward I. □ **107** 46 20N 63 20W
Prince Edward Is. **3** 45 15 S 39 0 E
Prince George **108** 53 55N 122 50W
Prince of Wales I. **104** 55 30N 133 0W
Prince of Wales Is. **97** 10 40 S 142 10 E
Prince Patrick I. **4** 77 0N 120 0W
Prince Regent Inlet **4** 73 0N 90 0W
Prince Rupert **108** 54 20N 130 20W
Princess Charlotte B. **97** 14 25 S 144 0 E
Princess Royal I. **108** 53 0N 128 40W
Princeton, Can. **108** 49 27N 120 30W
Princeton, Ill., U.S.A. **116** 41 25N 89 25W
Princeton, Ind., U.S.A. **114** 38 20N 87 35W
Princeton, Ky., U.S.A. **114** 37 6N 87 55W
Princeton, Mo., U.S.A. **116** 40 23N 93 35W
Princeton, N.J., U.S.A. **114** 40 18N 74 40W
Princeton, W. Va., U.S.A. **114** 37 21N 81 8W
Principe Chan. **108** 53 28N 130 0W
Principe da Beira **126** 12 20 S 64 30W
Principe, I. de **79** 1 37N 7 27 E
Prineville **118** 44 17N 120 50W
Prins Albert **92** 33 12 S 22 2 E
Prins Harald Kyst **5** 70 0 S 35 1 E
Prinsesse Astrid Kyst **5** 70 45 S 12 30 E
Prinsesse Ragnhild Kyst **5** 70 15 S 27 30 E
Prior, C. **30** 43 34N 8 17W
Priozersk **52** 61 2N 30 7 E
Pripet = Pripyat → **54** 51 20N 30 9 E
Pripet Marshes = Polesye **54** 52 0N 28 10 E

Pripyat Quillabamba

Pripyat → 54 51 20N 30 9 E
Prislop, Pasul 46 47 37N 25 15 E
Pristen 55 51 15N 36 44 E
Priština 42 42 40N 21 13 E
Pritchard 115 30 47N 88 5W
Pritzwalk 24 53 10N 12 11 E
Privas 21 44 45N 4 37 E
Priverno 40 41 29N 13 10 E
Privolzhsk 55 57 23N 41 16 E
Privolzhskaya Vozvyshennost 55 51 0N 46 0 E
Privolzhskiy 55 51 25N 46 3 E
Privolzhye 55 52 52N 48 33 E
Priyutnoye 57 46 12N 43 40 E
Prizren 42 42 13N 20 45 E
Prizzi 40 37 44N 13 24 E
Prnjavor 42 44 52N 17 43 E
Probolinggo 73 7 46 S 113 13 E
Prochowice 28 51 17N 16 20 E
Procida 40 40 46N 14 0 E
Proddatur 70 14 45N 78 30 E
Proença-a-Nova 31 39 45N 7 54W
Progreso 120 21 20N 89 40W
Prokhladnyy 57 43 50N 44 2 E
Prokletije 44 42 30N 19 45 E
Prokopyevsk 58 54 0N 86 45 E
Prokuplje 42 43 16N 21 36 E
Proletarskaya 57 46 42N 41 50 E
Prome = Pyè 67 18 45N 95 30 E
Prophet → 108 58 48N 122 40W
Propriá 127 10 13 S 36 51W
Propriano 21 41 41N 8 52 E
Proserpine 97 20 21 S 148 36 E
Prosna 28 51 1N 18 30 E
Prosser 118 46 11N 119 52W
Prostějov 27 49 30N 17 9 E
Prostki 28 53 42N 22 25 E
Proston 99 26 8 S 151 32 E
Proszowice 27 50 13N 20 16 E
Protection 117 37 16N 99 30W
Próti 45 37 5N 21 32 E
Provadiya 43 43 12N 27 30 E
Provence 21 43 40N 5 46 E
Providence, Ky., U.S.A. 114 37 25N 87 46W
Providence, R.I., U.S.A. 114 41 50N 71 28W
Providence Bay 106 45 41N 82 15W
Providence Mts. 119 35 0N 115 30W
Providencia, I. de 121 13 25N 81 26W
Provideniya 59 64 23N 173 18W
Provins 19 48 33N 3 15 E
Provo 118 40 16N 111 37W
Provost 109 52 25N 110 20W
Prozor 42 43 50N 17 34 E
Prud'homme 109 52 20N 105 54W
Prudnik 28 50 20N 17 38 E
Prüm 25 50 14N 6 22 E
Pruszcz Gd. 28 54 17N 18 40 E
Pruszków 28 52 9N 20 49 E
Prut → 46 46 3N 28 10 E
Pruzhany 54 52 33N 24 28 E
Prvič 39 44 55N 14 47 E
Prydz B. 5 69 0S 74 0 E
Pryor 117 36 17N 95 20W
Przasnysz 28 53 2N 20 45 E
Przedbórz 28 51 6N 19 53 E
Przedecz 28 52 20N 18 53 E
Przemyśl 27 49 50N 22 45 E
Przeworsk 27 50 6N 22 32 E
Przewóz 28 51 28N 14 57 E
Przhevalsk 58 42 30N 78 20 E
Przysuchla 28 51 22N 20 38 E
Psakhná 45 38 34N 23 35 E
Psará 45 38 37N 25 38 E
Psathoúra 44 39 30N 24 12 E
Psel → 56 49 5N 33 20 E
Pserimos 45 36 56N 27 12 E
Pskov 54 57 50N 28 25 E
Psunj 42 45 25N 17 19 E
Pszczyna 27 49 59N 18 58 E
Pteleón 45 39 3N 22 57 E
Ptich → 54 52 9N 28 52 E
Ptolemais 44 40 30N 21 43 E
Ptuj 39 46 28N 15 50 E
Ptujska Gora 39 46 23N 15 47 E
Puán 124 37 30 S 62 45W
Pucallpa 126 8 25 S 74 30W
Pucheng 77 27 59N 118 31 E
Pucheni 46 45 12N 25 17 E
Pučišće 39 43 22N 16 43 E
Puck 28 54 45N 18 23 E
Pucka, Zatoka 28 54 30N 18 40 E
Pudozh 52 61 48N 36 32 E
Pudukkottai 70 10 28N 78 47 E
Puebla 120 19 0N 98 10W
Puebla □ 120 18 30N 98 0W
Puebla de Alcocer 31 38 59N 5 14W
Puebla de Cazalla, La 31 37 10N 5 20W
Puebla de Don Fadrique 33 37 58N 2 25W
Puebla de Don Rodrigo 31 39 5N 4 37W
Puebla de Guzmán 31 37 37N 7 15W
Puebla de los Infantes, La 31 37 47N 5 24W
Puebla de Montalbán, La 30 39 52N 4 22W
Puebla de Sanabria 30 42 4N 6 38W
Puebla de Trives 30 42 20N 7 10W
Puebla del Caramiñal 30 42 37N 8 56W
Puebla, La 32 39 46N 3 1 E
Pueblo 116 38 20N 104 40W
Pueblo Bonito 119 36 4N 107 57W
Pueblo Hundido 124 26 20 S 70 5W
Puelches 124 38 5 S 65 51W
Puelén 124 37 32 S 67 38W
Puente Alto 124 33 32 S 70 35W
Puente del Arzobispo 30 39 48N 5 10W
Puente-Genil 31 37 22N 4 47W
Puente la Reina 32 42 40N 1 49W
Puenteareas 30 42 10N 8 28W
Puentedeume 30 43 24N 8 10W
Puentes de Garcia Rodriguez 30 43 27N 7 50W
Puerco → 119 34 22N 107 50W
Puerta, La 33 38 22N 2 45W
Puerto Aisén 128 45 27 S 73 0W
Puerto Armuelles 121 8 20N 82 51W
Puerto Ayacucho 126 5 40N 67 35W
Puerto Barrios 120 15 40N 88 32W
Puerto Bermejo 124 26 55 S 58 34W
Puerto Bermúdez 126 10 20 S 75 0W
Puerto Bolívar 126 3 19 S 79 55W
Puerto Cabello 126 10 28N 68 1W
Puerto Cabezas 121 14 0N 83 30W
Puerto Capaz = Jebba 82 35 11N 4 43W
Puerto Carreño 126 6 12N 67 22W
Puerto Castilla 121 16 0N 86 0W
Puerto Chicama 126 7 45 S 79 20W
Puerto Coig 128 50 54 S 69 15W
Puerto Cortes 121 8 55N 84 0W
Puerto Cortés 120 15 51N 88 0W
Puerto Cumarebo 126 11 29N 69 30W
Puerto de Santa María 31 36 36N 6 13W
Puerto del Rosario 80 28 30N 13 52W
Puerto Deseado 128 47 55 S 66 0W
Puerto Heath 126 12 34 S 68 39W
Puerto Juárez 120 21 11N 86 49W
Puerto La Cruz 126 10 13N 64 38W
Puerto Leguízamo 126 0 12 S 74 46W
Puerto Libertad 120 29 55N 112 41W
Puerto Lobos 128 42 0 S 65 3W
Puerto Lumbreras 33 37 34N 1 48W
Puerto Madryn 128 42 48 S 65 4W
Puerto Maldonado 126 12 30 S 69 10W
Puerto Mazarrón 33 37 34N 1 15W
Puerto Montt 128 41 28 S 73 0W
Puerto Morelos 120 20 49N 86 52W
Puerto Natales 128 51 45 S 72 15W
Puerto Padre 121 21 13N 76 35W
Puerto Páez 126 6 13N 67 28W
Puerto Peñasco 120 31 20N 113 33W
Puerto Pinasco 124 22 36 S 57 50W
Puerto Pirámides 128 42 35 S 64 20W
Puerto Plata 121 19 48N 70 45W
Puerto Princesa 73 9 46N 118 45 E
Puerto Quellón 128 43 7 S 73 37W
Puerto Quepos 121 9 29N 84 6W
Puerto Real 31 36 33N 6 12W
Puerto Rico ■ 121 18 15N 66 45W
Puerto Sastre 124 22 2 S 57 55W
Puerto Suárez 126 18 58 S 57 52W
Puerto Vallarta 120 20 36N 105 15W
Puerto Wilches 126 7 21N 73 54W
Puertollano 31 38 43N 4 7W
Puertomarin 30 42 48N 7 36W
Pueyrredón, L. 128 47 20 S 72 0W
Pugachev 55 52 0N 48 49 E
Puge 90 4 45 S 33 11 E
Puget Sd. 118 47 15N 122 30W
Puget-Théniers 21 43 58N 6 53 E
Púglia □ 41 41 0N 16 30 E
Pugu 90 6 55 S 39 4 E
Pui 46 45 30N 23 4 E
Puieşti 46 46 25N 27 33 E
Puig Mayor, Mte. 32 39 48N 2 47 E
Puigcerdá 32 42 24N 1 50 E
Puigmal 32 42 23N 2 7 E
Puisaye, Collines de 19 47 34N 3 18 E
Puiseaux 19 48 11N 2 30 E
Puka 44 42 2N 19 53 E
Pukaki L. 101 44 4 S 170 1 E
Pukatawagan 109 55 45N 101 20W
Pukekohe 101 37 12 S 174 55 E
Pukou 77 32 7N 118 38 E
Pula 40 39 0N 9 0 E
Pula (Pola) 39 44 54N 13 57 E
Pulaski, N.Y., U.S.A. 114 43 32N 76 9W
Pulaski, Tenn., U.S.A. 115 35 10N 87 0W
Pulaski, Va., U.S.A. 114 37 4N 80 49W
Pulawy 28 51 23N 21 59 E
Pulgaon 68 20 44N 78 21 E
Pulicat, L. 70 13 40N 80 15 E
Puliyangudi 70 9 11N 77 24 E
Pullman 118 46 49N 117 10W
Pulog, Mt. 73 16 40N 120 50 E
Puloraja 72 4 55N 95 24 E
Pułtusk 28 52 43N 21 6 E
Pumlumon Fawr 13 52 29N 3 47W
Puna 126 19 45 S 65 28W
Puná, I. 126 2 55 S 80 5W
Punakha 69 27 42N 89 52 E
Punalur 70 9 0N 76 56 E
Punasar 68 27 6N 73 6 E
Punata 126 17 32 S 65 50W
Punch 69 33 48N 74 4 E
Pune 70 18 29N 73 57 E
Pungue, Ponte de 91 19 0S 34 0 E
Puning 77 23 20N 116 12 E
Punjab □ 68 31 0N 76 0 E
Puno 126 15 55 S 70 3W
Punta Alta 128 38 53 S 62 4W
Punta Arenas 128 53 10 S 71 0W
Punta de Díaz 124 28 0 S 70 45W
Punta Gorda, Belize 120 16 10N 88 45W
Punta Gorda, U.S.A. 115 26 55N 82 0W
Puntarenas 121 10 0N 84 50W
Punto Fijo 126 11 50N 70 13W
Punxsutawney 114 40 56N 79 0W
Puqi 77 29 40N 113 50 E
Puquio 126 14 45 S 74 10W
Pur → 58 67 31N 77 55 E
Purace, Vol. 126 2 21N 76 23W
Puračić 42 44 33N 18 28 E
Purari → 98 7 49 S 145 0 E
Purbeck, Isle of 13 50 40N 2 5W
Purcell 117 35 0N 97 25W
Purchena Tetica 33 37 21N 2 21W
Puri 69 19 50N 85 58 E
Purli 68 18 50N 76 35 E
Purmerend 16 52 30N 4 58 E
Purna → 70 19 6N 77 2 E
Purnea 69 25 45N 87 31 E
Pursat 71 12 34N 103 50 E
Purukcahu 72 0 35 S 114 35 E
Purulia 69 23 17N 86 24 E
Purus → 126 3 42 S 61 28W
Půrvomay 43 42 8N 25 17 E
Purwakarta 73 6 35 S 107 29 E
Purwodadi, Jawa, Indon. 73 7 51 S 110 0 E
Purwodadi, Jawa, Indon. 73 7 7 S 110 55 E
Purwokerto 73 7 25 S 109 14 E
Purworedjo 73 7 43 S 110 2 E
Pus → 70 19 55N 77 55 E
Pusad 70 19 56N 77 36 E
Pusan 76 35 5N 129 0 E
Pushchino 59 54 10N 158 0 E
Pushkin 54 59 45N 30 25 E
Pushkino, R.S.F.S.R., U.S.S.R. 55 51 16N 47 0 E
Pushkino, R.S.F.S.R., U.S.S.R. 55 56 2N 37 49 E
Püspökladány 27 47 19N 21 6 E
Pustoshka 54 56 20N 29 30 E
Puszczykowo 28 52 18N 16 49 E
Putahow L. 109 59 54N 100 40W
Putao 67 27 28N 97 30 E
Putaruru 101 38 2 S 175 50 E
Putbus 24 54 19N 13 29 E
Puţeni 46 45 49N 27 42 E
Puthein Myit → 67 15 56N 94 18 E
Putian 77 25 23N 119 0 E
Putignano 41 40 50N 17 5 E
Puting, Tanjung 72 3 31 S 111 46 E
Putlitz 24 53 15N 12 3 E
Putna 46 47 50N 25 33 E
Putna → 46 45 42N 27 26 E
Putnam 113 41 55N 71 55W
Putnok 27 48 18N 20 26 E
Putorana, Gory 59 69 0N 95 0 E
Puttalam Lagoon 70 8 15N 79 45 E
Putten 16 52 16N 5 36 E
Puttgarden 24 54 28N 11 15 E
Puttur 70 12 46N 75 12 E
Putumayo → 126 3 7 S 67 58W
Putussibau 72 0 50N 112 56 E
Puy-de-Dôme 20 45 46N 2 57 E
Puy-de-Dôme □ 20 45 47N 3 0 E
Puy-de-Sancy 20 45 32N 2 48 E
Puy-Guillaume 20 45 57N 3 29 E
Puy, Le 20 45 3N 3 52 E
Puy l'Évêque 20 44 31N 1 9 E
Puyallup 118 47 10N 122 22W
Puyang 76 35 40N 115 1 E
Puylaurens 20 43 35N 2 0 E
Puyôo 20 43 33N 0 56W
Pwani □ 90 7 0 S 39 0 E
Pweto 91 8 25 S 28 51 E
Pwllheli 12 52 54N 4 26W
Pya-ozero 52 66 5N 30 58 E
Pyana → 55 55 30N 46 0 E
Pyapon 67 16 20N 95 40 E
Pyasina → 59 73 30N 87 0 E
Pyatigorsk 57 44 2N 43 6 E
Pyatikhatki 56 48 28N 33 38 E
Pydna 44 40 20N 22 34 E
Pyinmana 67 19 45N 96 12 E
Pyŏngyang 76 39 0N 125 30 E
Pyote 117 31 34N 103 5W
Pyramid L. 118 40 0N 119 30W
Pyramids 86 29 58N 31 9 E
Pyrénées 20 42 45N 0 18 E
Pyrenees = Pyrénées 20 42 45N 0 18 E
Pyrénées-Atlantiques □ 20 43 15N 1 0W
Pyrénées-Orientales □ 20 42 35N 2 26 E
Pyrzyce 28 53 10N 14 55 E
Pyshchug 55 58 57N 45 47 E
Pytalovo 54 57 5N 27 55 E
Pyttegga 47 62 13N 7 42 E
Pyu 67 18 30N 96 28 E
Pyzdry 28 52 11N 17 42 E

Q

Qabalān 62 32 8N 35 17 E
Qabātiyah 62 32 25N 35 16 E
Qaidam Pendi 75 37 0N 95 0 E
Qa'iya 64 24 33N 43 15 E
Qal' at Shajwa 86 25 2N 38 57 E
Qala-i-Jadid (Spin Baldak) 68 31 1N 66 25 E
Qalāt 65 32 15N 66 58 E
Qal'at al Akhḑar 64 28 0N 37 10 E
Qal'at al Mu'azzam 64 27 45N 37 31 E
Qal'at Saura 64 26 10N 38 40 E
Qal'eh-ye Now 65 35 0N 63 5 E
Qalqīlya 62 32 12N 34 58 E
Qalyûb 86 30 12N 31 11 E
Qam 62 32 36N 35 43 E
Qamar, Ghubbat al 63 16 20N 52 30 E
Qamruddin Karez 68 31 45N 68 20 E
Qāna 62 33 12N 35 17 E
Qâra 86 29 38N 26 30 E
Qarachuk 64 37 0N 42 2 E
Qārah 64 29 55N 40 3 E
Qardud 87 10 20N 29 56 E
Qarqan 75 38 5N 85 20 E
Qarqan He → 75 39 30N 88 30 E
Qarrasa 87 14 38N 32 5 E
Qasim 64 26 0N 43 0 E
Qāsim 62 32 59N 36 2 E
Qaşr Bū Hadi 83 31 1N 16 45 E
Qaşr-e Qand 65 26 15N 60 45 E
Qasr Farâfra 86 27 0N 28 1 E
Qatar ■ 65 25 30N 51 15 E
Qattâra 86 30 12N 27 3 E
Qattâra Depression = Qattâra, Munkhafed el 86 29 30N 27 30 E
Qattâra, Munkhafed el 86 29 30N 27 30 E
Qāyen 65 33 40N 59 10 E
Qazvin 64 36 15N 50 0 E
Qena 86 26 10N 32 43 E
Qena, Wadi → 86 26 12N 32 44 E
Qeshm 65 26 55N 56 10 E
Qezi'ot 62 30 52N 34 26 E
Qian Xian 77 34 31N 108 15 E
Qianshan 77 30 37N 116 35 E
Qianxi 77 27 3N 106 3 E
Qianyang 77 27 18N 110 10 E
Qijiang 77 28 57N 106 35 E
Qila Safed 66 29 0N 61 30 E
Qila Saifulla 68 30 45N 68 17 E
Qilian Shan 75 38 30N 96 0 E
Qin Ling = Qinling Shandi 77 33 50N 108 10 E
Qin'an 77 34 48N 105 40 E
Qingdao 76 36 5N 120 20 E
Qinghai □ 75 36 0N 98 0 E
Qinghai Hu 75 36 40N 100 10 E
Qingjiang, Jiangsu, China 77 33 30N 119 2 E
Qingjiang, Jiangxi, China 77 28 4N 115 29 E
Qingliu 77 26 11N 116 48 E
Qingshuihe 76 39 55N 111 35 E
Qingyang 76 36 2N 107 55 E
Qingyuan 77 23 40N 112 59 E
Qinhuangdao 76 39 56N 119 30 E
Qinling Shandi 77 33 50N 108 10 E
Qinyang 77 35 7N 112 57 E
Qinyuan 76 36 29N 112 20 E
Qinzhou 75 21 58N 108 38 E
Qiongshan 77 19 51N 110 26 E
Qiongzhou Haixia 77 20 10N 110 15 E
Qiqihar 75 47 26N 124 0 E
Qiryat 'Anavim 62 31 49N 35 7 E
Qiryat Ata 62 32 47N 35 6 E
Qiryat Bialik 62 32 50N 35 5 E
Qiryat Gat 62 31 32N 34 46 E
Qiryat Ḥayyim 62 32 49N 35 4 E
Qiryat Mal'akhi 62 31 44N 34 44 E
Qiryat Shemona 62 33 13N 35 35 E
Qiryat Yam 62 32 51N 35 4 E
Qishan 77 22 52N 120 25 E
Qishon → 62 32 49N 35 2 E
Qishrān 86 20 14N 40 2 E
Qitai 75 44 2N 89 35 E
Qiyahe 76 53 0N 120 35 E
Qiyang 77 26 35N 111 50 E
Qizan 87 16 57N 42 34 E
Qizān 63 17 0N 42 20 E
Qom 65 34 40N 51 0 E
Qomolangma Feng (Mt. Everest) 75 28 0N 86 45 E
Qondūz 65 36 50N 68 50 E
Qondūz □ 65 36 50N 68 50 E
Qu Jiang → 77 30 1N 106 24 E
Qu Xian, Sichuan, China 77 30 48N 106 58 E
Qu Xian, Zhejiang, China 75 28 57N 118 54 E
Quackenbrück 24 52 40N 7 59 E
Quakertown 113 40 27N 75 20W
Quambatook 99 35 49 S 143 34 E
Quambone 99 30 57 S 147 53 E
Quan Long = Ca Mau 71 9 7N 105 8 E
Quanan 117 34 20N 99 45W
Quandialla 99 34 1 S 147 47 E
Quang Ngai 71 15 13N 108 58 E
Quang Yen 71 20 56N 106 52 E
Quantock Hills 13 51 8N 3 10W
Quanzhou, Fujian, China 75 24 55N 118 34 E
Quanzhou, Guangxi Zhuangzu, China 77 25 57N 111 5 E
Quaraí 124 30 15 S 56 20W
Quarré-les-Tombes 19 47 21N 4 0 E
Quartu Sant' Elena 40 39 15N 9 10 E
Quartzsite 119 33 44N 114 16W
Quatsino 108 50 30N 127 40W
Quatsino Sd. 108 50 25N 127 58W
Qubab = Mishmar Ayyalon 62 31 52N 34 57 E
Qūchān 65 37 10N 58 27 E
† Que Que 91 18 58 S 29 48 E
Queanbeyan 97 35 17 S 149 14 E
Québec 107 46 52N 71 13W
Québec □ 107 50 0N 70 0W
Quedlinburg 24 51 47N 11 9 E
Queen Alexandra Ra. 5 85 0 S 170 0 E
Queen Charlotte 108 53 15N 132 2W
Queen Charlotte Is. 108 53 20N 132 10W
Queen Charlotte Str. 108 51 0N 128 0W
Queen Elizabeth Is. 102 76 0N 95 0W
Queen Elizabeth Nat. Park 90 0 0 S 30 0 E
Queen Mary Coast 5 70 0 S 95 0 E
Queen Maud G. 104 68 15N 102 30W
Queen Maud Ra. 5 86 0 S 160 0W
Queens Chan. 96 15 0 S 129 30 E
Queenscliff 97 38 16 S 144 39 E
Queensland □ 97 22 0 S 142 0 E
Queenstown, Austral. 97 42 4 S 145 35 E
Queenstown, N.Z. 101 45 1 S 168 40 E
Queenstown, S. Afr. 92 31 52 S 26 52 E
Queguay Grande → 124 32 9 S 58 9W
Queimadas 127 11 0 S 39 38W
Quela 88 9 10 S 16 56 E
Quelimane 91 17 53 S 36 58 E
Quelpart = Cheju Do 77 33 29N 126 34 E
Quemado, N. Mex., U.S.A. 119 34 17N 108 28W
Quemado, Tex., U.S.A. 117 28 58N 100 35W
Quemú-Quemú 124 36 3 S 63 36W
Quequén 124 38 30 S 58 30W
Querétaro 120 20 40N 100 23W
Querétaro □ 120 20 30N 100 0W
Querfurt 24 51 22N 11 33 E
Querqueville 18 49 40N 1 42W
Quesada 33 37 51N 3 4W
Queshan 77 32 55N 114 2 E
Quesnel 108 53 0N 122 30W
Quesnel → 108 52 58N 122 29W
Quesnel L. 108 52 30N 121 20W
Quesnoy, Le 19 50 15N 3 38 E
Questa 119 36 45N 105 35W
Questembert 18 47 40N 2 28W
Quetico Prov. Park 106 48 30N 91 45W
Quetta 66 30 15N 66 55 E
* Quetta □ 66 30 15N 66 55 E
Quezaltenango 120 14 50N 91 30W
Quezon City 73 14 38N 121 0 E
Qui Nhon 71 13 40N 109 13 E
Quiaca, La 124 22 5 S 65 35W
Quibaxe 88 8 24 S 14 27 E
Quibdo 126 5 42N 76 40W
Quiberon 18 47 29N 3 9W
Quick 108 54 36N 126 54W
Quickborn 24 53 42N 9 52 E
Quiet L. 108 61 5N 133 5W
Quiindy 124 25 58 S 57 14W
Quilán, C. 128 43 15 S 74 30W
Quilengues 89 14 12 S 14 12 E
Quilimarí 124 32 5 S 71 30W
Quilino 124 30 14 S 64 29W
Quillabamba 126 12 50 S 72 50W

* Now part of Baluchistan □

† Renamed Kwekwe

Quillagua Red Rock, L.

Quillagua 124 21 40S 69 40W
Quillaicillo 124 31 17S 71 40W
Quillan 20 42 53N 2 10E
Quillebeuf 18 49 28N 0 30E
Quillota 124 32 54S 71 16W
Quilmes 124 34 43S 58 15W
Quilon 70 8 50N 76 38E
Quilpie 97 26 35S 144 11E
Quilpué 124 33 5S 71 33W
Quilua 91 16 17S 39 54E
Quimili 124 27 40S 62 30W
Quimper 18 48 0N 4 9W
Quimperlé 18 47 53N 3 33W
Quincy, Calif., U.S.A. 118 39 56N 121 0W
Quincy, Fla., U.S.A. 115 30 34N 84 34W
Quincy, Ill., U.S.A. 116 39 55N 91 20W
Quincy, Mass., U.S.A. 114 42 14N 71 0W
Quincy, Wash., U.S.A. 118 47 22N 119 56W
Quines 124 32 13S 65 48W
Quinga 91 15 49S 40 15E
Quingey 19 47 7N 5 52E
Quintana de la Serena 31 38 45N 5 40W
Quintana Roo □ 120 19 0N 88 0W
Quintanar de la Orden 32 39 36N 3 5W
Quintanar de la Sierra 32 41 57N 2 55W
Quintanar del Rey 33 39 21N 1 56W
Quintero 124 32 45S 71 30W
Quintin 18 48 26N 2 56W
Quinto 32 41 25N 0 32W
Quinyambie 99 30 15S 141 0E
Quipar → 33 38 15N 1 40W
Quirihue 124 36 15S 72 35W
Quirindi 99 31 28S 150 40E
Quiroga 30 42 28N 7 18W
Quissac 21 43 55N 4 0E
Quissanga 91 12 24S 40 28E
Quitilipi 124 26 50S 60 13W
Quitman, Ga., U.S.A. 115 30 49N 83 35W
Quitman, Miss., U.S.A. 115 32 2N 88 42W
Quitman, Tex., U.S.A. 117 32 48N 95 25W
Quito 126 0 15S 78 35W
Quixadá 127 4 55S 39 0W
Quixaxe 91 15 17S 40 4E
Qul'ân, Jazâ'ir 86 24 22N 35 31E
Qumrân 62 31 43N 35 27E
Quneitra 62 33 7N 35 48E
Quoin Pt. 92 34 46S 19 37E
Quondong 99 33 6S 140 18E
Quorn 97 32 25S 138 0E
Qurein 87 13 30N 34 50E
Qûs 86 25 55N 32 50E
Quseir 86 26 7N 34 16E
Qusrah 62 32 5N 35 20E
Quthing 93 30 25S 27 36E
Qytet Stalin (Kuçove) 44 40 47N 19 57E

R

Råå 49 56 0N 12 45E
Raab 26 48 21N 13 39E
Raahe 50 64 40N 24 28E
Ra'ananna 62 32 12N 34 52E
Raasay 14 57 25N 6 4W
Raasay, Sd. of 14 57 30N 6 8W
Rab 39 44 45N 14 45E
Raba 73 8 36S 118 55E
Rába → 27 47 38N 17 38E
Raba → 27 50 8N 20 30E
Rabaçal → 30 41 30N 7 12W
Rabah 85 13 5N 5 30E
Rabai 90 3 50S 39 31E
Rabastens, Hautes-Pyrénées, France 20 43 25N 0 10E
Rabastens, Tarn, France 20 43 50N 1 43E
Rabat, Malta 36 35 53N 14 25E
Rabat, Moroc. 82 34 2N 6 48W
Rabaul 94 4 24S 152 18E
Rabbit → 108 59 41N 127 12W
Rabbit Lake 109 53 8N 107 46W
Rabbitskin → 108 61 47N 120 42W
Râbigh 64 22 50N 39 5E
Rabka 27 49 37N 19 59E
Rača 42 44 14N 21 0E
Răcale 41 39 57N 18 6E
Racalmuto 40 37 25N 13 41E
Răcășdia 42 44 59N 21 36E
Racconigi 38 44 47N 7 41E
Race, C. 107 46 40N 53 5W
Rach Gia 71 10 5N 105 5E
Raciąż 28 52 46N 20 10E
Racibórz 27 50 7N 18 18E
Racine 114 42 41N 87 51W
Radama, Nosy 93 14 0S 47 47E
Radama, Saikanosy 93 14 16S 47 53E
Radan 42 42 59N 21 29E
Rădăuţi 46 47 50N 25 59E
Radbuza → 26 49 35N 13 5E
Räde 47 59 21N 10 53E
Radeburg 24 51 6N 13 55E
Radeče 39 46 5N 15 14E
Radekhov 54 50 25N 24 32E
Radew → 28 54 2N 15 52E
Radford 114 37 8N 80 32W
Radhanpur 68 23 50N 71 38E
Radhwa, Jabal 64 24 34N 38 18E
Radiska → 42 41 38N 20 37E
Radisson 109 52 30N 107 20W
Radium Hill 97 32 30S 140 42E
Radium Hot Springs 108 50 35N 116 2W
Radja, Kepulauan 73 0 30S 130 00E
Radków 28 50 30N 16 24E
Radlin 27 50 3N 18 29E
Radna 42 46 7N 21 41E
Radnevo 43 42 17N 25 58E
Radnice 26 49 51N 13 35E
Radnor Forest 13 52 17N 3 10W
Radolfzell 25 47 44N 8 58E
Radom 28 51 23N 21 12E
Radom □ 28 51 30N 21 0E
Radomir 42 42 37N 23 4E
Radomka → 28 51 31N 21 11E
Radomsko 28 51 5N 19 28E
Radomyshl 54 50 30N 29 12E
Radomysl Wielki 27 50 14N 21 15E
Radoszyce 28 51 4N 20 15E
Radoviš 42 41 38N 22 28E
Radovljica 39 46 22N 14 12E
Radstadt 26 47 24N 13 28E
Radstock 13 51 17N 2 25W
Răducăneni 46 46 58N 27 54E
Raduša 42 42 7N 21 15E
Radviliškis 54 55 49N 23 33E
Radville 109 49 30N 104 15W
Radymno 27 49 59N 22 52E
Radzanów 28 52 56N 20 8E
Radziejów 28 52 40N 18 30E
Radzymin 28 52 25N 21 11E
Radzyń Chełmiński 28 53 23N 18 55E
Radzyń Podlaski 28 51 47N 22 37E
Rae 108 62 50N 116 3W
Rae Bareli 69 26 18N 81 20E
Rae Isthmus 105 66 40N 87 30W
Raeren 16 50 41N 6 7E
Raeside, L. 96 29 20S 122 0E
Raetihi 101 39 25S 175 17E
Rafaela 124 31 10S 61 30W
Rafah 86 31 18N 34 14E
Rafai 90 4 59N 23 58E
Raffadali 40 37 23N 13 29E
Rafḥā 64 29 35N 43 35E
Rafsanjān 65 30 30N 56 5E
Ragag 87 10 59N 24 40E
Raglan, Austral. 98 23 42S 150 49E
Raglan, N.Z. 101 37 55S 174 55E
Ragunda 48 63 6N 16 23E
Ragusa 41 36 56N 14 42E
Raha 73 4 55S 123 0E
Rahad al Bardī 81 11 20N 23 40E
Rahad, Nahr ed → 87 14 28N 33 31E
Rahden 24 52 26N 8 36E
Raheita 87 12 46N 43 4E
Rahimyar Khan 68 28 30N 70 25E
Raichur 70 16 10N 77 20E
Raiganj 69 25 37N 88 10E
Raigarh, Madhya Pradesh, India 69 21 56N 83 25E
Raigarh, Orissa, India 70 19 51N 82 6E
Raiis 64 23 33N 38 43E
Raijua 73 10 37S 121 36E
Railton 99 41 25S 146 28E
Rainbow Lake 108 58 30N 119 23W
Rainier 118 46 4N 123 0W
Rainier, Mt. 118 46 50N 121 50W
Rainy L. 109 48 42N 93 10W
Rainy River 109 48 43N 94 29W
Raipur 69 21 17N 81 45E
Raja, Kepulauan 73 0 30S 129 40E
Raja, Ujung 72 3 40N 96 25E
Rajahmundry 70 17 1N 81 48E
Rajang → 72 2 30N 112 0E
Rajapalaiyam 70 9 25N 77 35E
Rajasthan □ 68 26 45N 73 30E
Rajasthan Canal 68 28 0N 72 0E
Rajbari 69 23 47N 89 41E
Rajgarh, Mad. P., India 68 24 2N 76 45E
Rajgarh, Raj., India 68 28 40N 75 25E
Rajgród 28 53 42N 22 42E
Rajhenburg 39 46 1N 15 29E
Rajkot 68 22 15N 70 56E
Rajmahal Hills 69 24 30N 87 30E
Rajnandgaon 69 21 5N 81 5E
Rajojooseppi 50 68 25N 28 30E
Rajpipla 68 21 50N 73 30E
Rajpura 68 30 25N 76 32E
Rajshahi 69 24 22N 88 39E
Rajshahi □ 69 25 0N 89 0E
Rakaia 101 43 45S 172 1E
Rakaia → 101 43 36S 172 15E
Rakan, Ra's 65 26 10N 51 20E
Rakaposhi 69 36 10N 74 25E
Rakha 86 18 25N 41 30E
Rakhni 68 30 4N 69 56E
Rakitovo 43 41 59N 24 5E
Rakkestad 47 59 25N 11 21E
Rakoniewice 28 52 10N 16 16E
Rakops 92 21 1S 24 28E
Rákospalota 27 47 30N 19 5E
Rakov 54 53 58N 26 59E
Rakovica 39 44 59N 15 38E
Rakovník 26 50 6N 13 42E
Rakovski 43 42 21N 24 57E
Rakvere 54 59 30N 26 25E
Raleigh 115 35 47N 78 39W
Raleigh B. 115 34 50N 76 15W
Ralja 42 44 33N 20 34E
Ralls 117 33 40N 101 20W
Ram → 108 62 1N 123 41W
Râm Allâh 62 31 55N 35 10E
Rama 62 32 56N 35 21E
Ramacca 41 37 24N 14 40E
Ramachandrapuram 70 16 50N 82 4E
Ramales de la Victoria 32 43 15N 3 28W
Ramanathapuram 70 9 25N 78 55E
Ramanetaka, B. de 93 14 13S 47 52E
Ramas C. 70 15 5N 73 55E
Ramat Gan 62 32 4N 34 48E
Ramat HaSharon 62 32 7N 34 50E
Ramatlhabama 92 25 37S 25 33E
Rambervillers 19 48 20N 6 38E
Rambipuji 73 8 12S 113 37E
Rambla, La 31 37 37N 4 45W
Rambouillet 19 48 40N 1 48E
Ramdurg 70 15 58N 75 22E
Rame Hd. 99 37 47S 149 30E
Ramea 107 47 28N 57 4W
Ramechhap 69 27 25N 86 10E
Ramelau 73 8 55S 126 22E
Ramenskoye 55 55 32N 38 15E
Ramgarh, Bihar, India 69 23 40N 85 35E
Ramgarh, Rajasthan, India 68 27 16N 75 14E
Ramgarh, Rajasthan, India 68 27 30N 70 36E
Rāmhormoz 64 31 15N 49 35E
Ramla 62 31 55N 34 52E
Ramlat Zalṭan 83 28 30N 19 30E
Ramlu 87 13 32N 41 40E
Ramme 49 56 30N 8 11E
Rammün 62 31 55N 35 17E
Ramnad = Ramanathapuram 70 9 25N 78 55E
Ramnäs 48 59 46N 16 12E
Ramon 55 51 55N 39 21E
Ramon, Har 62 30 30N 34 38E
Ramona 119 33 1N 116 56W
Ramore 106 48 30N 80 25W
Ramos → 120 25 35N 105 3W
Ramoutsa 92 24 50S 25 52E
Rampart 104 65 0N 150 15W
Rampur, H.P., India 68 31 26N 77 43E
Rampur, Mad. P., India 68 23 25N 73 53E
Rampur, Orissa, India 69 21 48N 83 58E
Rampur, U.P., India 68 28 50N 79 5E
Rampura 68 24 30N 75 27E
Rampurhat 69 24 10N 87 50E
Ramree Kyun 67 19 0N 94 0E
Ramsey, Can. 106 47 25N 82 20W
Ramsey, U.K. 12 54 20N 4 21W
Ramsgate 13 51 20N 1 25E
Ramsjö 48 62 11N 15 37E
Ramtek 69 21 20N 79 15E
Ramu → 98 4 0S 144 41E
Ramvik 48 62 49N 17 51E
Ranaghat 69 23 15N 88 35E
Ranahu 68 25 55N 69 45E
Ranau 72 6 2N 116 40E
Rancagua 124 34 10S 70 50W
Rance → 18 48 34N 1 59W
Rance, Barrage de la 18 48 30N 2 3W
Rancheria → 108 60 13N 129 7W
Ranchester 118 44 57N 107 12W
Ranchi 69 23 19N 85 27E
Rancu 46 44 32N 24 15E
Rand 100 35 33S 146 32E
Randan 20 46 2N 3 21E
Randazzo 41 37 53N 14 56E
Randers 49 56 29N 10 1E
Randers Fjord 49 56 37N 10 20E
Randfontein 93 26 8S 27 45E
Randolph, Mass., U.S.A. 113 42 10N 71 3W
Randolph, N.Y., U.S.A. 112 42 10N 78 59W
Randolph, Utah, U.S.A. 118 41 43N 111 10W
Randolph, Vt., U.S.A. 113 43 55N 72 39W
Randsburg 119 35 22N 117 44W
Randsfjorden 47 60 15N 10 25E
Råne älv → 50 65 50N 22 20E
Rangaunu B. 101 34 51S 173 15E
Rångedala 49 57 47N 13 9E
Rangeley 114 44 58N 70 33W
Rangely 118 40 3N 108 53W
Ranger 117 32 30N 98 42W
Rangia 67 26 28N 91 38E
Rangiora 101 43 19S 172 36E
Rangitaiki → 101 37 54S 176 49E
Rangitata → 101 43 45S 171 15E
Rangkasbitung 73 6 22S 106 16E
Rangon → 67 16 28N 96 40E
Rangoon 67 16 45N 96 20E
Ranibennur 70 14 35N 75 30E
Raniganj 69 23 40N 87 5E
Ranipet 70 12 56N 79 23E
Rankin 117 31 16N 101 56W
Rankin Inlet 104 62 30N 93 0W
Rankins Springs 99 33 49S 146 14E
Rannoch, L. 14 56 41N 4 20W
Rannoch Moor 14 56 38N 4 48W
Ranobe, Helodranon' i 93 23 3S 43 33E
Ranohira 93 22 29S 45 24E
Ranomafana, Tamatave, Madag. 93 18 57S 48 50E
Ranomafana, Tuléar, Madag. 93 24 34S 47 0E
Ranong 71 9 56N 98 40E
Ransiki 73 1 30S 134 10E
Rantau 72 2 56S 115 9E
Rantauprapat 72 2 15N 99 50E
Rantemario 73 3 15S 119 57E
Rantīs 62 32 4N 35 3E
Rantoul 114 40 18N 88 10W
Ranum 49 56 54N 9 14E
Ranwanlenau 92 19 37S 22 49E
Raohe 76 46 47N 134 0E
Raon l'Étape 19 48 24N 6 50E
Raoui, Erg er 82 29 0N 2 0W
Rapa Iti 95 27 35S 144 20W
Rapallo 38 44 21N 9 12E
Rapang 73 3 45S 119 55E
Rāpch 65 25 40N 59 15E
Rapid → 108 59 15N 129 5W
Rapid City 116 44 0N 103 0W
Rapid River 114 45 55N 87 0W
Rapides des Joachims 106 46 13N 77 43W
Rapla 54 59 1N 24 52E
Rarotonga 95 21 30S 160 0W
Ra's al Khaymah 65 25 50N 56 5E
Ra's al-Unuf 83 30 25N 18 15E
Ras Bânâs 81 23 57N 35 59E
Ras Dashen 87 13 8N 38 26E
Ras el Ma 82 34 26N 0 50W
Ras Mallap 86 29 18N 32 50E
Ra's Tannūrah 64 26 40N 50 10E
Râs Timirist 84 19 21N 16 30W
Rasa, Punta 128 40 50S 62 15W
Raseiniai 54 55 25N 23 5E
Rashad 87 11 55N 31 0E
Rashîd 86 31 21N 30 22E
Rashîd, Masabb 86 31 22N 30 17E
Rasht 64 37 20N 49 40E
Rasipuram 70 11 30N 78 15E
Raška 42 43 19N 20 39E
Rason, L. 96 28 45S 124 25E
Rașova 46 44 15N 27 55E
Rasovo 43 43 42N 23 17E
Rasra 69 25 50N 83 50E
Rass el Oued 83 35 57N 5 2E
Rasskazovo 55 52 35N 41 50E
Rastatt 25 48 50N 8 12E
Rastu 46 43 53N 23 16E
Raszków 28 51 43N 17 40E
Rat Buri 71 13 30N 99 54E
Rat Is. 104 51 50N 178 15E
Rat River 108 61 7N 112 36W
Ratangarh 68 28 5N 74 35E
Rath 69 25 36N 79 37E
Rath Luirc (Charleville) 15 52 21N 8 40W
Rathdrum, Ireland 15 52 57N 6 13W
Rathdrum, U.S.A. 118 47 50N 116 58W
Rathenow 24 52 38N 12 23E
Rathkeale 15 52 32N 8 57W
Rathlin I. 15 55 18N 6 14W
Rathlin O'Birne I. 15 54 40N 8 50W
Ratibor = Racibórz 27 50 7N 18 18E
Rätikon 26 47 0N 9 55E
Ratlam 68 23 20N 75 0E
Ratnagiri 70 16 57N 73 18E
Ratnapura 70 6 40N 80 20E
Raton 117 37 0N 104 30W
Ratten 26 47 28N 15 44E
Rattray Hd. 14 57 38N 1 50W
Rättvik 48 60 52N 15 7E
Ratz, Mt. 108 57 23N 132 12W
Ratzeburg 24 53 41N 10 46E
Raub 71 3 47N 101 52E
Rauch 124 36 45S 59 5W
Raufarhöfn 50 66 27N 15 57W
Raufoss 47 60 44N 10 37E
Raukumara Ra. 101 38 5S 177 55E
Rauland 47 59 43N 8 0E
Rauma 51 61 10N 21 30E
Rauma → 47 62 34N 7 43E
Raundal 47 60 40N 6 37E
Raung 73 8 8S 114 4E
Raurkela 69 22 14N 84 50E
Rava Russkaya 54 50 15N 23 42E
Ravanusa 40 37 16N 13 58E
Rāvar 65 31 20N 56 51E
Ravena 113 42 28N 73 49W
Ravenna, Italy 39 44 28N 12 15E
Ravenna, Nebr., U.S.A. 116 41 3N 98 58W
Ravenna, Ohio, U.S.A. 112 41 11N 81 15W
Ravensburg 25 47 48N 9 38E
Ravenshoe 97 17 37S 145 29E
Ravensthorpe 96 33 35S 120 2E
Ravenswood, Austral. 98 20 6S 146 54E
Ravenswood, U.S.A. 114 38 58N 81 47W
Ravi → 68 30 35N 71 49E
Ravna Gora 39 45 24N 14 50E
Ravna Reka 42 43 59N 21 35E
Rawa Mazowiecka 28 51 46N 20 12E
Rawalpindi 66 33 38N 73 8E
Rawāndūz 64 36 40N 44 30E
Rawang 71 3 20N 101 35E
Rawdon 106 46 3N 73 40W
Rawene 101 35 25S 173 32E
Rawicz 28 51 36N 16 52E
Rawka → 28 52 9N 20 8E
Rawlinna 96 30 58S 125 28E
Rawlins 118 41 50N 107 20W
Rawlinson Range 96 24 40S 128 30E
Rawson 128 43 15S 65 0W
Ray 116 48 21N 103 6W
Ray, C. 107 47 33N 59 15W
Rayachoti 70 14 4N 78 50E
Rayadrug 70 14 40N 76 50E
Rayagada 70 19 15N 83 20E
Raychikhinsk 59 49 46N 129 25E
Raymond, Can. 108 49 30N 112 35W
Raymond, U.S.A. 118 46 45N 123 48W
Raymondville 117 26 30N 97 50W
Raymore 109 51 25N 104 31W
Rayne 117 30 16N 92 16W
Rayong 71 12 40N 101 20E
Rayville 117 32 30N 91 45W
Raz, Pte. du 18 48 2N 4 47W
Ražana 42 44 6N 19 55E
Ražanj 42 43 40N 21 31E
Razdelna 43 43 13N 27 41E
Razdel'naya 56 46 50N 30 2E
Razdolnoye 56 45 46N 33 29E
Razelm, Lacul 46 44 50N 29 0E
Razgrad 43 43 33N 26 34E
Razlog 43 41 53N 23 28E
Razmak 68 32 45N 69 50E
Razole 70 16 36N 81 48E
Ré, Île de 20 46 12N 1 30W
Reading, U.K. 13 51 27N 0 57W
Reading, U.S.A. 114 40 20N 75 53W
Realicó 124 35 0S 64 15W
Réalmont 20 43 48N 2 10E
Ream 71 10 34N 103 39E
Rebais 19 48 50N 3 10E
Rebi 73 6 23S 134 7E
Rebiana 83 24 12N 22 10E
Rebun-Tō 74 45 23N 141 2E
Recanati 39 43 24N 13 32E
Recaş 42 45 46N 21 30E
Recherche, Arch. of the 96 34 15S 122 50E
Rechitsa 54 52 13N 30 15E
Recife 127 8 0S 35 0W
Recklinghausen 24 51 36N 7 10E
Reconquista 124 29 10S 59 45W
Recreo 124 29 25S 65 10W
Recz 28 53 16N 15 31E
Red →, Can. 109 50 24N 96 48W
Red →, Minn., U.S.A. 116 48 10N 97 0W
Red →, Tex., U.S.A. 117 31 0N 91 40W
Red Bank 113 40 21N 74 4W
Red Bay 107 51 44N 56 25W
Red Bluff 118 40 11N 122 11W
Red Bluff L. 117 31 59N 103 58W
Red Cloud 116 40 8N 98 33W
Red Deer 108 52 20N 113 50W
Red Deer →, Alta., Can. 109 50 58N 110 0W
Red Deer →, Man., Can. 109 52 53N 101 1W
Red Deer L. 109 52 55N 101 20W
Red Indian L. 107 48 35N 57 0W
Red Lake 109 51 3N 93 49W
Red Lake Falls 116 47 54N 96 15W
Red Lodge 118 45 10N 109 10W
Red Oak 116 41 0N 95 10W
Red Rock 106 48 55N 88 15W
Red Rock, L. 116 41 30N 93 15W

Red Sea Röbel

Red Sea 63 25 0N 36 0 E
Red Sucker L 109 54 9N 93 40W
Red Tower Pass = Turnu Rosu P. 46 45 33N 24 17 E
Red Wing 116 44 32N 92 35W
Reda 28 54 40N 18 19 E
Redbridge 13 51 35N 0 7 E
Redcar 12 54 37N 1 4W
Redcliff 109 50 10N 110 50W
Redcliffe 99 27 12 S 153 0 E
Reddersburg 92 29 41 S 26 10 E
Redding 118 40 30N 122 25W
Redditch 13 52 18N 1 57W
Redfield 116 45 0N 98 30W
Redknife → 108 61 14N 119 22W
Redlands 119 34 0N 117 11W
Redmond 118 44 19N 121 11W
Redon 18 47 40N 2 6W
Redonda 121 16 58N 62 19W
Redondela 30 42 15N 8 38W
Redondo 31 38 39N 7 37W
Redondo Beach 119 33 52N 118 26W
Redrock Pt. 108 62 11N 115 2W
Redruth 13 50 14N 5 14W
Redvers 109 49 35N 101 40W
Redwater 108 53 55N 113 6W
Redwood 113 44 18N 75 48W
Redwood City 119 37 30N 122 15W
Redwood Falls 116 44 30N 95 2W
Ree, L. 15 53 35N 8 0W
Reed City 114 43 52N 85 30W
Reed, L 109 54 38N 100 30W
Reeder 116 46 7N 102 52W
Reedley 119 36 36N 119 27W
Reedsburg 116 43 34N 90 5W
Reedsport 118 43 45N 124 4W
Reefton 101 42 6 S 171 51 E
Reftele 49 57 11N 13 35 E
Refugio 117 28 18N 97 17W
Rega → 28 54 10N 15 18 E
Regalbuto 41 37 40N 14 38 E
Regavim 62 32 32N 35 2 E
Regen 25 48 58N 13 9 E
Regen → 25 49 2N 12 6 E
Regensburg 25 49 1N 12 7 E
Réggio di Calábria 41 38 7N 15 38 E
Réggio nell' Emilia 38 44 42N 10 38 E
Regina 109 50 27N 104 35W
Registro 125 24 29 S 47 49W
Reguengos de Monsaraz 31 38 25N 7 32W
Rehar → 69 23 55N 82 40 E
Rehoboth 92 23 15 S 17 4 E
Rehovot 62 31 54N 34 48 E
Rei-Bouba 81 8 40N 14 15 E
Reichenbach 24 50 36N 12 19 E
Reid River 98 19 40 S 146 48 E
Reidsville 115 36 21N 79 40W
Reigate 13 51 14N 0 11W
Reillo 32 39 54N 1 53W
Reims 19 49 15N 4 0 E
Reina 62 32 43N 35 18 E
Reina Adelaida, Arch. 128 52 20 S 74 0W
Reinbeck 116 42 18N 92 0W
Reindeer → 109 55 36N 103 11W
Reindeer I. 109 52 30N 98 0W
Reindeer L. 109 57 15N 102 15W
Reine, La 32 48 50N 79 30W
Reinga, C. 101 34 25 S 172 43 E
Reinosa 30 43 2N 4 15W
Reinosa, Paso 30 42 56N 4 10W
Reitz 93 27 48 S 28 29 E
Reivilo 92 27 36 S 24 8 E
Rejmyra 49 58 50N 15 55 E
Rejowiec Fabryczny 28 51 5N 23 17 E
Reka → 39 45 40N 14 0 E
Rekinniki 59 60 51N 163 40 E
Rekovac 42 43 51N 21 3 E
Reliance 109 63 0N 109 20W
Remad, Oued → 82 33 28N 1 20W
Rémalard 18 48 26N 0 47 E
Remanso 127 9 41 S 42 4W
Remarkable, Mt. 99 32 48 S 138 10 E
Rembang 73 6 42 S 111 21 E
Remchi 82 35 2N 1 26W
Remeshk 65 26 55N 58 50 E
Remetea 46 46 45N 25 29 E
Remich 16 49 32N 6 22 E
Remiremont 19 48 0N 6 36 E
Remo 87 6 48N 41 20 E
Remontnoye 57 46 34N 43 37 E
Remoulins 21 43 55N 4 35 E
Remscheid 24 51 11N 7 12 E
Rena 47 61 8N 11 20 E
Rena → 47 61 8N 11 23 E
Rende 41 39 19N 16 11 E
Rendina 45 39 4N 21 58 E
Rendsburg 24 54 18N 9 41 E
Rene 59 66 2N 179 25W
Renfrew, Can. 106 45 30N 76 40W
Renfrew, U.K. 14 55 52N 4 24W
Rengat 72 0 30 S 102 45 E
Rengo 124 34 24 S 70 50W
Renhuai 77 27 48N 106 24 E
Reni 56 45 28N 28 15 E
Renigunta 70 13 38N 79 30 E
Renk 81 11 50N 32 50 E
Renkum 16 51 58N 5 43 E
Renmark 97 34 11 S 140 43 E
Rennell Sd. 108 53 23N 132 35W
Renner Springs T.O. 96 18 20 S 133 47 E
Rennes 18 48 7N 1 41W
Rennes, Bassin de 18 48 12N 1 33W
Rennesøy 47 59 6N 5 43 E
Reno 118 39 30N 119 50W
Reno → 39 44 37N 12 17 E
Renovo 114 41 20N 77 47W
Rensselaer, Ind., U.S.A. 114 40 57N 87 10W
Rensselaer, N.Y., U.S.A. 113 42 38N 73 41W
Rentería 32 43 19N 1 54W
Renton 118 47 30N 122 9W
Réo 84 12 28N 2 35W
Réole, La 20 44 35N 0 1W
Reotipur 69 25 33N 83 45 E
Repalle 70 16 2N 80 45 E
Répcelak 27 47 24N 17 1 E
Republic, Mich., U.S.A. 114 46 25N 87 59W
Republic, Wash., U.S.A. 118 48 38N 118 42W
Republican → 116 39 3N 96 48W
Republican City 116 40 9N 99 20W
Repulse B., Antarct. 5 64 30 S 99 30 E
Repulse B., Austral. 97 20 31 S 148 45 E
Repulse Bay 105 66 30N 86 30W
Requena, Peru 126 5 5 S 73 52W
Requena, Spain 33 39 30N 1 4W
Resele 48 63 20N 17 5 E
Resen 42 41 5N 21 0 E
Reserve, Can. 109 52 28N 102 39W
Reserve, U.S.A. 119 33 50N 108 54W
Resht = Rasht 64 37 20N 49 40 E
Resistencia 124 27 30 S 59 0W
Reşiţa 42 45 18N 21 53 E
Resko 28 53 47N 15 25 E
Resolution I., Can. 105 61 30N 65 0W
Resolution I., N.Z. 101 45 40 S 166 40 E
Ressano Garcia 93 25 25 S 32 0 E
Reston 109 49 33N 101 6W
Reszel 28 54 4N 21 10 E
Retalhuleu 120 14 33N 91 46W
Reteag 46 47 10N 24 0 E
Retenue, Lac de 91 11 0 S 27 0 E
Rethel 19 49 30N 4 20 E
Rethem 24 52 47N 9 25 E
Réthimnon 45 35 18N 24 30 E
Réthimnon □ 45 35 23N 24 28 E
Rétiers 18 47 55N 1 25W
Retortillo 30 40 48N 6 21W
Rétság 27 47 58N 19 10 E
Réunion 3 22 0 S 56 0 E
Reus 32 41 10N 1 5 E
Reuss → 25 47 16N 8 24 E
Reuterstadt Stavenhagen 24 53 41N 12 54 E
Reutlingen 25 48 28N 9 13 E
Reutte 26 47 29N 10 42 E
Reval = Tailinn 54 59 29N 24 58 E
Revda 52 56 48N 59 57 E
Revel 20 43 28N 2 0 E
Revelganj 69 25 50N 84 40 E
Revelstoke 108 51 0N 118 10W
Reventazón 126 6 10 S 81 0W
Revigny 19 48 50N 5 0 E
Revilla Gigedo, Is. 95 18 40N 112 0W
Revillagigedo I. 108 55 50N 131 20W
Revin 19 49 55N 4 39 E
Revuè → 91 19 50 S 34 0 E
Rewa 69 24 33N 81 25 E
Rewari 68 28 15N 76 40 E
Rexburg 118 43 55N 111 50W
Rey Malabo 88 3 45N 8 50 E
Rey, Rio del → 85 4 30N 8 48 E
Reykjahliô 50 65 40N 16 55W
Reykjanes 50 63 48N 22 40W
Reykjavík 50 64 10N 21 57 E
Reynolds 109 49 40N 95 55W
Reynolds Ra. 96 22 30 S 133 0 E
Reynoldsville 112 41 5N 78 58W
Reynosa 120 26 5N 98 18W
Rezā'īyeh 64 37 40N 45 0 E
Rezā'īyeh, Daryācheh-ye 64 37 50N 45 30 E
Rezekne 54 56 30N 27 17 E
Rezovo 43 42 0N 28 0 E
Rgotina 42 44 1N 22 17 E
Rhamnus 45 38 12N 24 3 E
Rharis, O. → 83 26 0N 5 4 E
Rhayader 13 52 19N 3 30W
Rheden 16 52 0N 6 3 E
Rhein 109 51 25N 102 15W
Rhein → 24 51 52N 6 20 E
Rhein-Main-Donau-Kanal 25 49 1N 11 27 E
Rheinbach 24 50 38N 6 54 E
Rheine 24 52 17N 7 25 E
Rheinland-Pfalz □ 25 50 0N 7 0 E
Rheinsberg 24 53 6N 12 52 E
Rheriss ,Oued → 82 30 50N 4 34W
Rheydt 24 51 10N 6 24 E
Rhin = Rhein → 24 51 52N 6 20 E
Rhinau 19 48 19N 7 43 E
Rhine = Rhein → 24 51 52N 6 20 E
Rhinelander 116 45 38N 89 29W
Rhino Camp 90 3 0N 31 22 E
Rhir, Cap 82 30 38N 9 54W
Rho 38 45 31N 9 2 E
Rhode Island □ 114 41 38N 71 37W
Rhodes = Ródhos 45 36 15N 28 10 E
Rhodes' Tomb 91 20 30 S 28 30 E
Rhodesia = Zimbabwe ■ 91 20 0 S 30 0 E
Rhodope Mts. = Rhodopi Planina 43 41 40N 24 20 E
Rhodopi Planina 43 41 40N 24 20 E
Rhondda 13 51 39N 3 30W
Rhône □ 21 45 54N 4 35 E
Rhône → 21 43 28N 4 42 E
Rhum 14 57 0N 6 20W
Rhumney 13 51 32N 3 7W
Rhyl 12 53 19N 3 29W
Ri-Aba 85 3 28N 8 40 E
Riachão 127 7 20 S 46 37W
Riaño 30 42 59N 5 0W
Rians 21 43 37N 5 44 E
Riansares → 32 39 32N 3 18W
Riasi 69 33 10N 74 50 E
Riau □ 72 0 0 102 35 E
Riau, Kepulauan 72 0 30N 104 20 E
Riaza 32 41 18N 3 30W
Riaza → 32 41 42N 3 55W
Riba de Saelices 32 40 55N 2 17W
Ribadavia 30 42 17N 8 8W
Ribadeo 30 43 35N 7 5W
Ribadesella 30 43 30N 5 7W
Ribas 32 42 19N 2 15 E
Ribble → 12 54 13N 2 20W
Ribe 49 55 19N 8 44 E
Ribeauvillé 19 48 10N 7 20 E
Ribécourt 19 49 30N 2 55 E
Ribeira 30 42 36N 8 58W
Ribeirão Prêto 125 21 10 S 47 50W
Ribemont 19 49 47N 3 27 E
Ribera 40 37 30N 13 13 E
Ribérac 20 45 15N 0 20 E
Riberalta 126 11 0 S 66 0W
Ribnica 39 45 45N 14 45 E
Ribnitz-Damgarten 24 54 14N 12 24 E
Ričany 26 50 0N 14 40 E
Riccarton 101 43 32 S 172 37 E
Riccia 41 41 30N 14 50 E
Riccione 39 44 0N 12 39 E
Rice L. 112 44 12N 78 10W
Rice Lake 116 45 30N 91 42W
Riceys, Les 19 47 59N 4 22 E
Rich 82 32 16N 4 30W
Rich Hill 117 38 5N 94 22W
Richards Bay 93 28 48 S 32 6 E
Richards L. 109 59 10N 107 10W
Richardson → 109 58 25N 111 14W
Richardton 116 46 56N 102 22W
Richelieu 18 47 0N 0 20 E
Richey 116 47 42N 105 5W
Richfield, Idaho, U.S.A. 118 43 2N 114 5W
Richfield, Utah, U.S.A. 119 38 50N 112 0W
Richford 113 45 0N 72 40W
Richibucto 107 46 42N 64 54W
Richland, Ga., U.S.A. 115 32 7N 84 40W
Richland, Oreg., U.S.A. 118 44 49N 117 9W
Richland, Wash., U.S.A. 118 46 15N 119 15W
Richland Center 116 43 21N 90 22W
Richlands 114 37 7N 81 49W
Richmond, N.S.W., Austral. 100 33 35 S 150 42 E
Richmond, Queens., Austral. 97 20 43 S 143 8 E
Richmond, N.Z. 101 41 20 S 173 12 E
Richmond, S. Afr. 93 29 51 S 30 18 E
Richmond, N. Yorks., U.K. 12 54 24N 1 43W
Richmond, Surrey, U.K. 13 51 28N 0 18W
Richmond, Calif., U.S.A. 118 37 58N 122 21W
Richmond, Ind., U.S.A. 114 39 50N 84 50W
Richmond, Ky., U.S.A. 114 37 40N 84 20W
Richmond, Mich., U.S.A. 112 42 47N 82 45W
Richmond, Mo., U.S.A. 116 39 15N 93 58W
Richmond, Tex., U.S.A. 117 29 32N 95 42W
Richmond, Utah, U.S.A. 118 41 55N 111 48W
Richmond, Va., U.S.A. 114 37 33N 77 27W
Richmond, Ra. 99 29 0 S 152 45 E
Richton 115 31 23N 88 58W
Richwood 114 38 17N 80 32W
Ricla 32 41 31N 1 24W
Riddarhyttan 48 59 49N 15 33 E
Ridgedale 109 53 0N 104 10W
Ridgeland 115 32 30N 80 58W
Ridgelands 98 23 16 S 150 17 E
Ridgetown 106 42 26N 81 52W
Ridgewood 113 40 59N 74 7W
Ridgway 114 41 25N 78 43W
Riding Mt. Nat. Park 109 50 50N 100 0W
Ried 26 48 14N 13 30 E
Riedlingen 25 48 9N 9 28 E
Rienza → 39 46 49N 11 47 E
Riesa 24 51 19N 13 19 E
Riesi 41 37 16N 14 4 E
Rieti 39 42 23N 12 50 E
Rieupeyroux 20 44 19N 2 12 E
Riez 21 43 49N 6 6 E
Rifle 118 39 40N 107 50W
Rifstangi 50 66 32N 16 12W
Rift Valley □ 90 0 20N 36 0 E
Rig Rig 81 14 13N 14 25 E
Riga 54 56 53N 24 8 E
Riga, G. of = Rīgas Jūras Līcis 54 57 40N 23 45 E
Rīgas Jūras Līcis 54 57 40N 23 45 E
Rigaud 113 45 29N 74 18W
Rigby 118 43 41N 111 58W
Rīgestān □ 65 30 15N 65 0 E
Riggins 118 45 29N 116 26W
Rignac 20 44 25N 2 16 E
Rigolet 107 54 10N 58 23W
Riihimäki 51 60 45N 24 48 E
Riiser-Larsen-halvøya 5 68 0 S 35 0 E
Rijau 85 11 8N 5 17 E
Rijeka 39 45 20N 14 21 E
Rijeka Crnojevica 42 42 24N 19 1 E
Rijn → 16 52 12N 4 21 E
Rijssen 16 52 19N 6 30 E
Rijswijk 16 52 4N 4 22 E
Rike 87 10 50N 39 53 E
Rila 43 42 7N 23 7 E
Rila Planina 42 42 10N 23 0 E
Riley 118 43 35N 119 33W
Rilly 19 49 11N 4 3 E
Rima → 85 13 4N 5 10 E
Rimah, Wadi ar → 64 26 5N 41 30 E
Rimavská Sobota 27 48 22N 20 2 E
Rimbey 108 52 35N 114 15W
Rimbo 48 59 44N 18 21 E
Rimforsa 49 58 6N 15 43 E
Rimi 85 12 58N 7 43 E
Rímini 39 44 3N 12 33 E
Rîmna → 46 45 36N 27 3 E
Rîmnicu Sărat 46 45 26N 27 3 E
Rîmnicu Vîlcea 46 45 9N 24 21 E
Rimouski 107 48 27N 68 30W
Rinca 73 8 45 S 119 35 E
Rinconada 124 22 26 S 66 10W
Rineanna 15 52 42N 85 7W
Ringarum 49 58 21N 16 26 E
Ringe 49 55 13N 10 28 E
Ringim 85 12 13N 9 10 E
Ringkøbing 49 56 5N 8 15 E
Ringling 118 46 16N 110 56W
Ringsaker 47 60 54N 10 45 E
Ringsjön 49 55 55N 13 30 E
Ringsted 49 55 25N 11 46 E
Ringvassøy 50 69 56N 19 15 E
Rinia 45 37 23N 25 13 E
Rinjani 72 8 24 S 116 28 E
Rinteln 24 52 11N 9 3 E
Rio Branco 126 9 58 S 67 49W
Río Branco 125 32 40 S 53 40W
Rio Brilhante 125 21 48 S 54 33W
Rio Claro, Brazil 125 22 19 S 47 35W
Rio Claro, Trin. 121 10 20N 61 25W
Río Colorado 128 39 0 S 64 0W
Río Cuarto 124 33 10 S 64 25W
Rio das Pedras 93 23 8 S 35 28 E
Rio de Janeiro 125 23 0 S 43 12W
Rio de Janeiro □ 125 22 50 S 43 0W
Rio do Sul 125 27 13 S 49 37W
Río Gallegos 128 51 35 S 69 15W
Río Grande 128 53 50 S 67 45W
Rio Grande 125 32 0 S 52 20W
Rio Grande → 117 25 57N 97 9W
Rio Grande City 117 26 23N 98 49W
Río Grande del Norte → 110 26 0N 97 0W
Rio Grande do Norte □ 127 5 40 S 36 0W
Rio Grande do Sul □ 125 30 0 S 53 0W
Rio Largo 127 9 28 S 35 50W
Rio Maior 31 39 19N 8 57W
Rio Marina 38 42 48N 10 25 E
Río Mulatos 126 19 40 S 66 50W
Río Muni □ 88 1 30N 10 0 E
Rio Negro 125 26 0 S 50 0W
Rio Pardo 125 30 0 S 52 30W
Río, Punta del 33 36 49N 2 24W
Río Segundo 124 31 40 S 63 59W
Río Tercero 124 32 15 S 64 8W
Rio Tinto 30 41 11N 8 34W
Rio Verde 127 17 50 S 51 0W
Río Verde 120 21 56N 99 59W
Rio Vista 118 38 11N 121 44W
Ríobamba 126 1 50 S 78 45W
Ríohacha 126 11 33N 72 55W
Rioja, La, Argent. 124 29 20 S 67 0W
Rioja, La, Spain 32 42 20N 2 20W
Rioja, La □ 124 29 30 S 67 0W
Riom 20 45 54N 3 7 E
Riom-ès-Montagnes 20 45 17N 2 39 E
Rion-des-Landes 20 43 55N 0 56W
Rionero in Vúlture 41 40 55N 15 40 E
Rioni → 57 42 5N 41 50 E
Rios 30 41 58N 7 16W
Riosucio 126 5 30N 75 40W
Riosucio 126 7 27N 77 7W
Riou L. 109 59 7N 106 25W
Rioz 19 47 25N 6 04 E
Riparia, Dora → 38 45 7N 7 24 E
Ripatransone 39 43 0N 13 45 E
Ripley, Can. 112 44 4N 81 35W
Ripley, N.Y., U.S.A. 112 42 16N 79 44W
Ripley, Tenn., U.S.A. 117 35 43N 89 34W
Ripoll 32 42 15N 2 13 E
Ripon, U.K. 12 54 8N 1 31W
Ripon, U.S.A. 114 43 51N 88 50W
Riposto 41 37 44N 15 12 E
Risan 42 42 32N 18 42 E
Riscle 20 43 39N 0 5W
Rishiri-Tō, Japan 74 45 11N 141 15 E
Rishiri-Tō, Japan 74 45 11N 141 15 E
Rishon le Ziyyon 62 31 58N 34 48 E
Rishpon 62 32 12N 34 49 E
Risle → 18 49 26N 0 23 E
Rîsnov 46 45 35N 25 27 E
Rison 117 33 57N 92 11W
Risør 47 58 43N 9 13 E
Ritchies Archipelago 71 12 5N 94 0 E
Riti 85 7 57N 9 41 E
Rittman 112 40 57N 81 48W
Ritzville 118 47 10N 118 21W
Riva Bella 18 49 17N 0 18W
Riva del Garda 38 45 53N 10 50 E
Rivadavia, Buenos Aires, Argent. 124 35 29 S 62 59W
Rivadavia, Mendoza, Argent. 124 33 13 S 68 30W
Rivadavia, Salta, Argent. 124 24 5 S 62 54W
Rivadavia, Chile 124 29 57 S 70 35W
Rivarolo Canavese 38 45 20N 7 42 E
Rivas 121 11 30N 85 50W
Rive-de-Gier 21 45 32N 4 37 E
River Cess 84 5 30N 9 32W
Rivera 125 31 0 S 55 50W
Riverdsale 92 34 7 S 21 15 E
Riverhead 114 40 53N 72 40W
Riverhurst 109 50 55N 106 50W
Riverina 97 35 30 S 145 20 E
Rivers 109 50 2N 100 14W
Rivers □ 85 5 0N 6 30 E
Rivers Inl. 108 51 40N 127 20W
Rivers, L. of the 109 49 49N 105 44W
Riverside, Calif., U.S.A. 119 34 0N 117 22W
Riverside, Wyo., U.S.A. 118 41 12N 106 57W
Riversleigh 98 19 5 S 138 40 E
Riverton, Austral. 99 34 10 S 138 46 E
Riverton, Can. 109 51 1N 97 0W
Riverton, N.Z. 101 46 21 S 168 0 E
Riverton, U.S.A. 118 43 1N 108 27W
Rives 21 45 21N 5 31 E
Rivesaltes 20 42 47N 2 50 E
Riviera 38 44 0N 8 30 E
Riviera di Levante 36 44 23N 9 15 E
Riviera di Ponente 36 43 50N 7 58 E
Rivière-à-Pierre 107 46 59N 72 11W
Rivière-au-Renard 107 48 59N 64 23W
Rivière-du-Loup 107 47 50N 69 30W
Rivière-Pentecôte 107 49 57N 67 1W
Rivoli 38 45 3N 7 31 E
Rivoli B. 99 37 32 S 140 3 E
Riyadh = Ar Riyāḍ 64 24 41N 46 42 E
Rize 64 41 0N 40 30 E
Rizhao 77 35 25N 119 30 E
Rizzuto, C. 41 38 54N 17 5 E
Rjukan 47 59 54N 8 33 E
Rjuven 47 59 9N 7 8 E
Roa, Norway 47 60 17N 10 37 E
Roa, Spain 30 41 41N 3 56W
Roag, L. 14 58 10N 6 55W
Roanne 21 46 3N 4 4 E
Roanoke, Ala., U.S.A. 115 33 9N 85 23W
Roanoke, Va., U.S.A. 114 37 19N 79 55W
Roanoke → 115 35 56N 76 43W
Roanoke I. 115 35 55N 75 40W
Roanoke Rapids 115 36 28N 77 42W
Roatán 121 16 18N 86 35W
Robbins I. 99 40 42 S 145 0 E
Robe → 15 53 38N 9 10W
Robe, Mt. 100 31 40 S 141 20 E
Röbel 24 53 24N 12 37 E

Robert Lee Rujen

Robert Lee 117 31 55N 100 26W
Roberts 118 43 44N 112 8W
Robertsganj 69 24 44N 83 4 E
Robertson 92 33 46 S 19 50 E
Robertson I. 5 65 15 S 59 30W
Robertsport 84 6 45N 11 26W
Robertstown 99 33 58 S 139 5 E
Roberval 107 48 32N 72 15W
Robeson Ch. 4 82 0N 61 30W
Robinson Crusoe I. 95 33 38 S 78 52W
Robinson Ranges 96 25 40 S 119 0 E
Robinvale 99 34 40 S 142 45 E
Robla, La 30 42 50N 5 41W
Roblin 109 51 14N 101 21W
Roboré 126 18 10 S 59 45W
Robson, Mt. 108 53 10N 119 10W
Robstown 117 27 47N 97 40W
Roc, Pointe du 18 48 50N 1 37W
Roca, C. da 31 38 40N 9 31W
Rocas, I. 127 4 0 S 34 1W
Rocca d'Aspidé 41 40 27N 15 10 E
Rocca San Casciano 39 44 3N 11 45 E
Roccalbegna 39 42 47N 11 30 E
Roccastrada 39 43 0N 11 10 E
Roccella Iónica 41 38 20N 16 24 E
Rocha 125 34 30 S 54 25W
Rochdale 12 53 36N 2 10W
Roche-Bernard, La 18 47 31N 2 19W
Roche-Canillac, La 20 45 12N 1 57 E
Roche, La 21 46 4N 6 19 E
Roche-sur-Yon, La 18 46 40N 1 25W
Rochechouart 20 45 50N 0 49 E
Rochefort, Belg. 16 50 9N 5 12 E
Rochefort, France 20 45 56N 0 57W
Rochefort-en-Terre 18 47 42N 2 22W
Rochefoucauld, La 20 45 44N 0 24 E
Rochelle 116 41 55N 89 5W
Rochelle, La 20 46 10N 1 9W
Rocher River 108 61 23N 112 44W
Rocheservière 18 46 57N 1 30W
Rochester, Austral. 100 36 22 S 144 41 E
Rochester, Can. 108 54 22N 113 27W
Rochester, U.K. 13 51 22N 0 30 E
Rochester, Ind., U.S.A. 114 41 5N 86 15W
Rochester, Minn., U.S.A. 116 44 1N 92 28W
Rochester, N.H., U.S.A. 114 43 19N 70 57W
Rochester, N.Y., U.S.A. 114 43 10N 77 40W
Rochester, Pa., U.S.A. 112 40 41N 80 17W
Rociana 31 37 19N 6 35W
Rociu 46 44 43N 25 2 E
Rock → 108 60 7N 127 7W
Rock Hill 115 34 55N 81 2W
Rock Island 116 41 30N 90 35W
Rock Port 116 40 26N 95 30W
Rock Rapids 116 43 25N 96 10W
Rock River 118 41 49N 106 0W
Rock Sound 121 24 54N 76 12W
Rock Sprs., Ariz., U.S.A. 119 34 2N 112 11W
Rock Sprs., Mont., U.S.A. 118 46 55N 106 11W
Rock Sprs., Tex., U.S.A. 117 30 2N 100 11W
Rock Sprs., Wyo., U.S.A. 118 41 40N 109 10W
Rock Valley 116 43 10N 96 17W
Rockall 8 57 37N 13 42W
Rockdale 117 30 40N 97 0W
Rockefeller Plat. 5 80 0 S 140 0W
Rockford 116 42 20N 89 0W
Rockglen 109 49 11N 105 57W
Rockhampton 97 23 22 S 150 32 E
Rockingham B. 98 18 5 S 146 10 E
Rockingham Forest 13 52 28N 0 42W
Rocklake 116 48 50N 99 13W
Rockland, Can. 113 45 33N 75 17W
Rockland, Idaho, U.S.A. 118 42 37N 112 57W
Rockland, Me., U.S.A. 107 44 6N 69 6W
Rockland, Mich., U.S.A. 116 46 40N 89 10W
Rocklands Reservoir 100 37 15 S 142 5 E
Rockmart 115 34 1N 85 2W
Rockport 117 28 2N 97 3W
Rockville, Conn., U.S.A. 113 41 51N 72 27W
Rockville, Md., U.S.A. 114 39 7N 77 10W
Rockwall 117 32 55N 96 30W
Rockwell City 116 42 20N 94 35W
Rockwood 115 35 52N 84 40W
Rocky Ford 116 38 7N 103 45W
Rocky Lane 108 58 31N 116 22W
Rocky Mount 115 35 55N 77 48W
Rocky Mountain House 108 52 22N 114 55W
Rocky Mts. 108 55 0N 121 0W
Rocky Pt. 96 33 30 S 123 57 E
Rocky River 112 41 30N 81 40W
Rockyford 108 51 14N 113 10W
Rocroi 19 49 55N 4 30 E
Rod 66 28 10N 63 5 E
Roda, La, Albacete, Spain 33 39 13N 2 15W
Roda, La, Sevilla, Spain 31 37 12N 4 46W
Rødberg 47 60 17N 8 56 E
Rødby 49 54 41N 11 23 E
Rødbyhavn 49 54 39N 11 22 E
Roddickton 107 50 51N 56 8W
Rødding 49 55 23N 9 3 E
Rødekro 49 55 4N 9 20 E
Rødenes 47 59 35N 11 34 E
Rodenkirchen 24 53 24N 8 26 E
Roderick I. 108 52 38N 128 22W
Rodez 20 44 21N 2 33 E
Rodholívas 44 40 55N 24 0 E
Rodhópi □ 44 41 5N 25 30 E
Ródhos 45 36 15N 28 10 E
Rodi Garganico 41 41 55N 15 53 E
Rodna 46 47 25N 24 50 E
Rodnei, Munţii 46 47 35N 24 35 E
Rodney 112 42 34N 81 41W
Rodney, C. 101 36 17 S 174 50 E
Rodniki 55 57 7N 41 47 E
Rodriguez 3 19 45 S 63 20 E
Rodstock, C. 96 33 12 S 134 20 E
Roe → 15 55 10N 6 59W
Roebling 113 40 7N 74 45W
Roebourne 96 20 44 S 117 9 E
Roebuck B. 96 18 5 S 122 20 E
Roermond 16 51 12N 6 0 E
Roes Welcome Sd. 105 65 0N 87 0W
Roeselare 16 50 57N 3 7 E
Rogachev 54 53 8N 30 5 E
Rogaçica 42 44 4N 19 40 E
Rogagua, L. 126 13 43 S 66 50W
Rogaland fylke □ 47 59 12N 6 20 E
Rogaška Slatina 39 46 15N 15 42 E
Rogatec 39 46 15N 15 46 E
Rogatica 42 43 47N 19 0 E
Rogatin 54 49 24N 24 36 E
Rogers 117 36 20N 94 5W
Rogers City 114 45 25N 83 49W
Rogerson 118 42 10N 114 40W
Rogersville 115 36 27N 83 1W
Roggan 106 54 25N 79 32W
Roggeveldberge 92 32 10 S 20 10 E
Roggiano Gravina 41 39 37N 16 9 E
Rogliano, France 21 42 57N 9 30 E
Rogliano, Italy 41 39 11N 16 20 E
Rogoaguado, L. 126 13 0 S 65 30W
Rogowo 28 52 43N 17 38 E
Rogozno 28 52 45N 16 59 E
Rogue → 118 42 30N 124 0W
Rohan 18 48 4N 2 45W
Rohrbach 19 49 3N 7 15 E
Rohri 68 27 45N 68 51 E
Rohri Canal 68 26 15N 68 27 E
Rohtak 68 28 55N 76 43 E
Roi Et 71 16 4N 103 40 E
Roisel 19 49 58N 3 6 E
Rojas 124 34 10 S 60 45W
Rojo, C. 120 21 33N 97 20W
Rokan → 72 2 0N 100 50 E
Rokeby 98 13 39 S 142 40 E
Rokiskis 54 55 55N 25 35 E
Rokitno 54 50 57N 35 56 E
Rokycany 26 49 43N 13 35 E
Rolândia 125 23 18 S 51 23W
Røldal 47 59 47N 6 50 E
Rolette 116 48 42N 99 50W
Rolla, Kansas, U.S.A. 117 37 10N 101 40W
Rolla, Mo., U.S.A. 117 37 56N 91 42W
Rolla, N. Dak., U.S.A. 116 48 50N 99 36W
Rollag 47 60 2N 9 18 E
Rolleston 98 24 28 S 148 35 E
Rollingstone 98 19 2 S 146 24 E
Rom 87 9 54N 32 16 E
Roma, Austral. 97 26 32 S 148 49 E
Roma, Italy 40 41 54N 12 30 E
Roman, Bulg. 43 43 8N 23 54 E
Roman, Romania 46 46 57N 26 55 E
Roman, U.S.S.R. 59 66 4N 112 14 E
Roman-Kosh, Gora 56 44 37N 34 15 E
Romana, La 121 18 27N 68 57W
Romanche → 21 45 5N 5 43 E
Romang 73 7 30 S 127 20 E
Români 86 30 59N 32 38 E
Romania ■ 46 46 0N 25 0 E
Romanija Planina 42 43 50N 18 45 E
Romano, Cayo 121 22 0N 77 30W
Romano di Lombardía 38 45 32N 9 45 E
Romanovka = Bessarabka 56 46 21N 28 58 E
Romans 21 45 3N 5 3 E
Romanshorn 25 47 33N 9 22 E
Romblon 73 12 33N 122 17 E
Rombo □ 90 3 10 S 37 30 E
Rome, Ga., U.S.A. 115 34 20N 85 0W
Rome, N.Y., U.S.A. 114 43 14N 75 29W
Rome = Roma 40 41 54N 12 30 E
Romeleåsen 49 55 34N 13 33 E
Romenay 21 46 30N 5 1 E
Romerike 47 60 7N 11 10 E
Romilly 19 48 31N 3 44 E
Romîni 46 44 59N 24 11 E
Rommani 82 33 31N 6 40W
Romney 114 39 21N 78 45W
Romney Marsh 13 51 0N 1 0 E
Romny 54 50 48N 33 28 E
Rømø 49 55 10N 8 30 E
Romodan 54 50 0N 33 15 E
Romodanovo 55 54 26N 45 23 E
Romont 25 46 42N 6 54 E
Romorantin-Lanthenay 19 47 21N 1 45 E
Romsdalen 47 62 25N 8 0 E
Rona 14 57 33N 6 0W
Ronan 118 47 30N 114 6W
Roncador, Cayos 121 13 32N 80 4W
Roncador, Serra do 127 12 30 S 52 30W
Roncesvalles, Paso 32 43 1N 1 19W
Ronceverte 114 37 45N 80 28W
Ronciglione 39 42 18N 12 12 E
Ronco → 39 44 24N 12 12 E
Ronda 31 36 46N 5 12W
Ronda, Serranía de 31 36 44N 5 3W
Rondane 47 61 57N 9 50 E
Rondônia □ 126 11 0 S 63 0W
Rondonópolis 127 16 28 S 54 38W
Rong, Koh 71 10 45N 103 15 E
Rong Xian 77 29 23N 104 22 E
Rong'an 77 25 14N 109 22 E
Ronge, L. la 109 55 6N 105 17W
Ronge, La 109 55 5N 105 20W
Rongshui 77 25 5N 109 12 E
Ronne Land 5 83 0 S 70 0W
Ronneby 49 56 12N 15 17 E
Ronse 16 50 45N 3 35 E
Roof Butte 119 36 29N 109 5W
Roorkee 68 29 52N 77 59 E
Roosendaal 16 51 32N 4 29 E
Roosevelt, Minn., U.S.A. 116 48 51N 95 2W
Roosevelt, Utah, U.S.A. 118 40 19N 110 1W
Roosevelt I. 5 79 30 S 162 0W
Roosevelt, Mt. 108 58 26N 125 20W
Roosevelt Res. 119 33 46N 111 0W
Ropczyce 27 50 4N 21 38 E
Roper → 96 14 43 S 135 27 E
Ropesville 117 33 25N 102 10W
Roque Pérez 124 35 25 S 59 24W
Roquebrou, La 20 44 58N 2 12 E
Roquefort 20 44 2N 0 20W
Roquefort-sur-Soulzon 20 43 58N 2 59 E
Roquemaure 21 44 3N 4 48 E
Roquetas 32 40 50N 0 30 E
Roquevaire 21 43 20N 5 36 E
Roraima □ 126 2 0N 61 30W
Roraima, Mt. 126 5 10N 60 40W
Rorketon 109 51 24N 99 35W
Røros 47 62 35N 11 23 E
Rorschach 25 47 28N 9 30 E
Rosa 91 9 33 S 31 15 E
Rosa, C. 83 37 0N 8 16 E
Rosa, Monte 25 45 57N 7 53 E
Rosal 30 41 57N 8 51W
Rosal de la Frontera 31 37 59N 7 13W
Rosalia 118 47 14N 117 25W
Rosans 21 44 24N 5 29 E
Rosario 124 33 0 S 60 40W
Rosário 127 3 0 S 44 15W
Rosario, Baja Calif. N., Mexico 120 30 0N 115 50W
Rosario, Durango, Mexico 120 26 30N 105 35W
Rosario, Sinaloa, Mexico 120 23 0N 105 52W
Rosario, Parag. 124 24 30 S 57 35W
Rosario de la Frontera 124 25 50 S 65 0W
Rosario de Lerma 124 24 59 S 65 35W
Rosario del Tala 124 32 20 S 59 10W
Rosário do Sul 125 30 15 S 54 55W
Rosarno 41 38 29N 15 59 E
Rosas 32 42 19N 3 10 E
Roscoe 116 45 27N 99 20W
Roscoff 18 48 44N 4 0W
Roscommon, Ireland 15 53 38N 8 11W
Roscommon, U.S.A. 114 44 27N 84 35W
Roscommon □ 15 53 40N 8 15W
Roscrea 15 52 58N 7 50W
Rose Blanche 107 47 38N 58 45W
Rose Harbour 108 52 15N 131 10W
Rose Pt. 108 54 11N 131 39W
Rose Valley 109 52 19N 103 49W
Roseau, Domin. 121 15 20N 61 24W
Roseau, U.S.A. 116 48 51N 95 46W
Rosebery 99 41 46 S 145 33 E
Rosebud, Austral. 100 38 21 S 144 54 E
Rosebud, U.S.A. 117 31 5N 97 0W
Roseburg 118 43 10N 123 20W
Rosedale, Austral. 98 24 38 S 151 53 E
Rosedale, U.S.A. 117 33 51N 91 0W
Rosemary 108 50 46N 112 5W
Rosenberg 117 29 30N 95 48W
Rosendaël 19 51 3N 2 24 E
Rosenheim 25 47 51N 12 9 E
Roseto degli Abruzzi 39 42 40N 14 2 E
Rosetown 109 51 35N 107 59W
Rosetta = Rashîd 86 31 21N 30 22 E
Roseville 118 38 46N 121 17W
Rosewood 99 27 38 S 152 36 E
Rosh Haniqra, Kefar 62 33 5N 35 5 E
Rosh Pinna 62 32 58N 35 32 E
Rosières 19 49 49N 2 43 E
Rosignano Marittimo 38 43 23N 10 28 E
Rosignol 126 6 15N 57 30W
Roşiori de Vede 46 44 9N 25 0 E
Rositsa 43 43 57N 27 57 E
Rositsa → 43 43 10N 25 30 E
Roskilde 49 55 38N 12 3 E
Roskilde Amtskommune □ 49 55 35N 12 5 E
Roskilde Fjord 49 55 50N 12 2 E
Roslavl 54 53 57N 32 55 E
Roslyn 99 34 29 S 149 37 E
Rosmaninhal 31 39 44N 7 5W
Røsnæs 49 55 44N 10 55 E
Rosolini 41 36 49N 14 58 E
Rosporden 18 47 57N 3 50W
Ross, Austral. 99 42 2 S 147 30 E
Ross, N.Z. 101 42 53 S 170 49 E
Ross Dependency □ 5 70 0 S 170 5W
Ross I. 5 77 30 S 168 0 E
Ross Ice Shelf 5 80 0 S 180 0W
Ross L. 118 48 50N 121 5W
Ross on Wye 13 51 55N 2 34W
Ross Sea 5 74 0 S 178 0 E
Rossan Pt. 15 54 42N 8 47W
Rossano Cálabro 41 39 36N 16 39 E
Rossburn 109 50 40N 100 49W
Rosseau 112 45 16N 79 39W
Rossignol, L., N.S., Can. 107 44 12N 65 10W
Rossignol, L., Qué., Can. 106 52 43N 73 40W
Rossland 108 49 6N 117 50W
Rosslare 15 52 17N 6 23W
Rosslau 24 51 52N 12 15 E
Rosso 84 16 40N 15 45W
Rossosh 57 50 15N 39 28 E
Rossport 106 48 50N 87 30W
Røssvatnet 50 65 45N 14 5 E
Rossville 98 15 48 S 145 15 E
Rosthern 109 52 40N 106 20W
Rostock 24 54 4N 12 9 E
Rostock □ 24 54 10N 12 30 E
Rostov, Don, U.S.S.R. 57 47 15N 39 45 E
Rostov, Moskva, U.S.S.R. 55 57 14N 39 25 E
Rostrenen 18 48 14N 3 21W
Roswell 117 33 26N 104 32W
Rosyth 14 56 2N 3 26W
Rota 31 36 37N 6 20W
Rotälven → 48 61 15N 14 3 E
Rotan 117 32 52N 100 30W
Rotenburg 24 53 6N 9 24 E
Roth 25 49 15N 11 6 E
Rothaargebirge 22 51 0N 8 20 E
Rothenburg ob der Tauber 25 49 21N 10 11 E
Rother → 13 50 59N 0 40 E
Rotherham 12 53 26N 1 21W
Rothes 14 57 31N 3 12W
Rothesay, Can. 107 45 23N 66 0W
Rothesay, U.K. 14 55 50N 5 3W
Roti 73 10 50 S 123 0 E
Roto 97 33 0 S 145 30 E
Rotondella 41 40 10N 16 30 E
Rotoroa, L. 101 41 55 S 172 39 E
Rotorua 101 38 9 S 176 16 E
Rotorua, L. 101 38 5 S 176 18 E
Rott → 25 48 26N 13 26 E
Rottenburg 25 48 28N 8 56 E
Rottenmann 26 47 31N 14 22 E
Rotterdam 16 51 55N 4 30 E
Rottumeroog 16 53 33N 6 34 E
Rottweil 25 48 9N 8 38 E
Rotuma 94 12 25 S 177 5 E
Roubaix 19 50 40N 3 10 E
Roudnice 26 50 25N 14 15 E
Rouen 18 49 27N 1 4 E
Rouillac 20 45 47N 0 4W
Rouleau 109 50 10N 104 56W
Round Mt. 97 30 26 S 152 16 E
Round Mountain 118 38 46N 117 3W
Roundup 118 46 25N 108 35W
Rousay 14 59 10N 3 2W
Rouses Point 113 44 58N 73 22W
Rousse, L'Île 21 42 37N 8 57 E
Roussillon, Isère, France 21 45 24N 4 49 E
Roussillon, Pyrénées-Or., France 20 42 30N 2 35 E
Rouxville 92 30 25 S 26 50 E
Rouyn 106 48 20N 79 0W
Rovaniemi 50 66 29N 25 41 E
Rovato 38 45 34N 10 0 E
Rovenki 57 48 5N 39 21 E
Rovereto 38 45 53N 11 3 E
Rovigo 39 45 4N 11 48 E
Rovinari 46 44 56N 23 10 E
Rovinj 39 45 5N 13 40 E
Rovno 54 50 40N 26 10 E
Rovnoye 55 50 52N 46 3 E
Rovuma → 91 10 29 S 40 28 E
Rowena 99 29 48 S 148 55 E
Rowley Shoals 96 17 30 S 119 0 E
Roxa 84 11 15N 15 45W
Roxas 73 11 36N 122 49 E
Roxboro 115 36 24N 78 59W
Roxborough Downs 98 22 30 S 138 45 E
Roxburgh 101 45 33 S 169 19 E
Roxen 49 58 30N 15 40 E
Roy, Mont., U.S.A. 118 47 17N 109 0W
Roy, N. Mex., U.S.A. 117 35 57N 104 8W
Roy, Le 117 38 8N 95 35W
Roya, Peña 32 40 25N 0 40W
Royal Oak 114 42 30N 83 5W
Royan 20 45 37N 1 2W
Roye 19 49 42N 2 48 E
Røyken 47 59 45N 10 23 E
Rožaj 42 42 50N 20 15 E
Różan 28 52 52N 21 25 E
Rozay 19 48 40N 2 56 E
Rozhishche 54 50 54N 25 15 E
Rozier, Le 20 44 13N 3 12 E
Rožňava 27 48 37N 20 35 E
Rozogi 28 53 48N 21 9 E
Rozoy-sur-Serre 19 49 40N 4 8 E
Rozwadów 28 50 37N 22 2 E
Rrësheni 44 41 47N 19 49 E
Rrogozhino 44 41 2N 19 50 E
Rtanj 42 43 45N 21 50 E
Rtishchevo 55 55 16N 43 50 E
Rúa 30 42 24N 7 6W
Ruacaná 92 17 20 S 14 12 E
Ruahine Ra. 101 39 55 S 176 2 E
Ruapehu 101 39 17 S 175 35 E
Ruapuke I. 101 46 46 S 168 31 E
Ruaus, Wadi → 83 30 26N 15 24 E
Rubeho Mts. 90 6 50 S 36 25 E
Rubezhnoye 56 49 6N 38 25 E
Rubh a' Mhail 14 55 55N 6 10W
Rubha Hunish 14 57 42N 6 20W
Rubicone → 39 44 8N 12 28 E
Rubino 84 6 4N 4 18W
Rubio 126 7 43N 72 22W
Rubtsovsk 58 51 30N 81 10 E
Ruby 104 64 40N 155 35W
Ruby L. 118 40 10N 115 28W
Ruby Mts. 118 40 30N 115 30W
Rubyvale 98 23 25 S 147 45 E
Rucava 54 56 9N 21 12 E
Ruciane-Nida 28 53 40N 21 32 E
Rud 47 60 1N 10 1 E
Ruda 49 57 6N 16 7 E
Ruda Śląska 28 50 16N 18 50 E
Ruden 24 54 13N 13 47 E
Rüdersdorf 24 52 28N 13 48 E
Rudewa 91 10 7 S 34 40 E
Rudkøbing 49 54 56N 10 41 E
Rudna 28 51 30N 16 17 E
Rudnichnyy 52 59 38N 52 26 E
Rudnik, Bulg. 43 42 36N 27 30 E
Rudnik, Poland 28 50 26N 22 15 E
Rudnik, Yugo. 42 44 8N 20 30 E
Rudnik, Yugo. 43 44 7N 20 35 E
Rudnogorsk 59 57 15N 103 42 E
Rudnya 54 54 55N 31 7 E
Rudnyy 58 52 57N 63 7 E
Rudo 42 43 41N 19 23 E
Rudolf, Ostrov 58 81 45N 58 30 E
Rudolstadt 24 50 44N 11 20 E
Rudozem 43 41 29N 24 51 E
Rudyard 114 46 14N 84 35W
Rue 19 50 15N 1 40 E
Ruelle 20 45 41N 0 14 E
Rufa'a 87 14 44N 33 22 E
Ruffec-Charente 20 46 2N 0 12 E
Rufiji □ 90 8 0 S 38 30 E
Rufiji → 90 7 50 S 39 15 E
Rufino 124 34 20 S 62 50W
Rufisque 84 14 40N 17 15W
Rufunsa 91 15 4 S 29 34 E
Rugao 77 32 23N 120 31 E
Rugby, U.K. 13 52 23N 1 16W
Rugby, U.S.A. 116 48 21N 100 0W
Rügen 24 54 22N 13 25 E
Rugles 18 48 50N 0 40 E
Ruhama 62 31 31N 34 43 E
Ruhengeri 90 1 30 S 29 36 E
Ruhla 24 50 53N 10 21 E
Ruhland 24 51 27N 13 52 E
Ruhr → 24 51 25N 6 44 E
Ruhuhu → 91 10 31 S 34 34 E
Rui'an 77 27 47N 120 40 E
Ruidosa 117 29 59N 104 39W
Ruidoso 119 33 19N 105 39W
Ruj 42 42 52N 22 42 E
Rujen 42 42 9N 22 30 E

Ruk St-Junien

Ruk	68	27 50N	68 42 E
Rukwa □	90	7 0S	31 30 E
Rukwa L.	90	8 0S	32 20 E
Rum Cay	121	23 40N	74 58W
Rum Jungle	96	13 0S	130 59 E
Ruma	42	45 0N	19 50 E
Rumāḩ	64	25 29N	47 10 E
Rumania = Romania ■	46	46 0N	25 0 E
Rumbêk	87	6 54N	29 37 E
Rumburk	26	50 57N	14 32 E
Rumford	114	44 30N	70 30W
Rumia	28	54 37N	18 25 E
Rumilly	21	45 53N	5 56 E
Rumoi	74	43 56N	141 39W
Rumonge	90	3 59S	29 26 E
Rumsey	108	51 51N	112 48W
Rumula	98	16 35S	145 20 E
Rumuruti	90	0 17N	36 32 E
Runan	77	33 0N	114 30 E
Runanga	101	42 25S	171 15 E
Runaway, C.	101	37 32S	178 2 E
Runcorn	12	53 20N	2 44W
Rungwa	90	6 55S	33 32 E
Rungwa →	90	7 36S	31 50 E
Rungwe	91	9 11S	33 32 E
Rungwe □	91	9 25S	33 32 E
Runka	85	12 28N	7 20 E
Runn	48	60 30N	15 40 E
Ruoqiang	75	38 55N	88 10 E
Rupa	67	27 15N	92 21 E
Rupar	68	31 2N	76 38 E
Rupat	72	1 45N	101 40 E
Rupea	46	46 2N	25 13 E
Rupert →	106	51 29N	78 45W
Rupert House = Fort Rupert	106	51 30N	78 40W
Rupsa	69	21 44N	89 30 E
Rur →	24	51 20N	6 0 E
Rurrenabaque	126	14 30S	67 32W
Rus →	33	39 30N	2 30W
Rusambo	91	16 30S	32 4 E
Rusape	91	18 35S	32 8 E
Ruschuk = Ruse	43	43 48N	25 59 E
Ruse	43	43 48N	25 59 E
Ruşeţu	46	44 57N	27 14 E
Rushden	13	52 17N	0 37W
Rushford	116	43 48N	91 46W
Rushville, Ill., U.S.A.	116	40 6N	90 35W
Rushville, Ind., U.S.A.	114	39 38N	85 22W
Rushville, Nebr., U.S.A.	116	42 43N	102 28W
Rushworth	100	36 32S	145 1 E
Rusken	49	57 15N	14 20 E
Russas	127	4 55S	37 50W
Russell, Can.	109	50 50N	101 20W
Russell, N.Z.	101	35 16S	174 10 E
Russell, U.S.A.	116	38 56N	98 55W
Russell L., Man., Can.	109	56 15N	101 30W
Russell L., N.W.T., Can.	108	63 5N	115 44W
Russellkonda	69	19 57N	84 42 E
Russellville, Ala., U.S.A.	115	34 30N	87 44W
Russellville, Ark., U.S.A.	117	35 15N	93 8W
Russellville, Ky., U.S.A.	115	36 50N	86 50W
Russi	39	44 21N	12 1 E
Russian S.F.S.R. □	59	62 0N	105 0 E
Russkaya Polyana	58	53 47N	73 53 E
Russkoye Ustie	4	71 0N	149 0 E
Rust	27	47 49N	16 42 E
Rustavi	57	41 30N	45 0 E
Rustenburg	92	25 41S	27 14 E
Ruston	117	32 30N	92 58W
Rutana	90	3 55S	30 0 E
Rute	31	37 19N	4 23W
Ruteng	73	8 35S	120 30 E
Ruth, Mich., U.S.A.	112	43 42N	82 45W
Ruth, Nev., U.S.A.	118	39 15N	115 1W
Rutherglen, Austral.	100	36 5S	146 29 E
Rutherglen, U.K.	14	55 50N	4 11W
Rutigliano	41	41 1N	17 0 E
Rutland I.	71	11 25N	92 40 E
Rutland Plains	98	15 38S	141 43 E
Rutledge →	109	61 4N	112 0W
Rutledge L.	109	61 33N	110 47W
Rutshuru	90	1 13S	29 25 E
Ruurlo	16	52 5N	6 24 E
Ruvo di Púglia	41	41 7N	16 27 E
Ruvu	90	6 49S	38 43 E
Ruvu →	90	6 23S	38 52 E
Ruvuma □	91	10 20S	36 0 E
Ruwenzori	90	0 30N	29 55 E
Ruyigi	90	3 29S	30 15 E
Ruzayevka	55	54 4N	45 0 E
Růžhevo Konare	43	42 23N	24 46 E
Ružomberok	27	49 3N	19 17 E
Rwanda ■	90	2 0S	30 0 E
Ry	49	56 5N	9 45 E
Ryakhovo	43	44 0N	26 18 E
Ryan, L.	14	55 0N	5 2W
Ryazan	55	54 40N	39 40 E
Ryazhsk	55	53 45N	40 3 E
Rybache	58	46 40N	81 20 E
Rybachiy Poluostrov	52	69 43N	32 0 E
*Rybinsk	55	58 5N	38 50 E
Rybinskoye Vdkhr.	55	58 30N	38 25 E
Rybnik	27	50 6N	18 32 E
Rybnitsa	56	47 45N	29 0 E
Rybnoye	55	54 45N	39 30 E
Rychwał	28	52 4N	18 10 E
Ryd	49	56 27N	14 42 E
Ryde	13	50 44N	1 9W
Rydöbruk	49	56 58N	13 7 E
Rydsnäs	49	57 47N	15 9 E
Rydułtowy	27	50 4N	18 23 E
Rydzyna	28	51 47N	16 39 E
Rye	13	50 57N	0 46 E
Rye →	12	54 12N	0 53W
Rye Patch Res.	118	40 38N	118 20W
Ryegate	118	46 21N	109 15W
Ryki	28	51 38N	21 56 E
Rylsk	54	51 36N	34 43 E
Rylstone	99	32 46S	149 58 E
Rymanów	27	49 35N	21 51 E
Ryn	28	53 57N	21 34 E
Rypin	28	53 3N	19 25 E
Ryūkyū Is. = Nansei-Shotō	74	26 0N	128 0 E
Rzepin	28	52 20N	14 49 E
Rzeszów	27	50 5N	21 58 E
Rzeszów □	27	50 10N	22 0 E
Rzhev	54	56 20N	34 20 E

S

Sa Dec	71	10 20N	105 46 E
Sa'ad (Muharraqa)	62	31 28N	34 33 E
Sa'ādatābād	65	30 10N	53 5 E
Saale →	24	51 57N	11 56 E
Saaler Bodden	24	54 20N	12 25 E
Saalfeld	24	50 39N	11 21 E
Saalfelden	26	47 25N	12 51 E
Saane →	25	46 23N	7 18 E
Saar (Sarre) →	19	49 42N	6 34 E
Saarbrücken	25	49 15N	6 58 E
Saarburg	25	49 36N	6 32 E
Saaremaa	54	58 30N	22 30 E
Saariselkä	50	68 16N	28 15 E
Saarland □	25	49 15N	7 0 E
Saarlouis	25	49 19N	6 45 E
Saba	121	17 42N	63 26W
Šabac	42	44 48N	19 42 E
Sabadell	32	41 28N	2 7 E
Sabagalet	72	1 36S	98 40 E
Sabah □	72	6 0N	117 0 E
Sábana de la Mar	121	19 7N	69 24W
Sábanalarga	126	10 38N	74 55W
Sabang	72	5 50N	95 15 E
Sabará	127	19 55S	43 46W
Sabarania	73	2 5S	138 18 E
Sabari →	70	17 35N	81 16 E
Sabasţiyah	62	32 17N	35 12 E
Sabattis	113	44 6N	74 40W
Sabáudia	40	41 17N	13 2 E
Sabhah	83	27 9N	14 29 E
Sabhah □	83	26 0N	14 0 E
Sabie	93	25 10S	30 48 E
Sabinal, Mexico	120	30 58N	107 25W
Sabinal, U.S.A.	117	29 20N	99 27W
Sabinal, Punta del	33	36 43N	2 44W
Sabinas	120	27 50N	101 10W
Sabinas Hidalgo	120	26 33N	100 10W
Sabine	117	29 42N	93 54W
Sabine →	117	30 0N	93 35W
Sabine L.	117	29 50N	93 50W
Sabinov	27	49 6N	21 5 E
Sabirabad	57	40 5N	48 30 E
Sabkhat Tāwurghā'	83	31 48N	15 30 E
Sablayan	73	12 50N	120 50 E
Sable, C., Can.	107	43 29N	65 38W
Sable, C., U.S.A.	121	25 13N	81 0W
Sable I.	107	44 0N	60 0W
Sablé-sur-Sarthe	18	47 50N	0 20W
Sables-d'Olonne, Les	20	46 30N	1 45W
Sabolev	59	54 20N	155 30 E
Sabor →	30	41 10N	7 7W
Sabou	84	12 1N	2 15W
Sabrātah	83	32 47N	12 29 E
Sabria	83	33 22N	8 45 E
Sabrina Coast	5	68 0S	120 0 E
Sabugal	30	40 20N	7 5W
Sabzevār	65	36 15N	57 40 E
Sabzvārān	65	28 45N	57 50 E
Sac City	116	42 26N	95 0W
Sacedón	32	40 29N	2 41W
Sachigo →	106	55 6N	88 58W
Sachigo, L.	106	53 50N	92 12W
Sachkhere	57	42 25N	43 28 E
Sacile	39	45 58N	12 30 E
Sackets Harbor	113	43 56N	76 7W
Säckingen	25	47 34N	7 56 E
Saco, Me., U.S.A.	115	43 30N	70 27W
Saco, Mont., U.S.A.	118	48 28N	107 19W
Sacramento	118	38 33N	121 30 E
Sacramento →	118	38 3N	121 56W
Sacramento Mts.	119	32 30N	105 30W
Sacratif, Cabo	33	36 42N	3 28W
Săcueni	46	47 20N	22 5 E
Sada	30	43 22N	8 15W
Sádaba	32	42 19N	1 12W
Sadani	90	5 58S	38 35 E
Sadao	71	6 38N	100 26 E
Sadasivpet	70	17 38N	77 59 E
Sadd el Aali	86	23 54N	32 54 E
Sade	85	11 22N	10 45 E
Sadimi	91	9 25S	23 32 E
Sado	74	38 0N	138 25 E
Sado →	31	38 29N	8 55W
Sado, Shima	74	38 15N	138 30 E
Sadon, Burma	67	25 28N	98 0 E
Sadon, U.S.S.R.	57	42 52N	43 58 E
Sæby	49	57 21N	10 30 E
Saegerstown	112	41 42N	80 10W
Saelices	32	39 55N	2 49W
Safaga	86	26 42N	34 0 E
Şafaha	86	26 25N	39 0 E
Šafárikovo	27	48 25N	20 20 E
Säffle	48	59 8N	12 55 E
Safford	119	32 50N	109 43W
Saffron Walden	13	52 2N	0 15 E
Safi	82	32 18N	9 20W
Safīd Kūh	65	34 45N	63 0 E
Safonovo	54	55 4N	33 16 E
Safranbolu	56	41 15N	32 41 E
Sag Harbor	113	40 59N	72 17W
Saga	73	2 40S	132 55 E
Saga □	74	33 15N	130 20 E
Sagala	84	14 9N	6 38W
Sagara	70	14 14N	75 6 E
Sagara, L.	90	5 20S	31 0 E
Saghīr, Zab al	64	35 10N	43 20 E
Sagil	75	50 15N	91 15 E
Saginaw	114	43 26N	83 55W
Saginaw B.	106	43 50N	83 40W
Sagleipie	84	7 0N	8 52W
Saglouc (Sugluk)	105	62 10N	74 40W
Sagone	21	42 7N	8 42 E
Sagone, G. de	21	42 4N	8 40 E
Sagra, La >	33	37 57N	2 35W
Sagres	31	37 0N	8 58W
Sagua la Grande	121	22 50N	80 10W
Saguache	119	38 10N	106 10W
Saguenay →	107	48 22N	71 0W
Sagunto	32	39 42N	0 18W
Sahaba	86	18 57N	30 25 E
Sahagún	30	42 18N	5 2W
Saham	62	32 42N	35 46 E
Saḩam al Jawlān	62	32 45N	35 55 E
Sahand, Kūh-e	64	37 44N	46 27 E
Sahara	82	23 0N	5 0 E
Saharanpur	68	29 58N	77 33 E
Saharien Atlas	82	33 30N	1 0 E
Sahasinaka	93	21 49S	47 49 E
Sahaswan	68	28 5N	78 45 E
Sahel, Canal du	84	14 20N	6 0W
Sahibganj	69	25 12N	87 40 E
Sahiwal	68	30 45N	73 8 E
Sahtaneh →	108	59 2N	122 28W
Sahuaripa	120	29 0N	109 13W
Sahuarita	119	31 58N	110 59W
Sahuayo	120	20 4N	102 43W
Sahy	27	48 4N	18 55 E
Saibai I.	98	9 25S	142 40 E
Sa'id Bundas	81	8 24N	24 48 E
Saïda	82	34 50N	0 11 E
Saīdābād	65	29 30N	55 45 E
Saïdia	82	35 5N	2 14W
Saidu	69	34 43N	72 24 E
Saignes	20	45 20N	2 31 E
Saigon = Thanh Bho Ho Chi Minh	71	10 46N	106 40 E
Saih-al-Malih	65	23 37N	58 31 E
Saijō	74	33 55N	133 11 E
Saikhoa Ghat	67	27 50N	95 40 E
Saiki	74	32 58N	131 51 E
Saillans	21	44 42N	5 12 E
Sailolof	73	1 7S	130 46 E
St. Abb's Head	14	55 55N	2 10W
St. Aegyd	26	47 52N	15 33 E
St-Affrique	20	43 57N	2 53 E
St-Agrève	21	45 0N	4 23 E
St-Aignan	18	47 16N	1 22 E
St. Alban's	107	47 51N	55 50W
St. Albans, U.K.	13	51 44N	0 19W
St. Albans, Vt., U.S.A.	114	44 49N	73 7W
St. Albans, W. Va., U.S.A.	114	38 21N	81 50W
St. Alban's Head	13	50 34N	2 3W
St. Albert	108	53 37N	113 32W
St-Amand	19	50 25N	3 26 E
St-Amand-en-Puisaye	19	47 32N	3 5 E
St-Amand-Mont-Rond	20	46 43N	2 30 E
St-Amarin	19	47 54N	7 0 E
St-Amour	21	46 26N	5 21 E
St-André-de-Cubzac	20	44 59N	0 26W
St-André-de-l'Eure	18	48 54N	1 16 E
St-André-les-Alpes	21	43 58N	6 30 E
St. André, Tanjona	93	16 11S	44 27 E
St. Andrew's	107	47 45N	59 15W
St. Andrews	14	56 20N	2 48W
St-Anicet	113	45 8N	74 22W
St. Ann B.	107	46 22N	60 25W
St. Anne	18	49 43N	2 11W
St. Anthony, Can.	107	51 22N	55 35W
St. Anthony, U.S.A.	118	44 0N	111 40W
St-Antonin-Noble-Val	20	44 10N	1 45 E
St. Arnaud	99	36 40S	143 16 E
St. Arthur	107	47 33N	67 46W
St. Asaph	12	53 15N	3 27W
St-Astier	20	45 8N	0 31 E
St-Aubin-du-Cormier	18	48 15N	1 26W
St. Augustin	93	23 33S	43 46 E
St-Augustin-Saguenay	107	51 13N	58 38W
St. Augustine	115	29 52N	81 20W
St. Austell	13	50 20N	4 48W
St-Avold	19	49 6N	6 43 E
St.-Barthélemy, I.	121	17 50N	62 50W
St. Bee's Hd.	12	54 30N	3 38 E
St-Benoît-du-Sault	20	46 26N	1 24 E
St. Bernard, Col du Grand	25	45 53N	7 11 E
St. Boniface	109	49 53N	97 5W
St-Bonnet	21	44 40N	6 5 E
St-Brévin-les-Pins	18	47 14N	2 10W
St-Brice-en-Coglès	18	48 25N	1 22W
St. Bride's	107	46 56N	54 10W
St. Bride's B.	13	51 48N	5 15W
St-Brieuc	18	48 30N	2 46W
St-Calais	18	47 55N	0 45 E
St-Cast	18	48 37N	2 18W
St. Catharines	106	43 10N	79 15W
St. Catherines I.	115	31 35N	81 10W
St. Catherine's Pt.	13	50 34N	1 18W
St-Céré	20	44 51N	1 54 E
St.-Cergue	25	46 27N	6 10 E
St-Cernin	20	45 5N	2 25 E
St-Chamond	21	45 28N	4 31 E
St. Charles, Ill., U.S.A.	114	41 55N	88 21W
St. Charles, Mo., U.S.A.	116	38 46N	90 30W
St-Chély-d'Apcher	20	44 48N	3 17 E
St-Chinian	20	43 25N	2 56 E
St. Christopher (St. Kitts)	121	17 20N	62 40W
St-Ciers-sur-Gironde	20	45 17N	0 37W
St. Clair, Mich, U.S.A.	112	42 47N	82 27W
St. Clair, Pa., U.S.A.	113	40 42N	76 12W
St. Clair, L.	106	42 30N	82 45W
St. Clairsville	112	40 5N	80 53W
St-Claud	20	45 54N	0 28 E
St. Claude	109	49 40N	98 20W
St-Claude	21	46 22N	5 52 E
St-Cloud	18	48 51N	2 12 E
St. Cloud, Fla., U.S.A.	115	28 15N	81 15W
St. Cloud, Minn., U.S.A.	116	45 30N	94 11W
St-Coeur de Marie	107	48 39N	71 43W
St. Croix	121	17 45N	64 45W
St. Croix →	116	44 45N	92 50W
St. Croix Falls	116	45 18N	92 22W
St-Cyprien	20	42 37N	3 0 E
St-Cyr	21	43 11N	5 43 E
St. David's, Can.	107	48 12N	58 52W
St. David's, U.K.	13	51 54N	5 16W
St. David's Head	13	51 55N	5 16W
St-Denis	19	48 56N	2 22 E
St-Denis-d'Orques	18	48 2N	0 17W
St-Dié	19	48 17N	6 56 E
St-Dizier	19	48 40N	5 0 E
St-Egrève	21	45 14N	5 41 E
St. Elias, Mt.	104	60 14N	140 50W
St Elias Mts.	108	60 33N	139 28W
St-Éloy-les-Mines	20	46 10N	2 51 E
St-Émilion	20	44 53N	0 9W
St-Étienne	21	45 27N	4 22 E
St-Étienne-de-Tinée	21	44 16N	6 56 E
St. Eugène	113	45 30N	74 28W
St. Eustatius	121	17 20N	63 0W
St-Félicien	106	48 40N	72 25W
St-Florent	21	42 41N	9 18 E
St-Florent-sur-Cher	19	46 59N	2 15 E
St-Florentin	19	48 0N	3 45 E
St-Flour	20	45 2N	3 6 E
St-Fons	21	45 42N	4 52 E
St. Francis	116	39 48N	101 47W
St. Francis →	117	34 38N	90 36W
St. Francis, C.	92	34 14S	24 49 E
St. Francis, L.	113	45 10N	74 22W
St. Francisville	117	30 48N	91 22W
St-Fulgent	18	46 50N	1 10W
St-Gabriel-de-Brandon	106	46 17N	73 24W
St-Gaudens	20	43 6N	0 44 E
St-Gengoux-le-National	21	46 37N	4 40 E
St-Geniez-d'Olt	20	44 27N	2 58 E
St. George, Austral.	97	28 1S	148 30 E
St. George, Berm.	121	32 24N	64 42W
St. George, Can.	107	45 11N	66 50W
St. George, S.C., U.S.A.	115	33 13N	80 37W
St. George, Utah, U.S.A.	119	37 10N	113 35W
St. George, C., Can.	107	48 30N	59 16W
St. George, C., U.S.A.	115	29 36N	85 2W
St-Georges	16	50 37N	5 20 E
St. George's	107	48 26N	58 31W
St. Georges	106	46 42N	72 35W
St-Georges	107	46 8N	70 40W
St. Georges	127	4 0N	52 0W
St. George's	121	12 5N	61 43W
St. George's B.	107	48 24N	58 53W
Saint George's Channel	98	4 10S	152 20 E
St. George's Channel	11	52 0N	6 0W
St-Georges-de-Didonne	20	45 36N	1 0W
St. Georges Head	100	35 12S	150 42 E
St-Germain	19	48 53N	2 5 E
St-Germain-Lembron	20	45 27N	3 14 E
St-Germain-de-Calberte	20	44 13N	3 48 E
St-Germain-des-Fossés	20	46 12N	3 26 E
St-Germain-du-Plain	19	46 42N	4 58 E
St-Germain-Laval	21	45 50N	4 1 E
St-Gers	20	45 18N	0 37W
St-Gervais, Haute Savoie, France	21	45 53N	6 42 E
St-Gervais, Puy de Dôme, France	20	46 4N	2 50 E
St-Gildas, Pte. de	18	47 8N	2 14W
St-Gilles-Croix-de-Vie	18	46 41N	1 55W
St-Gilles-du-Gard	21	43 40N	4 26 E
St-Girons	20	42 59N	1 8 E
St. Goar	25	50 12N	7 43 E
St-Gualtier	18	48 39N	1 26 E
St-Guénolé	18	47 49N	4 23W
St. Helena, Atl. Oc.	7	15 55S	5 44W
St. Helena, U.S.A.	118	38 29N	122 30W
St. Helenabaai	92	32 40S	18 10 E
St. Helens, U.K.	12	53 28N	2 44W
St. Helens, U.S.A.	118	45 55N	122 50W
St. Helier	18	49 11N	2 6W
St-Hilaire	18	48 35N	1 7W
St-Hippolyte	19	47 20N	6 50 E
St-Hippolyte-du-Fort	20	43 58N	3 52 E
St-Honoré	19	46 54N	3 50 E
St-Hubert	16	50 2N	5 23 E
St-Hyacinthe	106	45 40N	72 58W
St. Ignace	114	45 53N	84 43W
St. Ignace I.	106	48 45N	88 0W
St. Ignatius	118	47 19N	114 8W
St-Imier	25	47 9N	6 58 E
St. Ives, Cambs., U.K.	13	52 20N	0 5W
St. Ives, Cornwall, U.K.	13	50 13N	5 29W
St-James	18	48 31N	1 20W
St. James	116	43 57N	94 40W
St. Jean	106	45 20N	73 20W
St-Jean	21	45 30N	5 10 E
St-Jean →	107	50 17N	64 20W
St. Jean Baptiste	109	49 15N	97 20W
St-Jean-d'Angély	20	45 57N	0 31W
St-Jean-de-Maurienne	21	45 16N	6 21 E
St-Jean-de-Luz	20	43 23N	1 39W
St-Jean-de-Monts	18	46 47N	2 4W
St-Jean-du-Gard	20	44 7N	3 52 E
St-Jean-en-Royans	21	45 1N	5 18 E
St-Jean, L.	107	48 40N	72 0W
St-Jean-Port-Joli	107	47 15N	70 13W
St-Jérôme, Qué., Can.	106	45 47N	74 0W
St-Jérôme, Qué., Can.	107	48 26N	71 53W
St. John, Can.	107	45 20N	66 8W
St. John, Kans., U.S.A.	117	37 59N	98 45W
St. John, N.D., U.S.A.	116	48 58N	99 40W
St. John →	107	45 15N	66 4W
St. John, C.	107	50 0N	55 32W
St. John's, Antigua	121	17 6N	61 51W
St. John's, Can.	107	47 35N	52 40W
St. Johns, Ariz., U.S.A.	119	34 31N	109 26W
St. Johns, Mich., U.S.A.	114	43 0N	84 31W
St. John's →	115	30 20N	81 30W
St. Johnsbury	114	44 25N	72 1W
St. Johnsville	113	43 0N	74 43W
St. Joseph, La., U.S.A.	117	31 55N	91 15W
St. Joseph, Mich., U.S.A.	114	42 5N	86 30W
St. Joseph, Mo., U.S.A.	116	39 46N	94 50W
St. Joseph →	114	42 7N	86 30W
St. Joseph, I.	106	46 12N	83 58W
St. Joseph, L.	106	51 10N	90 35W
St-Jovite	106	46 8N	74 38W
St-Juéry	20	43 55N	2 12 E
St-Julien	21	46 8N	6 5 E
St-Julien-Chapteuil	21	45 2N	4 4 E
St-Julien-du-Sault	19	48 1N	3 17 E
St-Junien	20	45 53N	0 55 E

*Renamed Andropov

St-Just-en-Chaussée	19	49 30N	2 25 E
St-Just-en-Chevalet	20	45 55N	3 50 E
St-Justin	20	43 59N	0 14W
St. Kilda, N.Z.	101	45 53 S	170 31 E
St. Kilda, U.K.	8	57 9N	8 34W
St. Kitts-Nevis ■	121	17 20N	62 40W
St. Laurent	109	50 25N	97 58W
St-Laurent	127	5 29N	54 3W
St-Laurent-du-Pont	21	45 23N	5 45 E
St-Laurent-en-Grandvaux	21	46 35N	5 58 E
St. Lawrence	107	46 54N	55 23W
St. Lawrence →	107	49 30N	66 0W
St. Lawrence, Gulf of	107	48 25N	62 0W
St. Lawrence I.	104	63 0N	170 0W
St. Leonard	107	47 12N	67 58W
St-Léonard-de-Noblat	20	45 49N	1 29 E
St. Lewis →	107	52 26N	56 11W
St-Lô	18	49 7N	1 5W
St-Louis	84	16 8N	16 27W
St. Louis, Mich., U.S.A.	114	43 27N	84 38W
St. Louis, Mo., U.S.A.	116	38 40N	90 12W
St. Louis →	116	47 15N	92 45W
St-Loup-sur-Semouse	19	47 53N	6 16 E
St. Lucia ■	121	14 0N	60 50W
St. Lucia, C.	93	28 32 S	32 29 E
St. Lucia Channel	121	14 15N	61 0W
St. Lucia, Lake	93	28 5 S	32 30 E
St. Lunaire-Griquet	107	51 31N	55 28W
St. Maarten	121	18 0N	63 5W
St-Maixent-l'École	20	46 24N	0 12W
St-Malo	18	48 39N	2 1W
St-Malo, G. de	18	48 50N	2 30W
St-Mandrier	21	43 4N	5 56 E
St-Marc	121	19 10N	72 41W
St-Marcellin	21	45 9N	5 20 E
St-Marcouf, Îs.	18	49 30N	1 10W
St. Maries	118	47 17N	116 34W
St-Martin, Charente-M., France	20	46 12N	1 22W
St-Martin, Pas-de-Calais, France	19	50 42N	1 38 E
St-Martin, I.	121	18 0N	63 0W
St. Martin L.	109	51 40N	98 30W
St-Martin-Vésubie	21	44 4N	7 15 E
St. Martins	107	45 22N	65 34W
St. Martinsville	117	30 10N	91 50W
St-Martory	20	43 9N	0 56 E
St. Mary B.	107	46 50N	53 50W
St. Mary Is.	70	13 20N	74 35 E
St. Mary Pk.	97	31 32 S	138 34 E
St. Marys, Austral.	97	41 35 S	148 11 E
St. Marys, Can.	112	43 20N	81 10W
St. Mary's, U.K.	13	49 55N	6 17W
St. Mary's, U.S.A.	114	40 33N	84 20W
St. Marys	114	41 27N	78 33W
St. Marys Bay	107	44 25N	66 10W
St. Mary's, C.	107	46 50N	54 12W
St. Mathews I. = Zadetkyi Kyun	71	10 0N	98 25 E
St-Mathieu, Pte. de	18	48 20N	4 45W
St-Maur-des-Fossés	19	48 48N	2 30 E
St-Maurice →	106	46 21N	72 31W
St-Médard-de-Guizières	20	45 1N	0 4W
St-Méen-le-Grand	18	48 11N	2 12W
St. Michaels	119	35 38N	109 5W
St. Michael's Mt.	13	50 7N	5 30W
St-Michel	21	45 15N	6 29 E
St-Mihiel	19	48 54N	5 30 E
St-Nazaire	18	47 17N	2 12W
St. Neots	13	52 14N	0 16W
St-Nicolas-de-Port	19	48 38N	6 18 E
St-Omer	19	50 45N	2 15 E
St. Ouen	19	48 50N	2 20 E
St-Ouen	19	50 2N	2 7 E
St-Pacome	107	47 24N	69 58W
St-Palais	20	45 40N	1 8W
St-Pamphile	107	46 58N	69 48W
St-Pardoux-la-Rivière	20	45 29N	0 45 E
St. Pascal	107	47 32N	69 48W
St. Paul, Can.	108	54 0N	111 17W
St. Paul, Ind. Oc.	3	30 40 S	77 34 E
St. Paul, Minn., U.S.A.	116	44 54N	93 5W
St. Paul, Nebr., U.S.A.	116	41 15N	98 30W
St-Paul-de-Fenouillet	20	42 50N	2 28 E
St. Paul, I.	107	47 12N	60 9W
St-Péray	21	44 57N	4 50 E
St-Père-en-Retz	18	47 11N	2 2W
St. Peter	116	44 21N	93 57W
St. Peter Port	18	49 27N	2 31W
St. Peters, N.S., Can.	107	45 40N	60 53W
St. Peters, P.E.I., Can.	107	46 25N	62 35W
St. Petersburg	115	27 45N	82 40W
St-Philbert-de-Grand-Lieu	18	47 2N	1 39W
St Pierre	107	46 46N	56 12W
St-Pierre-d'Oléron	20	45 57N	1 19W
St-Pierre-Église	18	49 40N	1 24W
St-Pierre-en-Port	18	49 48N	0 30 E
St-Pierre et Miquelon □	107	46 55N	56 10W
St-Pierre, L.	106	46 12N	72 52W
St-Pierre-le-Moûtier	19	46 47N	3 7 E
St.-Pierre-sur-Dives	18	49 2N	0 1W
St.-Pol	19	50 21N	2 20 E
St-Pol-de-Léon	18	48 41N	4 0W
St-Pol-sur-Mer	19	51 1N	2 20 E
St-Pons	20	43 30N	2 45 E
St-Pourçain-sur-Sioule	20	46 18N	3 18 E
St-Quay-Portrieux	18	48 39N	2 51W
St-Quentin	19	49 50N	3 16 E
St-Rambert-d'Albon	21	45 17N	4 49 E
St-Raphaël	21	43 25N	6 46 E
St. Regis, Mont., U.S.A.	118	47 20N	115 3W
St. Regis, N.Y., U.S.A.	113	44 39N	74 34W
St-Rémy-de-Provence	21	43 48N	4 50 E
St-Renan	18	48 26N	4 37W
St-Saëns	18	49 41N	1 16 E
St-Sauveur-en-Puisaye	19	47 37N	3 12 E
St-Sauveur-le-Vicomte	18	49 23N	1 32W
St-Savin	20	46 34N	0 50 E
St-Savinien	20	45 53N	0 42W
St. Sebastien, Tanjon' i	93	12 26 S	48 44 E
St-Seine-l'Abbaye	19	47 26N	4 47 E
St-Sernin	20	43 54N	2 35 E
St-Servan-sur-Mer	18	48 38N	2 0W
St-Sever	20	43 46N	0 34W
St-Sever-Calvados	18	48 50N	1 3W
St-Siméon	107	47 51N	69 54W
St. Stephen	107	45 16N	67 17W
St-Sulpice-Laurière	20	46 3N	1 29 E
St-Sulpice-la-Pointe	20	43 46N	1 41 E
St-Thégonnec	18	48 31N	3 57W
St. Thomas, Can.	106	42 45N	81 10W
St. Thomas, W. Indies	121	18 21N	64 55W
St-Tite	106	46 45N	72 34W
St-Tropez	21	43 17N	6 38 E
St. Troud = Sint Truiden	16	50 48N	5 10 E
St-Vaast-la-Hougue	18	49 35N	1 17W
St-Valéry	19	50 10N	1 38 E
St-Valéry-en-Caux	18	49 52N	0 43 E
St-Vallier	21	45 11N	4 50 E
St-Vallier-de-Thiey	21	43 42N	6 51 E
St-Varent	18	46 53N	0 13W
St. Vincent	6	18 0N	26 1W
St. Vincent ■	121	13 10N	61 10W
St-Vincent-de-Tyrosse	20	43 39N	1 18W
St. Vincent, G.	97	35 0 S	138 0 E
St. Vincent Passage	121	13 30N	61 0W
St. Vincent, Tanjona	93	21 58 S	43 20 E
St-Vith	16	50 17N	6 9 E
St-Yrieux-la-Perche	20	45 31N	1 12 E
Ste-Adresse	18	49 31N	0 5 E
Ste-Agathe-des-Monts	106	46 3N	74 17W
Ste Anne de Beaupré	107	47 2N	70 58W
Ste-Anne-des-Monts	107	49 8N	66 30W
Ste-Énimie	20	44 22N	3 26 E
Ste-Foy-la-Grande	20	44 50N	0 13 E
Ste. Genevieve	116	37 59N	90 2W
Ste-Hermine	20	46 32N	1 4W
Ste-Livrade-sur-Lot	20	44 24N	0 36 E
Ste-Marguerite →	107	50 9N	66 36W
Ste Marie	121	14 48N	61 1W
Ste-Marie-aux-Mines	19	48 10N	7 12 E
Ste-Marie de la Madeleine	107	46 26N	71 0W
Ste-Maure-de-Touraine	18	47 7N	0 37 E
Ste-Maxime	21	43 19N	6 39 E
Ste-Menehould	19	49 5N	4 54 E
Ste-Mère-Église	18	49 24N	1 19W
Ste-Rose	121	16 20N	61 45W
Ste.-Rose du lac	109	51 4N	99 30W
Saintes	20	45 45N	0 37W
Saintes, Île des	121	15 50N	61 35W
Saintes-Maries-de-la-Mer	21	43 26N	4 26 E
Saintonge	20	45 40N	0 50W
Sairang	67	23 50N	92 45 E
Sairecábur, Cerro	124	22 43 S	67 54W
Saitama □	74	36 25N	139 30 E
Sajama	126	18 7 S	69 0W
Sajan	42	45 50N	20 20 E
Sajószentpéter	27	48 12N	20 44 E
Sakai	74	34 30N	135 30 E
Sakākah	64	30 0N	40 8 E
Sakami, L.	106	53 15N	77 0W
Sâkâne, 'Erg i-n	82	20 30N	1 30W
Sakania	91	12 43 S	28 30 E
Sakarya →	56	41 7N	30 39 E
Sakata	74	38 55N	139 50 E
Sakeny →	93	20 0 S	45 25 E
Sakété	85	6 40N	2 45 E
Sakhalin, Ostrov	59	51 0N	143 0 E
Sakhi Gopal	69	19 58N	85 50 E
Sakhnīn	62	32 52N	35 12 E
Saki	56	45 9N	33 34 E
Sakiai	54	54 59N	23 0 E
Sakołow Małopolski	28	50 10N	22 9 E
Sakon Nakhon	71	17 10N	104 9 E
Sakrand	68	26 10N	68 15 E
Sakri	68	21 2N	74 20 E
Sakskøbing	49	54 49N	11 39 E
Sal →	57	47 31N	40 45 E
Šal'a	27	48 10N	17 50 E
Sala	48	59 58N	16 35 E
Sala Consilina	41	40 23N	15 35 E
Sala-y-Gómez	95	26 28 S	105 28W
Salaberry-de-Valleyfield	106	45 15N	74 8W
Saladas	124	28 15 S	58 40W
Saladillo	124	35 40 S	59 55W
Salado →, Buenos Aires, Argent.	124	35 44 S	57 22W
Salado →, La Pampa, Argent.	128	37 30 S	67 0W
Salado →, Santa Fe, Argent.	124	31 40 S	60 41W
Salado →, Mexico	120	26 52N	99 19W
Salaga	85	8 31N	0 31W
Sălaj □	46	47 15N	23 0 E
Salala, Liberia	84	6 42N	10 7W
Salala, Sudan	86	21 17N	36 16 E
Salālah	63	16 56N	53 59 E
Salamanca, Chile	124	31 46 S	70 59W
Salamanca, Spain	30	40 58N	5 39W
Salamanca, U.S.A.	114	42 10N	78 42W
Salamanca □	30	40 57N	5 40W
Salamis	45	37 56N	23 30 E
Salar de Atacama	124	23 30 S	68 25W
Salar de Uyuni	126	20 30 S	67 45W
Sălard	46	47 12N	22 3 E
Salas	30	43 25N	6 15W
Salas de los Infantes	32	42 2N	3 17W
Salatiga	73	7 19 S	110 30 E
Salavat	52	53 21N	55 55 E
Salaverry	126	8 15 S	79 0W
Salawati	73	1 7 S	130 52 E
Salayar	73	6 7 S	120 30 E
Salazar →	32	42 40N	1 20W
Salbris	19	47 25N	2 3 E
Salcia	46	43 56N	24 55 E
Salcombe	13	50 14N	3 47W
Saldaña	30	42 32N	4 48W
Saldanha	92	33 0 S	17 58 E
Saldanhabaai	92	33 6 S	18 0 E
Saldus	54	56 38N	22 30 E
Sale	97	38 6 S	147 6 E
Salé	82	34 3N	6 48W
Sale	12	53 26N	2 19W
Salebabu	73	3 55N	126 40 E
Salekhard	58	66 30N	66 35 E
Salem, India	70	11 40N	78 11 E
Salem, Ind., U.S.A.	114	38 38N	86 6W
Salem, Mass., U.S.A.	114	42 29N	70 53W
Salem, Mo., U.S.A.	117	37 40N	91 30W
Salem, N.J., U.S.A.	114	39 34N	75 29W
Salem, Ohio, U.S.A.	114	40 52N	80 50W
Salem, Oreg., U.S.A.	118	45 0N	123 0W
Salem, S.D., U.S.A.	116	43 44N	97 23W
Salem, Va., U.S.A.	114	37 19N	80 8W
Salemi	40	37 49N	12 47 E
Salernes	21	43 34N	6 15 E
Salerno	41	40 40N	14 44 E
Salerno, G. di	41	40 35N	14 45 E
Salfit	62	32 5N	35 11 E
Salford	12	53 30N	2 17W
Salgir →	56	45 38N	35 1 E
Salgótarján	27	48 5N	19 47 E
Salies-de-Béarn	20	43 28N	0 56W
Salina, Italy	41	38 35N	14 50 E
Salina, U.S.A.	116	38 50N	97 40W
Salina Cruz	120	16 10N	95 10W
Salinas, Brazil	127	16 10 S	42 10W
Salinas, Chile	124	23 31 S	69 29W
Salinas, Ecuador	126	2 10 S	80 58W
Salinas, U.S.A.	119	36 40N	121 41W
Salinas →, Mexico	120	16 28N	90 31W
Salinas →, U.S.A.	119	36 45N	121 48W
Salinas Ambargasta	124	29 0 S	65 0W
Salinas, B. de	121	11 4N	85 45W
Salinas, C. de	33	39 16N	3 4 E
Salinas (de Hidalgo)	120	22 30N	101 40W
Salinas Grandes	124	30 0 S	65 0W
Salinas, Pampa de las	124	31 58 S	66 42W
Saline →, Ark., U.S.A.	117	33 10N	92 8W
Saline →, Kans., U.S.A.	116	38 51N	97 30W
Salinópolis	127	0 40 S	47 20W
Salins	19	46 57N	5 53 E
Salins-les-Bains	19	46 58N	5 52 E
Salir	31	37 14N	8 2W
Salisbury, Austral.	99	34 46 S	138 40 E
Salisbury, U.K.	13	51 4N	1 48W
Salisbury, Md., U.S.A.	114	38 20N	75 38W
Salisbury, N.C., U.S.A.	115	35 20N	80 29W
* Salisbury, Zimb.	91	17 43 S	31 2 E
Salisbury Plain	13	51 13N	1 50W
Săliște	46	45 45N	23 56 E
Salka	85	10 20N	4 58 E
Salle, La	116	41 20N	89 6W
Sallent	32	41 49N	1 54 E
Salles-Curan	20	44 11N	2 48 E
Salling	49	56 40N	8 55 E
Sallisaw	117	35 26N	94 45W
Sallom Junction	86	19 17N	37 6 E
Salmerón	32	40 33N	2 29W
Salmo	108	49 10N	117 20W
Salmon	118	45 12N	113 56W
Salmon →, Can.	108	54 3N	122 40W
Salmon →, U.S.A.	118	45 51N	116 46W
Salmon Arm	108	50 40N	119 15W
Salmon Falls	118	42 48N	114 59W
Salmon Res.	107	48 05N	56 00W
Salmon River Mts.	118	45 0N	114 30W
Salo	51	60 22N	23 10 E
Salò	38	45 37N	10 32 E
Salobreña	31	36 44N	3 35W
Salome	119	33 51N	113 37W
Salon-de-Provence	21	43 39N	5 6 E
Salonica = Thessaloniki	44	40 38N	22 58 E
Salonta	46	46 49N	21 42 E
Salop = Shropshire □	13	52 36N	2 45W
Salor →	31	39 39N	7 3W
Salou, Cabo	32	41 3N	1 10 E
Salsacate	124	31 20 S	65 5W
Salses	20	42 50N	2 55 E
Salsette I.	70	19 5N	72 50 E
Salsk	57	46 28N	41 30 E
Salso →	41	37 6N	13 55 E
Salsomaggiore	38	44 48N	9 59 E
Salt →, Can.	108	60 0N	112 25W
Salt →, U.S.A.	119	33 23N	112 18W
Salt Creek	99	36 8 S	139 38 E
Salt Fork →	117	36 37N	97 7W
Salt Lake City	118	40 45N	111 58W
Salt Range	68	32 30N	72 25 E
Salta	124	24 57 S	65 25W
Salta □	124	24 48 S	65 30W
Saltcoats	14	55 38N	4 47W
Saltee Is.	15	52 7N	6 37W
Saltfjorden	50	67 15N	14 10 E
Saltholm	49	55 38N	12 43 E
Salthólmavík	50	65 24N	21 57W
Saltillo	120	25 30N	100 57W
Salto, Argent.	124	34 20 S	60 15W
Salto, Uruguay	124	31 27 S	57 50W
Salton Sea	119	33 20N	115 50W
Saltpond	85	5 15N	1 3W
Saltsjöbaden	49	59 15N	18 20 E
Saltspring	108	48 54N	123 37W
Saltville	114	36 53N	81 46W
Saluda →	115	34 0N	81 4W
Salûm	86	31 31N	25 7 E
Salûm, Khâlig el	86	31 30N	25 9 E
Salur	70	18 27N	83 18 E
Saluzzo	38	44 39N	7 29 E
Salvador, Brazil	127	13 0 S	38 30W
Salvador, Can.	109	52 10N	109 32W
Salvador, L.	117	29 46N	90 16W
Salvaterra de Magos	31	39 1N	8 47W
Sálvora, Isla	30	42 30N	8 58W
Salwa	65	24 45N	50 55 E
Salween →	67	16 31N	97 37 E
Salyany	53	39 10N	48 50 E
Salyersville	114	37 45N	83 4W
Salza →	26	47 40N	14 43 E
Salzach →	26	48 12N	12 56 E
Salzburg	26	47 48N	13 2 E
Salzburg □	26	47 15N	13 0 E
Salzgitter	24	52 13N	10 22 E
Salzwedel	24	52 50N	11 11 E
Sam Neua	71	20 29N	104 0 E
Sam Ngao	71	17 18N	99 0 E
Sam Rayburn Res.	117	31 15N	94 20W
Sama	58	60 12N	60 22 E
Sama de Langreo	30	43 18N	5 40W
Samagaltai	59	50 36N	95 3 E
Samales Group	73	6 0N	122 0 E
Samalkot	70	17 3N	82 13 E
Samâlût	86	28 20N	30 42 E
Samana	68	30 10N	76 13 E
Samanga	91	8 20 S	39 13 E
Samangán □	65	36 15N	68 3 E
Samangwa	90	4 23 S	24 10 E
Samar	73	12 0N	125 0 E
Samarai	98	10 39 S	150 41 E
Samaria = Shōmrōn	62	32 15N	35 13 E
Samarinda	72	0 30 S	117 9 E
Samarkand	58	39 40N	66 55 E
Sāmarrā"	64	34 16N	43 55 E
Samastipur	69	25 50N	85 50 E
Samatan	20	43 29N	0 55 E
Samba	90	4 38 S	26 22 E
Sambalpur	69	21 28N	84 4 E
Sambar, Tanjung	72	2 59 S	110 19 E
Sambas	72	1 20N	109 20 E
Sambava	93	14 16 S	50 10 E
Sambawizi	91	18 24 S	26 13 E
Sambhal	68	28 35N	78 37 E
Sambhar	68	26 52N	75 6 E
Sambiase	41	38 58N	16 16 E
Sambonifacio	38	45 24N	11 16 E
Sambor, Camb.	71	12 46N	106 0 E
Sambor, U.S.S.R.	54	49 30N	23 10 E
Sambre →	16	50 27N	4 52 E
Sambuca di Sicilia	40	37 39N	13 6 E
Samburu □	90	1 10N	37 0 E
Samchŏk	76	37 30N	129 10 E
Same	90	4 2 S	37 38 E
Samer	19	50 38N	1 44 E
Samfya	91	11 22 S	29 31 E
Sámi	45	38 15N	20 39 E
Samna	86	25 12N	37 17 E
Samnū	83	27 15N	14 55 E
Samo Alto	124	30 22 S	71 0W
Samobor	39	45 47N	15 44 E
Samoëns	21	46 5N	6 45 E
Samokov	43	42 18N	23 33 E
Samoorombón, Bahía	124	36 5 S	57 20W
Samorogouan	84	11 21N	4 57W
Sámos	45	37 45N	26 50 E
Samos	30	42 44N	7 20W
Samoš	42	45 13N	20 49 E
Samotharáki	44	39 48N	19 31 E
Samothráki	44	40 28N	25 28 E
Samoylovka	55	51 12N	43 43 E
Sampa	84	8 0N	2 36W
Sampacho	124	33 20 S	64 50W
Sampang	73	7 11 S	113 13 E
Samper de Calanda	32	41 11N	0 28W
Sampit	72	2 34 S	113 0 E
Sampit, Teluk	72	3 5 S	113 3 E
Samra	64	25 35N	41 0 E
Samsø	49	55 50N	10 35 E
Samsø Bælt	49	55 45N	10 45 E
Samsun	64	41 15N	36 22 E
Samsun Dağı	45	37 45N	27 10 E
Samtredia	57	42 7N	42 24 E
Samui, Ko	71	9 30N	100 0 E
Samur →	57	41 53N	48 32 E
Samusole	91	10 2 S	24 0 E
Samut Prakan	71	13 32N	100 40 E
Samut Sakhon	71	13 31N	100 13 E
Samut Songkhram (Mekong)	71	13 24N	100 1 E
Samwari	68	28 30N	66 46 E
San	84	13 15N	4 57W
San →	27	50 45N	21 51 E
San Adrián, C. de	30	43 21N	8 50W
San Agustin, C.	73	6 20N	126 13 E
San Agustín de Valle Fértil	124	30 35 S	67 30W
San Ambrosio	95	26 28 S	79 53W
San Andreas	118	38 0N	120 39W
San Andrés, I. de	121	12 42N	81 46W
San Andres Mts.	119	33 0N	106 45W
San Andrés Tuxtla	120	18 30N	95 20W
San Angelo	117	31 30N	100 30W
San Antonio, Chile	124	33 40 S	71 40W
San Antonio, N. Mex., U.S.A.	119	33 58N	106 57W
San Antonio, Tex., U.S.A.	117	29 30N	98 30W
San Antonio →	117	28 30N	96 50W
San Antonio Abad	33	38 59N	1 19 E
San Antonio, C., Argent.	124	36 15 S	56 40W
San Antonio, C., Cuba	121	21 50N	84 57W
San Antonio, C. de	33	38 48N	0 12 E
San Antonio de los Baños	121	22 54N	82 31W
San Antonio de los Cobres	124	24 10 S	66 17W
San Antonio Oeste	128	40 40 S	65 0W
San Augustine	117	31 30N	94 7W
San Bartolomeo in Galdo	41	41 23N	15 2 E
San Benedetto	38	45 2N	10 57 E
San Benedetto del Tronto	39	42 57N	13 52 E
San Benito	117	26 5N	97 39W
San Bernardino	119	34 7N	117 18W
San Bernardino Str.	73	13 0N	125 0 E
San Bernardo	124	33 40 S	70 50W
San Bernardo, I. de	126	9 45N	75 50W
San Blas	120	26 4N	108 46W
San Blas, C.	115	29 40N	85 12W
San Borja	126	14 50 S	66 52W
San Buenaventura	120	27 5N	101 32W
San Carlos, Argent.	124	33 50 S	69 0W
San Carlos, Chile	124	36 10 S	72 0W
San Carlos, Mexico	120	29 0N	100 54W
San Carlos, Nic.	121	11 12N	84 50W
San Carlos, Phil.	73	10 29N	123 25 E
San Carlos, Uruguay	125	34 46 S	54 58W
San Carlos, U.S.A.	119	33 24N	110 27W
San Carlos, Amazonas, Venez.	126	1 55N	67 4W
San Carlos, Cojedes, Venez.	126	9 40N	68 36W
San Carlos = Butuku-Luba	85	3 29N	8 33 E
San Carlos de Bariloche	128	41 10 S	71 25W
San Carlos de la Rápita	32	40 37N	0 35 E
San Carlos del Zulia	126	9 1N	71 55W
San Carlos L.	119	33 15N	110 25W
San Cataldo	40	37 30N	13 58 E
San Celoni	32	41 42N	2 30 E
San Clemente, Chile	124	35 30 S	71 29W
San Clemente, Spain	33	39 24N	2 25W
San Clemente, U.S.A.	119	33 29N	117 36W
San Clemente I.	119	32 53N	118 30W
San Constanzo	39	43 46N	13 5 E

* Renamed Harare

San Cristóbal Santéramo in Colle

San Cristóbal, Argent. 124 30 20 S 61 10W
San Cristóbal, Dom. Rep. 121 18 25N 70 6W
San Cristóbal, Venez. 126 16 50N 92 40W
San Cristóbal de las Casas 120 16 50N 92 33W
San Damiano d'Asti 38 44 51N 8 4 E
San Daniele del Friuli 39 46 10N 13 0 E
San Demétrio Corone 41 39 34N 16 22 E
San Diego, Calif., U.S.A. 119 32 43N 117 10W
San Diego, Tex., U.S.A. 117 27 47N 98 15W
San Diego, C. 128 54 40 S 65 10W
San Donà di Piave 39 45 38N 12 34 E
San Elpídio a Mare 39 43 16N 13 41 E
San Estanislao 124 24 39 S 56 26W
San Esteban de Gormaz 32 41 34N 3 13W
San Felice sul Panaro 38 44 51N 11 9 E
San Felipe, Chile 124 32 43 S 70 42W
San Felipe, Mexico 120 31 0N 114 52W
San Felipe, Venez. 126 10 20N 68 44W
San Feliu de Guíxols 32 41 45N 3 1 E
San Feliu de Llobregat 32 41 23N 2 2 E
San Félix 95 26 23 S 80 0W
San Fernando, Chile 124 34 30 S 71 0W
San Fernando, Mexico 120 30 0N 115 10W
San Fernando, Luzon, Phil. 73 16 40N 120 23 E
San Fernando, Luzon, Phil. 73 15 5N 120 37 E
San Fernando, Spain 31 36 28N 6 17W
San Fernando, Trin. 121 10 20N 61 30W
San Fernando, U.S.A. 119 34 15N 118 29W
San Fernando → 120 24 55N 98 10W
San Fernando de Apure 126 7 54N 67 15W
San Fernando de Atabapo 126 4 3N 67 42W
San Fernando di Púglia 41 41 18N 16 5 E
San Francisco, Argent. 124 31 30 S 62 5W
San Francisco, U.S.A. 119 37 47N 122 30W
San Francisco → 119 32 59N 109 22W
San Francisco de Macorîs 121 19 19N 70 15W
San Francisco del Monte de Oro 124 32 36 S 66 8W
San Francisco del Oro 120 26 52N 105 50W
San Francisco Javier 33 38 42N 1 26 E
San Francisco, Paso de 124 27 0 S 68 0W
San Fratello 41 38 1N 14 33 E
San Gavino Monreale 40 39 33N 8 47 E
San Gil 126 6 33N 73 8W
San Gimignano 38 43 28N 11 3 E
San Giórgio di Nogaro 39 45 50N 13 13 E
San Giórgio Iónico 41 40 27N 17 23 E
San Giovanni Bianco 38 45 52N 9 40 E
San Giovanni in Fiore 41 39 16N 16 42 E
San Giovanni in Persiceto 39 44 39N 11 12 E
San Giovanni Rotondo 41 41 41N 15 42 E
San Giovanni Valdarno 39 43 32N 11 30 E
San Giuliano Terme 38 43 45N 10 26 E
San Gottardo, Paso del 25 46 33N 8 33 E
San Grcángelo 40 40 14N 16 14 E
San Gregorio 125 32 37 S 55 40W
San Guiseppe Iato 40 37 57N 13 11 E
San Ignacio, Boliv. 126 16 20 S 60 55W
San Ignacio, Parag. 124 26 52 S 57 3W
San Ignacio, Laguna 120 26 50N 113 11W
San Ildefonso, C. 73 16 0N 122 1 E
San Isidro 124 34 29 S 58 31W
San Javier, Misiones, Argent. 125 27 55 S 55 5W
San Javier, Santa Fe, Argent. 124 30 40 S 59 55W
San Javier, Boliv. 126 16 18 S 62 30W
San Javier, Chile 124 35 40 S 71 45W
San Javier, Spain 33 37 49N 0 50W
San Joaquin → 119 37 4N 121 51W
San Jorge 124 31 54 S 61 50W
San Jorge, Bahía de 120 31 20N 113 20W
San Jorge, Golfo 128 46 0 S 66 0W
San Jorge, G. de 32 40 50N 0 55W
San José, Boliv. 126 17 53 S 60 50W
San José, C. Rica 121 10 0N 84 2W
San José, Guat. 120 14 0N 90 50W
San José, Mexico 120 25 0N 110 50W
San Jose, Luzon, Phil. 73 15 45N 120 55 E
San Jose, Mindoro, Phil. 73 12 27N 121 4 E
San Jose, Panay, Phil. 73 10 50N 122 5 E
San José 33 38 55N 1 18 E
San Jose, Calif., U.S.A. 119 37 20N 121 53W
San Jose, N. Mex., U.S.A. 119 35 26N 105 30W
San Jose → 119 34 58N 106 7W
San José de Feliciano 124 30 26 S 58 46W
San José de Jáchal 124 30 15 S 68 46W
San José de Mayo 124 34 27 S 56 40W
San José de Ocune 126 4 15N 70 20W
San José del Cabo 120 23 0N 109 40W
San José del Guaviare 126 2 35N 72 38W
San Juan, Argent. 124 31 30 S 68 30W
San Juan, Dom. Rep. 121 18 45N 72 45W
San Juan, Mexico 120 21 20N 102 50W
San Juan, Phil. 73 8 25N 126 20 E
San Juan, Pto. Rico 121 18 28N 66 8W
San Juan □ 124 31 9 S 69 0W
San Juan →, Argent. 124 32 20 S 67 25W
San Juan →, Nic. 121 10 56N 83 42W
San Juan →, U.S.A. 119 37 20N 110 20W
San Juan Bautista, Parag. 124 26 37 S 57 6W
San Juan Bautista, Spain 33 39 5N 1 31 E
San Juan, C. 88 1 5N 9 20 E
San Juan Capistrano 119 33 29N 117 40W
San Juan de los Morros 126 9 55N 67 21W
San Juan del Norte, B. de 121 11 0N 83 40W
San Juan del Puerto 31 37 20N 6 50W
San Juan del Río 120 20 25N 100 0W
San Juan del Sur 121 11 20N 85 51W
San Juan Mts. 119 38 30N 108 30W
San Julián 128 49 15 S 67 45W
San Just, Sierra de 32 40 45N 0 49W
San Justo 124 30 47 S 60 30W
San Lázaro, C. 120 24 50N 112 18W
San Lázaro, Sa. de 120 23 25N 110 0W
San Leandro 119 37 40N 122 6W
San Leonardo 32 41 51N 3 5W
San Lorenzo, Argent. 124 32 45 S 60 45W
San Lorenzo, Ecuador 126 1 15N 78 50W
San Lorenzo, Parag. 124 25 20 S 57 32W
San Lorenzo → 120 24 15N 107 24W
San Lorenzo de la Parrilla 32 39 51N 2 22W
San Lorenzo de Morunys 32 42 8N 1 35 E
San Lorenzo, I., Mexico 120 28 35N 112 50W
San Lorenzo, I., Peru 126 12 7 S 77 15W
San Lorenzo, Mt. 128 47 40 S 72 20W
San Lucas, Boliv. 126 20 5 S 65 7W
San Lucas, Mexico 120 27 10N 112 14W
San Lucas, C. de 120 22 50N 110 0W
San Lúcido 41 39 18N 16 3 E
San Luis, Argent. 124 33 20 S 66 20W
San Luis, U.S.A. 119 37 3N 105 26W
San Luis □ 124 34 0 S 66 0W
San Luis de la Paz 120 21 19N 100 32W
San Luis, I. 120 29 58N 114 26W
San Luis Obispo 119 35 21N 120 38W
San Luis Potosí 120 22 9N 100 59W
San Luis Potosí □ 120 22 10N 101 0W
San Luis Río Colorado 120 32 29N 114 58W
San Luis, Sierra de 124 32 30 S 66 10W
San Marco Argentano 41 39 34N 16 8 E
San Marco dei Cavoti 41 41 20N 14 50 E
San Marco in Lámis 41 41 43N 15 38 E
San Marcos, Guat. 120 14 59N 91 52W
San Marcos, Mexico 120 27 13N 112 6W
San Marcos, U.S.A. 117 29 53N 98 0W
San Marino 39 43 56N 12 25 E
San Marino ■ 39 43 56N 12 25 E
San Martín 124 33 5 S 68 28W
San Martín de Valdeiglesias 30 40 21N 4 24W
San Martín, L. 128 48 50 S 72 50W
San Martino de Calvi 38 45 57N 9 41 E
San Mateo, Spain 32 40 28N 0 10 E
San Mateo, U.S.A. 119 37 32N 122 19W
San Matías 126 16 25 S 58 20W
San Matías, Golfo 128 41 30 S 64 0W
San Matías, G. of 122 41 30 S 64 0W
San Miguel, El Sal. 120 13 30N 88 12W
San Miguel, Spain 33 39 3N 1 26 E
San Miguel, U.S.A. 119 35 45N 120 42W
San Miguel → 126 13 52 S 63 56W
San Miguel de Salinas 33 37 59N 0 47W
San Miguel de Tucumán 124 26 50 S 65 20W
San Miguel del Monte 124 35 23 S 58 50W
San Miniato 38 43 40N 10 50 E
San Narciso 73 15 2N 120 3 E
San Nicolás de los Arroyas 124 33 25 S 60 10W
San Nicolas I. 119 33 16N 119 30W
San Pablo 124 21 43 S 66 38W
San Paolo di Civitate 41 41 44N 15 16 E
San Pedro, Buenos Aires, Argent. 125 26 30 S 54 10W
San Pedro, Jujuy, Argent. 124 24 12 S 64 55W
San-Pédro 84 4 50N 6 33W
San Pedro □ 124 24 0 S 57 0W
San Pedro →, Chihuahua, Mexico 120 28 20N 106 10W
San Pedro →, Nayarit, Mexico 120 21 45N 105 30W
San Pedro →, U.S.A. 119 33 0N 110 50W
San Pedro de Atacama 124 22 55 S 68 15W
San Pedro de Jujuy 124 24 12 S 64 55W
San Pedro de las Colonias 120 25 50N 102 59W
San Pedro de Lloc 126 7 15 S 79 28W
San Pedro de Macorís 121 18 30N 69 18W
San Pedro del Paraná 124 26 43 S 56 13W
San Pedro del Pinatar 33 37 50N 0 50W
San Pedro Mártir, Sierra 120 31 0N 115 30W
San Pedro Mixtepec 120 16 2N 97 7W
San Pedro Ocampo = Melchor Ocampo 120 24 52N 101 40W
San Pedro, Pta. 124 25 30 S 70 38W
San Pedro, Sierra de 31 39 18N 6 40W
San Pedro Sula 120 15 30N 88 0W
San Pedro,Pta. 124 25 30 S 70 38W
San Pietro, I. 40 39 9N 8 17 E
San Pietro Vernótico 41 40 28N 18 0 E
San Quintin 73 16 1N 120 56 E
San Rafael, Argent. 124 34 40 S 68 21W
San Rafael, Calif., U.S.A. 118 37 59N 122 32W
San Rafael, N. Mex., U.S.A. 119 35 6N 107 58W
San Ramón de la Nueva Orán 124 23 10 S 64 20W
San Remo 38 43 48N 7 47 E
San Roque, Argent. 124 28 25 S 58 45W
San Roque, Spain 31 36 17N 5 21W
San Rosendo 124 37 16 S 72 43W
San Saba 117 31 12N 98 45W
San Salvador 120 13 40N 89 10W
San Salvador de Jujuy 124 24 10 S 64 48W
San Salvador I. 121 24 0N 74 32W
San Sebastián, Argent. 128 53 10 S 68 30W
San Sebastián, Spain 32 43 17N 1 58W
San Serverino Marche 39 43 13N 13 10 E
San Simon 119 32 14N 109 16W
San Stéfano di Cadore 39 46 34N 12 33 E
San Valentin, Mte. 128 46 30 S 73 30W
San Vicente de Alcántara 31 39 22N 7 8W
San Vicente de la Barquera 30 43 23N 4 29W
San Vincenzo 38 43 6N 10 29 E
San Vito 40 39 26N 9 32 E
San Vito al Tagliamento 39 45 55N 12 50 E
San Vito, C. 40 38 11N 12 41 E
San Vito Chietino 39 42 19N 14 27 E
San Vito dei Normanni 41 40 40N 17 40 E
San Ygnacio 117 27 6N 99 24W
Sana' 63 15 27N 44 12 E
Sana → 39 45 3N 16 23 E
Sanaba 84 12 25N 3 47W
Sanabria, La 30 42 0N 6 30W
Sanâfir 86 27 55N 34 37 E
Sanaga → 88 3 35N 9 38 E
Sanak I. 104 53 30N 162 30W
Sanana 73 2 5 S 125 59 E
Sanand 68 22 59N 72 25 E
Sanandaj 64 35 18N 47 1 E
Sanandita 124 21 40 S 63 45W
Sanary 21 43 7N 5 48 E
Sanawad 68 22 11N 76 5 E
Sancergues 19 47 10N 2 54 E
Sancerre 19 47 20N 2 50 E
Sancerrois, Coll. du 19 47 20N 2 40 E
Sancha He → 77 26 48N 106 7 E
Sanchor 68 24 45N 71 55 E
Sanco, Pt. 73 8 15N 126 24 E
Sancoins 19 46 47N 2 55 E
Sancti-Spíritus 121 21 52N 79 33W
Sand → 93 22 25 S 30 5 E
Sand Springs 117 36 12N 96 5W
Sandah 86 20 35N 39 32 E
Sandakan 72 5 53N 118 4 E
Sandan 71 12 46N 106 0 E
Sandanski 43 41 35N 23 16 E
Sandaré 84 14 40N 10 15W
Sanday 14 59 15N 2 30W
Sande, Möre og Romsdal, Norway 47 62 15N 5 27 E
Sande, Sogn og Fjordane, Norway 47 61 20N 5 47 E
Sandefjord 47 59 10N 10 15 E
Sandeid 47 59 33N 5 52 E
Sanders 119 35 12N 109 25W
Sanderson 117 30 5N 102 30W
Sandfly L. 109 55 43N 106 6W
Sandgate 99 27 18 S 153 3 E
Sandia 126 14 10 S 69 30W
Sandıklı 64 38 30N 30 20 E
Sandnes 47 58 50N 5 45 E
Sandness 14 60 18N 1 38W
Sandoa 88 9 41 S 23 0 E
Sandomierz 28 50 40N 21 43 E
Sandover → 97 21 43 S 136 32 E
Sandoway 67 18 20N 94 30 E
Sandpoint 118 48 20N 116 34W
Sandringham 12 52 50N 0 30 E
Sandslån 48 63 2N 17 49 E
Sandspit 108 53 14N 131 49W
Sandstone 96 27 59 S 119 16 E
Sandusky, Mich., U.S.A. 106 43 26N 82 50W
Sandusky, Ohio, U.S.A. 114 41 25N 82 40W
Sandvig 49 55 18N 14 48 E
Sandviken 48 60 38N 16 46 E
Sandwich B., Can. 107 53 40N 57 15W
Sandwich B., S. Afr. 92 23 25 S 14 20 E
Sandwich, C. 98 18 14 S 146 18 E
Sandwich Group 5 57 0 S 27 0W
Sandwip Chan. 67 22 35N 91 35 E
Sandy C., Queens., Austral. 97 24 42 S 153 15 E
Sandy C., Tas., Austral. 97 41 25 S 144 45 E
Sandy Cr. → 118 41 15N 109 47W
Sandy L. 106 53 2N 93 0W
Sandy Lake 106 53 0N 93 15W
Sandy Narrows 109 55 5N 103 4W
Sanford, Fla., U.S.A. 115 28 45N 81 20W
Sanford, Me., U.S.A. 113 43 28N 70 47W
Sanford, N.C., U.S.A. 115 35 30N 79 10W
Sanford → 96 27 22 S 115 53 E
Sanford Mt. 104 62 30N 143 0W
Sanga 91 12 22 S 35 21 E
Sanga → 88 1 5 S 17 0 E
Sanga-Tolon 59 61 50N 149 40 E
Sangamner 70 19 37N 74 15 E
Sangar 59 64 2N 127 31 E
Sangasanga 72 0 36 S 117 13 E
Sange 90 6 58 S 28 21 E
Sangeang 73 8 12 S 119 6 E
Sanger 119 36 41N 119 35W
Sangerhausen 24 51 28N 11 18 E
Sanggan He → 76 38 12N 117 15 E
Sanggau 72 0 5N 110 30 E
Sangihe, Kepulauan 73 3 0N 126 0 E
Sangihe, P. 73 3 45N 125 30 E
Sangkapura 72 5 52 S 112 40 E
Sangli 70 16 55N 74 33 E
Sangmélina 88 2 57N 12 1 E
Sangonera → 33 37 59N 1 4W
Sangre de Cristo Mts. 117 37 0N 105 0W
Sangro → 39 42 14N 14 32 E
Sangudo 108 53 50N 114 54W
Sangüesa 32 42 37N 1 17W
Sanguinaires, Îs. 21 41 51N 8 36 E
Sangzhi 77 29 25N 110 12 E
Sanhala 84 10 3N 6 51W
Sanish 116 48 0N 102 30W
Sanje 90 0 49 S 31 30 E
Sanjiang 77 25 48N 109 37 E
Sankaranayinarkovil 70 9 10N 77 35 E
Sankeshwar 70 16 23N 74 32 E
Sankt Andra 26 46 46N 14 50 E
Sankt Blasien 25 47 47N 8 7 E
Sankt Gallen 25 47 26N 9 22 E
Sankt Gallen □ 25 47 25N 9 22 E
Sankt Gotthard P. = San Gottardo, Paso del 25 46 33N 8 33 E
Sankt Ingbert 25 49 16N 7 6 E
Sankt Johann, Salzburg, Austria 26 47 22N 13 12 E
Sankt Johann, Tirol, Austria 26 47 30N 12 25 E
Sankt Moritz 25 46 30N 9 50 E
Sankt Olof 49 55 37N 14 8 E
Sankt Pölten 26 48 12N 15 38 E
Sankt Valentin 26 48 11N 14 33 E
Sankt Veit 26 46 54N 14 22 E
Sankt Wendel 25 49 27N 7 9 E
Sankt Wolfgang 26 47 43N 13 27 E
Sankuru → 88 4 17 S 20 25 E
Sanlúcar de Barrameda 31 36 46N 6 21W
Sanlúcar la Mayor 31 37 26N 6 18W
Sanluri 40 39 35N 8 55 E
Sanmenxia 77 34 47N 111 12 E
Sannaspos 92 29 6 S 26 34 E
Sannicandro Gargánico 41 41 50N 15 34 E
Sannidal 47 58 55N 9 15 E
Sannieshof 92 26 30 S 25 47 E
Sanok 27 49 35N 22 10 E
Sanquhar 14 55 21N 3 56W
Sansanding Dam 84 13 48N 6 0W
Sansepolcro 39 43 34N 12 8 E
Sanshui 75 23 10N 112 56 E
Sanski Most 39 44 46N 16 40 E
Sant' Ágata de Goti 41 41 6N 14 30 E
Sant' Ágata di Militello 41 38 2N 14 8 E
Santa Ana, Boliv. 126 13 50 S 65 40W
Santa Ana, Ecuador 126 1 16 S 80 20W
Santa Ana, El Sal. 120 14 0N 89 31W
Santa Ana, Mexico 120 30 31N 111 8W
Santa Ana, U.S.A. 119 33 48N 117 55W
Sant' Ángelo Lodigiano 38 45 14N 9 25 E
Sant' Antíoco 40 39 2N 8 30 E
Sant' Arcángelo di Romagna 39 44 4N 12 26 E
Santa Bárbara, Mexico 120 26 48N 105 50W
Santa Bárbara, Spain 32 40 42N 0 29 E
Santa Barbara 119 34 25N 119 40W
Santa Bárbara, Mt. 33 37 23N 2 50W
Santa Catalina 120 25 40N 110 50W
Santa Catalina, G. of 119 33 0N 118 0W
Santa Catalina I. 119 33 20N 118 30W
Santa Catarina □ 125 27 25 S 48 30W
Santa Catarina, I. de 125 27 30 S 48 40W
Santa Caterina Villarmosa 41 37 37N 14 1 E
Santa Cecília 125 26 56 S 50 18W
Santa Clara, Cuba 121 22 20N 80 0W
Santa Clara, Calif., U.S.A. 119 37 21N 122 0W
Santa Clara, Utah, U.S.A. 119 37 10N 113 38W
Santa Clara de Olimar 125 32 50 S 54 54W
Santa Clara Pk. 119 35 58N 106 45W
Santa Clotilde 126 2 33 S 73 45W
Santa Coloma de Farnés 32 41 50N 2 39 E
Santa Coloma de Gramanet 32 41 27N 2 13 E
Santa Comba 30 43 2N 8 49W
Santa Croce Camerina 41 36 50N 14 30 E
Santa Croce di Magliano 41 41 43N 14 59 E
Santa Cruz, Argent. 128 50 0 S 68 32W
Santa Cruz, Boliv. 126 17 43 S 63 10W
Santa Cruz, Chile 124 34 38 S 71 27W
Santa Cruz, C. Rica 121 10 15N 85 35W
Santa Cruz, Phil. 73 14 20N 121 24 E
Santa Cruz, Calif., U.S.A. 119 36 55N 122 1W
Santa Cruz, N. Mexico, U.S.A. 119 35 59N 106 1W
Santa Cruz □ 126 17 43 S 63 10W
Santa Cruz → 128 50 10 S 68 20W
Santa Cruz de Mudela 33 38 39N 3 28W
Sta. Cruz de Tenerife 80 28 28N 16 15W
Santa Cruz del Retamar 30 40 8N 4 14W
Santa Cruz del Sur 121 20 44N 78 0W
Santa Cruz do Rio Pardo 125 22 54 S 49 37W
Santa Cruz do Sul 125 29 42 S 52 25W
Santa Cruz I. 119 34 0N 119 45W
Santa Cruz, Is. 94 10 30 S 166 0 E
Santa Domingo, Cay 121 21 25N 75 15W
Santa Elena, Argent. 124 30 58 S 59 47W
Santa Elena, Ecuador 126 2 16 S 80 52W
Santa Elena, C. 121 10 54N 85 56W
Sant' Eufémia, Golfo di 41 38 50N 16 10 E
Santa Eulalia 33 38 59N 1 32 E
Santa Fe, Argent. 124 31 35 S 60 41W
Santa Fe, Spain 31 37 11N 3 43W
Santa Fe, U.S.A. 119 35 40N 106 0W
Santa Fé □ 124 31 50 S 60 55W
Santa Filomena 127 9 6 S 45 50W
Santa Genoveva 120 23 18N 109 52W
Santa Inés 31 38 32N 5 37W
Santa Inés, I. 128 54 0 S 73 0W
Santa Isabel, Argent. 124 36 10 S 66 54W
Santa Isabel, Brazil 127 11 45 S 51 30W
Santa Isabel = Rey Malabo 85 3 45N 8 50 E
Santa Isabel, Pico 85 3 36N 8 49 E
Santa Lucía, Corrientes, Argent. 124 28 58 S 59 5W
Santa Lucía, San Juan, Argent. 124 31 30 S 68 30W
Santa Lucía, Spain 33 37 35N 0 58W
Santa Lucia 124 34 27 S 56 24W
Santa Lucia Range 119 36 0N 121 20W
Santa Margarita, Argent. 124 38 28 S 61 35W
Santa Margarita, Mexico 120 24 30N 111 50W
Santa Margherita 38 44 20N 9 11 E
Santa María 124 26 40 S 66 0W
Santa Maria, Brazil 125 29 40 S 53 48W
Santa Maria, Spain 32 39 38N 2 47 E
Santa Maria, U.S.A. 119 34 58N 120 29W
Santa Maria, Zambia 91 11 5 S 29 58 E
Santa María → 120 31 0N 107 14W
Santa María, Bahía de 120 25 10N 108 40W
Santa Maria, Cabo de 31 36 58N 7 53W
Santa Maria Capua Vetere 41 41 3N 14 15 E
Santa Maria da Vitória 127 13 24 S 44 12W
Santa María del Oro 120 25 58N 105 20W
Santa Maria di Leuca, C. 41 39 48N 18 20 E
Santa María la Real de Nieva 30 41 4N 4 24W
Santa Marta, Colomb. 126 11 15N 74 13W
Santa Marta, Spain 31 38 37N 6 39W
Santa Marta Grande, C. 125 28 43 S 48 50W
Santa Marta, Ría de 30 43 44N 7 45W
Santa Marta, Sierra Nevada de 126 10 55N 73 50W
Santa Maura = Levkás 45 38 40N 20 43 E
Santa Monica 119 34 0N 118 30W
Santa Olalla, Huelva, Spain 31 37 54N 6 14W
Santa Olalla, Toledo, Spain 30 40 2N 4 25W
Sant' Onofrio 41 38 42N 16 10 E
Santa Paula 119 34 20N 119 2W
Santa Pola 33 38 13N 0 35W
Santa Rita 119 32 50N 108 0W
Santa Rosa, La Pampa, Argent. 124 36 40 S 64 17W
Santa Rosa, San Luis, Argent. 124 32 21 S 65 10W
Santa Rosa, Boliv. 126 10 36 S 67 20W
Santa Rosa, Brazil 125 27 52 S 54 29W
Santa Rosa, Calif., U.S.A. 118 38 26N 122 43W
Santa Rosa, N. Mexico, U.S.A. 117 34 58N 104 40W
Santa Rosa de Copán 120 14 47N 88 46W
Santa Rosa de Río Primero 124 31 8 S 63 20W
Santa Rosa I., Calif., U.S.A. 119 34 0N 120 6W
Santa Rosa I., Fla., U.S.A. 115 30 23N 87 0W
Santa Rosa Mts. 118 41 45N 117 30W
Santa Rosalía 120 27 20N 112 20W
Santa Sofia 39 43 57N 11 55 E
Santa Sylvina 124 27 50 S 61 10W
Santa Tecla = Nueva San Salvador 120 13 40N 89 25W
Santa Teresa 124 33 25 S 60 47W
Santa Teresa di Riva 41 37 58N 15 21 E
Santa Teresa Gallura 40 41 14N 9 12 E
Santa Vitória do Palmar 125 33 32 S 53 25W
Santadi 40 39 5N 8 42 E
Santai 75 31 5N 104 58 E
Santana, Coxilha de 125 30 50 S 55 35W
Santana do Livramento 125 30 55 S 55 30W
Santanayi 33 39 20N 3 5 E
Santander 30 43 27N 3 51W
Santander □ 30 43 25N 4 0W
Santander Jiménez 120 24 11N 98 29W
Santaquin 118 40 0N 111 51W
Santarém, Brazil 127 2 25 S 54 42W
Santarém, Port. 31 39 12N 8 42W
Santarém □ 31 39 10N 8 40W
Santaren Channel 121 24 0N 79 30W
Santéramo in Colle 41 40 48N 16 45 E

Santerno
Scunthorpe

Santerno → 39 44 10N 11 38 E
Santhia 38 45 20N 8 10 E
Santiago, Brazil 125 29 11 S 54 52W
Santiago, Chile 124 33 24 S 70 40W
Santiago, Panama 121 8 0N 81 0W
Santiago □ 124 33 30 S 70 50W
Santiago de Compostela 30 42 52N 8 37W
Santiago de Cuba 121 20 0N 75 49W
Santiago de los Cabelleros 121 19 30N 70 40W
Santiago del Estero 124 27 50 S 64 15W
Santiago del Estero □ 124 27 40 S 63 15W
Santiago do Cacém 31 38 1N 8 42W
Santiago Ixcuintla 120 21 50N 105 11W
Santiago Papasquiaro 120 25 0N 105 20W
Santiago, Punta de 85 3 12N 8 40 E
Santiaguillo, L. de 120 24 50N 104 50W
Santillana del Mar 30 43 24N 4 6W
Santipur 69 23 17N 88 25 E
Santisteban del Puerto 33 38 17N 3 15W
Santo Amaro 127 12 30 S 38 43W
Santo Anastácio 125 21 58 S 51 39W
Santo André 125 23 39 S 46 29W
Santo Ângelo 125 28 15 S 54 15W
Santo Antonio 127 15 50 S 56 0W
Santo Corazón 126 18 0 S 58 45W
Santo Domingo, Dom. Rep. 121 18 30N 64 54W
Santo Domingo, Baja Calif. N., Mexico 120 30 43N 116 2W
Santo Domingo, Baja Calif. S., Mexico 120 25 32N 112 2W
Santo Domingo, Nic. 121 12 14N 84 59W
Santo Domingo de la Calzada 32 42 26N 2 57W
Santo Stéfano di Camastro 41 38 1N 14 22 E
Santo Stino di Livenza 39 45 45N 12 40 E
Santo Tirso 30 41 21N 8 28W
Santo Tomás 126 14 26 S 72 8W
Santo Tomé 125 28 40 S 56 5W
Santo Tomé de Guayana 126 8 22N 62 40W
Santoña 30 43 29N 3 27W
Santos 125 24 0 S 46 20W
Santos Dumont 125 22 55 S 43 10W
Santos, Sierra de los 31 38 7N 5 12W
Şanūr 62 32 22N 35 15 E
Sanvignes-les-Mines 19 46 40N 4 18 E
Sanyuan 77 34 35N 108 58 E
Sanza Pombo 88 7 18 S 15 56 E
São Anastácio 125 22 0 S 51 40W
São Bartolomeu de Messines 31 37 15N 8 17W
São Borja 125 28 39 S 56 0W
São Bras d'Alportel 31 37 8N 7 37W
São Carlos 125 22 0 S 47 50W
São Cristóvão 127 11 1 S 37 15W
São Domingos 127 13 25 S 46 19W
São Francisco 127 16 0 S 44 50W
São Francisco → 127 10 30 S 36 24W
São Francisco do Sul 125 26 15 S 48 36W
São Gabriel 125 30 20 S 54 20W
São Gonçalo 125 22 48 S 43 5W
Sao Hill 91 8 20 S 35 12 E
São João da Boa Vista 125 22 0 S 46 52W
São João da Pesqueira 30 41 8N 7 24W
São João del Rei 125 21 8 S 44 15W
São João do Araguaia 127 5 23 S 48 46W
São João do Piauí 127 8 21 S 42 15W
São José do Rio Prêto 125 20 50 S 49 20W
São José dos Campos 125 23 7 S 45 52W
São Leopoldo 125 29 50 S 51 10W
São Lourenço 125 22 7 S 45 3W
São Lourenço → 127 17 53 S 57 27W
São Luís Gonzaga 125 28 25 S 55 0W
São Luís (Maranhão) 127 2 39 S 44 15W
São Marcos → 127 18 15 S 47 37W
São Marcos, B. de 127 2 0 S 44 0W
São Martinho 30 40 18N 8 8W
São Mateus 127 18 44 S 39 50W
São Miguel 8 37 33N 25 27W
São Paulo 125 23 32 S 46 37W
São Paulo □ 125 22 0 S 49 0W
Sao Paulo, I. 6 0 50N 31 40W
São Pedro do Sul 30 40 46N 8 4W
São Roque, C. de 127 5 30 S 35 16W
São Sebastião do Paraíso 125 20 54 S 46 59W
São Sebastião, I. de 125 23 50 S 45 18W
São Teotónio 31 37 30N 8 42W
São Tomé 79 0 10N 6 39 E
São Tomé, C. de 125 22 0 S 40 59W
São Vicente 125 23 57 S 46 23W
São Vicente, Cabo de 31 37 0N 9 0W
Saona, I. 121 18 10N 68 40W
Saône → 19 45 44N 4 50 E
Saône-et-Loire □ 19 46 25N 4 50 E
Saonek 73 0 22 S 130 55 E
Saoura, O. → 82 29 0N 0 55W
Sápai 44 41 2N 25 43 E
Saparua 73 3 33 S 128 40 E
Sapele 85 5 50N 5 40 E
Sapelo I. 115 31 28N 81 15W
Sapiéntza 45 36 45N 21 43 E
Sapone 85 12 3N 1 35W
Saposoa 126 6 55 S 76 45W
Sapozhok 55 53 59N 40 41 E
Sapphire Mts. 118 46 20N 113 45W
Sapporo 74 43 0N 141 21 E
Sapri 41 40 5N 15 37 E
Sapudi 73 7 2 S 114 17 E
Sapulpa 117 36 0N 96 0W
Saqqez 64 36 15N 46 20 E
Sar-e Pol 65 36 10N 66 0 E
Sar Planina 42 42 10N 21 0 E
Sara 84 11 40N 3 53W
Sarāb 64 38 0N 47 30 E
Saragossa = Zaragoza 32 41 39N 0 53W
Saraguro 126 3 35 S 79 16W
Saraipalli 69 21 20N 82 59 E
Sarajevo 42 43 52N 18 26 E
Saralu 46 44 43N 28 10 E
Saran 86 19 35N 40 30 E
Saran, G. 72 0 30 S 111 25 E
Saranac Lake 114 44 20N 74 10W
Saranda, Alb. 44 39 52N 19 55 E
Saranda, Tanz. 90 5 45 S 34 59 E
Sarandí del Yi 125 33 18 S 55 38W
Sarandí Grande 124 33 44 S 56 20W
Sarangani B. 73 6 0N 125 13 E
Sarangani Is. 73 5 25N 125 25 E
Sarangarh 69 21 30N 83 5 E
Saransk 55 54 10N 45 10 E
Sarapul 52 56 28N 53 48 E
Sarasota 115 27 20N 82 30W
Saratoga 118 41 30N 106 48W
Saratoga Springs 114 43 5N 73 47W
Saratov 55 51 30N 46 2 E
Saravane 71 15 43N 106 25 E
Sarawak □ 72 2 0N 113 0 E
Saraya 84 12 50N 11 45W
Sarbāz 65 26 38N 61 19 E
Sarbīsheh 65 32 30N 59 40 E
Sârbogârd 27 46 50N 18 40 E
Sarca → 38 45 52N 10 52 E
Sardalas 83 25 50N 10 34 E
Sardarshahr 68 28 30N 74 29 E
Sardegna 40 39 57N 9 0 E
Sardhana 68 29 9N 77 39 E
Sardinia = Sardegna 40 39 57N 9 0 E
Sarengrad 42 45 14N 19 16 E
Saréyamou 84 16 7N 3 10W
Sargasso Sea 6 27 0N 72 0W
Sargent 116 41 42N 99 24W
Sargodha 68 32 10N 72 40 E
* Sargodha □ 68 31 50N 72 0 E
Sarh 81 9 5N 18 23 E
Sarhro, Djebel 82 31 6N 5 0W
Sārī 65 36 30N 53 4 E
Sária 45 35 54N 27 17 E
Sarida → 62 32 4N 34 45 E
Sarikamiş 64 40 22N 42 35 E
Sarikei 72 2 8N 111 30 E
Sarina 97 21 22 S 149 13 E
Sariñena 32 41 47N 0 10W
Sarīr Tibasti 83 22 50N 18 30 E
Sarita 117 27 14N 97 49W
Sariyer 43 41 10N 29 3 E
Sark 18 49 25N 2 20W
Sarkad 27 46 47N 21 23 E
Sarlat-la-Canéda 20 44 54N 1 13 E
Sarles 116 48 58N 99 0W
Sărmaşu 46 46 45N 24 13 E
Sarmi 73 1 49 S 138 44 E
Sarmiento 128 45 35 S 69 5W
Särna 48 61 41N 13 8 E
Sarnano 39 43 2N 13 17 E
Sarnen 25 46 53N 8 13 E
Sarnia 106 42 58N 82 23W
Sarno 41 40 48N 14 35 E
Sarnowa 28 51 39N 16 53 E
Sarny 54 51 17N 26 40 E
Särö 49 57 31N 11 57 E
Sarolangun 72 2 19 S 102 42 E
Saronikós Kólpos 45 37 45N 23 45 E
Saronno 38 45 38N 9 2 E
Saros Körfezi 44 40 30N 26 15 E
Sárospatak 27 48 18N 21 33 E
Sarosul Românesc 42 45 34N 21 43 E
Sarova 55 54 55N 43 19 E
Sarpsborg 47 59 16N 11 12 E
Sarracín 32 42 15N 3 45W
Sarralbe 19 48 55N 7 1 E
Sarre = Saar → 19 49 7N 7 4 E
Sarre, La 106 48 45N 79 15W
Sarre-Union 19 48 55N 7 4 E
Sarrebourg 19 48 43N 7 3 E
Sarreguemines 19 49 1N 7 4 E
Sarriá 30 42 49N 7 29W
Sarrión 32 40 9N 0 49W
Sarro 84 13 40N 5 15W
Sarstedt 24 52 13N 9 50 E
Sartène 21 41 38N 8 58 E
Sarthe □ 18 47 58N 0 10 E
Sarthe → 18 47 33N 0 31W
Sartilly 18 48 45N 1 28W
Sartynya 58 63 22N 63 11 E
Sarum 86 21 11N 39 10 E
Sarūr 65 23 17N 58 4 E
Sárvár 27 47 15N 16 56 E
Sarvestān 65 29 20N 53 10 E
Särvfjället 48 62 42N 13 30 E
Sárviz → 27 46 24N 18 41 E
Sary-Tash 58 39 44N 73 15 E
Sarych, Mys. 56 44 25N 33 45 E
Saryshagan 58 46 12N 73 38 E
Sarzana 38 44 5N 9 59 E
Sarzeau 18 47 31N 2 48W
Sasa 62 33 2N 35 23 E
Sasabeneh 63 7 59N 44 43 E
Sasaram 69 24 57N 84 5 E
Sasca Montană 42 44 50N 21 45 E
Sasebo 74 33 10N 129 43 E
Saser Mt. 69 34 50N 77 50 E
Saskatchewan □ 109 54 40N 106 0W
Saskatchewan → 109 53 37N 100 40W
Saskatoon 109 52 10N 106 38W
Saskylakh 59 71 55N 114 1 E
Sasnovka 55 56 20N 51 4 E
Sasolburg 93 26 46 S 27 49 E
Sasovo 55 54 25N 41 55 E
Sassandra 84 5 0N 6 8W
Sassandra → 84 4 58N 6 5W
Sássari 40 40 44N 8 33 E
Sassnitz 24 54 29N 13 39 E
Sasso Marconi 39 44 22N 11 12 E
Sassocorvaro 39 43 47N 12 30 E
Sassoferrato 39 43 26N 12 51 E
Sassuolo 38 44 31N 10 47 E
Sástago 32 41 19N 0 21W
Sastown 84 4 45N 8 27W
Sasumua Dam 90 0 45 S 36 40 E
Sasyk, Ozero 46 45 45N 30 0 E
Sata-Misaki 74 30 59N 130 40 E
Satadougou 84 12 25N 11 25W
Satanta 117 37 30N 101 0W
Satara 70 17 44N 73 58 E
Satilla → 115 30 59N 81 28W
Satka 52 55 3N 59 1 E
Satkhira 69 22 43N 89 8 E
Satmala Hills 70 20 15N 74 40 E
Satna 69 24 35N 80 50 E
Sator 39 44 11N 16 37 E
Sátoraljaújhely 27 48 25N 21 41 E
Satpura Ra. 68 21 25N 76 10 E
Satrup 24 54 39N 9 38 E
Sattenapalle 70 16 25N 80 6 E
Satu Mare 46 47 46N 22 55 E
Satui 72 3 50 S 115 27 E
Satumare □ 46 47 45N 23 0 E
Satun 71 6 43N 100 2 E
Saturnina → 126 12 15 S 58 10W
Sauce 124 30 5 S 58 46W
Saucillo 120 28 1N 105 17W
Sauda 47 59 40N 6 20 E
Sauðarkrókur 50 65 45N 19 40W
Saudi Arabia ■ 64 26 0N 44 0 E
Sauerland 24 51 0N 8 0 E
Saugeen → 112 44 30N 81 22W
Saugerties 114 42 4N 73 58W
Saugues 20 44 58N 3 32 E
Sauherad 47 59 25N 9 15 E
Saujon 20 45 41N 0 55W
Sauk Center 116 45 42N 94 56W
Sauk Rapids 116 45 35N 94 10W
Saulgau 25 48 4N 9 32 E
Saulieu 19 47 17N 4 14 E
Sault 21 44 6N 5 24 E
Sault Ste. Marie, Can. 106 46 30N 84 20W
Sault Ste. Marie, U.S.A. 114 46 27N 84 22W
Saumlaki 73 7 55 S 131 20 E
Saumur 18 47 15N 0 5W
Saunders C. 101 45 53 S 170 45 E
Saunders I. 5 57 48 S 26 28W
Saurbær, Borgarfjarðarsýsla, Iceland 50 64 24N 21 35W
Saurbær, Eyjafjarðarsýsla, Iceland 50 65 27N 18 13W
Sauri 85 11 42N 6 44 E
Saurimo 88 9 40 S 20 12 E
Sauveterre 20 43 25N 0 57W
Sauzé-Vaussais 20 46 8N 0 8 E
Sava 39 40 28N 17 32 E
Sava → 39 44 50N 20 26 E
Savage 116 47 27N 104 20W
Savai'i 101 13 28 S 172 24W
Savalou 85 7 57N 1 58 E
Savane 91 19 37 S 35 8 E
Savanna 116 42 5N 90 10W
Savanna la Mar 121 18 10N 78 10W
Savannah, Ga., U.S.A. 115 32 4N 81 4W
Savannah, Mo., U.S.A. 116 39 55N 94 46W
Savannah, Tenn., U.S.A. 115 35 12N 88 18W
Savannah → 115 32 2N 80 53W
Savannakhet 71 16 30N 104 49 E
Savant L. 106 50 16N 90 44W
Savant Lake 106 50 14N 90 40W
Savantvadi 70 15 55N 73 54 E
Savanur 70 14 59N 75 21 E
Savda 68 21 9N 75 56 E
Savé 85 8 2N 2 29 E
Save → 20 43 47N 1 17 E
Sāveh 64 35 2N 50 20 E
Savelugu 85 9 38N 0 54W
Savenay 18 47 20N 1 55W
Saverdun 20 43 14N 1 34 E
Saverne 19 48 39N 7 20 E
Savigliano 38 44 39N 7 40 E
Savigny-sur-Braye 18 47 53N 0 49 E
Saviñao 30 42 35N 7 38W
Savio → 39 44 19N 12 20 E
Šavnik 42 42 59N 19 10 E
Savoie □ 21 45 26N 6 35 E
Savona 38 44 19N 8 29 E
Savonlinna 52 61 52N 28 53 E
Sävsjö 49 57 20N 14 40 E
Sävsjøström 49 57 1N 15 25 E
Sawahlunto 72 0 40 S 100 52 E
Sawai 73 3 0 S 129 5 E
Sawai Madhopur 68 26 0N 76 25 E
Sawara 74 35 55N 140 30 E
Sawatch Mts. 119 38 30N 106 30W
Sawdā, Jabal as 83 28 51N 15 12 E
Sawel, Mt. 15 54 48N 7 5W
Sawfajjin, W. 83 31 46N 14 30 E
Sawknah 81 29 4N 15 47 E
Sawmills 91 19 30 S 28 2 E
Sawu 73 10 35 S 121 50 E
Sawu Sea 73 9 30 S 121 50 E
Sawyerville 113 45 20N 71 34W
Saxby → 98 18 25 S 140 53 E
Saxony, Lower = Niedersachsen □ 24 52 45N 9 0 E
Saxton 112 40 12N 78 18W
Say 85 13 8N 2 22 E
Saya 85 9 30N 3 18 E
Sayabec 107 48 35N 67 41W
Sayán 126 11 8 S 77 12W
Sayan, Vostochnyy 59 54 0N 96 0 E
Sayan, Zapadnyy 59 52 30N 94 0 E
Sayasan 57 42 56N 46 15 E
Saydā 64 33 35N 35 25 E
Şayghān 65 35 10N 67 55 E
Sayḩut 63 15 12N 51 10 E
Saynshand 75 44 55N 110 11 E
Sayre, Okla., U.S.A. 117 35 20N 99 40W
Sayre, Pa., U.S.A. 114 42 0N 76 30W
Sayula 120 19 50N 103 40W
Sayville 113 40 45N 73 7W
Sazan 44 40 30N 19 20 E
Sázava → 26 49 53N 14 24 E
Sazin 69 35 35N 73 30 E
Sazlika → 43 41 59N 25 50 E
Sbeïtla 83 35 12N 9 7 E
Scaër 18 48 2N 3 42W
Scafell Pikes 12 54 26N 3 14W
Scalea 41 39 49N 15 47 E
Scalpay 14 57 51N 6 40W
Scandia 108 50 20N 112 0W
Scandiano 38 44 36N 10 40 E
Scandinavia 9 64 0N 12 0 E
Scansano 39 42 40N 11 20 E
Scapa Flow 14 58 52N 3 6W
Scarborough, Trin. 121 11 11N 60 42W
Scarborough, U.K. 12 54 17N 0 24W
Scarpe → 19 50 31N 3 27 E
Scēdro 39 43 6N 16 43 E
Scenic 116 43 49N 102 32W
Schaal See 24 53 40N 10 57 E
Schaffhausen □ 25 47 42N 8 36 E
Schagen 16 52 49N 4 48 E
Schärding 26 48 27N 13 27 E
Scharhörn 24 53 58N 8 24 E
Scharnitz 26 47 23N 11 15 E
Scheessel 24 53 10N 9 33 E
Schefferville 107 54 48N 66 50W
Scheibbs 26 48 1N 15 9 E
Schelde → 16 51 15N 4 16 E
Schenectady 114 42 50N 73 58W
Scherfede 24 51 32N 9 2 E
Schesslitz 25 49 59N 11 2 E
Scheveningen 16 52 6N 4 16 E
Schiedam 16 51 55N 4 25 E
Schiermonnikoog 16 53 30N 6 15 E
Schifferstadt 25 49 22N 8 23 E
Schiltigheim 19 48 35N 7 45 E
Schio 39 45 42N 11 21 E
Schirmeck 19 48 29N 7 12 E
Schladming 26 47 23N 13 41 E
Schlei → 24 54 45N 9 52 E
Schleiden 24 50 32N 6 26 E
Schleiz 24 50 35N 11 49 E
Schleswig 24 54 32N 9 34 E
Schleswig-Holstein □ 24 54 10N 9 40 E
Schlüchtern 25 50 20N 9 32 E
Schmalkalden 24 50 43N 10 28 E
Schmölin 24 50 54N 12 22 E
Schmölln 24 53 15N 14 6 E
Schneeberg, Austria 26 47 47N 15 48 E
Schneeberg, Ger. 24 50 35N 12 39 E
Schofield 116 44 54N 89 39W
Schönberg, Rostock, Ger. 24 53 50N 10 55 E
Schönberg, Schleswig-Holstein, Ger. 24 54 23N 10 20 E
Schönebeck 24 52 2N 11 42 E
Schongau 25 47 49N 10 54 E
Schöningen 24 52 8N 10 57 E
Schortens 24 53 37N 7 51 E
Schouten I. 99 42 20 S 148 20 E
Schouten, Kepulauan 73 1 0 S 136 0 E
Schouwen 16 51 43N 3 45 E
Schramberg 25 48 12N 8 24 E
Schrankogl 26 47 3N 11 7 E
Schreiber 106 48 45N 87 20W
Schrobenhausen 25 48 33N 11 16 E
Schruns 26 47 5N 9 56 E
Schuler 109 50 20N 110 6W
Schumacher 106 48 30N 81 16W
Schurz 118 38 57N 118 48W
Schuyler 116 41 30N 97 3W
Schuylkill Haven 113 40 37N 76 11W
Schwabach 25 49 19N 11 3 E
Schwäbisch Gmünd 25 48 49N 9 48 E
Schwäbisch Hall 25 49 7N 9 45 E
Schwäbische Alb 25 48 30N 9 30 E
Schwabmünchen 25 48 11N 10 45 E
Schwandorf 25 49 20N 12 7 E
Schwarmstedt 24 52 41N 9 37 E
Schwarzach → 26 46 56N 12 35 E
Schwärze 24 52 50N 13 49 E
Schwarzenberg 24 50 31N 12 49 E
Schwarzwald 25 48 0N 8 0 E
Schwaz 26 47 20N 11 44 E
Schwedt 24 53 4N 14 18 E
Schweinfurt 25 50 3N 10 12 E
Schweizer Reneke 92 27 11 S 25 18 E
Schwerin 24 53 37N 11 22 E
Schwerin □ 24 53 35N 11 20 E
Schweriner See 24 53 45N 11 26 E
Schwetzingen 25 49 22N 8 35 E
Schwyz 25 47 2N 8 39 E
Schwyz □ 25 47 2N 8 39 E
Sciacca 40 37 30N 13 3 E
Scicli 41 36 48N 14 41 E
Scie, La 107 49 57N 55 36W
Scilla 41 38 18N 15 44 E
Scilly, Isles of 13 49 55N 6 15W
Ścinawa 28 51 25N 16 26 E
Scione 44 39 57N 23 36 E
Scioto → 114 38 44N 83 0W
Scobey 116 48 47N 105 30W
Scone, Austral. 99 32 5 S 150 52 E
Scone, U.K. 14 56 25N 3 26W
Scordia 41 37 19N 14 50 E
Scoresbysund 4 70 20N 23 0W
Scorno, Punta dello 40 41 7N 8 23 E
Scotia, Calif., U.S.A. 118 40 36N 124 4W
Scotia, N.Y., U.S.A. 113 42 50N 73 58W
Scotia Sea 5 56 5 S 56 0W
Scotland 116 43 10N 97 45W
Scotland □ 13 57 0N 4 0W
Scotland Neck 115 36 6N 77 32W
Scott 5 77 0 S 165 0 E
Scott, C. 5 71 30 S 168 0 E
Scott City 116 38 30N 100 52W
Scott Glacier 5 66 15 S 100 5 E
Scott I. 5 67 0 S 179 0 E
Scott Inlet 105 71 0N 71 0W
Scott Is. 108 50 48N 128 40W
Scott L. 109 59 55N 106 18W
Scott Reef 96 14 0 S 121 50 E
Scottburgh 93 30 15 S 30 47 E
Scottdale 112 40 8N 79 35W
Scottsbluff 116 41 55N 103 35W
Scottsboro 115 34 40N 86 0W
Scottsburg 114 38 40N 85 46W
Scottsdale 97 41 9 S 147 31 E
Scottsville, Ky., U.S.A. 115 36 48N 86 10W
Scottsville, N.Y., U.S.A. 112 43 2N 77 47W
Scottville, Austral. 98 20 33 S 147 49 E
Scottville, U.S.A. 114 43 57N 86 18W
Scranton 114 41 22N 75 41W
Scugog, L. 112 44 10N 78 55W
Scunthorpe 12 53 35N 0 38W

* Now part of Punjab □

Scusciuban Shāhrūd

Scusciuban	63	10 18N	50 12 E
Sea Breeze	112	43 12N	77 32W
Seaford, Austral.	100	38 10S	145 11 E
Seaford, U.S.A.	114	38 37N	75 36W
Seaforth	106	43 35N	81 25W
Seagraves	117	32 56N	102 30W
Seal →	109	58 50N	97 30W
Seal Cove	107	49 57N	56 22W
Seal L.	107	54 20N	61 30W
Sealy	117	29 46N	96 9W
Searchlight	119	35 31N	114 55W
Searcy	117	35 15N	91 45W
Searles L.	119	35 47N	117 17W
Seaside	118	45 59N	123 55W
Seaspray	99	38 25S	147 15 E
Seattle	118	47 41N	122 15W
Seaview Ra.	97	18 40S	145 45 E
Sebastián Vizcaino, Bahía	120	28 0N	114 30W
Sebastopol	118	38 24N	122 49W
Sebastopol = Sevastopol	56	44 35N	33 30 E
Sebderat	87	15 26N	36 42 E
Sebdou	82	34 38N	1 19W
Sebeş	46	45 58N	23 34 E
Sebeşului, Munţii	46	45 36N	23 40 E
Sebewaing	114	43 45N	83 27W
Sebezh	54	56 14N	28 22 E
Sébi	84	15 50N	4 12W
Şebinkarahisar	56	40 22N	38 28 E
Sebiş	46	46 23N	22 13 E
Sebkhet Te-n-Dghâmcha	84	18 30N	15 55W
Sebkra Azzel Mati	82	26 10N	0 43 E
Sebkra Mekerghene	82	26 21N	1 30 E
Sebnitz	24	50 58N	14 17 E
Sebou, Oued →	82	34 16N	6 40W
Sebring, Fla., U.S.A.	115	27 30N	81 26W
Sebring, Ohio, U.S.A.	112	40 55N	81 2W
Sebringville	112	43 24N	81 4W
Sebta = Ceuta	82	35 52N	5 19W
Sebuku	72	3 30S	116 25 E
Sebuku, Teluk	72	4 0N	118 10 E
Sečanj	42	45 25N	20 47 E
Secchia →	38	44 4N	11 0 E
Sechelt	108	49 25N	123 42W
Sechura, Desierto de	126	6 0S	80 30W
Seclin	19	50 33N	3 2 E
Secondigny	18	46 37N	0 26W
Sečovce	27	48 42N	21 40 E
Secretary I.	101	45 15S	166 56 E
Secunderabad	70	17 28N	78 30 E
Sedalia	116	38 40N	93 18W
Sedan, Austral.	99	34 34S	139 19 E
Sedan, France	19	49 43N	4 57 E
Sedan, U.S.A.	117	37 10N	96 11W
Sedano	32	42 43N	3 49W
Seddon	101	41 40S	174 7 E
Seddonville	101	41 33S	172 1 E
Sede Ya'aqov	62	32 43N	35 7 E
Sedgewick	108	52 48N	111 41W
Sedhiou	84	12 44N	15 30W
Sedičany	26	49 40N	14 25 E
Sedico	39	46 8N	12 6 E
Sedienie	43	42 16N	24 33 E
Sedley	109	50 10N	104 0W
Sedom	62	31 5N	35 20 E
Sedova, Pik	58	73 29N	54 58 E
Sedrata	83	36 7N	7 31 E
Sedro Woolley	118	48 30N	122 15W
Seduva	54	55 45N	23 45 E
Sędziszów Małapolski	27	50 5N	21 45 E
Seebad Ahlbeck	24	53 56N	14 10 E
Seefeld	26	47 19N	11 13 E
Seehausen	24	52 52N	11 43 E
Seeheim	92	26 50S	17 45 E
Seekoe →	92	30 18S	25 1 E
Seelaw	24	52 32N	14 22 E
Se'elim, Nahal	62	31 21N	35 24 E
Sées	18	48 38N	0 10 E
Seesen	24	51 53N	10 10 E
Sefadu	84	8 35N	10 58W
Séfeto	84	14 8N	9 49W
Sefrou	82	33 52N	4 52W
Sefwi Bekwai	84	6 10N	2 25W
Seg-ozero	54	63 0N	33 10 E
Segamat	71	2 30N	102 50 E
Segarcea	46	44 6N	23 43 E
Segbwema	84	8 0N	11 0W
Seget	73	1 24S	130 58 E
Segezha	52	63 44N	34 19 E
Segueur, O. →	82	32 4N	2 4 E
Segid	87	16 55N	42 0 E
Segonzac	20	45 36N	0 14W
Segorbe	32	39 50N	0 30W
Ségou	84	13 30N	6 16W
Segovia	30	40 57N	4 10W
Segovia = Coco →	121	15 0N	83 8W
Segovia □	30	40 55N	4 10W
Segré	18	47 40N	0 52W
Segre →	32	41 40N	0 43 E
Séguéla	84	7 55N	6 40W
Seguin	117	29 34N	97 58W
Segundo	117	37 12N	104 50W
Segundo →	124	30 53S	62 44W
Segura →	33	38 6N	0 54W
Segura, Sierra de	33	38 5N	2 45W
Sehore	68	23 10N	77 5 E
Sehwan	68	26 28N	67 53 E
Şeica Mare	46	46 1N	24 7 E
Seiland	50	70 25N	23 15 E
Seiling	117	36 10N	98 56W
Seille →, Moselle, France	19	49 7N	6 11 E
Seille →, Saône-et-Loire, France	21	46 31N	4 57 E
Sein, Î. de	18	48 2N	4 52W
Seinäjoki →	50	62 40N	22 45 E
Seine →	18	49 26N	0 26 E
Seine, B. de la	18	49 40N	0 40W
Seine-et-Marne □	19	48 45N	3 0 E
Seine-Maritime □	18	49 40N	1 0 E
Seine-Saint-Denis □	19	48 58N	2 24 E
Seini	46	47 44N	23 21 E
Seistan	65	30 50N	61 0 E
Seistan-Baluchestān □	65	27 0N	62 0 E
Sejerø	49	55 54N	11 9 E
Sejerø Bugt	49	55 53N	11 15 E
Sejny	28	54 6N	23 21 E
Seka	87	8 10N	36 52 E
Sekayu	72	2 51S	103 51 E
Seke	90	3 20S	33 31 E
Sekenke	90	4 18S	34 11 E
Sekiu	118	48 16N	124 18W
Sekken Veøy	47	62 45N	7 30 E
Sekondi-Takoradi	84	4 58N	1 45W
Sekuma	92	24 36S	23 50 E
Selah	118	46 44N	120 30W
Selama	71	5 12N	100 42 E
Selangor □	71	3 20N	101 30 E
Selárgius	40	39 14N	9 14 E
Selaru	73	8 9S	131 0 E
Selb	25	50 9N	12 9 E
Selby, U.K.	12	53 47N	1 5W
Selby, U.S.A.	116	45 34N	100 2W
Selca	39	43 20N	16 50 E
Selden	116	39 33N	100 39W
Seldovia	104	59 30N	151 45W
Sele →	41	40 27N	14 58 E
Selemdzha →	59	51 42N	128 53 E
Selenge →	75	49 25N	103 59 E
Selenica	44	40 33N	19 39 E
Selenter See	24	54 19N	10 26 E
Sélestat	19	48 16N	7 26 E
Seletan, Tg.	72	4 10S	114 40 E
Seletin	46	47 50N	25 12 E
Selevac	42	44 28N	20 52 E
Selfridge	116	46 3N	100 57W
Sélibabi	84	15 10N	12 15W
Seliger, Oz.	54	57 15N	33 0 E
Seligman	119	35 17N	112 56W
Şelim	57	40 30N	42 46 E
Selîma, El Wâhât el	86	21 22N	29 19 E
Selinda Spillway	92	18 35S	23 10 E
Selinoús	45	37 35N	21 37 E
Selizharovo	54	56 51N	33 27 E
Selje	47	62 3N	5 22 E
Seljord	47	59 30N	8 40 E
Selkirk, Can.	109	50 10N	96 55W
Selkirk, U.K.	14	55 33N	2 50W
Selkirk I.	109	53 20N	99 6W
Selkirk Mts.	108	51 15N	117 40W
Selles-sur-Cher	19	47 16N	1 33 E
Sellières	19	46 50N	5 32 E
Sells	119	31 57N	111 57W
Sellye	27	45 52N	17 51 E
Selma, Ala., U.S.A.	115	32 30N	87 0W
Selma, Calif., U.S.A.	119	36 39N	119 39W
Selma, N.C., U.S.A.	115	35 32N	78 15W
Selmer	115	35 9N	88 36W
Selo	44	41 10N	25 53 E
Selongey	19	47 36N	5 10 E
Selowandoma Falls	91	21 15S	31 50 E
Selpele	73	0 1S	130 5 E
Selsey Bill	13	50 44N	0 47W
Seltz	19	48 48N	8 4 E
Selu	73	7 32S	130 55 E
Selukwe	91	19 40S	30 0 E
Sélune →	18	48 38N	1 22W
Selva, Argent.	124	29 50S	62 0W
Selva, Italy	39	46 33N	11 46 E
Selva, Spain	32	41 13N	1 8 E
Selva, La	32	42 0N	2 45 E
Selvas	126	6 30S	67 0W
Selwyn L.	109	60 0N	104 30W
Selwyn P.O.	97	21 32S	140 30 E
Selwyn Ra.	97	21 10S	140 0 E
Seman →	44	40 45N	19 50 E
Semara	82	26 48N	11 41W
Semarang	73	7 0S	110 26 E
Semau	73	10 13S	123 22 E
Sembabule	90	0 4S	31 25 E
Sémé	84	15 4N	13 41W
Semeih	87	12 43N	30 53 E
Semenov	55	56 43N	44 30 E
Semenovka, Ukraine S.S.R., U.S.S.R.	54	52 8N	32 36 E
Semenovka, Ukraine S.S.R., U.S.S.R.	56	49 37N	33 10 E
Semeru	73	8 4S	112 55 E
Semiluki	55	51 41N	39 2 E
Seminoe Res.	118	42 0N	107 0W
Seminole, Okla., U.S.A.	117	35 15N	96 45W
Seminole, Tex., U.S.A.	117	32 41N	102 38W
Semiozernoye	58	52 22N	64 8 E
Semipalatinsk	58	50 30N	80 10 E
Semirara Is.	73	12 0N	121 20 E
Semisopochnoi	104	52 0N	179 40W
Semitau	72	0 29N	111 57 E
Semiyarskoye	58	50 55N	78 23 E
Semmering Pass	26	47 41N	15 45 E
Semnān	65	35 55N	53 25 E
Semnān □	65	36 0N	54 0 E
Semois →	16	49 53N	4 44 E
Semporna	73	4 30N	118 33 E
Semuda	72	2 51S	112 58 E
Semur-en-Auxois	19	47 30N	4 20 E
Sen →	71	13 45N	105 12 E
Sena	91	17 25S	35 0 E
Sena Madureira	126	9 5S	68 45W
Senador Pompeu	127	5 40S	39 20W
Senai	71	1 38N	103 38 E
Senaja	72	6 45N	117 3 E
Senanga	92	16 2S	23 14 E
Senatobia	117	34 38N	89 57W
Sendafa	87	9 11N	39 3 E
Sendai, Kagoshima, Japan	74	31 50N	130 20 E
Sendai, Miyagi, Japan	74	38 15N	140 53 E
Sendamangalam	70	11 17N	78 17 E
Sendeling's Drift	92	28 12S	16 52 E
Sendenhorst	24	51 50N	7 49 E
Sendurjana	68	21 32N	78 17 E
Senec	27	48 12N	17 23 E
Seneca, Oreg., U.S.A.	118	44 10N	119 2W
Seneca, S.C., U.S.A.	115	34 43N	82 59W
Seneca Falls	114	42 55N	76 50W
Seneca L.	114	42 40N	76 58W
Senegal ■	84	14 30N	14 30W
Senegal →	84	15 48N	16 32W
Senekal	93	28 30S	27 36 E
Senftenberg	24	51 30N	14 1 E
Senga Hill	91	9 19S	31 11 E
Senge Khambab (Indus) →	68	28 40N	70 10 E
Sengerema □	90	2 10S	32 20 E
Sengiley	55	53 58N	48 46 E
Sengkang	73	4 8S	120 1 E
Sengua →	91	17 7S	28 5 E
Senhor-do-Bonfim	127	10 30S	40 10W
Senica	27	48 41N	17 25 E
Senigállia	39	43 42N	13 12 E
Senio →	39	44 35N	12 15 E
Senise	40	40 6N	16 15 E
Senj	39	45 0N	14 58 E
Senja	50	69 25N	17 30 E
Senlis	19	49 13N	2 35 E
Senmonorom	71	12 27N	107 12 E
Sennâr	87	13 30N	33 35 E
Senneterre	106	48 25N	77 15W
Senniquelle	84	7 19N	8 38W
Senno	54	54 45N	29 43 E
Sennori	40	40 49N	8 36 E
Senonches	18	48 34N	1 2 E
Senorbì	40	39 33N	9 8 E
Senožeče	39	45 43N	14 3 E
Sens	19	48 11N	3 15 E
Senta	42	45 55N	20 3 E
Sentein	20	42 53N	0 58 E
Sentery	90	5 17S	25 42 E
Sentinel	119	32 45N	113 13W
Sentolo	73	7 55S	110 13 E
Senya Beraku	85	5 28N	0 31W
Seo de Urgel	32	42 22N	1 23 E
Seohara	68	29 15N	78 33 E
Seoni	69	22 5N	79 30 E
Seoriuarayan	69	21 45N	82 34 E
Seoul = Sŏul	76	37 31N	127 6 E
Separation Point	107	53 37N	57 25W
Sepik →	98	3 49S	144 30 E
Sępólno Krajeńskie	28	53 26N	17 30 E
Sepone	71	16 45N	106 13 E
Sepopa	92	18 49S	22 12 E
Sepopol	28	54 16N	21 2 E
Sept-Îles	107	50 13N	66 22W
Septemvri	43	42 13N	24 6 E
Septimus	98	21 13S	148 47 E
Sepúlveda	30	41 18N	3 45W
Sequeros	30	40 31N	6 2W
Sequim	118	48 3N	123 9W
Sequoia Nat. Park	119	36 30N	118 30W
Serafimovich	57	49 36N	42 43 E
Seraing	16	50 35N	5 32 E
Seram	73	3 10S	129 0 E
Seram Sea	73	2 30S	128 30 E
Serampore	69	22 44N	88 21 E
Serang	73	6 8S	106 10 E
Serasan	72	2 29N	109 4 E
Seravezza	38	43 59N	10 13 E
Serbia = Srbija	42	43 30N	21 0 E
Sercaia	46	45 49N	25 9 E
Serdo	87	11 56N	41 14 E
Serdobsk	55	52 28N	44 10 E
Seredka	54	58 12N	28 10 E
Seregno	38	45 40N	9 12 E
Seremban	71	2 43N	101 53 E
Serena, La, Chile	124	29 55S	71 10W
Serena, La, Spain	31	38 45N	5 40W
Serengeti □	90	2 0S	34 30 E
Serengeti Plain	90	2 40S	35 0 E
Sereth = Siret →	46	47 58N	26 5 E
Sergach	55	55 30N	45 30 E
Serge →	32	41 54N	0 50 E
Sergino	58	62 30N	65 38 E
Sergipe □	127	10 30S	37 30W
Seria	72	4 37N	114 23 E
Serian	72	1 10N	110 31 E
Seriate	38	45 42N	9 43 E
Seribu, Kepulauan	72	5 36S	106 33 E
Sérifontaine	19	49 20N	1 45 E
Sérifos	45	37 9N	24 30 E
Sérignan	20	43 17N	3 17 E
Sermaize-les-Bains	19	48 47N	4 54 E
Sermata	73	8 15S	128 50 E
Sérmide	39	45 0N	11 17 E
Sernovodsk	55	53 54N	51 16 E
Serny Zavod	58	39 59N	58 50 E
Serock	28	52 31N	21 4 E
Serón	33	37 20N	2 29W
Serós	32	41 27N	0 24 E
Serov	58	59 29N	60 35 E
Serowe	92	22 25S	26 43 E
Serpa	31	37 57N	7 38 E
Serpeddi, Punta	40	39 19N	9 18 E
Serpentara	40	39 8N	9 38 E
Serpis →	33	38 59N	0 9W
Serpukhov	55	54 55N	37 28 E
Serra San Bruno	41	38 31N	16 23 E
Serracapriola	41	41 47N	15 12 E
Serradilla	30	39 50N	6 9W
Sérrai	44	41 5N	23 31 E
Sérrai □	44	41 5N	23 37 E
Serramanna	40	39 26N	8 56 E
Serrat, C.	83	37 14N	9 10 E
Serre-Poncon, Barrage de	21	44 22N	6 20 E
Serres	21	44 26N	5 43 E
Serrezuela	124	30 40S	65 20W
Serrinha	127	11 39S	39 0W
Sersale	41	39 1N	16 44 E
Sertã	30	39 48N	8 6W
Sertânia	127	8 5S	37 20W
Sertanópolis	125	23 4S	51 2W
Serua	73	6 18S	130 1 E
Serui	73	1 53S	136 10 E
Serule	92	21 57S	27 20 E
Sérvia	44	40 9N	21 58 E
Sese Is.	90	0 20S	32 20 E
Sesepe	73	1 30S	127 59 E
Sesfontein	92	19 7S	13 39 E
Sesheke	92	17 29S	24 13 E
Sesia →	38	45 5N	8 37 E
Sesimbra	31	38 28N	9 6W
Sessa Aurunca	40	41 14N	13 55 E
Sestao	32	43 18N	3 0W
Sesto S. Giovanni	38	45 32N	9 14 E
Sestos	44	40 16N	26 23 E
Sestri Levante	38	44 17N	9 22 E
Sestrières	38	44 58N	6 56 E
Sestrunj	39	44 10N	15 0 E
Sestu	40	39 18N	9 6 E
Sète	20	43 25N	3 42 E
Sete Lagôas	127	19 27S	44 16W
Sétif	83	36 9N	5 26 E
Setonaikai	74	34 20N	133 30 E
Settat	82	33 0N	7 40W
Setté-Cama	88	2 32S	9 45 E
Séttimo Tor	38	45 9N	7 46 E
Setting L.	109	55 0N	98 38W
Settle	12	54 5N	2 18W
Settlement Pt.	115	26 40N	79 0W
Setto Calende	38	45 44N	8 37 E
Setúbal	31	38 30N	8 58W
Setúbal □	31	38 25N	8 35W
Setúbal, B. de	31	38 40N	8 56W
Seugne →	20	45 42N	0 32W
Seul, Lac-Rés.	106	50 25N	92 30W
Seulimeum	72	5 27N	95 15 E
Sevan	57	40 33N	44 56 E
Sevan, Ozero	57	40 30N	45 20 E
Sevastopol	56	44 35N	33 30 E
Seven Sisters	108	54 56N	128 10W
Sever →	31	39 40N	7 32W
Sévérac-le-Château	20	44 20N	3 5 E
Severn →, Can.	106	56 2N	87 36W
Severn →, U.K.	13	51 35N	2 38W
Severn L.	106	53 54N	90 48W
Severnaya Zemlya	59	79 0N	100 0 E
Severnyye Uvaly	52	58 0N	48 0 E
Severo-Kurilsk	59	50 40N	156 8 E
Severo-Yeniseyskiy	59	60 22N	93 1 E
Severočeský □	26	50 30N	14 0 E
Severodinsk	52	64 27N	39 58 E
Severodonetsk	57	48 58N	38 30 E
Severomoravský □	27	49 38N	17 40 E
Severomorsk	52	69 5N	33 27 E
Severouralsk	52	60 9N	59 57 E
Sevier	119	38 39N	112 11W
Sevier →	119	39 10N	113 6W
Sevier L.	118	39 0N	113 20W
Sevilla	31	37 23N	6 0W
Sevilla □	31	37 25N	5 30W
Seville = Sevilla	31	37 23N	6 0W
Sevlievo	43	43 2N	25 3 E
Sevnica	39	46 2N	15 19 E
Sèvre-Nantaise →	18	47 12N	1 33W
Sèvre Niortaise →	20	46 18N	1 8W
Sevsk	54	52 10N	34 30 E
Seward, Alaska, U.S.A.	104	60 6N	149 26W
Seward, Nebr., U.S.A.	116	40 55N	97 6W
Seward Pen.	104	65 0N	164 0W
Sewell	124	34 10S	70 23W
Sewer	73	5 53S	134 40 E
Sewickley	112	40 33N	80 12W
Sexsmith	108	55 21N	118 47W
Seychelles ■	3	5 0S	56 0 E
Seyðisfjörður	50	65 16N	14 0W
Seym →	54	51 27N	32 34 E
Seymchan	59	62 54N	152 30 E
Seymour, Austral.	99	37 0S	145 10 E
Seymour, Conn., U.S.A.	113	41 23N	73 5W
Seymour, Ind., U.S.A.	114	39 0N	85 50W
Seymour, Tex., U.S.A.	117	33 35N	99 18W
Seymour, Wis., U.S.A.	114	44 30N	88 20W
Seyne	21	44 21N	6 22 E
Seyne-sur-Mer, La	21	43 7N	5 52 E
Seyssel	21	45 57N	5 50 E
Sežana	39	45 43N	13 41 E
Sézanne	19	48 40N	3 40 E
Sezze	40	41 30N	13 3 E
Sfax	83	34 49N	10 48 E
Sfintu Gheorghe	46	45 52N	25 48 E
Sha Xian	77	26 23N	117 45 E
Shaanxi □	77	35 0N	109 0 E
Shaba	90	8 0S	25 0 E
† Shabani	91	20 17S	30 2 E
Shabla	43	43 31N	28 32 E
Shabunda	90	2 40S	27 16 E
Shache	75	38 20N	77 10 E
Shackleton	5	78 30S	36 1W
Shackleton Ice Shelf	5	66 0S	100 0 E
Shackleton Inlet	5	83 0S	160 0 E
Shaddad	86	21 25N	40 2 E
Shadrinsk	58	56 5N	63 32 E
Shaffa	85	10 30N	12 6 E
Shafter, Calif., U.S.A.	119	35 32N	119 14W
Shafter, Tex., U.S.A.	117	29 49N	104 18W
Shaftesbury	13	51 0N	2 12W
Shagamu	85	6 51N	3 39 E
Shah Bunder	68	24 13N	67 56 E
* Shah Faisalabad	68	31 30N	73 5 E
Shahabad, Andhra Pradesh, India	70	17 10N	76 54 E
Shahabad, Punjab, India	68	30 10N	76 55 E
Shahabad, Raj., India	68	25 15N	77 11 E
Shahabad, Ut. P., India	69	27 36N	79 56 E
Shāhābād, Kermanshāhān, Iran	64	34 10N	46 30 E
Shāhābād, Khorāsān, Iran	65	37 40N	56 50 E
Shahada	68	21 33N	74 30 E
Shahadpur	68	25 55N	68 35 E
Shahapur	70	15 50N	74 34 E
Shahdād	65	30 30N	57 40 E
Shahdadkot	68	27 50N	67 55 E
Shahganj	69	26 3N	82 44 E
Shaḫḫāt	81	32 48N	21 54 E
Shāhī	65	36 30N	52 55 E
Shahjahanpur	69	27 54N	79 57 E
Shahpur, Mad. P., India	68	22 12N	77 58 E
Shahpur, Mysore, India	70	16 40N	76 48 E
Shahpūr	64	38 12N	44 45 E
Shahpur	68	28 46N	68 27 E
Shahpura	69	23 10N	80 45 E
Shahr Kord	65	32 15N	50 55 E
Shahrezā	65	32 0N	51 55 E
Shahrig	68	30 15N	67 40 E
Shāhrūd	65	36 30N	55 0 E

* *Renamed Faisalabad*

† *Renamed Zvishavane*

Shahsād, Namakzār-e Siliguri

Shahsād, Namakzār-e 65 30 20N 58 20 E
Shahsavār 65 36 45N 51 12 E
Shaibara 86 25 26N 36 47 E
Shaikhabad 66 34 2N 68 45 E
Shajapur 68 23 27N 76 21 E
Shakargarh 68 32 17N 75 10 E
Shakawe 92 18 28 S 21 49 E
Shaker Heights 112 41 29N 81 36W
Shakhty 57 47 40N 40 16 E
Shakhunya 55 57 40N 46 46 E
Shaki 85 8 41N 3 21 E
Shakopee 116 44 45N 93 30W
Shala, L. 87 7 30N 38 30 E
Shallow Lake 112 44 36N 81 5W
Sham, J. ash 65 23 10N 57 5 E
Shamâl Dârfûr □ 87 15 0N 25 0 E
Shamâl Kordofân □ 87 15 0N 30 0 E
Shamattawa 109 55 51N 92 5W
Shamattawa → 106 55 1N 85 23W
Shambe 87 7 8N 30 46 E
Shambu 87 9 32N 37 3 E
Shamgong Dzong 69 27 13N 90 35 E
Shamīl 65 27 30N 56 55 E
Shamkhor 57 40 50N 46 0 E
Shamli 68 29 32N 77 18 E
Shammar, Jabal 64 27 40N 41 0 E
Shamo, L. 87 5 45N 37 30 E
Shamokin 114 40 47N 76 33W
Shamrock 117 35 15N 100 15W
Shan □ 67 21 30N 98 30 E
Shanan → 87 8 0N 40 20 E
Shanchengzhen 76 42 20N 125 20 E
Shandong □ 76 36 0N 118 0 E
Shang Xian 77 33 50N 109 58 E
Shangalowe 91 10 50 S 26 30 E
Shangani 91 19 41 S 29 20 E
Shangani → 91 18 41 S 27 10 E
Shangbancheng 76 40 50N 118 1 E
Shangcheng 77 31 47N 115 26 E
Shangchuan Dao 77 21 40N 112 50 E
Shangdu 76 41 30N 113 30 E
Shanggao 77 28 17N 114 55 E
Shanghai 75 31 15N 121 26 E
Shangqiu 77 34 26N 115 36 E
Shangrao 75 28 25N 117 59 E
Shangshui 77 33 42N 114 35 E
Shangsi 77 22 8N 107 58 E
Shangyou 77 25 48N 114 32 E
Shangzhi 76 45 22N 127 56 E
Shani 85 10 14N 12 2 E
Shaniko 118 45 0N 120 50W
Shannon, Greenl. 4 75 10N 18 30W
Shannon, N.Z. 101 40 33 S 175 25 E
Shannon → 15 52 35N 9 30W
Shansi = Shanxi □ 76 37 0N 112 0 E
Shantar, Ostrov Bolshoy 59 55 9N 137 40 E
Shantou 75 23 18N 116 40 E
Shantung = Shandong □ 76 36 0N 118 0 E
Shanxi □ 76 37 0N 112 0 E
Shanyang 77 33 31N 109 55 E
Shaoguan 75 24 48N 113 35 E
Shaowu 75 27 22N 117 28 E
Shaoxing 75 30 0N 120 35 E
Shaoyang 75 27 14N 111 25 E
Shapinsay 14 59 2N 2 50W
Shaqrā', Si. Arab. 64 25 15N 45 16 E
Shaqrā', Yemen, S. 63 13 22N 45 44 E
Sharafa (Ogr) 87 11 59N 27 7 E
Sharavati → 70 14 20N 74 25 E
Sharbot Lake 113 44 46N 76 41W
Shark B. 96 25 55 S 113 32 E
Sharm el Sheikh 86 27 53N 34 15 E
Sharon, Mass., U.S.A. 113 42 5N 71 11W
Sharon, Pa., U.S.A. 114 41 18N 80 30W
Sharon, Plain of = Hasharon 62 32 12N 34 49 E
Sharon Springs 116 38 54N 101 45W
Sharp Pt. 98 10 58 S 142 43 E
Sharpe L. 109 54 5N 93 40W
Sharpsville 112 41 16N 80 28W
Shary 64 27 14N 43 29 E
Sharya 55 58 22N 45 20 E
Shasha 87 6 29N 35 59 E
Shashemene 87 7 13N 38 33 E
Shashi 75 30 25N 112 14 E
Shashi → 91 21 14 S 29 20 E
Shasta, Mt. 118 41 30N 122 12W
Shasta Res. 118 40 50N 122 15W
Shatsk 55 54 0N 41 45 E
Shattuck 117 36 17N 99 55W
Shatura 55 55 34N 39 31 E
Shaumyani 57 41 22N 41 45 E
Shaunavon 109 49 35N 108 25W
Shaw → 96 20 21 S 119 17 E
Shaw I. 98 20 30 S 149 2 E
Shawan 75 44 34N 85 50 E
Shawanaga 112 45 31N 80 17W
Shawano 114 44 45N 88 38W
Shawinigan 106 46 35N 72 50W
Shawnee 117 35 15N 97 0W
Shayib el Banat, Bebel 86 26 59N 33 29 E
Shchekino 55 54 1N 37 34 E
Shcherbakov = Rybinsk 55 58 5N 38 50 E
Shchigri 55 51 55N 36 58 E
Shchors 54 51 48N 31 56 E
Shchuchiosk 58 52 56N 70 12 E
She Xian 77 29 50N 118 25 E
Shebekino 55 50 28N 36 54 E
Shebele, Wabi → 87 2 0N 44 0 E
Sheboygan 114 43 46N 87 45W
Shechem 62 32 13N 35 21 E
Shediac 107 46 14N 64 32W
Sheelin, Lough 15 53 48N 7 20W
Sheep Haven 15 55 12N 7 55W
Sheerness 13 51 26N 0 47 E
Sheet Harbour 107 44 56N 62 31W
Shefar'am 62 32 48N 35 10 E
Sheffield, U.K. 12 53 23N 1 28W
Sheffield, Ala., U.S.A. 115 34 45N 87 42W
Sheffield, Mass., U.S.A. 113 42 6N 73 23W
Sheffield, Pa., U.S.A. 112 41 42N 79 3W
Sheffield, Tex., U.S.A. 117 30 42N 101 49W
Shegaon 68 20 48N 76 47 E
Sheho 109 51 35N 103 13W
Shehojele 87 10 40N 35 9 E
Sheikhpura 69 25 9N 85 53 E
Shek Hasan 87 12 5N 35 58 E
Shekhupura 68 31 42N 73 58 E
Sheki 57 41 10N 47 5 E
Sheksna → 55 59 0N 38 30 E
Shelburne, N.S., Can. 107 43 47N 65 20W
Shelburne, Ont., Can. 106 44 4N 80 15W
Shelburne, U.S.A. 113 44 23N 73 15W
Shelburne B. 97 11 50 S 142 50 E
Shelburne Falls 113 42 36N 72 45W
Shelby, Mich., U.S.A. 114 43 34N 86 27W
Shelby, Mont., U.S.A. 118 48 30N 111 52W
Shelby, N.C., U.S.A. 115 35 18N 81 34W
Shelby, Ohio, U.S.A. 112 40 52N 82 40W
Shelbyville, Ill., U.S.A. 116 39 25N 88 45W
Shelbyville, Ind., U.S.A. 114 39 30N 85 42W
Shelbyville, Tenn., U.S.A. 115 35 30N 86 25W
Sheldon 116 43 6N 95 40W
Sheldrake 107 50 20N 64 51W
Shelikhova, Zaliv 59 59 30N 157 0 E
Shell Creek Ra. 118 39 15N 114 30W
Shell Lake 109 53 19N 107 2W
Shellbrook 109 53 13N 106 24W
Shellharbour 97 34 31 S 150 51 E
Shelling Rocks 15 51 45N 10 35W
Shelon → 54 58 10N 30 30 E
Shelton, Conn., U.S.A. 113 41 18N 73 7W
Shelton, Wash., U.S.A. 118 47 15N 123 6W
Shemakha 57 40 38N 48 37 E
Shenandoah, Iowa, U.S.A. 116 40 50N 95 25W
Shenandoah, Pa., U.S.A. 114 40 49N 76 13W
Shenandoah, Va., U.S.A. 114 38 30N 78 38W
Shenandoah → 114 39 19N 77 44W
Shenchi 76 39 8N 112 10 E
Shencottah 70 8 59N 77 18 E
Shendam 85 8 49N 9 30 E
Shendî 87 16 46N 33 22 E
Shendurni 70 20 39N 75 36 E
Sheng Xian 77 29 35N 120 50 E
Shëngjergji 44 41 17N 20 10 E
Shëngjini 44 41 50N 19 35 E
Shenmëria 44 42 7N 20 13 E
Shenmu 76 38 50N 110 29 E
Shenqiucheng 77 33 24N 115 2 E
Shensi = Shaanxi □ 77 35 0N 109 0 E
Shenyang 76 41 48N 123 27 E
Shepetovka 54 50 10N 27 10 E
Shephelah = Hashefela 62 31 30N 34 43 E
Shepparton 97 36 23 S 145 26 E
Sheqi 77 33 12N 112 57 E
Sherada 87 7 18N 36 30 E
Sherborne 13 50 56N 2 31W
Sherbro I. 84 7 30N 12 40W
Sherbrooke 107 45 28N 71 57W
Sherda 83 20 7N 16 46 E
Shereik 86 18 44N 33 47 E
Sheridan, Ark., U.S.A. 117 34 20N 92 25W
Sheridan, Col., U.S.A. 116 39 44N 105 3W
Sheridan, Wyo., U.S.A. 118 44 50N 107 0W
Sherkot 68 29 22N 78 35 E
Sherman 117 33 40N 96 35W
Sherpur 69 25 0N 90 0 E
Sherridon 109 55 8N 101 5W
Sherwood, N.D., U.S.A. 116 48 59N 101 36W
Sherwood, Tex., U.S.A. 117 31 18N 100 45W
Sherwood Forest 12 53 5N 1 5W
Sheslay 108 58 17N 131 52W
Sheslay → 108 58 48N 132 5W
Shethanei L. 109 58 48N 97 50W
Shetland □ 14 60 30N 1 30W
Shetland Is. 14 60 30N 1 30W
Shevaroy Hills 70 11 58N 78 12 E
Shewa □ 87 9 33N 38 10 E
Shewa Gimira 87 7 4N 35 51 E
Sheyenne 116 47 52N 99 8W
Sheyenne → 116 47 5N 96 50W
Shibām 63 16 0N 48 36 E
Shibîn El Kôm 86 30 31N 30 55 E
Shibîn el Qanâtir 86 30 19N 31 19 E
Shibogama L. 106 53 35N 88 15W
Shibushi 74 31 25N 131 8 E
Shidao 76 36 50N 122 25 E
Shiel, L. 14 56 48N 5 32W
Shiga □ 74 35 20N 136 0 E
Shigaib 81 15 5N 23 35 E
Shiguaigou 76 40 52N 110 15 E
Shihchiachuangi = Shijiazhuang 76 38 2N 114 28 E
Shijaku 44 41 21N 19 33 E
Shijiazhuang 76 38 2N 114 28 E
Shikarpur, India 68 28 17N 78 7 E
Shikarpur, Pak. 68 27 57N 68 39 E
Shikoku 74 33 30N 133 30 E
Shikoku □ 74 33 30N 133 30 E
Shikoku-Sanchi 74 33 30N 133 30 E
Shilabo 63 6 22N 44 32 E
Shilka 59 52 0N 115 55 E
Shilka → 59 53 20N 121 26 E
Shillelagh 15 52 46N 6 32W
Shillong 67 25 35N 91 53 E
Shilo 62 32 4N 35 18 E
Shilong 75 23 5N 113 52 E
Shilovo 55 54 25N 40 57 E
Shimabara 74 32 48N 130 20 E
Shimada 74 34 49N 138 10 E
Shimane □ 74 35 0N 132 30 E
Shimanovsk 59 52 15N 127 30 E
Shimizu 74 35 0N 138 30 E
Shimodate 74 36 20N 139 55 E
Shimoga 70 13 57N 75 32 E
Shimoni 90 4 38 S 39 20 E
Shimonoseki 74 33 58N 131 0 E
Shimpuru Rapids 92 17 45 S 19 55 E
Shimsha → 70 13 15N 77 10 E
Shimsk 54 58 15N 30 50 E
Shin, L. 14 58 7N 4 30W
Shin-Tone → 74 35 44N 140 51 E
Shinano → 74 36 50N 138 30 E
Shīndand 65 33 12N 62 8 E
Shingleton 106 46 25N 86 33W
Shingū 74 33 40N 135 55 E
Shinkafe 85 13 8N 6 29 E
Shinyanga 90 3 45 S 33 27 E
Shinyanga □ 90 3 50 S 34 0 E
Shio-no-Misaki 74 33 25N 135 45 E
Ship I. 117 30 16N 88 55W
Shipehenski Prokhod 43 42 45N 25 15 E
Shippegan 107 47 45N 64 45W
Shippensburg 114 40 4N 77 32W
Shiprock 119 36 51N 108 45W
Shiqian 77 27 32N 108 13 E
Shiqma, N. → 62 31 37N 34 30 E
Shiquan 77 33 5N 108 15 E
Shīr Kūh 65 31 39N 54 3 E
Shīrāz 65 29 42N 52 30 E
Shirbin 86 31 11N 31 32 E
Shire → 91 17 42 S 35 19 E
Shiretoko-Misaki 74 44 21N 145 20 E
Shiringushi 55 53 51N 42 46 E
Shiriya-Zaki 74 41 25N 141 30 E
Shirol 70 16 47N 74 41 E
Shirpur 68 21 21N 74 57 E
Shīrvān 65 37 30N 57 50 E
Shishmanova 43 42 58N 23 12 E
Shisur 63 17 30N 54 0 E
Shitai 77 30 12N 117 25 E
Shivali (Sirkali) 70 11 15N 79 41 E
Shivpuri 68 25 26N 77 42 E
Shivta 62 30 53N 34 40 E
Shiwei 76 51 19N 119 55 E
Shixing 77 24 46N 114 5 E
Shiyata 86 29 25N 25 7 E
Shizuishan 76 39 15N 106 50 E
Shizuoka 74 35 0N 138 24 E
Shizuoka □ 74 35 15N 138 40 E
Shklov 54 54 16N 30 15 E
Shkoder = Shkodra 44 42 6N 19 1 E
Shkodra 44 42 6N 19 20 E
Shkodra □ 44 42 25N 19 20 E
Shkumbini → 44 41 5N 19 50 E
Shmidt, O. 59 81 0N 91 0 E
Shoal Lake 109 50 30N 100 35W
Shoalhaven → 100 34 54 S 150 42 E
Shoeburyness 13 51 31N 0 49 E
Sholapur 70 17 43N 75 56 E
Shologontsy 59 66 13N 114 0 E
Shomera 62 33 4N 35 17 E
Shōmrōn 62 32 15N 35 13 E
Shongopovi 119 35 49N 110 37W
Shoranur 70 10 46N 76 19 E
Shorapur 70 16 31N 76 48 E
Shoshone 118 43 0N 114 27W
Shoshone L. 118 44 30N 110 40W
Shoshone Mts. 118 39 30N 117 30W
Shoshong 92 22 56 S 26 31 E
Shoshoni 118 43 13N 108 5W
Shostka 54 51 57N 33 32 E
Shouyang 76 37 54N 113 8 E
Show Low 119 34 16N 110 0W
Shpola 56 49 1N 31 30 E
Shreveport 117 32 30N 93 50W
Shrewsbury 12 52 42N 2 45W
Shrivardhan 70 18 4N 73 3 E
Shropshire □ 13 52 36N 2 45W
Shuangcheng 76 45 20N 126 15 E
Shuangliao 76 43 29N 123 30 E
Shuangyashan 76 46 28N 131 5 E
Shucheng 77 31 28N 116 57 E
Shu'eib, Wadi 62 31 54N 35 38 E
Shuguri Falls 91 8 33 S 37 22 E
Shujalpur 68 23 18N 76 46 E
Shulan 76 44 28N 127 0 E
Shule 75 39 25N 76 3 E
Shumagin Is. 104 55 0N 159 0W
Shumerlya 55 55 30N 46 25 E
Shumikha 58 55 10N 63 15 E
Shunchang 77 26 54N 117 48 E
Shunde 77 22 42N 113 14 E
Shungay 57 48 30N 46 45 E
Shungnak 104 66 55N 157 10W
Shuo Xian 76 39 20N 112 33 E
Shūr → 65 28 30N 55 0 E
Shurma 55 56 58N 50 21 E
Shūsf 65 31 50N 60 5 E
Shūshtar 64 32 0N 48 50 E
Shuswap L. 108 50 55N 119 3W
Shuwaykah 62 32 20N 35 1 E
Shuya 55 56 50N 41 28 E
Shwebo 67 22 30N 95 45 E
Shwegu 67 24 15N 96 26 E
Shweli → 67 23 45N 96 45 E
Shyok 69 34 15N 78 12 E
Shyok → 69 35 13N 75 53 E
Si Kiang = Xi Jiang → 75 22 5N 113 20 E
Si Racha 71 13 10N 100 48 E
Siah 64 22 0N 47 0 E
Siahan Range 66 27 30N 64 40 E
Siaksrinderapura 72 0 51N 102 0 E
Sialkot 68 32 32N 74 30 E
Siam = Thailand ■ 71 16 0N 102 0 E
Siam, G. of 71 11 30N 101 0 E
Sian = Xi'an 77 34 15N 109 0 E
Siantan, P. 72 3 10N 106 15 E
Sīāreh 65 28 5N 60 14 E
Siargao 73 9 52N 126 3 E
Siasi 73 5 34N 120 50 E
Siátista 44 40 15N 21 33 E
Siau 73 2 50N 125 25 E
Siauliai 54 55 56N 23 15 E
Siaya □ 90 0 0N 34 20 E
Siazan 57 41 3N 49 10 E
Sibâi, Gebel el 86 25 45N 34 10 E
Sibari 41 39 47N 16 27 E
Sibay 52 52 42N 58 39 E
Sibaya, L. 93 27 20 S 32 45 E
Šibenik 39 43 48N 15 54 E
Siberia 60 60 0N 100 0 E
Siberut 72 1 30 S 99 0 E
Sibi 68 29 30N 67 54 E
Sibil 73 4 59 S 140 35 E
Sibiti 88 3 38 S 13 19 E
Sibiu 46 45 45N 24 9 E
Sibiu □ 46 45 50N 24 15 E
Sibley, Iowa, U.S.A. 116 43 21N 95 43W
Sibley, La., U.S.A. 117 32 34N 93 16W
Sibolga 72 1 42N 98 45 E
Sibsagar 67 27 0N 94 36 E
Sibu 72 2 18N 111 49 E
Sibuco 73 7 20N 122 10 E
Sibuguey B. 73 7 50N 122 45 E
Sibutu 73 4 45N 119 30 E
Sibutu Passage 73 4 50N 120 0 E
Sibuyan 73 12 25N 122 40 E
Sibuyan Sea 73 12 30N 122 20 E
Sicamous 108 50 49N 119 0W
Siccus → 99 31 42 S 139 25 E
Sichuan □ 75 31 0N 104 0 E
Sicilia 41 37 30N 14 30 E
Sicilia, Canale di 40 37 25N 12 30 E
Sicilian Channel = Sicilia, Canale di 40 37 25N 12 30 E
Sicily = Sicilia 41 37 30N 14 30 E
Sicuani 126 14 21 S 71 10W
Siculiana 40 37 20N 13 23 E
Šid 42 45 8N 19 14 E
Sidamo □ 87 5 0N 37 50 E
Sidaouet 85 18 34N 8 3 E
Siddipet 70 18 0N 78 51 E
Sidéradougou 84 10 42N 4 12W
Siderno Marina 41 38 16N 16 17 E
Sidheros, Ákra 45 35 19N 26 19 E
Sidhirókastron 44 41 13N 23 24 E
Sidhpur 68 23 56N 72 25 E
Sîdi Abd el Rahmân 86 30 55N 29 44 E
Sîdi Barrâni 86 31 38N 25 58 E
Sidi-bel-Abbès 82 35 13N 0 39W
Sidi Bennour 82 32 40N 8 25W
Sidi Haneish 86 31 10N 27 35 E
Sidi Kacem 82 34 11N 5 49W
Sidi Moussa, O. → 82 26 58N 3 54 E
Sidi Omar 86 31 24N 24 57 E
Sidi Slimane 82 34 16N 5 56W
Sidi Smaïl 82 32 50N 8 31W
Sidlaw Hills 14 56 32N 3 10W
Sidley, Mt. 5 77 2 S 126 2W
Sidmouth 13 50 40N 3 13W
Sidmouth, C. 98 13 25 S 143 36 E
Sidney, Can. 108 48 39N 123 24W
Sidney, Mont., U.S.A. 116 47 42N 104 7W
Sidney, N.Y., U.S.A. 114 42 18N 75 20W
Sidney, Ohio, U.S.A. 114 40 18N 84 6W
Sidoarjo 73 7 30 S 112 46 E
Sidra, G. of = Khalīj Surt 35 31 40N 18 30 E
Siedlce 28 52 10N 22 20 E
Siedlce □ 28 52 0N 22 0 E
Sieg → 24 50 46N 7 7 E
Siegburg 24 50 48N 7 12 E
Siegen 24 50 52N 8 2 E
Siem Reap 71 13 20N 103 52 E
Siena 39 43 20N 11 20 E
Sieniawa 27 50 11N 22 38 E
Sieradź 28 51 37N 18 41 E
Sieraków 28 52 39N 16 2 E
Sierck-les-Bains 19 49 26N 6 20 E
Sierpc 28 52 55N 19 43 E
Sierra Blanca, N. Mex., U.S.A. 119 33 20N 105 54W
Sierra Blanca, Tex., U.S.A. 119 31 11N 105 17W
Sierra City 118 39 34N 120 42W
Sierra Colorada 128 40 35 S 67 50W
Sierra de Yeguas 31 37 7N 4 52W
Sierra Gorda 124 22 50 S 69 15W
Sierra Leone ■ 84 9 0N 12 0W
Sierra Mojada 120 27 19N 103 42W
Sierre 25 46 17N 7 31 E
Sif Fatima 83 31 6N 8 41 E
Sífnos 45 37 0N 24 45 E
Sifton 109 51 21N 100 8W
Sifton Pass 108 57 52N 126 15W
Sig 82 35 32N 0 12W
Sigdal 47 60 4N 9 38 E
Sigean 20 43 2N 2 58 E
Sighetul Marmatiei 46 47 57N 23 52 E
Sighişoara 46 46 12N 24 50 E
Sigli 72 5 25N 96 0 E
Siglufjörður 50 66 12N 18 55W
Sigma 73 11 29N 122 40 E
Sigmaringen 25 48 5N 9 13 E
Signakhi 57 41 40N 45 57 E
Signy I. 5 60 45 S 45 56W
Signy-l'Abbaye 19 49 40N 4 25 E
Sigsig 126 3 0 S 78 50W
Sigtuna 48 59 36N 17 44 E
Sigüenza 32 41 3N 2 40W
Siguiri 84 11 31N 9 10W
Sigulda 54 57 10N 24 55 E
Sigurd 119 38 49N 112 0W
Sihanoukville = Kompong Som 71 10 40N 103 30 E
Sihui 77 23 20N 112 40 E
Si'īr 62 31 35N 35 9 E
Siirt 64 37 57N 41 55 E
Sijarira Ra. 91 17 36 S 27 45 E
Sikar 68 27 33N 75 10 E
Sikasso 84 11 18N 5 35W
Sikeston 117 36 52N 89 35W
Sikhote Alin, Khrebet 59 46 0N 136 0 E
Sikiá. 44 40 2N 23 56 E
Síkinos 45 36 40N 25 8 E
Sikkani Chief → 108 57 47N 122 15W
Sikkim □ 69 27 50N 88 30 E
Siklós 27 45 50N 18 19 E
Sil → 30 42 27N 7 43W
Sila, La 41 39 15N 16 35 E
Silandro 38 46 38N 10 48 E
Silat az Zahr 62 32 19N 35 11 E
Silba 39 44 24N 14 41 E
Silchar 67 24 49N 92 48 E
Silcox 109 57 12N 94 10W
Siler City 115 35 44N 79 30W
Sileru → 70 17 49N 81 24 E
Silesia = Slask 22 51 0N 16 30 E
Silet 82 22 44N 4 37 E
Silgarhi Doti 69 29 15N 81 0 E
Silghat 67 26 35N 93 0 E
Silifke 64 36 22N 33 58 E
Siliguri 69 26 45N 88 25 E

Siling Co Sobótka

Siling Co 75 31 50N 89 20 E
Siliqua 40 39 20N 8 49 E
Silistra 43 44 6N 27 19 E
Siljan, L. 48 60 55N 14 45 E
Silkeborg 49 56 10N 9 32 E
Sillajhuay, Cordillera 126 19 46 S 68 40W
Sillé-le-Guillaume 18 48 10N 0 8W
Siloam Springs 117 36 15N 94 31W
Silogui 72 1 10 S 9 0 E
Silsbee 117 30 20N 94 8W
Silute 54 55 21N 21 33 E
Silva Porto = Bié 89 12 22 S 16 55 E
Silver City, Panama 120 9 19N 79 53W
Silver City, N. Mex., U.S.A. 119 32 50N 108 18W
Silver City, Nev., U.S.A. 118 39 15N 119 48W
Silver Cr. ~ 118 43 16N 119 13W
Silver Creek 114 42 33N 79 9W
Silver Lake 118 43 9N 121 4W
Silverton, Austral. 100 31 52 S 141 10 E
Silverton, Colo., U.S.A. 119 37 51N 107 45W
Silverton, Tex., U.S.A. 117 34 30N 101 16W
Silves 31 37 11N 8 26W
Silvi 39 42 32N 14 5 E
Silvies ~ 118 43 22N 118 48W
Silvretta Gruppe 25 46 50N 10 6 E
Silwa Bahari 86 24 45N 32 55 E
Silwâd 62 31 59N 35 15 E
Silz 26 47 16N 10 56 E
Sim, C. 82 31 26N 9 51W
Simanggang 72 1 15N 111 32 E
Simard, L. 106 47 40N 78 40W
Simărtin 46 46 19N 25 58 E
Simba 90 2 10 S 37 36 E
Simbach 25 48 16N 13 3 E
Simbo 90 4 51 S 29 41 E
Simcoe 106 42 50N 80 20W
Simcoe, L. 106 44 25N 79 20W
Simenga 59 62 42N 108 25 E
Simeto ~ 41 37 25N 15 10 E
Simeulue 72 2 45N 95 45 E
Simferopol 56 44 55N 34 3 E
Sími 45 36 35N 27 50 E
Simikot 69 30 0N 81 50 E
Simitli 42 41 52N 23 7 E
Simla 68 31 2N 77 9 E
Şimleu-Silvaniei 46 47 17N 22 50 E
Simmern 25 49 59N 7 32 E
Simmie 109 49 56N 108 6W
Simojärvi 50 66 5N 27 3 E
Simojoki ~ 50 65 35N 25 1 E
Simonette ~ 108 55 9N 118 15W
Simonstown 92 34 14 S 18 26 E
Simontornya 27 46 45N 18 33 E
Simpang, Indon. 72 1 16 S 104 5 E
Simpang, Malay. 71 4 50N 100 40 E
Simplon Pass 25 46 15N 8 0 E
Simplon Tunnel 25 46 15N 8 7 E
Simpson Des. 97 25 0 S 137 0 E
Simrishamn 49 55 33N 14 22 E
Simunjan 72 1 25N 110 45 E
Simushir, Ostrov 59 46 50N 152 30 E
Sina ~ 70 17 30N 75 55 E
Sinabang 72 2 30N 96 24 E
Sinadogo 63 5 50N 47 0 E
Sinai = Es Sînâ' 86 29 0N 34 0 E
Sinai, Mt. = Mûsa, G. 86 28 32N 33 59 E
Sinaia 46 45 21N 25 38 E
Sinaloa 120 25 50N 108 20W
Sinaloa □ 120 25 0N 107 30W
Sinalunga 39 43 12N 11 43 E
Sinan 77 27 56N 108 13 E
Sînandrei 46 45 52N 21 13 E
Sīnāwan 83 31 0N 10 37 E
Sincelejo 126 9 18N 75 24W
Sinclair 118 41 47N 107 10W
Sinclair Mills 108 54 5N 121 40W
Sincorá, Serra do 127 13 30 S 41 0W
Sind 68 26 0N 68 30 E
Sind Sagar Doab 68 32 0N 71 30 E
Sindal 49 57 28N 10 10 E
Sindangan 73 8 10N 123 5 E
Sindangbarang 73 7 27 S 107 1 E
Sinde 91 17 28 S 25 51 E
Sinegorski 57 48 0N 40 52 E
Sinelnikovo 56 48 25N 35 30 E
Sines 31 37 56N 8 51W
Sines, Cabo de 31 37 58N 8 53W
Sineu 32 39 38N 3 1 E
Sinfra 84 6 35N 5 56W
Singa 87 13 10N 33 57 E
Singanallur 70 11 2N 77 1 E
Singaparna 73 7 23 S 108 4 E
Singapore ■ 71 1 17N 103 51 E
Singapore, Straits of 71 1 15N 104 0 E
Singaraja 72 8 6 S 115 10 E
Singen 25 47 45N 8 50 E
Singida 90 4 49 S 34 48 E
Singida □ 90 6 0 S 34 30 E
Singitikós Kólpos 44 40 6N 24 0 E
Singkaling Hkamti 67 26 0N 95 39 E
Singkawang 72 1 0N 108 57 E
Singkep 72 0 30 S 104 20 E
Singleton 97 32 33 S 151 0 E
Singleton, Mt. 96 29 27 S 117 15 E
Singö 48 60 12N 18 45 E
Singoli 68 25 0N 75 22 E
Siniátsikon, Óros 44 40 25N 21 35 E
Siniscóla 40 40 35N 9 40 E
Sinj 39 43 42N 16 39 E
Sinjai 73 5 7 S 120 20 E
Sinjajevina, Planina 42 42 57N 19 22 E
Sinjār 64 36 19N 41 52 E
Sinjil 62 32 3N 35 15 E
Sinkat 86 18 55N 36 49 E
Sinkiang Uighur = Xinjiang Uygur □ 75 42 0N 86 0 E
Sinnai 40 39 18N 9 13 E
Sinnar 70 19 48N 74 0 E
Sinni ~ 41 40 9N 16 42 E
Sînnicolau Maré 42 46 5N 20 39 E
Sinnuris 86 29 26N 30 31 E
Sinoe, L. 46 44 35N 28 50 E
Sinoia 91 17 20 S 30 8 E
Sinop 64 42 1N 35 11 E
Sinskoye 59 61 8N 126 48 E
Sint Maarten 121 18 0N 63 5W
Sint Niklaas 16 51 10N 4 9 E
Sint Truiden 16 50 48N 5 10 E
Sîntana 46 46 20N 21 30 E
Sintang 72 0 5N 111 35 E
Sinton 117 28 1N 97 30W
Sintra 31 38 47N 9 25W
Sinŭiju 76 40 5N 124 24 E
Sinyukha ~ 56 48 3N 30 51 E
Siocon 73 7 40N 122 10 E
Siófok 27 16 39 S 23 36 E
Sioma 92 16 25 S 23 28 E
Sion 25 46 14N 7 20 E
Sioux City 116 42 32N 96 25W
Sioux Falls 116 43 35N 96 40W
Sioux Lookout 106 50 10N 91 50W
Šipan 42 42 45N 17 52 E
Siping 76 43 8N 124 21 E
Sipiwesk L. 109 55 5N 97 35W
Sipora 72 2 18 S 99 40 E
Siquia ~ 121 12 10N 84 20W
Siquijor 73 9 12N 123 35 E
Sir Edward Pellew Group 97 15 40 S 137 10 E
Sira 70 13 41N 76 49 E
Siracusa 41 37 4N 15 17 E
Sirajganj 69 24 25N 89 47 E
Sirakoro 84 12 41N 9 14W
Sirasso 84 9 16N 6 6W
Siret 46 47 55N 26 5 E
Siret ~ 46 47 58N 26 5 E
Şiria 42 46 16N 21 38 E
Sirino, Monte 41 40 7N 15 50 E
Sirkali (Shivali) 70 11 15N 79 41 E
Sírna. 45 36 22N 26 42 E
Sirohi 68 24 52N 72 53 E
Široki Brijeg 42 43 21N 17 36 E
Sironj 68 24 5N 77 39 E
Síros 45 37 28N 24 57 E
Sirsa 68 29 33N 75 4 E
Sirsi 70 14 40N 74 49 E
Siruela 31 38 58N 5 3W
Sisak 39 45 30N 16 21 E
Sisaket 71 15 8N 104 23 E
Sisante 33 39 25N 2 12W
Sisargas, Islas 30 43 21N 8 50W
Sishen 92 27 47 S 22 59 E
Sishui 77 34 48N 113 15 E
Sisipuk L. 109 55 45N 101 50W
Sisophon 71 13 38N 102 59 E
Sisseton 116 45 43N 97 3W
Sissonne 19 49 34N 3 51 E
Sistema Central 30 40 40N 5 55W
Sistema Iberico 32 41 0N 2 10W
Sisteron 21 44 12N 5 57 E
Sisters 118 44 21N 121 32W
Sitamarhi 69 26 37N 85 30 E
Sitapur 69 27 38N 80 45 E
Siteki 93 26 32 S 31 58 E
Sitges 32 41 17N 1 47 E
Sithoniá 44 40 0N 23 45 E
Sitia 45 35 13N 26 6 E
Sitka 104 57 9N 135 20W
Sitoti 92 23 15 S 23 40 E
Sitra 86 28 40N 26 53 E
Sittang ~ 67 17 10N 96 58 E
Sittang Myit ~ 67 17 20N 96 45 E
Sittard 16 51 0N 5 52 E
Sittensen 24 53 17N 9 32 E
Sittona 87 14 25N 37 23 E
Situbondo 73 7 45 S 114 0 E
Sivaganga 70 9 50N 78 28 E
Sivagiri 70 9 16N 77 26 E
Sivakasi 70 9 24N 77 47 E
Sivana 68 28 37N 78 6 E
Sīvand 65 30 5N 52 55 E
Sivas 64 39 43N 36 58 E
Siverek 64 37 50N 39 19 E
Sivomaskinskiy 52 66 40N 62 35 E
Sivrihisar 64 39 30N 31 35 E
Sîwa 86 29 11N 25 31 E
Sîwa, El Wâhât es 86 29 10N 25 30 E
Siwalik Range 69 28 0N 83 0 E
Siwan 69 26 13N 84 21 E
Siyâl, Jazâ'ir 86 22 49N 36 12 E
Sizewell 13 52 13N 1 38 E
Sjælland 49 55 30N 11 30 E
Sjællands Odde 49 56 0N 11 15 E
Själevad 48 63 18N 18 36 E
Sjarinska Banja 42 42 45N 21 38 E
Sjenica 42 43 16N 20 0 E
Sjoa 47 61 41N 9 33 E
Sjöbo 49 55 37N 13 45 E
Sjösa 49 58 47N 17 4 E
Skadarsko Jezero 42 42 10N 19 20 E
Skadovsk 56 46 17N 32 52 E
Skagafjörður 50 65 54N 19 35W
Skagastølstindane 47 61 28N 7 52 E
Skagen 49 57 43N 10 35 E
Skagern 48 59 0N 14 20 E
Skagerrak 49 57 30N 9 0 E
Skagway 104 59 23N 135 20W
Skaidi 50 70 26N 24 30 E
Skala Podolskaya 56 48 50N 26 15 E
Skalat 54 49 23N 25 55 E
Skalbmierz 28 50 20N 20 25 E
Skalica 27 48 50N 17 15 E
Skalni Dol = Kamenyak 43 43 24N 26 57 E
Skals 49 56 34N 9 24 E
Skanderborg 49 56 2N 9 55 E
Skånevik 47 59 43N 5 53 E
Skänninge 49 58 24N 15 5 E
Skanör 49 55 24N 12 50 E
Skantzoúra 45 39 5N 24 6 E
Skara 49 58 25N 13 30 E
Skaraborgs län □ 49 58 20N 13 30 E
Skardu 69 35 20N 75 44 E
Skarrild 49 55 58N 8 53 E
Skarszewy 28 54 4N 18 25 E
Skaryszew 28 51 19N 21 15 E
Skarzysko Kamienna 28 51 7N 20 52 E
Skattungbyn 48 61 10N 14 56 E
Skebokvarn 48 59 7N 16 45 E
Skeena ~ 108 54 9N 130 5W
Skeena Mts. 108 56 40N 128 30W
Skegness 12 53 9N 0 20 E
Skeldon 126 5 55N 57 20W
Skellefte älv ~ 50 64 45N 21 10 E
Skellefteå 50 64 45N 20 58 E
Skelleftehamn 50 64 47N 20 59 E
Skender Vakuf 42 44 29N 17 22 E
Skene 49 57 30N 12 37 E
Skerries, The 12 53 27N 4 40W
Skhíza 45 36 41N 21 40 E
Skhoinoúsa 45 36 53N 25 31 E
Skhwaner, Pegunungan 72 1 0 S 112 30 E
Ski 47 59 43N 10 52 E
Skíathos 45 39 12N 23 30 E
Skibbereen 15 51 33N 9 16W
Skiddaw 12 54 39N 3 9W
Skien 47 59 12N 9 35 E
Skierniewice 28 51 58N 20 10 E
Skierniewice □ 28 52 0N 20 10 E
Skikda 83 36 50N 6 58 E
Skillingaryd 49 57 27N 14 5 E
Skillinge 49 55 30N 14 16 E
Skillingmark 48 59 48N 12 1 E
Skinári, Ákra 45 37 56N 20 40 E
Skipton, Austral. 99 37 39 S 143 40 E
Skipton, U.K. 12 53 57N 2 1W
Skiropoúla 45 38 50N 24 21 E
Skíros 45 38 55N 24 34 E
Skivarp 49 55 26N 13 34 E
Skive 49 56 33N 9 2 E
Skjåk 47 61 52N 8 22 E
Skjálfandafljót ~ 50 65 59N 17 25W
Skjálfandi 50 66 5N 17 30W
Skjeberg 47 59 12N 11 12 E
Skjern 49 55 57N 8 30 E
Skoczów 27 49 49N 18 45 E
Skodje 47 62 30N 6 43 E
Škofja Loka 39 46 9N 14 19 E
Skoghall 48 59 20N 13 30 E
Skoki 28 52 40N 17 11 E
Skole 54 49 3N 23 30 E
Skópelos 45 39 9N 23 47 E
Skopin 55 53 55N 39 32 E
Skopje 42 42 1N 21 32 E
Skórcz 28 53 47N 18 30 E
Skottfoss 47 59 12N 9 30 E
Skovorodino 59 54 0N 125 0 E
Skowhegan 107 44 49N 69 40W
Skownan 109 51 58N 99 35W
Skradin 39 43 52N 15 53 E
Skreanäs 49 56 52N 12 35 E
Skrwa ~ 28 52 35N 19 32 E
Skull 15 51 32N 9 40W
Skultorp 49 58 24N 13 51 E
Skunk ~ 116 40 42N 91 7W
Skuodas 54 56 21N 21 45 E
Skurup 49 55 28N 13 30 E
Skutskär 49 60 37N 17 25 E
Skvira 56 49 44N 29 40 E
Skwierzyna 28 52 33N 15 30 E
Skye 14 57 15N 6 10W
Skykomish 118 47 43N 121 16W
Skyros = Skíros 45 38 52N 24 37 E
Slagelse 49 55 23N 11 19 E
Slamet, G. 72 7 16 S 109 8 E
Slaney ~ 15 52 52N 6 45W
Slangerup 49 55 50N 12 11 E
Slănic 46 45 14N 25 58 E
Slankamen 42 45 8N 20 15 E
Slano 42 42 48N 17 53 E
Slantsy 54 59 7N 28 5 E
Slany 26 50 13N 14 6 E
Slask 22 51 0N 16 30 E
Slate Is. 106 48 40N 87 0W
Slatina 46 44 28N 24 22 E
Slaton 117 33 27N 101 38W
Slave ~ 108 61 18N 113 39W
Slave Coast 85 6 0N 2 30 E
Slave Lake 108 55 17N 114 43W
Slave Pt. 108 61 11N 115 56W
Slavgorod 58 53 1N 78 37 E
Slavinja 42 43 9N 22 50 E
Slavkov (Austerlitz) 27 49 10N 16 52 E
Slavnoye 54 54 24N 29 15 E
Slavonska Požega 42 45 20N 17 40 E
Slavonski Brod 42 45 11N 18 0 E
Slavuta 54 50 15N 27 2 E
Slavyansk 56 48 55N 37 36 E
Slavyansk-na-Kubani 56 45 15N 38 11 E
Sława 28 51 52N 16 2 E
Sławno 28 54 20N 16 41 E
Sławoborze 28 53 55N 15 42 E
Sleaford 12 53 0N 0 22W
Sleat, Sd. of 14 57 5N 5 47W
Sleeper Is. 105 58 30N 81 0W
Sleepy Eye 116 44 15N 94 45W
Sleman 73 7 40 S 110 20 E
Slemon L. 108 63 13N 116 4W
Ślesin 28 52 22N 18 14 E
Slidell 117 30 20N 89 48W
Sliedrecht 16 51 50N 4 45 E
Slieve Aughty 15 53 4N 8 30W
Slieve Bloom 15 53 4N 7 40W
Slieve Donard 15 54 10N 5 57W
Slieve Gullion 15 54 8N 6 26W
Slieve Mish 15 52 12N 9 50W
Slievenamon 15 52 25N 7 37W
Sligo 15 54 17N 8 28W
Sligo □ 15 54 10N 8 35W
Sligo B. 15 54 20N 8 40W
Slite 51 57 42N 18 48 E
Sliven 43 42 42N 26 19 E
Slivnitsa 42 42 50N 23 0 E
Sljeme 39 45 57N 15 58 E
Sloansville 113 42 45N 74 22W
Slobodskoy 52 58 40N 50 6 E
Slobozia, Ialomiţa, Romania 46 44 34N 27 23 E
Slobozia, Valahia, Romania 46 44 30N 25 14 E
Slocan 108 49 48N 117 28W
Slochteren 16 53 12N 6 48 E
Slöinge 49 56 51N 12 42 E
Słomniki 28 50 16N 20 4 E
Slonim 54 53 4N 25 19 E
Slough 13 51 30N 0 35W
Slovakia = Slovensko 27 48 30N 19 0 E
Slovakian Ore Mts. = Slovenské Rudohorie 27 48 45N 20 0 E
Slovenia = Slovenija 39 45 58N 14 30 E
Slovenija □ 39 45 58N 14 30 E
Slovenj Gradec 39 46 31N 15 5 E
Slovenska Bistrica 39 46 24N 15 35 E
Slovenská Socialisticka Republika □ 27 48 30N 10 0 E
Slovenské Rudohorie 27 48 45N 20 0 E
Slovensko □ 27 48 30N 19 0 E
Słubice 28 52 22N 14 35 E
Sluch ~ 54 51 37N 26 38 E
Sluis 16 51 18N 3 23 E
Slunchev Bryag 43 42 40N 27 41 E
Slunj 39 45 6N 15 33 E
Słupca 28 52 15N 17 52 E
Słupia ~ 28 54 35N 16 51 E
Słupsk 28 54 30N 17 3 E
Słupsk □ 28 54 15N 17 30 E
Slurry 92 25 49 S 25 42 E
Slutsk 54 53 2N 27 31 E
Slyne Hd. 15 53 25N 10 10W
Slyudyanka 59 51 40N 103 40 E
Smålandsfarvandet 49 55 10N 11 20 E
Smalandsstenar 49 57 9N 13 24 E
Smalltree L. 109 61 0N 105 0W
Smallwood Reservoir 107 54 20N 63 10W
Smarje 39 46 15N 15 34 E
Smart Syndicate Dam 92 30 45 S 23 10 E
Smeaton 109 53 30N 104 49W
Smederevo 42 44 40N 20 57 E
Smederevska Palanka 42 44 22N 20 58 E
Smela 56 49 15N 31 58 E
Smethport 112 41 50N 78 28W
Smidovich 59 48 36N 133 49 E
Smigiel 28 52 1N 16 32 E
Smiley 109 51 38N 109 29W
Smilyan 43 41 29N 24 46 E
Smith 108 55 10N 114 0W
Smith ~ 108 59 34N 126 30W
Smith Arm 104 66 15N 123 0W
Smith Center 116 39 50N 98 50W
Smith Sund 4 78 30N 74 0W
Smithburne ~ 98 17 3 S 140 57 E
Smithers 108 54 45N 127 10W
Smithfield, Madag. 93 30 9 S 26 30 E
Smithfield, N.C., U.S.A. 115 35 31N 78 16W
Smithfield, Utah, U.S.A. 118 41 50N 111 50W
Smiths Falls 106 44 55N 76 0W
Smithton 99 40 53 S 145 6 E
Smithtown 99 30 58 S 152 48 E
Smithville, Can. 112 43 6N 79 33W
Smithville, U.S.A. 117 30 2N 97 12W
Smoky ~ 108 56 10N 117 21W
Smoky Falls 106 50 4N 82 10W
Smoky Hill ~ 116 39 3N 96 48W
Smoky Lake 108 54 10N 112 30W
Smøla 47 63 23N 8 3 E
Smolensk 54 54 45N 32 0 E
Smolikas, Óros 44 40 9N 20 58 E
Smolník 27 48 43N 20 44 E
Smolyan 43 41 36N 24 38 E
Smooth Rock Falls 106 49 17N 81 37W
Smoothstone L. 109 54 40N 106 50W
Smorgon 54 54 20N 26 24 E
Smulţi 46 45 57N 27 44 E
Smyadovo 43 43 2N 27 1 E
Smyrna = İzmir 64 38 25N 27 8 E
Snaefell 12 54 18N 4 26W
Snaefellsjökull 50 64 45N 23 46W
Snake ~ 118 46 12N 119 2W
Snake I. 99 38 47 S 146 33 E
Snake L. 109 55 32N 106 35W
Snake Ra. 118 39 0N 114 30W
Snake River 118 44 10N 110 42W
Snake River Plain 118 43 13N 113 0W
Snarum 47 60 1N 9 54 E
Snedsted 49 56 55N 8 32 E
Sneek 16 53 2N 5 40 E
Snejbjerg 49 56 8N 8 54 E
Snezhnoye 57 48 0N 38 58 E
Sněžka 26 50 41N 15 50 E
Snežnik 39 45 36N 14 35 E
Sniadowo 28 53 2N 22 0 E
Sniardwy, Jezioro 28 53 48N 21 50 E
Snigirevka 56 47 2N 32 49 E
Snina 27 49 0N 22 9 E
Snizort, L. 14 57 33N 6 28W
Snøhetta 47 62 19N 9 16 E
Snohomish 118 47 53N 122 6W
Snonuten 47 59 31N 6 50 E
Snow Hill 114 38 10N 75 21W
Snow Lake 109 54 52N 100 3W
Snowbird L. 109 60 45N 103 0W
Snowdon 12 53 4N 4 8W
Snowdrift 109 62 24N 110 44W
Snowdrift ~ 109 62 24N 110 44W
Snowflake 119 34 30N 110 4W
Snowshoe Pk. 118 48 13N 115 41W
Snowtown 99 33 46 S 138 14 E
Snowville 118 41 59N 112 47W
Snowy ~ 97 37 46 S 148 30 E
Snowy Mts. 99 36 30 S 148 20 E
Snyatyn 56 48 30N 25 50 E
Snyder, Okla., U.S.A. 117 34 40N 99 0W
Snyder, Tex., U.S.A. 117 32 45N 100 57W
Soahanina 93 18 42 S 44 13 E
Soalala 93 16 6 S 45 20 E
Soanierana-Ivongo 93 16 55 S 49 35 E
Soap Lake 118 47 23N 119 31W
Sobat, Nahr ~ 87 9 22N 31 33 E
Soběslav 26 49 16N 14 45 E
Sobhapur 68 22 47N 78 17 E
Sobinka 55 56 0N 40 0 E
Sobótka 28 50 54N 16 44 E

Sobrado Spragge

Sobrado 30 43 2N 8 2W
Sobral 127 3 50S 40 20W
Sobreira Formosa 31 39 46N 7 51W
Soča → 39 46 20N 13 40E
Sochaczew 28 52 15N 20 13E
Soch'e = Shache 75 38 20N 77 10E
Sochi 57 43 35N 39 40E
Société, Is. de la 95 17 0S 151 0W
Society Is. = Société, Is. de la 95 17 0S 151 0W
Socompa, Portezuelo de 124 24 27S 68 18W
Socorro, Colomb. 126 6 29N 73 16W
Socorro, U.S.A. 119 34 4N 106 54W
Socotra 63 12 30N 54 0E
Socúellmos 33 39 16N 2 47W
Soda L. 119 35 7N 116 2W
Soda Plains 69 35 30N 79 0E
Soda Springs 118 42 40N 111 40W
Söderfors 48 60 23N 17 25E
Söderhamn 48 61 18N 17 10E
Söderköping 48 58 31N 16 20E
Södermanlands län □ 48 59 10N 16 30E
Södertälje 48 59 12N 17 39E
Sodiri 81 14 27N 29 0E
Sodo 87 7 0N 37 41E
Södra Vi 49 57 45N 15 45E
Sodražica 39 45 45N 14 39E
Sodus 112 43 13N 77 5W
Soekmekaar 93 23 30S 29 55E
Soest, Ger. 24 51 34N 8 7E
Soest, Neth. 16 52 9N 5 19E
Sofádhes 44 39 20N 22 4E
Sofara 84 13 59N 4 9W
Sofia = Sofiya 43 42 45N 23 20E
Sofia → 93 15 27S 47 23E
Sofievka 56 48 6N 33 55E
Sofiiski 59 52 15N 133 59E
Sofikón 45 37 47N 23 3E
Sofiya 43 42 45N 23 20E
Sogad 73 10 30N 125 0E
Sogakofe 85 6 2N 0 39E
Sogamoso 126 5 43N 72 56W
Sögel 24 52 50N 7 32E
Sogn og Fjordane fylke □ 47 61 40N 6 0E
Sognefjorden 47 61 10N 5 50E
Sohâg 86 26 33N 31 43E
Soignies 16 50 35N 4 5E
Soira, Mt. 87 14 45N 39 30E
Soissons 19 49 25N 3 19E
Sōja 74 34 40N 133 45E
Sojat 68 25 55N 73 45E
Sok → 55 53 24N 50 8E
Sokal 54 50 31N 24 15E
Söke 45 37 48N 27 28E
Sokelo 91 9 55S 24 36E
Sokhós 44 40 48N 23 22E
Sokki, Oued In → 82 29 30N 3 42E
Sokna 47 60 16N 9 50E
Soknedal 47 62 57N 10 13E
Soko Banja 42 43 40N 21 51E
Sokodé 85 9 0N 1 11E
Sokol 55 59 30N 40 5E
Sokolac 42 43 56N 18 48E
Sokółka 28 53 25N 23 30E
Sokolo 84 14 53N 6 8W
Sokolov 26 50 12N 12 40E
Sokołów Małpolski 27 50 12N 22 7E
Sokołów Podlaski 28 52 25N 22 15E
Sokoły 28 52 59N 22 42E
Sokoto 85 13 2N 5 16E
Sokoto □ 85 12 30N 5 0E
Sokoto → 85 11 20N 4 10E
Sol Iletsk 52 51 10N 55 0E
Sola 47 58 53N 5 36E
Sola → 27 50 4N 19 15E
Solai 90 0 2N 36 12E
Solana, La 33 38 59N 3 14W
Solano 73 16 31N 121 15E
Solares 30 43 23N 3 43W
Solberga 49 57 45N 14 43E
Solca 46 47 40N 25 50E
Solec Kujawski 28 53 5N 18 14E
Soledad, U.S.A. 119 36 27N 121 16W
Soledad, Venez. 126 8 10N 63 34W
Solent, The 13 50 45N 1 25W
Solenzara 21 41 53N 9 23E
Solesmes 19 50 10N 3 30E
Solfonn 47 60 2N 6 57E
Soligalich 55 59 5N 42 10E
Soligorsk 54 52 51N 27 27E
Solikamsk 58 59 38N 56 50E
Solila 93 21 25S 46 37E
Solimões → = Amazonas → 126 2 15S 66 30W
Solingen 24 51 10N 7 4E
Sollebrunn 49 58 8N 12 32E
Sollefteå 48 63 12N 17 20E
Sollentuna 48 59 26N 17 56E
Sóller 32 39 46N 2 43E
Solling 24 51 44N 9 36E
Solna 48 59 22N 18 1E
Solnechnogorsk 55 56 10N 36 57E
Sologne 19 47 40N 2 0E
Solok 72 0 45S 100 40E
Sololá 120 14 49N 91 10E
Solomon Is. ■ 94 6 0S 155 0E
Solomon, N. Fork → 116 39 29N 98 26W
Solomon Sea 98 7 0S 150 0E
Solomon, S. Fork → 116 39 25N 99 12W
Solomon's Pools = Birak Sulaymān 62 31 42N 35 7E
Solon 75 46 32N 121 10E
Solon Springs 116 46 19N 91 47W
Solor 73 8 27S 123 0E
Solotcha 55 54 48N 39 53E
Solothurn 25 47 13N 7 32E
Solothurn □ 25 47 18N 7 40E
Solsona 32 42 0N 1 31E
Solt 27 46 45N 19 1E
Solta 39 43 24N 16 15E
Soltānābād 65 36 29N 58 5E
Soltāniyeh 64 36 20N 48 55E
Soltau 24 52 59N 9 50E
Soltsy 54 58 10N 30 30E
Solund 47 61 5N 4 50E
Solunska Glava 42 41 44N 21 31E
Solvay 114 43 5N 76 17W
Sölvesborg 49 56 5N 14 35E
Solvychegodsk 52 61 21N 46 56E
Solway Firth 12 54 45N 3 38W
Solwezi 91 12 11S 26 21E
Somali Rep. ■ 63 7 0N 47 0E
Sombe Dzong 69 27 13N 89 8E
Sombernon 19 47 20N 4 40E
Sombor 42 45 46N 19 9E
Sombra 112 42 43N 82 29W
Sombrerete 120 23 40N 103 40W
Sombrero 121 18 37N 63 30W
Somers 118 48 4N 114 18W
Somerset, Berm. 121 32 16N 64 55W
Somerset, Can. 109 49 25N 98 39W
Somerset, Colo., U.S.A. 119 38 55N 107 30W
Somerset, Ky., U.S.A. 114 37 5N 84 40W
Somerset, Mass., U.S.A. 113 41 45N 71 10W
Somerset, Pa., U.S.A. 112 40 1N 79 4W
Somerset □ 13 51 9N 3 0W
Somerset East 92 32 42S 25 35E
Somerset I. 104 73 30N 93 0W
Somerset West 92 34 8S 18 50E
Somersworth 113 43 15N 70 51W
Somerton 119 32 35N 114 47W
Somerville 113 40 34N 74 36W
Someş → 46 47 15N 23 45E
Someşul Mare → 46 47 18N 24 30E
Somma Lombardo 38 45 41N 8 42E
Somma Vesuviana 41 40 52N 14 23E
Sommariva 99 26 24S 146 36E
Sommatino 40 37 20N 14 0E
Somme □ 19 50 0N 2 20E
Somme, B. de la 18 50 14N 1 33E
Sommen 49 58 12N 15 0E
Sommen, L. 49 58 0N 15 15E
Sommepy-Tahure 19 49 15N 4 31E
Sömmerda 24 51 10N 11 8E
Sommesous 19 48 44N 4 12E
Sommières 21 43 47N 4 6E
Somogy □ 27 46 19N 17 30E
Somogyszob 27 46 18N 17 20E
Sompolno 28 52 26N 18 30E
Somport, Paso 32 42 48N 0 31W
Somport, Puerto de 32 42 48N 0 31W
Son, Norway 47 59 32N 10 42E
Son, Spain 30 42 43N 8 58W
Son La 71 21 20N 103 50E
Sonamukhi 69 23 18N 87 27E
Soncino 38 45 24N 9 52E
Sondags → 92 33 44S 25 51E
Sóndalo 38 46 20N 10 20E
Sønder Omme 49 55 50N 8 54E
Sønder Ternby 49 57 31N 9 58E
Sønderborg 49 54 55N 9 49E
Sønderjyllands Amtskommune □ 49 55 10N 9 10E
Sondershausen 24 51 22N 10 50E
Sóndrio 38 46 10N 9 53E
Sone 91 17 23S 34 55E
Sonepat 68 29 0N 77 5E
Sonepur 69 20 55N 83 50E
Song Cau 71 13 27N 109 18E
Song Xian 77 34 12N 112 8E
Songea 91 10 40S 35 40E
Songea □ 91 10 30S 36 0E
Songeons 19 49 32N 1 50E
Songhua Hu 76 43 35N 126 50E
Songhua Jiang → 75 47 45N 132 30E
Songjiang 77 31 1N 121 12E
Songkhla 71 7 13N 100 37E
Songling 76 48 2N 121 9E
Songpan 75 32 40N 103 30E
Songtao 77 28 11N 109 10E
Songwe 90 3 20S 26 16E
Songwe → 91 9 44S 33 58E
Songzi 77 30 12N 111 45E
Sonkovo 55 57 50N 37 5E
Sonmiani 66 25 25N 66 40E
Sonnino 40 41 25N 13 13E
Sono → 127 9 58S 48 11W
Sonora, Calif., U.S.A. 119 37 59N 120 27W
Sonora, Texas, U.S.A. 117 30 33N 100 37W
Sonora □ 120 29 0N 111 0W
Sonora → 120 28 50N 111 33W
Sonora P. 118 38 17N 119 35W
Sonsomate 120 13 43N 89 44W
Sonthofen 25 47 31N 10 16E
Soo Junction 114 46 20N 85 14W
Soochow = Suzhou 75 31 19N 120 38E
Sopi 73 2 34N 128 28E
Sopo, Nahr → 87 8 40N 26 30E
Sopot, Poland 28 54 27N 18 31E
Sopot, Yugo. 42 44 29N 20 30E
Sopotnica 42 41 23N 21 13E
Sopron 27 47 45N 16 32E
Sop's Arm 107 49 46N 56 56W
Sør-Rondane 5 72 0S 25 0E
Sør-Trøndelag fylke □ 47 63 0N 10 0E
Sora 40 41 45N 13 36E
Sorada 70 19 45N 84 26E
Sorah 68 27 13N 68 56E
Söråker 48 62 30N 17 32E
Sorano 39 42 40N 11 42E
Sorata 126 15 50S 68 40W
Sorbas 33 37 6N 2 7W
Sorel 106 46 0N 73 10W
Sorento 99 38 22S 144 47E
Soreq, N. → 62 31 57N 34 43E
Soresina 38 45 17N 9 51E
Sorgono 40 40 01N 9 06E
Sorgues 21 44 1N 4 53E
Soria 32 41 43N 2 32W
Soria □ 32 41 46N 2 28W
Soriano 124 33 24S 58 19W
Soriano nel Cimino 39 42 25N 12 14E
Sorkh, Kuh-e 65 35 40N 58 30E
Sorø 49 55 26N 11 32E
Soro 84 10 9N 9 48W
Sorocaba 125 23 31S 47 27W
Sorochinsk 52 52 26N 53 10E
Soroki 56 48 8N 28 12E
Soroksár 27 47 24N 19 9E
Soron 68 27 55N 78 45E
Sorong 73 0 55S 131 15E
Soroti 90 1 43N 33 35E
Sørøya 50 70 40N 22 30E
Sørøyane 47 62 25N 5 32E
Sørøysundet 50 70 25N 23 0E
Sorraia → 31 38 55N 8 53W
Sorrento 41 40 38N 14 23E
Sorris Sorris 92 21 0S 14 46E
Sorsele 50 65 31N 17 30E
Sorso 40 40 50N 8 34E
Sorsogon 73 13 0N 124 0E
Sortavala 52 61 42N 30 41E
Sortino 41 37 9N 15 1E
Sorvizhi 55 57 52N 48 32E
Sos 32 42 30N 1 13W
Soscumica, L. 106 50 15N 77 27W
Sosna → 55 52 42N 38 55E
Sosnogorsk 52 63 37N 53 51E
Sosnovka, R.S.F.S.R., U.S.S.R. 55 53 13N 41 24E
Sosnovka, R.S.F.S.R., U.S.S.R. 59 54 9N 109 35E
Sosnowiec 28 50 20N 19 10E
Sospel 21 43 52N 7 27E
Šoštanj 39 46 23N 15 4E
Sosva 52 59 10N 61 50E
Soto la Marina → 120 23 40N 97 40W
Soto y Amío 30 42 46N 5 53W
Sotteville-lès-Rouen 18 49 24N 1 5E
Sotuta 120 20 29N 89 43W
Souanké 88 2 10N 14 3E
Soúdhas, Kólpos 45 35 25N 24 10E
Souflion 44 41 12N 26 18E
Souillac 20 44 53N 1 29E
Souk-Ahras 83 36 23N 7 57E
Souk el Arba du Rharb 82 34 43N 5 59W
Sŏul 76 37 31N 126 58E
Soulac-sur-Mer 20 45 30N 1 7W
Soultz 19 48 57N 7 52E
Soúnion, Ákra 45 37 37N 24 1E
Sour el Ghozlane 83 36 10N 3 45E
Sources, Mt. aux 93 28 45S 28 50E
Sourdeval 18 48 43N 0 55W
Soure, Brazil 127 0 35S 48 30W
Soure, Port. 30 40 4N 8 38W
Souris, Man., Can. 109 49 40N 100 20W
Souris, P.E.I., Can. 107 46 21N 62 15W
Souris → 109 49 40N 99 34W
Soúrpi 45 39 6N 22 54E
Sousa 127 6 45S 38 10W
Sousel, Brazil 127 2 38S 52 29W
Sousel, Port. 31 38 57N 7 40W
Souss, O. → 82 30 27N 9 31W
Sousse 83 35 50N 10 38E
Soustons 20 43 45N 1 19W
Souterraine, La 20 46 15N 1 30E
South Africa, Rep. of, ■ 89 32 0S 17 0E
South America 122 10 0S 60 0W
South Atlantic Ocean 7 20 0S 10 0W
South Aulatsivik I. 107 56 45N 61 30W
South Australia □ 96 32 0S 139 0E
South Baldy, Mt. 119 34 6N 107 27W
South Bend, Ind., U.S.A. 114 41 38N 86 20W
South Bend, Wash., U.S.A. 118 46 44N 123 52W
South Boston 115 36 42N 78 58W
South Branch 107 47 55N 59 2W
South Brook 107 49 26N 56 5W
South Buganda □ 90 0 15S 31 30E
South Carolina □ 115 33 45N 81 0W
South Charleston 114 38 20N 81 40W
South China Sea 71 10 0N 113 0E
South Dakota □ 116 45 0N 100 0W
South Downs 13 50 53N 0 10W
South East C. 97 43 40S 146 50E
South-East Indian Rise 94 43 0S 80 0E
South Esk → 14 56 44N 3 3W
South Foreland 13 51 7N 1 23E
South Fork → 118 47 54N 113 15W
South Gamboa 120 9 4N 79 40W
South Georgia 5 54 30S 37 0W
South Glamorgan □ 13 51 30N 3 20W
South Grafton 99 29 41S 152 57E
South Haven 114 42 22N 86 20W
South Henik, L. 109 61 30N 97 30W
South Honshu Ridge 94 23 0N 143 0E
South Horr 90 2 12N 36 56E
South I., Kenya 90 2 35N 36 35E
South I., N.Z. 101 44 0S 170 0E
South Invercargill 101 46 26S 168 23E
South Knife → 109 58 55N 94 37W
South Korea ■ 76 36 0N 128 0E
South Loup → 116 41 4N 98 40W
South Mashonaland □ 91 18 0S 31 30E
South Milwaukee 114 42 50N 87 52W
South Molton 13 51 1N 3 50W
South Nahanni → 108 61 3N 123 21W
South Negril Pt. 121 18 14N 78 30W
South Orkney Is. 5 63 0S 45 0W
South Pass 118 42 20N 108 58W
South Passage 96 26 07S 113 09E
South Pines 115 35 10N 79 25W
South Pittsburg 115 35 1N 85 42W
South Platte → 116 41 7N 100 42W
South Pole 5 90 0S 0 0E
South Porcupine 106 48 30N 81 12W
South River, Can. 106 45 52N 79 23W
South River, U.S.A. 113 40 27N 74 23W
South Ronaldsay 14 58 46N 2 58W
South Sandwich Is. 7 57 0S 27 0W
South Saskatchewan → 109 53 15N 105 5W
South Seal → 109 58 48N 98 8W
South Sentinel I. 71 11 1N 92 16E
South Shetland Is. 5 62 0S 59 0W
South Shields 12 54 59N 1 26W
South Sioux City 116 42 30N 96 24W
South Taranaki Bight 101 39 40S 174 5E
South Thompson → 108 50 40N 120 20W
South Twin I. 106 53 7N 79 52W
South Tyne → 12 54 46N 2 25W
South Uist 14 57 20N 7 15W
South West Africa = Namibia ■ 92 22 0S 18 9E
South West C. 99 43 34S 146 3E
South Yemen ■ 63 15 0N 48 0E
South Yorkshire □ 12 53 30N 1 20W
Southampton, Can. 106 44 30N 81 25W
Southampton, U.K. 13 50 54N 1 23W
Southampton, U.S.A. 114 40 54N 72 22W
Southampton I. 105 64 30N 84 0W
Southbridge, N.Z. 101 43 48S 172 16E
Southbridge, U.S.A. 113 42 4N 72 2W
Southeast Pacific Basin 95 16 30S 92 0W
Southend 109 56 19N 103 22W
Southend-on-Sea 13 51 32N 0 42E
Southern □, Malawi 91 15 0S 35 0E
Southern □, S. Leone 84 8 0N 12 30W
Southern □, Zambia 91 16 20S 26 20E
Southern Alps 101 43 41S 170 11E
Southern Cross 96 31 12S 119 15E
Southern Indian L. 109 57 10N 98 30W
Southern Ocean 5 62 0S 60 0E
Southern Uplands 14 55 30N 3 3W
Southington 113 41 37N 72 53W
Southold 113 41 4N 72 26W
Southport, Austral. 97 27 58S 153 25E
Southport, U.K. 12 53 38N 3 1W
Southport, U.S.A. 115 33 55N 78 0W
Southwestern Pacific Basin 94 42 0S 170 0W
Southwold 13 52 19N 1 41E
Soutpansberge 93 23 0S 29 30E
Souvigny 20 46 33N 3 10E
Sovata 46 46 35N 25 3E
Sovetsk, Lithuania, U.S.S.R. 54 55 6N 21 50E
Sovetsk, R.S.F.S.R., U.S.S.R. 55 57 38N 48 53E
Sovetskaya 57 49 1N 42 7E
Sovetskaya Gavan 59 48 50N 140 0E
Sovicille 39 43 16N 11 12E
Sovra 42 42 44N 17 34E
Sōya-Misaki 74 45 30N 142 0E
Soyo 88 6 13S 12 20E
Sozh → 54 51 57N 30 48E
Sozopol 43 42 23N 27 42E
Spa 16 50 29N 5 53E
Spain ■ 29 40 0N 5 0W
Spalding, Austral. 99 33 30S 138 37E
Spalding, U.K. 12 52 47N 0 9W
Spalding, U.S.A. 116 41 45N 98 27W
Spangereid 47 58 3N 7 9E
Spangler 112 40 39N 78 48W
Spaniard's Bay 107 47 38N 53 20W
Spanish 106 46 12N 82 20W
Spanish Fork 118 40 10N 111 37W
Spanish Town 121 18 0N 76 57W
Sparks 118 39 30N 119 45W
Sparta, Ga., U.S.A. 115 33 18N 82 59W
Sparta, Wis., U.S.A. 116 43 55N 90 47W
Sparta = Spárti 45 37 5N 22 25E
Spartanburg 115 35 0N 82 0W
Spartansburg 112 41 48N 79 43W
Spartel, C. 82 35 47N 5 56W
Spárti 45 37 5N 22 25E
Spartivento, C., Calabria, Italy 41 37 56N 16 4E
Spartivento, C., Sard., Italy 40 38 52N 8 50E
Spas-Demensk 54 54 20N 34 0E
Spas-Klepiki 55 55 10N 40 10E
Spassk-Dalniy 59 44 40N 132 48E
Spassk-Ryazanskiy 55 54 24N 40 25E
Spátha, Akra 45 35 42N 23 43E
Spatsizi → 108 57 42N 128 7W
Spearfish 116 44 32N 103 52W
Spearman 117 36 15N 101 10W
Speers 109 52 43N 107 34W
Speightstown 121 13 15N 59 39W
Speke Gulf 90 2 20S 32 50E
Spenard 104 61 11N 149 50W
Spence Bay 104 69 32N 93 32W
Spencer, Idaho, U.S.A. 118 44 18N 112 8W
Spencer, Iowa, U.S.A. 116 43 5N 95 19W
Spencer, N.Y., U.S.A. 113 42 14N 76 30W
Spencer, Nebr., U.S.A. 116 42 52N 98 43W
Spencer, W. Va., U.S.A. 114 38 47N 81 24W
Spencer B. 92 25 30S 14 47E
Spencer, C. 97 35 20S 136 53E
Spencer G. 97 34 0S 137 20E
Spencerville 113 44 51N 75 33W
Spences Bridge 108 50 25N 121 20W
Spenser Mts. 101 42 15S 172 45E
Sperkhiós → 45 38 57N 22 3E
Sperrin Mts. 15 54 50N 7 0W
Spessart 25 50 10N 9 20E
Spétsai 45 37 15N 23 10E
Spey → 14 57 26N 3 25W
Speyer 25 49 19N 8 26E
Speyer → 25 49 19N 8 27E
Spézia, La 38 44 8N 9 50E
Spezzano Albanese 41 39 41N 16 19E
Spiekeroog 24 53 45N 7 42E
Spielfeld 39 46 43N 15 38E
Spiez 25 46 40N 7 40E
Spili 45 35 13N 24 31E
Spilimbergo 39 46 7N 12 53E
Spinazzola 41 40 58N 16 5E
Spind 47 58 6N 6 53E
Spineni 46 44 43N 24 37E
Spirit Lake 118 47 56N 116 56W
Spirit River 108 55 45N 118 50W
Spiritwood 109 53 24N 107 33W
Spišská Nová Ves 27 48 58N 20 34E
Spišské Podhradie 27 49 0N 20 48E
Spital 26 47 42N 14 18E
Spithead 13 50 43N 1 5W
Spittal 26 46 48N 13 31E
Spitzbergen = Svalbard 4 78 0N 17 0E
Split 39 43 31N 16 26E
Split L. 109 56 8N 96 15W
Splitski Kanal 39 43 31N 16 20E
Splügenpass 25 46 30N 9 20E
Spofford 117 29 10N 100 27W
Spokane 118 47 45N 117 25W
Spoleto 39 42 46N 12 47E
Spooner 116 45 49N 91 51W
Sporádhes 45 39 0N 24 30E
Sporyy Navolok, Mys 58 75 50N 68 40E
Spragge 106 46 15N 82 40W

Sprague Suceava

Sprague 118 47 18N 117 59W
Sprague River 118 42 28N 121 31W
Spratly, I. 72 8 20N 112 0 E
Spray 118 44 50N 119 46W
Spree → 24 52 32N 13 13 E
Spring City 118 39 31N 111 28W
Spring Mts. 119 36 20N 115 43W
Spring Valley, Minn., U.S.A. 116 43 40N 92 23W
Spring Valley, N.Y., U.S.A. 113 41 7N 74 4W
Springbok 92 29 42 S 17 54 E
Springburn 101 43 40 S 171 32 E
Springdale, Can. 107 49 30N 56 6W
Springdale, Ark., U.S.A. 117 36 10N 94 5W
Springdale, Wash., U.S.A. 118 48 1N 117 50W
Springe 24 52 12N 9 35 E
Springer 117 36 22N 104 36W
Springerville 119 34 10N 109 16W
Springfield, Can. 112 42 50N 80 56W
Springfield, N.Z. 101 43 19 S 171 56 E
Springfield, Colo., U.S.A. 117 37 26N 102 40W
Springfield, Ill., U.S.A. 116 39 48N 89 40W
Springfield, Mass., U.S.A. 114 42 8N 72 37W
Springfield, Mo., U.S.A. 117 37 15N 93 20W
Springfield, Ohio, U.S.A. 114 39 58N 83 48W
Springfield, Oreg., U.S.A. 118 44 2N 123 0W
Springfield, Tenn., U.S.A. 115 36 35N 86 55W
Springfield, Vt., U.S.A. 113 43 20N 72 30W
Springfontein 92 30 15 S 25 40 E
Springhill 107 45 40N 64 4W
Springhouse 108 51 56N 122 7W
Springhurst 99 36 10 S 146 31 E
Springs 93 26 13 S 28 25 E
Springsure 97 24 8 S 148 6 E
Springvale, Austral. 98 23 33 S 140 42 E
Springvale, U.S.A. 113 43 28N 70 48W
Springville, N.Y., U.S.A. 114 42 31N 78 41W
Springville, Utah, U.S.A. 118 40 14N 111 35W
Springwater 109 51 58N 108 23W
Spruce-Creek 112 40 36N 78 9W
Spur 117 33 28N 100 50W
Spurn Hd. 12 53 34N 0 8 E
Spuž 42 42 32N 19 10 E
Spuzzum 108 49 37N 121 23W
Squam L. 113 43 45N 71 32W
Squamish 108 49 45N 123 10W
Square Islands 107 52 47N 55 47W
Squillace, Golfo di 41 38 43N 16 35 E
Squinzano 41 40 27N 18 1 E
Sragen 73 7 28 S 110 59 E
Srbac 42 45 7N 17 30 E
Srbija □ 42 43 30N 21 0 E
Srbobran 42 45 32N 19 48 E
Sre Umbell 71 11 8N 103 46 E
Srebrnica 42 44 10N 19 18 E
Sredinnyy Khrebet 59 57 0N 160 0 E
Središče 39 46 24N 16 17 E
Sredna Gora 43 42 40N 24 20 E
Sredne Tambovskoye 59 50 55N 137 45 E
Srednekolymsk 59 67 27N 153 40 E
Srednevilyuysk 59 63 50N 123 5 E
Sredni Rodopi 43 41 40N 24 45 E
Šrem 28 52 6N 17 2 E
Sremska Mitrovica 42 44 59N 19 33 E
Sremski Karlovci 42 45 12N 19 56 E
Sretensk 59 52 10N 117 40 E
Sri Lanka ■ 70 7 30N 80 50 E
Sriharikota, I. 70 13 40N 80 20 E
Srikakulam 70 18 14N 83 58 E
Srinagar 66 34 5N 74 50 E
Sripur 69 24 14N 90 30 E
Srirangam 70 10 54N 78 42 E
Srirangapatnam 70 12 26N 76 43 E
Srivilliputtur 70 9 31N 77 40 E
Środa Śląska 28 51 10N 16 36 E
Środa Wielkopolski 28 52 15N 17 19 E
Srokowo 28 54 13N 21 31 E
Srpska Crnja 42 45 38N 20 44 E
Srpska Itabej 42 45 35N 20 44 E
Staaten → 98 16 24 S 141 17 E
Staberhuk 24 54 23N 11 18 E
Stade 24 53 35N 9 31 E
Staðarhólskirkja 50 65 23N 21 58W
Städjan 48 61 56N 12 52 E
Stadlandet 47 62 10N 5 10 E
Stadskanaal 16 53 4N 6 55 E
Stadthagen 24 52 20N 9 14 E
Stadtlohn 24 52 0N 6 52 E
Stadtroda 24 50 51N 11 44 E
Stafafell 50 64 25N 14 52W
Staffa 14 56 26N 6 21W
Stafford, U.K. 12 52 49N 2 9W
Stafford, U.S.A. 117 38 0N 98 35W
Stafford □ 12 52 53N 2 10W
Stafford Springs 113 41 58N 72 20W
Stagnone 40 37 50N 12 28 E
Staines 13 51 26N 0 30W
Stainz 26 46 53N 15 17 E
Stalač 42 43 43N 21 28 E
Stalingrad = Volgograd 57 48 40N 44 25 E
Staliniri = Tskhinvali 57 42 14N 44 1 E
Stalino = Donetsk 56 48 0N 37 45 E
Stalinogorsk = Novomoskovsk 55 54 5N 38 15 E
Stalowa Wola 28 50 34N 22 3 E
Stalybridge 12 53 29N 2 4W
Stamford, Austral. 98 21 15 S 143 46 E
Stamford, U.K. 13 52 39N 0 29W
Stamford, Conn., U.S.A. 114 41 5N 73 30W
Stamford, Tex., U.S.A. 117 32 58N 99 50W
Stamps 117 33 22N 93 30W
Stanberry 116 40 12N 94 32W
Standerton 93 26 55 S 29 7 E
Standish 114 43 58N 83 57W
Stanford 118 47 11N 110 10W
Stange 47 60 43N 11 5 E
Stanger 93 29 27 S 31 14 E
Stanišić 42 45 56N 19 10 E
Stanislav = Ivano-Frankovsk 54 49 0N 24 40 E
Stanisławów 28 52 18N 21 33 E
Stanke Dimitrov 42 42 17N 23 9 E
Stanley, Austral. 99 40 46 S 145 19 E
Stanley, N.B., Can. 107 46 20N 66 44W
Stanley, Sask., Can. 109 55 24N 104 22W
Stanley, Falk. Is. 128 51 40 S 59 51W
Stanley, Idaho, U.S.A. 118 44 10N 114 59W
Stanley, N.D., U.S.A. 116 48 20N 102 23W
Stanley, N.Y., U.S.A. 112 42 48N 77 6W
Stanley, Wis., U.S.A. 116 44 57N 91 0W
Stanley Res. 70 11 50N 77 40 E
Stann Creek 120 17 0N 88 13W
Stanovoy Khrebet 59 55 0N 130 0 E
Stanthorpe 97 28 36 S 151 59 E
Stanton 117 32 8N 101 45W
Staples 116 46 21N 94 48W
Stapleton 116 41 30N 100 31W
Staporków 28 51 9N 20 31 E
Star City 109 52 50N 104 20W
Stara-minskaya 57 46 33N 39 0 E
Stara Moravica 42 45 50N 19 30 E
Stara Pazova 42 45 0N 20 10 E
Stara Planina 43 43 15N 23 0 E
Stara Zagora 43 42 26N 25 39 E
Starachowice 28 51 3N 21 2 E
Starashcherbinovskaya 57 46 40N 38 53 E
Staraya Russa 54 57 58N 31 23 E
Starbuck I. 95 5 37 S 155 55W
Stargard 24 53 29N 13 19 E
Stargard Szczeciński 28 53 20N 15 0 E
Stari Bar 42 42 7N 19 13 E
Stari Trg 39 45 29N 15 7 E
Staritsa 54 56 33N 35 0 E
Starke 115 30 0N 82 10W
Starkville, Colo., U.S.A. 117 37 10N 104 31W
Starkville, Miss., U.S.A, 115 33 26N 88 48W
Starnberg 25 48 0N 11 20 E
Starnberger See 25 47 55N 11 20 E
Starobelsk 57 49 16N 39 0 E
Starodub 54 52 30N 32 50 E
Starogard 28 53 59N 18 30 E
Starokonstantinov 56 49 48N 27 10 E
Starosielce 28 53 8N 23 5 E
Start Pt. 13 50 13N 3 38W
Stary Sącz 27 49 33N 20 35 E
Staryy Biryuzyak 57 44 46N 46 50 E
Staryy Chartoriysk 54 51 15N 25 54 E
Staryy Kheydzhan 59 60 0N 144 50 E
Staryy Krym 56 45 3N 35 8 E
Staryy Oskol 55 51 19N 37 55 E
Stassfurt 24 51 51N 11 34 E
Staszów 28 50 33N 21 10 E
State College 114 40 47N 77 49W
Staten I. 113 40 35N 74 10W
Staten, I. = Los Estados, I. de 128 54 40 S 64 30W
Statesboro 115 32 26N 81 46W
Statesville 115 35 48N 80 51W
Staunton, Ill., U.S.A. 116 39 0N 89 49W
Staunton, Va., U.S.A. 114 38 7N 79 4W
Stavanger 47 58 57N 5 40 E
Stavelot 16 50 23N 5 55 E
Staveren 16 52 53N 5 22 E
Stavern 47 59 0N 10 1 E
Stavre 48 62 51N 15 19 E
Stavropol 57 45 5N 42 0 E
Stavroúpolis 44 41 12N 24 45 E
Stawell 97 37 5 S 142 47 E
Stawell → 98 20 20 S 142 55 E
Stawiski 28 53 22N 22 9 E
Stawiszyn 28 51 56N 18 4 E
Stayner 112 44 25N 80 5W
Steamboat Springs 118 40 30N 106 50W
Stębark 28 53 30N 20 10 E
Stebleva 44 41 18N 20 33 E
Steele 116 46 56N 99 52W
Steelton 114 40 17N 76 50W
Steelville 117 37 57N 91 21W
Steen River 108 59 40N 117 12W
Steenvoorde 19 50 48N 2 33 E
Steenwijk 16 52 47N 6 7 E
Steep Pt. 96 26 08 S 113 8 E
Steep Rock 109 51 30N 98 48W
Ştefănesti 46 47 44N 27 15 E
Stefanie L. = Chew Bahir 87 4 40N 36 50 E
Stefansson Bay 5 67 20 S 59 8 E
Stege 49 55 0N 12 18 E
Steiermark □ 26 47 26N 15 0 E
Steigerwald 25 49 45N 10 30 E
Steinbach 109 49 32N 96 40W
Steinfort 16 49 39N 5 55 E
Steinheim 24 51 50N 9 6 E
Steinhuder Meer 24 52 48N 9 20 E
Steinkjer 50 63 59N 11 31 E
Stellaland 92 26 45 S 24 50 E
Stellarton 107 45 32N 62 30W
Stellenbosch 92 33 58 S 18 50 E
Stemshaug 47 63 19N 8 44 E
Stendal 24 52 36N 11 50 E
Stensele 50 65 3N 17 8 E
Stenstorp 49 58 17N 13 45 E
Stepanakert 53 39 40N 46 25 E
Stephan 116 48 30N 96 53W
Stephens Creek 99 31 50 S 141 30 E
Stephens I. 108 54 10N 130 45W
Stephenville, Can. 107 48 31N 58 35W
Stephenville, U.S.A. 117 32 12N 98 12W
Stepnica 28 53 38N 14 36 E
Stepnoi = Elista 57 46 16N 44 14 E
Stepnyak 58 52 50N 70 50 E
Steppe 60 50 0N 50 0 E
Stereá Ellas □ 45 38 50N 22 0 E
Sterkstroom 92 31 32 S 26 32 E
Sterling, Colo., U.S.A. 116 40 40N 103 15W
Sterling, Ill., U.S.A. 116 41 45N 89 45W
Sterling, Kans., U.S.A. 116 38 17N 98 13W
Sterling City 117 31 50N 100 59W
Sterling Run 112 41 25N 78 12W
Sterlitamak 52 53 40N 56 0 E
Sternberg 24 53 42N 11 48 E
Šternberk 27 49 45N 17 15 E
Stettin = Szczecin 28 53 27N 14 27 E
Stettiner Haff 24 53 50N 14 25 E
Stettler 108 52 19N 112 40W
Steubenville 114 40 21N 80 39W
Stevens Port 116 44 32N 89 34W
Stevenson L. 109 53 55N 96 0W
Stevns Klint 49 55 17N 12 28 E
Stewart, B.C., Can. 108 55 56N 129 57W
Stewart, N.W.T., Can. 104 63 19N 139 26W
Stewart, I. 128 54 50 S 71 15W
Stewart I. 101 46 58 S 167 54 E
Stewiacke 107 45 9N 63 22W
Steynsburg 92 31 15 S 25 49 E
Steyr 26 48 3N 14 25 E
Steyr → 26 48 17N 14 15 E
Steytlerville 92 33 17 S 24 19 E
Stia 39 43 48N 11 41 E
Stigler 117 35 19N 95 6W
Stigliano 41 40 24N 16 13 E
Stigsnæs 49 55 13N 11 18 E
Stigtomta 49 58 47N 16 48 E
Stikine → 104 56 40N 132 30W
Stilfontein 92 26 50 S 26 50 E
Stilis 45 38 55N 22 47 E
Stillwater, Minn., U.S.A. 116 45 3N 92 47W
Stillwater, N.Y., U.S.A. 113 42 55N 73 41W
Stillwater, Okla., U.S.A. 117 36 5N 97 3W
Stillwater Mts. 118 39 45N 118 6W
Stilwell 117 35 52N 94 36W
Stimfalías, L. 45 37 51N 22 27 E
Štip 42 41 42N 22 10 E
Stíra 45 38 9N 24 14 E
Stiring-Wendel 19 49 12N 6 57 E
Stirling, Austral. 98 17 12 S 141 35 E
Stirling, Can. 108 49 30N 112 30W
Stirling, U.K. 14 56 7N 3 57W
Stirling Ra. 96 34 23 S 118 0 E
Stittsville 113 45 15N 75 55W
Stockach 25 47 51N 9 01 E
Stockaryd 49 57 19N 14 36 E
Stockerau 27 48 24N 16 12 E
Stockett 118 47 23N 111 7W
Stockholm 48 59 20N 18 3 E
Stockholms län □ 48 59 30N 18 20 E
Stockinbingal 100 34 30 S 147 53 E
Stockport 12 53 25N 2 11W
Stockton, Austral. 100 32 50 S 151 47 E
Stockton, Calif., U.S.A. 119 38 0N 121 20W
Stockton, Kans., U.S.A. 116 39 30N 99 20W
Stockton, Mo., U.S.A. 117 37 40N 93 48W
Stockton-on-Tees 12 54 34N 1 20W
Stockvik 48 62 17N 17 23 E
Stoczek Łukowski 28 51 58N 22 0 E
Stöde 48 62 28N 16 35 E
Stogovo 42 41 31N 20 38 E
Stoke-on-Trent 12 53 1N 2 11W
Stokes Bay 106 45 0N 81 28W
Stokes Pt. 99 40 10 S 143 56 E
Stokkseyri 50 63 50N 21 2W
Stokksnes 50 64 14N 14 58W
Stolac 42 43 8N 17 59 E
Stolberg 24 50 48N 6 13 E
Stolbovaya, R.S.F.S.R., U.S.S.R. 55 55 10N 37 32 E
Stolbovaya, R.S.F.S.R., U.S.S.R. 59 64 50N 153 50 E
Stolbovoy, Ostrov 59 56 44N 163 14 E
Stolbtsy 54 53 30N 26 43 E
Stolin 54 51 53N 26 50 E
Stolnici 46 44 31N 24 48 E
Ston 42 42 51N 17 43 E
Stonehaven 14 56 58N 2 11W
Stonehenge 98 24 22 S 143 17 E
Stonewall 109 50 10N 97 19W
Stonington I. 5 68 11 S 67 0W
Stony L., Man., Can. 109 58 51N 98 40W
Stony L., Ont., Can. 112 44 30N 78 0W
Stony Rapids 109 59 16N 105 50W
Stony Tunguska = Tunguska, Nizhnyaya → 59 65 48N 88 4 E
Stopnica 28 50 27N 20 57 E
Stora Gla 48 59 30N 12 30 E
Stora Karlsö 49 57 17N 17 59 E
Stora Lulevatten 50 67 10N 19 30 E
Stora Sjöfallet 50 67 29N 18 40 E
Storavan 50 65 45N 18 10 E
Stördal 47 63 28N 10 56 E
Store Bælt 49 55 20N 11 0 E
Store Creek 99 32 54 S 149 6 E
Store Heddinge 49 55 18N 12 23 E
Støren 47 63 3N 10 18 E
Storfjorden 47 62 25N 6 30 E
Storm B. 97 43 10 S 147 30 E
Storm Lake 116 42 35N 95 11W
Stormberg 92 31 16 S 26 17 E
Stormsrivier 92 33 59 S 23 52 E
Stornoway 14 58 12N 6 23W
Storozhinets 56 48 14N 25 45 E
Storsjö 48 62 49N 13 5 E
Storsjöen, Hedmark, Norway 47 60 20N 11 40 E
Storsjöen, Hedmark, Norway 47 61 30N 11 14 E
Storsjön, Gävleborg, Sweden 48 60 35N 16 45 E
Storsjön, Jämtland, Sweden 48 62 50N 13 8 E
Storstrøms Amt. □ 49 54 50N 11 45 E
Storuman 50 65 5N 17 10 E
Storuman,sjö 50 65 13N 16 50 E
Storvik 48 60 35N 16 33 E
Stoughton 109 49 40N 103 0W
Stour →, Dorset, U.K. 13 50 48N 2 7W
Stour →, Here. & Worcs., U.K. 13 52 25N 2 13W
Stour →, Suffolk, U.K. 13 51 55N 1 5 E
Stour (Gt. Stour) → 13 51 15N 1 20 E
Stourbridge 13 52 28N 2 8W
Stout, L. 109 52 0N 94 40W
Stowmarket 13 52 11N 1 0 E
Strabane 15 54 50N 7 28W
Strabane □ 15 54 45N 7 25W
Stracin 42 42 13N 22 2 E
Stradella 38 45 4N 9 20 E
Strahan 97 42 9 S 145 20 E
Strakonice 26 49 15N 13 53 E
Straldzha 43 42 35N 26 40 E
Stralsund 24 54 17N 13 5 E
Strand, Norway 47 61 17N 11 17 E
Strand, S. Afr. 92 34 9 S 18 48 E
Stranda 47 62 19N 6 58 E
Strandebarm 47 60 17N 6 0 E
Strandvik 47 60 9N 5 41 E
Strangford, L. 15 54 30N 5 37W
Strängnäs 48 59 23N 17 2 E
Stranraer 14 54 54N 5 0W
Strasbourg, Can. 109 51 4N 104 55W
Strasbourg, France 19 48 35N 7 42 E
Strasburg, Ger. 24 53 30N 13 44 E
Strasburg, U.S.A. 116 46 12N 100 9W
Stratford, Austral. 100 37 59 S 147 7 E
Stratford, Can. 106 43 23N 81 0W
Stratford, N.Z. 101 39 20 S 174 19 E
Stratford, Calif., U.S.A. 119 36 10N 119 49W
Stratford, Conn., U.S.A. 113 41 13N 73 8W
Stratford, Tex., U.S.A. 117 36 20N 102 3W
Stratford-on-Avon 13 52 12N 1 42W
Strath Spey 14 57 15N 3 40W
Strathalbyn 99 35 13 S 138 53 E
Strathclyde □ 14 56 0N 4 50W
Strathcona Prov. Park 108 49 38N 125 40W
Strathmore, Austral. 98 17 50 S 142 35 E
Strathmore, Can. 108 51 5N 113 18W
Strathmore, U.K. 14 56 40N 3 4W
Strathnaver 108 53 20N 122 33W
Strathpeffer 14 57 35N 4 32W
Strathroy 106 42 58N 81 38W
Strathy Pt. 14 58 35N 4 0W
Stratton, U.K. 12 51 41N 1 45W
Stratton, U.S.A. 116 39 20N 102 36W
Straubing 25 48 53N 12 35 E
Straumnes 50 66 26N 23 8W
Strausberg 24 52 40N 13 52 E
Strawberry Res. 118 40 10N 111 7W
Strawn 117 32 36N 98 30W
Strážnice 27 48 54N 17 19 E
Streaky Bay 96 32 48 S 134 13 E
Streator 116 41 9N 88 52W
Středočeský □ 26 49 55N 14 30 E
Středoslovenský □ 27 48 30N 19 15 E
Streeter 116 46 39N 99 21W
Streetsville 112 43 35N 79 42W
Strehaia 46 44 37N 23 10 E
Strelcha 43 42 25N 24 19 E
Strelka 59 58 5N 93 3 E
Strésa 38 45 52N 8 28 E
Strezhevoy 58 60 42N 77 34 E
Střibro 26 49 44N 13 0 E
Strickland → 98 7 35 S 141 36 E
Strimón → 44 40 46N 23 51 E
Strimonikós Kólpos 44 40 33N 24 0 E
Strofádhes 45 37 15N 21 0 E
Strombacka 48 61 58N 16 44 E
Strómboli 41 38 48N 15 12 E
Stromeferry 14 57 20N 5 33W
Stromness 14 58 58N 3 18W
Ströms vattudal 50 64 15N 14 55 E
Strömsnäsbruk 49 56 35N 13 45 E
Strömstad 48 58 55N 11 15 E
Strömsund 50 63 51N 15 35 E
Stróngoli 41 39 16N 17 2 E
Stronsay 14 59 8N 2 38W
Stronsburg 116 41 7N 97 36W
Stropkov 27 49 13N 21 39 E
Stroud 13 51 44N 2 12W
Stroud Road 99 32 18 S 151 57 E
Stroudsburg 113 40 59N 75 15W
Struer 49 56 30N 8 35 E
Struga 42 41 13N 20 44 E
Strugi Krasnyye 54 58 21N 29 1 E
Strumica 42 41 28N 22 41 E
Strumica → 42 41 20N 22 22 E
Struthers, Can. 106 48 41N 85 51W
Struthers, U.S.A. 114 41 6N 80 38W
Stryama 43 42 16N 24 54 E
Stryi 54 49 16N 23 48 E
Stryker 108 48 40N 114 44W
Stryków 28 51 55N 19 33 E
Strzegom 28 50 58N 16 20 E
Strzelce Krajeńskie 28 52 52N 15 33 E
Strzelce Opolskie 28 50 31N 18 18 E
Strzelecki Cr. → 97 29 37 S 139 59 E
Strzelin 28 50 46N 17 2 E
Strzelno 28 52 35N 18 9 E
Strzybnica 28 50 28N 18 48 E
Strzyżów 27 49 52N 21 47 E
Stuart, Fla., U.S.A. 115 27 11N 80 12W
Stuart, Nebr., U.S.A. 116 42 39N 99 8W
Stuart → 108 54 0N 123 35W
Stuart L. 108 54 30N 124 30W
Stuart Range 96 29 10 S 134 56 E
Stuart Town 100 32 44 S 149 4 E
Stubbekøbing 49 54 53N 12 9 E
Stuben 26 47 10N 10 8 E
Studen Kladenets, Yazovir 43 41 37N 25 30 E
Stugun 48 63 10N 15 40 E
Stühlingen 25 47 44N 8 26 E
Stull, L. 109 54 24N 92 34W
Stung Treng 71 13 31N 105 58 E
Stupart → 109 56 0N 93 25W
Stupino 55 54 57N 38 2 E
Sturgeon B. 109 52 0N 97 50W
Sturgeon Bay 114 44 52N 87 20W
Sturgeon Falls 106 46 25N 79 57W
Sturgeon L., Alta., Can. 108 55 6N 117 32W
Sturgeon L., Ont., Can. 106 50 0N 90 45W
Sturgeon L., Ont., Can. 112 44 28N 78 43W
Sturgis, Mich., U.S.A. 114 41 50N 85 25W
Sturgis, S.D., U.S.A. 116 44 25N 103 30W
Sturkö 49 56 5N 15 42 E
Štúrovo 27 47 48N 18 41 E
Sturt Cr. → 96 20 8 S 127 24 E
Stutterheim 92 32 33 S 27 28 E
Stuttgart, Ger. 25 48 46N 9 10 E
Stuttgart, U.S.A. 117 34 30N 91 33W
Stuyvesant 113 42 23N 73 45W
Stykkishólmur 50 65 2N 22 40W
Styr → 54 52 7N 26 35 E
Styria = Steiermark □ 26 47 26N 15 0 E
Su Xian 77 33 41N 116 59 E
Suakin 86 19 8N 37 20 E
Suaqui 120 29 12N 109 41W
Subang 73 6 34 S 107 45 E
Subi 72 2 58N 108 50 E
Subiaco 39 41 56N 13 5 E
Subotica 42 46 6N 19 49 E
Success 109 50 28N 108 6W
Suceava 46 47 38N 26 16 E

HIA

Suceava Tabatinga, Serra da

Suceava □ 46 47 37N 25 40 E
Suceava → 46 47 38N 26 16 E
Sucha-Beskidzka 27 49 44N 19 35 E
Suchan 28 53 18N 15 18 E
Suchedniów 28 51 3N 20 49 E
Suchitoto 120 13 56N 89 0W
Suchou = Suzhou 75 31 18N 120 36 E
Süchow = Xuzhou 77 34 18N 117 10 E
Suchowola 28 53 33N 23 3 E
Suck → 15 53 17N 8 18W
Suckling, Mt. 98 9 49 S 148 53 E
Sucre 126 19 0 S 65 15W
Sućuraj 39 43 10N 17 8 E
Sud-Ouest, Pte. du 107 49 23N 63 36W
Sud, Pte. 107 49 3N 62 14W
Suda → 55 59 0N 37 40 E
Sudair 64 26 0N 45 0 E
Sudak 56 44 51N 34 57 E
Sudan 117 34 4N 102 32W
Sudan ■ 81 15 0N 30 0 E
Suday 55 59 0N 43 0 E
Sudbury 106 46 30N 81 0W
Sûdd 87 8 20N 30 0 E
Süderbrarup 24 54 38N 9 47 E
Süderlügum 24 54 50N 8 55 E
Süderoog-Sand 24 54 27N 8 30 E
Sudetan Mts. = Sudety 27 50 20N 16 45 E
Sudety 27 50 20N 16 45 E
Sudi 91 10 11 S 39 57 E
Sudirman, Pegunungan 73 4 30 S 137 0 E
Suditi 46 44 35N 27 38 E
Sudogda 55 55 55N 40 50 E
Sudr 86 29 40N 32 42 E
Sudzha 54 51 14N 35 17 E
Sueca 33 39 12N 0 21W
Suedala 49 55 30N 13 15 E
Sueur, Le 116 44 25N 93 52W
Suez = El Suweis 86 28 40N 33 0 E
Suez Canal = Suweis, Qanâl es 86 31 0N 33 20 E
Sûf 62 32 19N 35 49 E
Şufaynah 64 23 6N 40 33 E
Suffield 109 50 12N 111 10W
Suffolk 114 36 47N 76 33W
Suffolk □ 13 52 16N 1 0 E
Sufuk 65 23 50N 51 50 E
Şugag 46 45 47N 23 37 E
Sugar City 116 38 18N 103 38W
Sugluk = Sagloue 105 62 30N 74 15W
Suhaia, L. 46 43 45N 25 15 E
Suhār 65 24 20N 56 40 E
Suhbaatar 75 50 17N 106 10 E
Suhl 24 50 35N 10 40 E
Suhl □ 24 50 37N 10 43 E
Sui Xian, Henan, China 77 34 25N 115 2 E
Sui Xian, Henan, China 77 31 42N 113 24 E
Suichang 77 28 29N 119 15 E
Suichuan 77 26 20N 114 32 E
Suide 76 37 30N 110 12 E
Suifenhe 76 44 25N 131 10 E
Suihua 75 46 32N 126 55 E
Suining, Hunan, China 77 26 35N 110 10 E
Suining, Sichuan, China 77 30 26N 105 35 E
Suiping 77 33 10N 113 59 E
Suippes 19 49 8N 4 30 E
Suir → 15 52 15N 7 10W
Suixi 77 21 19N 110 18 E
Suizhong 76 40 21N 120 20 E
Sujangarh 68 27 42N 74 31 E
Sujica 42 43 52N 17 11 E
Sukabumi 73 6 56 S 106 50 E
Sukadana, Kalimantan, Indon. 72 1 10 S 110 0 E
Sukadana, Sumatera, Indon. 72 5 5 S 105 33 E
Sukaradja 72 2 28 S 110 25 E
Sukarnapura = Jayapura 73 2 37 S 140 38 E
Sukhindol 43 43 11N 25 10 E
Sukhinichi 54 54 8N 35 10 E
Sukhona → 52 60 30N 45 0 E
Sukhumi 57 43 0N 41 0 E
Sukkur 68 27 42N 68 54 E
Sukkur Barrage 68 27 40N 68 50 E
Sukma 70 18 24N 81 45 E
Sukovo 42 43 4N 22 37 E
Sukunka → 108 55 45N 121 15W
Sula → 54 49 40N 32 41 E
Sula, Kepulauan 73 1 45 S 125 0 E
Sulaiman Range 68 30 30N 69 50 E
Sulak → 57 43 20N 47 34 E
Sulam Tsor 62 33 4N 35 6 E
Sulawesi □ 73 2 0 S 120 0 E
Sulechów 28 52 5N 15 40 E
Sulęcin 28 52 26N 15 10 E
Sulejów 28 51 26N 19 53 E
Sulejówek 28 52 13N 21 17 E
Sulima 84 6 58N 11 32W
Sulina 46 45 10N 29 40 E
Sulingen 24 52 41N 8 47 E
Suliţa 46 47 39N 26 59 E
Sulitälma 50 67 17N 17 28 E
Sulitjelma 50 67 9N 16 3 E
Sułkowice 27 49 50N 19 49 E
Sullana 126 4 52 S 80 39W
Sullivan, Ill., U.S.A. 116 39 40N 88 40W
Sullivan, Ind., U.S.A. 114 39 5N 87 26W
Sullivan, Mo., U.S.A. 116 38 10N 91 10W
Sullivan Bay 108 50 55N 126 50W
Sully-sur-Loire 19 47 45N 2 20 E
Sulmierzyce 28 51 37N 17 32 E
Sulmona 39 42 3N 13 55 E
Sulphur, La., U.S.A. 117 30 13N 93 22W
Sulphur, Okla., U.S.A. 117 34 35N 97 0W
Sulphur Pt. 108 60 56N 114 48W
Sulphur Springs 117 33 5N 95 36W
Sulphur Springs, Cr. → 117 32 12N 101 36W
Sultan 106 47 36N 82 47W
Sultanpur 69 26 18N 82 4 E
Sultsa 52 63 27N 46 2 E
Sulu Arch. 73 6 0N 121 0 E
Sulu Sea 73 8 0N 120 0 E
Sululta 87 9 10N 38 43 E
Suluq 83 31 44N 20 14 E
Sulzbach 25 49 18N 7 4 E
Sulzbach-Rosenberg 25 49 30N 11 46 E
Sumalata 73 1 0N 122 31 E
Sumampa 124 29 25 S 63 29W
Sumatera □ 72 0 40N 100 20 E
Sumatera Barat □ 72 1 0 S 100 0 E
Sumatera Selatan □ 72 3 30 S 104 0 E
Sumatera Utara □ 72 2 0N 99 0 E
Sumatra 118 46 38N 107 31W
Sumatra = Sumatera □ 72 0 40N 100 20 E
Sumba 73 9 45 S 119 35 E
Sumba, Selat 73 9 0 S 118 40 E
Sumbawa 72 8 26 S 117 30 E
Sumbawa Besar 72 8 30 S 117 26 E
Sumbawanga □ 90 8 0 S 31 30 E
Sumbing 73 7 19 S 110 3 E
Sumburgh Hd. 14 59 52N 1 17W
Sumedang 73 6 49 S 107 56 E
Sümeg 27 46 59N 17 20 E
Sumenep 73 7 3 S 113 51 E
Sumgait 57 40 34N 49 38 E
Summer L. 118 42 50N 120 50W
Summerland 108 49 32N 119 41W
Summerside 107 46 24N 63 47W
Summerville, Ga., U.S.A. 115 34 30N 85 20W
Summerville, S.C., U.S.A. 115 33 2N 80 11W
Summit Lake 108 54 20N 122 40W
Summit Pk. 119 37 20N 106 48W
Sumner 116 42 49N 92 7W
Sumperk 27 49 59N 17 0 E
Sumter 115 33 55N 80 22W
Sumy 54 50 57N 34 50 E
Sunart, L. 14 56 42N 5 43W
Sunburst 118 48 56N 111 59W
Sunbury, Austral. 99 37 35 S 144 44 E
Sunbury, U.S.A. 114 40 50N 76 46W
Sunchales 124 30 58 S 61 35W
Suncho Corral 124 27 55 S 63 27W
Sunchon 77 34 52N 127 31 E
Suncook 113 43 8N 71 27W
Sunda Is. 94 5 0 S 105 0 E
Sunda Kecil, Kepulauan 72 7 30 S 117 0 E
Sunda, Selat 72 6 20 S 105 30 E
Sundance 116 44 27N 104 27W
Sundarbans, The 69 22 0N 89 0 E
Sundargarh 69 22 4N 84 5 E
Sundays = Sondags → 92 33 44 S 25 51 E
Sundbyberg 48 59 22N 17 58 E
Sunderland, Can. 112 44 16N 79 4W
Sunderland, U.K. 12 54 54N 1 22W
Sunderland, U.S.A. 113 42 27N 72 36W
Sundre 108 51 49N 114 38W
Sundridge 106 45 45N 79 25W
Sunds 49 56 13N 9 1 E
Sundsjö 48 62 59N 15 9 E
Sundsvall 48 62 23N 17 17 E
Sungaigerong 72 2 59 S 104 52 E
Sungailiat 72 1 51 S 106 8 E
Sungaipakning 72 1 19N 102 0 E
Sungaipenuh 72 2 1 S 101 20 E
Sungaitiram 72 0 45 S 117 8 E
Sungari = Songhua Jiang → 76 47 45N 132 30 E
Sungei Patani 71 5 38N 100 29 E
Sungei Siput 71 4 51N 101 6 E
Sungguminasa 73 5 17 S 119 30 E
Sunghua Chiang = Songhua Jiang → 76 47 45N 132 30 E
Sungikai 87 12 20N 29 51 E
Sungtao Hu 77 19 20N 109 35 E
Sungurlu 56 40 12N 34 21 E
Sunja 39 45 21N 16 35 E
Sunndalsøra 47 62 40N 8 33 E
Sunne 48 59 52N 13 5 E
Sunnfjord 47 61 25N 5 18 E
Sunnyside, Utah, U.S.A. 118 39 34N 110 24W
Sunnyside, Wash., U.S.A. 118 46 24N 120 2W
Sunray 117 36 1N 101 47W
Sunshine 100 37 48 S 144 52 E
Suntar 59 62 15N 117 30 E
Sunyani 84 7 21N 2 22W
Suoyarvi 52 62 12N 32 23 E
Supai 119 36 14N 112 44W
Supaul 69 26 10N 86 40 E
Superior, Ariz., U.S.A. 119 33 19N 111 9W
Superior, Mont., U.S.A. 118 47 15N 114 57W
Superior, Nebr., U.S.A. 116 40 3N 98 2W
Superior, Wis., U.S.A. 116 46 45N 92 5W
Superior, L. 111 47 40N 87 0W
Supetar 39 43 25N 16 32 E
Suphan Buri 71 14 14N 100 10 E
Suphan Daği 64 38 54N 42 48 E
Supraśl 28 53 13N 23 19 E
Suq al Jum'ah 83 32 58N 13 12 E
Sūq ash Shūyukh 64 30 53N 46 28 E
Suqian 77 33 54N 118 8 E
Sūr, Leb. 62 33 19N 35 16 E
Sūr, Oman 65 22 34N 59 32 E
Sur, Pt. 119 36 18N 121 54W
Sura → 55 56 6N 46 0 E
Surabaja = Surabaya 73 7 17 S 112 45 E
Surabaya 73 7 17 S 112 45 E
Surahammar 48 59 43N 16 13 E
Suraia 46 45 40N 27 25 E
Surakarta 73 7 35 S 110 48 E
Surakhany 57 40 25N 50 1 E
Surandai 70 8 58N 77 26 E
Šurany 27 48 6N 18 10 E
Surat, Austral. 99 27 10 S 149 6 E
Surat, India 68 21 12N 72 55 E
Surat Thani 71 9 6N 99 20 E
Suratgarh 68 29 18N 73 55 E
Suraz 28 52 57N 22 57 E
Surazh, Byelorussia, U.S.S.R. 54 55 25N 30 44 E
Surazh, R.S.F.S.R., U.S.S.R. 54 53 5N 32 27 E
Surduc 46 47 15N 23 25 E
Surduc Pasul 46 45 21N 23 23 E
Surdulica 42 42 41N 22 11 E
Sûre → 16 49 44N 6 31 E
Surendranagar 68 22 45N 71 40 E
Surgères 20 46 7N 0 47W
Surgut 58 61 14N 73 20 E
Suri 69 23 50N 87 34 E
Surianu 46 45 33N 23 31 E
Suriapet 70 17 10N 79 40 E
Şūrīf 62 31 40N 35 4 E
Surigao 73 9 47N 125 29 E
Surin 71 14 50N 103 34 E
Surinam ■ 127 4 0N 56 0W
Suriname → 127 5 50N 55 15W
Surmene 57 41 0N 40 1 E
Surovikino 57 48 32N 42 55 E
Surprise L. 108 59 40N 133 15W
Surrey □ 13 51 16N 0 30W
Sursee 25 47 11N 8 6 E
Sursk 55 53 3N 45 40 E
Surt 83 31 11N 16 39 E
Surt, Al Hammadah al 83 30 0N 17 50 E
Surt, Khalīj 83 31 40N 18 30 E
Surtsey 50 63 20N 20 30W
Suruga-Wan 74 34 45N 138 30 E
Susa 38 45 8N 7 3 E
Susâ → 49 55 20N 11 42 E
Sušac 39 42 46N 16 30 E
Susak 39 44 30N 14 18 E
Süsangerd 64 31 35N 48 6 E
Susanino 59 52 50N 140 14 E
Susanville 118 40 28N 120 40W
Sušice 26 49 17N 13 30 E
Susquehanna → 114 39 33N 76 5W
Susquehanna Depot 113 41 55N 75 36W
Susques 124 23 35 S 66 25W
Sussex, Can. 107 45 45N 65 37W
Sussex, U.S.A. 113 41 12N 74 38W
Sussex, E. □ 13 51 0N 0 20 E
Sussex, W. □ 13 51 0N 0 30W
Sustut → 108 56 20N 127 30W
Susuman 59 62 47N 148 10 E
Susunu 73 3 20 S 133 25 E
Susz 28 53 44N 19 20 E
Şuţeşti 46 45 13N 27 27 E
Sutherland, S. Afr. 92 32 33 S 20 40 E
Sutherland, U.S.A. 116 41 12N 101 11W
Sutherland Falls 101 44 48 S 167 46 E
Sutherland Pt. 97 28 15 S 153 35 E
Sutherlin 118 43 28N 123 16W
Sutivan 39 43 23N 16 30 E
Sutlej → 68 29 23N 71 3 E
Sutton, Can. 113 45 6N 72 37W
Sutton, U.S.A. 116 40 40N 97 50W
Sutton → 106 55 15N 83 45W
Sutton-in-Ashfield 12 53 7N 1 20W
Suttor → 98 21 36 S 147 2 E
Suva 94 18 6 S 178 30 E
Suva Gora 42 41 45N 21 3 E
Suva Planina 42 43 10N 22 5 E
Suva Reka 42 42 21N 20 50 E
Suvo Rudište 42 43 17N 20 49 E
Suvorov 55 54 7N 36 30 E
Suvorov Is. = Suwarrow Is. 95 13 15 S 163 30W
Suvorovo 43 43 20N 27 35 E
Suwałki 28 54 8N 22 59 E
Suwałki □ 28 54 0N 22 30 E
Suwannee → 115 29 18N 83 9W
Suwanose Jima 74 29 26N 129 30 E
Suwarrow Is. 95 15 0 S 163 0W
Suweis, Khalîg el 86 28 40N 33 0 E
Suweis, Qanâl es 86 31 0N 32 20 E
Suwŏn 76 37 17N 127 1 E
Suzdal 55 56 29N 40 26 E
Suze, La 18 47 54N 0 2 E
Suzhou 75 31 19N 120 38 E
Suzu-Misaki 74 37 31N 137 21 E
Suzuka 74 34 55N 136 36 E
Suzzara 38 45 0N 10 45 E
Svalbard 4 78 0N 17 0 E
Svalbarð 50 66 12N 15 43W
Svalöv 49 55 57N 13 8 E
Svanvik 50 69 25N 30 3 E
Svappavaara 50 67 40N 21 03 E
Svarstad 47 59 27N 9 56 E
Svartisen 50 66 40N 13 50 E
Svartvik 48 62 19N 17 24 E
Svatovo 56 49 35N 38 11 E
Svay Rieng 71 11 9N 105 45 E
Sveio 47 59 33N 5 23 E
Svenborg 49 55 4N 10 35 E
Svene 47 59 45N 9 31 E
Svenljunga 49 57 29N 13 5 E
Svenstrup 49 56 58N 9 50 E
Sverdlovsk, R.S.F.S.R., U.S.S.R. 52 56 50N 60 30 E
Sverdlovsk, Ukraine S.S.R., U.S.S.R. 57 48 5N 39 37 E
Sverdrup Is. 4 79 0N 97 0W
Svetac 39 43 3N 15 43 E
Sveti Ivan Zelina 39 45 57N 16 16 E
Sveti Jurij 39 46 14N 15 24 E
Sveti Lenart 39 46 36N 15 48 E
Sveti Nikola, Prokhad 42 43 27N 22 6 E
Sveti Nikole 42 41 51N 21 56 E
Sveti Rok 39 40 1N 9 6 E
Sveti Trojica 39 46 37N 15 50 E
Svetlogorsk 54 52 38N 29 46 E
Svetlograd 57 45 25N 42 58 E
Svetlovodsk 54 49 2N 33 13 E
Svetozarevo 42 44 5N 21 15 E
Svidník 27 49 20N 21 37 E
Svilaja Pl. 39 43 49N 16 31 E
Svilajnac 42 44 15N 21 11 E
Svilengrad 43 41 49N 26 12 E
Svir → 52 60 30N 32 48 E
Svishtov 43 43 36N 25 23 E
Svisloch 54 53 3N 24 2 E
Svitava → 27 49 30N 16 37 E
Svitavy 27 49 47N 16 28 E
Svobodnyy 59 51 20N 128 0 E
Svoge 43 42 59N 23 23 E
Svolvær 50 68 15N 14 34 E
Svratka → 27 49 11N 16 38 E
Svrljig 42 43 25N 22 6 E
Swabian Alps = Schäbischer Alb 25 48 30N 9 30 E
Swain Reefs 97 21 45 S 152 20 E
Swainsboro 115 32 38N 82 22W
Swakopmund 92 22 37 S 14 30 E
Swale → 12 54 5N 1 20W
Swan → 96 32 3 S 115 45 E
Swan Hill 97 35 20 S 143 33 E
Swan Hills 108 54 42N 115 24W
Swan Islands 121 17 22N 83 57W
Swan L. 109 52 30N 100 40W
Swan River 109 52 10N 101 16W
Swanage 13 50 36N 1 59W
Swansea, Austral. 99 33 3 S 151 35 E
Swansea, U.K. 13 51 37N 3 57W
Swartberge 92 33 20 S 22 0 E
Swartruggens 92 25 39 S 26 42 E
Swarzędz 28 52 25N 17 4 E
Swastika 106 48 7N 80 6W
Swatow = Shantou 76 23 18N 116 40 E
Swaziland ■ 93 26 30 S 31 30 E
Sweden ■ 50 67 0N 15 0 E
Swedru 85 5 32N 0 41W
Sweet Home 118 44 26N 122 25W
Sweetwater 117 32 30N 100 28W
Sweetwater → 118 42 31N 107 2W
Swellendam 92 34 1 S 20 26 E
Swider → 28 52 6N 21 14 E
Świdnica 28 50 50N 16 30 E
Świdnik 28 51 13N 22 39 E
Świdwin 28 53 47N 15 49 E
Świebodzice 28 50 51N 16 20 E
Świebodzin 28 52 15N 15 31 E
Świecie 28 53 25N 18 30 E
Świętokrzyskie, Góry 28 51 0N 20 30 E
Swift Current 109 50 20N 107 45W
Swiftcurrent → 109 50 38N 107 44W
Swilly, L. 15 55 12N 7 35W
Swindle, I. 108 52 30N 128 35W
Swindon 13 51 33N 1 47W
Swinemünde = Świnoujście 28 53 54N 14 16 E
Świnoujście 28 53 54N 14 16 E
Switzerland ■ 25 46 30N 8 0 E
Swords 15 53 27N 6 15W
Syasstroy 54 60 5N 32 15 E
Sychevka 54 55 59N 34 16 E
Syców 28 51 19N 17 40 E
Sydney, Austral. 97 33 53 S 151 10 E
Sydney, Can. 107 46 7N 60 7W
Sydney, U.S.A. 116 41 12N 103 0W
Sydney Mines 107 46 18N 60 15W
Sydprøven 4 60 30N 45 35W
Sydra G. of = Surt, Khalīj 35 31 40N 18 30 E
Syke 24 52 55N 8 50 E
Syktyvkar 52 61 45N 50 40 E
Sylacauga 115 33 10N 86 15W
Sylarna 50 63 2N 12 13 E
Sylhet 67 24 54N 91 52 E
Sylt 24 54 50N 8 20 E
Sylvan Lake 108 52 20N 114 03W
Sylvania 115 32 45N 81 37W
Sylvester 115 31 31N 83 50W
Sym 58 60 20N 88 18 E
Syracuse, Kans., U.S.A. 117 38 0N 101 46W
Syracuse, N.Y., U.S.A. 114 43 4N 76 11W
Syrdarya → 58 46 3N 61 0 E
Syria ■ 64 35 0N 38 0 E
Syriam 69 16 44N 96 19 E
Syrian Desert 60 31 0N 40 0 E
Syul'dzhyukyor 59 63 14N 113 32 E
Syutkya 43 41 50N 24 16 E
Syzran 55 53 12N 48 30 E
Szabolcs-Szatmár □ 27 48 2N 21 45 E
Szamocin 28 53 2N 17 7 E
Szamos → 27 48 7N 22 20 E
Szaraz → 27 46 28N 20 44 E
Szarvas 27 46 50N 20 38 E
Szazhalombatta 27 47 20N 18 58 E
Szczawnica 27 49 26N 20 30 E
Szczebrzeszyn 28 50 42N 22 59 E
Szczecin 28 53 27N 14 27 E
Szczecin □ 28 53 25N 14 32 E
Szczecinek 28 53 43N 16 41 E
Szczekocimy 28 50 38N 19 48 E
Szczucin 28 50 18N 21 4 E
Szczuczyn 28 53 36N 22 19 E
Szczytno 28 53 33N 21 0 E
Szechwan = Sichuan □ 75 31 0N 104 0 E
Szécsény 27 48 7N 19 30 E
Szeged 27 46 16N 20 10 E
Szeghalom 27 47 1N 21 10 E
Székesfehérvár 27 47 15N 18 25 E
Szekszárd 27 46 22N 18 42 E
Szendrö 27 48 24N 20 41 E
Szentendre 27 47 39N 19 4 E
Szentes 27 46 39N 20 21 E
Szentgotthárd 27 46 58N 16 19 E
Szentlörinc 27 46 3N 18 1 E
Szerencs 27 48 10N 21 12 E
Szigetvár 27 46 3N 17 46 E
Szikszó 27 48 12N 20 56 E
Szkwa → 28 53 11N 21 43 E
Szlichtyngowa 28 51 42N 16 15 E
Szob 27 47 48N 18 53 E
Szolnok 27 47 10N 20 15 E
Szolnok □ 27 47 15N 20 30 E
Szombathely 27 47 14N 16 38 E
Szprotawa 28 51 33N 15 35 E
Sztum 28 53 55N 19 1 E
Sztutowo 28 54 20N 19 15 E
Szubin 28 53 1N 17 45 E
Szydłowiec 28 51 15N 20 51 E
Szypliszki 28 54 17N 23 2 E

T

Tabacal 124 23 15 S 64 15W
Tabaco 73 13 22N 123 44 E
Tabagné 84 7 59N 3 4W
Ţābah 64 26 55N 42 38 E
Tabar Is. 98 2 50 S 152 0 E
Tabarca, Isla de 33 38 17N 0 30W
Tabarka 83 36 56N 8 46 E
Ţabas, Khorāsān, Iran 65 33 35N 56 55 E
Ţabas, Khorāsān, Iran 65 32 48N 60 12 E
Tabasará, Serranía de 121 8 35N 81 40W
Tabasco □ 120 17 45N 93 30W
Tabatinga, Serra da 127 10 30 S 44 0W

Tabelbala, Kahal de Tarp

Tabelbala, Kahal de **82** 28 47N 2 0W
Tabelkaza **80** 29 50N 0 55 E
Taber **108** 49 47N 112 8W
Tabernas **33** 37 4N 2 26W
Tabernes de Valldigna **33** 39 5N 0 13W
Tablas **73** 12 25N 122 2 E
Table B. **107** 53 40N 56 25W
Table Mt. **92** 34 0S 18 22 E
Table Top, Mt. **98** 23 24S 147 11 E
Tábor **26** 49 25N 14 39 E
Tabor **62** 32 42N 35 24 E
Tabora **90** 5 2S 32 50 E
Tabora □ **90** 5 0S 33 0 E
Tabou **84** 4 30N 7 20W
Tabrīz **64** 38 7N 46 20 E
Tabuenca **32** 41 42N 1 33W
Tabūk **64** 28 23N 36 36 E
Tacheng **75** 46 40N 82 58 E
Tach'ing Shan = Daqing Shan **76** 40 40N 111 0 E
Tachov **26** 49 47N 12 39 E
Tácina → **41** 38 57N 16 55 E
Tacloban **73** 11 15N 124 58 E
Tacna **126** 18 0S 70 20W
Tacoma **118** 47 15N 122 30W
Tacuarembó **125** 31 45S 56 0W
Tademaït, Plateau du **82** 28 30N 2 30 E
Tadent, O. → **83** 22 25N 6 40 E
Tadjerdjeri, O. → **83** 26 0N 8 0W
Tadjerouna **82** 33 31N 2 3 E
Tadjettaret, O. → **83** 21 20N 7 22 E
Tadjmout, Atlas, Alg. **82** 33 52N 2 30 E
Tadjmout, Sahara, Alg. **82** 25 37N 3 48 E
Tadjoura **87** 11 50N 42 55 E
Tadjoura, Golfe de **87** 11 50N 43 0 E
Tadmor **101** 41 27S 172 45 E
Tadoule, L. **109** 58 36N 98 20W
Tadoussac **107** 48 11N 69 42W
Tadzhik S.S.R. □ **58** 35 30N 70 0 E
Taegu **76** 35 50N 128 37 E
Taejŏn **76** 36 20N 127 28 E
Tafalla **32** 42 30N 1 41W
Tafar **87** 6 52N 28 15 E
Țafas **62** 32 44N 36 5 E
Tafassasset, O. → **83** 22 0N 9 57 E
Tafelbaai **92** 33 35S 18 25 E
Tafelney, C. **82** 31 3N 9 51W
Tafermaar **73** 6 47S 134 10 E
Taffermit **82** 29 37N 9 15W
Tafí Viejo **124** 26 43S 65 17W
Tafiré **84** 9 4N 5 4W
Tafnidilt **82** 28 47N 10 58W
Tafraoute **82** 29 50N 8 58W
Taft, Phil. **73** 11 57N 125 30 E
Taft, Calif., U.S.A. **119** 35 9N 119 28W
Taft, Tex., U.S.A. **117** 27 58N 97 23W
Taga Dzong **69** 27 5N 89 55 E
Taganrog **57** 47 12N 38 50 E
Taganrogskiy Zaliv **56** 47 0N 38 30 E
Tagânt **84** 18 20N 11 0W
Tagbilaran **73** 9 39N 123 51 E
Tággia **38** 43 52N 7 50 E
Taghrīfat **83** 29 5N 17 26 E
Taghzout **82** 33 30N 4 49W
Tagish **108** 60 19N 134 16W
Tagish L. **104** 60 10N 134 20W
Tagliacozzo **39** 42 4N 13 13 E
Tagliamento → **39** 45 38N 13 5 E
Táglio di Po **39** 45 0N 12 12 E
Tagomago, I. de **33** 39 2N 1 39 E
Taguatinga **127** 12 16S 42 26W
Tagula I. **98** 11 30S 153 30 E
Tagum (Hijo) **73** 7 33N 125 53 E
Tagus = Tajo → **29** 39 44N 5 50W
Tahakopa **101** 46 30S 169 23 E
Tahala **82** 34 0N 4 28W
Tahan, Gunong **71** 4 34N 102 17 E
Tahat **83** 23 18N 5 33 E
Tāherī **65** 27 43N 52 20 E
Tahiti **95** 17 37S 149 27W
Tahoe City **118** 39 12N 120 9W
Tahoe, L. **118** 39 0N 120 9W
Tahoua **85** 14 57N 5 16 E
Tahta **86** 26 44N 31 32 E
Tahulandang **73** 2 27N 125 23 E
Tahuna **73** 3 38N 125 30 E
Taï **84** 5 55N 7 30W
Tai Hu **75** 31 5N 120 10 E
Tai Shan **76** 36 25N 117 20 E
Tai'an **76** 36 12N 117 8 E
Taibei **75** 25 4N 121 29 E
Taibus Qi **76** 41 54N 115 22 E
T'aichung = Taizhong **75** 24 10N 120 38 E
Taidong **75** 22 43N 121 9 E
Taieri → **101** 46 3S 170 12 E
Taiga Madema **83** 23 46N 15 25 E
Taigu **76** 37 28N 112 30 E
Taihang Shan **76** 36 0N 113 30 E
Taihape **101** 39 41S 175 48 E
Taihe **77** 26 47N 114 52 E
Taihu **77** 30 22N 116 20 E
Taijiang **77** 26 39N 108 21 E
Taikang, Heilongjiang, China **76** 46 50N 124 25 E
Taikang, Henan, China **77** 34 5N 114 50 E
Taikkyi **69** 17 20N 96 0 E
Tailai **76** 46 23N 123 24 E
Tailem Bend **99** 35 12S 139 29 E
Tailfingen **25** 48 15N 9 1 E
Taimyr = Taymyr **59** 75 0N 100 0 E
Taimyr, Oz. **59** 74 20N 102 0 E
Tain **14** 57 49N 4 4W
Tainan **77** 23 17N 120 18 E
Taínaron, Ákra **45** 36 22N 22 27 E
Taining **77** 26 54N 117 9 E
T'aipei = Taibei **75** 25 4N 121 29 E
Taiping **71** 4 51N 100 44 E
Taishan **77** 22 14N 112 41 E
Taishun **77** 27 30N 119 42 E
Taita □ **90** 4 0S 38 30 E
Taita Hills **90** 3 25S 38 15 E
Taitao, Pen. de **128** 46 30S 75 0W
Taivalkoski **50** 65 33N 28 12 E
Taiwan ■ **75** 24 0N 121 0 E
Taïyetos Óros **45** 37 0N 22 23 E
Taiyib → **62** 31 55N 35 17 E
Taiyiba **62** 32 36N 35 27 E
Taiyuan **76** 37 52N 112 33 E
Taizhong **77** 24 12N 120 35 E
Taizhou **77** 32 28N 119 55 E
Ta'izz **63** 13 35N 44 2 E
Tajarḥī **83** 24 21N 14 28 E
Tajo → **31** 38 40N 9 24W
Tajumulco, Volcán de **120** 15 2N 91 50W
Tājūrā **83** 32 51N 13 21 E
Tak **71** 16 52N 99 8 E
Takada **74** 37 7N 138 15 E
Takaka **101** 40 51S 172 50 E
Takamatsu **74** 34 20N 134 5 E
Takanabe **74** 32 8N 131 30 E
Takaoka **74** 36 47N 137 0 E
Takapuna **101** 36 47S 174 47 E
Takasaki **74** 36 20N 139 0 E
Takatsuki **74** 34 51N 135 37 E
Takaungu **90** 3 38S 39 52 E
Takayama **74** 36 18N 137 11 E
Takefu **74** 35 50N 136 10 E
Takengeun **72** 4 45N 96 50 E
Takeo **71** 10 59N 104 47 E
Tåkern **49** 58 22N 14 45 E
Tākestān **64** 36 0N 49 40 E
Takhar □ **65** 36 40N 70 0 E
Takla L. **108** 55 15N 125 45W
Takla Landing **108** 55 30N 125 50W
Takla Makan **60** 39 0N 83 0 E
Takla Makan = Taklimakan Shamo **75** 38 0N 83 0 E
Taklimakan Shamo **75** 38 0N 83 0 E
Taku → **108** 58 30N 133 50W
Takua Pa **71** 7 18N 9 59 E
Takum **85** 7 18N 9 36 E
Tala **125** 34 21S 55 46W
Talagante **124** 33 40S 70 50W
Talaïnt **82** 29 41N 9 40W
Talak **85** 18 0N 5 0 E
Talamanca, Cordillera de **121** 9 20N 83 20W
Talara **126** 4 38S 81 18 E
Talas **58** 42 30N 72 13 E
Talasea **98** 5 20S 150 2 E
Talata Mafara **85** 12 38N 6 4 E
Talaud, Kepulauan **73** 4 30N 127 10 E
Talavera de la Reina **30** 39 55N 4 46W
Talayan **73** 6 52N 124 24 E
Talbert, Sillon de **18** 48 53N 3 5W
Talbot, C. **96** 13 48S 126 43 E
Talbragar → **99** 32 12S 148 37 E
Talca **124** 35 28S 71 40W
Talca □ **124** 35 20S 71 46W
Talcahuano **124** 36 40S 73 10W
Talcher **69** 21 0N 85 18 E
Talcho **85** 14 44N 3 28 E
Taldy Kurgan **58** 45 10N 78 45 E
Țalesh, Kūhhā-ye **64** 39 0N 48 30 E
Talfīt **62** 32 5N 35 17 E
Talguharai **86** 18 19N 35 56 E
Tali Post **87** 5 55N 30 44 E
Taliabu **73** 1 45S 125 0 E
Talibon **73** 10 9N 124 20 E
Talihina **117** 34 45N 95 1W
Talikoti **70** 16 29N 76 17 E
Taling Sung **71** 15 5N 99 11 E
Taliwang **72** 8 50S 116 55 E
Talkeetna **104** 62 20N 150 9W
Tall **62** 33 0N 35 6 E
Tall 'Afar **64** 36 22N 42 27 E
Tall 'Asūr **62** 31 59N 35 17 E
Talla **86** 28 5N 30 43 E
Talladega **115** 33 28N 86 2W
Tallahassee **115** 30 25N 84 15W
Tallangatta **99** 36 15S 147 19 E
Tallarook **99** 37 5S 145 6 E
Tällberg **48** 60 51N 15 2 E
Tallering Pk. **96** 28 6S 115 37 E
Tallinn **54** 59 22N 24 48 E
Tallulah **117** 32 25N 91 12W
Țallūzā **62** 32 17N 35 18 E
Tălmaciu **46** 45 38N 24 19 E
Talmest **82** 31 48N 9 21W
Talmont **20** 46 27N 1 37W
Talnoye **56** 48 50N 30 44 E
Taloda **68** 21 34N 74 11 E
Talodi **87** 10 35N 30 22 E
Talovaya **55** 51 6N 40 45 E
Talsi **54** 57 10N 22 30 E
Talsinnt **82** 32 33N 3 27W
Taltal **124** 25 23S 70 33W
Taltson → **108** 61 24N 112 46W
Taltson L. **109** 61 30N 110 15W
Talwood **99** 28 29S 149 29 E
Talyawalka Cr. → **99** 32 28S 142 22 E
Tama **116** 41 56N 92 37W
Tamale **85** 9 22N 0 50W
Taman **56** 45 14N 36 41 E
Tamanar **82** 31 1N 9 46W
Tamano **74** 34 29N 133 59 E
Tamanrasset **83** 22 50N 5 30 E
Tamanrasset, O. → **82** 22 0N 2 0 E
Tamaqua **113** 40 46N 75 58W
Tamar → **13** 50 33N 4 15W
Tamarite de Litera **32** 41 52N 0 25 E
Tamási **27** 46 40N 18 18 E
Tamaské **85** 14 49N 5 43 E
Tamaulipas □ **120** 24 0N 99 0W
Tamaulipas, Sierra de **120** 23 30N 98 20W
Tamazula **120** 24 55N 106 58W
Tamba-Dabatou **84** 11 50N 10 40W
Tambacounda **84** 13 45N 13 40W
Tambelan, Kepulauan **72** 1 0N 107 30 E
Tambo **98** 24 54S 146 14 E
Tambo de Mora **126** 13 30S 76 8W
Tambohorano **93** 17 30S 43 58 E
Tambora **72** 8 12S 118 5 E
Tambov **55** 52 45N 41 28 E
Tambre → **30** 42 49N 8 53W
Tambuku **73** 7 8S 113 40 E
Tamburâ **87** 5 40N 27 25 E
Tâmchekket **84** 17 25N 10 40W
Tamega → **30** 41 5N 8 21W
Tamelelt **82** 31 50N 7 32W
Tamenglong **67** 25 0N 93 35 E
Tamerza **83** 34 23N 7 58 E
Tamgak, Mts. **80** 19 12N 8 35 E
Tamiahua, Laguna de **120** 21 30N 97 30W
Tamil Nadu □ **70** 11 0N 77 0 E
Tamluk **69** 22 18N 87 58 E
Tammerfors = Tampere **51** 61 30N 23 50 E
Tammisaari **51** 60 0N 23 26 E
Țammūn **62** 32 18N 35 23 E
Tämnaren **48** 60 10N 17 25 E
Tamo Abu, Pegunungan **72** 3 10N 115 0 E
Tampa **115** 27 57N 82 38W
Tampa B. **115** 27 40N 82 40W
Tampere **51** 61 30N 23 50 E
Tampico **120** 22 20N 97 50W
Tampin **71** 2 28N 102 13 E
Tamri **82** 30 49N 9 50W
Tamrida = Hadibu **63** 12 35N 54 2 E
Tamsagbulag **75** 47 14N 117 21 E
Tamsalu **54** 59 11N 26 8 E
Tamsweg **26** 47 7N 13 49 E
Tamu **67** 24 13N 94 12 E
Tamuja → **31** 39 38N 6 29W
Tamworth, Austral. **97** 31 7S 150 58 E
Tamworth, U.K. **13** 52 38N 1 41W
Tan-tan **82** 28 29N 11 1W
Tana **50** 70 26N 28 14 E
Tana →, Kenya **90** 2 32S 40 31 E
Tana →, Norway **50** 70 30N 28 23 E
Tana, L. **87** 13 5N 37 30 E
Tana River **90** 2 0S 39 30 E
Tanafjorden **50** 70 45N 28 25 E
Tanagro → **41** 40 35N 15 25 E
Tanahbala **72** 0 30S 98 30 E
Tanahgrogot **72** 1 55S 116 15 E
Tanahjampea **73** 7 10S 120 35 E
Tanahmasa **72** 0 12S 98 39 E
Tanahmerah **73** 6 5S 140 16 E
Tanakura **74** 37 10N 140 20 E
Tanami Des. **96** 18 50S 132 0 E
Tanana **104** 65 10N 152 15W
Tanana → **104** 65 9N 151 55W
Tananarive = Antananarivo **93** 18 55S 47 35 E
Tanannt **82** 31 54N 6 56W
Tánaro → **38** 45 1N 8 47 E
Tanaunella **40** 40 42N 9 45 E
Tancarville **18** 49 29N 0 28 E
Tanchŏn **76** 40 27N 128 54 E
Tanda, U.P., India **68** 28 57N 78 56 E
Tanda, U.P., India **69** 26 33N 82 35 E
Tanda, Ivory C. **84** 7 48N 3 10W
Tandag **73** 9 4N 126 9 E
Tandaia **91** 9 25S 34 15 E
Tăndărei **46** 44 39N 27 40 E
Tandaué **92** 16 58S 18 5 E
Tandil **124** 37 15S 59 6W
Tandil, Sa. del **124** 37 30S 59 0W
Tandlianwala **68** 31 3N 73 9 E
Tando Adam **68** 25 45N 68 40 E
Tandou L. **99** 32 40S 142 5 E
Tandsbyn **48** 63 0N 14 45 E
Tandur **70** 19 11N 79 30 E
Tane-ga-Shima **74** 30 30N 131 0 E
Taneatua **101** 38 4S 177 1 E
Tanen Tong Dan **67** 16 30N 98 30 E
Tanew → **28** 50 29N 22 16 E
Tanezrouft **82** 23 9N 0 11 E
Tanga **88** 5 5S 39 2 E
Tanga □ **90** 5 20S 38 0 E
Tanga Is. **98** 3 20S 153 15 E
Tangail **69** 24 15N 89 55 E
Tanganyika, L. **90** 6 40S 30 0 E
Tanger **82** 35 50N 5 49W
Tangerang **73** 6 12S 106 39 E
Tangerhütte **24** 52 26N 11 50 E
Tangermünde **24** 52 32N 11 57 E
Tanggu **76** 39 2N 117 40 E
Tanggula Shan **75** 32 40N 92 10 E
Tanghe **77** 32 47N 112 50 E
Tangier = Tanger **82** 35 50N 5 49W
Tangkak **71** 2 18N 102 34 E
Tangorin P.O. **98** 21 47S 144 12 E
Tangshan **76** 39 38N 118 10 E
Tanguiéta **85** 10 35N 1 21 E
Tanimbar, Kepulauan **73** 7 30S 131 30 E
Taninges **21** 46 7N 6 36 E
Tanjay **73** 9 30N 123 5 E
Tanjore = Thanjavur **70** 10 48N 79 12 E
Tanjung **72** 2 10S 115 25 E
Tanjungbalai **72** 2 55N 99 44 E
Tanjungbatu **72** 2 23N 118 3 E
Tanjungkarang **72** 5 20S 105 10 E
Tanjungpandan **72** 2 43S 107 38 E
Tanjungpinang **72** 1 5N 104 30 E
Tanjungpriok **73** 6 8S 106 55 E
Tanjungredeb **72** 2 9N 117 29 E
Tanjungselor **72** 2 55N 117 25 E
Tank **68** 32 14N 70 25 E
Tänndalen **48** 62 33N 12 18 E
Tannis Bugt **49** 57 40N 10 15 E
Tannu-Ola **59** 51 0N 94 0 E
Tano → **84** 5 7N 2 56W
Tanout **85** 14 50N 8 55 E
Tanta **86** 30 45N 30 57 E
Tantoyuca **120** 21 21N 98 10W
Tantung = Dandong **76** 40 10N 124 20 E
Tantūra = Dor **62** 32 37N 34 55 E
Tanuku **70** 16 45N 81 44 E
Tanumshede **49** 58 42N 11 20 E
Tanunda **99** 34 30S 139 0 E
Tanur **70** 11 1N 75 52 E
Tanus **20** 44 8N 2 19 E
Tanzania ■ **90** 6 40S 34 0 E
Tanzilla → **108** 58 8N 130 43W
Tao'an **76** 45 22N 122 40 E
Taormina **41** 37 52N 15 16 E
Taos **119** 36 28N 105 35W
Taoudenni **82** 22 40N 3 55W
Taoudrart, Adrar **82** 24 25N 2 24 E
Taounate **82** 34 25N 4 41W
Taourirt, Alg. **82** 26 37N 0 20 E
Taourirt, Moroc. **82** 34 25N 2 53W
Taouz **82** 30 53N 4 0W
Taoyuan, China **77** 28 55N 111 16 E
Taoyuan, Taiwan **77** 25 0N 121 13 E
Tapa **54** 59 15N 25 50 E
Tapa Shan = Daba Shan **75** 31 50N 109 20 E
Tapachula **120** 14 54N 92 17W
Tapah **71** 4 12N 101 15 E
Tapajós → **127** 2 24S 54 41W
Tapaktuan **72** 3 15N 97 10 E
Tapanui **101** 45 56S 169 18 E
Tapauá → **126** 5 40S 64 21W
Tapeta **84** 6 29N 8 52W
Tapia **30** 43 34N 6 56W
Tápiószele **27** 47 25N 19 55 E
Tapirapecó, Serra **126** 1 10N 65 0W
Tapolca **27** 46 53N 17 29 E
Tappahannock **114** 37 56N 76 50W
Tapti → **68** 21 8N 72 41 E
Tapuaenuku, Mt. **101** 42 0S 173 39 E
Tapul Group **73** 5 35N 120 50 E
Taquara **125** 29 36S 50 46W
Taquari → **126** 19 15S 57 17W
Tar Island **108** 57 03N 111 40W
Tara, Austral. **99** 27 17S 150 31 E
Tara, Can. **112** 44 28N 81 9W
Tara, U.S.S.R. **58** 56 55N 74 24 E
Tara, Zambia **91** 16 58S 26 45 E
Tara →, U.S.S.R. **58** 56 42N 74 36 E
Tara →, Yugo. **42** 43 21N 18 51 E
Tarabagatay, Khrebet **58** 48 0N 83 0 E
Tarābulus, Leb. **64** 34 31N 35 50 E
Tarābulus, Libya **83** 32 49N 13 7 E
Tarahouahout **83** 22 41N 5 59 E
Tarakan **72** 3 20N 117 35 E
Tarakit, Mt. **90** 2 2N 35 10 E
Taralga **99** 34 26S 149 52 E
Taranagar **68** 28 43N 74 50 E
Taranaki □ **101** 39 5S 174 51 E
Tarancón **32** 40 1N 3 1W
Taranga **68** 23 56N 72 43 E
Taranga Hill **68** 24 0N 72 40 E
Táranto **41** 40 30N 17 11 E
Táranto, G. di **41** 40 0N 17 15 E
Tarapacá **126** 2 56S 69 46W
Tarapacá □ **124** 20 45S 69 30W
Tarare **21** 45 54N 4 26 E
Tararua Range **101** 40 45S 175 25 E
Tarascon, Ariège, France **20** 42 50N 1 37 E
Tarascon, Bouches-du-Rhône, France **21** 43 48N 4 39 E
Tarashcha **56** 49 30N 30 31 E
Tarat **80** 25 55N 9 3 E
Tarat, Bj. **83** 26 13N 9 18 E
Tarauacá **126** 8 6S 70 48W
Tarauacá → **126** 6 42S 69 48W
Taravo → **21** 41 42N 8 49 E
Tarawera **101** 39 2S 176 36 E
Tarawera L. **101** 38 13S 176 27 E
Tarazona **32** 41 55N 1 43W
Tarazona de la Mancha **33** 39 16N 1 55W
Tarbat Ness **14** 57 52N 3 48W
Tarbert, Strathclyde, U.K. **14** 55 55N 5 25W
Tarbert, W. Isles, U.K. **14** 57 54N 6 49W
Tarbes **20** 43 15N 0 3 E
Tarboro **115** 35 55N 77 30W
Tarbrax **98** 21 7S 142 26 E
Tarbū **83** 26 0N 15 5 E
Tarcento **39** 46 12N 13 12 E
Tarcoola **96** 30 44S 134 36 E
Tarcoon **99** 30 15S 146 43 E
Tardets-Sorholus **20** 43 8N 0 52W
Tardoire → **20** 45 52N 0 14 E
Taree **97** 31 50S 152 30 E
Tarentaise **21** 45 30N 6 35 E
Tarf, Ras **82** 35 40N 5 11W
Tarf Shaqq al Abd **86** 26 50N 36 6 E
Tarfa, Wadi el → **86** 28 25N 30 50 E
Tarfaya **80** 27 55N 12 55W
Targon **20** 44 44N 0 16W
Targuist **82** 34 59N 4 14W
Tărhăus **46** 46 40N 26 8 E
Tărhăus, Munții **46** 46 39N 26 7 E
Tarhbalt **82** 30 39N 5 20W
Tarhit **82** 30 58N 2 0W
Tarhūnah **83** 32 27N 13 36 E
Tarib, Wadi → **86** 18 30N 43 23 E
Tarifa **31** 36 1N 5 36W
Tarija **124** 21 30S 64 40W
Tarija □ **124** 21 30S 63 30W
Tariku → **73** 2 55S 138 26 E
Tarim He → **75** 39 30N 88 30 E
Tarim Pendi **75** 40 0N 84 0 E
Tarime □ **90** 1 15S 34 0 E
Taritatu → **73** 2 54S 138 27 E
Tarka → **92** 32 10S 26 0 E
Tarkastad **92** 32 0S 26 16 E
Tarkhankut, Mys **56** 45 25N 32 30 E
Tarko Sale **58** 64 55N 77 50 E
Tarkwa **84** 5 20N 2 0W
Tarlac **73** 15 29N 120 35 E
Tarm **49** 55 56N 8 31 E
Tarma **126** 11 25S 75 45W
Tarn □ **20** 43 49N 2 8 E
Tarn → **20** 44 5N 1 6 E
Tarn-et-Garonne □ **20** 44 8N 1 20 E
Tarna → **27** 47 31N 19 59 E
Tårnby **49** 55 37N 12 36 E
Tarnica **27** 49 4N 22 44 E
Tarnobrzeg **28** 50 35N 21 41 E
Tarnobrzeg □ **28** 50 40N 22 0 E
Tarnogród **28** 50 22N 22 45 E
Tarnów **27** 50 3N 21 0 E
Tarnów □ **27** 50 0N 21 0 E
Tarnowskie Góry **28** 50 27N 18 54 E
Táro → **38** 45 0N 10 15 E
Tarong **99** 26 47S 151 51 E
Taroom **97** 25 36S 149 48 E
Taroudannt **82** 30 30N 8 52W
Tarp **24** 54 40N 9 25 E

Tarpon Springs Thaon

Tarpon Springs	**115**	28 8N	82 42W
Tarquínia	**39**	42 15N	11 45 E
Tarqūmiyah	**62**	31 35N	35 1 E
Tarragona	**32**	41 5N	1 17 E
Tarragona □	**32**	41 0N	1 0 E
Tarrasa	**32**	41 34N	2 1 E
Tárrega	**32**	41 39N	1 9 E
Tarrytown	**113**	41 5N	73 52W
Tarshiha = Me'ona	**62**	33 1N	35 15 E
Tarso Emissi	**83**	21 27N	18 36 E
Tarso Ourari	**83**	21 27N	17 27 E
Tarsus	**64**	36 58N	34 55 E
Tartagal	**124**	22 30S	63 50W
Tartas	**20**	43 50N	0 49W
Tartna Point	**99**	32 54S	142 24 E
Tartu	**54**	58 20N	26 44 E
Tarṭūs	**64**	34 55N	35 55 E
Tarussa	**55**	54 44N	37 10 E
Tarutao, Ko	**71**	6 33N	99 40 E
Tarutung	**72**	2 0N	98 54 E
Tarvisio	**39**	46 31N	13 35 E
Tarz Ulli	**83**	25 32N	10 8 E
Tasāwah	**83**	26 0N	13 30 E
Taschereau	**106**	48 40N	78 40W
Taseko →	**108**	52 4N	123 9W
Tasgaon	**70**	17 2N	74 39 E
Tash-Kumyr	**58**	41 40N	72 10 E
Ta'shan	**87**	16 31N	42 33 E
Tashauz	**58**	41 49N	59 58 E
Tashi Chho Dzong = Thimphu	**69**	27 31N	89 45 E
Tashkent	**58**	41 20N	69 10 E
Tashtagol	**58**	52 47N	87 53 E
Tasikmalaya	**73**	7 18S	108 12 E
Tåsjön	**50**	64 15N	16 0 E
Taskan	**59**	62 59N	150 20 E
Taskopru	**56**	41 30N	34 15 E
Tasman B.	**101**	40 59S	173 25 E
Tasman Mts.	**101**	41 3S	172 25 E
Tasman Pen.	**97**	43 10S	148 0 E
Tasman Sea	**94**	36 0S	160 0 E
Tasmania □	**97**	42 0S	146 30 E
Tăşnad	**46**	47 30N	22 33 E
Tassil Tin-Rerhoh	**82**	20 5N	3 55 E
Tassili n-Ajjer	**83**	25 47N	8 1 E
Tassili-Oua-n-Ahaggar	**83**	20 41N	5 30 E
Tasu Sd.	**108**	52 47N	132 2W
Tata, Hung.	**27**	47 37N	18 19 E
Tata, Moroc.	**82**	29 46N	7 56W
Tatabánya	**27**	47 32N	18 25 E
Tatahouine	**83**	32 57N	10 29 E
Tatar A.S.S.R. □	**52**	55 30N	51 30 E
Tatarbunary	**56**	45 50N	29 39 E
Tatarsk	**58**	55 14N	76 0 E
* Tatarskiy Proliv	**59**	54 0N	141 0 E
Tateyama	**74**	35 0N	139 50 E
Tathlina L.	**108**	60 33N	117 39W
Tathra	**99**	36 44S	149 59 E
Tatinnai L.	**109**	60 55N	97 40W
Tatnam, C.	**109**	57 16N	91 0W
Tatra = Tatry	**27**	49 20N	20 0 E
Tatry	**27**	49 20N	20 0 E
Tatta	**68**	24 42N	67 55 E
Tatuí	**125**	23 25S	47 53W
Tatum	**117**	33 16N	103 16W
Tat'ung = Datong	**76**	40 6N	113 12 E
Tatura	**100**	36 29S	145 16 E
Tatvan	**64**	38 31N	42 15 E
Taubaté	**125**	23 0S	45 36W
Tauberbischofsheim	**25**	49 37N	9 40 E
Taucha	**24**	51 22N	12 31 E
Tauern	**26**	47 15N	12 40 E
Tauern-tunnel	**26**	47 0N	13 12 E
Taufikia	**87**	9 24N	31 37 E
Taumarunui	**101**	38 53S	175 15 E
Taumaturgo	**126**	8 54S	72 51W
Taung	**92**	27 33S	24 47 E
Taungdwingyi	**67**	20 1N	95 40 E
Taunggyi	**67**	20 50N	97 0 E
Taungup	**67**	18 51N	94 14 E
Taungup Pass	**67**	18 40N	94 45 E
Taunsa Barrage	**68**	30 42N	70 50 E
Taunton, U.K.	**13**	51 1N	3 7W
Taunton, U.S.A.	**114**	41 54N	71 6W
Taunus	**25**	50 15N	8 20 E
Taupo	**101**	38 41S	176 7 E
Taupo, L.	**101**	38 46S	175 55 E
Taurage	**54**	55 14N	22 16 E
Tauranga	**101**	37 42S	176 11 E
Tauranga Harb.	**101**	37 30S	176 5 E
Taurianova	**41**	38 22N	16 1 E
Taurus Mts. = Toros Dağlari	**64**	37 0N	35 0 E
Tauste	**32**	41 58N	1 18W
Tauz	**57**	41 0N	45 40 E
Tavda	**58**	58 7N	65 8 E
Tavda →	**58**	59 20N	63 28 E
Taverny	**19**	49 2N	2 13 E
Taveta	**90**	3 23S	37 37 E
Taveuni	**101**	16 51S	179 58W
Tavignano →	**21**	42 7N	9 33 E
Tavira	**31**	37 8N	7 40W
Tavistock, Can.	**112**	43 19N	80 50W
Tavistock, U.K.	**13**	50 33N	4 9W
Tavolara	**40**	40 55N	9 40 E
Távora →	**30**	41 8N	7 35W
Tavoy	**71**	14 2N	98 12 E
Taw →	**13**	17 37S	177 55 E
Tawas City	**114**	44 16N	83 31W
Tawau	**72**	4 20N	117 55 E
Tawitawi	**73**	5 10N	120 0 E
Tāwurgha'	**83**	32 1N	15 2 E
Tay →	**14**	56 37N	3 38W
Tay, Firth of	**14**	56 25N	3 8W
Tay, L.	**14**	56 30N	4 10W
Tay Ninh	**71**	11 20N	106 5 E
Tayabamba	**126**	8 15S	77 16W
Taylakovy	**58**	59 13N	74 0 E
Taylor, Can.	**108**	56 13N	120 40W
Taylor, Ariz., U.S.A.	**119**	34 28N	110 5W
Taylor, Nebr., U.S.A.	**116**	41 46N	99 23W
Taylor, Pa., U.S.A.	**113**	41 23N	75 43W
Taylor, Tex., U.S.A.	**117**	30 30N	97 30W
Taylor Mt.	**119**	35 16N	107 36W
Taylorville	**116**	39 32N	89 20W
Taymā'	**64**	27 35N	38 45 E
Taymyr, P-ov.	**59**	75 0N	100 0 E
Tayport	**14**	56 27N	2 52W
Ṭayr Zibnā	**62**	33 14N	35 23 E
Tayshet	**59**	55 58N	98 1 E
Tayside □	**14**	56 25N	3 30W
Taytay	**73**	10 45N	119 30 E
Taz →	**58**	67 32N	78 40 E
Taza	**82**	34 16N	4 6W
Tazenakht	**82**	30 35N	7 12W
Tazin →	**109**	60 26N	110 45W
Tazin L.	**109**	59 44N	108 42W
Tazoult	**83**	35 29N	6 11 E
Tazovskiy	**58**	67 30N	78 44 E
Tbilisi (Tiflis)	**57**	41 43N	44 50 E
Tchad (Chad) ■	**81**	12 30N	17 15 E
Tchad, L.	**81**	13 30N	14 30 E
Tch'ang-k'ing = Changqing	**75**	29 35N	106 35 E
Tchaourou	**85**	8 58N	2 40 E
Tch'eng-tou = Chengdu	**75**	30 38N	104 2 E
Tchentlo L.	**108**	55 15N	125 0W
Tchibanga	**88**	2 45S	11 0 E
Tchin Tabaraden	**85**	15 58N	5 56 E
Tczew	**28**	54 8N	18 50 E
Te Anau, L.	**101**	45 15S	167 45 E
Te Aroha	**101**	37 32S	175 44 E
Te Awamutu	**101**	38 1S	175 20 E
Te Kuiti	**101**	38 20S	175 11 E
Te Puke	**101**	37 46S	176 22 E
Te Waewae B.	**101**	46 13S	167 33 E
Teaca	**46**	46 55N	24 30 E
Teague	**117**	31 40N	96 20W
Teano	**41**	41 15N	14 1 E
Teapa	**120**	18 35N	92 56W
Teba	**31**	36 59N	4 55W
Tebakang	**72**	1 6N	110 30 E
Teberda	**57**	43 30N	41 46 E
Tébessa	**83**	35 22N	8 8 E
Tebicuary →	**124**	26 36S	58 16W
Tebingtinggi, Bengkulu, Indon.	**72**	3 38S	103 9 E
Tebingtinggi, Sumatera Utara, Indon.	**72**	3 20N	99 9 E
Tébourba	**83**	36 49N	9 51 E
Téboursouk	**83**	36 29N	9 10 E
Tebulos	**57**	42 36N	45 17 E
Tech →	**20**	42 36N	3 3 E
Techiman	**84**	7 35N	1 58W
Techirghiol	**46**	44 4N	28 32 E
Tecuala	**120**	22 23N	105 27W
Tecuci	**46**	45 51N	27 27 E
Tecumseh	**114**	42 1N	83 59W
Tedzhen	**58**	37 23N	60 31 E
Tees →	**12**	54 36N	1 25W
Teesside	**12**	54 37N	1 13W
Teeswater	**112**	43 59N	81 17W
Tefé	**126**	3 25S	64 50W
Tegal	**73**	6 52S	109 8 E
Tegelen	**16**	51 20N	6 9 E
Tegernsee	**25**	47 43N	11 46 E
Teggiano	**41**	40 24N	15 32 E
Teghra	**69**	25 30N	85 34 E
Tegid, L.	**12**	52 53N	3 38W
Tegina	**85**	10 5N	6 11 E
Tegucigalpa	**121**	14 5N	87 14W
Tehachapi	**119**	35 11N	118 29W
Tehachapi Mts.	**119**	35 0N	118 40W
Tehamiyam	**86**	18 20N	36 32 E
Tehilla	**86**	17 42N	36 6 E
Téhini	**84**	9 39N	3 40W
Tehrān	**65**	35 44N	51 30 E
Tehrān □	**65**	35 0N	49 30 E
Tehuacán	**120**	18 30N	97 30W
Tehuantepec	**120**	16 21N	95 13W
Tehuantepec, Golfo de	**120**	15 50N	95 0W
Tehuantepec, Istmo de	**120**	17 0N	94 30W
Teich, Le	**20**	44 38N	0 59W
Teifi →	**13**	52 4N	4 14W
Teign →	**13**	50 41N	3 42W
Teignmouth	**13**	50 33N	3 30W
Teil, Le	**21**	44 33N	4 40 E
Teilleul, Le	**18**	48 32N	0 53W
Teiuş	**46**	46 12N	23 40 E
Teixeira Pinto	**84**	12 3N	16 0W
Tejo →	**31**	38 40N	9 24W
Tekamah	**116**	41 48N	96 22W
Tekapo, L.	**101**	43 53S	170 33 E
Tekax	**120**	20 11N	89 18W
Tekeli	**58**	44 50N	79 0 E
Tekeze →	**87**	14 20N	35 50 E
Tekija	**42**	44 42N	22 26 E
Tekirdağ	**64**	40 58N	27 30 E
Tekkali	**70**	18 37N	84 15 E
Tekoa	**118**	47 19N	117 4W
Tekouiât, O. →	**82**	22 25N	2 35 E
Tel Adashim	**62**	32 30N	35 17 E
Tel Aviv-Yafo	**62**	32 4N	34 48 E
Tel Lakhish	**62**	31 34N	34 51 E
Tel Megiddo	**62**	32 35N	35 11 E
Tel Mond	**62**	32 15N	34 56 E
Tela	**120**	15 40N	87 28W
Télagh	**82**	34 51N	0 32W
Telanaipura = Jambi	**72**	1 38S	103 37 E
Telavi	**57**	42 0N	45 30 E
Telciu	**46**	47 25N	24 24 E
Telegraph Cr.	**108**	58 0N	131 10W
Telekhany	**54**	52 30N	25 46 E
Telemark fylke □	**47**	59 25N	8 30 E
Telén	**124**	36 15S	65 31W
Teleneshty	**46**	47 35N	28 24 E
Teleño	**30**	42 23N	6 22W
Teleorman □	**46**	44 0N	25 0 E
Teleorman →	**46**	44 15N	25 20 E
Teles Pires →	**126**	7 21S	58 3W
Telescope Peak	**119**	36 6N	117 7W
Teletaye	**85**	16 31N	1 30 E
Telford	**12**	52 42N	2 31W
Telfs	**26**	47 19N	11 4 E
Telgte	**24**	51 59N	7 46 E
Télimélé	**84**	10 54N	13 2W
Telkwa	**108**	54 41N	127 5W
Tell City	**114**	38 0N	86 44W
Tellicherry	**70**	11 45N	75 30 E
Telluride	**119**	37 58N	107 48W
Telok Anson	**71**	4 3N	101 0 E
Telom →	**71**	4 20N	101 46 E
Telpos Iz	**52**	63 35N	57 30 E
Telsen	**128**	42 30S	66 50W
Telšiai	**54**	55 59N	22 14 E
Teltow	**24**	52 24N	13 15 E
Telukbetung	**72**	5 29S	105 17 E
Telukbutun	**72**	4 13N	108 12 E
Telukdalem	**72**	0 33N	97 50 E
Tema	**85**	5 41N	0 0 E
Temanggung	**73**	7 18S	110 10 E
Temax	**120**	21 10N	88 50W
Tembe	**90**	0 16S	28 14 E
Tembeling →	**71**	4 20N	102 23 E
Tembleque	**32**	39 41N	3 30W
Tembuland	**93**	31 35S	28 0 E
Teme →	**13**	52 23N	2 15W
Temecula	**119**	33 26N	117 6W
Temerloh	**71**	3 27N	102 25 E
Temir	**58**	49 21N	57 3 E
Temirtau, Kazakh, U.S.S.R.	**58**	50 5N	72 56 E
Temirtau, R.S.F.S.R., U.S.S.R.	**58**	53 10N	87 30 E
Témiscaming	**106**	46 44N	79 5W
Temma	**99**	41 12S	144 48 E
Temnikov	**55**	54 40N	43 11 E
Temo →	**40**	40 20N	8 30 E
Temora	**99**	34 30S	147 30 E
Temosachic	**120**	28 58N	107 50W
Tempe	**119**	33 26N	111 59W
Tempino	**72**	1 42S	103 30 E
Témpio Pausania	**40**	40 53N	9 6 E
Temple	**117**	31 5N	97 22W
Temple B.	**97**	12 15S	143 3 E
Templemore	**15**	52 48N	7 50W
Templeton →	**98**	21 0S	138 40 E
Templin	**24**	53 8N	13 31 E
Temryuk	**56**	45 15N	37 24 E
Temska →	**42**	43 17N	22 33 E
Temuco	**128**	38 45S	72 40W
Temuka	**101**	44 14S	171 17 E
Tenabo	**120**	20 2N	90 12W
Tenaha	**117**	31 57N	94 25W
Tenali	**70**	16 15N	80 35 E
Tenancingo	**120**	19 0N	99 33W
Tenango	**120**	19 7N	99 33W
Tenasserim	**71**	12 6N	99 3 E
Tenasserim □	**71**	14 0N	98 30 E
Tenay	**21**	45 55N	5 30 E
Tenby	**13**	51 40N	4 42W
Tendaho	**87**	11 48N	40 54 E
Tende	**21**	44 5N	7 35 E
Tende, Col de	**21**	44 9N	7 32 E
Tendelti	**87**	13 1N	31 55 E
Tendjedi, Adrar	**83**	23 41N	7 32 E
Tendrara	**82**	33 3N	1 58W
Teneida	**86**	25 30N	29 19 E
Ténéré	**85**	19 0N	10 30 E
Tenerife	**80**	28 15N	16 35W
Ténès	**82**	36 31N	1 14 E
Teng →	**71**	20 30N	98 10 E
Teng Xian, Guangxi Zhuangzu, China	**77**	23 21N	110 56 E
Teng Xian, Shandong, China	**77**	35 5N	117 10 E
Tengah □	**73**	2 0S	122 0 E
Tengah Kepulauan	**72**	7 5S	118 15 E
Tengchong	**75**	25 0N	98 28 E
Tenggara □	**73**	3 0S	122 0 E
Tenggarong	**72**	0 24S	116 58 E
Tengiz, Ozero	**58**	50 30N	69 0 E
Tenille	**115**	32 58N	82 50W
Tenkasi	**70**	8 55N	77 20 E
Tenke, Congo	**91**	11 22S	26 40 E
Tenke, Zaïre	**91**	10 32S	26 7 E
Tenkodogo	**85**	11 54N	0 19W
Tenna →	**39**	43 12N	13 47 E
Tennant Creek	**96**	19 30S	134 15 E
Tennessee □	**111**	36 0N	86 30W
Tennessee →	**114**	34 30N	86 20W
Tennsift, Oued →	**82**	32 3N	9 28W
Tenom	**72**	5 4N	115 57 E
Tenosique	**120**	17 30N	91 24W
Tenryū-Gawa →	**74**	35 39N	137 48 E
Tent L.	**109**	62 25N	107 54W
Tenterfield	**97**	29 0S	152 0 E
Teófilo Otoni	**127**	17 50S	41 30W
Teotihuacán	**120**	19 44N	98 50W
Tepa	**73**	7 52S	129 31 E
Tepalcatepec →	**120**	18 35N	101 59W
Tepelena	**44**	40 17N	20 2 E
Tepic	**120**	21 30N	104 54W
Teplice	**26**	50 40N	13 48 E
Tepoca, C.	**120**	30 20N	112 25W
Tequila	**120**	20 54N	103 47W
Ter →	**32**	42 0N	3 12 E
Ter Apel	**16**	52 53N	7 5 E
Téra	**85**	14 0N	0 45 E
Tera →	**30**	41 54N	5 44W
Téramo	**39**	42 40N	13 40 E
Terang	**99**	38 15S	142 55 E
Terazit, Massif de	**83**	20 2N	8 30 E
Terceira	**8**	38 43N	27 13W
Tercero →	**124**	32 58S	61 47W
Terdal	**70**	16 33N	75 3 E
Terebovlya	**54**	49 18N	25 44 E
Teregova	**46**	45 10N	22 16 E
Terek →, U.S.S.R.	**56**	43 55N	47 30 E
Terek →, U.S.S.R.	**57**	44 0N	47 30 E
Terembone Cr. →	**99**	30 25S	148 50 E
Terengganu □	**71**	4 55N	103 0 E
Tereshka →	**55**	51 48N	46 26 E
Teresina	**127**	5 9S	42 45W
Terespol	**28**	52 5N	23 37 E
Terewah L.	**99**	29 52S	147 35 E
Terges →	**31**	37 49N	7 41W
Tergnier	**19**	49 40N	3 17 E
Terhazza	**82**	23 38N	5 22W
Terlizzi	**41**	41 8N	16 32 E
Terme	**56**	41 11N	37 0 E
Termez	**58**	37 15N	67 15 E
Términi Imerese	**40**	37 58N	13 42 E
Términos, Laguna de	**120**	18 35N	91 30W
Térmoli	**39**	42 0N	15 0 E
Ternate	**73**	0 45N	127 25 E
Terneuzen	**16**	51 20N	3 50 E
Terney	**59**	45 3N	136 37 E
Terni	**39**	42 34N	12 38 E
Ternitz	**26**	47 43N	16 2 E
Ternopol	**54**	49 30N	25 40 E
Terra Nova B.	**5**	74 50S	164 40 E
Terrace	**108**	54 30N	128 35W
Terrace Bay	**106**	48 47N	87 5W
Terracina	**40**	41 17N	13 12 E
Terralba	**40**	39 42N	8 38 E
Terranuova Bracciolini	**39**	43 31N	11 35 E
Terrasini Favarotta	**40**	38 10N	13 4 E
Terrasson	**20**	45 7N	1 19 E
Terre Haute	**114**	39 28N	87 24W
Terrebonne B.	**117**	29 15N	90 28W
Terrecht	**82**	20 10N	0 10W
Terrell	**117**	32 44N	96 19W
Terrenceville	**107**	47 40N	54 44W
Terrick Terrick	**98**	24 44S	145 5 E
Terry	**116**	46 47N	105 20W
Terschelling	**16**	53 25N	5 20 E
Terter →	**57**	40 35N	47 22 E
Teruel	**32**	40 22N	1 8W
Teruel □	**32**	40 48N	1 0W
Tervel	**43**	43 45N	27 28 E
Tervola	**50**	66 6N	24 49 E
Teryaweyna L.	**99**	32 18S	143 22 E
Tešanj	**42**	44 38N	17 59 E
Teseney	**87**	15 5N	36 42 E
Tesha →	**55**	55 38N	42 9 E
Teshio-Gawa →	**74**	44 53N	141 45 E
Tešica	**42**	43 27N	21 45 E
Tesiyn Gol →	**75**	50 40N	93 20 E
Teslić	**42**	44 37N	17 54 E
Teslin	**104**	60 10N	132 43W
Teslin →	**108**	61 34N	134 35W
Teslin L.	**108**	60 15N	132 57W
Tessalit	**85**	20 12N	1 0 E
Tessaoua	**85**	13 47N	7 56 E
Tessin	**24**	54 2N	12 28 E
Tessit	**85**	15 13N	0 18 E
Test →	**13**	51 7N	1 30W
Testa del Gargano	**41**	41 50N	16 10 E
Teste, La	**20**	44 37N	1 8W
Têt	**27**	47 30N	17 33 E
Têt →	**20**	42 44N	3 2 E
Tetachuck L.	**108**	53 18N	125 55W
Tetas, Pta.	**124**	23 31S	70 38W
Tete	**91**	16 13S	33 33 E
Tete □	**91**	15 15S	32 40 E
Teterev →	**54**	51 1N	30 5 E
Teterow	**24**	53 45N	12 34 E
Teteven	**43**	42 58N	24 17 E
Tethul →	**108**	60 35N	112 12W
Tetiyev	**56**	49 22N	29 38 E
Teton →	**118**	47 58N	111 0W
Tétouan	**82**	35 35N	5 21W
Tetovo	**42**	42 1N	21 2 E
Tetuán = Tétouan	**82**	35 30N	5 25W
Tetyushi	**55**	54 55N	48 49 E
Teuco →	**124**	25 35S	60 11W
Teulada	**40**	38 59N	8 47 E
Teulon	**109**	50 23N	97 16W
Teun	**73**	6 59S	129 8 E
Teutoburger Wald	**22**	52 5N	8 20 E
Tevere →	**39**	41 44N	12 14 E
Teverya	**62**	32 47N	35 32 E
Teviot →	**14**	55 21N	2 51W
Tewantin	**99**	26 27S	153 3 E
Tewkesbury	**13**	51 59N	2 8W
Texada I.	**108**	49 40N	124 25W
Texarkana, Ark., U.S.A.	**117**	33 25N	94 0W
Texarkana, Tex., U.S.A.	**117**	33 25N	94 3W
Texas	**99**	28 49S	151 9 E
Texas □	**117**	31 40N	98 30W
Texas City	**117**	29 20N	94 55W
Texel	**16**	53 5N	4 50 E
Texhoma	**117**	36 32N	101 47W
Texline	**117**	36 26N	103 0W
Texoma L.	**117**	34 0N	96 38W
Teykovo	**55**	56 55N	40 30 E
Teyvareh	**65**	33 30N	64 24 E
Teza →	**55**	56 32N	41 53 E
Teziutlán	**120**	19 50N	97 22W
Tezpur	**67**	26 40N	92 45 E
Tezzeron L.	**108**	54 43N	124 30W
Tha-anne →	**109**	60 31N	94 37W
Tha Nun	**71**	8 12N	98 17 E
Thaba Putsoa	**93**	29 45S	28 0 E
Thabana Ntlenyana	**93**	29 30S	29 16 E
Thabazimbi	**93**	24 40S	27 21 E
Thabor, Mt.	**21**	45 7N	6 34 E
Thai Nguyen	**71**	21 35N	105 55 E
Thailand (Siam) ■	**71**	16 0N	102 0 E
Thakhek	**71**	17 25N	104 45 E
Thal	**66**	33 28N	70 33 E
Thal Desert	**68**	31 10N	71 30 E
Thala	**83**	35 35N	8 40 E
Thala La	**67**	28 25N	97 23 E
Thallon	**99**	28 39S	148 49 E
Thalwil	**25**	47 17N	8 35 E
Thame →	**13**	51 35N	1 8W
Thames	**101**	37 7S	175 34 E
Thames →, Can.	**106**	42 20N	82 25W
Thames →, U.K.	**13**	51 30N	0 35 E
Thames →, U.S.A.	**113**	41 18N	72 9W
Thamesford	**112**	43 4N	81 0W
Thamesville	**112**	42 33N	81 59W
Thāmit, W.	**83**	30 51N	16 14 E
Thana	**70**	19 12N	72 59 E
Thanesar	**68**	30 1N	76 52 E
Thanet, I. of	**13**	51 21N	1 20 E
Thang Binh	**71**	15 50N	108 20 E
Thangool	**98**	24 38S	150 42 E
Thanh Hoa	**71**	19 48N	105 46 E
Thanjavur (Tanjore)	**70**	10 48N	79 12 E
Thanlwin Myit →	**67**	20 0N	98 0 E
Thann	**19**	47 48N	7 5 E
Thaon	**19**	48 15N	6 25 E

* *Renamed Sakhalinskiy Zaliv*

Thar Tocina

Thar (Great Indian) Desert **68** 28 0N 72 0 E
Tharad **68** 24 30N 71 44 E
Thargomindah **97** 27 58 S 143 46 E
Tharrawaddy **67** 17 38N 95 48 E
Thasopoúla **44** 40 49N 24 45 E
Thásos, Greece **44** 40 50N 24 42 E
Thásos, Greece **44** 40 40N 24 40 E
Thatcher, Ariz., U.S.A. **119** 32 54N 109 46W
Thatcher, Colo., U.S.A. **117** 37 38N 104 6W
Thaton **67** 16 55N 97 22 E
Thau, Étang de **20** 43 23N 3 36 E
Thaungdut **67** 24 30N 94 40 E
Thayer **117** 36 34N 91 34W
Thayetmyo **67** 19 20N 95 10 E
Thazi **67** 21 0N 96 5 E
The Bight **121** 24 19N 75 24W
The Dalles **118** 45 40N 121 11W
The English Company's Is. **97** 11 50 S 136 32 E
The Flatts **121** 32 16N 64 45W
The Frome → **99** 29 8 S 137 54 E
The Granites **96** 20 35 S 130 21 E
The Grenadines, Is. **121** 12 40N 61 20W
The Hague = s'-Gravenhage **16** 52 7N 4 14 E
The Hamilton → **96** 26 40 S 135 19 E
The Johnston Lakes **96** 32 25 S 120 30 E
The Macumba → **97** 27 52 S 137 12 E
The Pas **109** 53 45N 101 15W
The Range **91** 19 2 S 31 2 E
The Rock **99** 35 15 S 147 2 E
The Salt Lake **99** 30 6 S 142 8 E
The Warburton → **99** 28 4 S 137 28 E
Thebes **86** 25 40N 32 35 E
Thebes = Thívai **45** 38 19N 23 19 E
Thedford, Can. **112** 43 9N 81 51W
Thedford, U.S.A. **116** 41 59N 100 31W
Theebine **99** 25 57 S 152 34 E
Theil, Le **18** 48 16N 0 42 E
Thekulthili L. **109** 61 3N 110 0W
Thelon → **109** 62 35N 104 3W
Thénezay **18** 46 44N 0 2W
Thenia **83** 36 44N 3 33 E
Thenon **20** 45 9N 1 4 E
Theodore **97** 24 55 S 150 3 E
Thérain → **19** 49 15N 2 27 E
Theresa **113** 44 13N 75 50W
Thermaïkos Kólpos **44** 40 15N 22 45 E
Thermopolis **118** 43 35N 108 10W
Thermopylae P. **45** 38 48N 22 35 E
Thesprotía □ **44** 39 27N 20 22 E
Thessalía □ **44** 39 30N 22 0 E
Thessalon **106** 46 20N 83 30W
Thessaloníki **44** 40 38N 22 58 E
Thessaloníki □ **44** 40 45N 23 0 E
Thessaly = Thessalía **44** 39 30N 22 0 E
Thetford **13** 52 25N 0 44 E
Thetford Mines **107** 46 8N 71 18W
Theunissen **92** 28 26 S 26 43 E
Thiámis → **44** 39 15N 20 6 E
Thiberville **18** 49 8N 0 27 E
Thibodaux **117** 29 48N 90 49W
Thicket Portage **109** 55 19N 97 42W
Thief River Falls **116** 48 15N 96 48W
Thiel Mts. **5** 85 15 S 91 0W
Thiene **39** 45 42N 11 29 E
Thiérache **19** 49 51N 3 45 E
Thiers **20** 45 52N 3 33 E
Thies **84** 14 50N 16 51W
Thiet **87** 7 37N 28 49 E
Thika **90** 1 1 S 37 5 E
Thikombia **101** 15 44 S 179 55W
Thille-Boubacar **84** 16 31N 15 5W
Thillot, Le **19** 47 53N 6 46 E
Thimphu (Tashi Chho Dzong) **69** 27 31N 89 45 E
Þingvallavatn **50** 64 11N 21 9W
Thionville **19** 49 20N 6 10 E
Thíra **45** 36 23N 25 27 E
Thirasía **45** 36 26N 25 21 E
Thirsk **12** 54 15N 1 20W
Thistle I. **96** 35 0 S 136 8 E
Thívai **45** 38 19N 23 19 E
Thiviers **20** 45 25N 0 54 E
Thizy **21** 46 2N 4 18 E
Þjórsá → **50** 63 47N 20 48W
Thlewiaza →, Man., Can. **109** 59 43N 100 5W
Thlewiaza →, N.W.T., Can. **109** 60 29N 94 40W
Thoa → **109** 60 31N 109 47W
Thoissey **21** 46 12N 4 48 E
Thomas, Okla., U.S.A. **117** 35 48N 98 48W
Thomas, W. Va., U.S.A. **114** 39 10N 79 30W
Thomas, L. **99** 26 4 S 137 58 E
Thomaston **115** 32 54N 84 20W
Thomasville, Ala., U.S.A. **115** 31 55N 87 42W
Thomasville, Ga., U.S.A. **115** 30 50N 84 0W
Thomasville, N.C., U.S.A. **115** 35 55N 80 4W
Thompson **109** 55 45N 97 52W
Thompson →, Can. **108** 50 15N 121 24W
Thompson →, U.S.A. **116** 39 46N 93 37W
Thompson Falls **118** 47 37N 115 20W
Thompson Landing **109** 62 56N 110 40W
Thompson Pk. **118** 41 0N 123 3W
Thompsons **119** 39 0N 109 50W
Thompsonville **113** 42 0N 72 37W
Thomson → **97** 25 11 S 142 53 E
Thomson's Falls = Nyahururu **90** 0 2N 36 27 E
Thon Buri **71** 13 43N 100 29 E
Thônes **21** 45 54N 6 18 E
Thonon-les-Bains **21** 46 22N 6 29 E
Thorez **57** 48 4N 38 34 E
Þórisvatn **50** 64 20N 18 55W
Þorlákshöfn **50** 63 51N 21 22W
Thornaby on Tees **12** 54 36N 1 19W
Thornbury **112** 44 34N 80 26W
Thorne Glacier **5** 87 30 S 150 0W
Thorold **112** 43 7N 79 12W
Þórshöfn **50** 66 12N 15 20W
Thouarcé **18** 47 17N 0 30W
Thouars **18** 46 58N 0 15W
Thrace = Thráki □ **44** 41 10N 25 30 E
Thráki □ **44** 41 9N 25 30 E
Thrakikón Pélagos **44** 40 30N 25 0 E
Three Forks **118** 45 55N 111 32W
Three Hills **108** 51 43N 113 15W
Three Hummock I. **99** 40 25 S 144 55 E
Three Lakes **116** 45 48N 89 10W
Three Points, C. **84** 4 42N 2 6W
Three Rivers **117** 28 30N 98 10W
Three Sisters, Mt. **118** 44 10N 121 46W
Throssell Ra. **96** 22 3 S 121 43 E
Thrun Pass **26** 47 20N 12 25 E
Thubun Lakes **109** 61 30N 112 0W
Thuddungra **100** 34 8 S 148 8 E
Thueyts **21** 44 41N 4 9 E
Thuin **16** 50 20N 4 17 E
Thuir **20** 42 38N 2 45 E
Thule, Antarct. **5** 59 27 S 27 19W
Thule, Greenl. **4** 77 40N 69 0W
Thun **25** 46 45N 7 38 E
Thunder B. **114** 45 0N 83 20W
Thunder Bay **106** 48 20N 89 15W
Thunersee **25** 46 43N 7 39 E
Thung Song **71** 8 10N 99 40 E
Thunkar **69** 27 55N 91 0 E
Thur → **25** 47 32N 9 10 E
Thurgau □ **25** 47 34N 9 10 E
Thüringer Wald **24** 50 35N 11 0 E
Thurles **15** 52 40N 7 53W
Thurloo Downs **99** 29 15 S 143 30 E
Thurn P. **25** 47 20N 12 25 E
Thursday I. **97** 10 30 S 142 3 E
Thurso, Can. **106** 45 36N 75 15W
Thurso, U.K. **14** 58 34N 3 31W
Thurston I. **5** 72 0 S 100 0W
Thury-Harcourt **18** 49 0N 0 30W
Thutade L. **108** 57 0N 126 55W
Thyborøn **49** 56 42N 8 12 E
Thylungra **99** 26 4 S 143 28 E
Thyolo **91** 16 7 S 35 5 E
Thysville = Mbanza Ngungu **88** 5 12 S 14 53 E
Ti-n-Barraouene, O. → **85** 18 40N 4 5 E
Ti-n-Medjerdam, O. → **82** 25 45N 1 30 E
Ti-n-Tarabine, O. → **83** 21 0N 7 25 E
Ti-n-Zaouatène **82** 20 0N 2 55 E
Tia **99** 31 10 S 150 34 E
Tian Shan **75** 43 0N 84 0 E
Tiandu **77** 18 18N 109 36 E
Tian'e **77** 25 1N 107 9 E
Tianhe **77** 24 48N 108 40 E
Tianjin **76** 39 8N 117 10 E
Tiankoura **84** 10 47N 3 17W
Tianshui **77** 34 32N 105 40 E
Tianyang **77** 23 42N 106 53 E
Tianzhen **76** 40 24N 114 5 E
Tiaret **82** 35 20N 1 21 E
Tiassalé **84** 5 58N 4 57W
Tibagi **125** 24 30 S 50 24W
Tibagi → **125** 22 47 S 51 1W
Tibati **85** 6 22N 12 30 E
Tiber = Tevere → **39** 41 44N 12 14 E
Tiber Res. **118** 48 20N 111 15W
Tiberias, L. = Kinneret, Yam **62** 32 45N 35 35 E
Tibesti **83** 21 0N 17 30 E
Tibet = Xizang □ **75** 32 0N 88 0 E
Tibiri **85** 13 34N 7 4 E
Ţibleş **46** 47 32N 24 15 E
Tibnīn **62** 33 12N 35 24 E
Tibooburra **97** 29 26 S 142 1 E
Tibro **49** 58 28N 14 10 E
Tiburón **120** 29 0N 112 30W
Tîchît **84** 18 21N 9 29W
Ticho **87** 7 50N 39 32 E
Ticino □ **25** 46 20N 8 45 E
Ticino → **38** 45 9N 9 14 E
Ticonderoga **114** 43 50N 73 28W
Ticul **120** 20 20N 89 31W
Tidaholm **49** 58 12N 13 55 E
Tiddim **67** 23 28N 93 45 E
Tideridjaouine, Adrar **82** 23 0N 2 15 E
Tidikelt **82** 26 58N 1 30 E
Tidjikja **84** 18 29N 11 35W
Tidore **73** 0 40N 127 25 E
Tiébissou **84** 7 9N 5 10W
Tiéboro **83** 21 20N 17 7 E
Tiel, Neth. **16** 51 53N 5 26 E
Tiel, Senegal **84** 14 55N 15 5W
Tieling **76** 42 20N 123 55 E
Tielt **16** 51 0N 3 20 E
Tien Shan = Tian Shan **75** 43 0N 84 0 E
Tien-tsin = Tianjin **76** 39 8N 117 10 E
T'ienching = Tianjin **76** 39 8N 117 10 E
Tienen **16** 50 48N 4 57 E
Tiénigbé **84** 8 11N 5 43W
Tientsin = Tianjin **76** 39 8N 117 10 E
Tierp **48** 60 20N 17 30 E
Tierra Amarilla, Chile **124** 27 28 S 70 18W
Tierra Amarilla, U.S.A. **119** 36 42N 106 33W
Tierra de Barros **31** 38 40N 6 30W
Tierra de Campos **30** 42 10N 4 50W
Tierra del Fuego, I. Gr. de **128** 54 0 S 69 0W
Tiétar → **30** 39 50N 6 1W
Tieté → **125** 20 40 S 51 35W
Tifarit **82** 26 9N 10 33W
Tiffin **114** 41 8N 83 10W
Tiflèt **82** 33 54N 6 20W
Tiflis = Tbilisi **57** 41 43N 44 50 E
Tifrah **62** 31 19N 34 42 E
Tifton **115** 31 28N 83 32W
Tifu **73** 3 39 S 126 24 E
Tigil **59** 57 49N 158 40 E
Tignish **107** 46 58N 64 2W
Tigre □ **87** 13 35N 39 15 E
Tigre → **126** 4 30 S 74 10W
Tigris = Dijlah, Nahr → **64** 31 0N 47 25 E
Tiguentourine **83** 27 52N 9 8 E
Tigveni **46** 45 10N 24 31 E
Tigyaing **67** 23 45N 96 10 E
Tigzerte, O. → **82** 28 10N 9 37W
Tih, Gebel el **86** 29 32N 33 26 E
Tihama **64** 22 0N 39 0 E
Tihodaine, Dunes de **83** 25 15N 7 15 E
Tijesno **39** 43 48N 15 39 E
Tījī **83** 32 0N 11 18 E
Tijuana **120** 32 30N 117 10W
Tikal **120** 17 13N 89 24W
Tikamgarh **68** 24 44N 78 50 E
Tikhoretsk **57** 45 56N 40 5 E
Tikhvin **54** 59 35N 33 30 E
Tikkadouine, Adrar **82** 24 28N 1 30 E
Tiko **85** 4 4N 9 20 E
Tikrīt **64** 34 35N 43 37 E
Tiksi **59** 71 40N 128 45 E
Tilamuta **73** 0 32N 122 23 E
Tilburg **16** 51 31N 5 6 E
Tilbury, Can. **106** 42 17N 82 23W
Tilbury, U.K. **13** 51 27N 0 24 E
Tilcara **124** 23 36 S 65 23W
Tilden, Nebr., U.S.A. **116** 42 3N 97 45W
Tilden, Tex., U.S.A. **117** 28 28N 98 33W
Tilemses **85** 15 37N 4 44 E
Tilemsi, Vallée du **85** 17 42N 0 15 E
Tilhar **69** 28 0N 79 45 E
Tilia, O. → **82** 27 32N 0 55 E
Tilichiki **59** 60 27N 166 5 E
Tiligul → **56** 47 4N 30 57 E
Tililane **82** 27 49N 0 6W
Tílissos **45** 35 2N 25 0 E
Till → **12** 55 35N 2 3W
Tillabéri **85** 14 28N 1 28 E
Tillamook **118** 45 29N 123 55W
Tillberga **48** 59 52N 16 39 E
Tillia **85** 16 8N 4 47 E
Tillsonburg **106** 42 53N 80 44W
Tílos **45** 36 27N 27 27 E
Tilpa **99** 30 57 S 144 24 E
Tilrhemt **82** 33 9N 3 22 E
Tilsit = Sovetsk **54** 55 6N 21 50 E
Tilt → **14** 56 50N 3 50W
Tilton **113** 43 25N 71 36W
Timagami L. **106** 47 0N 80 10W
Timanskiy Kryazh **52** 65 58N 50 5 E
Timaru **101** 44 23 S 171 14 E
Timashevsk **57** 45 35N 39 0 E
Timau, Italy **39** 46 35N 13 0 E
Timau, Kenya **90** 0 4N 37 15 E
Timbákion **45** 35 4N 24 45 E
Timbedgha **84** 16 17N 8 16W
Timber Lake **116** 45 29N 101 6W
Timboon **99** 38 30 S 142 58 E
Timbuktu = Tombouctou **84** 16 50N 3 0W
Timdjaouine **82** 21 37N 4 30 E
Timelloulíne **83** 29 22N 8 55 E
Timétrine Montagnes **85** 19 25N 1 0W
Timfi Óros **44** 39 59N 20 45 E
Timfristós, Óros **45** 38 57N 21 50 E
Timhadit **82** 33 15N 5 4W
Tîmia **85** 18 4N 8 40 E
Timimoun **82** 29 14N 0 16 E
Timimoun, Sebkha de **82** 28 50N 0 46 E
Timiş □ **42** 45 40N 21 30 E
Timiş → **46** 45 30N 21 0 E
Timişoara **42** 45 43N 21 15 E
Timmins **106** 48 28N 81 25W
Timok → **42** 44 10N 22 40 E
Timon **127** 5 8 S 42 52W
Timor **73** 9 0 S 125 0 E
Timor □ **73** 9 0 S 125 0 E
Timor Sea **97** 10 0 S 127 0 E
Tin Alkoum **83** 24 42N 10 17 E
Tin Gornai **85** 16 38N 0 38W
Tin Gornaï → **85** 20 30N 4 35 E
Tîna, Khalîg el **86** 31 20N 32 42 E
Tinaca Pt. **73** 5 30N 125 25 E
Tinafak, O. → **83** 27 10N 7 0 E
Tinca **46** 46 46N 21 58 E
Tinchebray **18** 48 47N 0 45W
Tindivanam **70** 12 15N 79 41 E
Tindouf **82** 27 42N 8 10W
Tinee → **21** 43 55N 7 11 E
Tineo **30** 43 21N 6 27W
Tinerhir **82** 31 29N 5 31W
Tinfouchi **82** 28 52N 5 49W
Tinglev **49** 54 57N 9 13 E
Tingo Maria **126** 9 10 S 75 54W
Tingsryd **49** 56 31N 15 0 E
Tinjoub **82** 29 45N 5 40W
Tinnoset **47** 59 55N 9 3 E
Tinnsjø **47** 59 55N 8 54 E
Tinogasta **124** 28 5 S 67 32W
Tinos **45** 37 33N 25 8 E
Tiñoso, C. **33** 37 32N 1 6W
Tintina **124** 27 2 S 62 45W
Tintinara **99** 35 48 S 140 2 E
Tinto → **31** 37 12N 6 55W
Tioga **112** 41 54N 77 9W
Tioman, Pulau **71** 2 50N 104 10 E
Tione di Trento **38** 46 3N 10 44 E
Tionesta **112** 41 29N 79 28W
Tior **87** 6 26N 31 11 E
Tioulilin **82** 27 1N 0 2W
Tipongpani **67** 27 20N 95 55 E
Tipperary **15** 52 28N 8 10W
Tipperary □ **15** 52 37N 7 55W
Tipton, U.K. **13** 52 32N 2 4W
Tipton, Calif., U.S.A. **119** 36 3N 119 19W
Tipton, Ind., U.S.A. **114** 40 17N 86 0W
Tipton, Iowa, U.S.A. **116** 41 45N 91 12W
Tiptonville **117** 36 22N 89 30W
Tiptur **70** 13 15N 76 26 E
Tirahart, O. **82** 23 45N 3 10 E
Tirân **65** 32 45N 51 8 E
Tirân **86** 27 56N 34 45 E
Tirana **44** 41 18N 19 49 E
Tirana-Durrësi □ **44** 41 35N 20 0 E
Tirano **38** 46 13N 10 11 E
Tiraspol **56** 46 55N 29 35 E
Tirat Karmel **62** 32 46N 34 58 E
Tirat Yehuda **62** 32 1N 34 56 E
Tirat Zevi **62** 32 26N 35 31 E
Tiratimine **82** 25 56N 3 37 E
Tirdout **85** 16 7N 1 5W
Tire **64** 38 5N 27 50 E
Tirebolu **64** 40 58N 38 45 E
Tiree **14** 56 31N 6 55W
Tîrgovişte **46** 44 55N 25 27 E
Tîrgu Frumos **46** 47 12N 27 2 E
Tîrgu-Jiu **46** 45 5N 23 19 E
Tîrgu Mureş **46** 46 31N 24 38 E
Tîrgu Neamţ **46** 47 12N 26 25 E
Tîrgu Ocna **46** 46 16N 26 39 E
Tîrgu Secuiesc **46** 46 0N 26 10 E
Tirich Mir **66** 36 15N 71 55 E
Tiriola **41** 38 57N 16 32 E
Tirna → **70** 18 4N 76 57 E
Tîrnava Mare → **46** 46 15N 24 30 E
Tîrnava Mică → **46** 46 17N 24 30 E
Tîrnăveni **46** 46 19N 24 13 E
Tírnavos **44** 39 45N 22 18 E
Tîrnova **46** 45 23N 22 1 E
Tirodi **69** 21 40N 79 44 E
Tirol □ **26** 47 3N 10 43 E
Tirschenreuth **25** 49 51N 12 20 E
Tirso → **40** 39 52N 8 33 E
Tirso, L. del **40** 40 8N 8 56 E
Tiruchchirappalli **70** 10 45N 78 45 E
Tiruchendur **70** 8 30N 78 11 E
Tiruchengodu **70** 11 23N 77 56 E
Tirumangalam **70** 9 49N 77 58 E
Tirunelveli (Tinnevelly) **70** 8 45N 77 45 E
Tirupati **70** 13 39N 79 25 E
Tiruppattur **70** 12 30N 78 30 E
Tiruppur **70** 11 5N 77 22 E
Tiruturaipundi **70** 10 32N 79 41 E
Tiruvadaimarudur **70** 11 2N 79 27 E
Tiruvallar **70** 13 9N 79 57 E
Tiruvannamalai **70** 12 15N 79 5 E
Tiruvarur **70** 10 46N 79 38 E
Tiruvatipuram **70** 12 39N 79 33 E
Tiruvottiyur **70** 13 10N 80 22 E
Tisa → **42** 45 15N 20 17 E
Tisdale **109** 52 50N 104 0W
Tishomingo **117** 34 14N 96 38W
Tisjön **48** 60 56N 13 0 E
Tisnaren **48** 58 58N 15 56 E
Tišnov **27** 49 21N 16 25 E
Tisovec **27** 48 41N 19 56 E
Tissemsilt **82** 35 35N 1 50 E
Tissint **82** 29 57N 7 16W
Tissø **49** 55 35N 11 18 E
Tista → **69** 25 23N 89 43 E
Tisza → **27** 46 8N 20 2 E
Tiszaföldvár **27** 47 0N 20 14 E
Tiszafüred **27** 47 38N 20 50 E
Tiszalök **27** 48 0N 21 10 E
Tiszavasvári **27** 47 58N 21 18 E
Tit, Ahaggar, Alg. **83** 23 0N 5 10 E
Tit, Tademait, Alg. **82** 27 0N 1 29 E
Tit-Ary **59** 71 55N 127 2 E
Titaguas **32** 39 53N 1 6W
Titel **42** 45 10N 20 18 E
Titicaca, L. **126** 15 30 S 69 30W
Titilagarh **70** 20 15N 83 11 E
Titiwa **85** 12 14N 12 53 E
Titograd **42** 42 30N 19 19 E
Titov Veles **42** 41 46N 21 47 E
Titova Korenica **39** 44 45N 15 41 E
Titovo Užice **42** 43 55N 19 50 E
Titule **90** 3 15N 25 31 E
Titusville, Fla., U.S.A. **115** 28 37N 80 49W
Titusville, Pa., U.S.A. **114** 41 35N 79 39W
Tivaouane **84** 14 56N 16 45W
Tivat **42** 42 28N 18 43 E
Tiveden **49** 58 50N 14 30 E
Tiverton **13** 50 54N 3 30W
Tivoli **39** 41 58N 12 45 E
Tiwī **65** 22 45N 59 12 E
Tiyo **87** 14 41N 40 15 E
Tizga **82** 32 1N 5 9W
Ti'zi N'Isli **82** 32 28N 5 47W
Tizi-Ouzou **83** 36 42N 4 3 E
Tizimín **120** 21 0N 88 1W
Tiznit **82** 29 48N 9 45W
Tjeggelvas **50** 66 37N 17 45 E
Tjirebon = Cirebon **73** 6 45 S 108 32 E
Tjöme **47** 59 8N 10 26 E
Tjörn **49** 58 0N 11 35 E
Tkibuli **57** 42 26N 43 0 E
Tkvarcheli **57** 42 47N 41 42 E
Tlahualilo **120** 26 20N 103 30W
Tlaxcala **120** 19 20N 98 14W
Tlaxcala □ **120** 19 30N 98 20W
Tlaxiaco **120** 17 18N 97 40W
Tlell **108** 53 34N 131 56W
Tlemcen **82** 34 52N 1 21W
Tleta Sidi Bouguedra **82** 32 16N 9 59W
Tlumach, U.S.S.R. **54** 48 46N 25 0 E
Tlumach, U.S.S.R. **56** 48 51N 25 0 E
Tłuszcz **28** 52 25N 21 25 E
Tlyarata **57** 42 9N 46 26 E
Tmassah **83** 26 19N 15 51 E
Tnine d'Anglou **82** 29 50N 9 50W
Toad → **108** 59 25N 124 57W
Toala **73** 1 30 S 121 40 E
Toamasina **93** 18 10 S 49 25 E
Toamasina □ **93** 18 0 S 49 0 E
Toay **124** 36 43 S 64 38W
Toba **74** 34 30N 136 51 E
Toba, Danau **72** 2 40N 98 50 E
Toba Kakar **68** 31 30N 69 0 E
Toba Tek Singh **68** 30 55N 72 25 E
Tobago **121** 11 10N 60 30W
Tobarra **33** 38 37N 1 44W
Tobelo **73** 1 45N 127 56 E
Tobermorey **98** 22 12 S 137 51 E
Tobermory, Can. **106** 45 12N 81 40W
Tobermory, U.K. **14** 56 37N 6 4W
Tobin L. **109** 53 35N 103 30W
Toboali **72** 3 0 S 106 25 E
Tobol **58** 52 40N 62 39 E
Toboli **73** 0 38 S 120 5 E
Tobolsk **58** 58 15N 68 10 E
Tobruk = Tubruq **81** 32 7N 23 55 E
Tobyhanna **113** 41 10N 75 25W
Tocantinópolis **127** 6 20 S 47 25W
Tocantins → **127** 1 45 S 49 10W
Toccoa **115** 34 32N 83 17W
Toce → **38** 45 56N 8 29 E
Tochigi **74** 36 25N 139 45 E
Tochigi □ **74** 36 45N 139 45 E
Tocina **31** 37 37N 5 44W

Tocopilla Treuenbrietzen

Tocopilla **124** 22 5S 70 10W
Tocumwal **99** 35 51S 145 31 E
Tocuyo → **126** 11 3N 68 23W
Todeli **73** 1 38S 124 34 E
Todenyang **90** 4 35N 35 56 E
Todi **39** 42 47N 12 24 E
Todos os Santos, Baía de **127** 12 48S 38 38W
Todos Santos **120** 23 27N 110 13W
Todtnau **25** 47 50N 7 56 E
Toecé **85** 11 50N 1 16W
Tofield **108** 53 25N 112 40W
Tofino **108** 49 11N 125 55W
Töfsingdalens nationalpark **48** 62 15N 12 44 E
Toftlund **49** 55 11N 9 2 E
Tofua **101** 19 45S 175 05W
Togba **84** 17 26N 10 12W
Togian, Kepulauan **73** 0 20S 121 50 E
Togliatti **55** 53 32N 49 24 E
Togo ■ **85** 6 15N 1 35 E
Togtoh **76** 40 15N 111 10 E
Toinya **87** 6 17N 29 46 E
Tojo **73** 1 20S 121 15 E
Tokaj **27** 48 8N 21 27 E
Tōkamachi **74** 37 8N 138 43 E
Tokanui **101** 46 34S 168 56 E
Tokar **81** 18 27N 37 56 E
Tokara Kaikyō **74** 30 0N 130 0 E
Tokarahi **101** 44 56S 170 39 E
Tokat **64** 40 22N 36 35 E
Tokelau Is. ■ **94** 9 0S 171 45W
Tokmak **58** 42 49N 75 15 E
Toko Ra. **98** 23 5S 138 20 E
Tokong **71** 5 27N 100 23 E
Tokushima **74** 34 4N 134 34 E
Tokushima □ **74** 34 15N 134 0 E
Tokuyama **74** 34 3N 131 50 E
Tōkyō **74** 35 45N 139 45 E
Tōkyō □ **74** 35 40N 139 30 E
Tolbukhin **43** 43 37N 27 49 E
Toledo, Spain **30** 39 50N 4 2W
Toledo, Ohio, U.S.A. **114** 41 37N 83 33W
Toledo, Oreg., U.S.A. **118** 44 40N 123 59W
Toledo, Wash., U.S.A. **118** 46 29N 122 51W
Toledo, Montes de **31** 39 33N 4 20W
Tolentino **39** 43 12N 13 17 E
Tolga, Alg. **83** 34 40N 5 22 E
Tolga, Norway **47** 62 26N 11 1 E
Toliara **93** 23 21S 43 40 E
Toliara □ **93** 21 0S 45 0 E
Tolima, Vol. **126** 4 40N 75 19W
Tolitoli **73** 1 5N 120 50 E
Tolkmicko **28** 54 19N 19 31 E
Tollarp **49** 55 55N 13 58 E
Tolleson **119** 33 29N 112 10W
Tolmachevo **54** 58 56N 29 51 E
Tolmezzo **39** 46 23N 13 0 E
Tolmin **39** 46 11N 13 45 E
Tolna **27** 46 25N 18 48 E
Tolna □ **27** 46 30N 18 30 E
Tolo **88** 2 55S 18 34 E
Tolo, Teluk **73** 2 20S 122 10 E
Tolochin **54** 54 25N 29 42 E
Tolosa **32** 43 8N 2 5W
Tolox **31** 36 41N 4 54W
Toluca **120** 19 20N 99 40W
Tom Burke **93** 23 5S 28 4 E
Tom Price **96** 22 40S 117 48 E
Tomah **116** 43 59N 90 30W
Tomahawk **116** 45 28N 89 40W
Tomar **31** 39 36N 8 25W
Tómaros Óros **44** 39 29N 20 48 E
Tomaszów Mazowiecki **28** 51 30N 19 57 E
Tombé **87** 5 53N 31 40 E
Tombigbee → **115** 31 4N 87 58W
Tombouctou **84** 16 50N 3 0W
Tombstone **119** 31 40N 110 4W
Tomé **124** 36 36S 72 57W
Tomelilla **49** 55 33N 13 58 E
Tomelloso **33** 39 10N 3 2W
Tomingley **99** 32 6S 148 16 E
Tomini **73** 0 30N 120 30 E
Tomini, Teluk **73** 0 10S 122 0 E
Tominian **84** 13 17N 4 35W
Tomiño **30** 41 59N 8 46W
Tommot **59** 59 4N 126 20 E
Tomnavoulin **14** 57 19N 3 18W
Toms River **113** 39 59N 74 12W
Tomsk **58** 56 30N 85 5 E
Tomtabacken **49** 57 30N 14 30 E
Tonalá **120** 16 8N 93 41W
Tonale, Passo del **38** 46 15N 10 34 E
Tonalea **119** 36 17N 110 58W
Tonantins **126** 2 45S 67 45W
Tonasket **118** 48 45N 119 30W
Tonawanda **114** 43 0N 78 54W
Tonbridge **13** 51 12N 0 18 E
Tondano **73** 1 35N 124 54 E
Tondela **30** 40 31N 8 5W
Tønder **49** 54 58N 8 50 E
Tondi **70** 9 45N 79 4 E
Tondi Kiwindi **85** 14 28N 2 02 E
Tondibi **85** 16 39N 0 14W
Tong Xian **76** 39 55N 116 35 E
Tonga ■ **101** 19 50S 174 30W
Tonga Trench **94** 18 0S 175 0W
Tongaat **93** 29 33S 31 9 E
Tongaland **93** 27 0S 32 0 E
Tongareva **95** 9 0S 158 0W
Tongatapu **101** 21 10S 174 0W
Tongcheng **77** 31 4N 116 56 E
Tongchuan **77** 35 6N 109 3 E
Tongdao **77** 26 10N 109 42 E
Tongeren **16** 50 47N 5 28 E
Tongguan **77** 34 40N 110 25 E
Tonghua **76** 41 42N 125 58 E
Tongio **99** 37 14S 147 44 E
Tongjiang, Heilongjiang, China **75** 47 40N 132 27 E
Tongjiang, Sichuan, China **77** 31 58N 107 11 E
Tongking = Tonkin, G. of **71** 20 0N 108 0 E
Tongliao **76** 43 38N 122 18 E
Tongling **77** 30 55N 117 48 E
Tonglu **77** 29 45N 119 37 E
Tongnan **77** 30 9N 105 50 E
Tongobory **93** 23 32S 44 20 E
Tongoy **124** 30 16S 71 31W
Tongren **75** 27 43N 109 11 E
Tongres = Tongeren **16** 50 47N 5 28 E
Tongue **14** 58 29N 4 25W
Tongue → **116** 46 24N 105 52W
Tongyu **76** 44 45N 123 4 E
Tongzi **77** 28 9N 106 49 E
Tonj **87** 7 20N 28 44 E
Tonk **68** 26 6N 75 54 E
Tonkawa **117** 36 44N 97 22W
Tonkin = Bac-Phan **71** 22 0N 105 0 E
Tonlé Sap **71** 13 0N 104 0 E
Tonnay-Charente **20** 45 56N 0 55W
Tonneins **20** 44 23N 0 19 E
Tonnerre **19** 47 51N 3 59 E
Tönning **24** 54 18N 8 57 E
Tonopah **119** 38 4N 117 12W
Tønsberg **47** 59 19N 10 25 E
Tonstad **47** 58 40N 6 45 E
Tonto Basin **119** 33 56N 111 27W
Tooele **118** 40 30N 112 20W
Toompine **99** 27 15S 144 19 E
Toonpan **98** 19 28S 146 48 E
Toora **99** 38 39S 146 23 E
Toora-Khem **59** 52 28N 96 17 E
Toowoomba **97** 27 32S 151 56 E
Top-ozero **52** 65 35N 32 0 E
Topalu **46** 44 31N 28 3 E
Topeka **116** 39 3N 95 40W
Topki **58** 55 20N 85 35 E
Topl'a → **27** 48 45N 21 45 E
Topley **108** 54 49N 126 18W
Toplica → **42** 43 15N 21 49 E
Toplița **46** 46 55N 25 20 E
Topocalma, Pta. **124** 34 10S 72 2W
Topock **119** 34 46N 114 29W
Topola **42** 44 17N 20 41 E
Topolčani **42** 41 14N 21 56 E
Topoľčany **27** 48 35N 18 12 E
Topoli **57** 47 59N 51 38 E
Topolnitsa → **43** 42 11N 24 18 E
Topolobampo **120** 25 40N 109 4W
Topolovgrad **43** 42 5N 26 20 E
Topolvățu Mare **42** 45 46N 21 41 E
Toppenish **118** 46 27N 120 16W
Topusko **39** 45 18N 15 59 E
Tor Bay **96** 35 5S 117 50 E
Torá **32** 41 49N 1 25 E
Tora Kit **87** 11 2N 32 36 E
Toraka Vestale **93** 16 20S 43 58 E
Torata **126** 17 23S 70 1W
Torbat-e Ḩeydārīyeh **65** 35 15N 59 12 E
Torbat-e Jām **65** 35 16N 60 35 E
Torbay, Can. **107** 47 40N 52 42W
Torbay, U.K. **13** 50 26N 3 31W
Tørdal **47** 59 10N 8 45 E
Tordesillas **30** 41 30N 5 0W
Tordoya **30** 43 6N 8 36W
Töreboda **49** 58 41N 14 7 E
Torey **59** 50 33N 104 50 E
Torfajökull **50** 63 54N 19 0W
Torgau **24** 51 32N 13 0 E
Torgelow **24** 53 40N 13 59 E
Torhout **16** 51 5N 3 7 E
Tori **87** 7 53N 33 35 E
Torigni-sur-Vire **18** 49 3N 0 58W
Torija **32** 40 44N 3 2W
Torin **120** 27 33N 110 15W
Toriñana, C. **30** 43 3N 9 17W
Torino **38** 45 4N 7 40 E
Torit **87** 4 27N 32 31 E
Torkovichi **54** 58 51N 30 21 E
Tormac **42** 45 30N 21 30 E
Tormentine **107** 46 6N 63 46W
Tormes → **30** 41 18N 6 29W
Tornado Mt. **108** 49 55N 114 40W
Torne älv → **50** 65 50N 24 12 E
Torneträsk **50** 68 24N 19 15 E
Tornio **50** 65 50N 24 12 E
Tornionjoki → **50** 65 50N 24 12 E
Tornquist **124** 38 8S 62 15W
Toro **30** 41 35N 5 24W
Torö **49** 58 48N 17 50 E
Toro, Cerro del **124** 29 10S 69 50W
Toro, Pta. **120** 9 22N 79 57W
Törökszentmiklós **27** 47 11N 20 27 E
Toroníios Kólpos **44** 40 5N 23 30 E
Toronto, Austral. **99** 33 0S 151 30 E
Toronto, Can. **106** 43 39N 79 20W
Toronto, U.S.A. **114** 40 27N 80 36W
Toronto, L. **120** 27 40N 105 30W
Toropets **54** 56 30N 31 40 E
Tororo **90** 0 45N 34 12 E
Toros Dağlari **64** 37 0N 35 0 E
Torpshammar **48** 62 29N 16 20 E
Torquay, Can. **109** 49 9N 103 30W
Torquay, U.K. **13** 50 27N 3 31W
Torquemada **30** 42 2N 4 19W
Torralba de Calatrava **31** 39 1N 3 44W
Torrão **31** 38 16N 8 11W
Torre Annunziata **41** 40 45N 14 26 E
Tôrre de Moncorvo **30** 41 12N 7 8W
Torre del Greco **41** 40 47N 14 22 E
Torre del Mar **31** 36 44N 4 6W
Torre-Pacheco **33** 37 44N 0 57W
Torre Pellice **38** 44 49N 7 13 E
Torreblanca **32** 40 14N 0 12 E
Torrecampo **31** 38 29N 4 41W
Torrecilla en Cameros **32** 42 15N 2 38W
Torredembarra **32** 41 9N 1 24 E
Torredonjimeno **31** 37 46N 3 57W
Torrejoncillo **30** 39 54N 6 28W
Torrelaguna **32** 40 50N 3 38W
Torrelavega **30** 43 20N 4 5W
Torremaggiore **41** 41 42N 15 17 E
Torremolinos **31** 36 38N 4 30W
Torrens Cr. → **98** 22 23S 145 9 E
Torrens Creek **98** 20 48S 145 3 E
Torrens, L. **97** 31 0S 137 50 E
Torrente **33** 39 27N 0 28W
Torrenueva **33** 38 38N 3 22W
Torréon **120** 25 33N 103 25W
Torreperogil **33** 38 2N 3 17W
Torres **120** 28 46N 110 47W
Torres Novas **31** 39 27N 8 33W
Torres Strait **97** 9 50S 142 20 E
Torres Vedras **31** 39 5N 9 15W
Torrevieja **33** 37 59N 0 42W
Torrey **119** 38 18N 111 25W
Torridge → **13** 50 51N 4 10W
Torridon, L. **14** 57 35N 5 50W
Torrijos **30** 39 59N 4 18W
Torrington, Conn., U.S.A. **114** 41 50N 73 9W
Torrington, Wyo., U.S.A. **116** 42 5N 104 8W
Torroella de Montgri **32** 42 2N 3 8 E
Torrox **31** 36 46N 3 57W
Torsås **49** 56 24N 16 0 E
Torsby **48** 60 7N 13 0 E
Torsö **49** 58 48N 13 45 E
Tortola **121** 18 19N 65 0W
Tórtoles de Esgueva **30** 41 49N 4 2W
Tortona **38** 44 53N 8 54 E
Tortoreto **39** 42 50N 13 55 E
Tortorici **41** 38 2N 14 48 E
Tortosa **32** 40 49N 0 31 E
Tortosa, C. **32** 40 41N 0 52 E
Tortosendo **30** 40 15N 7 31W
Tortue, Î. de la **121** 20 5N 72 57W
Tortuga, La **126** 11 0N 65 22W
Ţorūd **65** 35 25N 55 5 E
Toruń **28** 53 0N 18 39 E
Toruń □ **28** 53 20N 19 0 E
Torup, Denmark **49** 57 5N 9 5 E
Torup, Sweden **49** 56 57N 13 5 E
Tory I. **15** 55 17N 8 12W
Torysa → **27** 48 39N 21 21 E
Torzhok **54** 57 5N 34 55 E
Tosa-Wan **74** 33 15N 133 30 E
Toscana **38** 43 30N 11 5 E
Toscano, Arcipelago **38** 42 30N 10 30 E
Tosno **54** 59 38N 30 46 E
Tossa **32** 41 43N 2 56 E
Tostado **124** 29 15S 61 50W
Tostedt **24** 53 17N 9 42 E
Tosya **64** 41 1N 34 2 E
Toszek **28** 50 27N 18 32 E
Totak **47** 59 40N 7 45 E
Totana **33** 37 45N 1 30W
Toten **47** 60 37N 10 53 E
Toteng **92** 20 22S 22 58 E
Tôtes **18** 49 41N 1 3 E
Tótkomlós **27** 46 24N 20 45 E
Totma **55** 60 0N 42 40 E
Totnes **13** 50 26N 3 41W
Totonicapán **120** 14 58N 91 12W
Totten Glacier **5** 66 45S 116 10 E
Tottenham, Austral. **99** 32 14S 147 21 E
Tottenham, Can. **112** 44 1N 79 49W
Tottori **74** 35 30N 134 15 E
Tottori □ **74** 35 30N 134 12 E
Touat **82** 27 27N 0 30 E
Touba **84** 8 22N 7 40W
Toubkal, Djebel **82** 31 0N 8 0W
Toucy **19** 47 44N 3 15 E
Tougan **84** 13 11N 2 58W
Touggourt **83** 33 10N 6 0 E
Tougué **84** 11 25N 11 50W
Toukmatine **83** 24 49N 7 11 E
Toul **19** 48 40N 5 53 E
Toulepleu **84** 6 32N 8 24W
Toulon **21** 43 10N 5 55 E
Toulouse **20** 43 37N 1 27 E
Toummo **83** 22 45N 14 8 E
Toummo Dhoba **83** 22 30N 14 31 E
Toumodi **84** 6 32N 5 4W
Tounassine, Hamada **82** 28 48N 5 0W
Toungoo **67** 19 0N 96 30 E
Touques → **18** 49 22N 0 8 E
Touquet-Paris-Plage, Le **19** 50 30N 1 36 E
Tour-du-Pin, La **21** 45 33N 5 27 E
Touraine **18** 47 20N 0 30 E
Tourcoing **19** 50 42N 3 10 E
Tournai **16** 50 35N 3 25 E
Tournan-en-Brie **19** 48 44N 2 46 E
Tournay **20** 43 13N 0 13 E
Tournon **21** 45 4N 4 50 E
Tournon-St-Martin **18** 46 45N 0 58 E
Tournus **21** 46 35N 4 54 E
Tours **18** 47 22N 0 40 E
Touside, Pic **83** 21 1N 16 29 E
Touwsrivier **92** 33 20S 20 0 E
Tovarkovskiy **55** 53 40N 38 14 E
Tovdal **47** 58 47N 8 10 E
Tovdalselva → **47** 58 15N 8 5 E
Towamba **99** 37 6S 149 43 E
Towanda **114** 41 46N 76 30W
Towang **67** 27 37N 91 50 E
Tower **116** 47 49N 92 17W
Towerhill Cr. → **98** 22 28S 144 35 E
Towner **116** 48 25N 100 26W
Townsend **118** 46 25N 111 32W
Townshend, C. **97** 22 18S 150 30 E
Townshend I. **97** 22 10S 150 31 E
Townsville **97** 19 15S 146 45 E
Towson **114** 39 26N 76 34W
Towyn **13** 52 36N 4 5W
Toyah **117** 31 20N 103 48W
Toyahvale **117** 30 58N 103 45W
Toyama **74** 36 40N 137 15 E
Toyama □ **74** 36 45N 137 30 E
Toyama-Wan **74** 37 0N 137 30 E
Toyohashi **74** 34 45N 137 25 E
Toyokawa **74** 34 48N 137 27 E
Toyonaka **74** 34 50N 135 28 E
Toyooka **74** 35 35N 134 48 E
Toyota **74** 35 3N 137 7 E
Tozeur **83** 33 56N 8 8 E
Trabancos → **30** 41 36N 5 15W
Traben Trarbach **25** 49 57N 7 7 E
Trabzon **64** 41 0N 39 45 E
Tracadie **107** 47 30N 64 55W
Tracy, Calif., U.S.A. **119** 37 46N 121 27W
Tracy, Minn., U.S.A. **116** 44 12N 95 38W
Tradate **38** 45 43N 8 54 E
Trafalgar **100** 38 14S 146 12 E
Trafalgar, C. **31** 36 10N 6 2W
Trăgħăn **83** 26 0N 14 30 E
Traian **46** 45 2N 28 15 E
Trail **108** 49 5N 117 40W
Trainor L. **108** 60 24N 120 17W
Tralee **15** 52 16N 9 42W
Tralee B. **15** 52 17N 9 55W
Tramore **15** 52 10N 7 10W
Tran Ninh, Cao Nguyen **71** 19 30N 103 10 E
Tranås **49** 58 3N 14 59 E
Trancas **124** 26 11S 65 20W
Tranche, La **20** 46 20N 1 26W
Tranche-sur-Mer, La **18** 46 20N 1 27W
Trancoso **30** 40 49N 7 21W
Tranebjerg **49** 55 51N 10 36 E
Tranemo **49** 57 30N 13 20 E
Trang **71** 7 33N 99 38 E
Trangahy **93** 19 7S 44 31 E
Trangan **73** 6 40S 134 20 E
Trangie **99** 32 4S 148 0 E
Trångsviken **48** 63 19N 14 0 E
Trani **41** 41 17N 16 24 E
Tranoroa **93** 24 42S 45 4 E
Tranquebar **70** 11 1N 79 54 E
Tranqueras **125** 31 13S 55 45W
Trans Nzoia □ **90** 1 0N 35 0 E
Transcona **109** 49 55N 97 0W
Transilvania **46** 46 19N 25 0 E
Transkei □ **93** 32 15S 28 15 E
Transtrand **48** 61 6N 13 20 E
Transvaal □ **92** 25 0S 29 0 E
Transylvania = Transilvania **46** 46 19N 25 0 E
Transylvanian Alps **46** 45 30N 25 0 E
Trápani **40** 38 1N 12 30 E
Trapper Peak **118** 45 56N 114 29W
Traralgon **97** 38 12S 146 34 E
Traryd **49** 56 35N 13 45 E
Trarza □ **84** 17 30N 15 0W
Trasacco **39** 41 58N 13 30 E
Trăscău, Munţii **46** 46 14N 23 14 E
Trasimeno, L. **39** 43 10N 12 5 E
Trat **71** 12 14N 102 33 E
Traun **26** 48 14N 14 15 E
Traunsee **26** 47 55N 13 50 E
Traunstein **25** 47 52N 12 40 E
Tråvad **49** 58 15N 13 5 E
Traveller's L. **99** 33 20S 142 0 E
Travemünde **24** 53 58N 10 52 E
Travers, Mt. **101** 42 1S 172 45 E
Traverse City **114** 44 45N 85 39W
Traverse Is. **5** 57 0S 28 0W
Travnik **42** 44 17N 17 39 E
Trazo **30** 43 0N 8 30W
Trbovlje **39** 46 12N 15 5 E
Trébbia → **38** 45 4N 9 41 E
Trebel → **24** 53 55N 13 1 E
Třebíč **26** 49 14N 15 55 E
Trebinje **42** 42 44N 18 22 E
Trebisacce **41** 39 52N 16 32 E
Trebišnica → **42** 42 47N 18 8 E
Trebišov **27** 48 38N 21 41 E
Trebižat → **42** 43 15N 17 30 E
Trebnje **39** 45 54N 15 1 E
Třeboň **26** 48 59N 14 48 E
Trebujena **31** 36 52N 6 11W
Trecate **38** 45 26N 8 42 E
Tredegar **13** 51 47N 3 16W
Tregaron **13** 52 14N 3 56W
Trégastel-Plage **18** 48 49N 3 31W
Tregnago **39** 45 31N 11 10 E
Tréguier **18** 48 47N 3 16W
Trégune **18** 47 51N 3 51W
Treherne **109** 49 38N 98 42W
Tréia **39** 43 20N 13 20 E
Treignac **20** 45 32N 1 48 E
Treinta y Tres **125** 33 16S 54 17W
Treis **25** 50 9N 7 19 E
Treklyano **42** 42 33N 22 36 E
Trekveld **92** 30 35S 19 45 E
Trelde Næs **49** 55 38N 9 53 E
Trelew **128** 43 10S 65 20W
Trélissac **20** 45 11N 0 47 E
Trelleborg **49** 55 20N 13 10 E
Trélon **19** 50 5N 4 6 E
Tremblade, La **20** 45 46N 1 8W
Tremiti **39** 42 8N 15 30 E
Tremonton **118** 41 45N 112 10W
Tremp **32** 42 10N 0 52 E
Trenary **114** 46 12N 86 59W
Trenche → **106** 47 46N 72 53W
Trenčín **27** 48 52N 18 4 E
Trenggalek **73** 8 5S 111 38 E
Trenque Lauquen **124** 36 5S 62 45W
Trent → **12** 53 33N 0 44W
Trentino-Alto Adige □ **38** 46 30N 11 0 E
Trento **38** 46 5N 11 8 E
Trenton, Can. **106** 44 10N 77 34W
Trenton, Mo., U.S.A. **116** 40 5N 93 37W
Trenton, N.J., U.S.A. **114** 40 15N 74 41W
Trenton, Nebr., U.S.A. **116** 40 14N 101 4W
Trenton, Tenn., U.S.A. **117** 35 58N 88 57W
Trepassey **107** 46 43N 53 25W
Tréport, Le **18** 50 3N 1 20 E
Trepuzzi **41** 40 26N 18 4 E
Tres Arroyos **124** 38 26S 60 20W
Três Corações **125** 21 44S 45 15W
Três Lagoas **127** 20 50S 51 43W
Tres Marías **120** 21 25N 106 28W
Tres Montes, C. **128** 46 50S 75 30W
Três Pontas **125** 21 23S 45 29W
Tres Puentes **124** 27 50S 70 15W
Tres Puntas, C. **128** 47 0S 66 0W
Três Rios **125** 22 6S 43 15W
Treska → **42** 42 0N 21 20 E
Treskavika Planina **42** 43 40N 18 20 E
Trespaderne **32** 42 47N 3 24W
Trets **21** 43 27N 5 41 E
Treuchtlingen **25** 48 58N 10 55 E
Treuenbrietzen **24** 52 6N 12 51 E

Treviglio Tyldal

Treviglio 38 45 31N 9 35 E
Trevinca, Peña 30 42 15N 6 46W
Treviso 39 45 40N 12 15 E
Trévoux 21 45 57N 4 47 E
Treysa 24 50 55N 9 12 E
Trgovište 42 42 20N 22 10 E
Triabunna 99 42 30S 147 55 E
Triánda 45 36 25N 28 10 E
Triaucourt-en-Argonne 19 48 59N 5 2 E
Tribsees 24 54 4N 12 46 E
Tribulation, C. 97 16 5S 145 29 E
Tribune 116 38 30N 101 45W
Tricárico 41 40 37N 16 9 E
Tricase 41 39 56N 18 20 E
Trichinopoly = Tiruchchirappalli 70 10 45N 78 45 E
Trichur 70 10 30N 76 18 E
Trida 99 33 1S 145 1 E
Trier 25 49 45N 6 37 E
Trieste 39 45 39N 13 45 E
Trieste, G. di 39 45 37N 13 40 E
Trieux → 18 48 50N 3 3W
Triggiano 41 41 4N 16 58 E
Triglav 39 46 21N 13 50 E
Trigno → 39 42 4N 14 48 E
Trigueros 31 37 24N 6 50W
Trikeri 45 39 6N 23 5 E
Trikhonis, Límni 45 38 34N 21 30 E
Tríkkala 44 39 34N 21 47 E
Tríkkala □ 44 39 41N 21 30 E
Trikora, Puncak 73 4 15S 138 45 E
Trilj 39 43 38N 16 42 E
Trillo 32 40 42N 2 35W
Trim 15 53 34N 6 48W
Trincomalee 70 8 38N 81 15 E
Trindade, I. 7 20 20S 29 50W
Trinidad, Boliv. 126 14 46S 64 50W
Trinidad, Colomb. 126 5 25N 71 40W
Trinidad, Cuba 121 21 48N 80 0W
Trinidad, Uruguay 124 33 30S 56 50W
Trinidad, U.S.A. 117 37 15N 104 30W
Trinidad, W. Indies 121 10 30N 61 15W
Trinidad & Tobago ■ 121 10 30N 61 20W
Trinidad → 120 17 49N 95 9W
Trinidad, I. 128 39 10S 62 0W
Trinitápoli 41 41 22N 16 5 E
Trinity, Can. 107 48 59N 53 55W
Trinity, U.S.A. 117 30 59N 95 25W
Trinity →, Calif., U.S.A. 118 41 11N 123 42W
Trinity →, Tex., U.S.A. 117 30 30N 95 0W
Trinity B., Austral. 97 16 30S 146 0 E
Trinity B., Can. 107 48 20N 53 10W
Trinity Mts. 118 40 20N 118 50W
Trinkitat 81 18 45N 37 51 E
Trino 38 45 10N 8 18 E
Trion 115 34 35N 85 18W
Trionto C. 41 39 38N 16 47 E
Triora 38 44 0N 7 46 E
Tripoli = Tarābulus, Leb. 64 34 31N 35 50 E
Tripoli = Tarābulus, Libya 83 32 58N 13 12 E
Tripolis 45 37 31N 22 25 E
Tripp 116 43 16N 97 58W
Tripura □ 67 24 0N 92 0 E
Trischen 24 54 3N 8 32 E
Tristan da Cunha 7 37 6S 12 20W
Trivandrum 70 8 41N 77 0 E
Trivento 41 41 48N 14 31 E
Trnava 27 48 23N 17 35 E
Trobriand Is. 98 8 30S 151 0 E
Trochu 108 51 50N 113 13W
Trodely I. 106 52 15N 79 26W
Troezen 45 37 25N 23 15 E
Trogir 39 43 32N 16 15 E
Troglav 39 43 56N 16 36 E
Trøgstad 47 59 37N 11 16 E
Tróia 41 41 22N 15 19 E
Troilus, L. 106 50 50N 74 35W
Troina 41 37 47N 14 34 E
Trois Fourches, Cap des 82 35 26N 2 58W
Trois-Pistoles 107 48 5N 69 10W
Trois-Riviéres 106 46 25N 72 34W
Troitsk 58 54 10N 61 35 E
Troitsko Pechorsk 52 62 40N 56 10 E
Trölladyngja 50 64 54N 17 16W
Trollhättan 49 58 17N 12 20 E
Trollheimen 47 62 46N 9 1 E
Troms fylke □ 50 68 56N 19 0 E
Tromsø 50 69 40N 18 56 E
Tronador 128 41 10S 71 50W
Trondheim 47 63 36N 10 25 E
Trondheimsfjorden 47 63 35N 10 30 E
Trönninge 49 56 37N 12 51 E
Trönö 48 61 22N 16 54 E
Tronto → 39 42 54N 13 55 E
Troon 14 55 33N 4 40W
Tropea 41 38 40N 15 53 E
Tropic 119 37 36N 112 4W
Tropoja 44 42 23N 20 10 E
Trossachs, The 14 56 14N 4 24W
Trostan 15 55 4N 6 10W
Trostberg 25 48 2N 12 33 E
Trostyanets 54 50 33N 34 59 E
Trotternish 14 57 32N 6 15W
Troup 117 32 10N 95 3W
Trout → 108 61 19N 119 51W
Trout L., N.W.T., Can. 108 60 40N 121 40W
Trout L., Ont., Can. 109 51 20N 93 15W
Trout Lake 106 46 10N 85 2W
Trout River 107 49 29N 58 8W
Trouville 18 49 21N 0 5 E
Trowbridge 13 51 18N 2 12W
Troy, Turkey 44 39 57N 26 12 E
Troy, Turkey 64 39 55N 26 20 E
Troy, Ala., U.S.A. 115 31 50N 85 58W
Troy, Idaho, U.S.A. 118 46 44N 116 46W
Troy, Kans., U.S.A. 116 39 47N 95 2W
Troy, Mo., U.S.A. 116 38 56N 90 59W
Troy, Montana, U.S.A. 118 48 30N 115 58W
Troy, N.Y., U.S.A. 114 42 45N 73 39W
Troy, Ohio, U.S.A. 114 40 0N 84 10W
Troyan 43 42 57N 24 43 E
Troyes 19 48 19N 4 3 E
Trpanj 42 43 1N 17 15 E
Trstena 27 49 21N 19 37 E
Trstenik 42 43 36N 21 0 E
Trubchevsk 54 52 33N 33 47 E
Trucial States = United Arab Emirates ■ 65 24 0N 54 30 E
Truckee 118 39 20N 120 11W
Trujillo, Hond. 121 16 0N 86 0W
Trujillo, Peru 126 8 6S 79 0W
Trujillo, Spain 31 39 28N 5 55W
Trujillo, U.S.A. 117 35 34N 104 44W
Trujillo, Venez. 126 9 22N 70 38W
Truk 94 7 25N 151 46 E
Trumann 117 35 42N 90 32W
Trumbull, Mt. 119 36 25N 113 8W
Trun 42 42 51N 22 38 E
Trun 18 48 50N 0 2 E
Trundle 99 32 53S 147 35 E
Trung-Phan 72 16 0N 108 0 E
Truro, Can. 107 45 21N 63 14W
Truro, U.K. 13 50 17N 5 2W
Trustrup 49 56 20N 10 46 E
Truth or Consequences 119 33 9N 107 16W
Trutnov 26 50 37N 15 54 E
Truyère → 20 44 38N 2 34 E
Tryavna 43 42 54N 25 25 E
Tryon 115 35 15N 82 16W
Tryonville 112 41 42N 79 48W
Trzcianka 28 53 3N 16 25 E
Trzciel 28 52 23N 15 50 E
Trzcińsko Zdrój 28 52 58N 14 35 E
Trzebiatów 28 54 3N 15 18 E
Trzebiez 28 53 38N 14 31 E
Trzebinia-Siersza 27 50 11N 19 18 E
Trzebnica 28 51 20N 17 1 E
Trzemeszno 28 52 33N 17 48 E
Tržič 39 46 22N 14 18 E
Tsageri 57 42 39N 42 46 E
Tsamandás 44 39 46N 20 21 E
Tsaratanana 93 16 47S 47 39 E
Tsaratanana, Mt. de 93 14 0S 49 0 E
Tsarevo = Michurin 43 42 9N 27 51 E
Tsarichanka 56 48 55N 34 30 E
Tsaritsáni 44 39 53N 22 14 E
Tsau 92 20 8S 22 22 E
Tsebrikovo 56 47 9N 30 10 E
Tselinograd 58 51 10N 71 30 E
Tsetserleg 75 47 36N 101 32 E
Tshabong 92 26 2S 22 29 E
Tshane 92 24 5S 21 54 E
Tshela 88 4 57S 13 4 E
Tshesebe 93 21 51S 27 32 E
Tshibeke 90 2 40S 28 35 E
Tshibinda 90 2 23S 28 43 E
Tshikapa 88 6 28S 20 48 E
Tshilenge 90 6 17S 23 48 E
Tshinsenda 91 12 20S 28 0 E
Tshofa 90 5 13S 25 16 E
Tshwane 92 22 24S 22 1 E
Tsigara 92 20 22S 25 54 E
Tsihombe 93 25 18S 45 29 E
Tsimlyansk 57 47 40N 42 6 E
Tsimlyanskoye Vdkhr. 57 48 0N 43 0 E
Tsinan = Jinan 76 36 38N 117 1 E
Tsineng 92 27 05S 23 05 E
Tsinga 44 41 23N 24 44 E
Tsinghai = Qinghai □ 75 36 0N 98 0 E
Tsingtao = Qingdao 76 36 5N 120 20 E
Tsinjomitondraka 93 15 40S 47 8 E
Tsiroanomandidy 93 18 46S 46 2 E
Tsivilsk 55 55 50N 47 25 E
Tsivory 93 24 4S 46 5 E
Tskhinali 53 42 22N 43 52 E
Tskhinvali 57 42 14N 44 1 E
Tsna → 55 54 55N 41 58 E
Tsodilo Hill 92 18 49S 21 43 E
Tsu 74 34 45N 136 25 E
Tsu L. 108 60 40N 111 52W
Tsuchiura 74 36 5N 140 15 E
Tsugaru-Kaikyō 74 41 35N 141 0 E
Tsumeb 92 19 9S 17 44 E
Tsumis 92 23 39S 17 29 E
Tsuruga 74 35 45N 136 2 E
Tsushima 74 34 20N 129 20 E
Tsvetkovo 56 49 8N 31 33 E
Tua → 30 41 13N 7 26W
Tual 73 5 38S 132 44 E
Tuam 15 53 30N 8 50W
Tuamotu Arch. 95 17 0S 144 0W
Tuamotu Ridge 95 20 0S 138 0W
Tuao 73 17 55N 122 22 E
Tuapse 57 44 5N 39 10 E
Tuatapere 101 46 8S 167 41 E
Tuba City 119 36 8N 111 18W
Tubac 119 31 37N 111 20W
Tuban 73 6 54S 112 3 E
Tubarão 125 28 30S 49 0W
Tūbās 62 32 20N 35 22 E
Tubau 72 3 10N 113 40 E
Tübingen 25 48 31N 9 4 E
Tubja, W. → 86 25 27N 38 45 E
Ṭubruq 81 32 7N 23 55 E
Tubuai Is. 95 25 0S 150 0W
Tucacas 126 10 48N 68 19W
Tuchodi → 108 58 17N 123 42W
Tuchola 28 53 33N 17 52 E
Tuchów 27 49 54N 21 1 E
Tucker's Town 121 32 17N 64 43W
Tucson 119 32 14N 110 59W
Tucumán □ 124 26 48S 66 2W
Tucumcari 117 35 12N 103 45W
Tucupita 126 9 2N 62 3W
Tucuruí 127 3 42S 49 44W
Tuczno 28 53 13N 16 10 E
Tudela 32 42 4N 1 39W
Tudela de Duero 30 41 37N 4 39W
Tudmur 64 34 36N 38 15 E
Tudor, Lac 107 55 50N 65 25W
Tudora 46 47 31N 26 45 E
Tuella → 30 41 30N 7 12W
Tufi 98 9 8S 149 19 E
Tuguegarao 73 17 35N 121 42 E
Tugur 59 53 44N 136 45 E
Tukangbesi, Kepulauan 73 6 0S 124 0 E
Tukarak I. 106 56 15N 78 45W
Tûkh 86 30 21N 31 12 E
Tukobo 84 5 1N 2 47W
Tūkrah 83 32 30N 20 37 E
Tuktoyaktuk 104 69 27N 133 2W
Tukums 54 57 2N 23 10 E
Tukuyu 91 9 17S 33 35 E
Tula, Hidalgo, Mexico 120 20 0N 99 20W
Tula, Tamaulipas, Mexico 120 23 0N 99 40W
Tula, Nigeria 85 9 51N 11 27 E
Tula, U.S.S.R. 55 54 13N 37 38 E
Tulak 65 33 55N 63 40 E
Tulancingo 120 20 5N 99 22W
Tulare 119 36 15N 119 26W
Tulare Lake 119 36 0N 119 53W
Tularosa 119 33 4N 106 1W
Tulbagh 92 33 16S 19 6 E
Tulcán 126 0 48N 77 43W
Tulcea 46 45 13N 28 46 E
Tulcea □ 46 45 0N 29 0 E
Tulchin 56 48 41N 28 49 E
Tulemalu L. 109 62 58N 99 25W
Tulgheş 46 46 58N 25 45 E
Tuli, Indon. 73 1 24S 122 26 E
Tuli, Zimb. 91 21 58S 29 13 E
Ṭūlkarm 62 32 19N 35 2 E
Tulla 117 34 35N 101 44W
Tullahoma 115 35 23N 86 12W
Tullamore, Austral. 99 32 39S 147 36 E
Tullamore, Ireland 15 53 17N 7 30W
Tulle 20 45 16N 1 46 E
Tullibigeal 99 33 25S 146 44 E
Tullins 21 45 18N 5 29 E
Tulln 26 48 20N 16 4 E
Tullow 15 52 48N 6 45W
Tullus 87 11 7N 24 31 E
Tully 98 17 56S 145 55 E
Ṭulmaythah 81 32 40N 20 55 E
Tulmur 98 22 40S 142 20 E
Tulnici 46 45 51N 26 38 E
Tulovo 43 42 33N 25 32 E
Tulsa 117 36 10N 96 0W
Tulsequah 108 58 39N 133 35W
Tulu Milki 87 9 55N 38 20 E
Tulu Welel 87 8 56N 34 47 E
Tulua 126 4 6N 76 11W
Tulun 59 54 32N 100 35 E
Tulungagung 72 8 5S 111 54 E
Tum 73 3 36S 130 21 E
Tuma 55 55 10N 40 30 E
Tuma → 121 13 6N 84 35W
Tumaco 126 1 50N 78 45W
Tumatumari 126 5 20N 58 55W
Tumba 48 59 12N 17 48 E
Tumba, L. 88 0 50S 18 0 E
Tumbarumba 99 35 44S 148 0 E
Tumbaya 124 23 50S 65 26W
Túmbes 126 3 37S 80 27W
Tumbwe 91 11 25S 27 15 E
Tumen 76 43 0N 129 50 E
Tumen Jiang → 76 42 20N 130 35 E
Tumeremo 126 7 18N 61 30W
Tumkur 70 13 18N 77 6 E
Tummel, L. 14 56 43N 3 55W
Tump 66 26 7N 62 16 E
Tumpat 71 6 11N 102 10 E
Tumsar 69 21 26N 79 45 E
Tumu 84 10 56N 1 56W
Tumucumaque, Serra 127 2 0N 55 0W
Tumut 97 35 16S 148 13 E
Tumwater 118 47 0N 122 58W
Tunas de Zaza 121 21 39N 79 34W
Tunbridge Wells 13 51 7N 0 16 E
Tuncurry 99 32 17S 152 29 E
Tunduru 91 11 8S 37 25 E
Tunduru □ 91 11 5S 37 22 E
Tundzha → 43 41 40N 26 35 E
Tune 47 59 16N 11 2 E
Tunga → 70 15 0N 75 50 E
Tunga Pass 67 29 0N 94 14 E
Tungabhadra → 70 15 57N 78 15 E
Tungabhadra Dam 70 15 0N 75 50 E
Tungaru 87 10 9N 30 52 E
Tungla 121 13 24N 84 21W
Tungnafellsjökull 50 64 45N 17 55W
Tungsten, Can. 108 61 57N 128 16W
Tungsten, U.S.A. 118 40 50N 118 10W
Tunguska, Nizhnyaya → 59 65 48N 88 4 E
Tunguska, Podkamennaya → 59 61 36N 90 18 E
Tuni 70 17 22N 82 36 E
Tunica 117 34 43N 90 23W
Tunis 83 36 50N 10 11 E
Tunis, Golfe de 83 37 0N 10 30 E
Tunisia ■ 83 33 30N 9 10 E
Tunja 126 5 33N 73 25W
Tunkhannock 113 41 32N 75 46W
Tunliu 76 36 13N 112 52 E
Tunnsjøen 50 64 45N 13 25 E
Tunungayualok I. 107 56 0N 61 0W
Tunuyán 124 33 35S 69 0W
Tunuyán → 124 33 33S 67 30W
Tunxi 75 29 42N 118 25 E
Tuolumne 119 37 59N 120 16W
Tuoy-Khaya 59 62 32N 111 25 E
Tupã 125 21 57S 50 28W
Tupelo 115 34 15N 88 42W
Tupik, U.S.S.R. 54 55 42N 33 22 E
Tupik, U.S.S.R. 59 54 26N 119 57 E
Tupinambaranas 126 3 0S 58 0W
Tupiza 124 21 30S 65 40W
Tupižnica 42 43 43N 22 10 E
Tupper 108 55 32N 120 1W
Tupper L. 114 44 18N 74 30W
Tupungato, Cerro 124 33 15S 69 50W
Tuquan 76 45 18N 121 38 E
Tuque, La 106 47 30N 72 50W
Túquerres 126 1 5N 77 37W
Tura, India 69 25 30N 90 16 E
Tura, U.S.S.R. 59 64 20N 100 17 E
Turaba, Wadi → 86 21 15N 41 32 E
Turabah 64 28 20N 43 15 E
Turaiyur 70 11 9N 78 38 E
Tūrān 65 35 39N 56 42 E
Turan 59 51 55N 95 0 E
Turayf 64 31 41N 38 39 E
Turbacz 27 49 30N 20 8 E
Turbe 42 44 15N 17 35 E
Turda 46 46 34N 23 47 E
Turégano 30 41 9N 4 1W
Turek 28 52 3N 18 30 E
Turfan = Turpan 75 43 58N 89 10 E
Turfan Depression = Turpan Hami 75 42 40N 89 25 E
Tŭrgovishte 43 43 17N 26 38 E
Turgutlu 64 38 30N 27 48 E
Turhal 56 40 24N 36 5 E
Turia → 33 39 27N 0 19W
Turiaçu 127 1 40S 45 19W
Turiaçu → 127 1 36S 45 19W
Turiec → 27 49 07N 18 55 E
Turin 108 49 47N 112 24W
Turin = Torino 38 45 3N 7 40 E
Turka 54 49 10N 23 2 E
Turkana □ 90 3 0N 35 30 E
Turkana, L. 90 3 30N 36 5 E
Turkestan 58 43 17N 68 16 E
Túrkeve 27 47 6N 20 44 E
Turkey ■ 64 39 0N 36 0 E
Turki 55 52 0N 43 15 E
Turkmen S.S.R. □ 58 39 0N 59 0 E
Turks Is. 121 21 20N 71 20W
Turks Island Passage 121 21 30N 71 30W
Turku 51 60 30N 22 19 E
Turkwe → 90 3 6N 36 6 E
Turlock 119 37 30N 120 55W
Turnagain → 108 59 12N 127 35W
Turnagain, C. 101 40 28S 176 38 E
Turneffe Is. 120 17 20N 87 50W
Turner 118 48 52N 108 25W
Turner Valley 108 50 40N 114 17W
Turners Falls 113 42 36N 72 34W
Turnhout 16 51 19N 4 57 E
Türnitz 26 47 55N 15 29 E
Turnor L. 109 56 35N 108 35W
Turnov 26 50 34N 15 10 E
Tŭrnovo 43 43 5N 25 41 E
Turnovo 43 43 5N 25 41 E
Turnu Măgurele 46 43 46N 24 56 E
Turnu Rosu Pasul 46 45 33N 24 17 E
Turnu-Severin 46 44 39N 22 41 E
Turobin 28 50 50N 22 44 E
Turon 117 37 48N 98 27W
Turpan 75 43 58N 89 10 E
Turpan Hami 75 42 40N 89 25 E
Turrës, Kalaja e 44 41 10N 19 28 E
Turriff 14 57 32N 2 28W
Tursha 55 56 55N 47 36 E
Tursi 41 40 15N 16 27 E
Turtle Hd. I. 98 10 56S 142 37 E
Turtle L., Can. 109 53 36N 108 38W
Turtle L., U.S.A. 116 45 22N 92 10W
Turtle Lake 116 47 30N 100 55W
Turtleford 109 53 23N 108 57W
Turukhansk 59 65 21N 88 5 E
Turun ja Porin lääni □ 51 60 27N 22 15 E
Turzovka 27 49 25N 18 35 E
Tuscaloosa 115 33 13N 87 31W
Tuscánia 39 42 25N 11 53 E
Tuscany = Toscana 38 43 28N 11 15 E
Tuscola, Ill., U.S.A. 114 39 48N 88 15W
Tuscola, Tex., U.S.A. 117 32 15N 99 48W
Tuscumbia 115 34 42N 87 42W
Tuskar Rock 15 52 12N 6 10W
Tuskegee 115 32 24N 85 39W
Tustna 47 63 10N 8 5 E
Tuszyn 28 51 36N 19 33 E
Tutayev 55 57 53N 39 32 E
Tuticorin 70 8 50N 78 12 E
Tutin 42 43 0N 20 20 E
Tutóia 127 2 45S 42 20W
Tutong 72 4 47N 114 40 E
Tutova → 46 46 20N 27 30 E
Tutrakan 43 44 2N 26 40 E
Tutshi L. 108 59 56N 134 30W
Tuttle 116 47 9N 100 00W
Tuttlingen 25 47 59N 8 50 E
Tutuala 73 8 25S 127 15 E
Tutuila 101 14 19S 170 50W
Tuva A.S.S.R. □ 59 51 30N 95 0 E
Tuvalu ■ 94 8 0S 178 0 E
Tuxpan 120 20 58N 97 23W
Tuxtla Gutiérrez 120 16 50N 93 10W
Tuy 30 42 3N 8 39W
Tuy Hoa 71 13 5N 109 10 E
Tuya L. 108 59 7N 130 35W
Tuyen Hoa 71 17 50N 106 10 E
Tuz Gölü 64 38 45N 33 30 E
Ṭūz Khurmātū 64 34 56N 44 38 E
Tuzla 42 44 34N 18 41 E
Tuzlov → 57 47 28N 39 45 E
Tvååker 49 57 4N 12 25 E
Tvedestrand 47 58 38N 8 58 E
Tvŭrditsa 43 42 42N 25 53 E
Twardogóra 28 51 23N 17 28 E
Tweed 112 44 29N 77 19W
Tweed → 14 55 42N 2 10W
Tweedsmuir Prov. Park 108 53 0N 126 20W
Twentynine Palms 119 34 10N 116 4W
Twillingate 107 49 42N 54 45W
Twin Bridges 118 45 33N 112 23W
Twin Falls 118 42 30N 114 30W
Twin Valley 116 47 18N 96 15W
Twisp 118 48 21N 120 5W
Twistringen 24 52 48N 8 38 E
Two Harbors 116 47 1N 91 40W
Two Hills 108 53 43N 111 52W
Two Rivers 114 44 10N 87 31W
Twofold B. 97 37 8S 149 59 E
Tychy 27 50 9N 18 59 E
Tyczyn 27 49 58N 22 2 E
Tydal 47 63 4N 11 34 E
Tykocin 28 53 13N 22 46 E
Tyldal 47 62 8N 10 48 E

Tyler Uvira

Tyler, Minn., U.S.A. **116** 44 18N 96 8W
Tyler, Tex., U.S.A. **117** 32 18N 95 18W
Týn nad Vltavou **26** 49 13N 14 26 E
Tynda **59** 55 10N 124 43 E
Tyne & Wear □ **12** 54 55N 1 35W
Tyne → **12** 54 58N 1 28W
Tynemouth **12** 55 1N 1 27W
Tynset **47** 62 17N 10 47 E
Tyre = Sūr **62** 33 12N 35 11 E
Tyrifjorden **47** 60 2N 10 8 E
Tyringe **49** 56 9N 13 35 E
Tyristrand **47** 60 5N 10 5 E
Tyrnyauz **57** 43 21N 42 45 E
Tyrol = Tirol **26** 47 3N 10 43 E
Tyrone **112** 40 39N 78 10W
Tyrrell → **100** 35 26 S 142 51 E
Tyrrell Arm **109** 62 27N 97 30W
Tyrrell, L. **99** 35 20 S 142 50 E
Tyrrell L. **109** 63 7N 105 27W
Tyrrhenian Sea **34** 40 0N 12 30 E
Tysfjorden **50** 68 7N 16 25 E
Tysnes **47** 60 1N 5 30 E
Tysnesøy **47** 60 0N 5 35 E
Tyssedal **47** 60 7N 6 35 E
Tystberga **49** 58 51N 17 15 E
Tyub Karagan, M. **57** 44 40N 50 19 E
Tyuleniy **57** 44 28N 47 30 E
Tyulgan **52** 52 22N 56 12 E
Tyumen **58** 57 11N 65 29 E
Tywi → **13** 51 48N 4 20W
Tzaneen **93** 23 47 S 30 9 E
Tzermiadhes Neápolis **46** 35 11N 25 29 E
Tzoumérka, Óros **44** 39 30N 21 26 E
Tzukong = Zigong **75** 29 15N 104 48 E

U

Uad Erni, O. → **82** 26 45N 10 47W
Uanda **98** 21 37 S 144 55 E
Uarsciek **63** 2 28N 45 55 E
Uasin □ **90** 0 30N 35 20 E
Uato-Udo **73** 9 7 S 125 36 E
Uatumã → **126** 2 26 S 57 37W
Uaupés **126** 0 8 S 67 5W
Ub **42** 44 28N 20 6 E
Ubá **125** 21 8 S 43 0W
Ubaitaba **127** 14 18 S 39 20W
Ubangi = Oubangi → **88** 1 0N 17 50 E
Ubauro **68** 28 15N 69 45 E
Ubaye → **21** 44 28N 6 18 E
Ube **74** 33 56N 131 15 E
Ubeda **33** 38 3N 3 23W
Uberaba **127** 19 50 S 47 55W
Uberlândia **127** 19 0 S 48 20W
Überlingen **25** 47 46N 9 10 E
Ubiaja **85** 6 41N 6 22 E
Ubombo **93** 27 31 S 32 4 E
Ubon Ratchathani **71** 15 15N 104 50 E
Ubondo **90** 0 55 S 25 42 E
Ubort → **54** 52 6N 28 30 E
Ubrique **31** 36 41N 5 27W
Ubundu **90** 0 22 S 25 30 E
Ucayali → **126** 4 30 S 73 30W
Uchi Lake **109** 51 5N 92 35W
Uchiura-Wan **74** 42 25N 140 40 E
Uchte **24** 52 29N 8 52 E
Uchur → **59** 58 48N 130 35 E
Ucluelet **108** 48 57N 125 32W
Ucuriş **46** 46 41N 21 58 E
Uda → **59** 54 42N 135 14 E
Udaipur **68** 24 36N 73 44 E
Udaipur Garhi **69** 27 0N 86 35 E
Udamalpet **70** 10 35N 77 15 E
Udbina **39** 44 31N 15 47 E
Uddeholm **48** 60 1N 13 38 E
Uddevalla **49** 58 21N 11 55 E
Uddjaur **50** 65 25N 21 15 E
Udgir **70** 18 25N 77 5 E
Udi **85** 6 23N 7 21 E
Údine **39** 46 5N 13 10 E
Udipi **70** 13 25N 74 42 E
Udmurt A.S.S.R. □ **52** 57 30N 52 30 E
Udon Thani **71** 17 29N 102 46 E
Udvoy Balkan **43** 42 50N 26 50 E
Udzungwa Range **91** 9 30 S 35 10 E
Ueckermünde **24** 53 45N 14 1 E
Ueda **74** 36 24N 138 16 E
Uedineniya, Os. **4** 78 0N 85 0 E
Uelen **59** 66 10N 170 0W
Uelzen **24** 53 0N 10 33 E
Uere → **88** 3 45N 24 45 E
Ufa **52** 54 45N 55 55 E
Ufa → **52** 54 40N 56 0 E
Uffenheim **25** 49 32N 10 15 E
Ugalla → **90** 5 8 S 30 42 E
Uganda ■ **90** 2 0N 32 0 E
Ugento **41** 39 55N 18 10 E
Ugep **85** 5 53N 8 2 E
Ugie **93** 31 10 S 28 13 E
Ugijar **33** 36 58N 3 7W
Ugine **21** 45 45N 6 25 E
Ugla **86** 25 40N 37 42 E
Uglegorsk **59** 49 5N 142 2 E
Uglich **55** 57 33N 38 20 E
Ugljane **39** 43 35N 16 46 E
Ugolyak **59** 64 33N 120 30 E
Ugra → **54** 54 30N 36 7 E
Ugûrchin **43** 43 6N 24 26 E
Uh → **27** 48 7N 21 25 E
Uherske Hradiště **27** 49 4N 17 30 E
Uhersky Brod **27** 49 1N 17 40 E
Úhlava → **26** 49 45N 13 24 E
Uhrichsville **114** 40 23N 81 22W
Uige **88** 7 30 S 14 40 E
Uiju **76** 40 15N 124 35 E
Uinta Mts. **118** 40 45N 110 30W
Uitenhage **92** 33 40 S 25 28 E
Uithuizen **16** 53 24N 6 41 E
Újfehértó **27** 47 49N 21 41 E

Ujhani **68** 28 0N 79 6 E
Ujjain **68** 23 9N 75 43 E
Újpest **27** 47 32N 19 6 E
Újszász **27** 47 19N 20 7 E
Ujung Pandang **73** 5 10 S 119 20 E
Uka **59** 57 50N 162 0 E
Ukara I. **90** 1 50 S 33 0 E
Ukerewe □ **90** 2 0 S 32 30 E
Ukerewe I. **90** 2 0 S 33 0 E
Ukholovo **55** 53 47N 40 30 E
Ukhrul **67** 25 10N 94 25 E
Ukhta **52** 63 55N 54 0 E
Ukiah **118** 39 10N 123 9W
Ukmerge **54** 55 15N 24 45 E
Ukrainian S.S.R. □ **56** 49 0N 32 0 E
Ukwi **92** 23 29 S 20 30 E
Ulaanbaatar **75** 47 54N 106 52 E
Ulaangom **75** 50 0N 92 10 E
Ulamba **91** 9 3 S 23 38 E
Ulan Bator = Ulaanbaatar **75** 47 54N 106 52 E
Ulan Ude **59** 51 45N 107 40 E
Ulanga □ **91** 8 40 S 36 50 E
Ulanów **28** 50 30N 22 16 E
Ulaya, Morogoro, Tanz. **90** 7 3 S 36 55 E
Ulaya, Tabora, Tanz. **90** 4 25 S 33 30 E
Ulcinj **42** 41 58N 19 10 E
Ulco **92** 28 21 S 24 15 E
Ulefoss **47** 59 17N 9 16 E
Ulëza **44** 41 46N 19 57 E
Ulfborg **49** 56 16N 8 20 E
Ulhasnagar **70** 19 15N 73 10 E
Uljma **42** 45 2N 21 10 E
Ulla → **30** 42 39N 8 44W
Ulladulla **99** 35 21 S 150 29 E
Ullånger **48** 62 58N 18 10 E
Ullapool **14** 57 54N 5 10W
Ullared **49** 57 8N 12 42 E
Ulldecona **32** 40 36N 0 20 E
Ullswater **12** 54 35N 2 52W
Ullung-do **76** 37 30N 130 30 E
Ulm **25** 48 23N 10 0 E
Ulmarra **99** 29 37 S 153 4 E
Ulmeni **46** 45 4N 26 40 E
Ulricehamn **49** 57 46N 13 26 E
Ulsberg **47** 62 45N 9 59 E
Ulsteinvik **47** 62 21N 5 53 E
Ulster □ **15** 54 35N 6 30W
Ulstrem **43** 42 1N 26 27 E
Ulubaria **69** 22 31N 88 4 E
Uluguru Mts. **90** 7 15 S 37 40 E
Ulungur He **75** 47 1N 87 24 E
Ulutau **58** 48 39N 67 1 E
Ulverston **12** 54 13N 3 7W
Ulverstone **97** 41 11 S 146 11 E
Ulvik **47** 60 35N 6 54 E
Ulya **59** 59 10N 142 0 E
Ulyanovsk **55** 54 20N 48 25 E
Ulyasutay (Javhlant) **75** 47 56N 97 28 E
Ulysses **117** 37 39N 101 25W
Umag **39** 45 26N 13 31 E
Umala **126** 17 25 S 68 5W
Uman **56** 48 40N 30 12 E
Umarkhed **70** 19 37N 77 46 E
Umatilla **118** 45 58N 119 17W
Umba **52** 66 50N 34 20 E
Umbertide **39** 43 18N 12 20 E
Umboi I. **98** 5 40 S 148 0 E
Umbrella Mts. **101** 45 35 S 169 5 E
Umbria □ **39** 42 53N 12 30 E
Ume älv → **50** 63 45N 20 20 E
Umeå **50** 63 45N 20 20 E
Umera **73** 0 12 S 129 37 E
Umfuli → **91** 17 30 S 29 23 E
Umgusa **91** 19 29 S 27 52 E
Umka **42** 44 40N 20 19 E
Umkomaas **93** 30 13 S 30 48 E
Umm al Arānib **83** 26 10N 14 43 E
Umm al Qaywayn **65** 25 30N 55 35 E
Umm Arda **87** 15 17N 32 31 E
Umm az Zamul **65** 22 42N 55 18 E
Umm Bel **87** 13 35N 28 0 E
Umm Dubban **87** 15 23N 32 52 E
Umm el Fahm **62** 32 31N 35 9 E
Umm Koweika **87** 13 10N 32 16 E
Umm Lajj **64** 25 0N 37 23 E
Umm Merwa **86** 18 4N 32 30 E
Umm Qays **62** 32 40N 35 41 E
Umm Rumah **86** 25 50N 36 30 E
Umm Ruwaba **87** 12 50N 31 20 E
Umm Sidr **87** 14 29N 25 10 E
Ummanz **24** 54 29N 13 9 E
Umnak **104** 53 20N 168 20W
Umniati → **91** 16 49 S 28 45 E
Umpang **71** 16 3N 98 54 E
Umpqua → **118** 43 42N 124 3W
Umrer **68** 20 51N 79 18 E
Umreth **68** 22 41N 73 4 E
Umshandige Dam **91** 20 10 S 30 40 E
* Umtali **91** 18 58 S 32 38 E
Umtata **93** 31 36 S 28 49 E
Umuahia **85** 5 33N 7 29 E
Umvukwe Ra. **91** 16 45 S 30 45 E
Umvukwes **91** 17 0 S 30 57 E
Umvuma **91** 19 16 S 30 30 E
Umzimvubu **93** 31 38 S 29 33 E
Umzingwane → **91** 22 12 S 29 56 E
Umzinto **93** 30 15 S 30 45 E
Una **68** 20 46N 71 8 E
Una → **39** 45 16N 16 55 E
Unac → **39** 44 30N 16 9 E
Unadilla **113** 42 20N 75 17W
Unalaska **104** 53 40N 166 40W
Uncastillo **32** 42 21N 1 8W
Uncía **126** 18 25 S 66 40W
Uncompahgre Pk. **119** 38 5N 107 32W
Unden **49** 58 45N 14 25 E
Underbool **99** 35 10 S 141 51 E
Undersaker **48** 63 19N 13 21 E
Undersvik **48** 61 36N 16 20 E
Undredal **47** 60 57N 7 6 E
Unecha **54** 52 50N 32 37 E
Ungarie **99** 33 38 S 146 56 E

* Renamed Mutare

Ungava B. **105** 59 30N 67 30W
Ungeny **56** 47 11N 27 51 E
Unggi **76** 42 16N 130 28 E
Ungwatiri **87** 16 52N 36 10 E
Uni **55** 56 44N 51 47 E
União da Vitória **125** 26 13 S 51 5W
Uniejów **28** 51 59N 18 46 E
Unije **39** 44 40N 14 15 E
Unimak **104** 55 0N 164 0W
Unimak Pass. **104** 53 30N 165 15W
Union, Miss, U.S.A. **117** 32 34N 89 14W
Union, Mo., U.S.A. **116** 38 25N 91 0W
Union, S.C., U.S.A. **115** 34 43N 81 39W
Union City, N.J., U.S.A. **113** 40 47N 74 5W
Union City, Ohio, U.S.A. **114** 40 11N 84 49W
Union City, Pa., U.S.A. **114** 41 53N 79 50W
Union City, Tenn., U.S.A. **117** 36 25N 89 0W
Union Gap **118** 46 38N 120 29W
Unión, La, Chile **128** 40 10 S 73 0W
Unión, La, El Sal. **120** 13 20N 87 50W
Unión, La, Spain **33** 37 38N 0 53W
Union, Mt. **119** 34 34N 112 21W
Union of Soviet Socialist Republics ■ **59** 60 0N 100 0 E
Union Springs **115** 32 9N 85 44W
Uniondale **92** 33 39 S 23 7 E
Uniontown **114** 39 54N 79 45W
Unionville **116** 40 29N 93 1W
Unirea **46** 44 15N 27 35 E
United Arab Emirates ■ **65** 23 50N 54 0 E
United Kingdom ■ **11** 55 0N 3 0W
United States of America ■ **111** 37 0N 96 0W
United States Trust Terr. of the Pacific Is. **94** 10 0N 160 0 E
Unity **109** 52 30N 109 5W
Universales, Mtes. **32** 40 18N 1 33W
Unjha **68** 23 46N 72 24 E
Unnao **69** 26 35N 80 30 E
Uno, Ilha **84** 11 15N 16 13W
Unst **14** 60 50N 0 55W
Unstrut → **24** 51 10N 11 48 E
Unuk → **108** 56 5N 131 3W
Ünye **56** 41 5N 37 15 E
Unzha **55** 58 0N 44 0 E
Unzha → **55** 57 30N 43 40 E
Upa → **27** 50 35N 16 15 E
Upata **126** 8 1N 62 24W
Upemba, L. **91** 8 30 S 26 20 E
Upernavik **4** 72 49N 56 20W
Upington **92** 28 25 S 21 15 E
Upleta **68** 21 46N 70 16 E
Upolu **101** 13 58 S 172 0W
Upper Alkali Lake **118** 41 47N 120 8W
Upper Arrow L. **108** 50 30N 117 50W
Upper Austria = Oberösterreich **26** 48 10N 14 0 E
Upper Foster L. **109** 56 47N 105 20W
Upper Hutt **101** 41 8 S 175 5 E
Upper Klamath L. **118** 42 16N 121 55W
Upper L. Erne **15** 54 14N 7 22W
Upper Lake **118** 39 10N 122 55W
Upper Musquodoboit **107** 45 10N 62 58W
Upper Red L. **116** 48 0N 95 0W
Upper Sandusky **114** 40 50N 83 17W
Upper Taimyr → **59** 74 15N 99 48 E
*Upper Volta ■ **84** 12 0N 1 0W
Upphärad **49** 58 9N 12 19 E
Uppsala **48** 59 53N 17 38 E
Uppsala län □ **48** 60 0N 17 30 E
Upstart, C. **98** 19 41 S 147 45 E
Upton **116** 44 8N 104 35W
Ur **64** 30 55N 46 25 E
Uracara **126** 2 20 S 57 50W
Urach **25** 48 29N 9 25 E
Urad Qianqi **76** 40 40N 108 30 E
Ural → **58** 47 0N 51 48 E
Ural, Mt. **99** 33 21 S 146 12 E
Ural Mts. = Uralskie Gory **52** 60 0N 59 0 E
Uralla **99** 30 37 S 151 29 E
Uralsk **52** 51 20N 51 20 E
Uralskie Gory **52** 60 0N 59 0 E
Urambo **90** 5 4 S 32 0 E
Urambo □ **90** 5 0 S 32 0 E
Urana **100** 35 15 S 146 21 E
Urandangie **97** 21 32 S 138 14 E
Uranium City **109** 59 34N 108 37W
Uravakonda **70** 14 57N 77 12 E
Urawa **74** 35 50N 139 40 E
Uray **58** 60 5N 65 15 E
Urbana, Ill., U.S.A. **114** 40 7N 88 12W
Urbana, Ohio, U.S.A. **114** 40 9N 83 44W
Urbana, La **126** 7 8N 66 56W
Urbánia **39** 43 40N 12 31 E
Urbel → **32** 42 21N 3 40W
Urbino **39** 43 43N 12 38 E
Urbión, Picos de **32** 42 1N 2 52W
Urcos **126** 13 40 S 71 38W
Urda, Spain **31** 39 25N 3 43W
Urda, U.S.S.R. **57** 48 52N 47 23 E
Urdinarrain **124** 32 37 S 58 52W
Urdos **20** 42 51N 0 35W
Urdzhar **58** 47 5N 81 38 E
Ure → **12** 54 20N 1 25W
Uren **55** 57 35N 45 55 E
Urengoy **58** 65 58N 28 25 E
Ures **120** 29 30N 110 30W
Urfa **64** 37 12N 38 50 E
Urfahr **26** 48 19N 14 17 E
Urgench **58** 41 40N 60 41 E
Uri □ **25** 46 43N 8 35 E
Uribia **126** 11 43N 72 16W
Urim **62** 31 18N 34 32 E
Uriondo **124** 21 41 S 64 41W
Urique → **120** 26 29N 107 58W
Urk **16** 52 39N 5 36 E
Urla **64** 38 20N 26 47 E
Urlati **46** 44 59N 26 15 E
Urmia = Rezā'īyeh **64** 37 40N 45 0 E
Urmia, L. = Rezā'īyeh, Daryācheh-ye **64** 37 30N 45 30 E
Uroševac **42** 42 23N 21 10 E
Urshult **49** 56 31N 14 50 E
Ursus **28** 52 12N 20 53 E

*Renamed Burkina Faso

Uruana **127** 15 30 S 49 41W
Uruapan **120** 19 30N 102 0W
Urubamba **126** 13 20 S 72 10W
Urubamba → **126** 10 43 S 73 48W
Uruçuí **127** 7 20 S 44 28W
Uruguai → **125** 26 0 S 53 30W
Uruguaiana **124** 29 50 S 57 0W
Uruguay ■ **124** 32 30 S 56 30W
Uruguay → **124** 34 12 S 58 18W
Urumchi = Ürümqi **75** 43 45N 87 45 E
Ürümqi **75** 43 45N 87 45 E
Urup → **57** 46 0N 41 10 E
Urup, Os. **59** 46 0N 151 0 E
Uryung-Khaya **59** 72 48N 113 23 E
Uryupinsk **55** 50 45N 41 58 E
Urzhum **55** 57 10N 49 56 E
Urziceni **46** 44 40N 26 42 E
Usa → **52** 65 67N 56 55 E
Uşak **64** 38 43N 29 28 E
Usakos **92** 22 0 S 15 31 E
Ušće **42** 43 30N 20 39 E
Usedom **24** 53 50N 13 55 E
Usfan **86** 21 58N 39 27 E
Ush-Tobe **58** 45 16N 78 0 E
Ushakova, O. **4** 82 0N 80 0 E
Ushant = Ouessant, Île d' **18** 48 25N 5 5W
Ushashi **90** 1 59 S 33 57 E
Ushat **87** 7 59N 29 28 E
Ushuaia **128** 54 50 S 68 23W
Ushumun **59** 52 47N 126 32 E
Usk → **13** 51 37N 2 56W
Uskedal **47** 59 56N 5 53 E
Üsküdar **64** 41 0N 29 5 E
Uslar **24** 51 39N 9 39 E
Usman **55** 52 5N 39 48 E
Usoke **90** 5 7 S 32 19 E
Usolye Sibirskoye **59** 52 48N 103 40 E
Usoro **85** 5 33N 6 11 E
Uspallata, P. de **124** 32 37 S 69 22W
Uspenskiy **58** 48 41N 72 43 E
Ussel **20** 45 32N 2 18 E
Ussuriysk **59** 43 48N 131 59 E
Ust-Aldan = Batamay **59** 63 30N 129 15 E
Ust Amginskoye = Khandyga **59** 62 42N 135 0 E
Ust-Bolsheretsk **59** 52 50N 156 15 E
Ust Buzulukskaya **55** 50 8N 42 11 E
Ust chaun **59** 68 47N 170 30 E
Ust-Donetskiy **57** 47 35N 40 55 E
Ust'-Ilga **59** 55 5N 104 55 E
Ust Ilimpeya = Yukti **59** 63 20N 105 0 E
Ust-Ilimsk **59** 58 3N 102 39 E
Ust Ishim **58** 57 45N 71 10 E
Ust-Kamchatsk **59** 56 10N 162 28 E
Ust-Kamenogorsk **58** 50 0N 82 36 E
Ust-Karenga **59** 54 25N 116 30 E
Ust Khayryuzova **59** 57 15N 156 45 E
Ust-Kut **59** 56 50N 105 42 E
Ust Kuyga **59** 70 1N 135 43 E
Ust-Labinsk **57** 45 15N 39 41 E
Ust Luga **54** 59 35N 28 20 E
Ust Maya **59** 60 30N 134 28 E
Ust-Mil **59** 59 40N 133 11 E
Ust-Nera **59** 64 35N 143 15 E
Ust-Nyukzha **59** 56 34N 121 37 E
Ust Olenek **59** 73 0N 119 48 E
Ust-Omchug **59** 61 9N 149 38 E
Ust Port **58** 69 40N 84 26 E
Ust Tsilma **52** 65 25N 52 0 E
Ust-Tungir **59** 55 25N 120 36 E
Ust Urt = Ustyurt, Plato **58** 44 0N 55 0 E
Ust Usa **52** 66 0N 56 30 E
Ust Vorkuta **58** 67 24N 64 0 E
Ustaoset **47** 60 30N 8 2 E
Ustaritz **20** 43 24N 1 27W
Uste **55** 59 35N 39 40 E
Ústí nad Labem **26** 50 41N 14 3 E
Ústí nad Orlicí **27** 49 58N 16 24 E
Ustica **40** 38 42N 13 10 E
Ustka **28** 54 35N 16 55 E
Ustroń **27** 49 43N 18 48 E
Ustrzyki Dolne **27** 49 27N 22 40 E
Ustye **59** 57 46N 94 37 E
Ustyurt, Plato **58** 44 0N 55 0 E
Ustyuzhna **55** 58 50N 36 32 E
Usu **75** 44 27N 84 40 E
Usuki **74** 33 8N 131 49 E
Usulután **120** 13 25N 88 28W
Usumacinta → **120** 17 0N 91 0W
Usure **90** 4 40 S 34 22 E
Uta **73** 4 33 S 136 0 E
Utah □ **118** 39 30N 111 30W
Utah, L. **118** 40 10N 111 58W
Ute Cr. **117** 35 21N 103 45W
Utena **54** 55 27N 25 40 E
Ütersen **24** 53 40N 9 40 E
Utete **90** 8 0 S 38 45 E
Uthai Thani **71** 15 22N 100 3 E
Utiariti **126** 13 0 S 58 10W
Utica, N.Y., U.S.A. **114** 43 5N 75 18W
Utica, Ohio, U.S.A. **112** 40 13N 82 26W
Utiel **32** 39 37N 1 11W
Utik L. **109** 55 15N 96 0W
Utikuma L. **108** 55 50N 115 30W
Utrecht, Neth. **16** 52 5N 5 8 E
Utrecht, S. Afr. **93** 27 38 S 30 20 E
Utrecht □ **16** 52 6N 5 7 E
Utrera **31** 37 12N 5 48W
Utsjoki **50** 69 51N 26 59 E
Utsunomiya **74** 36 30N 139 50 E
Uttar Pradesh □ **69** 27 0N 80 0 E
Uttaradit **71** 17 36N 100 5 E
Uttoxeter **12** 52 53N 1 50W
Ütze **24** 52 28N 10 11 E
Uusikaarlepyy **50** 63 32N 22 31 E
Uusikaupunki **51** 60 47N 21 25 E
Uva **52** 56 59N 52 13 E
Uvac → **42** 43 35N 19 40 E
Uvalde **117** 29 15N 99 48W
Uvarovo **55** 51 59N 42 14 E
Uvat **58** 59 5N 68 50 E
Uvinza **90** 5 5 S 30 24 E
Uvira **90** 3 22 S 29 3 E

Uvs Nuur Verdigre

Uvs Nuur	75	50 20N	92 30 E
Uwajima	74	33 10N	132 35 E
Uweinat, Jebel	86	21 54N	24 58 E
Uxbridge	112	44 6N	79 7W
Uxin Qi	76	38 50N	109 5 E
Uxmal	120	20 22N	89 46W
Uyandi	59	69 19N	141 0 E
Uyo	85	5 1N	7 53 E
Uyuni	126	20 28S	66 47W
Uzbek S.S.R. □	58	41 30N	65 0 E
Uzen	53	43 27N	53 10 E
Uzen, Bol. →	55	50 0N	49 30 E
Uzen, Mal. →	55	50 0N	48 30 E
Uzerche	20	45 25N	1 34 E
Uzès	21	44 1N	4 26 E
Uzh →	54	51 15N	30 12 E
Uzhgorod	54	48 36N	22 18 E
Uzlovaya	55	54 0N	38 5 E
Uzunköprü	43	41 16N	26 43 E
V			
Vaal →	92	29 4S	23 38 E
Vaaldam	93	27 0S	28 14 E
Vaalwater	93	24 15S	28 8 E
Vaasa	50	63 6N	21 38 E
Vaasan lääni □	50	63 2N	22 50 E
Vabre	20	43 42N	2 24 E
Vác	27	47 49N	19 10 E
Vacaria	125	28 31S	50 52W
Vacaville	118	38 21N	122 0W
Vaccarès, Étang de	21	43 32N	4 34 E
Vach →	58	60 45N	76 45 E
Vache, Î.-à-	121	18 2N	73 35W
Väddö	48	59 55N	18 50 E
Vadnagar	68	23 47N	72 40 E
Vado Lígure	38	44 16N	8 26 E
Vadodara	68	22 20N	73 10 E
Vadsø	50	70 3N	29 50 E
Vadstena	49	58 28N	14 54 E
Vaduz	25	47 8N	9 31 E
Værøy	50	67 40N	12 40 E
Vagney	19	48 1N	6 43 E
Vagnhärad	48	58 57N	17 33 E
Vagos	30	40 33N	8 42W
Váh →	27	47 55N	18 0 E
Vahsel B.	5	75 0S	35 0W
Vaigach	58	70 10N	59 0 E
Vaigai →	70	9 15N	79 10 E
Vaiges	18	48 2N	0 30W
Vaihingen	25	48 55N	8 58 E
Vaijapur	70	19 58N	74 45 E
Vaikam	70	9 45N	76 25 E
Vailly Aisne	19	49 25N	3 30 E
Vaippar →	70	9 0N	78 25 E
Vaison	21	44 14N	5 4 E
Vajpur	68	21 24N	73 17 E
Vakarel	43	42 35N	23 40 E
Vaksdal	47	60 29N	5 45 E
Vál	27	47 22N	18 40 E
Val-d'Ajol, Le	19	47 55N	6 30 E
Val-de-Marne □	19	48 45N	2 28 E
Val-d'Oise □	19	49 5N	2 10 E
Val d'Or	106	48 7N	77 47W
Val Marie	109	49 15N	107 45W
Valadares	30	41 5N	8 38W
Valahia	46	44 35N	25 0 E
Valais □	25	46 12N	7 45 E
Valandovo	42	41 19N	22 34 E
Valašské Meziříčí	27	49 29N	17 59 E
Valáxa	45	38 50N	24 29 E
Vâlcani	42	46 0N	20 26 E
Valcheta	128	40 40S	66 8W
Valdagno	39	45 38N	11 18 E
Valdahon, Le	19	47 8N	6 20 E
Valday	54	57 58N	33 9 E
Valdayskaya Vozvyshennost	54	57 0N	33 30 E
Valdeazogues →	31	38 45N	4 55W
Valdemarsvik	49	58 14N	16 40 E
Valdepeñas, Ciudad Real, Spain	31	38 43N	3 25W
Valdepeñas, Jaén, Spain	31	37 33N	3 47W
Valderaduey →	30	41 31N	5 42W
Valderrobres	32	40 53N	0 9 E
Valdés, Pen.	128	42 30S	63 45W
Valdez	104	61 14N	76 17W
Valdivia	128	39 50S	73 14W
Valdobbiádene	39	45 53N	12 0 E
Valdosta	115	30 50N	83 20W
Valdoviño	30	43 36N	8 8W
Valdres	47	60 55N	9 28 E
Vale, U.S.A.	118	44 0N	117 15W
Vale, U.S.S.R.	57	41 30N	42 58 E
Valea lui Mihai	46	47 32N	22 11 E
Valença, Brazil	127	13 20S	39 5W
Valença, Port.	30	42 1N	8 34W
Valença do Piauí	127	6 20S	41 45W
Valençay	19	47 9N	1 34 E
Valence	21	44 57N	4 54 E
Valence-d'Agen	20	44 8N	0 54 E
Valencia, Spain	33	39 27N	0 23W
Valencia, Venez.	126	10 11N	68 0W
Valencia □	33	39 20N	0 40W
Valencia, Albufera de	33	39 20N	0 27W
Valencia de Alcántara	31	39 25N	7 14W
Valencia de Don Juan	30	42 17N	5 31W
Valencia del Ventoso	31	38 15N	6 29W
Valencia, G. de	33	39 30N	0 20 E
Valenciennes	19	50 20N	3 34 E
Văleni	46	44 15N	24 45 E
Valensole	21	43 50N	5 59 E
Valentia Hr.	15	51 56N	10 17W
Valentia I.	15	51 54N	10 22W
Valentim, Sa. do	127	6 0S	43 30W
Valentine, Nebr., U.S.A.	116	42 50N	100 35W
Valentine, Tex., U.S.A.	117	30 36N	104 28W
Valenza	38	45 2N	8 39 E
Våler	47	60 41N	11 50 E
Valera	126	9 19N	70 37W
Valga	54	57 44N	26 0 E
Valguarnera Caropepe	41	37 30N	14 22 E
Valier	118	48 25N	112 9W
Valinco, G. de	21	41 40N	8 52 E
Valjevo	42	44 18N	19 53 E
Valkenswaard	16	51 21N	5 29 E
Vall de Uxó	32	39 49N	0 15W
Valla	48	59 2N	16 20 E
Valladolid, Mexico	120	20 40N	88 11W
Valladolid, Spain	30	41 38N	4 43W
Valladolid □	30	41 38N	4 43W
Vallata	41	41 3N	15 16 E
Valldemosa	32	39 43N	2 37 E
Valle	47	59 13N	7 33 E
Valle d'Aosta □	38	45 45N	7 22 E
Valle de Arán	32	42 50N	0 55 E
Valle de Cabuérniga	30	43 14N	4 18W
Valle de la Pascua	126	9 13N	66 0W
Valle de Santiago	120	20 25N	101 15W
Valle Fértil, Sierra del	124	30 20S	68 0W
Valle Hermoso	120	25 35N	97 40W
Vallecas	30	40 23N	3 41W
Vallejo	118	38 12N	122 15W
Vallenar	124	28 30S	70 50W
Valleraugue	20	44 6N	3 39 E
Vallet	18	47 10N	1 15W
Valletta	36	35 54N	14 30 E
Valley City	116	46 57N	98 0W
Valley Falls	118	42 33N	120 16W
Valleyview	108	55 5N	117 17W
Valli di Comácchio	39	44 40N	12 15 E
Vallimanca, Arroyo	124	35 40S	59 10W
Vallo della Lucánia	41	40 14N	15 16 E
Vallon	21	44 25N	4 23 E
Vallorbe	25	46 42N	6 20 E
Valls	32	41 18N	1 15 E
Vallsta	48	61 31N	16 22 E
Valmaseda	32	43 11N	3 12W
Valmiera	54	57 37N	25 29 E
Valmont	18	49 45N	0 30 E
Valmontone	40	41 48N	12 55 E
Valmy	19	49 5N	4 45 E
Valnera, Mte.	32	43 9N	3 40W
Valognes	18	49 30N	1 28W
Valona = Vlóra	44	40 32N	19 28 E
Valongo	30	41 8N	8 30W
Valpaços	30	41 36N	7 17W
Valparaíso, Chile	124	33 2S	71 40W
Valparaíso, Mexico	120	22 50N	103 32W
Valparaiso	114	41 27N	87 2W
Valparaíso □	124	33 2S	71 40W
Valpovo	42	45 39N	18 25 E
Valréas	21	44 24N	5 0 E
Vals	25	46 39N	9 11 E
Vals →	92	27 23S	26 30 E
Vals-les-Bains	21	44 42N	4 24 E
Vals, Tanjung	73	8 26S	137 25 E
Valsbaai	92	34 15S	18 40 E
Valskog	48	59 27N	15 57 E
Válta	44	40 3N	23 25 E
Valtellina	38	46 9N	9 55 E
Valuyki	55	50 10N	38 5 E
Valverde del Camino	31	37 35N	6 47W
Valverde del Fresno	30	40 15N	6 51W
Vama	46	47 34N	25 42 E
Vámos	45	35 24N	24 13 E
Vamsadhara →	70	18 21N	84 8 E
Van	64	38 30N	43 20 E
Van Alstyne	117	33 25N	96 36W
Van Bruyssel	107	47 56N	72 9W
Van Buren, Can.	107	47 10N	67 55W
Van Buren, Ark., U.S.A.	117	35 28N	94 18W
Van Buren, Me., U.S.A.	115	47 10N	68 1W
Van Buren, Mo., U.S.A.	117	37 0N	91 0W
Van der Kloof Dam	92	30 04S	24 40 E
Van Diemen, C.	97	16 30S	139 46 E
Van Diemen G.	96	11 45S	132 0 E
Van Gölü	64	38 30N	43 0 E
Van Horn	117	31 3N	104 55W
Van Reenen P.	93	28 22S	29 27 E
Van Rees, Pegunungan	73	2 35S	138 15 E
Van Tassell	116	42 40N	104 3W
Van Tivu	70	8 51N	78 15 E
Van Wert	114	40 52N	84 31W
Vanavara	59	60 22N	102 16 E
Vancouver, Can.	108	49 15N	123 10W
Vancouver, U.S.A.	118	45 44N	122 41W
Vancouver I.	108	49 50N	126 0W
Vandalia, Ill., U.S.A.	116	38 57N	89 4W
Vandalia, Mo., U.S.A.	116	39 18N	91 30W
Vandeloos Bay	70	8 0N	81 45 E
Vanderbijlpark	93	26 42S	27 54 E
Vandergrift	114	40 36N	79 33W
Vanderhoof	108	54 0N	124 0W
Vanderlin I.	97	15 44S	137 2 E
Vandyke	98	24 10S	147 51 E
Vänern	49	58 47N	13 30 E
Vänersborg	49	58 26N	12 19 E
Vang Vieng	71	18 58N	102 32 E
Vanga	90	4 35S	39 12 E
Vangaindrano	93	23 21S	47 36 E
Vanguard	109	49 55N	107 20W
Vanier	106	45 27N	75 40W
Vanimo	98	2 42S	141 21 E
Vanivilasa Sagara	70	13 45N	76 30 E
Vaniyambadi	70	12 46N	78 44 E
Vankarem	59	67 51N	175 50 E
Vankleek Hill	106	45 32N	74 40W
Vanna	50	70 6N	19 50 E
Vännäs	50	63 58N	19 48 E
Vannes	18	47 40N	2 47W
Vanoise, Massif de la	21	45 25N	6 40 E
Vanrhynsdorp	92	31 36S	18 44 E
Vanrook	98	16 57S	141 57 E
Vans, Les	21	44 25N	4 7 E
Vansbro	48	60 32N	14 15 E
Vanse	47	58 6N	6 41 E
Vansittart B.	96	14 3S	126 17 E
Vanthli	68	21 28N	70 25 E
Vanua Levu	101	16 33S	179 15 E
Vanua Mbalavu	101	17 40S	178 57W
Vanwyksvlei	92	30 18S	21 49 E
Vanylven	47	62 5N	5 33 E
Vapnyarka	56	48 32N	28 45 E
Var □	21	43 27N	6 18 E
Var →	21	43 39N	7 12 E
Vara	49	58 16N	12 55 E
Varada →	70	15 0N	75 40 E
Varades	18	47 25N	1 1W
Varaita →	38	44 49N	7 36 E
Varaldsøy	47	60 6N	5 59 E
Varallo	38	45 50N	8 13 E
Varanasi (Benares)	69	25 22N	83 0 E
Varangerfjorden	50	70 3N	29 25 E
Varaždin	39	46 20N	16 20 E
Varazze	38	44 21N	8 36 E
Varberg	49	57 6N	12 20 E
Vardar →	42	40 35N	22 50 E
Varde	49	55 38N	8 29 E
Varde Å	49	55 35N	8 19 E
Varel	24	53 23N	8 9 E
Varena	54	54 12N	24 30 E
Varennes-sur-Allier	20	46 19N	3 24 E
Vareš	42	44 12N	18 23 E
Varese	38	45 49N	8 50 E
Varese Ligure	38	44 22N	9 33 E
Vårgårda	49	58 2N	12 49 E
Varginha	125	21 33S	45 25W
Vargön	49	58 22N	12 20 E
Varhaug	47	58 37N	5 41 E
Variadero	117	35 43N	104 17W
Varillas	124	24 0S	70 10W
Väring	49	58 30N	14 0 E
Värmeln	48	59 35N	12 54 E
Värmlands län □	48	60 0N	13 20 E
Varna	43	43 13N	27 56 E
Varna →	70	16 48N	74 32 E
Värnamo	49	57 10N	14 3 E
Varnsdorf	26	50 55N	14 35 E
Värö	49	57 16N	12 11 E
Vars	113	45 21N	75 21W
Varteig	47	59 23N	11 12 E
Varvarin	42	43 43N	21 20 E
Varzaneh	65	32 25N	52 40 E
Varzi	38	44 50N	9 12 E
Varzo	38	46 12N	8 15 E
Varzy	19	47 22N	3 20 E
Vas □	27	47 10N	16 55 E
Vasa	50	63 6N	21 38 E
Vasa Barris →	127	11 10S	37 10W
Vásárosnamény	27	48 9N	22 19 E
Vascão →	31	37 31N	7 31W
Vaşcău	46	46 28N	22 30 E
Vascongadas	32	42 50N	2 45W
Väse	48	59 23N	13 52 E
Vasht = Khāsh	65	28 14N	61 14 E
Vasilevichi	54	52 15N	29 50 E
Vasilikón	45	38 25N	23 40 E
Vasilkov	54	50 7N	30 15 E
Vaslui	46	46 38N	27 42 E
Vaslui □	46	46 30N	27 45 E
Väsman	48	60 9N	15 5 E
Vassar, Can.	109	49 10N	95 55W
Vassar, U.S.A.	114	43 23N	83 33W
Västerås	49	59 37N	16 38 E
Västerbottens län □	50	64 58N	18 0 E
Västernorrlands län □	48	63 30N	17 30 E
Västervik	49	57 43N	16 43 E
Västmanlands län □	48	59 45N	16 20 E
Vasto	39	42 8N	14 40 E
Vasvár	27	47 3N	16 47 E
Vatan	19	47 4N	1 50 E
Vathí, Itháki, Greece	45	38 18N	20 40 E
Vathí, Sámos, Greece	45	37 46N	27 1 E
Váthia	45	36 29N	22 29 E
Vatican City ■	39	41 54N	12 27 E
Vaticano, C.	40	38 40N	15 48 E
Vatin	42	45 12N	21 20 E
Vatnajökull	50	64 30N	16 48W
Vatnås	47	59 58N	9 37 E
Vatne	47	62 33N	6 38 E
Vatneyri	50	65 35N	24 0W
Vatoa	101	19 50S	178 13W
Vatoloha, Mt.	93	17 52S	47 48 E
Vatomandry	93	19 20S	48 59 E
Vatra-Dornei	46	47 22N	25 22 E
Vättern	49	58 25N	14 30 E
Vaucluse □	21	44 3N	5 10 E
Vaucouleurs	19	48 37N	5 40 E
Vaud □	25	46 35N	6 30 E
Vaughan	119	34 37N	105 12W
Vaughn	118	47 37N	111 36W
Vaupés →	126	0 2N	67 16W
Vauvert	21	43 42N	4 17 E
Vauxhall	108	50 5N	112 9W
Vava'u	101	18 36S	174 0W
Vavincourt	19	48 49N	5 12 E
Vavoua	84	7 23N	6 29W
Vaxholm	48	59 25N	18 20 E
Växjö	49	56 52N	14 50 E
Vaygach, Ostrov	58	70 0N	60 0 E
Vazovgrad	43	42 39N	24 45 E
Vechta	24	52 47N	8 18 E
Vechte →	16	52 34N	6 6 E
Vecilla, La	30	42 51N	5 27W
Vecsés	27	47 26N	19 19 E
Vedaraniam	70	10 25N	79 50 E
Veddige	49	57 17N	12 20 E
Vedea →	46	44 0N	25 20 E
Vedia	124	34 30S	61 31W
Vedra, I. del	33	38 52N	1 12 E
Veendam	16	53 5N	6 52 E
Veenendaal	16	52 2N	5 34 E
Vefsna →	50	65 48N	13 10 E
Vega, Norway	50	65 40N	11 55 E
Vega, U.S.A.	117	35 18N	102 26W
Vega, La	121	19 20N	70 30W
Vegadeo	30	43 27N	7 4W
Vegafjorden	50	65 37N	12 0 E
Vegesack	24	53 10N	8 38 E
Veggli	47	60 3N	9 9 E
Veghel	16	51 37N	5 32 E
Vegorritis, Limni	44	40 45N	21 45 E
Vegreville	108	53 30N	112 5W
Vegusdal	47	58 32N	8 10 E
Veii	39	42 0N	12 24 E
Vejen	49	55 30N	9 9 E
Vejer de la Frontera	31	36 15N	5 59W
Vejle	49	55 43N	9 30 E
Vejle Fjord	49	55 40N	9 50 E
Vela Luka	39	42 59N	16 44 E
Velanai I.	70	9 45N	79 45 E
Velarde	119	36 11N	106 1W
Velasco	117	29 0N	95 20W
Velasco, Sierra de.	124	29 20S	67 10W
Velay, Mts. du	20	45 0N	3 40 E
Velddrif	92	32 42S	18 11 E
Velebit Planina	39	44 50N	15 20 E
Velebitski Kanal	39	44 45N	14 55 E
Veleka →	43	42 4N	27 58 E
Velenje	39	46 23N	15 8 E
Velestínon	44	39 23N	22 43 E
Veleta, La	31	37 1N	3 22W
Vélez	126	6 1N	73 41W
Velež	42	43 19N	18 2 E
Vélez Blanco	33	37 41N	2 5W
Vélez Málaga	31	36 48N	4 5W
Vélez Rubio	33	37 41N	2 5W
Velhas →	127	17 13S	44 49W
Velika	42	45 27N	17 40 E
Velika Gorica	39	45 44N	16 5 E
Velika Gradište	42	44 46N	21 29 E
Velika Kapela	39	45 10N	15 5 E
Velika Kladuša	39	45 11N	15 48 E
Velika Morava →	42	44 43N	21 3 E
Velika Plana	42	44 20N	21 1 E
Velikaya →	54	57 48N	28 20 E
Velikaya Lepetikha	56	47 2N	33 58 E
Veliké Kapušany	27	48 34N	22 5 E
Velike Lašče	39	45 49N	14 45 E
Veliki Backa Kanal	42	45 45N	19 15 E
Veliki Jastrebac	42	43 25N	21 30 E
Veliki Popović	42	44 8N	21 18 E
Veliki Ustyug	52	60 47N	46 20 E
Velikiye Luki	54	56 25N	30 32 E
Velikonda Range	70	14 45N	79 10 E
Velikoye, Oz.	55	55 15N	40 10 E
Velingrad	43	42 4N	23 58 E
Velino, Mte.	39	42 10N	13 20 E
Velizh	54	55 36N	31 11 E
Velké Karlovice	27	49 20N	18 17 E
Velke Meziřici	26	49 21N	16 1 E
Vel'ký ostrov Žitný	27	48 5N	17 20 E
Vellar →	70	11 30N	79 36 E
Velletri	40	41 43N	12 43 E
Vellinge	49	55 29N	13 0 E
Vellore	70	12 57N	79 10 E
Velsen-Noord	16	52 27N	4 40 E
Velsk	52	61 10N	42 5 E
Velten	24	52 40N	13 11 E
Velva	116	48 6N	100 56W
Velvendós	44	40 15N	22 6 E
Vembanad Lake	70	9 36N	76 15 E
Veme	47	60 14N	10 7 E
Ven	49	55 55N	12 45 E
Vena	49	57 31N	16 0 E
Venado	120	22 56N	101 10W
Venado Tuerto	124	33 50S	62 0W
Venafro	41	41 28N	14 3 E
Venarey-les-Laumes	19	47 32N	4 26 E
Venaria	38	45 6N	7 39 E
Venčane	42	44 24N	20 28 E
Vence	21	43 43N	7 6 E
Vendas Novas	31	38 39N	8 27W
Vendée □	18	46 50N	1 35W
Vendée →	18	46 20N	1 10W
Vendée, Collines de	18	46 35N	0 45W
Vendeuvre-sur-Barse	19	48 14N	4 28 E
Vendôme	18	47 47N	1 3 E
Vendrell	32	41 10N	1 30 E
Vendsyssel	49	57 22N	10 0 E
Véneta, Laguna	39	45 23N	12 25 E
Véneto □	39	45 40N	12 0 E
Venev	55	54 22N	38 17 E
Venézia	39	45 27N	12 20 E
Venézia, Golfo di	39	45 20N	13 0 E
Venezuela ■	126	8 0N	65 0W
Venezuela, Golfo de	126	11 30N	71 0W
Vengurla	70	15 53N	73 45 E
Vengurla Rocks	70	15 55N	73 22 E
Venice = Venézia	39	45 27N	12 20 E
Vénissieux	21	45 43N	4 53 E
Venkatagiri	70	14 0N	79 35 E
Venkatapuram	70	18 20N	80 30 E
Venlo	16	51 22N	6 11 E
Vennesla	47	58 15N	8 0 E
Venraij	16	51 31N	6 0 E
Venta de Cardeña	31	38 16N	4 20W
Venta de San Rafael	30	40 42N	4 12W
Ventana, Punta de la	120	24 4N	109 48W
Ventana, Sa. de la	124	38 0S	62 30W
Ventersburg	92	28 7S	27 9 E
Ventimíglia	38	43 50N	7 39 E
Ventnor	13	50 35N	1 12W
Ventotene	40	40 48N	13 25 E
Ventoux	21	44 10N	5 17 E
Ventspils	54	57 25N	21 32 E
Ventuarí →	126	3 58N	67 2W
Ventura	119	34 16N	119 18W
Vera, Argent.	124	29 30S	60 20W
Vera, Spain	33	37 15N	1 51W
Veracruz	120	19 10N	96 10W
Veracruz □	120	19 0N	96 15W
Veraval	68	20 53N	70 27 E
Verbánia	38	45 56N	8 43 E
Verbicaro	41	39 46N	15 54 E
Vercelli	38	45 19N	8 25 E
Verchovchevo	56	48 32N	34 10 E
Verdalsøra	50	63 48N	11 30 E
Verde →, Argent.	128	41 56S	65 5W
Verde →, Chihuahua, Mexico	120	26 29N	107 58W
Verde →, Oaxaca, Mexico	120	15 59N	97 50W
Verde →, Veracruz, Mexico	120	21 10N	102 50W
Verde →, Parag.	124	23 9S	57 37W
Verde, Cay	121	23 0N	75 5W
Verden	24	52 58N	9 18 E
Verdhikoúsa	44	39 47N	21 59 E
Verdigre	116	42 38N	98 0W

Verdon Visoko

Verdon → 21 43 43N 5 46 E
Verdon-sur-Mer, Le 20 45 33N 1 4W
Verdun 19 49 12N 5 24 E
Verdun-sur-le Doubs 19 46 54N 5 0 E
Vereeniging 93 26 38 S 27 57 E
Vérendrye, Parc Prov. de la 106 47 20N 76 40W
Verga, C. 84 10 30N 14 10W
Vergara 32 43 9N 2 28W
Vergato 38 44 18N 11 8 E
Vergemont 98 23 33 S 143 1 E
Vergemont Cr. → 98 24 16 S 143 16 E
Vergennes 113 44 9N 73 15W
Vergt 20 45 2N 0 43 E
Verín 30 41 57N 7 27W
Veriña 30 43 32N 5 43W
Verkhnedvinsk 54 55 45N 27 58 E
Verkhnevilyuysk 59 63 27N 120 18 E
Verkhneye Kalinino 59 59 54N 108 8 E
Verkhniy Baskunchak 57 48 14N 46 44 E
Verkhovye 55 52 55N 37 15 E
Verkhoyansk 59 67 35N 133 25 E
Verkhoyanskiy Khrebet 59 66 0N 129 0 E
Verlo 109 50 19N 108 35W
Verma 47 62 21N 8 3 E
Vermenton 19 47 40N 3 42 E
Vermilion 109 53 20N 110 50W
Vermilion →, Alta., Can. 109 53 22N 110 51W
Vermilion →, Qué., Can. 106 47 38N 72 56W
Vermilion, B. 117 29 45N 91 55W
Vermilion Bay 109 49 51N 93 34W
Vermilion Chutes 108 58 22N 114 51W
Vermilion L. 116 47 53N 92 25W
Vermillion 116 42 50N 96 56W
Vermont □ 114 43 40N 72 50W
Vernal 118 40 28N 109 35W
Verner 106 46 25N 80 8W
Verneuil-sur-Avre 18 48 45N 0 55 E
Vernon, Can. 108 50 20N 119 15W
Vernon, France 18 49 5N 1 30 E
Vernon, U.S.A. 117 34 10N 99 20W
Vero Beach 115 27 39N 80 23W
Véroia 44 40 34N 22 12 E
Verolanuova 38 45 20N 10 5 E
Véroli 40 41 43N 13 24 E
Verona 38 45 27N 11 0 E
Veropol 59 65 15N 168 40 E
Versailles 19 48 48N 2 8 E
Vert, C. 84 14 45N 17 30W
Vertou 18 47 10N 1 28W
Vertus 19 48 54N 4 0 E
Verulam 93 29 38 S 31 2 E
Verviers 16 50 37N 5 52 E
Vervins 19 49 50N 3 53 E
Verwood 109 49 30N 105 40W
Verzej 39 46 34N 16 13 E
Veselí nad Lužnicí 26 49 12N 14 43 E
Veseliye 43 42 18N 27 38 E
Veselovskoye Vdkhr. 57 47 0N 41 0 E
Veshenskaya 57 49 35N 41 44 E
Vesle → 19 49 23N 3 38 E
Vesoul 19 47 40N 6 11 E
Vessigebro 49 56 58N 12 40 E
Vest-Agder fylke □ 47 58 30N 7 15 E
Vestby 47 59 37N 10 45 E
Vestfjorden 50 67 55N 14 0 E
Vestfold fylke □ 47 59 15N 10 0 E
Vestmannaeyjar 50 63 27N 20 15W
Vestmarka 47 59 56N 11 59 E
Vestnes 47 62 39N 7 5 E
Vestone 38 45 43N 10 25 E
Vestsjællands Amtskommune □ 49 55 30N 11 20 E
Vestspitsbergen 4 78 40N 17 0 E
Vestvågøy 50 68 18N 13 50 E
Vesuvio 41 40 50N 14 22 E
Vesuvius, Mt. = Vesuvio 41 40 50N 14 22 E
Vesyegonsk 55 58 40N 37 16 E
Veszprém 27 47 8N 17 57 E
Veszprém □ 27 47 5N 17 55 E
Vésztő 27 46 55N 21 16 E
Vetapalem 70 15 47N 80 18 E
Vetlanda 49 57 24N 15 3 E
Vetluga 55 57 53N 45 45 E
Vetluzhskiy 55 57 17N 45 12 E
Vetovo 43 43 42N 26 16 E
Vetralia 39 42 20N 12 2 E
Vetren 43 42 15N 24 3 E
Vettore, Monte 39 42 49N 13 16 E
Veurne 16 51 5N 2 40 E
Vevey 25 46 28N 6 51 E
Vévi 44 40 47N 21 38 E
Veynes 21 44 32N 5 49 E
Veys 64 31 30N 49 0 E
Vézelise 19 48 30N 6 5 E
Vézère → 20 44 53N 0 53 E
Vezhen 43 42 50N 24 20 E
Viacha 126 16 39 S 68 18W
Viadana 38 44 55N 10 30 E
Viana, Brazil 127 3 13 S 45 0W
Viana, Spain 32 42 31N 2 22W
Viana del Bollo 30 42 11N 7 6W
Viana do Alentejo 31 38 17N 7 59W
Viana do Castelo 30 41 42N 8 50W
Vianna do Castelo □ 30 41 50N 8 30W
Vianópolis 127 16 40 S 48 35W
Viar → 31 37 36N 5 50W
Viaréggio 38 43 52N 10 13 E
Viaur → 20 44 8N 1 58 E
Vibank 109 50 20N 103 56W
Vibo Valéntia 41 38 40N 16 5 E
Viborg 49 56 27N 9 23 E
Vibraye 18 48 3N 0 44 E
Vic-en-Bigorre 20 43 24N 0 3 E
Vic-Fézensac 20 43 47N 0 19 E
Vic-sur-Cère 20 44 59N 2 38 E
Vic-sur-Seille 19 48 45N 6 33 E
Vicenza 39 45 32N 11 31 E
Vich 32 41 58N 2 19 E
Vichuga 55 57 12N 41 55 E
Vichy 20 46 9N 3 26 E
Vicksburg, Mich., U.S.A. 114 42 10N 85 30W
Vicksburg, Miss., U.S.A. 117 32 22N 90 56W
Vico del Gargaro 41 41 54N 15 57 E
Vico, L. di 39 42 20N 12 10 E
Viçosa 127 9 28 S 36 14W
Victor, Colo., U.S.A. 116 38 43N 105 7W
Victor, N.Y., U.S.A. 112 42 58N 77 24W
Victor Harbour 97 35 30 S 138 37 E
Victoria, Argent. 124 32 40 S 60 10W
Victoria, Camer. 88 4 1N 9 10 E
Victoria, Can. 108 48 30N 123 25W
Victoria, Chile 128 38 13 S 72 20W
* Victoria, Guin. 84 10 50N 14 32W
Victoria, H. K. 75 22 16N 114 15 E
Victoria, Malay. 72 5 20N 115 14 E
Victoria, Kans., U.S.A. 116 38 52N 99 8W
Victoria, Tex., U.S.A. 117 28 50N 97 0W
Victoria □, Austral. 97 37 0 S 144 0 E
Victoria □, Zimb. 91 21 0 S 31 30 E
Victoria → 96 15 10 S 129 40 E
Victoria Beach 109 50 40N 96 35W
Victoria de las Tunas 121 20 58N 76 59W
Victoria Falls 91 17 58 S 25 52 E
Victoria, Grand L. 106 47 31N 77 30W
Victoria Harbour 106 44 45N 79 45W
Victoria I. 104 71 0N 111 0W
Victoria, L. 90 1 0 S 33 0 E
Victoria Ld. 5 75 0 S 160 0 E
Victoria, Mt. 98 8 55 S 147 32 E
Victoria Nile → 90 2 14N 31 26 E
Victoria Res. 107 48 20N 57 27W
Victoria River Downs 96 16 25 S 131 0 E
Victoria Taungdeik 67 21 15N 93 55 E
Victoria West 92 31 25 S 23 4 E
Victoriaville 107 46 4N 71 56W
Victorica 124 36 20 S 65 30W
Victorville 119 34 32N 117 18W
Vicuña 124 30 0 S 70 50W
Vicuña Mackenna 124 33 53 S 64 25W
Vidalia 115 32 13N 82 25W
Vidauban 21 43 25N 6 27 E
Vidigueira 31 38 12N 7 48W
Vidin 42 43 59N 22 50 E
Vidio, Cabo 30 43 35N 6 14W
Vidisha (Bhilsa) 68 23 28N 77 53 E
Vidöstern 49 57 5N 14 0 E
Vidra 46 45 56N 26 55 E
Viduša 42 42 55N 18 21 E
Vidzy 54 55 23N 26 37 E
Viechtach 25 49 5N 12 53 E
Viedma 128 40 50 S 63 0W
Viedma, L. 128 49 30 S 72 30W
Vieira 30 41 38N 8 8W
Viella 32 42 43N 0 44 E
Vien Pou Kha 71 20 45N 101 5 E
Vienenburg 24 51 57N 10 35 E
Vienna 117 37 29N 88 54W
Vienna = Wien 27 48 12N 16 22 E
Vienne 21 45 31N 4 53 E
Vienne □ 20 46 30N 0 42 E
Vienne → 18 47 13N 0 5 E
Vientiane 71 17 58N 102 36 E
Vientos, Paso de los 121 20 0N 74 0W
Viersen 24 51 15N 6 23 E
Vierwaldstättersee 25 47 0N 8 30 E
Vierzon 19 47 13N 2 5 E
Vieste 40 41 52N 16 14 E
Vietnam ■ 71 19 0N 106 0 E
Vieux-Boucau-les-Bains 20 43 48N 1 23W
Vif 21 45 5N 5 41 E
Vigan 73 17 35N 120 28 E
Vigan, Le 20 44 0N 3 36 E
Vigévano 38 45 18N 8 50 E
Vigia 127 0 50 S 48 5W
Vignacourt 19 50 1N 2 15 E
Vignemale, Pic du 20 42 47N 0 10W
Vigneulles 19 48 59N 5 40 E
Vignola 38 44 29N 11 0 E
Vigo 30 42 12N 8 41W
Vigo, Ría de 30 42 15N 8 45W
Vihiers 18 47 10N 0 30W
Vijayadurg 70 16 30N 73 25 E
Vijayawada (Bezwada) 70 16 31N 80 39 E
Vikedal 47 59 30N 5 55 E
Viken 49 58 39N 14 20 E
Vikersund 47 59 58N 10 2 E
Viking 108 53 7N 111 50W
Vikna 50 64 55N 10 58 E
Vikramasingapuram 70 8 40N 76 47 E
Viksjö 48 62 45N 17 26 E
Vikulovo 58 56 50N 70 40 E
Vila Aiferes Chamusca 93 24 27 S 33 0 E
Vila Caldas Xavier 91 14 28 S 33 0 E
Vila Coutinho 91 14 37 S 34 19 E
Vila da Maganja 91 17 18 S 37 30 E
Vila de João Belo = Xai-Xai 93 25 6 S 33 31 E
Vila de Junqueiro 91 15 25 S 36 58 E
Vila de Manica 91 18 58 S 32 59 E
Vila de Rei 31 39 41N 8 9W
Vila do Bispo 31 37 5N 8 53W
Vila do Chibuto 93 24 40 S 33 33 E
Vila do Conde 30 41 21N 8 45W
Vila Fontes 91 17 51 S 35 24 E
Vila Franca de Xira 31 38 57N 8 59W
Vila Gamito 91 14 12 S 33 0 E
Vila Gomes da Costa 93 24 20 S 33 37 E
Vila Luisa 93 25 45 S 32 35 E
Vila Machado 91 19 15 S 34 14 E
Vila Mouzinho 91 14 48 S 34 25 E
Vila Nova de Foscôa 30 41 5N 7 9W
Vila Nova de Ourém 31 39 40N 8 35W
Vila Novo de Gaia 30 41 4N 8 40W
Vila Paiva de Andrada 91 18 44 S 34 2 E
Vila Pouca de Aguiar 30 41 30N 7 38W
Vila Real 30 41 17N 7 48W
Vila Real de Santo António 31 37 10N 7 28W
Vila Vasco da Gama 91 14 54 S 32 14 E
Vila Velha 125 20 20 S 40 17W
Vila Verissimo Sarmento 88 8 7 S 20 38 E
Vila Viçosa 31 38 45N 7 27W
Vilaboa 30 42 21N 8 39W
Vilaine → 18 47 30N 2 27W
Vilanculos 93 22 1 S 35 17 E
Vilar Formosa 30 40 38N 6 45W
Vilareal □ 30 41 36N 7 35W
Vilaseca-Salou 32 41 7N 1 9 E
Vîlcea □ 46 45 0N 24 10 E
Vileyka 54 54 30N 26 53 E
Vilhelmina 50 64 35N 16 39 E
Vilhena 126 12 40 S 60 5W
Viliga 59 61 36N 156 56 E
Viliya → 54 55 54N 23 53 E
Viljandi 54 58 28N 25 30 E
Vilkovo 56 45 28N 29 32 E
Villa Abecia 124 21 0 S 68 18W
Villa Ahumada 120 30 38N 106 30W
Villa Ana 124 28 28 S 59 40W
Villa Ángela 124 27 34 S 60 45W
Villa Bella 126 10 25 S 65 22W
Villa Bens = Tarfaya 80 27 55N 12 55W
Villa Cañás 124 34 0 S 61 35W
Villa Cisneros = Dakhla 80 23 50N 15 53W
Villa Colón 124 31 38 S 68 20W
Villa Constitución 124 33 15 S 60 20W
Villa de María 124 29 55 S 63 43W
Villa Dolores 124 31 58 S 65 15W
Villa Guillermina 124 28 15 S 59 29W
Villa Hayes 124 25 0 S 57 20W
Villa Iris 124 38 12 S 63 12W
Villa María 124 32 20 S 63 10W
Villa Mazán 124 28 40 S 66 30W
Villa Minozzo 38 44 21N 10 30 E
Villa Montes 124 21 10 S 63 30W
Villa Ocampo 124 28 30 S 59 20W
Villa Ojo de Agua 124 29 30 S 63 44W
Villa San Giovanni 41 38 13N 15 38 E
Villa San José 124 32 12 S 58 15W
Villa San Martín 124 28 15 S 64 9W
Villa Santina 39 46 25N 12 55 E
Villablino 30 42 57N 6 19W
Villacañas 32 39 38N 3 20W
Villacarlos 32 39 53N 4 17 E
Villacarriedo 32 43 14N 3 48W
Villacarrillo 33 38 7N 3 3W
Villacastín 30 40 46N 4 25W
Villach 26 46 37N 13 51 E
Villaciado 40 39 27N 8 45 E
Villada 30 42 15N 4 59W
Villadiego 30 42 31N 4 1W
Villadóssola 38 46 4N 8 16 E
Villafeliche 32 41 10N 1 30W
Villafranca 32 42 17N 1 46W
Villafranca de los Barros 31 38 35N 6 18W
Villafranca de los Caballeros 33 39 26N 3 21W
Villafranca del Bierzo 30 42 38N 6 50W
Villafranca del Cid 32 40 26N 0 16W
Villafranca del Panadés 32 41 21N 1 40 E
Villafranca di Verona 38 45 20N 10 51 E
Villagarcía de Arosa 30 42 34N 8 46W
Villagrán 120 24 29N 99 29W
Villaguay 124 32 0 S 59 0W
Villaharta 31 38 9N 4 54W
Villahermosa, Mexico 120 18 0N 92 50W
Villahermosa, Spain 33 38 46N 2 52W
Villaines-la-Juhel 18 48 21N 0 20W
Villajoyosa 33 38 30N 0 12W
Villalba 30 43 26N 7 40W
Villalba de Guardo 30 42 42N 4 49W
Villalcampo, Pantano de 30 41 31N 6 0W
Villalón de Campos 30 42 5N 5 4W
Villalpando 30 41 51N 5 25W
Villaluenga 30 40 2N 3 54W
Villamanán 30 42 19N 5 35W
Villamartín 31 36 52N 5 38W
Villamayor 32 39 50N 2 59W
Villamblard 20 45 2N 0 32 E
Villanova Monteleone 40 40 30N 8 28 E
Villanueva 119 35 16N 105 23W
Villanueva de Castellón 33 39 5N 0 31W
Villanueva de Córdoba 31 38 20N 4 38W
Villanueva de la Fuente 33 38 42N 2 42W
Villanueva de la Serena 31 38 59N 5 50W
Villanueva de la Sierra 30 40 12N 6 24W
Villanueva de los Castillejos 31 37 30N 7 15W
Villanueva del Arzobispo 33 38 10N 3 0W
Villanueva del Duque 31 38 20N 5 0W
Villanueva del Fresno 31 38 23N 7 10W
Villanueva y Geltrú 32 41 13N 1 40 E
Villaodrid 30 43 20N 7 11W
Villaputzu 40 39 28N 9 33 E
Villar del Arzobispo 32 39 44N 0 50W
Villar del Rey 31 39 7N 6 50W
Villarcayo 32 42 56N 3 34W
Villard-Bonnet 21 45 14N 5 53 E
Villard-de-Lans 21 45 3N 5 33 E
Villarino de los Aires 30 41 18N 6 23W
Villarosa 41 37 36N 14 9 E
Villarramiel 30 42 2N 4 55W
Villarreal 32 39 55N 0 3W
Villarrica, Chile 128 39 15 S 72 15W
Villarrica, Parag. 124 25 40 S 56 30W
Villarrobledo 33 39 18N 2 36W
Villarroya de la Sierra 32 41 27N 1 46W
Villarrubia de los Ojos 33 39 14N 3 36W
Villars 21 46 0N 5 2 E
Villarta de San Juan 33 39 15N 3 25W
Villasayas 32 41 24N 2 39W
Villaseca de los Gamitos 30 41 2N 6 7W
Villastar 32 40 17N 1 9W
Villatobas 32 39 54N 3 20W
Villavicencio, Argent. 124 32 28 S 69 0W
Villavicencio, Colomb. 126 4 9N 73 37W
Villaviciosa 30 43 32N 5 27W
Villazón 124 22 0 S 65 35W
Ville-Marie 106 47 20N 79 30W
Ville Platte 117 30 45N 92 17W
Villedieu 18 48 50N 1 12W
Villefort 20 44 28N 3 56 E
Villefranche 19 47 19N 1 46 E
Villefranche-de-Lauragais 20 43 25N 1 44 E
Villefranche-de-Rouergue 20 44 21N 2 2 E
Villefranche-du-Périgord 20 44 38N 1 5 E
Villefranche-sur-Saône 21 45 59N 4 43 E
Villel 32 40 14N 1 12W
Villemaur 19 48 14N 3 40 E
Villemur-sur-Tarn 20 43 51N 1 31 E
Villena 33 38 39N 0 52W
Villenauxe 19 48 36N 3 30 E
Villenave 20 44 46N 0 33W
Villeneuve, France 19 48 42N 2 25 E
Villeneuve, Italy 38 45 40N 7 10 E
Villeneuve-l'Archevêque 19 48 14N 3 32 E
Villeneuve-lès-Avignon 21 43 57N 4 49 E
Villeneuve-sur-Allier 20 46 40N 3 13 E
Villeneuve-sur-Lot 20 44 24N 0 42 E
Villeréal 20 44 38N 0 45 E
Villers-Bocage 18 49 3N 0 40W
Villers-Bretonneux 19 49 50N 2 30 E
Villers-Cotterêts 19 49 15N 3 4 E
Villers-Outreaux 19 50 2N 3 18 E
Villers-sur-Mer 18 49 21N 0 2W
Villersexel 19 47 33N 6 26 E
Villerupt 19 49 28N 5 55 E
Villerville 18 49 26N 0 5 E
Villiers 93 27 2 S 28 36 E
Villingen 25 48 4N 8 28 E
Villingen-Schwenningen 25 48 3N 8 29 E
Villisca 116 40 55N 94 59W
Villupuram 70 11 59N 79 31 E
Vilna 108 54 7N 111 55W
Vilnius 54 54 38N 25 19 E
Vils 26 47 33N 10 37 E
Vils → 25 48 38N 13 11 E
Vilsbiburg 25 48 27N 12 23 E
Vilshofen 25 48 38N 13 11 E
Vilskutskogo, Proliv 59 78 0N 103 0 E
Vilusi 42 42 44N 18 34 E
Vilvoorde 16 50 56N 4 26 E
Vilyuy → 59 64 24N 126 26 E
Vilyuysk 59 63 40N 121 35 E
Vimercate 38 45 38N 9 25 E
Vimiosa 30 41 35N 6 31W
Vimmerby 49 57 40N 15 55 E
Vimoutiers 18 48 57N 0 10 E
Vimperk 26 49 3N 13 46 E
Viña del Mar 124 33 0 S 71 30W
Vinaroz 32 40 30N 0 27 E
Vincennes 114 38 42N 87 29W
Vinchina 124 28 45 S 68 15W
Vindel älven → 50 63 55N 19 50 E
Vindeln 50 64 12N 19 43 E
Vinderup 49 56 29N 8 45 E
Vindhya Ra. 68 22 50N 77 0 E
Vineland 114 39 30N 75 0W
Vinga 42 46 0N 21 14 E
Vingnes 47 61 7N 10 26 E
Vinh 71 18 45N 105 38 E
Vinhais 30 41 50N 7 0W
Vinica, Hrvatska, Yugo. 39 46 20N 16 9 E
Vinica, Slovenija, Yugo. 39 45 28N 15 16 E
Vinita 117 36 40N 95 12W
Vinkovci 42 45 19N 18 48 E
Vinnitsa 56 49 15N 28 30 E
Vinson Massif 5 78 35 S 85 25W
Vinstra 47 61 37N 9 44 E
Vinton, Iowa, U.S.A. 116 42 8N 92 1W
Vinton, La., U.S.A. 117 30 13N 93 35W
Vințu de Jos 46 46 0N 23 30 E
Viöl 24 54 32N 9 12 E
Vipava 39 45 51N 13 58 E
Vipiteno 39 46 55N 11 25 E
Viqueque 73 8 52 S 126 23 E
Vir 39 44 17N 15 3 E
Virac 73 13 30N 124 20 E
Virago Sd. 108 54 0N 132 30W
Virajpet 70 12 10N 75 50 E
Viramgam 68 23 5N 72 0 E
Viranşehir 64 37 13N 39 45 E
Virarajendrapet = Virajpet 70 12 10N 75 50 E
Viravanallur 70 8 40N 77 30 E
Virden 109 49 50N 100 56W
Vire 18 48 50N 0 53W
Vire → 18 49 20N 1 7W
Virgenes, C. 128 52 19 S 68 21W
Virgin →, Can. 109 57 2N 108 17W
Virgin →, U.S.A. 119 36 50N 114 10W
Virgin Gorda 121 18 30N 64 26W
Virgin Is. 121 18 40N 64 30W
Virginia, S. Afr. 92 28 8 S 26 55 E
Virginia, U.S.A. 116 47 30N 92 32W
Virginia □ 114 37 45N 78 0W
Virginia Beach 114 36 54N 75 58W
Virginia City, Mont., U.S.A. 118 45 18N 111 58W
Virginia City, Nev., U.S.A. 118 39 19N 119 39W
Virginia Falls 108 61 38N 125 42W
Virginiatown 106 48 9N 79 36W
Virieu-le-Grand 21 45 51N 5 39 E
Virje 42 46 4N 16 59 E
Viroqua 116 43 33N 90 57W
Virovitica 42 45 51N 17 21 E
Virpazar 42 42 14N 19 6 E
Virserum 49 57 20N 15 35 E
Virton 16 49 35N 5 32 E
Virtsu 54 58 32N 23 33 E
Virudunagar 70 9 30N 78 0 E
Vis 39 43 0N 16 10 E
Vis Kanal 39 43 4N 16 5 E
Visalia 119 36 25N 119 18W
Visayan Sea 73 11 30N 123 30 E
Visby 49 57 37N 18 18 E
Viscount Melville Sd. 4 74 10N 108 0W
Visé 16 50 44N 5 41 E
Višegrad 42 43 47N 19 17 E
Viseu, Brazil 127 1 10 S 46 5W
Viseu, Port. 30 40 40N 7 55W
Viseu □ 30 40 40N 7 55W
Vişeu de Sus 46 47 45N 24 25 E
Vishakhapatnam 70 17 45N 83 20 E
Vishnupur 69 23 8N 87 20 E
Visikoi I. 5 56 43 S 27 15W
Visingsö 49 58 2N 14 20 E
Viskafors 49 57 37N 12 50 E
Vislanda 49 56 46N 14 30 E
Vislinskil Zaliv (Zalew Wislany) 28 54 20N 19 50 E
Visnagar 68 23 45N 72 32 E
Višnja Gora 39 45 58N 14 45 E
Viso del Marqués 33 38 32N 3 34W
Viso, Mte. 38 44 38N 7 5 E
Visoko 42 43 58N 18 10 E

* Renamed Limbe

Visp Wangdu

Visp **25** 46 17N 7 52 E
Visselhövede **24** 52 59N 9 36 E
Vistonikos, Ormos **44** 41 0N 25 7 E
Vistula = Wisła → **28** 54 22N 18 55 E
Vit → **43** 43 30N 24 30 E
Vitanje **39** 46 25N 15 18 E
Vitebsk **54** 55 10N 30 15 E
Viterbo **39** 42 25N 12 8 E
Viti Levu **101** 17 30 S 177 30 E
Vitiaz Str. **98** 5 40 S 147 10 E
Vitigudino **30** 41 1N 6 26W
Vitim **59** 59 28N 112 35 E
Vitim → **59** 59 26N 112 34 E
Vitina **45** 37 40N 22 10 E
Vitina **42** 43 17N 17 29 E
Vitória **127** 20 20 S 40 22W
Vitoria **32** 42 50N 2 41W
Vitória da Conquista **127** 14 51 S 40 51W
Vitória de São Antão **127** 8 10 S 35 20W
Vitré **18** 48 8N 1 12W
Vitry-le-François **19** 48 43N 4 33 E
Vitsi, Óros **44** 40 40N 21 25 E
Vitteaux **19** 47 24N 4 30 E
Vittel **19** 48 12N 5 57 E
Vittória **41** 36 58N 14 30 E
Vittório Véneto **39** 45 59N 12 18 E
Vitu Is. **98** 4 50 S 149 25 E
Viver **32** 39 55N 0 36W
Vivero **30** 43 39N 7 38W
Viviers **21** 44 30N 4 40 E
Vivonne **20** 46 25N 0 15 E
Vizcaíno, Desierto de **120** 27 40N 113 50W
Vizcaíno, Sierra **120** 27 30N 114 0W
Vizcaya □ **32** 43 15N 2 45W
Vizianagaram **70** 18 6N 83 30 E
Vizille **21** 45 5N 5 46 E
Viziňada **39** 45 20N 13 46 E
Viziru **46** 45 0N 27 43 E
Vizovice **27** 49 12N 17 56 E
Vizzini **41** 37 9N 14 43 E
Vjosa → **44** 40 37N 19 42 E
Vlaardingen **16** 51 55N 4 21 E
Vlădeasa **46** 46 47N 22 50 E
Vladicin Han **42** 42 42N 22 1 E
Vladimir **55** 56 15N 40 30 E
Vladimir Volynskiy **54** 50 50N 24 18 E
Vladimirci **42** 44 36N 19 45 E
Vladimirovac **42** 45 1N 20 53 E
Vladimirovka, R.S.F.S.R., U.S.S.R. **57** 48 27N 46 10 E
Vladimirovka, R.S.F.S.R., U.S.S.R. **57** 44 45N 44 41 E
Vladimirovo **43** 43 32N 23 22 E
Vladislavovka **56** 45 15N 35 15 E
Vladivostok **59** 43 10N 131 53 E
Vlasenica **42** 44 11N 18 59 E
Vlašić **42** 44 19N 17 37 E
Vlašim **26** 49 40N 14 53 E
Vlasinsko Jezero **42** 42 44N 22 22 E
Vlasotinci **42** 42 59N 22 7 E
Vlieland **16** 53 16N 4 55 E
Vlissingen **16** 51 26N 3 34 E
Vlóra **44** 40 32N 19 28 E
Vlóra □ **44** 40 12N 20 0 E
Vlorës, Gjiri i **44** 40 29N 19 27 E
Vltava → **26** 50 21N 14 30 E
Vobarno **38** 45 38N 10 30 E
Voćin **42** 45 37N 17 33 E
Vöcklabruck **26** 48 1N 13 39 E
Vodice **39** 43 47N 15 47 E
Vodňany **26** 49 9N 14 11 E
Vodnjan **39** 44 59N 13 52 E
Vogelkop = Doberai, Jazirah **73** 1 25 S 133 0 E
Vogelsberg **24** 50 37N 9 15 E
Voghera **38** 44 59N 9 1 E
Vohibinany **93** 18 49 S 49 4 E
Vohimarina **93** 13 25 S 50 0 E
Vohimena, Tanjon' i **93** 25 36 S 45 8 E
Vohipeno **93** 22 22 S 47 51 E
Voi **90** 3 25 S 38 32 E
Void **19** 48 40N 5 36 E
Voinești, Iași, Romania **46** 47 5N 27 27 E
Voinești, Prahova, Romania **46** 45 5N 25 14 E
Voiotía □ **45** 38 20N 23 0 E
Voiron **21** 45 22N 5 35 E
Voisey B. **107** 56 15N 61 50W
Voitsberg **26** 47 3N 15 9 E
Voiviïs Límni **44** 39 30N 22 45 E
Vojens **49** 55 16N 9 18 E
Vojmsjön **50** 64 55N 16 40 E
Vojnik **38** 46 18N 15 19 E
Vojnió **39** 45 19N 15 43 E
Vojvodina, Auton. Pokrajina □ **42** 45 20N 20 0 E
Vokhma **55** 59 0N 46 45 E
Vokhma → **55** 56 20N 46 20 E
Vokhtoga **55** 58 46N 41 8 E
Volary **26** 48 54N 13 52 E
Volborg **116** 45 50N 105 44W
Volcano Is. **94** 25 0N 141 0 E
Volchansk **55** 50 17N 36 58 E
Volchayevka **59** 48 40N 134 30 E
Volchya → **56** 48 0N 37 0 E
Volda **47** 62 9N 6 5 E
Volga **55** 57 58N 38 16 E
Volga → **57** 48 30N 46 0 E
Volga Hts. = Privolzhskaya V. S. **53** 51 0N 46 0 E
Volgodonsk **57** 47 33N 42 5 E
Volgograd **57** 48 40N 44 25 E
Volgogradskoye Vdkhr. **55** 50 0N 45 20 E
Volgorechensk **55** 57 28N 41 14 E
Volissós **45** 38 29N 25 54 E
Volkach **25** 49 52N 10 14 E
Völkermarkt **26** 46 39N 14 39 E
Volkhov **54** 59 55N 32 15 E
Volkhov → **54** 60 8N 32 20 E
Völklingen **25** 49 15N 6 50 E
Volkovysk **54** 53 9N 24 30 E
Volksrust **93** 27 24 S 29 53 E
Vollenhove **16** 52 40N 5 58 E
Vol'n'ansk **56** 47 55N 35 29 E
Volnovakha **56** 47 35N 37 30 E
Volochanka **59** 71 0N 94 28 E
Volodarsk **55** 56 12N 43 15 E
Vologda **55** 59 10N 40 0 E
Volokolamsk **55** 56 5N 35 57 E
Volokonovka **55** 50 33N 37 52 E
Vólos **44** 39 24N 22 59 E
Volosovo **54** 59 27N 29 32 E
Volozhin **54** 54 3N 26 30 E
Volsk **55** 52 5N 47 22 E
Volta → **85** 5 46N 0 41 E
Volta, L. **85** 7 30N 0 15 E
Volta Redonda **125** 22 31 S 44 5W
Volterra **38** 43 24N 10 50 E
Voltri **38** 44 25N 8 43 E
Volturara Áppula **41** 41 30N 15 2 E
Volturno → **41** 41 1N 13 55 E
Volubilis **82** 34 2N 5 33W
Volujak **42** 43 53N 17 47 E
Vólvi, L. **44** 40 40N 23 34 E
Volzhsk **55** 55 57N 48 23 E
Volzhskiy **57** 48 56N 44 46 E
Vondrozo **93** 22 49 S 47 20 E
Vónitsa **45** 38 53N 20 58 E
Voorburg **16** 52 5N 4 24 E
Vopnafjörður **50** 65 45N 14 40W
Vorarlberg □ **26** 47 20N 10 0 E
Vóras Óros **44** 40 57N 21 45 E
Vorbasse **49** 55 39N 9 6 E
Vorderrhein → **25** 46 49N 9 25 E
Vordingborg **49** 55 0N 11 54 E
Voreppe **21** 45 18N 5 39 E
Voriai Sporádhes **45** 39 15N 23 30 E
Vórios Evvoïkos Kólpos **45** 38 45N 23 15 E
Vorkuta **52** 67 48N 64 20 E
Vorma → **47** 60 9N 11 27 E
Vorona → **55** 51 22N 42 3 E
Voronezh, R.S.F.S.R., U.S.S.R. **55** 51 40N 39 10 E
Voronezh, Ukraine, U.S.S.R. **54** 51 47N 33 28 E
Voronezh → **55** 51 56N 37 17 E
Vorontsovo-Aleksandrovskoye = Zelenokumsk **57** 44 30N 44 1 E
Voroshilovgrad **57** 48 38N 39 15 E
Vorovskoye **59** 54 30N 155 50 E
Vorskla → **56** 48 50N 34 10 E
Võru **54** 57 48N 26 54 E
Vorupør **49** 56 58N 8 22 E
Vosges **19** 48 20N 7 10 E
Vosges □ **19** 48 12N 6 20 E
Voskopoja **44** 40 40N 20 33 E
Voskresensk **55** 55 19N 38 43 E
Voskresenskoye **55** 56 51N 45 30 E
Voss **47** 60 38N 6 26 E
Vostochnyy Sayan **59** 54 0N 96 0 E
Vostok I. **95** 10 5 S 152 23W
Votice **26** 49 38N 14 39 E
Votkinsk **52** 57 0N 53 55 E
Votkinskoye Vdkhr. **52** 57 30N 55 0 E
Vouga → **30** 40 41N 8 40W
Vouillé **18** 46 38N 0 10 E
Voulte-sur-Rhône, La **21** 44 48N 4 46 E
Vouvray **18** 47 25N 0 48 E
Voúxa, Ákra **45** 35 37N 23 32 E
Vouzela **30** 40 43N 8 7W
Vouziers **19** 49 22N 4 40 E
Voves **19** 48 15N 1 38 E
Voxna **48** 61 20N 15 40 E
Vozhe Oz. **52** 60 45N 39 0 E
Vozhgaly **55** 58 9N 50 11 E
Voznesenka **59** 56 40N 95 3 E
Voznesensk **56** 47 35N 31 21 E
Voznesenye **52** 61 0N 35 45 E
Vráble **27** 48 15N 18 16 E
Vraćevšnica **42** 44 2N 20 34 E
Vrådal **47** 59 20N 8 25 E
Vraka **44** 42 8N 19 28 E
Vrakhnéïka **45** 38 10N 21 40 E
Vrancea □ **46** 45 50N 26 45 E
Vrancei, Munții **46** 46 0N 26 30 E
Vrangelya, Ostrov **59** 71 0N 180 0 E
Vranica **42** 43 55N 17 50 E
Vranje **42** 42 34N 21 54 E
Vranjska Banja **42** 42 34N 22 1 E
Vranov **27** 48 53N 21 40 E
Vransko **39** 46 17N 14 58 E
Vratsa **43** 43 13N 23 30 E
Vrbas **42** 45 40N 19 40 E
Vrbas → **42** 45 8N 17 29 E
Vrbnik **39** 45 4N 14 40 E
Vrbovec **39** 45 53N 16 28 E
Vrbovsko **39** 45 24N 15 5 E
Vrchlabí **26** 50 38N 15 37 E
Vrede **93** 27 24 S 29 6 E
Vredefort **92** 27 0 S 26 22 E
Vredenburg **92** 32 51 S 18 0 E
Vredendal **92** 31 41 S 18 35 E
Vrena **49** 58 54N 16 41 E
Vrgorac **42** 43 12N 17 20 E
Vrhnika **39** 45 58N 14 15 E
Vriddhachalam **70** 11 30N 79 20 E
Vrïdi **84** 5 15N 4 3W
Vrindaban **68** 27 37N 77 40 E
Vrnograč **39** 45 10N 15 57 E
Vrondádhes **45** 38 25N 26 7 E
Vrpolje **42** 45 13N 18 24 E
Vršac **42** 45 8N 21 18 E
Vrsacki Kanal **42** 45 15N 21 0 E
Vryburg **92** 26 55 S 24 45 E
Vryheid **93** 27 45 S 30 47 E
Vsetín **27** 49 20N 18 0 E
Vucha → **43** 42 10N 24 26 E
Vučitrn **42** 42 49N 20 59 E
Vught **16** 51 38N 5 20 E
Vukovar **42** 45 21N 18 59 E
Vulcan, Can. **108** 50 25N 113 15W
Vulcan, Romania **46** 45 23N 23 17 E
Vulcan, U.S.A. **114** 45 46N 87 51W
Vulcano **41** 38 25N 14 58 E
Vŭlchedruma **43** 43 42N 23 27 E
Vulci **39** 42 23N 11 37 E
Vulkaneshty **56** 45 35N 28 30 E
Vunduzi → **91** 18 56 S 34 1 E
Vung Tau **71** 10 21N 107 4 E
Vŭrbitsa **43** 42 59N 26 40 E
Vurshets **43** 43 15N 23 23 E
Vutcani **46** 46 26N 27 59 E
Vuyyuru **70** 16 28N 80 50 E
Vyara **68** 21 8N 73 28 E
Vyasniki **55** 56 10N 42 10 E
Vyatka → **52** 56 30N 51 0 E
Vyatskiye Polyany **52** 56 5N 51 0 E
Vyazemskiy **59** 47 32N 134 45 E
Vyazma **54** 55 10N 34 15 E
Vyborg **52** 60 43N 28 47 E
Vychegda → **52** 61 18N 46 36 E
Vychodné Beskydy **27** 49 30N 22 0 E
Východočeský □ **26** 50 20N 15 45 E
Východoslovenský □ **27** 48 50N 21 0 E
Vyg-ozero **52** 63 30N 34 0 E
Vyksa **55** 55 19N 42 11 E
Vypin **70** 10 10N 76 15 E
Vyrnwy, L. **12** 52 48N 3 30W
Vyshniy Volochek **54** 57 30N 34 30 E
Vyškov **27** 49 17N 17 0 E
Vysoké Mýto **27** 49 58N 10 10 E
Vysokovsk **55** 56 22N 36 30 E
Vysotsk **54** 51 43N 26 32 E
Vyšší Brod **26** 48 37N 14 19 E
Vytegra **52** 61 0N 36 27 E

W

W.A.C. Bennett Dam **108** 56 2N 122 6W
Wa **84** 10 7N 2 25W
Waal → **16** 51 59N 4 30 E
Wabakimi L. **106** 50 38N 89 45W
Wabana **107** 47 40N 53 0W
Wabasca **108** 55 57N 113 56W
Wabash **114** 40 48N 85 46W
Wabash → **114** 37 46N 88 2W
Wabeno **114** 45 25N 88 40W
Wabi → **87** 7 45N 40 50 E
Wabigoon L. **109** 49 44N 92 44W
Wabowden **109** 54 55N 98 38W
Wąbrzeźno **28** 53 16N 18 57 E
Wabuk Pt. **106** 55 20N 85 5W
Wabush **107** 52 55N 66 52W
Wabuska **118** 39 9N 119 13W
Wächtersbach **25** 50 16N 9 18 E
Waco **117** 31 33N 97 5W
Waconichi, L. **106** 50 8N 74 0W
Wad Ban Naqa **87** 16 32N 33 9 E
Wad Banda **87** 13 10N 27 56 E
Wad el Haddad **87** 13 50N 33 30 E
Wad en Nau **87** 14 10N 33 34 E
Wad Hamid **87** 16 30N 32 45 E
Wâd Medanî **87** 14 28N 33 30 E
Waddān **83** 29 9N 16 10 E
Waddān, Jabal **83** 29 0N 16 15 E
Waddeneilanden **16** 53 25N 5 10 E
Waddenzee **16** 53 6N 5 10 E
Waddington **113** 44 51N 75 12W
Waddington, Mt. **108** 51 23N 125 15W
Waddy Pt. **99** 24 58 S 153 21 E
Wadena, Can. **109** 51 57N 103 47W
Wadena, U.S.A. **116** 46 25N 95 8W
Wädenswil **25** 47 14N 8 40 E
Wadesboro **115** 35 2N 80 2W
Wadhams **108** 51 30N 127 30W
Wādī ash Shāṭi' **83** 27 30N 15 0 E
Wādī Banī Walīd **83** 31 49N 14 0 E
Wadi Gemâl **86** 24 35N 35 10 E
Wadi Halfa **86** 21 53N 31 19 E
Wadi Masila **63** 16 30N 49 0 E
Wadi Şabāḩ **64** 23 50N 48 30 E
Wadlew **28** 51 31N 19 23 E
Wadowice **27** 49 52N 19 30 E
Wadsworth **118** 39 38N 119 22W
Wafrah **64** 28 33N 47 56 E
Wageningen **16** 51 58N 5 40 E
Wager B. **105** 65 26N 88 40W
Wager Bay **105** 65 56N 90 49W
Wagga Wagga **97** 35 7 S 147 24 E
Waghete **73** 4 10 S 135 50 E
Wagin **96** 33 17 S 117 25 E
Wagon Mound **117** 36 1N 104 44W
Wagoner **117** 36 0N 95 20W
Wagrowiec **28** 52 48N 17 11 E
Wahai **73** 2 48 S 129 35 E
Wahiawa **110** 21 30N 158 2W
Wahoo **116** 41 15N 96 35W
Wahpeton **116** 46 20N 96 35W
Wai **70** 17 56N 73 57 E
Waiau → **101** 42 47 S 173 22 E
Waiawe Ganga → **70** 6 15N 81 0 E
Waibeem **73** 0 30 S 132 59 E
Waiblingen **25** 48 49N 9 20 E
Waidhofen, Niederösterreich, Austria **26** 48 49N 15 17 E
Waidhofen, Niederösterreich, Austria **26** 47 57N 14 46 E
Waigeo **73** 0 20 S 130 40 E
Waihi **101** 37 23 S 175 52 E
Waihou → **101** 37 15 S 175 40 E
Waika **90** 2 22 S 25 42 E
Waikabubak **73** 9 45 S 119 25 E
Waikaremoana **101** 38 42 S 177 12 E
Waikari **101** 42 58 S 172 41 E
Waikato → **101** 37 23 S 174 43 E
Waikerie **99** 34 9 S 140 0 E
Waikokopu **101** 39 3 S 177 52 E
Waikouaiti **101** 45 36 S 170 41 E
Waimate **101** 44 45 S 171 3 E
Wainganga → **69** 18 50N 79 55 E
Waingapu **73** 9 35 S 120 11 E
Wainwright, Can. **109** 52 50N 110 50W
Wainwright, U.S.A. **104** 70 39N 160 1W
Waiouru **101** 39 28 S 175 41 E
Waipara **101** 43 3 S 172 46 E
Waipawa **101** 39 56 S 176 38 E
Waipiro **101** 38 2 S 178 22 E
Waipu **101** 35 59 S 174 29 E
Waipukurau **101** 40 1 S 176 33 E
Wairakei **101** 38 37 S 176 6 E
Wairarapa, L. **101** 41 14 S 175 15 E
Wairoa **101** 39 3 S 177 25 E
Waitaki → **101** 44 56 S 171 7 E
Waitara **101** 38 59 S 174 15 E
Waitsburg **118** 46 15N 118 0W
Waiuku **101** 37 15 S 174 45 E
Wajima **74** 37 30N 137 0 E
Wajir **90** 1 42N 40 5 E
Wajir □ **90** 1 42N 40 20 E
Wakasa-Wan **74** 35 40N 135 30 E
Wakatipu, L. **101** 45 5 S 168 33 E
Wakaw **109** 52 39N 105 44W
Wakayama **74** 34 15N 135 15 E
Wakayama-ken □ **74** 33 50N 135 30 E
Wake Forest **115** 35 58N 78 30W
Wake I. **94** 19 18N 166 36 E
Wakefield, N.Z. **101** 41 24 S 173 5 E
Wakefield, U.K. **12** 53 41N 1 31W
Wakefield, Mass., U.S.A. **113** 42 30N 71 3W
Wakefield, Mich., U.S.A. **116** 46 28N 89 53W
Wakema **67** 16 30N 95 11 E
Wakkanai **74** 45 28N 141 35 E
Wakkerstroom **93** 27 24 S 30 10 E
Wakool **99** 35 28 S 144 23 E
Wakool → **99** 35 5 S 143 33 E
Wakre **73** 0 19 S 131 5 E
Wakuach L. **107** 55 34N 67 32W
Walamba **91** 13 30 S 28 42 E
Wałbrzych **28** 50 45N 16 18 E
Walbury Hill **13** 51 22N 1 28W
Walcha **99** 30 55 S 151 31 E
Walcheren **16** 51 30N 3 35 E
Walcott **118** 41 50N 106 55W
Wałcz **28** 53 17N 16 27 E
Wald **25** 47 17N 8 56 E
Waldbröl **24** 50 52N 7 36 E
Waldeck **24** 51 12N 9 4 E
Walden, Colo., U.S.A. **118** 40 47N 106 20W
Walden, N.Y., U.S.A. **113** 41 32N 74 13W
Waldport **118** 44 30N 124 2W
Waldron, Can. **109** 50 53N 102 35W
Waldron, U.S.A. **117** 34 52N 94 4W
Waldshut **25** 47 37N 8 12 E
Walembele **84** 10 30N 1 58W
Wales □ **11** 52 30N 3 30W
Walewale **85** 10 21N 0 50W
Walgett **97** 30 0 S 148 5 E
Walgreen Coast **5** 75 15 S 105 0W
Walhalla, Austral. **99** 37 56 S 146 29 E
Walhalla, U.S.A. **109** 48 55N 97 55W
Walker **116** 47 4N 94 35W
Walker L., Man., Can. **109** 54 42N 95 57W
Walker L., Qué., Can. **107** 50 20N 67 11W
Walker L., U.S.A. **118** 38 56N 118 46W
Walkerston **98** 21 11 S 149 8 E
Walkerton **112** 44 10N 81 10W
Wall **116** 44 0N 102 14W
Walla Walla **118** 46 3N 118 25W
Wallabadah **98** 17 57 S 142 15 E
Wallace, Idaho, U.S.A. **118** 47 30N 116 0W
Wallace, N.C., U.S.A. **115** 34 44N 77 59W
Wallace, Nebr., U.S.A. **116** 40 51N 101 12W
Wallaceburg **106** 42 34N 82 23W
Wallachia = Valahia **46** 44 35N 25 0 E
Wallal **99** 26 32 S 146 7 E
Wallaroo **97** 33 56 S 137 39 E
Wallasey **12** 53 26N 3 2W
Walldürn **25** 49 34N 9 23 E
Wallerawang **99** 33 25 S 150 4 E
Wallingford, U.K. **13** 51 40N 1 15W
Wallingford, U.S.A. **113** 41 27N 72 50W
Wallis Arch. **94** 13 18 S 176 10W
Wallowa **118** 45 40N 117 35W
Wallowa, Mts. **118** 45 20N 117 30W
Wallsend, Austral. **99** 32 55 S 151 40 E
Wallsend, U.K. **12** 54 59N 1 30W
Wallula **118** 46 3N 118 59W
Wallumbilla **99** 26 33 S 149 9 E
Walmer **92** 33 57 S 25 35 E
Walmsley, L. **109** 63 25N 108 36W
Walney, Isle of **12** 54 5N 3 15W
Walnut Ridge **117** 36 7N 90 58W
Walsall **13** 52 36N 1 59W
Walsenburg **117** 37 42N 104 45W
Walsh **117** 37 28N 102 15W
Walsh → **98** 16 31 S 143 42 E
Walsh P.O. **98** 16 40 S 144 0 E
Walsrode **24** 52 51N 9 37 E
Waltair **70** 17 44N 83 23 E
Walterboro **115** 32 53N 80 40W
Walters **117** 34 25N 98 20W
Waltershausen **24** 50 53N 10 33 E
Waltham **113** 42 22N 71 12W
Waltham Sta. **106** 45 57N 76 57W
Waltman **118** 43 8N 107 15W
Walton **113** 42 12N 75 9W
Walvisbaai **92** 23 0 S 14 28 E
Wamba, Kenya **90** 0 58N 37 19 E
Wamba, Zaïre **90** 2 10N 27 57 E
Wamego **116** 39 14N 96 22W
Wamena **73** 4 4 S 138 57 E
Wampsville **113** 43 4N 75 42W
Wamsasi **73** 3 27 S 126 7 E
Wana **68** 32 20N 69 32 E
Wanaaring **99** 29 38 S 144 9 E
Wanaka L. **101** 44 33 S 169 7 E
Wan'an **77** 26 26N 114 49 E
Wanapiri **73** 4 30 S 135 59 E
Wanapitei L. **106** 46 45N 80 40W
Wanbi **99** 34 46 S 140 17 E
Wanda Shan **76** 46 0N 132 0 E
Wanderer **91** 19 36 S 30 1 E
Wandiwash **70** 12 30N 79 30 E
Wandoan **97** 26 5 S 149 55 E
Wang Kai (Ghâbat el Arab) **87** 9 3N 29 23 E
Wang Saphung **71** 17 18N 101 46 E
Wanga **90** 2 58N 29 12 E
Wangal **73** 6 8 S 134 9 E
Wanganella **99** 35 6 S 144 49 E
Wanganui **101** 39 56 S 175 3 E
Wangaratta **97** 36 21 S 146 19 E
Wangdu **76** 38 40N 115 7 E

Wangerooge	**24**	53 47N	7 52 E
Wangi	**90**	1 58 S	40 58 E
Wangiwangi	**73**	5 22 S	123 37 E
Wangjiang	**77**	30 10N	116 42 E
Wangqing	**76**	43 12N	129 42 E
Wankaner	**68**	22 35N	71 0 E
* Wankie	**91**	18 18 S	26 30 E
* Wankie Nat. Park	**92**	19 0 S	26 30 E
Wanless	**109**	54 11N	101 21W
Wanning	**77**	18 48N	110 22 E
Wannon →	**100**	37 38 S	141 25 E
Wanquan	**76**	40 50N	114 40 E
Wanxian	**75**	30 42N	108 20 E
Wanyuan	**77**	32 4N	108 3 E
Wanzai	**77**	28 7N	114 30 E
Wapakoneta	**114**	40 35N	84 10W
Wapato	**118**	46 30N	120 25W
Wapawekka L.	**109**	54 55N	104 40W
Wappingers Falls	**113**	41 35N	73 56W
Wapsipinicon →	**116**	41 44N	90 19W
Waranga Res.	**100**	36 32 S	145 5 E
Warangal	**70**	17 58N	79 35 E
Waratah	**99**	41 30 S	145 30 E
Waratah B.	**99**	38 54 S	146 5 E
Warburg	**24**	51 29N	9 10 E
Warburton	**99**	37 47 S	145 42 E
Warburton →	**97**	28 4 S	137 28 E
Ward	**101**	41 49 S	174 11 E
Ward →	**99**	26 28 S	146 6 E
Ward Cove	**108**	55 25N	132 43W
Ward Hunt, C.	**98**	8 2 S	148 10 E
Wardak □	**65**	34 0N	68 0 E
Warden	**93**	27 50 S	29 0 E
Wardha	**68**	20 45N	78 39 E
Wardlow	**108**	50 56N	111 31W
Ware, Can.	**108**	57 26N	125 41W
Ware, U.S.A.	**113**	42 16N	72 15W
Wareham	**113**	41 45N	70 44W
Waren	**24**	53 30N	12 41 E
Warendorf	**24**	51 57N	8 0 E
Warialda	**97**	29 29 S	150 33 E
Wariap	**73**	1 30 S	134 5 E
Warka	**28**	51 47N	21 12 E
Warkopi	**73**	1 12 S	134 9 E
Warley	**13**	52 30N	2 0W
Warm Springs, Mont., U.S.A.	**118**	46 11N	112 48W
Warm Springs, Nev., U.S.A.	**119**	38 16N	116 32W
Warman	**109**	52 19N	106 30W
Warmbad, Namibia	**92**	28 25 S	18 42 E
Warmbad, S. Afr.	**93**	24 51 S	28 19 E
Warmeriville	**19**	49 20N	4 13 E
Warnambool Downs	**98**	22 48 S	142 52 E
Warnemünde	**24**	54 9N	12 5 E
Warner	**108**	49 17N	112 12W
Warner Range, Mts.	**118**	41 30 S	120 20W
Warner Robins	**115**	32 41N	83 36W
Warnow →	**24**	54 6N	12 9 E
Warora	**70**	20 14N	79 1 E
Warracknabeal	**100**	36 9 S	142 26 E
Warragul	**99**	38 10 S	145 58 E
Warrego →	**97**	30 24 S	145 21 E
Warrego Ra.	**97**	24 58 S	146 0 E
Warren, Austral.	**99**	31 42 S	147 51 E
Warren, Ark., U.S.A.	**117**	33 35N	92 3W
Warren, Minn., U.S.A.	**116**	48 12N	96 46W
Warren, Ohio, U.S.A.	**114**	41 18N	80 52W
Warren, Pa., U.S.A.	**114**	41 52N	79 10W
Warrenpoint	**15**	54 7N	6 15W
Warrensburg	**116**	38 45N	93 45W
Warrenton, S. Afr.	**92**	28 9 S	24 47 E
Warrenton, U.S.A.	**118**	46 11N	123 59W
Warrenville	**99**	25 48 S	147 22 E
Warri	**85**	5 30N	5 41 E
Warrina	**96**	28 12 S	135 50 E
Warrington, U.K.	**12**	53 25N	2 38W
Warrington, U.S.A.	**115**	30 22N	87 16W
Warrnambool	**97**	38 25 S	142 30 E
Warroad	**116**	48 54N	95 19W
Warsa	**73**	0 47 S	135 55 E
Warsaw, Ind., U.S.A.	**114**	41 14N	85 50W
Warsaw, N.Y., U.S.A.	**112**	42 46N	78 10W
Warsaw, Ohio, U.S.A.	**112**	40 20N	82 0W
Warsaw = Warszawa	**28**	52 13N	21 0 E
Warstein	**24**	51 26N	8 20 E
Warszawa	**28**	52 13N	21 0 E
Warszawa □	**28**	52 30N	21 0 E
Warta	**28**	51 43N	18 38 E
Warta →	**28**	52 35N	14 39 E
Waru	**73**	3 30 S	130 36 E
Warud	**68**	21 30N	78 16 E
Warwick, Austral.	**97**	28 10 S	152 1 E
Warwick, U.K.	**13**	52 17N	1 36W
Warwick, U.S.A.	**114**	41 43N	71 25W
Warwick □	**13**	52 20N	1 30W
Wasa	**108**	49 45N	115 50W
Wasaga Beach	**112**	44 31N	80 1W
Wasatch, Ra.	**118**	40 30N	111 15W
Wasbank	**93**	28 15 S	30 9 E
Wasco, Calif., U.S.A.	**119**	35 37N	119 16W
Wasco, Oreg., U.S.A.	**118**	45 36N	120 46W
Waseca	**116**	44 3N	93 31W
Wasekamio L.	**109**	56 45N	108 45W
Wash, The	**12**	52 58N	0 20 E
Washago	**112**	44 45N	79 20W
Washburn, N.D., U.S.A.	**116**	47 17N	101 0W
Washburn, Wis., U.S.A.	**116**	46 38N	90 55W
Washington, D.C., U.S.A.	**114**	38 52N	77 0W
Washington, Ga., U.S.A.	**115**	33 45N	82 45W
Washington, Ind., U.S.A.	**114**	38 40N	87 8W
Washington, Iowa, U.S.A.	**116**	41 20N	91 45W
Washington, Mo, U.S.A.	**116**	38 35N	91 1W
Washington, N.C., U.S.A.	**115**	35 35N	77 1W
Washington, N.J., U.S.A.	**113**	40 45N	74 59W
Washington, Pa., U.S.A.	**114**	40 10N	80 20W
Washington, Utah, U.S.A.	**119**	37 10N	113 30W
Washington □	**118**	47 45N	120 30W
† Washington I., Pac. Oc.	**95**	4 43N	160 25W
Washington I., U.S.A.	**114**	45 24N	86 54W
Washington Mt.	**114**	44 15N	71 18W
Wasian	**73**	1 47 S	133 19 E
Wasilków	**28**	53 12N	23 13 E
Wasior	**73**	2 43 S	134 30 E
Waskaiowaka, L.	**109**	56 33N	96 23W
Waskesiu Lake	**109**	53 55N	106 5W
Wasm	**86**	18 2N	41 32 E
Wassenaar	**16**	52 8N	4 24 E
Wasserburg	**25**	48 4N	12 15 E
Wasserkuppe	**24**	50 30N	9 56 E
Wassy	**19**	48 30N	4 58 E
Waswanipi	**106**	49 40N	76 29W
Waswanipi, L.	**106**	49 35N	76 40W
Watangpon	**73**	4 29 S	120 25 E
Water Park Pt.	**98**	22 56 S	150 47 E
Water Valley	**117**	34 9N	89 38W
Waterberg, Namibia	**92**	20 30 S	17 18 E
Waterberg, S. Afr.	**93**	24 14 S	28 0 E
Waterbury, Conn., U.S.A.	**114**	41 32N	73 0W
Waterbury, Vt., U.S.A.	**113**	44 22N	72 44W
Waterbury L.	**109**	58 10N	104 22W
Waterdown	**112**	43 20N	79 53W
Waterford, Can.	**112**	42 56N	80 17W
Waterford, Ireland	**15**	52 16N	7 8W
Waterford □	**15**	52 10N	7 40W
Waterford Harb.	**15**	52 10N	6 58W
Waterhen L., Man., Can.	**109**	52 10N	99 40W
Waterhen L., Sask., Can.	**109**	54 28N	108 25W
Waterloo, Belg.	**16**	50 43N	4 25 E
Waterloo, Ont., Can.	**106**	43 30N	80 32W
Waterloo, Qué., Can.	**113**	45 22N	72 32W
Waterloo, S. Leone	**84**	8 26N	13 8W
Waterloo, Ill., U.S.A.	**116**	38 22N	90 6W
Waterloo, Iowa, U.S.A.	**116**	42 27N	92 20W
Waterloo, N.Y., U.S.A.	**112**	42 54N	76 53W
Watersmeet	**116**	46 15N	89 12W
Waterton Lakes Nat. Park	**108**	49 5N	114 15W
Watertown, Conn., U.S.A.	**113**	41 36N	73 7W
Watertown, N.Y., U.S.A.	**114**	43 58N	75 57W
Watertown, S.D., U.S.A.	**116**	44 57N	97 5W
Watertown, Wis., U.S.A.	**116**	43 15N	88 45W
Waterval-Boven	**93**	25 40 S	30 18 E
Waterville, Can.	**113**	45 16N	71 54W
Waterville, Me., U.S.A.	**107**	44 35N	69 40W
Waterville, N.Y., U.S.A.	**113**	42 56N	75 23W
Waterville, Pa., U.S.A.	**112**	41 19N	77 21W
Waterville, Wash., U.S.A.	**118**	47 38N	120 1W
Watervliet	**114**	42 46N	73 43W
Wates	**73**	7 53 S	110 6 E
Watford, Can.	**112**	42 57N	81 53W
Watford, U.K.	**13**	51 38N	0 23W
Watford City	**116**	47 50N	103 23W
Wathaman →	**109**	57 16N	102 59W
Watkins Glen	**114**	42 25N	76 55W
Watling I. = San Salvador	**121**	24 0N	74 40W
Watonga	**117**	35 51N	98 24W
Watrous, Can.	**109**	51 40N	105 25W
Watrous, U.S.A.	**117**	35 50N	104 55W
Watsa	**90**	3 4N	29 30 E
Watseka	**114**	40 45N	87 45W
Watson	**109**	52 10N	104 30W
Watson Lake	**104**	60 6N	128 49W
Watsonville	**119**	36 55N	121 49W
Wattwil	**25**	47 18N	9 6 E
Watuata = Batuata	**73**	6 12 S	122 42 E
Watubela, Kepulauan	**73**	4 28 S	131 35 E
Wau	**98**	7 21 S	146 47 E
Waubamik	**112**	45 27N	80 1W
Waubay	**116**	45 22N	97 17W
Waubra	**99**	37 21 S	143 39 E
Wauchope	**99**	31 28 S	152 45 E
Wauchula	**115**	27 35N	81 50W
Waugh	**109**	49 40N	95 11W
Waukegan	**114**	42 22N	87 54W
Waukesha	**114**	43 0N	88 15W
Waukon	**116**	43 14N	91 33W
Wauneta	**116**	40 27N	101 25W
Waupaca	**116**	44 22N	89 8W
Waupun	**116**	43 38N	88 44W
Waurika	**117**	34 12N	98 0W
Wausau	**116**	44 57N	89 40W
Wautoma	**116**	44 3N	89 20W
Wauwatosa	**114**	43 6N	87 59W
Wave Hill	**96**	17 32 S	131 0 E
Waveney →	**13**	52 24N	1 20 E
Waverley	**101**	39 46 S	174 37 E
Waverly, Iowa, U.S.A.	**116**	42 40N	92 30W
Waverly, N.Y., U.S.A.	**114**	42 0N	76 33W
Wavre	**16**	50 43N	4 38 E
Wâw	**87**	7 45N	28 1 E
Waw al Kabir	**81**	25 20N	17 20 E
Wâw al Kabîr	**83**	25 20N	16 43 E
Wâw an Nāmūs	**83**	24 55N	17 46 E
Wawa, Can.	**106**	47 59N	84 47W
Wawa, Nigeria	**85**	9 54N	4 27 E
Wawa, Sudan	**86**	20 30N	30 22 E
Wawanesa	**109**	49 36N	99 40W
Wawoi →	**98**	7 48 S	143 16 E
Waxahachie	**117**	32 22N	96 53W
Waxweiler	**25**	50 6N	6 22 E
Wayabula Rau	**73**	2 29N	128 17 E
Wayatinah	**99**	42 19 S	146 27 E
Waycross	**115**	31 12N	82 25W
Wayi	**87**	5 8N	30 10 E
Wayne, Nebr., U.S.A.	**116**	42 16N	97 0W
Wayne, W. Va., U.S.A.	**114**	38 15N	82 27W
Waynesboro, Ga., U.S.A.	**115**	33 6N	82 1W
Waynesboro, Miss., U.S.A.	**115**	31 40N	88 39W
Waynesboro, Pa., U.S.A.	**114**	39 46N	77 32W
Waynesboro, Va., U.S.A.	**114**	38 4N	78 57W
Waynesburg	**114**	39 54N	80 12W
Waynesville	**115**	35 31N	83 0W
Waynoka	**117**	36 38N	98 53W
Wâzin	**83**	31 58N	10 40 E
Wazirabad	**68**	32 30N	74 8 E
Wda →	**28**	53 25N	18 29 E
We	**72**	5 51N	95 18 E
Weald, The	**13**	51 7N	0 9 E
Wear →	**12**	54 55N	1 22W
Weatherford, Okla., U.S.A.	**117**	35 30N	98 45W
Weatherford, Tex., U.S.A.	**117**	32 45N	97 48W
Weaverville	**118**	40 44N	122 56W
Webb City	**117**	37 9N	94 30W
Webster, Mass., U.S.A.	**113**	42 4N	71 54W
Webster, N.Y., U.S.A.	**112**	43 11N	77 27W
Webster, S.D., U.S.A.	**116**	45 24N	97 33W
Webster, Wis., U.S.A.	**116**	45 53N	92 25W
Webster City	**116**	42 30N	93 50W
Webster Green	**116**	38 38N	90 20W
Webster Springs	**114**	38 30N	80 25W
Weda	**73**	0 21N	127 50 E
Weda, Teluk	**73**	0 30N	127 50 E
Weddell I.	**128**	51 50 S	61 0W
Weddell Sea	**5**	72 30 S	40 0W
Wedderburn	**99**	36 26 S	143 33 E
Wedge I.	**96**	30 50 S	115 11 E
Wedgeport	**107**	43 44N	65 59W
Wedza	**91**	18 40 S	31 33 E
Wee Waa	**99**	30 11 S	149 26 E
Weed	**118**	41 29N	122 22W
Weedsport	**113**	43 3N	76 35W
Weedville	**112**	41 17N	78 28W
Weemelah	**99**	29 2 S	149 15 E
Weenen	**93**	28 48 S	30 7 E
Weener	**24**	53 10N	7 23 E
Weert	**16**	51 15N	5 43 E
Wegierska-Gorka	**27**	49 36N	19 7 E
Wegliniec	**28**	51 18N	15 10 E
Węgorzewo	**28**	54 13N	21 43 E
Węgrów	**28**	52 24N	22 0 E
Wei He →, Hebei, China	**76**	36 10N	115 45 E
Wei He →, Shaanxi, China	**77**	34 38N	110 15 E
Weida	**24**	50 47N	12 3 E
Weiden	**25**	49 40N	12 10 E
Weifang	**76**	36 44N	119 7 E
Weihai	**76**	37 30N	122 6 E
Weilburg	**24**	50 28N	8 17 E
Weilheim	**25**	47 50N	11 9 E
Weimar	**24**	51 0N	11 20 E
Weinan	**77**	34 31N	109 29 E
Weingarten	**25**	47 49N	9 39 E
Weinheim	**25**	49 33N	8 40 E
Weipa	**97**	12 40 S	141 50 E
Weir →, Austral.	**99**	28 20 S	149 50 E
Weir →, Can.	**109**	56 54N	93 21W
Weir River	**109**	56 49N	94 6W
Weirton	**112**	40 23N	80 35W
Weiser	**118**	44 10N	117 0W
Weishan	**77**	34 47N	117 5 E
Weissenburg	**25**	49 2N	10 58 E
Weissenfels	**24**	51 11N	12 0 E
Weisswasser	**24**	51 30N	14 36 E
Wéitra	**26**	48 41N	14 54 E
Weiyuan	**76**	35 7N	104 10 E
Weiz	**26**	47 13N	15 39 E
Weizhou Dao	**77**	21 0N	109 5 E
Wejherowo	**28**	54 35N	18 12 E
Wekusko	**109**	54 30N	99 45W
Wekusko L.	**109**	54 40N	99 50W
Welby	**109**	50 33N	101 29W
Welch	**114**	37 29N	81 36W
Weldya	**87**	11 50N	39 34 E
Welega □	**87**	9 25N	34 20 E
Welkite	**87**	8 15N	37 42 E
Welkom	**92**	28 0 S	26 50 E
Welland	**106**	43 0N	79 15W
Welland →	**12**	52 43N	0 10W
Wellesley Is.	**97**	16 42 S	139 30 E
Wellin	**16**	50 5N	5 6 E
Wellingborough	**13**	52 18N	0 41W
Wellington, Austral.	**97**	32 35 S	148 59 E
Wellington, Can.	**106**	43 57N	77 20W
Wellington, N.Z.	**101**	41 19 S	174 46 E
Wellington, S. Afr.	**92**	33 38 S	18 57 E
Wellington, U.K.	**13**	50 58N	3 13W
Wellington, Col., U.S.A.	**116**	40 43N	105 0W
Wellington, Kans., U.S.A.	**117**	37 15N	97 25W
Wellington, Nev., U.S.A.	**118**	38 47N	119 28W
Wellington, Ohio, U.S.A.	**112**	41 9N	82 12W
Wellington, Tex., U.S.A.	**117**	34 55N	100 13W
Wellington □	**101**	40 8 S	175 36 E
Wellington, I.	**128**	49 30 S	75 0W
Wellington, L.	**99**	38 6 S	147 20 E
Wellington (Telford)	**12**	52 42N	2 31W
Wells, Norfolk, U.K.	**12**	52 57N	0 51 E
Wells, Somerset, U.K.	**13**	51 12N	2 39W
Wells, Me., U.S.A.	**113**	43 18N	70 35W
Wells, Minn., U.S.A.	**116**	43 44N	93 45W
Wells, Nev., U.S.A.	**118**	41 8N	115 0W
Wells Gray Prov. Park	**108**	52 30N	120 15W
Wells L.	**96**	26 44 S	123 15 E
Wells River	**113**	44 9N	72 4W
Wellsboro	**114**	41 45N	77 20W
Wellsburg	**112**	40 15N	80 36W
Wellsville, Mo., U.S.A.	**116**	39 4N	91 30W
Wellsville, N.Y., U.S.A.	**114**	42 9N	77 53W
Wellsville, Ohio, U.S.A.	**114**	40 36N	80 40W
Wellsville, Utah, U.S.A.	**118**	41 35N	111 59W
Wellton	**119**	32 39N	114 6W
Welmel, Wabi →	**87**	5 38N	40 47 E
Wełna →	**28**	52 46N	17 32 E
Welo □	**87**	11 50N	39 48 E
Wels	**26**	48 9N	14 1 E
Welshpool	**13**	52 40N	3 9W
Welwyn	**109**	50 20N	101 30W
Wem	**12**	52 52N	2 45W
Wembere →	**90**	4 10 S	34 15 E
Wen Xian	**77**	32 43N	104 36 E
Wenatchee	**118**	47 30N	120 17W
Wenchang	**77**	19 38N	110 42 E
Wenchi	**84**	7 46N	2 8W
Wenchow = Wenzhou	**75**	28 0N	120 38 E
Wendell	**118**	42 50N	114 42W
Wendeng	**76**	37 15N	122 5 E
Wendesi	**73**	2 30 S	134 17 E
Wendo	**87**	6 40N	38 27 E
Wendover	**118**	40 49N	114 1W
Wengcheng	**77**	24 22N	113 50 E
Wenlock	**98**	13 6 S	142 58 E
Wenlock →	**97**	12 2 S	141 55 E
Wensu	**75**	41 15N	80 10 E
Wentworth	**97**	34 2 S	141 54 E
Wenut	**73**	3 11 S	133 19 E
Wenxi	**77**	35 20N	111 10 E
Wenzhou	**75**	28 0N	120 38 E
Weott	**118**	40 19N	123 56W
Wepener	**92**	29 42 S	27 3 E
Werda	**92**	25 24 S	23 15 E
Werdau	**24**	50 45N	12 20 E
Werder, Ethiopia	**63**	6 58N	45 1 E
Werder, Ger.	**24**	52 23N	12 56 E
Werdohl	**24**	51 15N	7 47 E
Wereilu	**87**	10 40N	39 28 E
Weri	**73**	3 10 S	132 38 E
Werne	**24**	51 38N	7 38 E
Werneck	**25**	49 59N	10 6 E
Wernigerode	**24**	51 49N	10 45 E
Werra →	**24**	51 26N	9 39 E
Werribee	**99**	37 54 S	144 40 E
Werrimull	**99**	34 25 S	141 38 E
Werris Creek	**99**	31 18 S	150 38 E
Wersar	**73**	1 30 S	131 55 E
Wertach →	**25**	48 24N	10 53 E
Wertheim	**25**	49 44N	9 32 E
Wertingen	**25**	48 33N	10 41 E
Wesel	**24**	51 39N	6 34 E
Weser →	**24**	53 33N	8 30 E
Wesiri	**73**	7 30 S	126 30 E
Wesleyville, Can.	**107**	49 8N	53 36W
Wesleyville, U.S.A.	**112**	42 9N	80 1W
Wessel Is.	**97**	11 10 S	136 45 E
Wesselburen	**24**	54 11N	8 53 E
Wessington	**116**	44 30N	98 40W
Wessington Springs	**116**	44 10N	98 35W
West	**117**	31 50N	97 5W
West B.	**117**	29 5N	89 27W
West Bend	**114**	43 25N	88 10W
West Bengal □	**69**	23 0N	88 0 E
West Branch	**114**	44 16N	84 13W
West Bromwich	**13**	52 32N	2 1W
West Chazy	**113**	44 49N	73 28W
West Chester	**114**	39 58N	75 36W
West Columbia	**117**	29 10N	95 38W
West Des Moines	**116**	41 30N	93 45W
West Falkland	**128**	51 40 S	60 0W
West Frankfurt	**116**	37 56N	89 0W
West Germany ■	**24**	52 0N	9 0 E
West Glamorgan □	**13**	51 40N	3 55W
West Hartford	**113**	41 45N	72 45W
West Haven	**113**	41 18N	72 57W
West Helena	**117**	34 30N	90 40W
West Ice Shelf	**5**	67 0 S	85 0 E
West Indies	**121**	15 0N	70 0W
West Looe	**13**	50 21N	4 29W
West Lorne	**112**	42 36N	81 36W
West Lunga →	**91**	13 6 S	24 39 E
West Magpie →	**107**	51 2N	64 42W
West Memphis	**117**	35 5N	90 11W
West Midlands □	**13**	52 30N	1 55W
West Monroe	**117**	32 32N	92 7W
West Moors	**12**	50 49N	1 50W
West Newton	**112**	40 14N	79 46W
West Nicholson	**91**	21 2 S	29 20 E
West Palm Beach	**115**	26 44N	80 3W
West Pittston	**113**	41 19N	75 49W
West Plains	**117**	36 45N	91 50W
West Point, Ga., U.S.A.	**115**	32 54N	85 10W
West Point, Miss., U.S.A.	**115**	33 36N	88 38W
West Point, Nebr., U.S.A.	**116**	41 50N	96 43W
West Point, Va., U.S.A.	**114**	37 35N	76 47W
West Pokot □	**90**	1 30N	35 15 E
West Road →	**108**	53 18N	122 53W
West Rutland	**114**	43 38N	73 0W
West Schelde → = Westerschelde	**16**	51 25N	3 25 E
West Siberian Plain	**60**	62 0N	75 0 E
West Sussex □	**13**	50 55N	0 30W
West-Terschelling	**16**	53 22N	5 13 E
West Virginia □	**114**	39 0N	81 0W
West-Vlaanderen □	**16**	51 0N	3 0 E
West Wyalong	**100**	33 56 S	147 10 E
West Yellowstone	**118**	44 47N	111 4W
West Yorkshire □	**12**	53 45N	1 40W
Westbrook, Maine, U.S.A.	**115**	43 40N	70 22W
Westbrook, Tex., U.S.A.	**117**	32 25N	101 0W
Westbury	**99**	41 30 S	146 51 E
Westby	**116**	48 52N	104 3W
Westerland	**24**	54 51N	8 20 E
Western □, Kenya	**90**	0 30N	34 30 E
Western □, Uganda	**90**	1 45N	31 30 E
Western □, Zambia	**91**	15 15 S	24 30 E
Western Australia □	**96**	25 0 S	118 0 E
Western Ghats	**70**	14 0N	75 0 E
Western Isles □	**14**	57 30N	7 10W
Western Samoa ■	**101**	14 0 S	172 0W
Westernport	**114**	39 30N	79 5W
Westerschelde →	**16**	51 25N	3 25 E
Westerstede	**24**	53 15N	7 55 E
Westerwald	**24**	50 39N	8 0 E
Westfield, Mass., U.S.A.	**113**	42 9N	72 49W
Westfield, N.Y., U.S.A.	**112**	42 20N	79 38W
Westfield, Pa., U.S.A.	**112**	41 54N	77 32W
Westhope	**116**	48 55N	101 0W
Westland □	**101**	43 33 S	169 59 E
Westland Bight	**101**	42 55 S	170 5 E
Westlock	**108**	54 9N	113 55W
Westmeath □	**15**	53 30N	7 30W
Westminster	**114**	39 34N	77 1W
Westmorland	**119**	33 2N	115 42W
Weston, Malay.	**72**	5 10N	115 35 E
Weston, Oreg., U.S.A.	**118**	45 50N	118 30W
Weston, W. Va., U.S.A.	**114**	39 3N	80 29W
Weston I.	**106**	52 33N	79 36W
Weston-super-Mare	**13**	51 20N	2 59W
Westport, Can.	**113**	44 40N	76 25W
Westport, Ireland	**15**	53 44N	9 31W
Westport, N.Z.	**101**	41 46 S	171 37 E
Westport, U.S.A.	**118**	46 48N	124 4W
Westray, Can.	**109**	53 36N	101 24W
Westray, U.K.	**14**	59 18N	3 0W
Westree	**106**	47 26N	81 34W
Westview	**108**	49 50N	124 31W
Westville, Ill., U.S.A.	**114**	40 3N	87 36W
Westville, Okla., U.S.A.	**117**	36 0N	94 33W
Westwood	**118**	40 26N	121 0W
Wetar	**73**	7 30 S	126 30 E
Wetaskiwin	**108**	52 55N	113 24W
Wethersfield	**113**	41 43N	72 40W
Wetteren	**16**	51 0N	3 53 E
Wetzlar	**24**	50 33N	8 30 E

** Renamed Hwange*

† Renamed Teraina

Wewak Workington

Wewak 98 3 38S 143 41 E
Wewaka 117 35 10N 96 35W
Wexford 15 52 20N 6 28W
Wexford □ 15 52 20N 6 25W
Wexford Harb. 15 52 20N 6 25W
Weyburn 109 49 40N 103 50W
Weyburn L. 108 63 0N 117 59W
Weyer 26 47 51N 14 40 E
Weyib → 87 7 15N 40 15 E
Weymouth, Can. 107 44 30N 66 1W
Weymouth, U.K. 13 50 36N 2 28W
Weymouth, U.S.A. 113 42 13N 70 53W
Weymouth, C. 97 12 37S 143 27 E
Whakatane 101 37 57S 177 1 E
Whale → 107 58 15N 67 40W
Whale Cove 104 62 11N 92 36W
Whales, B. of 5 78 0S 165 0W
Whalsay 14 60 22N 1 0W
Whangamomona 101 39 8S 174 44 E
Whangarei 101 35 43S 174 21 E
Whangarei Harbour 101 35 45S 174 28 E
Wharfe → 12 53 55N 1 30W
Wharfedale 12 54 7N 2 4W
Wharton, N.J., U.S.A. 113 40 53N 74 36W
Wharton, Pa., U.S.A. 112 41 31N 78 1W
Wharton, Tex., U.S.A. 117 29 20N 96 6W
Wheatland 116 42 4N 104 58W
Wheatley 112 42 6N 82 27W
Wheaton 116 45 50N 96 29W
Wheeler, Oreg., U.S.A. 118 45 50N 123 57W
Wheeler, Tex., U.S.A. 117 35 29N 100 15W
Wheeler → 109 57 25N 105 30W
Wheeler Pk., N. Mex., U.S.A. 119 36 34N 105 25W
Wheeler Pk., Nev., U.S.A. 119 38 57N 114 15W
Wheeling 114 40 2N 80 41W
Whernside 12 54 14N 2 24W
Whidbey I. 108 48 15N 122 40W
Whidbey Is. 96 34 30S 135 3 E
Whiskey Gap 108 49 0N 113 3W
Whiskey Jack L. 109 58 23N 101 55W
Whistler 115 30 50N 88 10W
Whitby, Can. 112 43 52N 78 56W
Whitby, U.K. 12 54 29N 0 37W
White →, Ark., U.S.A. 117 33 53N 91 3W
White →, Colo., U.S.A. 118 40 8N 109 41W
White →, Ind., U.S.A. 114 38 25N 87 44W
White →, S.D., U.S.A. 116 43 45N 99 30W
White B. 107 50 0N 56 35W
White Bear Res. 107 48 10N 57 5W
White Bird 118 45 46N 116 21W
White Butte 116 46 23N 103 19W
White City 116 38 50N 96 45W
White Cliffs 99 30 50S 143 10 E
White Deer 117 35 30N 101 8W
White Hall 116 39 25N 90 27W
White Haven 113 41 3N 75 47W
White I. 101 37 30S 177 13 E
White L., Can. 113 45 18N 76 31W
White L., U.S.A. 117 29 45N 92 30W
White Mts., Calif., U.S.A. 119 37 30N 118 15W
White Mts., N.H., U.S.A. 113 44 15N 71 15W
White Nile = Nîl el Abyad → 87 15 38N 32 31 E
White Nile Dam 87 15 24N 32 30 E
White Otter L. 106 49 5N 91 55W
White Pass 104 59 40N 135 3W
White Plains 113 41 2N 73 44W
White River, Can. 106 48 35N 85 20W
White River, S. Afr. 93 25 20S 31 00 E
White River, U.S.A. 116 43 34N 100 45W
White River Junc. 113 43 38N 72 20W
White Russia = Byelorussian S.S.R. □ 54 53 30N 27 0 E
White Sea = Beloye More 52 66 30N 38 0 E
White Sulphur Springs, Mont., U.S.A. 118 46 35N 110 54W
White Sulphur Springs, W. Va., U.S.A. 114 37 50N 80 16W
White Volta (Volta Blanche) → 85 9 10N 1 15W
Whitecliffs 101 43 26S 171 55 E
Whitecourt 108 54 10N 115 45W
Whiteface 117 33 35N 102 40W
Whitefield 113 44 23N 71 37W
Whitefish 118 48 25N 114 22W
Whitefish L. 109 62 41N 106 48W
Whitefish Pt. 114 46 45N 85 0W
Whitegull, L. 107 55 27N 64 17W
Whitehall, Mich., U.S.A. 114 43 21N 86 20W
Whitehall, Mont., U.S.A. 118 45 52N 112 4W
Whitehall, N.Y., U.S.A. 113 43 32N 73 28W
Whitehall, Wis., U.S.A. 116 44 20N 91 19W
Whitehaven 12 54 33N 3 35W
Whitehorse 104 60 43N 135 3W
Whitehorse, Vale of 13 51 37N 1 30W
Whiteman Ra. 98 5 55S 150 0 E
Whitemark 99 40 7S 148 3 E
Whitemouth 109 49 57N 95 58W
Whiteplains 84 6 28N 10 40W
Whitesail, L. 108 53 35N 127 45W
Whitesboro, N.Y., U.S.A. 113 43 8N 75 20W
Whitesboro, Tex., U.S.A. 117 33 40N 96 58W
Whiteshell Prov. Park 109 50 0N 95 40W
Whitetail 116 48 54N 105 15W
Whiteville 115 34 20N 78 40W
Whitewater 114 42 50N 88 45W
Whitewater Baldy, Mt. 119 33 20N 108 44W
Whitewater L. 106 50 50N 89 10W
Whitewood, Austral. 98 21 28S 143 30 E
Whitewood, Can. 109 50 20N 102 20W
Whitfield 99 36 42S 146 24 E
Whithorn 14 54 44N 4 25W
Whitianga 101 36 47S 175 41 E
Whitman 113 42 4N 70 55W
Whitmire 115 34 33N 81 40W
Whitney 106 45 31N 78 14W
Whitney, Mt. 119 36 35N 118 14W
Whitney Pt. 113 42 19N 75 59W
Whitstable 13 51 21N 1 2 E
Whitsunday I. 97 20 15S 149 4 E
Whittier 104 60 46N 148 48W
Whittlesea 99 37 27S 145 9 E
Whitwell 115 35 15N 85 30W
Wholdaia L. 109 60 43N 104 20W
Whyalla 97 33 2S 137 30 E
Whyjonta 99 29 41S 142 28 E
Wiarton 106 44 40N 81 10W
Wiawso 84 6 10N 2 25W
Wiazów 28 50 50N 17 10 E
Wibaux 116 47 0N 104 13W
Wichita 117 37 40N 97 20W
Wichita Falls 117 33 57N 98 30W
Wick 14 58 26N 3 5W
Wickenburg 119 33 58N 112 45W
Wickett 117 31 37N 102 58W
Wickham, C. 99 39 35S 143 57 E
Wickliffe 112 41 36N 81 29W
Wicklow 15 53 0N 6 2W
Wicklow □ 15 52 59N 6 25W
Wicklow Hd. 15 52 59N 6 3W
Wicklow Mts. 15 53 0N 6 30W
Widawa 28 51 27N 18 51 E
Widawka 28 51 7N 19 36 E
Widnes 12 53 22N 2 44W
Więcbork 28 53 21N 17 30 E
Wiedenbrück 24 51 52N 8 15 E
Wiek 24 54 37N 13 17 E
Wielbark 28 53 24N 20 55 E
Wieleń 28 52 53N 16 9 E
Wieliczka 27 50 0N 20 5 E
Wieluń 28 51 15N 18 34 E
Wien 27 48 12N 16 22 E
Wiener Neustadt 27 47 49N 16 16 E
Wieprz →, Koszalin, Poland 28 54 26N 16 35 E
Wieprz →, Lublin, Poland 28 51 34N 21 49 E
Wierden 16 52 22N 6 35 E
Wieruszów 28 51 19N 18 9 E
Wiesbaden 25 50 7N 8 17 E
Wiesental 25 49 15N 8 30 E
Wigan 12 53 33N 2 38W
Wiggins, Colo., U.S.A. 116 40 16N 104 3W
Wiggins, Miss., U.S.A. 117 30 53N 89 9W
Wight, I. of 13 50 40N 1 20W
Wigry, Jezioro 28 54 2N 23 8 E
Wigtown 14 54 52N 4 27W
Wigtown B. 14 54 46N 4 15W
Wil 25 47 28N 9 3 E
Wilamowice 27 49 55N 19 9 E
Wilber 116 40 34N 96 59W
Wilberforce 112 45 2N 78 13W
Wilberforce, C. 97 11 54S 136 35 E
Wilburton 117 34 55N 95 15W
Wilcannia 97 31 30S 143 26 E
Wilcox 112 41 34N 78 43W
Wildbad 25 48 44N 8 32 E
Wildeshausen 24 52 54N 8 25 E
Wildon 26 46 52N 15 31 E
Wildrose 116 48 36N 103 11W
Wildspitze 26 46 53N 10 53 E
Wildwood 114 38 59N 74 46W
Wilga → 28 51 52N 21 18 E
Wilhelm II Coast 5 68 0S 90 0 E
Wilhelm Mt. 98 5 50S 145 1 E
Wilhelm-Pieck-Stadt Guben 24 51 59N 14 48 E
Wilhelmsburg, Austria 26 48 6N 15 36 E
Wilhelmsburg, Ger. 24 53 28N 10 1 E
Wilhelmshaven 24 53 30N 8 9 E
Wilhelmstal 92 21 58S 16 21 E
Wilkes Barre 114 41 15N 75 52W
Wilkes Land 5 69 0S 120 0 E
Wilkes Sub-Glacial Basin 5 75 0S 130 0 E
Wilkesboro 115 36 10N 81 9W
Wilkie 109 52 27N 108 42W
Wilkinsburg 112 40 26N 79 50W
Willamina 118 45 9N 123 32W
Willandra Billabong Creek → 99 33 22S 145 52 E
Willapa, B. 118 46 44N 124 0W
Willard, N. Mex., U.S.A. 119 34 35N 106 1W
Willard, Utah, U.S.A. 118 41 28N 112 1W
Willcox 119 32 13N 109 53W
Willemstad 121 12 5N 69 0W
William → 109 59 8N 109 19W
Williams 119 35 16N 112 11W
Williams Lake 108 52 10N 122 10W
Williamsburg, Ky., U.S.A. 115 36 45N 84 10W
Williamsburg, Pa., U.S.A. 112 40 27N 78 14W
Williamsburg, Va., U.S.A. 114 37 17N 76 44W
Williamson, N.Y., U.S.A. 112 43 14N 77 15W
Williamson, W. Va., U.S.A. 114 37 46N 82 17W
Williamsport 114 41 18N 77 1W
Williamston 115 35 50N 77 5W
Williamstown, Austral. 99 37 51S 144 52 E
Williamstown, Mass., U.S.A. 113 42 41N 73 12W
Williamstown, N.Y., U.S.A. 113 43 25N 75 54W
Williamsville 117 37 0N 90 33W
Willimantic 113 41 45N 72 12W
Williston, S. Afr. 92 31 20S 20 53 E
Williston, Fla., U.S.A. 115 29 25N 82 28W
Williston, N.D., U.S.A. 116 48 10N 103 35W
Williston L. 108 56 0N 124 0W
Willits 118 39 28N 123 17W
Willmar 116 45 5N 95 0W
Willoughby 112 41 38N 81 26W
Willow Bunch 109 49 20N 105 35W
Willow L. 108 62 10N 119 8W
Willow Lake 116 44 40N 97 40W
Willow River 108 54 6N 122 28W
Willow Springs 117 37 0N 92 0W
Willowlake → 108 62 42N 123 8W
Willowmore 92 33 15S 23 30 E
Willows, Austral. 98 23 39S 147 25 E
Willows, U.S.A. 118 39 30N 122 10W
Wills Cr. → 98 22 43S 140 2 E
Wills Pt. 117 32 42N 95 57W
Willunga 99 35 15S 138 30 E
Wilmette 114 42 6N 87 44W
Wilmington, Austral. 99 32 39S 138 7 E
Wilmington, Del., U.S.A. 114 39 45N 75 32W
Wilmington, Ill., U.S.A. 114 41 19N 88 10W
Wilmington, N.C., U.S.A. 115 34 14N 77 54W
Wilmington, Ohio, U.S.A. 114 39 27N 83 50W
Wilpena Cr. → 99 31 25S 139 29 E
Wilsall 118 45 59N 110 40W
Wilson 115 35 44N 77 54W
Wilson → 99 27 38S 141 24 E
Wilson, Mt. 119 37 55N 108 3W
Wilson's Promontory 97 38 55S 146 25 E
Wilster 24 53 55N 9 23 E
Wilton, U.K. 13 51 5N 1 52W
Wilton, U.S.A. 116 47 12N 100 47W
Wiltshire □ 13 51 20N 2 0W
Wiltz 16 49 57N 5 55 E
Wiluna 96 26 36S 120 14 E
Wimereux 19 50 45N 1 37 E
Wimmera 97 36 30S 142 0 E
Wimmera → 99 36 8S 141 56 E
Winam G. 90 0 20S 34 15 E
Winburg 92 28 30S 27 2 E
Winchendon 113 42 40N 72 3W
Winchester, U.K. 13 51 4N 1 19W
Winchester, Conn., U.S.A. 113 41 53N 73 9W
Winchester, Idaho, U.S.A. 118 46 11N 116 32W
Winchester, Ind., U.S.A. 114 40 10N 84 56W
Winchester, Ky., U.S.A. 114 38 0N 84 8W
Winchester, Mass., U.S.A. 113 42 28N 71 10W
Winchester, N.H., U.S.A. 113 42 47N 72 22W
Winchester, Tenn., U.S.A. 115 35 11N 86 8W
Winchester, Va., U.S.A. 114 39 14N 78 8W
Wind → 118 43 8N 108 12W
Wind River Range 118 43 0N 109 30W
Windber 114 40 14N 78 50W
Windermere, L. 12 54 20N 2 57W
Windfall 108 54 12N 116 13W
Windflower L. 108 62 52N 118 30W
Windhoek 92 22 35S 17 4 E
Windischgarsten 26 47 42N 14 21 E
Windom 116 43 48N 95 3W
Windorah 97 25 24S 142 36 E
Window Rock 119 35 47N 109 4W
Windrush → 13 51 48N 1 35W
Windsor, Austral. 99 33 37S 150 50 E
Windsor, N.S., Can. 107 44 59N 64 5W
Windsor, Newf., Can. 107 48 57N 55 40W
Windsor, Ont., Can. 106 42 18N 83 0W
Windsor, U.K. 13 51 28N 0 36W
Windsor, Col., U.S.A. 116 40 33N 104 45W
Windsor, Conn., U.S.A. 113 41 50N 72 40W
Windsor, Mo., U.S.A. 116 38 32N 93 31W
Windsor, N.Y., U.S.A. 113 42 5N 75 37W
Windsor, Vt., U.S.A. 114 43 30N 72 25W
Windsorton 92 28 16S 24 44 E
Windward Is., Atl. Oc. 121 13 0N 63 0W
Windward Is., Pac. Oc. 95 18 0S 149 0W
Windward Passage = Vientos, Paso de los 121 20 0N 74 0W
Windy L. 109 60 20N 100 2W
Winefred L. 109 55 30N 110 30W
Winejok 87 9 1N 27 30 E
Winfield 117 37 15N 97 0W
Wingen 99 31 54S 150 54 E
Wingham, Austral. 99 31 48S 152 22 E
Wingham, Can. 106 43 55N 81 20W
Winifred 118 47 30N 109 28W
Winisk 106 55 20N 85 15W
Winisk → 106 55 17N 85 5W
Winisk L. 106 52 55N 87 22W
Wink 117 31 49N 103 9W
Winkler 109 49 10N 97 56W
Winklern 26 46 52N 12 52 E
Winlock 118 46 29N 122 56W
Winneba 85 5 25N 0 36W
Winnebago 116 43 43N 94 8W
Winnebago L. 114 44 0N 88 20W
Winnemucca 118 41 0N 117 45W
Winnemucca, L. 118 40 25N 119 21W
Winner 116 43 23N 99 52W
Winnetka 114 42 8N 87 46W
Winnett 118 47 2N 108 21W
Winnfield 117 31 57N 92 38W
Winnibigoshish L. 116 47 25N 94 12W
Winnipeg 109 49 54N 97 9W
Winnipeg → 109 50 38N 96 19W
Winnipeg Beach 109 50 30N 96 58W
Winnipeg, L. 109 52 0N 97 0W
Winnipegosis 109 51 39N 99 55W
Winnipegosis L. 109 52 30N 100 0W
Winnipesaukee, L. 113 43 38N 71 21W
Winnsboro, La., U.S.A. 117 32 10N 91 41W
Winnsboro, S.C., U.S.A. 115 34 23N 81 5W
Winnsboro, Tex., U.S.A. 117 32 56N 95 15W
Winokapau, L. 107 53 15N 62 50W
Winona, Miss., U.S.A. 117 33 30N 89 42W
Winona, Wis., U.S.A. 116 44 2N 91 39W
Winooski 114 44 31N 73 11W
Winschoten 16 53 9N 7 3 E
Winsen 24 53 21N 10 11 E
Winslow 119 35 2N 110 41W
Winsted 113 41 55N 73 5W
Winston-Salem 115 36 7N 80 15W
Winter Garden 115 28 33N 81 35W
Winter Haven 115 28 0N 81 42W
Winter Park 115 28 34N 81 19W
Winterberg 24 51 12N 8 30 E
Winters 117 31 58N 99 58W
Winterset 116 41 18N 94 0W
Wintersville 112 40 22N 80 38W
Winterswijk 16 51 58N 6 43 E
Winterthur 25 47 30N 8 44 E
Winthrop, Minn., U.S.A. 116 44 31N 94 25W
Winthrop, Wash., U.S.A. 118 48 27N 120 6W
Winton, Austral. 97 22 24S 143 3 E
Winton, N.Z. 101 46 8S 168 20 E
Winton, N.C., U.S.A. 115 36 25N 76 58W
Winton, Pa., U.S.A. 113 41 27N 75 33W
Wintzenheim 19 48 4N 7 17 E
Wipper → 24 51 17N 11 10 E
Wirral 12 53 25N 3 0W
Wisbech 12 52 39N 0 10 E
Wisconsin □ 116 44 30N 90 0W
Wisconsin → 116 43 0N 91 15W
Wisconsin Dells 116 43 38N 89 45W
Wisconsin Rapids 116 44 25N 89 50W
Wisdom 118 45 37N 113 27W
Wishaw 14 55 46N 3 55W
Wishek 116 46 20N 99 35W
Wisła 27 49 38N 18 53 E
Wisła → 28 54 22N 18 55 E
Wisłok → 27 50 13N 22 32 E
Wisłoka → 27 50 27N 21 23 E
Wismar 24 53 53N 11 23 E
Wisner 116 42 0N 96 46W
Wissant 19 50 52N 1 40 E
Wissembourg 19 49 2N 7 57 E
Wistoka → 27 49 50N 21 28 E
Wisznice 28 51 48N 23 13 E
Witbank 93 25 51S 29 14 E
Witdraai 92 26 58S 20 48 E
Witham → 12 53 3N 0 8W
Withernsea 12 53 43N 0 2 E
Witkowo 28 52 26N 17 45 E
Witney 13 51 47N 1 29W
Witnossob → 92 26 55S 20 37 E
Wittdün 24 54 38N 8 23 E
Witten 24 51 26N 7 19 E
Wittenberg 24 51 51N 12 39 E
Wittenberge 24 53 0N 11 44 E
Wittenburg 24 53 30N 11 4 E
Wittenoom 96 22 15S 118 20 E
Wittingen 24 52 43N 10 43 E
Wittlich 25 50 0N 6 54 E
Wittmund 24 53 39N 7 45 E
Wittow 24 54 37N 13 21 E
Wittstock 24 53 10N 12 30 E
Witzenhausen 24 51 20N 9 50 E
Wkra → 28 52 27N 20 44 E
Władysławowo 28 54 48N 18 25 E
Wlen 28 51 0N 15 39 E
Wlingi 73 8 5S 112 25 E
Włocławe □ 28 52 50N 19 10 E
Włocławek 28 52 40N 19 3 E
Włodawa 28 51 33N 23 31 E
Włoszczowa 28 50 50N 19 55 E
Woburn 113 42 31N 71 7W
Wodonga 99 36 5S 146 50 E
Wodzisław Śląski 27 50 1N 18 26 E
Woerth 19 48 57N 7 45 E
Woëvre, Plaine de la 19 49 15N 5 45 E
Wokam 73 5 45S 134 28 E
Woking 108 55 35N 118 50W
Wolbrom 28 50 24N 19 45 E
Wołczyn 28 51 1N 18 3 E
Woldegk 24 53 27N 13 35 E
Wolf → 108 60 17N 132 33W
Wolf Creek 118 47 1N 112 2W
Wolf L. 108 60 24N 131 40W
Wolf Point 116 48 6N 105 40W
Wolfe I. 106 44 7N 76 20W
Wolfenbüttel 24 52 10N 10 33 E
Wolfenden 108 52 0N 119 25W
Wolfsberg 26 46 50N 14 52 E
Wolfsburg 24 52 27N 10 49 E
Wolgast 24 54 3N 13 46 E
Wolhusen 25 47 4N 8 4 E
Wolin, Poland 28 53 50N 14 37 E
Wolin, Poland 28 54 0N 14 40 E
Wollaston, Islas 128 55 40S 67 30W
Wollaston L. 109 58 7N 103 10W
Wollaston Pen. 104 69 30N 115 0W
Wollondilly → 100 34 12S 150 18 E
Wollongong 97 34 25S 150 54 E
Wolmaransstad 92 27 12S 26 13 E
Wolmirstedt 24 52 15N 11 35 E
Wołomin 28 52 19N 21 15 E
Wołów 28 51 20N 16 38 E
Wolseley, Austral. 99 36 23S 140 54 E
Wolseley, Can. 109 50 25N 103 15W
Wolseley, S. Afr. 92 33 26S 19 7 E
Wolstenholme Fjord 4 76 0N 70 0W
Wolsztyn 28 52 8N 16 5 E
Wolvega 16 52 52N 6 0 E
Wolverhampton 13 52 35N 2 6W
Wondai 97 26 20S 151 49 E
Wonder Gorge 91 14 40S 29 0 E
Wongalarroo L. 99 31 32S 144 0 E
Wŏnju 76 37 22N 127 58 E
Wonosari 73 7 58S 110 36 E
Wŏnsan 76 39 11N 127 27 E
Wonthaggi 97 38 37S 145 37 E
Woocalla 99 31 42S 137 12 E
Wood Buffalo Nat. Park 108 59 0N 113 41W
Wood L. 109 55 17N 103 17W
Wood Lake 116 42 38N 100 14W
Woodbridge 112 43 47N 79 36W
Woodburn 99 29 6S 153 23 E
Woodend 99 37 20S 144 33 E
Woodland 118 38 40N 121 50W
Woodlark I. 98 9 10S 152 50 E
Woodpecker 108 53 30N 122 40W
Woodridge 109 49 20N 96 9W
Woodroffe, Mt. 96 26 20S 131 45 E
Woodruff, Ariz., U.S.A. 119 34 51N 110 1W
Woodruff, Utah, U.S.A. 118 41 30N 111 4W
Woods, L., Austral. 96 17 50S 133 30 E
Woods, L., Can. 107 54 30N 65 13W
Woods, L. of the 109 49 15N 94 45W
Woodside 100 38 31S 146 52 E
Woodstock, Austral. 98 19 35S 146 50 E
Woodstock, N.B., Can. 107 46 11N 67 37W
Woodstock, Ont., Can. 106 43 10N 80 45W
Woodstock, U.K. 13 51 51N 1 20W
Woodstock, Ill., U.S.A. 116 42 17N 88 30W
Woodstock, Vt., U.S.A. 113 43 37N 72 31W
Woodsville 113 44 10N 72 0W
Woodville, N.Z. 101 40 20S 175 53 E
Woodville, U.S.A. 117 30 45N 94 25W
Woodward 117 36 24N 99 28W
Woolamai, C. 99 38 30S 145 23 E
Woombye 99 26 40S 152 55 E
Woomera 97 31 30S 137 10 E
Woonona 100 34 21S 150 54 E
Woonsocket 114 42 0N 71 30W
Woonsockett 116 44 5N 98 15W
Wooramel → 96 25 47S 114 10 E
Wooster 114 40 48N 81 55W
Worcester, S. Afr. 92 33 39S 19 27 E
Worcester, U.K. 13 52 12N 2 12W
Worcester, Mass., U.S.A. 114 42 14N 71 49W
Worcester, N.Y., U.S.A. 113 42 35N 74 45W
Wörgl 26 47 29N 12 3 E
Workington 12 54 39N 3 34W

Worksop Yining

Worksop 12 53 19N 1 9W
Workum 16 52 59N 5 26 E
Worland 118 44 0N 107 59W
Wormhoudt 19 50 52N 2 28 E
Worms 25 49 37N 8 21 E
Wörth 25 49 1N 12 24 E
Wortham 117 31 48N 96 27W
Wörther See 26 46 37N 14 10 E
Worthing 13 50 49N 0 21W
Worthington 116 43 35N 95 36W
Wosi 73 0 15 S 128 0 E
Wou-han = Wuhan 75 30 31N 114 18 E
Wour 83 21 14N 16 0 E
Wowoni 73 4 5 S 123 5 E
Wozniki 28 50 35N 19 4 E
Wrangell 104 56 30N 132 25W
Wrangell, I. 108 56 20N 132 10W
Wrangell Mts. 104 61 40N 143 30W
Wrath, C. 14 58 38N 5 0W
Wray 116 40 8N 102 18W
Wrekin, The 12 52 41N 2 35W
Wrens 115 33 13N 82 23W
Wrexham 12 53 5N 3 0W
Wriezen 24 52 43N 14 9 E
Wright, Can. 108 51 52N 121 40W
Wright, Phil. 73 11 42N 125 2 E
Wrightson, Mt. 119 31 43N 110 56W
Wrigley 104 63 16N 123 37W
Wrocław 28 51 5N 17 5 E
Wrocław □ 28 51 0N 17 0 E
Wronki 28 52 41N 16 21 E
Września 28 52 21N 17 36 E
Wschowa 28 51 48N 16 20 E
Wu Jiang → 75 29 40N 107 20 E
Wuchang 76 44 55N 127 5 E
Wuchuan 77 28 25N 108 3 E
Wuding He → 76 37 2N 110 23 E
Wugang 77 26 44N 110 35 E
Wugong Shan 77 27 30N 114 0 E
Wuhan 75 30 31N 114 18 E
Wuhsi = Wuxi 75 31 33N 120 18 E
Wuhu 75 31 22N 118 21 E
Wukari 85 7 51N 9 42 E
Wulehe 85 8 39N 0 0
Wuliaru 73 7 27 S 131 0 E
Wulumuchi = Ürümqi 75 43 45N 87 45 E
Wum 85 6 24N 10 2 E
Wuning 77 29 17N 115 5 E
Wunnummin L. 106 52 55N 89 10W
Wunsiedel 25 50 2N 12 0 E
Wunstorf 24 52 26N 9 29 E
Wuntho 67 23 55N 95 45 E
Wuping 77 25 5N 116 5 E
Wuppertal, Ger. 24 51 15N 7 8 E
Wuppertal, S. Afr. 92 32 13 S 19 12 E
Wuqing 76 39 23N 117 4 E
Wurung 98 19 13 S 140 38 E
Würzburg 25 49 46N 9 55 E
Wurzen 24 51 21N 12 45 E
Wushan 77 31 7N 109 54 E
Wustrow 24 54 4N 11 33 E
Wutach → 25 47 37N 8 15 E
Wutongqiao 75 29 22N 103 50 E
Wuwei, Anhui, China 77 31 18N 117 54 E
Wuwei, Gansu, China 75 37 57N 102 34 E
Wuxi, Jiangsu, China 75 31 33N 120 18 E
Wuxi, Sichuan, China 77 31 23N 109 35 E
Wuxing 77 30 51N 120 8 E
Wuyi, Hebei, China 76 37 46N 115 56 E
Wuyi, Zhejiang, China 77 28 52N 119 50 E
Wuyi Shan 75 27 0N 117 0 E
Wuying 76 47 53N 129 56 E
Wuyo 85 10 23N 11 50 E
Wuyuan 76 41 2N 108 20 E
Wuzhai 76 38 54N 111 48 E
Wuzhi Shan 75 18 45N 109 45 E
Wuzhong 76 38 2N 106 12 E
Wuzhou 75 23 30N 111 18 E
Wyaaba Cr. → 98 16 27 S 141 35 E
Wyalusing 113 41 40N 76 16W
Wyandotte 114 42 14N 83 13W
Wyandra 97 27 12 S 145 56 E
Wyangala Res. 100 33 54 S 149 0 E
Wyara, L. 99 28 42 S 144 14 E
Wycheproof 99 36 0 S 143 17 E
Wye → 13 51 36N 2 40W
Wyk 24 54 41N 8 33 E
Wymondham 13 52 45N 0 42W
Wymore 116 40 10N 96 40W
Wynberg 92 34 2 S 18 28 E
Wyndham, Austral. 96 15 33 S 128 3 E
Wyndham, N.Z. 101 46 20 S 168 51 E
Wyndmere 116 46 23N 97 7W
Wynne 117 35 15N 90 50W
Wynnum 99 27 27 S 153 9 E
Wynyard 109 51 45N 104 10W
Wyoming □ 110 42 48N 109 0W
Wyong 99 33 14 S 151 24 E
Wyrzysk 28 53 10N 17 17 E
Wysoka 28 53 13N 17 2 E
Wysokie 28 50 55N 22 40 E
Wysokie Mazowieckie 28 52 55N 22 30 E
Wyszków 28 52 36N 21 25 E
Wyszogród 28 52 23N 20 9 E
Wytheville 114 37 0N 81 3W

X

Xai-Xai 93 25 6 S 33 31 E
Xainza 75 30 58N 88 35 E
Xangongo 92 16 45 S 15 0 E
Xanten 24 51 40N 6 27 E
Xánthi 44 41 10N 24 58 E
Xánthi □ 44 41 10N 24 58 E
Xapuri 126 10 35 S 68 35W
Xau, L. 92 21 15 S 24 44 E
Xavantina 125 21 15 S 52 48W
Xenia 114 39 42N 83 57W
Xi Jiang → 75 22 5N 113 20 E
Xi Xian 76 36 41N 110 58 E
Xiachengzi 76 44 40N 130 18 E
Xiachuan Dao 77 21 40N 112 40 E
Xiaguan 75 25 32N 100 16 E
Xiajiang 77 27 30N 115 10 E
Xiamen 75 24 25N 118 4 E
Xi'an 77 34 15N 109 0 E
Xianfeng 77 29 40N 109 8 E
Xiang Jiang → 75 28 55N 112 50 E
Xiangfan 75 32 2N 112 8 E
Xiangning 76 35 58N 110 50 E
Xiangtan 75 27 51N 112 54 E
Xiangxiang 77 27 43N 112 28 E
Xiangyang 75 32 1N 112 8 E
Xiangyin 77 28 38N 112 54 E
Xiangzhou 77 23 58N 109 40 E
Xianju 77 28 51N 120 44 E
Xianyang 77 34 20N 108 40 E
Xiao Hinggan Ling 75 49 0N 127 0 E
Xiaogan 77 30 52N 113 55 E
Xiapu 75 26 54N 119 59 E
Xichang 75 27 51N 102 19 E
Xichuan 77 33 0N 111 30 E
Xieng Khouang 71 19 17N 103 25 E
Xifeng 77 27 7N 106 42 E
Xigazê 75 29 5N 88 45 E
Xihe 77 34 2N 105 20 E
Xiliao He → 76 43 32N 123 35 E
Xilin 77 24 30N 105 6 E
Xilókastron 45 38 4N 22 43 E
Xin Xian 76 38 22N 112 46 E
Xinavane 93 25 2 S 32 47 E
Xinbin 76 41 40N 125 2 E
Xincheng 77 24 5N 108 39 E
Xinfeng 77 25 27N 114 58 E
Xing'an 75 25 38N 110 40 E
Xingan 77 27 46N 115 20 E
Xingcheng 76 40 40N 120 45 E
Xingguo 77 26 21N 115 21 E
Xinghua 77 32 58N 119 48 E
Xinghua Wan 77 25 15N 119 20 E
Xingning 77 24 3N 115 42 E
Xingren 75 25 24N 105 11 E
Xingshan 77 31 15N 110 45 E
Xingtai 76 37 3N 114 32 E
Xingu → 127 1 30 S 51 53W
Xingyang 77 34 45N 112 52 E
Xinhua 77 27 42N 111 13 E
Xiniás, L. 45 39 2N 22 12 E
Xining 75 36 34N 101 40 E
Xinjiang 76 35 34N 111 11 E
Xinjiang Uygur Zizhiqu □ 75 42 0N 86 0 E
Xinjin 76 39 25N 121 58 E
Xinle 76 38 25N 114 40 E
Xinmin 76 41 59N 122 50 E
Xinning 77 26 28N 110 50 E
Xinxiang 77 35 18N 113 50 E
Xinyang 75 32 6N 114 3 E
Xinzheng 77 34 20N 113 45 E
Xinzhou 77 19 43N 109 17 E
Xinzhu 75 24 49N 120 57 E
Xiongyuecheng 76 40 12N 122 5 E
Xiping 77 33 22N 114 0 E
Xique-Xique 127 10 50 S 42 40W
Xiuyan 76 40 18N 123 11 E
Xixabangma Feng 67 28 20N 85 40 E
Xixiang 77 33 0N 107 44 E
Xizang □ 75 32 0N 88 0 E
Xuancheng 77 30 56N 118 43 E
Xuan'en 77 30 0N 109 30 E
Xuanhan 77 31 18N 107 38 E
Xuanhua 76 40 40N 115 2 E
Xuchang 77 34 2N 113 48 E
Xuguit Qi 76 49 17N 120 44 E
Xunke 76 49 35N 128 27 E
Xupu 77 27 53N 110 32 E
Xuwen 77 20 20N 110 10 E
Xuyong 77 28 10N 105 22 E
Xuzhou 77 34 18N 117 10 E

Y

Ya 'Bad 62 32 27N 35 10 E
Yaamba 98 23 8 S 150 22 E
Ya'an 75 29 58N 103 5 E
Yaapeet 99 35 45 S 142 3 E
Yabassi 85 4 30N 9 57 E
Yabelo 87 4 50N 38 8 E
Yablanitsa 43 43 2N 24 5 E
Yablonovy Khrebet 59 53 0N 114 0 E
Yabrīn 64 23 17N 48 58 E
Yacheng 77 18 22N 109 6 E
Yacuiba 124 22 0 S 63 43W
Yadgir 70 16 45N 77 5 E
Yadkin → 115 35 23N 80 3W
Yadrin 55 55 57N 46 12 E
Yagaba 85 10 14N 1 20W
Yagodnoye 59 62 33N 149 40 E
Yagoua 88 10 20N 15 13 E
Yagur 62 32 45N 35 4 E
Yahila 90 0 13N 24 28 E
Yahk 108 49 6N 116 10W
Yahuma 88 1 0N 23 10 E
Yajua 85 11 27N 12 49 E
Yakima 118 46 42N 120 30W
Yakima → 118 47 0N 120 30W
Yako 84 12 59N 2 15W
Yakoruda 43 42 1N 23 29 E
Yakut A.S.S.R. □ 59 62 0N 130 0 E
Yakutat 104 59 29N 139 44W
Yakutsk 59 62 5N 129 50 E
Yala 71 6 33N 101 18 E
Yalabusha → 117 33 30N 90 12W
Yalboroo 98 20 50 S 148 40 E
Yale 112 43 9N 82 47W
Yalgoo 96 28 16 S 116 39 E
Yalinga 88 6 33N 23 10 E
Yalkubul, Punta 120 21 32N 88 37W
Yalleroi 98 24 3 S 145 42 E
Yallourn 97 38 10 S 146 18 E
Yalong Jiang → 75 26 40N 101 55 E
Yalpukh, Oz. 46 45 30N 28 41 E
Yalta 56 44 30N 34 10 E
Yalu Chiang → 76 41 30N 126 30 E
Yalu He → 76 46 56N 123 30 E
Yalu Jiang → 76 40 0N 124 22 E
Yalutorovsk 58 56 41N 66 12 E
Yam Kinneret 62 32 45N 35 35 E
Yamagata 74 38 15N 140 15 E
Yamagata □ 74 38 30N 140 0 E
Yamaguchi 74 34 10N 131 32 E
Yamaguchi □ 74 34 20N 131 40 E
Yamal, Poluostrov 58 71 0N 70 0 E
Yamama 64 24 5N 47 30 E
Yamanashi □ 74 35 40N 138 40 E
Yamantau 52 54 20N 57 40 E
Yamantau, Gora 52 54 15N 58 6 E
Yamba 99 29 26 S 153 23 E
Yâmbiô 87 4 35N 28 16 E
Yambol 43 42 30N 26 36 E
Yamdena 73 7 45 S 131 20 E
Yamil 85 12 53N 8 4 E
Yamma-Yamma, L. 97 26 16 S 141 20 E
Yampa → 118 40 37N 108 59W
Yampi Sd. 96 16 8 S 123 38 E
Yampol 56 48 15N 28 15 E
Yamrat 85 10 11N 9 55 E
Yamrukchal 43 42 44N 24 52 E
Yamuna (Jumna) → 68 25 30N 81 53 E
Yamzho Yumco 75 28 48N 90 35 E
Yan 85 10 5N 12 11 E
Yan → 70 9 0N 81 10 E
Yana → 59 71 30N 136 0 E
Yanac 99 36 8 S 141 25 E
Yanai 74 33 58N 132 7 E
Yanam 70 16 47N 82 15 E
Yan'an 76 36 35N 109 26 E
Yanaul 52 56 25N 55 0 E
Yanbu 'al Baḩr 64 24 0N 38 5 E
Yancannia 99 30 12 S 142 35 E
Yanchang 76 36 43N 110 1 E
Yancheng, Henan, China 77 33 35N 114 0 E
Yancheng, Jiangsu, China 77 33 23N 120 8 E
Yanchi 76 37 48N 107 20 E
Yanchuan 76 36 51N 110 10 E
Yanco 100 34 38 S 146 27 E
Yandaran 98 24 43 S 152 6 E
Yanfolila 84 11 11N 8 9W
Yangambi 90 0 47N 24 20 E
Yangch'ü = Taiyuan 76 37 52N 112 33 E
Yangchun 75 22 11N 111 48 E
Yanggao 76 40 21N 113 55 E
Yangi-Yer 58 40 17N 68 48 E
Yangjiang 75 21 50N 110 59 E
Yangquan 76 37 58N 113 31 E
Yangshan 77 24 30N 112 40 E
Yangshuo 77 24 48N 110 29 E
Yangtze Kiang = Chang Jiang → 75 31 20N 121 52 E
Yangxin 77 29 50N 115 12 E
Yangzhou 77 32 21N 119 26 E
Yanhee Res. 71 17 30N 98 45 E
Yanji 76 42 59N 129 30 E
Yankton 116 42 55N 97 25W
Yanna 99 26 58 S 146 0 E
Yanonge 90 0 35N 24 38 E
Yanqi 75 42 5N 86 35 E
Yanqing 76 40 30N 115 58 E
Yanshan 77 28 15N 117 41 E
Yantabulla 99 29 21 S 145 0 E
Yantai 76 37 34N 121 22 E
Yanting 77 31 11N 105 24 E
Yantra → 43 43 40N 25 37 E
Yanzhou 76 35 35N 116 49 E
Yao 81 12 56N 17 33 E
Yaoundé 88 3 50N 11 35 E
Yap 94 9 31N 138 6 E
Yapen 73 1 50 S 136 0 E
Yapen, Selat 73 1 20 S 136 10 E
Yappar → 98 18 22 S 141 16 E
Yaqui → 120 27 37N 110 39W
Yar 55 58 14N 52 5 E
Yar-Sale 58 66 50N 70 50 E
Yaraka 97 24 53 S 144 3 E
Yarangüme 64 37 35N 29 8 E
Yaransk 55 57 22N 47 49 E
Yaratishky 54 54 3N 26 0 E
Yare → 13 52 36N 1 28 E
Yarensk 52 61 10N 49 8 E
Yarfa 86 24 40N 38 35 E
Yari → 126 0 20 S 72 20W
Yarkand = Shache 75 38 20N 77 10 E
Yarker 113 44 23N 76 46W
Yarkhun → 69 36 17N 72 30 E
Yarmouth 107 43 50N 66 7W
Yarmuk → 62 32 38N 35 34 E
Yarmūk → 62 32 42N 35 40 E
Yaroslavl 55 57 35N 39 55 E
Yarra → 100 37 50 S 144 53 E
Yarram 99 38 29 S 146 9 E
Yarraman 99 26 50 S 152 0 E
Yarranvale 99 26 50 S 145 20 E
Yarras 99 31 25 S 152 20 E
Yarrawonga 100 36 0 S 146 0 E
Yartsevo, R.S.F.S.R., U.S.S.R. 54 55 6N 32 43 E
Yartsevo, R.S.F.S.R., U.S.S.R. 59 60 20N 90 0 E
Yasawa Group 101 17 00 S 177 23 E
Yaselda → 54 52 7N 26 28 E
Yashi 85 12 23N 7 54 E
Yasinovataya 56 48 7N 37 57 E
Yasinski, L. 106 53 16N 77 35W
Yasothon 71 15 50N 104 10 E
Yass 97 34 49 S 148 54 E
Yas'ur 62 32 54N 35 10 E
Yatağn 45 37 20N 28 10 E
Yates Center 117 37 53N 95 45W
Yathkyed L. 109 62 40N 98 0W
Yatsushiro 74 32 30N 130 40 E
Yatta Plateau 90 2 0 S 38 0 E
Yaṭṭah 62 31 27N 35 6 E
Yauyos 126 12 19 S 75 50W
Yaval 68 21 10N 75 42 E
Yavari → 126 4 21 S 70 2W
Yavne 62 31 52N 34 45 E
Yavorov 54 49 55N 23 20 E
Yawatahama 74 33 27N 132 24 E
Yawri B. 84 8 22N 13 0W
Yazd (Yezd) 65 31 55N 54 27 E
Yazdān 65 33 30N 60 50 E
Yazoo → 117 32 35N 90 50W
Yazoo City 117 32 48N 90 28W
Ybbs 26 48 12N 15 4 E
Ye Xian 76 37 8N 119 57 E
Yebbi-Souma 83 21 7N 17 54 E
Yebyu 67 14 15N 98 13 E
Yecla 33 38 35N 1 5W
Yedintsy 56 48 9N 27 18 E
Yefremov 55 53 8N 38 3 E
Yegorlyk → 57 46 33N 41 40 E
Yegorlykskaya 57 46 35N 40 35 E
Yegoryevsk 55 55 27N 38 55 E
Yegros 124 26 20 S 56 25W
Yehuda, Midbar 62 31 35N 35 15 E
Yei 87 4 9N 30 40 E
Yei, Nahr → 87 6 15N 30 13 E
Yelabuga 52 55 45N 52 4 E
Yelan 55 50 55N 43 43 E
Yelan-Kolenovski 55 51 16N 41 4 E
Yelandur 70 12 6N 77 0 E
Yelanskoye 59 61 25N 128 0 E
Yelarbon 99 28 33 S 150 38 E
Yelatma 55 55 0N 41 45 E
Yelets 55 52 40N 38 30 E
Yélimané 84 15 9N 10 34W
Yell 14 60 35N 1 5W
Yell Sd. 14 60 33N 1 15W
Yellamanchilli (Elamanchili) 70 17 33N 82 50 E
Yellow Mt. 100 32 31 S 146 52 E
Yellow Sea 76 35 0N 123 0 E
Yellowhead P. 108 52 53N 118 25W
Yellowknife 108 62 27N 114 29W
Yellowknife → 104 62 31N 114 19W
Yellowstone → 116 47 58N 103 59W
Yellowstone L. 118 44 30N 110 20W
Yellowstone National Park 118 44 35N 110 0W
Yellowtail Res. 118 45 6N 108 8W
Yelnya 54 54 35N 33 15 E
Yelsk 54 51 50N 29 10 E
Yelvertoft 98 20 13 S 138 45 E
Yelwa 85 10 49N 4 41 E
Yemen ■ 63 15 0N 44 0 E
Yenakiyevo 56 48 15N 38 15 E
Yenangyaung 67 20 30N 95 0 E
Yenda 99 34 13 S 146 14 E
Yendéré 84 10 12N 4 59W
Yendi 85 9 29N 0 1W
Yenisaía 44 41 1N 24 57 E
Yenisey → 58 71 50N 82 40 E
Yeniseysk 59 58 27N 92 13 E
Yeniseyskiy Zaliv 58 72 20N 81 0 E
Yenne 21 45 43N 5 44 E
Yenotayevka 57 47 15N 47 0 E
Yenyuka 59 57 57N 121 15 E
Yeo, L. 96 28 0 S 124 30 E
Yeola 70 20 0N 74 30 E
Yeotmal 70 20 20N 78 15 E
Yeovil 13 50 57N 2 38W
Yepes 32 39 55N 3 39W
Yeppoon 97 23 5 S 150 47 E
Yeráki 45 37 0N 22 42 E
Yerbent 58 39 30N 58 50 E
Yerbogachen 59 61 16N 108 0 E
Yerevan 57 40 10N 44 31 E
Yerla → 70 16 50N 74 30 E
Yermak 58 52 2N 76 55 E
Yermakovo 59 52 25N 126 20 E
Yermo 119 34 58N 116 50W
Yerofey Pavlovich 59 54 0N 122 0 E
Yershov 55 51 22N 48 16 E
Yerushalayim 62 31 47N 35 10 E
Yerville 18 49 40N 0 53 E
Yes Tor 13 50 41N 3 59W
Yesnogorsk 55 54 32N 37 38 E
Yeso 117 34 29N 104 37W
Yessentuki 57 44 0N 42 53 E
Yessey 59 68 29N 102 10 E
Yeste 33 38 22N 2 19W
Yeu, I. d' 18 46 42N 2 20W
Yevlakh 57 40 39N 47 7 E
Yevpatoriya 56 45 15N 33 20 E
Yevstratovskiy 55 50 11N 39 45 E
Yeya → 57 46 40N 38 40 E
Yeysk 56 46 40N 38 12 E
Yhati 124 25 45 S 56 35W
Yhú 125 25 0 S 56 0W
Yi → 124 33 7 S 57 8W
Yi Xian 76 41 30N 121 22 E
Yialí 45 36 41N 27 11 E
Yi'allaq, G. 86 30 21N 33 31 E
Yiáltra 45 38 51N 22 59 E
Yianisádhes 45 35 20N 26 10 E
Yiannitsa 44 40 46N 22 24 E
Yibin 75 28 45N 104 32 E
Yichang 75 30 40N 111 20 E
Yicheng 76 35 42N 111 40 E
Yichuan 76 36 2N 110 10 E
Yichun, Heilongjiang, China 75 47 44N 128 52 E
Yichun, Jiangxi, China 77 27 48N 114 22 E
Yidhá 44 40 35N 22 53 E
Yidu 76 36 43N 118 28 E
Yihuang 77 27 30N 116 12 E
Yijun 76 35 28N 109 8 E
Yilan, China 76 46 19N 129 34 E
Yilan, Taiwan 75 24 51N 121 44 E
Yilehuli Shan 76 51 20N 124 20 E
Yimianpo 76 45 7N 128 2 E
Yinchuan 76 38 30N 106 15 E
Ying He → 77 32 30N 116 30 E
Ying Xian 76 39 32N 113 10 E
Yingcheng 77 30 56N 113 35 E
Yingde 77 24 10N 113 25 E
Yingkou 76 40 37N 122 18 E
Yingshan 77 30 41N 115 32 E
Yingshang 77 32 38N 116 12 E
Yingtan 75 28 12N 117 0 E
Yining 75 43 58N 81 10 E

Yinjiang Zikhron Ya'Aqov

Yinjiang 77 28 1N 108 21 E
Yinkanie 99 34 22S 140 17 E
Yinnietharra 96 24 39S 116 12 E
Yioúra, Greece 44 39 23N 24 10 E
Yioúra, Greece 45 37 32N 24 40 E
Yipinglang 75 25 10N 101 52 E
Yirga Alem 87 6 48N 38 22 E
Yirshi 76 47 18N 119 49 E
Yishan 75 24 28N 108 38 E
Yíthion 45 36 46N 22 34 E
Yitong 76 43 13N 125 20 E
Yitulihe 76 50 38N 121 34 E
Yixing 77 31 21N 119 48 E
Yiyang, Henan, China 77 34 27N 112 10 E
Yiyang, Hunan, China 75 28 35N 112 18 E
Yizhang 77 25 27N 112 57 E
Yizre'el 62 32 34N 35 19 E
Ylitornio 50 66 19N 23 39 E
Ylivieska 50 64 4N 24 28 E
Yngaren 49 58 50N 16 35 E
Ynykchanskiy 59 60 15N 137 35 E
Yoakum 117 29 20N 97 20W
Yog Pt. 73 14 6N 124 12 E
Yogan 85 6 23N 1 30 E
Yogyakarta 73 7 49S 110 22 E
Yoho Nat. Park 108 51 25N 116 30W
Yojoa, L. de 120 14 53N 88 0W
Yokadouma 88 3 26N 15 6 E
Yokkaichi 74 35 0N 136 38 E
Yoko 85 5 32N 12 20 E
Yokohama 74 35 27N 139 28 E
Yokosuka 74 35 20N 139 40 E
Yola 85 9 10N 12 29 E
Yolaina, Cordillera de 121 11 30N 84 0W
Yonago 74 35 25N 133 19 E
Yong Peng 71 2 0N 103 3 E
Yong'an 77 25 59N 117 25 E
Yongchun 77 25 16N 118 20 E
Yongding 77 24 43N 116 45 E
Yongfeng 77 27 20N 115 22 E
Yongfu 77 24 59N 109 59 E
Yonghe 76 36 46N 110 38 E
Yongji 77 34 52N 110 28 E
Yongshun 77 29 2N 109 51 E
Yongxin 77 26 58N 114 15 E
Yongxing 77 26 9N 113 8 E
Yongxiu 77 29 2N 115 42 E
Yonibana 84 8 30N 12 19W
Yonkers 114 40 57N 73 51W
Yonne □ 19 47 50N 3 40 E
Yonne → 19 48 23N 2 58 E
Yoqne'am 62 32 40N 35 6 E
York, Austral. 96 31 52S 116 47 E
York, U.K. 12 53 58N 1 7W
York, Ala., U.S.A. 115 32 30N 88 18W
York, Nebr., U.S.A. 116 40 55N 97 35W
York, Pa., U.S.A. 114 39 57N 76 43W
York, C. 97 10 42S 142 31 E
York, Kap 4 75 55N 66 25W
York Sd. 96 14 50S 125 5 E
Yorke Pen. 97 34 50S 137 40 E
Yorkshire Wolds 12 54 0N 0 30W
Yorkton 109 51 11N 102 28W
Yorktown 117 29 0N 97 29W
Yosemite National Park 119 38 0N 119 30W
Yoshkar Ola 55 56 38N 47 55 E
Yŏsu 77 34 47N 127 45 E
Yotvata 62 29 55N 35 2 E
You Jiang → 75 23 22N 110 3 E
Youbou 108 48 53N 124 13W
Youghal 15 51 58N 7 51W
Youghal B. 15 51 55N 7 50W
Youkounkoun 84 12 35N 13 11W
Young, Austral. 97 34 19S 148 18 E
Young, Can. 109 51 47N 105 45W
Young, Uruguay 124 32 44S 57 36W
Young, U.S.A. 119 34 9N 110 56W
Younghusband Pen. 99 36 0S 139 25 E
Youngstown, Can. 109 51 35N 111 10W
Youngstown, N.Y., U.S.A. 112 43 16N 79 2W
Youngstown, Ohio, U.S.A. 114 41 7N 80 41W
Youngsville 112 41 51N 79 21W
Youssoufia 82 32 16N 8 31W
Youyang 77 28 47N 108 42 E
Youyu 76 40 10N 112 20 E
Yozgat 64 39 51N 34 47 E
Ypané → 124 23 29S 57 19W
Yport 18 49 45N 0 15 E
Ypres = Ieper 16 50 51N 2 53 E
Ypsilanti 114 42 18N 83 40W
Yreka 118 41 44N 122 40W
Ysleta 119 31 45N 106 24W
Yssingeaux 21 45 9N 4 8 E
Ystad 49 55 26N 13 50 E
Ythan → 14 57 26N 2 12W
Ytterhogdal 48 62 12N 14 56 E
Ytyk-Kel 59 62 30N 133 45 E
Yu Shan 75 23 30N 120 58 E
Yu Xian, Hebei, China 76 39 50N 114 35 E
Yu Xian, Henan, China 77 34 10N 113 28 E
Yuan Jiang → 75 28 55N 111 50 E
Yuanling 75 28 29N 110 22 E
Yuanyang 75 23 10N 102 43 E
Yuba City 118 39 12N 121 37W
Yucatán □ 120 21 30N 86 30W
Yucatán, Canal de 121 22 0N 86 30W
Yucca 119 34 56N 114 6W
Yucheng 76 36 55N 116 32 E
Yuci 76 37 42N 112 46 E
Yudino, R.S.F.S.R., U.S.S.R. 55 55 51N 48 55 E
Yudino, R.S.F.S.R., U.S.S.R. 58 55 10N 67 55 E
Yudu 77 25 59N 115 30 E
Yueqing 77 28 9N 120 59 E
Yueyang 77 29 21N 113 5 E
Yugan 77 28 43N 116 37 E
Yugoslavia ■ 37 44 0N 20 0 E
Yuhuan 77 28 9N 121 12 E
Yujiang 77 28 10N 116 43 E
Yukhnov 54 54 44N 35 15 E
Yukon Territory □ 104 63 0N 135 0W
Yukti 59 63 26N 105 42 E
Yule → 96 20 41S 118 17 E
Yuli 85 9 44N 10 12 E
Yülin 77 18 10N 109 31 E
Yulin, Guangxi Zhuangzu, China 77 22 40N 110 8 E
Yulin, Shaanxi, China 76 38 20N 109 30 E
Yuma, Ariz., U.S.A. 119 32 45N 114 37W
Yuma, Colo., U.S.A. 116 40 10N 102 43W
Yuma, B. de 121 18 20N 68 35W
Yumbe 90 3 28N 31 15 E
Yumbi 90 1 12S 26 15 E
Yumen 75 39 50N 97 30 E
Yun Xian 75 32 50N 110 46 E
Yungas 126 17 0S 66 0W
Yungay 124 37 10S 72 5W
Yunhe 77 28 8N 119 33 E
Yunlin 77 23 42N 120 30 E
Yunnan □ 75 25 0N 102 0 E
Yunquera de Henares 32 40 47N 3 11W
Yunta 99 32 34S 139 36 E
Yunxiao 77 23 59N 117 18 E
Yur 59 59 52N 137 41 E
Yurgao 58 55 42N 84 51 E
Yuribei 58 71 8N 76 58 E
Yurimaguas 126 5 55S 76 7W
Yurya 55 59 1N 49 13 E
Yuryev-Polskiy 55 56 30N 39 40 E
Yuryevets 55 57 25N 43 2 E
Yuscarán 121 13 58N 86 45W
Yushu, Jilin, China 76 44 43N 126 38 E
Yushu, Qinghai, China 75 33 5N 96 55 E
Yuyao 77 30 3N 121 10 E
Yuzha 55 56 34N 42 1 E
Yuzhno-Sakhalinsk 59 46 58N 142 45 E
Yvelines □ 19 48 40N 1 45 E
Yverdon 25 46 47N 6 39 E
Yvetot 18 49 37N 0 44 E

Z

Zaandam 16 52 26N 4 49 E
Zab, Monts du 83 34 55N 5 0 E
Žabalj 42 45 21N 20 5 E
Žabari 42 44 22N 21 15 E
Zabarjad 86 23 40N 36 12 E
Zabaykalskiy 59 49 40N 117 25 E
Zabid 63 14 0N 43 10 E
Ząbkowice Śląskie 28 50 35N 16 50 E
Žabljak 42 43 18N 19 7 E
Zabłudów 28 53 0N 23 19 E
Žabno 27 50 9N 20 53 E
Zābol 65 31 0N 61 32 E
Zābolī 65 27 10N 61 35 E
Zabré 85 11 12N 0 36W
Zabrze 28 50 18N 18 50 E
Zabul □ 65 32 0N 67 0 E
Zacapa 120 14 59N 89 31W
Zacatecas 120 22 49N 102 34W
Zacatecas □ 120 23 30N 103 0W
Zacatecoluca 120 13 29N 88 51W
Zacoalco 120 20 14N 103 33W
Zadar 39 44 8N 15 14 E
Zadawa 85 11 33N 10 19 E
Zadetkyi Kyun 72 10 0N 98 25 E
Zadonsk 55 52 25N 38 56 E
Zafora 45 36 5N 26 24 E
Zafra 31 38 26N 6 30W
Zafriya 62 31 59N 34 51 E
Żagań 28 51 39N 15 22 E
Zagazig 86 30 40N 31 30 E
Zaghouan 83 36 23N 10 10 E
Zaglivérion 44 40 36N 23 15 E
Zaglou 82 27 17N 0 3W
Zagnanado 85 7 18N 2 28 E
Zagorá 44 39 27N 23 6 E
Zagora 82 30 22N 5 51W
Zagórów 28 52 10N 17 54 E
Zagorsk 55 56 20N 38 10 E
Zagórz 27 49 30N 22 14 E
Zagreb 39 45 50N 16 0 E
Zāgros, Kudhā-ye 65 33 45N 47 0 E
Žagubica 42 44 15N 21 47 E
Zaguinaso 84 10 1N 6 14W
Zagyva → 27 47 5N 20 4 E
Zāhedān 65 29 30N 60 50 E
Zahirabad 70 17 43N 77 37 E
Zahlah 64 33 52N 35 50 E
Zahna 24 51 54N 12 47 E
Zahrez Chergui 82 35 0N 3 30 E
Zahrez Rharbi 82 34 50N 2 55 E
Zaïr 82 29 47N 5 51W
Zaïre → 88 6 4S 12 24 E
Zaïre, Rep. of ■ 88 3 0S 23 0 E
Zaječar 42 43 53N 22 18 E
Zakamensk 59 50 23N 103 17 E
Zakataly 57 41 38N 46 35 E
Zakavkazye 57 42 0N 44 0 E
Zākhū 64 37 10N 42 50 E
Zákinthos 45 37 47N 20 57 E
Zaklików 28 50 46N 22 7 E
Zakopane 27 49 18N 19 57 E
Zakroczym 28 52 26N 20 38 E
Zala □ 27 46 42N 16 50 E
Zala → 27 46 43N 17 16 E
Zalaegerszeg 27 46 53N 16 47 E
Zalakomár 27 46 33N 17 10 E
Zalalövö 27 46 51N 16 35 E
Zalamea de la Serena 31 38 40N 5 38W
Zalamea la Real 31 37 41N 6 38W
Zalău 46 47 12N 23 3 E
Zalazna 55 58 39N 52 31 E
Žalec 39 46 16N 15 10 E
Zaleshchiki 56 48 45N 25 45 E
Zalewo 28 53 50N 19 41 E
Zalingei 81 12 51N 23 29 E
Zaltan, Jabal 83 28 46N 19 45 E
Zambeke 90 2 8N 25 17 E
Zambeze → 91 18 55S 36 4 E
Zambezi 89 13 30S 23 15 E
Zambezi = Zambeze → 91 18 55S 36 4 E
Zambezia □ 91 16 15S 37 30 E
Zambia ■ 89 15 0S 28 0 E
Zamboanga 73 6 59N 122 3 E
Zambrów 28 52 59N 22 14 E
Zametchino 55 53 30N 42 30 E
Zamora, Mexico 120 20 0N 102 21W
Zamora, Spain 30 41 30N 5 45W
Zamora □ 30 41 30N 5 46W
Zamość 28 50 43N 23 15 E
Zamość □ 28 50 40N 23 10 E
Zamzam, W. 83 31 0N 14 30 E
Zan 85 9 26N 0 17W
Zanaga 88 2 48S 13 48 E
Záncara → 33 39 18N 3 18W
Zandvoort 16 52 22N 4 32 E
Zanesville 114 39 56N 82 2W
Zangue → 91 17 50S 35 21 E
Zanjan 64 36 40N 48 35 E
Zannone 40 40 58N 13 2 E
Zante = Zákinthos 45 37 47N 20 54 E
Zanthus 96 31 2S 123 34 E
Zanzibar 90 6 12S 39 12 E
Zanzūr 83 32 55N 13 1 E
Zaouiet El-Kala = Bordj Omar Driss 83 28 4N 6 40 E
Zaouiet Reggane 82 26 32N 0 3 E
Zapadna Morava → 42 43 38N 21 30 E
Zapadnaya Dvina 54 56 15N 32 3 E
Zapadnaya Dvina → 54 57 4N 24 3 E
Západné Beskydy 27 49 30N 19 0 E
Zapadni Rodopi 43 41 50N 24 0 E
Zapadočeský □ 26 49 35N 13 0 E
Západoslovenský □ 27 48 30N 17 30 E
Zapala 128 39 0S 70 5W
Zapaleri, Cerro 124 22 49S 67 11W
Zapata 117 26 56N 99 17W
Zapatón → 31 39 0N 6 49W
Zapodnyy Sayan 59 52 30N 94 0 E
Zapolyarnyy 52 69 26N 30 51 E
Zaporozhye 56 47 50N 35 10 E
Zapponeta 41 41 27N 15 57 E
Zara 64 39 58N 37 43 E
Zaragoza, Coahuila, Mexico 120 28 30N 101 0W
Zaragoza, Nuevo León, Mexico 120 24 0N 99 46W
Zaragoza, Spain 32 41 39N 0 53W
Zaragoza □ 32 41 35N 1 0W
Zarand 65 30 46N 56 34 E
Zărandului, Munţii 46 46 14N 22 7 E
Zaranj 65 30 55N 61 55 E
Zarasai 54 55 40N 26 20 E
Zarate 124 34 7S 59 0W
Zaraysk 55 54 48N 38 53 E
Zarembo I. 108 56 20N 132 50W
Zaria 85 11 0N 7 40 E
Zarisberge 92 24 30S 16 15 E
Zárkon 44 39 38N 22 6 E
Żarów 28 50 56N 16 29 E
Zarqā' → 62 32 10N 35 37 E
Zaruma 126 3 40S 79 38W
Żary 28 51 37N 15 10 E
Zarza de Alange 31 38 49N 6 13W
Zarza de Granadilla 30 40 14N 6 3W
Zarza, La 31 37 42N 6 51W
Zarzaîtine 83 28 15N 9 34 E
Zarzis 83 33 31N 11 2 E
Zas 30 43 4N 8 53W
Zashiversk 59 67 25N 142 40 E
Zaskar Mountains 69 33 15N 77 30 E
Zastron 92 30 18S 27 7 E
Žatec 26 50 20N 13 32 E
Zator 27 49 59N 19 28 E
Zavala 42 42 50N 17 59 E
Zavarāh 65 33 29N 52 28 E
Zavetnoye 57 47 13N 43 50 E
Zavidovići 42 44 27N 18 13 E
Zavitinsk 59 50 10N 129 20 E
Zavodoski 5 56 0S 27 45W
Zavolzhsk 55 57 30N 42 10 E
Zavolzhye 55 56 37N 43 26 E
Zawadzkie 28 50 37N 18 28 E
Zawichost 28 50 48N 21 51 E
Zawidów 28 51 1N 15 1 E
Zawiercie 28 50 30N 19 24 E
Zāwiyat al Bayḍā 81 32 30N 21 40 E
Zawyet Shammâs 86 31 30N 26 37 E
Zâwyet Um el Rakham 86 31 18N 27 1 E
Zâwyet Ungeîla 86 31 23N 26 42 E
Zāyandeh → 65 32 35N 52 0 E
Zayarsk 59 56 12N 102 55 E
Zaysan 58 47 28N 84 52 E
Zaysan, Oz. 58 48 0N 83 0 E
Zaytā 62 32 23N 35 2 E
Zāzamt, W. 83 30 29N 14 30 E
Zazir, O. → 83 22 0N 5 40 E
Zázrivá 27 49 16N 19 7 E
Zbarazh 54 49 43N 25 44 E
Zbąszyń 28 52 14N 15 56 E
Zbąszynek 28 52 16N 15 51 E
Zblewo 28 53 56N 18 19 E
Zdolbunov 54 50 30N 26 15 E
Ždrelo 42 44 16N 21 28 E
Zduńska Wola 28 51 37N 18 59 E
Zduny 28 51 39N 17 21 E
Zeballos 108 49 59N 126 50W
Zebediela 93 24 20S 19 7 E
Zeebrugge 16 51 19N 3 12 E
Zeehan 97 41 52S 145 25 E
Zeeland □ 16 51 30N 3 50 E
Ze'elim 62 31 13N 34 32 E
Zeerust 92 25 31S 26 4 E
Zefat 62 32 58N 35 29 E
Zegdou 82 29 51N 4 45W
Zege 87 11 43N 37 18 E
Zégoua 84 10 32N 5 35W
Zehdenick 24 52 59N 13 20 E
Zeila 63 11 21N 43 30 E
Zeist 16 52 5N 5 15 E
Zeitz 24 51 3N 12 9 E
Żelechów 28 51 49N 21 54 E
Zelengora 42 43 22N 18 30 E
Zelenika 42 42 27N 18 37 E
Zelenodolsk 55 55 55N 48 30 E
Zelenogradsk 54 54 53N 20 29 E
Zelenokumsk 57 44 24N 43 53 E
Zelënyy 57 48 6N 50 45 E
Zeleznik 42 44 43N 20 23 E
Zell, Baden, Ger. 25 47 42N 7 50 E
Zell, Rhld-Pfz., Ger. 25 50 2N 7 11 E
Zell am See 26 47 19N 12 47 E
Zella Mehlis 24 50 40N 10 41 E
Zelów 28 51 28N 19 14 E
Zelzate 16 51 13N 3 47 E
Zembra, I. 83 37 5N 10 56 E
Zémio 90 5 2N 25 5 E
Zemlya Frantsa Iosifa 4 81 0N 55 0 E
Zemmora 82 35 44N 0 51 E
Zemoul, O. → 82 29 15N 7 0W
Zemun 42 44 51N 20 25 E
Zengbe 85 5 46N 13 4 E
Zenica 42 44 10N 17 57 E
Zenina 82 34 30N 2 37 E
Žepče 42 44 28N 18 2 E
Zeraf, Bahr ez → 87 9 42N 30 52 E
Zerbst 24 51 59N 12 8 E
Zerhamra 82 29 58N 2 30W
Żerków 28 52 4N 17 32 E
Zermatt 25 46 2N 7 46 E
Zernez 25 46 42N 10 7 E
Zernograd 57 46 52N 40 19 E
Zerqani 44 41 30N 20 20 E
Zestafoni 57 42 6N 43 0 E
Zetel 24 53 25N 7 57 E
Zeulenroda 24 50 39N 12 0 E
Zeven 24 53 17N 9 19 E
Zévio 38 45 23N 11 10 E
Zeya 59 53 48N 127 14 E
Zeya → 59 53 13N 127 35 E
Zêzere → 31 39 28N 8 20W
Zgierz 28 51 50N 19 27 E
Zgorzelec 28 51 10N 15 0 E
Zhabinka 54 52 13N 24 2 E
Zhailma 58 51 37N 61 33 E
Zhangguangcai Ling 76 45 0N 129 0 E
Zhanghua 75 24 6N 120 29 E
Zhangjiakou 76 40 48N 114 55 E
Zhangping 77 25 17N 117 23 E
Zhangpu 77 24 8N 117 35 E
Zhangwu 76 42 43N 123 52 E
Zhangye 75 38 50N 100 23 E
Zhangzhou 75 24 30N 117 35 E
Zhanhua 76 37 40N 118 8 E
Zhanjiang 75 21 15N 110 20 E
Zhanyi 75 25 38N 103 48 E
Zhanyu 76 44 30N 122 30 E
Zhao Xian 76 37 43N 114 45 E
Zhao'an 77 23 41N 117 10 E
Zhaoping 77 24 11N 110 48 E
Zhaoqing 77 23 0N 112 20 E
Zhaotong 75 27 20N 103 44 E
Zhaoyuan 76 37 20N 120 23 E
Zharkovskiy 54 55 56N 32 19 E
Zhashkov 56 49 15N 30 5 E
Zhdanov 56 47 5N 37 31 E
Zhecheng 77 34 7N 115 20 E
Zhejiang □ 75 29 0N 120 0 E
Zheleznodorozhny 52 62 35N 50 55 E
Zheleznogorsk 54 52 22N 35 23 E
Zheleznogorsk-Ilimskiy 59 56 34N 104 8 E
Zheltyye Vody 56 48 21N 33 31 E
Zhen'an 77 33 27N 109 9 E
Zhenfeng 77 25 22N 105 40 E
Zheng'an 77 28 32N 107 27 E
Zhengding 76 38 8N 114 32 E
Zhenghe 77 27 20N 118 50 E
Zhengyang 77 32 37N 114 22 E
Zhengyangguan 77 32 30N 116 29 E
Zhengzhou 77 34 45N 113 34 E
Zhenjiang 75 32 11N 119 26 E
Zhenlai 76 45 50N 123 5 E
Zhenning 77 26 4N 105 45 E
Zhenyuan, Gansu, China 76 35 35N 107 30 E
Zhenyuan, Guizhou, China 75 27 4N 108 21 E
Zherdevka 55 51 56N 41 29 E
Zhigansk 59 66 48N 123 27 E
Zhigulevsk 55 53 28N 49 30 E
Zhijiang 75 27 27N 109 42 E
Zhirnovsk 55 50 57N 44 49 E
Zhitomir 54 50 20N 28 40 E
Zhizdra 54 53 45N 34 40 E
Zhlobin 54 52 55N 30 0 E
Zhmerinka 56 49 2N 28 2 E
Zhodino 54 54 5N 28 17 E
Zhokhova, Ostrov 59 76 4N 152 40 E
Zhong Xian 77 30 21N 108 1 E
Zhongdian 75 27 48N 99 42 E
Zhongshan 77 22 26N 113 20 E
Zhongwei 76 37 30N 105 12 E
Zhongxiang 77 31 12N 112 34 E
Zhoushan Dao 77 28 5N 122 10 E
Zhouzhi 77 34 10N 108 12 E
Zhovtnevoye 56 46 54N 32 3 E
Zhuanghe 76 39 40N 123 0 E
Zhucheng 76 36 0N 119 27 E
Zhugqu 77 33 40N 104 30 E
Zhuji 77 29 40N 120 10 E
Zhukovka 54 53 35N 33 50 E
Zhumadian 75 32 59N 114 2 E
Zhuo Xian 76 39 28N 115 58 E
Zhupanovo 59 53 40N 159 52 E
Zhushan 77 32 15N 110 13 E
Zhuxi 77 32 25N 109 40 E
Zhuzhou 75 27 49N 113 12 E
Ziarat 68 30 25N 67 49 E
Zibo 76 36 47N 118 3 E
Zidarovo 43 42 20N 27 24 E
Ziębice 28 50 37N 17 2 E
Zielona Góra 28 51 57N 15 31 E
Zielona Góra □ 28 51 57N 15 30 E
Zierikzee 16 51 40N 3 55 E
Ziesar 24 52 16N 12 19 E
Zifta 86 30 43N 31 14 E
Zigey 81 14 43N 15 50 E
Zigong 75 29 15N 104 48 E
Zigui 75 31 0N 110 40 E
Ziguinchor 84 12 35N 16 20W
Zikhron Ya'Aqov 62 32 34N 34 56 E

Zile	64 40 15N 35 52 E	Ziz, Oued ↷	
Žilina	27 49 12N 18 42 E	Zizhong	82 31 40N 4 15W
Zillah	83 28 30N 17 33 E	Zlarin	77 29 48N 104 47 E
Zillertaler Alpen	26 47 6N 11 45 E	Zlatar, Hrvatska, Yugo.	39 43 42N 15 49 E
Zima	59 54 0N 102 5 E	Zlatar, Srbija, Yugo.	39 46 5N 16 3 E
Zimane, Adrar in	82 22 10N 4 30 E	Zlataritsa	42 43 25N 19 47 E
Zimapán	120 20 54N 99 20W	Zlatibor	43 43 2N 25 55 E
Zimba	91 17 20S 26 11 E	Zlatitsa	42 43 45N 19 43 E
Zimbabwe	91 20 16S 30 54 E	Zlatna	43 42 41N 24 7 E
Zimbabwe ■	91 20 0S 30 0 E	Zlatograd	46 46 8N 23 11 E
Zimnicea	46 43 40N 25 22 E	Zlatoust	43 41 22N 25 7 E
Zimovniki	57 47 10N 42 25 E	Zletovo	52 55 10N 59 40 E
Zinder	85 13 48N 9 0 E	Žlitan	42 41 59N 22 17 E
Zinga	91 9 16S 38 49 E	Złocieniec	83 32 32N 14 35 E
Zingst	24 54 24N 12 45 E	Złoczew	28 53 30N 16 1 E
Ziniaré	85 12 35N 1 18W	Zlot	28 51 24N 18 35 E
Zinjibār	63 13 5N 45 23 E	Złotoryja	42 44 1N 22 0 E
Zinkgruvan	49 58 50N 15 6 E	Złotów	28 51 8N 15 55 E
Zinnowitz	24 54 5N 13 54 E	Złoty Stok	28 53 22N 17 2 E
Zion Nat. Park	119 37 25N 112 50W	Zmeinogorsk	28 50 27N 16 53 E
Zipaquirá	126 5 0N 74 0W	Żmigród	58 51 10N 82 13 E
Zippori	62 32 45N 35 16 E	Zmiyev	28 51 28N 16 53 E
Zirc	27 47 17N 17 42 E	Znamenka	56 49 39N 36 27 E
Žiri	39 46 5N 14 5 E	Znamensk	56 48 45N 32 30 E
Žirje	39 43 39N 15 42 E	Žnin	54 54 37N 21 17 E
Zirko	65 25 0N 53 40 E	Znojmo	28 52 51N 17 44 E
Zirl	26 47 17N 11 14 E	Zoar	26 48 50N 16 2 E
Zisterdorf	27 48 33N 16 45 E	Zobia	92 33 30S 21 26 E
Zitácuaro	120 19 28N 100 21W	Zogno	90 3 0N 25 59 E
Zitava ↷	27 48 14N 18 21 E	Zolochev	38 45 49N 9 41 E
Žitište	42 45 30N 20 32 E	Zolotonosha	54 49 45N 24 51 E
Zitsa	44 39 47N 20 40 E	Zomba	56 49 39N 32 5 E
Zittau	24 50 54N 14 47 E	Zongo	91 15 22S 35 19 E
Zitundo	93 26 48S 32 47 E	Zonguldak	88 4 20N 18 35 E
Živinice	42 44 27N 18 36 E	Zorgo	56 41 28N 31 50 E
Ziway, L.	87 8 0N 38 50 E	Zorita	85 12 15N 0 35W
Zixi	77 27 45N 117 4 E	Zorleni	31 39 17N 5 39W
Ziyang	77 32 32N 108 31 E	Zornitsa	46 46 14N 27 44 E
			43 42 23N 26 58 E

Zorra Island	120 9 18N 79 52W	Zunyi	75 27 42N 106 53 E
Zorritos	126 3 43S 80 40W	Županja	42 45 4N 18 43 E
Zory	27 50 3N 18 44 E	Zuqar	87 14 0N 42 40 E
Zorzor	84 7 46N 9 28W	Żur	42 12 13N 20 34 E
Zossen	24 52 13N 13 28 E	Zürich	25 47 22N 8 32 E
Zou Xiang	77 35 30N 116 58 E	Zürich □	25 47 26N 8 40 E
Zouar	83 20 30N 16 32 E	Zürichsee	25 47 18N 8 40 E
Zouérate	80 22 44N 12 21W	Zuromin	28 53 4N 19 51 E
Zousfana, O. ↷	82 31 28N 2 17W	Zuru	85 11 20N 5 11 E
Zoutkamp	16 53 20N 6 18 E	Żut	39 43 52N 15 17 E
Zrenjanin	42 45 22N 20 23 E	Zutphen	16 52 9N 6 12 E
Zuarungu	85 10 49N 0 46W	Zuwārah	83 32 58N 12 1 E
Zuba	85 9 11N 7 12 E	Zuyevka	55 58 25N 51 10 E
Zubair, Jazāir	87 15 0N 42 10 E	Žužemberk	39 45 52N 14 56 E
Zubia	31 37 8N 3 33W	Zvenigorodka	56 49 4N 30 56 E
Zubtsov	54 56 10N 34 34 E	Zverinogolovskoye	58 54 23N 64 40 E
Zuénoula	84 7 34N 6 3W	Zvezdets	43 42 6N 27 26 E
Zuera	32 41 51N 0 49W	Zvolen	27 48 33N 19 10 E
Zuetina	83 30 58N 20 7 E	Zvonce	42 42 57N 22 34 E
Zufar	63 17 40N 54 0 E	Zvornik	42 44 26N 19 7 E
Zug	25 47 10N 8 31 E	Zwedru (Tchien)	84 5 59N 8 15W
Zugdidi	57 42 30N 41 55 E	Zweibrücken	25 49 15N 7 20 E
Zugersee	25 47 7N 8 35 E	Zwenkau	24 51 13N 12 19 E
Zugspitze	25 47 25N 10 59 E	Zwettl	26 48 35N 15 9 E
Zuid-Holland □	16 52 0N 4 35 E	Zwickau	24 50 43N 12 30 E
Zuidhorn	16 53 15N 6 23 E	Zwiesel	25 49 1N 13 14 E
Zújar	33 37 34N 2 50W	Zwischenahn	24 53 12N 8 1 E
Zújar ↷	31 39 1N 5 47W	Zwoleń	28 51 21N 21 36 E
Zújar, Pantano del	31 38 55N 5 35W	Zwolle, Neth.	16 52 31N 6 6 E
Zula	87 15 17N 39 40 E	Zwolle, U.S.A.	117 31 38N 93 38W
Zulpich	24 50 41N 6 38 E	Żychlin	28 52 15N 19 37 E
Zululand	93 43 19N 2 15 E	Żymoetz ↷	108 54 33N 128 31W
Zumaya	32 43 19N 2 15W	Żyrardów	28 52 3N 20 28 E
Zumbo	91 15 35S 30 26 E	Żyrya	57 40 20N 50 15 E
Zummo	85 9 51N 12 59 E	Zyryanka	59 65 45N 150 51 E
Zungeru	85 9 48N 6 8 E	Zyryanovsk	58 49 43N 84 20 E
Zunhua	76 40 18N 117 58 E	Żywiec	27 49 42N 19 10 E
Zuni	119 35 7N 108 57W		

Recent Place Name Changes

The following place name changes have recently occurred.
The new names are on the maps but the former names are in the index.

India

Former name	New name
Ambarnath	Amarnath
Arrah	Ara
Aruppukottai	Aruppukkottai
Barrackpur	Barakpur
Berhampore	Baharampur
Bokharo Steel City	Bokaro
Budge Budge	Baj Baj
Burdwam	Barddhaman
Chapra	Chhapra
Cooch Behar	Koch Bihar
Dohad	Dahod
Dhulia	Dhule
English Bazar	Ingraj Bazar
Farrukhabad-cum-Fatehgarh	Fategarh
Ferozepore	Firozpur
Gadag-Batgeri	Gadag
Gudiyatam	Gudiyattam
Hardwar	Haridwar
Hooghly-Chinsura	Chunchura
Howrah	Haora
Hubli-Dharwar	Dharwad
Kadayanallur	Kadaiyanallur
Manaar, Gulf of	Mannar, Gulf of
Maunath Bhanjan	Mau
Mehsana	Mahesana
Midnapore	Medinipur
Monghyr	Munger
Morvi	Morbi
Nabadwip	Navadwip
Nander	Nanded
Palayancottai	Palayankottai
Purnea	Purnia
Rajnandgaon	Raj Nandgaon
Santipur	Shantipur
Serampore	Shrirampur
Siliguri	Shiliguri
Sonepat	Sonipat
South Suburban	Behala

Iran

Former name	New name
Bandar-e Pahlavi	Bandar-e Anzalī
Bandar-e Shāh	Bandar-e Torkeman
Bandar-e Shahpur	Bandar-e Khomeynī
Dezh Shāhpūr	Marīvan
Gach Sārān	Gachsārān
Herowābād	Khalkhāl
Kermānshāh	Bakhtārān
Naft-e Shāh	Naftshahr
Rezaˀīyeh	Orūmīyeh
Rezaˀīyeh, Daryācheh-ye	Orūmīyeh, Daryācheh-ye
Shāhābād	Āshkhāneh
Shāhābād	Eslāmābad-e Gharb
Shāhī	Qāˀemshahr
Shahrezā	Qomsheh
Shāhrud	Emāmrūd
Shahsavār	Tonekābon
Solţāniyeh	Saˀīdīyeh

Mozambique

Former name	New name
Augusto Cardosa	Metangula
Entre Rios	Malema
Malvérnia	Chicualacuala
Miranda	Macalogue
Olivença	Lupilichi
Vila Alferes Chamusca	Guijá
Vila Caldas Xavier	Muende
Vila Coutinho	Ulonguè
Vila Fontes	Caia
Vila de Junqueiro	Gurué
Vila Luísa	Marracuene
Vila Paiva de Andrada	Gorongoza

Zimbabwe

Former name	New name
Balla Balla	Mbalabala
Belingwe	Mberengwa
Chipinga	Chipinge
Dett	Dete
Enkeldoorn	Chivhu
Essexvale	Esigodini
Fort Victoria	Masvingo
Gwelo	Gweru
Hartley	Chegutu
Gatooma	Kadoma
Inyazura	Nyazura
Marandellas	Marondera
Mashaba	Mashava
Melsetter	Chimanimani
Mrewa	Murewa
Mtoko	Mutoko
Nuanetsi	Mwenezi
Que Que	Kwekwe
Salisbury	Harare
Selukwe	Shurugwi
Shabani	Zvishavane
Sinoia	Chinhoyi
Somabula	Somabhula
Tjolotjo	Tsholotsho
Umvuma	Mvuma
Umtali	Mutare
Wankie	Hwange

Maps, Illustrations and Index printed in Great Britain by George Philip Printers Ltd., London